# THE ROUTLEDGE HANDBOOK OF SELF-DETERMINATION AND SECESSION

*The Routledge Handbook of Self-Determination and Secession* explores the various debates surrounding the issues of self-determination and secession, and the legal, political, and normative implications they give rise to.

Offering a broad survey of the state of the sub-discipline today, the chapters are divided into seven key parts: an Introduction, Self-Determination, Explaining and Justifying Secession, Secession Strategies, Counter-Secession Strategies, International Law and Secession, and Constitutional Law and Secession. The authors, from a range of disciplinary backgrounds, explore all the recent approaches to secession and self-determination based on strategic interaction of major actors in a secession process.

This handbook will be of great interest to students and researchers from a variety of disciplines including politics and international relations, security studies, and law.

**Ryan D. Griffiths** is Associate Professor in the Department of Political Science at Syracuse University, USA.

**Aleksandar Pavković** is Honorary Associate Professor in the School of Social Sciences at Macquarie University, Australia.

**Peter Radan** is Honorary Professor of Law at Macquarie University, Australia. He is also a Fellow of the Australian Academy of Law.

# THE ROUTLEDGE HANDBOOK OF SELF-DETERMINATION AND SECESSION

*Edited by Ryan D. Griffiths,*
*Aleksandar Pavković and Peter Radan*

Routledge
Taylor & Francis Group

LONDON AND NEW YORK

Designed cover image: © Getty Images

First published 2023
by Routledge
4 Park Square, Milton Park, Abingdon, Oxon OX14 4RN

and by Routledge
605 Third Avenue, New York, NY 10158

*Routledge is an imprint of the Taylor & Francis Group, an informa business*

*British Library Cataloguing-in-Publication Data*
A catalogue record for this book is available from the British Library

ISBN: 978-0-367-47811-7 (hbk)
ISBN: 978-0-367-69246-9 (pbk)
ISBN: 978-1-003-03659-3 (ebk)

DOI: 10.4324/9781003036593

Typeset in Bembo
by Apex CoVantage, LLC

# CONTENTS

Contents

# PREFACE

Self-determination and secession are important dynamics in international and domestic politics. Self-determination, as an idea of self-rule, still shapes the goals and aspirations of numerous political movements around the world. Secession, as both a process of leaving an existing state and its endpoint, a new state, is responsible for much more than altering our maps; it is also a common source of conflict. These dynamics are the subject of this handbook, which provides an interdisciplinary collection on the latest research. The theoretical, conceptual, and practical dimensions of self-determination and secession are examined by scholars from a range of disciplines, including history, philosophy, politics, international relations, and law.

The handbook is divided into seven parts. In the first introductory part, a set of scholars describe the meaning, emergence, and history of self-determination and secession. Part II focuses on the normative and legal implications of self-determination across a set of domains. Part III includes a set of chapters that explore the causes and justifications for secession. In Parts IV and V, the authors examine two different but related sides of the dynamics of secession: the strategies of secessionist movements and the counter-secession strategies of states. These developing research areas are in dialogue with one another. Part VI of the volume centers on the relationship between international law and secession. Following that, Part VII covers the domestic and constitutional legal side of secession. This survey of current research on self-determination and secession is certainly not exhaustive. For example, it contains no specific case studies of the processes of self-determination or secession. While this was a result of the editorial decision, the absence of a detailed exploration of popular mobilization for secession and of the role of nationalist ideologies in this process possibly reflects a current absence of research focused on these topics.

# NOTES ON CONTRIBUTORS

**Uriel Abulof** is Associate Professor of Politics at Tel-Aviv University, Israel. He studies the politics of fear, happiness and hope, nationalism and ethnic conflicts, and introducing "political existentialism". He has published over 60 peer-reviewed academic articles, and several books and edited volumes.

**Glen Anderson** is Senior Lecturer in Law at Newcastle Law School, Australia. He has published in prestigious journals on secessionism, self-determination, the Trendtex principle, property law, and trusts.

**Kristin M. Bakke** is Professor in the Department of Political Science at University College London, UK, and Associated Research Professor at the Peace Research Institute, Oslo, Norway. Her research explores states' responses to opposition movements, self-determination struggles, and post-war state-building.

**Karlo Basta** is Lecturer in Politics and International Relations at the University of Edinburgh, UK. His research is on comparative nationalism, institutional change, and the politics of time and events.

**Felicitas Benziger** is an MPhil/PhD candidate at Middlesex University London, UK, researching on self-determination of peoples in the context of supranationalism.

**Eiki Berg** is Professor of International Relations at the University of Tartu, Estonia. He has published widely on sovereignty and territoriality issues, and on different aspects of de facto state dynamics. In 2012, he received the National Science Award in the field of Social Sciences.

**Helge Blakkisrud** is Assistant Professor of Russian and Post-Soviet Studies at the University of Oslo, Norway, and Senior Researcher at the Norwegian Institute of International Affairs. His research interests include nation- and state-building in Russia and Eurasia, hereunder in the region's internationally unrecognized de facto states.

**Elisenda Casañas-Adam** is Lecturer in Public Law and Human Rights and Associate Director of the Edinburgh Centre for Constitutional Law at Edinburgh Law School, UK. Her main research interests lie in the comparative analysis of public law, focusing on multinational constitutionalism, referendums and self-determination, and the protection of human rights in multi-level systems.

**Joshua Castellino** is Executive Director of Minority Rights Group and former (founding) Dean of the Law School at Middlesex University, UK, where he retains his Chair. He holds visiting positions at the University of Oxford, UK, College of Europe, Belgium, and National University of Ireland, Galway, and sits on governing boards of civil society organizations in several countries.

**Kathleen Gallagher Cunningham** is Professor in the Department of Government and Politics at the University of Maryland, USA, and Research Professor at the Peace Research Institute Oslo, Norway. Her primary research interests include self-determination, secession, civil war, and nonviolent resistance.

**Bohumil Doboš** is Assistant Professor at the Institute of Political Studies in the Faculty of Social Sciences at Charles University, Czech Republic. His research interest lies in the field of geopolitics with a focus on violent non-state actors (mainly in sub-Saharan Africa), development of territorial political units, and astropolitics and space security.

**Feike E. M. Fliervoet** is a PhD candidate at the European University Institute, Italy, and Lecturer at the Institute of Political Science at Leiden University, the Netherlands. Her dissertation focuses on cohesion and fragmentation in secessionist movements. Her broader research interests include questions of sovereignty and self-determination, civil war, political violence, and rebel governance.

**Thomas D. Grant** is Fellow of the Lauterpacht Centre for International Law at the University of Cambridge, UK, and a former designee (US National Group) to the Permanent Court of Arbitration.

**Ryan D. Griffiths** is Associate Professor in the Department of Political Science at Syracuse University, USA. His research focuses on the dynamics of secession and the study of sovereignty, state systems, and international orders.

**Caroline Hall** works in operations for a non-profit in Washington, D.C., USA, where she loves watching community-led organizations in separatist regions thrive.

**Roman J. Hoyos** is Professor of Law at Southwestern Law School in Los Angeles, California, USA, where he teaches courses on property and constitutional law. He is currently working on secession in American law.

**R. Joseph Huddleston** is Assistant Professor in the School of Diplomacy and International Relations at Seton Hall University, USA. He studies diplomacy by self-determination movements, dynamics in intrastate conflict, and conflict research design.

**Alyn James Johnson** is Principal of Public Law Solutions, a firm that specializes in constitutional and administrative law in Toronto, Canada. He has taught both law and literature at the university level. His legal publications include numerous articles and blogs on constitutional structure, judicial review, and the delegation of legislative power. His previous work in English literature focused on racism, postcolonialism, and modernism.

**Andreas Juon** is Postdoctoral Fellow in the International Conflict Research group at ETH Zurich, Switzerland, where he investigates majority backlashes against minority accommodation. In his most recent publications, he considers the contradictory consequences of power-sharing institutions for democratic quality and democratization.

**Argyro Kartsonaki** is a researcher at the IFSH at the University of Hamburg, Germany. Her research interests include secession, peace processes, and peace agreements design.

**James Ker-Lindsay** is Research Associate at LSEE-Research on Southeast Europe at the European Institute at the London School of Economics and Political Science, UK, and Visiting Professor at the University of Kent, UK. His work focuses on conflict, peace and security, and secession and recognition.

**Peter Krause** is Associate Professor of Political Science at Boston College, USA, and Research Affiliate with the MIT Security Studies Program, USA. His research focuses on Middle East politics, political violence, and national movements.

**Shpend Kursani** is Lecturer in International Relations at the Johan Skytte Institute of Political Studies at the University of Tartu, Estonia. His research focuses on self-determination, secession, recognition, and state-making.

**Suzanne Lalonde** is Professor of Public International Law and the Law of the Sea at the Law Faculty of the Université de Montréal, Canada. Her research and publications (in both French and English) focus on core international legal principles, in particular those pertaining to sovereignty and the determination of boundaries on land and at sea.

**Costas Laoutides** is Associate Professor in International Relations in the School of Humanities and Social Science at Deakin University in Melbourne, Australia. His research focuses on minority oppression, ethnopolitical violence, and territorial separatism.

**David MacDonald** is Full Professor in the Political Science Department at the University of Guelph, Canada. His primary research is on comparative Indigenous–settler relations in western settler states, focusing on Canada and Aotearoa New Zealand.

**Caitlin McCulloch** is Associate Political Scientist at RAND Corporation, USA. Her work focuses on domestic contexts of war, security cooperation, and the impact of environmental change on conflict. Prior to joining RAND, she was a Fulbright researcher (2016–2017) and Peace Corps volunteer (2011–2013) in the Republic of Georgia.

**Aileen McHarg** is Professor of Public Law and Human Rights at Durham University, UK. She writes on a range of topics in UK and Scots public law but has particular expertise on devolution and the territorial constitution. Amongst other things, she is Joint General Editor of the journal *Public Law* and Co-Chair of the British-Irish chapter of the International Society of Public Law.

**Sean Mueller** is Assistant Professor at the Institute of Political Studies at the University of Lausanne, Switzerland. His main research areas are Swiss and comparative federalism as well as subnational politics and multi-level governance more broadly.

**Diego Muro** is Senior Lecturer at the School of International Relations at the University of St Andrews, UK, and Senior Research Fellow at the Barcelona Centre for International Affairs (CIDOB), Spain. His research is centrally concerned with the relationship between identity politics, secession, and political violence, with a comparative-historical focus on Europe.

**Thomas D. Musgrave** is Senior Lecturer in the School of Law at the University of Wollongong, Australia, where he teaches Australian constitutional law and public international law. He is a member of the Law Society of Ontario, Canada.

**Rowan Nicholson** teaches and researches in international law and public law. His other research interests include the status of Indigenous Australians. He has worked on cases before the International Court of Justice about genocide and border disputes and previously served as Co-Director of the Sydney Centre for International Law at the University of Sydney, Australia. He is now at Flinders University, Australia.

**Zoran Oklopcic** is Associate Professor in the Department of Law and Legal Studies at Carlton University, in Ottawa, Canada. Until recently his research focused on the vocabulary of peoplehood in the context of state formation at the intersection of three disciplines: constitutional theory, normative political theory, and international law.

**Aleksandar Pavković** is Honorary Associate Professor in the School of Social Sciences at Macquarie University, Australia. His research interests span over various manifestations of secession and state fragmentation such as, more recently, declarations of independence, national anthems, and patriotism.

**Scott Pegg** is Professor in the Department of Political Science at Indiana University–Purdue University Indianapolis (IUPUI), USA.

**Matt Qvortrup** is Professor of Political Science at Coventry University, UK, and Visiting Professor at the Australian National University College of Law. An expert in referendums, he is Editor-in-Chief of *European Political Science Review*. A political scientist as well as a lawyer, he is the author of more than a dozen books on referendums.

**Peter Radan** is Honorary Professor of Law at Macquarie University, Australia. He is also a Fellow of the Australian Academy of Law. His principal area of research has been in the field of secession, but he has also published, and teaches in, the areas of contact law and equity and trusts.

**Martin Riegl** is Assistant Professor and Academic Coordinator of the Geopolitical Studies program at the Institute of Political Studies at Charles University, Czech Republic. He is professionally interested in the process of political fragmentation, the geopolitics of international recognition, the global transformation of power, and the geopolitics of sub-Saharan Africa.

**Philip G. Roeder** is Professor of Political Science at the University of California, San Diego, USA. His current research is on constitutional provisions designed in response to national secessionism.

**Brad R. Roth** is Professor of Political Science and Law at Wayne State University, USA. He has written widely on questions of sovereignty, self-determination, democracy, human rights, and international criminal justice. From 2010 to 2018, he served as one of three American Branch representatives to the International Law Association's Committee on Recognition/ Non-Recognition of States and Governments.

**Nicholas Sambanis** is Presidential Distinguished Professor of Political Science and Director of the Identity & Conflict Lab at the University of Pennsylvania, USA. He writes on inter-group conflict, ranging from everyday forms of discrimination to violent protests and civil wars.

**Lee J. M. Seymour** is Associate Professor in the Department of Political Science at the Université de Montréal, Canada. His work focuses on political violence, civil war, and self-determination.

**David S. Siroky** is Professor of Government at the University of Essex, UK. He studies conflict, cooperation, and collective action in politics and economics. His work has been recognized with several awards, including the Deil S. Wright Best Paper Award from the American Political Science Association's section on Federalism and Intergovernmental Relations.

**Nikos Skoutaris** is Associate Professor in EU Law at the University of East Anglia, UK. His research interests lie in the intersection between EU law, comparative constitutional law, and conflict resolution theory. He has published extensively on issues related to secession in the EU. He has acted as an adviser to the European parliamentary group of the European United Left/ Nordic Green Left for Brexit-related issues.

**Milena Sterio** is The Charles R. Emrick Jr.–Calfee Halter & Griswold Professor of Law at the Cleveland-Marshall College of Law, USA, where she specializes in international law, human rights, and international criminal Law. In 2013, she was a Fulbright Scholar in Baku, Azerbaijan, where she studied secession issues related to the disputed Nagorno-Karabakh province.

**Timothy William Waters** is Professor at the Maurer School of Law at Indiana University, USA, and Associate Director of the Center for Constitutional Democracy. He writes on war crimes and state formation.

**Rivka Weill** is Professor of Law at the Harry Radzyner Law School at Reichman University, Israel. She was a clerk and legal adviser for the President of the Supreme Court of Israel, Aharon Barak.

**Yan Xiang** is Professor of Law School of Wuhan University, China, where she teaches Western legal history. As Deputy Director of the Human Rights Institute of Wuhan University and the Director of the Center for Protection the Rights of Disadvantaged Citizens, with volunteers from the WHU Law School, she offers free legal service to vulnerable groups. Her research concerns the protection of human rights.

**Yawen Zhang** is a PhD student at the Law School of Wuhan University. Her research interests include the history of foreign constitutional law.

# PART I

# Introduction

# 1

# THE MEANING OF
# SELF-DETERMINATION

*Rowan Nicholson*

At the height of the decolonization movement, the United Nations General Assembly declared that "[a]ll peoples have the right to self-determination" (UNGA 1960: para. 2). Almost identical assertions appear in human rights covenants, judicial decisions interpreting customary international law, government statements, and secessionist manifestos. But these assertions, even if correct in an abstract sense, are misleading. Their applicability to "all" peoples suggests that self-determination has a stable, universal meaning. In reality, it has multiple manifestations that have little in common apart from an affinity, sometimes close but sometimes more distant, with the idea of a capacity for free will. For some peoples, self-determination is a powerful tool that can be used to construct a new State; for others, it is a looser principle with less concrete legal consequences; and in some circumstances, it may simply play a rhetorical role.

The purpose of this chapter is to elucidate the meaning of self-determination. Six manifestations of it will be discussed: self-determination as a moral or political idea, external self-determination, internal self-determination, self-determination as indigenous autonomy, self-determination as a right against intervention, and economic self-determination. The chapter will conclude by considering whether the term can be given an all-embracing definition despite this variety – and despite any other manifestations of self-determination that may exist or might emerge in future, since these six may not be exhaustive of the possibilities.

## Self-determination as a moral or political idea

The term "self-determination" has roots in moral philosophy. In the seventeenth century, John Locke used it to allude to a capacity for free will, in particular the freedom to commit acts that engender guilt (Locke 1689: part iv.xvii). In the eighteenth century, Immanuel Kant wrote that a being's "will is conceived as a capacity of determining itself to action"; he went on to use the term – in German, *Selbstbestimmung* – in his discussion of that capacity (Kant 2005: 86).

Self-determination has essentially retained this meaning in moral and political thought: the capacity of a self for free will. This is the first manifestation of it that will be discussed.

It is true that Locke and Kant were thinking of individuals, whereas in later political usage whole nations or peoples are also described as exercising self-determination. This, however, is a transposition of the Kantian idea of individual self-determination (Morgan 1988: 357–358). The transposition can be observed in a primeval form in the 1790s, when revolutionary France

DOI: 10.4324/9781003036593-2

organized plebiscites – expressions of popular free will – to justify the annexation of territories such as Alsace (Cassese 1995: 11–13). The rise of nationalism in the course of the nineteenth century made the transposition more plausible. In nationalist ideology, "the members of a nation reach freedom and fulfilment by cultivating the peculiar identity of their own nation and by sinking their own persons in the greater whole of the nation"; in other words, each individual, "in pursuit of self-determination, wills himself as the member of a nation" (Kedourie 1966: 73, 80). The capacity for free will is thus transposed from individuals to the greater whole.

Nowadays, it is rare to describe this greater whole as a nation. That is partly because the word "nation" can be loaded or ambiguous. Sometimes it means a State or another State-like formal institution; sometimes, as here, it denotes a more fuzzily delineated group of individuals that a State or nationalist movement might claim to represent (Nicholson 2019: 1–3).

In the context of self-determination, it is more common to refer to such a group as a people. And it is significant that the word "people", which in ordinary English can be grammatically plural, is in this context often singular. Instead of saying that people (plural) *have* self-determination or *are* entitled to it, commentators often say that *a* people (singular) *has* or *is*. This fits with the notion that self-determination is the capacity for free will of the people itself – an undifferentiated, unitary entity – and not shorthand for the many distinct free wills of its individual members. At first glance, to an international lawyer, there is nothing strange about this. A State is also treated as a single unit, a self, with a will of its own. But the will of a State is a transparent legal fiction. In the world of flesh and blood, the expressions of will that are attributed to a State consist of words or actions by various individual officials who are deemed to represent the State according to established rules. For example, "Heads of State, Heads of Government and Ministers for Foreign Affairs" are "considered as representing their State" for "the purpose of performing all acts relating to the conclusion of a treaty" (Vienna Convention 1969: art. 7; see also ARSIWA 2001: arts. 4–11). The free will of a people is also a fiction or construction of a sort, but a much less transparent one. It is difficult to separate from nationalist ideology – or else, in the case of a people that is not considered to be a nation, from some other conception of identity that defines which individuals are subsumed into the greater whole. Since a people's free will is often expressed through a plebiscite or other democratic process, to that extent it may be similarly difficult to separate from ideas about democracy.

Typically, those who invoke self-determination in a political sense are not asserting in the abstract that a people has a general capacity for free will. They are asserting that a people has a capacity for free will over specific questions. In the 1910s, two political figures helped to shape what these questions tend to be: the leaders of revolutionary Russia and of the United States.

Vladimir Lenin developed his view of self-determination in the years leading up to the revolutions of 1917 (see especially Lenin 1964). The international lawyer Antonio Cassese, tracing Lenin's influence on later Soviet declarations and ultimately on the UN Charter, has distinguished between several circumstances in which, according to Lenin, a principle of self-determination applied (Cassese 1995: 14–19). Self-determination applied to the allocation of territories after inter-State armed conflict; it applied to colonies; and it also applied to non-colonized peoples – who, like colonized peoples, were entitled to secede from their existing States and create new States of their own but who, unlike colonized peoples, were expected to achieve that through a plebiscite rather than violence. These circumstances have something in common. In each case, the specific question over which a people could exercise its free will was the question of which State was to govern that people: a choice about external status.

Almost contemporaneously, President Woodrow Wilson presented his conception of self-determination in his "Fourteen Points" speech about US aims in the First World War (Wilson 1918). For him, as for Lenin and despite their contrasting ideologies, self-determination could involve choices about external status. One difference is that Wilson did not suggest that even colonized peoples could effectuate that choice by violence; he insisted merely on "a strict observance of the principle" that their interests "must have equal weight with the equitable claims" of the colonizing States that administered their territories (Wilson 1918: point V). Another difference – and a point that will prove important – is that Wilson suggested that self-determination could involve an additional choice: a people's right to determine its own form of government (Cassese 1995: 20). He argued accordingly that Russia ought to have an "unembarrassed opportunity for the independent determination of her own political development and national policy" (Wilson 1918: point VI). That might be described as a choice about internal development. If it is objected that this phrase is rather vague – it could refer to many things, from participation in political processes to selection of an economic model – then it will be seen that the vagueness of the language reflects a vagueness in the concept.

The first of several definitions of self-determination can now be formulated. In the sense of moral philosophy, it is an individual's capacity for free will. In a political sense, it is the same capacity transposed from an individual to a greater whole, a nation or people, which is treated as a single self with a single free will; typically, it refers to a people's capacity to make choices about external status or internal development. This is a very broad definition. Much more could be said about the details of self-determination as understood by Locke, Kant, the French and Russian revolutionaries, Wilson, and others. But for the rest of this chapter, moral and political ideas will be left behind in favor of a focus on the legal meanings of the term.

## External self-determination

In 1920, the League of Nations appointed a committee of jurists, the first of two bodies, to consider a dispute between Sweden and Finland about the Aaland Islands. The committee observed that "the principle of self-determination of peoples plays an important part in modern political thought" and had inspired explicit provisions in a number of treaties; but it explained that, in the absence of such a treaty, "the right of disposing of national territory is essentially an attribute of the sovereignty of every State" and "International Law does not recognise the right of national groups" to secede "by the simple expression of a wish" (ICJ 1920: 5). The "principle of self-determination of peoples" could "be called into play" only in circumstances such as revolution and war that are "obscure and uncertain from a legal point of view" and that, "to a large extent, cannot be met by the application of the normal rules of positive law" (ICJ 1920: 6). In other words, even after being championed and elaborated upon by Lenin and Wilson, self-determination was not immediately transformed from a political idea into a legal right in a strict sense.

That changed in the early decades after the Second World War, when a rule crystallized into customary international law that gave certain peoples a right to secede (ICJ 2019: paras 144–161). This is the meaning of self-determination that most international lawyers have in mind when they use the term without further qualification. If they add a qualifier, they call it "external" self-determination (Secession Reference 1998: para. 26). Its meaning is not exactly the same as that of the earlier political idea. It differs in at least three respects.

First, choices about internal development are not relevant here; this chapter will not return to that idea until it moves on to other manifestations of self-determination. External self-determination, as the phrase implies, relates to choices about external status. According to the Friendly Relations Declaration of 1970, the options that a people may choose include the establishment of a new State, free association with or integration into an existing State, and "emergence into any other political status freely determined by a people" (UNGA 1970: principle *e*).

A second difference is that external self-determination can be described in strict legal terms as a right, including a right to choose to create a new State. That is unlike self-determination in a moral or political sense, which was described earlier as a capacity.

A right to choose to create a new State is not the same as an actual power to create one; a people cannot, merely by voting in a plebiscite, instantly or mechanically bring a new State into being (Nicholson 2019: 173). To implement the people's choice, a new formal institution must generally be constructed, which may involve drafting a constitution, selecting leaders, and so on. This new institution will be expected to comply with the ordinary rule that a State must have a population, a territory, a government, and independence (or, as that last requirement is sometimes more clumsily expressed, a "capacity to enter into relations with the other States": Montevideo Convention 1933: art 1). External self-determination shapes the operation of this rule in complex ways; it also interacts with recognition – which, in limited circumstances, may be able to provide an alternative path to statehood – and with the principle that no law arises from unlawfulness (Nicholson 2019: 171–187). The critical point, however, is that external self-determination does not fully replace the ordinary rules about statehood.

The most direct legal consequence of a right to external self-determination is that existing States acquire a correlative duty. The duty is to "respect" the right or, more actively, "to promote, through joint and separate action, realization of the principle of equal rights and self-determination of peoples" (UNGA 1970: principle *e*). For an existing State that administers the territory of a people possessing a right to external self-determination, this may amount to a duty to organize a plebiscite or to help to construct a new institution. If the administering State refuses to comply, it will commit a breach of international law that might attract condemnation or even trigger a response by other States or the United Nations. The obligations have been described as "a sort of time-bomb" in that the administering State "has to fulfil them knowing that by this action it will eventually have to relinquish its title" over the territory (Cassese 1995: 187). It is in this sense that external self-determination is a legal right.

This can be seen as an extension of the political meaning of self-determination as a capacity for free will: the law facilitates and vindicates a people's freely made choice. Moreover, the idea that a people has a right – and therefore a distinct legal personality – is consistent with the political idea that a people is a single self. An alternative term used by international lawyers that emphasizes its unitary nature is "self-determination unit" (e.g. Crawford 2006: 124–125). But the fact that external self-determination is a right in a strict legal sense radically changes the meaning of the term. The term now carries, embedded within it, an elaborate structure of conditional statements about what things ought to be done and what will happen if they are not done.

There is a final respect in which the meaning of external self-determination differs from the political meaning of the term. The catalyst for its emergence as a legal right was the movement for Western powers to withdraw from their colonies in Africa, Asia, and elsewhere. This still restricts its field of application. It applies to two established categories of peoples.

One is colonized peoples (Secession Reference 1998: paras 131–132). Historically, these included the peoples of mandate or trust territories, most of which were former German colonies that had been confiscated after the First World War to be administered by other States; they also include the peoples of other Western colonies, which the United Nations calls "non-self-governing territories" (UNC 1945: ch. XI). Of the many former non-self-governing territories, most are now independent and only a few remain, mainly small islands.

The other established category embraces peoples that are "subject to alien subjugation, domination or exploitation outside a colonial context" (Secession Reference 1998: para. 133). The Palestinian people is the most prominent example, albeit one that is complicated by various idiosyncrasies (compare ICJ 2004: para. 88). Another possible example, though highly debatable, is the people of what is now Bangladesh. When it sought to secede from Pakistan in 1971, India argued in the UN Security Council that in substance, even if not in a technical sense, the territory was non-self-governing and had been held "under colonial rule" (UNSC 1971: paras 168, 185; Salmon 1973). In any case, this non-colonized category is small and peripheral; external self-determination primarily applies to colonized peoples. In this respect, it is narrower than the political idea of self-determination as understood by the likes of Wilson, which extended, for example, to European peoples such as the Poles who were living within multi-ethnic States (Wilson 1918: point XIII).

It can be concluded that the meaning of external self-determination is a natural development from the meaning of self-determination as a moral or political idea but is, nonetheless, significantly narrower. It relates to free will, but only over a specific question, external status. Instead of being a loose capacity, it is a right in a strict legal sense with established legal consequences. And it is vested only in a limited class of peoples, primarily colonized peoples.

There remains a little more to say about who falls into that limited class, but it is intertwined with the concept of internal self-determination, which is the next topic for discussion.

## Internal self-determination

In *Reference re Secession of Quebec*, the Supreme Court of Canada considered the possibility that the province of Québec might secede from Canada. The decision provides a useful synthesis of aspects of the international law of self-determination. The court observed that

> sources of international law establish that the right to self-determination of a people is normally fulfilled through *internal* self-determination – a people's pursuit of its political, economic, social and cultural development within the framework of an existing state. A right to *external* self-determination . . . arises in only the most extreme of cases
> *(Secession Reference 1998: para. 126, emphasis in original).*

The court identified the two categories that have already been described: the established categories of colonized and non-colonized peoples with a right to external self-determination. But it added that, according to some commentators, that right might also arise in a third circumstance:

> the underlying proposition is that, when a people is blocked from the meaningful exercise of its right to self-determination internally, it is entitled, as a last resort, to exercise it by secession. . . . [This] parallels the other two recognized situations in that the ability of a people to exercise its right to self-determination internally is somehow being totally frustrated
> *(Secession Reference 1998: paras 134–135).*

The court emphasized that it was debatable whether this proposition was correct.

This is one respect in which internal self-determination is legally consequential. A people, despite falling outside the two established categories of external self-determination units, may have an entitlement to internal self-determination. This entitlement is usually limited to choices about internal development – about political, economic, social, or cultural development within an existing State – as distinct from external status. However, in an exceptional circumstance, debatably, the entitlement may be transmogrified into a right to external self-determination. The examples invoked in the debate about this proposition, such as Kosovo or Bangladesh, tend to feature allegations of crimes against humanity or other grave wrongs (e.g. Pellet 2015). Since vindicating a people's choice about external status can be seen as a remedy for wrongs like these, it is linked with the notion of "remedial secession" (ICJ 2010: para. 82).

Just as it is difficult to be certain about this proposition, it is also difficult to be certain about the other possible legal consequences of internal self-determination.

For now, the self-determination of indigenous peoples, such as the First Nations, Inuit, and Métis within Québec, will be left aside. So will the self-determination of the people of an existing State as a whole, such as the people of Canada. Although both are sometimes considered under the umbrella of internal self-determination, the focus of the present discussion is on the internal self-determination of other peoples within existing States. These might include the people of a subunit of a State, such as the people of Québec; they might also include various ethnic, linguistic, religious, or racial groups within existing States. In his seminal work on self-determination, Cassese conducts a search for legal rules about internal self-determination that might apply to peoples of these kinds, and he struggles to find very many (Cassese 1995: 101–140). He distinguishes between rules in a strict sense and principles of a looser nature.

In connection with racial groups, Cassese points to persuasive evidence of a rule in the strict sense. Drawing on State practice on apartheid South Africa and Rhodesia, both of which discriminated against their black majorities, he concludes that "racial groups have the right to take part in the national decision-making process"; he adds, however, that international law provides little guidance about how this right is to be implemented, other than to affirm that it is not a right to secede and that the creation of putatively independent entities that perpetuate racial discrimination, such as the Bantustans established by South Africa, "can in no way be regarded as a proper way of realizing self-determination" (Cassese 1995: 124). There may also be other rules in the strict sense that relate to internal self-determination. For instance, it has been suggested that where "there are one or more groups within a State constituting one or more ethnic, religious or language communities, they have the right to recognition of their identity under international law" (Badinter Commission 1991: para. 2).

Cassese also points to a looser legal principle articulated by the International Court of Justice (ICJ): "the principle of self-determination, defined as the need to pay regard to the freely expressed will of peoples" (ICJ 1975: para. 59). This principle aligns closely with the political meaning of self-determination that was introduced earlier, with the difference that it plays a somewhat nebulous normative role within the international legal system. Cassese writes of it:

> Clearly, this principle poses a very loose standard; it does not define either the *units of self-determination* or *areas or matters* to which it applies, or the *means or methods* of its implementation. In particular, it does not specify whether self-determination should have an *internal* or *external* dimension. . . . The principle simply sets out general guidelines for State behaviour and therefore acts as a sort of overarching standard for international relations.
>
> *(Cassese 1995: 128, emphasis in original)*

In the context of external self-determination and of the internal self-determination of certain groups, the principle is effectively supplanted by more specific rules. But the loose principle may be the only applicable legal standard in some other cases (Cassese 1995: 132).

The uncertainties about the international law of internal self-determination are such that it is hard to pin down a definition of the term. One of the few things that can be said for sure is that it relates to choices about internal development, and to that extent it is anchored in the familiar idea that a people has a capacity for free will. But the paucity of guidance on what options may be chosen and on when and how choices may be made, among other things, means that the connection to free will seems hazier and more distant than in the case of external self-determination. And whereas external self-determination is undoubtedly a legal right, internal self-determination appears to have a mélange of functions: it provides a possible precondition for the acquisition of a right to external self-determination; it is a free-standing right of some groups; and it is an aspect of a looser but more widely applicable legal principle.

## Self-determination as indigenous autonomy

Some characteristics of indigenous peoples for purposes of international law can be drawn from a 1989 treaty of the International Labour Organization. They are "peoples in independent countries"; they "are regarded as indigenous on account of their descent from the populations which inhabited" a country "at the time of conquest or colonisation or the establishment of present state boundaries"; they "retain some or all of their own social, economic, cultural and political institutions"; and a "fundamental criterion" is "[s]elf-identification as indigenous" (ILO 1989: art. 1). On the one hand, then, indigenous peoples resemble the colonized peoples that are accorded a right to external self-determination: they tend to have suffered dispossession and exploitation by European empires such as the Spanish or British or ensuing settler societies such as the United States. On the other hand, they also share characteristics with the ethnic and other groups that are generally restricted to internal self-determination: they tend, nowadays, to form minorities within their traditional territories. This may partly explain why the meaning of self-determination in the context of indigenous peoples appears to be slightly different from both external and internal self-determination as those terms are otherwise understood.

In submissions to a UN Working Group on Indigenous Populations in the 1980s, some indigenous representatives interpreted self-determination as entailing something akin to a choice about external status. For example, one declaration made jointly by several indigenous organizations proclaimed that "[n]o State shall assert any jurisdiction over an indigenous people or its territory, except in accordance with the freely expressed wishes of the nation or people concerned" (WGIP 1985: annex 4, 1).

The UN Declaration on the Rights of Indigenous Peoples of 2007 goes nowhere near this far. It provides that indigenous peoples have a "right to self-determination" by virtue of which "they freely determine their political status and freely pursue their economic, social and cultural development"; a separate provision then clarifies that this cannot be "construed as authorizing" any action that would impair the territorial integrity of existing States (UNGA 2007: arts. 3, 46(1)). That is to say, it does not offer a choice about external status. But the declaration offers something more than choices about development such as those entailed by internal self-determination. It offers a right to autonomy. As Marc Weller explains, following a review of the extent to which ethnic and other minorities are entitled to autonomy,

> international commitments to autonomy outside of the context of Indigenous rights have been rather sparse. While some governments have granted autonomy . . . [such as the autonomy of the Aaland Islands within Finland], there is no firm obligation to satisfy demands for self-governance in this way.
>
> Indigenous people, on the other hand, have this entitlement without question. The Declaration is very explicit in this respect.
>
> *(Weller 2018: 144)*

In the most explicit of the relevant provisions, the declaration provides that, "in exercising their right to self-determination", indigenous peoples "have the right to autonomy or self-government in matters relating to their internal and local affairs, as well as ways and means for financing their autonomous functions" (UNGA 2007: art. 4). Perhaps the closest analogue to this that has been mentioned up to now is the right of racial groups to take part in a State's decision-making process. Even that, however, does not amount to an entitlement of the kind in this provision: a right to autonomous institutions that are distinct from those of the State as a whole.

The declaration is not in itself binding and is not necessarily reflected in binding rules of customary international law (though some have suggested that Article 3, the provision affirming in general terms that indigenous peoples have a right to self-determination, does accord with custom; Scheinin and Åhrén 2018: 64). That notwithstanding, it suggests a meaning of self-determination that falls somewhere in between external and internal self-determination as they are otherwise understood. It treats indigenous peoples as singular entities with a capacity for free will, and it gives them a right to exercise that free will by means of autonomy.

## Self-determination as a right against intervention

Self-determination bears yet another meaning in the context of the self-determination of the people of an existing State as a whole. This might be linked with the allusions in the UN Charter to "the principle of equal rights and self-determination of peoples" (UNC 1945: arts 1(2), 55). A committee involved in drafting the Charter explained that "the principle of equal rights of peoples and that of self-determination are two complementary parts of one standard of conduct"; that respect for it "is a basis for the development of friendly relations" among nations and "one of the measures to strengthen universal peace"; and that it entails "a free and genuine expression of the will of the people, which avoids cases of the alleged expression of the popular will, such as those used for their own ends by [Nazi] Germany and [Fascist] Italy" (UNCIO 1945: 396). James Crawford observes that this seems to mean self-determination in the sense of "the right of the people of a State to choose its own form of government without external intervention"; elsewhere, he affirms that in the case of an existing State – excluding for this purpose any part of the State whose people is a distinct external self-determination unit, such as a colony – the principle "normally takes the well-known form of the rule preventing intervention in the internal affairs of a State, a central element of which is the right of the people to choose for themselves their own form of government" (Crawford 2006: 114, 126).

This could be interpreted as a logical adaptation of the right to external self-determination to a different situation. In some cases, especially where a people with that right rejects secession in favor of integration or association with an existing State, there may be some doubt about whether the right has been exhausted. For example, the French territory of New Caledonia was removed from the UN list of non-self-governing territories in 1947 but was reinstated in 1986 (UNGA 1986). And in 1998, its people were given up to three opportunities to vote about its status (Nouméa Accord 1998). But where a people chooses to secede and establish a new State, there can be no doubt: the idea that it retains a right to external self-determination, understood as embracing a right to secede, becomes nonsensical. The people has made a once-and-for-all choice. Making that choice, however, does not extinguish the people's broader entitlement to self-determination. It evolves into an entitlement of the people of the newly established State to continue to vindicate the choice by making ongoing choices about other matters; it becomes an entitlement to *maintain* independence, as distinct from acquiring independence.

As logical as this may be, self-determination in this sense has some puzzling features. The first concerns the identity of the legal person who holds the right to self-determination.

If one were to take literally the idea that the people of an existing State has a right to choose its own form of government, then one might expect that right to be opposable to the State in a similar manner to individual human rights. In other words, one might expect the State to have a correlative duty to respect the right. The right would, on that view, amount to something like a right to democracy. This is conceivable but far from established:

> it is difficult to discern any consistent action taken in the international arena to protect the rights of peoples subjected to authoritarian or despotic governments, and based on the principle that such governments are in violation of their people's right to self-determination.
>
> *(Cassese 1995: 102)*

On the contrary, since self-determination in this sense is said to take "the well-known form of the rule preventing intervention in the internal affairs of a State" (Crawford 2006: 126), it can more readily be invoked by authoritarian States in order to *resist* international efforts to promote democracy. Consider the remarks of the ICJ in reply to an allegation that Nicaragua had reneged on a commitment to hold free elections and had taken steps towards a communist dictatorship: "adherence by a State to any particular doctrine", explained the court, "does not constitute a violation of customary international law", and "to hold otherwise would make nonsense of the fundamental principle of State Sovereignty . . . and the freedom of choice of the political, social, economic and cultural system of a State". Nor could the court "contemplate the creation of a new rule opening up a right of intervention by one State against another on the ground that the latter has opted for some particular ideology or political system" (ICJ 1986: para. 263).

Possibly, then, the right of self-determination in this context, though putatively vested in the people of a State as a whole, is in practice exercised by the State itself and is opposable to other States. There is little evidence that the people is treated as a distinct legal person; it appears to be effectively absorbed into the legal personality of the State. That is a point of difference between this meaning of self-determination and the other meanings that have been discussed, all of which clearly treat peoples as singular entities with their own free wills.

Related to this is another puzzling feature of self-determination in the context of the people of an existing State. The rule against intervention in internal affairs, especially in peacetime, has a long pedigree in international law. Emmer de Vattel wrote in the eighteenth century that "we should not only refrain from usurping the territory of others; we should also respect it, and abstain from every act contrary to the rights of the sovereign" (Vattel 2008: part II.93). And at the start of the twentieth century, Lassa Oppenheim affirmed that States had a duty to abstain "from any act which contains a violation of another State's independence or territorial and personal supremacy" and that "there is no doubt" that "intervention is as a rule forbidden by the Law of Nations which protects the International Personality of the States" (Oppenheim 1905: parts 125, 134). In short, the rule predates the emergence into international law of any conception of self-determination. Moreover, as illustrated by the passage from the ICJ about Nicaragua quoted earlier, the rule is frequently expressed in language other than that of self-determination. This raises the question of what difference it makes to say that the peoples of existing States have a right to self-determination. Does it add anything at all, in practice, to the rights that international law has vested in States for hundreds of years?

Solving the puzzles of self-determination in the context of the peoples of existing States is beyond the scope of this chapter. Still, there are grounds for suspecting that, in this context, its main function is "rebranding": imbuing something old with new significance. By association with other meanings of self-determination, it evokes the idea that peoples are singular entities with a capacity for free will; but in practice, it may simply refer to an established right of States: their right not to be subjected to intervention by other States in their internal affairs.

## Economic self-determination

A full discussion of the various human rights treaties and other international instruments that refer to self-determination is also beyond the scope of this chapter (but see, e.g., Saul et al. 2014). In general, they might be interpreted as referring to self-determination in one of the senses already discussed or in some combination of those senses. But one aspect of the two covenants of 1966 – the International Covenant on Economic, Social and Cultural Rights and the International Covenant on Civil and Political Rights – is worthy of separate discussion: "economic" self-determination.

The covenants provide, in familiar language, that "[a]ll peoples have the right of self-determination", by virtue of which "they freely determine their political status and freely pursue their economic, social and cultural development"; but they then immediately add:

> All peoples may, for their own ends, freely dispose of their natural wealth and resources without prejudice to any obligations arising out of international economic co-operation, based upon the principle of mutual benefit, and international law. In no case may a people be deprived of its own means of subsistence.
>
> *(ICESCR 1966: art. 1; ICCPR 1966: art. 1)*

The Human Rights Committee has described this in a general comment as "a particular aspect of the economic content of the right of self-determination" (HRC 1984).

In other instruments, there is some slippage between the notion that this is a right of peoples and – echoing what was observed about self-determination as a right against intervention – the notion that it is a right of States. For example, in a resolution of 1962, the General Assembly alluded both to the "right of peoples and nations to permanent sovereignty over their natural resources" and to the "inalienable right of all States freely to dispose of their natural wealth and resources" (UNGA 1962). However, the idea of economic self-determination does not appear to be restricted either to existing States or to their peoples. Some administering States have devolved the power to make economic choices to the peoples of colonized or occupied territories while retaining political control; and references to economic development also form part of formulations of internal self-determination and of the self-determination of indigenous peoples, including the formulations that were cited earlier (see Saul et al. 2014: 59).

A capacity for free will is ingrained in the idea of economic self-determination: it vindicates choices made by peoples or States about the disposition of wealth and resources.

## An all-embracing definition?

The idea of economic self-determination illustrates a point of broader relevance to this chapter: that the boundaries between the various manifestations of self-determination are blurry. Would it make more sense to treat economic self-determination not as an idea for separate discussion, but merely as an aspect of external, internal, or indigenous self-determination or of the right against intervention? Equally, would it make more sense to treat all these things not as discrete rights or rules or whatever else they may be, but as applications to specific situations of a single, unified legal concept, the loose principle mentioned by Cassese? And is there always a practical difference between that principle, with its nebulous normative role, and the similarly nebulous political meaning of self-determination? To this can be added the numerous uncertainties about the law of self-determination that have been mentioned, along with some other complexities that have been only touched upon: the possibility that yet other manifestations of it may exist or might emerge in future and the relationship between customary and treaty law on the topic.

The blurriness, uncertainties, and complexities are not random; they form a pattern. The pattern results from the transposition of self-determination – described at the beginning of this chapter – from a moral idea applicable to one type of self, an individual, to a political or legal idea applicable to another type of self, a nation or people treated as a singular entity.

Peoples, unlike individuals, are very indeterminate things. An illustration of the difficulty of identifying a people, what has been called the "onion problem", is Yugoslavia as it existed as a State in the early 1990s (Koskenniemi 1994: 260). The outermost layer of the onion was the Yugoslav people as a whole, which might have been defined as the people of an existing State or, alternatively, by at least a degree of common history. Next came the peoples of subunits of the State – Croatia, Serbia, Slovenia, and so on – which nursed nationalist movements of their own. And after that came, for example, the ethnic Serb minority within the borders of Croatia, which might be treated either as a people in itself or as part of a larger, ethnic conception of the Serb people. As this suggests, any attempt to produce a general definition or description of a people for purposes of self-determination is likely to be controversial, because it is likely to conflict with other claims to peoplehood. Such attempts as have been made tend to be impracticably vague (e.g. IME 1990: 7–8). Martti Koskenniemi comments, in light of this indeterminacy, that

> a generally formulated right or a principle such as "self-determination" . . . seems to convey a value that most people will immediately endorse. The more concrete it is made, however – that is, the more it is applied as a right of this or that entity – the more controversial it starts to appear, with the result, finally, that it becomes useless when it seems most needed: in a dispute about the boundaries of a particular "self" against another.
>
> *(Koskenniemi 1994: 264)*

This problem with a generally formulated right or principle, he adds, does not render the law of self-determination "non-existent or useless"; what it means is that the law "cannot be kept apart from political priorities in particular situations, such as giving priority to decolonising pursuits over attempts to maintain European imperiums" (Koskenniemi 1994: 265–266). The pattern that can be observed is consistent with this.

Self-determination takes its most legally concrete forms where there is the least controversy about the boundaries of the peoples entitled to it. Reflecting the priority of decolonization, colonized peoples – a comparatively uncontroversial category, inasmuch as the United Nations maintains a list of relevant territories – are entitled to self-determination in the sense of a legal right to make choices about external status: a powerful tool that can be used to construct a new State. A few non-colonized peoples have this right too. Self-determination also takes a concrete form in the context of the peoples of existing States, though there are grounds for suspecting that this simply amounts to rebranding the established right against intervention.

Other manifestations of self-determination are more beset by blurriness, uncertainties, and complexities. To some extent this is true of indigenous and economic self-determination. But the extreme case here is the internal self-determination of ethnic minorities, of the peoples of subunits such as Québec, and of various other peoples within existing States, a concept that somehow involves choices about internal development but that oscillates between functioning as a precondition, as a right, and as an aspect of a nebulous legal principle. One of the paradoxes of self-determination is that, nowadays, the term seems to be used the most frequently in these contexts. That is because the process of decolonization largely burned itself out in the late twentieth century, meaning that few opportunities remain to invoke the more concrete notion of external self-determination. Perhaps, however, the fact that self-determination *can* function in a concrete way strengthens its rhetorical value in other contexts. When secessionist movements invoke it, for example, their audiences may be led to imagine that it extends as far as a right to secession in international law even when that is extremely dubious.

What room does this leave for an all-embracing definition of self-determination?

It has proven difficult to advance beyond the very first definition that was presented in this chapter: the capacity of a self for free will or, in Kant's phrase, "a capacity of determining itself to action" (Kant 2005: 86). Everything else is contingent. In particular, the components of this all-embracing definition – self, capacity, and free will – take on different meanings in different circumstances. In political and legal usage, the self appears to be the most stable of the components: it refers not to an individual but to a group of individuals, a people, that is treated as a single entity. But this stability is only apparent, because the entities described as peoples are so heterogenous that the description is almost useless without further elaboration. Depending on who the people is, the significance of having a capacity also varies drastically: in some cases, it is a right in a strict legal sense; usually it is something looser. As for the notion of free will, in practice it seldom refers to the exercise of will over any question whatsoever: it may refer specifically to a choice about secession or another external status, or to choices about internal development, or to indigenous autonomy, or to the conduct of internal affairs without intervention by other States, or to choices about the disposition of wealth and resources.

On an all-embracing but highly abstract definition, it is hard to deny that "[a]ll peoples have the right to self-determination" (UNGA 1960: para. 2). It may often be politically useful to speak in these universal terms. But at a less abstract level, none of the many functions of self-determination is truly universal. Much greater meaning can be wrung out of the concept when one specifies exactly which manifestation of it one has in mind.

# References

ARSIWA 2001, Articles on Responsibility of States for Internationally Wrongful Acts, 2001, *Yearbook of the International Law Commission*, 2(2): 26.

Badinter Commission 1991, Opinion No 2, *International Law Reports*, 92: 167.

Cassese, A. 1995, *Self-Determination of Peoples: A Legal Reappraisal*, Cambridge: Cambridge University Press.

Crawford, J. 2006, *The Creation of States in International Law*, 2nd ed., Oxford: Oxford University Press.

HRC 1984, Human Rights Committee 1984, General Comment No 12, in Compilation of General Comments and General Recommendations Adopted by Human Rights Treaty Bodies, UN Doc. HRI/GEN/1/Rev. 9 (Vol. I): 183.

ICCPR 1966, International Covenant on Civil and Political Rights, *United Nations Treaty Series*, 999: 1.

ICESCR 1966, International Covenant on Economic, Social and Cultural Rights, *United Nations Treaty Series*, 993: 3.

ICJ 1920, International Committee of Jurists, 1920, Report Upon the Legal Aspects of the Aaland Islands Question 1920, *League of Nations Official Journal*, Special Supplement No. 3.

ICJ 1975, International Court of Justice, *Western Sahara (Advisory Opinion)*, *International Court of Justice Reports*, 12.

ICJ 1986, International Court of Justice, *Military and Paramilitary Activities in and against Nicaragua (Nicaragua v. United States of America)*, *International Court of Justice Reports*, 14.

ICJ 2004, International Court of Justice, *Legal Consequences of the Construction of a Wall in the Occupied Palestinian Territory (Advisory Opinion)*, *International Court of Justice Reports*, 136.

ICJ 2010, International Court of Justice, *Accordance with International Law of the Unilateral Declaration of Independence in Respect of Kosovo (Advisory Opinion)*, *International Court of Justice Reports*, 403.

ICJ 2019, International Court of Justice, *Legal Consequences of the Separation of the Chagos Archipelago from Mauritius in 1965 (Advisory Opinion)*, *International Court of Justice Reports*, 95.

ILO 1989, International Labour Organization, Convention Concerning Indigenous and Tribal Peoples in Independent Countries 1989, *United Nations Treaty Series*, 1650: 383.

IME 1990, International Meeting of Experts on Further Study of the Concept of the Rights of Peoples 1990, Final Report and Recommendations, Unesco Doc. SNS-89/CONF.602/7.

Kant, I. 2005, *Groundwork for the Metaphysics of Morals*, trans. T. K. Abbott & L. Denis, Peterborough, Ontario: Broadview Press (original work published 1785).

Kedourie, E. 1966, *Nationalism*, 3rd ed., London: Hutchinson.

Koskenniemi, M. 1994, National Self-Determination Today: Problems of Legal Theory and Practice, *International and Comparative Law Quarterly*, 43: 241–269.

Lenin, V. I. 1964, The Socialist Revolution and the Right of Nations to Self-Determination, in *Collected Works*, vol. 22, London: Lawrence & Wishart: 143 (original work published 1916).

Locke, J. 1689, *An Essay Concerning Human Understanding*, London.

Montevideo Convention 1933, Montevideo Convention on the Rights and Duties of States, *League of Nations Treaty Series*, 165: 19.

Morgan, E. M. 1988, The Imagery and Meaning of Self-Determination, *New York University Journal of International Law and Politics*, 20(2): 355–404.

Nicholson, R. 2019, *Statehood and the State-Like in International Law*, Oxford: Oxford University Press.

Nouméa Accord 1998, *Australian Indigenous Law Reporter*, 7: 88.

Oppenheim L. F. L. 1905, *International Law*, vol. I, London: Longmans, Green, & Co.

Pellet, A. 2015, Kosovo: The Questions Not Asked: Self-Determination, Secession, and Recognition, in M. Milanović & M. Wood (eds.), *The Law and Politics of the Kosovo Advisory Opinion*, Oxford: Oxford University Press: 268.

Salmon, J. 1973, Naissance et reconnaissance du Bangla-Desh, in J. Tittel (ed.), *Multitudo legum ius unum: Festschrift für Wilhelm Wengler*, vol. 1, Berlin: Interrecht: 467–490.

Saul, B., Kinley, D., & Mowbray, J. 2014, *The International Covenant on Economic, Social and Cultural Rights: Commentary, Cases, and Materials*, Oxford: Oxford University Press.

Secession Reference 1998, Supreme Court of Canada, *Reference re Secession of Quebec* [1998] 2 S.C.R. 217.

Scheinin, M. & Åhrén, M. 2018, Relationship to Human Rights, and Related International Instruments, in J. Hohmann & M. Weller (eds.), *The UN Declaration on the Rights of Indigenous Peoples: A Commentary*, Oxford: Oxford University Press: 63.

UNC 1945, United Nations Charter, 1945, <www.un.org/en/about-us/un-charter/full-text>

UNCIO 1945, United Nations Conference on International Organization, *Documents*, vol. VI, New York: United Nations Information Organizations.

UNGA 1960, United Nations General Assembly, Declaration on the Granting of Independence to Colonial Countries and Peoples, Resolution 1514 (XV), 14 December.

UNGA 1962, United Nations General Assembly, Resolution 1803 (XVII), 14 December.

UNGA 1970, United Nations General Assembly, Declaration on Principles of International Law Concerning Friendly Relations and Co-Operation Among States in Accordance With the Charter of the United Nations, Annex to Resolution 2625 (XXV), 24 October.

UNGA 1986, United Nations General Assembly, Resolution 41/41A, 2 December.

UNGA 2007, United Nations General Assembly, United Nations Declaration on the Rights of Indigenous Peoples, Annex to Resolution 61/295, 13 September.

UNSC 1971, United Nations Security Council, *Official Records*, 1606th Meeting, 4 December, UN Doc. S/PV.1606.

Vattel, E. de 2008, *The Law of Nations*, eds. B. Kapossy & R. Whatmore, Indianapolis: Liberty Fund (original work published 1758).

Vienna Convention 1969, Vienna Convention on the Law of the Treaties, 23 May, 1155 U.N.T.S. 331.

Weller, M. 2018, Self-Determination of Indigenous Peoples: Articles 3, 4, 5, 18, 23, and 46(1), in J. Hohmann & M. Weller (eds.), *The UN Declaration on the Rights of Indigenous Peoples: A Commentary*, Oxford: Oxford University Press: 115.

Wilson, W. 1918, *Address of the President of the United States, Delivered at a Joint Session of the Two Houses of Congress, January 8, 1918*, Washington: US Government Printing Office.

WGIP 1985, Working Group on Indigenous Populations, Study of the Problem of Discrimination against Indigenous Populations, UN Doc. E/CN.4/Sub.2/1985/22.

# 2

# THE EMERGENCE AND EVOLUTION OF SELF-DETERMINATION

*Uriel Abulof*

## Introduction

A little over a century ago, global politics changed: on February 11, 1918, US President Woodrow Wilson named "Self-determination" an "imperative principle" and injected it, as a cure, into the political heart of a world engulfed in its first global war. A month following his Fourteen Points speech (January 8, 1918), Wilson consecrated this concept as the moral cornerstone of the international society, embarking on a crusade to "make the world safe for democracy."

Self-determination, however, did not emerge then and there, but centuries earlier. Employing historical conceptual analysis (Palonen 2002), this article excavates the genesis of self-determination, focusing on intellectual and political developments leading up to the last century. The importance of this conceptual genealogy goes beyond accurately detailing how self-determination came to be. The history of self-determination so deeply entwines with the history of modern (political) philosophy and practice that tracing self-determination helps us reveal key trends and tensions that still define, indeed haunt, our world today. Here I analyze the emergence of this pivotal principle, both theoretically and historically.

Theoretically, I argue that self-determination is a political response to "the disenchantment of the world." The modern withdrawal of the divine from politics created an existential legitimacy crisis. When sacred scriptures barely prescribe our public lives – what should? What should politics look like when based upon human freedom and civil liberties? Self-determination emerged as an answer, a way for modern people to appropriate their politics. I suggest that self-determination outlines a distinctively modern path for political power, based less on force and fear, more on popular willpower. Self-determination emerged as a political *speech-act*, a performative utterance (Austin 1975) that manifests the people's capacity, and right, to will polities into existence. Indeed, if modern statecraft were witchcraft, "self-determination" would be its spell, cast to re-chart borders, to wreck states, and to erect new ones. Conducting "normative concept analysis" (Abulof 2015b) on self-determination reveals its putative power as a world-making word; partaking in the language of legitimation, it does not merely describe reality, but purports to change it too (Abulof 2016a).

Historically, I show self-determination as exceptionally protean – a highly volatile, yet volitional principle, its pendulum oscillating through a series of curious conversions: From religious to secular, from philosophical to political, from ideational to practical, from individual

DOI: 10.4324/9781003036593-3

to collective, from communist to national, from liberal to totalitarian – and, sometimes, back again.

I identity and analyze three formative, ideational-discursive phases in the emergence of self-determination: Enlightenment (from theology to humanism), communism (its Marxist roots and socialist fruits), and Wilsonianism (liberal internationalism for global democratic peace). While we usually regard self-determination as inherently secular, it in fact emerged as a theological principle ascribed not to man but to God. I unearth the very first appearance of "self-determination" in the English Church's discourse in 1666, and suggest that subsequent Enlightenment thinkers humanized self-determination, not least for their politics. Communists turned self-determination into a principle of nationalism; Marx employed it to leverage the European Spring of Nations, and Lenin used it strategically to lead, via nationalism, to socialism. Finally, in the twilight of World War I, Wilson propagated self-determination as a vehicle for democracy and peace, worldwide, while his aides and allies tried to curb it.

Throughout, a fascinating pattern emerges: Self-determination is a treacherous principle. English churchmen applied it to forestall the advent of human freedom and its political effects, precisely what subsequent Enlightenment thinkers used it to advance. Communists employed it to intercept or else harness nationalism, but nationalists outdid them in their own language game. Liberals tried to appropriate self-determination to dismantle its authoritarian explosiveness, but the rise of Nazism blew up the ground on which they stood. Self-determination is a double-edged principle (Abulof and Cordell 2016).

## Common ground, midair: self-determination's specious power

In principle, whether the modern nation-state is a "sleeping beauty" awaiting history's kiss, or a "Frankenstein's monster" fabricated by devious elites, its first expression is "self-determination." After all, what justifies the inter*national* system but national self-determination? This justificatory concept effectively "provide[s] the political power and the moral meaning to the idea of an international society" (Hurrell 2007: 121). Arguably, "no phrase has had greater political resonance in the last one hundred years than 'self-determination'" (Weitz 2015: 462), and "there may be no other term in modern political discourse which is used with more emotion and passion" (Neuberger 2001: 391). Thus, while most self-determination scholars employ diplomatic (e.g. Lynch 2002), normative (Archibugi 2003), and legal (Vidmar 2009) perspectives, here I complement these important vistas by focusing on self-determination discourse (e.g. Fisch 2015).

The most striking aspect of self-determination discourse is that it defies the great ideological divides of the twentieth century. Self-determination is the only normative common ground of the century's leading ideologies: liberalism, socialism, and nationalism. It was the single shared principle to which FDR, Joseph Stalin, and Adolf Hitler subscribed – in words, though rarely in action. The concept so dominated twentieth-century political discourse that no prominent leader from any camp dared speak against it. This may have prompted Hannum (1996: 27) to conclude, "Perhaps no contemporary norm of international law has been so vigorously promoted or so widely accepted as the right of all peoples to self-determination." Why so? What makes this principle so appealing to modern people, and politics? Does this common ground truly hold?

The answer lies in the very nature of politics. Scholars typically regard politics as the public struggle over power – power over people. Power, in turn, is the capacity to control, "to produce effects or outcomes that would not otherwise have occurred," getting our way despite possible resistance (Wrong 1995: xx). Setting aside the "soft power" of persuasion and passion (and the generalized notion of the "power *to*"), what creates power *over* people?

There are two familiar paths to such power: force and fear. You may act because one forces you to, or for fearing that they might hurt you if you don't. Superior force can coerce action, while fear can achieve the same effect without direct contact. The two familiar paths of power – force and fear – correspond with the two familiar facets of liberty – non-interference and non-domination, respectively (Pettit 1997). Force is interference, while domination instills fear of retribution. This is no surprise; power and liberty intensively entwine, both being about control. Power is about the *capacity* to control; liberty is about *who* controls *what* (or *ought* to control) – corresponding with Berlin's (2002: 36) positive and negative liberties, respectively.

But there is another, more elusive, path to power over people: the will. Occasionally, we yield without being forced or afraid – we comply simply because others will it. Between hard and soft power, will is a liminal, often neglected, category of control. In Milgram's (1974) famous studies on "obedience to authority," the experimenter neither forced nor intimidated the participants, but merely expressed his resolute will; his clout was enough for most participants to obey. Real-world examples abound, e.g., Stalinist USSR cultivating "blind obedience to the will of the Leader" (Medvedev and Shriver 1989: 652).

Still, not every will is power; in fact, this rarely happens. The epitome of commanding willpower is God. Orthodox Jews typically observe Shabbat because God supposedly wants them to. Inquiring "so what – why do you do what God wants you to?" makes little sense to them. The divine will itself suffices for believers. An omnipotent God can obviously force His way, or instill fear, but arguably, neither force nor fear (not even persuasion) is needed. Submission is sublimated through the sublime. Two purported qualities make this will so powerful: God is inherently good and utterly independent. His virtuousness is innate and eternal, his independence literal: God depends on nothing but Himself, a "first cause" willing worlds through words into existence.

In the historical analysis provided in this chapter, I propose that this divine ideal of the will underpins self-determination's mass appeal. People have employed self-determination to enshrine their own collective, human, willpower. They framed self-determination as inherently good, thus morally incontestable (by all modern ideologies). Such self-determination is not merely about getting independence; it *is* independence. Thus construed, independence constitutes the third meaning of liberty. Arguably, being released from coercion (non-interference) or exempt from potential intimidation (non-domination), is not enough to be fully liberated. One also needs to be able to determine things by one*self*. Thus framed, self-determination is a self-contained principle.

The ideal of divine-like willpower bedevils self-determination. Crawford (2001: 7) once commented that "the 'right of self-determination of peoples' is perhaps the most controversial and contested of the many controversial and contested terms in the vocabulary of international law." Why so? Partly because *ideal* self-determination cannot be a qualified right at all; as an assertion of will, self-determination requires no one's permission. In fact, if you need authorization, you lack self-determination, effectively turning "the right of self-determination" into an antinomy.

People, however, had to realize, the hard way, that they are no God. They are not innately good, if only for the obvious reason they keep debating what is good. And they are not utterly independent. If anything, quite the opposite: humans are fundamentally dependent. The common ground of self-determination is thus suspended midair.

This realization, however inconscient, of human limitations drives the attempts to square the circle. The result: turning self-determination into a right, a principle perforce predicated on the intents and capacities of others. Appending right to the principle made it clear: Determination is as much others' as the self's; in fact, in political matters, others determine the self, much more than the other way around.

The allure of self-determination's omnipotence, however, has not vanished with its legal qualification. In trying to fulfill that powerful promise, thinkers and practitioners turned national self-determination into the prime speech-act of modern politics. Some utterances, Austin (1975) notes, do not merely describe; they act. Going beyond content (semantics) to context (pragmatics), words can endow meaning (a locutionary act) with realized intent (an illocutionary act) to affect the listeners' beliefs or behaviors (a perlocutionary act). For example: meaningful speech ("I now pronounce you husband and wife"), with an intent (to wed), can have a social effect (marriage).

National self-determination, I submit, is a political speech-act: a performative, deliberate utterance seeking, occasionally having, sociopolitical effects. It does so by allying prescription with persuasion (illocutionary with perlocutionary act): self-determination does not merely suggest what ought to be done but generates and galvanizes the agent who ought to do it – the "self," *the people.*

For millennia, the political answer to *"who* controls *what?"* was clear: the state controls (and ought to control) the people; politics was thus more about *"what* controls *whom."* The idea/l of self-determination challenged that traditional outlook, substituting people for God as the source of political legitimacy (Connor 2002). Indeed, "self-determination is an ending process of self-identification" (Allotr 1993: 204), with potentially profound political implications. Accordingly, individuals can determine their social identity, *inter alia* their peoplehood, and the people can determine their polity. "And God said, Let there be light: and there was light" (Genesis 1:3), and through self-determination, people – and peoples – tried to follow suit. Like the independent good God, people could now proclaim "Let there be state (our state!)," and expect it to happen.

By establishing the people-turn-nation – whether ethnic or civic – as the "master" of political meanings and actions, self-determination legitimates a world of nation-states – where national boundaries should make state borders, not the other way around. Self-determination thus reveals, and seeks to rectify, the "nation-state mismatch": the incongruence between national boundaries and state borders. "We, the people" should be calling the political shots, spelling states into a legitimate existence.

The speech-act of self-determination, however, is no metaphysical spell. Between the ideal and the real, self-determination ended up submerged in a precarious paradox. "On the surface it seemed reasonable: let the people decide," Sir Ivor Jennings (1956: 56) commented, "It was in fact ridiculous, because the people cannot decide until someone decides who are the people." States readily dispensed with this ridicule to become that decisive "someone." Rather than a collective human agent (a people), an anthropomorphized structure (the state) came to determine, and effectively tame, self-determination (Abulof 2020). Moreover, though backing *democracy,* self-determination often boosted autocracy. Extolling the sacred "will of the people," autocrats could purport to know what the people truly want, and need – reflecting their higher, better, selves – thus "coercing others for the own sake" (Berlin 2002: 179).

## Enlightenment: deification and humanization

Self-determination appears thoroughly secular, and today it certainly is. This brief section is the first study to set the record straight, revealing self-determination's theological origins amidst Enlightenment. This "origin story" bears not only historical but theoretical and contemporary importance too – helping us better understand the principle's appeal and troubles, and its current trajectory.

Self-determination was born in 1666, during *annus mirabilis*, Isaac Newton's year of wonders. The English physicist, only 23 at the time, used the closure of Cambridge University by a pandemic outbreak to observe an apple falling from a tree to bring the Scientific Revolution to a magnificent conclusion. At the same time, not too far away, Samuel Parker, a 26-year-old English churchman, was troubled by another, more biblical, fall, and coined the term "self-determination" to make his case.

It was a pious case for reconciling God's dominion with civil sovereignty. A devotee of the Stuart Restoration (1660–1688) that reinstated British monarchy, Parker came close on the high heels of Hobbes, and his *Leviathan*'s plea for a monarch-led social contract. And like his pre-eminent contemporary, Parker too was trying to figure out a way out of the wounded woods planted by the English Civil War (1642–1651) and the ongoing, often violent, civil and religious clashes that engulfed his country.

Parker sensed something sinister ensuing in the wake of the Scientific Revolution and the coming Enlightenment. Liberty was on the rise, in principle if not in practice, undermining the supremacy of God's will with subversive assertions about human moral agency embodied in people's independent will. Parker took pains to show that this was a dangerous chimera, and "self-determination" was his key.

For Parker (1666: 30–31), God alone possesses the true "power of self-determination." Man's liberty falters since people, like other animals, are always, somehow, in need, and so are never entirely liberated. "Divine will," on the other hand, "has Power and Dominion over its own actions, and that can be determined only by its own intrinsic energy," that is, proceeding from "a choosing and self-determining Principle." What God self-determines is independently and inherently good, and thus constitutes the only fountain and foundation for authority, expressed through monarchy – absolute and patriarchal. Antithetically, human conscience provides a poor moral guidance, and must submit to the magistrate which should alone, for peace's sake, direct social life.

Parker's thesis reverberated soon after the publication of his 1666 polemic treatise. In 1674–1675, in parallel, and possibly in a concerted effort, several English clergymen and theologians started to employ "self-determination" in their politico-religious treatises. Matthew Scrivener (1674: 309), Joseph Truman (1675: 80), Richard Baxter (1675: 223), and others followed Parker by making self-determination a rhetorical device to reaffirm the superiority of God's will, and the inferiority of people – to both God and His monarchical agents (Jewell 2004).

Then came John Locke, and self-determination took a humanistic turn. Locke read Parker's works, and in 1670 he composed his response. Though brief and unpublished, it may be decisive in Locke's intellectual evolution. Here Locke developed, likely for the very first time, his criticism of absolute, patriarchal authority, which Parker espoused, and here he made his radical case that "all government, whether monarchical or other, is only from the consent of the people" (cited in Marshall 1994: 75). Locke's 1670 response to Parker may be read as an unpublished draft for his seminal *Two Treatises of Government* (1689), foreshadowing his attack on Sir Robert Filmer's *Patriarcha* in the first treatise, his social contract theory in the second.

In the very same year, concluding his *An Essay Concerning Human Understanding*, Locke (1775 [1689]: 293) looked at self-determination and upended Parker's argument – on rational-theological grounds. Believing that men's actions are punishable by a just God creates a nexus "between guilt and a power to do otherwise; between a power to do otherwise and freedom; and between freedom and self-determination," eventually revealing "connexion between men and self-determination." Thus, "men can determine themselves," bearing the heavy responsibly of their freedom. However religiously inspired, Locke's argument effectively jostled God from the domain of self-determination.

"Dare to know" (*Sapere aude*) was of course Immanuel Kant's Enlightenment credo, and for the German philosopher, self-determination drives that daring pursuit – and justifies it too. It is possible that Kant employed "self-determination" (*Selbstbestimmung* in German) unaware of its century-old English genesis. It is also possible that Kant encountered self-determination in Locke's 1689 *Human Understanding*, either directly or, more likely, through Johann Nicolaus Tetens (aka the "German Locke"), who followed the English thinker's take on self-consciousness (Kitcher 2011).

For Kant, self-determination is humanity's ultimate goal. Humans are endowed with the freedom of the will to choose and act. But choosing is not enough. Free will's real challenge lies in attaining autonomy (or self-legislation, which Kant employs interchangeably with self-determination), that is, in choosing independently of other people and one's own inclinations. When freedom becomes a spontaneous, independent reason, self-determining itself turns autonomous – choosing by rational, thus universal, laws that serve a high goal. In Kant's (2011: 82–85) words, "The will is thought as a capacity to determine itself to action," and "what serves the will as the objective ground of its self-determination is the end."

But what ground, what goal, is good enough for such an ideal self-determination? Kant's (2011: 84–85) categorical imperative takes a teleological leap. The end is humanity itself: "a human being and generally every rational being *exists* as an end in itself, *not merely as a means*." Crucially, humanity is "an absolute worth . . . an *end in itself*," because it can create ends. For Kant, "humanity is nothing other than the capacity to choose ends" (Guyer 2005: 154, emphasis in original).

Capable of giving to itself universal laws, humanity at its autonomous best becomes *the* self-determining subject. If Parker deified self-determination through God, Kant comes close to deifying humanity through self-determination – exercising independent, universal will. And if Locke upended Parker's argument, Kant overturned it. Humans are surely not as self-caused as God, but they can be self-willed.

Still, we must recall, Kant's self-confidence is Enlightenment's swan song, resorting to universal "pure reason" to uphold its promise. The promise of self-determination was borne by an idealized version of universal humanity, endowed with independent "pure reason," not actual humans amidst changing sociopolitical circumstances.

It was G.W.F. Hegel, at the heels of Kant, who socialized self-determination. Hegel employed the concept explicitly, and quite frequently, to address the metaphysical, moral and practical conundrums of human freedom. Self-determination is the gist of full, moral, freedom, for "Morality means that the subject in its freedom posits out of itself the determinations of the good, the ethical and what is right" (cited in Duquette 2003: 81).

For Hegel, self-determination perforce involves people who are socially embedded, thus responsible for others (Church 2012). Society and its politics, however, imbues self-determination with existential paradoxes, which, Hegel believed, Rousseau expressed most clearly. Both the suggestions that "man is born free" and that people should "be forced to be free" fly in the face of self-determination, which should be wholly volitional and independent. But how can that ideal become real, when man is nonetheless "everywhere . . . in chains"? In the wake of the Enlightenment's maculate conception of self-determination, could a more meticulous politicization of this principle help?

## Communism: nationalization

While Parker, Locke, Kant, and Hegel turned to self-determination for both theo-philosophical and political reasons, a more vigorous (secular) politicization of "self-determination" transpired in the second half of the nineteenth century. The globalization of modern political thought, including nationalism, started earlier (Armitage 2013) with revolutions in England (1688), the United States (1775–1783) and France (1789), echoing in the first partition of Poland (1772) and in the Latin American wars of independence, but none explicitly referred to "self-determination."

The Revolutions of 1848 marked the *nationalization* of political self-determination, tellingly transpiring through communism. The year that saw the publication of the *Manifesto of the Communist Party* also saw the *Manifesto to the European Peoples*, issued by the 1848 Prague Slavic Congress, avowing the "equal rights of all nations" to liberty. Can Marxism and nationalism coalesce? Marx certainly thought they might, if the hierarchy between class and nation is clear, favoring the former. For Marx and Engels, the "popular sovereignty" of the French Revolution was largely bourgeois, sidestepping the proletariat. Dissolving this smoke screen, the *Communist Manifesto* thus proclaims: "the worker has no country." The events of 1848 suggested the possibility of creating this country by riding the rising tide of nationalism.

This was no small task, as tensions between the socialist imperative and the nationalist creed became apparent. Self-determination became the conceptual springboard for this move. Marx famously turned Hegel's spiritual dialectics material, but he also turned "self-determination" far more political, and national. The first usage of the phrase came in Marx's 1865 *Proclamation on the Polish Question*, "[assuring] to Poland the right of self-determination which belongs to every nation" (cited in Carr 1985 [1950]: 416; see also Connor 1969). But is it truly the right of "every nation"? Poland was an easy case, part of the struggle against the reactionary Tsar. What about other (potential) peoples?

Marx and Engels preferred large, economically viable units, and accordingly believed that self-determination should be reserved for "nations," big peoples like Germans and Poles, not "nationalities," smaller communities, like Serbs and Czechs, that should remain part of a bigger state. This is the first, but certainly not the last, sign of what would become the hallmark of the politics of self-determination: the attempts to tame, indeed domesticate, it (Fisch 2015). Indeed, turning self-determination national through Marx(ism) was a means towards the ultimate end: the proletarian revolution.

Engels's postscript to the 1893 Italian edition of the *Manifesto* is revealing: "if the Revolution of 1848 was not a socialist revolution, it paved the way, prepared the ground for the latter," since "without restoring autonomy and unity to each nation, it will be impossible to achieve the international union of the proletariat" (Marx and Engels [1848] 1898). Overall, in communism, both formative and mature, "formal support for the right of national self-determination in the abstract, coupled with very selective support for national movements in the realm of action" (Connor 1984: 20).

Self-determination took center stage at the Second International Socialist Congress in London (1896), which declared that "it stands for the full right of all nations to self-determination [*Selbstbestimmungsrecht*] and expresses its sympathy for the workers of every country now suffering under the yoke of military, national or other absolutism." The theme is later evoked, with Lenin's support, in the 1903 First Program of the Russian Social Democratic Labor Party (RSDLP), declaring, "All nationalities forming the state have the right to self-determination."

This is the backdrop for the ensuing inner-socialist debate about self-determination. Rosa Luxemburg, a leading Marxist theorist and revolutionary, played a key role. In a series of articles on *The National Question and Autonomy*, Luxemburg ([1908–1909] 1976), denounced the 1903 RSDLP platform. With the secessionist Polish case in mind, she depicted the right to self-determination as a *bourgeois* nationalism, which might endanger socialist internationalism (namely, promoting socialism in all countries). This principle, Luxemburg argues, is nothing but "a metaphysical formula which leaves the determination of the nationality question up to each of the nationalities according to their whims," and she sarcastically comments, "The 'right' of a nation to freedom is only worth as much as the 'right' of each man to eat off gold plates." When Luxemburg writes, "The actual possibility of 'self-determination' for all ethnic groups or otherwise defined nationalities is a utopia," one clearly senses it is dystopia she has in mind. That too was to be become a leitmotif of self-determination politics: viewing this principle as dangerously naïve, an ideal that puts the real at risk.

Stalin ([1913] 1954, emphasis in original) adds another interesting facet to early socialist discourse on self-determination, stating unequivocally: "The right of self-determination means that only the nation itself has the right to determine its destiny . . . It has the right to complete secession. Nations are sovereign, and all nations have equal rights." Yet, the taming of self-determination quickly surfaces: "No demand of a nation which is striving for self-determination will 'contradict the precise meaning' of the Social-Democratic programme." Speaking in the name of "the interests of the proletariat," Stalin eventually rejected both cultural autonomy and full secession, instead concluding that "*regional autonomy is an essential element* in the solution of the national question."

Lenin's ([1916] 1964) position was different, seeing self-determination as not only compatible with, but in fact a precondition for, the international socialist revolution:

> It would be a betrayal of socialism to refuse to implement the self-determination of nations under socialism . . . We say: In order that we may have the strength to accomplish the socialist revolution and overthrow the bourgeoisie, the workers must unite more closely and this close union is promoted by the struggle for self-determination.

Contra Engels's distinction between qualified and unqualified peoples, and Stalin rejecting, in both words and action, self-determination as (potential) secession, Lenin ([1914] 1971) held that "it would be wrong to interpret the right to self-determination as meaning anything but the right to existence as a separate state," and not just as an "autonomous nation."

Applying self-determination to all nations, big and small, ethnic and civic – all the way through to full sovereignty – gave this original, ideal self-determination its popular appeal. The socialist move turned self-determination from an intellectual "act of speech" into a political speech-act – from signifying an idea into a principle powerful enough to mobilize people for changing political reality. But for Lenin, it was already part of a larger scheme: "By conceding all, or rather, by seeming to concede all to nationalism, one in fact was promoting internationalism . . . support for the slogan of self-determination, rather than acting as a stimulant to nationalism, would prove to be an anesthetic" (Connor 1984: 34) – to check self-determination, allow it to blossom.

The fall of the Tsarist regime in March 1917 signaled the ascendance of Lenin's proactive and extensive interpretation of self-determination. Partly as a way to overtrump the doctrine of self-determination as propagated by others, Lenin elevated the concept from the realm of intellectual polemics into international diplomacy (Connor 1984: 33). The Bolshevik *Declaration of the Rights of the Peoples of Russia* (November 2, 1917) emphasized "the right of the peoples of Russia to free self-determination, even to the point of separation and the formation of an independent state" (Nation 1918: 817). The concept was harnessed by the Bolsheviks to target the Provisional Government, which finally announced that it too sought to attain "a durable peace on the basis of the right of nations to decide their own destinies" (cited in Musgrave 1997: 17).

The Russian announcements were followed by declarations of independence by non-Russian groups. Self-determination was explicitly invoked. For example, upon the Bolshevik *Declaration*, Finland proclaimed independence, which the Soviet government recognized a month later. Meanwhile, Ukrainian President Vinichenko's proclamation of autonomy on November 20, 1917, was followed by his plea for inclusion in the January 1918 German–Russian peace negotiations at Brest-Litovsk, arguing from the outset that peace "must assure to every people, even the smallest, full and unlimited national self-determination" (Horne and Austin 1920: 25). It is in this context, in the twilight of World War I, that self-determination became a more pronounced national speech-act: explicitly invoking self-determination, peoples asserted collective identities, and polities sought political ends.

The first leader to explicitly subscribe to national self-determination, Lenin was also the first to (ab)use it to further his state's territorial interests at the expense of other peoples – and to become torn by the growing gap between the principle and its practice. Lenin and his disciples learned to attach a "great strategic value . . . to being identified as stalwart defenders of self-determination of the Afro-Asian peoples" (Connor 1984: 33). At the same time, as in the conquest of the borderlands, Lenin was willing to subordinate his notion of self-determination to Soviet interests, and, above all, the cause of the proletarian revolution.

And yet, in the twilight of his reign, amidst Stalin's attempt to subject Georgia to Moscow – Lenin still held to his ideal self-determination. In his "Last Testament" letter on *The Question of Nationalities or "Autonomisation,"* Lenin ([1922] 1964) observed,

> It is quite natural that in such circumstances the "freedom to secede from the union" by which we justify ourselves will be a mere scrap of paper, unable to defend the non-Russians from the onslaught of that really Russian man, the Great-Russian chauvinist, in substance a rascal and a tyrant, such as the typical Russian bureaucrat is.

## Wilson: propagation and democratization

Marx turned self-determination national, Lenin made it a powerful speech-act, and Wilson universalized it – rendering it, in word and deed, a *universal* principle of global politics headed towards the promised global land of peaceful liberal democracy. Was Wilson influenced directly by Lenin, or is there a missing link between the two?

I suggest one possible link. The first liberal leader to explicitly speak of national self-determination was not Woodrow Wilson, but the British premier Lloyd George. Outlining the three grand "British War Aims" on January 5, 1918, George (1918) posited the principle as the cornerstone of the second aim: "a territorial settlement must be secured, based on the right of self-determination or the consent of the governed" (cited in Doumanis 2016: 121). It is reasonable to assume that Lloyd George was familiar with the socialist rhetoric on self-determination, and although I lack conclusive evidence, that Wilson was influenced by Lloyd George.

Either way, Wilson's famous "Fourteen Points" speech (January 8, 1918) made no explicit reference to "self-determination." Shortly after Lloyd George's war aims speech, Wilson employed the exact phrase for the first time. In an address delivered on February 11, 1918, before a joint session of the US Congress, Wilson declared: "National aspirations must be respected; peoples may now be dominated and governed only by their own consent. 'Self-determination' is not a mere phrase. It is an imperative principle of actions which statesmen will henceforth ignore at their peril."

Lenin and Wilson were ideologically apart, but both saw national self-determination as a key strategy – not a mere tactic – to an even greater goal. For Lenin, nationalism was a prerequisite for socialist internationalism; for Wilson, for a democratic interstate peace (Smith 2017). Unaware of its potential resonance in Europe and beyond, and without due planning, Wilson uttered "self-determination" not as a program but as a creed, utilized to augment the war efforts, helping to "make the world safe for democracy" (Lynch 2002). Wilson thus accused the Germans of undermining "the ideals of justice and humanity and liberty, the principle of the free self-determination of nations upon which all the modern world insists" (April 6, 1918; New York Times 1918: 277).

Wilson's propaganda machine was pivotal in transforming self-determination into a universal speech-act, paradoxically employing "the conscious and intelligent manipulation" of the unconscious self to market self-determination (Bernays 1928; see also Hamilton 2020). But whether self-determination tapped into the conscious or the unconscious of people, it resonated wide and deep, boosted in practice by the Allied powers' military gains. Importantly, self-determination is color-blind, with "no 'racial' connotations," and could thus be embraced by everyone (Kohn 1958: 536).

Seemingly overnight, worldwide calls for political action were made in the name of self-determination. Uttering the words mattered: invoking self-determination, a people can become a nation, presumably entitled to independence. Collective identity and the collective's polity was now predicated on a specific speech. Manela (2007) traced the immense and immediate impact that "the Wilsonian moment" had on colonized societies in Egypt, India, China, and Korea. Uprisings, reform movements, and revolutions were carried out under the banner of self-determination. By universalizing self-determination, the "Wilsonian moment" arguably enthroned the will of the people "at the center of the discourse of legitimacy in international relations," establishing "the self-determining nation-state as the only legitimate political form throughout the globe" (Manela 2007: 5).

In a matter of months, a phrase conceived by the English Church, humanized by Enlightenment intellectuals, and nationalized at the hands of socialist thinkers, became a pervasive, near-universal principle, invoked by politicians, diplomats, and publics alike, reshaping world politics. Wilson himself was astounded at the upshot of his words, at the popular and deep chords they struck, and the political implications. Most revealing was his meeting in Paris (June 11, 1919) with Frank Walsh, chairman of the American Commission on Irish Independence, and worth presenting at some length. Walsh pleaded:

> Mr. President, when you uttered those words declaring that all nations had a right to self-determination . . . you voiced the aspirations of countless millions of people that had been saying them to each other, and begging governments that oppressed them to recognize them. When you, as head of the most powerful nation in the world, uttered them, and they received the assent of the representatives of all the nations, it became a fact, Mr. President. Those people are imbued with the principle. They may be killed trying to vindicate it, but they can no longer be kept in subjection by the action of diplomats, government officials, or even governments. They are freed now.

Were they? Words alone, even speech-acts, however politically potent, cannot liberate people or peoples. Turning self-determination's illocutionary ideal into perlocutionary reality – a world of self-determining nation-states – required both vision *and* force. Walsh correctly saw self-determination as giving voice to hitherto silent millions, and recognized that by US might "it became a fact," but people with power did not necessarily favor such a principle, and Wilson started to realize this:

> You have touched on the great metaphysical tragedy of today. My words have raised hope in the hearts of millions of people. It is my wish that they have that; but could you imagine that you could revolutionize the world at once, could you imagine that those peoples could come into that at once? . . . When I gave utterance to those words,

I said them without a knowledge that nationalities existed, which are coming to us day after day . . . No one knows the feelings that are inside of me while I am meeting with these people and discussing these things . . . It distresses me. But I believe, as you gentlemen do, in Divine Providence, and I am in His hands, and I don't care what happens me individually. I believe these things and I know that countless millions of other people believe them

*(United States Senate 1919: 838).*

Wilson's poignant confession for raising "hope in the hearts of millions . . . without a knowledge that nationalities existed" is a humbling reminder of the limitations of a visionary leadership. Wilson initially saw nation through the American civic, liberal lens, sidestepping ethnonationalism (Lynch 2002: 425), but he seems to have eventually realized his mistake: Nations are often ethnic, and ideal self-determination promises them too, even if they are illiberal or antiliberal, the right to become independent. The Wilsonian propagation of self-determination succeeded; its liberal democratization often failed.

Equally revealing is Wilson's resort to "Divine Providence": fearing that this humanized principle was getting out of hand, Wilson *unwittingly* returned to its Godly origins. Are humans too fallible to self-determine themselves, let alone their politics?

Several thinkers and politicians believed they were. Disillusionment with self-determination had already revealed itself at the 1919 Paris Peace Conference: "the British and American delegations were anxious to confine self-determination to Europe, while the French and Italian delegations would have preferred to confine it to Utopia" (Cobban 1970: 66). Indeed, like the socialists, liberal leaders too have partaken in the curbing self-determination, and if self-determination is a principle of political hope, its chronicles also chart constant frustrations, often igniting violence, sometimes leading to despair.

Most remarkable is the lament by Robert Lansing (1921: 97–98), Wilson's own Secretary of State. Like Wilson, Lansing too realized that "the phrase [self-determination] is simply loaded with dynamite"; unlike Wilson, however, Lansing resolutely proclaimed that "this principle is dangerous to peace and stability," by "putting such ideas into the minds of certain races."

Wilson died in 1924, Lansing in 1928, a year before the Great Depression and the global calamity in its wake. Was self-determination a culprit in the making of World War II? We may never know, because ultimately, from the very ascendance of self-determination, Lansing's lament effectively prevailed over Wilson's hopeful vision.

The chronicles of the past century show why and how (Abulof 2016b, 2020; Fisch 2015). Self-determination repeatedly showed itself to be a precarious principle. Wilson used self-determination, intending its confinement to liberal democratic hands, Lansing to avoid its spread to "certain races," and Hitler to create *Lebensraum* for one such race. Cold War leaders used it to undermine the moral standing of their rival, and anti-colonialist leaders to keep their new states' territorial integrity. Today, liberals turn to self-determination to prevent ethnonationalism from tearing apart the benevolent post–World War II Leviathans, autocrats to excuse the territorial appetite. In the process, self-determination, reframed by Enlightenment thinkers to empower humanity, has become the battleground of powerful states seeking mastery over peoples.

## Conclusions

This chapter has traced the emergence of self-determination, theoretically and historically, focusing on the principle's less familiar yet formative period. I showed how self-determination became a defining principle of modern politics, of people's efforts to appropriate authority (legitimate power) that was once considered God's. The attempt, I submit, was only half successful: God was partly dethroned, but people failed to ascend to the seat of absolute legitimacy. The modern state, emerging as an intermediary Leviathan, often aided civil liberties but further demonstrated the human failure to attain a divinelike willpower – innately good and independent.

Self-determination has been a confused, and confusing, compass (Abulof 2015a). Mishandling self-determination, modern states may have pulled the normative rug from beneath their own feet, suspending the interstate system in mid-air. The taming of self-determination has effectively curbed the establishment of new states and the re-charting of borders, based on ethnonational grids. The "nation-state mismatch" lingers. And yet, the domestication of self-determination has not killed nationalism; it has recently revived in the West and abides in the rest. All along, mishandling self-determination has undermined the political legitimacy of established states and regimes, exposing both state-holders and stateless peoples to mounting crises. Thus, every crisis that inflicts the state Leviathan, whether moral or material, becomes, in the modern era, an occasion for reviving self-determination.

Treating (ethno)nationalism like a whack-a-mole game is unlikely to produce better results in the future. Like a grinning Cheshire cat, and not unlike religion, nationalism too occasionally seems to disappear here, only to surface later elsewhere. Perhaps cultivating self-determination as a principle of choice, rather than of control, could pave a path out of this impasse, but that would require seeing states, old and new, as means to human ends, not the other way around. True, divinelike self-determination is a chimera: people are morally flawed and inherently dependent. But they have the freedom to choose their dependencies.

# References

Abulof, U. (2015a). The Confused Compass: From Self-Determination to State-Determination. *Ethnopolitics* 14 (5), pp. 488–497.

Abulof, U. (2015b). Normative Concepts Analysis: Unpacking the Language of Legitimation. *International Journal of Social Research Methodology* 18 (1), pp. 73–89.

Abulof, U. (2016a). Public Political Thought: Bridging the Sociological: Philosophical Divide in the Study of Legitimacy. *The British Journal of Sociology* 67 (2), pp. 371–391.

Abulof, U. (2016b). We the Peoples? The Strange Demise of Self-Determination. *European Journal of International Relations* 22 (3), pp. 536–565.

Abulof, U. (2020). Taming Self-Determination: The Trials of a Political Speech-Act. *International Political Science Review* 41 (5), pp. 622–637.

Abulof, U., and K. Cordell. (2016). *Self-Determination in the Early Twenty-First Century: A Double Edged Concept.* New York: Routledge.

Allotr, P. (1993). Self-Determination: Absolute Right or Social Poetry? In *Modern Law of Self-Determination*, ed. C. Tomuschat. Boston: M. Nijhoff Publishers.

Archibugi, D. (2003). A Critical Analysis of the Self-Determination of Peoples: A Cosmopolitan Perspective. *Constellations* 10 (4), pp. 488–505.

Armitage, David. (2013). *Foundations of Modern International Thought.* New York: Cambridge University Press.

Austin, J.L. (1975). *How to Do Things with Words.* 2nd ed. Oxford: Clarendon Press.

Baxter, R. (1675). *A Treatise of Self-Denial: By Richard Baxter, Pastor of the Church at Kederminster.* 2nd ed. London: printed by Robert White, for Nevil Simmons at the Princes Arms in Saint Pauls Church-yard.

Berlin, I. (2002). *Liberty: Incorporating Four Essays on Liberty.* Edited by H. Hardy and I. Harris. Oxford: Oxford University Press.

Bernays, E.L. (1928). *Propaganda.* New York: H. Liveright.

Carr, E.H. 1985 [1950]. *The Bolshevik Revolution, 1917–1923.* New York: W.W. Norton.

Church, J. (2012). G.W.F. Hegel on Self-Determination and Democratic Theory. *American Journal of Political Science* 56 (4), pp. 1021–1039.

Cobban, A. (1970). *The Nation State and National Self-Determination.* New York: Crowell.

Connor, W.F. (1969). The Ethnic Dilemma in Marxist-Leninist Doctrine. *World Affairs* 132 (1), pp. 5–12.

Connor, W.F. (1984). *The National Question in Marxist-Leninist Theory and Strategy*. Princeton, NJ: Princeton University Press.

Connor, W.F. (2002). Nationalism and Political Illegitimacy. In *Ethnonationalism in the Contemporary World: Walker Connor and the Study of Nationalism*, ed. D. Conversi. New York: Routledge.

Crawford, J. (2001). The Right of Self-Determination in International Law: Its Development and Future. In *People's Rights*, ed. P. Alston. New York: Oxford University Press.

Doumanis, Nicholas. (2016). *The Oxford Handbook of European History, 1914–1945*. Oxford Handbooks. New York: Oxford University Press.

Duquette, D.A. (ed.). (2003). *Hegel's History of Philosophy: New Interpretations*. Albany, NY: State University of New York Press.

Fisch, J. (2015). *The Right of Self-Determination of Peoples: The Domestication of an Illusion*. Translated by A. Mage. New York, NY: Cambridge University Press.

Guyer, P. (2005). *Kant's System of Nature and Freedom: Selected Essays*. New York: Oxford University Press.

Hamilton, J.M. (2020). *Manipulating the Masses: Woodrow Wilson and the Birth of American Propaganda*. Baton Rouge: Louisiana State University Press.

Hannum, H. (1996). *Autonomy, Sovereignty, and Self-Determination: The Accommodation of Conflicting Rights*. Rev. ed. Philadelphia: University of Pennsylvania Press.

Horne, C.F., and W.F. Austin. (1920). *The Great Events of the Great War: A Comprehensive and Readable Source Record of the World's Great War*. New York: J. J. Little & Ives co.

Hurrell, A. (2007). *On Global Order: Power, Values, and the Constitution of International Society*. New York: Oxford University Press.

Jennings, I. (1956). *The Approach to Self-Government*. Cambridge: University Press.

Jewell, J. (2004). *Authority's Advocate: Samuel Parker, Religion, and Politics in Restoration England*. Tallahassee: The Florida State University.

Kant, I. (2011). *Groundwork of the Metaphysics of Morals: A German-English Edition*. Translated by M.J. Gregor. New York: Cambridge University Press.

Kitcher, P. (2011). *Kant's Thinker*. New York: Oxford University Press.

Kohn, H. (1958). The United Nations and National Self-Determination. *The Review of Politics* 20 (4), pp. 526–545.

Lansing, R. (1921). *The Peace Negotiations, a Personal Narrative*. New York: Houghton Mifflin Company.

Lenin, V.I. ([1914] 1971). *The Right of Nations to Self-Determination*. Translated by B. Isaacs. Moscow: Progress Publishers.

Lenin, V.I. ([1916] 1964). The Discussion on Self-Determination Summed Up. In *Collected Works*. Vol. 22. Moscow: Progress Publishers.

Lenin, V.I. ([1922] 1964). The Question of Nationalities or "Autonomisation." In *Collected Works*. Vol. 36. Moscow: Progress Publishers.

Locke, J. 1775 [1689]. *An Essay Concerning Human Understanding in Four Books*. 17th ed. London: John Beecroft.

Luxemburg, R., and H.B. Davis. [1908–1909] 1976. *The National Question: Selected Writings*. New York: Monthly Review Press.

Lynch, A. (2002). Woodrow Wilson and the Principle of "National Self-Determination": A Reconsideration. *Review of International Studies* 28 (2), pp. 419–436.

Manela, E. (2007). *The Wilsonian Moment: Self-Determination and the International Origins of Anticolonial Nationalism*. New York: Oxford University Press.

Marshall, J. (1994). *John Locke: Resistance, Religion, and Responsibility*. Cambridge; New York: Cambridge University Press.

Marx, K., and F. Engels. [1848] 1898. *Manifesto of the Communist Party*. 2nd ed. New York: The National Executive Committee of the Socialist Labor Party.

Medvedev, R.A., and G. Shriver. (1989). *Let History Judge: The Origins and Consequences of Stalinism*. Rev. and expanded ed. New York: Columbia University Press.

Milgram, S. (1974). *Obedience to Authority; an Experimental View*. 1st ed. New York: Harper & Row.

Musgrave, T.D. (1997). *Self-Determination and National Minorities*. New York: Oxford University Press.

Nation, The. (1918). *Declaration of the Rights of the Peoples of Russia, Volume 107 (#2791), December 28, 1918*. New York: J.H. Richards.

Neuberger, B. (2001). National Self-Determination: A Theoretical Discussion. *Nationalities Papers* 29 (3), pp. 391–418.

New York Times. (1918). *The New York Times Current History of the European War*. Vol. 14 (Janury–March 1918). New York: New York Times Co.

Palonen, K. (2002). The History of Concepts as a Style of Political Theorizing. *European Journal of Political Theory* 1 (1), pp. 91–106.

Parker, S. (1666). *An Account of the Nature and Extent of the Divine Dominion & Goodnesse Especially as They Refer to the Origenian Hypothesis Concerning the Preexistence of Soul*. Oxford: W. Hall for R. Davis.

Pettit, P. (1997). *Republicanism: A Theory of Freedom and Government*. New York: Oxford University Press.

Scrivener, M. (1674). *A Course of Divinity, or, an Introduction to the Knowledge of the True Catholick Religion*. London: Tho. Roycroft for Robert Clavil.

Smith, T. (2017). *Why Wilson Matters: The Origin of American Liberal Internationalism and Its Crisis Today*. Princeton: Princeton University Press.

Stalin, J. [1913] 1954. *Marxism and the National Question*. Moscow: Foreign Languages Pub. House.

Truman, J. (1675). *A Discourse of Natural and Moral Impotency*. 2nd ed. London: Printed for Robert Clavel, and Are to Be Sold at the Sign of the Peacock . . .

United States Senate. (1919). Report of Interview in Paris between the President of the United States and the American Commission on Irish Independence. In *Treaty of Peace with Germany: Hearings before the Committee on Foreign Relations*. Washington, DC: US Congress.

Vidmar, J. (2009). International Legal Responses to Kosovo's Declaration of Independence. *Vanderbilt Journal of Transnational Law* 42 (3), pp. 779–851.

Weitz, E.D. (2015). Self-Determination: How a German Enlightenment Idea Became the Slogan of National Liberation and a Human Right. *The American Historical Review* 120 (2), pp. 462–496.

Wrong, D.H. (1995). *Power: Its Forms, Bases, and Uses*. New Brunswick, NJ: Transaction Publishers.

# 3

# THE MEANING OF SECESSION

*Peter Radan*

## Introduction

When the United Nations (UN) came into existence in 1945, it had 51 member States. By 2022 that number had nearly tripled to 193 member States. How many of these new member States were the product of secession is a much-debated issue in the scholarly literature. At the heart of this debate lies disagreement over the definition of secession. At one end of the spectrum in the debate, narrow definitions mean that very few of these new member States were the product of secession. At the other end of the spectrum, broad definitions see the great majority of these new member States as the product of secession. However, what is notable is that the majority of scholars, in overlooking the need to detail the bases upon which their definitions are built, have produced what Anderson criticises as being "arbitrary definition[s] devoid of justification" (Anderson 2013: 344).

The lack of consensus over the definition of secession has significant practical implications. For example, there is considerable debate about whether there exists a right of secession in international law (see further, Roth in Chapter 32, this volume). That debate essentially revolves around whether international law recognises the existence of what Anderson refers to as "unilateral non-colonial secession" (Anderson 2017). That debate does not deal with, nor should be seen as dealing with, other types of State creation that come within some of the broader definitions of secession. However, international law does regulate State creation in some of these other types of State creation.

## Definitions of secession

The word "secession" has its roots in the Latin words *se*, meaning "apart", and *cedere*, meaning "to go". Secession is thus associated with leaving or withdrawing from some place. This means, in effect, that secession is a *process*, and a State created as a result of that process is the *outcome* of that process (Coppieters 2003: 4–5). Kohen aptly notes that "[s]ecession is not an instant fact. It always implies a complex series of claims and decisions, negotiations and/or struggle, which may – or may not – lead to the creation of a new State" (Kohen 2006: 14). The process of secession starts when representatives of a population that is settled in a territory proclaim, usually by means of a declaration of independence, a new State on that territory (see further, Kartsonaki and Pavković, Chapter 20, this volume). Invariably, recognition of statehood is sought from existing States. In international law, the function of recognition is a controversial issue. According to the declaratory theory on recognition, recognition has no role to play in the creation of a State, with recognition being simply another State's formal acknowledgment of the existence of the new State. On the other hand, according to the constitutive theory on recognition, widespread recognition of a State creates the State (Crawford 2006: 19–28). Whatever the merits are of these competing theories, it is widely accepted that, in the context of State creation by secession, recognition by States of a seceding territorial entity has at least some part to play in achieving statehood (Dugard & Raič 2006: 99). That this is so is effectively conceded by secessionists themselves. Historically, international recognition of statehood has been the major foreign policy goal of any secessionist movement (Crawford 2006: 376). For example, recognition by India, a significant regional power, of Bangladesh in 1971 was crucial to the success of the latter's secession from Pakistan (Crawford 2006: 141). Conversely, the failure of the Turkish Republic of Northern Cyprus to gain widespread recognition of its attempt, initiated in 1983, to secede from Cyprus, means that the outcome of statehood is yet to be achieved (*Loizidou -v.- Turkey*, 1996: 471).

In the literature as to which instances of State creation come within the process of secession, the scholarly literature, as noted earlier, reveals a wide spectrum of views and thus significantly different definitions of secession.

A narrow definition of secession is propounded by Crawford, who defines it as "the creation of a State by the use or threat of force without the consent of the former sovereign" (Crawford 2006: 375). Crawford's reference to "the former sovereign" means that secession includes departures of a territorial community from within a State's territory or from its colonial entities. It can be noted that other scholars maintain that the opposition of the "the former sovereign" is an element of secession (for example, Kohen 2006: 3; Dugard 2003: 89). In requiring opposition to secession from "the former sovereign", Crawford's definition implies the continuation of "the former sovereign" once secession has occurred. In the context of a territorial community seeking to withdraw from within a State (the "host State"), when taken together with the requirement of the use or threat of force by the secessionist movement, the opposition and continuation of the host State means that Crawford's definition excludes from secession many cases of State creation, such as the States that emerged from the dissolutions of the Soviet Union, Czechoslovakia, and Yugoslavia during what Buchanan refers to as an "age of secession" following the collapse of the Berlin Wall in 1989 (Buchanan 1997: 301). Nor, as is discussed in this chapter, does Crawford include within the scope of secession the creation of many, but not all, of the States resulting from the process of decolonisation. Thus, when writing in 2006, Crawford argued that the only example of State creation by secession, outside the context of decolonisation, after the UN was created in 1945 was that of Bangladesh's withdrawal from Pakistan in 1971 (Crawford 2006: 415). Since 2006, the only instance of State creation by secession that falls within Crawford's definition in that context is that of Kosovo's secession from Serbia in 2008. Although Kosovo has not, as of mid-2022, been admitted as a member State of the UN, it can be regarded as a State given that it has been recognised as such by 119 States.

Crawford's definition reflects a widely accepted and continuing negative attitude towards secession. This attitude derives from two sources.

The first is the almost universal desire of States to preserve their territorial integrity (see further, Weill, Chapter 36, this volume). In the case of the United States, one of the most powerful and influential States, hostility to secession is further underpinned as a result of its experience with the secessions of 11 of its states that ignited the Civil War of 1861–1865. Brandon proffers a number of factors that explain this hostility. One is that secession is perceived as constituting disloyalty to the United States, bordering on treason. Another is that secession led to the most destructive war in the history of the United States to that point of time, which, according to the most recent estimates, led to the loss of at least 750,000 lives (Hacker 2011: 311). The final, and arguably most important, factor is that the secessions of the 11 states that constituted the Confederate States of America for four years were all associated with the defence and perpetuation of slavery (Brandon 1998: 167).

A second source for the negative attitude towards secession stems from the UN Charter, which prohibits member States from threatening or using force "against the territorial integrity or political independence of any state" (UNC 1945: art 2(4)). It was thus, unsurprising that, in 1970, UN Secretary-General U Thant said that the UN "has never accepted and does not accept and I do not believe will ever accept the principle of secession of part of its Member State[s]" (quoted in Anderson 2013: 344). Although Bangladesh's secession from Pakistan in 1971 and admission to the UN in 1974, disproved U Thant's assertion, the negativity towards secession was still evident in the nuanced words of one of his successors when, in 1992, Secretary-General Boutros Boutros-Ghali said that "if every ethnic, religious or linguistic group claimed statehood, there would be no limit to fragmentation, and peace, security and economic well-being for all would become ever more difficult to achieve" (Boutros-Ghali 1992: para. 17). The consequence of this widely held negative view of secession is reflected in Crawford's narrow definition of secession and also explains why, although many of the 142 States created after 1945 and duly admitted to the UN, are, notwithstanding that they looked very much like cases of State creation through the process of secession, categorised as being something else.

A broader definition of secession that encompasses some of the forms of State creation that Crawford excludes from his definition, is provided by Anderson, who defines secession as "[t]he withdrawal of territory (colonial or non-colonial) from part of an existing state to create a new state" (Anderson 2013: 344). Implicit in this definition is that because secession relates only to territory forming "part of an existing state", Anderson's definition, like that of Crawford's, implies the continuation of the host State once secession has occurred. An even broader definition of secession would include within its scope all of the instances of State creation that fall outside Crawford's definition. Such a definition is proffered by Radan, who defines secession as "the creation of a new State upon territory previously forming part of, or being a colonial entity of, an existing State" (Radan 2008: 18).

The first point of distinction between the definitions proffered by Anderson and Radan, on the one hand, and Crawford's narrow definition, on the other, concerns opposition to secession from the host State. This requirement, outside the context of decolonisation, means that Bangladesh and Kosovo are the only cases of State creation since 1945 that fall within Crawford's definition of secession. Thus, although Eritrea's claim to statehood was initially opposed by Ethiopia, but not at the time the Eritrean State was recognised, what started out as an attempt at secession is not a case of secession according to Crawford's definition. Nor is South Sudan's withdrawal from Sudan a case of secession within Crawford's definition, because, although Sudan initially opposed the secession of South Sudan, in 2011 South Sudan gained its independence with the consent of Sudan as the result of an agreement reached in 2005. And, given that the host State did not survive in the cases of the negotiated dissolutions of the Soviet Union and Czechoslovakia and the factual dissolution of Yugoslavia in the 1990s, none of the new States that emerged from these dissolutions fall within Crawford's definition of secession.

An argument in favour of Crawford's requirement that for State creation to be an instance of secession, it must be opposed, at all times, by the host State is that if the host State, either at the outset or eventually, consents to part of its territory becoming a new State, this presents no problem for international law because the consent will inevitably result in widespread recognition from other States, and, more importantly, admission of the newly created State to the UN. However, Radan contests Crawford's insistence that secession is properly confined to cases where secession is, at all times, opposed by the host State. He argues that it makes no sense to regard something that starts out as an attempt to secede and ends up with the creation of a new State as not constituting secession, simply because the host State either did not oppose it at all or withdrew its initial opposition before the process of State creation was completed. For him, if what starts out as an attempt at secession eventually leads to the creation of a new State, then it is properly defined as an instance of secession (Radan 2008: 26–27).

It should be noted that, in a co-authored opinion on the possibility of the independence of Scotland from the United Kingdom, Crawford proffered a definition of secession that omitted the element of opposition from the host State. This definition stated secession was "the process by which a group seeks to separate itself from the state to which it belongs and to create a new state on part of that state's territory. It is essentially a unilateral process" (Crawford & Boyle 2012: para. 22.1). In referring to the creation of a new State "on part of" the host State's territory, this definition implies the continued existence of the host State. Pursuant to this definition, Eritrea and South Sudan are included as instances of secession (Crawford & Boyle 2012: paras 58, 62). However, the reference to secession being "essentially a unilateral process" excluded the consensual creation of new States from the "dissolution" of the Soviet Union (Crawford & Boyle 2012: para. 57) and the creation of the new States of the Czech Republic and Slovakia pursuant to the negotiated dissolution of Czechoslovakia (Crawford & Boyle 2012: paras 74–78). In relation to the dissolution of Czechoslovakia, this is described as a case of "negotiated independence" which was defined as "[a] bilateral and consensual process by which a state confers independence on a territory and people by legislative or other means" (Crawford & Boyle 2012: para. 22.2). In accordance with this definition, the dissolution of the Soviet Union would also constitute an instance of a "negotiated independence", rather than secession, notwithstanding that it was agreed that Russia was regarded as the continuation of, and successor State to, the Soviet Union, whereas neither the Czech Republic nor Slovakia were the continuation of, and successor State to, Czechoslovakia.

The creation of States from Yugoslavia starting in the mid-1990s is a complex one in terms of whether these States were instances of secession within either of Crawford's earlier definition of secession or his subsequent, somewhat broader, definition. The creation of new States out of Yugoslavia arose in three different contexts. The last of them in point of time was the aforementioned secession of Kosovo from Serbia in 2008, which none of Crawford, Anderson, and Radan would deny was an instance of secession. The second context is the secession of Montenegro from the State Union of Serbia and Montenegro (previously known as the Federal Republic of Yugoslavia from 1992 to 2003 and admitted as a member State of the UN on 1 November 2000). Following a referendum vote in favour of secession in May 2006, Montenegro proclaimed its independence on 3 June 2006. Two days later, Serbia adopted a declaration asserting that Serbia maintained the legal identity and the UN membership of the State Union of Serbia and Montenegro. This claim was accepted and Serbia, as the successor state to the State Union of Serbia and Montenegro, has continued on as a UN member State ever since. Because Montenegro's independence was not contested or opposed by Serbia, its independence would not constitute a secession within Crawford's first definition of secession. However, it is an instance of secession pursuant to Crawford's later definition of secession (Crawford & Boyle 2012: para. 59), as well as those proffered by Anderson (Anderson 2013: 354) and Radan.

The third, but first chronologically, context of the creation of new States from Yugoslavia is the creation of Croatia, Slovenia, Bosnia and Hercegovina, and the Former Yugoslav Republic of Macedonia (North Macedonia since 2019) in the wake of their recognition by the European

Community in the early 1990s (see further, Grant, Chapter 34, this volume). Both Crawford (in both of his definitions) and Anderson argue that these four States were the product of the dissolution of, rather than the secession from, Yugoslavia. In making the argument here, Anderson refers to two key events. The first was the ruling of the Badinter Arbitration Commission on 29 November 1991, in its *Opinion No 1*, that Yugoslavia was "in the process of dissolution" (Trifunovska 1994: 417). The second event was UN Security Council Resolution 757 of 30 May 1992, which noted that the claim by the remaining part of Yugoslavia, by then renamed as the Federal Republic of Yugoslavia, that it be the successor to, and automatically continue the membership of, what was referred to as the "former" Yugoslavia, had "not been generally accepted" (Trifunovska 1994: 594). For Anderson, the creation of the aforementioned four States to emerge from Yugoslavia was the product of dissolution, rather than secession, because the Federal Republic of Yugoslavia was not seen as the continuation of, or successor to, Yugoslavia. This was in contrast to the situation with the break-up of the Soviet Union in 1991 where Russia was accepted as the continuation of, and successor to, the Soviet Union. This meant, according to Anderson, that the Soviet Union, unlike Yugoslavia, "had experienced multiple secessions without also experiencing dissolution" (Anderson 2013: 384). On the other hand, for Radan, who regards the creation of these four States as instances of secession, the key event was the Badinter Arbitration Commission's *Opinion No 8*, delivered on 4 July 1992. Although the Commission had, as previously noted, ruled that Yugoslavia had been, since 29 November 1991, "in the process of dissolution", it was only on 4 July 1992 that it ruled that Yugoslavia "no longer exists" and that "it no longer has legal personality" (Trifunovska 1994: 635–636). On the basis of this ruling, because the Commission had made its recommendations on the international recognition of the four Yugoslav republics before 4 July 1992, that is at a time when, according to Radan, Yugoslavia "was a state whose existence was beyond doubt and which had not come to an end", the recognition of these four republics as States was the result of their "secession from [Yugoslavia] rather than recognition of new states arising from the debris of a near-failed state" (Radan 2002: 216). Dugard also rejects the argument that because a state, such as Yugoslavia, is dissolved, that new States that emerge from the dissolved State are not instances of secession. He dismisses the Badinter Commission ruling on the dissolution of Yugoslavia as "not convincing" and argues that "[t]he dissolution of Yugoslavia in 1991 may be categorized as a case of secession on the part of Slovenia, Croatia, Bosnia–Herzegovina and Macedonia from Yugoslavia" (Dugard 2003: 94).

The second point of distinction between the definitions proffered by Anderson and Radan, on the one hand, and Crawford's narrow definition, on the other, is the latter's requirement that secession be achieved pursuant to the use or threat of force. Radan argues that there is no reason why the use or threat of force should be an element of any defintion of secession because it is only concerned with the *means* by which secession is achieved. He argues that an attempt at secession that achieves the outcome of independent statehood is a secession whether or not it involves the use or threat of force (Radan 2008: 30). Furthermore, if one accepts Crawford's argument that secession requires opposition of the host State, then the element of the use or threat of force is superfluous, because a secessionist demand from a territiorial community which is opposed by the host State implies that, if necessary, force will be used in order for the territorial community to become a new State.

The third, and final, point of distinction between the definitions proffered by Anderson and Radan, on the one hand, and Crawford's narrow definition is the latter's exclusion from secession of some, but not all, of the States created as a result of decolonisation. However, Radan and Anderson regard all instances of decolonisation leading to independent statehood as examples of secession.

Following World War II, decolonisation led to the creation of many new States from what were formally referred to as either non-self-governing territories (UNC 1945: chapter 11) or trust territories (UNC 1945: chapters 12 and 13). Some scholars exclude all cases of decolonisation from their definitions of secession (see, for example, Dahlitz 2003: 6–7; Higgins 2003: 35; Kohen 2006: 14). However, Crawford takes a less absolute position by including as examples of secession cases of statehood resulting from "the forcible seizure of independence by the territory in question" and excluding those resulting from "the grant of independence by the previous sovereign" (Crawford 2006: 330). It is on the basis of there being forcible independence from their colonial masters that Crawford observed that, during the nineteenth century, "secession was the most conspicuous and probably the most common method of the creation of new States" (Crawford 2006: 375). Amongst the examples Crawford uses to illustrate this point are the States created from former Spanish colonies in Central and South America and the secessions of Greece from the Ottoman Empire and of Belgium from the Netherlands. Much the same could be said for the creation of new States along the eastern seaboard of North America that declared their independence from the British Empire pursuant to their Declaration of Independence in 1776, which Armitage refers to as "the first formal secession proclamation in world history" (Armitage 2010: 48). However, for reasons outlined earlier in relation to the use or threat of force, Radan argues there is no merit in making a distinction between forcible and consensual State creation in the decolonisation context and that all cases of decolonisation that lead to the creation of a new State are instances of secession (Radan 2008: 25).

What can be said about decolonisation is that, unlike secession from within an existing State, the process of decolonisation has, since the end of World War II, been generally welcomed and supported. Hostility to colonialism led the UN General Assembly to issue two resolutions in 1960 that legitimised decolonisation as falling within the principle of the self-determination of peoples. The first called for "immediate steps" to be taken towards colonial entities attaining "complete independence and freedom" (UNGA 1960a: para. 5). In regulating the process of decolonisation, the second resolution spoke in terms of the "evolution and progress" towards reaching a full measure of self-government by one of three means, namely, "(a) [e]mergence as a sovereign independent State; (b) [f]ree association with an independent State; or (c) [i]ntegration with an independent State" (UNGA 1960b: Annex, Principles I & VI). The practice of the UN pursuant to these resolutions has been to strongly prefer independent statehood for colonial entities (Crawford 2006: 629). Whether this positive attitude towards State creation through decolonisation is a sufficient basis to exclude it from the scope of any definition of secession is contested by Coggins, who argues that, although "anti-colonial secessions and non-colonial secessions have different inherent characteristics and conflict dynamics, both types ultimately sought to separate from an existing state to create a new one" (Coggins 2011: 26). Finally, Anderson argues that, on the basis of decisions of the International Court of Justice in cases such as the *Western Sahara Case* (ICJ 1975), "metropolitan [i.e., colonial] powers possess sovereignty throughout their colonial territories" with the consequence that "colonial territories should . . . be classified as constituent parts of the metropolitan power" (Anderson 2013: 376–377). This leads him to conclude that because colonial territories are "subject to the overarching sovereignty of their metropolitan power . . . any withdrawal of this sovereignty to create a new state is secession" (Anderson 2013: 379).

## Is irredentism secession?

An issue discussed in some of the scholarly literature on State creation and secession is that of whether irredentism, which involves the withdrawal of territory from one State and its incorporation into another State, comes within the definition of secession. Some definitions of secession include irredentism within its scope. For example, the *International Encyclopedia of the Social Sciences* defines the secession as "the act of withdrawing territory from a state and converting it into an independent state or joining it to another state" (IESS 2022; see also Dahlitz 2003: 6; Raič 2002: 308; Haverland 1987: 384). However, most scholars take the view that irredentism is distinct from secession because it results in the incorporation of the departing territory from a targeted State into another, often adjoining, State, rather than the creation of a new State (Ambrosio 2001: 2; Radan 2008: 22–23; Anderson 2013: 370–373). Another point of distinction between secession and irredentism relates to the numbers of parties involved in each of these processes. If irredentism involves a territorial community within State A being incorporated into State B, three parties are involved, namely the irredentist State (State B), which is usually the sponsor of the irredentist claim, the State targeted by the irredentist State (State A), and the territorial community within the targeted State (Brubaker 1996: 4–6). However, secessionist claims involve only two parties, namely, the State from which secession is sought and the territorial community within that State that wishes to withdraw from it. Although irredentism and secession are distinct, the distinction is not always clear-cut in practice, as is illustrated by the attempted secession of the Republic of Serb Krajina (Krajina) from Croatia during the early 1990s. Although the Serbs of Croatia declared their independence from Croatia and applied to the European Community for the recognition of Krajina as an independent State in late 1991, it was clear that their preference was to remain part of Yugoslavia. Although what remained of Yugoslavia at that time declined to formally recognise Krajina, it nevertheless committed itself to acting as protector of the Krajina Serbs and acted as their principal backer until 1995, when Krajina's attempt at secession was finally crushed (Radan 2018). Although there were clear irredentist sentiments in this case, Krajina is best viewed as an instance of attempted secession, given that it applied for recognition as a State and that what remained of Yugoslavia never formally declared any irredentist claims to the Serb populated regions of Croatia.

## Conclusion

This chapter has detailed a number of definitions of secession. On the one hand, there is the narrow definition proffered by Crawford, the effect of which is that relatively few cases of State creation since 1945 come within his definition of secession. On the other hand, the broader definitions proffered by Anderson and Radan include a much greater number of instances of State creation since 1945 within their definitions, with Radan's definition being the broadest. What is common to all of these definitions is that they involve the creation of a new State or States over territory which was either part of a State or over which a State exercised sovereignty. From a legal perspective the creation of these new States is the subject of legal regulation. This regulation comes within one of two contexts. The first is the creation of new States as a result of decolonisation which is, as detailed in the chapter, regulated by the two UN General Assembly resolutions adopted in 1960. Decolonisation is largely complete with, as of mid-2022, no trust territories and only 17 non-self-governing territories. Of these Non-Self-governing territories, the largest (266,000 sq. km.) and most populous (612,000), and most contentious, is Western Sahara. The remaining 16 are all small islands with a combined area of 27,421 sq. km. and a total population of 1,110,029 (UN 2022).

The second context of State creation is the creation of a new State or States out of an existing State. Although the domestic constitutional law of many States precludes secession from the State, a very small number of States' constitutions do set out procedures by which secession from that State is possible (Radan 2020: 40–44). From the perspective of international law, State creation pursuant to agreement such as occurred with the dissolutions of Czechoslovakia and the Soviet Union, as well as the creation of Eritrea out of Ethiopia and South Sudan out of Sudan, present no legal problems because all relevant parties agreed to the creation of the new States or State. However, where a territorial community within a State seeks to create a new State and it is contested by the host State, the question of the existence of a legal right to do so is, as noted in this chapter, a subject of debate, with many scholars arguing that, in appropriate circumstances a right of remedial secession exists in international law (see further, Roth, Chapter 32, this volume). In this context, it is only such instances of State creation that fall within Crawford's narrow definition of secession. However, other instances of State creation resulting from the departure of a territorial community from an existing State fall within the broad definitions of secession proffered by Radan, because he takes the view that whether the departure is consensual or contested, the result is the same, namely the departure of a territorial community from a State that ends with the creation of a new State.

# References

Ambrosio, T. 2001, *Irredentism, Ethnic Conflict and International Politics*, Westport: Praeger Publishers.
Anderson, G. 2013, "Secession in International Law: What Are We Talking About?", *Loyola of Los Angeles International and Comparative Law Review*, 35: 343–388.
Anderson, G. 2017, "Unilateral Non-Colonial Secession and Internal Self-Determination: A Right of Newly Seceded Peoples to Democracy?", *Arizona Journal of International & Comparative Law*, 34: 1–63.
Armitage, D. 2010, "Secession and Civil War", in D. H. Doyle (ed.), *Secession as an International Phenomenon: From America's Civil War to Contemporary Separatist Movements*, Athens: University of Georgia Press: 37–55.
Boutros-Ghali, B. 1992, *An Agenda for Peace, Preventive Diplomacy, Peacemaking and Peace-Keeping*, New York: United Nations.
Brandon, M. E. 1998, *Free in the World: American Slavery and Constitutional Failure*, Princeton: Princeton University Press.
Brubaker, R. 1996, *Nationalism Reframed, Nationhood and the National Question in the New Europe*, Cambridge: Cambridge University Press.
Buchanan, A. 1997, "Self-Determination, Secession and the Rule of Law", in R. McKim & J. McMahan (eds.), *The Morality of Nationalism*, New York: Oxford University Press: 301–323.
Coggins, B. L. 2011, "The History of Secession: An Overview", in A. Pavković & P. Radan (eds.), *The Ashgate Research Companion to Secession*, Farnham: Ashgate Publishing Ltd: 23–43.
Coppieters, B. 2003, "Introduction", in B. Coppieters & R. Sakwa (eds.), *Contextualizing Secession, Normative Studies in a Comparative Perspective*, Oxford: Oxford University Press: 1–21.
Crawford, J. 2006, *The Creation of States in International Law*, 2nd ed., Oxford: Clarendon Press.
Crawford, J. & Boyle, A. 2012, *Opinion: Referendum on the Independence of Scotland – International Law Aspects*, <https://assets.publishing.service.gov.uk/government/uploads/system/uploads/attachment_data/file/79408/Annex_A.pdf>
Dahlitz, J. 2003, "Introduction", in J. Dahlitz (ed.), *Secession and International Law: Conflict Avoidance – Regional Appraisals*, The Hague: TMC Asser Press: 1–10.
Dugard, J. 2003, "A Legal Basis for Secession – Relevant Principles and Rules", in J. Dahlitz (ed.), *Secession and International Law: Conflict Avoidance – Regional Appraisals*, The Hague: TMC Asser Press: 898–896.
Dugard, J. & Raič, D. 2006, "The Role of Recognition in the Law and Practice of Secession", in M. G. Kohen (ed.), *Secession, International Law Perspectives*, Cambridge: Cambridge University Press: 94–137.
Hacker, J. D. 2011, "A Census-Based Count of the Civil War Dead", *Civil War History*, 57: 307–348.
Haverland, C. 1987, "Secession", in R. Bernhardt (ed.), *Encyclopedia of Public International Law, Instalment 10: States, Responsibility of States, International Law and Municipal Law*, North-Holland: Elsevier Science Publishers: 384–389.
Higgins, R. 2003, "Self-Determination and Secession", in J. Dahlitz (ed.), *Secession and International Law: Conflict Avoidance – Regional Appraisals*, The Hague: TMC Asser Press: 21–38.
ICJ 1975, "International Court of Justice, 1975, Advisory Opinion of the International Court of Justice on the Western Sahara", *International Court of Justice Reports* 12.
IESS 2022, *International Encyclopedia of the Social Sciences*, <www.encyclopedia.com/social-sciences-and-law/political-science-and-government/political-science-terms-and-concepts/secession>

Kohen, M. G. 2006, "Introduction", in M. G. Kohen (ed.), *Secession, International Law Perspectives*, Cambridge: Cambridge University Press: 1–20.

Loizidou -v.- Turkey 1996, "European Court of Human Rights", *Loizidou -v.- Turkey*, 108 I. L. R. 445.

Radan, P. 2002, *The Break-Up of Yugoslavia in International Law*, London: Routledge.

Radan, P. 2008, "Secession: A Word in Search of a Meaning", in A. Pavković & P. Radan (eds.), *On the Way to Statehood: Secession and Globalisation*, Ashgate: Aldershot: 17–32.

Radan, P. 2018, "Republika Srpska Krajina and the Right of Peoples to Self Determination", *Istorija 20.veka*, 36(1): 9–34.

Radan, P. 2020, "Secessionist Referendums in International and Domestic Law", in M. Qvortrup (ed.), *Nationalism, Referendums and Democracy: Voting on Ethnic Issues and Independence*, 2nd ed., London: Routledge: 33–46.

Raič, D. 2002, *Statehood and the Law of Self-Determination*, The Hague: Kluwer Law International.

Trifunovska, S. 1994, *Yugoslavia Through Documents: From its Creation to Its Dissolution*, Dordrecht: Martinus Nijhoff Publishers.

UN 2022, "United Nations", *United Nations and Decolonization: Non-Self-Governing Territories*, www.un.org/dppa/decolonization/en/nsgt

UNC 1945, *United Nations Charter*, www.un.org/en/about-us/un-charter/full-text

UNGA 1960a, United Nations General Assembly, Declaration on the Granting of Independence to Colonial Countries and Peoples, Resolution 1514 (XV), 14 December.

UNGA 1960b, United Nations General Assembly, Principles Which Should Guide Members in Determining Whether or Not an Obligation Exists to Transmit the Information Called for in Article 73(e) of the Charter of the United Nations, annex to Resolution 1541 (XV), 15 December.

# PART II

# Self-determination

# 4

# WHO ARE THE "PEOPLES" ENTITLED TO THE RIGHT OF SELF-DETERMINATION?

*Glen Anderson*

It is commonly understood that international law bestows a right of self-determination on "peoples", but less understood is precisely who the "peoples" are. The governing pillars of the law of self-determination – treaties and declaratory General Assembly resolutions – fail to provide an obvious answer. This is problematic, as the law of self-determination is widely accepted as taking effect in the decolonization context and is increasingly considered as having application in the non-colonial context, most particularly via a qualified right to unilateral non-colonial (UNC) secession (Anderson 2016: 1234–1235; Anderson 2015: 8–13). The present chapter addresses this problem by positing a legally informed definition of the "peoples".

An initial caveat is necessary, namely, that attempts to define the "peoples" are necessarily fraught with difficulty, due to the deliberately nebulous nature of international legal instruments. It is no accident that the law of self-determination is less precise than it might otherwise be, as attempting to forge consensus among States on the content of any international instrument requires latitude for self-serving interpretation. This tendency is only exacerbated in the context of self-determination, which has the ability to qualify, and in some cases override, two of the most sacrosanct principles of the Westphalian international order: the sovereignty and territorial integrity of States.

The present chapter focuses on the textual law of self-determination, as expressed in treaties and declaratory General Assembly resolutions, to ascertain – within sensible tolerances – who the "peoples" are. Orthodox canons of textual interpretation are employed. Whenever possible, key words and phrases are construed according to their "ordinary" meaning, with regard for the particular instrument's "object and purpose", as laid down by Article 31(1) of the 1969 Vienna Convention on the Law of Treaties (Vienna Convention). When key words and phrases remain "ambiguous or obscure", resort will also be made to the *travaux préparatoires* (preparatory work, normally of a documentary nature) and *procès verbaux* (preparatory work, documenting oral debate), as enumerated by the Vienna Convention in Article 32(a).

## Treaties

Three treaties especially bear upon the definition of "peoples": the United Nations (UN) Charter, the International Covenant on Economic, Social and Cultural Rights (UNGA 1966a) and the International Covenant on Civil and Political Rights (UNGA 1966b).

DOI: 10.4324/9781003036593-6

## *The United Nations Charter*

The treaty law (and legal) origins of the self-determination of peoples can be traced to the UN Charter (Duursma 1996: 12; Radan 2002: 30; Anderson 2016: 1204). The opening sentence of the Charter's preamble begins with the phrase "[w]e, the peoples of the United Nations" and concludes by pledging the organization to the "economic and social advancement of all peoples." Leaving aside the issue of the legal status of the Charter's preamble generally,[1] these opening remarks do not offer any precise insight to the meaning of "peoples". Despite this, "peoples" was used as a general descriptor for potential subjects of the organization and must, therefore, include the entire population of States.

Article 1(2) provides the first mention of "self-determination of peoples", stating that the UN's purpose is:

> To develop friendly relations among nations based on respect for the principle of equal rights and self-determination of peoples, and to take other appropriate measures to strengthen universal peace.

Clearly, there is a nexus between "nations" and "equal rights and self-determination of peoples". It is unclear, however, exactly what this nexus implies. It is possible that Article 1(2) is suggesting that nations and peoples are synonymous. Equally, it is possible that nations and peoples are not strictly synonymous, and simply overlap in certain contexts. The most that can be determined from Article 1(2) is that it does not suggest that a nation cannot be a people.

Article 55 pledges member States to promote (emphasis added):

> [C]onditions of stability and well being which are necessary for peaceful and friendly relations among *nations* based on respect for the equal rights and self-determination of peoples.

Article 55 reiterates the nexus between "nations" and the "equal rights and self-determination of peoples" contained in Article 1(2). Beyond this, however, Article 55 offers nothing further.

Article 73 provides:

> Members of the United Nations which have or assume responsibilities for the administration of territories whose peoples have not yet attained a full measure of self-government recognize the principle that the interests of the inhabitants of these territories are paramount, and accept as a sacred trust the obligation to promote to the utmost, within the system of international peace and security established by the present Charter, the well-being of the inhabitants of these territories.

Article 73 describes the populations of non-self-governing territories as "peoples" and "inhabitants" interchangeably. As Radan has noted, the term "inhabitants" must therefore include the entire population of a colonial territory. He also reasons that because the terms "inhabitants" and "peoples" are used interchangeably, the use of the term "peoples" in Article 73 must refer to the entire population of a non-self-governing territory (Radan 2002: 31).

As Radan has also noted, however, Article 73 uses the plural term "peoples" in preference to the singular "people," and this opens the *additional* possibility that more than one people may inhabit a non-self-governing territory (Radan 2002: 31). This interpretation is supported by examination of Article 73(b), which pledges member States:

[T]o develop self-government, to take due account of the political aspirations of the peoples, and to assist them in the progressive development of their free political institutions, according to the particular circumstances of each territory and its peoples and their varying stages of advancement.

The phrase "each territory and its peoples", with its use of the singular "territory" followed by the plural "peoples", indicates that more than one people may inhabit a non-self-governing territory (Radan 2002: 31).

This interpretation is further supported by examination of Article 76(b), which pledges member States:

[T]o promote the political, economic, social, and educational advancement of the inhabitants of the trust territories, and their progressive development towards self-government or independence as may be appropriate to the particular circumstances of each territory and its peoples and the freely expressed wishes of the peoples concerned, and as may be provided by the terms of each trusteeship agreement.

As with Articles 73 and 73(b), the phrase "each territory and its peoples" with its use of the singular "territory" followed by the plural "peoples" indicates that more than one people may inhabit a non-self-governing territory (Radan 2002: 31–32).

If, therefore, as indicated by Articles 73, 73(b) and 76(b), more than one people can inhabit a non-self-governing territory, this raises the question of whether peoples in such a context constitute nations. Article 73(a) would seem to support such an inference, mandating "due respect for the *culture* of the peoples concerned" (emphasis added). As Radan has observed, "[t]he reference to culture echoes some aspects of the definition of a nation", thereby suggesting that more than one nation may inhabit a non-self-governing territory (Radan 2002: 31).

Bearing this in mind, the use of the term "peoples" in any context within the Charter – if it is to be consistently interpreted – must include nations. *A priori*, given that many States are recognized as possessing a multinational character, it follows that more than one people can exist within a State.

The Charter's *travaux préparatoires* and *procès verbaux* also support a broad interpretation of the term "peoples". The former, for example, indicates that the term "nation" as employed in Articles 1(2) and 55 includes a variety of political entities, including "colonies, mandates, protectorates . . . quasi [S]tates [and] [S]tates" (UNCIO 1945–1952: vol. XVIII, 657). The *travaux préparatoires* also indicates that the term "peoples" was intended to apply to nations, particularly those that were non-self-governing in eastern Europe, meaning that peoples are not necessarily States (UNCIO 1945–1952: vol. VI, 296). Indeed, the Belgian delegation suggested that the term "peoples" could mean "national groups which do not identify themselves with the population of a State" (UNCIO 1945–1952: vol. VI, 296).[2] The *procès verbaux* reinforces this analysis, with the drafting committee concluding that Article 1(2) applied to "[S]tates" and "nations":

[W]hat is intended by paragraph 2 is to proclaim the equal rights of peoples as such, consequently their right to self-determination. Equality of rights therefore extends in the Charter to [S]tates [and] nations.

(UNCIO 1945–1952: vol. VI, 704)

The drafting committee thus ruled out any interpretation of "peoples" strictly synonymous with the entire population of a State or non-self-governing territory (Quane 1998: 542).

This flexible interpretation was confirmed by the UN Secretariat, which after analyzing the Charter's text as a whole, concluded that the term "peoples" referred to "groups of human beings who may or may not, comprise [S]tates or *nations*" (UNCIO 1945–1952: vol. XVIII, 658, emphasis added). Various scholars have reached similar conclusions (Radan 2002: 30–32; Franck 1998: 744; Cristescu 1981: para. 262; Quane 1998: 543; Ofuatey-Kodjoe 1995: 354).

Examination of the UN Charter therefore indicates that "peoples" are not necessarily synonymous with the entire population of a State or non-self-governing territory and may include sub-State national groups and national groups within non-self-governing territories.

## International covenants on human rights

In December 1966 the UN General Assembly unanimously adopted the International Covenant on Economic, Social and Cultural Rights (Economic Rights Covenant) and the International Covenant on Civil and Political Rights (Civil Rights Covenant).

Article 1(1) is identical for both covenants and provides:

> All peoples have the right to self-determination. By virtue of that right they freely determine their political status and freely pursue their economic, social and cultural development.

Determining the definition of "peoples" from examination of Article 1(1), however, is problematic. It is unclear whether peoples are the entire population of States, non-self-governing territories, or nations. What is clear is that "*all* peoples have the right to self-determination" (emphasis added) and this suggests that the term "peoples" is of broad and general applicability (Šuković 1972: 344).

Article 1(2) is also identical for both covenants and provides that "[a]ll peoples may, for their own ends, freely dispose of their natural wealth and resources". The same paragraph continues that under no circumstances can a people be deprived of its own means of subsistence. Once again, however, it is unclear exactly what the term "peoples" means. Although inferentially reaffirming that "*all* peoples" (emphasis added) have the right to self-determination, it is difficult to determine whether peoples are States, non-self-governing territories or nations.

Article 1(3) is also identical for both covenants and provides:

> The States Parties to the present Covenant, including those having responsibility for the administration of Non-Self-Governing and Trust Territories, shall promote the realization of the right of self-determination, and shall respect that right, in conformity with the provisions of the Charter of the United Nations.

Examination of Article 1(3) also fails to yield any conclusive definition of the term "peoples". One important factor does emerge, however, namely, that all States parties are to "promote the realization of the right to self-determination" and that this includes "those having responsibility for the administration of Non-Self-Governing Territories and Trust Territories". Thus, although Article 1(3) does not mention "peoples", it does link self-determination with non-self-governing and trust territories. The use of the word "including", however, prior to the mention of such territories, strongly implies that self-determination is not *exclusively* applicable to metropolitan powers, but also States without responsibility for non-self-governing territories. This naturally raises the possibility that the self-determination of peoples applies to groups beyond the non-self-governing context. This is buttressed by consideration of Article 1(1), which declares "[a]*ll* peoples have the right to self-determination" (emphasis added).

Article 1(3) also draws an explicit link between its content and the UN Charter, declaring that States parties shall respect the right to self-determination "in conformity with the provisions of the Charter of the United Nations". It is likely that this phrase affirms the definition of the term "peoples" deduced from the Charter, namely, that it is not necessarily synonymous with the entire population of a State or non-self-governing territory and may include sub-State national groups and national groups within non-self-governing territories.

That the term "peoples" is applicable beyond the non-self-governing context is confirmed by the covenants' *travaux préparatoires*, which indicate that during the drafting of common Article 1, a consensus emerged that "peoples" could exist in a non-colonial context (Bossuyt 1987: 32, 44–45; Summers 2007: 163). This view has been reiterated by the Human Rights Committee, which in General Comment 12 remarked:

> [T]he obligations [under Article 1] exist irrespective of whether a people entitled to self-determination depends on a State party to the Covenant or not [i.e., applies to colonial and non-colonial peoples alike]. It follows that all State parties to the Covenant should take positive action to facilitate realization of and respect for the right of peoples to self-determination.
>
> *(HRC 1984: para. 6)*

It follows that self-determination is applicable to *"all* State parties" (emphasis added) and that peoples must therefore exist beyond the colonial context.

Examination of the Covenants' *travaux préparatoires* also reveals that the term "peoples" includes nations, with several States advocating nationalist definitions of the term, such as "large compact national groups", "a group inhabiting a compact territory to which [each individual] belongs ethnically, culturally, historically or otherwise" and "racial units inhabiting well-defined territories" (Šuković 1972: 32). These definitions strongly indicate that sub-State national groups and national groups within non-self-governing territories must be included with the interpretation of the term "peoples".

Article 2(1) of the Civil Rights Covenant also sheds light – if only inferentially – on the meaning of "peoples" within common Article 1 of the Covenants:

> Each State Party to the present Covenant undertakes to respect and to ensure to all individuals within its territory and subject to its jurisdiction the rights recognized in the present Covenant, without distinction of any kind, such as race, colour, sex, language, religion, political or other opinion, national or social origin, property, birth or other status.

The phrase "all individuals within its territory" is significant. When juxtaposed with the terminology of common Article 1, it is apparent that a people and "all individuals" within a State's territory are not necessarily synonymous. If the term "people" was strictly synonymous with all the individuals of a State – i.e., the entire population – then Article 2(1) would have used the expression "to ensure the people within its territory". The fact that Article 2(1) is dealing with individual rights, while Article 1 is dealing with group rights, does not negate this interpretation. This is because any group is necessarily comprised of individuals, and when referring to groups of individuals to whom individual rights are applicable, a descriptor for the collective will be employed, such as "all individuals within its territory". If the expressions "peoples" and "all inhabitants" were strictly synonymous, then logically both articles would have used identical terminology (Radan 2002: 47). Thus, the differing terminology between common Article 1 and Article 2(1) of the Civil Rights Covenant suggests that a "people" and "all the inhabitants" of a State are not necessarily synonymous. When this conclusion is combined with the analysis originating from interpretation of common Article 1 and the covenants' *travaux préparatoires*, it seems probable that the term "peoples" is not necessarily synonymous with the entire population of a State or non-self-governing territory and may include sub-State national groups and national groups within non-self-governing territories.

This interpretation is reinforced by the Human Rights Committee, which, in General Comment 12, requests that States "describe the constitutional and political processes which in practice allow the exercise of [the] right [of self-determination]" (HRC 1984: para. 4). As various scholars have argued, the reference to a State's internal constitution and political processes strongly suggests that the right to self-determination can be exercised by groups *within* a State (Radan 2002: 48; McCorquodale 1995a: 98). This is confirmed by Britain's reporting to the Committee, which treated the Scottish, Welsh and Irish nations as separate peoples (McCorquodale 1995b: 294–298).

A final provision often cited as bearing upon the meaning of "peoples" within the Covenants is Article 27 of the Civil Rights Covenant, which provides:

> In those States in which ethnic, religious or linguistic minorities exist, persons belonging to such minorities shall not be denied the right, in community with the other members of their group, to enjoy their own culture, to profess and practice their own religion, or to use their own language.

It has been suggested by Cassese that Article 27 indicates that a minority cannot be a people, as minorities are not endowed with political, economic or social autonomy. Cassese then extrapolates that if a minority within a State cannot be a people, the meaning of "peoples" within the Covenants must be strictly synonymous with the entire population of a State (Cassese 1995: 61–62). As the text of Article 27 makes clear, however, the rights described therein are exercisable by individuals and not groups (Jonathan 1995: 917; Radan 2002: 49). Thus, simply because Article 27 does not confer any political, economic or social autonomy upon minorities does not prove that the term "peoples" is strictly synonymous with the entire population of a State. Rather, Article 27 should be read as only appropriating rights to individuals who are members of a minority. Significantly, there is no reason evident within the covenants to suggest that a minority may not also be a sub-State national group. *A priori*, there is no reason evident within the covenants to suggest that a minority may not be a people. Equally, however, it is possible that a minority may *not* be a people, particularly when a given minority is not a nation (Radan 2002: 49). In short, there is no reason to assume, as Cassese does, that Article 27 in some way restricts the definition of "peoples" as used in common Article 1. It is most likely that the terms "minority" and "peoples" although overlapping, denote two separate concepts – a conclusion that is unsurprising given the use of two distinct terminologies in common Article 1 and Article 27 of the Civil Rights Covenant.

Examination of the Economic Rights Covenant and Civil Rights Covenant thus indicates, on balance, that the term "peoples" is not necessarily synonymous with the entire population of a State or non-self-governing territory and may include sub-State national groups and national groups within non-self-governing territories.

## Legal effect of treaties

Once signed and ratified by States, treaties are binding under the principle of *pacta sunt servanda*. The meaning of "peoples" deduced from the UN Charter, Economic Rights Covenant and Civil Rights Covenant is therefore binding on signatory States.

## Declaratory General Assembly resolutions

Four declaratory General Assembly resolutions especially impact upon the definition of "peoples": the Declaration on the Granting of Independence to Colonial Countries and Peoples (UNGA 1960a), the Declaration on Principles of International Law Concerning Friendly Relations and Co-Operation Among States in Accordance With the Charter of the United Nations (UNGA 1970), the Declaration on the Occasion of the Fiftieth Anniversary of the United Nations (UNGA 1995) and the United Nations Declaration on the Rights of Indigenous Peoples (UNGA 2007).

### *Declaration on the Granting of Independence to Colonial Countries and Peoples*

The first declaratory General Assembly resolution to mention the right of peoples to self-determination was the 1960 Declaration on the Granting of Independence to Colonial Countries and Peoples (Colonial Declaration), which in Article 1 provides:

> The subjugation of peoples to alien subjugation, domination and exploitation constitutes a denial of fundamental human rights, is contrary to the Charter of the United Nations and is an impediment to the promotion of world peace and cooperation.
>
> *(UNGA 1960a: art. 1)*

Article 1 stipulates that the "subjugation, domination and exploitation" of peoples, which may include situations in addition to colonialism, such as, *inter alia*, apartheid and foreign occupation, is illegal. *A priori*, Article 1 *may* indicate that "peoples" can be used to describe groups beyond the colonial context.

Article 2 of the Colonial Declaration provides:

> All peoples have the right to self-determination; by virtue of that right they freely determine their political status and freely pursue their economic, social and cultural development.
>
> *(UNGA 1960a: art. 2)*

Article 2 begins with the inclusive phrase "all peoples have the right to self-determination", which indicates that "peoples" is a term of broad and general applicability. It follows that "peoples" probably refers to the entire population of States and non-self-governing territories (Tomuschat 1993: 2). This is supported by the fact that the Colonial Declaration was the first instrument after the UN Charter to discuss the right of peoples to self-determination, and it would therefore seem likely that the term "peoples" would be ascribed a similar meaning to that seminal instrument. No explicit guidance is given within Article 2 as to whether sub-State national groups and national groups within non-self-governing territories also constitute peoples. Such a finding would be *likely*, however, as Article 2 does make reference to "cultural development", which resembles some aspects of the definition of a nation.

Article 4 of the Colonial Declaration provides:

> All armed action or repressive measures of all kinds directed against dependent peoples shall cease in order to enable them to exercise peacefully and freely their right to complete independence, and the integrity of their national territory shall be respected.
>
> *(UNGA 1960a: art. 4)*

Article 4 uses the term "dependent peoples" when outlawing repressive measures designed to prevent the attainment of independence. It will be recalled that Articles 1 and 2 do not employ the term "dependent peoples", using instead the less specific term "peoples." Although not entirely certain, there may be a distinction between "dependent peoples" and "peoples" more generally; otherwise, Article 4 would have used the term "peoples". *A priori*, the term "peoples" *may* refer to peoples in the non-colonial context.

Article 6 of the Colonial Declaration provides:

> Any attempt aimed at the partial or total disruption of the national unity and the territorial integrity of a country is incompatible with the purposes and principle of the Charter of the United Nations.
>
> *(UNGA 1960a: art. 6)*

Trying to determine the impact of Article 6 – if it indeed impacts at all – on the meaning of "peoples" is problematic. Various scholars, for example, have interpreted Article 6 as implying that a "people" must refer to the entire population of a non-self-governing territory (Cassese 1995: 72–73; Ofuatey-Kodjoe 1995: 358). This is because it outlaws "[a]ny attempt aimed at the partial or total disruption of the national unity and territorial integrity of a *country*" (emphasis added). Inherent in this position is that the word "country" must refer exclusively to the entire population of a non-self-governing territory.[3] However, even if this interpretation of "country" is accepted *arguendo*, it still does not follow that Article 6 implies a "people" must constitute the entire population of a non-self-governing territory. As Radan has explained:

> The fundamental concern of the [Colonial] Declaration, made abundantly clear by its provisions, is the independence from foreign rule of all peoples in non-self-governing and trust territories. Sovereignty and political power were to be vested in the colonial peoples to the exclusion of the UN members administering such territories pursuant to Chapters XI and XII of the Charter. The Declaration's provisions on continued territorial integrity of colonial territories simply meant that former multinational colonial territories became multinational States. In fact, the Declaration's provisions on the continued territorial integrity of colonial territories was recognition of the fact that these territories were usually populated by a number of different peoples or nations. Mindful of the bloodshed and dislocation that had occurred in the decolonization of British India, the UN members, in drafting the Declaration, found it necessary to insist on the continued territorial integrity of former colonial territories.
>
> *(Radan 2002: 39)*

*A priori*, Article 6 does not limit the definition of "peoples" to the entire population of non-self-governing territories; rather, it only specifies that such territories, should they comprise multiple national groups, must become multinational States.

Article 7 of the Colonial Declaration provides:

> All States shall observe faithfully and strictly the provisions of the Charter of the United Nations, the Universal Declaration of Human Rights and the present Declaration on the basis of equality, non-interference in the internal affairs of all States, and respect for the sovereign rights of all peoples and their territorial integrity.
>
> *(UNGA 1960a: art. 7)*

Article 7 is especially difficult to construe. It begins by addressing the obligations therein to "States" and continues by confirming the norm of non–interference in the internal affairs of "States," a norm established by Article 2(7) of the UN Charter. It then directs all States to respect the "sovereign rights of all peoples and their territorial integrity". It is possible that Article 7 is suggesting that the term "peoples" is applicable in a non–colonial context, i.e., that States should not interfere in the internal affairs of other States. Equally, however, it is possible that the term "peoples" is applicable in a colonial context, i.e., that non–self–governing peoples should be granted their "sovereign rights" and be permitted to achieve independence, or free association/independence with an existing state (UNGA 1960b: Principle 6). Article 7 does not, therefore, shed any definitive light on the definition of "peoples".

The Colonial Declaration was complemented by General Assembly Resolution 1541 (UNGA 1960b). Given the interconnection between both instruments, it is appropriate to consider the meaning of "peoples" within Resolution 1541, even though, strictly speaking, it is not a declaratory General Assembly resolution.

The first mention of "peoples" in Resolution 1541 occurs in Principle 1, which notes that "[a]n obligation exists to transmit information under Article 73e of the Charter in respect of such territories whose peoples have not yet attained a full measure of self-government". The wording of Principle 1 is ambiguous, indicating that the inhabitants, or entire population of a non-self-governing territory, may be a people. By virtue of its use of double plurals, however, Principle 1 leaves open the possibility that the entire inhabitants of a non-self-governing territory may comprise more than one people.

Principle 2 of Resolution 1541 provides:

> Chapter XI of the Charter embodies the concept of Non-Self-Governing Territories in a dynamic state of evolution and progress towards a "full measure of self-government". As soon as a territory and its peoples attain a full measure of self-government, the obligation ceases. Until this comes about, the obligation to transmit information under Article 73e continues.
>
> *(UNGA 1960b: Principle 2)*

Principle 2 indicates that the entire inhabitants of a non-self-governing territory may comprise more than one people, using the phrase "a territory and its peoples".[4] This supports the view, derived from Article 2 of the Colonial Declaration and its reference to "cultural development", that national groups within non-self-governing territories are included within the term "peoples".

Principle 7 of Resolution 1541 declares:

> (a) Free association should be the result of a free and voluntary choice made by the peoples of the territory concerned expressed through informed and democratic processes. It should be one which respects the individuality and the cultural characteristics of the territory and its peoples, and retains for the peoples of the territory which is associated with an independent State the freedom to modify the status of that territory through the expression of their will by democratic means and through constitutional processes.
>
> (b) The associated territory should have the right to determine its internal constitution without outside interference in accordance with due constitutional processes and the freely expressed wishes of the people. This does not preclude consultations as appropriate or necessary under the terms of the free association agreed upon.
>
> *(UNGA 1960b: Principle 7)*

Principle 7, paragraph (a) indicates that the inhabitants of a non-self-governing territory can comprise more than one people, using the expressions "peoples of the territory" and "territory and its peoples." Strangely, however, this terminology – which is consistent with Principle 2 – is not replicated in Principle 7, paragraph (b), which in the first sentence uses the term "territory" (singular) followed by the phrase "wishes of the people" (singular). According to Principle 7, paragraph (b), therefore, only one people can inhabit a non-self-governing territory. This is a significant drafting inconsistency which casts doubt on whether national groups within non-self-governing territories are captured by the expression "peoples".

Principle 8 of Resolution 1541 states:

> Integration with an independent State should be on the basis of complete equality between the peoples of the erstwhile Non-Self-Governing Territory and those of the independent country with which it is integrated. The peoples of both territories should have equal status and rights of citizenship and equal guarantees of fundamental rights and freedoms without any distinction or discrimination: both should have equal rights and opportunities for representation and effective participation at all levels in the executive, legislative and judicial organs of government.
>
> *(UNGA 1960b: Principle 8)*

Principle 8 indicates that more than one people may inhabit a non-self-governing territory, as evidenced by the phrase "peoples [plural] of the erstwhile Non-Self-Governing Territory [singular]". This supports the view, derived from Article 2 of the Colonial Declaration and its reference to "cultural development", that national groups within non-self-governing territories are included within the term "peoples".

Significantly, Principle 8 also indicates that peoples may exist in a non-colonial context, as indicated by its opening sentence, "Integration with an independent State should be on the basis of complete equality between the peoples of the erstwhile Non-Self-Governing Territory and those of the independent country with which it is integrated." The placement of the word "independent" prior to the word "country" strongly indicates that the term "country" refers to independent States. This meaning is supported by analysis of Principle 4, which provides that "Prima facie there is an obligation to transmit information in respect of a territory which is geographically separate and is distinct ethnically and/or culturally from the country administering it." The phrase "country administering it" clearly suggests that metropolitan powers, which are independent States, are countries.

Principle 8 continues in its second sentence to note that "[t]he peoples of both territories [i.e., the peoples of the erstwhile Non-Self-Governing Territory and those of the independent country with which it is integrated] should have equal rights of citizenship and equal guarantees of fundamental rights." The second sentence therefore reaffirms that "peoples" may exist in a non-colonial context, by virtue of the phrase "the peoples of both territories". Given that Principle 8 indicates that more than one people may inhabit a non-self-governing territory, and that peoples may exist in a colonial and non-colonial context, it is likely that more than one people may inhabit a State. This is supported by close analysis of the opening sentence of Principle 8, which provides "integration with an independent State should be on the basis of complete equality between the peoples of the erstwhile Non-Self-Governing Territory and *those* of the independent country with which it is integrated" (emphasis added). The use of the word "those" indicates pluralism, suggesting that more than one people may inhabit a State. *A priori*, "peoples" probably also refers to sub-State national groups.

The final paragraphs warranting examination are contained in Principle 9, which provide:

Integration should come about in the following circumstances:

(a) The integrating territory should have attained an advanced stage of self-government with free political institutions, so that its peoples would have the capacity to make a responsible choice through informed and democratic processes;

(b) The integration should be the result of the freely expressed wishes of the territory's peoples acting with full knowledge of the change in their status.

*(UNGA 1960b: Principle 9)*

Principle 9, paragraph (a) indicates that more than one people may inhabit a non-self-governing territory, as evidenced by the use of the term "territory" (singular) with the phrase "its peoples" (plural). Paragraph (b) confirms this position, using the phrase "territory's peoples". Principle 9, paragraphs (a) and (b) thus support the view, derived from Article 2 of the Colonial Declaration and its reference to "cultural development", that national groups within non-self-governing territories are included within the term "peoples".

Examination of the Colonial Declaration and accompanying Resolution 1541 therefore indicates that the term "peoples" is employed in a manner consistent with the UN Charter, namely, that it is not necessarily synonymous with the entire population of a State or non-self-governing territory and may include sub-State national groups and national groups within non-self-governing territories.

Finally, it is apposite to note that the broad meaning of "peoples" deduced throughout the preceding discussion, particularly the view that the Colonial Declaration captures peoples in a non-colonial context, is a controversial one. Quane, for example, after examining the meaning of "peoples" within the Colonial Declaration, has concluded:

Support for this narrow interpretation [of] "peoples" [i.e., confined to the colonial context] can be found in the overall context, the title and the object and purpose of the resolution. Furthermore, the overwhelming majority of representatives who spoke during the debate on the Resolution addressed themselves solely to the position of colonial peoples.

*(Quane 1998: 548)*

This position, however, overlooks the "plain and ordinary meaning"[5] of the term "peoples" derived from close analysis of the provisions within the Colonial Declaration and accompanying Resolution 1541. Furthermore, it also requires that the Colonial Declaration – the first declaratory General Assembly resolution to expound upon the topic of "peoples" – propounds a different meaning of "peoples" to that contained within the UN Charter. As demonstrated here, a close analysis of the Colonial Declaration and accompanying Resolution 1541 does *not* suggest a definition of "peoples" inconsistent with the Charter.

### *Declaration on Principles of International Law Concerning Friendly Relations and Co-Operation Among States in Accordance With the Charter of the United Nations*

The Declaration on Principles of International Law Concerning Friendly Relations and Co-Operation Among States in Accordance With the Charter of the United Nations (Friendly

Relations Declaration) was adopted by the UN General Assembly in October 1970. As the name suggests, it enumerates principles of international law concerning friendly relations and cooperation among States. Principle 5, paragraph 1 of the Friendly Relations Declaration provides:

> By virtue of the principle of equal rights and self-determination of peoples enshrined in the Charter of the United Nations, all peoples have the right freely to determine, without external interference, their political status and to pursue their economic, social and cultural development, and every State has the duty to respect this right in accordance with the provisions of the Charter.
>
> *(UNGA 1970: Principle 5 para. 1)*

Paragraph 1 begins by linking the word "peoples" with the UN Charter, which inferentially suggests that "peoples" is employed in a manner consistent with that seminal treaty, namely, that a people is not necessarily synonymous with the entire population of a State or non-self-governing territory and may include sub-State national groups and national groups within non-self-governing territories.

This interpretation is buttressed by analysis of the paragraph's overall text, which mentions "State[s]" and "peoples", thereby indicating separate concepts. Paragraph 1 also mentions "cultural development", which resembles some aspects of the definition of a nation. Additionally, paragraph 1 declares that "*all* peoples" (emphasis added) enjoy the right to self-determination, which indicates that "peoples" is an expression of broad and general applicability, extending to the colonial and non-colonial context (Šuković 1972: 346).

A similar conclusion is reached by examination of paragraph 2, which again links the word "peoples" with the UN Charter and mentions "State[s]" and "peoples" as distinct concepts. Furthermore, sub-paragraph 2(b) indicates that peoples may exist in a colonial context, and then supplements this with the addendum that "subjection of peoples to alien subjugation, domination and exploitation" is contrary to the UN Charter. Unless the latter phrase is pleonastic, it indicates that peoples can also exist in a non-colonial context, as situations of "alien subjugation, domination and exploitation" are not, by definition, confined exclusively to the colonial context.

Paragraph 4 reiterates, *mutatis mutandis*, the content of Principle 6 of Resolution 1541 regarding the methods by which a people may exercise their right to external self-determination.[6] However unlike Principle VI, the paragraph does not explicitly seek to limit the application of its content to colonial peoples. This difference is crucial, as it arguably opens the possibility for paragraph 4 to apply to non-colonial peoples. Paragraph 4 would therefore appear to comport with the meaning of "peoples" as deduced from paragraphs 1 and 2.

Paragraph 5 deals with the duty of "States" to refrain from action which would deprive "peoples" of their right to self-determination, and by so doing reaffirms that States and peoples are two distinct concepts. Furthermore, if it is accepted that paragraphs 1, 2 and 4 imply that peoples can exist in a colonial and non-colonial context, it follows that the directive contained in paragraph 5 must also apply to peoples in a colonial and non-colonial setting.

Paragraph 6 deals exclusively with peoples in a colonial context, as indicated by the opening phrase, "The territory of a colony or other Non-Self-Governing Territory has, under the Charter, a status separate and distinct from the territory of the State administering it." The fact that paragraph 6 confines its purpose to colonial peoples is significant for the fact that the paragraphs preceding it do *not*. This is further evidence that the preceding paragraphs – 1, 2, 4 and 5 – refer to peoples *beyond* the colonial context.

Paragraph 6 continues by noting that "such separate and distinct status under the Charter shall exist until the people of the colony or Non-Self-Governing Territory have exercised their right to self-determination". Crucially, paragraph 6 would seem to indicate that only one people can exist within a non-self-governing territory, as the plural "peoples" is not employed. It will be recalled that this drafting is inconsistent with the UN Charter, Articles 73, 73(b) and 76(b), and Resolution 1541, Principles 2, 7(a), 8 and 9, all of which indicate that more than one people may inhabit a non-self-governing territory. Bearing this in mind, the failure of paragraph 6 to use the plural term "peoples" probably constitutes a drafting error.

Paragraph 7 arguably moves beyond the colonial context when employing the term "peoples", providing:

> Nothing in the foregoing paragraphs shall be construed as authorizing or encouraging any action which would dismember or impair, totally or in part, the territorial integrity or political unity of sovereign and independent States conducting themselves in compliance with the principle of equal rights and self-determination of peoples as described above and thus possessed of a government representing the whole people belonging to the territory without distinction as to race, creed or colour.
>
> *(UNGA 1970: Principle 5 para. 7)*

Paragraph 7 links its content to "sovereign and independent States", which would seem to refer to "States" and not non-self-governing territories. Although it might be argued that metropolitan powers are "States" responsible for non-self-governing territories, this appears not to be the primary objective of paragraph 7. This reasoning is not negated by the subsequent phrase "States conducting themselves in compliance with the principle of equal rights and self-determination of peoples as described above", which necessarily requires that all other paragraphs before paragraph 7 must be considered, as paragraphs 1, 2, 4 and 5 indicate that peoples can exist in a colonial and a non-colonial context. Only paragraph 6 restricts its discussion of peoples to the non-self-governing or colonial context. Therefore, paragraph 7 is probably addressing its comments to sovereign States, which by implication confirms the applicability of the term "peoples" to the non-colonial context.

Paragraph 7 does, however, contain some drafting glitches. This is because although it applies the term "peoples" to the non-colonial context, taken literally, it indicates that only one people can constitute a sovereign State. This is revealed by the phrase "thus possessed of a government representing the whole *people* belonging to the territory" (emphasis added). If it is accepted that "peoples" may refer to sub-State national groups and national groups within non-self-governing territories, as indicated by the UN Charter, Articles 73, 73(b) and 76(b) and Resolution 1541, Principles 2, 7(a), 8 and 9, it would seem that the drafting of paragraph 7 is erroneous, as the phrase "whole people belonging to the territory" suggests that there may only be one people within a State. Moreover, the phrase "without distinction as to race, creed or colour", which proceeds the phrase "whole people belonging to the territory" suggests that States are non-monolithic and comprise sub-State groups (Radan 2002: 60; Duursma 1996: 25). Paragraph 7 should perhaps have used the phrase "thus possessed of a government representing *all peoples* belonging to the territory without distinction as to race, creed or colour." Use of the plural "peoples" would, it is submitted, bring paragraph 7 unambiguously into line with prior instruments, including the UN Charter, with which the Friendly Relations Declaration was drafted to be in accordance, as indicated by the latter's extended title – Declaration on Principles of International Law Concerning Friendly Relations and Co-Operation Among States *in Accordance With the Charter of the United Nations* (emphasis added).

Despite some ambiguous tendencies, particularly those detected in Principle 5, paragraphs 6 and 7, on balance, it is submitted that the term "peoples" is employed by the Friendly Relations

Declaration in a manner consistent with earlier UN instruments, namely, that it is not necessarily synonymous with the entire population of a State or non-self-governing territory, and may include sub-State national groups and national groups within non-self-governing territories.

Finally, the textual content of the Friendly Relations Declaration has been vicariously incorporated into subsequent declaratory General Assembly resolutions, such the Manila Declaration on the Peaceful Settlement of International Disputes (UNGA 1982: art. 11(6)), the Declaration on the Enhancement of the Effectiveness of the Principle of Refraining from the Threat or Use of Force in International Relations (UNGA 1987: art. 3), and Article 3 of the Declaration on the Prevention and Removal of Disputes and Situations Which May Threaten International Peace and Security and on the Role of the United Nations in This Field (UNGA 1988: art. 3). The same can also be said with respect to Article 7 of the non-declaratory – but nonetheless legally significant – Definition of Aggression (UNGA 1974: art. 7). These instruments can therefore be said to apply the same definition of "peoples".

## The Declaration on the Occasion of the Fiftieth Anniversary of the United Nations

In October 1995 the General Assembly adopted the Declaration on the Occasion of the Fiftieth Anniversary of the United Nations (Fiftieth Anniversary Declaration) which, in Article 1, provides that the UN will:

> Continue to reaffirm the right of self-determination of all peoples, taking into account the particular situation of peoples under colonial or other forms of alien domination or foreign occupation, and recognize the right of peoples to take legitimate action in accordance with the Charter of the United Nations to realize their inalienable right to self-determination. This shall not be construed as authorizing or encouraging any action that would dismember or impair, totally or in part, the territorial integrity or political unity of sovereign and independent States conducting themselves in compliance with the principle of equal rights and self-determination of peoples and thus possessed of a government representing the whole people belonging to the territory without distinction of any kind.
>
> (UNGA 1995: art. 1)

Article 1 contains two sentences. The first specifies that "all peoples" have the right to self-determination, which suggests that "peoples" is a term of broad and general applicability. This interpretation is confirmed by the remainder of the first sentence, which recognizes the "particular situation of peoples under colonial or other forms of alien domination or foreign occupation." The phrase "colonial . . . domination" refers to colonial situations of the type targeted and defined in the Colonial Declaration and accompanying Resolution 1541. The phrase "alien domination", although including colonial situations, is necessarily broader, extending to the non-colonial context where peoples are subjected to alien or foreign rule. The phrase "foreign domination" most likely refers to situations of foreign occupation and exploitation, and therefore includes peoples in a colonial and non-colonial context. The first sentence of Article 1 thus indicates that peoples may exist in a colonial and non-colonial context. It fails, however, to indicate whether peoples are necessarily synonymous with the entire population of a State or non-self-governing territory, or may also include sub-State national groups and national groups within non-self-governing territories. No explicit reference is made, for example, to the articulation of the "self-determination of peoples" in any earlier UN instruments, such as the

Friendly Relations Declaration. Nonetheless, given the long lineage of the phrase "self-determination of peoples" within declaratory General Assembly resolutions, all of which indicate that
"peoples" may include sub-State national groups and national groups within non-self-governing
territories, it is highly likely that "peoples", as employed in Article 1 of the Fiftieth Anniversary
Declaration, has a commensurate meaning.

The second sentence of Article 1 reiterates, *mutatis mutandis*, Principle 5, paragraph 7 of the
Friendly Relations Declaration, with an *a contrario* reading revealing that only those "sovereign
and independent States conducting themselves in compliance with the principle of equal rights
and self-determination of peoples and thus possessed of a government representing the whole
people belonging to the territory without distinction of any kind" will be guaranteed their
"territorial integrity or political unity". The second sentence of Article 1 thus links its content
to "sovereign and independent States" – not non-self-governing territories.

As with Principle 5, paragraph 7 of the Friendly Relations Declaration, however, the second sentence of Article 1 of the Fiftieth Anniversary Declaration does contain some drafting
irregularities. This is because, if taken literally, it indicates that only one people can comprise a
sovereign State. This is revealed by the phrase, "thus possessed of a government representing the
whole *people* belonging to the territory" (emphasis added). The use of the singular "people" as
opposed to the plural "peoples" can most likely be attributed to the fact that the second sentence
of Article 1 was based on Principle 5, paragraph 7 of the Friendly Relations Declaration. If,
however, it is accepted that "peoples" can refer to sub-State national groups and national groups
within non-self-governing territories, as indicated by instruments antedating the Friendly Relations Declaration, such as the UN Charter, Articles 73, 73(b) and 76(b), and Resolution 1541,
Principles 2, 7(a), 8 and 9, it would seem that the drafting of Article 1 is incorrect, as the phrase
"whole people" suggests there can only be one people within a state. Moreover, the phrase
"without distinction of any kind", which proceeds the phrase "whole people belonging to the
territory", suggests that States are non-monolithic and comprise sub-State groups. On balance,
therefore, the phrase "whole people" most likely represents a drafting error.

Thus, although Article 1 of the Fiftieth Anniversary Declaration is not without ambiguities,
particularly those detected in the second sentence, on balance, it is submitted that the term
"peoples" is employed in a manner consistent with earlier UN instruments, namely, that it is
not necessarily synonymous with the entire population of a State or non-self-governing territory and may include sub-State national groups and national groups within non-self-governing
territories.

## United Nations Declaration on the Rights of Indigenous Peoples

In September 2007, the General Assembly adopted the United Nations Declaration on the
Rights of Indigenous Peoples (Indigenous Declaration), which in Article 2 declares:

> Indigenous peoples and individuals are free and equal to other peoples and individuals
> and have the right to be free from any kind of discrimination, in the exercise of their
> rights, in particular, that based on their indigenous origin or identity.
>
> *(UNGA 2007: art. 2)*

Article 2 suggests that indigenous peoples constitute a particular type of people, and furthermore, that indigenous peoples can be distinguished by their "indigenous origin or identity".
Given that indigenous groups – as ordinarily understood – reside within sovereign States, it is
highly probable that "indigenous peoples" constitute sub-State national groups.

Article 46(1) provides further insight as to the meaning of "peoples", specifying:

> Nothing in this Declaration may be interpreted as implying for any State, people, group or person any right to engage in any activity or to perform any act contrary to the Charter of the United Nations.
>
> *(UNGA 2007: art. 46(1))*

Article 46(1) intimates that States and peoples are not necessarily synonymous, as indicated by the adjacent listing of "State[s]" and "people[s]". Given that indigenous groups reside within sovereign States, it is likely that "indigenous peoples" comprise sub-State national groups.

The view that indigenous peoples constitute sub-State national groups is supported by Article 9, which provides:

> Indigenous peoples and individuals have the right to belong to an indigenous community or *nation*, in accordance with the traditions and customs of the community or nation concerned. No discrimination of any kind may arise from the exercise of such a right.
>
> *(UNGA 2007: art. 9, emphasis added)*

The linkage between "peoples" and "nations" was also inferentially supported by indigenous representatives involved in the Declaration's drafting, who argued:

> There can be no doubt that we are peoples with distinct historical, political and cultural identities and will remain so. We are united by our histories as distinct societies, as well as by our languages, laws and traditions. . . . Indigenous peoples are unquestionably peoples in every legal, political, social, cultural and ethnological meaning of the term. It would be discriminatory, illogical and unscientific to identify us in the United Nations Declaration [Indigenous Declaration] . . . as anything less than peoples.
>
> *(CHR 2000: 2)*

The reference to criteria such as unique history, social organization, language, laws and traditions – all of which allude to the definition of a nation – strongly indicates that indigenous peoples are nations.

The Indigenous Declaration therefore suggests that "indigenous peoples" are one type of peoples and that States and peoples are not necessarily synonymous. Examination of Article 9 strongly suggests that indigenous peoples typically constitute sub-State national groups.

## *Legal effect of declaratory General Assembly resolutions*

Generally, declaratory General Assembly resolutions gain legal effect via customary law (Anderson 2013: 379–388, 394, 438). However, as intimated by the International Court of Justice (ICJ) in *Nicaragua v. the United States of America* (ICJ 1986), the textual content of such resolutions will only satisfy the requirement of *opinio juris*, and thus enjoy perfection under customary law, when accompanied by concomitant State practice in terms of physical acts and omissions (ICJ 1986: Paras 188, 189, 192, 202, 205; Anderson 2013: 386–387). This would generally require that the law of self-determination is applicable to (1) States as a whole, (2) non-self-governing territories, (3) sub-State national groups and (4) national groups within non-self-governing territories. Is this reflected in State practice? Without undertaking an exhaustive empirical analysis, the answer is probably "yes". There is strong evidence that self-determination has an internal dimension – meaning it is applicable within sovereign States (Anderson 2017: 63). This extends to sub-State groups, as indicated by State reporting to the Human Rights Committee in accordance with General Comment 12 (McCorquodale 1995b: 294–298). Self-determination has also been applied to allow unilateral colonial (UC) secession from metropolitan powers, and perhaps – at least in the case of deliberate and sustained human rights abuses *in extremis* – unilateral non-colonial (UNC) secession (Anderson 2016: 1234–1235; Anderson 2015: 8–13, 23–30). The latter is borne out by examination of acts of recognition in relation to Bangladesh, Croatia and Kosovo (Anderson 2015: 31–40). There is therefore no reason to think that the meaning of "peoples" deducible from declaratory General Assembly resolutions is incommensurate with State practice in terms of physical acts and omissions.

## Conclusion

Using orthodox methods of textual interpretation laid down by ss 31(1) and 32(a) of the 1969 Vienna Convention on the Law of Treaties, a consistent definition of the term "peoples" emerges from international treaties and declaratory General Assembly resolutions, namely that "peoples" are not necessarily synonymous with the entire population of a State or non-self-governing territory and may include sub-State national groups and national groups within non-self-governing territories. This definition allows the law of self-determination to apply in a variety of contexts, not simply – as some scholars and States' representatives might suggest – in the decolonization context, or with respect to the entire population of a sovereign State. This view is reinforced by the Indigenous Declaration, which applies to indigenous peoples within sovereign States.

It would seem that the term "peoples" is, in certain settings, interrelated with the concept of nations, or national groupings, although most of the international instruments analysed in this chapter do not provide the definition of a nation. Some useful guidance on the legal meaning of a nation, however, is furnished by the Indigenous Declaration, which in Article 9 states (emphasis added):

> Indigenous peoples and individuals have the right to belong to an indigenous community or *nation*, in accordance with the traditions and customs of the community or nation concerned.

The Indigenous Declaration thus suggests that nations are associated with "traditions and customs", thereby echoing the romantic definition of nation, namely, a distinct cultural group identified by shared language, religion, ethnicity and history.

In conclusion, the term "peoples" can be ascribed a legal definition encompassing: (1) the entire population of a State; (2) the entire population of a non-self-governing territory; (3) sub-State national groups; and (4) national groups within non-self-governing territories. In the case of (3) and (4), the term "peoples" broadly correlates with the romantic definition of a nation. However, (1) and (2) *may* also correlate with the romantic definition of a nation in the event of a unitary nation-State or non-self-governing territory. To be clear, though, in (1) and (2) the term "peoples" is capable of referring to the entire population of a multinational State or non-self-governing territory. Context is therefore key – the term "peoples" does not have a singular definition under international law, but can instead refer to a variety of groups in different situations.

# Notes

1 Article 31(2) of the Vienna Convention on the Law of Treaties provides that "[t]he context for the purpose of the interpretation of a treaty shall comprise, in addition to the text . . . its preamble and annexes".

2 The Belgian delegation proposed an amendment to remove the ambiguity which referred to "the essential rights and equality of the states, and of the peoples' right to self-determination" (UNCIO 1945–1952: vol. VI, 300).

3 The word "country" is not defined within the Colonial Declaration, and only appears once in Article 6. It is possible, and indeed probable, therefore, that it was included to denote both the territory of a non-self-governing territory and the territory of States. This flexible interpretation is confirmed by close analysis of an accompanying General Assembly resolution (UNGA 1960b), which in Principle 9 declares: "Integration with an independent State should be on the basis of complete equality between the peoples of the erstwhile Non-Self-Governing Territory and those of the independent country with which it is integrated". *A priori*, the term "country" does not exclusively refer to non-self-governing territories and may also include States.

4 Similar terminology is contained in Articles 73, 73(b) and 76(b) of the UN Charter.

5 As mandated by Article 31(1) of the 1969 Vienna Convention on the Law of Treaties.

6 Principle 6 of General Assembly Resolution 1541 (XV), states "[a] Non-Self-Governing Territory can be said to have reached a full measure of self-government by: (a) Emergence as a sovereign independent State; (b) Free association with an independent State; or (c) Integration with an independent State" (UNGA 1960b: Principle 6).

# References

Anderson, G. 2013, "Unilateral Non-Colonial Secession in International Law and Declaratory General Assembly Resolutions: Textual Content and Legal Effects", *Denver Journal of International Law and Policy*, 41(3): 345–395.

Anderson, G. 2015, "Unilateral Non-Colonial Secession and the Criteria for Statehood in International Law", *Brooklyn Journal of International Law*, 41(1): 1–98.

Anderson, G. 2016, "A Post-Millennial Inquiry into the United Nations Law of Self-Determination: A Right to Unilateral Non-Colonial Secession?", *Vanderbilt Journal of Transnational Law*, 49(5): 1183–1254.

Anderson, G. 2017, "Unilateral Non-Colonial Secession and Internal Self-Determination: A Right of Newly Seceded Peoples to Democracy", *Arizona Journal of International and Comparative Law*, 34(1): 1–64.

Bossuyt, M. J. 1987, *Guide to the "Travaux Préparatoires" of the International Covenant on Civil and Political Rights*, Martinus Nijhoff Publishers: Dordrecht.

Cassese, A. 1995, *Self-Determination of Peoples: A Legal Reappraisal*, Cambridge University Press: Cambridge.

CHR 2000, Commission on Human Rights, Fifty-Sixth Session, Item 15 (Position of Indigenous Peoples in Regard to the Use of the Term Indigenous Peoples in the United Nations Draft Declaration for the Rights of Indigenous Peoples), 22 February.

Cristescu, A. 1981, *The Right to Self-Determination: Historical and Current Developments on the Basis of United Nations Instruments*, United Nations: New York.

Duursma, J. 1996, *Fragmentation and the International Relations of Micro-States*, Cambridge University Press: Cambridge.

Franck, T. M. 1998, "Legitimacy in the International System", *American Journal of International Law*, 82(4): 705–759.

HRC 1984, Human Rights Committee, CCPR General Comment No. 12, Article 1 (Right to Self-determination), Right to Self-Determination of Peoples, 13 March.

ICJ 1986, "International Court of Justice", *Military and Paramilitary Activities in and against Nicaragua (Nicaragua v. United States of America)*, International Court of Justice Reports 14.

Jonathan, G. C. 1995, "Human Rights Covenants", in R. Bernhardt (ed.), *Encyclopedia of Public International Law*, Vol. 2, North-Holland: Amsterdam: 915–922.

McCorquodale, R. 1995a, "Negotiating Sovereignty: The Practice of the United Kingdom in Regard to the Right of Self-Determination", *British Yearbook of International Law*, 66(1): 283–331.

McCorquodale, R. 1995b, "The Right to Self-Determination", in D. Harris & S. Joseph (eds.), *The International Covenant on Civil and Political Rights and United Kingdom Law*, Clarendon Press: Oxford: 91–119.

Ofuatey-Kodjoe, W. 1995, "Self-Determination", in O. Schachter & C. C. Joyner (eds.), *United Nations Legal Order, Volume 1*, Cambridge University Press: Cambridge: 349–389.

Quane, H. 1998, "The United Nations and the Evolving Right to Self-Determination", *International and Comparative Law Quarterly*, 47(3): 537–572.

Radan, P. 2002, *The Break-Up of Yugoslavia and International Law*, Routledge: London.

Šuković, O. 1972, "Principle of Equal Rights and Self-Determination of Peoples", in M. Šahović (ed.), *Principles of International Law Concerning Friendly Relations and Cooperation*, The Institute of International Politics and Economics: Belgrade: 323–373.

Summers, J. 2007, *Peoples and International Law: How Nationalism and Self-Determination Shape a Contemporary Law of Nations*, Martinus Nijhoff Publishers: Leiden.

Tomuschat, C. 1993, "Self-Determination in a Post-Colonial World", in C. Tomuschat (ed.), *Modern Law of Self-Determination*, Martinus Nijhoff Publishers: Dordrecht: 1–20.

UNCIO 1945–1952, *United Nations Documents of the Conference on International Organization*, 18 Vols, San Francisco.

UNGA 1960a, United Nations General Assembly, Declaration on the Granting of Independence to Colonial Countries and Peoples, Resolution 1514 (XV), 14 December.

UNGA 1960b, United Nations General Assembly, Principles Which Should Guide Members in Determining Whether or Not an Obligation Exists to Transmit the Information Called for in Article 73(e) of the Charter of the United Nations, annex to Resolution 1541 (XV), 15 December.

UNGA 1966a, United Nations General Assembly, International Covenant on Economic, Social and Cultural Rights, Resolution 2200 (XXI), 16 December.

UNGA 1966b, United Nations General Assembly, International Covenant on Civil and Political Rights, Resolution 2200 (XXI), 16 December.

UNGA 1970, United Nations General Assembly, Declaration on Principles of International Law Concerning Friendly Relations and Co-Operation Among States in Accordance With the Charter of the United Nations, Resolution 2625 (XXV), 24 October.

UNGA 1974, United Nations General Assembly, Definition of Aggression, Resolution 3314 (XXIX), 14 December.

UNGA 1982, United Nations General Assembly, Manila Declaration on the Peaceful Settlement of International Disputes, Resolution 37/10, 15 November.

UNGA 1987, United Nations General Assembly, Declaration on the Enhancement of the Effectiveness of the Principle of Refraining from the Threat or Use of Force in International Relations, Resolution 42/22, 18 November.

UNGA 1988, United Nations General Assembly, Declaration on the Prevention and Removal of Disputes and Situations Which May Threaten International Peace and Security and on the Role of the United Nations in This Field, Resolution 43/51, 5 December.

UNGA 1995, United Nations General Assembly, Declaration on the Occasion of the Fiftieth Anniversary of the United Nations, Resolution 50/6, 24 October.

UNGA 2007, United Nations General Assembly, United Nations Declaration on the Rights of Indigenous Peoples, Resolution 61/295, 13 September.

# 5

# SELF-DETERMINATION AND DECOLONIZATION

*Costas Laoutides*

## Introduction

The end of the First World War has been the apex of imperial expansion when the last major redrawing of the colonial map favoured the victors of the Great War. Yet such expansion lacked legitimate control in the eyes of at least some parts of the populations under imperial rule. The time before and during the Paris Peace Conference was marked by the promotion of the principle of self-determination by the then president of the United States Woodrow Wilson, who defended a new form of political organization based on democratic self-rule. This prospect increased the aspirations of nationalists across the colonial world who believed that the road to independence "passed through Paris" (Manela 2007, p. 12). The disappointment in the colonies from the shortcomings in the Versailles Peace Treaty regarding the principle of self-determination led to the mobilization of anti-colonial protest movements which enjoyed widespread support (Simpson 2018). Although decolonization based on self-determination harks back to the American and Haitian Revolutions in the late eighteenth and early nineteenth centuries, this chapter is mainly concerned with the second wave of the decolonization process that took place in the second half of the twentieth century. Two reasons underscore this choice. First, the latter process liberated more than 1.1 billion people who were under imperial rule at the end of the Second World War. This estimate incorporates populations in the 1946 list of non-self-governing territories by the United Nations (UNGA Resolution 66(I)) as well as populations under colonial rule in India, Burma and Algeria that were not included in the General Assembly list. Second, post-1945 self-determination of the peoples was gradually institutionalized in the United Nations' legal framework, and it thus underpinned the decolonization process within the emerging framework of human rights protection in international politics. The increasing importance of self-determination as an institutional norm was also reflected by its incorporation in key documents of regional international organizations such as the Conference for the Security and Cooperation in Europe (later OSCE) and the Organization of African Unity (later African Union).

The chapter is divided in three parts. Part one traces the origins of self-determination and its two basic formulations at the end of the First World War. Part two explores the institutionalization and interpretation of the principle within the decolonization context after 1945, whilst part three touches on the issue of self-determination beyond the colonial context and its ramification for contemporary international politics.

DOI: 10.4324/9781003036593-7

## Background: self-determination by the end of the First World War

The first step in unpacking the relation of self-determination with decolonization is to explore the evolution of self-determination in political thought and practice. Since the seventeenth century, individual self-determination has been linked with free will and free agency. Self-determining individuals are autonomous free agents with respect to some of their actions; if one is free, this means one is self-determined (Chappell 2005). This proposition, commonly met in the works of John Locke, Jean-Jacques Rousseau and Immanuel Kant, suggests that humans with self-imposed norms determine themselves as free and moral beings (Beran 1998; Kedourie 1993). Because individuals make choices based on reason that are informed by moral values, self-determination makes individuals humans. As moral agents, humans have a duty to respect the self-determination of all other humans. This interaction generates a right to individual self-determination (Weitz 2015).

The transition from the individual to collective self-determination in a colonial context is found in the American Declaration of Independence of 1776 that begins with a reference to the need of "one people to dissolve the political bands which have connected them with another" and declares:

> We hold these truths to be self-evident, that all men are created equal, that they are endowed by their Creator with certain unalienable Rights, that among these are Life, Liberty and the pursuit of Happiness. That to secure these rights, Governments are instituted among Men, deriving their just powers from the consent of the governed. That whenever any Form of Government becomes destructive of these ends, it is the Right of the People to alter or to abolish it, and to institute new Government.

For the drafters of the American Declaration, self-determination was directly linked to the abolition of forms of government that do not have the consent of the governed.

Gradually in the nineteenth century, collective self-determination was invested with the principle of nationality. Several nineteenth-century thinkers such as Johann Gottfried Herder, Giuseppe Mazzini, Ernest Renan and Otto Bauer argued that the collective where the individuals can pursue self-determination and protect their individual rights is their autonomous nation (Heraclides 2020; Weitz 2015). Individuals could be free only in a community that shares a common culture; thus, individual self-determination and collective, national, self-determination are inseparable.

John Stuart Mill (1863/1910, p. 360) summarizes this line of thought:

> Where the sentiment of nationality exists in any force, there is a prima facie case for uniting all the members of the nationality under the same government, and a government to themselves apart . . . Free institutions are next to impossible in a country made up of different nationalities.

For Mill, free institutions are directly linked with collective self-government based on nationality. The idea that only nations can claim collective self-determination was perceived as universal truth without the need for further qualification. The unquestionable character of national self-determination was further manifested in the notion of independent statehood (French & Gutman 1974). The independent territorial state is the locus where national self-determination is realized and self-government is achieved (Waters 2020, p. 20; Waters, Chapter 9, this volume).

## Wilson, Lenin, and the League of Nations

By the end of the First World War two versions of the principle of national self-determination have been clearly formulated. The first was associated with then US President Woodrow Wilson, who promoted the principle of nationalities as one of the main pillars for the post-war international order closely linked to popular sovereignty and majority rule (Throntveit 2011). The Wilsonian conception of self-determination was based on democratic theory, and it was the logical corollary of self-rule and the consent of the governed (Lynch 2002, pp. 424–425). For Wilson, self-determination required that peoples of each state be granted the right freely to select state authorities and political leaders. Self-determination meant self-government, and accordingly, people subjected to colonial control had the right to self-rule.

At the international level, Wilson advocated four different variants of the principle of self-determination. First, he suggested the right of each people to choose the form of government under which they would live. The second version of self-determination was related to the restructuring of central Europe in accordance with national desires. Wilson was confident that if the principle was implemented correctly, the risk of renewed global conflict would be significantly reduced, and, therefore, he insisted that self-determination should be the guiding principle when it came to dividing the Ottoman and Austro-Hungarian empires and redrawing the map of Europe. Third, he championed self-determination as a criterion governing territorial change, and fourth, he took self-determination into account for the purpose of settling colonial claims. However, in his view, self-determination should not be the sole or even the paramount yardstick in this area, but ought to be reconciled with the interests of colonial powers (de Carvalho, Leira & Hobson 2011, pp. 750–751). Hence, the emancipatory character of self-determination in colonial contexts was compromised (Kernek 1982, pp. 243–245).

Wilson's principles were employed by activists in anti-colonial movements, which erupted during wartime political and economic turmoil. Often such revolts were based on a wider critique of imperialism and capitalism as the sources of economic exploitation and colonialism (Manela 2007). Wilson, however, in tune with the political thought of the time, was treating nationalism and democracy as almost synonymous terms with the nation-state to be regarded as the political expression of the democratic will of the people (Mayall 1990). The principle of self-determination had a dual role. It was seen as the principle for international re-organization in the post–First World War order, and it was the principle to guide popular governance within states. Nevertheless, the range of application of the new political framework was limited to Europe with little leeway for expanding the principle in the colonial space of the imperial powers of the time (Manela 2007). Independent statehood was appropriate for those considered fit in racial and civilizational terms (Linklater 2016). This was also confirmed by scholars of international law advocating a selective application of the new principle in "civilized nations", as Bluntschli (1895/2000, pp. 92–93) argued:

> Not every people is capable of maintaining a State, and only a people of political capacity can claim to become an independent nation. The incapable need the guidance of other and more gifted nations; the weak must combine with others or submit to the protection of strong powers.

Wilson's view on self-determination was also disruptive to anti-colonial movements who based their claims on transnational solidarities, like religion, that transcended notions of nationality (Simpson 2018).

The second version of the principle of national self-determination originates in Marxist thought. Similar to other progressive thinkers, Marx recognized the need for collective control as means to overcome the alienation that make humans "debased, enslaved, forsaken, despicable being[s]" (Marx 2005, p. 182). His proposal for gaining and exercising collective control place emphasis on social rather than political autonomy (Forst 2017). Self-determination is emancipatory for the working class rather than the nation, yet Marx and Engels saw the national liberation movements as the transitional phase from bourgeoisie dominated to a classless socialist society. In 1896 at its Congress in London, the Second Socialist International affirmed the right of nations to self-determination and opposition to colonialism.

The leader of the Russian Revolution, Vladimir Lenin, took his cue from nineteenth-century Marxist thought and suggested that the right of self-determination should be established as a general criterion for the liberation of peoples. Following Marx and Engels, Lenin believed that nationalism was a phenomenon of the capitalist era and would disappear with capitalism itself. He viewed the creation of nation-states as a necessary step in the historical evolution towards a socialist society. In his book *On Imperialism*, the principle of self-determination thus became an explanatory tool in his primary economic analysis of imperial expansion (Mayer 1964). According to Lenin, self-determination would lead to the liberation of oppressed peoples that would contribute to the success of the socialist revolution (Lenin 1916/1969). In this light nationalism was a progressive force that would facilitate the transition from feudalism to capitalism. However, once this point was reached and capitalism was fully developed, as was the case in Western Europe and North America, nationalism become an oppressive impediment to the advancement towards socialism (Jones 1990). Lenin envisioned self-determination as having three components. First, it could be invoked by national groups who wished to decide on their own destiny autonomously. Second, it was a principle to be applied in the aftermath of military conflicts between sovereign states, for the allocation of territories to one or another power. Third, it was an anti-colonial postulate designed to lead to the liberation of all colonized territories. In the colonial and semi-colonial areas of the world where capitalism had not yet penetrated at all, the situation was totally different. Here the necessary capitalist phase had first to be achieved before the goals of the proletariat could be attained. The proletariat should, therefore, co-operate with bourgeois elements in such countries in order to create a nation-state, since this was a necessary precursor of the socialist state. The socialist cause and the interest in the revolution always took priority over the principle (Lenin 1969, p. 167; Cassese 1995, p. 18). The principle was valued as a tactical instrument which would remain useful as long as it promoted the ends of the class struggle (Laoutides 2015). Writing in Pravda on 21 February 1918 in favour of the Brest-Litovsk peace treaty, Lenin asks rhetorically: "Who should be put first, the right of nations to self-determination, or socialism?" And he answers: "Socialism" (cited in Cassese 1995, p. 18).

Lenin's and Wilson's views differed in three respects: first is the different political and ideological origins of their theory of self-determination. Second, their views differed with regard to the recognition of self-determination by the international community as the principle that guarantees political autonomy. This is a development of Wilson's understanding of self-determination, which transcends its essentially "domestic" and internal dimension as envisaged by Lenin. Third, their views differed with regard to the implementation of self-determination. Wilson did not envisage self-determination as giving rise to a right of waging violent revolutions. Whereas Lenin called for the immediate liberation of those living under colonial rule, Wilson championed "orderly liberal reformism" (Lynch 2002). Lenin saw self-determination as a revolutionary principle for radically redistributing power within existing states or granting independence both to those nationalities oppressed by central governments and peoples subject to colonialism. This concept called into question not only the internal structure of the states, but also that of the international community, since it granted recognition at the international level to nations and peoples governed by "oppressive structures". On the other hand, Wilson perceived self-determination as a political and normative postulate to be employed in a non-violent fashion under international law (Manela 2007).

After the Paris Peace Conference in 1919, the principle was applied only on the defeated side of the Great War. Borders changed, some countries expanded their territories like Romania and Greece, whilst new independent states appeared such as Poland, Czechoslovakia and the Baltic nations. Yet, despite the excitement that was generated in imperial colonies before and during the Peace Conference for the change that self-determination could bring to colonial peoples, the principle was not extended to the colonies, and finally it was not incorporated in the Covenant of the League of Nations. It appeared that not all peoples were entitled to the same principle (Manela 2007). During the interwar period a number of movements in the imperial space, such as in India and French Indochina, continued to promote their aspirations and demands for liberation on the basis of self-determination either as liberal postulate or a Marxist principle.

## Self-determination in the post-1945 world order

The implementation of the principle in European affairs provided the nationalist movements in the Arab world, in colonial Asia and in Central America with a precedent, even if it had no immediate counterpart on the legal plane (Buchheit 1978; Cassese 1995; Musgrave 1997). The minority rights regime, as an integral part of the League of Nations, was introduced with the aim to maintain international peace and to serve as a means of evading the acceptance of self-determination as an international legal principle (Green 1970; Kymlicka 1989, 1995; Jackson-Preece 2005; Nickel 1997; Thornberry 1990, 1991). It should not, therefore, be surprising that the principle was to a very large extent subordinated to other concerns when it came to making peace treaties with the defeated. It was implicitly an acceptance of exclusiveness and aggressive nationalism, since the arrangements of 1919 had been drawn on national lines, thus giving the revisionists the opportunity to employ co-national minorities as agents for promoting their revisionist agenda (Brownlie 1970, p. 97; Cobban 1945, p. 38). The ambiguous and inconsistent application of the principle which lacked a clarified legal standing became a catalyst in the hands of diplomats and propagandists who subsequently handed over the task to the generals. The most profound expression of this ambiguity was the claim for *Selbstbestimmungsrecht* (the right to self-determination) through the 1930s by the Nazis, who maintained that the rights of Germany as a nation had been violated by the terms of the Treaty of Versailles and that German minorities in Central and Eastern Europe have been victimized and persecuted. To address this injustice, National Socialist Germany offered its own solution – the Aryan racial community who could determine itself disregarding the existence of other communities (Weitz 2015).

Discussions during the Second World War regarding the new world order established the need for a new organization that would play the leading role in the maintenance of international peace and security. As early as 1941 in the first draft of the Atlantic Charter, the prelude to the United Nations, the idea of self-determination was proclaimed as a general standard governing territorial changes as well as a principle concerning the free choice of rulers in every sovereign state (Grenville 1974, pp. 198–210). The Allied powers pledged to "respect the right of all peoples to choose the form of government under which they will live" and "see sovereign rights and self-government restored to those who have been forcibly deprived of them" (Atlantic Charter 1941).

Anti-colonial leaders employed the Atlantic Charter in their efforts to promote their liberation struggle. In October 1941 the Premier of British Burma and fervent nationalist U Saw travelled to London and demanded that the British government apply the third clause of the Atlantic Charter, the right to self-determination, to Burma (Charney 2009). This was followed by the demand of the Anti-Fascist People's Freedom League in Burma, on 16 May 1945, "that the right of national self-determination shall be applied forthwith to Burma" (Tinker 1986, p. 463). A few months later, on 2 September 1945, Ho Chi Minh declared Vietnam's independence stating that "we are convinced that the Allied nations, which at Tehran and San Francisco have acknowledged the principles of self-determination and equality of nations, will not refuse to acknowledge the independence of Vietnam" (Ho Chi Minh 1967, p. 143).

Still, the long debate on whether self-determination ought to be included in the UN Charter was an indication of the uneasiness that the prospect of collective self-determination caused at the international level from the early stages of its formation. Before entering in the final draft of the UN Charter at the San Francisco talks in 1945, the principle was discussed extensively among the delegates; not all of them were amenable to the idea of incorporating self-determination in the Charter (Cassese 1995, pp. 39–41; Russell 1958, pp. 811–813; Sureda 1973, p. 99). After 1941 the United States, as the emerging superpower, sought to incorporate self-determination as a basic principle of global order with a narrowed scope and meaning. The focus of US officials was on interpreting self-determination as popular self-rule, rather than as a right held by all colonized peoples. Britain, as a colonial power, insisted that "rights" inhered in individuals and not in collectivities, and that self-determination was a principle, not a right, and thus would not impose any legal obligations on states (Simpson 2018). Both powers, therefore, worked to delete references to self-determination in the UN Charter, but finally, after pressure from Latin America countries as well as the Soviet Union and its allies, the United States and European powers agreed to its inclusion.

The principle was included in Articles 1(2), 55 and 57 of the Charter. The general and cryptic reference to self-determination of the peoples led to a debate around the main features of the content and the character of the concept (Calogeropoulos-Stratis 1973, pp. 168–173; Cot & Pellet 1991, pp. 1070–1083; Driessen 1992, pp. 118–124; Gayim 1990, pp. 21–26; UNCIO 1945, vol. VI, pp. 455, 704).

According to Cassese (1995, p. 42) states were unable to define self-determination with a positive content. Based on the debate preceding the adoption of Article 1(2), it could be inferred in negative terms only. Self-determination did not mean: (1) the right of a minority or an ethnic or national group to secede from a sovereign country (2) the right of a colonial people to achieve political independence; for these people self-determination could only mean "self-government," (3) the right of the people of a sovereign state to choose freely its rulers through regular, democratic and free elections; (4) the right of two or more nations, belonging either to a sovereign country or to two sovereign countries, to merge. The lack of positive content for self-determination in the early stages of the UN life led to the suggestion that states should grant self-government as much as possible to the communities over which they exercised jurisdiction.

Another feature was that the principle was considered as a means of furthering the development of friendly relations among states, and therefore, it was regarded as a component of the world peace architecture. This conception imposed a certain limitation to the power of the principle as an independent value and, consequently, could be easily set aside when its fulfilment involved the possibility of conflict and war between states. Finally, since self-determination was envisaged in a loose fashion, the Charter did not impose direct and immediate legal obligations on member states in this area. It rather seems to have endorsed the gradual devolution of government power, but nor sovereignty, to the colonies.

In the discussion of the trusteeship system, self-determination played an oblique role, although Article 76(b) does include a reference to the "freely expressed wishes of the people concerned". However, the arrangements were to be based on the free conclusion of agreements. The general issue of non-self-governing territories, other than trust territories, was dealt with sparsely in Chapter XI of the Charter, where there is no reference to self-determination (Russell 1958, p. 831). The UN practice gave to Chapter XI an infusion of the principle of self-determination as part of the overall "law of the Charter." Once the Charter was in force, it became increasingly difficult to deny the legal content of the principle (Brownlie 1970, p. 98). Despite the limitations and the implicit character of the rules, the adoption of the UN Charter could be described as a victory for the principle of self-determination since it matured from a political principle to a standard legal norm.

The vagueness with which self-determination was included in the UN Charter also implies another major problem: not only is there no attempt to define the precise application of self-determination, and, thus, to regulate it; but, crucially, there is no reference to the inter-state workings of self-determination. The vague definition of self-determination at this point also triggered a series of competing interpretations in the years that followed the end of the Second World War.

A major point of contention between UN member states was the degree to which the self-determination of the peoples was associated with the protection and promotion of human rights. In the years following the Second World War, socialist countries along with many recently independent Third World countries became the most active advocates of anti-colonial self-determination. Two different views were developed within the anti-colonial bloc at the UN, between the self-determination secured through "sovereignty" and the self-determination achieved by "democracy". The sovereignty argument of self-determination viewed protection of individual human rights as a secondary issue that would follow the achievement of independence. Accordingly, the creation of a postcolonial democracy is not a prerequisite for the realization of independent statehood. This view was encapsulated in the way the socialist bloc adopted and developed Lenin's thesis on self-determination as a primarily anti-colonial principle. Hence, self-determination meant the liberation of the peoples subject to racist regimes, colonial domination and their effects (Mojekwu 1980; Ouguergouz & Tehindrazanarivelo 2006). This approach placed emphasis on the right to external self-determination, whilst maintaining an implicit link between self-determination and the principles of sovereign equality of states and non-interference in domestic affairs. On the other hand, advocates of a democratic self-determination placed individual human rights and self-determination on the same level. Political freedom and self-determination were mutually dependent. Speaking at the United Nations General Assembly Third Committee in the early 1950s, the Afghan Ambassador to the UN Abdul Rahman Pazhwak described colonialism as "a flagrant violation of the most sacred rights of the individual", and further asserted that "in depriving peoples of their rights to govern themselves, colonial Powers had often violated the right to life and liberty and many other fundamental rights of the individual" (Burke 2010, p. 40). Democratic anti-colonial nationalism was epitomized by the anti-colonial struggle in countries like India, Indonesia and Pakistan. In this light, the approach to self-determination was associated with two interrelated issues: the fight against colonialism and racism, and the struggle against any form of neo-colonialism that aims at the exploitation of a country's natural resources.

Within this highly confrontational environment, the articulation of an "international bill of rights" which would satisfy the desire for a new world order was put forward. The first step towards this end was the Universal Declaration of Human Rights, which was adopted by the UN in 1948. Article 21(3) of the Declaration stated that "the will of the people shall be the basis of the authority of government", which did not add anything substantial to the various positions taken on the content and scope of the self-determination of the peoples but the basis of democratic rule (Musgrave 1997).

During the 1950s, despite its internal disagreements, the anti-colonial bloc contrived to transform self-determination into a universal principle with a more radical character. The United States and the European colonial powers opposed the new formulation of the principle promoted by the anti-colonial bloc by insisting that the provisions of the principle in the UN Charter were set out broadly without imposing any specific obligations for the member states (Cassese 1995). Subsequently, they tried to disconnect their colonial rule to discussions about human rights at the UN. During the debates for the introduction of a resolution on self-determination as a human right in November 1950, the European imperial powers attempted to avoid any human rights promises to the populations outside the metropolitan space by promoting a special colonial clause in the draft human rights covenant. The clause, if adopted, would have allowed the imperial powers to exclude their colonies from claiming the rights in the covenant (Burke 2010). Paradoxically, on 4 November 1950 in Rome, the same European countries would sign the European Convention on Human Rights, setting out the most robust system for the protection of human rights in Europe (ECHR 1950). The double standards employed by the colonial powers were based on a very questionable argument, suggesting that "backward" indigenous inhabitants were not ready for European human rights (Burke 2010, p. 40). Such arguments continued to circulate in the context of the Cold War even by powers such as the United States that were trying to sustain a defence of self-determination in favour of oppressed peoples under Soviet control, whilst at the same time they were trying not to undermine the ties with their allies which were also colonial powers. In a conversation with Netherlands Ambassador J. H. van Roijen in 1962 about the self-determination of West New Guinea (Western Papua), then US President John Kennedy, asserting the right of self-determination of West Berliners, argued:

> Oh that is entirely different because there are something like two and a quarter million West Berliners where there are only seven hundred thousand of those Papuans. Moreover, the West Berliners are *highly civilized* and *highly cultured*, whereas those inhabitants of West New Guinea are living, as it were, in the Stone Age.
>
> *(Webster 2013, p. 9, emphasis added)*

The discussion concerning an international covenant on human rights led to the decision to draft two separate covenants, one dealing with civil and political rights, and the other with economic and social rights. Gradually it became clear that despite the opposition by the European powers and the United States, the overwhelming majority of the UN members, that increased rapidly, supported the inclusion of a right to self-determination in the two human rights covenants and that they aspired to an extension of the norm to the realm of economic and cultural sovereignty (Simpson 2018).

After a long debate between the United States and its European allies and the USSR and its socialist allies supported by many newly independent states, a provision on self-determination was included in common Article 1 of the two international covenants. Summing up the relevant points of the discussion on the role of the principle in these covenants, it could be argued that self-determination was a precondition of other individual human rights whilst also upholding ideas of both internal and external self-determination: democracy and representative government, and sovereign independence for "peoples" (Crawford 1988; Thornberry 1989). In this context, self-determination took shape for the first time in an international treaty and was interpreted as an individual non-absolute right which was not limited only to the achievement of independence, but furthered the establishment of a democratic process within the state in question. The provisions of the covenants attributed more specific content to the concept and, therefore, strengthened Chapters XI and XII of the UN Charter (Buchheit 1978; Cassese 1995). However, while the text supported the view that the covenants embody universal principles, the recently decolonized states managed effectively to limit the scope to the colonial situation; the right "freely to determine their political status" was a mechanism to facilitate the process of decolonization and thus to clearly demarcate the content of self-determination (Whelan 1992).

The turning point for the institutionalization of self-determination in the United Nations was the adoption of the UN General Assembly Resolutions 1514 and 1541 in 1960, the "Year of Africa", when more than a dozen French colonies became independent. These resolutions were coupled by the two international covenants on human rights in 1966 and the 1970 "Declaration of the Principles of International Law" (UNGA Resolution 2625) marked a turning point in the evolution of self-determination claims, simultaneously expanding them. It extended the definition of self-determination from an act of colonial emancipation to a process linked to representative government (Simpson 2018).

The practice of the UN, as reflected in the UN documents, led to the conclusion that since the 1960s the world community had been stepping towards the articulation of general standards in which this right is applicable (by the majority, one man one vote) only to colonies (Hannum 1990, pp. 36; Pomerance 1982, pp. 13–15). On this basis the International Court of Justice acknowledged self-determination as a fully-fledged right. In its legal opinion regarding both the Namibian and the Western Saharan cases, self-determination was declared not just as a guiding principle, but as a legal right that could be invoked by its holders to claim separate statehood and sovereign independence (Crawford 2006, pp. 122–123).

The content of the UN legal regulation could be summarized as follows:

1 All peoples subject to colonial rule or foreign occupations have a right to self-determination.
2 The right concerns only the choice of the international status of the people and the territory they inhabit.
3 The principle of territorial integrity overrides any territorial claims by the people of the region that aspires to self-determination.
4 The procedures for materializing the right vary depending on the outcome of the exercise. Therefore, according to whether a colony would (a) end up as an independent state, (b) form an association with an independent state or (c) integrate into an independent state, the procedures oscillate between the adoption of formal democratic processes to ascertain the will of the population and the absence of any such process to ascertain the will of the inhabitants.
5 The right can be exercised only once.

Accordingly, the key elements in the UN's understanding of the self-determination of the people were the emphasis on colonial peoples as the subject of right. Such peoples were territorially defined with the borders of these communities to be drawn from the colonial administrative demarcations. In other words, borders made peoples as coherent political units. Subsequently, the colonial borders defined the space where independent statehood would be realised (see Waters, Chapter 9, this volume).

## Self-determination beyond the colonial context

The view that self-determination means self-determination of colonies or occupied territories was adopted by the majority of UN members in an attempt to maintain the territorial integrity of the states, and, thereby, keep Pandora's Box firmly closed (Hannum 1990, p. 36). The fear of an endless creation of states has been captured in 1972 by then US President Richard Nixon, who in a conversation with the Secretary of State Henry Kissinger about "more self-determination in Africa", Nixon replied, "Yeah. Goddamn. Just think, 42 countries in Africa. 42 countries. That's ridiculous" (Simpson 2012, p. 675). Colonial self-determination has been defended by states and scholars, and international practice has also validated the established perception of the principle (Cristescu 1981, para. 279; Gros Espiell 1980, para. 90; Higgins 1994, pp. 115–116; Michalska 1991, pp. 78–83; Quane 1998, p. 571; Shaw 1978, pp. 147, 153). However, this interpretation of self-determination does not reflect the diversity of opinion between the member states in the UN regarding the scope and the subject of the principle. Several countries were keen on establishing a dimension of the right to self-determination beyond the colonial context based on a remedial understanding of the concept as a last resort for clear cases of ongoing oppression (Buchheit 1978, pp. 81–93). It was believed and proposed within the UN bodies that populations considered as a minority within a state should be assured certain guarantees which would secure their development and well-being as a constituent part of the political society to which they belonged (Tomuchat 2006, p. 26). Such a line of thought attempts to address a de-colonial legacy of making authoritarian states protected under the principle of non-intervention. At a meeting of the drafting committee for UNGA Resolution 2625 in 1967, the Burmese delegate representing the military junta that had taken power in 1962 claimed that the UN "had clearly and incontrovertibly established" that self-determination "was relevant only to colonialism and was to be specifically applied in the promotion of independence of peoples under colonial domination" (Burke 2010, p. 57). It was against such views that the extension of self-determination beyond decolonization was contemplated.

A number of scholars and jurists suggested that the right to self-determination cannot only be confined to colonies, but ought to be extended, beyond the colonial context, to metropolitan territories where the inhabitants do not share in the government of the region or the state (Brownlie 1970, pp. 601–602; Buchheit 1978, p. 81; Crawford 2006, pp. 99–102; Musgrave 1997, pp. 62–90). Based on the "consent of the governed", according to these analyses, the UN implicitly provided a justification for legitimate action against illegitimate authority. However, until the end of the Cold War international practice limited the cases of application to only one, namely Bangladesh (Cassese 1995, pp. 108–121; Hannum 1990, pp. 35, 453; Kimminich 1993, pp. 91–94; Musgrave 1997, pp. 76, 191–192; Pomerance 1982, p. 39). It is evident that the idea of self-determination as independent statehood outside the colonial space was not outlawed because this would be incompatible with the concept of "the consent of the governed". However, secession is understood in a conservative fashion as a last resort since the international community wishes to avoid further stirrings of separatist sentiments (Tomuchat 2006).

The willingness by some countries to incorporate the norm of self-determination beyond decolonization is evident in the Helsinki Final Act of the Conference on Security and Cooperation in Europe (CSCE 1975), which echoed the link between individual human rights and collective self-determination marked in the UN practice (Higgins 2003). Principle VII of the Final Act commits member states to the protection of human rights including the rights and fundamental freedoms of persons belong to national minorities, and Principle VIII reaffirmed that "all peoples always have the right, in full freedom, to determine, when and as they wish, their internal and external political status, without external interference, and to pursue as they wish their political, economic, social and cultural development" (Higgins 2003). A view shared among scholars and practitioners is that the drafters of the Final Act wanted a text where self-determination would not imply secession yet would allow for change of borders in Europe (Heraclides 2020; Sadigbayli 2013). The friction was coming from the tension between not recognizing the right to self-determination to national groups found in many European countries – such recognition could lead to secessionist claims – and keeping open the possibility for the unification of Germany (Hazewinkel 2007). To this end the final text combined the acknowledgement that frontiers of states can change peacefully (Principle I) with the protection of individual rights of members of national minorities (Principle VII) and the right to self-determination (Principle VIII).

From a different angle, it has been suggested that the right to external self-determination could never be considered as an exclusive right of colonial peoples (Tomuchat 1993, pp. 2–3; Henrard 2000, p. 288). It is a right applicable to all peoples as it is evident by the formal declaration of protest by the Federal Republic of Germany and the Netherlands against the Indian Government. The latter put forward a reservation concerning the ratification of the two International Covenants on Human, Civil and Political Rights by stating that self-determination in common Article 1 was to be understood as a right solely of "peoples under foreign domination" (Raič 2002, p. 235; UNICESCR 1966/1979, p. 5).[1] In their objection, the Netherlands asserted that:

> The right of self-determination as embodied in the Covenants is conferred upon all peoples. This follows not only from the very language of article 1 common to the two Covenants but as well from the most authoritative statement of the law concerned, i.e., the Declaration on Principles of International Law concerning Friendly Relations and Co-operation among States in accordance with the Charter of the United Nations. Any attempt to limit the scope of this right or to attach conditions not provided for in the relevant instruments would undermine the concept of self-determination itself and would thereby seriously weaken its universally acceptable character.
>
> *(UNICESCR 1966/1981, p. 15)*

Similarly, Germany objected to India's reservation, emphasizing

> the right of self-determination as enshrined in the Charter of the United Nations and as embodied in the Covenants applies to all peoples and not only to those under foreign domination. All peoples, therefore, have the inalienable right freely to determine their political status and freely to pursue their economic, social and cultural development . . . any limitation of their applicability to all nations is incompatible with the object and purpose of the Covenants.
>
> *(UNICESCR 1966/1980, p. 12)*

The Human Rights Committee in 1984 also defended this position when it made a general comment on Article 1 of the International Covenant on Civil and Political Rights by which it confirmed that self-determination is a right of all peoples (Hannum 1990, pp. 43–44; Henrard 2000, p. 290).

In the same fashion, the European Community through the representative of the United Kingdom, acting on behalf of the member states, declared to the Third Committee of the UN General Assembly in 1986:

> In accordance with the principles set out in the Charter, the common first article of both International Covenants proclaims the right to self-determination. It is important to remember that, under the Covenants, self-determination is a right of peoples. It applies with equal force to all peoples, without discrimination . . . Self-determination

is not a single event – one revolution or one election. The exercise of this right is a continuous process. If peoples are to, in the words of the Covenants, "freely determine their political status and freely pursue their economic, social and cultural development," they must have regular opportunities to choose their government and their social systems freely, and to change them when they so wish.

*(Marston 1986, pp. 487, 516)*

These positions indicated the evolution of self-determination of the peoples as a principle that is applicable in a non-colonial context. The decolonization process under UN auspices is close to completion as nearly two million people are still under 17 non-self-governing territories, whilst the end of the Cold War in 1989 was a turning point about the applicability of self-determination outside the colonial space (Pellet 1992). The unification of Germany as well as the break-up of the former Yugoslavia and the Soviet Union were tectonic shifts that signalled the need to articulate collective self-determination as a norm that would regulate the (re-)forming of polities.

## Note

1   The second date indicates the year of reservation and ratification by India.

## References

*Atlantic Charter* 1941, 14 August, The Avalon Project, available at https://avalon.law.yale.edu/wwii/atlantic.asp [accessed 15 July 2021].

Beran, H. 1998, "A Democratic Theory of Political Self-Determination for a New World Order," in P.B. Lehning (ed.), *Theories of Secession*, London: Routledge.

Bluntschli, J.K. 1895/2000, *The Theory of the State*, Kitchener: Batoche Books.

Brownlie, I. 1970, "An Essay in the History of the Principle of Self-Determination," in C.H. Alexandrowicz (ed.), *Studies in the History of the Law of Nations*, Grotian Society Papers 1968, The Hague: Nijhoff.

Buchheit, L. 1978, *Secession: The Legitimacy of Self-Determination*, New Haven, CT: Yale University Press.

Burke, R. 2010, "'Transforming the Ends into the Means': The Third World and Right to Self-Determination," in R. Burke (ed.), *Decolonization and the Evolution of International Human Rights*, Philadelphia: University of Pennsylvania Press.

Calogeropoulos-Stratis, S. 1973, *Le Droit des peuples à disposer d'eux-mêmes*, Brussels: Bruylant.

Cassese, A. 1995, *Self-Determination of Peoples: A Legal Appraisal*, Cambridge: Cambridge University Press.

Chappell, V. 2005, "Self-Determination,"., in C. Mercer and E. O'Neill (eds.), *Early Modern Philosophy: Mind, Matter, and Metaphysics*, Oxford: Oxford University Press.

Charney, M.W. 2009, *A History of Modern Burma*, Cambridge: Cambridge University Press.

Cobban, A. 1945, *National Self-Determination*, Oxford: Oxford University Press.

Conference on Security and Cooperation in Europe (CSCE) (1975), Final Act, Helsinki, available at: https://www.osce.org/files/f/documents/5/c/39501.pdf [accessed 26 August 2021].

Cot, J.-P. & Pellet, A. 1991, *La Charte des Nations Unies*, 2nd edition, Paris: Economica.

Crawford, J. 1988, "The Rights of Peoples: 'Peoples' or Governments?," in J. Crawford (ed.), *The Rights of Peoples*, Oxford: Clarendon Press, 136–147.

Crawford, J. 2006, *The Creation of States in International Law*, 2nd ed., Cambridge: Cambridge University Press.

Cristescu, A. 1981, "The Right to Self-Determination: Historical and Current Development on the Basis of UN Instruments," U.N.Doc. E/CN.4/Sub.2/404/Rev.1, available at: https://digitallibrary.un.org/record/25252?ln=en 9 [accessed 25 August 2021].

De Carvalho, B., Leira, H. & Hobson, J.M. 2011, "The Big Bangs of IR: The Myths That Your Teachers Still Tell You about 1648 and 1919," *Millennium: Journal of International Studies*, 39(3): 735–758.

Driessen, B. 1992, *The Concept of a Nation in International Law*, The Hague: T.M.C. Asser Instituut.

European Convention on Human Rights 1950, available at www.echr.coe.int/documents/convention_eng.pdf [accessed 8 August 2021].

Forst, R. 2017, "Noumenal Alienation: Rousseau, Kant and Marx on the Dialectics of Self-Determination," *Kantian Review*, 22(4): 523–551.

French, S., & Gutman, S. 1974, "The Principle of Self-determination," in V. Held, S. Morgenbesser, and T. Nagel (eds.), *Philosophy, Morality, and International Affairs*, New York: Oxford University Press.

Gayim, E. 1990, *The Principle of Self-Determination: A Study of Its Historical and Contemporary Legal Evolution*, Norwegian Centre for Human Rights. Publication Series, no. 5, Oslo: University of Oslo.

Green, L. 1970, "Protection of Minorities in the League of Nations and the United Nations," in A. Gottlieb (ed.), *Human Rights, Federalism and Minorities*, Toronto: Canadian Institute of International Affairs.

Grenville, J.A.S. 1974, *The Major International Treaties: 1914–1973 – A History and Guide with Texts*, London: Stein and Day.

Gros Espiell, H. 1980, "The Right to Self-Determination: Implementation of United Nations Resolutions," U.N.Doc. E/CN.4/Sub.2/405/Rev.1, available at: https://digitallibrary.un.org/record/13664?ln=en [accessed 25 August 2021].

Hannum, H. 1990, *Autonomy, Sovereignty and Self-Determination: The Accommodation of Conflicting Rights*, Philadelphia: University of Pennsylvania Press.

Hazewinkel, H.J. 2007, "Self-Determination, Territorial Integrity and the OSCE," *Helsinki Monitor: Security and Human Rights*, 18(4): 289–302.

Henrard, K. 2000, *Devising an Adequate System of Minority Protection: Individual Human Rights, Minority Rights, and the Right to Self-Determination*, The Hague: Nijhoff.

Heraclides, A. 2020, "Self-Determination and Secession: The Normative Discourse Yesterday and Today," in M. Riegl and B. Doboš (eds.), *Perspectives on Secession: Theory and Case Studies*, Cham, Switzerland: Springer.

Higgins, R. 1994, *Problems and Process: International Law and How We Use It*, Oxford: Clarendon Press.

Higgins, R. 2003, "Self-Determination and Secession," in J. Duhlitz (ed.), *Secession and International Law: Conflict Avoidance, Regional Appraisals*, New York and Geneva: United Nations Publications.

Ho Chi Minh 1967, "Declaration of Independence of the Democratic Republic of Vietnam," in B.B. Fall (ed.), *Ho Chi Minh On Revolution Selected Writings: 1920–1966*, New York and London: Praeger.

Jackson-Preece, J. 2005, *Minority Rights: Between Diversity and Community*, Cambridge: Polity Press.

Jones, R.A. 1990, *The Soviet Concept of "Limited Sovereignty" from Lenin to Gorbachev: The Brezhnev Doctrine*. New York: St. Martin's Press.

Kedourie, E. 1993, *Nationalism*, 4th ed., London: Blackwell.

Kernek, S.J. 1982, "Woodrow Wilson and National Self-Determination along Italy's Frontier: A Study of the Manipulation of Principles in the Pursuit of Political Interests," *Proceedings of the American Philosophical Society*, 126(4): 243–300.

Kimminich, O. 1993, "A 'Federal' Right of Self-Determination," in C. Tomuchat (ed.), *The Modern Law of Self-Determination*, The Hague: Nijhoff.

Kymlicka, W. 1989, *Liberalism, Community, and Culture*, Oxford: Oxford University Press.

Kymlicka, W. 1995, *Multicultural Citizenship: A Liberal Theory of Minority Right*, Oxford: Oxford University Press.

Laoutides, C. 2015, *Self-Determination and Collective Responsibility in the Secessionist Struggle*, Abington: Routledge.

Lenin, V. 1917/1969, *Imperialism: The Highest Stage of Capitalism: A Popular Outline*, Beijing: Peking Press.

Linklater, A. 2016, "The 'Standard of Civilisation' in World Politics,'" *Human Figurations*, 5(2), available at: http://hdl.handle.net/2027/spo.11217607.0005.205 [accessed 15 November 2021].

Lynch, A. 2002, "Woodrow Wilson and the Principle of 'National Self-Determination': A Reconsideration," *Review of International Studies*, 28(2): 419–436.

Manela, E. 2007, *The Wilsonian Moment: Self-Determination and the International Origins of Anti-Colonialism*, Oxford: Oxford University Press.

Marston, G. 1986, "United Kingdom Materials on International Law: Survey," *British Yearbook of International Law*, 57: 487–654.

Marx, K. 2005, "Contribution to the Critique of Hegel's Philosophy of Law", in K. Marx and F. Engels (eds.), *Collected Works, vol. 3, Marx and Engels: 1843–1844* (trans. J. Cohen et al.), New York: International Publishers.

Mayall, J. 1990, *Nationalism and International Society*, Cambridge: Cambridge University Press.

Mayer, A.J. 1964, *Wilson versus Lenin: Political Origins of the New Diplomacy: 1917–18*, New York: Meridian Books.

Michalska, A. 1991, "Rights of Peoples to Self-Determination in International Law," in W. Twining (ed.), *Issues of Self-Determination*, Aberdeen: Aberdeen University Press.

Mill, J.S. 1863/1910, *Utilitarianism, Liberty, Representative Government*, London: J.M Dent & Sons.

Mojekwu, C. 1980, "Self-Determination: The African Perspective," in Y. Alexander and R. Friedlander (eds.), *Self-Determination: National, Regional and Global Dimensions*, Boulder, CO: Westview Press.

Musgrave, T.D. 1997, *Self-Determination and National Minorities*, Oxford: Oxford University Press.

Nickel, J.W. 1997, "Group Agency and Group Rights," in I. Shapiro and W. Kymlicka (eds.), *Ethnicity and Group Rights* (Nomos XXXIX), New York: New York University Press.

Ouguergouz, F., & Tehindrazanarivelo, D.L. 2006, "The Question of Secession in Africa," in M.G. Kohen (ed.), *Secession: International Law Perspectives*, Cambridge: Cambridge University Press.

Pellet, A. 1992, "The Opinions of the Badinter Arbitration Committee: A Second Breath for the Self-Determination of Peoples," *European Journal of International Law*, 3(1): 178–185.

Pomerance, M. 1982, *Self-Determination in Law and Practice: The New Document in the United Nations*, The Hague: Nijhoff.

Quane, H. 1998, "The United Nations and the Evolving Right to Self-Determination," *International and Comparative Law Quarterly*, 47(3): 537–572.

Raič, D. 2002, *Statehood and the Law of Self-Determination*, The Hague: Nijhoff.

Russell, R.B. 1958, *A History of the United Nations Charter: The Role of the United States, 1940–45*, Washington: Brookings Institution.

Sadigbayli, R. 2013, "Codification of the Inviolability of Frontiers Principle in the Helsinki Final Act: Its Purpose and Implications for Conflict Resolution," *Security and Human Rights*, 24(3–4): 392–417.

Shaw, M.N. 1978, "The Western Sahara Case," *British Yearbook of International Law* 49: 119–154.

Simpson, B. 2012, "The United States and the Curious History of Self-Determination," *Diplomatic History*, 36(4): 675–694.

Simpson, B. 2018, "Self-Determination and Decolonization," in M. Thomas and A.S. Thompson (eds.), *The Oxford Handbook of the Ends of Empire*, Oxford: Oxford University Press.

Sureda, R. 1973, *The Evolution of the Right of Self-Determination: A Study of United Nations Practice*, Leiden: Sijthoff.

Thornberry, P. 1991, *International Law and the Rights of Minorities*, Oxford: Clarendon Press.

Thornberry, P. 1990, *The Rights of Ethnic Minorities in International Law*, Oxford: Clarendon Press.

Thornberry, P. 1989, "Self-Determination, Minorities, Human Rights: A Review of International Instruments," *International Comparative Law Quarterly*, 38(4): 867–889.

Throntveit, T. 2011, "The Fable of the Fourteen Points: Woodrow Wilson and National Self-Determination," *Diplomatic History*, 35(3): 445–481.

Tinker, H. 1986, "Burma's Struggle for Independence: The Transfer of Power Thesis Re-Examined," *Modern Asian Studies*, 20(3): 461–481.

Tomuchat, C. 1993, "Self-Determination in a Post-Colonial World," in C. Tomuchat (ed.), *Modern Law of Self-Determination,* Dordrecht: Martinus Nijhoff.

Tomuchat, C. 2006, "Secession and Self-Determination," in M.G. Kohen (ed.), *Secession: International Law Perspectives*, Cambridge: Cambridge University Press.

United Nations Conference on International Organization (UNCIO) (1945), Documents, vol. VI, available at: https://digitallibrary.un.org/record/1300969?ln=en [accessed 14 November 2021].

United Nations International Covenant on Economic, Social and Cultural Rights (UNICESCR) (1966), *United Nations Treaty Series*, vol. 993, C.N.781.2001.TREATIES-6, available at: https://treaties.un.org/Pages/ViewDetails.aspx?src=TREATY&mtdsg_no=IV-3&chapter=4&clang=_en#EndDec [accessed 20 November 2021].

Waters, T.W. 2020, *Boxing Pandora: Rethinking Borders, States, and Secession in a Democratic World*, New Haven: Yale University Press.

Webster, D. 2013, "Self-Determination Abandoned: The Road to the New York Agreement on West New Guinea (Papua), 1960–62," *Indonesia*, 95: 9–24.

Weitz, E.D. 2015, "Self-Determination: How a German Enlightenment Idea Became the Slogan of National Liberation and a Human Right," *American Historical Review*, 120(2): 462–496.

Whelan, A. 1992, "Self-Determination and Decolonization: Foundations for the Future," *Irish Studies in International Affairs*, 3(4): 25–51.

# 6

# SELF-DETERMINATION AND THE USE OF FORCE

*Rowan Nicholson*

The first purpose enumerated in the Charter of the United Nations is to "maintain international peace and security"; the second, in part, is to "develop friendly relations" based on respect for the "self-determination of peoples" (UNC 1945: art. 1). These purposes are reflected in rules that occupy the highest position in the hierarchy of international law: a rule obliging States to refrain from the use of force and a rule entitling peoples to self-determination. Few other features of the law in the UN era have the same importance. But if these two purposes are both so valued by the community of States, and if the corresponding rules are both so robust, what happens when they both apply to the same set of facts? Do the rules come into conflict such that one rule ultimately prevails over the other – revealing, perhaps, what States *truly* value? Or is any conflict an illusion? The questions are not purely theoretical. They have been raised by Portugal's refusal to relinquish its African colonies, by India's actions in Bangladesh and Goa, and by other events. They may become relevant again in future.

The answers, this chapter will suggest, vary from one scenario to another. The chapter will begin with some preliminary matters. Then it will survey scenarios in which the law of self-determination and the law on the use of force interact: where an administering State uses force against a people, where representatives of a people use force in a war of national liberation, and where a foreign State uses force either to facilitate secession or to annex territory.

## Actors, chorus, and setting

The scenarios that will be examined in this chapter feature a recurring cast of actors: peoples and States. They also feature what might called a chorus: the wider community of other States that are not directly involved. The scenarios will be examined within the setting of international law – in other words, by considering what legal rules apply – as distinct from looking at them from a historical perspective or through the lens of a theory of international relations.

A few words must be said about each of these things, beginning with the actors.

It will be evident that the concept of a people is politically and legally contested (Anderson: Chapter 4, this volume). But this chapter will focus on the established subset of peoples who have a right to self-determination in the strongest sense: a right to *external* self-determination. This is a right to choose to create a new State – that is, to secede – or, less often, to acquire another political status such as free association or integration with an existing State (UNGA

DOI: 10.4324/9781003036593-8

1970a: principle *e*). It vests in peoples of colonized territories; in certain other oppressed peoples, such as those under foreign military occupation; and possibly also, though there is uncertainty about this, in peoples that are prevented from pursuing their political, economic, social, and cultural development within the framework of an existing State (Secession Reference 1998: paras 131–138). There are also other types of peoples and other types of self-determination, but they are not connected with changes to external political status, and hence they tend not to raise such difficult questions about the use of force on the international stage (though on the use of force internally against peoples such as black South Africans, see Cassese 1995: 197).

The other actors in the scenarios are States. All States have a duty to respect external self-determination and to promote its realization (UNGA 1970a: principle *e*). They also have a duty to "refrain in their international relations from the threat or use of force against the territorial integrity or political independence of any state, or in any other manner inconsistent with the Purposes of the United Nations" (UNC 1945: 2(4)), subject to exceptions where force is authorized by the Security Council or used in self-defence (UNC 1945: arts 42, 51).

Whereas some States act in lead roles in the scenarios, the majority of States merely observe and comment upon the action, like the chorus in a classical Greek drama. The importance of this chorus of States is as follows. The interaction between self-determination and the use of force has not given rise to a large body of case law, a treaty, or an attempt at codification. But it has prompted State practice and *opinio iuris* (acceptance that the practice is law): the two elements of rules of customary international law. In particular, it has prompted resolutions by organs of the United Nations that express approval or disapproval of actions or that make assertions about the law. Such resolutions, even if not legally binding in themselves, "can, in certain circumstances, provide evidence important for establishing the existence" of a customary rule (ICJ 1996: para. 70). The weight of a resolution depends on various factors, including its wording, any surrounding debates and explanations, and the size of the majority in favour (ILC 2018: commentary to conclusion 12, para. 6). It is, therefore, often the chorus that indicates how customary international law deals with the complex interaction between self-determination and the use of force – though it will be seen that the chorus sometimes speaks discordantly or cryptically.

There remain a couple of characteristics of international law that require introduction. One is a distinction between two types of legal questions that will be raised by the scenarios. Some questions are about whether a particular action by an entity, such as a use of force, is *unlawful* in the sense that the action is prohibited by international law. Another way to say that an action is unlawful is to say that the entity has a duty not to do it or that the action breaches a right of another entity (Nicholson 2019: 12–19). Other questions are about whether an action, whether lawful or not, has consequences that are *valid* in the eyes of international law. Relevant consequences include the creation of a new State and the transfer of territory from one State to another. Questions about lawfulness and validity are interrelated. Some rules of international law reflect the principle that no law arises from unlawfulness (*ex iniuria ius non oritur*). That principle says that if an action is unlawful, then that taints certain consequences of the action such that international law will treat them as invalid. It will be seen in this chapter, however, that the two types of questions are still distinct and may be resolved in contrasting ways.

Also relevant is the notion of peremptory norms (*ius cogens*). A peremptory norm is a customary rule "from which no derogation is permitted and which can be modified only by a subsequent norm of general international law having the same character" (Vienna Convention 1969: art. 53). This means that if there is a conflict between a peremptory norm and another rule – whether that rule derives from custom, a treaty, or elsewhere – then the peremptory norm prevails. Only a tiny number of norms are widely accepted as being peremptory, but these include the prohibition on the use of force and the right to self-determination (ARSIWA 2001: commentary to art. 26). The fact that both these rules occupy the highest position within the hierarchy is what makes their interaction so complex, because it cannot be resolved by saying that peremptory norms prevail over other rules. The two rules are often cited to illustrate the possibility that two peremptory norms might conflict. For instance, Brian Lepard writes:

> [P]roblems arise where one asserted norm of *jus cogens*, such as a prohibition of the nondefensive use of force, conflicts with another putative *jus cogens* norm, such as a right to self-determination. The traditional definition of *jus cogens* norms as allowing no derogation whatsoever leaves us at an impasse and cannot address this kind of conflict successfully. As Ian Brownlie asks by way of example: "If a state uses force to implement the principle of self-determination, is it possible to assume that one aspect of *jus cogens* is more significant than another?"
>
> *(Lepard 2010: 250, quoting from Brownlie 2008: 512)*

This chapter will return to that issue in its conclusion.

## An administering State uses force

In the first scenario, a State administers the territory of a people with a right to external self-determination – typically, a colonized territory – and uses force against the people in order to preserve its control. On the one hand, the prohibition on the use of force generally applies to the use of force by States *against other States*, which means that it is generally lawful for States to use force internally for purposes such as suppressing revolt (Corten 2010: 126–197). On the other hand, this particular internal use of force may prevent the people from exercising its right to external self-determination. This raises the question of whether the law of self-determination modifies the law on force such that the administering State's use of force may be unlawful.

This is one point on which the chorus has made its view fairly clear. The Friendly Relations Declaration, a resolution passed by the UN General Assembly in 1970, proclaims that "[e]very State has the duty to refrain from any forcible action which deprives peoples . . . of their right to self-determination and freedom and independence" (UNGA 1970a: principle *e*; Rosenstock 1971: 732–733).

There is room to debate how far this goes. The United States, while expressing support for the declaration, clarified that in its view, the text "did not limit the right of an Administering Authority to use appropriate police measures in the territories for which it was responsible" (UNGA 1970b: para. 25). Indonesia, whose people had "bitter memories" of colonial rule by the Netherlands, replied that "[p]olice action with regular military troops armed with tanks, bombers and guns . . . were actually full-scale military operations" and that "[i]mposing 'law and order' in such situations meant imposing 'colonial law and order', that is the law of the jungle and the order of prisons" (UNGA 1970c: para. 75). But the prohibition certainly applies in extreme cases of colonial violence. Thus, in the 1970s, the UN Security Council called on Portugal – at that time governed by an authoritarian regime that was hostile to decolonization – to cease its "military operations" and "acts of repression" against the peoples of its colonies of Angola, Guinea-Bissau, Cape Verde, and Mozambique and "to enter into negotiations" with a view to permitting them "to exercise their right self-determination" (UNSC 1972).

There is also room to debate *why* it is unlawful for an administering State to use force in a way that deprives a people of its right to self-determination. There are two interpretations.

One interpretation is that this is a consequence of the rule that States must refrain "in their international relations" from the use of force "against the territorial integrity . . . of any state" (UNC 1945: art. 2(4)). Another of the principles articulated in the Friendly Relations Declaration is that a colonized territory "has a status separate and distinct from the territory of the State administering it" (UNGA 1970a: principle *e*). That suggests that the relations between the State and the people qualify as "international relations". The fact remains, however, that the people's territory is not actually a separate State, which means that it cannot be said that a use of force against the people qualifies as a use of force against the territorial integrity of a State.

The more convincing interpretation is that, as James Crawford concludes, a use of force by an administering State against a people "is not a use of force against the territorial integrity and political independence of a State, though it will be in another manner inconsistent with the purposes of the United Nations" (Crawford 2006: 137). In other words, in this scenario, the law of self-determination creates an additional, free-standing prohibition on the use of force.

This scenario played out many times in the era of decolonization after the Second World War. Portugal and the Netherlands have already been mentioned. The United Kingdom used force to suppress revolts such as the Mau Mau Uprising in Kenya and the Malayan Emergency; and France also used force in some colonies, most notably against the insurgency in Algeria (Shipway 2008: 140–172; Gray 2018: 68). Today, the scenario is less topical. But there is one ongoing dispute to which it is potentially, albeit debatably, relevant. As a matter of international law, Taiwan is usually considered to be part of China rather than a separate State, but it governs itself outside the control of the authorities on Mainland China. Some scholars have suggested that its people has a right to external self-determination (see e.g. Huang 2001). Since it does not fall into the established categories of colonized or oppressed peoples, this suggestion rests on a highly controversial view of the law. But if correct, it would provide an argument to the effect that Mainland China cannot lawfully use force to take control of Taiwan (on this and other arguments to similar effect, see Crawford 2006: 220; Gray 2018: 74).

## Representatives of a people use force

If the chorus has made its view fairly clear about the use of force by the administering State, its members have spoken discordantly about the use of force by the people's own representatives. This scenario occurs when a national liberation movement mounts an insurgency or war, as in some of the cases alluded to in the previous discussion, such as Algeria and Portuguese Africa (Corten 2010: 135–149; Wilson 1988). There are three questions to consider here: whether the movement can lawfully use force; whether a foreign State can lawfully assist it; and, regardless of the answers to those first two questions, whether the movement can validly bring a new State into being.

The General Assembly resolutions that relate to the first question – whether the movement can lawfully use force – are sometimes ambiguous and sometimes unambiguous.

The ambiguous resolutions tend to use the terms "legitimacy" and "struggle". For example, in 1965, the General Assembly recognized "the legitimacy of the struggle by the peoples under colonial rule to exercise their right to self-determination and independence" (UNGA 1965). Similarly, in 1974, it reaffirmed "the legitimacy of the struggle of the Namibian people by all means at their disposal against the illegal occupation of their country by South Africa" (UNGA 1974a). The same year, the General Assembly adopted the Definition of Aggression, which refers to "peoples forcibly deprived" of "the right to self-determination, freedom and independence" and then affirms "the right of these peoples to struggle to that end" (UNGA 1974b: art. 7). But "legitimacy" is not a technical legal term and does not necessarily mean the same thing as lawfulness. The word "struggle" is also deliberately ambiguous. As Christine Gray observes, it "was taken by some states to mean armed struggle and by other states" – including the European colonial powers and the United States – "to mean peaceful struggle", with the result that "consensus was attained only at the price of ambiguity" (Gray 2018: 69). That makes it difficult to draw any inference about the lawfulness of the use of force.

Other resolutions refer unambiguously to a right of peoples to, for instance, "wage both political and armed struggle" (e.g. UNGA 1981: principle III(b)). But these unambiguous resolutions did not achieve consensus among States, in particular among both colonial powers and former colonies, and hence have limited value as evidence of customary international law (Gray 2018: 71; UN 1981: 145–149). Once again, it is difficult to draw any inference.

Despite this, it is still possible to answer the question about whether national liberation movements can lawfully use force by reference to established general principles.

The prohibition on the use of force applies to the use of force *by States*, which means that it has little to say about the use of force by a non-State entity such as a national liberation movement. International law does not explicitly regulate such a use of force (Crawford 2006: 135–136). And where international law is silent about an action by an entity, the "default" rule is that the action is lawful in the sense that the action is not prohibited by law (that is to say, even if the entity lacks a positive right to do the action, the entity lacks a duty to refrain from doing the action: Nicholson 2019: 30–32). Since there is no applicable prohibition of force with which the right to self-determination could come into conflict in this scenario, there is no need to look to the General Assembly to clarify how any such conflict must be resolved.

A national liberation movement can, then, lawfully use force.

There are caveats to this. One is that it is a statement solely about international law. Any insurgency will, by its nature, be treated as unlawful by the domestic law of the State against which it is directed. Another is that international law does have things to say about the conduct of a national liberation movement *during the course* of hostilities. The movement may have a duty to comply with rules of international humanitarian law about protecting individuals (PAGC 1977: arts 1(4), 96(3); Abi-Saab 1979). But those rules do not concern the question of whether the use of force is in itself lawful or unlawful.

The second question raised by this scenario is whether a foreign State, perhaps sympathetic to the cause of national liberation, can lawfully assist the movement.

Outside the context of self-determination, assisting insurgents may be unlawful. If it goes so far as to involve the actual threat or use of force, then it is captured by the prohibition reflected in Article 2(4) of the United Nations Charter (UN Charter). But even if it does not go that far, it may be prohibited by the related but wider principle of non-intervention. In *Nicaragua v. United States*, the International Court of Justice (ICJ) held that this principle prohibits a State from intervening in the internal or external affairs of another State when the intervention "uses methods of coercion in regard to" choices such as "the choice of a political, economic, social and cultural system, and the formulation of foreign policy" (ICJ 1986: para. 205). It added that the "element of coercion . . . is particularly obvious in the case of an intervention which uses force, either in the direct form of military action, or in the indirect form of support for subversive or terrorist armed activities within another State" (ICJ 1986: para. 205). The United States had breached the prohibition of non-intervention "by training, arming, equipping, financing and supplying" an insurgency against Nicaragua known as the Contras (ICJ 1986: paras 108, 293(3)).

In *Nicaragua v. United States*, however, the ICJ clarified that it was "not here concerned with the process of decolonization" (ICJ 1986: para. 206). Judge Schwebel, who dissented, criticized this remark on the ground that "the Court may be understood as inferentially endorsing an exception to the prohibition of intervention, in favour of the legality of intervention in the promotion of the so-called 'wars of liberation', or, at any rate, some such wars" (ICJ 1986: 351). Such an exception would presumably be based on the possession of a right to external self-determination.

It is unclear how far such any such exception extends. The same resolutions of the General Assembly that refer ambiguously to the "struggle" for self-determination and to its "legitimacy" also use ambiguous language to describe assistance by foreign States. The resolution from 1965 quoted earlier invited "all States to provide material and moral assistance to the national liberation movements in colonial Territories" (UNGA 1965). The Definition of Aggression refers to the "right of peoples . . . to seek and receive support, in accordance with the principles of the Charter and in conformity" with the Colonial Declaration (UNGA 1974b: art. 7). The Colonial Declaration – a resolution that made a major contribution to the crystallization of the right to external self-determination into customary international law (ICJ 2019: para. 153) – makes no reference at all to assistance or support by foreign States (UNGA 1960a).

On a broad view, there is an exception permitting states to "provide economic, political and logistical support to liberation movements, as well as sending arms and ammunitions" (though they are "not allowed to overstep this threshold in helping liberation movements" by using force themselves, a point that will be discussed in the next part of this chapter; Cassese 1995: 199–200). On a narrower view, "[s]upport that may be given to a national liberation movement may be humanitarian, political or economic" but not "military" (Corten 2010: 148).

The third question raised by this scenario is the clearest and potentially the most important. This question is not about the lawfulness of the use of force but, rather, about the validity of its consequences. Can a national liberation movement validly create a new State, even though it has used force, and even if foreign States intervene by assisting it?

Practice confirms that it can. For example, in the 1960s and 1970s, a movement in Guinea-Bissau waged a war of national liberation against Portugal and received assistance from foreign States, but those facts did not stop Guinea-Bissau from becoming a new State (Crawford 2006: 139). Indeed, international law imposes certain requirements before a new State can emerge, which typically entail a high level of control over territory, and it appears that these requirements are actually *less onerous* in a case like Guinea-Bissau (Bryant et al. 1974; Nicholson 2019: 180–184). In such a case, a people has resorted to force to fulfil its right to external self-determination, but at the same time the administering State is unlawfully using force to deny that right. International law, in effect, is adjusted in favour of the people.

An ongoing dispute that raises the questions just discussed is the one about Palestine. The people of Palestine has a right to external self-determination on the basis that it is subject to foreign military occupation (ICJ 2004: especially paras 88, 118). In the past, the General Assembly has urged States "to extend their support to the Palestinian people through its sole and legitimate representative, the Palestine Liberation Organization, in its struggle to regain its right to self-determination and independence" (UNGA 1986: para. 33). More recent resolutions have omitted words such as "struggle", which may reflect a shift of emphasis away from the use of force by the Palestinians (e.g. UNGA 2020). The applicability to Palestine of this body of law is also complicated by the Palestinian claim – which is accepted by the majority of States and the General Assembly – that Palestine already qualifies as a State (UNGA 2012).

## A foreign State uses force to facilitate secession

To some extent, the disagreement in the General Assembly summarized in the previous part of this chapter was not really about the use of force by a national liberation movement. It was about the possibility that a *foreign State* might use force against the administering State. If customary international law went further than saying that national liberation movements could lawfully use force and receive assistance, in the sense that the force and the assistance were not prohibited, if the law also said that such movements had a positive *right* to use force, then that might have entailed "a dangerous consequence: third States could have claimed to act in collective self-defence in order to send troops to fight against the colonial Power", which "could have produced highly undesirable consequences for world peace" (Cassese 1995: 198; see also Dugard 1967). More generally, there are questions about how the law of self-determination and the law on force interact when a foreign State uses force against the administering State.

Two scenarios can be distinguished here, based on the aims and consequences of the use of force by the foreign State. These will be discussed in separate parts of the chapter.

In one of these scenarios, the foreign State uses force against the administering State in order to facilitate the creation of a new State in fulfilment of a people's right to external self-determination. The scenario is sometimes illustrated by India's successful use of force against Pakistan to facilitate the secession of Bangladesh from Pakistan in 1971. Bangladesh – or, as it was known before its secession, East Pakistan – is, however, problematic as an illustration. The problem is that its people did not fit squarely into the subset of peoples with a right to external self-determination. There are two ways its people might be squeezed in.

First, there is the argument actually made by India. It was observed earlier that colonized peoples and certain other oppressed peoples have a right to external self-determination. Among the clearest exemplars are the peoples of the colonized territories that are listed by the UN as "non-self-governing" (UNC 1945: ch. XI; Secession Reference 1998: paras 131–132). In 1960, the General Assembly resolved to treat as *prima facie* non-self-governing "a territory which is geographically separate and is distinct ethnically and/or culturally from the country administering it" (UNGA 1960b: principle IV). Geographically, East Pakistan was about 1,800 kilometres from the rest of Pakistan. Ethnically and culturally, its mostly Bengali population shared the Islamic religion with the rest of Pakistan but in other respects was distinct. In the Security Council, India argued that Pakistan was attempting "to hold under colonial rule 75 million persons whom they have exploited for 23 years" and that if the General Assembly's indicators were applied, then East Pakistan could be declared "a non-self-governing territory" (UNSC 1971: paras 168, 185). Arguably, the similarities between East Pakistan and colonized territories might have sufficed for its people to qualify for a right to external self-determination. But the fact remains that it was never on the UN list of non-self-governing territories, and other States did not endorse India's attempt to expand the subset of peoples with the right.

Second, it was also observed earlier that peoples might acquire the right if prevented from pursuing their political, economic, social, and cultural development within the framework of an existing State. Ved P. Nanda, writing shortly after the secession of Bangladesh, put its people forward as an example of this. Citing the "deprivation of human rights" by Pakistan, its "use of excessive force . . . to stifle dissent", and allegations of genocide, he argued that "a decision can be made to place the demands of self-determination above those of 'territorial integrity' and of a 'non-interventionist' stand" (Nanda 1972: 336). But there is uncertainty – indeed, great political and scholarly controversy – about whether a people can ever acquire a right to external self-determination in these circumstances (Secession Reference 1998: paras 134–138).

Despite being problematic as an illustration, Bangladesh can at least offer hints about how the law of self-determination and the law on force might interact in this scenario.

One question is whether it is lawful for a foreign State to use force against the administering State to facilitate secession. This raises the "dangerous consequence" mentioned at the start of this discussion (Cassese 1995: 198). India's use of force against Pakistan to facilitate the secession of Bangladesh, since it was not clearly in self-defence and was not authorized by the

Security Council, was on its face unlawful. The case offers little reason to think that a right to external self-determination – if the people of East Pakistan even had one – could have undone that unlawfulness. Many States criticized India's use of force as a breach of the UN Charter (Okeke 1974: 142–157). Thomas Franck and Nigel Rodley concluded that "the Bangladesh case, although containing important mitigating factors in India's favor, does not constitute the basis for a definable, workable, or desirable new rule of law which, in the future, would make certain kinds of unilateral military interventions permissible" (Franck 1973: 276).

What, then, about the validity of the consequences in this scenario? If a foreign State uses force to facilitate the creation of a new State, can a new State validly emerge?

Outside the context of self-determination, the answer is generally no. Consider the example of Cyprus. In 1974, Turkey used force against Cyprus and occupied the northern part of the island; then in 1983, with Turkey's support, an entity calling itself the Turkish Republic of Northern Cyprus purported to secede from Cyprus and become a new State (Crawford 2006: 143–147). The Security Council described its purported secession as "legally invalid", called on all States "to respect the sovereignty, independence, [and] territorial integrity" of the existing State of Cyprus, and called on them "not to recognize" any purported new State (UNSC 1983). Even in the absence of a special rule covering this situation, an entity such as the Turkish Republic of Northern Cyprus will often struggle to meet the requirements that international law imposes before a new State can emerge. In particular, since it is likely to be heavily dependent on the State whose use of force facilitated its creation, it will struggle to meet the requirement that it be independent (compare Manchukuo, a puppet entity created in 1931 that was dependent on Japan; League of Nations 1933: 72). But in any case, there appears to be a special rule. The rule is to the effect that, if an entity is created by an unlawful use of force, it is precluded from qualifying as a new state (Nicholson 2019: 165–168). This reflects a wider principle that tends to invalidate the consequences of a breach of a peremptory norm (Orakhelashvili 2006: 218–223; see also ARSIWA 2001: art. 41).

The question here is whether the outcome differs if the creation of a new State would ful-fil a people's right to external self-determination. The example of Bangladesh hints that the outcome might differ. Unlike in cases such as the Turkish Republic of Northern Cyprus, the Security Council did not declare the secession of Bangladesh invalid and did not call on States not to recognize it. Many States did recognize it during 1972, despite Pakistani objections, and these included major powers with diverse ideological dispositions: India, the Soviet Union, the United Kingdom, France, the United States, and others (Nanda 1972: 336). This is evidence that Bangladesh was able to acquire statehood unilaterally – meaning without the consent of its parent State, Pakistan – as a consequence of the use of force by India. An explanation given by Jean Salmon is that, "if the act of force creating Bangladesh was unlawful, the result is not," because it followed other violence that impeded the people from exercising self-determination (this author's translation of Salmon 1973: 490; compare Crawford 2006: 140–143). That is to say, where a people's right to external self-determination is being forcibly denied, there may be an exception to the rule that a new State cannot validly be created by a use of force.

Beyond the problematic case of Bangladesh, support for the existence of this exception might be drawn from the words of the Definition of Aggression. It provides that "[n]othing in this Declaration", including in particular the provision that defines which acts constitute aggres-sion, "could in any way prejudice the right to self-determination, freedom and independence . . . of peoples forcibly deprived of that right . . . particularly peoples under colonial and racist regimes or other forms of alien domination" (UNGA 1974b: art. 7; see also the further discus-sion of this scenario and related issues in Nicholson 2019: 180–187).

Subject to the lingering uncertainty about this exception, this scenario – in which a for-eign State uses force to facilitate the creation of a new State in fulfilment of a right to external self-determination – offers the clearest insight so far into the interaction between the law of self-determination and the law on force. Neither body of law gives way to the other in its primary sphere of operation. On the one hand, an otherwise-unlawful use of force remains unlawful, even though it serves to fulfil the right to self-determination. On the other hand, an otherwise-valid fulfilment of that right may remain valid, even though it depends on the use of force.

## A foreign State uses force to annex territory

The final scenario also involves the use of force against an administering State by a foreign State, but the potential consequences are different. Recall that the creation of a new State is not the only possible outcome of an exercise of external self-determination; a people may instead opt for integration with an existing State (UNGA 1970a: principle *e*). In this scenario, a foreign State uses force, occupies the territory inhabited by the people, and purports to integrate that territory into its own in fulfilment of the people's right to external self-determination.

Again, India offers an example. In 1961, it invaded and purported to annex the Portuguese colonial territory of Goa, an enclave surrounded by Indian territory (along with two smaller Portuguese colonial enclaves, Daman and Diu; see generally Trinidad 2018: 188–195).

India defended its actions on two interwoven grounds. One was that Goa was not Portuguese territory at all but rather "an integral part of India" that had been "illegally occupied" by Portugal for 450 years, from which it followed that India was not using force against the territorial integrity of another State (UNSC 1961a: paras 46, 60). Quincy Wright observed in a comment on the episode that this interpretation of the term "territorial integrity" (which appears in Article 2(4) of the UN Charter) would have the untenable consequence that "attacks would be permissible in every boundary dispute", and he added that the better view is that "territorial integrity means *de facto* possession, not *de jure* title" (Wright 1962: 623). In any case, this argument by India did not concern self-determination. The other argument that India made did. It argued that Portugal was in breach of the duty to respect self-determination and that India was entitled to assist in the liberation of the people of Goa (Higgins 1963: 187 n. 90).

The Security Council – divided by the politics of the Cold War and decolonization – failed to respond coherently. On one side, a resolution deploring India for using force unlawfully received majority support, including from France, the United Kingdom, the United States, and China (at that time, represented by the government on Taiwan), but it was vetoed by the Soviet Union; on the other side, a resolution that was supportive of India received votes from Ceylon, Egypt, Liberia, and the Soviet Union but was rejected by the majority (see Higgins 1963: 187; Trinidad 2018: 191–193). The General Assembly responded with a resolution that condemned Portugal for non-compliance with the law of self-determination, but it did not say anything clear about the use of force and purported annexation by India (UNGA 1961).

Similarly to the case of Bangladesh, and despite the muted reaction from the organs of the United Nations, there is little reason to think that the law of self-determination or India's allegation about illegal occupation could have turned an otherwise-unlawful use of force into a lawful one (Cassese 1995: 199). In Wright's summary of the legal position,

> Goa was under the administration of Portugal, Portugal was under the obligation to promote self-government in the territory, and the General Assembly was competent to see that this obligation was fulfilled, but India had no legal right to invade and annex the territory.
>
> *(Wright 1962: 626)*

But this scenario raises a different question of validity from that raised by Bangladesh. Until the middle of the twentieth century, international law acknowledged military conquest as a valid means of acquiring territory. Nowadays, the rule outside the context of self-determination is that, if a State purports to annex territory by the use of force, the purported annexation is both unlawful and invalid (UNGA 1970a: principle *a*; ICJ 2004: para. 87). This reflects the wider principle, mentioned earlier, that tends to invalidate the consequences of a breach of a peremptory norm (Orakhelashvili 2006: 218–223). The question here is whether there is an exception in the case of a colonial enclave such as Goa whose people have a right to external self-determination. Such an exception might permit what is, in substance, a military conquest on the premise that it fulfils the desire of the people for integration.

Although there is some support for this idea (see e.g. Dugard 1987: 116; Orakhelashvili 2006: 222–223), there are also some uncertainties about what happened with Goa.

First, it is uncertain that the annexation of Goa actually did qualify as the fulfilment of the right to external self-determination. The essence of self-determination is the idea that a people has a capacity for free will; in this context, it entitles peoples "freely to determine, without external interference, their political status" (UNGA 1970a: principle *e*). Jawaharlal Nehru, the Indian prime minister, suggested before the invasion that if the people of Goa wished to remain separate from India, then he would not bring Goa into India by force. But Nehru was also quoted as saying that India would not tolerate Portugal's presence regardless of what the Goans wanted (see the quotations compiled in Trinidad 2018: 189). After the invasion, consistent with the latter position, India did not hold a vote to actually ascertain what the Goans wanted. Moreover, some of the speeches made during the Security Council debate suggested that, in the absence of such a vote, the annexation could not fulfil the right to external self-determination. Chile – which voted for the resolution that deplored India for using force unlawfully – argued that "the parties to the dispute should take into consideration the wishes of the inhabitants" and that "[i]f India were to take possession tomorrow of the territories it claims today, it could have no satisfaction, because it would not have integrated them into its own territory by honourable and lawful means" (UNSC 1961b: para. 30). Jamie Trinidad concludes that Goa is a case not of the fulfilment but of the *denial* of external self-determination, and he explains:

> India's problem was that it was unwilling to accept any outcome other than the absorp-
> tion of Goa, Daman and Diu. If it had proclaimed a willingness to hold a self-deter-
> mination referendum . . . its arguments in the Security Council would have seemed
> less transparently self-serving. Its failure to conduct a popular consultation was perhaps
> connected with its reluctance to do so in Kashmir, rather than to any anxiety that the
> populations of Goa, Daman and Diu would vote against a merger with India.
>
> *(Trinidad 2018: 194)*

There remains a second uncertainty. It is not clear on what legal basis India did validly annex Goa. Portugal continued to object until, following a revolution, its new government retrospectively recognized the annexation by treaty (Treaty on Recognition 1974: art. 1). One possible interpretation of the case is that India validly acquired the territory only on the basis of that act of consent by Portugal (though, even on that interpretation, self-determination may have played a role in allowing "illegality to be more readily accommodated though the processes of recognition": Crawford 2006: 138).

Other cases relevant to any military conquest exception are even more problematic.

In 1974, Indonesia invaded another Portuguese colonial territory whose people had a right to external self-determination, East Timor (see generally Strating 2014). This time, the invaders presented themselves as complying with the formalities of the law of self-determination. In 1976, in advance of purporting to annex the territory, they set up a people's assembly that opted for integration with Indonesia (Krieger 1997: 44). But this was dismissed as propaganda rather than a genuine choice; according to the former Australian consul in East Timor, the "elections" to the assembly were "openly rigged, with Timorese being rounded up by Indonesian troops and escorted to polling booths where their votes were cast under the careful scrutiny of the occupation forces" (Dunn 2003: 257–258). Other States, with the notable exception of Australia, treated the purported annexation as invalid in accordance with the ordinary rule about military conquest (ICJ 1995: paras 14–17). This interpretation was vindicated in 1999, when the people of East Timor were finally able to exercise their right to external self-determination and voted overwhelmingly for the creation of a new State (Special Committee 2000: paras 4–12).

A more recent case that may appear relevant is Crimea. In 2014, Russia used force to facilitate the purported secession of Crimea from Ukraine and then, within a matter of days, purported to annex it – actions that other States condemned as unlawful and invalid (UNGA 2014). Russia invoked self-determination to justify those actions, but the people of Crimea lacked an established right to external self-determination (Grant 2015: 54–58).

One is left to speculate about what international law might say in a clear case. Would the law of self-determination prevail over the rule about military conquest? The assurance in the Definition of Aggression that there can be no prejudice to the right to self-determination, quoted earlier in relation to Bangladesh, might at least hint that the answer is yes.

## Conclusion

This chapter began by asking what happens when the prohibition on the use of force and the right to external self-determination both apply to the same set of facts. It will be evident by now that there is no single answer to that question. Furthermore, the answers that have been given in this chapter – some confidently, some speculatively – are highly heterogenous:

- If an administering State uses force internally against a people with a right to external self-determination, then the law of self-determination turns that otherwise-lawful use of force into an unlawful one. In other words, far from coming into conflict with it, *the law of self-determination enlarges the sphere of operation of the prohibition on force.*
- If a national liberation movement – representative of a people – uses force against the administering State, then that use of force is lawful anyway, because only States are prohibited from using force. In this respect, *neither body of law modifies the other.*
- If a foreign State assists such a movement, then the law of self-determination appears to turn that otherwise-unlawful intervention into a lawful one. The extent of this exception is unclear. But note that, on any view, this does not mean that the law of self-determination prevails over the law on force in the strict sense. It means that *the law of self-determination may prevail over the related but wider principle of non-intervention.*
- If a national liberation movement uses force to secede, and even if a foreign State assists it, then that use of force will not invalidate the creation of a new State. Indeed, on the premise that the administering State is unlawfully using force to deny self-determination, *the two bodies of law combine so as to make the creation of a new State less onerous.*
- If a foreign State uses force against the administering State to facilitate either secession or annexation in fulfilment of a right to external self-determination, then that use of force remains unlawful. On that question of lawfulness, *the prohibition on force prevails.*

- If a foreign State uses force against the administering State to facilitate either secession or annexation in fulfilment of a right to external self-determination, then there is at least some reason to think that the use of force might not invalidate the creation of a new State or the annexation of the territory. On those questions of validity, it is possible, though not certain, that *the fulfilment of the right to external self-determination prevails*.

This chapter also posed some further questions about the nature of the interaction between the relevant rules. Do they come into conflict such that one rule ultimately prevails over the other – revealing, perhaps, what States *truly* value? Or is any conflict an illusion? And it was observed that their status as peremptory norms heightens the complexity of these questions.

In most of the scenarios, the rules are not, strictly speaking, in conflict.

The only true conflicts that occur are in the scenarios in which a foreign State uses force against the administering State to facilitate secession or annexation in fulfilment of a right to external self-determination. The conflict arises because of the principle that tends to invalidate the consequences of a breach of a peremptory norm, including – ordinarily – any consequential secession or annexation. But even here, it is not as simple as saying that one of the two rules ultimately prevails over the other. It would be more accurate to say that each rule prevails over the other within its own primary sphere of operation. The peremptory norm prohibiting the use of force prevails on the question of whether the use of force is unlawful. But the peremptory norm entitling a people to external self-determination may prevail on the question of whether that right can validly be fulfilled by means of a consequential change of status.

# References

Abi-Saab, G. 1979, "Wars of National Liberation and the Geneva Conventions and Protocols", *Collected Courses of the Hague Academy of International Law*, 165: 363.

ARSIWA 2001, "Articles on Responsibility of States for Internationally Wrongful Acts, 2001", *Yearbook of the International Law Commission*, 2(2): 26.

Brownlie, I. 2008, *Principles of Public International Law*, 7th ed., Oxford: Oxford University Press.

Bryant, B., et al. 1974, "Recognition of Guinea (Bissau)", *Harvard International Law Journal*, 15: 482.

Cassese, A. 1995, *Self-Determination of Peoples: A Legal Reappraisal*, Cambridge: Cambridge University Press.

Corten, O. 2010, *The Law against War: The Prohibition on the Use of Force in Contemporary International Law*, trans. C. Sutcliffe, Oxford: Hart.

Crawford, J. 2006, *The Creation of States in International Law*, 2nd ed., Oxford: Oxford University Press.

Dugard, J. 1967, "The Organisation of African Unity and Colonialism: An Inquiry into the Plea of Self-Defence as a Justification for the Use of Force in the Eradication of Colonialism", *International and Comparative Law Quarterly*, 16: 157.

Dugard, J. 1987, *Recognition and the United Nations*, Cambridge: Grotius.

Dunn, J. 2003, *East Timor: A Rough Passage to Independence*, Sydney: Longueville Books.

Franck, T. M. & Rodley, N. S. 1973, "After Bangladesh: The Law of Humanitarian Intervention by Military Force", *American Journal of International Law* 67: 275.

Grant, T. 2015, *Aggression against Ukraine: Territory, Responsibility, and International Law*, New York: Palgrave Macmillan.

Gray, C. 2018, *International Law and the Use of Force*, 4th ed., Oxford: Oxford University.

Higgins, R. 1963, *The Development of International Law Through the Political Organs of the United Nations*, Oxford: Oxford University Press.

Huang, E. T. 2001, "The Evolution of the Concept of Self-Determination and the Right of the People of Taiwan to Self-Determination", *New York International Law Review*, 14: 167.

ICJ 1986, International Court of Justice, *Military and Paramilitary Activities in and against Nicaragua (Nicaragua v. United States of America)*, *International Court of Justice Reports* 14.

ICJ 1995, International Court of Justice, *East Timor (Portugal v. Australia)*, *International Court of Justice Reports* 90.

ICJ 1996, International Court of Justice, *Legality of the Threat or Use of Nuclear Weapons (Advisory Opinion)*, *International Court of Justice Reports* 226.

ICJ 2004, International Court of Justice, *Legal Consequences of the Construction of a Wall in the Occupied Palestinian Territory (Advisory Opinion)*, *International Court of Justice Reports* 136.

ICJ 2019, International Court of Justice, *Legal Consequences of the Separation of the Chagos Archipelago from Mauritius in 1965 (Advisory Opinion)*, *International Court of Justice Reports* 95.

ILC 2018, International Law Commission, "Conclusions on Identification of Customary International Law", 2018, UN Doc. A/73/10.

Krieger, H. (ed.) 1997, *East Timor and the International Community: Basic Documents*, Cambridge: Cambridge University Press.

League of Nations 1933, "Report Provided for in Article 15(4) of the Covenant on Manchuria", *League of Nations Official Journal Special Supplement*, 112: 56.

Lepard, B. D. 2010, *Customary International Law: A New Theory with Practical Applications*, Cambridge: Cambridge University Press.

Nanda, V. P. 1972, "Self-Determination in International Law: The Tragic Tale of Two Cities – Islamabad (West Pakistan) and Dacca (East Pakistan)", *American Journal of International Law*, 66: 321.

Nicholson, R. 2019, *Statehood and the State-Like in International Law*, Oxford: Oxford University Press.

Okeke, C. N. 1974, *Controversial Subjects of Contemporary International Law: An Examination of the New Entities of International Law and Their Treaty-Making Capacity*, Rotterdam: Rotterdam University Press.

Orakhelashvili, A. 2006, *Peremptory Norms in International Law*, Oxford: Oxford University Press.

PAGC 1977, "Protocol Additional to the Geneva Conventions, 1977", *United Nations Treaty Series*, 1125: 3.

Rosenstock, R. 1971, "The Declaration of Principles of International Law Concerning Friendly Relations: A Survey", *American Journal of International Law*, 65: 713.

Salmon, J. 1973, "Naissance et reconnaissance du Bangla-Desh", in J. Tittel (ed.), *Multitudo legum ius unum: Festschrift für Wilhelm Wengler, vol. 1*, Berlin: Interrecht: 467–490.

Secession Reference 1998, Supreme Court of Canada, *Reference re Secession of Quebec* [1998] 2 S.C.R. 217.

Shipway, M. 2008, *Decolonization and Its Impact: A Comparative Approach to the End of the Colonial Empires*, Oxford: Blackwell.

Special Committee 2000, Special Committee on the Situation with Regard to the Implementation of the Declaration on the Granting of Independence to Colonial Countries and Peoples, 2000, "East Timor: Working Paper Prepared by the Secretariat", UN Doc. A/AC.109/2000/12.

Strating, R. 2014, "Contested Self-Determination: Indonesia and East Timor's Battle over Borders, International Law and Ethnic Identity", *Journal of Pacific History*, 49: 469.

Treaty on Recognition 1974, "Treaty on Recognition of India's Sovereignty over Goa, Daman, Diu, Dadra and Nagar Haveli, 1974", *United Nations Treaty Series*, 982: 158.

Trinidad, J. 2018, *Self-Determination in Disputed Colonial Territories*, Cambridge: Cambridge University Press.

UN 1981, United Nations, *Yearbook of the United Nations* 35.

UNC 1945, United Nations Charter, www.un.org/en/about-us/un-charter/full-text

UNGA 1960a, United Nations General Assembly, Declaration on the Granting of Independence to Colonial Countries and Peoples, Resolution 1514 (XV), 14 December.

UNGA 1960b, United Nations General Assembly, Principles Which Should Guide Members in Determining Whether or Not an Obligation Exists to Transmit the Information Called for in Article 73(e) of the Charter of the United Nations, annex to Resolution 1541 (XV), 15 December.

UNGA 1961, United Nations General Assembly, Resolution 1699 (XVI), 19 December.

UNGA 1965, United Nations General Assembly, Resolution 2105 (XX), 20 December.

UNGA 1970a, United Nations General Assembly, Declaration on Principles of International Law Concerning Friendly Relations and Co-Operation Among States in Accordance With the Charter of the United Nations, annex to Resolution 2625 (XXV), 24 October.

UNGA 1970b, United Nations General Assembly, *Official Records*, Sixth Committee, 1180th Meeting, 24 September 1970, UN Doc. A/C.6/SR.1180.

UNGA 1970c, United Nations General Assembly, *Official Records*, Sixth Committee, 1182nd Meeting, 25 September 1970, UN Doc. A/C.6/SR.1180.

UNGA 1974a, United Nations General Assembly, Resolution 3295 (XXIX), 13 December.

UNGA 1974b, United Nations General Assembly, Definition of Aggression, annex to Resolution 3314 (XXIX), 14 December.

UNGA 1981, United Nations General Assembly, Declaration on the Inadmissibility of Intervention and Interference in the Internal Affairs of States, annex to Resolution 36/103, 9 December.

UNGA 1986, United Nations General Assembly, Resolution 41/101, 4 December.

UNGA 2012, United Nations General Assembly, Resolution 67/19, 29 November.

UNGA 2014, United Nations General Assembly, Resolution 68/262, 27 March.

UNGA 2020, United Nations General Assembly, Resolution 75/172, 16 December.

UNSC 1961a, United Nations Security Council, *Official Records*, 987th Meeting, 18 December, UN Doc. S/PV.987.

UNSC 1961b, United Nations Security Council, *Official Records*, 988th Meeting, 18 December, UN Doc. S/PV.988.

UNSC 1971, United Nations Security Council, *Official Records*, 1606th Meeting, 4 December, UN Doc. S/PV.1606.

UNSC 1972, United Nations Security Council, Resolution 322, 22 November.

UNSC 1983, United Nations Security Council, Resolution 541, 18 November.

Vienna Convention 1969, Vienna Convention on the Law of the Treaties, 23 May, 1155 U.N.T.S. 331.

Wilson, H. 1988, *International Law and the Use of Force by National Liberation Movements*, Oxford: Clarendon Press.

Wright, Q. 1962, "The Goa Incident", *American Journal of International Law*, 56: 617.

# 7

# MINORITIES, SELF-DETERMINATION, AND SECESSION

*Felicitas Benziger and Joshua Castellino*

## Introduction

For international law researchers, the right to self-determination remains the gift that keeps on giving. Despite its long pedigree (Fisch 2015: Part II), as of the writing of this chapter, core issues such as the determination of its legal subject (peoples) and the norm's precise content beyond the United Nations' (UN) decolonization practices remain debated and controversial. The key issue that underpins much of the controversy is the question of whether the right to self-determination for a "people" includes the right to secede. Thus, while scholars and practitioners may or may not include secession as an integral part of the "right of self-determination", the idea of a "right" to secession forces a fundamental clash with the well-honed and founding principle of safeguards for a State's territorial integrity (Brilmayer 1991).

Attempts to "regulate" and determine fixed contours for what may seem the amorphous concept of self-determination thus inevitably focus on "who" could be deemed a "people" and what means could be used to achieve such self-determination. This chapter addresses the first question, seeking to explore the extent to which "minorities" are implicated as a group (perhaps as "peoples") in the possibility, if not the right to secede. Rather than seeking to define "peoples", this chapter will focus instead on "minorities" in a bid, first, to test the extent to which they may fit the criteria of "peoplehood" and, second, to explore whether there is evidence in norm creation and State practice for any discernible conclusion to the question of the relationship of minorities to secession.

The definitions of peoples proposed range from being so general as to apply to virtually all cases of a new independent State being established, to being so restrictive as to apply only in very limited circumstances. Anderson, for example, suggests that any "withdrawal of territory (colonial or non-colonial) from part of an existing state to create a new state" be a case of secession (Anderson 2013: 5), thereby implying that the inhabitants living in that territory could be deemed a "people". Christakis, on the other hand, holds that secession necessarily involves a unilateral act on the side of the seceding party (Christakis 2012), which assumes that any diversity in that population is subsumed into a monolithic "people" unified by that desire. Crawford supports the narrowest definition of secession, arguing that "secession" presupposes a threat or the use of force (Crawford 2006: 375). Crawford presents secession as aligned to Anderson's

DOI: 10.4324/9781003036593-9

definition, which, it could be argued, privileges the "territory over the people" in contrast to Judge Dillard's opinion validating "people over territory" (ICJ 1975: 114). If it is incontestable that secession designates the separation – consensual or not – of a part of a State's territory in the process of becoming a sovereign State itself (Van den Driest 2013: 6), it remains open as to who that separation is designed to serve.

In exploring the relationship of minorities to secession, the ambiguous legal status of self-determination of peoples as a norm of international law plays an important role. While it crystallized as a near indisputable claim in the context of UN decolonization, its status and content in other fields of international law remains uncertain (Hilpold 2012: 51). Of course, even in the context of decolonization, the assumption that self-determination could effectively flow on the basis of colonially demarcated boundary lines relegated groups to becoming minorities in the emerging sovereign States (Allen & Castellino 2003: 20–22; Shahabuddin 2019: 335, 339, 342, 343). Thus, while self-determination was seen as emancipatory for the many, it effectively transferred sovereignty to majorities (or powerful minorities) within established boundary lines, irrespective of the histories of the communities within that newly emerged jurisdiction. The overt reliance on the sacrosanct nature of boundaries in international law, coupled with strict constitutional legal regimes in emerging States, foreclosed secession and, often as a consequence, the right of self-determination to groups, irrespective of their historic claim to being a people or a nation.

In more recent decades there has been leeway in the interpretation of the right to indigenous peoples' self-determination. Indigenous peoples' articulation of rights, relevant jurisprudence, and scholarship embeds the right to self-determination of peoples in its widest human right context, highlighting interconnection with other rights provided for in the UN Declaration on Indigenous Peoples' Rights and the two human rights covenants (Charters & Stavenhagen 2009). Overall, the indigenous right to self-determination, in contrast to the self-determination exercised during decolonization, places an emphasis on the "internal dimension" of self-determination, with many courts pronouncing legal opinions on the matter that deliberately avoid the issues of secession, instead restricting self-determination to a means to access other rights on the basis of effective equality (Anaya 2009: 186–189). This segregates self-determination into a right exercised against colonization of the salt-water type, from other exercises seeking active transfer of sovereignty over a territory on the basis of "nationhood". This internal self-determination is thereby understood as not involving questions of statehood, but rather focusing on governance processes. In a generally accepted hierarchy over legitimacy, indigenous peoples are presumed to have the strongest claims, but even for these communities, secession is deemed beyond reach (Daes 2008: 17, 23, 24). For "minorities" deemed to have a lesser claim to self-determination, the right is rarely discussed other than as an obligation upon the State to design means of effective political participation. Of course, the unilateral occupation of Ukraine by Russia in 2022 on the basis of the protection of Russian linguistic minorities in the East – thereby extending the earlier Crimean occupation – may be the exception, but its credibility is too contested to discuss with any credence. In theory, therefore, the only potential scenario that may justify a secessionist claim for minorities is "remedial self-determination", less on the basis of the doctrine of *jus resistendi ac secessionis*, but more on the basis of self-defence in the face of gross violations of human rights.

To unravel some of these issues, this chapter starts by distinguishing and assessing the claim of "peoples", "indigenous peoples", and "minorities" as possible right bearers of self-determination. Part of the latter section will be an assessment of the impact of colonial boundaries on the right to self-determination of minorities, with special regard to the role of *uti possidetis*, and the doctrine of remedial secession as grounds for secessionist claims under the right to self-determination of peoples beyond the context of decolonization.

## Self-determination as a contested norm for "peoples", "indigenous peoples", and minorities

When pursuing the question of whether or not a people holds a right to secede based on the right or principle of self-determination, the specific context in which self-determination operates must be considered. Today, it is widely accepted among scholars in international law that self-determination in the context of decolonization, for example, has a distinct content from, say, in the context of indigenous peoples' rights (Åhrén 2016). This is based on two primary reasons. First, self-determination of peoples as a norm of international law does not possess a strictly defined content (Knop 2002: 1, 2), or, as Ratner puts it, is a political tenet dressed up as law (Ratner 1996: 590). In scholarship and jurisprudence, different approaches have emerged in an attempt to tame the legal concept and application of the self-determination of peoples. These approaches vary from distinguishing its application according to different topical situations to differentiating its modes of implementation. Thus, Hofbauer's division of self-determination in four different sub-categories – political, economic, social, and cultural self-determination (Hofbauer 2016: 69) – is useful in fostering an understanding of what self-determination as a norm can comprise but is unhelpful in determining its substantive legal content. The second approach of differentiating between the ways in which self-determination can be exercised is reflected in the Supreme Court of Canada decision in *Reference re Secession of Quebec*, where the Court distinguished between internal and external self-determination. Internal self-determination was interpreted as covering "a people's pursuit of its political, economic, social and cultural development within the framework of an existing state" (Secession Reference 1998: para. 126). External self-determination, "potentially" including claims to secession, was viewed by the Court as an option that "arises in only the most extreme of cases and, even then, under carefully defined circumstances" (Secession Reference 1998: para. 126). Besides secession, the Court regarded the other options for the establishment of independent States in the process of decolonization as set out in UN General Assembly Resolution 2625 XXV of 24 October 1970 (Friendly Relations Declaration) as possible avenues in cases involving external self-determination (Secession Reference 1998: para. 126). Thus, rather than defining the content of the norm, the designations "internal" and "external" were adopted to describe how the right could be exercised, not what it embodied (Raič 2002: 227). It remains questionable whether the two modes of implementation can be clearly distinguished. For example, one could consider domestic independence referenda to be a case of internal self-determination, since the procedural rules embedding the referendum would often be established in constitutional law (Levrat 2017: 8). Alternatively, one could base it on the argument that in such a situation, the relationship between a State and its citizens *inter se* is at issue (van den Driest 2013: 60). In either case, this would appear to fall within the contours of internal self-determination. By contrast, it could be argued that a successful secessionist movement, even if formally initiated under domestic law regulations, will eventually touch upon relations to third States, hence becoming a case of external self-determination (Weller 2017). This question was also raised in *Reference re Secession of Quebec*, where the Court was asked whether Québec could unilaterally secede under international law (Secession Reference 1998: paras 16–23). The Court's interpretation touched on Canada's domestic law, thereby drawing sustenance under the category of internal rather than external self-determination (Secession Reference 1998: paras 16–23). This illustrates the difficulty of distinguishing between the two modes of implementation.

It is this ambiguity on the content and application of self-determination of peoples as an international law norm that led Crawford to designate it as *lex obscura* (Crawford 2001: 10). Yet, it is not only the content of the norm that is shrouded in mystery; the obscurity surrounding the content of self-determination of peoples is related to its disputed legal nature in international law. As Cassese proposes, there are grounds to assume that self-determination of peoples as international norm has a multi-layered existence (Cassese 1995: 315–320). In the context of decolonization, extensive practice and jurisprudence furthered the crystallization of the right to self-determination as an evident claim-right (Erk 2012). However, this cannot be said about international law in general, in the context of which Cassese proposed to consider self-determination as a general law principle (Cassese 1995: 126–140). An important characteristic for any claim-right is the clear definition of its legal subject (Erk 2012: 4, 5). Unlike in other areas of international law, in the context of decolonization it is clear that the subjects of the colonial right to self-determination are the inhabitants of former colonies, who are deemed to exercise that right as a *quasi-nation* irrespective of their pre-existence in that meter (Oeter 2012: para. 23). Thus, in the decolonization context, the definition and identification of "peoples" are intrinsically linked to the territorial unit in question.

In terms of implementation of the right to self-determination, three possible outcomes were envisaged in the successful exercise of self-determination, namely, integration, association with another State, or independence (as secession from the colonial entity) (Oeter 2012: paras 28–38). The territorial delineation of the emerging State was beyond dispute in the eyes of the international community – the principle of *uti possidetis* ensured that the former colonial boundaries become the new frontiers of the independent State (Peters 2014: 98). Beyond decolonization, these aspects remain uncertain (Castellino 2014: 27, 28). The two main approaches to defining "peoples" in general international law either ignore how territories may be formative of identities – this approach may be regarded as "borrowed" from how peoplehood in the context of UN decolonization was determined – or seek to designate an entity as a "people" based on certain common features, such as language, history, ethnic identity, and/or religion. The latter comes very close to the definition of minorities (Wright 1999: 627), only leaving aside the factor that a minority, from an etymological point of view, is numerically inferior to the rest of the population of a State defined within territorial borders. The literature (for example, Kolb 2013) suggests that it is nearly impossible to define "peoples" in abstract terms, leaving the potential claim-right without its most important characteristic: a defined right holder. Furthermore, legitimate concerns remain about transferring external aspects of the colonial right to self-determination to other situations in international law (Hilpold 2012: 51), leaving the implementation questions of the right outside decolonization contexts uncertain.

While there remains disagreement regarding what self-determination incorporates when not applied to former colonial "peoples", this is also reflected in questions over secession. Some scholars view secession as merely declaratory, referring to the factual process by which a territory achieves independent statehood regardless of its context and means (Anderson 2017), while others suggest that secession necessarily involves the prior threat or use of force (Crawford 2006: 375). Still, others question whether territories achieving independence in the process of decolonization are cases of secession at all (Higgins 2003: 35).

Perhaps the most sophisticated context in which self-determination is operational in State practice and *opinio juris* today is in the realm of indigenous peoples' rights. This context reflects the versatility of self-determination and its utility depending on its context of application. Similar to the colonial right to self-determination, it identifies a clear rights holder viz. indigenous peoples, while drawing inspiration from the notion of peoplehood. Of course, as with a people, determining who qualifies as "indigenous peoples" remains an issue that has produced a considerable body of literature (Castellino & Doyle 2018). However, unlike "peoples" in general, and also in a departure of the decolonization approach to the definition of "peoples", in the identification of indigenous peoples, emphasis is placed on the subjective element of self-identification as indigenous peoples (Daes 2008: 10), although this leaves some disputes open. The most widely accepted working formula in that regard remains Cobo's definition:

> Indigenous communities, peoples and nations are those which, having a historical continuity with pre-invasion and pre-colonial societies that developed on their territories, consider themselves distinct from other sectors of the societies now prevailing in those territories, or parts of them. They form at present non-dominant sectors of society and are determined to preserve, develop and transmit to future generations their ancestral territories, and their ethnic identity, as the basis of their continued existence as peoples, in accordance with their own cultural patterns, social institutions and legal systems.
>
> *(Cobo 1986: para. 379)*

Again, while combining objective and subjective (self-identification) criteria, this working definition draws heavily on the connection to territory. Interestingly, from the perspective of minorities, the distinct definition of indigenous peoples was pursued with the intention of separating indigenous peoples from the notion of minorities in international law, as the latter are usually denied access to the right to self-determination beyond rights to political participation (Daes 2009: 54–68).

Unlike the right to self-determination exercised in decolonization, it is widely accepted that the indigenous right to self-determination is not geared towards external self-determination, placing emphasis on its internal dimension, encompassing self-government and autonomy (Doyle 2015: 125). States' concerns that indigenous self-determination would construct grounds to secede have often proved a major "stumbling block" in progressing indigenous peoples' rights (Daes 2008: 1). As configured currently, secession is not explicitly ruled out, with indigenous peoples actively seeking the right to "represent themselves on the international level" (Åhrén 2016: 6.1). But, in general, indigenous self-determination does not envisage a right of secession leading to independent statehood. Of course, as with any other situation, remedial secession could, as discussed later in this chapter, prove to be an exception. This interpretation puts indigenous peoples on a similar footing to peoples in international law – but, in line with the protection of territorial integrity, it has also proved an important step towards access to rights directed towards self-government and autonomy.

## Minorities and secession

The question of minorities' accessing a right to self-determination similar to those pertaining to indigenous peoples remains far more vexed for a variety of reasons. The definition of minorities is contested (Barten 2015: 2, 6). However, there is broad consensus that the attempt by Capotorti in 1977 may be adequate. He posits minorities as:

A group numerically inferior to the rest of the population of a State, in a non-dominant position, whose members – being nationals of the State – possess ethnic, religious or linguistic characteristics differing from those of the rest of the population and show, if only implicitly, a sense of solidarity, directed towards preserving their culture, traditions, religion or language.

*(Capotorti 1979: para. 568)*

Of course, this definition immediately raises questions about how minorities may be distinguished from "peoples" or "indigenous peoples", with the primary criteria being the territorial unit against which they are set. Thus, depending on the approach chosen to define these groups, many scholars come to the justifiable conclusion that the differences between peoples, indigenous peoples, and minorities may be marginal (Barten 2015: 19, 20; Pentassuglia 2002: 307, 308).

As an original axis around which international law itself evolved and one of the first of groups with protected characteristics, minorities would seem well placed to assert strong rights including self-determination. Yet, despite vocal claims to that effect, State practice generally denies minorities the "right" to claim/articulate their case in terms of secession (Costa 2003: 63, 64). Even where successful, the groups that may have laid claims to self-determination as "minorities" quickly become recognized as "peoples" once the secession was completed. Thus, in Bangladesh, Timor Leste, South Sudan, and Eritrea in a more classical context, and in Croatia, Slovenia, North Macedonia, Montenegro, arguably Bosnia and Herzegovina, and the vexed question of Kosovo in a context of the dissolution of a State, the claimants eventually were described as nations once self-determination has materialized through secession. This contrasts with other situations where groups deemed "minorities" under domestic law make claims to secession based on historical nationhood. Thus, Catalans, Basques, Scots, Chechens, Uygurs, Tibetans, Kurds, West Papuans, Kashmiris, Tamils, and Nagas have had claims to secession foreclosed by strictures and machinations in domestic law. There are also key questions about groups that are minorities in one State, with a kin population in an adjoining State. This applies to Inner Mongolia, Kosovo, Sunnis in Iraq and Iran, Kurds in Syria, Turkey, and Iran, Baluchis in Pakistan and Iran, and other situations, some of which may maintain submerged dreams of statehood through secession. In continents like Africa, where boundary lines were established in a particularly arbitrary manner, their sanctification as sacrosanct resulted in the construction of new entities that were agnostic to the shared histories and identities of the communities upon that territory. For many communities in Africa, the arrival of colonizers was tragic, but their departure, leaving behind relics of new identities deemed permanent, condemned them to a lesser status, often subjected to the permanent sovereignty and subjugation of tribes to which they may have been historically antagonistic (Nugent & Asiwaju 1996).

The principle of *uti possidetis* effectively enabled many minority situations to emerge, with their voices often deliberately submerged as a means to eschew the risk of secession (Mnyongani 2008: 466, 471, 473–474, 475). The adherence to former colonial boundaries, drawn on the basis of delineation of colonial interests among themselves rather than through historical ebbs and driven by ethnic, linguistic, cultural, or even religious grounds that frame an identity, led to the establishment of incoherent postcolonial states (Shahabuddin 2019: 337). Assertions by minorities of identity and outreaches to the claim of "nations" to determine their own future were dismissed as separatist and tribal, with many of the new States embarking on a process of *nation building*, sometimes drawing on a composite inclusive identity, and other times by simply projecting the dominate tribal identity upon the State and treating all who deviated from it as "anti-national"

(Castellino 2014: 33; Mnyongani 2008: 471). The result was an often conflict-loaded path to sovereign statehood for many new, postcolonial states in Africa with similar echoes elsewhere (Shastri & Wilson 2001). The Nigerian civil war between 1967 and 1970 following the secession of what was then the Republic of Biafra, the Congo Crisis between 1960 and 1965, and the Eritrean–Ethiopian conflict are examples of the significant impact the seemingly arbitrary drawing of boundaries had. As in Latin America, in the case of the African continent as a whole, the imposition/adoption of the nation-state mentality and notions of Westphalian sovereignty of States proved to be an obstacle to the aspirations of many minorities (for example, the Southern Cameroons: Chiatoh 2019: 629–653). In other cases, the former colonial boundaries, imposed to delineate the new States' territories, created minorities that found themselves liable to being rendered stateless as a result of this process of State creation. The current plight of the Rohingya, as highlighted prior to the genocide by the UN High Commissioner for Human Rights in 2017, is a painful reminder that fissures in human society can be exploited to cause the significant harm international law seeks to prevent (Al Hussein 2017; Shahabuddin 2019: 334–358).

In contrast to peoples, and even indigenous peoples, the questions that arise concern what minorities are, how they differ from the other two entities dealt with so far, and what that means regarding claims to secession pursuant to the right to self-determination. The matter is not simply one of mere terminology, but entails substantive legal consequences. Since in international law self-determination is restricted to "peoples", minorities are traditionally denied access to the fruits of self-determination (United Nations Guide for Minorities 2021). Fear of anarchy and a constant process of State fragmentation remain the primary reasons for this reservation. With international law seeking to walk the tightrope between order and justice, there remains a bias towards the former, in the hope that it will maintain peace through stability (Pentassuglia 2002: 303, 308).

The intrinsic link between minorities and peoples in the context of self-determination was established early in the history of the more modern discussion of self-determination in the wake of World War I. This connection was explicitly acknowledged by the Committee of Jurists in *Aaland Islands*. The dispute revolved around the question whether the inhabitants of the Aaland Islands, which prior to Russian and later Finnish governance were part of Sweden, had a right to secede from Finland and merge with Sweden based on the principle of self-determination of peoples. Two reports resulted from the proceedings, the first stemming from the Committee of Jurists, who dealt with the question of whether or not the issue was one of international or rather domestic (national) law, and the second from the Committee of Rapporteurs, who were entrusted with the merits of the case. The Committee of Jurists said:

> The principle recognising the rights of peoples to determine their political fate . . . must be brought into line with that of the protection of minorities; both have a common object – to assure to some national Group the maintenance and free development of its social, ethnical or religious characteristics.
>
> *(ICJ 1920: 4)*

The Rapporteurs, on the other hand, came to a conclusion which from today's perspective seems almost revolutionary:

> The separation of a minority from the State of which it forms a part and its incorporation in another State can only be considered as an altogether exceptional solution, a last resort when the State lacks either the will or the power to enact and apply just and effective guarantees.
>
> *(ICR 1921: 317, 318)*

Thus, the Committee of Rapporteurs confirmed that under strict circumstances, namely a situation in which the respective minority cannot otherwise safeguard its interests, recourse to secession as an exercise of self-determination of peoples may be possible. Notwithstanding this seemingly revolutionary finding, the reports must be considered in their entirety. Both reports endorse the significance of territorial sovereignty as an essential characteristic of a sovereign State several times and confirm the priority of territorial sovereignty over competing claims arising under the principle of self-determination (ICJ 1920: 3, 5; ICR 1921: 317, 318). Finland's and the Aaland Islands' long histories were also considered (ICJ 1920: 5–9). Consequently, the reports must be viewed as decisions on an individual case not readily transferrable to other contexts. Nonetheless, the Aaland Islands dispute was the first time a judicial body considered a minority group as potentially possessing a right to secede under the principle of self-determination.

However, international law subsequently developed in a contrary direction on the question of the secession of minorities. Today, there is considerable evidence towards the position that minorities do not have a right to secede from their existing State on the basis of the principle of self-determination (van den Driest 2013: 297–298). In fact, it could be argued more controversially, that the "right of self-determination" does not apply to minorities, and as a consequence, there can be no right to secession under that rubric (Castellino 2014: 38). In terms of international human rights law, it could instead be said that minorities have the right to non-discrimination in access of individual rights, a distinct right to political participation in conjunction with members of their community, and a somewhat contested group right as a "minority" which would enable them to protect, preserve, and transmit their existence to their descendants. Despite this, there have been instances, as indicated earlier, where minorities have exercised political action to create new States.

## Impact of colonial boundaries

From the perspective of minorities, it could be argued that the process of decolonization was a key determinant in their relationship with any potential claim to self-determination (including secession). The principle of *uti possidetis*, derived from Roman law (Allen & Castellino 2003: 20), while not offering a foundation for substantive legal claims let alone having any effect on the legality of the process of State creation (Peters 2014: 101), was of paramount significance within decolonization, more specifically concerning quests for secession, where the principle was relevant with regards to the territorial delimitation of future States. As a principle of international law, *uti possidetis* must be classified as an international legal principle, despite not falling within the ambit of the "general principles of law recognized by civilized nations" (Peters 2014: 99, 100). The International Court of Justice (ICJ) first confirmed the principle in international law in the *Frontier Dispute* case (ICJ 1986: para. 23). As Peters succinctly summarized, *uti possidetis* serves the objective of preventing forcible acquisition of territories so as to protect the territorial status quo (Peters 2014: 115). The ICJ went even further in *Frontier Dispute*, observing that more than protecting territorial integrity, *uti possidetis* ultimately gives newly established States the ambit to consolidate power and assert their sovereignty as international States (ICJ 1986: para. 26). While the principle emerged against the background of decolonization in Latin America (1910–1925) (Allen & Castellino 2003: 20), it has been extended well beyond decolonization. Thus, the Badinter Commission referred to the principle in relation to the dissolution of Yugoslavia in the 1990s, treating it as a default provision subsidiary to any agreements reached between the parties concerned (Pellet 1992: 184).

In relation to secession as an outcome of self-determination, an immediately relevant question is whether *uti possidetis* protects the newly emerged State from external as well as internal challenges to its territorial integrity. The doctrine was originally formulated in the context of foreclosing Latin America to *reconquista* from the Spanish, while internal claims against the entities from other newly emerged entities remained in abeyance (Shaw 1996: 98–100). However non-State actors, in that case indigenous peoples, who in many cases were not numerical minorities, were not even considered in the equation. During the post–World War II era of decolonization (1945–1990), the norm was considered to specifically guarantee the jurisdiction of the new government to the entirety of the territory. Thus, *uti possidetis* explicitly elevated and anointed a single authority in a given territorial unit, validating it as the new State's legitimate government. This immediately stifled secessionist movements from within the new State, while emerging constitutional legal processes solidified that position in domestic law. As Nesi states:

> [T]he norm aims to avoid disputes over territorial delimitations. In this respect, the *uti possidetis* doctrine arguably meets two needs: it prevents boundary disputes, and it deters the local exploitation of weaknesses and disorders in newly created States which are often vulnerable to secessionist actions.
>
> *(Nesi 2018: para. 9)*

Peters validates the ICJ's observation that *uti possidetis* was, *inter alia*, also envisaged as preventing "fratricidal struggles" potentially pitting minorities against the new rulers, that were simmering post withdrawal of colonial administration (Peters 2014: 119).

History shows that the aspiration of preventing such struggles through *uti possidetis* was not wholly successful. Thus, the impact of the principle of *uti possidetis* on secession as an exercise of self-determination remains an interesting question. This question is examined in two different scenarios: pre- and post-secession. The relevant question in the pre-secession context is whether the principle in and of itself allows for secession in any form. The arbitrary implementation of boundaries under the principle of *uti possidetis* did not always take place in accordance with the interests of the communities concerned, be they nations, indigenous peoples, or minorities (Allen & Castellino 2003: 21, 22). Rather, the doctrine effectively subsumes them into a single unit of a "peoples" even where the evidence for their congruence with this concept is nebulous (ibid). Thus, cause and effect became confused. The right to self-determination ostensibly engaged the legal grounds for the unit to secede from the colonial ruler. Yet the principle of *uti possidetis* effectively determined the parameters for that secession. Ideally, if application of the principle was adhered to more closely, it ought to have been called upon as a subsidiary agreement between States, after secession had successfully taken place. Worded differently, the secession in question would answer the question regarding "if", while *uti possidetis* would concern itself with addressing "how" such a process could be embarked upon with a view to establishing the territorial, and possibly maritime (Lone 2012), delimitation of the newly emerged State. In the post-secession context the relevant question is when – that is to say, in what cases – the principle would apply. *Uti possidetis* emerged against the background of the decolonization of Spanish and Portuguese America mainly with a view to demarcating one emerging entity from its neighbour. This was then transmitted, via the decision of the Organization of African Unity (Cairo Resolution 1964), to becoming a principle along which African decolonization proceeded (Allen & Castellino 2003: 21, 22). The Badinter Commission, in its opinion in the dissolution of Yugoslavia, found the principle useful and applicable beyond decolonization, at least in cases where the emerging entities could reach no other agreement (Pellet 1992: 184). The break-up of the Soviet Union and emergence of post-Soviet States also followed this principle despite those boundaries having been drawn to accommodate Soviet control, leaving deep-seated, so-called frozen conflicts, and disparate minorities in one entity that could have been accommodated into a different "peoples" were boundary realignments possible. The attempted agglomeration of Russia itself through a forcible reunification of Russian minorities in Ukraine also presents the specter of self-determination arguments on minorities (Laurinavičiūtė 2015: 66–75), a situation reiterated by the events in 2022. (see further Felicitas Benziger, A Closer Look at Recent Self-Determination Issues in Eastern Europe (IntLawGrrls 26 September 2022) at <https://ilg2.org/2022/09/26/a-closer-look-at-recent-self-determination-issues-in-eastern-europe/> accessed 8 December 2022.

## Gross violations of human rights and remedial self-determination

Of course, notwithstanding the negation of minorities' "right" to secession in the literature, the instance where State practice has shown exceptions is in the context of so-called "remedial secession". Remedial secession departs from the broader notion of self-determination as a norm of international law that is interconnected with the international human rights system. Thus, the doctrine draws sustenance from the idea that in the context of gross violations of human rights perpetrated against a territorially distinct community, often a disenfranchised minority, secession may simply prove an *ultima ratio* remedy to prevent further egregious abuse. Thus, remedial secession could be understood as a unilateral act that takes place without the consent of the "parent" State (van den Driest 2013: 7).

Arguments that develop and articulate the doctrine of remedial secession usually reference UN General Assembly Resolution 2625 XXV of 1970, also called the Friendly Relations Declaration. That Declaration's "saving clause" (Spijkers 2011: 404) states:

> Nothing in the foregoing paragraphs shall be construed as authorizing or encouraging any action which would dismember or impair, totally or in part, the territorial integrity or political unity of sovereign and independent States conducting themselves in compliance with the principle of equal rights and self-determination of peoples as described above and thus possessed of a government representing the whole people belonging to the territory without distinction as to race, creed or colour.

The decisive question for the application of the doctrine of remedial secession in practice is under what circumstances a group may be entitled to secede from a State based on the right to self-determination. Crawford proposes that unilateral secession as a legally neutral act is not based on "any right conferred by international law" (Crawford 2006: 388). Yet, irrespective of the unilateral nature of the act of remedial secession, it would still directly contradict the *jus cogens* norm of territorial integrity. (However, since the ICJ's Kosovo Advisory Opinion stated that the "scope of the principle of territorial integrity is confined to the sphere of relations between States", some scholars have pointed out that it may be questionable whether non-State actors could violate the principle at all (ICJ 2010: para. 80; Wilde 2011: 303). Remedial secession, like any other form of secession, would breach the fundamental rule concerning the inviolability of a State's territorial integrity. In fact, it would directly breach the first part of the saving clause quoted earlier. Yet, three factors need to be further flagged: first, that this form of self-determination is hostile to the parent State more than other forms of secession and usually occurs in the midst of hostilities; second, that it seeks to rely on growing and giving sustenance to the idea that compliance with principles of international laws requires a State to conduct itself in a particular manner; and third, that a threshold exists that may endanger a community, through risk or experience of gross human rights violations, including ethnic cleansing, crimes against humanity, or potentially even genocide. Of course, the text of the Friendly Relations Declaration, as scholars of self-determination are all too familiar with, provides sustenance for the doctrine of remedial secession, while simultaneously upholding the importance of territorial integrity.

In the context of the interplay of the issues of minority rights and secession, the reiteration of the principle of territorial integrity in UN General Assembly Resolution 3314 (XXIX) defining aggression is also relevant, as is the ICJ's Kosovo Advisory Opinion, which weighs territorial integrity against other factors. Supporters of the doctrine of remedial secession agree that an overriding interest can be called into question only in cases of serious and persistent injustices (Cassese 1995: 119–120).

The case law on the doctrine of remedial secession has not been fully developed, even though pleadings have been submitted for judicial consideration. Thus, in the written submissions leading to the ICJ's Kosovo Advisory Opinion, a number of States, above all the Netherlands, included references to the doctrine of remedial secession (ICJ 2010: para. 3.6). Despite such input, the ICJ chose to avoid touching the contentious issue of remedial secession. This is also mirrored in a general lack of practice with regards to the doctrine in international law (Vidmar 2010).

While the Kosovo Declaration of Independence is often discussed in relation to remedial secession, its "fit" into this category can be questioned since the act took place after the human rights situation for Kosovars significantly improved (Oeter 2015: 63–65). Thus, the act was not an imminent act of self-defence in the face of a marauding army, but rather a considered decision not to stay within the fold of a sovereign State on the basis of gross human rights violations that had already occurred. Also, while it is unquestionable that Kosovars were a minority in Serbia and Montenegro at the time of the action, their credentials within that category were tempered by being a kin-minority to a community across a border that formed an existing State (Albania). In that regard, it may also be emphasized that uncertainties over the definition of "peoples" appear to bear less importance in the context of the doctrine of remedial secession (authors supporting the doctrine are divided on the question of the legal subject (see Van den Driest 2013: 115–117). Rather, the strength of the doctrine often stems from an ethnic, religious, or linguistic difference between the entity and the parent State, although the trigger actions would need to go considerably beyond the entrenchment of structural discrimination to cross the perceived threshold where secession may come into play. The Bangladeshi example is probably a clearer picture of such a form of secession. In this case, the ethno-linguistically different Bengali people in East Pakistan faced regular discrimination despite being at par in terms of numbers with their West Pakistani counterparts, seceded in the face of an armed action by the State of Pakistan in the aftermath of an election that the Awami League, the political party turned national liberation movement, mobilized on grounds of linguistic rights (Islam 1985).

## Conclusion

This chapter explored minorities' potential claims to self-determination with a focus on the contested question of secession. Traditionally, secession – while it remains disputed whether this label really suits the context – was justified when exercised within the right to self-determination held by colonial peoples in their efforts to determine their political future with particular attention to questions of statehood. In that context, the entity "people" is defined in territorial terms: a people eligible to exercise the colonial right to self-determination are inhabitants of former colonies. Outside the decolonization context, attempts to "domesticate" the elusive entity "peoples" as potential right holders has proven difficult. Theoretical approaches can be divided in two categories: the territorial approach and the approach placing emphasis on "objective" features such as language, common history, religious, and other similar categories that may or may not facilitate distinguishing certain groups from others. By way of comparison, the widely accepted working definition applied to the identification of indigenous peoples emphasizes their special relation to the territory while also considering various other facets, including questions of culture, that distinguish indigenous peoples from others. One particularity that emerged in the area of indigenous peoples' rights, however, is the accentuation of self-identification by the group themselves as a necessary subjective criterion. While this criterion is deemed essential in identifying indigenous peoples, it is usually not considered to the same extent when "peoples" in general international law are being discussed. Recognition as a people is the necessary threshold requirement to access a right to self-determination, which is often viewed as the precondition for any secessionist claims. Despite there being strong grounds for the argument that ultimately the lines separating "peoples", "indigenous peoples", and "minorities" are thin, practice in international law supports the controversial conclusion that a right to self-determination does not apply to minorities at all. Instead, it could be said that minorities hold certain rights broadly grounded in international human rights law. This includes the right to non-discrimination in accessing individual rights, a distinct right to political participation, the rights to practice, propagate, disseminate, and especially to transmit facets of their identity including religion and culture to future generations, and potential collective rights as a recognized protected group, "a minority", to protect their current existence and to safeguard this for their descendants. In exploring a potential right to secede accessible to minorities, the only currently available option in theory remains the path of "remedial secession", which stems less from the emphasis on the entity as "peoples" and more on the notion of a state of emergency that may arise for any oppressed group. However, this legal concept remains highly controversial with virtually no practice in international law, thereby leaving it more a theoretical idea rather than a viable option to pursue. Despite this, while minorities have no right to secession under international law or domestic law, there have been, as this chapter has shown, instances where minorities have exercised political action to create new States.

# References

Åhrén, M. 2016, *Indigenous Peoples' Status in the International Legal System*, Oxford: Oxford University Press.

Al Hussein, Z. R. 2017, *The Rohingya Statement*, <www.ohchr.org/EN/NewsEvents/Pages/DisplayNews.aspx?NewsID=%EF%99%85%EF%99%85%EF%99%87%EF%99%8B%EF%99%8B&LangID=E>

Allen, S. & Castellino, J. 2003, "Reinforcing Territorial Regimes: Uti Possidetis and the Right to Self-Determination in Modern International Law", *Amicus Curiae*, 48: 20–25.

Anaya, S. J. 2009, "The Right of Indigenous Peoples to Self-Determination in the Post-Colonial Era", in C. Charters & R. Stavenhagen (eds.), *Making the Declaration Work: The United Nations Declaration on the Rights of Indigenous Peoples*, Copenhagen: International Work Group for Indigenous Affairs: 184–199.

Anderson, G. 2013, "Secession in International Law: What Are We Talking About?", *Loyola of Los Angeles International and Comparative Law Review*, 35: 343–388.

Anderson, G. 2017, "Unilateral Non-Colonial Secession and Internal Self-Determination: A Right of Newly Seceded Peoples to Democracy", *Arizona Journal of International & Comparative Law*, 34: 1–63.

Barten, U. 2015, "What's in a Name: Peoples, Minorities, Indigenous Peoples, Tribal Groups and Nations", *Journal on Ethnopolitics and Minority Issues in Europe*, 14 (1): 1–25.

Brilmayer, L. 1991, "Secession and Self Determinations: A Territorial Interpretation", *Yale Journal of International Law*, 16: 177–202.

Cairo Resolution 1964, Organization of African Unity, *Cairo Resolution*, reproduced in I. Brownlie I (ed.) 1971, *Basic Documents on African Affairs*, Oxford: Clarendon Press: 360.

Capotorti, F. 1979, *Study on the Rights of Persons Belonging to Ethnic, Religious and Linguistic Minorities*, E/CN.4/Sub.2/384/Rev.1.

Cassese, A. 1995, *Self-Determination of Peoples: A Legal Reappraisal*, Cambridge: Cambridge University Press.

Castellino, J. 2014, "International Law and Self-Determination: Peoples, Indigenous Peoples, and Minorities", in C. Walter, A. von Ungern-Sternberg & K. Abushov (eds.), *Self-Determination and Secession in International Law*, Oxford: Oxford University Press: 27–44.

Castellino, J. & Doyle, C. 2018, "Who Are 'Indigenous Peoples'? An Examination of Concepts Concerning Group Membership in the UNDRIP", in J. Hohmann & M. Weller (eds.), *The UN Declaration on the Rights of Indigenous Peoples: A Commentary*, Oxford: Oxford University Press: 7–37.

Charters, C. & Stavenhagen, R. (eds.), 2009, *Making the Declaration Work: The United Nations Declaration on the Rights of Indigenous Peoples*, Copenhagen: International Work Group for Indigenous Affairs.

Chiatoh, V. M. 2019, "Self-Determination and Integrity: Southern Cameroons and the Republic of Cameroon", *African Journal of International and Comparative Law*, 27: 629–653.

Christakis, T. 2012, "Secession", in *Oxford Bibliographies*, <www-oxfordbibliographies-com. ezproxy.mdx.ac.uk/view/document/obo-9780199796953/obo-9780199796953-0044. xml?rskey=YufGa8&result=1&q=theodore+christakis+secession#firstMatch>

Cobo, M. 1986, *Study of the Problem of Discrimination against Indigenous Populations*, UN Doc. E/CN.4/Sub.2/1986/7/Add.4

Costa, J. 2003, "On Theories of Secession: Minorities, Majorities and the Multinational State", *Critical Review of International Social and Political Philosophy*, 6: 63–90.

Crawford, J. 2001, *The Right to Self-Determination in International Law: Its Developments and Future*, Oxford: Oxford University Press.

Crawford, J. 2006, *The Creation of States in International Law*, 2nd ed., Oxford: Oxford University Press.

Daes, E.-I. 2008, "An Overview of the History of Indigenous Peoples: Self-Determination and the United Nations", *Cambridge Review of International Affairs*, 21: 7–26.

Daes, E.-I. 2009, "The Contribution of the Working Group on Indigenous Populations to the Genesis and Evolution of the UN Declaration on the Rights of Indigenous Peoples", in C. Charters & R. Stavenhagen (eds.), *Making the Declaration Work: The United Nations Declaration on the Rights of Indigenous Peoples*, Copenhagen: International Work Group for Indigenous Affairs: 48–76.

Doyle, C. M. 2015, *Indigenous Peoples, Title to Territory and Resources: The Transformative Role of Free Prior & Informed Consent*, London: Routledge.

Erk, C. 2012, "What Makes a Right a Human Right? The Philosophy of Human Rights", in W. Schweidler (ed.), *Human Rights and Natural Law. An Intercultural Philosophical Perspective*, Sankt Augustin: Academia Verlag: 101–131.

Fisch, J. 2015, *The Right to Self-Determination of Peoples: The Domestication of an Illusion*, Cambridge: Cambridge University Press.

Higgins, R. 2003, "Self-Determination and Secession", in J. Dahlitz (ed.), *Secession and International Law: Conflict Avoidance – Regional Appraisals*, The Hague: T. M. C. Asser Press: 21–38.

Hilpold, P. 2012, "Secession in International Law: Does The Kosovo Opinion Require a Re-Assessment of This Concept?", in P. Hilpold (ed.), *Kosovo and International Law*, Leiden: Brill Nijhoff: 47–78.

Hofbauer, J. A. 2016, *Sovereignty in the Exercise of the Right to Self-Determination*, Leiden: Brill Nijhoff.

ICJ 1975, International Court of Justice, Advisory Opinion of the International Court of Justice on the Western Sahara, *International Court of Justice Reports* 12.

ICJ 1986, International Court of Justice, *Case Concerning the Frontier Dispute (Burkina Faso/Republic of Mali)*, *International Court of Justice Reports* 554.

ICJ 2010, International Court of Justice, *Accordance with International Law of the Unilateral Declaration of Independence in Respect of Kosovo*, Advisory Opinion International Court of Justice Reports 403

ICJ 1920, International Committee of Jurists, "Advisory Opinion Upon the Legal Aspects of the Aaland Islands Question", *League of Nations Official Journal*, Special Supplement No. 3: 2.

ICR 1921, International Commission of Rapporteurs, "Report: The Aaland Islands Question", League of Nations Council Document B7: 21/68/106.

Islam, M. R. 1985, "Secessionist Self-Determination: Some Lessons from Katanga, Biafra and Bangladesh", *Journal of Peace Research*, 22: 211–221.

Knop, K. 2002, *Diversity and Self-Determination in International Law*, Cambridge: Cambridge University Press.

Kolb, R. 2013, "Autodétermination et 'Sécession-Remède' en Droit International Public", in M.C. Bassiouni (ed.), *The Global Community Yearbook of International Law and Jurisprudence: Global Trends: Law, Policy & Justice Essays in Honour of Professor Giuliana Ziccardi Capaldo*, New York: Oxford University Press: 57–77.

Laurinavičiūtė, L. 2015, "The Relevance of Remedial Secession in the Post-Soviet 'Frozen Conflicts'", *International Comparative Jurisprudence*, 1: 66–75.

Levrat, N. 2017, *The Right to National Self-Determination within the EU: A Legal Investigation*, EUborders Working Paper 08.

Lone, F. 2012, "Uti Possidetis Juris", in *Oxford Bibliographies*, <www-oxfordbibliographies-com. ezproxy.mdx.ac.uk/view/document/obo-9780199796953/obo-9780199796953-0065. xml?rskey=njBPDy&result=1&q=Uti+Possidetis+Iuris#obo-9780199796953–0065-div2–0001>

Mnyongani, F. D. 2008, "Between a Rock and a Hard Place: The Right to Self-Determination versus Uti Possidetis in Africa", *Comparative & International Law Journal of Southern Africa*, 41: 463–479.

Nesi, G. 2018, "Uti Possidetis Doctrine", in *Oxford Public International Law*, <https://opil-ouplaw-com.ezproxy.mdx.ac.uk/view/10.1093/law:epil/9780199231690/law-9780199231690-e1125?rskey=CdzHIb&result=1&prd=OPIL>

Nugent, P. & Asiwaju, A. I. (eds.), 1996, *African Boundaries: Barriers, Conduits and Opportunities*, London: Pinter Publishers.

Oeter, S. 2012, "Self-Determination", in B. Simma, D.-E. Khan, G. Nolte, A. Paulus & N. Wessendorf (eds.), *The Charter of the United Nations: A Commentary, Volume I*, Oxford: Oxford University Press: 313–329.

Oeter, S. 2015, "The Kosovo Case: An Unfortunate Precedent", in *Zeitschrift für ausländisches öffentliches Recht*, <www.zaoerv.de/75_2015/75_2015_1_a_51_74.pdf>

Pellet, A. 1992, "The Opinions of the Badinter Arbitration Committee: A Second Breath for the Self-Determination of Peoples", *European Journal of International Law*, 3: 178–185.

Pentassuglia, G. 2002, "State Sovereignty, Minorities and Self-Determination: A Comprehensive Legal View", *International Journal on Minority and Group Rights*, 9: 303–324.

Peters, A. 2014, "The Principle of *Uti Possidetis Juris*: How Relevant Is It for Secession?", in C. Walter, A. von Ungern-Sternberg, & K. Abushov (eds.), *Self-Determination and Secession in International Law*, Oxford: Oxford University Press: 95–137.

Raič, D. 2002, *Statehood and the Law of Self-Determination*, The Hague: Kluwer Law International.

Ratner, S. R. 1996, "Drawing a Better Line: Uti Possidetis and the Borders of New States", *American Journal of International Law*, 90: 590–624.

Secession Reference 1998, Supreme Court of Canada, *Reference re Secession of Quebec* [1998] 2 S.C.R. 217.

Shahabuddin, M. 2019, "Post-Colonial Boundaries in International Law, and the Making of the Rohingya Crisis in Myanmar", *Asian Journal of International Law*, 9: 334–358.

Shastri, A. & Wilson, A. J. 2001, *The Post-Colonial States of South Asia: Democracy, Identity, Development and Security*, London: Routledge.

Shaw, M. N. 1996, "The Heritage of States: The Principle of *Uti Possidetis Juris* Today", *British Yearbook of International Law*, 61: 75–154.

Spijkers, O. 2011, *The United Nations, the Evolution of Global Values and International Law*, Antwerp: Intersentia.

United Nations Guide for Minorities 2021, Pamphlet No. 4: Human Rights Treaty Bodies and Complaint Mechanisms, <www.ohchr.org/EN/Issues/Minorities/Pages/MinoritiesGuide.aspx>

van den Driest, S. F. 2013, *Remedial Secession: A Right to External Self-Determination as a Remedy to Serious Injustices?*, Antwerp: Intersentia.

Vidmar, J. 2010, "Remedial Secession in International Law: Theory and (Lack of) Practice", *St Antony's International Review*, 6: 37–56.

Weller, M. 2017, *Secession and Self-Determination in Western Europe: The Case of Catalonia*,

Wilde, R. 2011, "Accordance with International Law of the Unilateral Declaration of Independence in Respect of Kosovo", *American Journal of International Law*, 105: 301–307.

Wright, J. 1999, "Minority Groups, Autonomy, and Self-Determination", *Oxford Journal of Legal Studies*, 19: 605–629.

# 8

# INDIGENOUS PEOPLES AND SELF-DETERMINATION IN SETTLER STATES

*David MacDonald**

## Introduction

Indigenous peoples, sometimes known collectively as the "fourth world," have endured hardships during centuries of colonialism. Currently, 40% of the world's countries contain Indigenous nations, who collectively comprise 476 million people, or 6% of the global population, and 19% of the extreme poor (World Bank 2022). While Indigenous peoples have been systematically marginalized in settler states, they have organized collectively to promote their inherent rights, domestically, across borders, and internationally through regional organizations and the United Nations. The UN Declaration on the Rights of Indigenous Peoples (adopted by the UN General Assembly in 2007) is a testament to many decades of deliberation, negotiation, and consensus decision-making, laying out a minimum standard of Indigenous rights. This chapter focuses on western settler states: Canada, the United States, Australia, Aotearoa New Zealand (collectively the CANZUS states). While self-determination and independent sovereign statehood often flow together, this Westphalian option is rarely requested by Indigenous peoples. Rather, the UNDRIP facilitates alternative expressions of self-determination that comprise (*inter alia*) forms of internal autonomy, input into decision-making within the state, the right to free prior and informed consent, treaty making and full participation in international organizations, and freer movement across state borders. The UNDRIP can play an important role in guaranteeing these and other inherent Indigenous rights, if it is recognized and implemented by settler states.

## Background

Indigenous peoples have in many cases been subjected to genocidal actions by colonizing states, which means their populations suffered dramatic demographic losses, have been alienated from the majority of their ancestral lands and waters, and may (through aggressive and coercive assimilation) have lost key aspects of their languages, spiritual practices, governance structures, and other indicia of group identity. Forcible transfer out of the group through residential schooling or the removal of children by child welfare agencies has reduced knowledge of Indigenous identities amongst some Indigenous peoples (MacDonald 2019). Within international politics, Indigenous peoples have been notable for their active exclusion. As Anishnaabe legal theorist

DOI: 10.4324/9781003036593-10

John Borrows notes: "For over 500 years, international law has prevented Indigenous Peoples from participating in the global order. Doctrines of discovery and theories of terra nullius considered Indigenous Peoples lower on the so-called scales of civilization" (2020: 12).

Due in large part to this long and complex history, and the continued realities of colonization, many Indigenous peoples do not seek an official legal definition of what it means to be Indigenous, given that establishing strict criteria could exclude some peoples from consideration. This is especially so in a climate where many governments want to avoid recognizing Indigenous peoples on their territory, perceiving their existence as a potential challenge to state sovereignty. Indeed, the power to define and thereby include or exclude is viewed with suspicion by many, and "definitions imposed by others" on Indigenous peoples are often seen as "not necessary or desirable" (Chen 2017). This marks a departure from other contributors to this volume who will favor clear criteria to identify who is and who is not a member of a particular type of group.

Of course, there are some commonly accepted criteria for identifying Indigenous peoples, which they have themselves developed through their own organizing. The United Nations (1981) identified Indigenous peoples by such attributes as being coherent "communities, peoples and nations," maintaining a "historical continuity with pre-invasion and pre-colonial societies that developed on their territories," and "consider[ing] themselves distinct from other sectors of the societies now prevailing on those territories, or parts of them." They are further identified as being non-dominant, seeking to "preserve, develop and transmit to future generations their ancestral territories, and their ethnic identity, as the basis of their continued existence as peoples, in accordance with their own cultural patterns, social institutions and legal system" (as cited in Castellino 2014: 33–34). To this we can add Article 1b of the International Labour Organization's *Convention Concerning Indigenous and Tribal Peoples in Independent Countries* (C169 1989), which identifies Indigenous peoples as tracing

> descent from the populations which inhabited the country, or a geographical region to which the country belongs, at the time of conquest or colonisation or the establishment of present state boundaries and who, irrespective of their legal status, retain some or all of their own social, economic, cultural and political institutions (UNHCR, 1989).

Peoples plural encompasses "diverse collectives" and can include different types of groups: "tribes, first peoples/nations, aboriginals, ethnic groups, adivasi, janajati, or occupational and geographical terms like hunter-gatherers, nomads, peasants, and hill people" (UNPFII 2021). Central to an understanding of Indigenous peoples is the recognition of their *sui generis* right to self-determination. The UN Expert Mechanism on the Rights of Indigenous Peoples identifies this right as "the inherent power to make binding agreements between themselves and other polities." This includes treaties and other agreements between Indigenous peoples and other types of government and institution (EMRIP 2018).

Recognition as a legal subject in international law often has political dimensions, given that states themselves often give themselves the legitimacy to either grant or withhold recognition. Likewise, conceptions of state sovereignty are also political, and as Bauder and Mueller (2021: 2) note, "sovereignty does not exist a priori." Instead, it is "claimed, asserted, and enacted by those who have the ability to do so." That power has accrued primarily to states. While decolonization proceeded in much of the world after 1945, Indigenous peoples in settler states were hampered by the UN's "salt water" thesis, an informal outcome of the Declaration on the Granting of Independence to Colonial Countries and Peoples passed in 1960. While promoting the right of self-determination to all peoples, the Declaration also forbade any "attempt aimed at the partial or total disruption of the national unity and the territorial integrity of a country." This asserted that colonies seeking independence as sovereign states had to be geographically separate from the colonizing power by a body of salt or blue water. In practice, only those colonies which were non-contiguous from the colonial metropole or colonizing power could claim independence under international law (Lightfoot and MacDonald 2020). Specifically, Resolution 1514 of the Declaration laid out rights to self-determination for "non-self governing territories" which were "geographically separate and is distinct ethnically and/or culturally from the country administering it" (Iorns 1992: 254).

Settler states are not defined in international law, but social scientists identify these as states where the majority of the population are descended from those who colonized and settled territories which were originally inhabited by Indigenous peoples. Processes of settlement were often violent, with European colonizers primarily focused on asserting control of territory, so that lands, waters, indeed anything that could be commodified as a natural resource was claimed by the state. Resource extraction for the benefit of the colonizing metropole (as in more standard understandings of colonialism) was less important than the control of territory and the imposition of foreign institutions to allow for settler dominance (Glenn 2015). Wolfe has referred to a "logic of elimination" as a key aspect of settler colonialism, where Indigenous societies are dissolved, to be replaced by "a new colonial society on the expropriated land base" (Wolfe 2006).

Settler states are often democratic, but the voting power of the settler majority is used to reduce the self-determining rights of Indigenous peoples. Settler states can thus promote narratives of being democratic, tolerant, open, affluent, and multicultural, while at the same time maintaining systems which actively and paternalistically suppress Indigenous peoples and their institutions (Bauder and Mueller 2021: 5–7). Gover identifies the "persistent lack of [I]ndigenous consent to settler governance" as "a defining constitutive flaw of settler statehood, one that undermines the liberal premises of a state's legitimacy" (2015: 346). Relations are increasingly characterized by "political bargains" between the state institutions and Indigenous governance entities and organizations, which are perceived as sub-national actors rather than those negotiating from an equal level of legitimacy (Gover 2015: 347).

The focus of this chapter is on states where the majority of settlers are of European origin. This is not to say that other states do not have Indigenous peoples who have been dominated by non-Indigenous majorities. This is true of many states, and the International Work Group for Indigenous Affairs documents the status of Indigenous peoples throughout the world, including Asia, Africa, Europe, and the Pacific. While CANZUS states do recognize the existence of Indigenous peoples and the need for (some) Indigenous rights, other countries are less forthcoming. For example, PR China does not recognize any Indigenous peoples, although it extends some autonomy to selected "ethnic minorities." Japan refuses to recognize the Okinawan Ryūkyūan people as Indigenous, although it has extended this recognition to the Ainu. Russia does not recognize any Indigenous peoples, deploying instead the term "Indigenous Minority Peoples" to extend some very basic rights to selected groups, numerically below a pre-determined threshold (IWGIA 2021: 195, 233, 546–547).

This chapter's focus is on cases where there are ethno-cultural differences between the dominant settler majority (of primarily European ancestry) and Indigenous peoples. Certainly intermarriage over centuries ensures that a proportion of Indigenous peoples also claim European, African, and other ancestries. There have been debates about "blood quantum" and the percentage of Indigenous "blood" being determinative of who should be considered Indigenous. There are political implications here, given that settler states have sometimes used a percentage of Indigenous "blood" (often 50% or higher) to self-servingly allocate certain rights to some Indigenous peoples while withholding them from others. While Indigenous identity can and has been racialized to some extent, it is also a political identity, tied to specific ancestors, families, communities, lands, languages, customs, spiritual practices, and other indicia of group identity (Axelsson and Sköld 2011; Gover 2016; Palmater 2011). The focus of this chapter is on the rights of Indigenous collective units to self-determination. The precise composition of those units (who is part or not a part of the unit) is a very large and complex discussion beyond the scope of this chapter.

## Colonization

The colonization of the Americas over five centuries involved multiple European powers (including Spain, Portugal, Holland, Great Britain, and France), deploying a range of means for enslaving, killing, and destroying the civilizations of Indigenous peoples, radically reducing their numbers. Processes of Christian conversion, forced assimilation, land theft, and many other activities led to the (at least partial) replacement of Indigenous forms of government and land stewardship with European forms. Indigenous peoples lost the vast majority of their lands. In Australia, colonization took place later, primarily in the eighteenth century, but this island continent was the locus of violence including frontier massacres, bounties, warfare, and other forms of violence. New Zealand was colonized in the nineteenth century and was also the scene of considerable violence (MacDonald 2008).

In European law, the so-called doctrine of discovery (denying non-Christians recognition as property owners and rational, self-governing peoples) proved central to legitimating the theft of Indigenous lands and the creation of settler states. In practice, as Miller et al. put it: "the discovering European nation gained real property rights to native lands and sovereign powers over native peoples and governments merely by finding lands unknown to other Europeans and planting their flag in the soil" (2010: 4). The original doctrine can be traced back to the fifth century AD, designed to legitimate a "worldwide papal jurisdiction" that allowed initially for the legitimation of the Crusades and the invasion of "infidel" lands. It would later be used by Spain and Portugal to legitimate the conquest of the Americas (Miller et al. 2010: 9).

Eventually, treaties were signed between representatives of the British crown and Indigenous leaders, and later between settler states and Indigenous peoples. The exception is Australia, which has no formal treaties with Indigenous peoples. Aotearoa New Zealand has one treaty, the 1840 Treaty of Waitangti, which covers the entire landmass of the country. Canada has over 70 treaties officially recognized between 1701 and 1923, with a further 25 "modern treaties" signed after this time (CIRNAC 2020). The United States negotiated and signed 368 treaties from 1777 to 1868 (Gover 2014). In all cases, treaties with Indigenous peoples were not land surrender agreements, nor did they imply consent to dissolve centuries of self-government. There are stark differences between the Indigenous language versions and oral understandings of treaty (to which Indigenous peoples acceded), and the English versions written down and disingenuously recognized under settler law (Krasowski 2019; Orange 2011).

Further, non-humans form a key aspect of how Indigenous self-determination is conceptualized and how treaties were agreed. Indigenous cosmologies encompass lands, waters, plants, and animals. Indigenous accounts of treaty and agreement making between European colonizers and Indigenous peoples involve wider sets of relations, and commensurate responsibilities. Heidi Kiiwetinepinesiik Stark (Turtle Mountain Ojibwe) articulates how treaties involved bringing newcomers into an already existing web of relationships with all creation, those "pre-existing relationships and responsibilities across Anishinaabe *aki* (the Earth) that were impacted by these agreements" (2017: 256). As she explains: "We spoke not only for the land, but also for the newcomers to this land. We vouched for these newcomers. In doing so we became responsible for Americans and Canadians, and how they would relate to aki" (2017: 268).

Many Indigenous scholars stress the unbreakable interrelationships between humans and everything around them. Nêhiyaw legal theorist Tracey Lindberg elaborates on the concept that "the earth is our mother" by describing an expanded understanding of Indigenous group identity, distinct from European conceptions: "Included within that familial relationship is the understanding that we have a relationship with the land that is reciprocal. It has cared for us. We must care for it" (Miller et al. 2010: 89–90). In her forward to the UN *State of the World's Indigenous Peoples* report, Anne Nuorgam (Sámi), Chair of the UN Permanent Forum on Indigenous Issues, highlights the inextricable ties between Indigenous peoples and lands, the source of their "cultural, spiritual, social and political identity and the foundation of traditional knowledge systems." Indeed, the denial of traditional land rights makes them "highly vulnerable to displacement, poverty, discrimination and marginalization" (UNDESAIP 2021: vii–viii). The return of lands and the ongoing relationship with lands are central to Indigenous identities and conceptions of self-determination. The need to care for the lands and waters means that full statehood on a smaller independent territory is generally not considered as the primary objective, especially if it means separation from much of the original ancestral land base.

## Indigenous organizing in favor of self-determination

Indigenous peoples have organized over centuries to promote their own rights. Anishinaabe political theorist Sheryl Lightfoot has traced a global Indigenous politics marked by mutual respect for difference, cooperation on common objectives, regular networking, and the sharing of best practices, strategies, and experiences. Indigenous diversity is extremely important to remember, especially in the ways people deal with settler states. Some Indigenous peoples practice traditional governance, while others have embraced more western-style institutions and procedures (Lightfoot 2018: 178). Borrows notes a range of Indigenous views over such issues as resource exploitation and use, international trade, and what constitutes Indigenous self-determination. Indeed: "Indigenous Peoples can be as politically diverse as other groups of people in the world," meaning that in practice there are "conflicting, convergent parallel and cross-cutting positions found within Indigenous communities" (2020: 18).

From the onset of European colonization, Indigenous peoples have asserted the right to be sovereign on their own territories, and they are clear that they never ceded the right to be sovereign, and never consented to interference in their own affairs by external political and other actors, including the governments of settler states in which they now reside (Åhrén 2021: 11). To this end, Indigenous peoples have been organizing internationally since the inception of the League of Nations, with well-known lobbying efforts in 1923 by Deskaheh of the Six Nations, who sought to have his people's sovereignty recognized (Young 2019). In 1924, Māori spiritual and political leader Tahupōtiki Wiremu Rātana lobbied the British monarch King George V to honor the Treaty of Waitangi. His delegation presented a petition with over 30,000 signatures to the League. This effort too did not produce much international recognition, but it did positively influence political rights for Māori domestically (NZ History 2021).

Concerted Indigenous activism began during the 1960s and 1970s, consonant with decolonization and civil rights movements around the world. The International Indian Treaty Council was formed in 1974, bringing together some 5,000 representatives from 98 Indigenous nations (IITC 2022). The IITC adopted a Declaration of Continuing Independence in that year, laying the basis for further action by other organizations. For example, the Canadian National Indian

Brotherhood followed this in 1975 with an international conference, where the World Council of Indigenous Peoples was formed (Young 2019: 393–394). By 1977, the IITC gained consultative status to the United Nations Economic and Social Council, which in 2011 was upgraded to general consultation status (IITC 2022). Currently, there are 16 organizations with consultative status, and the influence of Indigenous peoples and organizations at the international level has grown.

While Lightfoot is clear that there is no singular Indigenous culture, she does highlight some common values and goals in many cases, which led to cooperation in a global Indigenous rights movement. This includes "the concept of a globally shared Indigenous identity that largely emerged as a result of the movement." As she explains: "This is a supranational layer of Indigenous identity added to the already complex web of kinship, tribal, and national identities that Indigenous people maintain." However, there has been no effort to create a homogenizing or universalizing movement. Indeed, the movement "deliberately aims to collectively secure the distinctiveness and singularity of individual Indigenous nations, cultures, and communities." She thus describes it as "a unifying (as distinct from unified) vision of Indigenous ontologies and composed of thoughtful and creatively strategic Indigenous political actors who represent the diversity of Indigenous Peoples and enact common Indigenous values in their transnational activities" (Lightfoot 2016: 74).

Barelli observes that Indigenous peoples have been able to leverage certain advantages at the international level. He isolates certain features: "the coalition's global dimension, its collective identity and its ability to skilfully exploit the opportunities for engagement provided by the international legal system." Indeed, he continues: "the fact that indigenous representatives sitting in UN rooms could speak on behalf of hundreds of millions of indigenous people affected both the force of their claims and the way in which the latter were perceived by States' representatives" (Barelli 2016: 145).

A milestone in Indigenous organization came in 1981, with the "Study on the Problem of Discrimination against Indigenous Populations," published by the UN Sub-Commission on Prevention of Discrimination and Protection of Minorities. The report inaugurated several decades of activism at the UN level. The Working Group on Indigenous Populations was created in 1982, providing Indigenous peoples with a forum for communicating with one another and for expressing concerns to the UN. By 1989, Convention 169 was introduced by the ILO, recognizing an Indigenous right to self-determination. Due to extensive lobbying and coordination, the UN agreed to develop certain organs to address the needs of Indigenous peoples. This included the formation of the Permanent Forum on Indigenous Issues in 2000 (a 16-member advisory body which reports to the Economic and Social Council), followed shortly after by the creation of the Special Rapporteur on the Rights of Indigenous Peoples, who reported to the Commission on Human Rights, then later to the Human Rights Council. In 2007, the five-member Expert Mechanism on the Rights of Indigenous Peoples (EMRIP) was created in Geneva, the same year that the UNDRIP was passed in the UN General Assembly. EMRIP also reports to the Human Rights Council (UNDESA 2021).

## The UN Declaration on the Rights of Indigenous Peoples

The genesis of the UN Declaration goes back to the 1970s, but Indigenous peoples did not have much influence at the UN until the 1980s. In 1984, the Fourth General Assembly of the World Council of Indigenous Peoples adopted a Declaration of Principles, with the first Principle stating: "All Indigenous Peoples have the right to self-determination." A further declaration the following year strengthened this right to "whatever degree of autonomy or self-government they choose," including their "political status," their "own economic, social, religious and cultural development," as well as "their own membership and/or citizenship, without external interference" (Daes 2009: 51). By 2007, the UN General Assembly passed the Declaration with 144 positive votes, 11 abstentions, and 4 voting against (Australia, New Zealand, Canada, and the United States). As Lightfoot and I have noted elsewhere, international law prior to the Declaration excluded Indigenous peoples in terms of their collective rights "to maintain such things as Indigenous culture, language, religion, identity, or their own educational systems in the face of assimilative pressures." At the same time, they did not have the rights to maintain their own lands as other peoples did after 1960 (Lightfoot and MacDonald 2017).

As Claire Charters (Ngāti Whakaue, Tūwharetoa, Ngā Puhi, Tainui) explains: "the Declaration goes some way towards mitigating international law's historical and Eurocentric bias against Indigenous Peoples and, also, clarifies the content of the body of law that is indigenous peoples' rights" (2009: 281). The Declaration is normatively very strong, as it relies on a decades-long process which was transparent, and subject to negotiation and consensus, ultimately passing through six different UN institutions (Charters 2009: 282). As Lightfoot has put it, the Declaration is a set of guidelines, its focus being to encourage Indigenous peoples and states to work together, to "recognize, negotiate and protect a variety of possible self-government or autonomy arrangements for Indigenous peoples, dealing with them as 'peoples,' even if not as states" (Lightfoot and MacDonald 2017).

Article 4 covers the right to "autonomy or self-government in matters relating to their internal or local affairs, as well as ways and means for financing their autonomous function." Indigenous peoples, according to Article 5, also have the right to "maintain and strengthen their distinct political, legal, economic, social and cultural institutions, while retaining their right to participate fully, in the life of the State." Article 23 closely parallels this with the right to "promote, develop and maintain their institutional structures and their distinctive customs, spirituality, traditions, procedures, practices and, in the cases where they exist, juridical systems or customs." So too does Article 18, which covers the right to develop and maintain Indigenous "decision-making institutions" through representatives chosen by themselves and according to their own procedures. Article 19 is particularly important, covering the need for states to obtain the "free, prior and informed consent" of Indigenous peoples, "before adopting and implementing legislative or administrative measures that may affect them" (UNDRIP 2008; Charters 2009: 291–292).

Indeed, FPIC is a cornerstone of the Declaration (which also builds on the UN Convention on Biological Diversity, and ILO Convention 169), obliging settler states, corporations, and other actors to fully engage with Indigenous peoples and to gain their consent before any development activities are contemplated on their traditional territories. Actors are to outline the costs and benefits of any planned activities, and to ensure the effective participation of Indigenous peoples in decision-making over issues that impact on them and their territories. The UN's FPIC *Manual for Project Practitioners* (2016) has highlighted very serious problems of environmental destruction and Indigenous land alienation, impoverishment, and death as a result of the unrestrained exploitation of resources on Indigenous territories. The process of obtaining consent is to be free of coercion, to be undertaken in culturally appropriate ways, with sufficient time for communities to discuss and deliberate in their own languages, and using their methods of decision-making. Additionally, "FPIC enables them to negotiate the conditions under which the project will be designed, implemented, monitored and evaluated." There is no guarantee of consent if actors undertake this process. Indigenous peoples can withhold consent, or provide consent and withdraw it at any stage if they are not happy with how the development has proceeded (2016: 13).

The UN Declaration might be seen as bringing Indigenous conceptions of sovereignty and self-determination front and center to the politics of settler states. At one level, the Declaration promotes the right of Indigenous self-determination, specifically Article 3: to "freely determine their political status and freely pursue their economic, social and cultural development." However, Article 46 states:

> Nothing in this Declaration may be interpreted as implying for any State, people, group or person any right to engage in any activity or to perform any act contrary to the Charter of the United Nations or construed as authorizing or encouraging any action which would dismember or impair, totally or in part, the territorial integrity or political unity of sovereign and independent States.
>
> *(Lightfoot 2016: 18; Scheinin and Åhrén 2018)*

Does this mean Indigenous peoples can form independent states, effectively seceding from settler states? For some Indigenous peoples, this option should remain on the table, either to exert leverage against settler states or to act as a guarantor of Indigenous rights as human rights. Other Indigenous nations, however, have rejected the need for this level of autonomy (Daes 2009: 69–70). Desire for full self-determination in principle often stems from past and present mistreatment by settler governments. The right can provide, Eide notes, "a bargaining position from which a reciprocal trust can develop between the indigenous and others in society." The idea is that "an internationally recognized right to self-determination" provides protection beyond the temporary promises or political whims of settler governments, allowing an international layer of monitoring and scrutiny, a way of appealing decisions that go against Indigenous interests domestically (Eide 2009: 41).

According to S. James Anaya (Apache and Purépecha), former UN Special Rapporteur on the Rights of Indigenous Peoples, Westphalian statehood can be seen as an outdated form of sovereignty, in an era when the world is "moving toward greater interconnectedness and decentralization," where formal state boundaries are less important to "the ordering of communities and authority." Further, he articulates a view of self-determination for Indigenous peoples as "full and equal participants at all levels in the construction and functioning of the governing institutions under which they live" (Anaya 2009: 188–189). Equally clear to Anaya is that Indigenous peoples have lost most of their land base through processes of colonization, so independence can not be based on the original lands, but only on a small portion of them. He is clear that existing on small parcels of land cut off from the rest of a former country will not benefit Indigenous peoples. Indeed: "full self-determination, in a real sense, does not justify – and may even be impeded by – a separate state" (Anaya 2009: 188).

In practice, most Indigenous nations do not have the population size, the economic power, or the territorial boundaries to make full sovereignty a viable proposition. Nor is it guaranteed in the Declaration, which is agnostic on this matter. As Weller notes, while the Declaration "does not establish a new, positive entitlement to secession for Indigenous peoples," it likewise does not "diminish their potential entitlement, should one exist, in general international law to form a new State" (Weller 2018: 26, 32). Barelli similarly notes that the Declaration has not changed the fact that "sub-national groups do not have a right to independence." Where it is new is to guarantee an Indigenous-specific right of self-determination within existing states. This is something innovative that did not exist before, except perhaps in limited cases through treaties (2011: 422–423).

## Types of self-determination for Indigenous peoples

As Dahl notes, the quest by Indigenous peoples for autonomy rarely results in challenges to the territorial integrity of the state within which they are located. There are some exceptions. The peoples of East Timor were successful in gaining their independence, something which has eluded West Papua and Western Sahara (2020: 9). However, this is unusual. Given that most Indigenous peoples do not seek full independence, much of the literature focuses instead on internal forms of self-determination. Dahl usefully makes differentiations between "breaking out" and "breaking in" strategies. The first is for Indigenous peoples to have their own autonomy on their own territories, or to possess forms of functional autonomy within the state. This could include specified rights, such as the right to special schools, services in their own languages, the right to speak their languages in legal proceedings, and their own legal proceedings. Exclusive or specific rights to hunt or fish might also be included here. The "break in" strategy concerns where Indigenous peoples and organizations work with the state and other official bodies to cooperate to change the overall focus of policymaking (Dahl 2020: 19).

This builds on Anaya's earlier terms "autonomous governance" and "participatory engagement." The first concerns Indigenous-specific institutions, while the second outlines Indigenous access to and influence over settler state decision-making, given than Indigenous peoples are "simultaneously distinct from, yet joined to, larger units of social and political interaction, units that may include indigenous federations, the states within which they live, and the global community itself" (Anaya 2009: 193).

Yap and Yu reference the seminal work of Erica-Irene Daes, who offers a useful definition of Indigenous self-determination, which includes "the freedom for Indigenous Peoples to live well, to live according to their own values and beliefs, and to be respected by their non-indigenous neighbours." She continues that

> the true test of self-determination is not whether Indigenous Peoples have their own institutions, legislative authorities, laws, police and judges. The true test of self-determination is whether Indigenous Peoples themselves actually feel that they have choices about their way of life.
>
> *(Yap and Yu 2018: 98)*

In practice, Indigenous nations are organized into a range of local and national institutions. In the United States, there are between 2.5 million and 6 million Indigenous peoples, many organized into some 574 Native American tribal entities which are federally recognized by the US government. Most have federally recognized homelands and have limited forms of inherent sovereignty, with some control over their own schools, police, and legal systems. However, Indigenous nations are also seen in US law as wards of the federal government, which exercises a guardianship function over tribal entities (Braun 2021: 570).

Distinctions need to be made between Indigenous people as individual members of an ethnic or cultural group with certain collective rights, and Indigenous people as peoples – as members of coherent and long-lasting political units which have historic and ongoing legal relationships with the central government. For example, within Canada's landmass are approximately 1.7 million Indigenous peoples, comprising 5% of the country's population. Of these, 744,855 are recognized as members of one of 634 First Nations, with 44.2% of these people living on reserves. There are also two other groups of Indigenous peoples: the Métis and Inuit. The latter two groups are not necessarily members of specific nations tied to specific territory as such (Galloway and Bascaramurty 2017). Having status means in most cases being subject to the *Indian Act*, a political instrument which has reduced the political power and numbers of Indigenous peoples by dividing them into "bands" and imposing on them a settler colonial administrative and political structure. While most bands have elected chief and council systems, these are not considered to be traditional forms of government (Palmater 2011: 166–167). The lands on which reserves are located are officially not owned by First Nations, but held in trust by the federal government through the crown. These lands represent a small fraction of the original land base of these nations, and sometimes were located far from their traditional territories. This was done deliberately in order to free up arable land for European settlement while simultaneously depriving Indigenous peoples of their political and economic power (Joseph 2018).

There are also different representative bodies, depending on what is being represented. For example, First Nations governments are represented by provincial and territorial advocacy organizations such as Chiefs of Ontario, Union of New Brunswick Indians, and the Assembly of Manitoba Chiefs. At the national level, the Assembly of First Nations lobbies the federal government on behalf of its member organizations. Such organizations do not represent everyone, and there are separate Métis and Inuit organizations such as the Métis National Council, the Inuit Tapiriit Kanatami, the Native Women's Association of Canada, and the Congress of Aboriginal Peoples (CAP). The CAP in particular is an umbrella organization that represents Métis and non-status Indians, as well as off-reserve status Indians and Southern Inuit Peoples. These organizations work at the local, national, and international levels (Norris 2021: 559–560).

The 1993 Nunavut Land Claim Agreement provided Inuit with control of 350,000 square kilometers, or about of 18% of what became the territory of Nunavut in 1999. A government was established at the same time which provides governing autonomy. However, the territory is still heavily dependent on federal transfer payments, and the remainder of the land is still under crown and private ownership. Canada has two other Inuit autonomies, in Nunatsiavut (Labrador) and Nunavik (Québec), as well as a range of agreements with First Nations (Dahl 2020: 22, 24).

Aotearoa New Zealand has representative organizations such as the National Māori Council, which represents Māori from across 16 districts around the country. There is also the Iwi Chairs Forum, which is similar to the AFN in that it brings together leaders from many of the iwi in the country. However, unlike the AFN, there is no National Chief to liaise regularly with settler governments, nor is there a large administrative staff to carry out work. Overall, Aotearoa New Zealand is divided into 13 rohe, or territories, with multiple iwi and hāpu within each. Some encompass enormous territory like Waipounamu and Rēkohu/Wharekauri (which comprises most of the South Island) to much smaller territories like Te Moana O Raukawa (a small part of the southern North Island). Little of these territories are owned or controlled by iwi, however. Within each rohe, certain iwi and hāpu are recognized as being mana whenua and exercising kaitiakitanga, or guardianship, over resources through an ethic of stewardship (Te Puni Kōkiri 2021). As part of the ongoing Treaty settlements process, iwi have formed Rūnanga, councils or administrative and institutional bodies that bring hāpu and one or more iwi together to promote political, economic, social, and other forms of development.

In Australia, the National Congress of Australia's First Peoples represents individual Indigenous people as well as organizations. Each state also has a land council comprised of representatives of local Indigenous nations: the United Ngunnawal Elders Council, Tasmanian Aboriginal Land and Sea Council, the Barengi Gadjin Land Council, and so on. The United States similarly has such organizations such as the National Congress of American Indians, and regional intertribal organizations such as the Affiliated Tribes of the Northwest Indians, Intertribal Council of Arizona, Midwest Alliance of Sovereign Tribes, and United Tribes of Michigan. These are examples of parallel autonomy, where, as Dahl explains: "indigenous autonomy exists in parallel to the national structures. While such autonomy can give an indigenous group collective and exclusive land rights within a certain territory, those groups keep their individual rights as citizens of the State" (Dahl 2020: 20). Overall, while these are subnational bodies, they can and do work with other Indigenous and other organizations at the international level.

Indigenous nations can also practice self-determination largely outside the framework of settler states. One example is the 2014 "Northern Tribes Buffalo Treaty," signed by representatives from 11 Indigenous nations in the United States and Canada. The first intertribal treaty to be signed on the Great Plains in over 150 years, the treaty covers 6.3 million acres of Indigenous-owned or managed lands, some straddling the border. The treaty allows for the restoration of the buffalo, which were almost entirely exterminated during the colonization of the Americas. Another example is the 2015 Tar Sands Treaty Alliance, an inter-Indigenous treaty (signed by 55 Indigenous First Nations and tribes) to halt the expansion of Tar Sands production and distribution in North America (Lightfoot and MacDonald 2017: 27–30).

At an individual level, members of the Haudenasaunee Confederacy, with territories in what is now Canada and the United States, have used their own travel documents and passports for over a century, peacefully asserting their right to self-determination as Haudenasaunee nationals and citizens. As Lightfoot observes, this case is a clear example of how "expressions of Indigenous peoples' self-determination need not be limited to a strict 'inside or outside' relationship with states or a 'one size fits all' approach." Indeed, this is a useful example of how concepts of borders and sovereignty can be peacefully negotiated and decolonized without threatening the integrity of settler states (Lightfoot 2021: 17, 20).

## Forms of international self-determination

Also important under the Declaration are international Indigenous rights, which are not confined to state borders. In practice, as Cambou notes, the Indigenous peoples, "in particular those divided by international borders, have the right to maintain and develop contacts, relations and cooperation with their own members as well as other peoples across borders" (2019: 189). Cross-border contacts are not to be impeded, and institutions which straddle several states are to be recognized and permitted. The previous section outlined some examples of these forms of self-determination in practice. Other examples include representative institutions internationally and the right to be included in decision-making by settler states in international agreements, when their interests are involved. Cambou identifies these "as external aspects of the right to self-determination to which Indigenous Peoples are also entitled" (2019: 189).

Another key aspect of Indigenous self-determination involves their right to international representation and communication outside the confines of settler states. This is clearly laid out and needs to be respected. This can operate against traditional norms of state sovereignty, which hold that international organizations and other states should not interfere in what are normally considered to be domestic affairs normally within the domestic jurisdiction of the state (Anaya 2009: 194). Henceforth, the international community will need to be far more attentive to violations of human rights under the UN Declaration. If states are infringing on the self-determination of Indigenous peoples within their borders, intervention of some kind may become necessary. International organs such as the Permanent Forum, the Expert Mechanism, and the office of the Special Rapporteur can and do continually monitor how states treat Indigenous peoples within their borders, regularly alerting the international community to Indigenous rights violations (Anaya 2009: 195).

Anaya's point is that states and the state system should be respected and maintained so long as it supports the self-determining rights of Indigenous peoples. The increase in global interconnectedness is to be encouraged. As Anaya puts it, while self-determination must include "confronting and reversing the legacies of empire, discrimination, and cultural suffocation," the focus should not include "vengefulness or spite for past evils," nor should it "foster divisiveness." Instead, there must be a concerted effort to "build a social and political order based on relations of mutual understanding and respect" (Anaya 2009: 196).

## Conclusion

COVID-19 further exposed the vulnerability of many Indigenous peoples to the pandemic. Indigenous peoples were subject to higher rates of food insecurity, poorer access to healthcare, and higher mortality rates than settlers (i.e. 10 times higher in the United States between the ages of 10 to 50, and 40% higher in Canada). Additionally, some governments used pandemic measures to reduce the civic space for Indigenous activism, while further encroaching on their rights (Mamo 2021: 8–9). At the same time, when Indigenous peoples had control over their own health policies, they were better able to navigate the pandemic. In Australia, for example, when Aboriginal community healthcare providers were able to provide culturally appropriate treatment, cases of infection were six times less than in other Indigenous communities (Mamo, 2021: 15).

Indigenous peoples continue to practice self-determination, despite challenges from settler states. The UN Declaration provides much-needed support for this effort. Canada recently passed Bill C-15, which pledges that the federal government must ensure that its laws are consistent with the Declaration, while similarly implementing an action plan to achieve the Declaration's objectives (Parliament of Canada, 2020). Canada has worked to incorporate the Declaration into its legislation, and New Zealand is similarly working on a process to do so.

As this chapter demonstrates, the journey for Indigenous peoples on the road to self-determination has been long, and can best be seen as a series of ongoing relationships with settler states. Most Indigenous peoples regard self-determination taking place alongside the existing territorial dimensions of settler states. They often seek their own forms of autonomy and self-government in the sense of internal self-determination, and they also seek autonomy in organizing regionally and internationally in pursuit of their rights. This can include relationships with other Indigenous peoples that work across state borders. For settler governments, the Declaration should be seen as an opportunity to strengthen and deepen productive and respectful relations with Indigenous peoples.

## Glossary

**Indigenous peoples**   non-dominant peoples who maintain historical continuity with pre-invasion and pre-colonial societies and ancestral territories, and consider themselves to be distinct from the dominant societies of countries in which they live.
**Settler states**   states where the majority of the population are descended from people who colonized and settled territories which were originally inhabited by Indigenous peoples.
**United Nations Declaration on the Rights of Indigenous Peoples (UNDRIP)**   adopted in 2007, it lays out a minimum international standard for the individual and collective rights of Indigenous peoples. The Declaration contains 23 clauses in its preamble and 46 articles.

## Note

*   My thanks to Sheryl Lightfoot, Jennifer Preston, Paul Joffe, Perry Bellegarde, Claire Charters, Moana Jackson, Margaret Mutu, Elsa Stamatopoulou, S. James Anaya, Broddi Sigurðarson, and Bradford Morse. This chapter is an outcome of SSHRC Grant 430413, and was written while I was a visiting scholar at Auckland Law School, University of Auckland/Te Whare Wānanga o Tāmaki Makaurau.

# References

Åhrén, M. (2021). Recognition of Indigenous Peoples' Rights to Lands, Territories and Resources. In *State of the World's Indigenous Peoples Volume V*. New York: United Nations. Available at: www.un.org/development/desa/indigenouspeoples/wp-content/uploads/sites/19/2021/03/State-of-Worlds-Indigenous-Peoples-Vol-V-Final.pdf (Accessed: 4 October 2021).

Anaya, S.J. (2009). The Right of Indigenous Peoples to Self-Determination in the Post-Declaration Era. In Charters, C. and Stavenhagen, R. (eds) *Making the Declaration Work*. Copenhagen, DK: International Work Group for Indigenous Affairs.

Axelsson, P. and Sköld, P. (2011). *Indigenous Peoples and Demography*. New York, NY: Berghan.

Barelli, M. (2011). Shaping Indigenous Self-Determination. *International Community Law Review*, 13(4), pp. 413–436.

Barelli, M. (2016). *Seeking Justice in International Law*. London: Routledge.

Bauder, H. and Mueller, R. (2021). Westphalian Vs. Indigenous Sovereignty. *Geopolitics*, 26(3), pp. 1–18.

Borrows, J. (2020). *Indigenous Diversities in International Investment and Trade*. Cambridge: Cambridge University Press.

Braun, S. (2021). The United States of America. In Mamo, D. (ed) *The Indigenous World*. Copenhagen, DK: International Work Group for Indigenous Affairs.

Cambou, D. (2019). The 2005 Draft Nordic Sámi Convention. In Corradi, G. et al. (eds) *Critical Indigenous Rights Studies*. New York: Routledge.

Castellino, J. (2014). International Law and Self-Determination. In Walter, C. et al. (eds) *Self-Determination and Secession in International Law*. Oxford: Oxford University Press.

Charters, C. (2009). The Legitimacy of the UN Declaration on the Rights of Indigenous Peoples. In Charters, C. and Stavenhagen, R. (eds) *Making the Declaration Work*. Copenhagen, DK: International Work Group for Indigenous Affairs.

Chen, W. (2017). *Indigenous Rights in International Law*. Oxford: Oxford University Press. Available at: https://oxfordre.com/internationalstudies/view/10.1093/acrefore/9780190846626.001.0001/acrefore-9780190846626-e-77 (Accessed: 4 October 2021).

Crown-Indigenous Relations and Northern Affairs Canada. (2020). *Treaties and Agreements*. Ottawa, ON: Government of Canada. Available at: www.rcaanc-cirnac.gc.ca/eng/1100100028574/1529354437231 (Accessed: 4 October 2021).

Daes, E. (2009). The Contribution of the Working Group on Indigenous Populations to the Genesis and Evolution of the UNDRIP. In Charters, C. and Stavenhagen, R. (eds) *Making the Declaration Work*. Copenhagen, DK: International Work Group for Indigenous Affairs.

Dahl, J. (2020). Study on Indigenous Peoples' Autonomies. In Dahl, J. et al. (eds) *Building Autonomies*. Copenhagen, DK: International Work Group for Indigenous Affairs.

Eide, A. (2009). The Indigenous Peoples, the Working Group on Indigenous Populations and the Adoption of the UNDRIP. In Charters, C. and Stavenhagen, R. (eds) *Making the Declaration Work*. Copenhagen, DK: International Work Group for Indigenous Affairs.

Expert Mechanism on the Rights of Indigenous Peoples Human. (2018). *Free, Prior and Informed Consent Report*. A/HRC/39/62. Available at: www.ohchr.org/en/issues/ipeoples/emrip/pages/studyfpic.aspx (Accessed: 4 October 2021).

Galloway, G. and Bascaramurty, D. (2017). Census 2016. *Globe and Mail*, 25 October. Available at: https://beta.theglobeandmail.com/news/national/census-2016-highlights-diversity-housing-indigenous/article36711216/?ref=www.theglobeandmail.com& (Accessed: 4 October 2021).

Glenn, E. (2015). Settler Colonialism as Structure. *Sociology of Race and Ethnicity* 1(1), pp. 54–74.

Gover, K. (2014). Nation to Nation. *American Indian Magazine*, 15(2). Available at: www.americanindianmagazine.org/story/nation-nation-treaties-between-united-states-and-american-indian-nations (Accessed: 4 October 2021).

Gover, K. (2015). 'CANZUS' and the UN Declaration on the Rights of Indigenous Peoples. *European Journal of International Law*, 26(2), pp. 345–373.

Gover, K. (2016). Indigenous Membership and Human Rights. In Lennox, C. and Short, D. (eds) *Handbook of Indigenous Peoples' Rights*. London: Routledge.

International Indian Treaty Council. (2022). *About IITC*. Available at: https://www.iitc.org/about-iitc/ (Accessed: 14 October 2022).

International Work Group for Indigenous Affairs. (2021). *The Indigenous World*. Copenhagen, DK: IWGIA. Available at: www.iwgia.org/en/resources/indigenous-world.html (Accessed: 4 October 2021).

Iorns, C. (1992). Indigenous Peoples and Self Determination. *Case Western Reserve Journal of International Law*, 24(2/3).

Joseph, R. (2018). *21 Things You May Not Know about the Indian Act*. Vancouver: Indigenous Relations Press.

Krasowski, S. (2019). *No Surrender*. Regina, SK: University of Regina Press.

Lightfoot, S. (2016). *Global Indigenous Politics*. New York, NY: Routledge.

Lightfoot, S. (2018). A Promise Too Far? In Hillmer, N. and Lagassé, P. (eds) *Justin Trudeau and Canadian Foreign Policy*. London: Palgrave.

Lightfoot, S. (2021). Decolonizing Self-Determination: Haudenosaunee Passports and Negotiated Sovereignty. *European Journal of International Relations*, 27(2), pp. 1–24.

Lightfoot, S. and MacDonald, D. (2017). Treaty Relations between Indigenous Peoples: Advancing Global Understandings of Self-Determination. *New Diversities*, 19(2), pp. 25–39.

Lightfoot, S. and MacDonald, D. (2020). The United Nations as Both Foe and Friend to Indigenous Peoples and Self-Determination. *E-International Relations*. March. Available at: www.e-ir.info/2020/03/12/the-un-as-both-foe-and-friend-to-indigenous-peoples-and-self-determination/ (Accessed: 4 October 2021).

MacDonald, D. (2008). *Identity Politics in the Age of Genocide*. London: Routledge.

MacDonald, D. (2019). *The Sleeping Giant Awakens*. Toronto: University of Toronto Press.

Mamo, D. (2021). Editorial. In Mamo, D. (ed) *The Indigenous World*. Copenhagen, DK: International Work Group for Indigenous Affairs.

Miller, R., Ruru, J., Behrendt, L. and Lindberg, T. (2010). *Discovering Indigenous Lands*. Oxford, UK: Oxford University Press.

Norris, M. (2021) Canada. In Mamo, D. (ed) *The Indigenous World*. Copenhagen, DK: International Work Group for Indigenous Affairs.

NZ History (2021). *The 1920s–1924 – Key Events*. New Zealand Ministry for Culture and Heritage. Available at: https://nzhistory.govt.nz/culture/the-1920s/1924 (Accessed: 4 October 2021).

Orange, C. (2011). *The Treaty of Waitangi*. Auckland: Bridget Williams.

Palmater, P. (2011). *Beyond Blood*. Vancouver, BC: University of British Columbia Press.

Parliament of Canada (2020). *BILL C-15*. Available at: https://parl.ca/DocumentViewer/en/43-2/bill/C-15/first-reading (Accessed: 4 October 2021).

Scheinin, M. and Åhrén, M. (2018). Relationship to Human Rights, and Related International Instruments. In Hohmann, J. and Weller, M. (eds.) *The UN Declaration on the Rights of Indigenous Peoples: A Commentary*. Oxford Scholarly Authorities on International Law. Available at: https://opil.ouplaw.com/view/10.1093/law/9780199673223.001.0001/law-9780199673223-chapter-4 (Accessed: 4 October 2021).

Stark, H.K. (2017). Changing the Treaty Question. In Borrows, J. and Coyle, M. (eds) *The Right Relationship*. Toronto, ON: University of Toronto Press.

Te Puni Kōkiri (2021). *Te Kāhui Māngai*. Wellington, NZ. Available at: www.tkm.govt.nz/ (Accessed: 4 October 2021).

United Nations Declaration on the Rights of Indigenous Peoples (2008). Available at: https://www.un-.org/development/desa/indigenouspeoples/declaration-on-the-rights-of-indigenous-peoples.html (Accessed: 30 October 2022).

United Nations Department of Economic and Social Affairs (2021). *Indigenous Peoples at the United Nations*. Available at: www.un.org/development/desa/indigenouspeoples/about-us.html (Accessed: 4 October 2021).

United Nations Department of Economic and Social Affairs Indigenous Peoples (2016). *Free Prior and Informed Consent*. New York: United Nations. Available at: www.un.org/development/desa/indigenouspeoples/publications/2016/10/free-prior-and-informed-consent-an-indigenous-peoples-right-and-a-good-practice-for-local-communities-fao/ (Accessed: 4 October 2021).

United Nations Department of Economic and Social Affairs Indigenous Peoples (2021). *State of the World's Indigenous Peoples Volume V*. New York: United Nations. Available at: www.un.org/development/desa/indigenouspeoples/wp-content/uploads/sites/19/2021/03/State-of-Worlds-Indigenous-Peoples-Vol-V-Final.pdf (Accessed: 4 October 2021).

United Nations High Commissioner for Refugees (1989). *Indigenous and Tribal Peoples Convention No. 169*. Available at: www.ohchr.org/en/professionalinterest/pages/indigenous.aspx (Accessed: 4 October 2021).

United Nations Permanent Forum On Indigenous Issues (2021). *Who Are Indigenous Peoples?*. New York: Secretariat of the Permanent Forum. Available at: www.un.org/esa/socdev/unpfii/documents/5session_factsheet1.pdf (Accessed: 4 October 2021).

Weller, M. (2018). Self-Determination of Indigenous Peoples. In Hohmann, J. and Weller, M. (eds) *The UN Declaration on the Rights of Indigenous Peoples: A Commentary*. Oxford Scholarly Authorities on International Law. Available at: https://opil.ouplaw.com/view/10.1093/law/9780199673223.001.0001/law-9780199673223-chapter-4 (Accessed: 4 October 2021).

Wolfe, P. (2006). Settler Colonialism and the Elimination of the Native. *Journal of Genocide Research*, 8(4), pp. 387–409.

World Bank. (2022). Indigenous Peoples. *World Bank*. Available at: https://www.worldbank.org/en/topic/indigenouspeoples (Accessed: 4 October 2022).

Yap, M. and Yu, E. (2018). Expressions of Indigenous Rights and Self-Determination from the Ground Up. In Howard-Wagner, D. et al. (eds) *The Neoliberal State*. Canberra: Australian National University Press.

Young, S. (2019). Re-Historicising Dissolved Identities. *London Review of International Law*, 7(3), pp. 377–408.

# 9

# THE MAP MAKES THE PEOPLE

## The territorial nature of self-determination

*Timothy William Waters**

*Peoples* self-determine, so what relationship does self-determination have to territory? Modern self-determination is strongly defined by, even subordinated to territory, in ways radically different from earlier, Wilsonian models. This change is significant: Self-determination no longer does much useful work in creating new states through secession, but instead is focused on internal qualities of the states we happen already to have. Although formally a right of peoples, it is more useful to think of self-determination as a right *of territories*, from which human communities benefit or not.

## Mapping self-determination's territorial meaning

What do we mean by territory? It might seem obvious enough – and the obvious, commonsensical understanding goes a long way – but it is helpful to define the term more closely.

Territory is not land; it is a political concept. Territory is physical space understood politically. When we speak of a country's 'territorial waters,' for example, we are identifying a space by its political status. This need not presuppose a *particular* political understanding – certainly, the legal fact called a state, however dominant, ain't necessarily so[1] – but *some* political theory necessarily underlies any description of the earth's surface as 'territory.'

Still, we shouldn't forget our naïve intuitions. The political meanings of territory reduce quite rapidly to that minimum – the control of human beings and resources in physical space – and woe to the theorist of sovereignty, let alone the statesman, who forgets the laws of physics and proximity. Physical space matters, so place matters, which is why we put political frames around space and call it territory.

A concept of territory may not be an absolutely essential part of political organization, but something like territory figures significantly in all complex systems. Even when candidates for non-territoriality are proposed – pre-colonial political structures in Southeast Asia, the *millet* system, papal authority or the Holy Roman Empire – they turn out to be anything but indifferent to the realities of governing people in politically defined physical space. And even though many human communities have no necessary territorial basis – churches, unions, conventions of Esperanto enthusiasts, global mafias and soccer hooligans – they inevitably coexist with authorities that are territorial.

Essential or not, the historical development of the modern state system has had territory at its center. Tillyean readings of how states formed assume territory as an almost irreducible feature – and often identify a time after which territoriality became entrenched, like a climax forest (see Tilly 1975, 1985: 169; see also Abramson 2017). Marxist theory predicted the withering away of the state – if not explicitly the end of territorial organization[2] – but nowhere has it worked out that way. The territorial state is the default today: "a State without a territory is not possible."[3] Perhaps it could have been otherwise, but it isn't otherwise now, and that's an historical development too.

Likewise, international law is predicated upon territorial units. Despite the blinding, brassy allure (or terror) of globalization and the insistent sirens of cosmopolitanism, global order remains overwhelmingly territorial in many, seemingly irreducible ways.[4] Of course, many specific *practices* of law and politics are not limited by geography,[5] but it is difficult to conceive seriously of a *system* without territorial units (though we shall try in the last section of this chapter).

So it is unsurprising that self-determination, in theory and especially in practice, has been closely bound to territory. Its territorial orientation simply marks it as consistent with – indeed, a central element in – the general model of international law and relations we happened to develop. Self-determination's concepts and commitments arose out of a historical context – late European modernity and the colonial-imperial era – and absorbed historically situated ideas of political identity that took the relationship of politics to place for granted. The particular form it assumed was the European territorial state.

Early theories of self-determination were, in effect, a response to the inadequacies of *jus emigrandi* as a strategy for negotiating political difference in European space. Pre-Westphalian treaties, such as the 1555 Peace of Augsburg, granted dissenting religious communities a right of exit. Exit is certainly better than being killed or trapped in a hostile state, but uprooting oneself is hardly ideal and doesn't admit the possibility that one might have as much claim to a place as the king – or an even better claim precisely because of who one is and where one is from.

If people were to stay where they were, then a stronger argument about having a right to stay was needed. The transition from divine and kingly claims of sovereignty to popular ones encouraged those more robust formulae: ideas like peoples, nations, and autochthony all circle around the political significance of what it means to be from, and of, a place.

So we find early articulations of self-determination linking identity to place – the linguistic community, the nation – and from there it isn't far to the idea of a people on *its* territory as the political legal basis for the state. National self-determination and popular sovereignty became the core conceptual challenges to divine and dynastic principles. And for related reasons, self-determination's entanglement with territory has contributed to its majoritarian and democratic tendencies in our time.

Self-determination is one of the frames we use to construct 'territory' – to determine political control of people and land, and to legitimate that control. That is what the theory says; the reality is almost precisely the opposite: Territory is what we use to construct self-determination.

## Two models of self-determination

Self-determination has had two great historical phases, with two different relationships to territory. In the pre-classical phase, self-determination could shape territories and move borders.[6] In the classical era in which we live, that relationship has flipped: Existing territories shape the right of self-determination. Is one better? Who can say – at least, let's see.

### *The pre-classical model: Wilsonian national self-determination*

In the pre-classical model, which we can date from the nineteenth century through the Wilsonian era,[7] human settlement is a pre- or extra-political fact, around which political borders are to be drawn. People whom we might reasonably call Italians live where they do, whether or not a political unit called Italy exists. And if it does not, it is to be drawn around them where they are.

This is a fiction, of course: no human settlement pre-exists the politics of the place where settlement happens. The very idea that some set of people are Italian, rather than French or Sicilian or Ladin or something else, is partly a function of territorial units whose governance shaped those identities.

But it is a fiction that pre-classical self-determination insists upon, with highly generative implications. Taken seriously, pre-classical self-determination breaks borders and reshapes territories: Objectively, qualitatively identifiable communities exist, and can claim the right to govern the places where they live.

In Wilson's Fourteen Points, all the themes of pre-classical self-determination are present: alignment of borders with national identity; national groups' autonomous development; historical justice; the need to sort the claims of multiple groups within a single state; and the demotion of colonial space (Wilson 1918). Present, too, are the challenges: the wild inconsistencies; the self-dealing *vae victis*; the need to identify what areas are 'indisputably' or 'clearly recognizable' as belonging to one nation or another; the use of words like 'undoubted' or 'impartial' signaling precisely the difficulties that arise as soon as one tries to apply such principles to actually inhabited spaces.

It is difficult to imagine Wilsonian self-determination without thinking about territory – certainly difficult to see what the point would have been. Which territory exactly was unclear, and in practice the model produced overlapping claims. But the two elements – people and territory – are analytically separate and exist in a clear causal relationship: peoples come first, units are the consequence of identifying peoples. Self-determination determines territory.

Nor, logically, would the causality necessarily stop. If a people's settlement patterns changed – whether through migration, assimilation, the emergence of new identities or some other process – then borders logically should change too. Exactly how was never clear, and since the Versailles system's protected new borders, self-determination's logic was abandoned in the moment it was adopted (*League of Nations* 1919, Art. 10). But then Wilsonian self-determination was a principle in principle, not so much in practice.

## Self-determination as legal order: the classical model

The new political principle didn't last long. A new, *legal* norm of self-determination introduced as part of the next postwar settlement radically altered the relationship of people to territory. In the pre-classical era, territory was a consequence of self-determination; the postwar order reversed that logic. In the pre-classical model, a people existed separately from the territory, and justified its existence. In the new, classical period, in which we still live, it is entirely otherwise: Territories exist, and define the people who in turn have the right to them.

The UN Charter declares self-determination a right of "peoples" (UN Charter 1945, Art. 1(2) and 55), though without actually defining a people, the content of the right or much else. But in short order – no later than the 1960 Colonial Declarations – self-determination became closely linked to decolonization and opposition to alien rule.[8]

Through decolonization, this new classical orthodoxy was expressly tied to territory. Unlike in the earlier Wilsonian version, the existence of a distinct territory, physically separated from the metropolitan state's territory (the so-called 'salt water thesis') became a necessary condition for identifying a colonial people possessed of self-determination.

And sometimes, seemingly, a sufficient condition too. The only other requirements were separate, asymmetrical rule and some ethnic or cultural difference between the non-self-governing and metropolitan populations.[9] But the territorial element predominated: There are no significant instances of colonial self-determination being successfully applied within the contiguous land borders of a state, even when significant racial or ethnic differences exist.[10]

This shift from a people-first to a territory-first orientation had important consequences. It produced a highly predictable set of cases, pre-identified on mid-century maps. It was no longer necessary, or even useful, to inquire deeply into the identity of the people. Now, a people was simply the population of an existing territory. Nor was it strictly necessary to inquire into their wishes; independence could usually be presumed, and only in a minority of cases were serious inquiries made or a fair referendum held.[11]

Most consequentially, self-determination became, in effect, a right of the territory – of the state. The territories in which post-war self-determination played out pre-existed. Identity no longer played as much of a role; Humans might still be the beneficiaries, but only inasmuch as they were subjects of an existing territory.[12] And, in the course of things, majorities benefitted more than minorities.

Over time, qualitative features have been attached to the classical core: Now self-determination implies not merely that territories should be independent, but that their governance should be democratic, rights-respecting and equally applied to all citizens. These moves are called 'internal self-determination,' and we'll turn to them shortly. But first we must consider a particular feature of the state system, to which self-determination is effectively subordinated, which shows how territory is central to modern self-determination – and defines it.

*Territorial integrity.* The UN Charter introduced another principle, territorial integrity, which protects states against changes to their territory against their will. Territorial integrity is closely linked to non-aggression (U.N. Charter Art. 2(4)), though it is a more expansive concept – it implicitly justifies states' protecting their integrity against *internal* threats as well.

It is anachronistic to speak of territorial *integrity* as a general norm prior to the prohibition of war. European states have long had well-developed theories of territory, but also understood that they might take territories from each other for many reasons. It is only with the postwar prohibition of aggression and the parallel promotion of human rights that 'integrity' was attached to territory. Territorial integrity as a legal norm dates only from the postwar era – the same moment when self-determination became a legal norm.

This is significant for how territory interacts with self-determination. In theory, territorial integrity and self-determination are in tension, since the former is conservative of units by definition, the latter not so. Indeed, this tension has been much observed.[13] But it does not exist.

So long as self-determination was understood as a principle of liberation or secession – as in the pre-classical, Wilsonian era – it was a challenge to states' territory and to imperialism. And in the early postwar period, when territorial integrity was first declared a legal principle *but also* colony after colony achieved independence, it might well have seemed that the tension between territorial integrity and self-determination was fundamental.

But this tension turned out to be contingent, and has disappeared almost entirely in the mature classical model. This was achieved by the very turn made to redefine self-determination away from its earlier impulses and towards a model based upon existing units.

Decolonization demonstrates how this seeming tension was actually a convergence. At first glance, decolonization seems to show the two principles quite at odds, since self-determination for colonial peoples broke the territory of the great empires. Yet it did so by making *existing* colonial units into states. Colonial liberation *looked like* a challenge to territorial integrity, but because colonial territories were already defined on the map, self-determination wasn't reshaping those units in light of the people living within them, the way pre-classical self-determination had tried. Classical self-determination is disruptive of the territorial integrity of *empire* – (at least, empires spread across salt water) – but not of *existing units* as such.

Indeed, it is telling that, as the decolonial model was being perfected, a rule developed that the imperial powers ought not to make any further changes to the borders of their colonies before independence – that the colonies' territorial integrity ought to be preserved.[14] The reason for this rule was practical – it aimed to prevent late-stage *divide et impera* – but it required unflinching commitment to the fiction of a pre-existing and indivisible self-determining 'people' that, in fact, often shared nothing except the experience of colonial subjugation. The irony is as inescapable as the borders.

Ironic or not, this rule helped ensure that the units on the colonial map became independent states with minimum alteration. It also figures into more recent, echoing disputes concerning Mayotte (separated from the Comorros following a referendum in which Mayotte was the only island voting to remain French),[15] and the Chagos archipelago.

The *Chagos* litigation demonstrates the hold of this territorially rigid rule on the shape of self-determination. The United Kingdom separated the Chagos Islands from Mauritius shortly before the latter's independence in 1968, removed the population and leased one of the islands to the United States for a military base while administering the archipelago as part of the British Indian Ocean Territory. In 2019, the International Court of Justice ruled that because of these actions, the United Kingdom had not lawfully completed the decolonization of Mauritius (*Chagos Opinion* 2019), violating both self-determination and the rule against late changes to colonial borders. It was a largely unimpeachable decision in doctrinal terms. But Chagos is over 2,000 kilometers from Mauritius, and its link with that island instead of some closer colonial possession (Sri Lanka, India, the Maldives) was a function of British imperial fiat. A case formally grounded on self-determination is only understandable as an assertion of territorial integrity.

The pre-independence territorial fixity rule shows that, even in the moment of supposedly maximal tension between territorial integrity and self-determination, these principles were in fact inexorably converging. And with their convergence, the generative substance of self-determination steadily drained away. Once the existing colonies were liberated, self-determination ceased to be able to generate or justify new units worthy of independence.

Indeed, once it had justified colonies' independence, self-determination in turn justified those new states' territorial integrity, since self-determination is a continuing right. Far from disrupting territory, classical self-determination reinforces and underpins the commitment to preserve existing units – that's the work it now does. The supposed tension between the two doctrines has been resolved by subordinating self-determination to territorial integrity.[16]

So, to sum: By basing the right to a state on human communities' shared qualities, pre-classical self-determination challenged the integrity of states' territory. But neither self-determination nor territorial integrity was yet a legal principle; that happened only with the new global order in 1945. The supposed tension between them was always more apparent than real, and resolved in favor of territorial integrity. Self-determination became the conservative justification for territorial integrity, applied to a finite set of units already in existence – states and colonies already on the map – and later to any units that, against the odds, came into existence thereafter.

Pre-classical self-determination could justify secession, and equally it could justify the fusion of units, where borders divided a biddable people. The present, classical model cannot easily be harnessed to change borders, or to answer any questions about the shape of units.[17] Classical self-determination has largely ceased to be a generator of new states. The doctrine's effects, if they are to be found, must be sought *inside* the states we already have. There, self-determination still shapes claims about democracy, rights and the quality of governance. Are these claims also affected by territorial considerations? Let's turn now to these internal forms of self-determination, and see.

## Internal self-determination's territorialized limits

A book on secession naturally focuses on external forms of self-determination. But there is a separate and more robust aspect of self-determination: the internal. Much contemporary practice and scholarship on self-determination is concerned with the *quality* of governance – democracy, human and minority rights, indigeneity – rather than new borders. It may not be immediately clear what territory has to do with these concerns – but in fact, territory is a vital organizing principle in internal self-determination too.

The logic of internal self-determination is straightforward and compelling: If a people governs itself, it ought actually to do so. This intuition was submerged during the decolonial period, when the urgency of independence from foreign and imperial domination provided its own justification and offered, seemingly, improvement in internal governance *per definitionem*.

But a doctrine as foundational and protean as self-determination is too useful to leave moribund; and after all, self-determination was never just a colonial matter, but a continuing right of all peoples. Besides, history continues: Having achieved external self-determination, a self-governing community might discover a natural interest in the quality of its governance. Or other states might wish to hold the new state's rulers to some standards: The appalling depredations of some postcolonial governments raised the question of why, exactly, local misrule was superior. Since the end of decolonization, self-determination's implicit purposes have increasingly become explicit: Especially from the late 1960s, there has been increasing attention to democratic and participatory aspects, though these were still an 'emerging' right as late as the 1990s (Franck 1992). Although secession crises occasionally generate attention, internal self-determination has been the field's dominant focus.

At first blush, this might seem to herald the *de*-territorialization of self-determination – the doctrine's immature 'external' phase giving way to a more sophisticated engagement with its true purposes. Yet the internal turn has not been a move away from territoriality. Internal self-determination's moves are all premised on doing their work within existing states – taking the territorial unit as given. Givens are often invisible, but that does not make them unimportant. Quite the opposite.

The turn to democracy illustrates the territorial underpinnings of internal self-determination. Democracy operates within existing state boundaries, its integrative and egalitarian impulses typically encouraging a focus on inclusion and equality.[18] This can be seen in electoral practice, which has tended towards a one-person, one-vote standard, in which racial, ethnic and other distinctions are minimized in favor of integration and participation.

Democratic processes assume a demos, and a demos is a function of its unit. Inclusion and participation look very different depending on who belongs to majority and minority, but that is entirely a question of demography and line drawing: With one set of borders, one majority is likely; but with different borders, a different one. This 'boundary problem' is a recognized and largely irreducible feature of democratic theory (see Whelan 1987: 13).[19]

Similarly with human and minority rights: human rights challenge states' sovereignty, but they do not challenge states' territorial integrity, or even address its demographic consequences. Human rights say surprisingly little about marginalization caused by bordered demography – the propriety of a state language, for example, or even state-sponsored religion. The choices that a state makes can radically disfavor certain groups without violating human rights.

Minority rights are even more subject to negotiation and interpretation within each existing state. And the very concept of minority rights is territorial – 'minority' being, by definition, that group which is not a self-determining people (Higgins 1994: 121–127). Minority rights aim to ameliorate a condition that exists solely because a bordered unit happens to enclose some numerically inferior community. Kosovo's Albanians were a minority in Serbia, a majority in independent Kosovo; in Serbia they were entitled to limited minority protections, but in Kosovo they enjoy the privileges of a majority. Minority rights are both an effort to ameliorate the democratic boundary problem and a function of it.

Democracy and rights assume a state, and then operate within the political and conceptual confines of that state. It is striking how little traction any of these doctrines offers for justifying border changes under almost any conditions, even when those conditions become quite terrible. The solution democracy offers is better democracy, within the borders already given; the solution rights offers is more rights better implemented, within those same borders. And if the demography of a particular state actually contributes to its problems, these moves – which are the stuff of internal self-determination – have almost nothing to say about that, because they are tools conceived to work on and within the state in the shape it already has.

The fixity, permanence and protected status of states' territories has important effects on other parts of the global system that self-determination supposedly addresses. Because territory is fixed, efforts to mitigate problems created by a territorial unit itself must usually be internal in nature. This is also true for many problems that, by their nature, are not contained within a single territory, such as climate change.

And even when the proverbial 'international community' intervenes, it does so to improve the situation *within* that state, almost never to create a new one. The territorial state – in particular, those units identified in 1945 – determines almost totally the field in which internal self-determination plays out. Rights, democracy and inclusive governance become not the goals of self-determination, but our only tools to mitigate the harsh rigidity that territorialized self-determination has imposed, because in practice there are no other.

## What's left of external self-determination: remedial secession

The deep territoriality of the international system has encouraged a focus on internal self-determination and discouraged the external kind. Indeed, it is difficult to imagine the vocabulary of 'internal' and 'external' even arising if not for the overriding importance of territorial integrity.

The point at which self-determination's internal focus and its almost vestigial external variant converge is remedial secession. Remedial secession is the doctrine that communities subjected to extremes of persecution and discrimination ought to have a protective remedy of independence. It provides a narrow pathway to statehood, but the narrowness of that path indicates how much self-determination has come to be defined, and cabined, by existing units – how much the doctrine is now a creature of territory.

The critical text underlying remedial secession is the UN General Assembly's 1970 Friendly Relations Declaration. It mostly reprises the principles of territorial integrity and non-interference – the closing orthodoxy of high decolonization – but includes a famous 'saving clause':

> Nothing in the foregoing paragraphs shall be construed as authorizing or encouraging any action which would dismember or impair, totally or in part, the territorial integrity or political unity of sovereign and independent States conducting themselves in compliance with the principle of equal rights and self-determination of peoples as

described above *and thus possessed of a government representing the whole people belonging to the territory without distinction* as to race, creed or colour.

(UN GA Res. 2625 1970, emphasis added)

Though one has to read it backwards, the clause suggests a limit to territorial integrity defined by internal self-determination. Territorial integrity is guaranteed for states "conducting themselves in compliance with the principle of equal rights and self-determination of peoples", implicitly defined as inclusive governance of the whole people without invidious distinctions. The phrasing begs the question of what protection a state's territorial integrity should receive if it *doesn't* respect these rights. From that question-begging, the doctrine of remedial secession has arisen.

In 1998, the Canadian Supreme Court announced a test for decent and inclusive treatment, even outside the colonial context; were a state to fail that test, secession might be a remedy (*Reference re Secession of Quebec* 1998). After the Kosovo crisis, this logic was further developed by the articulation of Responsibility to Protect, in which grave violations of human rights or extreme harms might trigger a right to intervene, with the (unacknowledged) implication that the remedy might be a new state.[20]

We have seen how the supposed tension between self-determination and territorial integrity is largely illusory. If there is any tension, it should appear in remedial secession, which breaks a sovereign unit because of a claim that internal self-determination had been denied. That looks like a revival of an old, Wilsonian logic.[21] Still, it is difficult to think of remedial secession's protections springing from self-determination as such – or to the degree they do, they mirror the profound transformations the doctrine has undergone, and reinforce just how much self-determination has been subordinated to the imperatives of territorial integrity.

The remedy of secession is offered to groups whose members have been denied equal rights as members of their existing state, on account of differences such as race or ethnicity. But these differences are not themselves the basis for self-determination, the way Wilson would have seen them. In fact they are supposed *not* to be taken into account: The harm remedial secession seeks to counter is exclusion from a general population, defined by a territory, in which race, ethnicity and religion are supposed to play no role.

This may be an attractive social vision, but it is one radically defined by the given of territory, in which self-determination does little work. A group benefitting from remedial secession does not have a credible self-determination claim *prior* to the events triggering its departure; it *becomes* a self-determining people only by seceding. We can describe the process this way: some minority has no self-determination claim other than membership in a territorially defined state; it is persecuted; as a remedy, it is given independence; as a consequence, it becomes a self-determining people, which otherwise it would not have been. It is only after escaping the state that the community becomes a people in the legal sense. This is radically different from the pre-classical model, which imagined a new state as the *consequence* of a *community's right*.

Rather than seeing remedial secession as a generative act of self-determination, it is more sensible to think of it as a humanitarian principle – springing from the logic of human rights – which can have territorial consequences *that in turn* create a new self-determination claim. As always in the classical period, the existence of a territorial unit decides the analysis, not the other way around.

Moreover, the rarity and narrowness of remedial secession actually reinforce the baseline normativity of the territorial system. There are almost no cases. The remedy is so rare, requiring such a high threshold, that it simply reminds us: The default, the space within which politics plays out, is the existing territorial state.

# Self-determination without territory: two problems

Finally, let's consider two doctrinal and practical problems that indicate the deep territoriality of self-determination: the self-determination of Indigenous peoples, and the problem of disappearing states.

## *Indigeneity: self-determination without a state (always within one)*

We may still be in the classical era of self-determination, but – as with the internal turn – the doctrine has not been static. Self-determination has expanded and been reshaped since decolonization, but expansion has made territoriality *more* central to the doctrine. This can be seen most clearly in indigenous peoples' rights.[22]

As the movement for indigenous rights developed, self-determination became its preferred mode; the Declaration on the Rights of Indigenous Peoples of 2007 is framed as an expression of self-determination (UN GA Res. 61/295: Arts. 3 & 4). It was a logical choice. Pre-classical self-determination relied on notions of autochthony, an intrinsic link to place – the old rhetoric of blood and soil. Such language was less favored in the postwar world, and less needed in the rigid decolonial model. But it was redeployed for indigeneity, which is explicitly grounded on descent, identity, culture and place.[23]

Indigenous self-determination identifies specific rights based on claims of a special relationship to physical space. Thus indigenous peoples have the right "to maintain and strengthen their distinctive spiritual relationship with their traditionally owned or otherwise occupied and used lands, territories, waters and coastal seas and other resources and to uphold their responsibilities to future generations in this regard" (UN GA Res. 61/295: Art. 25). States have limited control over indigenous lands, concerning hazardous waste disposal, military operations and strategic development (UN GA Res. 61/295: Arts. 29, 30 and 32). Indigenous peoples have the right to engage in cross-border cooperation (UN GA Res. 61/295: Art. 36), and a right to "restitution or other compensation for territories of which they were deprived without their consent" (UN GA Res. 61/295 Art. 28).

The extent to which indigenous rights are actually grounded on self-determination is ambiguous, and many are not specifically territorial in nature. But how much *all* indigenous rights are *limited* by territorial imperatives is made clear in the final article:

> Nothing in this Declaration may be interpreted as implying for any State, people, group or person any right to engage in any activity or to perform any act . . . construed as authorizing or encouraging any action which would dismember or impair, totally or in part, the territorial integrity or political unity of sovereign and independent States.
> *(UN GA Res. 61/295: Art. 46.1)*

This is an insurance policy against expansive claims by indigenous peoples – and the price of acceptance. But that this is the price, and this the insurance, tells us what we need to know, because the risk being insured against is what anyone familiar with the history and logic of self-determination would suppose: that self-determining peoples should get states.

Thus, the confirmation that indigenous communities are self-determining peoples, with more limited rights, is inextricably tied to territorial integrity. The whole conceptual move – extending self-determination to a group without any right to a state – demonstrates how thoroughly self-determination has been subordinated to territory.

It is only because self-determination had already been so thoroughly neutered as a generative principle that its application to indigenous peoples was politically possible. Under the earlier, pre-classical model, calling some community a self-determining people would have led, inexorably, to the conclusion that it deserved a state. But once self-determination came to be a right whose *external* benefits were enjoyed only by the whole populations of existing units, the doctrine became available in deracinated, internalized form, to new classes of 'peoples.'

Thus, indigeneity places territory squarely at its center in two ways. Indigenous peoples' self-determining rights are expressly constructed on territorially grounded identities, giving indigenous groups the right to control physical spaces. But indigenous rights are expressly limited so as in no way to affect the territorial integrity of existing states. The self-determination right of the state's whole population is territorial too, and its territoriality trumps. Indigeneity may "challenge the very idea of the modern nation-state itself" (Gausset, Kenrick and Gibb 2011), but legal indigeneity *as self-determination* has been constructed – like the broader doctrine – in obedience to the imperatives of territorial integrity.

## Not withering away, but sinking: disappearance

The existence of a self-determining people shouldn't require territory. A people justifies the distribution and governance of territory, not the other way around. That's not really how it works, but in theory it should be possible to imagine self-determining peoples without territory.

Certainly it is possible to imagine a people without a *state*. We've just seen that with indigenous peoples, but the possibility has always been there: After all, the whole point of pre-classical self-determination was to justify giving a state to some people, like the Poles, that didn't yet have one. Still, Poles' statelessness was a kind of injustice, to be corrected within the nation-state paradigm. So what about a fully self-determining people not possessing any territory at all? Can we imagine that, and would we find it useful to do so, or troubling?

This is not a hypothetical question. The total, physical disappearance of some existing states' territory might occur within the lifetimes of some readers of this book (Alexander and Simon 2014; McAdam 2012).[24] If some low-lying Pacific atoll, presently possessed of a seat in the United Nations, were to become uninhabitable – to revert to the status of rocks incapable of sustaining human life or sink entirely beneath the waves – its sinking would raise, as it were, a question: Can the state still exist without its territory? And would its citizens continue to be a legal people?

We must imagine that the population has not perished (interesting as it would be to consider the rights of an extinct people), but has departed – perhaps an exigent evacuation, more likely a slow migration. Has the state's population dispersed widely, and so ceased to exhibit the coherence we expect of a community? Or has it resettled *en masse*, perhaps in the territory of a sympathetic neighbor – or even against that neighbor's wishes? We might well find ourselves wishing to affirm its continuity, rather than just regret its passing.

Imaginative and humane solutions might be found to preserve the real and juridical state: cession of a small piece of land in a neighboring state to preserve a physical territory; or a presumption of state continuity[25] to preserve the state's identity, institutions and citizenship – a nomadic state, a new Sovereign Military Order of Malta. The possibilities are as abundant as the available metaphors and inevitable dissertation topics.

And there is the former territory itself. We might preserve the state's rights to its resources, especially its territorial waters, exclusive economic zone and seabed as if the land were still there, the same way that sudden shifts in the course of a river do not alter sovereignty of the land now on the wrong side of what is otherwise a border. It would be territorial rights without territory – rights based on the memory of territory: the ultimate test of intertemporal law.

As for the actual people, humanitarian considerations might counsel for a generous interpretation to preserve their community. Foremost among those would be the human right of self-determination. As we have seen, the very logic of self-determination should allow for peoples without land. The bare fact that they had land, and now lost it, should not necessarily render them stateless or strip them of peoplehood, any more than occupation or unjust expulsion does.

Such moves are conceivable, but none are automatic, and it's not clear they would or even should happen. Other states would have economic, strategic and legal interests. For example, the disappearance of habitable dry land might expand neighboring states' territorial waters, EEZs and seabeds, where those had been blocked by the now-disappeared state.

But moves to preserve the territorial status quo or the legal identity of a population rendered *gens nullius* would look increasingly like legal fictions, because that is what they would be. Maintaining rights to a territorial sea and EEZ based on submerged land not only looks dubious legally, but also practically, since the newly non-territorial sovereign would have a hard time policing its seas.

This, in fact, reminds us that even notionally absolute sovereignty over physical space is a deputization of shared global interests, and that the sovereign owes some minimal duties to other sovereigns, and through them, to the humans who benefit from those sovereignties (*Island of Palmas* 1928: 839). If a sovereign can no longer exercise those functions in fact, the fiction weakens too.

So while sympathy and legal creativity might preserve the rights of a disappeared unit, doing so would also reveal the predominant logic of the system. Whether it would challenge that logic or reinforce it is another question. However comforting it might be to imagine how a sinking atoll could liberate us from the grip of antiquated territorialism, it is likelier that the increasingly implausible accommodations we'd have to make would instead force us to rethink the importance not of territory, but of peoples. Nomadic self-determining communities may sound attractively post-modern and cosmopolitan, but the reality – bereft of a base, lacking resources, living at the sufferance of other powers – wouldn't feel like the vanguard of anything. It sounds like what Hannah Arendt warned against.

As well it should. This is a question about self-determination, but also the broader order of which self-determination is a part. If the system of international law and relations were not so illimitably territorial, the sinking of a whole country would still be a humanitarian challenge – even a tragedy – but not a legal problem. Without our focus on territory, we might calmly say that such a state continued, because its people persisted, even if they lived elsewhere.

The implausibility of saying that calmly tells us what we need to know about our world as it is. Sinking islands don't make the territorial nature of the state any less important. Quite the contrary, they force us to recognize how central territory is to the system we have – in ways that are historically contingent, powerfully present, and that irreducibly reflect the deepest patterns of how we humans live.

## Notes

\* Thanks to Prof. Sean Müller for valuable comments.
1 See Crawford (2006: 5) ("A State is not a fact in the sense that a chair is a fact; it is a fact in that sense . . . [of] a legal status attaching to a certain state of affairs by virtue of certain rules or practices"). And see Ruggie (1993).
2 Engels (1947: 341) ("The state is not 'abolished.' *It dies out*.") (emphasis in original).
3 Oppenheim, *International Law*, vol. 1, 8th ed. 1955, p. 451, cited in Shaw (1982: 61) (adding: "statehood is inconceivable in the absence of a reasonably defined geographical base").

4 See, e.g., Sassen (2002, 2008). Sassen's focus on the place-centered nature of political organization sensibly challenges more literal global and cosmopolitan notions. The processes of globalization are happening in and through institutions and doctrines designed for territorial states. As we'll see, that includes self-determination's rigid embrace of territorial integrity.

5 See, e.g., Raustiala (2005: 2559) ("the last century has witnessed a transformation of legal spatiality" including moves away from purely territorial applications of law).

6 Borders are discussed separately in Lalonde, Chapter 33, this volume.

7 Lenin's contributions to self-determination are equally significant and in many respects more influential on the subsequent, classical phase of the doctrine. See Lenin (1972).

8 Self-determination was never an exclusively colonial doctrine. It applied to peoples – soon clarified as "all peoples" (UN GA Res. 1514) and therefore justified the independence of all states, not just colonies. Laoutides discusses decolonization in Chapter 5, this volume.

9 See, e.g., UN GA Res. 1541: Annex, Principle IV (identifying a non-self-governing territory under the UN Charter as "a territory which is geographically separate and is distinct ethnically and/or culturally from the country administering it"). Note the verbal slippage: Territories are not ethnically distinct; people are.

10 A few colonies were contiguous, such as Southwest Africa. But that colony's original position vis-à-vis Germany fit the salt-water standard; South Africa's mandate came with qualifications. In general, requiring territorial separation excluded distinct (sometimes asymmetrically governed) societies such as Native American tribes and Tibetans.

11 Independence was not the only outcome that might achieve a 'full measure of self-government': 'Free association' or integration with another state was also possible (UN GA Res. 1541: Annex Principle VI). When territories opted for association or integration, greater scrutiny was applied and some form of referendum or consultation typically required.

12 We must not take this to its literal extreme: An *empty* territory cannot claim statehood; some humans have to live there. But *their* status is defined by the territory, not the other way around. Thanks to Professor Sean Müller for this point.

13 See, e.g., *Frontier Dispute* 1986: para. 25 (discussing the apparent conflict between self-determination and *uti possidetis*; Shaw (1982: 70–71) ("Perhaps the major principle of international law that would appear to have challenged the dominant territorial doctrine with success has been that of self-determination").

14 UN GA Res. 1514: Art. 4 ("the integrity of [dependent peoples'] national territory shall be respected").

15 See, e.g., UN GA Res. 47/9 (noting that "the results of the referendum . . . were to be considered on a global basis and not island by island").

16 See, e.g., *Frontier Dispute* 1986: para. 25 (resolving the apparent conflict in favor of territorial integrity); Shaw (1982: 70–71) ("[I]t is to be wondered how far indeed the principle of self-determination has affected the territorial basis of international law. The answer, it appears, is not to a substantial extent. The territorial framework of the non-self-governing entity has been, with only a few exceptions, substantially accepted as the identification pattern for the exercise of the right to self-determination").

17 See Meisels (2009: 114–115) ("[T]he liberal doctrine of self-determination does not supply us with sufficient answers to territorial questions. . . . In contested cases, the question of whether or not the disputed territory is in fact a separate unit, a 'given territory,' with its own relevant majority and minority, is often itself the crucial issue").

18 There are countervailing tendencies, especially models supporting multiculturalism or diversity, and equity perspectives can encourage differential treatment to ameliorate harmful differences; but the general orientation is clear.

19 Müller makes similar, more detailed arguments in his chapter on majoritarianism (Chapter 18, this volume).

20 Both the formal Responsibility to Protect doctrine approved by the Security Council and General Assembly and leading interpretations are silent about one of the likeliest implications of military intervention. See Waters (2016: 317–318, 320–324).

21 Or the belated extension of the decolonial norm to non-colonial settings: Decolonization was opposed to asymmetric governance of racially different territories; denying participation in governance based on race sounds similar. But decolonization was presumptive, whereas remedial secession requires considerably more 'evidence,' including extreme violence.

22 Indigeneity is addressed in MacDonald, Chapter 8, this volume.

23 Autochthony is often associated with traditionally or formerly dominant groups, indigeneity with marginalized communities (Gausset, Kenrick and Gibb 2011: 135). But this distinction is politicized,

poorly policed, and often analytically unhelpful (see Pelican 2009). Both terms imply claims of political priority based on identity linked to specific places: humans can be racial or ethnic anywhere, but only indigenous or autochthonous in relation to a particular place.

24 Whether entire states will literally sink is an open question – many atolls have actually grown over the last 40 years – but climate-related threats may nonetheless render some pelagic states uninhabitable ('Moving story' 2021: 30–31).

25 See, e.g., United Nations High Commissioner on Refugees (2011: para. 30) ("there is a general presumption of continuity of statehood and international legal personality . . . it was confirmed that statehood is not lost automatically with the loss of habitable territory").

# References

Abramson, S. 2017. The Economic Origins of the Territorial State. *International Organization* 71: 97.

Alexander, H. and J. Simon. 2014. Sinking into Statelessness. *Tilburg Law Review* 19: 20.

Chagos Opinion 2019. *Legal Consequences of the Separation of the Chagos Archipelago from Mauritius in 1965 (Advisory Opinion)*, International Court of Justice Reports 95.

Crawford, J. 2006. *The Creation of States in International Law*, 2nd ed. Oxford: Clarendon Press.

Engels, F. 1947. *Anti-Dühring: Herr Eugen Dühring's Revolution in Science*, translated by E. Burns. Moscow: Progress Publishers.

Franck, T. M. 1992. The Emerging Right to Democratic Governance. *American Journal of International Law* 86: 46.

Frontier Dispute 1986. International Court of Justice, *Case Concerning the Frontier Dispute (Burkina Faso/ Republic of Mali)*, International Court of Justice Reports 554.

Gausset, Q., Kenrick, J. and Gibb, R. 2011. Indigeneity and Autochthony: A Couple of False Twins? *Social Anthropology* 19: 135.

Higgins, R. 1994. *Problems and Process: International Law and How We Use It*. Oxford: Clarendon Press.

Island of Palms 1928. Permanent Court of Arbitration (Max Huber Arbitrator), *Island of Palmas (or Miangas) (The Netherlands/The United States of America)*, Reports of International Arbitral Awards XI: 1.

League of Nations 1919. *Covenant of the League of Nations*, 28 April.

Lenin, V. I. 1972. The Right of Nations to Self-Determination. In V. I. Lenin (ed.), *Lenin's Collected Works*, Vol. 20, translated by B. Isaacs and J. Fineberg. Moscow: Progress Publishers.

McAdam, J. 2012. *Climate Change, Forced Migration and International Law*. Oxford: Oxford University Press.

Meisels, T. 2009. *Territorial Rights*, 2nd ed. Dordrecht: Springer.

Moving Story 2021. Moving story. *The Economist*, 7 August, pp. 30–31.

Pelican, M. 2009. Complexities of Indigeneity and Autochthony: An African Example. *American Ethnologist* 36: 52.

Raustiala, K. 2005. The Geography of Justice. *Fordham Law Review* 73: 2501.

Ruggie, J. G. 1993. Territoriality and Beyond: Problematizing Modernity in International Relations. *International Organization* 47: 139.

Sassen, S. 2002. *The Global City*, 2nd ed. Princeton: Princeton University Press.

Sassen, S. 2008. *Territory, Authority, Rights: From Medieval to Global Assemblages*, 2nd ed. Princeton: Princeton University Press.

Reference re Secession of Quebec 1998. Supreme Court of Canada, *Reference re Secession of Quebec* [1998] 2 S.C.R. 217; [1998] 2 I.L.M. 1340.

Shaw, M.N. 1982. Territory in International Law. *Netherlands Yearbook of International Law* 13: 61.

Tilly, C. 1975. *The Formation of National States in Western Europe*. Princeton: Princeton University Press.

Tilly, C. 1985. War Making and State Making as Organized Crime. In P. Evans et al. (eds.), *Bringing the State Back In*. Cambridge: Cambridge University Press: 169.

UN Charter 1945. *United Nations Charter*. www.un.org/en/about-us/un-charter/full-text.

UN GA Res. 1514 1960. United Nations General Assembly, Declaration on the Granting of Independence to Colonial Countries and Peoples, Resolution 1514 (XV), 14 December.

UN GA Res 1541 1960. United Nations General Assembly, Principles Which Should Guide Members in Determining Whether or Not an Obligation Exists to Transmit the Information Called for in Article 73(e) of the Charter of the United Nations, annex to Resolution 1541 (XV), 15 December.

UN GA Res. 2625 1970. United Nations General Assembly, Declaration on Principles of International Law Concerning Friendly Relations and Co-Operation Among States in Accordance With the Charter of the United Nations, annex to Resolution 2625 (XXV), 24 October.

UN GA Res 47/9 1992. United Nations General Assembly, Question of the Comorian Island of Mayotte, U.N. Doc. A/Res/47/9, 27 October.

UN GA Res. 61/295 2007. United Nations General Assembly, United Nations Declaration on the Rights of Indigenous Peoples, annex to Resolution 61/295, 13 September.

UNHCR 2011. United Nations High Commissioner on Refugees, *Summary of Deliberations on Climate Change and Displacement.* <www.unhcr.org/4da2b5e19.pdf>.

Waters, T.W. 2016. The Spear Point and the Ground Beneath: Territorial Constraints on the Logic of Responsibility to Protect. *International Relations* 30: 314.

Whelan, F.G. 1987. Prologue: Democratic Theory and the Boundary Problem. *Nomos*, 25: 13.

Wilson, W. 1918. Speech to Joint Session of Congress, 8 January. https://wwi.lib.byu.edu/index.php/President_Wilson%27s_Fourteen_Points.

# PART III

# Explaining and justifying secession

# 10

# THE CAUSES OF SECESSION

*Diego Muro*

## Introduction

The majority of existing states are the product of secession. During the twentieth century the number of states quadrupled from 50 to almost 200, and the states born as a result of a secession (including decolonisation) represent around 70% of existing sovereign entities (Coggins 2011a: 28). Historically, the process of breaking away from a central political authority and being internationally recognised was a violent one (Sambanis 2011), but there were also gradual and non-violent paths towards political independence. Examples of peaceful secession include the secession of Norway from Sweden in 1905, Iceland from Denmark in 1944 and Singapore from the Malaysian Federation in 1965. Technically, the separation of Slovakia from Czechoslovakia in 1993 was a case of partition, whereas the independence of Soviet republics in the aftermath of the Cold War was a case of dissolution (of the USSR). More recently, there have been various other attempts to secede through the world, with the well-known cases of Québec, Scotland and Catalonia grabbing many of the headlines. Secession has re-emerged as a force to be reckoned with, and some scholars argue that we live in an 'age of secession' (Griffiths 2016).

Political science has studied secession at length, but it is unclear why some nations want a state of their own. What are the drivers of state birth? And what are the mechanisms that can prevent state death? Regrettably, we do not have a comprehensive theory of why states are born (Wood 1981: 107). The absence of an all-encompassing theory is partly due to the fact that experts disagree on what the causes of secession truly are. This chapter will identify some of the drivers behind claims for independence and will distinguish between underlying and proximate causes. In essence, underlying causes identify long-term preconditions and are examined in abstract terms. By contrast, proximate causes are about short-term precipitants and help us explain why something happened in the way it happened.

The main aim of this chapter is to use a grievance approach to enquire into the causes of secession. This approach sustains that individuals mobilise over issues of identity (ethnicity, religion, class, etc.) rather than over economics. People who see themselves belonging to the same national community can still perform a cost-benefit analysis in examining the potential rewards of secession, but they are mostly guided by a desire to improve the situation of the nation to which they belong. Whether the causes of secession are mostly economic or political, the chapter will argue that the common element is the existence of a grievance.

DOI: 10.4324/9781003036593-13

The rest of the chapter is organised as follows. The first section provides a working definition of secession and distinguishes between normative and explanatory theories. The second section analyses the scholarly literature on cultural roots, institutional incentives and economic interests that enable secession. The third section focuses on the proximate causes of secession, and a fourth section examines the roles played by politically motivated elites. The chapter concludes with a summary and some observations about the implications of this analysis for the future study of secession.

## Terminology and theories

This chapter follows Peter Radan in defining secession as 'the creation of a new [internationally recognised] state upon existing territory previously forming part of, or being a colonial entity of, an existing sovereign state' (Radan 2008: 18). The definition assumes the existence of a host or parent state as well as a minority group that attempts to secede, which is often a territorially based group with distinct historical and cultural identity. Other authors define the term secession differently (Crawford 2006) and, unsurprisingly, this is part of the reason why there is no comprehensive theory on secession. It is difficult to harmonise research agendas when there is no consensus on how to define the object of study.

Secession has been a topic for academic investigation for decades, but a coherent and comprehensive definition has escaped the field. Authors working on the topic sometimes refer to 'self-determination', 'independence', 'sovereignty' or 'regionalism', but also 'sub-state politics', 'nationalism' or 'separatism'. These terms emphasise slightly different aspects of the phenomenon, but they all struggle to come to terms with the relationship between legitimacy and politics. For example, being labelled a 'separatist' promotes condemnation of the actor and reflects the ideological or political bias of the labeller. The word has intrinsically negative connotations, and it is applied to opponents by those who subscribe a pro-state view of the situation. Secessionist groups also select names for themselves that consciously eschew the pejorative overtones of separatism and favour terms such as 'nationalist', 'democratic' or 'pro-independence'.

Definitions of secession naturally tend to mirror the disciplines of those who devise them, and experts sometimes opt for a definition that suits their purposes, from adopting a legal framework through which to design policy responses to approaching the phenomenon from a entirely academic point of view. Needless to say, the definitional problem is not unusual in the social sciences, where very few designations are widely accepted. A notable exception would be provided by Max Weber, who famously defined the state as the 'human community that (successfully) claims the monopoly of the legitimate use of physical force within a given territory' (Weber 1919). The label 'secession' is also used to cover a wide range of cases. A basic distinction could be made between pro-independence groups that use violence versus those who use peaceful means. Logically, it is not possible to identify a single set of causes that is common to all these cases of secession, and targeted explanations grounded in empirical evidence are required. For example, the perception of injustice felt by minority nations will vary in each case, not to mention the legality, legitimacy and/or permissibility of the act of secession. The need to use a variety of tools to interpret specific cases leads scholars of secession to become 'omnivorous', as they need to absorb the literatures from the fields of economics, sociology, international relations, historical studies, political psychology and, especially, nationalism studies.

Theories of secession can be divided into two large groups of theoretical approaches which can be called 'normative' and 'explanatory' (Requejo & Sanjaume-Calvet 2021). The first group of normative theories is mostly concerned with the ethical justification of secession and focuses on four key aspects: 'What' (is legitimate), 'Where' (can political divorce happen), 'When' (should it happen) and 'Who' (is the political actor that can decide). With important variations, political philosophers interested in the 4W (What-Where-When-Who) identify the acceptable conditions under which secession can be legitimate (Sanjaume-Calvet 2012). Normative theories identify plausible situations in which breaking away might be morally justified. These can be military occupation, instances of ethnic cleansing or genocide, violation of self-rule accords, etc. For example, Kosovo's declaration of independence in February 2008 and the NATO-led humanitarian intervention that made it possible were justified as a way to prevent further human rights abuses by the Serbian forces against ethnic Kosovo Albanians. At the same time, a subgroup of normative theories (remedial-right) has also warned of the danger for endless strategic bargaining of minorities against majority rule and 'limitless political fragmentation' (Buchanan 1991: 49), which could endanger the democratic process. Some of the scholars who have developed a normative approach to the morality of political divorce include Buchanan (1991), Tamir (1993), Moore (1998), Kymlicka (2001) and Seymour (2007), to name a few.[1]

A second group of theories is 'explanatory' and focuses on why secession happens, not whether it is a rightful or legitimate tool to remedy a certain grievance. This body of research is mainly empirical and tries to reveal a causal mechanism between independent and dependent variables. The goal of this second group of theories is to identify the processes or pathways through which secession is brought into being. They explain an outcome (e.g., secession) by offering a hypothesis about the causation that typically brings it about. Ultimately, the goal is to figure out why things happen and offer valid explanations of its causes, which can be of an economic, political, social or cultural nature. Very often, these theories are based on a notion of 'relative deprivation', which refers to the experience of being deprived of something that one believes oneself to be entitled to. As conceptualised by Ted Robert Gurr, relative deprivation theory suggests that as the perceived discrepancy between 'ought' and 'is' increases, the intensity of discontent also increases. However, not all those who suffer become activists, nor does political action always reflect objective social or economic deprivation. Discontent, frustration or grievance caused by unjust deprivation or differential treatment, in return, increases the likelihood of ethnic mobilisation in various forms (Gurr 1970). Interestingly, secessionist movements tend to combine both normative appeals and perceived deprivation in their public pronouncements and political arguments (Griffiths & Muro 2020).

The remainder of this chapter will focus on this second group of explanatory theories and will distinguish between 'underlying' and 'proximate' causes. In order to understand the difference between underlying and proximate causes, it might be useful to cite an example from the classical world. In his book *History of the Peloponnesian War*, the historian Thucydides provided a rich account of why Sparta and Athens went to war in 431–404 BCE. The ancient war arose not simply from specific grievances, he argued, but from a longer process of growing power and influence of the Athenian Empire that inspired fear among the Spartans, making the war inevitable. Thucydides mentions four publicly mentioned grievances which help the reader understand the war's outbreak. The events that sparked the war between the two powers mostly refer to issues of how Athens treated its allies and neutral cities and, more generally, to the regional balance of power in the Greek world. But the key point to remember is that, even if those regional disputes had been resolved, Athenians and Spartans would have still gone to war with each other. According to the Athenian Historian and General, *war was inevitable* (Thucydides 1972: 49).

Thucydides distinguished between two types of explanations: proximate and underlying causes. The four particular grievances just mentioned were 'proximate causes' or grounds for complaint, and they account for why the war happened when it did, in the way it did. The underlying cause (and the 'truest reason', according to Thucydides) was Sparta's fear of Athens, and this explains why conflict between the two city-states could not be avoided. Thucydides believed that the Peloponnesian War, which eventually brought the end of the golden age of ancient Greece, was inevitable because when a rising power is confronted by another power, they would inevitably wage war against each other to further or protect their interests. The conceptual distinction between underlying and proximate causes remains useful, as analysts struggle to differentiate between long-term preconditions and short-term precipitants of key historical events.

## The underlying causes of secession

Political scientists tend to focus on underlying causes because they provide us with better advice on how to prepare for the future. These are background preconditions (such as the existence of a regional identity or a homeland) that positively encourage the emergence of secessionist claims. By contrast, 'proximate causes' or specific grievances are widely available in any country and have the potential to activate or trigger existing preconditions. The contemporary world is not short of examples where societies are unjust, economic inequalities persist or resources are unevenly distributed. There are also numerous examples where the voices of indigenous groups and national minorities are excluded from central government decisions (Sorens 2012). But this does not mean that political actors will be willing to take action to remedy grievances and address these power imbalances. A perception of injustice may be the force behind secessionist movements (Moore 1998; Seymour 2007) but in order for collective 'interests' to be mobilised politically, the 'passions' of specific individuals are also necessary (Dion 1996). As the final sub-section on elites will explain, it is often the case that dissatisfied political entrepreneurs first identify a set of cleavages that affect a subset of the population, and then the masses accept such cleavages as salient.

But returning to our object of study, this sub-section focuses on the underlying causes of secession. These are the permissive conditions that make secession likely in the future but have little predictive power on their own. Underlying causes create an environment in which pro-independence claims can be made, but these preconditions need to be combined with more specific institutional settings and actors to be 'activated' by elites. To paraphrase Thucydides, the 'truest reasons' are often embedded in the narrative of the incidents leading up to crisis, and for researchers, the challenge is to distinguish causes from appearances to understand a political actor's reason for acting.

The empirical literature on secession has produced three broad sets of explanations for the emergence of pro-independence movements in liberal democracies. Most of these approaches generalise beyond a particular case and focus on a nationalist ideology, social movement or political party at sub-state level who aims to break away from the host state using peaceful means. A very substantial part of this literature comes from the field of nationalism studies, as secessionists often assume the existence of a nation, which can be defined as 'a named population sharing a historic territory, common myths and historical memories, a mass public culture, a common economy and common legal rights and duties for its members' (Smith 1995: 57). Needless to say, the central government has an important role to play in deciding how to respond to a collective demand for formal withdrawal with a strategy that ranges from meeting the demands in full or in part, or ignoring them (Cunningham 2013; Ker-Lindsay 2014). The kind of interaction between the multinational state, which risks its own dissolution, and the stateless nation,[2] which is a territorially based group with a distinct cultural and historical identity, will determine whether the nationalist movement becomes secessionist or not (Siroky, Mueller & Hechter 2016).

A first strand of research focuses on ethnic politics and the social bases of political cleavages. Scholars working on comparative regionalism and territorial politics have studied nationalist parties as expression of distinctive cultural and linguistic identities, which resisted the imposition of uniform rules and institutions from the centre and, when successful, were able to demand distinctive treatment and decentralising reforms. The so-called centre-periphery cleavage was key to explaining how party systems of several European democracies had been shaped from their inception (Lipset & Rokkan, 1967; Rokkan 1970), sometimes with the late emergence of ethno-cultural forces to challenge the established state-wide or national-level political parties. The territorial shape of the state was therefore a reflection of the degree to which centralising elites were able to override resistance from peripheral territories. Where centralisation was less successful, a centre-periphery cleavage would generate distinctive regionalist political parties which would hinder the 'nationalisation' of electoral competition (Caramani 2004). When it came to explaining dynamics of secession in advanced democracies, ethnicity and/or national identity was often highlighted as a key determinant (Hale 2000; Hechter 1992). A similar argument was put forward by proponents of the 'ethnic outbidding model', which argued that parties in ethnically heterogeneous societies appealed to voters on the basis of their ethnic identity rather than other social identities, such as class (Chandra 2005; Rabushka & Shepsle 1972). According to Jason Sorens, multiple factors influence how secession emerges. He found that 'geography, irredentist potential, past autonomy, kin ties with another secessionist group, . . . of secessionist groups in the country, and relative size are all factors that influence the likelihood of secession' (Sorens 2012: 53–54). Besides the salience of the ethnonational cleavage, the costs and benefits of independence also depend on 'the central government's ability to commit credibly to adopting policies beneficial to the community' (Sorens 2012: 6).[3]

A second strand of comparative politics research has been dominated by rationalist approaches. The key to understanding the institutional workings of a multinational state was no longer about fixed identities and long-held cleavages but on incentive structures (e.g., federal systems, decentralised states, etc.). Rational choice theory suggests that human behaviour results from rational individuals seeking to maximise their utility functions. It tends to stress economic motives and strives for parsimony by making a few simple assumptions about utility preferences. Hence, the study of nationalist politics has been dominated by a rational choice institutionalist framework that focuses on the role of formal institutional structures in determining the levels of territorial differentiation in party systems. For example, Chhibber and Kollman (2009) argued that decentralising reforms create incentives for politicians to organise at the sub-state level because that is where the levers of power are. Other work showed how decentralising reforms affect party organisations, by changing the incentive structures facing party actors and altering the functional usefulness of particular territorial structures (Van Biezen & Hopkin 2006). Last but not least, Brancatti argued that decentralised states can also increase ethnic conflict and secessionism indirectly by encouraging the growth of regional parties and incentivising ethnonationalist tensions. In short, decentralisation can strengthen regional political parties as it provides them with the resources (and incentives) they need to engage in ethnic conflict and secessionism (Brancatti 2006). The finding is important because it limits the healing power of some institutional tools of conflict management (e.g., ethnofederalism or territorial power-sharing) to manage and resolve ethnic and national conflict.

A third strand of research focused on economic interests as direct preconditions (Bartkus 1999; Zarkovic 1992). Horowitz (1985) first stressed the importance of economic-interest perspectives and psychological determinants in explaining ethnic conflict. In his framework, inhabitants of the poorest regions were more likely to embrace movements of independence. However, in the standard political economy framework, demands for secession respond to the interests of rich territories to protect themselves from the redistributive pressures imposed by the central state. For example, Sambanis and Milanovic (2011) proposed an economic explanation whereby richer regions are more likely to want greater autonomy. At the individual level, support for secession also increased amongst individuals interested in attaining greater personal welfare following independence. This proposition assumes that people will desire secession if they expect to profit personally from this state of affairs (Hechter 1992: 276). More generally, pressures for territorial fragmentation reflect the declining usefulness of national states as organising units in a more globalised economy (Alesina & Spolaore 2003). In the case of the European Union, regional integration offered regions an alternative to the nation-state (Jolly 2015) and 'if there was ever an environment that favoured small states, surely it is modern Western Europe' (Griffiths et al. 2015).

These three perspectives assumed the existence of a dissatisfied minority and a relatively straightforward understanding of the causal relationships between economic interests, ethnic and national identities and institutional arrangements. Economic interests were seen as unproblematic, social identities as given and institutional arrangements as incentive structures. However, economic approaches cannot explain why there is support for secession in cases where there are no clear economic gains after independence (e.g., Montenegro, Moldova, Québec, etc.). Likewise, ethnic approaches cannot account for rapid changes in the national self-identification or respondents. For example, support for Catalan independence experienced a dramatic growth from 20% to 42% between 2009 and 2019 even though it was not possible to detect a shift of a similar magnitude in the economy, institutions or self-reported identity of Catalans.[4] In addition, the variation in strength of secessionist forces across cases and over time is not particularly well predicted by these variables. In order to account for why support for independence fluctuates, one needs to examine both reasons to redress grievances but also opportunities. The competitive dynamics of the secessionist movement, the internal balance of power among groups and the existence of an hegemonic actor are also at the foundation of the success of groups and the movements of which they are part (Krause 2017; Zuber & Szöcsik 2015). In short, the existence of a dissatisfied minority is a necessary but not sufficient cause of secession, and it is essential to identify the triggers or proximate causes of secessionist mobilisation.

The following section will complement standard accounts that see secessionist movements as either driven by ethnic identities and ambitious regional political entrepreneurs, or as responses to territorially distinctive economic interests. It will argue that such demands for independence are the product of the underlying causes (or preconditions) and proximate causes (or precipitants).

## The proximate causes of secession

The existing literature on secession does a commendable job of reviewing the permissive conditions or underlying factors or that make some situations particularly prone to state break-up, but it is weak when it comes to identifying the catalytic factors – the triggers or proximate causes – of secession. In other words, we know a lot of things that are true about secession, but we do not know when they are going to be true. The result is that we know a lot less about the causes of secession than one would guess from looking at the size of the literature on the subject.

An evident starting point is that secession often happens in multinational states, and more often than not, when there has been an attempt by a majority group to impose cultural homogenisation. Modern states that have successfully adopted nation-building policies to assimilate existing populations into a common national culture often lack minority nationalist movements (Anderson 1991; Eisenstadt & Rokkan 1973; Gellner 1983). Where that one-to-one correspondence exists and there are homogenised populations, there is no minority nationalism and, as a result, no attempt to withdraw from the parent state. However, these 'pure' cases of nation-state are rare, for the boundaries of the state rarely coexist with the boundaries of the nation. By contrast, most contemporary states are either multi-ethnic, multinational or even multi-religious, and they need to respond to accommodation demands for greater autonomy and recognition. In some instances, national minorities have been the main target of the nation-building policies adopted by modern states, which try to fuse nationhood and statehood. In short, the attempt to assimilate ethnonational heterogeneity is the key reason why secession is intimately linked to the multinational state (Costa 2003; Seymour 2007).

Accordingly, a first proximate cause of secession is the reaction to state formation (Roeder 2007; Webb 2015). As argued by Michael Hechter, the demands of national minorities are typically a reaction to, or a by-product of, state nation-building (Hechter 2000). It is common to find minority nationalism (and secession) in states whose nation-building interventions failed to impose a single national identity. There are multiple examples of 'weak nationalisation' in Europe, where even old states like France achieved national unity much later than is commonly supposed. According to Eugene Weber, the 'unity of mind and feeling' required for a sense of nationhood was scarcely present in France before the turn of the twentieth century (Weber 1976: 95). This argument would also apply to European empires, which failed to impose a national identity on their colonies. After World War II, indigenous rebellions energised by nationalism would end colonialism with the help of the two new superpowers, both of which had taken positions against colonialism. But reactions against homogenisation could also be found in regions free from colonial rule, such as South Sudan, which resisted attempts of 'Arabisation' and 'Islamicisation' by the central government. Following independence in 1956, the country was essentially divided on the basis of ethnicity, language and religion. And yet, the Sudanese government 'sought to unify the country and create a single Sudanese nation where none had existed before' (Christopher 2011: 127). The dynamics of secession and counter-secession ultimately bring together state elites representing majority nationalism with regional elites representing minority nationalism.

The need to accommodate national diversity often results in new institutions, which is a second proximate cause or precipitant. In order to manage the power imbalance between majority and minority nationalism, states often design institutions that give power and voice to these constituent groups, while trying to be proportionate. These political and constitutional arrangements (federation, devolution, decentralisation, consociationalism, self-government, etc.) try to accommodate national diversity fairly. The common wisdom is that national harmony is the result of a fair distribution of political power. Political decentralisation is often seen as a mechanism to distribute power justly and reduce nationalist tensions in democratic settings. Conventionally, decentralisation brings the government closer to the people, increases opportunities to participate in government and gives groups control over their political, social and economic affairs. However, there is also research that argues that decentralisation can reinforce regionally based ethnic identities, producing legislation that discriminates against ethnic or religious groups in the country (Brancatti 2006).

The third proximate cause are crises. These triggering events may range from political transitions (where the balance of power can shift) to the collapse of state authority (where new actors can emerge more freely). However, economic crises are often the setting in which a secessionist crisis unfolds. There may be economic recessions or depressions, scarcity of resources, fast-paced modernisation processes or economic discrimination. For example, the ethnic tensions in Xinjiang are not only religious but also economic. Since the 1990s there has been a perception that Han Chinese immigrants have taken over the natural resources and land of Xinjiang, which belong to the Uygurs as the original owners (Mackerras 2001: 298). Needless to say, the potential to use these social problems and economic resentment rests not only in the hands of secessionists. States can also use these economic crises to blame some ethnic group or national group for whatever political and economic disparity the country is experiencing.

The issues that can trigger mass mobilisation may be of a political, social, cultural or economic nature but they do not happen on their own. In order for causes to be transformed into undisputable examples of discrimination, elites are necessary. These political entrepreneurs define the issues worth fighting and create political movements with their own institutions, ideologies, and socialisation processes. The following section will focus on elites as the fourth proximate cause.

## The role of elites

No secession is truly spontaneous. Whereas discontent and resentment are a 'must have' for any political movement, mobilisation cannot take place without elite intervention. The role of elites is to make sense of existing dissatisfaction and frame it into a persuasive narrative of national decline and rebirth. To a large extent, the role of elites is to provide discursive ammunition for the 'awakening' of the nation, the mobilisation of its people and the inevitable process of claim-making. While declaring to represent the interest of the minority group, the role of intellectuals, activists and politicians is not only to define the ills (and cure) for the nation but also to inspire confidence amongst their followers and lead them to action. In short, the main role of elites is to lead.

Theories of relative deprivation often assume that grievances are abundant in complex societies. Secessionist movements advance a variety of arguments for why they deserve independence. These may include a history of conflict with the state, illegal occupation or the democratic right to choose independence, among others (Griffiths & Martinez 2020a). These grievances are all important preconditions for secession, but any attempt to understand support for independence needs to take into account the question of elite initiation, which is an intervening variable. But what do secessionist elites want? And what are the types of messages they typically put forward?

A critical point to note is that secessionist elites are not interested in political accommodation or the institutional reform of the existing polity and want to exit from the host state. They have concluded that the status quo is detrimental to their nation and want to create a new sovereign state that is internationally recognised. As argued by Karlo Basta in Chapter 28, this volume, 'in order to endorse secession, people must first find it *necessary*'. Hence, secessionist leaders have to describe the political system not only as inadequate to channel the aspirations of the minority nation but incapable of regeneration. In Basta's own words, 'secessionist narratives must portray the institutional status quo not only as insupportable from the perspective of the potential seceding community, but *irreparable at any future point*' (Basta, Chapter 28, this volume). The option of future reform needs to be eradicated in order to convince moderates with dual identities, who may be happy with a greater degree of self-government, to support the creation of a new independent state (Muro & Vlaskamp 2016).

Secessionist elites are not unique in their social construction of reality. As a matter of fact, the structure of secessionist messages is rather typical of nationalist movements. According to Levinger and Lytle (2003), the rhetoric of national mobilisation is often made of three components – images of an idealised past, exaggerated depictions of a degraded present, and a utopian future condition – that are supposed to address the current decline. These three elements form a 'rhetorical triad' that constitutes an effective instrument for motivating mass political mobilisation. The structure of this discursive instrument is again not new, and it can be traced to ancient Greece and the idea of a lost 'golden age', which was developed by Hesiod in his poem 'Works and Days'. But the important element here is not the nostalgia for an idealised past but the potential for motivating mass political movements. In the words of Levinger and Lytle, the 'rhetorical triad' emphasises the links between identify formation and political mobilisation and suggest that 'narratives of communal decline and redemption play a central role in defining the agendas of nationalist movements' (Levinger & Lytle 2003: 175)

And what do elites want? The range of possible claims is vast, and it is impossible to provide an exhaustive list. Demands range from greater recognition of the national status of the minority community and the improvement of existing institutional arrangements, to a more comprehensive control of economic and/or social policy, greater fiscal resources or the celebration of a binding referendum on independence. Whereas the strategic goal of secessionists is always the same (e.g., the creation of a sovereign state), they often disagree on what tactical moves need to be made to realise their end goal. Secessionist movements often suffer fragmentation and ideological splits simply because they disagree on what is the most effective road path towards political independence (Krause 2017). Whereas some want to walk the shortest distance between two points, others believe that a non-linear and slower route allows the movement to increase support, prevent polarisation and maintain foreign support for the cause, which is essential for international recognition (Coggins 2011; Basta 2021).

It is often the case that elites first identify cleavages and the masses accept them as salient. But why do the followers follow? In the words of Fearon and Laitin (2000), 'a major puzzle in this story is why ethnic publics follow leaders down paths that seem to serve elite power interests most of all'. Unfortunately, the literature often becomes speculative when explaining this connection between elites and masses. References to myths, legends and elite manipulation are often mentioned to account for why masses follow their leader. Researchers often use discourse analysis to expose how political entrepreneurs use emotions to connect with sympathisers to legitimise their claims. 'Modernist' scholars of nationalism and followers of an instrumental view of nationalism assume that political entrepreneurs manipulate and instrumentalise national grievances for their own benefit only. But given that elites all over the world employ ethnic or national grievances of one kind or another, why do these appeals resonate in some places but not others?

Elite messages can resonate amongst followers only when political entrepreneurs are broadcasting on a wavelength to which the masses are attuned. Complete manipulation is difficult to envisage, but this is not to say that it is essential for elite message to be completely truthful.

Whether the grievance involves the worsening of relations between national groups, antagonistic policies by the state, unjust policies or an economic crisis, the followers need to identify a 'kernel of truth' in the secessionist message in order to be mobilised. The key point is that there is a communion of wills, which once again raises the issue about the legitimacy and support of secessionist claims. What is needed is a window of opportunity where both bottom-up and top-down processes meet. In the language of social movements, it will be necessary for a 'political opportunity structure' to present itself to the catalysing elites.

It is important to note that any secessionist crisis is a dyadic relationship between political actors claiming to represent the minority nation and forces who act on behalf of the multinational state (Griffiths & Muro 2020). State institutions are neither black boxes nor simple instruments of sanctioned power, but self-interested actors actively pursuing their own territorial integrity and survival. Central governments are sometimes willing to accommodate minority demands (e.g., decentralisation) but a secessionist escalation is often resisted in the strongest terms possible. In the absence of a general theory of accommodation in multinational states, it is vital to examine the institutions that constrain political action as well as the political dynamics that lead to political outcomes (Basta 2021: 11; Krause 2017; Zuber & Szöcsik 2015).

## Conclusion

The chapter has reviewed the drivers of secession and has distinguished between two types of causes: 'proximate' and 'underlying'. Underlying causes make secession by minority groups more likely. These background conditions involve institutional, economic, political and cultural grievances, distorted group histories, and perceived discriminations of all kinds. By contrast, the proximate causes are the catalytic factors that escalate an ethnonationalist confrontation into a secessionist crisis. The chapter has focused mostly on underlying grievances, which are the main focus of political science research. But a key takeaway point is that underlying causes create an enabling environment that, alone, is of no explanatory value but when in conjunction with proximate causes, may have explanatory value as to why some ethnonational groups make claims in favour of political independence. Overall, the chapter centred on explanatory theories of secession and excluded normative ones, which are mostly interested in describing the right to secede as a moral right.

Existing theories of sub-state nationalism and secession do a good job of explaining why independence movements arise in particular regions with ethnic or linguistic heterogeneity, but they are less successful in explaining why support for independence changes over time. Rationalist, economic and institutionalist theories can successfully account for long-term nationalist views, but they cannot explain why support for independence might change swiftly. In short, standard accounts based on economic interests, institutional incentives and cultural roots do not do a very good job of explaining the dramatic growth of pro-independence movements, which suggests that precipitant factors are also essential. Furthermore, it cannot explain why secessionist conflicts have broken out in some places but not others, and it cannot explain why some disputes are more violent and harder to resolve than others.

The chapter also made the point that grievances have no agency on their own. Secessionist standoffs are triggered by the actions of domestic elites, not mass unrest, or some uncontrollable form of primitivism or regional mass emotion. The observation of specific leaders (and their behaviour) is crucial to understanding the role of the explanatory variables identified in this chapter. The issues that affect national minorities matter, of course, but private resources and interests require careful examination. In other words, the emphasis on empirical reasoning that is typical of political science needs to be combined with the thick description and detail of historical research in order to understand why some nationalist claims become secessionist and others don't. The actions of particular individuals, movements and states can often account for these variations. In addition to mixed research methods, it is crucial to examine the interactions between regional and global powers in the international context. A full understanding of the leverage and influence of the more than 60 secessionist movements around the world requires a thorough examination of the relations taking place at the local, regional, national and international levels.

Secessionist movements 'voice' different grievances depending on the state they confront. In turn, state responses to demands for independent statehood range from accommodation to violent repression and even war (as in the case of Chechnya). After all, secession involves the loss to the parent state not only of a population but also a territory, and potentially everything located in that territory, which can include natural resources, industry and economic infrastructure. At the same time, the ability of secessionist leaders to successfully argue why they deserve independence – despite contestation – will determine whether the government's actions result in demobilisation or backlash. Ultimately, state break-up is a relational act that brings the state and the secessionist movement into conflict with each other. The situation is never entirely in the singular control of any of these competing actors that frequently leads to an emboldening of relations. Secessionist campaigns are sometimes studied in isolation, but a comprehensive view of the spiral involving these two self-interested actors requires studying both the forces of secession and counter-secession (Griffiths & Muro 2020).

There is no single cause of secession, or even a common set of causes. Different combinations of preconditions and precipitants are necessary to provide a fine-grained account of secessionist claim-making on the ground. Researchers of secession will do well to equip themselves with the abstract tools of the social sciences and the specific instruments of historical research to further advance the research agenda and identify the underlying and proximate causes in each historical setting. Secession is better understood as emerging from a process of interaction between different actors than as a mechanical cause-and-effect relationship. Future researchers will not be short of examples to examine where political conditions create long-standing feelings of indignity and frustration. We can be sure that stateless nations will continue to challenge the state's authority, advance their claims and push further for the creation of new sovereign states.

## Notes

1 Normative theories of secession are often divided into primary and remedial theories. For a comprehensive review, see Moore (1998) and Pavkovic and Radan (2007). A new typology of secessionist theories has been put forward by Marc Sanjaume-Calvet (2020).
2 According to Montserrat Guibernau, stateless nations are 'cultural communities sharing a common past, attached to a clearly demarcated territory, and wishing to decide upon their political future which lack a state of their own' (Guibernau 1999: 1).
3 There is a type of approach to ethnic and national conflict that assumes some kind of primitivism between ethnic groups in conflict. The key assumption here is that some sort of ancient hatred or perennial antagonism between competing groups makes conflict inevitable. For a critique of primitive theories, see Mann (2005, pp. 18–23).
4 Barometer of Public Opinion from the Catalan Government's Survey Institute (CEO): https://ceo. gencat.cat/es/barometre/. See also Muro and Lago (2020).

## References

Alesina, A. & Spolaore, E. (2003) *The Size of Nations*. Cambridge & London: MIT.
Anderson, B. (1991) *Imagined Communities: Reflections on the Origins and Spread of Nationalism*. London: Verso.
Bartkus, V.O. (1999) *The Dynamics of Secession*. Cambridge: Cambridge University Press.
Basta, K. (2021) *The Symbolic State: Minority Recognition, Majority Backlash, and Secession in Multinational Countries*. Montreal & Kingston: McGill-Queen's University Press.
Brancatti, D. (2006) 'Decentralization: Fueling the Fire or Dampening the Flames of Ethnic Conflict and Secessionism?', *International Organization*, 60 (3), pp. 651–685.
Buchanan, A. (1991). *The Morality of Political Divorce from Port Sumter to Lithuania and Quebec*. Oxford: Westview Press.
Caramani, D. (2004) *The Nationalization of Politics: The Formation of National Electorates and Party Systems in Western Europe*. Cambridge: Cambridge University Press.
Chandra, K. (2005) 'Ethnic Parties and Democratic Stability', *Perspectives on Politics*, 3(2), pp. 235–252.
Chhibber, P. & Kollman, K. (2009) *The Formation of National Party Systems: Federalism and Party Competition in Canada, Great Britain, India, and the United States*. Princeton: Princeton University Press.
Christopher, A.J. (2011) 'Secession and South Sudan: An African Precedent for the Future?', *South African Geographical Journal*, 93 (2), pp. 125–132.
Coggins, B.R. (2011) 'Friends in High Places: International Politics and the Emergence of States from Secessionism', *International Organization*, 65 (3), pp. 433–367.
Coggins, B.R. (2011a) 'The History of Secession: An Overview', in Pavkovic, A. and Radan, P. (eds.) *The Ashgate Research Companion to Secession*. London: Routledge, pp. 24–43.
Costa, J. (2003) 'On Theories of Secession: Minorities, Majorities and the Multinational State', *CRISPP*, 6 (2), pp. 63–90.

Crawford, J. (2006) *The Creation of State in International Law*. Oxford: Oxford University Press.

Cunningham, K.G. (2013) *Inside the Politics of Self-Determination*. Oxford: Oxford University Press.

Dion, S. (1996) 'Why Secession Is So Difficult in Well-Established Democracies', *British Journal of Political Science*, 26 (2), pp. 269–283.

Eisenstadt, S. & Rokkan, S. (eds.) (1973) *Building States and Nations*. London: Sage.

Fearon, J. and Laitin, D. (2000) 'Violence and the Social Construction of Ethnic Identity', *International Organization*, 54, pp. 845–877.

Gellner, E. (1983) *Nations and Nationalism*. Ithaca: Cornell University Press.

Griffiths, R. (2016) *Age of Secession*. Cambridge: Cambridge University Press.

Griffiths, R. & Muro, D. (2020) *Strategies of Secession and Counter-Secession*. London: Rowman & Littlefield Publishers/ECPR Press.

Griffiths, R.D., Guillén Álvarez, P. & Martínez i Coma, F. (2015) 'Between the Sword and the Wall: Spain's Limited Options for Catalan Secessionism', *Nations and Nationalism*, 21 (3), pp. 43–61.

Griffiths, R.D. & Martinez, A. (2020a) 'Local Conditions and the Demand for Independence: A Dataset of Secessionist Grievances', *Nations and Nationalism*, 27(2), pp. 580–590.

Guibernau, M. (1999) *Nations without States: Political Communities in the Global Age*. Cambridge: Polity Press.

Gurr, T.R. (1970) *Why Men Rebel*. Princeton: Princeton University Press.

Hale, H.E. (2000) 'The Parade of Sovereignties: Testing Theories of Secession in the Soviet Setting', *British Journal of Political Science*, 30 (1), pp. 31–56.

Hechter, M. (1992) 'The Dynamics of Secession', *Acta Sociologica*, 35, pp. 267–283.

Hechter, M. (2000) *Containing Nationalism*. Oxford: Oxford University Press.

Horowitz, D. (1985) *Ethnic Groups in Conflict: Theories, Patterns, Policies*. Berkeley, CA: University of California Press.

Jolly, S.K. (2015) *The European Union and the Rise of Regionalist Parties: New Comparative Politics*. Ann Arbor: University of Michigan Press.

Ker-Lindsay, J. (2014) 'Understanding State Responses to Secession', *Peacebuilding*, 2 (1), pp. 28–44.

Krause, P. (2017) *Rebel Power: Why National Movements Compete, Fight, and Win*. Cornell: Cornell University Press.

Kymlicka, W. (2001) *Politics in the Vernacular: Nationalism, Multiculturalism and Citizenship*. Oxford: Oxford University Press.

Levinger, M. & and Lytle, P.F. (2003) 'Myth and Mobilisation: The Triadic Structure of Nationalist Rhetoric. *Nations and Nationalism*, 7 (2), pp. 175–194.

Lipset, S.M. & Rokkan, S. (1967) 'Party Systems and Voter Alignments: Cross-National Perspectives'. [Contributors: Robert R. Alford And others]. *International Yearbook of Political Behavior Research*. New York: Free Press. Radan 2008.

Mackerras, C. (2001) 'Xinjiang at the Turn of the Century: The Causes of Separatism', *Central Asian Survey*, 20 (3), pp. 289–303.

Mann, M. (2005) *The Dark Side of Democracy: Explaining Ethnic Cleansing*. New York: Cambridge University Press.

Moore, M. (ed.) (1998). *National Self-Determination and Secession*. Nova York: Oxford University Press.

Muro, D. & Lago, I. (2020) *The Oxford Handbook of Spanish Politics*. Oxford: Oxford University Press.

Muro, D. & Vlaskamp, M.C. (2016) 'How Do Prospects of EU Membership Influence Support for Secession? A Survey Experiment in Catalonia and Scotland', *West European Politics*, 39 (6), pp. 1115–1138.

Pavkovic, A. & Radan, P. (2007). *Creating New States: Theory and Practice of Secession*. Aldershot, UK: Ashgate.

Rabushka, A. & Shepsle, K.A. (1972) *Politics in Plural Societies: A Theory of Democratic Instability*. Columbus, OH: Charles E. Merrill.

Radan, Peter. (2008) 'Secession: A Word in Search of a Meaning', in Radan, Peter and Pavkovic, Aleksandar (eds.) *On the Way to Statehood: Secession and Globalization*. Burlington, Vermont: Ashgate.

Requejo, F. & Sanjaume-Calvet, J. (2021) 'Explaining Secessionism: What Do We Really Know about It?', *Politics and Governance*, 9 (4), pp. 371–375.

Roeder, P.G. (2007). *Where Nation-States Come from: Institutional Change in the Age of Nationalism*. Princeton: Princeton University Press.

Rokkan, Stein. (1970). *Citizens, Elections, Parties. Approaches to the Comparative Study of the Processes of Development*. Oslo: Scandinavian University Books, Universitetsforlaget.

Sambanis, N. & Milanovic, B. (2011) 'Explaining the Demand for Sovereignity', *Policy Research Working Paper*, 5888, The World Bank.

Sanjaume-Calvet, M. (2012) 'La secessió a la ciència política', *Revisa del Centre d'Estudis Jordi Pujol*, 12, pp. 32–42.

Sanjaume-Calvet, M. (2020) 'Moralism in Theories of Secession: A Realist Perspective', *Nations and Nationalism*, 26 (2), pp. 323–343.

Seymour, M. (2007) 'Secession as a Remedial Right', *Inquiry*, 50 (4), pp. 395–423.

Siroky, D.S., Mueller, S., & Hechter, M. (2016) 'Center-Periphery Bargaining in the Age of Democracy', *Swiss Political Science Review*, 22 (4), pp. 439–453.

Smith, A.D. (1995) *Nations and Nationalism in a Global Era*. Cambridge, UK: Polity.

Sorens, J. (2012) *Secessionism: Identity, Interest and Strategy*. Montreal: McGill's-Queen's University Press.

Tamir, Y. (1993) *Liberal Nationalism*. Princeton, NJ: Princeton University Press.

Thucydides (1972) *History of the Peloponnesian War*. London & New York: Penguin Classics.

Van Biezen, I. & Hopkin, J. (2006) *Party Organization in Multi-level Contexts*. Manchester: Manchester University Press.

Weber, E. (1976) *Peasants into Frenchmen: The Modernization of Rural France, 1870–1914*. Stanford: Stanford University Press.

Weber, M. (1919) *Politics as Vocation*. Philadelphia: Fortress Press.

Webb, M.J. (2015) 'The Importance of Predecessor Centers of Sovereignty and Processes of State Formation in Explaining Secession', *Defense & Security Analysis*, 31 (1), pp. 22–34.

Wood, J.R. (1981) 'Secession: A Comparative Analytical Framework', *Canadian Journal of Political Science*, 14 (1), pp. 107–134.

Zarkovic Bookman, M. (1992) *The Economics of Secession*. Nova York: Palgrave.

Zuber, C.I. & Szöcsik, E. (2015) 'Ethnic Outbidding and Nested Competition: Explaining the Extremism of Ethnonational Minority Parties in Europe', *European Journal of Political Research*, 54, pp. 784–801. https://ejpr.onlinelibrary.wiley.com/doi/abs/10.1111/1475-6765.12105

# 11

# THE LIFECYCLE OF SECESSION

## Interactions, processes and predictions

*Nicholas Sambanis and David S. Siroky*

Secession – much of it violent – has been a recurrent refrain in modern world history. New nation-states have often come from the convulsive fall of empires, the dissolution of federations, or the forcible unification of governed and ungoverned territories. Violence has often been the price of freedom and what has earned many nations the right to be recognized as sovereign entities. Secessionist violence involves acts of personal sacrifice, but also mass atrocities against populations that are targeted to be eliminated, cleansed, or expelled from the nation's imagined homeland. History has sometimes condemned such violence, usually when secessionists were defeated, or glorified it, following a victory that (re)creates a sovereign state and nurtures the nation's solidarity, buttressed by its own myths about the nation's violent birth. Secessionist sentiment is expressed in movements, protests, or claims for greater self-determination by groups or 'distinct communities' that often feel excluded, marginalized, or too culturally distinct to remain incorporated in a larger political entity. While self-determination struggles are frequently seen as justified and glorified from within, secession typically appears unjustified, destabilizing, and costly to the non-secessionist segments of the country, to external states, and to international organizations.[1]

For Abraham Lincoln, as a recently sworn-in American president, Southern secessionism was "the essence of anarchy", a violation of the constitutional provisions protecting the majority from a tyrannical and discontented minority (Lincoln 1861a). Once mobilized, popular sentiment in favor of secession can become a force that disintegrates empires and integrates nations. As such, secessionism presents a challenge that invites a swift response from the state. In Lincoln's words, it is a challenge that "no government can possibly endure" (Lincoln 1861b).[2] Where secessionist sentiment takes hold, state-sponsored violence frequently follows, just as it did in the American context in 1861. The US Civil War over secession was so bloody that it killed roughly as many Americans in four years as have died in all other foreign and domestic wars collectively since the American Revolutionary War.[3]

The American experience is not unique, however. Indeed, most states in the world have experienced secession in their own country in some form at some point, at least once and sometimes more frequently. More than a few dozen states are still in the midst of separatist struggles today, both in the developed world (e.g., Canada, France, Spain, the United Kingdom) and in the developing world (e.g., Cameroon, Georgia, Indonesia, Ukraine). Societies that experience separatism have been unable to forge an underlying social consensus regarding the appropriate

DOI: 10.4324/9781003036593-14

limits of state authority, and norms and responsibilities of citizenship are contested among different social groups. These failures may be due to deep cultural cleavages or to historically contingent failures in state-building and nation-building. Paraphrasing Ernest Gellner's famous metaphor, we can think of societies with separatist groups as 'wild gardens' in which a shared national culture was never cultivated.

This chapter investigates the 'lifecycle of secession', that is, the four main stages through which self-determination movements may pass, from emergence and consolidation to escalation and recognition. As a political phenomenon, the desire for self-determination and the pursuit of secession underpin many modern civil wars; and civil wars are now – and have been for some time – the primary challenge to international peace and security, not to mention one of the greatest problems domestically in countries plagued by it for economic prosperity, solidarity, development and democracy.[4] Predicting when, where and which demands for self-determination will emerge, consolidate, turn violent and gain recognition is thus a crucial task for everyone concerned with international security and world order as well as for those focused on democracy and development. To make accurate predictions, we therefore focus on theories and analyses that speak to the *when* and *where* of these disparate stages in the lifecycle of secession. As our review illustrates, most of the literature has emphasized description and explanation over prediction. One clear direction for future research would therefore be to recalibrate scholarship on secession toward a greater balance between the goals of description, explanation and prediction.

Self-determination, separatism, secession and nationalism are topics that have inspired vast literatures in political science, sociology, history, psychology and economics. Although our collective intuitions have been honed by prior contributions to those literatures, much can be gained from reviewing and integrating theoretical insights to motivate a more robust predictive framework for the study of secession. There is, alas, no unifying theory or canonical model that predicts which groups will make self-determination claims and which will remain quiescent, which self-determination movements will turn violent, or which ones will secure recognition. In the course of examining key insights, we aim to weave together a review and synthesis of what we do arguably know – and how confident we can be in our knowledge – and to think about secession in terms of how 'means and motives' operate (and in some cases interact) at different stages in the lifecycle of secession. This approach, we hope, may usefully inform future theorizing, analysis and prediction.

Thus far, civil wars – defined as large-scale armed conflicts between the government of a sovereign state and domestic opposition groups fighting over political goals – have been analyzed through the prism of a deceptively simple typology organized around the division between "greed and grievance".[5] That approach, introduced in a seminal article by Collier and Hoeffler (2004), has served as something of an organizing principle for the quantitative study of civil war for the past two decades. There are several reasons that we believe the 'greed and grievance' distinction has outlived its analytical utility, and why a new framework would be potentially more valuable for the next era in the study of secession.

The 'greed and grievance' is a typology developed for civil wars in general rather than for secessionist conflicts specifically. As a result, the particularities of secessionist wars – and their distinct causes based in self-determination claims on the basis of territorial indigeneity, which other civil wars lack – have often been lost when they are lumped together with other types of political violence in quantitative studies. Second, 'greed' and 'grievance' are actually both 'motives' for individual behavior and collective action. This demand-focused typology therefore omits all the 'means' for mobilization and the capacity for collective action that have been the focus of so many studies. Sometimes, it is true, 'greed' is treated as a resource or an opportunity. However, thinking more carefully about 'greed', it is clear that it is really just another motive like grievances. Moreover, greed is a motive that seems to be much more relevant in non-secessionist civil wars. Third, and perhaps most counterproductive, 'greed' and 'grievance' have often been treated as competing rather than interactive and sometimes mutually reinforcing explanations. To redress this issue, we propose a fresh heuristic based on the interaction of means and motives during the lifecycle of secession with the goal of improving the predictive accuracy of our models.

## Means and motives

Our proposed framework emphasizes the basic distinction between *means* and *motives* during the lifecycle of secession.[6] Explanations that focus on the 'motives' for mobilization typically emphasize the reasons that make secessionist movements appealing to the masses. We discuss several kinds of motives, including those generated by modernization, economic inequality, political exclusion, psychological processes, and cultural differences. Most of the early literature on secession focused on motives in the form of economic, political and cultural 'grievances', while the past 20 years of scholarship has paid more attention to factors that in our framework relate to the 'means of mobilization'. These often include natural and other resources that can fuel and fund separatism, organizational capacity for mass mobilization, a favorable political opportunity structure, geography and institutions for collective action.

Scholars who emphasize the 'means' perspective believe that the key to understanding mobilization lies in factors that make collective action *feasible*, such as the group's ability to acquire resources to mobilize people toward accomplishing the group's goals (McAdam 1983; McCarthy and Zald 1977; Skocpol 1979; Tilly 1978), and resources for leaders to offer selective incentives (Buhaug et al. 2011; Regan and Norton 2005), a large pool of fighters (Dube and Vargas 2013), low opportunity costs for rebellion (Besley and Persson 2011; Collier and Hoeffler 2004; Miguel, Satyanath and Sergenti 2004), low state capacity (Besley and Persson 2009; Migdal 1988), natural resource and ethnic group concentration (Morelli and Rohner 2015), dense forests (Siroky and Dzutsev 2015), mountainous terrain (Fearon and Laitin 2003), and a favorable external environment with support by regional actors (Bormann, Sambanis and Toukan 2021). Much of the later wave of literature on civil war downplayed motives. Working on the assumption that motives are latent and abundant, these studies granted more attention to the set of conditions ('the means') that favor or render feasible violent mobilization. Recently, numerous scholars have advanced claims that implicitly or explicitly (using other terms) recognize the importance of both means and motives, and some studies that we discuss in this chapter have pointed to specific interactions which we believe should be emphasized even more in future studies.

Our framework builds on these efforts and uses the lens of motives and means for mobilization not only to assess what we know about secession, but also to bring together disparate studies and findings. In order to generate robust, multidimensional theories and reliable predictions of where and when secessionist violence will occur, we will need not only the predictive algorithms, but also an analytical framework that explores how means and motives interact at each stage in the lifecycle of secession. There should be renewed attention not only to the additive effects of means and motives, but also to dynamics and interactions. The first step is to identify studies that would help to move the field in this direction, for each stage in the lifecycle of secession, and then to examine which specific motives and means interact to produce collective action, and then to encode this information into predictive models.

An increasing number of studies of 'civil wars' have recognized the fundamental dynamics and interactions that bridge the motives and means perspectives on conflict. For instance, Østby et al. (2011) examine the interplay between scarcity and grievances, and Basedau et al. (2017) look at the interaction of resources and political inequalities. Kuhn and Weidmann (2015) explore how different types of inequalities affect both an ethnic group's 'willingness' and 'opportunity' to fight, while Sambanis and Milanovic (2014) explain violent secessionism as the expression of excess demand for self-determination, created by different configurations of regional power, resources and inequality. Siroky et al. (2020) show how the interaction of relative deprivation and relative mobilization capacity interact to produce collective violence. There are many other studies in this spirit that emphasize and assess one or more crucial interaction between motives and means in generating war and conflict.

Too often in the past, theories of secession have attempted to establish a hierarchy between means and motives. Some scholars have noted that grievances (motives) are too widespread and static to account for variable and rare collective action. As a result, they concentrate instead on the resource capacity and political opportunities for mass mobilization in favor of secession. Others have observed that many separatist groups are quite resource-poor, however. These scholars show how —despite the lack of adequate means for collective action – grievances largely account for why and when groups mobilize. Both sides in these debates have offered valuable insights, but it stands to reason that group conflict is actually most likely when a group has *both* the strong grievances to motivate it and sufficient mobilization capacity for collective action. Just as these motives are necessary for the emergence of self-determination movements, so too are the means needed for their consolidation and escalation. Both dimensions remain crucial throughout the lifecycle of secession, but we conjecture that the relative importance between them shifts over time toward the means of mobilization and away from the motives that caused the movements to emerge in the first instance. Our framework proposes a systematic way to analyze these dynamics, with the ultimate goal of creating predictive models for each stage in the lifecycle of secession, and by improving our ability to anticipate violent escalation hopefully saving more human lives.

## The lifecycle of secession

A standard approach in the social sciences treats secession as a binary phenomenon – it either occurs or it does not. While this approach certainly makes some sense, it clearly obscures by lumping together all the distinct stages in what we refer to in this chapter as 'the lifecycle of secession'. As a result, it necessarily limits our understanding of the transformation of self-determination claims from nonviolence to violence, and prevents us from addressing a range of pertinent questions that fall in between. This chapter breaks with this conventional practice by considering the entire process of secession, starting from the emergence of demands for self-determination, through separatist war and up to recognition. This more dynamic approach allows us to explore whether means and motives – and *which* means and motives – interact at each stage in the process of secession.

We highlight four stages of this process-driven approach: *emergence, consolidation, escalation* and *recognition*. Emergence refers to the expression of group claims for self-determination out of a population of potential self-determination movements (any territorially concentrated group can potentially make claims for greater autonomy). Emergence implies that latent sentiment for self-determination leads to the formation of organizations, parties or groups that make public claims for ethno-territorial autonomy or independence. Consolidation refers to the period of non-violent activity (protest, petitions, recruitment, coalition formation) by self-determination movements (SDMs). Escalation refers to the switch from non-violent claim-making to secessionist violence. Recognition refers to acquiring international status as a new country by already existing ones, and then joining the United Nations with all attendant rights and responsibilities.

Our approach aims to reorient scholarly attention to the unique features of each stage in the lifecycle of secession and the transitions from one stage to the next. These dynamics cannot be addressed in the usual way, that is, with slow-moving or static, monadic and structural explanations. The interactions between the groups seeking greater self-determination and the state from which they seek greater independence, together with the wider regional and international context, must be brought into greater focus. Previous examples of *processual* analyses that focus on the dynamics of secessionist conflict have taken a country-specific approach, typically focused on large, politically important countries such as China, Russia, India or Nigeria. Those countries have seen their fair share of conflict and separatism, and therefore a lot has been written about them. However, as Gellner (1983: 45) noted, 'for every effective nationalism, there are *n* potential ones . . . which do not bother to struggle, which fail to activate their potential nationalism, which do not even try'. While some global quantitative analyses have sought to address this imbalance and have offered key insights, major limitations remain, not only concerning causality but also regarding prediction.

There is no easy fix for this problem. Our goal in this chapter is to focus attention on studies and findings about secession that bring us closer to theorizing the *processes* and *interactions*. Quantitative modeling must incorporate these processes and interactions between 'motives' and 'means' – and evaluate their relative contributions – in order to improve prediction at each stage in the secessionist process. Few studies have systematically distinguished and examined stages or interactions, and those that have done one or the other have not done so with the aim of improving prediction.

We analyze claims for self-determination as emerging from a conscious effort to improve the welfare of a group. Thinking about the costs and benefits – and what self-determination is 'worth' to individuals – naturally brings into focus economic theories of secession. Yet a deficiency of an economic approach – much like the focus on quantitative studies of 'civil war' – is that it sees nothing special in *separatist* civil war – individual participation is motivated by the same cost-benefit calculations that might also explain violent crime or participation in protests or riots. Separatists in some economic studies are largely indistinguishable from criminals, bandits, rebels or pirates. The role of state legitimacy, relative deprivation, ethnic identity, and emotional as well as symbolic attachments rarely if ever enter into economic thinking about secession.

At the same time, political theories of separatist war due to 'grievances', motivated, for example, by political exclusion or ethnic differences, might over-predict the outcome; at some level, almost all claims for self-determination are motivated by such grievances, as critics have rightly observed. But why do some grievances produce mass mobilization while others remain elite affairs? Why are some violent and others not? Why do some escalate from peaceful to violent secession? Are the factors that predict the emergence of demands for secession the same as those that predict the escalation of self-determination movements (SDMs) to violence, or those that account for their international recognition as new states? While there are many compelling answers to these questions in the literature already, not enough studies focus on dynamics, processes and prediction. This chapter proposes a fresh way to organize the large, sprawling quantitative literature on secession, and thereby aims to provide a solid foundation for future studies on secessionist dynamics, processes and predictions. Our contribution focuses on the core *motives* and *means*, along with their interactions, at each step in the lifecycle of secession – *emergence, consolidation, escalation, recognition*.

## Emergence

The first stage in the lifecycle of secession is the *emergence* of a claim-making self-determination movement. The implicit baseline for comparison when analyzing the emergence stage is all the other ethnic or ethno-territorial groups that do not make self-determination claims. Generally, writers have argued that the emergence requires, at a minimum, a distinct cultural community, and usually a territorial basis. Beyond these basic necessary conditions, a variety of theories have been proposed, but most of what has been written on this subject can be classified as adopting an approach focused more on the motives or the means for emergence, while a few (in our view, not enough) studies underscore the interactions between them as key to the materialization of self-determination movements.

System-level and macro-historical explanations are important in understanding global and regional patterns – spikes and slumps in the emergence of SDMs over time – but typically fail to shed much light on cross-group and cross-national differences. "[While] the powerful ideology of self-determination helps explain the emergence of a political environment hospitable to territorially divisive claims", Horowitz points out (1981: 166), "it cannot explain which groups will take up the cause". In other words, a permissive international environment – one in which security and prosperity would not be significantly diminished by exiting the current polity, or one in which an international norm favoring self-determination exists (e.g., Griffiths 2016)[7] – is likely to induce a greater frequency of separatist movements and might induce the transformation of latent sentiment for SDMs into actual claim-making movements. But such systemic variables are less likely to predict particular instances of secession emerging, or to explain the timing of such movements arising or escalating. In short, a permissive international environment provides an opportunity that some groups – but not others, due to the absence of motives, means or both – will seize to form SDMs.

Hechter (2000) also provides a different macro-historical account, with greater specificity in explaining which groups will seek secession, where and when. He argues that nationalist or separatist movements have tended to emerge only where and when there was a shift to direct rule which challenged traditional authority structures and powerholders in peripheral areas of multinational polities. Against the background of this shift to direct rule, the ideology of nationalism and self-determination affords legitimacy to nascent secessions. A related argument emphasizes the regional diffusion of SDMs (e.g., Cunningham and Sawyer 2017), observing that effective secessions inspire other groups to also seek it and legitimize their efforts. Such spillovers enhance each individual group's means to mobilize, creating a permissive regional environment for secession.

Such perspectives for secession do not go far enough in explaining which groups will seek SDM or when their movements will emerge. Moving down to the regional and group levels brings us closer to the action. Focusing on the means for secessionist mobilization, for example, Jenne et al. (2007) shows that the relative power of groups plays a critical role in the emergence of secession, which is much more likely among 'strong' than 'weak' groups. In addition to 'power', much of the literature has focused on the role of wealth as an indicator of relative position, sometimes using the region and at other times taking the group as the primary unit of analysis. As Wallerstein (1961: 88) noted: "inevitably, some regions will be richer (less poor) than others, and claims to power combined with relative wealth make the case for secession strong". On average studies have indeed found that regions in advanced democracies with higher income levels – as well as recent histories of independence and larger populations – were more likely to pursue secession (Sorens 2005). Berkowitz (1997) created a model of the relationship between changes in regional income and secessionist pressures in the periphery within a fiscal federation, and then assessed it using developments over time in the peripheral Russian regions of Bashkortostan, Chechnia, Tatarstan and Sakha (Yakutia), which have experienced significant income gains and losses during the transition to a market economy.

Horowitz (1981: 172) also emphasized relative positions, but considered both the group's and the region's power simultaneously, writing: "the interplay of relative group position and relative regional position determines the emergence of separatism". This led him to suggest that secession was most likely to emerge in the developing world amid 'backward groups' in 'backward regions' rather than amid powerful and rich regions and groups.[8] Backwardness may be endogenous to neglect – a condition that often applies to peripheral regions of weaker states – but it is not the distance *per se* that renders secession possible or desirable among backward groups so much as the economic and political neglect from the central government – what Cederman and co-authors (e.g., 2013) have labeled 'political exclusion'. Backwardness may therefore be related to motives – especially grievances resulting from exclusion, poverty and inequality – as much as, if not more than, means.

Most of these structural accounts assume that the ethnic groups in question are geographically concentrated, without which the emergence of separatism is much less likely (e.g., Toft 2003). Geographic factors – not only concentration, but others such as mountainous terrain or dense forests – are largely constants and therefore have done little to shed light on the variable phenomenon of interest – the emergence of secession – and are unlikely to help us predict the future location, timing or scale of particular secessions. At best, they facilitate tendencies that are driven by non-geographic factors. Scholars also need to study the reason for attachment to the land – whether economic, strategic or symbolic motives contribute to secessionist mobilization. For example, Kelle (2017) suggests groups are more likely to call for self-rule when they attach symbolic meaning to their territory than when they assign strategic or material relevance to their land. The reason, she suggests, is that symbolic attachments have positive effects on group solidarity and cohesion, which facilitates mobilization. In general, geography has been highlighted mostly because it provides the means for groups to mobilize for secession, but the reasons for attachment to the land can shed light on the motives for secessionist mobilization.

One of the most important areas of research on the emergence of secession has focused on institutions. Perhaps nowhere is this more visible than in the study of secession from the former Soviet Union, where much of the early literature focused on the institutional means that some groups, but not others, had to exploit for establishing their claims to secession. Roeder (1991) assessed the rise of assertive ethnofederalism in the Soviet Union, and focused on the role of federal institutions in explaining variation in protests, and in understanding the assertiveness of relatively advantaged ethnic groups. Gorenburg (2003) also argued that the Soviet state structure played a primary role in the rise of nationalist movements. Pre-existing ethnic institutions profoundly influenced the means available to secessionist movement leaders and shaped their separatist behavior. Hale's work (2000) also examined why some ethnic regions pursued secession from the former Soviet Union, whereas others strove to save the same multinational state. Bringing together means and motives perspectives, Hale argued that regions were more likely to be separatist when they were less assimilated, increasing the demand for more autonomy, and were both wealthier and possessed a high level of self-rule, which afforded the means for mobilization. Smith (2013) focuses on comparing these Soviet ethnofederalism legacies with other regions to assess their external validity. Without challenging the emphasis on institutions per se, Grigoryan (2012) criticizes the argument that the ethnofederal designs of the Soviet Union and Yugoslavia were at the root of the violent conflicts after the breakup of the countries. He contends that these ethnofederal designs were themselves the results of previous nationalist mobilizations in the Russian empire and the Balkans. In short, the institutions were endogenous to prior mobilization.

Regardless of prior ethnofederal institutions, the process of democratization can itself created new motivations for the emergence of separatist movements by generating greater demand among citizens for nationalist politics. Giuliano (2006), for instance, shows how secessionism emerged in the former USSR from bottom-up motivations. Ethnofederal countries experiencing democratization were more likely to experience secession because regional leaders acquired new incentives to seek secession in response to local constituencies who demanded it and whose support they needed to stay in office. In a later book, Giuliano (2011) links these elite incentives with mass participation, arguing that the ability of nationalist leaders to persuade others to connect their material interests with the fate of the nation is what led to mobilization in some – but not all – Russian republics. At the same time, her study shows that alternative accounts based on religion, language, cultural difference, demography and economic development all fail to deliver.

The non-emergence of secession is the other side of the same coin. Since states have a common interest in supporting international institutions and rules to prevent secessionism because they are themselves often vulnerable to secessionism, Jackson and Rosberg (1982) suggested that many states (in Africa, particularly) have avoided lending support to secessionist demands abroad. In some cases, this has arguably prevented the emergence and consolidation of secession. Saideman (1997) re-examines this issue, sometimes known as the Pandora's box of secession. Rather than vulnerability to secession at home, his study shows that ethnic ties with groups at home do more to explain external state behavior vis-à-vis secessionists in neighboring countries. The fall of Yugoslavia, the Nigerian civil war, and the crisis in Congo are used to illustrate this motive-oriented argument about why external states do or do not lend support to secessionists abroad. The non-emergence of secession, then, is largely a story about how some groups that possess the motives to secede lack the external means to do so.

All told, the literature on the emergence of secession has provided key insights but has chiefly focused mostly on structure rather than process, has privileged either means or motives over their interactions, and has concentrated on understanding and explaining rather than predicting. Future research could therefore benefit from recalibrating the study of the emergence of secession towards processes, interactions and predictions, which are also relevant to the 'consolidation' stage – the second stage in the lifecycle of secession.

## Consolidation

Not all ethnic groups mobilize for secession, and among those who do, only a small number are able to consolidate themselves and sustain a political presence over time. Many movements disappear soon after they emerge, and this pattern has received scant attention compared to studies of the emergence of secessionist claims or the outbreak of secessionist war. As with the emergence of secessionist claims, the interaction between different motives and means shapes whether SDMs are able to consolidate and establish themselves over time.

In this stage, motives remain important, but whether a movement consolidates itself is increasingly about the means of mobilization. For example, Sorens (2011) emphasizes the role of natural resources in movement consolidation, and Capoccia et al. (2012) argue that demands for autonomy or secession tend to be more resilient when religious organizations, which afford greater capacity, make these demands. One reason religious organizations may have this effect is laid out in Hechter and Okamoto (2001), which focuses on the mechanisms that produce sustained minority group collective action. They argue that the prevention of free riding, the establishment of institutional arrangements producing demand for greater autonomy, and the development of distinctive social identities are the three keys to group solidarity and collective action.

This builds on Olson's seminal work (1965), which challenged the assumption, common at the time, that if all members of a group share common interests, then they will act collectively to achieve them regardless of the group's size. Olson's argument implies that secession depend on group size, since collective action in pursuit of common interests that require the provision of public goods will induce more free-riding as the size of the group grows. Olson (1971: 28) calls this 'the exploitation of the great by the small'. Optimality can be obtained only when the marginal costs are equal to the marginal benefits. This suggests that even when and where secessionist movements do emerge, due to the efforts of a small number of committed people, it will not be able to consolidate and sustain itself unless the free-rider problem is addressed. In the absence of selective incentives, or another solution, groups will fail to further their common interest (e.g., independence), and the movement will likely disappear over time. While small groups tend to provide public goods sub-optimally, larger groups often fail to produce them at all. Hechter's work on group solidarity (1987), as a prerequisite for sustained collective action, argues that the conjunction of dependence on the group for collective goods and the group's capacity to monitor and sanction members for noncompliance with obligations and norms determines whether a secessionist group will become a consolidated political force over time (Hechter and Pfaff 2020). In other words, the motivation for individuals to remain a member of the group and the group's means to keep members in line is what shapes group solidarity and the consolidation of secessionist movements.

Also thinking about consolidation in terms of the means for enhancing organizational cohesion and group solidarity, Roeder (2018) asks how some secessionist campaigns manage to sustain themselves over time and establish secession as the only perceived viable option, while others falter and lose ground to non-secessionist groups. The answer lies in the ability of campaigns to coordinate expectations within their population on a common purpose. The strategy of programmatic coordination, drawing on Lenin's language, makes independence the only possible option and renders the status quo untenable; in some cases, it justifies the use of violence.

Though most studies have focused on the country-level, region-level or group-level, it is also possible to see the interactions between means and motives in micro-level studies focused on individuals. For example, Hierro and Queralt (2021) investigate individual preferences on secession. Examining original survey data from Catalonia, they find that individuals who are excluded from public insurance because they are unemployed, as well as those who work in sectors and companies specialized in the host state market, are generally against secession. By contrast, those who specialize in foreign markets do not oppose independence. Their findings speak to the interaction of motives and means at the individual level, and underscore the importance of the role of risk associated with labor market asset specificity, building on Boix (2003), as a predictor of preferences for and against secession in secessionist regions.

Overall, the literature on the consolidation stage focuses on the means a bit more than on the motives in secessionist conflict. More of the literature on consolidation also examines processes as opposed to structures, which we view as positive. However, very little of this literature emphasizes interactions and almost none of it is explicitly predictive, both of which merit greater attention in future research. The next stage – escalation – has devoted somewhat more consideration to these two issues.

## Escalation

The vast majority of SDMs are peaceful; only a small number resort to violence in pursuit of their claims for more autonomy (Sambanis, Germann and Schädel 2018). At the same time, SDMs seeking outright secession and independence are much more likely to use violence. Most of the literature has focused on these violent cases, yet the differences between violent and nonviolent SDMs remain understudies and therefore still quite poorly understood. The decision to use violence in pursuit of autonomy marks a qualitative shift in an SDM (Germann and Sambanis 2021), which merits its own theorizing and analysis in the lifecycle of secession.

Violent conflict arises due to many reasons, but primary among them are the failure of state-building nationalism, the imposition of alien rule that is perceived illegitimate by an aspiring nation, the shift from indirect to direct rule (Hechter 2000, 2013), the political exclusion of territorially concentrated ethnic groups (Cederman et al. 2015), and lost autonomy (Siroky and Cuffe 2015). Most of these accounts emphasize motives, but often bring in means as a key component of the argument, though not necessarily in an interactive manner. For instance, Siroky and Cuffe (2015: 8) argue:

> Retracted or lost autonomy provides a strong motive and need not significantly diminish the group's collective action capacity. Moreover, it considerably weakens the government's ability to make credible commitments that might otherwise prevent tensions from escalating . . . thereby increasing the probability of [violent] secession.

Accounts of conflict escalation from nonviolence to violence invariably focus on how the state responds to group claims. The difficulty consists in predicting which groups will make what type of claims in anticipation of the state's response. One prominent line of thinking focuses squarely on the state's strategy and conceptualizes it in light of the potential reputational effects that its current approach may have for future secessions. The reputational theory provides a story of escalation that centers on the motives for the state to escalate. Walter (2006, 2009) is probably most closely associated with this argument, contending that leaders are less likely to make concessions if they are concerned with establishing a reputation for strength; and they will be more concerned with building such a reputation if there are many ethnic groups that could potentially 'emerge' as future secessionists. That concern will lead states to take a hardline attitude, refusing to talk with claim-making groups as a strategy to dissuade others from making more costly claims in the future. Although this reputational logic might apply in some settings, Nilsson (2010) criticizes the theory. He finds that weaker rebel groups are more likely to reach a negotiated settlement with the government when the number of warring parties *increases*. Using global data on territorial concessions from 1989 to 2004, however, Forsberg (2013) finds no support for the claim that granting territorial concessions to an ethnic group spurs new separatist conflicts, either within or across borders.

While some scholars posit that governments tend to oppose secessionist demands to establish reputations that will hopefully prevent setting a precedent for others, Griffiths (2015) contends that administrative organization is a third option for states to handle secession demands: governments can use administrative lines to decide for which regions they should recognize secession rights – and for which regions they should not – without fear of setting a precedent for others and hurting their reputation. Sambanis, Germann and Schädel (2018) use a more expansive dataset on SDMs than those used by previous studies, and find no empirical support for the reputational theory of separatist conflict (B. Walter 2006). Specifically, they show that the number of other ethnic groups in a certain state that might potentially secede does not increase the probability of that state using violence against any particular SDM making claims nonviolently.

Instead of reputations, Cunningham (2011) argues that what determines whether secessionists receive concessions – or are confronted with state violence – is their internal structure. Internally divided SDMs – i.e., those that are *less* consolidated – are *more* likely to obtain concessions than those that are more united, yet concessions to unitary groups are more successful at resolving these disputes. This suggests that concessions are part of the bargaining process, and not merely a tool to resolve disputes. Butt (2017) argues that external security – and not internal structure or

reputation building – is what shapes whether or not states use violence against peripheral secessionist movements. When leaders believe that the potential state emerging from the secession
will pose a greater threat to state security than the violent secession movement itself, then it is
more likely to use violence in an effort to squelch it. This account puts the emphasis squarely on
the state, and brings us back to the motivations for escalation – in this case, secessionist violence
is motivated by concerns about future external security.

Basta (2021) focuses explicitly on multinational states (e.g., Belgium, Bosnia, Iraq), and shows
that how central governments respond to self-determination demands, and with what political
consequences, is not only material but also symbolic. That is, in order to explain escalation after
the political economy demands of ethno-territorial groups have been satisfied, it is necessary to
consider the symbolic claims and counterclaims of majority and minority communities. Lecours
(2021) distinguishes between static and dynamic autonomy in regions within liberal democracies
(Catalonia, Scotland, Flanders, South Tyrol, Basque, Québec, Puerto Rico), and argues that
variation in separatism over time is shaped by the extent to which autonomy (i.e., concessions)
evolves to accomodate shifting identity, interests and circumstances. Dynamic autonomy stems
secession, while static autonomy stimulates it.

Among several different 'means' explanations for secessionist conflict, natural resource endow-
ments have received extensive attention in the literature on violent escalation. For instance,
Lujala (2009) explores the effect of natural resources on the severity of armed civil conflict and
finds that secessionist conflicts in areas with hydrocarbon production are *the most severe*, while
Hunziker and Cederman (2017) demonstrate that oil resources have a significant and robust
impact on the probability of secessionist conflict escalation.

Other means-oriented theories emphasize institutions. Cederman et al. (2015) provide
empirical evidence that both power-sharing and territorial autonomy have a strong conflict-pre-
venting impact in circumstances where there is no previous dispute history. In post-conflict settings, however, only inclusion in power-sharing arrangements at the central level of government
reduces the probability of conflict recurrence, while post-conflict regional autonomy is most
likely 'too little, too late'. Siroky and Cuffe (2015) suggest groups that have lost autonomy tend
to have both strong capacity and incentive to pursue secession, whereas those that have never
experienced autonomous institutional arrangements are unlikely to mobilize because they lack
collective action capacity. Germann and Sambanis (2021) use a two-step approach to examine
connections between lost autonomy and political exclusion, on the one hand, and the emergence and escalation of (non-)violent separatist claims, on the other. Their analysis finds that
both political exclusion and lost autonomy are significantly correlated with the escalation of
nonviolent claims for self-determination into violence, while lost autonomy is also a significant
correlate of the emergence of nonviolent separatist claims.

Bakke (2015) shows that devolved governance – including regional autonomy arrangements
and federalism – does not always preserve peace in states facing self-determination demands.
Through in-depth case studies of Chechnya, Punjab and Québec, as well as a statistical
cross-country analysis, she argues that the effects of policy, fiscal and political decentralization are
conditional on the traits of the societies they (are meant to) govern. Specifically, she highlights
three dimensions – the ethnic composition of a given unit such as republic, province or state;
how much wealth it has; and the political connection between the center and periphery – that
modify the effects of decentralization on violent secession.

Also emphasizing center-periphery relations, Lacina (2015) argues that ethnic groups sharing
the periphery with the most powerful ethnic group in their country are less likely to be violent
separatists. "Violent separatism", she writes, "is the product of interactions between a central
government and competing ethnic groups in the periphery". Rebellions do not typically arise

from ethnic groups that have better access to the central executive compared to their neighbors in the periphery, since the center is likely to choose policies for the periphery that correspond to the favored group's interests. The lack of motivating grievances translates into a lower probability of separatist violence, which can also be deterred by a strong and clear central commitment to opposing interests in the periphery. Buhaug (2006) emphasizes the strength of the rebel group relative to the state as key to explaining whether aggrieved groups that resort to violence in order to redress their grievance seek to overthrow the ruling government or instead pursue secession. Beardsley, Cunningham, and White (2017) bring in the role of the UNSC's involvement in self-determination disputes, which their study demonstrates can substantially dampen the propensity for disputes between self-determination movements and their respective governments to escalate to civil war.

Finally, several studies make clear interactive arguments that bring together 'motives' and 'means' to explain violent secession, which we see a very welcome development. For instance, Cunningham (2013) argues that, compared to conventional politics, secessionist war is more likely to happen when self-determination groups are internally fragmented and larger, and when they have kin groups in adjoining states, face economic discrimination, demand independence and function in poorer countries. In other words, secessionist civil war is more likely when there is an explosive mix of both motives and means. Cederman, Wimmer and Min (2010) also bring 'means' and 'motives' together in demonstrating that ethnic groups tend to get involved in conflict with the government when they are excluded from state power, have higher mobilizing capacity and have experienced conflict in the past. This study indicates that motives are critical in all stages of secession, especially the emergence phase, whereas the means for mobilization appear to gain in relative importance as the movement-state interactions escalate into violent secession.

A final study by Breslawski and Ives (2019) directs our attention to ideology to bridge the motives and means perspectives, and illustrates how they interact inter-temporally. Factions with a strong religious ideology have incentives to use violence because the use of violence allows them to show their religious credentials in transnational networks to secure weapons, support and funding. On this count, motives based in a strong ideology combine with the means of mobilization to explain violent secession.

This brings secession to the last stage in the lifecycle of secession – international recognition and independence. What predicts whether an SDM will eventually be admitted to the 'club of nations'?

## Recognition (independence)

The final stage in the lifecycle of a secession, for those movements that make it that far, is to become a new state. Easier said than done. The key is international recognition – the secret to joining the 'club of nations' – and not only or necessarily military victory on the battlefield. Crucial to examining secession is therefore the study of when and why aspiring states gain formal recognition from existing countries, and therefore also why some states refuse to extend recognition in certain cases.

External politics as a 'means' to recognition are crucial here, even more so than in earlier stages. As Horowitz (1981: 167) wrote: "whether a secessionist movement will achieve its aims . . . is determined largely by international politics, by the balance of interests and forces that extend beyond the state" (cf. Birch 1978). Coggins (2011, 2014) conducted one of the earlier explorations of state birth in international relations, and introduced an international-level model of state emergence. The means to gain recognition can also be internal. An internally focused 'means' account assesses the role of violence in recognition. Griffiths and Wasser (2019) introduce data on all secessionist movements between 1900 and 2006, and on the institutional and extra-institutional methods that secessionists have used from 1946 to 2011. No secessionist movement challenging a contiguous state has won its sovereignty, they show, without using institutional methods, either exclusively or in combination with extra-institutional methods. In short, there is no evidence that violence helps a secessionist movement to gain independence, whereas 'friends in high places' appears consistently helpful.

Recognition – even years later – is often not universal, with many states withholding recognition and the aspiring state held in a legal limbo. Looking more closely at current cases of contested recognition, Mirilovic and Siroky (2015, 2017, 2020) emphasize the motives of external states to extend and withhold recognition. They argue that transnational religious ties push external states toward recognition of secessionist states, for ideational reasons and for future alliance formation; whereas domestic religious regulations deter states from extending recognition, for fear of sending the wrong signal to domestic religious minorities. When these factors point in opposite directions, the former dominates in influence. Testing this theory, the authors find supportive evidence from contested recognitions around the world: e.g., Kosovo (2017), Palestine and Israel (2015) and Western Sahara (2020).

All of these analyses, however, are static. Recognition is a dynamic process that evolves over time and entails interactions with great power interests. Using new time series data, Siroky, Popovic and Mirilovic (2021) analyze the timing of recognition, asking why some states extend recognition to unilateral secessions quickly, while others delay it. Whereas previous studies have emphasized great power convergence, this study demonstrates the critical role of great power division in shaping recognition dynamics. Using unique data on Kosovo's recognition, the authors show that countries in the US sphere of influence – and receiving US military and financial aid – were more likely to recognize Kosovo, whereas countries under Russian influence – receiving arms and aid – tended to delay their recognition of this new state-like entity. The article quantifies this 'great power effect' on international recognition and demonstrates its diminishing returns over time as recognition disputes become protracted.

Recognition is a bit of a moving target. As Fabry (2012) argues, there is limited empirical evidence that unilateral secession tends to become internationally legitimate, and in other work, Fabry (2010) suggests that international society has adapted its understanding of recognition over time. This has made the means of attaining recognition through unilateral secession increasingly elusive, with Kosovo being a glaring exception to this general rule of thumb. Similarly, Huddleston (2020) sees recognition in a more fluid, continuous manner that evolves over time. He conceptualizes national sovereignty as a changing and continuous *process*, mirrored in foreign policy decisions short of legal recognition. The study suggests that diplomatic recognition, extant violence, separatist victory and sour relations between third-party countries and incumbent states positively influence the latent sovereignty of separatist groups, whereas concerns that sovereignty will create a precedent negatively influences it. Recognition not only is an outcome that secessionists seek to achieve, but it can also contribute to making disputes more intractable. Shelef and Zeira (2017) demonstrate that the international recognition of statehood by the UN General Assembly (UNGA) influences mass attitudes of groups in conflict toward territorial compromise by simultaneously reducing mass support for concessions on the territorial terms of partition while raising support for partition as a strategy of conflict resolution.

The recognition stage can be fruitfully analyzed from the perspective of the motives that drive states to extend and withhold recognition, along with the means needed to attain international recognition, namely external support by a large number of states. Most self-determination movements never arrive at this phase, and it is noteworthy that most of the motives and many of the internal means that were important for prior phases are largely irrelevant at this stage, and that new factors take on mounting weight.

## Conclusion

Secession is not just an event; it is also a process that can be characterized as a series of stylized stages. In this chapter, we have emphasized four key stages in the 'lifecycle of secession': emergence, consolidation, escalation and recognition. Within each phase, the majority of studies can be analytically classified into two groups: those focused on motives, and those emphasizing the means, for secession. We propose that the field could benefit from more focus on the interplay between these two perspectives and on emphasizing such interactions in pursuit of more accurate predictive models. Our review suggests that the relative importance of motives is greater in the early phases of secession, and that the significance of means increases as the self-determination movement advances through the stages towards recognition and statehood.

Secession continues to represent a key challenge to international peace and security. While most of the literature is understandably focused on *explaining* secession, establishing causality in many of the arguments summarized in this chapter is often difficult, given the complexities of cross-country or cross-group comparisons. More attention to prediction in future research on secession could yield significant benefits. Knowing when, where and which demands for self-determination will emerge, consolidate, turn violent and gain recognition is valuable to both scholars and policymakers. Predictions will be more accurate if we can explore factors that influence how and when SDMs transition from one stage of the lifecycle of secession to another. Identifying the four steps – and organizing the relevant literature along a 'means' and 'motives' typology of variables – is only a first step of course.

The framework that we have introduced and explored briefly in this chapter is focused not only on which means and motives operate during different stages of the lifecycle of secession, but also on how they may interact. In addition to recognizing the existence of these critical interactions, they must also be further theorized and utilized in future research to predict secessionist dynamics and processes. The next crucial step is to assess how these particular motives and means interact to produce collective action at each stage in the lifecycle of secession. We hope that in some small way this framework – based on the interaction of means and motives throughout the lifecycle of secession – contributes not only to organizing the large literature on secession and civil war, but also to the growth of studies emphasizing dynamics, processes and predictions.

## Notes

1  There is a large normative and philosophical literature on the moral justification for secession, on philosophical grounds and in terms of international law, that we do not directly engage with in this study. See, for example, Beran (1984) and Buchanan (2004).
2  At the time of this speech, 11 of 13 states had already ratified the Secession Ordinances of 13 Confederate States.
3  Estimates for deaths during the American Civil War (less often called the War between the States, or the War of Northern Aggression) range, but most estimates are above 620,000, which is also roughly the estimate for American battle-deaths in all other wars together: World War I, World War II, Korea, Vietnam, the Revolutionary War, the War of 1812, the Mexican–American War, the Iraq–Afghanistan War, the Spanish–American War, the Gulf War.
4  In their macro-historical analysis of patterns of state violence in the last 200 years, Wimmer and Min (2006) show that the risk of war was higher around periods of imperial expansion and dissolution and that, following the formation of new states, the risk of revolutionary war in those states was high. Since 1945, the majority of cases of violent ethnic conflict involves demands for regional autonomy, self-determination or secession Cederman, Wimmer and Min (2010); Sambanis and Zinn (2004).

5 Deceiving because greed is, in fact, also a grievance, e.g., when a rich region seeks secession because it does not wish to share its wealth; and, moreover, because both grievance and greed are motives, thus the typology entirely leaves out the key components related to the means for rebellion – e.g., resource mobilization and political opportunities.
6 While we focus in this chapter on applying this framework to secession, we believe that it also would represent an improvement for the study of civil war in general.
7 Also see Fazal and Griffiths (2014), which suggests that normative, security and economic changes in the international system have made secessionism more likely, since these changes have increased the benefits of independence more than its costs.
8 Horowitz defines backward and advanced (1981: 170) as follows:

> An advanced group is one that has benefited from opportunities in education and nonagricultural employment. Typically, it is represented above the mean in number of secondary-school and university graduates; in bureaucratic, commercial, and professional employment; and in per capita income. Certain stereotypes are commonly associated with these attributes. Advanced groups are generally regarded by themselves and others as highly motivated, diligent, intelligent, and dynamic. . . . Backward groups, less favorably situated on the average in terms of educational attainment, high-salaried employment, and per capita income, tend to be stereotyped as indolent, ignorant, and not disposed to achievement.

# References

Bakke, K. (2015). *Decentralization and Intrastate Struggles: Chechnya, Punjab, and Québec.* New York: Cambridge University Press.

Basedau, M., J. Fox, J. Pierskalla, G. Strüver, and J. Vüllers. (2017). Does Discrimination Breed Grievances: And Do Grievances Breed Violence? New Evidence from an Analysis of Religious Minorities in Developing Countries. *Conflict Management and Peace Science* 34(3), pp. 217–239.

Basta, K. (2021). *The Symbolic State.* Montreal: McGill-Queen's University Press.

Beardsley, K., D. Cunningham, and P. White. (2017). Resolving Civil Wars before They Start: The UN Security Council and Conflict Prevention in Self-Determination Disputes. *British Journal of Political Science* 47(3), pp. 675–697.

Beran, H. (1984). A Liberal Theory of Secession. *Political Studies* 32(1), pp. 21–31.

Berkowitz, D. (1997). Regional Income and Secession: Center-Periphery Relations in Emerging Market Economies. *Regional Science and Urban Economics* 27(1), pp. 17–45.

Besley, T., and T. Persson. (2009). The Origins of State Capacity: Property Rights, Taxation and Politics. *American Economic Review*, 99(4), pp. 1218–1244.

Besley, T., and T. Persson. (2011). The Logic of Political Violence. *The Quarterly Journal of Economics* 126(3), pp. 1411–1445.

Birch, Anthony H. (1978). Minority Nationalist Movements and Theories of Political Integration. *World Politics* 30, 325

Boix, C. (2003). *Democracy and Redistribution* (Cambridge Studies in Comparative Politics). Cambridge: Cambridge University Press.

Bormann, N., N. Sambanis, and M. Toukan. (2021). Outside Options: Power-Sharing in the Shadow of External Intervention after Civil War, Typescript. https://ncbormann.github.io/publication/outside_options/Outside_Options-200630.pdf

Breslawski, J., and B. Ives. (2019). Killing for God? Factional Violence on the Transnational Stage. *Journal of Conflict Resolution* 63(3), pp. 617–643.

Buchanan, A. (2004) *Justice, Legitimacy, and Self-Determination: Moral Foundations for International Law.* Oxford: Oxford University Press.

Buhaug, H. (2006). Relative Capability and Rebel Objective in Civil War. *Journal of Peace Research* 43(6), pp. 691–708.

Buhaug, H., K. S. Gleditsch, H. Holtermann, G. Østby, and A. F. Tollefsen. (2011). It's the Local Economy, Stupid! Geographic Wealth Dispersion and Conflict Outbreak Location. *Journal of Conflict Resolution* 55(5), pp. 814–840.

Butt, A. I. (2017). *Secession and Security: Explaining State Strategy against Separatists.* Ithaca, NY: Cornell University Press.

Capoccia, G., L. Sáez, and E. Rooij. (2012). When State Responses Fail: Religion and Secessionism in India 1952–2002. *The Journal of Politics* 74(4), pp. 1010–1022.

Cederman, L., S. Hug, A. Schädel, and J. Wucherpfennig. (2015). Territorial Autonomy in the Shadow of Future Conflict: Too Little, Too Late? *American Political Science Review* 109(2), pp. 354–370.

Cederman, L., A. Wimmer, and B. Min. (2010). Why Do Ethnic Groups Rebel? New Data and Analysis. *World Politics* 62(1), pp. 87–119. doi:10.1017/S0043887109990219

Cederman, Lars-Erik, Kristian Skrede Gleditsch, and Halvard Buhaug. (2013). *Inequality, Grievances, and Civil War*. New York, NY: Cambridge University Press.

Coggins, B. (2011) Friends in High Places: International Politics and the Emergence of States from Secessionism. *International Organization* 65(3), pp. 433–467.

Coggins, Bridget L. (2014). *Power Politics and State Formation in the Twentieth Century: The Dynamics of Recognition*. Cambridge University Press.

Collier, P., and A. Hoeffler. (2004) Greed and Grievance in Civil War. *Oxford Economic Papers* 56(4), pp. 563–595.

Cunningham, K.G. (2011). Divide and Conquer or Divide and Concede: How Do States Respond to Internally Divided Separatists? *American Political Science Review* 105(2), pp. 275–297.

Cunningham, K.G. (2013). Understanding Strategic Choice: The Determinants of Civil War and Nonviolent Campaign in Self-Determination Disputes. *Journal of Peace Research* 50(3), pp. 291–304.

Cunningham, K.G., and K. Sawyer. (2017). Is Self-Determination Contagious? A Spatial Analysis of the Spread of Self-Determination Claims. *International Organization* 71(3), pp. 585–604.

Dube, O., and J. Vargas. (2013). Commodity Price Shocks and Civil Conflict: Evidence from Colombia. *The Review of Economic Studies* 80(4), pp. 1384–1421.

Fabry, M. (2010). *Recognizing States: International Society and the Establishment of New States Since 1776*. Oxford: Oxford University Press.

Fabry, M. (2012). The Contemporary Practice of State Recognition: Kosovo, South Ossetia, Abkhazia, and Their Aftermath. *Nationalities Papers: The Journal of Nationalism and Ethnicity* 40(5), pp. 661–676.

Fazal, T., and R. Griffiths. (2014). Membership Has Its Privileges: The Changing Benefits of Statehood. *International Studies Review* 16(1), pp. 79–106.

Fearon, J., and D. Laitin. (2003). Ethnicity, Insurgency, and Civil War. *American Political Science Review* 97(1), pp. 75–90.

Forsberg, E. (2013). Do Ethnic Dominoes Fall? Evaluating Domino Effects of Granting Territorial Concessions to Separatist Groups. *International Studies Quarterly* 57(2), pp. 329–340.

Gellner, Ernest. (1983). *Nations and Nationalism*. Paris: Payot.

Germann, M., and N. Sambanis. (2021). Political Exclusion, Lost Autonomy, and Escalating Conflict over Self-Determination. *International Organization* 75(1), pp. 178–203. doi:10.1017/S0020818320000557

Giuliano, E. (2006). Secessionism from the Bottom Up: Democratization, Nationalism, and Local Accountability in the Russian Transition. *World Politics* 58(2), pp. 276–310.

Giuliano, E. (2011). *Constructing Grievance: Ethnic Nationalism in Russia's Republics*. Ithaca, NY: Cornell University Press.

Gorenburg, D. (2003). *Minority Ethnic Mobilization in the Russian Federation*. Cambridge: Cambridge University Press.

Griffiths, R. (2015). Between Dissolution and Blood: How Administrative Lines and Categories Shape Secessionist Outcomes. *International Organization* 69(3), pp. 731–751.

Griffiths, R. (2016). *Age of Secession*. Cambridge: Cambridge University Press.

Griffiths, R., and L. Wasser. (2019). Does Violent Secessionism Work? *Journal of Conflict Resolution* 63(5), pp. 1310–1336.

Grigoryan, A. (2012). Ethnofederalism, Separatism, and Conflict: What Have We Learned from the Soviet and Yugoslav Experiences? *International Political Science Review* 33(5), pp. 520–538.

Hale, H. (2000). The Parade of Sovereignties: Testing Theories of Secession in the Soviet Setting. *British Journal of Political Science* 30(1), pp. 31–56. doi:10.1017/S0007123400000028

Hechter, M. (1987). *Principles of Group Solidarity*. Berkeley: University of California Press.

Hechter, M. (2000). *Containing Nationalism*. Oxford: Oxford University Press.

Hechter, M. (2013). *Alien Rule*. Cambridge: Cambridge University Press.

Hechter, M., and D. Okamoto. (2001). Political Consequences of Minority Group Formation. *Annual Review of Political Science* 4(1), pp. 189–215.

Hierro, M., and D. Queralt. (2021). The Divide over Independence: Explaining Preferences for Secession in an Advanced Open Economy. *American Journal of Political Science* 65(2), pp. 422–442.

Horowitz, D. (1981). Patterns of Ethnic Separatism. *Comparative Studies in Society and History* 23(2), pp. 165–195.

Huddleston, J. (2020). Continuous Recognition: A Latent Variable Approach to Measuring International Sovereignty of Self-Determination Movements. *Journal of Peace Research* 57(6), pp. 789–800.

Hunziker, P., and L. Cederman. (2017). No Extraction without Representation: The Ethno-Regional Oil Curse and Secessionist Conflict. *Journal of Peace Research* 54(3), pp. 365–381.

Jackson, R., and C. Rosberg. (1982). Why Africa's Weak States Persist: The Empirical and the Juridical in Statehood. *World Politics* 35(1), pp. 1–24.

Jenne, E., S. Saideman, and W. Lowe. (2007). Separatism as a Bargaining Posture: The Role of Leverage in Minority Radicalization. *Journal of Peace Research* 44(5), pp. 539–558.

Kelle, F. L. (2017). To Claim or Not To Claim? How Territorial Value Shapes Demands for Self-Determination. *Comparative Political Studies* 50(7), pp. 992–1020.

Kuhn, P. and N. Weidmann. (2015) Unequal We Fight: Between-and Within-Group Inequality and Ethnic Civil War. *Political Science Research and Methods* 3(3), pp. 543–568.

Lacina, B. (2015). Periphery versus Periphery: The Stakes of Separatist War. *The Journal of Politics* 77(3), pp. 692–706.

Lecours, A. (2021). *Nationalism, Secessionism and Autonomy*. Oxford: Oxford University Press.

Lincoln, A. (1861a). First Inaugural Address, March 4. Washington, DC.

Lincoln, A. (1861b). Gradual Abolishment of Slavery: Message from the President of the United States, in Relation to Co-Operating with Any State for the Gradual Abolishment of Slavery.

Lujala, P. (2009). Deadly Combat over Natural Resources: Gems, Petroleum, Drugs, and the Severity of Armed Civil Conflict. *Journal of Conflict Resolution* 53(1), pp. 50–71.

McAdam, D. (1983). Tactical Innovation and the Pace of Insurgency. *American Sociological Review* 48, pp. 735–754.

McCarthy, J., and M. Zald. (1977). Resource Mobilization and Social Movements: A Partial Theory. *American Journal of Sociology* 82(6), pp. 1212–1241.

Migdal, J. (1988). Vision and Practice: The Leader, the State, and the Transformation of Society. *International Political Science Review* 9(1), pp. 23–41.

Miguel, E., Satyanath, S., and Sergenti, E. (2004). Economic Shocks and Civil Conflict: An Instrumental Variables Approach. *Journal of Political Economy* 112(4), pp. 725–753.

Mirilovic, N., and D. Siroky. (2015). Two States in the Holy Land? International Recognition and the Israeli-Palestinian Conflict. *Politics and Religion* 8(2), pp. 263–285.

Mirilovic, N., and D. Siroky. (2017). International Recognition and Religion: A Quantitative Analysis of Kosovo's Contested Status. *International Interactions* 43(4), pp. 668–687. doi:10.1080/03050629.2017.1 227805

Mirilovic, N., and D. Siroky. (2020). International Recognition, Religion, and the Status of Western Sahara. *Acta Politica* 56(3), pp. 1–19.

Morelli, M., and D. Rohner. (2015). Resource Concentration and Civil Wars. *Journal of Development Economics* 117, pp. 32–47.

Nilsson, D. (2010). Turning Weakness into Strength: Military Capabilities, Multiple Rebel Groups and Negotiated Settlements. *Conflict Management and Peace Science* 27(3), pp. 253–271.

Olson, Mancur (1971[1965]). *The Logic of Collective Action: Public Goods and the Theory of Groups* (Revised ed.). Cambridge, MA: Harvard University Press.

Østby, G., H. Urdal, M. Tadjoeddin, S. M. Murshed, and H. Strand. (2011). Population Pressure, Horizontal Inequality and Political Violence: A Disaggregated Study of Indonesian Provinces, 1990–2003. *The Journal of Development Studies* 47(3), pp. 377–398.

Regan, P., and D. Norton. (2005). Greed, Grievance, and Mobilization in Civil Wars. *Journal of Conflict Resolution* 49(3), pp. 319–336.

Roeder, P. (1991). Soviet Federalism and Ethnic Mobilization. *World Politics* 43(2), pp. 196–232.

Roeder, P. (2018). *National Secession: Persuasion and Violence in Independence Campaigns*. Ithaca, NY: Cornell University Press.

Saideman, S. (1997). Explaining the International Relations of Secessionist Conflicts: Vulnerability versus Ethnic Ties. *International Organization* 51(4), pp. 721–753.

Sambanis, N., M. Germann, and A. Schädel. (2018). SDM: A New Data Set on Self-Determination Movements with an Application to the Reputational Theory of Conflict. *Journal of Conflict Resolution* 62(3), pp. 656–686.

Sambanis, N., and B. Milanovic. (2014). Explaining Regional Autonomy Differences in Decentralized Countries. *Comparative Political Studies* 47(13), pp. 1830–1855.

Shelef, N., and Y. Zeira. (2017). Recognition Matters! UN State Status and Attitudes toward Territorial Compromise. *Journal of Conflict Resolution* 61(3), pp. 537–563.

Siroky, D., and J. Cuffe. (2015). Lost Autonomy, Nationalism and Separatism. *Comparative Political Studies* 48(1), pp. 3–34.

Siroky, D., and V. Dzutsev. (2015). The Empire Strikes Back: Ethnicity, Terrain, and Indiscriminate Violence in Counterinsurgencies. *Social Science Quarterly* 96(3), pp. 807–829.

Siroky, D., M. Popovic, and N. Mirilovic. (2021). Unilateral Secession, Great Power Contestation and International Recognition. *Journal of Peace Research*, 58(5), pp. 1049–1067.

Siroky, D., C. Warner, G. Filip-Crawford, A. Berlin, and S. Neuberg. (2020). Grievances and Rebellion: Comparing Relative Deprivation and Horizontal Inequality. *Conflict Management and Peace Science* 37(6), pp. 694–715.

Siroky, David, and Valery Dzutsati. (2015). The Empire Strikes Back: Ethnicity, Terrain, and Indiscriminate Violence in Counterinsurgencies. *Social Science Quarterly* 96(3): 807–829.

Skocpol, T. (1979). *States and Social Revolutions*. Cambridge: Cambridge University Press.

Smith, B. (2013). Separatist Conflict in the Former Soviet Union and Beyond: How Different Was Communism? *World Politics* 65(2), pp. 350–381.

Sorens, J. (2005). The Cross-Sectional Determinants of Secessionism in Advanced Democracies. *Comparative Political Studies* 38(3), pp. 304–326.

Sorens, J. (2011). Mineral Production, Territory, and Ethnic Rebellion: The Role of Rebel Constituencies. *Journal of Peace Research* 48(5), pp. 571–585.

Tilly, C. (1978). *From Mobilization to Revolution* (pp. xiii + 349). Reading, MA: Addison-Wesley.

Toft, Duffy Monica. (2003). *The Geography of Ethnic Violence: Identity, Interests, and the Indivisibility of Territory*. Princeton: Princeton University Press.

Wallerstein, I. (1961). *Africa: The Politics of Independence*. New York: Vintage Books.

Walter, B. (2006). Information, Uncertainty, and the Decision to Secede. *International Organization* 60(1), pp. 105–135. doi:10.1017/S0020818306060048

Walter, B. (2009). *Reputation and Civil War: Why Separatist Conflicts Are So Violent*. New York: Cambridge University Press.

Walter, Barbara F. (2006). Building Reputation: Why Governments Fight Some Separatists But Not Others. *American Journal of Political Science* 50(2), pp. 313–330.

Wimmer, A., and B. Min. (2006). From Empire to Nation-State: Explaining Wars in the Modern World, 1816–2001. *American Sociological Review* 71(6), pp. 867–897.

# 12

# THE CAUSES AND CONSEQUENCES OF FRAGMENTATION IN SECESSIONIST MOVEMENTS

*Feike E. M. Fliervoet and Lee J. M. Seymour*

Media accounts and conventional understandings of separatist conflict sometimes treat ethnona-tional groups as natural and coherent entities representing contested but otherwise unproblema-tized territories and populations seeking statehood. We often find references to the "Southerners" who fought for the independence of South Sudan, the "Kurdish separatists" waging a rebellion against Turkey, or the "Tamil insurgents" seeking an independent homeland in northern Sri Lanka. Such shorthand labels gloss over the complexity of these groups' identities as well as the divergent political strategies and projects they pursue.

In the same way that the "groupness" of ethnic groups is too often taken for granted (Brubaker 2004), secessionist movements are too frequently treated as the actors representing the people in whose name they claim to be fighting. Indeed, ethnonationalist movements are regularly equated with the one organization that most vocally – or, often, most violently – claims political leadership of the group: "Southerners" in South Sudan were thus synonymous with the Sudan People's Liberation Movement/Army (SPLM/A), Kurds in Turkey with the Turkish Worker's Party (*Partîya Karkerên Kurdistanê*, PKK), and Tamils in Sri Lanka with the Liberation Tigers of Tamil Eelam (LTTE). Less well known are the numerous rival organ-izations, violent and nonviolent, that have been part of each struggle. In each of the three aforementioned examples, as well as many others, factionalism, infighting, and shifting alliances have been a key dynamic shaping the course of the separatist struggle. Competition between these organizations, the diverse identities and ideologies around which they mobilize and the political strategies and aims that accompany them, complicate our understanding of self-deter-mination conflicts. Above all, they underscore that conflicts can seldom be reduced to a dyadic conflict between a unified government and opposition locked in a contest over the status of a territory and population.

Indeed, the fragmentation of secessionist movements seems counterintuitive insofar as a group's claim on the right to secession hinges on a certain unity of purpose. This is underscored in nationalist discourse and ideology that insists on the importance of nationalist unity in secur-ing the group's survival and realizing the national project. The conceptual failure to problematize the internal politics of self-determination can have important real-world consequences. Indeed, many have linked influential scholarship around wars such as those in Bosnia or Iraq to policies

DOI: 10.4324/9781003036593-15

that promote political projects rooted in exclusionary and violent forms of nationalism that marginalize moderate voices and more inclusive identities (Campbell 1998; Caspersen 2011; Jenne 2012).

This chapter surveys a wave of recent research that has sought to unpack the internal politics of secessionist groups, much of it drawing from research on multiparty civil wars. While the literature on the causes of rebel fragmentation has expanded considerably in recent years, this work includes studies of rebels with secessionist aims along with those seeking power at the center, and rebels with more parochial aims of defending local communities. Indeed, "new, new" civil wars (Walter 2017), marked by the increased prominence of transnational aims and identities of insurgents who mobilize peripheral or marginalized local communities, increasingly blur the boundaries between these traditional categories of conflicts. The distinction between territorial and governmental conflicts, that is, those in which the main "incompatibility" or "master cleavage" is between groups seeking independence or autonomy on the one hand, versus groups seeking to control the state on the other, is blurrier in syncretic conflicts in places such as Libya, Somalia, Mali, or Chechnya, where the transnational aims of Islamist groups mixes with local identities, whether ethnic, sectarian, tribal, or clan, in complex ways. Almost invariably, conflict among actors over aims and identities are central axes of contention within these ethnonationalist movements.

While research on fragmentation is diverse, a common thread in this work takes movements not as coherent actors, but as ongoing and internally contested political projects. This shifts the focus from the dyadic relationship between central governments and these opposition movements, to what has variously been termed factionalism, fractionalization, and fragmentation. In what follows, we first examine how scholars have sought to conceptualize fragmentation. We then review literature on the causes and dynamics of fragmentation, both in self-determination movements and organizations. The chapter concludes by taking stock of this research and suggesting avenues for future research.

## Fragmentation in conflicts of self-determination

Ontologically, much of the recent work on fragmentation pushes back against assumptions of "groupness" that permeate the study of ethnonationalist conflict. This assumption is common in quantitative work that conceptualizes separatist conflict in terms of contested relations between governments and "minorities at risk," or employs ethnic groups as the basis for coding cross-national datasets. The assumption that governments and rebels are unitary actors is also common in rationalist work that takes bargaining and commitment problems to be fundamental to the dynamics of secessionism modeled as a series of strategic choices. Finally, policy prescriptions that advise partition along ethnic lines as a solution to ethnic security dilemmas also evidence this assumption of groupness.

In critiquing this work by unpacking the groupness assumption, typically by looking at the internal politics of the opposition, scholars have focused on different *units of analysis*. First, some work has investigated *individual* patterns of behavior that undermine the cohesiveness of nationalist organizations. Much of this work has focused on what Stathis Kalyvas (2008) termed "ethnic defection," where individuals choose to align with the state against his or her own ethnic group, and wider processes of collective "identity shifts" as new categories of belonging loyal to the state emerge. Second, there is a strand of research that takes the *organization* or *armed group* as its unit of analysis and focuses on variations in cohesion and discipline (e.g. Staniland 2014). Third, there is a body of literature that looks at the interaction between different organizations, taking the nationalist or ethnic *movement* as the point of departure (e.g. Cunningham 2014;

Krause 2017). Finally, scholars have analyzed interactions among ethnic groups but accompanied them with attention to internal processes of fractionalization (Christia 2012), sometimes without necessarily abandoning commitments to primordialist groupness assumptions that treat ethnic identities and boundaries as fixed.

For those seeking to explain fragmentation on the side of nationalist opposition, this diversity in the units of analysis precludes any consensus on conceptualization and related questions of indicators and measures. Most quantitative studies on fragmentation rely on a simple count of the number of rebel organizations involved in a conflict, but several scholars have convincingly argued that a multidimensional conceptualization of fragmentation is necessary. Perhaps the most influential conceptualization sees fragmentation varying across movements in terms of the number of organizations, the institutional linkages between them, and their relative power (Bakke et al. 2012). In this conceptualization, the greater the number of organizations within a movement, the thinner the institutions or "rules of the game" promoting coordination and cooperation between them; and the more power that is diffused among them, the greater the degree of fragmentation. Many movements vary over time across all three dimensions. Taking the Palestinian movement example, the institutional structure of the Palestinian Liberation Organization (PLO), and to a lesser extent the Palestinian Authority, have mitigated deep divisions among the numerous factions that have struggled for the liberation of Palestine during certain phases of this long conflict. At times, power within the movement has been concentrated in Fatah, allowing this organization to act as the movement's hegemon; at other times, power was dispersed across Fatah and rival organizations such as Hamas, Islamic Jihad, and others, creating a fragmented movement prone to infighting.

Better data is being produced that allows researchers to analyze these complex linkages between different aspects of fragmentation. For instance, Dowd (2015) takes into account the number of actors in a conflict as well as the proportion of violence that can be attributed to each of them, in order to reflect the relative strength of different groups. In order to do greater justice to the relationships between different organizations involved in a conflict or political campaign, other scholars have compiled datasets on the pre-war origins of rebel groups, including their parent organizations (Braithwaite and Cunningham 2020), and the methods and tactics used by different nonviolent and violent actors that seek political change (Chenoweth et al. 2018).

It is worth noting that given the greater material resources and institutional coherence of the state, most research has focused on the dynamics of fragmentation in the opposition. There is nonetheless a tradition of work examining how divisions within the state shape the course of conflicts. Ian Lustick (1993), for instance, examines how the delicate balance states have to strike between threats of civic unrest, defections from ruling coalitions, and ideological hegemony influenced the contraction of imperial frontiers in the face of nationalist opposition in Ireland, Algeria, and Palestine. Similarly, Hendrik Spruyt (2005) uses partisan and constitutional vetoes and civilian control over the military to explain patterns of decolonization. Examining the link between federal institutions and conflict, Kristin Bakke (2015) points to political ties between elites at different levels of decentralized states as a key factor. Finally, Kathleen Gallagher Cunningham (2014) offers a rare study that examines the interaction of divisions within states and self-determination movements, finding that fragmented movements are more likely to receive concessions from the state, while in turn moderate levels of internal divisions within the state allow governments to commit more credibly to agreements to settle conflicts.

More recent work has looked at the security apparatus specifically, most notably the burgeoning literature on "pro-government militias" and the ways their prominent role in many conflicts undercuts the Weberian ideal of a unitary state exercising a monopoly on violence (Carey et al. 2013; Jentzsch et al. 2015). Yelena Biberman (2018), for instance, shows how

India's counterinsurgency in Kashmir and Turkey's conflict against Kurdish separatists relies on diverse groups of local collaborators to navigate the local population. Relatedly, another recent focus has been the importance of security force defections in shaping the success of nonviolent campaigns (Albrecht and Ohl 2016; Chenoweth and Stephan 2011; Dworschak 2020). In secessionist conflicts, however, nonviolent strategies are much less likely to be successful where ethnic differences between the government incumbent and challengers impede government defections and widespread mobilization (Pischedda 2020).

## The causes of fragmentation

Given the counterintuitive nature of fragmentation in secessionist movements, there has been a recent surge in scholarship seeking to identify its causes. Most of this work focuses on the causes of fragmentation in insurgent *organizations* rather than *movements*, thus seeking to explain *organizational splintering* rather than *movement fractionalization*. While the boundaries between movements and organizations are often blurred, we follow the convention of treating movements as the broadest level of mobilization, typically encompassing multiple, distinct organizations whose sense of common purpose and solidarity is highly variable. We will first discuss the scholarship on fragmentation at the movement level, followed by an overview of the literature explaining fragmentation at the level of the organization.

### *Fragmentation in movements*

First of all, Kathleen Gallagher Cunningham (2014) presents a theory of self-determination politics in which she argues that the fragmentation of self-determination movements is an effect of their interactions with the state. On the one hand, she finds that state accommodation leads to self-determination movements becoming more cohesive due to the cooptation of more moderate organizations by the state. On the other hand, the use of violence by the state (and more specifically, the onset of civil war) leads to self-determination movements becoming more fragmented, though this effect does not persist over time. Importantly, however, Cunningham suggests that these dynamics might differ for movements that have secessionist aims – but this expectation is not empirically assessed.

Seymour et al. (2016) build on Cunningham's earlier findings in their study of the causes of movement fragmentation, in which they argue that the number of organizations that make up a specific ethno-political movement is primarily determined by what they label "competitive dynamics" in a dual contest. These dynamics refer to competition both *within* the movement (i.e., an increase in the diversity of demands between factions) and *between* the movement and the state it contests (i.e., the degree of state repression or accommodation, and the onset of civil war). Their analysis finds several other variables not related to competitive dynamics to have a fragmenting effect, including the occurrence of mediation efforts, the presence of foreign fighters, greater state capacity (measured by GDP per capita), democracy, and group size.

Investigating the causes of fragmentation in armed opposition movements more broadly, Fjelde and Nilsson (2018) argue that the risk of movement fragmentation also depends on the presence of barriers to entry for nascent rebel groups. They find that when incumbent groups have strong social networks with either an ethnic or leftist base, the risk of fragmentation is lower. This effect is not present when incumbent groups have a strong religious base. These results suggest that, compared to other rebel groups, secessionist movements mobilized around an ethnic identity should be more likely to remain cohesive. In line with the results of Seymour et al. (2016), Fjelde and Nilsson further find that the risk of fragmentation increases when groups are accommodated by the government through either negotiations or democratic concessions; however, they do not find that government repression increases fragmentation.

Other authors argue that there is a relationship between repression and movement structure, however. In their article on the effect of repression on nationalist movement unity, McLauchlin and Pearlman (2012) demonstrate that it can either have a fragmenting or cohering effect depending on members' satisfaction with the movement's institutional arrangements prior to the onset of repression. In their case studies of the Iraqi Kurdish and Palestinian nationalist movements, they indeed find that state repression "amplifies trends in cooperation or conflict existent in a movement before the onset of repression" (McLauchlin and Pearlman 2012: 41). This suggests that state policies are likely to be a trigger, rather than a root cause, of movement cohesion and fragmentation. Lawrence (2010) also addresses the effects of repression on the fragmentation of nationalist movements, and finds that leadership repression, in particular, generates a power struggle within the movement that is likely to result in fragmentation.

Beyond the context of separatism, Mosinger (2018) presents an alternative theory to explain fragmentation in rebel movements, focusing on the rebels' relations with their civilian constituency. He hypothesizes that movements composed primarily of stationary rebel groups are less likely to be fragmented, because they cultivate closer relationships with the civilian population. In addition, he predicts that a curvilinear relationship exists between civilian grievances (operationalized as ethnic discrimination) and rebel fragmentation, in which the probability of rebel fragmentation is higher at intermediate levels of grievance. At more extreme levels of civilian grievance, the emergence of broad civilian networks is expected to prevent the emergence of splinter groups. His findings support both hypotheses: "roving" rebel movements are more likely to fragment than stationary movements, and an increase in ethnic discrimination initially spurs rebel fragmentation, but this relationship reverses at very high levels of civilian grievance.

Several of Mosinger's control variables are also significant, some of which are in line with the aforementioned studies while others are contradictory. Consistent with the results of Seymour et al. (2016) and Fjelde and Nilsson (2018), democracy is found to increase rebel fragmentation. However, Mosinger's findings contradict those of Seymour and colleagues when it comes to the effect of state capacity, as he finds a negative relationship between GDP per capita and rebel fragmentation. In addition, while Seymour and colleagues did not find a significant relationship between external support and movement fragmentation, Mosinger demonstrates that the disaggregation of external support does yield significant results: fungible support such as weapons and funds are associated with higher levels of rebel fragmentation, whereas non-fungible support in the form of a territorial sanctuary encourages rebel unification. Additional variables related to conflict intensity and mountainous terrain are also found to significantly increase rebel fragmentation.

## *Organizational splintering*

Although the literature directly addressing the causes of movement fragmentation is relatively sparse, valuable insights are also provided by the closely related literature on organizational splintering. Indeed, if a secessionist organization experiences a split, the overall number of organizations in the secessionist movement increases – thus causing movement fragmentation. The explanations for organizational splintering can broadly be divided into three categories: (1) organizational structure and leadership; (2) battlefield outcomes and tactics; and (3) relations with third parties.

Paul Staniland (2012b, 2014) has developed one of the most influential explanations for organizational splintering in the first category, arguing that the pre-existing social networks on which insurgent organizations are built determine the degree of organizational cohesion. He demonstrates that if there are strong prewar horizontal ties between leaders as well as strong vertical ties between leaders and local communities within a social base, the insurgent organization mobilizing said base is more likely to maintain cohesion. Divided social bases, on the other hand, are likely to result in fragmented organizations that fail to achieve organizational control at both the central and local levels. Eric Mosinger (2019) builds on Staniland's work by arguing that the wartime networks of rebel organizations – i.e., recruitment networks and organizational networks – also affect organizational cohesion: if changes occur in these networks, for example through the influx of new recruits, this is likely to alter the balance of power between rebel leaders, generating leadership disputes that can in turn lead to organizational splits.

Several other scholars have further investigated the role of the rebel leadership in maintaining organizational cohesion. When it comes to the structure of the leadership, Asal et al. (2012) find that ethnopolitical organizations with competing leadership structures are at a greater risk to split, and Burch and Ochreiter (2020) similarly conclude that organizations with a weak central command have a higher probability of splintering. The latter further find that rebel organizations with a high mobilization capacity are more likely to experience splits. Austin Doctor (2020) shows that leadership quality also matters: he finds that rebel leaders with combat experience are more likely to maintain organizational cohesion, whereas rebel leaders with political experience are more likely to witness organizational fragmentation.

A second group of authors explains organizational splintering based on the strategies adopted by rebel groups, and the extent to which these strategies translate into military success or failure. When it comes to rebel organizations' military achievements, both Fotini Christia and Michael Woldemariam find that battlefield outcomes are a key determinant of organizational integrity. First of all, Christia (2012) finds that poor battlefield performance is likely to trigger group fractionalization, particularly when losses are asymmetric across subgroups. While splitting at a time of weakness may seem counterintuitive, Christia demonstrates that it is a rational decision made by a subgroup to ensure its own survival. Woldemariam (2016, 2018) reaches the same conclusion, but adds that battlefield gains, too, can increase the likelihood of fragmentation. Military successes result in lowered perceptions of external threat, and therefore reduce the survival concerns of rebel subgroups. As such, the likelihood increases that unresolved differences rise to the surface, and that conflicts emerge over the distribution of (future) spoils. A key implication of Woldemariam's argument is that organizational cohesion is expected only in the event of battlefield stalemates.

Different strategies and tactics of rebel groups in civil war, along with the identity bases they mobilize, also matter for their cohesion. As Nagel and Doctor (2020) show, sexual violence increases the risk of organizational splintering. The perpetration of sexual violence actually promotes cohesion at the battalion level, but in doing so, it shifts fighters' allegiance from the organization to the fighting unit. Lieutenants subsequently feel emboldened to split from the organization, because they are confident that their subordinate battalions will follow them. Examining Islamist groups that mobilize around local versus global identities in Somalia and Iraq, Aisha Ahmad (2016) shows that global Islamists are better able than groups relying on ethnic or tribal identities to maintain cohesion.

When it comes to rebel groups' relations with third parties, Henning Tamm (2016, 2019) finds that it is not the number but the policies of external sponsors that matter for organizational cohesion. State sponsors can allocate their resources strategically to either reinforce or undermine the balance of power in an organization, and as such affect its integrity: if a state creates a more equal balance of power between the current faction leader and a rival, this makes an organizational split more likely. In such a scenario, "the rival becomes strong enough to defy the leader but remains too weak to overthrow him" (Tamm 2016: 599), and will therefore break away to create a faction of its own. If an external patron creates or reinforces an imbalance of power either in favor of the existing leader or its main rival, the organization will remain intact, but in the latter case it is more likely to experience an internal coup. Brandon Ives (2021) argues instead that the ethnic links between a rebel group and its external sponsor determine whether or not external support results in organizational splintering: those rebel groups that receive support from a state with whom they share ethnic ties are at lower risk to split.

Not surprisingly, given the focus on interactions with the state in explaining movement fragmentation, numerous scholars also link the state to patterns of organizational splintering. As demonstrated by Duursma and Fliervoet (2021), rebel groups are at a greater risk to split if they engage in peace talks with the government. This is also the case if negotiations with the state are conducted in the presence of an external mediator (Olson Lounsbery and Cook 2011). While Olson Lounsbery (2016) further expects foreign military intervention on behalf of the government to increase the likelihood of rebel splintering, this expectation is not supported empirically.

## The consequences of fragmentation

Perhaps most fundamentally, scholars have been interested in fragmentation for its profound effects on different conflict processes, with research focusing on several areas of interest. In this section, we focus on an (incomplete) list of four key areas: (1) shifts to and from violence and conflict recurrence; (2) specific patterns and repertoires of violence; (3) alliances and alignments; and (4) survival and success.

First, fragmentation has been linked to shifts to and from violence as well as conflict recurrence. Prior to violence, bargaining between a state and a fragmented movement increases uncertainty and generates commitment problems in ways that tend to lead to violence against the state (Cunningham 2013). Another key dynamic looks at escalating demands, with organizations within a fragmented movement making increasingly radical claims to attract the attention of the government, bolster internal cohesion, and outbid rivals, all while increasing civil war risk (Vogt et al. 2021). Violence itself can be a way of outbidding more moderate rivals, improving the faction's standing within a fragmented group in ways that drive escalation and diffusion of violence (Cunningham et al. 2012).

Downstream, fragmentation also shapes the exit from violent conflict, particularly processes of bargaining, accommodation, and mediation that play critical roles in conflict resolution. David Cunningham (2011) observes that the number of rebel groups is a strong determinant of conflict duration, a finding largely explained by the ways in which multiparty conflicts complicate bargaining processes. Indeed, much attention has focused on these bargaining processes and the various ways fragmentation influences the likelihood of concessions, how far these go in meeting demands, and the probability that these settlements resolve violence in the longer term. The social movements literature has long looked at "radical flank effects," or the contradictory effects that radical activists have on more moderate counterparts (e.g. Freeman 1975; Haines 1988). Kathleen Cunningham (2014) finds over 200 instances of states accommodating self-determination movements, linking a state's willingness to accommodate self-determination movement demands to levels of fragmentation in arguing that states strategically use concessions to moderate factions as a way of weakening their adversaries and learning about movement preferences.

Once a conflict settlement is reached, fragmentation can also shape the prospects that the agreement holds. The large literature on "spoiling" behavior attempts to explain the frequent failure of peace accords to prevent conflict relapse through a focus on hardline factions that have incentives to disrupt conflict resolution efforts (Stedman 1997). Wendy Pearlman (2009) argues that internal political contestation in fragmented movements is a key process in the emergence of spoilers, showing how smaller Palestinian factions undercut Israeli–Palestinian peace processes. While existing explanations emphasize the importance of the terms of the deal with Israel in explaining contestation within the Palestinian self-determination movement, Pearlman argues that many of these groups "were no less motivated by their struggle over representation of the Palestinian cause" (Pearlman 2009: 80). Such dynamics vastly complicate the work of mediation and engagement in peace processes. In the conflict in Mali, for instance, the fragmentation of armed groups vastly complicated the work of UN mediators and proved to be a key impediment to implementing the 2015 Bamako Agreement: new armed groups and splinters repeatedly emerged, using violence to push for inclusion in the process; this violence allowed the government to abjure responsibility for rampant insecurity; and factionalism promoted a focus on rent-seeking and individual perks (Boutellis and Zahar 2017).

Beyond rivalry between factions, these same dynamics also sow divisions within communities in ways that render them susceptible to renewed violence. In a study of how Dinka communities in Sudan experienced the war leading to the secession of South Sudan, for instance, Luka Biong Deng (2010) argues that those experiencing "exogenous" counterinsurgency warfare saw deepened and strengthened social bonds. In contrast, those riven by internecine violence between co-ethnic Dinka militias experienced a loss of social capital. These sorts of dynamics help explain why fragmentation in civil wars increases the odds of conflict recurrence downstream (Rudloff and Findley 2016).

Second, fragmentation also explains important patterns of violence within separatist civil wars. Not coincidentally, countries locked into seemingly perpetual multiparty violence such as South Sudan, Somalia, Afghanistan, and now Syria are plagued by rebel splits and state breakdown. The fragmentation of armed groups is generally associated with a range of violent behaviors as discipline and control break down, leading to the escalation and diffusion of violence and longer wars. In the most extreme cases, such fragmentation can lead to the emergence of different sides in a civil war, each pursuing a different set of claims in battles against both the government and other armed groups. In Syria or Afghanistan, for instance, numerous ethnonationalist and Islamist groups fight one another and the government, mobilizing around different ideologies and identities in pursuit of distinct political agendas. Indeed, recent work has extended the initial interest in inter-rebel violence among nationalist armed groups to Islamist groups mobilizing around ideological and religious identities (Hafez 2020).

As evidenced by the aforementioned survey of work on organizational splintering, splits within and between factions are almost invariably accompanied by violence and create the conditions for further instability and infighting. Costantino Pischedda's work (2018, 2020) finds that rebels, particularly when mobilizing from the same ethnic group, are prone to infighting when windows of opportunity emerge to eliminate rivals, or when weak groups launch desperate attacks against stronger rivals in the face of deteriorating power balances. Jonah Schulhofer-Wohl (2020) shows how "on-side fighting" in Syria between aligned armed groups is shaped by both short-term survival considerations and the achievement of longer-term political objectives, and is thus most likely to emerge among rebels when threats by the regime abate. Analyzing social media posts by Syrian armed groups to track how ideology shapes infighting among over 30 armed groups, Gade et al. (2019) demonstrate instead that power asymmetry and ideological distance correlate with a higher probability of infighting in this remarkably factionalized conflict.

The escalation of violent competition within and between different groups and sides almost always has deleterious effects for the security of civilians. Recent work expands the focus from civilian victimization and targeting to examine how fragmentation is linked to adverse behaviors such as sexual violence (Nagel and Doctor 2020) and child recruitment (Faulkner and Doctor 2021). The latter study, for instance, uses the recent FORGE dataset to demonstrate that splinter groups are more likely to recruit child soldiers to overcome the constraints on recruitment and ensure their immediate survival.

Fratricidal violence between factions within armed groups is a key mechanism leading to what Paul Staniland (2012a) terms "fratricidal flipping," or ethnic defection to align with the state for protection. Several recent studies have investigated how these pro-regime armed groups can drive violence, particularly against civilians. Huseyn Aliyev and Emil Souleimanov (2019), for instance, find that "co-ethnic militias," recruited by the state to fight rebels mobilizing from the same ethnic group, tend to target civilians less than non-ethnic militia. Another study by Abbs et al. (2020) finds that ethno-political ties between the state and a militia aligned with it polarizes ethnic communities in ways conducive to longer and more intense conflicts.

Third, in the context of multiparty civil wars we often observe fluid alliances between factions and groups. Several explanations for the alliance choices of armed groups exist in the literature, ranging from realist power balancing, to ideology, to wider structural factors. Examining wars in Bosnia and Afghanistan, Fotini Christia (2012) demonstrates how cycles of fractionalization perpetuate cycles of conflict as elites continually reassess power balances, using pre-existing cleavages within groups to either split from or attempt to take over their armed group. These dynamics of within-group fractionalization combine with patterns of repeated alliance breakdown and side switching according to a balance of power logic as armed groups "ally or affiliate with the weaker side in an anarchic all-out civil war to balance the distribution of power" (Christia 2012: 34). Whereas Christia's argument considers identity narratives and ideas to be malleable to the dictates of power, Emily Gade and colleagues (2019) show how ideological homophily conditions the alliance choices of Syrian factions who cooperate with groups that share their moral visions and political projects. Finally, in their article on the causes of fragmentation in the Syrian rebel movement, Walther and Pedersen (2020) argue that the repeated fracturing of rebel alliances among Syrian rebel groups is a second-order effect of conflict dynamics outside of the rebels' control. More specifically, their analysis demonstrates that the political environment in which the rebellion emerged was not conducive to the emergence of a coherent opposition movement. In the absence of pre-existing organizations through which the popular uprising could be coordinated (cf. Staniland 2014), Syrian discontent gave rise to a spontaneous and diffuse rebellion.

A related literature looks at alignments among factions in civil wars, focusing on the specific question of side-switching. Seymour (2014) traces the highly fluid alignments of armed groups in Southern Sudan and Darfur to local political rivalries that incite actors to collaborate in exchange for external support and patronage in ways reflective of militarized bargaining in what Alex de Waal (2015) terms Sudan's political marketplace. A quantitative study by Sabine Otto (2018) demonstrates that capacity matters as much as incentives, with armed groups that are the product of prior splits are better positioned to switch sides due to their greater levels of cohesiveness.

Fourth, and perhaps most fundamentally, the dynamics surveyed here matter for the key outcomes of ethnonationalist conflict, namely survival and success. With regard to the former, Akcinaroglu (2012) suggests that fragmentation increases the chances of survival for all factions involved in a conflict because it decreases the likelihood of each rebel group's defeat. As governments become militarily divided when facing multiple rebel groups simultaneously, they fail to eliminate even the weakest organizations. Mahoney (2017) finds instead that a group's size is a key predictor of its longevity following fragmentation, as larger core groups are more likely to survive than splinter factions. Evan Perkoski (2019) rather argues that the internal politics of splits shape the odds of organizational survival: studying the contrasting fates of republican splinter groups in Northern Ireland, he shows how groups forming around single issues have survival advantages linked to their ability to attract more homogeneous, preference-aligned recruits. Research on terrorist group longevity by Phillips (2015) suggests a different mechanism in which conflict between armed actors contributes to their survival more directly, as it encourages civilians to take sides and inspires innovation.

Regarding the outcomes of separatist conflicts, Peter Krause's book *Rebel Power* (2017) argues that the structure of nationalist movements explains nothing less than the variable success of independence struggles. Specifically, through case studies of Algerian, Irish, Zionist, and Palestinian movements, Krause argues that those led by hegemonic movements vastly stronger than their rivals were able to attain independence. The same conditioning effect of unity on the odds of success has also been found in non-violent resistance. In a micro-sociological study of mobilizations in Tunisia and Bahrain during the Arab Spring, Isabel Bramsen (2018) finds unity among both protestors and the regime to be a crucial factor alongside the timing of escalation.

## Where to from here?

The research surveyed in this chapter has greatly advanced our understanding of secessionist conflict, demonstrating conclusively that the internal politics of movements and actors matters for how conflicts begin, how they unfold, and how they end. Nonetheless, a number of important questions remain. First, a significant limitation of the literature on secessionist movement fragmentation is that it investigates this process only in *ongoing* civil wars. It thus focuses on circumstances in which collaboration is inherently difficult – yet separatist movements evince different patterns of cohesion and fragmentation both before civil wars erupt and after they are over, and even after having emerged from them somehow "victoriously." The Chechens, for example, won their first war with Russia in August 1996, but nonetheless fractured shortly afterwards as different factions turned against the government as well as each other. Future research should adopt a much broader timeframe that covers all of these phases, allowing for an assessment of whether a secessionist movement is susceptible to different fragmentary forces in different "lifecycles" – i.e., *ante-, in-,* and *post-bellum*. Second, the rationalist orientation of much of the work surveyed in this chapter raises questions about how the identities and ideologies of groups shape these processes, particularly beyond the dominant frame of ethnonationalism. Despite exciting research on the gendered dimensions of civil war, for instance, there has been little work on the intersection of fragmentation processes and gendered ideologies and identities. Third, the existing literature is currently skewed towards the investigation of cases with a high degree of fragmentation, paying much less attention to cases that have avoided or overcome internal conflict. Future research should pay heed to those movements that have achieved (different forms of) cohesion in order to identify the causes and consequences of movement unity (c.f. Fliervoet, forthcoming) and different "pathways to militant consolidation" (Hafez et al. 2021). Finally, while fragmentation is justly regarded as a process generally detrimental to important outcomes in peace and security, and as a significant barrier to conflict resolution, cohesive groups and movements can lay the basis for authoritarian transitions that impede the sorts of political pluralism and vibrant civil societies conducive to democracy and human rights. Further research is needed on the relationship between patterns of wartime fragmentation and cohesion, on the one hand, and the post-conflict regimes instated by movements emerging from separatist conflicts.

# References

Abbs, L., Clayton, G. and Thomson, A. (2020) 'The ties that bind: Ethnicity, pro-government militia, and the dynamics of violence in civil war', *Journal of Conflict Resolution*, 64(5), pp. 903–932. doi: 10.1177/0022002719883684.

Ahmad, A. (2016) 'Going global: Islamist competition in contemporary civil wars', *Security Studies*, 25(2), pp. 353–384. doi: 10.1080/09636412.2016.1171971.

Akcinaroglu, S. (2012) 'Rebel interdependencies and civil war outcomes', *Journal of Conflict Resolution*, 56(5), pp. 879–903. doi: 10.1177/0022002712445741.

Albrecht, H. and Ohl, D. (2016) 'Exit, resistance, loyalty: Military behavior during unrest in authoritarian regimes', *Perspectives on Politics*, 14(1), pp. 38–52. doi: 10.1017/S1537592715003217.

Aliyev, H. and Souleimanov, E. A. (2019) 'Ethnicity and conflict severity: Accounting for the effect of co-ethnic and non-ethnic militias on battlefield lethality', *Third World Quarterly*, 40(3), pp. 471–487. doi: 10.1080/01436597.2018.1545568.

Asal, V., Brown, M. and Dalton, A. (2012) 'Why split? Organizational splits among ethnopolitical organizations in the Middle East', *Journal of Conflict Resolution*, 56(1), pp. 94–117. doi: 10.1177/0022002711429680.

Bakke, K. M. (2015) *Decentralization and intrastate struggles: Chechnya, Punjab, and Québec*. New York: Cambridge University Press.

Bakke, K. M., Cunningham, K. G. and Seymour, L. J. M. (2012) 'A plague of initials: Fragmentation, cohesion, and infighting in civil wars', *Perspectives on Politics*, 10(2), pp. 265–283. doi: 10.1017/s1537592712000667.

Biberman, Y. (2018) 'Self-defense militias, death squads, and state outsourcing of violence in India and Turkey', *Journal of Strategic Studies*. Routledge, 41(5), pp. 751–781. doi: 10.1080/01402390.2016.1202822.

Biong Deng, L. (2010) 'Social capital and civil war: The Dinka communities in Sudan's civil war', *African Affairs*, 109(435), pp. 231–250. doi: 10.1093/afraf/adq001.

Boutellis, A. and Zahar, M.-J. (2017) *A process in search of peace: Lessons from the inter-Malian agreement*. New York: International Peace Institute. Available at: www.ipinst.org/wp-content/uploads/2017/06/IPI-Rpt-Inter-Malian-AgreementFinalRev.pdf [Accessed 7/18/2021].

Braithwaite, J. M. and Cunningham, K. G. (2020) 'When organizations rebel: Introducing the foundations of rebel group emergence (FORGE) dataset', *International Studies Quarterly*, 64(1), pp. 183–193. doi: 10.1093/isq/sqz085.

Bramsen, I. (2018) 'How civil war succeeds (or not): Micro-dynamics of unity, timing, and escalatory actions', *Peace & Change*, 43(1), pp. 61–89. doi: 10.1111/pech.12274.

Brubaker, R. (2004) *Ethnicity without groups*. Cambridge, MA: Harvard University Press.

Burch, M. and Ochreiter, L. (2020) 'The emergence of splinter factions in intrastate conflict', *Dynamics of Asymmetric Conflict*, 13(1), pp. 47–66. doi: 10.1080/17467586.2019.1650385.

Campbell, D. (1998) *National deconstruction: Violence, identity, and justice in Bosnia*. Minneapolis: University of Minnesota Press.

Carey, S. C., Mitchell, N. J. and Lowe, W. (2013) 'States, the security sector, and the monopoly of violence: A new database on pro-government militias', *Journal of Peace Research*, 50(2), pp. 249–258. doi: 10.1177/0022343312464881.

Caspersen, N. (2011) 'Democracy, nationalism and (lack of) sovereignty: The complex dynamics of democratisation in unrecognised states', *Nations and Nationalism*, 17(2), pp. 337–356. doi: 10.1111/j.1469-8129.2010.00471.x.

Chenoweth, E., Pinckney, J. and Lewis, O. (2018) 'Days of rage: Introducing the NAVCO 3.0 dataset', *Journal of Peace Research*, 55(4), pp. 524–534. doi: 10.1177/0022343318759411.

Chenoweth, E. and Stephan, M. J. (2011) *Why civil resistance works: The strategic logic of nonviolent conflict*. New York: Columbia University Press.

Christia, F. (2012) *Alliance formation in civil wars*. New York: Cambridge University Press.

Cunningham, D. E. (2011) *Barriers to peace in civil war*. Cambridge: Cambridge University Press.

Cunningham, K. G. (2013) 'Actor fragmentation and civil war bargaining: How internal divisions generate civil conflict', *American Journal of Political Science*, 57(3), pp. 659–672. doi: 10.1111/ajps.12003.

Cunningham, K. G. (2014) *Inside the politics of self-determination*. New York: Oxford University Press.

Cunningham, K. G., Bakke, K. M. and Seymour, L. J. M. (2012) 'Shirts today, skins tomorrow: Dual contests and the effects of fragmentation in self-determination disputes', *Journal of Conflict Resolution*, 56(1), pp. 67–93. doi: 10.1177/0022002711429697.

de Waal, A. (2015) *The real politics of the Horn of Africa: Money, war and the business of power*. Cambridge: Polity Press.

Doctor, A. C. (2020) 'A motion of no confidence: Leadership and rebel fragmentation', *Journal of Global Security Studies*, 5(4), pp. 598–616. doi: 10.1093/jogss/ogz060.

Dowd, C. (2015) 'Actor proliferation and the fragmentation of violent groups in conflict', *Research and Politics*, 2(4). doi: 10.1177/2053168015607891.

Duursma, A. and Fliervoet, F. (2021) 'Fueling factionalism? The impact of peace processes on rebel group fragmentation in civil wars', *Journal of Conflict Resolution*, 65(4), pp. 788–812. doi: 10.1177/0022002720958062.

Dworschak, C. (2020) 'Jumping on the bandwagon: Differentiation and security defection during conflict', *Journal of Conflict Resolution*, 64(7–8), pp. 1335–1357. doi: 10.1177/0022002720904763.

Faulkner, C. M. and Doctor, A. C. (2021) 'Rebel fragmentation and the recruitment of child soldiers', *International Studies Quarterly*, 65(3), pp. 647–659. doi: 10.1093/isq/sqab031.

Fjelde, H. and Nilsson, D. (2018) 'The rise of rebel contenders: Barriers to entry and fragmentation in civil wars', *Journal of Peace Research*, 55(5), pp. 551–565. doi: 10.1177/0022343318767497.

Fliervoet, F. E. M. (forthcoming) *Friends or foes? Explaining cohesion in secessionist movements*. Ph.D. thesis, European University Institute.

Freeman, J. (1975) *The politics of women's liberation: A case study of an emerging social movement and its relation to the policy process*. New York: David McKay.

Gade, E. K., Gabbay, M., Hafez, M. M. and Kelly, Z. (2019) 'Networks of cooperation: Rebel alliances in fragmented civil wars', *Journal of Conflict Resolution*, 63(9), pp. 2071–2097. doi: 10.1177/0022002719826234.

Gade, E. K., Hafez, M. M. and Gabbay, M. (2019) 'Fratricide in rebel movements: A network analysis of Syrian militant infighting', *Journal of Peace Research*, 56(3), pp. 321–335. doi: 10.1177/0022343318806940.

Hafez, M. M. (2020) 'Fratricidal rebels: Ideological extremity and warring factionalism in civil wars', *Terrorism and Political Violence*, 32(3), pp. 604–629. doi: 10.1080/09546553.2017.1389726.

Hafez, M. M., Gade, E. K. and Gabbay, M. (2021) 'Consolidation of nonstate armed actors in fragmented conflicts: Introducing an emerging research program', *Studies in Conflict and Terrorism*, forthcoming. doi: https://doi.org/10.1080/1057610X.2021.2013751

Haines, H. H. (1988) *Black radicals and the civil rights mainstream, 1954–1970*. Knoxville: University of Tennessee Press.

Ives, B. (2021) 'Ethnic external support and rebel group splintering', *Terrorism and Political Violence*, 33(7), pp. 1546–1566. doi: 10.1080/09546553.2019.1636035.

Jenne, E. K. (2012) 'When will we part with partition theory? Flawed premises and improbable longevity of the theory of ethnic partition', *Ethnopolitics*, 11(3), pp. 255–267. doi: 10.1080/17449057.2011.587956.

Jentzsch, C., Kalyvas, S. N. and Schubiger, L. I. (2015) 'Militias in civil wars', *Journal of Conflict Resolution*, 59(5), pp. 755–769. doi: 10.1177/0022002715576753.

Kalyvas, S. N. (2008) 'Ethnic defection in civil war', *Comparative Political Studies*, 41(8), pp. 1043–1068. doi: 10.1177/0010414008317949.

Krause, P. (2017) *Rebel power: Why national movements compete, fight, and win*. Ithaca: Cornell University Press.

Lawrence, A. (2010) 'Triggering nationalist violence: Competition and conflict in uprisings against colonial rule', *International Security*, 35(2), pp. 88–122. doi: 10.1162/ISEC_a_00019.

Lustick, I. S. (1993) *Unsettled states, disputed lands: Britain and Ireland, France and Algeria, Israel and the West Bank-Gaza*. Ithaca: Cornell University Press.

Mahoney, C. W. (2017) 'Splinters and schisms: Rebel group fragmentation and the durability of insurgencies', *Terrorism and Political Violence*, 32(2), pp. 345–364. doi: 10.1080/09546553.2017.1374254.

McLauchlin, T. and Pearlman, W. (2012) 'Out-group conflict, in-group unity?: Exploring the effect of repression on intramovement cooperation', *Journal of Conflict Resolution*, 56(1), pp. 41–66. doi: 10.1177/0022002711429707.

Mosinger, E. S. (2018) 'Brothers or others in arms? Civilian constituencies and rebel fragmentation in civil war', *Journal of Peace Research*, 55(1), pp. 62–77. doi: 10.1177/0022343316675907.

Mosinger, E. S. (2019) 'Balance of loyalties: Explaining rebel factional struggles in the Nicaraguan revolution', *Security Studies*, 28(5), pp. 935–975. doi: 10.1080/09636412.2019.1662481.

Nagel, R. U. and Doctor, A. C. (2020) 'Conflict-related sexual violence and rebel group fragmentation', *Journal of Conflict Resolution*, 64(7–8), pp. 1226–1253. doi: 10.1177/0022002719899443.

Olson Lounsbery, M. (2016) 'Foreign military intervention, power dynamics, and rebel group cohesion', *Journal of Global Security Studies*, 1(2), pp. 127–141. doi: 10.1093/jogss/ogw004.

Olson Lounsbery, M. and Cook, A. H. (2011) 'Rebellion, mediation, and group change: An empirical investigation of competing hypotheses', *Journal of Peace Research*, 48(1), pp. 73–84. doi: 10.1177/0022343310390256.

Otto, S. (2018) 'The grass is always greener? Armed group side switching in civil wars', *Journal of Conflict Resolution*. doi: 10.1177/0022002717693047.

Pearlman, W. (2009) 'Spoiling inside and out: Internal political contestation and the Middle East peace process', *International Security*, 33(3), pp. 79–109. doi: 10.1162/isec.2009.33.3.79.

Perkoski, E. (2019) 'Internal politics and the fragmentation of armed groups', *International Studies Quarterly*, 63(4), pp. 876–889. doi: 10.1093/isq/sqz076.

Phillips, B. J. (2015) 'Enemies with benefits? Violent rivalry and terrorist group longevity', *Journal of Peace Research*, 52(1), pp. 62–75. doi: 10.1177/0022343314550538.

Pischedda, C. (2018) 'Wars within wars: Why windows of opportunity and vulnerability cause inter-rebel fighting in internal conflicts', *International Security*, 43(1), pp. 138–176. doi: 10.1162/isec_a_00322.

Pischedda, C. (2020) *Conflict among rebels: Why insurgent groups fight each other.* New York: Columbia University Press.

Rudloff, P. and Findley, M. G. (2016) 'The downstream effects of combatant fragmentation on civil war recurrence', *Journal of Peace Research*, 53(1), pp. 19–32. doi: 10.1177/0022343315617067.

Schulhofer-Wohl, J. (2020) 'On-side fighting in civil war: The logic of mortal alignment in Syria', *Rationality and Society*, 32(4), pp. 402–460. doi: 10.1177/1043463120966989.

Seymour, L. J. M. (2014) 'Why factions switch sides in civil wars: Rivalry, patronage, and realignment in Sudan', *International Security*, 39(2), pp. 92–131. doi: 10.1162/ISEC_a_00179.

Seymour, L. J. M., Bakke, K. M. and Cunningham, K. G. (2016) 'E pluribus unum, ex uno plures: Competition, violence, and fragmentation in ethnopolitical movements', *Journal of Peace Research*, 53(1), pp. 3–18. doi: 10.1177/0022343315605571.

Spruyt, H. (2005) *Ending empire: Contested sovereignty and territorial partition.* Ithaca: Cornell University Press.

Staniland, P. (2012a) 'Between a rock and a hard place: Insurgent fratricide, ethnic defection, and the rise of pro-state paramilitaries', *Journal of Conflict Resolution*, 56(1), pp. 16–40. doi: 10.1177/0022002711429681.

Staniland, P. (2012b) 'Organizing insurgency: Networks, resources, and rebellion in South Asia', *International Security*, 37(1), pp. 142–177. doi: 10.1162/ISEC_a_00091.

Staniland, P. (2014) *Networks of rebellion: Explaining insurgent cohesion and collapse.* Ithaca: Cornell University Press.

Stedman, S. J. (1997) 'Spoiler problems in peace processes', *International Security*, 22(2), pp. 5–53.

Tamm, H. (2016) 'Rebel leaders, internal rivals, and external resources: How state sponsors affect insurgent cohesion', *International Studies Quarterly*, 60(4), pp. 599–610. doi: 10.1093/isq/sqw033.

Tamm, H. (2019) 'In the balance: External troop support and rebel fragmentation in the Second Congo War', *Journal of Strategic Studies*. doi: 10.1080/01402390.2019.1701442.

Vogt, M., Gleditsch, K. S. and Cederman, L.-E. (2021) 'From claims to violence: Signaling, outbidding, and escalation in ethnic conflict', *Journal of Conflict Resolution*, 65(7–8), pp. 1278–1307. doi: 10.1177/0022002721996436.

Walter, B. F. (2017) 'The new new civil wars', *Annual Review of Political Science*, 20(1), pp. 469–486. doi: 10.1146/annurev-polisci-060415-093921.

Walther, O. J. and Pedersen, P. S. (2020) 'Rebel fragmentation in Syria's civil war', *Small Wars and Insurgencies*, 31(3), pp. 445–474. doi: 10.1080/09592318.2020.1726566.

Woldemariam, M. (2016) 'Battlefield outcomes and rebel cohesion: Lessons from the Eritrean independence war', *Terrorism and Political Violence*, 28(1), pp. 135–156. doi: 10.1080/09546553.2014.886575.

Woldemariam, M. (2018) *Insurgent fragmentation in the Horn of Africa: Rebellion and its discontents.* Cambridge: Cambridge University Press.

# 13

# GEOPOLITICS OF SECESSION

## Secession in the international setting

*Martin Riegl and Bohumil Doboš**

## Introduction

What determines the outcome of attempted (non-consensual) secessions? How do the members of the international community respond to secession? Why do some entities achieve international recognition while the majority are crushed by central governments? "Why are some entities recognized as states while others not?" (Stokes 2019, p. 102).

This chapter aims to explore the role of geopolitical factors in the outcomes of non-consensual secessionist bids in the post-1945 environment. It argues that the outcomes have been decided by international politics (Horowitz 1985), which has thus far failed to develop clear procedural rules for resolving secessions (Rich 1993). While conventional wisdom, largely based on the norms of territorial integrity and non-intervention, postulates external players to refrain from supporting centrifugal tendencies in other states, practical politics tells a different story.

We present a geopolitical pattern explaining why some entities win the status of independent statehood, and other entities' campaigns fall by the wayside. We argue that the outcome of secession is framed within a geopolitical pattern determined by a combination of the geopolitical process of secession, principles of international law, right of self-determination, and territorial integrity (McConnell 2009, p. 344). Today, the principle of external self-determination is granted only to entities still bound by a colonial regime, reflecting the shift of self-determination from a negative right to a positive one as observed by M. Fabry (2010). Exceptions to this general principle are the cases of separation based on mutual agreement, residual non-self-governing territories, selective cases of remedial secession, and, potentially, occupations, as mentioned by M. Sterio (2013).

Secessionist bids occur largely in unfavorable strategic environments and must struggle to gain any recognition from generally unwilling members of the international community. Subject as they are to these conditions, secessionists are forced to operate in the context of external players' involvement. Thus, secessionist entities possess limited room for maneuver in their attempts to win relevant external support, especially that of greater powers better able to shape the de facto and de jure outcome of secession.

DOI: 10.4324/9781003036593-16

# Unilateral secession and its international recognition: variety of approaches

> Throughout much of the Cold War, therefore, it was taken as a given that unilateral acts of secession were ultimately destined to failure. The almost complete absence of any successful act of unilateral secession appeared to make the subject of secession and recognition a relatively uninteresting subject of investigation for most IR scholars . . . The end of the Cold War, and the collapse of the Soviet Union and Yugoslavia, inevitably reignited interest in the issue of secession and state dissolution.
>
> *(Ker-Lindsay 2017, pp. 2–3)*

Later, the unilateral secession of Kosovo and members of the international community's response in 2008 attracted enormous scholarly attention (Berg 2009; Geldenhuys 2009; Fabry 2010; Sterio 2010; Christakis 2011; Sakwa and Pavković 2011; Economides 2013; Wolf and Rodt 2013; Fazal and Griffiths 2014; Griffiths 2016; Buzard et al. 2017). L. De Vries et al. (2019) focused on the specific logic of secession in Africa, S. Pegg and E. Berg (2016) analyzed diplomatic channels between the United States and Abkhazia, Nagorno-Karabakh, TRNC, and Somaliland. Similarly, A. Cooley and L. A. Mitchell (2010) wrote on US engagement with Abkhazia. J. Ker-Lindsay (2015) presented a valuable theoretical study showing that extensive engagement does not signify recognition and that the intent is crucial.

E. Berg and R. Toomla (2009) analyzed Taiwan and Kosovo's engagement with the UN members. J. K. Lindsay (2017) published a fascinating in-depth study of back-room negotiations in the context of TRNC's quest for recognition. Since then, other interesting publications on the recognition of states, historical relations between secession and recognition, systemic changes and the role of external players, have emerged (Malešević and Ó Dochartaigh 2011; Berg 2009; Geldenhuys 2009; Fabry 2010; Sterio 2010, 2013; Christakis 2011; Coggins 2011; Pavković and Radan 2011; Berg and Mölder 2012; Economides 2013; Wolf and Rodt 2013; Fazal and Griffiths 2014; Fazal and Griffiths 2014; Griffiths 2016; Ker-Lindsay 2017; Riegl and Doboš 2018; Newman and Visoka 2018; Fabry 2020; Newman 2020; Sterio 2020).

T. M. Fazal and R. D. Griffiths (2014) presented a systemic explanation of the increasing number of secessionist bids, and R. D. Griffiths (2016: 5, 11) presented a theory predicting governmental responses to independence quests and the emergence of secessionist conflicts. As pointed out by J. Ker-Lindsay and E. Berg (2018), the role of major powers (geopolitics) in the process of international recognition is now receiving wider scholarly attention (see also Coggins 2014; Ker-Lindsay 2017, 2018; Riegl and Doboš 2018), including the evolution of international norms regarding recognition over the past centuries (Fabry 2010). Furthermore, the body of literature on the strategic aspects of secession is growing (Coggins 2014; Fazal and Griffiths 2014). The pertaining problem is that there is no single theory that offers a universal explanation for all secessions (Pavković and Radan 2007, p. 191).

## Types of fragmentation

The political map is shaped by both centripetal and centrifugal forces. The global political space reached the point of greatest aggregation (in terms of number of sovereign states) in 1912 (Griffiths 2016, pp. 1–2) and has, over the course of the intervening century, fragmented in a gradual but relentless fashion. The UN members' approach to the varying forms of non-consensual disintegration has differed wildly over the years, with its responses to secession lacking consistency.

As such, it is of the utmost importance to examine the terminological and definitional debate and understand how the nuances affect the study of the phenomena.

The fragmentation of political space can take several forms, each with important political, legal, or security consequences. In this context, the precise form of political fragmentation plays an essential role in shaping the international community's willingness to accept the quest as legitimate. As R. D. Griffiths (2016, p. 6) argues: "labels such as 'decolonization' and dissolution [are] primarily legal ones used to sort out which secessionist movements have the right to independence". The practical implications of this are paramount for secessionist entities, as the categorization of political fragmentation as secession, irredenta, expulsion, dissolution, anti-colonial secession largely determines the international community's approach.

While voluntary integrative processes are perceived, by and large, as a positive phenomenon, the same cannot be said of non-consensual political fragmentation which is usually cast in a poor light. Even the agreed-upon dissolution of Czechoslovakia was a source of major security concern (of potential violent escalation) in Europe. However, the engines of political disintegration are not a homogenous set of processes.

While the process of decolonization enjoyed the active support of the UN members, various authors have disagreed on the distinction between decolonization and secession (or dissolution). For R. D. Griffiths and L. M. Wasser (2018, p. 5) decolonization and dissolution both fall under the category of secession, B. Coggins (2014, p. 65) differentiates secession from decolonization when the central government consents to or even actively enforces the process; otherwise, she speaks about anti-colonial secession. P. Rosůlek (2014, pp. 32–33) introduced an innovative term, "secession through decolonization". However, most authors make a clear distinction between two processes (Graham and Horne 2012, p. 6). A. Pavković and P. Radan (2007, p. 2; 2011, p. 2), and A. Pavković (2020, p. 162) argue that territories under the colonial regime do not encompass an integral territory of the metropolitan and possess differing population characteristics, though they share a similar end goal – the creation of new states. Sometimes Micronesia, Marshall Islands, and Palau are wrongly categorized as freely associated states in line with A/RES/1541 (e.g., Rezwani 2016), which is the result of a semantic resemblance and a failure to comprehend the international-legal status of these Pacific states.

Outside the bounds of decolonization, the wider anti-secessionist attitude of the international community has become a kind of conventional wisdom, but there are several other identifiable types of non-consensual political fragmentation – secession violating self-determination and secession outside of decolonization (Crawford 2006). The latter situation represents the most common category and possesses important geopolitical consequences for movements attempting to achieve new independent statehood and is not satisfactorily regulated by international law (Sterio 2015, p. 305). While the declaration of independence by the South African Bantustans (Bophuthatswana, Ciskei, Transkei, and Venda) was fiercely opposed by the UN members, the expulsion – by some authors considered as the situation of negotiated secession (e.g., Chou 2011) – of Singapore was internationally accepted and, likewise, cases of partition are generally rather unproblematic in the eyes of the members of international community (Geldenhuys 2009, p. 36). The post–Cold War disintegration of multi-ethnic empires brought to discussion terms such as dissolution, disintegration, or multiple secession. Conversely, the debate on partitioning attracted only a little scholarly attention.

## Self-determination and secession

According to J. Crawford (2006, pp. 415, 417), there is no recognition of a unilateral right to secede. The two geopolitical processes of decolonization and secession (McConnell 2009) are closely linked with the principles of self-determination and territorial integrity. Historically, both geopolitical processes profoundly transformed the political map of the world. While secession was "the most common way for creation of new states prior to 1914" (Crawford 2006, p. 375), since 1945 the most common way of state creation has been through the process of decolonization – "a total of 96 new states has been created as a result of the process" (Christopher 2002, p. 213). When considering these processes, neither can be empirically analyzed separately from the principle of self-determination. While the eradication of colonialism is understood as a fundamental agenda and goal of the UN, self-determination has served as its guiding conceptual framework (Castellino 2011, p. 117). The often stark dichotomy between the legal principles of self-determination and territorial integrity has often led to conceptual confusion (Castellino 2011, p. 119).

E. Berg (2009, p. 223) rightly noted that much of the confusion surrounding the notion of self-determination is a reflection of the lack of consensus as to whether it is a political principle or a legal right. While the concept of self-determination was designed to provide a conceptual framework of independence for territories under the colonial regime, it continues to be an important source of legitimization in the strategies of secessionists. Similarly, to many national liberation movements, self-determination appeals are one of the sharpest items in their legitimacy strategies toolbox, alongside claims of oppression, effective statehood, and historical traditions of statehood (see Lynch 2004). "While international law embraces the right to self-determination for all people, and while this right can effectively translate into remedial secession, international law positively allows for this outcome only in the case of decolonization and, perhaps, occupation" (Sterio 2015, p. 299).

The inherent conflict between self-determination and territorial integrity has an important geopolitical dimension, as secession is the most common (14 out of 26) form of political fragmentation resulting in the creation of contested states (unrecognized entities) (Geldenhuys 2009, p. 293). The empirical practice shows that since the 1950s, the implementation of the principle of territorial integrity has almost universally prevailed over the principle of self-determination, with the notable exception of the decolonization process (Fabry 2020, p. 42). Nonetheless, this, as observed by A. Pavković, has not prevented the appearance of violent conflicts. According to him, non-consensual secession presents a breach of the territorial integrity and can result into an intra-state conflict when armed forces are deployed (Pavković 2020, p. 161).

As discussed by G. Visoka et al. (2020, p. 3) neither international law nor world politics provides the regulative rules or institutional mechanisms to standardize the practice of state recognition despite its crucial role in shaping world politics. As the result,

> [a]ll separatist movements operate, expand or shrink in a given and changing geopolitical context. One has to look at geopolitics to understand why some political entities become independent states while others of the same size and importance do not. It is geopolitics that helps us to explain why some secessionist movements are tolerated and others violently crushed.
>
> *(Malešević and Ó Dochartaigh 2011, p. 232)*

Also, for M. Sterio (2013, p. 66), geopolitical interests, particularly those of the great powers, consistently prevail over international norms.

> [T]he great powers (being) supportive of East Timor, Kosovo, and South Sudan, and not of Chechnya, the Georgian provinces, or Tibet? One plausible explanation, albeit

cynical one, is that the great powers seem intent on helping groups, movements, and states when it is in their own geopolitical interest to do so.

*(Sterio 2013, p. 66).*

It is a widely accepted belief that the international community favors the principle of territorial integrity over that of self-determination in order to preserve its stability, thereby denying would-be states the right to secession (Summers 2020, p. 133). However, such a reading lacks depth, and greater insight into the nuances surrounding the members of the international community's dealing with the various forms of secession is needed. The territories under the colonial regime (secession in compliance with self-determination) frequently enjoyed the active diplomatic support of the UN member states – from regional bodies and the UN. Thus, it can be argued, the colonial territories operated in a strategically favorable environment (Griffiths and Wasser 2018, p. 8). Even if the colonial power put a stop to any attempts to exercise self-determination, these territories found willing external support in their quest for independence even in cases where they failed to meet the criteria of de facto statehood (Crawford 2006, pp. 383–384). Resolution 1514 marked the beginning of a transformative era in the geopolitical order, and its prohibition of any disruption of the territorial integrity of ex-colonies represented a major geopolitical restructuring of the political space (Fabry 2011, p. 258). However, despite this, it was not a coherently applied practice, and several violations of this rule can be identified in the post-1945 world. This was especially true when independence ambitions clashed with geostrategic interests, both direct and indirect, of the great powers. Unfortunate entities that found themselves within this strategic environment often quickly discovered that it was not beneficial to their quests for independence.

The British Princely States, Eritrea, Western Sahara, and East Timor are just some examples of would-be states that found themselves caught in the tides of unfavorable strategic situations. M. J. Peterson (2020, p. 211) analyzed four situations, both voluntary and involuntary, when territories under the colonial regime failed to obtain independence within their colonial borders:

1   The incorporation of small colonies into a larger state with a plausible historical claim to their territory (Goa).
2   The merger of two separate colonies into a single new state (Togo, Somalia).
3   The division of one large colony into two states (the British Raj).
4   The voluntary continuation of a dependent relationship with a larger state by the population of a small colony which is, for example, the case of New Caledonia.

Territories and populations under the colonial regime failed to achieve their desired status when: (1) substantial external control over a strategically positioned and important would-be state was at stake – Anguilla; (2) the metropole opted to integrate a territory into its administrative system – Mayotte; (3) decolonization would have led to extreme fragmentation – as in the case of the Princely states of British India; and (4) there was an involuntary takeover by stronger state, usually a neighbor, such as Eritrea, East Timor (Christopher 2002, pp. 213–218).

Contrary to the territories under the colonial regime pursuing secession in accordance with the principle of self-determination, secession from a colonial power could equally be seen to violate the principle of self-determination, as was the case with Rhodesia, whereupon a far less favorable strategic environment would manifest itself. The same logic can be applied to cases of expulsion that violated the principle of self-determination (South African Bantustans) in the eyes of the members of the international community. J. Crawford (2006, pp. 384–388) in this respect differentiates between three situations linked to the relation of secession and self-determination:

(1) secession in furtherance of self-determination; (2) secession in violation of self-determination, as in the case of Rhodesia; and (3) secession outside the colonial context. Similarly, entities described by Ivanel 2015) as puppet states – including the State of Manchukuo, the Turkish Republic of Northern Cyprus, Abkhazia, South Ossetia, Donetsk, and Luhansk People's Republic – are approached by the members of the international community as illegitimate since their externally driven nature represents a breach of international norms.

As noted by A. Heraclides (1991), the members of the international community approach cases which can be defined as partition in a different manner to secession, although there is no clear line of division between the two. The partition of entities that merged voluntarily exist in a sort of international legal limbo since the entities lost or consumed their right to self-determination (e.g., the mergers of Somaliland with Somalia, Zanzibar with Tanganyika, and Gambia with Senegal). Nevertheless, in these cases the international community showed little of the reluctance they demonstrated in the cases of secession occurring in violation of self-determination or outside the context of decolonization. This was largely due to the difference between partition and secession being profound (consensual dismemberment versus non-consensual departure); in the case of a partition, granting international recognition to the new state is usually unproblematic (Geldenhuys 2009, p. 36).

Contrary to the experiences had by those would-be states created by less acceptable processes, entities born as result of dissolution encountered a more "constructive approach" from the members of the international community. C. Laoutides (2020, p. 65) argues that the UN members treated entities born out of the disintegration of the USSR and the SFRY as acts of decolonization in order to balance strategic interests and normative landscape. According to R. D. Griffiths (2020, p. 141) dissolution was an innovative approach and legal solution devised to conceptually distinguish the situation in the USSR and the SFRY from unilateral secessions. Laoutides's argument helps to explain why these entities achieved full recognition and the UN membership, while the vast majority of unilateral secessions failed to achieve their desired goal. As noted, for as long as there is no universal mechanism to reconcile the UN principles of territorial integrity and self-determination, secessionist conflicts are destined to be governed by geopolitical expediency (Sakwa and Pavković 2011, p. 155).

The broadest range of entities, and the most heterogenous in terms of their internal characteristics and in terms of the external diplomatic support they are offered, fall into the category of non-consensual (unilateral) secession, which in only the most exceptional circumstances attained international recognition. This suggests the existence of the anti-secessionist regime (McGarry 2004; Crawford 2006; Berg 2009, p. 224), established during the Cold War, which precluded successful secessionist activities especially in the core areas of the geostrategic realms. Though some authors indicate its easing (Huliaras 2002, p. 157) in the post–Cold War geopolitical restructuring (with the entry of more than 20 new entities into the system of states), a primary interest of the members of the international community is still the prevention of the fragmentation of the political space (Berg 2009; Fabry 2012; Ker-Lindsay 2013; Caspersen 2015). Indeed, for J. Crawford (2006, pp. 415, 417), rather than the weakening in the post–Cold War era, the practice has instead been reinforced.

We can observe a clear continuity between the Cold War and post–Cold War strategic environment, as codified in several documents including the 1975 Helsinki Final Act, the 1990 Charter of Paris, and the 1990 Copenhagen Document, that reveals a continuation of the practices of the colonial period that have thus far inhibited secession (Fabry 2011, p. 257).

The UN and regional bodies clearly support the territorial integrity of their members over the principle of self-determination outside the process of decolonization. "The UN has never accepted and does not accept, and I do not believe will ever accept, the principle of secession of a part of its Member State" (U Thant 1970). As stated by B. Coggins (2011, p. 39), "little has changed in the UN's approach to secessionism in the last 60 years. The UN has consistently maintained that the right to self-determination does not imply a right to secession". However, in spite of this, it is possible to empirically observe important nuances in the UN member's approach to post-1945 unilateral declarations of entities which can be generally categorized as secessions.

## Types and levels of external involvement

To understand the geopolitical logic of unilateral secession, an assessment of the role played by external actors in their provision of both political diplomatic and tangible support to both sides is essential. This support can be driven by a variety of different interests (ideological, strategic, etc.) (see Jackson and Rosberg 1982; Saideman 1997, 2001; Bélanger et al. 2005; Paquin 2010; Fazal and Griffiths 2014). While the supply of tangible external support is a relatively common practice, high-level political diplomatic support (international recognition) is a far rarer phenomenon (Paquin 2010, pp. 8, 27–28). The role played by geopolitics in determining the level of external support an entity receives has attracted increasing amounts of scholarly attention in recent years. M. Fabry (2011, p. 252) and B. Coggins (2011, pp. 38, 2014) researched the role of third parties' involvement in secessionist conflicts. M. Sterio (2013), R. D. Griffiths (2016), and J. Ker-Lindsay (2017) have emphasized the role of great powers (sometimes called "superpowers" by the authors). M. Sterio (2013) defined four criteria that are the precondition of any successful self-determination: (1) That the entity has suffered heinous human rights abuses; (2) the central government of its parent state is relatively weak; (3) the international community has already become involved through some kind of international administration of the secessionist territory; and (4) that it enjoys the support of most of the great powers. However, in the eyes of, J. Ker-Lindsay (2017, p. 8) the academic literature on this topic still remains rather limited.

A. Heraclides (1990, 1991) analyzed the types (tangible and political-diplomatic) and levels (escalation ladder) of external support in secessionist conflicts. To analyze the international community's approach, a modified version of Heraclides's (1990, p. 368) model concerning the types and levels of tangible and political-diplomatic support was applied. It includes:

1   High-level tangible support (ranging from the provision of arms to direct military involvement and inter-state war).
2   Limited tangible support, including (a) medium-level tangible support (extended non-military forms of involvement), and (b) low-level tangible support (such as humanitarian involvement).
3   High-level political–diplomatic recognition (international recognition);
4   Limited political-diplomatic support, sub-divided into (a) medium-level political-diplomatic support (assertions that that the breakaway entity has a right for self-determination, or veto on a UN SC resolution), and (b) low-level political-diplomatic support (such as expressions of concern regarding the conflict).

## The involvement of the external parties: an overview

The secessionist dreams of independence continue to be a major source of political disputes, tensions, and armed conflicts based on the unresolved tensions between the two opposed principles of self-determination and territorial integrity. As a result of the international community's failure to find a common approach for handling secessionist claims, the door has been left open for external players to use cases of secession to pursue their own geostrategic interests, often based on subjective normative justifications. A dataset of 89 cases of non-consensual secessions taking place between 1946 and 2019 was identified by one of the authors of this chapter. The dataset includes cases which can also be classified as irredenta (South Ossetia), expulsion (South African Bantustans), and dissolution (SFRY).

The interests of third parties behind the provision of either political-diplomatic and/or tangible support to secessionist entities (but also to the central governments) are diverse in nature but can be generally classified as either strategic, ideological, economic, or domestic within the various geopolitical contexts of the twentieth century i.e., World War II, the Cold War, the decolonization process, and other, more specific regional contexts.

Thus, external assistance provided both to secessionist entities and those central governments facing the breakaway elements reflected the interests and calculations of players, both local and far-off, reaching across the world regions and spanning different geopolitical contexts.

Some secessionist entities such as Rwenzururu United Kingdom in Uganda or Free State of Caprivi Strip in Namibia were suppressed without any external engagement. Other secessions were characterized by activities of a single actor pursuing their interests in the region such as in the case of the United Suvadive Republic, whose fate was dictated by the UK's geopolitical interests in the Indian Ocean; or the Union Island who found themselves a pawn in Barbados' aims to boost the Caribbean Commonwealth (McIntyre 1991, p. 142). Likewise, the Second East Turkestan Republic (Patrick 2010) and Mahabad (Koohi-Kamali 2003; Roosevelt 1947; Edmonds 1971) both became tools used by the Soviet government, in the first case with the aim of weakening an ideologically hostile government in China and in the latter to gather influence in the Middle Eastern region.

However, many other cases of secession were not single-player events and developed into sources of major world tension as the incompatible goals of a multitude of regional and global actors clashed. For example, by supporting the geostrategically important South Sudan, situated as it was close to the Red Sea, Israel aimed to weaken an ally of Egypt, while Iraq supported the Sudanese central government due to their joint chemical weapon production efforts.

In Katanga, the external actors providing political-diplomatic as well as tangible support were driven by a wide range of concerns and interests. Belgium's support was driven by its economic interests and the presence of Belgian settlers. France, on the other hand, feared that a precedent would be set for a potential UN intervention in Algeria though its own economic interests undoubtedly also played a role (Heraclides 1991, p. 72). Belgium, initially the key provider of materiel assistance for the Katanga secessionists, was later replaced by France, which provided arms, rockets, combat aircraft, and mercenary recruitment from a base in Brazzaville. Furthermore, France permitted Katangese to use airspace in Equatorial Africa, represented Katangese interests at the UN by condemning the UN involvement, or refused to pay for the UN's Congo operation. A significant amount of tangible support (money, arms, advisors) was provided by the Federation of Nyasaland and Rhodesia, fearing a threat of communism and international isolation. The UK also played an important role, which under H. Macmillan's government abstained or vetoed crucial UN resolutions and, even more importantly, allowed Sir Roy Wellensky (the Prime Minister of the Federation of Rhodesia and Nyasaland) to provide, in his own words, all necessary and legally possible support. Sir Wellensky was motivated largely by the strategic threat posed by the potential fall of key areas of Africa into the communist sphere of influence, racial "solidarity", and, more importantly, by the psychological state of a shared siege mentality with Katanga. However, he did not get the British government's approval to deploy troops from the British-ruled Central African Federation. Also, the decision of the South African government to provide tangible as well as diplomatic support, for example through noncompliance with the UN embargo on copper, was driven by the fear of a regional domino effect. Portugal assisted Katanga by allowing the export of arms, recruitment of mercenaries, purchase of aircraft via Portuguese Angola, and the export of copper through Angola; denied overflight rights to the UN planes; and rejected the stationing of the UN observers. Some conservative African states were sympathetic towards Katanga – namely Malagashy Republic, Cameroon, the Central African Republic (CAR), Ivory Coast, Niger, and Tunisia. Germany, Luxembourg, and Israel supplied Katanga with a limited amount of arms, while Italy and Greece, due to their settler populations, also voiced limited diplomatic support (Crowley 1963, p. 68; Heraclides 1991, pp. 64–65, 69–78; Saideman 1997, p. 732; Crawford 2006, p. 406; Villafana 2012, p. 54; Larmer and Kennes 2019, p. 372).

In Eritrea, the Communist Bloc's assistance to the entity was firstly provided in the context of their anti-Americanism (US support to the Haile Selassie regime) and anti-Zionism (attempt to stretch Muslim control over the whole of the Red Sea) conjoined with the prospect of garnering strategic influence in the region. The USSR strove to penetrate into the region and to secure access to warm seas first by support to Eritrea and Somalia, and later to Ethiopia's territorial integrity following the coup by the leftist Derg, led by Mengistu Haile Mariam. Israel's involvement, on the contrary, was predicated on a desire to prevent Muslim countries from dominating the Red Sea region (Heraclides 1991; Yohannes 1991).

On the other side, external support for the central government in Ethiopia clearly followed the logic of Cold War relations. Prior to the 1974 coup, the United States recognized the strategic importance of the Horn of Africa and supported efforts to secure Ethiopian access to the sea, so as to counter the dominance of potentially hostile Arab regimes over the Red Sea. The UK involved itself in order to maintain strategic dominance in the Mediterranean and Red Seas and presented a plan to divide the territory between Ethiopia and Sudan (Tesfagiorgios 2011, p. 61). France's opposition to Eritrea's independence was based on fears about the nationalist awakening in its colonies (Yohannes 1991).

In the post–Cold War period, external support has been also characterized by its geopolitical interests, no matter which official justifications have been presented. External support granted to secessionist entities in the Caucasus should be understood within a complex geopolitical web involving not only the crude resources in the Caspian basin and the related infrastructure projects, but also Russia's overarching strategy to counter the enlargement of NATO. In Moldova, the Pridnestrovian Moldavian Republic helps to separate the geopolitical space of the eastern Slavic world from the enlarging NATO and EU by destabilizing Moldova and potentially Ukraine if needed as well. The entity's existence would allow Russia to exert pressure on Ukraine's southern flank if needed, so in essence the conflict and the continued survival of Transnistria is largely at Russia's geopolitical convenience as it controls the entity via economic and military means (Bencic and Hodor 2011, pp. 411–413). An analysis of such cases confirms the observations of S. Malesević and N. Ó Dochartaigh (2011, p. 231) that it is the geopolitical context that decides which secessionist entities manage to win independence or at least manage *de facto* separation from its parent entity.

## Normative frameworks for recognition, inconsistently applied

Strong external support for the right to external self-determination within the decolonization process has been nowhere near universal. One case in point is Western Sahara (Sahrawi Arab Democratic Republic). The entity was formally decolonized in the wake of Spain's retreat in 1975 but was almost simultaneously conquered by Moroccan and Mauritanian troops. While Mauritania withdrew its forces in 1979, Morocco has remained in the territory until the present day. Morocco has been targeted by the Sahrawi insurgency group Polisario, which fights for the independence of Western Sahara. However, as it was an important NATO ally, Morocco was supported throughout the Cold War by its Western allies, an unsurprising fact given that Polisario was a leftist, Soviet-backed organization (Mundy 2009; Novais 2009). The support continued in the post–Cold War era and, in spite of plausible self-determination (decolonization) claims by the Sahrawi authorities, Morocco showed no inclination to abandon the West Saharan territory (see Mundy 2009; Zunes and Mundy 2010; Riegl and Doboš 2017).

An interesting case combining the normative and geopolitical dimensions is the comparison between the differing levels of international recognition received by Kosovo and Abkhazia. Both of these entities were established through a unilateral secession backed by an external patron. In the first case, the patron was the United States; in the second, Russia. Both entities achieved a state of *de facto* independence from their parent states – Serbia and Georgia – in the 1990s and firstly secured some form of limited international recognition in 2008. Nonetheless, as of March 2021, Kosovo enjoys the recognition of 98 states, Abkhazia by only 5 countries, and 6 if we generously interpret the stance of Vanuatu.

The greater willingness of the UN members to accept Kosovan statehood is rooted in normative arguments, as unlike Abkhazia, it is not widely perceived as a puppet state (Ivanel 2015: 46–47). One needs to note also that the United States has been able to mobilize many more states to recognize Kosovo as a result of its much greater alliance-building capacity compared to that of Russia. Thus, while both demonstrated the capacity to successfully intervene and ensure the *de facto* independence of the entities, formally parts of Serbia and Georgia, respectively, their ability to win international recognition for the fledgling states has differed greatly (Doboš and Riegl 2020).

A similar distinction has been visible in the international approach to the dissolution of federations. On the one hand, we can identify the dissolution of the Socialist Federative Republic of Yugoslavia in the first half of the 1990s. While opposed by the central government, in the end, based on the European Community's and the United States' reading of the situation, the dissolution was accepted with new countries of the Western Balkans becoming fully recognized and entering the UN (Rich 1993). Despite occurring roughly concurrently, the dissolution of the Somali Federation was never internationally accepted. Despite the voluntary merger of former British and Italian Somalia following decolonization in 1960 and Somaliland's 1991 unilateral decision to leave the entity, such a move was not accepted by either the UN or the African Union (Lewis 2011; Hoehne 2019). Given the greater importance of the Western Balkans to the global powers compared to the Horn of Africa, the Somali conflict was ignored rather than solved even though the principle of dissolution was applicable in both situations. Thus, we can identify different approaches to normatively analogous processes related to the specific type of fragmentation that favors one outcome over another, leading to different outcomes of otherwise conceptually similar processes.

## Conclusion

Based on our research, there are 89 post-1945 secessionist entities – a dataset that includes the breakaway entities (secession, irredenta, expulsion, dissolution) seeking independence (by detaching part of the territory), militarily opposed by the central government and/or by member(s) of the United Nations in the period between 1946 and 2019. Out of that list, 20 achieved full recognition and UN membership, 56 entities did not receive any recognition, 6 of them were breakaway entities (4 cases of expulsion, 2 unilateral secessions) that achieved patron recognition only, and 2 of them achieved wider international recognition. Twenty-seven seceded entities failed to win recognition (high-level diplomatic support) but enjoyed limited (medium or low-level) political-diplomatic support. Eighteen entities received medium and 9 entities low-level political diplomatic support, while 31 entities received no diplomatic support at all. To measure the level of recognition, the following classification is applied: none (0), patron (1), limited (up to 10), wide (more than 10 but not sufficient to qualify for UN membership), full (sufficient for UN admission). However, the absence of political-diplomatic support from the international community's members does not mean that the same members will not aid secessionist entities by providing tangible support. A total of 33 secessionist entities were provided high-level tangible support, an additional 7 entities received limited tangible support (medium tangible support in case of 3 entities and 4 entities received low-level tangible support).

To correctly understand the international community member's approach, it is necessary to consider the "sub-categories" of unilateral secession. Of the secessionist entities, 37% achieved high-level diplomatic support, and the same percentage received tangible support. Out of 89 secessionist entities, 20 achieved UN membership (22.5%), but when cases of dissolution are excluded, the number is only 2 (2.25%). In this context, C. Laoutides's (2020, p. 65) interpretation of the international community's treatment of entities born out of the disintegration of the USSR and the SFRY as acts of *de facto* decolonization in order to balance strategic interests and the normative landscape seems like an accurate assessment. In a similar way R. D. Griffiths (2020: 141) perceives dissolution as an innovative approach allowing to make a conceptual distinction between the situation in the USSR and the SFRY from unilateral secessions.

This chapter's analysis suggests a geopolitical pattern based on the combination of geopolitical processes, principles of international law, and geopolitical interests of external players. While the success of a secessionist attempt depends greatly on the type of secession (for example, dissolution or simple unilateral secession), it cannot be said that the members of the international community would follow any norms, legal or otherwise, in all instances. In general, the treatment of any secession as an act of decolonization engenders a more favorable strategic context compared to that of unilateral secession. This helps us to understand the logic of the general approach to independence quests and thus the strategic environment in which secessionist entities operate. Additionally, this general geopolitical pattern must be framed within the larger geopolitical context, combining the strategic relevance of secessionist entity to external players and their ability and willingness to assert their interests, which largely shape the outcome of secessionist attempts. For this reason, secessionists must attempt to navigate a complex maze of dynamically developing competing interests, norms, and situational conditions (Stokes 2019: 119). While high-level tangible support may enable secessionists to win *de facto* independence, *de jure* status requires a broader support of the members of international community. As explained by M. Fabry (2020, p. 38), not all UN members have the same diplomatic weight, as the UN Security Council's permanent members represent an elite club of gatekeepers and their disagreement prevents an entity from entering the UN. In the end, it is easier to prevent a secession from succeeding in getting international recognition than to ensure that it succeeds in this quest, further highlighting the general opposition to the fragmentation of the political map.

## Note

* This study was supported by the Charles University Research Programme "Progres" Q18 – *Social Sciences: From Multidisciplinarity to Interdisciplinarity*.

## References

Bencic, A., Hodor, T. I. 2011, Transdniestria, Ethnic Conflict or Geopolitical Interests?, in Mircea, B., Horga, I. & Sorin, S. (eds.). Ethnicity, Confession and Intercultural Dialogue at the European Union's East Border. MPRA Paper (44082): 407–421.

Bélanger, L., Duchesne, É. and Paquin, J. 2005, 'Foreign Interventions and Secessionist Movements: The Democratic Factor', *Canadian Journal of Political Science*, 38(2): 435–462.

Berg, E. 2009, 'Re-Examining Sovereignty Claims in Changing Territorialities: Reflections from "Kosovo Syndrome"', *Geopolitics*, 14(2): 219–234.

Berg, E. & Mölder, M. 2012, 'Who Is Entitled to "Earn Sovereignty"? Legitimacy and Regime Support in Abkhazia and Nagorno-Karabakh', *Nations and Nationalism*, 18(3): 527–545.

Berg, E. & Toomla, R. 2009, 'Forms of Normalization in the Quest for de facto statehood', *The International Spectator*, 44(4): 27–45.

Buzard, K., Graham, B. A. T. & Horne, B., 2017, 'Unrecognized States: A Theory of Self-Determination and Foreign Influence,' *Journal of Law Economics and Organization*, 33(3): 578–611.

Caspersen, N. 2015, 'The pursuit of international recognition after Kosovo', *Global Governance*, 21(3): 393–412.

Castellino, J. 2011, 'The UN Principle of Self-Determination and Secession from Decolonized States: Katanga and Biafra', in A. Pavković & P. Radan (eds.), *The Ashgate Research Companion to Secession*. Farnham: Ashgate, 117–130.

Chou, B. K. P. 2011, 'Case Study 6: Singapore: Expulsion or Negotiated Secession?', in A. Pavković & P. Radan (eds.), *The Ashgate Research Companion on Secession*. Farnham: Ashgate, 479–482.

Christakis, T. 2011, 'The ICJ Advisory Opinion on Kosovo: Has International Law Something to Say about Secession?', *Leiden Journal of International Law*, 24(1): 73–86.

Christopher, A. J. 2002, 'Decolonisation without Independence', *GeoJournal*, 56(3): 213–224.

Coggins, B. 2011, 'The History of Secession: An Overview', in A. Pavković & P. Radan (eds.), *The Ashgate Research Companion on Secession*. Farnham: Ashgate, 23–43.

Coggins, B. 2014, *Power Politics and State Formation in the Twentieth Century: The Dynamics of Recognition*. Cambridge: Cambridge University Press.

Cooley, A. & Mitchell, L.A. 2010, 'Engagement without Recognition: A New Strategy toward Abkhazia and Eurasia´s Unrecognized States', *The Washington Quarterly*, 33(4): 59–73.

Crawford, J. 2006, *The Creation of States in International Law*. Oxford: Clarendon Press.

Crowley, D.T. 1963, 'Politics and Tribalism in the Katanga', *The Western Political Quarterly*, 16(1): 68–78.

De Vries, L., Englebert, P. & Schomerus, M. (eds.) 2019. *Secessionism in African Politics Aspiration, Grievance, Performance, Disenchantment*. London: Palgrave MacMillan.

Doboš, B. & Riegl, M. 2020, 'Neomedievalism and International Recognition: Explaining the Level of Recognition via Networking', in M. Riegl & B. Doboš (eds.), *Perspectives on Secession: Theory and Case Studies*. Cham: Springer, 57–72.

Economides, S. 2013, 'Kosovo, Self-Determination and the International Order', *Europe-Asia Studies* 65(5): 823–836.

Edmonds, C.J. 1971, 'Kurdish Nationalism', *Journal of Contemporary History*, 6(1): 87–107.

Fabry, M. 2010, *Recognizing States: International Society and the Establishment of New States Since 1776*. Oxford: Oxford University Press.

Fabry, M. 2011, 'International Involvement in Secessionist Conflict: From the 16th Century to the Present', in A. Pavković & P. Radan (eds.), *The ashgate research companion to secession*. Farnham: Ashgate, 251–266.

Fabry, M. 2012, 'The Contemporary Practice of State Recognition: Kosovo, South Ossetia, Abkhazia, and their aftermath', *Nationalities Papers*, 40(5): 661–676.

Fabry, M. 2020, 'The Evolution of State Recognition', in G. Visoka, J. Doyle & E. Newman (eds.), *Routledge Handbook of State Recognition*. London and New York: Routledge, 37–47.

Fazal, T. M., & Griffiths, R. D. 2014, 'Membership Has Its Privileges: The Changing Benefits of Statehood', *International Studies Review*, 16(1): 79–106.

Geldenhuys, D. 2009, *Contested States in World Politics*. London: Palgrave MacMillan.

Graham, B. A. T. & Horne, B. 2012, *Unrecognized States: A Theory of Self-Determination and Foreign Influence*. Los Angeles: University of Southern California.

Griffiths, R. D. 2016, *The Age of Secession: The International and Domestic Determinants of State Birth*. Cambridge: Cambridge University Press.

Griffiths, R. D. 2020, 'Dynamics of Secession and State Birth', in G. Visoka, J. Doyle & E. Newman, E. (eds.), *Routledge Handbook of State Recognition*. London and New York: Routledge, 138–147.

Griffiths, R. D. & Wasser, L. M. 2018, 'Does Violent Secession Work?', *Journal of Conflict Resolution*, 63(5): 1–27.

Heraclides, A. 1990, 'Secessionist Minorities and External Involvement', *International Organization*, 44(3): 341–378.

Heraclides, A. 1991, *The Self-Determination of Minorities in International Politics*. London: Frank Cass.

Hoehne, M. V. 2019, 'Against the Grain: Somaliland's Secession from Somalia', in L. de Vries, P. Englebert & M. Schomerus (eds.), *Secessionism in African Politics: Aspiration, Grievance, Performance, Disenchantment*. Cham: Palgrave Macmillan, 229–262.

Horowitz, D.H. 1985, *Ethnic Groups in Conflict*. Berkeley, Los Angeles, London: California University Press.

Huliaras, A. 2002, 'The Viability of Somaliland: Internal Constraints and Regional Geopolitics', *Journal of Contemporary African Studies*, 20(2): 157–182.

Ivanel, B. 2015, 'Puppet States: A Growing Trend of Covert Occupation', in T. D. Gill (ed.), *Yearbook of International Humanitarian Law*. Cham: Springer, 43–65.

Jackson, R.H. & Rosberg, C. 1982, 'Why Africa's Weak States Persist: The Empirical and the Juridical in Statehood', *World Politics*, 35(1): 1–24.

Ker-Lindsay, J. 2013, 'Preventing the emergence of self-determination as an norm of secession: an assessment of the Kosovo 'unique case' argument', *Europe-Asia Studies*, 65(5): 837–856.

Ker-Lindsay, J. 2015, 'Engagement without Recognition: The Limits of Diplomatic Interaction with Contested States', *International Affairs*, 91(2): 267–285.

Ker-Lindsay, J. 2017, 'Secession and Recognition in Foreign Policy', in M. Balikov & W. R. Thompson (eds.), *Oxford Research Encyclopedia of Politics*. Oxford: Oxford University Press, 1–18.

Ker-Lindsay, J. 2018, 'The Stigmatisation of de facto States: Disapproval and "engagement without recognition"', *Ethnopolitics*, 17(4): 362–372.

Ker-Lindsay, J. & Berg, E. 2018, 'Introduction: A Conceptual Framework for Engagement with de facto States,' *Ethnopolitics*, 17(4): 335–342.

Koohi-Kamali, F. 2003, *The Political Development of the Kurds in Iran: Pastoral Nationalism*. New York: Palgrave MacMillan.

Laoutides, C. 2020, 'Self-Determination and the Recognition of States', in G. Visoka, J. Doyle & E. Newman (eds.), *Routledge Handbook of State Recognition*. London and New York: Routledge, 59–70.

Larmer, M. & Kennes, E. 2019, 'Katanga's Secessionism in the Democratic Republic of Congo', in L. de Vries, P. Englebert & M. Schomerus (eds.), *Secessionism in African Politics: Aspiration, Grievance, Performance, Disenchantment*. Cham: Palgrave Macmillan, 361–391.

Lewis, I. 2011, *Understanding Somalia and Somaliland: Culture, History, Society*. New York: Columbia University Press.

Lynch, D. 2004, *Engaging Eurasia's Separatist States: Unresolved Conflicts and De Facto States*. Washington, DC: United States Institute of Peace Press.

Malešević, S. & Ó Dochartaigh, N. 2011, 'Secession and Political Violence', in A. Pavković and P. Radan (eds.), *The Ashgate Research Companion to Secession*. Fahrnam: Ashgate, 228–251.

McConnell, F. 2009, 'De facto, Displaced, Tacit: The Sovereign Articulations of the Tibetan Government-in-Exile' *Political Geography*, 28(6): 343–352.

McGarry, J. 2004, 'Foreword: De facto States and the International Order', in T. Bahcheli, B. Bartmann & H. Srebrnik (eds.), *De Facto States: The Quest for Sovereignty*. London and New York: Routledge.

McIntyre, W. D. 1991, The Significance of the Commonwealth, 1965–90. Cambridge Imperial and Post-Colonial Studies Series. Houndmills, Basingstoke, Hampshire: Palgrave MacMillan.

Mundy, J. 2009, 'Out with the Old, in with the New: Western Sahara back to Square One?', *Mediterranean Politics*, 14(1): 115–122.

Newman, E. & Visoka, G. 2018, 'The Foreign Policy of State Recognition: Kosovo's Diplomatic Strategy to Join International Society', *Foreign Policy Analysis*, 14(3): 367–387.

Newman, E. (2020). State Recognition in a Transitional International Order. In Visoka, G., Doyle & J., Newman, E. (eds.). *Routledge Handbook of State Recognition*. London, New York: Routledge. Pp. 109-122.

Novais, R. A. 2009, 'An Unfinished Process: The Western Sahara as a Post-Scriptum of the Colonial Period', *Africana Studia*, 12: 59–66.

Paquin, J. 2010, *A Stability-Seeking Power: U.S. Foreign Policy and Secessionist Conflicts*, Montreal, Kingston, London, Ithaca: McGill-Queen's University Press.

Patrick, S. M. 2010, *The Uyghur Movement China's Insurgency in Xinjiang*. Fort Leavenworth: School of Advanced Military Studies.

Pavković, A. 2020, 'Recognition of Unilateral Secession', in G. Visoka, J. Doyle & E. Newman (eds.), *Routledge Handbook of State Recognition*. London and New York: Routledge, 161–173.

Pavković, A. & Radan, P. 2007, *Creating New States: Theory and Practice of Secession*. Aldershot: Ashgate.

Pavković, A. & Radan, P. 2011, 'Introduction', in A. Pavković & P. Radan (eds.), *The Ashgate Research Companion to Secession*. Burlington: Ashgate, 1–7.

Pegg, S. & Berg, E. 2016, 'Lost and Found: The WikiLeaks of *De Facto* State: Great Power Relations', *International Studies Perspectives* 17(3): 267–286.

Peterson, M. J. 2020, 'Recognition of Governments', in G. Visoka, J. Doyle & E. Newman (eds.), *Routledge Handbook of State Recognition*. London, New York: Routledge, 205–219.

Rezwani, D. A. 2016, 'Partial Independence Beats Full Independence', Territory, Politics, Governance, 4(3): 269–296.

Rich, R. 1993, 'Recognition of States: The Collapse of Yugoslavia and the Soviet Union', *European Journal of International Law*, 4(2): 36–65.

Riegl, M. & Doboš, B. 2018, 'Power and Recognition: How (Super)Powers Decide the International Recognition Process', *Policy and Politics*, (46)3: 442–471.

Roosevelt, A. 1947, 'The Kurdish Republic of Mahabad', *Middle East Journal*, 1(3): 247–269.

Rosůlek, P. 2014, *Politický secesionismus & etické teorie. Allen Buchanan a jeho kritici*. Brno: Barrister & Principal.

Saideman, S. M. 1997, 'Explaining the International Relations of Secessionist Conflicts: Vulnerability versus Ethnic Ties', *International Organization*, 51(4): 721–753.

Saideman, S. M. 2001, The Ties That Divide: Ethnic Politics, Foreign Policy, and International Conflict. New York: Columbia University Press.

Sakwa, R. & Pavković, A. 2011, 'Secession as a Way of Dissolving Federations: The USSR and Yugoslavia', in A. Pavković & P. Radan (eds.), *The Ashgate Research Companion to Secession*. Burlington: Ashgate, 147–170.

Sterio, M. 2010, 'On the Right to External Self-Determination: "Selfistans," Secession, and the Great Powers' Rule', *Minnesota Journal of International Law*, 19(1): 137–176.

Sterio, M. 2013, *The Right to Self-Determination under International Law: "Selfistans", Secession and the Rule of the Great Powers*. New York: Routledge.

Sterio, M. 2015, 'Self-Determination and Secession Under International Law: The New Framework', *ILSA Journal of International & Comparative Law*, 21(2): 293–306.

Sterio, M. 2020, 'Power Politics and State Recognition', in G. Visoka, J. Doyle & E. Newman (eds.), *Routledge Handbook of State Recognition*. London, New York: Routledge, 82–98.

Stokes, D. 2019, 'Political opportunities and the quest for political recognition in Tibet, Taiwan, and Palestine', *International Review of Sociology*, 29(1): 102–124.

Summers, J. 2020, 'Pathways to Independence and Recognition', in G. Visoka, J. Doyle & E. Newman (eds.), *Routledge Handbook of State Recognition*. London and New York: Routledge, 125–137.

Tesfagiorgios, M. 2011, *Eritrea*. Santa Barbara, Denver, Oxford: ABC – Clio.

U Thant. 1970, Secretary-General's Press Conference in Dakar, Senegal. *UN Monthly Chronicle*.

Villafana, F.R. 2012, *Cold War in the Congo: The Confrontation of Cuban Military Forces, 1960–1967*. New Brunswick, London: Transaction Publishers.

Visoka, G., Newman, E. & Doyle, J. 2020, 'Introduction: Statehood and Recognition in World Politics', in G. Visoka, J. Doyle & E. Newman (eds.), *Routledge Handbook of State Recognition*. London, New York: Routledge, 1–21.

Wolff, S. & Rodt, A. P. 2013, 'Self-Determination after Kosovo', *Euro-Asian Studies*, 65(5): 799–822.

Yohannes, O. 1991, *Eritrea: A Pawn in World Politics*. Gainesville: University of Florida Press.

Zunes, S. & Mundy, J. 2010, *Western Sahara: War Nationalism And Conflict Irresolution*. New York: Syracuse University Press.

# 14

# DEBATING THE RIGHT TO SECEDE

## Normative theories of secession

*Argyro Kartsonaki*

This chapter's purpose is to provide a theoretical background for understanding various approaches to secession. It does not defend any right to secession or any particular theory as being the most appropriate to assign such a right.

Secessionist attempts usually entail some form of conflict, sometimes violent, sometimes latent conflict that has its roots either in history or in contemporary issues of democratic rights and representation. Due to the lurking or obvious impact secession has domestically and internationally, secessionists need to present moral underpinnings that would legitimize the struggle for independence. Secessionist attempts need to be marketed to gain positive visibility in order to maximize their chances of success. For this purpose, it has become necessary to deploy normative arguments in support of secession.

Normative theories justifying secession provide the necessary normative arguments to secessionist groups to support their demands. As Kartsonaki and Pavković show in their chapter (Chapter 20, this volume), normative arguments in various forms dominate declarations of independence, especially in cases of unilateral secessions. In an effort to legitimize their claims both internally and externally, secessionists appeal, among others, to norms pertaining to either violations of human rights and other established rights under international law, or the commitments of the seceding-seeking state to honour the principles of liberal democracy in their new state. Through these norms, they seek to justify their demands and gain support for their claim for independent statehood.

Another reason why norms are important is that secession as a phenomenon needs to be somehow understood. Who has the right to secede? What justifies secession? Normative theories provide a framework for analysis that facilitates the understanding of secession by answering these and other related questions. Normative theories, by setting the conditions for a justified secession indirectly – and sometimes directly – discuss issues relating to the nature of nationhood, the limits of statehood and state authority and the power of collective identity, developing this field of political theory. Normative theories also contextualize basic human rights, including the freedom of choice, the right to self-determination and the very right to freedom, discussing the morality of law and contributing to the field of applied ethics.

Contemporary normative theories of secession focus on the question of who holds the right to secede or to whom this right is to be assigned. They usually do not attempt to address

DOI: 10.4324/9781003036593-17

the question of how the process of seceding is to be regulated or how to avoid the violence, which often accompanies or precedes secession. Hence, they are neither conflict management theories nor theories of political or organizational regulation of secession processes. Moreover, although most normative theories include a set of conditions for the right to be exercised, their focal point continues to be a theoretical justification of the right to secede rather than its implementation.

This chapter presents the most prominent normative theories of secession. It begins with remedial theories, and then it continues to choice theories, followed by national theories of secession. Afterwards, it presents three alternative theories: a territorial approach to secession, a multi-levelled one and a realist one. The conclusion of this chapter is that all theories fail to address the key questions they pose as to who holds the right to secede, and why they hold this right. There is also the lurking and unanswered question of whether there is such a right at all, and who would assign and/or enforce it. These questions are probably bound to remain unanswered due to the variety of secessionist groups in terms of characteristics and justifications, and the nature of the international environment where secessions (seek to) take place.

## Remedial theories of secession

In a nutshell, remedial secession (or just cause) theory proposes that a people may have or should have the right to secede if they have been subject to some form of major injustices by their host state. This focus on the harms that a people has suffered as the sole source of legitimization of secession is what distinguishes remedial secession theories and differentiates them from other theoretical approaches to secession. The debate on remedial secession has been predominantly a moral, philosophical, and legal one, and as a result, various proposals were made as to when a people would acquire the right to remedial secession. As there has not been a unified approach among theorists of what constitutes an injustice that would give to a people the right to remedial secession, this section, as well as the next ones, presents positions put forward by selected theorists of secession.

Allen Buchanan is perhaps the most cited scholar as a pioneer of the modern political and philosophical discussion on the morality of secession. He put forward a "remedial right only" theory of secession, arguing that a people has a general right to secede if and only if it had suffered certain injustices by the host state. In such cases, secession is seen as an appropriate remedy of last resort (Buchanan 1991, 1997). In most of his work, he proposes two main justifications for remedial secession: first, systematic and long-standing human rights violations that threaten the physical survival of the group, and second, unjust annexation of territory. Later, he also considered a further justification for remedial secession when the host state has violated self-government agreements between a minority group and the host state (Buchanan 2004).

Another theory of remedial secession was proposed by Birch (1984). Birch did not label his theory as remedial, but formulated it as a response to Beran's liberal theory, which will be mentioned in the following section on choice theories. In essence, Birch's theory was a remedial one, starting with the main point that groups are not entitled to opt out of a democratically governed state unless any of the following four circumstances occur. First, similar to Buchanan, he deemed unjust annexation to be one of these special circumstances that would legitimize secession, in particular in cases where the population of the seceding region has continuously expressed their discontent to their inclusion into the host state. The second circumstance would be the failure of the host state to protect the basic rights and security of the population. In that case, the host state would not necessarily be the perpetrator of abuses. However, unwillingness or incompetence to act in a manner that would protect the seceding population would also be enough to justify secession. Third, systematic and structured neglect of the political and economic interests of the seceding region by the host state would render secession justifiable. Finally, fourth, the rejection of a settlement proposed by the seceding region that would aim to protect its essential interests and might have been outvoted by a national majority would be a reason that would legitimize secession (Birch 1984). Birch argued that if any of these conditions is met and if the majority of the voters in the region are in support of this action, then the region should have the right to secede.

Costa (2003) developed an approach to secession as part of the broader debate on minority rights within a multinational state. He did not defend the right to secession per se and stressed that there are other ways to achieve self-determination within the borders of the state. However, he viewed the adoption of multinational arrangements as a matter of justice, and therefore he claimed that inability to protect the rights of minorities with meaningful "multinational arrangements" should be considered a valid reason for secession. By "meaningful multinational arrangements," he meant institutional measures that would guarantee the equality between the different national groups through extensive territorial self-government and/or through power-sharing arrangements. Should the host state fail to adopt such measures, then the national minority should have the right to secession.

In his work examining the morality of the Georgian–Abkhaz Conflict, Coppieters (2003) argued that it is possible to apply the "just war" (*jus ad bellum*) criteria of just cause, legitimate authority, right intentions, last resort, proportionality, and chance of success to determine to what extent secession is morally justified. Coppieters reinterpreted these criteria in order to apply them to secessionist conflicts. Thus, in this context, "just cause" would mean that secession would be necessary in order to redress or prevent a grave injustice, for example, military occupation, colonization, oppression or exploitation. "Last resort" refers to the lack of other alternatives able to settle the incompatibility in the form of minority rights or federalism, or the possibility of achieving independence according to mutually agreed procedures. "Legitimate authority" obliges the secessionists to abide by the principles of popular representation, the rule of law, democracy and minority rights, while "right intentions" relate to the first principle of "just cause" that secession would redress or prevent a severe injustice. "Proportionality" requires that the total cost of unilateral secession will not exceed the expected benefits, and finally, the "chance of success" relates to the assessment of the realistic likelihood that the seceding entity gains international recognition. Coppieters based this analogy between just war and unilateral secession on the perceived structural similarities these two acts have, i.e., that they both deal with exceptions to general moral rules, and that both aim to impose one's political will on their adversary outside a commonly accepted legal framework.

Overall, remedial secession theories posit that a group that defines itself as a distinct people should have the right to secession if it has been the victim of abuses by the host state. However, what these abuses are that would offer the right to secession has been subject to interpretation by legal and political theory scholars. As a summary, the following reasons, or their combinations, have been put forward as justifying remedial secession: physical abuses and threats to the groups' survival; unjust annexation of the claimed territory by the host state; violations of agreements or of status (from the part of the host state); and remedial secession as a last resort when all other means of cooperation and attempts to accommodate the secessionists' demands have failed. Remedial secession therefore is inherently connected to a sense of justice and undoing of a wrong, whether it is threats to physical safety of this particular population or unjust annexation of the territory this population claims as its own.

## Choice theories of secession

An alternative to remedial secession theories are the choice theories of secession. Various names have been attributed to these theories: choice theories (Pavković and Radan 2007), primary-right theories (Buchanan 1991, 1997, 2004), democratic theories (Beran 1998) or liberal theories (Beran 1984). This chapter will use the term "choice theories" because the matter of having a choice over the status of a group's government arrangements is the essence of this approach. As the name suggests, choice theories propose that groups should have the right to secession, should they choose to. This right is independent of whether the group has suffered injustices or whether these groups form a "people" (whether this mean nations, minority or any kind of community that shares a common consciousness of self-identification). Instead, as the primary consideration is the value of group self-determination, and as Speetzen and Wellman (2011) put it, "any group able and willing to perform the functions necessary for political legitimacy has a primary right to secede" (Speetzen and Wellman 2011: 415).

One of the first scholars to elaborate on choice theories of secession was Harry Beran (1984, 1988, 1998). Built on the basic principles of liberalism, such as freedom, sovereignty and majority rule, he argued that "secession should be permitted, where it is possible, because a separatist group desires secession strongly enough to engage successfully in the organized sociopolitical activities necessary to achieve it." He defended this right against the remedial approach by arguing that "to permit secession only on moral grounds such as oppression or a right to national self-determination, but not on the ground that it is deeply desired and pursued by adequate political action, seems to be incompatible with the arguments of liberty, sovereignty and majority rule" (Beran 1984: 28).

Beran described the ideal society as a "voluntary scheme" (1984: 24) formed by citizens, who voluntarily have bound themselves to the restraints of the state as a form of organization of the human society. Although the dissolution of this state has not been foreseen by liberalism, Beran argues that for a state to resemble, as closely as possible, a voluntary scheme would mean that the unity of the state itself is voluntary. Therefore, secession should be permitted where it is possible. Consequently, if there are separatist groups, they should have the right to a referendum in the territory they claim. That way, the majority of people living in the specific area would have the opportunity to determine their political society.

Despite his seemingly overtly permissive view on secession, Beran also set six conditions according to which secession should not be permitted: First, if the group that wishes to secede is not sufficiently large to assume the basic responsibilities of an independent state. Second, if the secessionist entity is not prepared to permit sub-groups within its borders to secede, even if such secession would be morally and practically feasible. Third, if the secessionist region is likely to exploit or oppress a sub-group within its borders that cannot in turn secede because of territorial dispersal or other reasons. Fourth, if the secessionists occupy an area that is not on the borders of the existing state, but in an area where an enclave would be created. Fifth, if it occupies an area that is culturally, economically or militarily essential to the existing state. Sixth, if it occupies an area which has a disproportionally high share of the economic resources of the existing state (Beran 1984). After applying these conditions to secessionist cases, it turns out that Beran's approach is quite restrictive, attributing the right to secession to only a few groups that would be able to fulfil those prerequisites.

Echoing the view of the state as voluntary association and setting conditions for a right to secede, Bossacoma Busquets (2020) defended a moral right to secession based on a hypothetical multinational contract between the state and its minority nations. This theoretical contract would also stipulate the right to secession if certain conditions emerged that spoke to the following seven principles: democracy, agreement and negotiation, need for liberal nationalism, respect for human rights and protection of minorities, territoriality, viability and compensation, and avoiding serious damage to third parties. Under his theory of "'justice as multinational fairness,' the more just the state treatment of minority nations is, the higher the requirements to secede ought to be" (Bossacoma Busquets 2020: 2). Bossacoma's work seeks to provide a framework to constitutionalize the right to secede in a way that would allow the accommodation of secessionist demands through consensual means rather than unilateral acts. Overall he advocates for an approach to secession that is governed by moral principles rather than power politics.

Gauthier (1994) has also written in support of voluntary political association, comparing secession to divorce and political association to marriage. He built his argument on the assumption that the right to association stems from the mutual desire of the parties to relate with one another, and on the condition that none of the parties desires to better its place by worsening the one of the fellow part. He also claimed that, as there is a "moral case for no-fault divorce, so there is a moral case for no-fault secession" (Gauthier 1994: 371).

Another scholar that presented a choice theory of secession was Wellman (2005), who suggested that the political abilities of a seceding group are the factors which should determine if its secession would be justified or not. He claimed that nationality and cultural characteristics are important only in cases where they support the implementation of the necessary political functions of the seceding region. Additionally, Wellman argued that it is not obligatory for secessions to occur within pre-existing internal borders of only one state. He claimed, for example, that in the case of the Kurds, whose population is scattered in four different states, secession would involve the breaking away from all four states and the subsequent unification of these territories into a new state. Similar to Beran, he recognized the instability that a permissive right to secession entails, and set a restraining condition by adding that secession should be permissible only if it would not undermine the political stability and the well-being of the citizens of the remaining state.

Furthermore, Copp proposed that a group would possess the right to secede only if it can qualify as a "society in a relevant sense" (Copp 1998: 228). According to him, a society in the relevant sense is

> a group comparable in size and in social and economic complexity to the population of a state; it has a multi-generational history; it is characterized by a relatively self-contained network of social relationships and by norms of cooperation and coordination that are salient to its members; it is comprehensive of the entire population of permanent residents of a relevant territory, with the exception of recent arrivals who may not yet fit into the group's network of social relationships.
>
> *(Copp 1998: 227–228)*

In addition, Copp (1998) asserted that even if a group has suffered injustices, it cannot have the right to secede unless it is both a political and a territorial society. He clarified that a society is political if all of its members have the firm will to constitute a state, and territorial if it occupies a certain area within which it can form a state.

In addition to remedial theories, Buchanan also referred to choice theories, calling them primary-right theories. He divided them into two main categories: ascriptive group theories, and plebiscitary/associative group theories. Ascriptive group theories refer to groups that share characteristics that are attributed to a person independently of their choice, such as ethnicity. They support that these groups whose membership is defined by ascriptive characteristics should have the international legal right to secede regardless of whether they have suffered any injustices or not (Buchanan 1997, 2004). Continuing to plebiscitary or associative group theories, they assert that it is not necessary for a group to share a common identity, nationality or any other ascriptive characteristics in order to have the right to secede. These theories are based on the "voluntary political choice" of a group, whose will is to form their own independent political unit. Thus, any group, no matter how heterogeneous, can qualify for the right to secede (Buchanan 1997, 2004).

The focal point of choice theories of secession is the ability of the seceding group to form a stable political society, and as such successfully perform the necessary political functions. This also pre-supposes that the new state will respect liberal values and will not harm regional stability. The freedom of choice and the viewing of the state as a form of political association that exists to safeguard the interests of its citizens, and the voluntary nature of the association of the population to the state, are of paramount importance in choice theories of secession. This means that in cases where the state loses the consent of (a part of) its population, then this part should have the right to secede, regardless of whether it forms a "people" or whether it has been subject to injustices.

## National theories of secession

The main position of the national theories (or communitarian theories) of secession is that *nations* are distinct units, and as such they should have a primary right to self-determination and, under certain conditions, the right to secession. National theories of secession are in the intersection of remedial and choice theories. The similarity with remedial theories lies in the argument that nations should have the inherent right to secede, similar to the claim of remedial secession that a people should have this right. Contrary to remedial secession theories, though, national theories do not presuppose that the nation should have its basic human rights violated in order to have the right to secede. It has this right just because it is a nation, independent of its status and treatment within the state, resembling to this point choice theories. National self-determination theories, however, are also different from choice theories that grant the right to secession to *every* politically organized group that desires secession independently of its national composition: according to national theories, the precondition for the right to secession is that the seceding group constitutes a nation.

The scholar who probably finds himself closer to the intersection of remedial and national theories of secession is Seymour (2007), who argued that nations have instrumental value, as they possess institutional identity and are autonomous sources of moral claims. Therefore, having the right to self-determination equals having the right to preserve their national identity. Seymour (2007) distinguished between internal and external self-determination and argued that minority nations should have a general primary right to internal self-determination. Should the host fail to grant them internal self-determination, they should then have the right to secede. Contrary to remedial theories, in particular Buchanan's approach, Seymour argued that the violations that would justify a right to secession should not necessarily reach the point of threats of physical safety, annexation of territories or the violation of previous intrastate autonomy arrangements, but they can also pertain to failure to secure fair representation or other forms of internal self-determination.

Another theorist of national theories of secession is David Miller (1997), who built his theory on the principle of nationality and set two criteria that a potential separatist group must initially meet in order to have a case to secede. First, the secessionist group should be a nation. He defined the nation as a group of people who recognize one another as belonging to the same community, who acknowledge special obligations to one another and who aspire to political autonomy, by virtue of characteristics that they believe they share. These are typically a common history, attachment to a geographical place and a public culture that differentiates them from their neighbours (Miller 1997: 266). Second, the group needs to have a valid historical claim on the demanded territory. If these first conditions are met, then other subsequent factors need to be taken into consideration – for example, the ethnic composition of the seceding group. As only few groups are nationally homogeneous, this means that the establishment of the new state will create a new minority. Thus, the future situation of this minority should be evaluated before the group obtains any right to secession. In addition, he claimed that the seceding group should not remove resources from the host state resources that have been jointly created, or leave the host state with insufficient resources to sustain itself, as both sides should have territory and resources to ground a viable community. Overall, Miller (1997) recognized that the breaking of a state raises a plethora of questions about historic identities, economic justice and minority rights, and he believed that an adequate theory of secession must address all these issues.

For Margalit and Raz, self-determination, as equal to secession, would be necessary in some circumstances for the protection of prosperity and dignity of what they called "encompassing groups," meaning groups sharing specific characteristics (Margalit and Raz 1990: 460). They added further that the secessionist-seeking encompassing group should constitute the majority in the claimed territory and that the new state should respect the fundamental interests of its inhabitants as well as those of other countries (Margalit and Raz 1990). Moreover, the decision to secede should be supported by the vast majority of its members, reflecting deep-rooted, long-lasting beliefs and not mere temporary aspiration. Finally, the right should be exercised in order to secure the prosperity and self-respect of the group. The attainment of those values appear to be at the core of their argument. Summing up their final argument, they assert that an encompassing group that constitutes the majority of the population in the relevant territory should have the right to self-government and secession, provided that the vital interests of self-respect and prosperity of directly or indirectly affected citizens are protected (Margalit and Raz 1990).

Finally, Moore argued that "a claim of a nation to political self-expression should amount to a defensible right, equal for all nations, and that this claim derives from the mere existence of a nation" (Moore 1997: 900). This right exists even in cases where this particular nation has not been victim of past or ongoing injustices. She elaborated her argument upon criticizing the legal application of the right to self-determination based on *uti possidetis juris* upon decolonization. She argued that applying the right to self-determination this way is narrow, unethical and unjust as it creates double standards among nations that should have the same political right to self-expression. Similar to the majority of theorists arguing for national self-determination, Moore (1997) also admitted that secession might not always be feasible or appropriate and proposed other forms of self-government and internal self-determination that could secure a nation's right to self-expression.

## Other normative theories of secession

The debate on normative theories of secession effectively ended around 2010. Afterwards, similar arguments were replicated and repeated without substantially adding to the aforementioned positions. This does not mean that research on secession ended. To the contrary, a wealth of scholarly literature has emerged investigating other aspects of secession and its implications, including international recognition, tactics of secession and counter-secession and also engagement without recognition (Coggins 2014; Griffiths 2021; Griffiths and Muro 2020; Ker-Lindsay 2018). Also, some normative approaches to secession were developed in either parallel or following the aforementioned theories. This section will present a territorial approach to secession, a multi-level one and a realist one.

Secessionist conflicts are by definition territorial; both the host state and the secessionists lay incompatible claims to exercise exclusive jurisdiction over the same piece of territory (Speetzen and Wellman 2011). However, this territorial nature of the demands for secession is only indirectly mentioned in the literature. In particular, the national self-determination theories take the attachment of an ethnic group to a certain territory for granted. Remedial secession implicitly refers to it by referring to unjust annexation of territory as legitimate justification for secession. Brilmayer (1991, 2015) made this connection of territory and secessionist demands explicit. She argued that a separatist movement needs to have a normatively sound claim to this particular piece of land in order to acquire the right to secession. Brilmayer saw secession as a remedy; however, the focal point of her thesis is the historical attachment to territory rather than any injustices the separatist groups would claim. She highlighted that the normative force behind secessionist arguments would derive from the right over a territory that many ethnic groups claim to possess. Without this legitimate claim over the territory, the group would not have the right to secede even in cases of mistreatment. She did not deny that minority groups might be victims of discriminatory policies that need to be addressed, but she stressed that the "remedy for maltreatment is better treatment by the current government," not secession, and these groups need to seek arrangements with the host state to protect their interests rather than pursue secession (Brilmayer 1991: 188).

Bauböck (2019) sought to present an alternative view to the concept of secession as a whole. He proposed a multi-levelled theory, where secession would also be relative to the context and the polities involved. He suggested that there are three levels of secession: first, when a territory seeks to upgrade its status either within the host state, such as by demanding self-government arrangements, or by seeking to break away and form an independent state. The second level of secession is when an institutionally defined unit within a state joins a different unit of the same institutional level within the host state; for example, when the Swiss municipality Moutier decided to leave the canton Berne and join the canton Jura. The third type of secession, would involve seceding without upgrading or realignment, e.g. the UK exit of the EU, where the UK ceases to be part of the EU, without changing its international status. Bauböck argued that secession from independent states is substantially legitimate if and only if territorial self-government rights of the seceding polity have been persistently violated and there is no alternative remedy. Thus, in essence, when speaking about secessionist groups as defined here in this volume, Bauböck appears to follow a particular interpretation of remedial secession, where secession would serve as last resort in cases where the host state has failed to establish what Costa (2003) has also named "meaningful multinational arrangements."

Finally, Sanjaume-Calvet (2020) formulated a normative view on secession informed by the realist tradition. He tried to combine normative considerations with an anti-utopian reasoning to build a realist theory of secession, where secession would draw its legitimacy from sources of empirical legitimacy internal to the context rather than external and universal. He sees secession as an option to be debated among the groups or units directly affected by it, and as such secession must be regarded as justified by the population involved, meaning the population of the whole state rather than only the seceding group. He also adds a morality clause following Pavković's "no irreparable harm principle" (Pavković 2011: 451). The purpose of secession should be to minimize violence and protect the seceding population from abuses commited by the host state before a declaration of independence or a secessionist attempt. Even in those cases, though, the violence that may be generated during secession should be limited and reparable.

Sanjaume-Calvet (2020) tried to develop an applied, contextual theory that would give centre stage to those involved in the political arena. His theory, unlike the previous ones, does not depend on a presumed assignment of the right of secession to any one group. It is based on the presumption of a domination-free political arena where debates, including debates on secession, can take place freely. This would require leaving open the possibility of negotiated secession, similar to the 2003 constitutional agreement between Serbia and Montenegro allowing for Montenegro's secession in 2006. His theory would remain inapplicable, though, for secessionist demands that take place in conditions where institutionalizing secession or even the discussion on institutionalizing secession would not be an option.

Sanjaume-Calvet maps a way to manage secession via constitutionalizing it as political option. A similar reasoning was also formulated by Weinstock (2000, 2001) with his procedural approach on how to regulate secession. In addition, there are various proposed ways on how to institutionalize self-determination, and by extension secession, both in political science and international law scholarship (Orentlicher 2003; Scharf 2003; Philpott 1995). All approaches, however, remain in the realm of theoretical debate, as there is no international law to regulate secession or supreme authority above the state to implement the suggested arrangements in cases of non-compliance.

## A critique to normative theories of secession

Normative theories advance our understanding of abstract notions. They contextualize basic human rights, debate issues relating to the nature of nationhood, the limits of statehood and state authority, and discuss the morality of secession. They contribute to the fields of political theory and of the theory of applied ethics.

However, they all have strong limitations that put in question their contribution beyond the theoretical realm. They all fail to answer the question of why a certain group would have a right to secede over another group and for whom they seek to construct such a right. Another related issue that remains unanswered concerns who is the recipient of these theories, i.e., for whom are these theories developed – state governments, separatist entities, policymakers, lawyers, or just theorists that theoretically discuss notions without any intention to apply this right? This section presents a critique towards each normative theory with the order presented earlier: remedial theories, choice theories and national theories of secession.

To begin with remedial secession, this strand of normative theories raises legal, moral and procedural questions. Legally, it has sparked a long-lasting debate on whether there is a (legal) right to remedial secession. This was also politically fuelled by the emergence of the Responsibility to Protect (R2P) doctrine and the widespread reference to Kosovo, as a case that allegedly manifested the existence of a right to remedial secession in conjunction with R2P (Borgen 2008; Anderson 2013; Roseberry 2013). Nonetheless, secession remains a grey area in international law, and there is no international law explicitly regulating secession (Crawford 2006; Mancini 2008). The absence of a specific law or court decision that explicitly regulates secession has led to diverse opinions regarding the existence and/or the applicability of remedial secession. These interpretations range from a complete denial of the existence of a right to remedial secession, to its outright acceptance as an established right derived by state practice (Kartsonaki 2020). However, even in the case of Kosovo and the widely cited opinion of the International Court of Justice on the legality of Kosovo's declaration of independence, the Court admitted that "differences existed regarding whether international law provides for a right of 'remedial secession' and, if so, in what circumstances" (ICJ 2010: §82). This opinion of the ICJ further strengthens the position that there is no explicit law to regulate remedial secession, leaving remedial secession in the sphere of theoretical debate rather than an established right.

Morally, remedial secession gives cause to various concerns. First, there is the issue of the creation of trapped minorities. An entity wishing to secede is rarely "utopian," namely democratic, ethnically homogenous, occupying a defined territory – without enclosed minorities – unanimously desiring independent statehood as the way to realize self-determination (Philpott 1995: 355). Secessionist regions might be illiberal, including (unwilling) minorities, and/or with a part of their population reluctant to secede (Philpott 1995). Although there is an argument to be made that the right to secession must be independent of its outcome, i.e., whether the secessionist state is viable, whether secession affects economic or strategic interests of its host state or whether the new state treats its trapped minority unjustly (Birch 1984: 602), it also seems immoral to disregard the issue of trapped minorities and reverse ethnic cleansing that tends to follow a secession, especially since justice is a fundamental premise of remedial secession.

A second moral problem arises because of the violence secessionist attempts may bring about. Secessionists' remedial claims to independence are often accompanied by violence and/or terrorist-like acts, especially in cases of unilateral secessions (Williams and Heymann 2004); the Basque ETA (Euskadi Ta Askatasuna/Basque Country and Freedom) and the separatist movements in Chechnya are only two examples (Kramer 2005). The Kosovo Liberation Army was also initially characterized as a terrorist group by the United States' special envoy to the Balkans Robert Gelbard (BBC 1998). Furthermore, many secessionist attempts resulted in violent conflict and waves of refugees and internally displaced persons. Conflicts have continued for years, and most times they have been brought to an end (if at all) after a bloody and decisive victory by one conflict side (Weller 2005). Hence, the alleged remedy of secession may have a very high cost in human suffering.

In terms of procedure, remedial secession seems to be reserved for "a people," i.e., only groups that form a collective that defines itself as distinct from, and within, the host state. This generates various problems. Not only is there no universally accepted definition of "a people," but remedial secession theories do not necessarily adhere to any of the existing ones. To elaborate further, there have been several attempts to define the term "people," for example inhabitants of a specific territory under colonial rule (Borgen 2008), or ethnic groups, sharing a common ethnicity, culture, language, religion, and social values (Sterio 2008). However, remedial secession does not presuppose the existence of a "people" in any of these terms. The paramount criterion is the presence of systematic injustices against the members of this group regardless of the characteristics of the group itself. What identifies the group, then, is the presence of injustices rather than any inherent characteristics the members of this group may have.

A second procedural problem is that of "proof" of injustices. Moore (2000: 230) noted that it is problematic that "a group must demonstrate that it has been wronged according to the criteria established by liberal conceptions of legitimate governance," pointing out that in illiberal regimes this might not be possible. The problem becomes more acute in the absence of a neutral arbitrator, both domestically and internationally, that would be able to decide on the validity of the claims to injustice or harm committed against the whole group. This ultimately leaves many groups, not only the minority ones, in illiberal regimes undefended against oppressive regimes, thus making remedial theories more restrictive than they seem to be.

A third procedural issue is that of "indeterminacy," referring to the difficulty in specifying the jurisdictional unit in which self-determination can occur (Moore 2000: 231). This refers, for example, to issues, such as who has the right to decide on secession (only the affected population or the citizens of the whole state), that remain unanswered. Similarly, there is the question on how to deal with abuses conducted against groups that are scattered across a state, rather than being concentrated in one particular region. Even if these groups hold a right to remedial secession, the mere geography would make it impossible to exercise that right. There are other alternatives, including cultural autonomy and fair representation in the electoral system, but history has shown that pluralitarian and majoritarian electoral systems usually serve to ensure the continuation of subordinate status of such minorities (McGarry and Moore 2011).

Choice theories also suffer from conceptual and procedural limitations. Conceptually, choice theories presuppose that secessions take place in liberal democratic contexts or that the seceding population will have access to democratic mechanisms. The concept of negotiations among secessionists and the host state aiming to find an optimum solution that respects the well-being of all parties involved is central in choice theories, as well as the view that the state is a voluntary association with exit clauses. This context, though, does not correspond to unilateral secessions, which by definition take place either without negotiations or after negotiations have failed. Also, unilateral secessions take place in constitutional frameworks that do not foresee, or do not honour as in the case of the former Yugoslavia, provisions in their constitutional structures that would allow secession.

Conceptually also, the marriage/divorce analogy is unable to address unilateral secessions. Unilateral secessions, by definition, pursue secession without the consent of the host state. This leaves open the question of who holds the right and who decides on the secession. If accepted that solely the inhabitants of the seceding territory are to choose, as opposed to the whole state, this leaves open the question on how to accommodate those individuals within the seceding group, who opted to remain within the union. Such issues do not arise in divorces, as the identity and will of the parties involved is not under question (Aronovitch 2000). Aronovitch (2000) also pointed out that even if no-fault secession would be acceptable, this would be a right possessed only by the seceding territory, not the host state. This would make the right to secession as political divorce one-sided only possessed by the one party of the union. There are also procedural issues; for example, in cases of divorce, non-compliance of one of the parties is settled in courts. There is, though, no international effective authority to enforce the terms of secession. These are some of the issues that turn the divorce/marriage analogy less relevant in cases of unilateral secessions.

In terms of procedure, choice theories assume that the right to secession belongs to the seceding group and that their choice should be demonstrated via democratic means, e.g. a referendum. The question that emerges is how to determine who would have the right to choose. There seems to be the assumption that all groups who would choose to opt out of the state as voluntary union would be entitled to that right. Conceptually, this leaves the holders of the right undefined, leading to problems with implementation, as a right cannot be assigned to an undefined group.

National theories of self-determination also suffer from the same conceptual problem as the previous theories: how to define the primary holder of the right to secession and how to define the nation. Moore (1997) proposed a solution to this by suggesting a subjective interpretation of this concept, rather than a description based on objective characteristics. This approach faces the problem of outside recognition of the nation: how does a group of people who claim to be a nation get to be recognized as such? The recognition of nationhood is inextricably linked to the question of justifiability of secession of the nations that seek recognition. In fact, the problem of recognition arises quite frequently in the debates about the justifiability of secession. For example, some of those who rejected the Bangladesh secession claimed that Bengalis were not a nation. Similarly, opponents of Bosnia and Herzegovina's independence claimed that Muslims or Bosniaks, the population who had a plurality in this (former) federal unit, were not a nation.

Finally, national theories of secession seem to suggest that the creation of ethnically homogenous states, where borders and nationality coincide, is *ethically* preferred to ethnically diverse states. Such an approach if taken literally can lead to systematic breach of human rights of the populations, which are forced out of such preferred homogenous states. In the same vein, national theories of secession apparently devalue the principles of pluralism, diversity and mutual recognition of diverse groups. These are founding principles on which many modern societies putatively abide to, but the right of secession, if granted only to single nations, implies that these should not (or cannot) be accepted as foundational principles.

## Concluding remarks

Each normative theory of secession advances certain moral arguments that would or should justify the independence of a group that fulfils a number of specified preconditions. Remedial secession emphasizes the presence of some form of injustices by the host state over the seceding-seeking population; choice theories prioritize the "will of the people" and the procedures of liberal democracy; whereas national theories put forward the nature of nations as distinct communities that should have the right to self-determination and secession.

All normative theories suffer from conceptual and procedural limitations. They inevitably fail to address the key questions of who the holder of the right to secede is and why this particular group, and not another one, has this right. The claim that there is a right to secession presupposes that there is a group definable either in terms of the characteristics of its members or in terms of the territory it occupies; the so-defined group would be then the holder of that right. However, normative theories fail to provide a universal definition to distinguish such groups. The variety in secession-seeking groups and their demands probably provides a good (but unacknowledged) reason for this failure. Moreover, the moral justifications put forward in each of these theories are partial, favouring one group over another, based on the favoured group's arbitrary (non-moral) qualities. Interestingly, despite the emphasis on the morality of secession, normative theories stipulate political or economic preconditions, rather than moral ones, that would enable a group to acquire this right.

Procedurally, they seem to imply that there is a supreme authority to regulate and assign a right to secession. In the case of choice theories, they also seem to take for granted that negotiations between host state and separatists are possible and that secessions take place in regimes that respect liberal democratic values. In that case, the supreme authority would be the constitutional framework of each country. This, however, would apply only to secessionist cases occurring in liberal, democratic contexts, where there is this constitutional option, leaving out secession taking place unilaterally. In such cases, in lieu of a supreme authority above the state and its constitutional framework, or a set of institutions to regulate, assign and enforce any right to secession, normative theories are bound to remain in the realm of theoretical debate.

## References

Anderson, G. 2013, 'Unilateral Non-Colonial Secession in International Law and Declaratory General Assembly Resolutions: Textual Content and Legal Effects', *Denver Journal of International Law and Policy*, 41: 345–395.
Aronovitch, H. 2000, 'Why Secession Is Unlike Divorce', *Public Affairs Quarterly*, 14: 27–37.
Bauböck, R. 2019, 'A Multilevel Theory of Democratic Secession', *Ethnopolitics*, 18: 227–246.
BBC. 1998, 'The KLA: Terrorists or Freedom Fighters?', http://news.bbc.co.uk/1/hi/world/europe/121818.stm
Beran, H. 1984, 'A Liberal Theory of Secession', *Political Studies*, 32: 21–31.
Beran, H. 1988, 'More Theory of Secession', *Political Studies*, 36: 316–323.
Beran, H. 1998, 'A Democratic Theory of Political Self-Determination for a New World Order', in P. Lehning (ed.), *Theories of Secession*, Routledge: New York: 33–60.
Birch, A. H. 1984, 'Another Liberal Theory of Secession', *Political Studies*, 32: 596–602.

Borgen, C. J. 2008, 'Kosovo's Declaration of Independence: Self-Determination, Secession and Recognition', *American Society of International Law*, ASIL INSIGHT: 1–5.

Bossacoma Busquets, P. 2020, *Morality and Legality of Secession: A Theory of National Self-Determination*, Palgrave Macmillan: Cham.

Brilmayer, L. 1991, 'Secession and Self-Determination: A Territorial Interpretation', *Yale Journal of International Law*, 16: 177–202.

Brilmayer, L. 2015, 'Secession and the Two Types of Territorial Claims', *ILSA Journal of International and Comparative Law*, 21: 325–331.

Buchanan, A. 1991, *Secession, the Morality of Political Divorce from Fort Sumter to Lithuania and Quebec*, Westview Press: Boulder, London.

Buchanan, A. 1997, 'Theories of Secession', *Philosophy and Public Affairs*, 26: 31–61.

Buchanan, A. 2004, *Justice, Legitimacy and Self-Determination*, Oxford University Press: Oxford.

Coggins, B. 2014, *Power Politics and State Formation in the Twentieth Century: The Dynamics of Recognition*, Cambridge University Press: New York.

Copp, D. 1998, 'International Law and Morality in the Theory of Secession', *The Journal of Ethics*, 2: 219–245.

Coppieters, B. 2003, 'War and Secession: A Moral Analysis of the Georgian: Abkhaz Conflict', in B. Coppieters & R. Sakwa (eds.), *Contextualing Secession*, Oxford University Press: Oxford: 187–212.

Costa, J. 2003, 'On Theories of Secession: Minorities, Majorities and the Multinational State', *Critical Review of International Social and Political Philosophy*, 6: 63–90.

Crawford, J. 2006, *The Creation of States in International Law*, Oxford University Press: New York.

Gauthier, D. 1994, 'Breaking Up: An Essay on Secession', *Canadian Journal of Philosophy*, 24: 357–371.

Griffiths, D. R. 2021, *Secession and the Sovereignty Game: Strategy and Tactics for Aspiring Nations*, Cornell University Press: Ithaca.

Griffiths, D. R. & Muro, D. (eds.) 2020, *Strategies of Secession and Counter-Secession*, Rowman and Littlefield International: London.

ICJ. 2010, 'Accordance with International Law of the Unilateral Declaration of Independence in Respect of Kosovo, Advisory Opinion, Reports 2010', 403–453.

Kartsonaki, A. 2020, 'Remedial Secession: Theory, Law and Reality', in R. D. Griffiths & D. Muro (eds.), *Strategies of Secession and Counter-Secession*, Rowman and Littlefield International: London: 31–51.

Ker-Lindsay, J. 2018. 'The Stigmatisation of De Facto States: Disapproval and "Engagement without Recognition"', *Ethnopolitics*, 17: 362–-372.

Kramer, M. 2005, 'Guerrilla Warfare, Counterinsurgency and Terrorism in the North Caucasus: The Military Dimension of the Russian: Chechen Conflict', *Europe-Asia Studies*, 57: 209–290.

Mancini, S. 2008, 'Rethinking the Boundaries of Democratic Secession: Liberalism, Nationalism, and the Right of Minorities to Self-Determination', *International Journal of Constitutional Law*, 6: 553–584.

Margalit, A. & Raz, J. 1990, 'National Self-Determination', *Journal of Philosophy*, LXXXVII: 439–461.

McGarry, J. & Moore, M. 2011, 'Secession and Domination', in A. Pavković & P. Radan (eds.), *The Ashgate Research Companion to Secession*, Ashgate: Farnham: 427–438.

Miller, D. 1997, 'Secession and the Principle of Nationality', *Canadian Journal of Philosophy*, 26: 261–282.

Moore, M. 1997, 'On National Self-Determination', *Political Studies*, XLV: 900–913.

Moore, M. 2000, 'The Ethics of Secession and a Normative Theory of Nationalism', *Canadian Journal of Law and Jurisprudence*, 13: 225–250.

Orentlicher, D. F. 2003, 'International Responses to Separatist Claims: Are Democratic Principles Relevant?', in S. Macedo & A. Buchanan (eds.), *Secession and Self-Determination*, New York University Press: New York: 19–49.

Pavković, A. 2011, 'The Right to Secede: Do We Really Need It?', in A. Pavković & P. Radan (eds.), *The Ashgate Research Companion to Secession*, Ashgate: Farnham: 439–452.

Pavković, A. & Peter Radan. 2007, *Creating New States: Theory and Practice of Secession*, Ashgate Publishing: Burlington.

Philpott, D. 1995, 'In Defense of Self-Determination', *Ethics*, 105: 352–385.

Roseberry, P. 2013, 'Mass Violence and the Recognition of Kosovo: Suffering and Recognition, 65:5', *Europe-Asia Studies*, 65: 857–873.

Sanjaume-Calvet, M. 2020, 'Moralism in Theories of Secession: A Realist Perspective', *Nations and Nationalism*, 26: 323–343.

Scharf, M. P. 2003, 'Earned Sovereignty: Juridical Underpinnings', *Denver Journal of International Law & Policy*, 31: 273–285.

Seymour, M. 2007, 'Secession as a Remedial Right', *Inquiry: An Interdisciplinary Journal of Philosophy*, 50: 395–423.

Speetzen, D. D. & Wellman, C. H. 2011, 'Choice Theories of Secession', in A. Pavković & P. Radan (eds.), *The Ashgate Research Companion to Secession*, Ashgate: Farnham: 413–526.

Sterio, M. 2010, 'On the Right to External Self-Determination: Selfistans, Secession, and the Great Powers' Rule', *Minnesota Journal of International Law*, 19: 137–176.

Weinstock, D. M. 2000, 'Towards a Pluralist Theory of Secession', *Canadian Journal of Law and Jurisprudence*, XIII.

Weinstock, D. M. 2001, 'Constitutionalising the Right to Secede', *The Journal of Political Philosophy*, 9: 182–203.

Weller, M. 2005, 'The Self-Determination Trap', *Ethnopolitics: Formerly Global Review of Ethnopolitics*, 4: 3–28.

Wellman, C. H. 2005, *A Theory of Secession*, Cambridge University Press: New York.

Williams, P. R. & Heymann, K. 2004, 'Earned Sovereignty: An Emerging Conflict Resolution Approach', *ILSA Journal of International and Comparative Law*, 10: 437–445.

# PART IV

# Secession strategies

# 15

# SECESSION AND THE STRATEGIC PLAYING FIELD

*Ryan D. Griffiths*

This chapter serves as a lead-in to Part IV of the volume that focuses on secessionist strategy, an important and developing research area connected by a set of core questions. In what ways do secessionists behave strategically, and can we identify recurring patterns? How do secessionists choose their methods, and how do those choices vary depending on context? Is it accurate to conceive of secession as taking place on a strategic playing field? Or does the game metaphor mischaracterize dynamics that are much more contingent and accidental in nature? These are the questions that my co-authors and I are focused on in this part of the volume. They are important questions with big implications, because secession is typically a form of rebellion. It is disruptive, polarizing, and often violent. Therefore, the ways in which secessionists operate, what they believe works, and how those beliefs are put into action are important topics of study.

This chapter has three sections. In the first, I describe the ways in which secessionist dynamics approximate a strategic playing field – what I have elsewhere called the sovereignty game (Griffiths 2021). As I show, this is a useful, if imperfect, metaphor. In section two, I show how strategic and tactical behavior varies across the diverse settings in which secessionist movements operate. I contend that there are recurring patterns to secessionist behavior and that actions are, to some extent, predictable depending on context. It is in section three that I revisit the game metaphor. That is, I show how the metaphor can be challenged and complicated for reasons pertaining to wishful thinking, imperfect information, mixed goals, and divided actors. One final note: my focus here is mostly on the strategy of secessionists, and less so on the state, their chief opponent. Although the relationship between secessionist movements and states is one of strategic interaction – and, indeed, the counter-strategies of states will loom in the background of my analysis – my chief focus will be on the secessionist side of that relationship. Part VI of this volume will bring the state into the center of the analysis.

## The strategic playing field

There are a number of ways in which the dynamics of secession constitute a strategic playing field. They have the characteristics of a game, though, as I discuss in this chapter, the kind of game is hard to determine. These characteristics include identifiable actors, a competitive tension between the actors, rules of the game, knowledge of the game, and a specification for how

DOI: 10.4324/9781003036593-19

resources can be used to achieve the objective. The primary actors in this game are secessionist movements and sovereign states. I define a secessionist movement as a "self-identified nation inside a sovereign state that seeks to separate and form a new [recognized] sovereign state," one with full membership in the United Nations (UN) (Griffiths 2016: 205). Sovereign states are simply the recognized independent states in the world, the full UN members.

The tension between these two actors comes down to the fact that secessionists desire sovereign recognition, an attribute that states both possess and guard. Let us take these points in turn. Secessionists aim to obtain sovereignty because it is valuable and carries privileges (Jackson 1990: 196; Fazal and Griffiths 2014). These privileges include the sovereign right to conduct your own affairs, and a legal identity with which member states can join international organizations and rest assured that their territorial integrity is backed by international law (Fabry 2010; Caspersen 2012). Meanwhile, states have a number of reasons to guard entry into their club, such as the concern that new states will be unstable, that they will swamp the membership of international organizations, and, perhaps most importantly, that any secession implies a territorial reduction for at least one existing state. For these reasons and others, states generally possess a status quo bias on the issue of secession. That said, preferences and the intensity of sentiment do vary among states, just as they do among secessionists.

The strategic playing field is shaped by formal and informal rules and practices. Perhaps the most important of these is the formal process of gaining sovereign recognition. In procedural terms, this is done by obtaining a full seat in the UN General Assembly. More than just a marker of legitimacy, this provides the state with a seat in the global parliament and a corresponding legal identity that is useful for a range of economic and diplomatic reasons. To join the UN, an aspiring nation tenders an application that is processed and submitted to the United Nations Security Council (UNSC) for a vote. Then, 9 of the 15 members have to vote in the affirmative without any vetoes from the five permanent members (P5): China, France, Russia, the United Kingdom, and the United States. An application that is approved by the Security Council is then subject to a vote in the General Assembly and has to secure a two-thirds majority. Once admitted applicants have declared that they will abide by the UN Charter, they can officially join the ranks of recognized sovereign states. One of the fascinating aspects of this institutional design is that it is states who decide who should be admitted, and that the P5 members have the ability to block any attempt. Different rules yield different games, and were the rules of admission to change or, for example, if the Security Council was reduced in power, then the strategic playing field would change.

There are various other rules and practices that shape secessionist behavior. One example is that third-party states, at least since 1945, are supposed to respect the wishes of the home state to withhold recognition until matters are worked out domestically. As such, the Scots and the Catalans are unlikely to be recognized until their home states, the United Kingdom and Spain, agree to the secession. Although recognition is sometimes granted in the absence of home state agreement, as it was initially with Bangladesh and currently is with Kosovo, it is a rare occurrence. This means that secessionists are going to have to reckon with their home state, the chief obstacle to their ambitions.

There are also rules and norms that simply make secessionist movements more likely to be accepted and supported by the international community. When a minority nation is the target of violence and/or human rights abuse by the state, and not seen as purveyors of violence and terrorism, then the international community is more likely to sympathize with their cause and pressure the home state. When an aspiring nation can successfully connect their case to decolonization, as the New Caledonians have, and the West Papuans have failed to do, then they effectively elevate their candidacy. Likewise, when a secessionist region can demonstrate through a legally sanctioned referendum that a clear majority favors independence, as the Bougainvilleans have, then they imbue their efforts with greater legitimacy.

Of course, a well-functioning game requires knowledge of the rules. It matters little that chess has clearly defined rules if one of the players is ignorant of them. In that regard, it should be noted that independence movements are not isolated actors operating without knowledge of the larger strategic playing field. On the contrary, they observe one another and are often quite networked. For example, the Catalan secessionists sent political strategists to Scotland in mid-2014 to gather tactical knowledge from the Scottish National Party (SNP) about how to target their independence message to different segments of the population. Similar relationships exist in other regions like, for example, among groups in Melanesia or mainland Southeast Asia. Although much of the networking is bilateral in nature, forums like the Unrepresented Nations and Peoples Organization (UNPO.org) provide opportunities for members to share experiences. Finally, advice on how to obtain sovereign statehood can also be acquired through diaspora networks, in-house legal counsel, non-governmental organizations, and consultancies like Independent Diplomat. These knowledge networks influence secessionist behavior. In her research on the topic, Reyko Huang found that secessionist rebels, "for whom international recognition is essential for attaining independent statehood," are more likely than other types of rebels to engage in international diplomacy (Huang 2016: 124). Similarly, Tanisha Fazal concluded that secessionists were more likely than other types of civil war combatants to conduct their actions in a manner that is consistent with international law (Fazal 2018). The reason for these patterns is straightforward: secessionists need to behave like proper states if they want to be recognized as such.

Given these parameters, what do secessionists actually do on the strategic playing field? I argue that at a very general strategic level, all secessionist movements are the same. There is only one international system, one UN they aim to join, and one entrance into it. To gain recognition, secessionists have to get their home state to remove its veto and/or go around the home state and enlist the help of the international community. In doing so, international support can be brought to bear on the home state. Indeed, in some cases, third-party states may even recognize the breakaway region in the absence of the home state's permission. Every secessionist movement engages with both its home state and the international community, though the balance between these two interlocutors can vary according to domestic and regional conditions. In fact, some regional organizations like the European Union and the African Union are particularly important in these dynamics. These are the primary contours of the strategic field.

Getting the home state and/or or the international community to make a change is where things get particularly interesting. Here, it is useful to differentiate between two categories of tactical behavior: compellence and normative appeal. These categories are analytically distinct. Compellence is about using assets in a directly confrontational way to force a change. In contrast, normative appeal is aimed at preferences. Here, secessionist movements make an emotive appeal to the population of the home state and the international community. Whereas the purpose of compellence is to make certain preferences costly, normative appeal means to change those preferences. These categories can be roughly mapped onto Steven Luke's three faces of power: direct action, agenda-setting, and belief shaping (Lukes 1974). Compellence is mostly about the first face; it is direct political action. Normative appeal is largely about the third face; it shapes beliefs and preferences. As I will detail, the second face is not completely absent, because by choosing certain tactics (e.g. nonviolent civil resistance), secessionists can limit the options for state response.

Secession is about a change from the status quo, one that results in new borders and the birth of a new state. To realize that change, secessionists need to compel the central government and/

or international community to recognize them as an independent sovereign state. As Thomas Schelling explained, compellence is a type of coercion aimed at forcing a target to do something that they would not otherwise do (Schelling 1966: 71–73). To bring about the desired change, the movement may engage in a set of tactics ranging from the use of outright violence to electoral competition to nonviolent forms of civil resistance that put pressure on the target. Bombings by Basque terrorists were acts that aimed to influence Spanish state policy. Winning a clear majority of the Scottish parliament can be used as a means to force London to negotiate. Nonviolent demonstrations and sit-ins in West Papua are a form of protest that is designed to put pressure on the Indonesian state. As I will detail, different movements will choose different compellence tactics depending on their setting.

The second category of tactics used by secessionists is to make a normative appeal to the hearts and minds of target populations. These appeals are meant to change attitudes and preferences on the issue. As the East Timorese demonstrated, the appeal to human rights can have a strong effect. Similarly, the bloody conflicts in Kosovo and Bangladesh were instrumental in raising international support that paved the way for independence. A different approach is to appeal to liberal democratic norms of legitimacy and argue for the right to choose. The Catalans have repeatedly demanded that the Spanish state give them a referendum on independence, as the United Kingdom has with Scotland.

Compellence and normative appeal can be used in tandem and often complement one another. For example, during its civil war with Papua New Guinea (PNG), Bougainville's leadership relied on their Sydney-based representative, Moses Havini, and his Bougainville Freedom Movement, to bring their cause to a global audience (Griffiths 2021). His efforts were conducted at the same time as secessionist forces fought the PNG army. Military leaders like Francis Ona and James Tanis attempted to compel the PNG government to negotiate by increasing the costs of noncompliance. Havini's diplomatic efforts gradually changed the preferences of the international community about the Bougainville conflict. Changing preferences can ultimately have a coercive effect on the home state because increased pressure is brought to bear through diplomatic channels, boycotts, embargoes, and other means. Although the end result is the same – convincing the home state and/or international community to make a change – the logic is different insofar as it directly targets preferences, even if costs are subsequently incurred as a result.

Let me finish this section by addressing two potential objections. The first is that I am imputing too much strategic thinking into secessionist action. Are secessionists so clear-eyed and rational that we can model their behavior using the language of Schelling? How well do they know the rules of the game? Although I will address these points in the final section of the chapter, suffice it to say that the game metaphor can go only so far. This is not chess, where the rules are perfectly and explicitly delimited. A better analogy is poker, given the importance of bluffing and reputation-building, but even there, the rules are ultimately fixed. The game that secessionists play is more open-ended that that. The playing field is fuzzy, but coherent enough to shape the play.

A second potential objection is that I am overstating the homogeneity of secessionist movements. After all, they come in all shapes and sizes, and, at close range, the realities of Scottish nationalism look rather different from those of Karen nationalism. But seen from a wide angle, all secessionist movements are playing on the same field. To gain recognition as a sovereign state, they need to get their home state and/or the international community to make a change. There are numerous local factors that define them, but their playing field is international. Therefore, at a general level, the strategy of secession is modular; it can be picked up and deployed by a diverse set of groups and, importantly, these groups watch and learn from one another. Their tactical choices are then calibrated and contextualized by local conditions.

## Tactical variation

If secessionist strategy is focused on getting the home state and international community to make a change, secessionist tactics are the more specific tools for getting to that end goal. I have outlined two categories of tactical behavior: compellence, and the appeal to norms. I will now discuss examples of these tactics and show how their use varies across different settings – that is, different kinds of movements. The sequence in which I describe these different kinds of movements follows from their structural relationship with the home state. Are the secessionists operating within a highly institutionalized, democratic state? How strong is the state, and what are its capabilities? Finally, is the secessionist region sundered from the state and governing in a de facto sense? The answers to these questions point to the kind of movement and its tactical options.

Movements that operate within highly institutionalized, democratic societies are faced with different tactical possibilities. At the strategic level, they are the same as any other movement insofar as they have to contend with their home state, persuade the international community, and apply to the UN. But their tactics differ in accordance with the institutional environment. Their main tactic of compellence is electoral capture – that is, using the democratic institutions of the state to pursue independence. Such movements often commit to nonviolent action as a means to build legitimacy and, in doing so, limit the response options of the state. Their primary normative appeal is that an identifiable nation should be able to choose its political fate via a democratic process (Beran 1998). Although these efforts are largely aimed at getting the home state to permit a referendum and give consent to independence, they, as the Catalans have shown, also attempt to court the international community in their efforts.

Democratized movements can be remarkably robust, with strong civil society organizations, deep financial support, and developed political parties. These are not clandestine movements that operate in the shadows, but politically engaged actors that compete in the public space. Although these movements have much going for them and are often the envy of other secessionists, the democratic process commits them to a struggle to win over the majority of the electorate. As the Scottish National Party has discovered, that is no easy task, especially in an advanced democracy where the opportunity cost of exit can be high.

A different and much more numerous kind of secessionist movement occurs in less democratic societies, where the breakaway nation is still connected institutionally to the state. I refer to these as combative movements, and examples include the Uighur, the Karen, and the West Papuans. Given their interconnectivity and potential for friction with the state, and their weakly institutionalized settings, they are often the location of violence and suppression. As a result, their chief normative argument will typically focus on the right to independent statehood in the face of human rights abuses by the state. That is, they will stress remedial rights in their appeals to the international community (Buchanan 1997). Although other normative arguments may be present, their setting simply raises the probability that the human rights argument will be utilized.

As the name suggests, the compellence tactics of combative movements tend to rely on confrontational, extra-institutional methods. The reason is simple; forming a secessionist political party and running for office requires that those paths are open. Where they are absent, and perhaps where the participants have little confidence in the integrity and legality of those institutions, secessionists will turn to extra-institutional methods. Such methods may focus on traditional applications of violence or forms of nonviolent civil resistance (Chenoweth and Stephan 2011; Griffiths and Wasser 2019). Although many movements employ violent and nonviolent methods simultaneously, I have argued that secessionist movements are more likely to choose violence as they approach parity with the government, as Bougainville did in the 1990s when it was able to fight the PNG forces to a hurting stalemate (Griffiths 2021). Nonviolent civil resistance can be an effective weapon, and it can blunt the ability of the state to respond with force, but it is the weapon of the weak. To be sure, this is a complex topic, but there is a relationship between the choice of these tactics and the strength of the movement relative to the state.

The third kind is the de facto state movement, a set that includes Abkhazia and Somaliland, among others. These are the least institutionally integrated. They are functional, breakaway regions that are denied international recognition. In each case, their home state has withheld its consent and successfully persuaded the international community to respect its territorial integrity. On one hand, these are success cases because they have won their independence on an empirical basis and effectively exited the larger state. For many movements like the Uighur, that alone would be a victory. On the other hand, their success at establishing de facto statehood has come at a cost. The secessionists have prevailed and established a state in empirical terms, but, as a result, reduced or minimized their points of contact with the home state. They cannot engage so easily in forms of civil disobedience or terrorism or electoral competition precisely because they have broken off and are typically separated from the home state by a militarized border like the line separating Artsakh from Azerbaijan. Instead of a complex situation of dual and overlapping sovereignty, the two sides are clearly separated by linear boundaries. In other words, they cannot compel the state to make a change because they have little direct leverage. Instead, they have to settle for defending the border and deterring the home state from attacking. Overall, de facto state movements develop a status quo bias that can end in a half step between reintegration and full independence (Caspersen 2012: 47).

Although de facto state movements can look passive and status quo biased where compellence is concerned, they are ardent practitioners in the art of normative appeal. These groups have strong incentives to appear state-like and engage in as much diplomatic behavior as possible. They cannot appeal so easily to norms regarding human rights or abuses by the state because they have so little contact with the state. Instead, they try to appeal to the normative argument that good governance and democratic values establish standards that warrant status as a sovereign state (Berg 2009). Essentially, they argue that they have earned their sovereignty.

Altogether, these three kinds show how differences in setting shape the tactical options available to secessionists. Movements in democratized settings are likely to pursue independence in a different way from those who maneuver in less democratic settings, or those who are sundered from the state and govern in a de facto sense. Of course, the boundaries between these kinds are fluid, and they could be parsed further.[1] For example, a small number of secessionist movements like New Caledonia and Western Sahara have argued, with some success, that they are entitled to independence via the path of decolonization. In terms of normative appeal, this is a particularly strong argument, one that is recognized by UN resolution (Sterio 2013: 11). Importantly, the compellence tactics of these movements vary considerably, because their settings can vary. Somaliland is a de facto state movement; West Papua is a weak combative movement; and New Caledonia is currently pursuing independence through the institutions of the French state. They occupy diverse settings but share a common normative appeal.

A different example is a sub-type of the democratized movement that exists among indigenous and aboriginal communities in countries like Australia and the United States. Examples include the Hawaiian sovereignty movement, the Lakotah, and the Murrawarri Republic. Like democratized movements, their compellence tactics are institutional in nature. But they often make different normative arguments regarding the fate of indigenous peoples in settler societies. Since these nations were not included under the ambit of decolonization, their legal representatives have typically challenged the legality of their forced inclusion in states like the United States and Australia. Their original sovereignty was never relinquished and is inherent.

To sum up, I have outlined the strategic playing field for secessionists, and the tactical variation that follows depending on setting. One thing that is missing in all of this is the other player:
the state. Although other chapters in this volume will discuss the counter-strategies of states, let
me make a few comments here as they relate to my framework. States also have strategies with
respect to secession; indeed, that is what completes the strategic playing field. But in many ways
these strategies are harder to discern, both because states may be less clear in their intentions,
and because counter-secession is very rarely their center of attention. Whereas secession is only
one of many issues for state governments, it is the central issue for a secessionist movement.

The overall strategy of states is in many ways the mirror image of the strategy of secession.
At the strategic level, states defend the perimeter by maintaining the veto, resisting pressure to
remove it, and weakening attempts by secessionists to compel and persuade others that their
cause is righteous. Although states use different tactics depending on context, there are features
that are common to all counter-secession efforts. Chief among them is the appeal to territorial
integrity. The international system is ultimately state-centric, and sovereign states are the key
actors. The default solution for any independence claim is to maintain the status quo, and it is
therefore incumbent on aspiring states to prove that their self-determination demands supersede
the need of the state to maintain its territorial integrity. In the collision between those competing normative demands, secessionists have numerous cards to play (decolonization, human
rights, etc.), but states have the ace: the principle that sovereign territory is inviolate.

Nevertheless, states often need to do more than simply stand behind their territorial integrity.
States engage in tactical behavior that is shaped by the same factors that influence secessionists:
the degree to which the independence movement is *de facto* independent, the regime type, and
the strength of the state. The issue of connectivity is a good starting point for the analysis because
*de facto* state movements interact with their home state in a fundamentally different way from
other movements. Their sunderance from the state removes their levers of compellence and
shifts the aim of the secessionists toward dissuasion. In some respects, states undergo the opposite
transformation. Just as they aim to dissuade when secessionists need to compel, they increasingly
need to compel as secessionists focus on dissuasion. As my co-authors discuss in this, some of the
most developed work on counter-secession strategy focuses on situations of de facto statehood
(Berg and Pegg 2020; Ker-Lindsay, Chapter 27, this volume), where states actively seek to isolate
the breakaway region and pressure it to give up its independence bid.

The tactical dynamics of secession change when the breakaway region is integrated into
the larger state. The next separating factor is the institutional structure of the state, because, as
argued earlier, movements in democratic settings are more likely to use the electoral process and
appeal to the right to choose. States, for their part, are more likely to respond in kind: to defeat
secessionist parties through elections and referenda, and to deny minority nations the right to
choose. Here, counter-secessionists often put forward arguments about legality and stability.
They may claim that secession is unconstitutional (Weill 2020), as the Spanish government has
done in reference to Catalonia, and they may accuse the secessionists of causing polarization,
division, and instability. Of course, a key feature of the game in societies like Canada and Spain
is the fact that both sides generally avoid using violence. Indeed, it is often explicitly ruled off
the table. As long as that remains the case, counter-secession tactics will mirror the tactics of
democratized movements.

Counter-secession tactics in non-democratic and/or under-institutionalized states typically
have a different character. Where the state is relatively strong, suppression is a common response.
For example, it is illegal to fly the Morning Star flag in West Papua, and Indonesian authorities
will arrest those who display it. For states like Myanmar or Papua New Guinea, where capacity
is more limited and breakaway regions in the periphery are relatively stronger, the government

is forced to accept a kind of informal autonomy. Both types are conflict-prone; it is the relative balance between the two sides that changes. States defend what they can, and they aim to deter secessionists from advancing their aims via the threat of punishment. The form of the punishment can vary, from detainment and incarceration to assassination and direct military engagement (Butt 2020). Importantly, these states will defend their territorial claim and fight on the diplomatic front, but there is some variation here. Stronger states that can suppress an independence movement will often maintain a kind of silence on the issue, but weaker states that are fighting harder to control the breakaway region are often forced to engage the international community.

The strategic playing field is created by the interaction between states and secessionist movements. Although this chapter has focused on secessionist action, the actions of the state are an important part of the dynamic. In a sense, they complete the dynamic because the predicted tactics for each secessionist kind develop in relation to the characteristics, capabilities, and tactics of the home state. These tactics are in many ways the mirror image of the tactics used by secessionists.

## Revisiting the game metaphor

In his groundbreaking 1969 article, Graham Allison provided a Rashomon-like conceptual analysis of the Cuban Missile Crisis (Allison 1969). Although we often assume that political and military contests are conducted in a strategic manner by rational actors – that, for example, John F. Kennedy was in a game of high-stakes chess with Nikita Khrushchev – there is much more going on. In fact, the same event can be seen in an entirely different light once we change our perspective and train our eyes on different key factors. For Allison, foreign policy is as much the product of organizational processes and bureaucratic politics as it is clear, rational strategic decision-making. In a somewhat similar manner, secession and the strategic playing field can also be seen from multiple perspectives. In this section, I complicate the game metaphor by discussing several common challenges.

One oft-heard critique of secessionist behavior is the perception that it is merely wishful thinking. It is said that secessionists are living out a pipe dream, that their declarations and pronouncements are the sound of one hand clapping, that their self-defeating desires will come to naught. As the journalist Josep Maria Marti Font put it,

> Catalans can feel that they have the moral high ground, talking about democracy, about our rights and how badly we are treated by Madrid, but we don't have an army, we don't have a treasury and we don't have anything except wishful thinking.
>
> *(Minder 2017: 300)*

The upshot of this view is that if secessionism is hope-driven, it is therefore irrational and, by extension, non-strategic.

I argue that while wishful thinking is commonly found among secessionists, it does not, on its own, undermine its strategic nature or call into question the game metaphor. After all, this is a pattern of thinking that is found in all games. Sports players will often overrate their chances, and they will believe in themselves that they can beat the odds. In this case, wishful thinking may be useful because it is motivational. However, wishful thinking is a well-known and pernicious problem with betting games, and here it is almost always regarded as a bad way to play. With respect to secession, wishful thinking is both good and bad, but it is usually present.

The value of wishful thinking is that it can infuse a cause with hope. Maintaining hope in the cause can help mobilize support, get people into the street, and fortify their nerves. In many cases, secessionism is a form of high-risk activism; in all cases, it is costly and time-consuming. It is a form of rebellion, and rebellion is a risky enterprise. Without a measure of hope at the core of the rebellion, it is likely to fade away. Of course, the downside to wishful thinking is that it can lead to poor tactical choices. It may inspire leaders to move too fast, make unwise choices, and pin their hopes on foreign assistance that is less likely to come then they realize. Overall, these are common aspects of the strategic playing field, but they do not undermine the game metaphor. On the contrary, they are part of the game.

There are other factors that challenge the game metaphor, or at least complicate it greatly. The first has to do with information. I stated previously that states and secessionist movements have knowledge of the game and its rules. But the game that secessionists play is fuzzier and more open-ended than a common sporting or parlor game because it is shaped by an evolving set of formal and informal rules and practices (Griffiths 2021). These rules and practices are not clearly specified or listed in a way that a practitioner could google on the internet, as they might if they prepared for a poker game. Moreover, the contours of the sovereignty game shapeshift over time, and sometimes they do so in reaction to how the game is played. As a result, all players maneuver in a setting that is characterized by incomplete information.

As an example of this problem, consider the 1998 Biak Massacre in West Papua, also known as Bloody Biak. This occurred as part of, and perhaps ended, what was known as the Papuan Spring, a period of hope following the fall of Suharto. In July of that year, West Papuans clamoring for independence gathered and hoisted the Morning Star flag on the water tower in Biak City. Six days later, the demonstrators were violently disbursed by the Indonesian military and more than 100 people were detained. According to reports, many of the detainees were beaten, raped, and murdered, and their mutilated bodies were dropped into the sea (Kirksey 2012: 48). In the wake of the massacre, the independence leader Filep Karma stated that he had operated under the belief that if they raised the Morning Star flag on the water tower and kept if aloft for 24 hours, then the UN would recognize their independence (Macleod 2015: 109–110). When they kept it up for 48 hours, and recognition did not come, and the Indonesian authorities still cracked down violently, Karma concluded that "this theory is not true." This story illustrates the problem of incomplete information, for as Karma tells it, they mistakenly believed that international support and recognition would follow from a specific action – in this case, raising the flag for 24 hours.

Although the Biak example is somewhat extreme, and the beliefs that motivated the action appear naïve, it highlights a problem that all secessionist movements share. They do not know the reservation price for international support. Catalan secessionists will often express their faith in the willingness of the European Union to step in should the tensions escalate. There is surely a point at which a prominent leader like Angela Merkel would apply pressure on the Spanish government to negotiate with Catalonia, but that point is unknown, perhaps even to Merkel. This information problem is amplified once we consider that international actors often have an incentive to not reveal their reservation price. By publicly stating the conditions under which Merkel would pressure Spanish Prime Minister Rajoy to negotiate with Catalonia, she would influence Catalan tactics. There is a potential moral hazard problem here, not to mention the fact that political leaders can damage their diplomatic relations.

There are numerous other ways in which secessionists simply have incomplete information. One striking similarity between the Scottish and New Caledonian independence referenda was the debate about whether each region would be better off as its own sovereign state. In both cases, the pro-independence side made arguments about their economic assets, their natural resources, and their ability to join regional trading organizations as well as the international community. For their part, the anti-independence side did their best to highlight the economic vulnerability of the potential state. Although both sides brought political and economic reports to bear in their arguments, it was very difficult to produce a reliable cost-benefit analysis. How would the new state arrange for debt repayment with the former central government? How would employee pensions be worked out? At what rate could the new state expect to join international organizations? This is not well-trodden ground, and there are no clear answers to these questions. To choose an independent state is to choose an uncertain future, and secessionists need to reduce that uncertainty just as the home state has reason to increase it. That uncertainty shapes preferences in a legal referendum like Scotland's, particularly among older and/or less risk-tolerant voters. It matters even more when the referendum and larger independence bid is considered illegal. In preparation for the September 27, 2015, Catalan Parliament elections, the pro-independence side stressed uncertainty reduction in their messaging to older voters.

The fog that permeates the strategic playing field can also be legalistic. In the early days of their independence bid, the Bougainvilleans attempted to portray their cause as one of unfulfilled decolonization. After all, they had been colonized, and their inclusion in Papua New Guinea was an artifact of European colonization. But they gradually learned that their cause did not fit the template for decolonization because they were not the right kind of colonial-administrative unit in 1975 – the critical date at which Papua New Guinea became independent – and thus they gradually shifted their normative appeal to focus on human rights.

I now turn to two final complicating factors that are mentioned elsewhere in this volume. One has to do with the fact that secessionists often have mixed objectives. Consider that each side in a game of chess has one player with one goal (to win). There is no alternative end goal, unless one values losing as equal to or greater than winning. In contrast, the sovereignty game is characterized by mixed objectives, and this can lead to poor tactical choices where the attainment of independence is concerned. It is important to remember that not all minority nations want independence. As Philip Roeder illustrates, secession campaigns are merely a subset of those groups who seek some form of increased local control (Roeder 2018: 24). Many groups modify their demands over time, moving back and forth between satisfaction, to wanting greater autonomy, to wanting sovereign independence, and so on. The objectives are mixed, and this influences tactical choices. If one only wants independence and is prepared to pay a high price for it, as some Catalan secessionists do, then confrontation and increased friction with the state is acceptable. But if one is prepared to settle for an autonomy arrangement, and may even rate that outcome as equal to or better than independence, as other Catalans prefer, then it would be less desirable to create conflict with the state that may remain your home.

A second but related problem is the tendency for division within an independence-seeking nation. There is a delightful scene in *Monty Python's Life of Brian* in which the John Cleese character tells an interested party that they are not the Judean People's Front, but rather the People's Front of Judea, the PFJ as he calls it, and that this is different from another group called the Judean Popular Peoples Front. In the banter that follows, one member of the PFJ gets tripped up on the name of their own group. I was reminded of this scene on several occasions when an actual secessionist, from Bougainville to West Papua to Catalonia, would describe the evolution of the different factions within their cause. Each secessionist movement consists of a constellation of actors who possess varying, sometimes conflicting objectives.

The are many reasons for this variation. Sometimes factions are rooted in competing clans or sub-regions of the potential breakaway region. For example, there is an old division among the

Iraqi Kurds between the Kurdistan Democratic Party, which centers on the Barzani tribe and is headquartered in Erbil, and the Patriotic Union of Kurdistan, which is led by the Talabani family from Sulaymaniyah. That division weakened support on the run-up to the 2017 independence referendum, because many Kurds from the area around Sulaymaniyah saw the bid as an initiative of the Barzani tribe, especially its leader, Massoud Barzani. Indeed, the perception of personal ambition can be a cause of division. Secessionists sometimes reported that they were turned off from the cause by the overly ambitious personas of people like Alex Salmond, Carles Puigdemont, and Rauf Denktash. Just as factions can form around the competing ambitions of different leaders, they can also form around competing methods. The Catalan political parties *Esquerra* and CUP were more comfortable with confrontation with Madrid than their counterparts in *Convergencia*. A regular source of factionalism is the question of violence. When PALIKA arose as a competing faction to the Caledonian Union as part of the Kanak independence effort in New Caledonia, it was over the matter of whether violence should be used.

There is now a vibrant literature on the effects of factionalism within self-determination groups (Cunningham 2014; Krause 2017). In a recent book, Roeder examined the strategic game played by different factions within a given minority nation (Roeder 2018). He argues that secessionist leaders need to win over a decisive majority of their platform population, and he analyzes why some groups prevail over others. In truth, many secessionist leaders are playing a two-level game, one faced inward toward in-group competitors, and one faced outward toward the state and the international community (Putnam 1998). One result of the internal game is that it complicates the external game. It leads to greater variation in tactical outcomes, and some of the choices may weaken the overall independence effort. In other words, when pursuing on objective in the internal game, an actor may choose a tactic that hinders the external game. It could, for example, make it harder for the state to negotiate a deal with secessionists because they are unorganized. In many cases, divisions within a secessionist effort are as bitter and violent as they are with the state.

Collectively, do these factors undermine the game metaphor and the notion that secessionists act strategically? The answer depends, in part, on what constitutes a game. This is not a board game, in which two unitary actors sit down and play in a circumscribed space according to clear, unchanging rules. Poker is a slightly better comparison given the elements of bluffing, hidden information, and reputation-building, but even that is ultimately a closed game insofar as the rules are static and the actors are unitary. The game played between secessionists and states is open-ended, protean, and somewhat vague. The endpoint is known, but the rules for getting there are not always so explicit. Furthermore, the players are internally divided and composed of multiple interests and goals. This is a complex and fuzzy game with very high stakes.

## Conclusion

In this chapter I have attempted to outline the strategic playing field for secessionists. In doing so, I have focused primarily on the secessionist side of what I call the sovereignty game. States are the other player in that game, and they have loomed in the background of my discussion. These two sides correspond to Parts IV and V of this volume. Each of the chapters contained in those sections takes a closer look at specific aspects of the game.

## Note

1 In Griffiths (2021), I identify six kinds of movements: (1) democratized, (2) indigenous legal, (3) weak combative, (4) strong combative, (5) de facto state, and (6) decolonial.

# References

Allison, G. T. (1969). Conceptual Models and the Cuban Missile Crisis. *American Political Science Review* 63(3), pp. 689–718.

Beran, H. (1998). A Democratic Theory of Political Self-Determination for a New World Order. In Percy Lehning (ed), *Theories of Secession*. New York: Routledge.

Berg, E. (2009). Re-Examining Sovereignty Claims in Changing Territorialities: Reflections from 'Kosovo Syndrome'. *Geopolitics* 14(2), pp. 219–234.

Berg, E. and Pegg, S. (2020). Do Parent State Strategies Matter in Resolving Secessionist Conflicts with De Facto States? In Ryan Griffiths and Diego Muro (eds), *Strategies of Secession and Counter-Secession*. London: ECPR Press.

Buchanan, A. (1997). Self-Determination, Secession, and the Rule of Law. In R. McKim and J. McMahan (eds), *The Morality of Nationalism*. Oxford: Oxford University Press.

Butt, A. (2020). State Strategy against Secessionists. In Ryan Griffiths and Diego Muro (eds), *Strategies of Secession and Counter-Secession*. London: ECPR Press.

Caspersen, N. (2012). *Unrecognized States: The Struggle for Sovereignty in the Modern International System*. Cambridge: Polity.

Chenoweth, E. and Stephan, M. J. (2011). *Why Civil Resistance Works: The Strategic Logic of Nonviolent Conflict*. New York: Columbia University Press.

Cunningham, K. G. (2014). *Inside the Politics of Self-Determination*. Oxford: Oxford University Press.

Fabry, M. (2010). *Recognizing States: International Society and the Establishment of New States since 1776*. Oxford: Oxford University Press.

Fazal, T. (2018). *Wars of Law: Unintended Consequences in the Regulation of Armed Conflict*. Ithaca: Cornell University Press.

Fazal, T. and Griffiths, R. (2014). Membership Has Its Privileges: The Changing Benefits of Statehood. *International Studies Review* 16(1), pp. 79–106.

Griffiths, R. D. (2016). *Age of Secession: The International and Domestic Determinants of State Birth*. Cambridge: Cambridge University Press.

Griffiths, R. D. (2021). *Secession and the Sovereignty Game: Strategy and Tactics for Aspiring Nations*. Ithaca: Cornell University Press.

Griffiths, R. D. and Wasser, L. M. (2019). Does Violent Secessionism Work? *Journal of Conflict Resolution* 63(5), pp. 1310–1336.

Huang, R. (2016). Rebel Diplomacy in Civil War. *International Security* 40(4), pp. 89–126.

Jackson, R. (1990). *Quasi-States: Sovereignty, International Relations, and the Third World*. Cambridge: Cambridge University Press.

Kirksey, E. (2012). *Freedom in Entangled Worlds: West Papua and the Architecture of Global Power*. Durham: Duke University Press.

Krause, P. (2017). *Rebel Power: Why Nationalist Movements Compete, Fight, and Win*. Ithaca: Cornell University Press.

Lukes, S. M. (1974). *Power: A Radical View*. London: MacMillan.

Macleod, J. (2015). *Merdeka and the Morning Star: Civil Resistance in West Papua*. Brisbane: University of Queensland Press.

Minder, R. (2017). *The Struggle for Catalonia: Rebel Politics in Spain*. London: Hurst and Company.

Putnam, R. D. (1998). Diplomacy and Domestic Politics: The Logic of Two-Level Games. *International Organization* 42(3), pp. 427–460.

Roeder, P. G. (2018). *National Secession: Persuasion and Violence in Independence Campaigns*. Ithaca: Cornell University Press.

Schelling, T. C. (1966). *Arms and Influence*. New Haven: Yale University Press.

Sterio, M. (2013). *The Right to Seld-Determinationa Under International Law: "Selfistans," Secession, and the Rule of the Great Powers*. London: Routledge.

Weill, R. (2020). Global Constitutional Strategies to Counter Secession. In Ryan Griffiths and Diego Muro (eds), *Strategies of Secession and Counter-Secession*. London: ECPR Press.

# 16

# STRATEGIC CHOICES FOR SECESSIONIST MOBILIZATION

*Philip G. Roeder*

The term *strategy*, derived from the Greek word for generalship, focuses on choices made by leaders but has been addressed fruitfully in academic research through two different lenses. With an emphasis on the conditions under which mobilization takes place, Karl W. Deutsch (1966), Miroslav Hroch (1985) in his earlier work, and Mark Beissinger (2002) identify the processes that characterize the mobilization of platform populations as nations.[1] The lessons for strategy are implicit rather than a key focus of these analyses. Alternatively, Hroch (2015) in his more recent work, Philip G. Roeder (2018), and Ryan D. Griffiths (2021)[2] shift the focus to the leaders of these campaigns, their options for mobilization of the platform population, and the constraints that shape the consequences that are likely to follow on each option. These two lenses provide insights into strategies of mobilization that complement one another.

A strategy of *mobilizing* for national secession aims to assemble, prepare, and deploy ideological, human, and material assets in order to achieve the goal of national independence for a claimed homeland (such as Bougainville, Scotland, or Tigray). The study of these strategies focuses on choices confronting leaders who seek to engage members of the much larger platform population on which each proposed state will be built. The members of this population may not always recognize that they are members of the platform, that the platform population has a homeland, that the platform population constitutes a nation with a right to sovereign statehood, that independence of the homeland will address many concerns of the platform population, or that their contributions to the cause will affect success in achieving the goal of independence.

The literature on national-secessionist mobilization commonly brackets two closely linked, yet distinct, dimensions of mobilization – one attitudinal and the other behavioral. *Attitudinal mobilization* refers to the subjective (cognitive, affective, and evaluative) changes that constitute national awakening or reawakening. *Behavioral mobilization* refers to the expanded numbers of participants in actions and escalating intensity of their actions to realize the goals of the national project. Nonetheless, the two emphases recognize the causal impact of each on the other. In addition, the literature distinguishes processes of mobilization that take place in society from those taking place in politics. In this chapter, the focus is on conscious choices by political actors (campaign leaders) to effect attitudinal and behavioral mobilization on behalf of the political goal of national independence for a people and its homeland.

DOI: 10.4324/9781003036593-20

## Lens 1: conditions of mobilization

Deutsch's *Nationalism and Social Communication* (1966) is the pioneering work in modern studies of nationalist mobilization. It searches for the social conditions that give rise to "complementarity of communications habits," which Deutsch sees as essential to the emergence of nations. Thus, his analysis stresses the societal context of attitudinal mobilization rather than the behavioral mobilization that takes place in politics. In Deutsch's (1966, p. 90) analysis, the information transmitted through social communication includes "knowledge, values, traditions, news, gossip, and commands." The attitudinal mobilization is part and parcel of the "social mobilization" that Deutsch (1961, pp. 493–494), in an earlier path-breaking essay, defines as "the process in which major clusters of old social, economic and psychological commitments are eroded or broken and people become available for new patterns of socialization and behavior." These subjective changes in society are seen as distinct from behavioral consequences in the realm of politics but set the stage for the political behaviors: "these changes tend to influence and sometimes to transform political behavior." Indeed, Deutsch (1961, p. 501) warns that "rapid social mobilization . . . may tend to strain or destroy the unity of states whose population is already divided into several groups with different languages or cultures or basic ways of life." In his analysis, this social mobilization enables more intensive communication within unassimilated populations – that is, populations not assimilated within the communications of the dominant community in the state – and thus sets the stage for their realignment with separatist nationalist movements. Yet Deutsch does not actually analyze the behavioral mobilization within these movements in the realm of politics.

Hroch's (1985, p. 13) *Social Preconditions of National Revival in Europe* provides insight into the class composition and social-developmental preconditions for "national agitation," which he defines as "activities directed towards increasing national consciousness." Yet this analysis stops short of a comparative analysis of the forms of agitation. Hroch (1985, p. 23) divides the chronology into three periods that he identifies as initial scholarly interest, subsequent patriotic agitation, and the rise of a mass national movement. He focuses his analysis on the second (Phase B, as he calls it), which is characterized by "the fermentation-process of national consciousness." He stresses that "the driving force in this era of national agitation was a group of patriots who . . . saw their mission as the spreading of national consciousness among the people."

Beissinger's (2002) magisterial *Nationalist Mobilization and the Collapse of the Soviet State* emphasizes the behavioral and political dimensions of mobilization. The analysis focuses on nationalist "action" that aggregates into what the "contentious politics" paradigm labels as "events" (McAdam, Tarrow, and Tilly 2001). In Beissinger's (2002, p. 27) analysis, the clustering of events becomes a "tide of nationalism," which comprises "multiple waves of nationalist mobilization whose content and outcome influence one another." Importantly, this behavior influences identities (that is, attitudinal mobilization) through processes that Beissinger (2002, pp. 147–148) refers to as "the mobilization of identity" and "fundamental transformation of identities." In Beissinger's (2002, pp. 8–9) case study, these events influenced "the ways in which both Russians and non-Russians thought about the Soviet state."

## *Implications for strategy*

Because the studies of nationalist mobilization by Deutsch (1966), Hroch (1985), and Beissinger (2002) focus on conditions, contexts, and macro-processes, we must infer lessons for the choices confronting national-secession leaders in these contexts. None of these studies can be faulted if I have drawn these implications improperly. Still, many of these implications have been reaffirmed, and many others have been expanded by recent work in economics, political science, and psychology on the tactics of what psychologists now label "social mobilization" (e.g., Rogers, Goldstein, and Fox 2018). Nevertheless, each is a hypothesis that should be continually challenged by new studies.

First and foremost are implications for *defining the platform* – that is, how leaders define the platform population and the territorial jurisdiction on behalf of which the national-secession project seeks sovereign independence. (In this way the strategic approach diverges from many analyses of national secessionism by treating the definitions of the platform population and homeland as matters of choice – albeit constrained choices.) The contextual studies suggest that leaders are more likely to be successful when they design their projects to focus on pre-existing identity communities that are already linked to projects for independent statehood and have traditions of activism on behalf of that goal. Todd Rogers, Noah J. Goldstein, and Craig R. Fox (2018, p. 370) underscore that "once a particular social identity has been made salient, people are more likely to behave consistently with what they believe to be the prototypical group behavior or with what they believe to be in the group's interests." To the extent that leaders have discretion, they are more likely to be successful when they define these nations and homelands to incorporate larger populations and on behalf of jurisdictions that are empowered within an ethnofederal state (Deutsch 1966, p. 128; Beissinger 2002, p. 144). It is more difficult to mobilize behind a nation and state that exist solely in the imagination, and easier to mobilize on behalf of existing jurisdictions around which identities have already coordinated and with the capabilities to protect, stage, and sustain collective action on behalf of its rights (Roeder 2007).

Second are implications for the *personalization of appeals* – that is, how the leaders frame their agenda of national and homeland rights in communications with the platform population. A key inference is for leaders to select a frame that speaks to the present consciousness of the people, recognizing that this may change as mobilization progresses (Beissinger 2002, p. 159). In this context, it may be important for leaders to begin in the initial stages of mobilization by framing the campaign's demands as less than complete independence – such as beginning with cultural and environmental protection or expanded autonomy rights (Beissinger 2002, p. 148). The message may be more effective in eliciting mobilization when it points to threats to the identity group or illegitimate deprivation of status (Rogers, Goldstein, and Fox 2018, pp. 364–373). And when the leader's operational objective is to use attitudinal mobilization in order to set the stage for behavioral mobilization, the leader is more likely to be successful when the message cultivates and deepens perceptions that participation is expected of "true" members of the platform population (injunctive and descriptive norms) and that one's standing within the community (accountability) depends on this.

Third are implications for the *targeting of appeals* – that is, choices concerning the parts of the platform population to target with mobilizational efforts. Leaders are more likely to be successful at attitudinal and behavioral mobilization when they target individuals in social networks and the influencers in those networks (Rogers, Goldstein, and Fox 2018, p. 373). The greatest potential appears to come from targeting urban populations and linguistically unassimilated populations (Deutsch 1966, p. 128; Beissinger 2002, pp. 136–137). Yet, the unassimilated often are found in rural settings, and the unassimilated urban population may define a very narrow base – such as recent countryside-to-city migrants. Still, the findings of these macro-studies imply that leaders will be more successful when they target socially mobilized segments of the unassimilated population, which may be identified by their residence in towns (rather than in the countryside or in cities), employment in non-agricultural sectors of the economy, attention to media, and subject to government exactions such as taxation or conscription (Deutsch 1966, p. 126). These findings also suggest that leaders may need to use various cues in identifying the influencers in these networks, such as targeting individuals in specific occupations such as politicians, property owners, or editors of newspapers (Deutsch 1966, pp. 101–104, 139). Teachers are critically important. Hroch (1985, p. 147) states in an unusually emphatic assertion, "The leaders of all the national movements sooner or later started to grasp the importance of the teachers as intermediaries in communication and instruments of patriotic agitation in the countryside." Leaders are also more likely to be successful when they can link with local officials who will be complicit in mounting or protecting large demonstrations of support (Beissinger 2002, p. 304). Yet, Hroch (1985, p. 155; 2015, pp. 125–126) stresses that national-secession leaders must know the particularities of their own societies since there are no universal cues applicable to all societies that would identify the specific occupations that should be targeted during nationalist agitation. In a still more careful targeting, leaders are more successful when they target those who share a common political vocabulary and symbology (Deutsch 1966, pp. 96–100).

Fourth are implications for *tactical choices* that link individual members of the platform population to the process of behavioral mobilization. Leaders are more likely to be successful at mobilization when they use events such as large-scale protests to "embolden" the platform population to express the goals of the national-secession project through further mobilization (Beissinger 2002, pp. 152–153, 296). While mass events may have a powerful impact on individuals, the leaders may need to establish cadres who can "personalize" the message of these events: "social mobilization will be more effective when interactions are made more person-to-person (rather than impersonal)" (Rogers, Goldstein, and Fox 2018, p. 362). Actual involvement by members of the targeted population – even in small ways initially – so as to "personalize" the events and deepen "feelings of synchrony" are ways that magnify this effect still more (Rogers, Goldstein, and Fox 2018, p. 364).[3]

Fifth are implications for *strategic planning* – an admonition for campaign leaders to take the long-term view that integrates each task of campaigning. Leaders are more successful when they treat each stage of the mobilization process as an investment in moving to a still higher level of mobilization, such as using events to coordinate and strengthen identification with the goal of independence within the platform population (Beissinger 2002, p. 154). Concessions won after earlier events (behavioral mobilization) should be institutionalized in ways that secure positions of power so as to give the campaign a place at the table to negotiate with the central government and to empower it with institutional weapons to coerce the central government to concede still more (Beissinger 2002, p. 402; Roeder 2007). At every stage of the mobilization process, leaders should seek to build within the platform population and central government a sense of the inevitability of independence (Beissinger 2002, p. 416).

And sixth are implications for *alliances*. Throughout the mobilization process, strategically minded leaders are more likely to be successful when they situate their struggle for independence of their platform population and homeland within the larger context of other platform populations and other causes. The leaders of smaller secessionist groups with limited capabilities and fewer opportunities may need to ride in the wake of larger and more powerful platform populations (Beissinger 2002, pp. 127–129). Within the homeland, the leaders may need to form strategic alliances with groups, such as environmentalists, with very different goals (Beissinger 2002, p. 389). They may need to stay attuned to opportunities for social appropriation of the resources of existing organizations to stage events and to sustain mobilization (McAdam, Tarrow, and Tilly 2001, pp. 47–48).

## Lens 2: mobilization as strategic choice

An alternative lens draws our attention to the strategic, operational, and tactical choices of the national-secession campaigns – and particularly to the options and constraints facing their leaders. Hroch's *European Nations: Explaining Their Formation* (2015, p. 266) gives special attention to "the decision making related to national identity" and presents insights into the forms of national agitation to develop national identity. In this analysis of attitudinal mobilization, Hroch (2015, p. 275) balances "efforts at national mobilization" against objective circumstances so that both strategic choice and contextual constraints are necessary, but neither is sufficient to explain the outcomes in different cases. Hroch draws our attention to the ways in which the leaders' nationalist agitation uses history and culture. In comments that prudently sidestep the debate whether a common national history or culture was a prerequisite for successful nationalisms, Hroch (2015, p. 163) observes that "a national history was one of the main arguments commonly used in the nineteenth century to achieve mobilization (and civic education) of one's national group, and to justify one's ethnic group's right to exist as a nation." In highlighting the "celebration of language" as a common theme in most movements, Hroch (2015, p. 205) notes that, "During national agitation it became a patriotic argument, which mainly addressed the members of the same ethnic group and urged them to cherish their mother tongue as one of the fundamental bonds guaranteeing their national identity." Hroch's analysis permits us to reframe the question from the necessary or sufficient conditions for mobilization to options and constraints on strategic choices to advance attitudinal mobilization. Similarly, Hroch (2015, pp. 235–263) notes how patriots in national agitation appropriated, or constructed from various existing elements, a national stereotype of what it meant to be a member of the nation; appropriated or built monuments, mythic figures, and historic personalities as icons of the nation; appropriated, revived, or invented rituals to celebrate the nation; and idealized the space and landscape of the homeland. Each of these is an operational choice that might advance attitudinal mobilization. Whether these are successful choices depends on the constraints that shape how the intended audience (platform population) receives these messages.

Roeder's *National Secession: Persuasion and Violence in Independence Campaigns* argues that many national-secession leaders learned their strategy either firsthand or secondhand from the writings of the Russian revolutionary Vladimir I. Lenin. These were first brought to secessionists through Soviet agencies but were then reinterpreted through the examples and publications of Algerian, Cuban, and Vietnamese revolutionaries and Ireland's secessionists. It was taught in university classrooms, off-campus study groups, and networks of revolutionaries (Sterling 1981, pp. 7–8, 13–16, 286–297; Romerstein 1986). This strategic influence was particularly apparent in some of the largest secessionist groups, including EPLF in Eritrea (Pool 2001, pp. 82–83), ETA in the Basque Country (Clark 1984, pp. 233–234), Fretilin in Timor Leste (Kingsbury 2009), IRA throughout Ireland (Sterling 1981, pp. 150–171), LTTE in Tamil Eelam (O'Ballance 1989, pp. 12, 15), PKK in Turkish Kurdistan (Romano 2006, p. 70), and Polisario in Western Sahara (Staff Researcher 2013).[4]

## Strategic challenges that shape responses

Roeder's (2018, p. 5) analysis stresses that the strategies of most national secessionists are shaped by a daunting strategic challenge – their own *operational weakness*. That is, national secessionists in most instances, most of the time, command far too few followers and resources to seize independence from a resistant central government. So, national secessionists must develop a strategy that emphasizes *strategic opportunism*. That is, national secessionists must prepare for circumstances when the central government is weakened to the point that it can resist no longer or foreign powers will intervene to impose separation. Yet, strategic preparations for these opportunities must operate under *forecast uncertainty*. That is, the national secessionists cannot forecast exactly when such opportunities will arise and what form they will take. Thus, secessionists must prepare a diverse toolkit of tactics. Over the long term, this will provide them with a flexible capacity to mobilize quickly with select tactics that are most likely at that moment to snatch power from an incapacitated central government or move a usually reluctant international community to intervention.

The response outlined in the widely circulated strategy is *programmatic coordination* so as to achieve *programmatic preemption*. Specifically, national-secession leaders begin the process of attitudinal mobilization and they build the organizational foundations for later behavioral mobilization that will permit them in an unexpected crisis to demonstrate to their own platform population, to the central government, and to the international community that the platform population is, indeed, united behind the goal of independence, that the proposed nation-state will be a viable state, and that any alternative proposals simply will not work. The strategy aims to build the attitudinal and organizational foundations for behavioral mobilization that convinces these others that granting independence is their only viable option.

Part of the strategic challenge for national secession leaders is *motivational heterogeneity* – that is, drawing together members of the platform population who see the goal of national independence in very different ways. *Enthusiasts* or true believers see national independence as a worthy end in itself, but many others see the struggle for and achievement of independence as means towards other ends. For *pragmatists*, independence promises opportunities for personal power and material gain. For *expressionists*, the struggle for independence offers an opportunity to engage in personally rewarding behaviors. For example, Hroch (1985, pp. 185–186) notes that during Phase B (Patriotic Agitation), successful European nationalist secessionists had to articulate in national terms the diverse interests of the constituents of the nation (e.g., Dion 1996; Lecours 2012, pp. 279–281; Meadwell 1993, p. 225). The campaign must link the program of independence to each of these constituencies but maintain a focus on independence as the common solution to their individual interests.

## *Attitudinal mobilization*

In the strategy to achieve programmatic preemption, as analyzed in Roeder (2018, pp. 67–91), attitudinal mobilization entails propagating the program for independence so as to coordinate members of the platform population around the belief that independence is both desirable and achievable. The strategy derived from the Marxist–Leninist tradition advises leaders to expend considerable energy on attitudinal mobilization of the platform population – particularly on the vanguard of this platform population (e.g., Kilcullen 2009, p. 34; Perritt 2008, pp. 25–35; Trapans 1991, p. 26). The activists who conduct this agitation and propaganda constitute essential parts of Hroch's "patriots." Hroch (1985, p. 23) elaborates on their role:

> between the manifestations of scholarly interest, on the one hand, and the mass diffusion of patriotic attitudes, on the other, . . . the driving force in this era of national agitation was a group of patriots who . . . saw their mission as the spreading of national consciousness among the people.

Campaign leaders may use this propagation of the program to reap five important benefits. First is *leadership unity*. Actual or anticipated attitudinal mobilization deters elites within the platform population from defecting from the independence project. It is the anticipation that a mobilized population is likely to reject alternative appeals that deters these defections even when members of these elites find their own commitment flagging. This is particularly important during the long periods when the goal of independence seems remote and after setbacks that call for rebuilding shattered campaigns. Second is *staff discipline*. This attitudinal mobilization (particularly political education classes for cadres) is critical to keeping the staff of the national-secession campaign motivated and focused on the common goal. The cadres in the field tailoring the message of independence to many particular audiences must be deterred from shifting the focus of their audiences away from the common goal (e.g., Pool 2001, p. 106). Third is *recruitment of pragmatists*. Attitudinal mobilization is essential to bringing pragmatists on board, by explaining to them why independence is the best way to serve their particular objectives. This requires tailoring a separate message for each interest, but with a common solution (e.g., Kaufman 2011, p. 953; Lieven 1993, p. 234; Meadwell 1993, p. 225; Romano 2006, p. 74). Fourth is *surge readiness*. Attitudinal mobilization is essential preparation for quick behavioral mobilization in future surge events when opportunities – sometimes unexpected opportunities – present themselves. The belief that independence will set things right has an energizing power (Hoffer 1951, p. 110; Skitka and Bauman 2008, pp. 31–33). The attitudinal mobilization is essential to preparation for the surges of behavioral mobilization that constitute the key "events" described in the contentious politics approach (McAdam, Tarrow, and Tilly 2001). And fifth is *tactical coordination*. In particular, attitudinal mobilization is essential to channeling the energies of expressionists who might otherwise use their activism in ways that undermine the message of the national-secession effort (e.g., Clark 1984, p. 158; Irish Republican Army 1956, Ch. 5; Kenny 2010, p. 536).

Yet the strategy of programmatic coordination also warns of the risks associated with over-zealous propagation. Leaders are constrained by the costs of propagation to limit the energy and resources spent on attitudinal mobilization. Moreover, extensive political education may alienate members of the platform population who take a more instrumental orientation to the independence campaign and who resist the tedium of time spent in political education meetings (e.g., Pool 2001, pp. 89–90, 99–101, 105).

## Building organizational foundations for mobilization

The tasks of attitudinal mobilization and preparation for behavioral mobilization require build-ing organizations to engage larger segments of the platform population (e.g., Chamberlain 2007, pp. 20, 33, 53; DeVotta 2004, p. 99; Erlich 1983, pp. 5–6; Hill 2002, pp. 43–46, 49–51; Iyob 1995, pp. 61–81; Kingsbury 2009, p. 43; Markakis 1987, pp. 67–68). This is a central theme that the Leninist tradition contributed to the national-secessionist strategy. A key objective of this organization building is to prepare the surge capacity that will bring a sudden and rapid mobili-zation of behavior such as voting, protesting outside government offices, erecting barricades in the streets, destroying governmental assets, or taking up positions of power within a new state. Roeder (2018, pp. 54–63) categorizes the organizational activities outlined in the strategy as three tasks – establishment of a core leadership, capacitation with a corps of cadres and activists who propagate the program, and association with the larger pool of potential participants in surge events.

*Organizational establishment* involves coordination among intellectuals to craft a program for independence, to limit alternative or competing programs, and to link these intellectuals with politicians who bring practical organizing and leadership skills (e.g., Krickus 1997, pp. 50–51; Lieven 1993, p. 224; Senn 1990, pp. 2, 7, 58; Trapans 1991, pp. 30–32). Each part of the estab-lishment task is daunting, since intellectuals often fall out among themselves and intellectuals and politicians often remain distrustful of one another. The campaign needs to keep all on board so as to keep them from defecting to competing projects. Practical politicians who turn to national secession for instrumental reasons such as their own political careers rather than true belief in independence may come over only when their prospects for a political career in the existing order begins to wane due to a collapsing central government (e.g., Zaheer 1994, pp. 125–126, 163–166). But they are also likely to be the first to defect to the side of the central government when the rewards for collaboration exceed those of secessionist activity.

*Organizational capacitation* is the task of building a corps of cadres and activists that can engage in attitudinal mobilization by propagating a message that reaches the larger population – often in face-to-face meetings such as pamphleteering, but at other times in anonymous actions such as demonstrative violence. The corps not only extends attitudinal mobilization within the platform population, but also prepares to take leadership positions within the platform population during future behavioral mobilization. These cadres and activists typically possess skills that many intellectuals and politicians lack, or lack the patience to carry out. The corps must be willing to sustain its propagation and training efforts even when the goal of independence appears to be remote, government crackdowns become severe, and the balance of costs and benefits in personal power or economic rewards is negative. The activities of this corps may be legal or illegal, violent or peaceful, but the strategy of programmatic coordination stresses that these activities must remain coordinated around the single goal of national independence. Most scholarly attention to this corps has focused on insurgents and terrorists, but typically the most important members are not engaged in violence. They are mostly unarmed civilians, such as journalists and publicists who write, print, and distribute the campaign's newspapers and pamphlets; teachers who conduct literacy and political-education courses in remote villages; and nurses who deliver babies safely and provide medical care to the ill and wounded (e.g., Clark 1984, p. 211; Díez Medrano 1995, p. 136; Pool 2001, p. 81). Even where members of this corps are willing to forego regular incomes for the cause, the larger the corps, the more expensive it will be to feed and house them, educate and drill them, maintain logistical support and communications with them, and monitor their behavior and sanction them when they go rogue (e.g., Markakis 1987, p. 113). These costs constrain leaders to limit the size of the corps.

*Organizational association* is the task of building a network of potential participants who constitute a reserve that can be mobilized into surges of behavioral mobilization. The Leninist tradition within the national-secessionist strategy proposes that this reserve be kept separate from the corps of cadres and activists by organizing this reserve through front organizations that the cadres and activists lead, without jeopardizing the professionalism of the corps. Due to forecast uncertainty, the leaders cannot know when opportunities will present themselves and what the nature of those opportunities will be. So, the preparation for more extensive behavioral mobilization presents five associational challenges that are highlighted by the strategy of programmatic preemption. First, the reserve must always be ready for behavioral mobilization, but not constantly in action. Second, maintaining this readiness requires seizing low-risk opportunities for action so as to drill and rehearse the activist reserve and possibly recruit still more members. Third, since the nature of the opportunities for a surge are uncertain, the cadres must prepare the reserve for a variety of future events such as voting, marching, or constructing barricades. Fourth, because the leaders should anticipate that a portion of the reserve will be unavailable at any particular time and for some forms of activity, and because the leaders need to use these events to convince the central government and international community that there is overwhelming support for the goal of independence, the campaign must create an oversized reserve throughout the platform population that unambiguously outnumbers supporters of remaining within the existing state. And fifth, in preparing for the long haul, the capacity to mobilize this reserve in surges must be matched by an ability to demobilize with as little damage to the campaign as possible (e.g., O'Ballance 1989, p. 119).

The number of people recruited to positions in the leadership, activist corps, and participatory reserve by true belief in the goal of independence as an end in itself is likely to be inadequate to demonstrate programmatic preemption. And the true believers (enthusiasts) often lack the skills needed to achieve programmatic preemption. Thus, campaign leaders typically must accept and manage some members who join in order to serve their power and economic interests (Wilson 1995, p. 34). This confronts national-secession leaders with a strategic dilemma: Those attracted by the expectation of personal gain from independence are essential to building and maintaining the overwhelming surge at the last critical moment, but these pragmatists potentially can subvert the campaign well before the goal of independence is achieved. Since the campaign typically offers few opportunities for gain during the long struggle, most pragmatists are unlikely to be attracted to the deprivations of working underground. For example, Hroch (1985, p. 134) finds in the initial periods of Europe's nationalist movements few major entrepreneurs, small-scale craft producers, or petty bourgeois among the patriots; these became prominent only in the final phase that he labels "the rise of a mass national movement" (also see Meadwell 1993, pp. 212–213). Yet, the need for their administrative, organizational, and political skills may require including a few even in leadership or staff positions and rewarding them with opportunities for near-term personal gain. The strategy warns of the danger that leaders face when these pragmatists enter the organization: pragmatists in these positions may lead the campaign toward compromise with the central government or even use their positions to pocket revolutionary taxes and extort payoffs in exchange for services and protection. Their self-serving actions may alienate large segments of the platform population and make potential recruits less likely to invest in the national-secession project due to cynicism about the motivation of those running the campaign.

## *Tactical choices in behavioral mobilization*

An essential part of the strategy of national secession is the choice among tactics to pursue the goal of independence. Although the most widely used tactics are peaceful, including election-eering, protests, and even clandestine subversion, most attention in the literature has focused on the choice of violence. For campaigns that have little prospect of defeating the central government in a contest of arms, the chief value of violence is in furthering attitudinal mobilization, building organizational strength, sparking surges of behavioral mobilization that constitute events, and signaling to the international community that independence is the only viable option (see, e.g., Byman 1998). That is, this violence is propaganda by other means.

As an investment in attitudinal mobilization in the larger population, violence has at least five benefits. First, it can be used to create the physical and psychological spaces to conduct intensive propaganda among members of the platform population. Villages that government officials vacate because they are "unsecured," at least for the nighttime hours, provide safe havens for meetings and political education to rally the platform and recruit activists (e.g., Romano 2006, pp. 88–89). Second, violence is a very visible signal to otherwise isolated members of the platform population that there are other members who also have grievances against the central government and support the cause of independence. In East Timor, for example, as Damien Kingsbury (2009, pp. 51–52) notes, violent acts served as "a beacon and the focal point for all facets of the independence movement." These actions are also unusually effective means of urging the platform population to take bold action alongside their co-nationals in the short term and means of recruiting a participatory reserve for the long run (e.g., Clark 1984, p. 49; Sullivan 1988, pp. 74, 92). Third, violence can be a way for campaign leaders to make a costly commitment to the platform population (and the international community) that the leaders will see the struggle for independence to its successful conclusion and not compromise with the central government. These serve as a signal to members of the platform population that investments in the campaign are more secure. Fourth, violence can provide a powerful signal to the platform population that the leaders know how to act like a state by protecting the platform population from coercion or at least avenging wrongs done to it. In the early stages of its struggle, John Sullivan (1988, p. 72) notes, ETA was "popular among large sections of the population, as it demonstrated ETA's power to strike back at the oppressor of the Basque people" (also see Clark 1984, p. 51; Kingsbury 2009, pp. 51–52; Romano 2006, p. 87). And fifth, violence can be a means for the campaign to demonstrate the promised rewards of independence when violence is used to redistribute property and power even before creation of a new state (Romano 2006, p. 75).

As an investment in organizational strength, violence can unify the leadership and strengthen its ties to its activist corps. Violence can recruit new cadres and activists to the campaign, deter defections among these staffers, and reassure these of the leadership's deep commitment to the cause of independence. Violence, such as bank robberies or raids of arsenals, can be a means to secure the resources to sustain the organization and its struggle. The organization-building role of violence is particularly strong in the literature on terrorism and civil wars (see Crenshaw 1981; Fearon and Laitin 2000; Fromkin 1975; Price 1977; Thornton 1964).

Yet, national-secession leaders typically find violence an imprudent choice. Opportunities for violence often recruit a particular type of expressionist who revels in burning down or blowing up things as ends in themselves (on expressive rewards from violence, see Schuessler 2000, p. ix; Wood 2003, pp. 18–19, 234–237). Campaign leaders typically need to limit such expressive action for at least four reasons: it alienates some members of the platform population, it exposes the campaign to retaliation from the central government, it builds a constituency within the campaign that will demand ever more opportunities to expand violence, and it introduces fissures into the campaign (e.g., English 2006, p. 382; Kingsbury 2009, pp. 55–56, 58). Violence can be costly to mount, and those costs rise sharply when a campaign seeks to maintain coordinated large-scale violence. As ETA learned, support for the militants and their families diverts resources from other propaganda activities that may be more efficient ways to produce attitudinal mobilization and to prepare for behavioral mobilization in a surge event. ETA also learned that violence provoked harsh governmental reprisals that destroyed the organization, killed or forced many of its leaders into exile and cadres into hiding, produced deep divisions in the Basque nationalist campaign, and alienated members of its platform population (Ahedo 2005, pp. 182–183, 185; Clark 1984, pp. 35–37, 41, 51–52; Sullivan 1988, pp. 36, 45, 74, 113, 135, 139).

## A strategy for demobilization?

The literature on national secession has only sporadically engaged the issue of demobilization and has given even less attention to its strategy – how leaders of national-secession campaigns might choose and manage this. Most of the attention in the literature has focused on demobilization as an objective decline in behaviors or as something done to rather than by campaigns. Tijen Demirel-Pegg (2017, p. 2) defines demobilization as "a decrease in the scale and scope of contentious collective action." Christian Davenport (2015, pp. 21, 299) offers a more expansive definition to embrace both attitudinal and behavioral demobilization, which includes termination of a national-secession campaign's institutions, loss of its members, termination or reduction in its behaviors, and fundamental shift in its goals. But his analysis focuses on how governmental repression might demobilize a campaign. In the New Africa campaign examined by Davenport (2015, pp. 238, 246, 248, 252) these governmental actions elicited self-destructive responses from the secessionist leaders, refocusing their attentions on internal disputes, sapping the campaign's energies at the expense of attitudinal and behavioral mobilization, and contributing to the collapse of the campaign. John Nagle's (2013) study of public opinion in Northern Ireland after 1998 suggests that behavioral demobilization may exact a price in attitudinal demobilization away from the goal of independence. In her analysis of what she labels "ideological deradicalization" (a form of attitudinal demobilization), Gyda Sindre (2018) explains that the Free Aceh Movement (GAM) shifted its goal from independence to regional autonomy within Indonesia as the result of internal divisions that arose as the movement grew and became organizationally complex, and as the leadership relaxed ideological controls over its new members. All three of these are studies of significant strategic failure: in the process of demobilization, national secessionists – that is, the enthusiasts still committed to independence – lost their roles in leading chief organizations, in shaping attitudes about independence among members of their platform populations, and in guiding behaviors in pursuit of that goal.

These studies set an important agenda for future research on strategies for demobilization – specifically, strategies that national-secession leaders who remain committed to the cause of independence may choose when they decide to demobilize the campaign's efforts. Further research might assess the effectiveness of different strategies of demobilization and how this effectiveness has varied with the different conditions prompting demobilization. As an analysis of strategies, the standard of effectiveness in this research should begin from the perspective of the leaders committed to independence and ask whether different strategic responses do more to preserve the likelihood of achieving the goal of independence. The conditions prompting leaders to choose to demobilize include situations when the current mobilizational activities overstretch the resources available to the campaign; produce a loss of leaders, staff, or members; or threaten the position of pro-independence leaders within the campaign. The best strategic response – best from the perspective of the remaining true believers – might be very different for each of these types of crises. For example, both ETA and the IRA pulled back when the intensity began to produce fissures in the organizations, to cause the organizations to lose members, and to make recruitment more difficult. Was this pullback a better means (compared to continuing the violence) to minimize any erosion in the prospects for independence? Demirel-Pegg (2017, p. 1) identifies catalysts that might produce one of these conditions that call for demobilization, including "severe repression, government concessions, countermobilization of opposition groups, [and] leadership changes." The best demobilization response for campaign leaders – that is, the response that does the least to diminish the prospects of achieving the goal of independence – may vary with each catalyst.

Further research is also needed on the specific types of demobilization. The literature does not define "attitudinal demobilization," but I would propose that this distinguish at least two dimensions – scaling back the propaganda efforts (such as fewer newspaper issues) and deemphasizing more extreme demands (such as suspending demands for an immediate referendum on independence). Empirical research may find it difficult to distinguish these, but it should not jump to the conclusion that silence from campaign leaders represents abandonment of the goal of independence rather than just a scaling back of propaganda efforts. Future research might identify how leaders attempt to accomplish each type of attitudinal demobilization with minimum damage to existing support for the goal of independence. New research might also distinguish behavioral demobilization from the decline of activism in the normal escalation–de-escalation tactical cycles (Demirel-Pegg 2017, p. 2). In Roeder's (2018, p. 62) analysis, the strategy of programmatic preemption derived from the Marxist–Leninist tradition idealized a billows-like capacity to expand and contract mobilization, but he does not offer many details on what the contraction of mobilization might mean in practice. Further research might assess whether nation-secession leaders have actually devised tactics for behavioral demobilization with minimum damage to attitudinal mobilization and minimum damage to the ability to resume behavioral mobilization at a later date when new opportunities arise.

*Philip G. Roeder*

# Notes

1 The term "platform population" refers to the collection of individuals that a national-secession campaign claims constitutes a nation, which is a population that purportedly has a right to a sovereign state of its own. The members of that platform population may not agree with these claims on their behalf.
2 I do not discuss Griffiths (2021), since he does a far better job of this in his chapter (Chapter 15, this volume).
3 The personalization and institutionalization of events are significant elements within the larger mechanism of brokerage, as identified by McAdam, Tarrow, and Tilly (2001, 26).
4 As Ted Robert Gurr and Jack A. Goldstone (1991, 335) note, this also provided strategic guidance in building decolonization/national-liberation movements in Vietnam, Cambodia, Zimbabwe, Nicaragua, Angola, Mozambique, Guinea-Bissau, Cape Verde, and Namibia.

# References

Ahedo, I. (2005). Political parties in the Basque Autonomous Community. In Gatti, G., Irazuzta, I. and Martínez de Albeniz, I. (eds) *Basque society: Structures, institutions, and contemporary life*. Reno: University of Nevada Center for Basque Studies, pp. 176–187.

Beissinger, M.R. (2002). *Nationalist mobilization and the collapse of the Soviet state*. New York: Cambridge University Press.

Byman, D. (1998). The logic of ethnic terrorism. *Studies in Conflict and Terrorism*, 21(2), pp. 149–169.

Chamberlain, E. (2007). *Faltering steps: Independence movements in East Timor: 1940s to the early 1970s*. Point Lonsdale, Victoria, Australia: Ernest Chamberlain.

Clark, R.P. (1984). *The Basque insurgents: ETA 1952–1980*. Madison: University of Wisconsin Press.

Crenshaw, M. (1981). The causes of terrorism. *Comparative Politics*, 13(4), pp. 379–399.

Davenport, C. (2015). *How Social Movements Die: Repression and Demobilization of the Republic of New Africa*. New York: Cambridge University Press.

Demirel-Pegg, T. (2017). The demobilization of protest campaigns. In Thompson, W.R. (ed.) *Oxford research encyclopedia of politics*. Available at: https://doi.org/10.1093/acreforce/9780190228637.013.251. (Accessed 29 March 2021).

Deutsch, K.W. (1961). Social mobilization and political development. *American Political Science Review*, 55(3), pp. 493–514.

Deutsch, K.W. (1966). *Nationalism and social communication: An inquiry into the foundations of nationality*, 2nd edn. Cambridge, MA: The MIT Press.

DeVotta, N. (2004). *Blowback: Linguistic nationalism, institutional decay, and ethnic conflict in Sri Lanka*. Stanford: Stanford University Press.

Díez Medrano, J. (1995). *Divided nations: Class, politics, and nationalism in the Basque Country and Catalonia*. Ithaca: Cornell University Press.

Dion, S. (1996). Why is secession difficult in well-established democracies? Lessons from Quebec. *British Journal of Political Science*, 26(2), pp. 269–283.

English, R. (2006). *Irish freedom: The history of nationalism in Ireland*. London: Pan Books.

Erlich, H. (1983). *The struggle over Eritrea, 1962–1978: War and revolution in the horn of Africa*. Stanford, CA: Hoover Institution Press.

Fearon, J.D. and Laitin, D.D. (2000). Violence and the social construction of ethnic identity. *International Organization*, 54(4), pp. 845–877.

Fromkin, D. (1975). The strategy of terrorism. *Foreign Affairs*, 53(4), pp. 683–698.

Griffiths, R.D. (2021). *Secession and the sovereignty game: Strategy and tactics for aspiring nations*. Ithaca: Cornell University Press.

Gurr, T.R. and Goldstone, J.A. (1991). Comparisons and policy implications. In Goldstone, J.A., Gurr, T.R. and Moshiri, F. (eds) *Revolutions of the late twentieth century*. Boulder: Westview Press, pp. 324–352.

Hill, H.M. (2002). *Stirrings of nationalism in East Timor: Fretilin 1974–78*. Otford, New South Wales, Australia: Otford Press.

Hoffer, E. (1951). *The true believer: Thoughts on the nature of mass movements*. New York: Harper & Row, Publishers.

Hroch, M. (1985). *Social preconditions of national revival in Europe: A comparative analysis of the social composition of patriotic groups among the smaller European nations*. New York: Cambridge University Press.

Hroch, M. (2015). *European nations: Explaining their formation*. New York: Verso.

Irish Republican Army (1956 [1985]). *Handbook for volunteers of the Irish Republican Army*. Boulder, CO: Paladin Press.

Iyob, R. (1995). *The Eritrean struggle for independence: domination, resistance, nationalism, 1941–1993*. New York: Cambridge University Press.

Kaufman, S.J. (2011). Symbols, frames, and violence: Studying ethnic war in the Philippines. *International Studies Quarterly*, 55(4), pp. 937–958.

Kenny, P.D. (2010). Structural integrity and cohesion in insurgent organizations: Evidence from protracted conflicts in Ireland and Burma. *International Studies Review*, 12(4), pp. 533–555.

Kilcullen, D. (2009). *The accidental guerrilla: Fighting small wars in the midst of a big one*. New York: Oxford University Press.

Kingsbury, D. (2009). *East Timor: The price of liberty*. New York: Palgrave Macmillan.

Krickus, R.J. (1997). *Showdown: The Lithuanian rebellion and the breakup of the Soviet empire*. Washington, DC: Brassey's.

Lecours, A. (2012). Sub-state nationalism in the western world: Explaining continued appeal. *Ethnopolitics*, 11(3), pp. 268–286.

Lieven, A. (1993). *The Baltic revolution: Estonia, Latvia, and Lithuania and the path to independence*. New Haven: Yale University Press.

Markakis, J. (1987). *National and class conflict in the horn of Africa*. New York: Cambridge University Press.

McAdam, D., Tarrow, S. and Tilly, C. (2001). *Dynamics of contention*. Cambridge: Cambridge University Press.

Meadwell, H. (1993). The politics of nationalism in Quebec. *World Politics*, 45(2), pp. 203–241.

Nagle, J. (2013). From secessionist mobilization to sub-state nationalism? assessing the impact of consociationalism and devolution on Irish nationalism in Northern Ireland. *Regional and Federal Studies*, 23(4), pp. 461–477.

O'Ballance, E. (1989). *The cyanide war: Tamil insurrection in Sri Lanka 1973–88*. London: Brassey's.

Perritt, H.H. (2008). *Kosovo liberation army: The inside story of an insurgency*. Urbana: University of Illinois Press.

Pool, D. (2001). *From guerrillas to government: The Eritrean people's liberation front*. Athens, OH: Ohio University Press.

Price, H.E. (1977). The strategy and tactics of revolutionary terrorism. *Comparative Studies in Society and History*, 19(1), pp. 52–66.

Roeder, P.G. (2007). *Where nation-states come from: Institutional change in the age of nationalism*. Princeton: Princeton University Press.

Roeder, P.G. (2018). *National secession: Persuasion and violence in independence campaigns*. Ithaca: Cornell University Press.

Rogers, T., Goldstein, N.J. and Fox, C.R. (2018). Social mobilization. *Annual Review of Psychology*, 69, pp. 157–181.

Romano, D. (2006). *The Kurdish nationalist movement: Opportunity, mobilization, and identity*. Cambridge: Cambridge University Press.

Romerstein, H. (1986). Political doctrine and apparatus. In Ra'anan, U. et al. (eds) *The hydra of carnage: the international linkages of terrorism and other low-intensity operations*. Lexington, MA: Lexington Books, pp. 59–75.

Schuessler, A.A. (2000). *The logic of expressive choice*. Princeton: Princeton University Press.

Senn, A.E. (1990). *Lithuania awakening*. Berkeley: University of California Press.

Sindre, G.M. (2018). From secessionism to regionalism: Intra-organizational change and ideological moderation within armed secessionist movements. *Political Geography*, 64, pp. 23–32.

Skitka, L.J. and Bauman, C.W. (2008). Moral conviction and political engagement. *Political Psychology*, 29(1), pp. 29–54.

Staff Researcher (2013). *War and insurgency in the Western Sahara*. Carlisle, PA: Strategic Studies Institute and U.S. War College Press.

Sterling, C. (1981). *The terror network: The secret war of international terrorism*. New York: Holt, Rinehart, and Winston.

Sullivan, J. (1988). *ETA and Basque nationalism: The fight for Euskadi 1890–1986*. New York: Routledge.

Thornton, T.P. (1964). Terror as a weapon of political agitation. In Eckstein, H. (ed) *Internal war*. Glencoe: Free Press of Glencoe, pp. 71–99.

Trapans, J.A. (1991). The sources of Latvia's popular movement. In Trapans, J.A. (ed) *Toward independence: The Baltic popular movements*. Boulder: Westview Press, pp. 25–41.

Wilson, J.Q. (1995). *Political organizations*. Princeton: Princeton University Press.

Wood, E.J. (2003). *Insurgent collective action and civil war in El Salvador*. Cambridge: Cambridge University Press.

Zaheer, H. (1994). *The separation of East Pakistan: the rise and realization of Bengali Muslim nationalism*. New York: Oxford University Press.

# 17

# REFERENDUMS AS INSTRUMENTS FOR SECESSION

*Matt Qvortrup*

"If the plebiscite decides for separatism, there is no more to be said about the political question" (Toynbee 1915: 251). Thus wrote the English historian Arnold Toynbee – an enthusiast for referendums to settle national and ethnic issues in 1915. Many of his contemporaries concurred, and in the aftermath of the First World War, long-standing issues of national self-determination were settled through 'plebiscites', as referendums tended to be called in those days (see Roshwald 2015 for an overview). After that, referendums have been increasingly used to resolve matters of secession and the creation of new States (Qvortrup 2022).

## Referendums on national and ethnic issues

Overall, one can distinguish between two types of referendums on ethnic and national issues. On the one hand, there are votes on transfers to another unit (irredentist referendums), on the other, there are referendums on secession (independence referendums). This chapter will focus on the latter.

Historically speaking, irredentist referendums were relatively common in the early part of the twentieth century but have become rarer since then, though some were held in the former Soviet Union (see Table 17.1).

Conversely, independence referendums have become more common since the Second World War, with a spike in the early 1990s.

But these votes have a long history. Three referendums on secession were held in 1861 in relation to the formation of the Confederate States of America. There, Texas, Virginia, and Tennessee submitted the decision to secede from the Union to the voters. In all cases, the voters opted for independence.[1] However, these referendums were unique, and it was another 45 years before the next independence referendum was held, namely the 1905 vote on Norwegian independence. The number of referendums on independence was also low in the following decades. Thus, there were no independence referendums in the 1920s, and in the 1930s, only two votes were held. Thus, in 1933 a vote was held on whether Western Australia should secede from Australia (a majority voted yes, but the vote was ignored by the state government, which had won the election on the same day and was opposed to secession). And in the Philippines a majority voted for a new secessionist constitution in 1935, which was a de facto vote for independence.

DOI: 10.4324/9781003036593-21

*Table 17.1* Irredentist referendums, 1527–2014

| | | |
|---|---|---|
| 1527 Burgundy | 1898 New South Wales | 1921 Sopron |
| 1791 Avignon | 1899 Western Australia | 1938 Austria (Anschluss) |
| 1792 Savoy | 1898 Queensland | 1947 Brigue |
| 1792 Nice | 1898 Victoria | 1948 Newfoundland |
| 1793 Moselle | 1899 New South Wales | 1948 Junagadh |
| 1798 Mulhouse | 1900 South Australia | 1949 Chandernagor |
| 1798 Geneva | 1909 Natal | 1955 Saarland |
| 1848 Lombardy | 1919 Aaland (Union with Sweden – | 1956 Togoland |
| 1848 Venice | not official) | 1961 Cameroun (two referendums |
| 1857 Moldova | 1919 Voralberg | in the two areas on unification) |
| 1860 Parma | 1920 Eupen | 1962 Singapore |
| 1860 Tuscany | 1920 South Schleswig | 1967 Afars |
| 1860 Sicily | 1920 North Schleswig/Sønderjylland | 1975 Sikim |
| 1860 Naples | 1920 Allenstein | 1991 Kourilles |
| 1860 Marche | 1920 Marienwerder | 1995 Transnistria (to join Russia) |
| 1860 Umbria | 1920 Klagenfurt | 2006 Transnistria |
| 1860 Savoy | 1921 Upper Silesia | 2014 Crimea |
| 1860 Nice | 1921 Tyrol | 2014 Donbas |
| 1898 Tasmania | | |

*Source*: Author's own study based on Centre for Research on Direct Democracy, 2020.

*Table 17.2* Secession referendums, 1944–1989 (those not leading to new States in bold)

| Parent Country | Seceding Country | Year | Turnout | Yes% |
|---|---|---|---|---|
| Denmark | Iceland | 1944 | 98 | 99 |
| China | Mongolia | 1945 | 98 | 64 |
| **Denmark** | **Faroe Islands** | **1946** | **50** | **64** |
| UK | Newfoundland | 1948 | 52 | 88 |
| France | Cambodia | 1955 | 100 | – |
| France | Guinea | 1958 | 97 | 95 |
| New Zealand | Western Samoa | 1961 | 86 | 77 |
| West Ind Fed | Jamaica | 1961 | 46 | 60 |
| France | Algeria | 1962 | 99 | 75 |
| Malaysia | Singapore | 1962 | 71 | 90 |
| UK | Malta | 1964 | 50 | 80 |
| USA | Micronesia | 1975 | 52 | 59 |
| **Canada** | **Québec** | **1980** | **85** | **41** |
| **Cyprus** | **Northern Cyprus** | **1985** | **78** | **70** |

*Source*: Author's own study based on Centre for Research on Direct Democracy, 2020.

Of the over 60 referendums on independence since 1860, 57 were held after 1944. The vast majority of these – 42 in total – were held in Europe (Qvortrup 2022). As shown in Table 17.2, there were 14 independence referendums in the four decades after World War II (Qvortrup 2022: 6).

This was a massive increase in the number of referendums compared to the previous decades. However, the number rose almost exponentially in the 1990s (see Table 17.3).

*Table 17.3* Secession referendums 1991–2019 (those not leading to new States in bold)

| Parent Country | Seceding Country | Year | Turnout | Yes Vote |
|---|---|---|---|---|
| USSR | Lithuania | 1991 | 91 | 84 |
| USSR | Estonia | 1991 | 77 | 83 |
| USSR | Latvia | 1991 | 74 | 88 |
| USSR | Georgia | 1991 | 98 | 90 |
| USSR | Ukraine | 1991 | 70 | 85 |
| **Georgia** | **South Ossetia** | **1991** | **98** | **90** |
| **Georgia** | **Abkhazia** | **1991** | **99** | **58** |
| Yugoslavia | Croatia | 1991 | 98 | 83 |
| **Croatia** | **Serbia** | **1991** | **98** | **83** |
| Yugoslavia | Macedonia | 1991 | 70 | 75 |
| USSR | Armenia | 1991 | 95 | 90 |
| **Bosnia** | **Serbia** | **1991** | **90** | **–** |
| **Serbia** | **Sandjak** | **1991** | **96** | **67** |
| Yugoslavia | Kosovo | 1991 | 99 | 87 |
| USSR | Turkmenistan | 1991 | 94 | 97 |
| **USSR** | **Karabagh** | **1991** | **N.A.** | **N.A.** |
| USSR | Uzbekistan | 1991 | 98 | 94 |
| **Macedonia** | **Albanians** | **1991** | **99** | **93** |
| **Moldova** | **Transnistria** | **1991** | **78** | **99** |
| Yugoslavia | Bosnia | 1992 | 99 | 64 |
| Yugoslavia | Montenegro | 1992 | 96 | 44 |
| **Georgia** | **South Ossetia** | **1992** | **NA** | **NA** |
| **Bosnia** | **Krajina** | **1992** | **99** | **64** |
| Ethiopia | Eritrea | 1993 | 99 | 98 |
| **Bosnia** | **Serbs** | **1993** | **96** | **92** |
| **USA** | **Puerto Rico** | **1993** | **48** | **73** |
| **USA** | **Palau** | **1993** | **64** | **68** |
| **Georgia** | **Abkhazia** | **1995** | **96** | **52** |
| **Québec** | **Cree** | **1995** | **95** | **75** |
| **Canada** | **Québec** | **1995** | **49** | **94** |
| **St Kitts and Nevis** | **Nevis** | **1998** | **57** | **61** |
| **USA** | **Puerto Rico** | **1998** | **50** | **71** |
| Indonesia | East Timor | 1999 | 78 | 94 |
| **Somalia** | **Somaliland** | **2001** | **–** | **97** |
| **New Zealand** | **Tokelau** | **2006** | | **95** |
| Yugoslavia | Montenegro | 2006 | 55 | 86 |
| Sudan | South Sudan | 2011 | 97 | 98 |
| **Britain** | **Scotland** | **2014** | **83** | **44** |
| **Iraq** | **Kurdistan** | **2017** | **72** | **92** |
| **Spain** | **Catalonia** | **2017** | **43** | **92** |
| **France** | **New Caledonia** | **2018** | **81** | **43** |
| **PNG** | **Bougainville** | **2019** | **87** | **98** |
| **France** | **New Caledonia** | **2020** | **85** | **46** |
| **France** | **New Caledonia** | **2021** | **43** | **4** |

*Source*: Author's own study based on Centre for Research on Direct Democracy, 2020.

And while the number of independence referendums dropped somewhat in the first two decades of the twenty-first century, the average number is still higher than it was in the 1970s and the 1980s. These tendencies beg the question: why did referendums on independence suddenly rise, and why there was a slight decline? Why, more precisely, did referendums increasingly become instruments of secession?

These are empirical questions that – as is often the case – are easier to pose than to answer. Given the relative paucity of independence referendums held over a relatively short period of time, it is debatable whether one can adequately analyse them using only quantitative techniques. (but see Mendez & Germann 2018). At the same time, relying on a purely qualitative approach risks that "the sample may be wildly unrepresentative" (Gerring 2008: 174). To understand the reasons for the use of referendums as instruments of secession requires one to draw on more recent techniques of comparative analysis that combine qualitative and quantitative analyses.

## Fuzzy Sets and referendums on independence

Fundamentally, one can distinguish between three types of referendums – those held in democracies, those held in autocracies, and those held in countries that fall in the intersection between the two. These can be analysed using a technique known as Fuzzy Sets Qualitative Comparative Analysis (fsQCA). This technique has been increasingly used in the social sciences to overcome the problem of representativeness in case studies and to counter the charge that pure quantitative analyses fail to appreciate the richness of qualitative – or *thick description* (Geertz 1973; Ragin 2008). Thus, using Fuzzy Sets, it is in theory possible to "have the best of both worlds; namely the precision that is prized by quantitative researchers and the use of substantive knowledge to calibrate measures that is central to qualitative research" (Ragin 2008: 182).

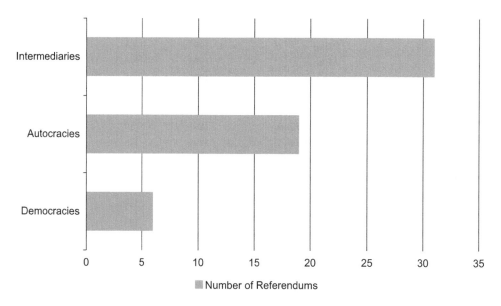

*Figure 17.1*  Number of independence referendums

*Source*: Author's own study based on Centre for Research on Direct Democracy, 2020.

Fuzzy Sets theory – as opposed to general set theory – is based on the assumption that there can be degrees of membership of a set. For example, countries can be more or less developed economically, or more or less democratic, and so on. Thus, when developing a crude Fuzzy Set, we can divide the countries into three categories, full democracies, autocracies, and countries that fall between the two, i.e., countries in transition using Polity-V scores.[2] This calibration can help us identify when and where referendums on independence (or secession) are likely to take place.

Doing this, we find that the vast majority of independence referendums are in countries that fall between the two (see Figure 17.1).

Perhaps surprisingly, there were a relatively high number of referendums in autocracies (19 in total). After all, dictatorships are premised on the assumption (or claim) that the ruler instinctively knows the will of the people. For this reason, there is little reason to ask them.

Conversely, there were a smaller number of independence referendums in democracies. So much for the idea that referendums are democratic. And, in any case, there is, as Dion has shown, very little appetite for secession in democratic countries (Dion 1996).

But by far the greatest number of votes were held in countries that were on the threshold of becoming democracies. A total of 31 referendums were held in countries that fall in the intermediary category, such as Yugoslavia and the Soviet Union in their final years.

Why this difference? What accounts for it? Why were there some referendums on independence in democracies, but many more in countries that were in the intermediate category of emerging – or semi-democracies?

The problem with referendums from an analytical point of view is that they are a case of what quantitative researchers call *Multiple Conjunctural Causation* (Rihoux 2008: 726) – that is, something that can be the result of many causes. For example, to use Rihoux's example, you can be fired from your job because you steal, because you have acted unprofessionally, or due to budget cuts (Rihoux 2008). In the same way, referendums can be caused by many different considerations.

The logic of holding an independence referendum in a period of transition is very different to holding one in a full democracy. In democracies, independence referendums are generally held for constitutional reasons, and to add legal legitimacy to the decision. In intermediary States, the reason for having referendums on independence are symbolic; to create a sense of unity.

## Referendums in transition countries

Why were more referendums held when countries are facing an existential crisis, and often after warlike situations? These referendums were held when things were in flux, and when the elites were not sure what the future held. Most of them were held in the aftermath of the fall of the Berlin Wall, at a time when commitment to democracy was taken for granted (Fukuyama 1989). At some level, these referendums can be seen to be part of an electoral calculus. As this author has put it elsewhere, the probability that an actor . . . will submit a national and ethnic issue to a vote depends on the relationship between the competition . . . the actor is facing and the . . . distance between the actor's preference point and the preference point of the median voter (Qvortrup 2022).

In other words, when politicians are under pressure, and the issue is a popular one, it is strategically prudent to put the matter to a vote. But there is also a deeper, almost metaphysical reason for holding a referendum on secession. This is often overlooked in the comparative literature, though, as we shall see, there is plenty of support for this in the case-study literature.

The fascinating thing about referendums is that they are simultaneously part of different discourses. The *official* discourse – as so often is the case – is formal, legal, and even idealistic. This perspective stresses the rule of law and lofty principles such as right of a people to self-determination. This sits alongside an instrumental or strategic logic, which is based on considerations of *Realpolitik*; and finally, the vote itself has a symbolic value.

Faced with the demand that they were "democratic", elites in areas that were on the threshold of democracy (such as Lithuania and Croatia in the early 1990s), opted for referendums to comply with the new paradigm of "government by the people". In doing so, they complied with the demands of the European Community, which made recognition conditional upon positive verdicts in referendums (Radan 2000; Rich 1993). This requirement has become standard in the referendums sponsored by the various States or international organisations. Thus, the 2001 Bougainville Peace Agreement included an "agreement to a constitutionally guaranteed referendum on Bougainville's political future to be held amongst Bougainvilleans 10–15 years after the establishment of the Autonomous Bougainville Government" (Bougainville Peace Agreement 2001). Likewise, the Comprehensive Peace Agreement in Sudan included a requirement that a referendum be held before possible secession by South Sudan, and a similar provision was part of the 2003 Comprehensive Peace Agreement in Sudan, which in Article 1.3 stated: "That the people of South Sudan have the right to self-determination, inter alia, through a referendum to determine their future status".

At one level, therefore, it seems that referendums are forced upon the would-be seceding nations to comply with some form of international commitment to democracy and government by the people. That such commitments were compatible with the conditionality paradigm (see Crawford 2000) is unlikely to be a coincidence. This paradigm required that aid was given in return for a commitment to holding free and fair elections. Thus, many of the referendums were held or planned at a time when overseas aid was conditional upon compliance with a (formally) democratic system of government. Yet, as Crawford, notes, this "commitment to the principles of human rights and democracy [was] at best partial" (Crawford 1997: 69). And, in any case, this requirement is not as burdensome as one might think.

To understand the logic – or the underlying essence – of referendums as instruments of secession, one needs to understand the rich context in which they are set. This means that one must look at the context of the referendums rather than try to engage in reductionism. As has been said, "it is not in our interest to bleach human behaviour of the very properties that interest us before we begin to examine it" (Geertz 1973: 17).

Hence, to understand referendums as instruments of secession, one needs to describe them in their multifaceted richness. And, as will be shown in this chapter, a main aspect of them is their "symbolic" aspect.

Referendums on independence exist not only as a vehicle for giving legitimacy to a vote, nor just because they fit with what is strategically and electorally prudent for rulers. Rather, they are also often held for internal and symbolic reasons.

Asking people to vote for independence can be seen as a way of consolidating and even cementing the feeling of a shared destiny. The vote in Bougainville in 2019 is a case in point. The vote was not about practical politics or independence. Most people had no clear idea of what that entailed. But they wanted to send a message. Thus, the main reason for holding a vote was that it provided meaning, and as such it can be analysed using the tools of ethnography as much as those of those of political economy. Clifford Geertz has noted that "the political processes of all nations are wider and deeper than the formal institutions designed to regulate them" (Geertz 1973: 316). This may be particularly true for independence referendums. Formally, these are held to regulate issues pertaining to national self-determination and ethnic complexity.

However, they are – as the previous quote from Bougainville suggests – more than merely on policy issues. Politics in general – and perhaps independence referendums in particular – are examples of this "politics of meaning" (Geertz 1973: 311). And this is nowhere better illustrated than in the sometimes (apparently) votes held in small places in the Caucasus with little prospect of ever becoming independent States.

From a "rational" perspective – i.e., if the aim is statehood and membership in the United Nations – the referendums in Donbas in Eastern Ukraine, South Ossetia (formally part of Georgia), and even North Cyprus are unlikely to achieve independence. However, as Dahlia Scheindlin found in a perceptive analysis, "the referendum process is not meaningless but symbolic; it fills the space between the actual and desired political reality for the entities who vote" (Scheindlin 2012: 65).

The main aim of the referendums in these cases is to "solidify the base", to use a term often used in electoral research of partisan supporters. Writing about the referendums in Transdniestria, Scheindlin observed that, "the small strip of Moldova across the Dniester River and bordering Ukraine had almost nothing resembling a coherent national or ethnic identity (Scheindlin 2012: 70). Yet, in this and other cases (Scheindlin cites Northern Cyprus and Nagorno-Karabakh), the referendums helped, "to forge peoplehood out of a diverse ethnic population" (Scheindlin 2012: 72).

The use of referendums can – to use a philosophical terminology introduced by Wittgenstein – be seen as a "language game", one in which the meaning of the word, broadly speaking, "gets its meaning in the context of its use" (Wittgenstein 2016: 262). Generally, in constitutional debates, and in democratic political theory, the referendum is part of a language game that emphasises choice and decision-making. However, in the context of a secession, it is also part of a symbolic discourse. This way of thinking about politics suggests that every political action "stands for something other than itself, and it also invokes an attitude, a set of impressions, or a pattern of events associated through time, through space, through logic, or through imagination with the symbol" (Edelman 1984: 6). This is particularly true for ethnonational referendums in general, and perhaps independence referendums in particular. As Scheindlin writes, "the actual goal of the referendum is less important than the political meaning that can be discovered from the process" (Scheindlin 2012: 75).

This symbolic importance of the referendum can also be observed historically. An example of this was arguably the case in Norway in 1905.

## Norway 1905

On 29 July 1905, the Norwegian Department of Ecclesiastical Affairs issued a statutory instrument – requiring Lutheran pastors to hold shorter sermons on Sunday, 13 August. On this particular Sunday, pastors were requested to "so arrange the service that it will be finished in good time before 1 pm" (quoted in Wambaugh 1920: 1069).

Given that church services started at 10 a.m., the request was not unreasonable, yet this is hardly a matter that needed government regulation. But 13 August was not just any Sunday. It was the day of the referendum on independence from the dual monarchy of Norway–Sweden, and the Norwegian government was taking nothing for granted. This was a national celebration of nationhood – and so was the referendum.

In the months before, matters had come to a head. The Norwegians were reluctant to pay roughly half of the costs of the dual monarchy's consulates, especially as most of them were in countries Norway did not trade with. After the Swedes did nothing, both chambers in the bicameral Norwegian *Stortinget* passed a unanimous resolution on establishing separate

Norwegian consulates. When the Swedish king, Oscar II, refused to sign the law, the Norwegian prime minister, Christian Michelsen, declared that the *Stortinget* immediately conferred the powers formerly vested in the monarch to themselves.

This hurt Swedish pride, especially among aristocrats. Some called for armed intervention. Yet, there were fears that an invasion would be a pretext for Russia (Sweden's eastern neighbour) to attack and, what was as important, the Swedish army was not skilled in what was likely to be years of guerrilla warfare in the Norwegian mountains. Furthermore, the Social Democrats and trade unions in Sweden were sympathetic towards the Norwegians.

The Swedes had maintained – correctly – that a unilateral declaration of independence was legally void, as Norway had freely agreed to enter into the dual monarchy. But this was politics rather than black-letter law, and Michelsen – a provincial shipping magnate from Bergen who had become prime minister – was out of his depth and had taken on a task he couldn't manage. Or so the Swedes believed.

The Swedes decided to call his bluff and challenge the Norwegians to hold a referendum. After a week of deliberations, the Swedish parliament issued a communique that called for a vote to ascertain the Norwegians' views. If the result showed the "unequivocal expression of the people's view of the matter [Norwegian independence]" then the Swedes would be willing to negotiate (Sweden's *Riksdag Till Kungun*, 28 July 1905, translated by the author).

Michelsen acted resolutely. The Swedes had underestimated him. Indeed, he had already secured support for a plebiscite on 23 July – five days before the Swedes officially issued their challenge. It is not entirely clear from the records and archives, but it seems that Michelsen got wind of the Swedish decision before it became official and secured support for a referendum before the Swedes threw down the constitutional gauntlet.

The Norwegians immediately began to organise the referendum. Only one day after the Swedish *Riksdag*'s ultimatum, the *Stortinget* issued a statutory instrument, which in considerable detail instructed municipal and parish-council officials that a referendum would be held "the 13th of August from one o clock in the afternoon" (Cirkulære Justitsministeriet 29 July 1905).

The Norwegian authorities showed no complacency and were keen that as many people as possible voted. Hence, the aforementioned request that pastors give short sermons. The would-be separatists showed attention to details, whatever else one thinks about their policy.

The result was astounding, as 99% voted for independence on a 85.6% turnout. The *Stortinget* sent notification to the Swedes. The latter sought reconciliation and sent a request to The Hague Tribunal. But Stockholm knew – not least because of the overwhelming result – that the game was up. They invited the Norwegians to negotiations in the Swedish border town of Karlstad on 31 July. The parties negotiated until 23 August, when it was agreed that the Norwegians would be granted independence subject to a number of largely cosmetic conditions. The Norwegians – albeit grudgingly – accepted. On 16 October, the [Swedish] *Riksdag* – after two months of negotiations – approved a government resolution to annul the Act of Union (Wambaugh 1920: 168). It should be clear from this example that the Norwegian referendum was *more* than a mere vote on a policy matter. But, of course, this was a long time ago. In 1905 Norway was a developing country, and in many ways similar to the countries that sought to break free from the Soviet Union or Yugoslavia in the 1990s.

On the face of it, the experiences from these countries (and from Norway in 1905) contrast with the logic of holding referendums in established democracies. Yet, as the following examples suggest, this impression might be in slight need of revision. Before a close examination of Catalonia, the cases of Québec and Scotland will be briefly considered.

## Québec and Scotland

Above all, neither the Parti Québécois (PQ) in Québec in 1980 and 1995 nor the Scottish National Party (SNP) in 2014 held referendums because this was demanded by an external body, as in the case in Bougainville, or in the former Yugoslavia. The Badinter Commission demanded referendums in Croatia and in Bosnia and Herzegovina. Slovenia held a referendum before any demands were made. Referendums in Krajina and in Republika Srpska were not held in response to any demands.

Formally, the logic of having a referendum in a democratic State is that this instrument allows voters to have their proverbial cake and eat it. They can vote for a party they like, but disagree with the same party on an important issue. This is what happened in Scotland. Thus, it has been reported that up to one-third of those who vote for the SNP do *not* support independence. Politically speaking, the SNP could have claimed that an election victory gave it a mandate. Indeed, this was the official position before 1999. However, as the SNP got closer to power – the party was on the fringes in the 1990s and before – it needed to have an electoral strategy that could appeal to a larger number of voters. Hence, the party changed its position and offered voters a choice; they could vote for a modern, progressive, centre-left party without committing themselves to a referendum. The voters then could have a say later on in a referendum.

This position was akin to the one adapted by the PQ, a secessionist party in the Francophone Canadian province that won its first election in 1976. The then party leader, René Lévesque, made a point of his party's position on the centre-left and was adamant that a vote for PQ was not *ipso facto* a mandate for a referendum (Pinard & Hamilton 1978).

At a theoretical level, it seems that the Scottish and Québécois nationalists granted referendums in the form of what A.V. Dicey called a 'People's veto' (Qvortrup 1999). From a more idealistic point of view, this strategy seems to conform to the unwritten rules of the game. Following referendums on independence in other developed countries, it was seen (almost) as a convention in the constitutional sense that declarations of independence were preceded by positive verdicts in referendums. Indeed, in the case of Québec, there were precedents for referendums in Iceland (1944) and Malta (1964). Likewise, in the Scottish case, there had been a referendum in Montenegro which was demanded by the European Union. Not having a referendum on independence would go against what James March and Johan P. Olsen call "the logic of appropriateness" (March & Olsen 2009: 479).

One should not *a priori* dismiss the importance of norms and the sense of "appropriateness", but electoral politics is more often than not a bare-knuckle fight. Without being able to quantify the feelings and motivations that account for human action, it seems that these referendums were also held because of a sense of the "logic of consequentiality" – that is, a more Machiavellian (or rational choice) sense of what was in the interest of the actors (Qvortrup 2022: 6).

To allow the voters to, politically speaking, have their cake and eat it, the SNP and the PQ were able to win elections – and then postpone the referendum to a later date. This was the strategy followed by First Minister Alex Salmond in Scotland before the referendum was held.

Why, then, was he holding a referendum which he was all but certain to lose? As the leader of a secessionist party whose very aim is to fight for an independent Scotland, he could not afford to offend the members. Many who join the SNP do so mainly because they want to win independence. For this reason, he had no choice but to hold a referendum. The logic of party politics demanded that the vote be held, as the party had won an election. If not now, then when?

Again, this is a case of the logic of consequentiality. Salmond wanted independence by secession from the United Kingdom. But he was also a party politician. The game that he was playing was not just one against the Unionists, still less just one against the government in London, but also one against hardliners in his party.

Thus, two kinds of logic exist, which are similar but not identical: the rallying of whole nations versus the rallying of the party faithful. In 'nations' within multi-ethnic States on the threshold of becoming democratic, forged nationhood is a tool for creating a sense of unity.

While legal norms and pressure from other States or international organisations are important for would-be territorial units that are contemplating referendums on secession or independence, it seems – on the basis of these examples – referendums on secession are held to mobilise parties that support independence. The example of Catalonia is a good illustration of this. A bit of context is necessary to understand the logic of how the referendum was used as an instrument to solidify the base among the Catalan secessionists.

## Catalonia

In 2017, a majority of the voters in Catalonia, an autonomous community within Spain, voted overwhelmingly for independence in what supporters called a referendum – but which opponents called an illegal and unconstitutional act. Over 92% voted in favour of the referendum question, which asked: "Do you want Catalonia to become an independent State in the form of a republic?" (Guidi & Casula 2019: 183).

This result was – on the face of it – reminiscent of the 1944 referendum in Iceland and the aforementioned vote in Norway – when similar majorities voted for independence from Denmark and Sweden respectively. However, the turnout in these referendums was considerably higher than in Catalonia. In both Iceland and Norway, it was more than 90%. In Catalonia, by contrast, only 43% of eligible voters turned out to vote (Guidi & Casula 2019: 183).

The long history of Catalonia is bitterly contested. Against this reality, this chapter will focus on the developments of the past century to understand the necessary context.

In 1913, a referendum was held in the municipalities of Catalonia, which led to the endorsement for setting up a deliberative body called *Mancomunitat de Catalunya* (Balcells 2015). At this stage the Spanish king had already endorsed a plan for Catalan autonomy, partly in response to the outrage caused by *la Setmana Tràgica* (a series of violent confrontations between the Spanish army and anarchists, socialists, and republicans of Barcelona). This only led to cosmetic changes.

As a result, in 1919, the Catalan assembly proposed the so-called *Projecte d'Estatut d'Autonomia de Catalunya de 1919*. This was largely in response to President Woodrow Wilson's apparent endorsement of the principle of self-determination of the people as a basis for the post–World War I settlement in Europe (Neuberger 2001). But the appeal came to naught. It was rejected by the *Cortes* (the Spanish parliament), and shortly thereafter, Spain became a dictatorship. The aspirations of the Catalans resurfaced again after the establishment of the Second Spanish Republic in 1931. The 1931 Constitution of Spain provided that that historical nations could hold referendums on further autonomy (Constitución española de 1931: Art 12).

Pursuant to this provision, referendums were held in Catalonia in 1931, in the Basque Country in 1933, and in Galicia in 1936. In all of these cases, the referendums were approved by nearly 100% of the voters. In all cases, the turnout was around 75%. Thus, there was a clear precedent for the referendums in Catalonia, the Basque Country, and Galicia that were held in 1979 and 1980. They took place after the restoration of democracy in Spain in the late 1970s.

In 1976, in the first democratically held statewide referendum in Spanish history, 97% of voters approved the transition to democracy. The agreement between the outgoing regime and the democratic parties paved the way for election of a constituent assembly in 1977, and the constitution of 1978, which established a semi-federal structure, but one where there were provisions for, "three historic nations – Catalonia, Galicia, and the Basque Country – to acquire regional governments with legislative powers" (Rourke, Hiskes, & Zirakzadeh 1992: 116).

There was a violent terrorist campaign in the Basque Country, where the separatist terrorist organisation *Euskadi Ta Askatasuna* (ETA) killed dozens of citizens every year. In Catalonia, by contrast, demands for outright independence were non-existent, and there were no examples of terrorist attacks. Indeed, several nationalist parties supported various governments in Madrid and were able to exert concessions from the right-wing central government.

After the socialist *Partido Socialista Obrero Español* (PSOE) came to power in 2004 tensions rose between the Partido Popular and its erstwhile Catalan allies.

The new socialist prime minister, Rodríguez Zapatero, had publicly promised to support a new statute of autonomy for Catalonia. Hence, a referendum was held in Catalonia on the so-called *Estatut d'Autonomia de Catalunya* (*Estatut*) in 2006. The new statute included references to a national anthem, but also – so claimed critics – impacted on the arrangement of transfers between Catalonia and other less prosperous provinces. The plan had been endorsed by all parties in the *Cortes* – with the exception of Partido Popular, which was opposed to any further decentralisation, and by the Catalan republican party, *Esquerra Republicana de Catalunya*, for the very opposite reasons.

But demands for greater autonomy were not limited to Catalonia. In February 2007, a vote was held on further autonomy in Andalucía (supported by 90% on a 35% voter turnout). This, however, was less controversial. The same could not be said for the developments in the Basque Country.

A vote had been scheduled in Spain's richest province for 2008 based on a statute that – according to critics – amounted to de facto independence. The Basque premier Juan Ibarretxe, who was also the leader of the moderate Basque national party *Euzko Alderdi Jeltzalea*, sought to fireproof himself against more radical elements of Basque nationalism. In this case, facing something that amounted to more than mere devolution, the referendum was denounced by both the (PSOE) and the Partido Popular. The two parties appealed the decision to hold the referendum to Spain's Constitutional Court, which found in their favour. The Basque leader appealed the decision to the European Court of Human Rights, which also ruled against him (El Pais, 23 February 2010).

The focus was now on Catalonia. While the *Estatut* was endorsed by just under 74% of those voting in the referendum in Catalonia in 2006, the turnout was only under 50%. The result, as in the case of the Basque Country, was appealed to the courts, in what was becoming a pattern.

The courts took their time. Finally, after four years of deliberation, The Constitutional Court ruled the statute unconstitutional, by a narrow 6–4 majority, and substantially rewrote it (Tribunal Constitucional 16th June 2010). This marked a turning point. When the Partido Popular formed a government in 2011, neither side had any incentive to reach a compromise. Electorally, seeking a conflict was a mechanism of solidifying the base.

With little support in Catalonia, Mariano Rajoy, the new Conservative prime minister, could use the showdown with Artur Mas, the premier of Catalonia, to rally his supporters around the Spanish flag. Likewise, Mas, the leader of the largest Catalan party, the previously relatively moderate *Convergència Democràtica de Catalunya* (CDC), became radicalised, not least as Rajoy's stance hardened opinion among Catalan nationalists. An estimated one million Catalans joined a protest in 2012. Much as Madrid and Barcelona disagreed, the conflict was an excellent mechanism for creating unity within the respective camps.

When Mas failed to win a majority in the provincial election, he was forced to rely on support from the more left-wing *Esquerra Republicana de Catalunya* (ERC). While CDC and ERC had won only 44% of the vote, the disproportionality of the electoral system meant that they had a narrow majority. They used this to organise a referendum in 2014. This was declared illegal by the Constitutional Court in October 2014. Mas instead organised a "consultation", which went ahead despite another ruling by the highest court. On 14 November 2014, 80% of those taking part supported independence, although the turnout (which was never officially provided by the provincial government) was below 41%.

As a result of the political instability that followed, Mas established the overtly separatist party *Junts pel Sí*. However, once again, the courts got involved. Mas was charged with misuse of public funds. In 2015, he was found guilty and barred from holding public office for ten years. His successor, Carles Puigdemont, swiftly moved to call yet another referendum on 9 June 2017. He stressed that the Catalans were willing to compromise, but that if the Spanish government would not give way, he would "hold it [the referendum] anyway" (quoted in Guidi & Casula 2019: 185). Thus, while claiming to be committed to compromise, he did not leave open the possibility of anything short of his ultimate goal.

Not everyone in his government was happy with this strategy. The escalation of tensions *within* the Catalan government led to the sacking of Jordi Baidget, the minister of enterprise and a moderate, on 3 July.

The referendum, once again, was declared illegal by the Courts. The Madrid government also used other techniques, not all of which were welcomed by international opinion. Ten days before the referendum, an estimated 10 million ballot papers were seized by national police. On the same day, 20 September, 14 public officials, including the finance secretary, were arrested. In a show of force that appeared heavy-handed, the Madrid government deployed 16,000 police officers to disrupt the vote.

Nevertheless, the referendum went ahead on 1 November 2017. And, as noted previously, the vast majority voted "yes". A few weeks later, the Catalan parliament declared independence. In response, the Spanish government imposed direct rule. Puigdemont fled to Belgium, and the Spanish government refused negotiations. The Spanish government received support from other European capitals, while several Catalan ministers were charged with sedition. This notwithstanding, the separatist parties won a slim majority of parliamentary seats (70 out of 135 seats) in the Catalan election on 21 December 2017. But they fell short of a majority in the popular vote, securing only 47.6% of the vote.

The demand for outright Catalan independence is a recent phenomenon. Previously, the demand had been for greater autonomy. This is what Catalan nationalists demanded (and got) after the referendum in 1931, and again in 1980, and, indeed, in 2006. However, the opposition from the Partido Popular hardened opinion. Playing to anti-Catalan feeling in many parts of Spain, the Partido Popular deliberately played hardball, and the Catalan government – also seeking to gain support – followed the same strategy.

## Conclusion

The rationale for holding independence referendums is an instance of what quantitative researchers call "Multiple Conjunctural Causation". These referendums are about politics, about law, and about the symbolism of national unity. This chapter has focused on the symbolic aspect of the use of these referendums.

Of the over 60 referendums on independence since 1860, 56 were held after 1944, and the majority of these were held after 1990. The vast majority of these – 42 in total – were held in Europe. The overwhelming plurality of these referendums were held in territorial units that were in transition to democracy, and after the breakdown of larger units such as the Soviet Union and the former Yugoslavia.

Undoubtedly, the new elites in these places acted strategically, but the main explanatory factor for holding referendums seems to be a symbolic one. Overall, votes on independence exist not only as a mechanism for providing support for independence, nor just because they fit with what is strategically and electorally prudent for rulers, but also, by asking people to vote for secession, to consolidate and cement the feeling of national unity. From a purely rational perspective, many of these referendums seem pointless, as they unlikely result in the formation of a new State. However, from a symbolic perspective, the very vote itself helps to create unity and is a part of a mental state formation process. Independence referendums "condense into one symbolic event . . . patriotic pride, remembrances of past glories or humiliations, promises of future greatness" (Edelman 1984: 6). The referendum hence becomes a myth, which – to use Malinowski's apt phrase – help weave the individual into "the social texture of his [or her] tribe" (Malinowski 1948: 93).

## Notes

1 In Tennessee, 104,913 (69%) voted for secession, while 47,238 voted against (Anderson 2013: 123). In Texas the figures were 44,317 (72%) for and 13,020 against (Anderson 2013: 116). In Virginia, 125,950 (86%) voted for and 20,373 against (Anderson 2013: 120).
2 Polity5 Project, Political Regime Characteristics and Transitions, 1800–2018 provides an annual, cross-national, time-series and polity-case formats coding democratic and autocratic "patterns of authority" and regime changes in all independent countries with total population greater than 500,000 in 2018 (167 countries in 2018).

## References

Anderson, L. M. 2013, *Federalism, Secession, and the American State, Divided*, New York: Routledge.
Balcells, A. 2015, *La Mancomunitat de Catalunya (1914); Centennial Symposium*, Barcelona: Institut d'Estudis Catalans.
Bougainville Peace Agreement 2001, <www.abg.gov.pg/peace-agreement>
Cirkulære Justitsministeriet 29 July 1905.
Constitución española de 1931.
Crawford, G. 1997, "Foreign aid and political conditionality: Issues of effectiveness and consistency", *Democratization*, 4(3): 69–108.
Crawford, G. 2000, *Foreign Aid and Political Reform: A Comparative Analysis of Democracy Assistance and Political Conditionality*, Basingstoke: Palgrave.
Dion, S. 1996, "Why is secession difficult in well-established democracies? Lessons from Quebec", *British Journal of Political Science*, 26(2): 269–283.
Edelman, M. 1984, *The Symbolic Uses of Politics*, Urbana: University of Illinois Press.
El Pais 2010, "Estrasburgo no admite el recurso del PNV sobre la anulación de la consulta soberanista", *El Pais*, 23rd Feb, A1.
Fukuyama, F. 1989, "The End of History?", *The National Interest*, 16: 3–18.
Geertz, C. 1973, *The Interpretation of Cultures*, New York: Basic books.
Gerring, J. 2008, "Case selection for case-study analysis: Qualitative and quantitative techniques", in J. M. Box-Steffensmeier, H. E. Brady & D. Collier (eds), *The Oxford Handbook of Political Methodology*, Oxford: Oxford University Press: 174–198.
Guidi, M. & Casula, M. 2019, "The Europeanization of the Catalan debate", in C. Closa, Margiotta & G. Martinico (eds), *Between Democracy and Law: The Amorality of Secession*, London: Routledge: 173–192.
Malinowski, B. 1948, *Magic, Science and Religion and Other Essays*, New York: The Free Press.
March, J. G. & Olsen, J. P. 2009, "The logic of appropriateness", in R. E. Goodin (ed), *The Oxford Handbook of Political Science*, Oxford: Oxford University Press: 478–497.
Mendez, F. & Germann, M. 2018, "Contested sovereignty: Mapping referendums on sovereignty over time and space", *British Journal of Political Science*, 48(1): 141–165.
Neuberger, B. 2001, "National self-determination: A theoretical discussion", *Nationalities Papers*, 29(3): 391–418.

Pinard, M. & Hamilton, R. 1978, "The Parti Québécois comes to power: An analysis of the 1976 Quebec election", *Canadian Journal of Political Science/Revue canadienne de science politique*, 11(4): 739–775.

Qvortrup, M. 1999, "A V Dicey: The referendum as the people's veto", *History of Political Thought*, 20(3): 531–546.

Qvortrup, M. 2022, I Want to Break Free: A Practical Guide to Making a New Country. Manchester: Manchester University Press.

Radan, P. 2000, "Post-secession international borders: A critical analysis of the opinions of the Badinter Arbitration Commission", *Melbourne University Law Review*, 24(1): 50–76.

Ragin, C. C. 2008, "Measurement versus calibration: A set-theoretic approach", in J. M. Box-Steffens-meier, H. E. Brady, & D. Collier (eds), *The Oxford Handbook of Political Methodology*, Oxford: Oxford University Press: 174–198.

Rich, R. 1993, "Recognition of states: The collapse of Yugoslavia and the Soviet Union", *European Journal of International Law*, 4(1): 36–65.

Rihoux, B. 2008, "Case-Oriented Configurational Research: Qualitative Comparative Analysis (Qca), Fuzzy Sets, and Related Techniques", in J. M. Box-Steffensmeier, H. E. Brady, & D. Collier (eds), *The Oxford Handbook of Political Methodology*, Oxford: Oxford University Press: 722–736.

Riksdag Till Kungen, 28th July, 1905 (Swedish Parliament letter to the King).

Roshwald, A. 2015, "The daily plebiscite as twenty-first-century reality?", *Ethnopolitics*, 14(5): 443–450.

Rourke, J. T., Hiskes, R. P. & Zirakzadeh, C. E. 1992, *Direct Democracy and International Politics: Deciding International Issues through Referendums*, Boulder: Lynne Rienner.

Scheindlin, D. 2012, "Phantom referendums in phantom states: Meaningless farce or a bridge to reality?", *Nationalism and Ethnic Politics*, 18(1): 65–87.

Toynbee, A. 1915, *Nationality and the war*, London: JM Dent & Sons.

*Tribunal Constitucional* 16th June 2010.

Wambaugh, S. 1920, *A Monograph on Plebiscites*, New York: Oxford University Press.

Wittgenstein, L. 2016, *Philosophische Untersuchungen*, Frankfurt aM: Suhrkamp.

# 18

# MAJORITARIANISM AND SECESSION

## An ambiguous but powerful relationship

*Sean Mueller*

Majoritarianism is an ideology centred on the organisation of political institutions and accompanying mechanisms of decision-making. The core ideas on which it rests are that governmental power should be as unrestrained as liberal-democratically possible, and that collectively binding decisions are taken by simple majority, which sometimes masks as a bare plurality (e.g. Sartori 1987, 134).[1] Ironically, majoritarianism of some sort is so deeply ingrained within liberal democracy that it has only rarely served as the exclusive object of theorising or – especially as of late – of advocating. More frequent are instances in which one of its many opposites is debated and indeed postulated, notably power-sharing or consensus democracy (e.g. Lijphart 2012), federalism (e.g. Burgess 2012; Gagnon 2021; Requejo 2010) and deliberative democracy (e.g. Gutmann & Thompson 2004).

The relationship of majoritarianism with secession is paradoxical. The former is for the latter both a key motivation to leave and a main obstacle to actually leaving, at the same time. As I will argue more fully in this chapter, the majoritarianism of existing nation-states such as Canada, Spain, or the United Kingdom (UK) is one of the main reasons why cultural minority groups such as the Québécois, Catalan or Scots want to secede. However, since fundamental changes to the nature of a political community need to be approved by (at least) a majority, and most often even by a super-majority (Schwartzberg 2014), majoritarianism also amounts to an almost insurmountable hurdle for such groups.

Yet the relationship of majoritarianism with secession is even more complex, for the former has served the latter both as a point of departure and of arrival: in wanting to leave behind a country that systematically ignores, oppresses, and even abuses a large minority, the new state dreamed of by secessionists should cater to the needs of the former minority (now the majority) and in turn overrule and ignore . . . the new minority! And just like already existing majoritarianism at the state level is an obstacle to leaving, so does the regionally projected majoritarianism obstruct the creating of a large enough support in society at both regional and state levels. Even civic nationalism, most prominently (and necessarily, given the virtual absence of an own language in the strict sense) encountered in Scotland (e.g. Arrighi 2019, 284), is of no help, for it, too, remains trapped in the majoritarian inclusion-exclusion dichotomy.

The purpose of this chapter, therefore, is twofold. At a theoretical level, the most important connections between majoritarianism and secession are spelled out for different dimensions in

DOI: 10.4324/9781003036593-22

the next section. The operation of these mechanisms is then investigated in four secessionist regions and the states of which they are (still) part: Catalonia and Spain, Flanders and Belgium, Québec and Canada, and Scotland and the UK.

## Defining democratic majoritarianism

A democracy is majoritarian to the extent that it maximises overall political power in the hands of a single person. Two logics converge: that of translating the will of a simple electoral majority as directly as possible into the composition of government (input), and that of maximising the impact of said government on state action (output). Ideally, then, elections are by first-past-the-post, where a plurality of votes suffices to win the only seat on offer in a constituency. Once in power, none of the usual constraints in either the governmental (e.g. a directly elected President next to the Prime Minister), partisan (coalitions), parliamentary (second chambers), direct-democratic (referendums), judicial, or federal dimension obtains (e.g. Bernauer & Vatter 2019; Lijphart 2012).

The person coming closest to such a state of affairs is a Prime Minister who is also leader of the parliamentary party with a majority of seats in the only chamber. In turn, majoritarian*ism* is the ideology advocating or defending such a political system and its behavioural outcome. Underlying both the institutional architecture and its political defence are supposedly democratic assumptions regarding interpersonal political equality ignoring, or even denying, the relevance of cultural group identities (Kymlicka 1995; Abizadeh 2021). However, the people are judged competent enough to elect its government, but not to express their political preferences directly using referendums; finally, the national parliament is held to be sovereign, meaning neither the judiciary nor lower-level governments can operate independently from but only trough it (Russell & Serban 2021, 10; Flinders et al. 2022).

## *Institutions . . .*

The institutional dimension of majoritarianism combines six main properties. All maximise majority rule through the absence of constraints. To begin with, *electoral* constraints are removed by relying on plurality voting such as first-past-the-post or two-round systems, where an absolute majority (50% + 1) is needed to gain a seat in parliament. While this typically transforms an electoral majority into a parliamentary majority, also an electoral plurality or even a minority (if ideally distributed over electoral districts of uneven size, as is the case in the US Senate: Ettinger 2019) might benefit from these rules. More generally, the permissiveness of an electoral system towards a multitude of parties can be assessed via the mean or median district magnitude (e.g. Neto & Cox 1997, 157): the smaller, the more majoritarian; the smallest being of course 1.

*Parliamentary* constraints arrive in the form of powerful second chambers or demanding investiture rules. Each of these poses a limit to either the translation of a bare plurality in the lower or only house, or of a majority in only one of two houses, into a governmental majority. Explicit demands for majority support before a new government can begin its mandate, as in Germany or Spain, are more demanding than "negative rules" according to which there has to be a majority against it lest it can assume office (Rasch et al. 2015, 17). In the latter case, even a parliamentary plurality – the party with the most seats, but short of 50% + 1 – may come to form the government if the opposing parties are unable to coordinate.

Within *government*, the electoral and/or parliamentary majority has full reign if its chief is also the head of state, as in presidential systems, or if the latter is purely ceremonial. In parliamentary and semi-presidential systems with an only symbolic head of state, neither the monarch nor an indirectly elected president nor even one that is directly elected (Duverger 1980) will act as an intra-executive check on the power of the prime minster. In both (semi-)presidential systems, when the president is also the leader of the parliamentary majority, and parliamentary systems, a fusion of executive and legislative powers occurs in the hands of the majority party – or, rather, in the hands of the person(s) directing that party.

*Direct-democratic* instruments will lead to compromises, and thereby contain the majority will, provided they bestow upon political minorities a meaningful veto and/or agenda setting powers (Vatter 2000, 174). Lacking those two components, the representative arena and parliamentary elections are all that counts. In the best case from the point of view of majoritarian democracy, only the government or a parliamentary majority can call a referendum where a simple majority is needed, thereby further cementing its grip on political power to the detriment of even a very large minority (cf. Morriss 2002, 190–192). The same can be said of *judicial review*: if strong as well as open to opposition parties and (organised) individuals, it can constrain the parliamentary and/or government majority of the day (e.g. Hall & Ura 2015; Macedo 2010) – the caveat being that judges themselves will typically have been appointed by some form of representative (super-)majority in the past. In other words: whether direct democracy and judicial review constrain or amplify and legitimise majority rule is an empirical question. Clearly many Catalans thought the latter was the case regarding the Spanish Constitutional Court's 2010 verdict (Mueller 2019, 147).

Finally, a democracy is all the more majoritarian the greater the amount of political power *centralised* at the state level, rather than being delegated to or retained at regional and local levels (Hooghe et al. 2016; Ladner et al. 2019). This alludes to what Stepan (1999) has called "demos-enabling", which here is reinterpreted as 'electoral, parliamentary, and/or governmental majority at state-level enabling'. For majoritarian decision-making to exploit its full potential, there can only be one majority: that calculated with the entire state and its singular national political community as reference points. Not considered here are undemocratic settings defined as, for instance, the absence of a real choice between at least two parties.

### ... And ideas

Having defined what majoritarian democracy looks like in terms of the institutional corset, we are now able to better understand its moral and political justifications. In theory, these can be divided into more or less explicit assumptions (of how society is) and goals (of how it should be). In practice, the two are often fused and barely separable – indeed, the core notion of interpersonal political equality is both an assumption and a goal, allowing one to hide behind the other when attacked on those terms: to the empirical reproach that not all citizens are in fact equally able or willing to participate in politics, majoritarianism can reply that democracy should enable but not force individuals to do so (hence the minimal, elitist understanding of democracy); while to the normative charge that there should be more to democracy than mere aggregation of votes, majoritarianists' reply can be political actor–centred in saying that ultimately it is individuals, or at least the groups they compose, that make democracy work.

Underlying the defence of the whole set or also individual components of majoritarian institutions is a view of society as composed of individuals with equal rights – nothing more, nothing less. If there was *more* to society than interpersonal equality, for instance inter-group equality, we could not defend the purely aggregative method of counting all votes equally but had to allow for "plural voting" (Mill 2001 [1861]) through the backdoor – for instance in the form of weighing votes by sub-state government and/or malapportionment (Rodden 2004). In turn, if there was *less* to majoritarianism than interpersonal equality, the ideology would cease to be democratic.

Thus, as it is defended by most adherents, the core value both postulated and assumed by majoritarian democrats is that all members of society count equally *a priori* (Abizadeh 2021, 5), i.e. before decisions are taken in elections, parliaments, or referendums. Note that in this way *majority* decisions are justified, but not actually those taken by pluralities. That is, the ideology purports to defend decisions taken by a popular majority, but ends up vindicating a parliamentary majority that may rest on a popular plurality. The secret hope of majoritarianism is not only that a parliamentary majority (in terms of seats) corresponds to a popular majority (in terms of votes cast), but also that the difference between majority and plurality disappears in a stable two-party system: In the UK, claim Rosenbluth and Shapiro (2018, 12), "the parties are large – only two, more or less – which forces them both to aim for the political middle. The electoral competition between them is a regular discipline to consider the interests of an electoral majority". By consequence, if one gains the upper hand over the other, it will automatically have secured a majority.[2]

At heart, then, majoritarianism is as monistic, hierarchical, and resolute as nationalism: there is only one majority (parliamentary and, ideally, also popular), and its will is superior to all other aggregations of preferences by virtue of numbers. All citizens are members of the same nation and, as such, count equally. But while this ideology may work well in culturally homogenous societies with cyclical major*ities* along multiple, primarily functional divisions (such as left-right), matters become more complicated in multinational societies. As is well known, here the risk is that cultural minorities also become permanent political minorities. That is all the more likely if state nationalism allies with majoritarianism, which is tempting, as it has the numbers on its side, if – but only if – we count only individuals, and not also cultural groups (Elster 1992, 24).

Members of the permanent minorities then face the choice between demanding and embracing non-majoritarian forms of democracy – such as federalism, if the group is territorially concentrated, or consociationalism, if it is not – or leaving and building their own, independent state. Ironically, as the next section shows, if the latter path is advocated, it often uses the exact same majoritarian arguments that have led to the minority being powerless in the first place: the right of "the majority" to decide and impose its will without restrictions.

## Case studies

Let us next look at four specific cases to observe the interplay of practiced and planned majoritarianisms at state and regional levels with secession. The contexts selected are the four usual suspects, i.e. those that have seen a significant push for secession or even an independence referendum: Catalonia, Flanders, Québec, and Scotland. The first two sub-sections look at majoritarianism at the state level, the remaining two at the regional level.

### *State-level institutions*

How majoritarian are Belgium, Canada, Spain, and the UK, as per the institutional and ideational definitions provided in the previous sections? Bernauer and Vatter (2019) provide one of the most encompassing and thorough summaries of majoritarian institutions at the country level – or what they call the four dimensions of "power diffusion". A first dimension measures the extent to which power is concentrated in the hands of a strong executive and indeed a single party commanding a parliamentary majority, while a second measures whether direct democracy is used in a pro- or counter-majoritarian fashion. It thus emerges that the UK, Canada, and Spain are majoritarian in both dimensions, Belgium only in the second. Bernauer and Vatter's

(2019) third dimension assesses the governmental system. All four countries are parliamentary democracies where only the legislative is directly elected and no other executive figure – least of all the merely symbolic monarch – rivals the triple-role of the Prime Minister as head of government, leader of the largest party, and, through that, also informal head of parliament.

Their fourth and final dimension relates to federalism. Figure 18.1 thus looks at the vertical dimension of power concentration and traces the evolution of self-rule and shared rule of the four selected regional units as provided by their state's framework. Self-rule refers to the amount of formal power over own, i.e. regional affairs (autonomy); shared rule assesses the extent to which regional governments or their representatives are given a say in state-wide decision (co-decision; Hooghe et al. 2016). Again, Belgium – and more particularly the Flemish region – stands out: not only in terms of the distance covered since 1970, but also in being alone in having significantly more shared rule than self-rule. In fact, while all four regions had about the same amount of regional self-rule by 2018 (80% or, in the case of Québec 100% of what the index assesses), the variation in shared rule is much greater: from 54% in Québec and Scotland to 79% in Catalonia and 96% in Flanders.

All four countries also have asymmetric bicameral systems, with only indirectly elected and appointed senators or, in the case of Spain, a mixture of sub-regional direct elections and indirect elections by the parliaments of the Autonomous Communities (Lijphart 2012). However, in none of the four countries is the second chamber the expression of regional governments, as in Germany, nor is it involved in the investiture of government, as in Italy. Their legitimacy and, by implication, also their effectiveness to curb majority rule is limited, too (Mueller et al. 2021). Both the parliamentary system and the almost exclusively representative character of the Belgian, British, Canadian, and Spanish political systems, with strong parliamentary party discipline (Field 2016; Kam 2009), reinforce their de facto unicameral nature further.

Finally, both judicial review and constitutional rigidity are strongest in Canada and weakest in the UK, with Belgium and Spain in the intermediate categories on both these indicators (Bernauer & Vatter 2019). However, constitutional rigidity and judicial review can also serve to cement the existing (majoritarian) order by raising the obstacles to change it further (e.g. Schwartzberg 2014). For it is one thing to have a rigid constitution that already guarantees a wide range of regional authority, with a strong supreme court to police it, as in Canada; but quite another matter altogether to want to move towards a more decentralised or even confederal system, as some in the UK, Spain, and Belgium desire.

Overall, then, the UK ends up as the most majoritarian political system: single party dominance at the state level is the norm, centralisation is high. And there are only weak checks on cabinet power in the form of direct democracy, a second chamber, judicial review, or super-majority requirements for constitutional change. Only the UK parliament is sovereign, which de facto means the party that controls a majority of seats in the House of Commons. At the other end of the scale – but not so very far either – we find Belgium (for proportional power diffusion and regional authority) and Canada (for judicial review, constitutional rigidity, and regional authority). Spain and Catalonia have more developed regional authority than the UK and Scotland, and judicial review and constitutional rigidity are also less majority-friendly at first sight, but state-level direct democracy and proportional power-sharing are equally lacking.

Ironically, the unfettered power of UK governments has also made them the most flexible in giving in to regionalist demands. If the party in power has promised devolution before the elections, it can deliver, such as Labour in 1997. If another party in power consents to holding a referendum on independence, it too can deliver (the Conservatives in 2014). By contrast, in Spain, judicial review – a counter-majoritarian feature, in principle – has stood in the way of expanding Catalan autonomy, in 2010 (Mueller 2019). Similarly, the high obstacles for

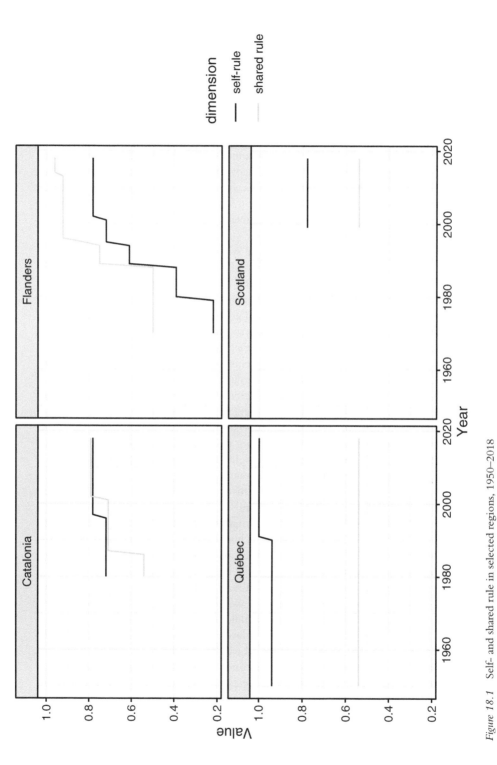

*Figure 18.1* Self- and shared rule in selected regions, 1950–2018

*Note:* Shown are normalised regional self- and shared rule scores, meaning that 1 corresponds to the maximum value possible.

*Source:* Author's own graph, with data from Hooghe et al. (2016) and Shair-Rosenfield et al. (2021).

constitutional reform in Canada have led to the failure of the 1987 Meech Lake Accord that had incorporated all of Québec's five demands for further self- and shared rule (Hueglin 2021, 224f). So while majoritarianism is generally oblivious to the preferences of minorities (by definition, for mere numerical ones, and depending on context, for cultural groups), it can on occasion become their ally. Moreover, institutional structures are only worth their societal acceptance and interpretation, as discussed next.

## Society and political parties

Beneath every institutional superstructure lie widely shared views and norms regarding the character of society. Particularly relevant in all our cases here is the extent to which society is considered to consist of just one nation as opposed to two or more. A first indicator of this arrives in the form of constitutional self-definitions. Thus, despite – or perhaps because of – the absence of a single codified basic law in the UK, the national status of Scotland (and Wales) is largely undisputed (cf. e.g. House of Commons 2015, 15). The Belgian constitution acknowledges that "Belgium is a federal State composed of Communities and Regions" (Art. 1), but at the same time insists that "All powers emanate from the Nation." (Art. 33). Even more ambivalent is the Spanish constitution: sovereignty belongs to "The Spanish Nation" and "Castilian is the official Spanish language" (preamble and Art. 3.1), but "nationalities" are equally recognised and "the other Spanish languages" can have co-official status at the regional level (Art.s and 3.2).

Nothing on "nation", neither in the singular nor in the plural, is contained in the Constitution of Canada. But that does not mean the question is resolved – far from it: the issue has been the object of fierce debates over many decades (e.g. Hueglin 2021, 291–299). Only in 2006 did the Canadian parliament approve a statement (with 266 to 16 votes) that "this House recognize that the Québécois form a nation within a united Canada". However, then Prime Minister Harper immediately qualified its significance by stating that he was "using the word nation in a cultural-sociological rather than in a legal sense" (CBC 2006).

The nationality question has also become the object of political and legal struggles in Spain (e.g. Brown & Cetrà 2020). Most significantly, the Spanish Constitutional Court ruled in 2010 that the words "nation" and "national reality" contained in the revised Catalan Autonomy Statute had no legal effect. This provided one of the sparks that ignited the secessionist fire. However, rather than being itself an independent cause for the growing political grievances of Catalan nationalists, the ruling is merely symptomatic of the fundamentally monistic understanding of the Spanish nation embraced by a large majority of Spaniards (cf. Mueller 2019).

This brings us to consider a second indicator for the mono- or plurinational character of a society: the party system. Requejo (2010, 277) has argued that for minority "nations" to qualify as such, they need to have both a distinct party system and at least one secessionist party within it. While it is perfectly feasible for a regional party system to be distinct in polarisation, fragmentation and/or any other dimension, the regular presence of at least one regional-nationalist party should suffice to indicate plurinationalism (Mazzoleni & Mueller 2016). All four countries assessed here have seen such parties emerge and persist both in national and regional elections. Thus, in 1991 was founded the *Bloc Québécois* (BQ), joining the ranks of similarly independentist parties such as *Esquerra Republicana de Catalunya* (ERC) and the Scottish National Party (SNP), both founded in the 1930s. In Flanders, the *Nieuw-Vlaamse Alliantie* (N-VA, founded in 2001) has become the biggest party not only regionally but also state-wide, although it shares the nationalist space with *Vlaams Belang* (VB, until 2004 *Vlaams Blok*).

To understand the salience of secessionism in society, Figure 18.2 plots the vote shares of these parties over the past federal or general elections in two ways: first, the votes gained by them as a percentage of all valid votes cast *in their own region*, and second, as a percentage of all valid votes cast *state-wide*. Focusing on the regional dimension first, the two most successful parties to date have been the N-VA and VB, which together scored a staggering 62% across the five Flemish provinces in 2007. Apart from this, however, the secessionist vote never surpasses 50% or, for the ERC, 25%.[3] Expressed in terms of state-wide support, all the scores are obviously much lower, given that all these parties compete only in their own region.[4] Furthermore, the size of their region matters, from Scotland and Catalonia (with 9% and 16% of all valid votes cast respectively), through Québec (a quarter), to Flanders (some two-thirds, in 2019).

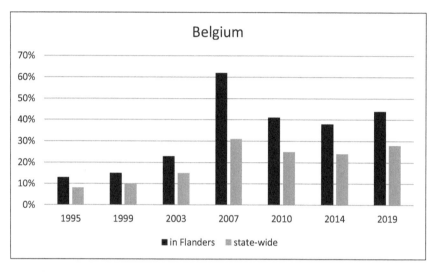

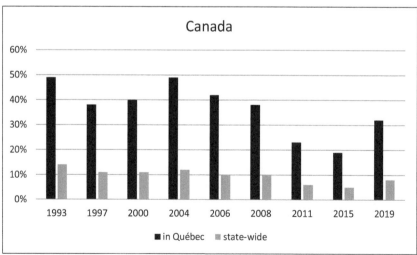

*Figure 18.2*   Regional and state-wide vote shares of secessionist parties in B, CAN, ESP and UK

*Note*: Shown are the vote shares of the ERC, N-VA + VB, BQ, and the SNP in federal/general elections as a percentage of all valid votes cast in the region (Flanders without Brussels) and overall.

*Source*: Author's own calculations and graphs with official electoral results from Belgium (Direction des Elections), Elections Canada, Spain (Ministerio del Interior) and the UK House of Commons Library.

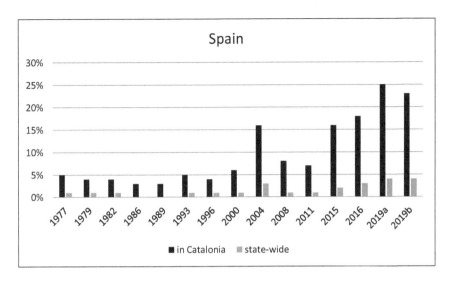

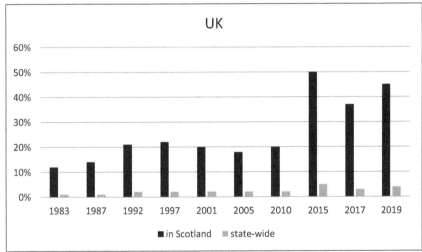

*Figure 18.2* (Continued)

We can now more fully appreciate how power concentration in the horizontal, "proportional" dimension works against some parties such as those advocating the secession of a particular region. In Canada, since 1960 all the state-wide governments have been single-party cabinets, and single-party *majority* cabinets for 73% of the time (Armingeon et al. 2020 and own updates). In the UK, single-party majority cabinets have even been in power for 85% of the time (ibid.). In Spain, single-party majority cabinets have been in power during only 40% of the time since 1977, whereas 55% of the time the top executive was formed by single-party *minorities* (ibid.). January 2020 has seen the first Spanish coalition government take power, albeit one that lacks a parliamentary majority. By contrast, in Belgium, coalitions have been the dominant mode, either of the minimal-winning (52% of the time between 1960 and 2021) or surplus type (42%; the rest are caretaker governments; ibid.).

Moreover, apart from the N-VA between 2014 and 2018, none of the secessionist parties surveyed here has ever formally participated in a state-wide government. However, the UK, Canada, and until recently also Spain were dominated by just two parties divided along the state-economy, i.e. left-right spectrum: a centre-right (Conservatives in Canada and the UK, the *Partido Popular* in Spain) versus a liberal (Canada) or centre-left party (Labour in the UK and Socialists in Spain). Each pair of parties not only alternated in the central executive, but also served a territorially integrative function by winning votes and seats in our four secessionist regions. In fact, for some state-wide parties the votes gained *in* the secessionist regions are quite important: the Spanish Socialists, for instance, gained an average of 12% of its seats in Catalonia between 1977 and November 2019 (Conservatives: 5%). Scotland was similarly once a Labour stronghold: between 1918 and 2010, some 14% of its Westminster seats came from there; since the general elections of 2015, however, Scottish Labour MPs have all but disappeared (Conservative equivalent, whole period: 6%). In Canada, too, Liberals are much more dependent on Québec than the Conservatives: between 1993 and 2019, some 18% of its seats were won there (and 22% in 2016 and 2019), compared to only 6% for the Conservative Party since its formation in 2003. So the majoritarian logic not only works to keep (numerical) minorities out, but also to keep cultural minority regions *in* the state-wide fold – especially from the side of political parties popular *there*.

Moreover, the fact that Canada and the UK rely on first-past-the-post for national parliamentary elections has, paradoxically, also served to artificially bolster the parliamentary presence of our secessionist parties, as shown in Table 18.1 (shaded cells). But the reverse is also true: despite scoring 6% of the state-wide vote, in 2015, the BQ obtained just 1% of the seats. The use of proportional rules in Spain and Flanders avoids both over- and under-representation. But although 1%, 2%, or 4% of seats might seem unimportant, in certain cases that suffices to be queen-maker (Mueller 2019). In January 2020, the investiture of the Spanish government would have failed anew had the 13 ERC MPs (and the 5 MPs from the Basque nationalist party *Euskal Herria Bildu*, together just 5% of seats) abstained (Cameron 2020).

*Table 18.1* State-wide vote and seats shares of secessionist parties, 1987–2019

| UK: SNP | | | CAN: BQ | | | ESP: ERC | | | Flanders: NV-A & VB | | |
|---|---|---|---|---|---|---|---|---|---|---|---|
| Year | Votes | Seats | Year | Votes | Seats | Year | Votes | Seats | Year | Votes | Seats |
| 1987 | 1% | 0.5% | 1993 | 14% | 18% | 1996 | 1% | 0.3% | | | |
| 1992 | 2% | 0.5% | 1997 | 11% | 15% | 2000 | 1% | 0.3% | | n.a. | |
| 1997 | 2% | 1% | 2000 | 11% | 13% | 2004 | 3% | 2% | 1995 | 8% | 7% |
| 2001 | 2% | 1% | 2004 | 12% | 18% | 2008 | 1% | 1% | 1999 | 10% | 10% |
| 2005* | 2% | 1% | 2006 | 10% | 17% | 2011 | 1% | 1% | 2003 | 15% | 13% |
| 2010 | 2% | 1% | 2008 | 10% | 16% | 2015 | 2% | 3% | 2007 | 31% | 31% |
| 2015 | 5% | 9% | 2011 | *6%* | *1%* | 2016 | 3% | 3% | 2010 | 25% | 26% |
| 2017 | 3% | 5% | 2015 | *5%* | *3%* | 2019a | 4% | 4% | 2014 | 24% | 24% |
| 2019 | 4% | 7% | 2019 | 8% | 9% | 2019b | 4% | 4% | 2019 | 28% | 29% |

*Notes*: The first column always indicates year of general or national election, the second the state-wide vote share, and the third the seat share in the Lower House on election day. Shaded cells = significant (2%+) overrepresentation compared to electoral score, bold = significant underrepresentation.

* Number of Scottish seats in the House of Commons reduced from 72 to 59.

*Source*: Author's own calculations; for data sources, see notes to Figures 18.2–18.4.

## *The regional level: current . . .*

How majoritarian are Catalonia, Flanders, Québec, and Scotland? Figure 18.3 shows the electoral fortunes of the largest parties in the parliaments of Québec and Scotland, taking into account vote and seat shares. Figure 18.4 does the same for the parliaments of Catalonia and Flanders. The horizontal line indicates the 50% mark above which a party can conveniently

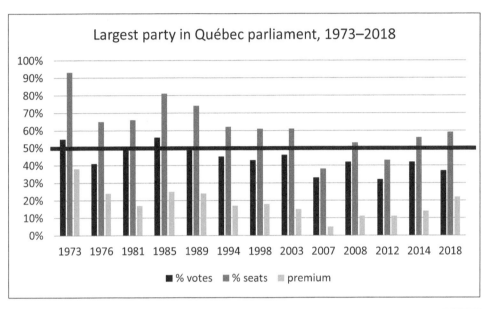

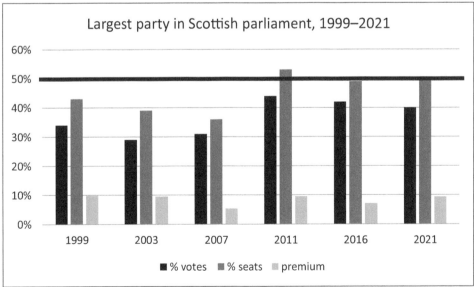

*Figure 18.3*  Largest parliamentary party in Québec and Scotland, 1973–2021

*Source*: Author's own calculations and graphs with official electoral results from Élections Québec and the UK House of Commons Library.

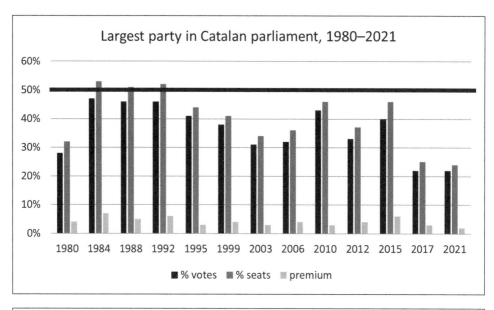

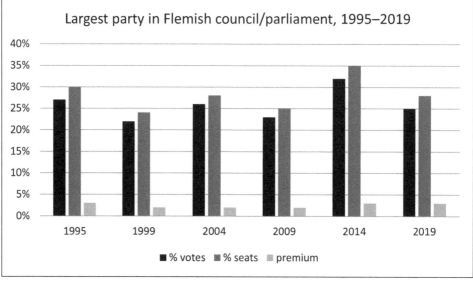

*Figure 18.4* Largest parliamentary party in Catalonia and Flanders, 1980–2021

*Source*: Author's own calculations and graphs with official electoral results from the Institut d'Estadística de Catalunya and Belgium (Direction des Élections).

form the regional government. All four regional political systems are parliamentary democracies with a single chamber.

From the comparison among these four, the following insights emerge. First, all four largely replicate the political systems of their encompassing states. Second, and as a consequence, Flanders is the least majoritarian: the proportional system has provided no single party with an absolute majority of seats, although here, too, the largest party is systematically favoured in the allocation of seats. Third, the Catalan party system seems to have left behind its period of almost hegemonic dominance (aided, between 1984 and 1992, by the electoral system) to resemble the fragmentation of Flanders.

Fourth, in majoritarian Québec, single-party governments are the rule, enabled not least by electoral "premiums" of up to 25% in 1985, and 38% in 1973 (18% on average; Scotland: 8%, Catalonia: 4%, Flanders: 3%). In 1998, the *Parti libéral du Québec* even won the most votes (43.6%), but obtained only 48 seats out of 125 (38%). In turn, the *Parti Québécois* (PQ), with 42.9%, won 76 seats (61%). So not only did the party with an electoral minority end up with a very comfortable parliamentary majority, but a secessionist party profited from the electoral system copied from the state-wide level. Fifth and finally, the majoritarian logic has also come to dominate in Scotland, despite the mixed-member proportionality system adopted in 1997 (Cairney & Widfeldt 2015; Matthews 2018).

Not by accident, then, have the only official independence referendums been held in Québec (1980: 40% yes; 1995: 49% yes) and Scotland (2014: 45% yes). They perfectly illustrate the paradoxical relationship of majoritarianism with secession. Majoritarianism is what enabled the single-party governments of Jacques Parizeau (PQ, 1994) and Alex Salmond (SNP, 2011) to take office alone despite securing mere pluralities of the vote (see Figure 18.3). In Scotland (and Wales), it also allowed the establishment of devolution itself, through the Labour government of 1997 (43% of the votes) and subsequent devolution referendums. By contrast, it was *a deviation* from simple majoritarianism that impeded Scottish devolution to begin already in 1979, since 40% of registered voters had to have voted favourably (Scottish Government 2013, 546). Next, in true majoritarian fashion, direct democracy was used to support governmental policy (Vatter 2000). Yet majoritarianism – more specifically the idea that a simple majority decides – was also responsible for *defeating* all three independence referendums. However slim the margin, the majority is always completely right and the minority totally wrong.

The same ambivalence, albeit in a different form, can be observed in Catalonia. The three nationalist-independentist parties combined scored just above 50% of seats in in the 2015, 2017, and 2021 regional elections, yet they won a popular majority (51%) only in 2021. Moreover, their success is territorially uneven: they comfortably won in the two smallest provinces, Lleida and Tarragona, but not in what is by far the largest area around the capital, Barcelona: here, they gained "only" between 45% and 46%, between 2015 and 2021. In other words, secessionists forces are weakest precisely in the province containing three quarters of the population – a clear majority. In fact, the largest *single* party coming out of the 2021 elections were the Catalan Socialists, who obtained 50,000 votes more than ERC but the same number of seats (33). So it was both in defiance of majoritarianism and by applying it at camp level that secessionists could retain executive power, through the investiture of Pere Aragonès (ERC) on 21 May 2021 by a vote of 74–61.[5]

## ... And projected

The final question to be asked concerns secessionist visions for the future. What projects are proposed by secessionists in our four cases? While it is obviously difficult to tell what would eventually be realised if any of these regions were to become independent, it is safe to assume that none would change its current political institutions. To the best of my knowledge, serious political reforms – of the parliamentary regime, electoral system, or the number and type of constituencies – are not on the agenda. These would also be difficult to justify, since in the event that secessionists were to succeed, it will have been possible only thanks to the existing institutions at the regional level (see the previous section).

Currently, neither do Québec secessionists advocate a move away from first-past-the-post, nor do their Flemish counterparties propose leaving proportionality behind. The *Parti Québécois* (2021) thus states the following: "*L'Assemblée nationale sera de même maintenue dans sa forme actuelle puisque les nouveaux pouvoirs qu'elle acquerra ne l'obligeront pas à modifier son mode de fonctionnement.*" ("The National Assembly [= Québec Parliament] will likewise be maintained in its current form since the new powers it will acquire do not require it to change its mode of operation.")[6] Nor do the European secessionists want to leave the EU – on the contrary, the N-VA envisions "a stronger Flanders in a stronger Europe".[7] However, all parties except the SNP (Scottish Government 2013, 45) advocate a republican form of government – most clearly here the ERC, which carries this aspect in its name and program: "La República que farem".[8] Finally, while the SNP promises to push for proportional elections to Westminster,[9] it seems quite happy with its own mixed-member proportional system, despite it not actually fostering "a more collegial approach to the sharing of executive power" (Matthews 2018, 349) and the high "premiums" it still pays to the largest party (up to 10%, see Figure 18.3).

In terms of the society and political community that are promised once independent, all four regions studied here are home to a mix of cultural and civic nationalists, with Québec's emphasis on French exclusivity forming one end of the continuum and Scotland the other. But make no mistake: the new countries will be home to the Catalan, Flemish, Scottish, and Québécois, respectively. It will be the majorities formed and confirmed within these new coordinates alone that shall determine who rules: "Independence means that the decisions about Scotland that are currently taken by governments at Westminster – often by governments that have been rejected by the majority of people in Scotland – will be taken here instead" (Scottish Government 2013, 374).

## Conclusion

This chapter has assessed the relationship between majoritarianism and secession. The former was defined as an ideology centred on the organisation of political institutions and accompanying mechanisms of decision-making, as follows: governmental power should be as unrestrained as liberal-democratically possible, and collectively binding decisions ought to be taken by a simple majority. A democracy is majoritarian to the extent that it maximises overall political power in the hands of a single person. Two logics thus converge: that of translating the will of a simple electoral majority as directly as possible into the composition of government (input), and that of maximising the impact of said government on state action (output). In the ideal-type majoritarian democracy, elections are by first-past-the-post, and once in power, none of the usual constraints in the governmental, partisan, parliamentary, direct-democratic, judicial, or federal dimensions exist: no directly elected president next to the Prime Minister, no need for coalitions, no second chamber, no referendums unless called by the government itself, a weak Supreme Court, and strong centralisation.

Several ambiguities and tensions were then revealed in the relationship of majoritarianism with secession. First, where majoritarianism is practiced and upheld at nation-state level, it *justifies demands* for secession. The majoritarian logic works on the basis of interpersonal equality, negating the political relevance of groups, and awards full power to whichever majority is formed. Without federal- or consociational-type deviations from strict majoritarian rule, structural minorities such as linguistic groups risk becoming permanently overruled to an extent that they stop identifying with that state. However, majoritarianism is also a *main obstacle*: the majority needs to either approve said deviations or let the minority and its territory go. The case of Scotland perfectly exemplifies this: devolution was granted by the Labour government of 1997, which came to power through a plurality of votes (43.2%). However, as of mid-2021, the Conservative government (elected, again, with a bare plurality of votes in 2019: 43.6%) has yet to agree to a second independence referendum. Such obstinacy further fuels the flames of regional grievances – especially since the current government owes only 2% of its 56% parliamentary majority to seats won in Scotland and is far from the most popular party there.

Second, the political parties most interested in keeping a secessionist region in the national fold are often those that depend on the support there to win power overall. The Liberals in Canada, the Socialists in Spain, and Labour in the UK have owed between 12% and 22% of their seats in the national parliament to electoral successes in Québec, Catalonia, and Scotland, respectively. The majoritarian need for these parties to *win regionally to govern nationally* pushes them to reconcile centrifugal and centripetal demands. However, at the end of the day they remain state-wide parties that need to cater to the whole country, not just one region. That centre-left parties have increasingly been marginalised in the Catalan and Scottish party systems thus does not bode well for their ability to manage centre–periphery tensions, nor for their governmental prospects. The Sanchez government approved in 2020, thanks only to the abstention of 13 ERC and 5 Basque nationalist MPs, would thus seem rather the end of an era and not the beginning of a new one.

Third, turning to the regional level, we often find practised *the exact same logic* that secessionists criticise as *unjust and oppressive* at the state level. The Catalan secessionists may have managed to secure a regional parliamentary majority over three successive elections (2015, 2017, and 2021), but only in the last one did they also a win a popular majority. Moreover, the largest area by far, the province of Barcelona, remains in the hands of non-nationalist parties. So applying the same majoritarian logic at the province or constituency level would deplete the "Catalan Republic" of three quarters of its current population. What is more, in having exercised and/ or demanding the "right to decide" on the future status of their region, secessionists in Québec, Scotland, and Catalonia all venerate the "will of the people" operationalised, again, as a simple majority at the regional level, with no deviations permitted. Either all go, or nobody goes. Recourse to referendums as plebiscites to bolster the governmental agenda of the day is typical for majoritarianism (Vatter 2000).

In all of this, the case of Flanders is exceptional in several regards. First, the region is populated and dominated by the cultural majority. So the majoritarian grievance of being permanently ignored on the basis of numbers does not function. Second, the entire party system is split linguistically, so no party needs to reconcile winning regionally and state-wide. That removes key centripetal actors present in the other three cases studied here. And in a final twist of irony, Flemish secessionists are the victims of *not enough* majoritarianism. For if the Belgian electoral system was based on first-past-the-post as in Canada or the UK, scoring as much as 25% of the state-wide vote (despite competing only in two-thirds of the country) would probably have been enough for the N-VA and the VB to impose their visions much earlier and forcefully. However, since the De Croo government formed in October 2020 is composed of no fewer than seven parties that together hold a parliamentary majority, those two largest parties are sidelined. Such coalitions are anything but majoritarian, confirming Belgium's place as a consensus democracy on the executive-parties dimension (Lijphart 2012; Bernauer & Vatter 2019). Lack of majoritarianism at the regional level also means that parties need to share power in coalitions there, which in Flanders they have done since the first ever direct elections of 1995. By contrast, recall that in the Québec of 1998 the *Parti Québécois* remained in power despite winning only a minority of votes, and that all the SNP governments since 2007 have had a mere plurality of votes (of between 31% and 44%; see Figure 18.3). As is known, both parties were able to subsequently call "all or nothing" independence referendums, whilst the Flemish secessionists have had to work through one state reform after the other to gradually increase their region's powers.

That they have done so rather successfully (see e.g. Figure 18.1) leads to a final thought: majoritarianism may turn out to be a curse in disguise. Although it serves as a main justification for secession if practised at the state level, it raises the obstacles to actually leaving to almost unreachable heights: a nation-state government favourably inclined enough to allow or at least tolerate an independence referendum, followed by a majority in a regional popular vote. In the latter, given that secessionists argue for a radical overhaul of current structures and a leap into the unknown, the odds will be decidedly stacked against them. Furthermore, although majoritarianism at the regional level enables effective governments also in the absence of popular majorities, it strengthens adversarial politics and contributes to polarisation and alienation (e.g. Mueller 2019). But so that the entire region is on board when departing, it would be in the interest of secessionists themselves to seek the support of more than just 50% + 1 of those voting.

## Notes

1 "Plurality" means more votes than anybody else (e.g. 45% vs. 30%, 20%, and 5%). "Majority" means 50% + 1 (if the total number of votes is uneven, else 50% rounded to the next integer) and is "simple" if only valid votes cast are counted and no quorum is specified.
2 With only two competitors, plurality and majority coincide. However, it is still possible that the winner of a popular plurality/majority ends up with a parliamentary minority, notably if constituencies are uneven in population size and voter preferences are unevenly distributed.
3 Especially after 2010, the ERC has been joined by other parties, notably *Junts per Catalunya*, in pursuing secession (Mueller 2019).
4 The ERC is an exception: it also stands in Valencia and the Balearic Islands. However, in 2019 it received less than 1% of its state-wide support outside of Catalonia. Similarly so the N-VA and VB: in 2019 they received just 2% of their state-wide vote in Brussels.
5 www.catalannews.com/politics/item/pere-aragones-becomes-132nd-catalan-president
6 https://pq.org/independance/#vie-politique
7 https://english.n-va.be/frequently-asked-questions#europe
8 www.esquerra.cat/ca/republica-que-farem
9 "We will continue to call for the first past the post voting system to be replaced at Westminster with proportional representation, so that every vote and every part of the country counts." www.snp.org/our-vision/constitution/

## References

Abizadeh, A. 2021, 'Counter-Majoritarian Democracy: Persistent Minorities, Federalism, and the Power of Numbers', *American Political Science Review*, 115:3, 742–756.
Armingeon, K., Engler, S., Leemann, L., et al. 2020, *Supplement to the Comparative Political Data Set: Government Composition 1960–2018*. Zurich: Institute of Political Science, University of Zurich.
Arrighi, J.-T. 2019, '"The People, Year Zero": Secessionism and Citizenship in Scotland and Catalonia', *Ethnopolitics* 18:3, 278–297.
Bernauer, J. & Vatter, A. 2019, *Power Diffusion and Democracy: Institutions, Deliberation and Outcomes*. Cambridge: Cambridge University Press.
Brown, S. & Cetrà, D. 2020, 'Why Stay Together? State Nationalism and Justifications for State Unity in Spain and the UK', *Nationalism and Ethnic Politics* 26:1, 46–65.
Burgess, M. 2012, *In Search of the Federal Spirit: New Comparative Empirical and Theoretical Perspectives*. Oxford: Oxford University Press.
Cairney, P. & Widfeldt A. 2015, 'Is Scotland a Westminster-Style Majoritarian Democracy or a Scandinavian-Style Consensus Democracy? A Comparison of Scotland, the UK and Sweden', *Regional & Federal Studies* 25:1, 1–18.
Cameron, D. R. 2020, 'With the Help of the Catalan Left, Sanchez Wins Investiture Vote in Spanish Congress', Yale Macmillan Center, at https://macmillan.yale.edu/news/help-catalan-left-sanchez-wins-investiture-vote-spanish-congress [27.6.2021].

CBC. 2006, 'House Passes Motion Recognizing Quebecois as Nation', at www.cbc.ca/news/canada/house-passes-motion-recognizing-quebecois-as-nation-1.574359 [27.6.2021].

Duverger, M. 1980, 'A New Political System Model: Semi-Presidential Government', *European Journal of Political Research* 8:2, 165–187.

Elster, J. 1992, 'On Majoritarianism and Rights', *East European Constitutional Review* 1:3, 19–24.

Ettinger, M. 2019, 'The Vastly Varying Importance of American Voters', at https://mettlinger.medium.com/the-vastly-varying-importance-of-american-voters-updated-and-revised-september-2019-cb-f15169b26b [1.3.2021].

Field, B. N. 2016, *Why Minority Governments Work: Multilevel Territorial Politics in Spain*, London: Palgrave Macmillan.

Flinders, M., Judge, D., Rhodes, R. A. W., & Vatter, A. 2022, 'Stretched But Not Snapped: A Response to Russell & Serban on Retiring the "Westminster Model"', *Government &Opposition* 57:2, 353–369.

Gagnon, A.-G. 2021, 'Multinational Federalism: Challenges, Shortcomings and Promises', *Regional & Federal Studies* 31:1, 99–114.

Gutmann, A. & Thompson, D. 2004, *Why Deliberative Democracy?*, Princeton, NJ: Princeton University Press.

Hall, M. E. K. & Ura, J. D. 2015, 'Judicial Majoritarianism', *The Journal of Politics* 77:3, 818–832.

Hooghe, L., Gary Marks, G., Schakel, A. H. et al. 2016, *Measuring Regional Authority: A Postfunctionalist Theory of Governance*, Volume 1, Oxford: Oxford University Press.

House of Commons. 2015, *The UK Constitution: A Summary, with Options for Reform*, London: Political and Constitutional Reform Committee.

Hueglin, T. O. 2021, *Federalism in Canada: Contested Concepts and Uneasy Balances*, Toronto: University of Toronto Press.

Kam, Ch. J. 2009, *Party Discipline and Parliamentary Politics*, Cambridge: Cambridge University Press.

Kymlicka, W. 1995, *Multicultural Citizenship: A Liberal Theory of Minority Rights*, Oxford: Oxford University Press.

Ladner, A., Keuffer, N., Baldersheim, H., Hlepas, N., Swianiewicz, P., Steyvers, K. & Navarro, C. 2019, *Patterns of Local Autonomy in Europe*, London: Palgrave Macmillan.

Lijphart, A. 2012, *Patterns of Democracy: Government Forms and Performance in Thirty-Six Countries*, 2nd ed., New Haven and London: Yale University Press.

Macedo, S. 2010, 'Against Majoritarianism: Democratic Values and Institutional Design', *Boston University Law Review* 90:2, 1029–1042.

Matthews, F. 2018, 'Does Decentralisation Make a Difference? Comparing the Democratic Performance of Central and Regional Governing Systems in the United Kingdom', *British Journal of Politics and International Relations* 20:2, 341–359.

Mazzoleni, O. & Mueller S. (eds.). 2016, *Regionalist Parties in Western Europe: Dimensions of Success*, London/New York: Routledge.

Mill, J. S. 2001 [1861], *Considerations on Representative Government*, Kitchener: Batoche Books.

Morriss, P. 2002, *Power: A Philosophical Analysis*, Manchester: Manchester University Press (reprint).

Mueller, S. 2019, 'Catalonia: The Perils of Majoritarianism', *Journal of Democracy* 30:2, 142–156.

Mueller, S., Vatter, A. & Dick, S. 2021, 'A New Index of Bicameralism: Taking Legitimacy Seriously', *Journal of Legislative Studies*, early view, doi:10.1080/13572334.2021.1996753

Neto, O. A. & Cox, G. 1997, 'Electoral Institutions, Cleavage Structures, and the Number of Parties', *American Journal of Political Science* 41:1, 149–174.

Rasch, B. E., Martin, S. & Cheibub, J. A. 2015, 'Investiture Rules and Government Formation', in Rasch, B.E., Martin, S. & Cheibub, J.A. (eds), *Parliaments and Government Formation: Unpacking Investiture Rules*, Oxford: Oxford University Press, 3–26.

Requejo, F. 2010, 'Federalism and Democracy: The Case of Minority Nations: A Federalist Defici', in Burgess, M. & Gagnon, A.-G. (eds), *Federal Democracies*, London: Palgrave, 275–298.

Rodden, J. 2004, 'Comparative Federalism and Decentralization: On Meaning and Measurement', *Comparative Politics* 36:4, 481–500.

Rosenbluth, F. M. & Shapiro, I. 2018, *Responsible Parties: Saving Democracy from Itself*, New Haven: Yale University Press.

Russell, M. & Serban, R. 2021, 'The Muddle of the "Westminster Model": A Concept Stretched Beyond Repair', *Government & Opposition* 56:4, 744–764.

Sartori, G. 1987, *The Theory of Democracy Revisited*, Chatham, NJ: Chatham House Publishers.

*Sean Mueller*

Schwartzberg, M. 2014, *Counting the Many: The Origins and Limits of Supermajority Rule*, Cambridge: Cambridge University Press.

Scottish Government. 2013, *Scotland's Future: Your Guide to an Independent Scotland*. Edinburgh: APS Group Scotland.

Shair-Rosenfield, S., Schakel, A. H., Niedzwiecki, S., Marks, G., Hooghe, L., & Chapman-Osterkatz, S. 2021, 'Language Difference and Regional Authority', *Regional & Federal Studies* 31:1, 73–97.

Stepan, A. 1999, 'Federalism and Democracy: Beyond the U.S. Model', *Journal of Democracy* 10: 19–34.

Vatter, A. 2000, 'Consensus and Direct Democracy: Conceptual and Empirical Linkages', *European Journal of Political Research* 38:2, 171–192.

# 19

# BEYOND 'CONSENSUAL' SECESSION? IMPLICIT DISTINCTIONS AND THE OBJECT(IVE)S OF CONSENT

*Zoran Oklopcic*

## Introduction

'Holy Roman Empire', as Voltaire allegedly observed, was a political entity of a special kind: neither holy, nor Roman, nor an empire. As it will hopefully become fully apparent by the end of this chapter, Voltaire's famous witticism deserves to be extended to 'consensual secession': a mode of state formation which, on closer inspection, appears to be neither really 'consensual' nor, for that matter, much of a 'secession' either. What distinguishes it from other forms of state formation which scholars treat as the instances of secession is not *consensus* about the fate of secessionists' demands among everyone concerned (cf. Williams 2015) but the acts which seem to be more accurately described either as *freely given permissions*, *externally extorted concessions*, or simply as the decisions to act in conformity with the applicable norms of the extant constitutional order. As indicated by the letters that populate the fourth column in Table 19.1, the outcomes which such acts bring about coincide not simply with the ascension of a previously separated territory to the rank of a fully sovereign state, but also with the *extinction* of the states to which such territories used to belong as one of their constituent parts.

We shall return to the examples from Table 19.1 in the final section of this chapter. In the meantime, we should begin by asking: Why should the incidents in which the extinction of the units which provide the referential frame for a particular mode of state formation be committed to memory as the instances of secession, and not territorial reconfiguration or state dissolution? What mental operations must the students of state formation perform in order to be able to decode the term 'consensual secession' as referring to an instance of state formation, in a way that appears minimally palatable? What is gained, and what is lost – in practical as well as analytical terms – by using the term 'consensual secession', and not those which can just as easily be used to capture its distinctive features?

DOI: 10.4324/9781003036593-23

Table 19.1 'Consensual secession'

| (I) Year | (II) Instance | (III) Host State Type | (IV) Host State Continues to Exist | (V) Government Consents Freely | (VI) Alternative Qualification |
|---|---|---|---|---|---|
| 1 | 1905 | NORWAY from Sweden | A two-member PERSONAL UNION | N | Y | THE DISSOLUTION of a personal union |
| 2 | 1918 | IRELAND from Britain | A 'UNION' STATE (formally unitary) | Y | Y/N | CONSTITUTIONAL DEVOLUTION + PEACE TREATY |
| 3 | 1944 | ICELAND from Denmark | A two-member PERSONAL UNION | Y | N | THE DISSOLUTION of a personal union the exercise of a right, guaranteed by the act of union |
| 4 | 1965 | SINGAPORE from Malaysia | A multi-member FEDERAL STATE | Y | Y | THE EXPULSION from a federal state; THE 'AMPUTATION' of the portion of the federal territory |
| 5 | 1993 | SLOVAKIA from Czechoslovakia | A two-member FEDERAL STATE | N | Y | THE DISSOLUTION of a federation |
| 6 | 2005 | MONTENEGRO from Serbia and Montenegro | A two-member QUASI-FEDERAL STATE | N | N | THE DISSOLUTION of a 'state union'; the exercise of a constitutional right |
| 7 | ? | QUÉBEC from Canada | A multi-member FEDERAL STATE | Y | Y* | THE RESTRICTION OF THE JURISDICTION of the Canadian constitutional order to a territory that excludes the territory of Québec as it resulted from constitutional negotiations via CONSTITUTIONAL AMENDMENT |

*Source:* Data for column V from Pavković and Radan (2007, 2011)

## (Consensual) secession: beyond territorial separation

When it comes to discriminating between the forces of good from the forces of evil in the context of conflicts over territorial sovereignty, much turns on how observers perceive the manner in which parties to the conflict sought to achieve their territorial aspirations. Identifying a state of affairs on the ground as an instance of a particular mode of state formation is of supreme importance for the success of competing aspirations. The same is the case, in a more indirect way, with terminological distinctions between different forms of state formation, which in turn give rise to the host of seemingly taxonomical questions.

Is the independence of Singapore the result of 'consensual secession', 'expulsion' or simply of constitutional 'devolution'? Is secession consensual or unilateral – if it occurs not with consent of a government of the host state that acts in conformity with extant constitutional norms, but with the consent of the representatives of a movement that prevailed in a civil war and which functions as a de facto government, and in conformity with a transitional agreement that effectively suspended the operation of the extant constitutional order, and under supervision of international organizations or foreign powers – as was the case with the secession of Eritrea from Ethiopia? Should the outcome of the process of territorial separation be seen as an instance of unilateral secession, of consensual secession or of mere 'exit' – and hence of no secession at all – if the process of separating unfolds in conformity with the provisions that regulate the process of withdrawal of member-states from a supranational political organization, such as the European Union?

On first look, the answers these questions elicit seem to be wholly dependent on one's definition of secession. The 'exit' of Britain from the European Union will count as the instance of secession if one defines it (as does the latest edition of the *Oxford English Dictionary*) as the act of 'formally withdrawing' from an 'alliance', 'federation', or some other kind 'political or religious organization' (OED 2020: online). And in turn, one will be compelled to reach the opposite conclusion if one's definition of secession corresponds with those that prevail in the contemporary scholarship on secession, where secession tends to appear either as the act of 'creation of a State by the use or threat of force without the consent of the former sovereign' (Crawford 2006, p. 375), or as 'the separation of part of the territory and population of an existing state, without the consent of that state' (Kattan 2018), or – as is the case in the contexts in which it occurs 'unilaterally' – as the 'withdrawal of a territory and its population from the jurisdiction of a state without the consent of the government of the state (or of the government which claims to represent the state)' (Anderson 2013, p. 353).

From the perspective of a would-be sovereign state, the object of the host state's consent can refer to at least three different things: (1) the withdrawal of an already existing 'territory' of a would-be state from the jurisdiction of a more encompassing one; (2) the withdrawal of an already existing 'territory' as well as – possibly – the creation of a new territorial unit 'upon the territory of the host state' *prior* to the formal 'withdrawal' of that 'unit' from a broader state; or (3) the separation of an identifiable part of the territory that would otherwise continue to belong to the host state – but only in the form of an already existing territorial unit, though not necessarily for the purpose of creating an independent state. Though each understanding of territorial separation hinges on a subtly different image of separating, each of them takes the existence of territory, as that what is being separated (from), for granted. What that is, exactly, is rarely confronted directly, explicitly and systematically.

'Even works dedicated to territoriality', as Ralf Michaels points out, 'rarely take time to discuss what territory means' (Michaels 2021). When they do, the concept of territory appeared as inextricably linked to both sovereignty, as well as geography: either as a 'geographical are[a] over which sovereignty . . . may be exercised' – or as simply as a 'land' 'in which sovereignty exists or may exist' (Shaw, quoted from Michaels 2021). If so, is the territory that the students of secession imagine as capable of being withdrawn from the host states' jurisdiction a 'geographical area' over which sovereignty exists? An affirmative answer to this question would immediately confront us with another, more elementary one: What makes the presumably existing 'geographical area' geographical?

For the purpose of this chapter, we fortunately don't need to confront this question. On the view that appears to prevail in contemporary scholarship on secession, territory is a pre-existing fragment of the earth's surface which we must choose to take for granted before we can reach the 'empirical' conclusion about who and where successfully claims a monopoly of physical force over a discrete set of individuals. On this view, territory is simply the spatial sphere of jurisdictionally comprehensive authority, exercised by the institutions belonging to an already existing, hierarchically organized administrative unit of a particular kind: (1) those whose institutions, as a totality, exercise comprehensive jurisdictional authority; (2) those which exist within a more encompassing, hierarchically organized, constitutional order; and (3) those which exist at the sub-state level of government *immediately beneath* the one colloquially referred to as 'of-central-government', 'domestic' or 'national'.

Beyond the two prevailing views – i.e. the one which, ultimately incoherently, reduces territory to a given geographical area, and the one which renders it coterminous with a pre-existing, legally defined sphere of spatial jurisdiction – a view which remains virtually absent from contemporary scholarship on secession is that of territory as 'an effect produced by state practices and technologies' (Neep 2017): i.e. as the totality of material effects produced by the regimes which (in regulating the behaviour of a highly predictable, sufficiently cooperative, relatively concentrated and fundamentally *sedentary* population) primarily rely on the technology of territoriality (cf. Mukerji 2010). The existence of such regimes presupposes the existence of a sufficient degree of not simply 'consent', but consent as 'diffuse support' for the ongoing continuation of a state understood as a territorial regime as a whole. From this it follows that the consent that distinguishes consensual from unilateral secession is always twofold: not only the consent of the government of the host state to secession, but also the 'consent' of those to be governed within a would-be state to be given away – literally se-ceded – by the government of the host state from the rest of that state. We will briefly explore the implications of this view of territory at the end of this chapter, but before we move on, another general point seems important enough to be emphasized.

## (Consensual) secession: beyond state formation

However qualified – as unilateral or as consensual – secession is a concept which we tend to understand in two distinct ways at the same time: (1) as an instance of territorial separation, and (2) as a mode of state formation. In contrast to 'territorial separation' which in the first case figures as the broader conceptual category of secession – its *genus proximum* – the 'territorial separation', implicit in the second case, that is one of the *differentiae* of secession: a characteristic feature which distinguishes it from other modes of state formation, such as partition. At a more abstract level, the secession that appears in the first case refers to territorial separation as the final outcome of the activities which preceded it, and which brought it about as their irreversible end result. The territorial separation that appears in the second case is a reference to the acts of separating, whose distinctive features turn the process of seceding into a distinct mode of state formation.

## Secession v. state dissolution

Against the backdrop of this distinction, the very possibility of secession as either consensual or as unilateral will inevitably appear as wholly dependent on one's more abstract notions of secession. From the perspective of those who approach secession as a reference to the *activities* characteristic of one particular form of state formation, the very *possibility* of such 'separation' hinges on the choices which – by the nature of things – can only be made *prospectively*. From the perspective of those who think of secession as the *culmination* of a process that results in the formation of an independent state, its identity as 'secession', partition or state dissolution can only be established *retrospectively*. Of the latter kind was James Crawford's verdict on the character of the process that led to the extinction of SFR Yugoslavia as a sovereign state – and whose 'dissolution' could only have been identified in retrospect, once it became obvious that the sequence of individual secessions from the federal centre ended up leaving no 'substantial central or federal component behind' (Crawford 2006, p. 390). The tenability of this verdict, as we will see in a moment, hinges not only on the persuasiveness of understanding of the principle of federalism in general, or the implications which that principle has for the functioning of the Yugoslav federal order, but also on the ways in which the federal order presents itself *visually* in the imagination of those who consider them as confronted with the prospect of secession.

## State disincorporation v. secession as separation

In contrast to a universe in which the act of joining into a federal union *literally* amounts to an act of *incorporation into* a new political *body* – which, on closer inspection, is exactly what made the 'union' between Texas and other American states 'complete', 'perpetual, and 'indissoluble' according to Justice Chase in *Texas v. White* (1868) (cf. Cushman 2018, p. 196) – the states that figure as the objects of secession, or (according to Crawford) as the by-products of state dissolution exist in two, not three dimensions. In a two-dimensional universe, secession is a reference to an act which, 'takes apart what was previously separately constructed . . . along the original line of unification', by 'using a previously organized mechanism' (O'Leary 2007) resembling, from that perspective, the motions used to *unplug* (a modular component from the rest of the mechanism) or to detach a coupon by tearing it apart from the rest of the movie ticket along the perforated line).

## Secession as separation v. partition as division

Thus conceived, secession stands in opposition not to state dissolution, but to partition, which results not in separation of an already existing territory from the one within which it already existed as an identifiable component, but in the formation of a brand new territory through the *division* of an already existing one, which, as Brendan O'Leary involves 'a fresh cut, a rip, a gash' or 'a slash' (O'Leary 2007, p. 886).

This gives rise to an important if, for the purposes of this inquiry, lateral question, which nonetheless deserves to be addressed in passing: If a seceding territory may seamlessly be detached from its environment, why we need to assume that the only way to divide it into parts is by tearing it apart? If it was possible to reconfigure a broader territorial configuration by detaching from it one of its modular fragments, why wouldn't it be possible to transform that fragment into a configuration of territorial modules? The procedure that allows the Kurds in Iraq to restructure the internal boundary of their region (which O'Leary himself uses as an example of internal boundary reconfigurations), or the one that is used in Switzerland, which relies on the system of so-called cascading referendums, should not be seen as a uniquely intra-state boundary-drawing solution. However impracticable internationally, these procedures ought to be seen as the proof of concept: demonstrating that the effect of 'partition' may be achieved in a structured manner, through a sequence of intra-unit, conditional, 'secessions', and showing – in practice – why secession-partition distinction cannot be sustained in theory.

## *(Orderly) devolution v. (consensual) secession*

Seen as a rhetorical device, secession is not only a mode of state formation which stands opposed to state dissolution, but also the one which is, in comparison to partition, less complicated, less nationalistic, less imposed, less violent and, overall, more presumptively legitimate. However understood, neither partition nor secession can be understood in isolation from all other modes of state formation. When it comes to consensual secession, those who deny its validity do so not simply because they consider the absence of consent of the host state the hallmark of secession as such, but also because they consider 'consensual secession' superfluous, in light of the already existing terms for the same mode of state formation, such as (constitutional) 'devolution'. Sometimes, this is reflected in etymology. The devolving that emerged from the Latin stem *de-* + *volvere* alludes not simply to the activity of transferring, but to the activity which causes that 'thing to pass from one person to another' by being *rolled* 'downward or onward'. Calling consensual secession 'devolution' is not to misunderstand the 'true' meaning of secession, but to point to something that the term 'consensual secession' can't: smoothness as a desirable characteristic of the process that culminates in the formation of a new state; the commendable manner in which state formation proceeds – smoothly, not abruptly, unpredictably, erratically or violently.

## Consensual secession: beyond the government's consent

When it comes to consensual secession, the 'consent' of the host state turns out to be the consent of *the government* of the host state, either in the form of (a) authoritative permission to act in ways that will result in the restriction of its spatial as personal jurisdiction, in conformity with the host state's constitution, or (b) as an unauthorized *permission* to violate the norms of the host state's constitutional order – amounting not to the 'giving of consent', but to high treason (if given by the officials of the state) or, at the very least, the abdication of a civic duty to uphold and defend the integrity of the national constitutional order. The governments that give their consent to secession in the name of the host state – to put it differently – may do so *in* conformity with, or in violation of not one, but two kinds of constitutional norms: those that govern the periodic transfer of political power within the host state, and those that govern the process of constitutional change, and of constitutional amendment in particular.

This complicates our notion of consensual secession as an instance of territorial withdrawal that enjoys the consent of the government of the host state, because materially constitutional as well as materially unconstitutional withdrawals from the host state may be *consented to* both by a de jure, as well as by a de facto, government of the host state. If so, the secession which contemporary scholars refer to as 'consensual' ought to be understood as a term which may refer to: (1) an act undertaken in conformity with the *permission* of the government of the host state; (b) an act which obtained the *recognition* of the host state before being recognized by the governments of other ones, or (c) an act envisaged by an *agreement*

i    between the authorized representatives of a wider state and the authentic representatives of the secessionist movement, implemented in conformity with the norms of the extant constitutional order (such as the one envisioned in the well-known and highly-regarded opinion of the Supreme Court of Canada, *Reference re Secession of Quebec*);

ii between the secessionists and the authoritative representatives of the host state, which – in clearing the way for secession – either formally suspends the application of otherwise applicable constitutional norms, or in some other way violates the binding norms of the domestic constitutional order (as would be the case with any agreement that would make it possible for Catalonia to secede from Spain, without satisfying the stringent conditions for constitutional amendment, as outlined in article 155 of the Spanish constitution);

iii between the secessionists and the representatives of the government of the host state who lack constitutional authority to enter into an agreement in the name of a wider state (as was the case with the agreements that set the stage for the secessions of Eritrea from Ethiopia in 1993, or South Sudan from Sudan in 2011);

iv between the representatives of the sub-state units within a broader state, who either lack the authority to enter into an agreement that leads to the termination of a broader state, or whose support among the populations of the about-to-become independent states is insufficient or uncertain (as was the case with the agreements that led to the dissolutions of the Soviet Union and Czechoslovakia).

Assuming that consensual forms of secession are less prima facie morally, politically or legally dubious than those scholars refer to unilaterally, it might be worth asking what makes them so from the perspective of the more specific 'agreements' referenced earlier. From that perspective, achieving consensual secession appears to be valuable (in the first case) because it conforms with the ideals of the rule of law and constitutional supremacy, implicit in the behaviour of governments that derive their authority from constitutional norms; or because it prevents the evil which would have ensued in its absence (as in the second case). The value of agreement in the third case – and of consent as a political ideal relevant in the context of different modes of state formation, more generally – is far from obvious, however.

## Consensual state formation: an (im)possible ideal

In *Webster's 1913 Dictionary*, 'consent' is defined as 'capable, deliberate, and voluntary agreement to or concurrence in some act or purpose implying physical and mental power and free action' (Webster's) – which is to say, by someone who had it their power to choose otherwise (Harrison 2003). Given freely, and manifested publicly, 'consent' is not just the formal expression of 'a felt willingness to agree with . . . what another person seeks or proposes' (Westen 2003, p. 5) but also of the one that it had been arrived at thoughtfully, which – in light of a resolute manner in which it had been expressed – can also counted on to be upheld into an indefinite future. When it comes to the early-modern imaginary of state formation, this meant that those who will have come together to establish a new political society by consenting to the terms stipulated in a social contract, will not be a random collection of individuals, but those who already 'like[d] each other . . . *so well*' (emphasis in original), or who, at the very minimum, have least 'apprehensions' toward each other (Locke 1690, s. 107).

What made this notion of consent seem applicable to the formation of spatially delineated political communities is not only the equivalence which its early adoptees (first and foremost in pre-and post-revolutionary America) drew between *revolution* (as the act of rebellion against tyranny) and *secession* (as a mode of its practical realization), but also the prevailing imagination of those communities as spatially unconstrained forms of government whose only purpose is the effective promotion of the common good of their covenanters (Skinner 1989, p. 115) – existing in a world in which their *emigres* may easily create new ones by agreement 'in any part of the world they can find free and unpossessed' (Locke 1690, s. 117).

In contrast to the communities which continue to exist in 'vacuis locis' (ibid.) and whose 'territorial' jurisdictions are wholly accidental to the authority that their governments exercise over explicitly or tacitly consenting individuals, the governments whose existence is presupposed by the idea of a fully sovereign and internationally recognized *state* exist as distinct both from the populations which they govern as well as from the territories as their notional receptacles. In a world devoid of empty spaces between such units, the lines that keep them apart from each other also function as semi-permeable membranes between those that are immediately adjacent (Sloterdijk 2016, pp. 236-7).

Though no longer able to exist as a directly applicable regulative ideal in a world where the formation of a new state immediately results in the territorial reconfiguration (or even extinction) of at least one among those that are already in existence, the idea of consent continued to inform the nineteenth-century imaginary of state formation under the name of 'common sympathies': a factor, which in the thought of John Stuart Mill, appeared as solely responsible for turning a 'portion of mankind' into a 'nationality', making those who belong to it not only 'co-operate with each other more willingly than with other people' but also 'desire to be under the same government' to the exclusion of all others (Mill 2015, p. 370).

Though unable to be translated into a rightful demand for political independence in the form of a sovereign state in a world in which such units exist as densely stacked against each other, Mill's 'sympathies' set the stage for the emergence of the 'principle of nationality' which made it possible to answer to the following questions even without the benefit of the ideals of consent and self: (1) *When* to establish politically autonomous territorial units? (As soon as the 'common sympathies' among a group of people become manifest.) (2) *How* to draw the boundaries of such units? (In a way which leaves as many of those who share the same sympathies included into, and as many of those who don't excluded from, a newly formed unit.) (3) *What* status should they enjoy within a worldwide legal order? (Ideally, as sovereign and fully independent states.)

## State formation and the varieties of consent

From a more historically panoramic perspective, however, the ideal of the concept of the government appears as desperately confused. In good part, this is due to the lack of effort to articulate its objects and objectives within a categorical apparatus that would include not only the attributes of contemporary territorial states, but also of those where it figured:

a    as the source from which a governments 'derive their just powers', and, by implication, as the foundation of a right, vested in the People as a whole, to abolish those that act against [their] purposes', and to 'institute' those that 'seem most likely to effect their Safety and Happiness' (Declaration of Independence 1776, p. 165);

b    as the foundation of a 'State', understood as 'the political community of free citizens, occupying a territory of defined boundaries, and organized under a government sanctioned and limited by a written constitution' (Texas v. White, US, Vol 74, 1868, p. 700);

c    as 'part of a constitutional theory which has, so far, been developed only or chiefly with regard to the adjustment or amendment of established systems of government', according to Woodrow Wilson, then Professor of Government at Princeton University (Wilson, quoted from Manela 2007, p. 35);

d    as the principle of international relations, from which it follows 'that no right anywhere exists to hand peoples about from sovereignty to sovereignty as if they were property' (ibid, p. 24);

e    as the basis of a lasting 'territorial settlement' in Europe after the end of the First World War, and coterminous with a 'right to self-determination' (Lloyd George 1918);

f    as equated with the 'good pleasure' of national minorities, and as such incompatible with the very idea of the State as a territorial and political unity (David Lloyd George, quoted from Manela 2007, p. 24; Commission of Rapporteurs 1921);

g    as alluded to in the references to the 'free expression' of the will and desires of the peoples of non-self-governing territories that haven't yet attained 'full measure of self-government', but entitled to attain independence without delay' (UNGA Resolutions 1514 and 1541);

h    as referring to the vast majority of the people in Kosovo, as one of the unique factors in support of recognizing the independence of Kosovo;

i    as equated with the 'ongoing agreement' of the people that live in Scotland, and considered the basis for their 'continuing participation' in the United Kingdom as a 'multi-national country whose constituent parts enjoy different constitutional settlements and rights' (Scottish Government 2019, p. 4);

j    as the basis for 'determin[ing] the territorial contours of a polity' informed by 'debate among all affected groups', as a superior alternative to 'the allotments made by hegemonic powers on the drawing board or in green rooms' (in Peters 2017);

k    as 'a value that is basic to the Canadian 'understanding of a free and democratic society', and a distinguishing feature of a system whose legitimacy in good part hinges on its capability to 'reflec[t] the aspirations of the people' (Reference re Secession of Quebec 1998: para. 67).

In the last case, it also puts that order under an obligation to give 'considerable weight . . . to 'the clear expression of 'clear majority of Quebecers that they no longer *wish* to remain in Canada' (Secession Reference 1998: para 92, emphasis added). This obligation – to give considerable weight to the clear expression of a demand for secession, supported by a clear regional majority – may be, as Neil Walker suggests, be understood as a direct correlate of a right to self-determination, which entitles a sub-state territorial people to expect to have its aspirations to live in an independent state to be taken seriously by the institutions of the host state's constitutional order (Walker 2018). In order to be able to comply with this expectation, however, such an order – as a whole – must be imagined as

1    *sensitive* enough to *register* large-scale shifts in what David Easton referred to as 'diffuse support' for the 'regime as a whole' among the population of Québec (Easton 1975);

2    *irritable* enough to be 'triggered' to react by a credible indication about the extent of popular support for secession among the people in Québec;

3    *responsive* enough to react to the expression of such desire by entering into constitutional negotiations, which may result in the significant restriction of Canada's spatial and personal jurisdiction.

Such constitutional negotiations wouldn't have been possible had the Supreme Court, as an organ of in charge of interpreting its constitution, not been as

4    *liberal-minded* enough about the meaning the foundational concepts of modern democratic state and liberal constitutionalism – in comparison with the approaches taken by other liberal democracies in similar situations – as well as

5    *relaxed* enough about the possibility that a successfully negotiated independence of one
     province doesn't put an end to a nation-wide constitutional crisis, but rather provides an
     impetus for the next round of territorial fragmentation.

On a closer look, interpretations such as Walker's are problematic not only because they encourage scholars and non-scholars alike to neglect the implications that the ideal of the consent has for the overall posture of democratically legitimate institutions, but also because: (a) they perpetuate a more general, yet highly spurious distinction between secession as a fact and self-determination as a fiction (distracting the experts and non-experts alike from the roles that specific mental schemata play in the imaginative constitution of secession as 'external' self-determination' or status elevation) and (b) because they contribute to the hegemony of the idea of a sovereign state as invariably substantive and not always as also an intermediary, instrumental objective of secessionist aspirations.

## (Consensual) secession beyond self-determination

As an act of self-*de*-termination, seceding is an act of defining the *boundaries of* (one) 'self', placing the *limits to* (one) 'self', identifying the *end(s) for* one(self), and, overall, of establishing *the terms of* one's existence. Inscribed into the Latin origins of 'determination', the limits, terms, ends and borders to which self-determination alludes are today ensconced into its two modes: the *internal*, where self-determination involves deciding the specific limitations to the exercise of collective political power, and exercising freedom to define collective political ends, free from external interference; and *external*, which is 'the result of a free and voluntary choice by the peoples of the territory concerned expressed through informed and democratic process' – and which culminates either in 'emergence' of a territory 'as a sovereign independent state', or in its 'free association with an independent state', or its 'integration with an independent state).

     Understood as the outcome of external self-determination that coincides with the *upgrade* in the legal status of a previously existing territorial unit, secession makes sense only if we imagine it against the backdrop of the political map of the world – which, in addition to the external, also represents the internal boundaries of sovereign states; and on which the said upgrade in status will be represented by the visual 'upgrade' of the boundaries of a self-determining unit: from a dotted line that signifies an administrative boundary of a sub-national unit, to a full line that separates an independent state from other independent states. The acts that must be undertaken for a successful transition from one to another in real life are well known. They include not just declaring independence or applying for membership in international organizations, but also setting obstacles to movement where otherwise there were none: either by erecting new border crossings as contemporary secessionists do when they manage to solidify their power over a given territory; or, by fortifying the camp on *Mons Sacer*, 'with stockade and trench' as historically first secessionists had done after they had collectively abandoned the confines of the city of Rome.

     Unlike most present-day Brexiteers, the plebeians who literally walked out through its gates chose to do so because they were willing to bet that leaving behind their livelihoods as bakers, shopkeepers, carpenters, or artisans, will soon prove so uncomfortable to the patricians whose daily needs they satisfied that it would compel them to accept their demands for constitutional reform. Though there are scholars who find similarities between their *secessio* and the political 'withdrawals' which we today think of as secessions, the literal exit of Roman plebeians from the city of Rome also deserves to be seen in a more existential light: not simply as an act of secession (as we understand it today), but also as a veritable act of se-*cession*, where those who – in 'withdrawing' from their workplaces – also made a conscious decision to *leave* their livelihoods that their work made possible, *behind*.

By and large, the students of secession chose to take the topography of the existing one for granted, but the time may have arrived to confront it as yet another contestable assumption. Secession, self-determination and consent will mean one thing in a world in which creating a new state constitutes a 'subtraction' from the territory of some other (Griffiths 2019, p. 145), and quite another meaning in a world in which 'humankind constitutes a manifold, a totality of interconnected processes' (Wolf 2010, p. 3) in which 'nations' and 'states' exist only as the references for the artefacts of human imagination. Yet even in a world devoid of sovereign states, the dreams of a radically better life will never be too distant from the dreams of radical jurisdictional reconfigurations. King Utopus in More's *Utopia* knew it all too well. Only after the feat of engineering that his subjects accomplished by building a 15-mile-long channel that separated his most recent territorial acquisition from the rest of the continent did an otherwise unremarkable peninsula he conquered turn into an island, which we know under the name of Utopia (Jameson 2005, p. 39).

## Consensual secession as a polemical conception

While the students of secession disagree about many things – about who, how, why, where and when is *morally justified* to pursue secession, about the existence or non-existence of a remedial right to secession, about the merits and demerits of constitutionalizing secession, about the rights of sub-state units to unilaterally separate from federations – they rarely, if ever, dispute the sensibility of 'secession' as an object of scholarly reflection, let alone about its *existence* as a 'watershed event' (Siroky 2013, p. 46) or a 'multifaceted phenomenon' (Coggins 2013, p. 24). In contrast to the alleged ridiculousness of self-determination – which implausibly proposes something that cannot be, that a people can 'decide' its fate even before it has been 'decided' into existence (by somebody else) – the 'secession' that appears in the scholarly debates about state formation is a fact of life, not an idea or a fiction. In this context, consensual secession appears to be, if not the most benign, then at least the least-worst mode of state formation. As long as a new state emerges on the basis of an agreement between those who appear to be authorized to defend the constitutional status quo, and those who appear to be authentically challenging it in the name of a discrete 'people', the legality of such agreement will simply be taken for granted. In contrast to unilateral secessions, whose legitimacy varies from situation to situation, secessions achieved consensually are legitimate *ex hypothesi*.

On closer inspection, the persuasiveness of this conclusion hinges on what we mean by secession in general, as well as on what in our imagination differentiates secession from other modes of state formation such as *state unification* (where a new state emerges as the outcome of an international agreement among sovereign states, which results in the extinction of their international legal personality); *state consolidation* (where a new state emerges through the concerted action of powerful states, administrative powers and international institutions); *state devolution* (where a new state emerges in conformity with the norms of a broader constitutional order) or *state dissolution* (where a new state emerges from the total extinction of the previous one).

On even closer inspection, the meaning of secession – and, *ceteris paribus*, the possibility of its 'consensual' variant – will inevitably also depend on (a) the interpretation of the general principles of international law (such as *uti possidetis juris*) as applicable or inapplicable to the situation at hand; (b) the identification of the salient features of constitutional orders of host states (as federal, or as non-federal-like); (c) the assumptions about the content of normative ideals, which make the operation of the constitutional organs of such states legitimate or illegitimate; (d) speculations about the intended functions of such orders' organs and conjectures about their typical functioning in the past; (e) preconceptions about the spatial and temporal properties of the orders that undergo radical constitutional transformation; and (f) the mental representations of the actual ways through which would-be independent entities become sovereign and independent states.

What typically figures as secession may also be taken as the instance of the *emergence* of an already existing territorial unit as a sovereign state, and its *assumption* to the position of an (internationally recognized) sovereign state; the *retraction* of the institutions of the host state from the territory of the about-to-become independent one, which in reality most often takes the form of their more or less violent *repulsion* by means of the *expulsion* of those who act in their name; or the *cession* of both the jurisdictional powers which the representatives of the seceding people, as well as of the individual and collective rights which its members enjoy, as the citizens of the host state, under its constitution. As for the instances of consensual secession (see Table 19.1), they can just as easily be re-described as an instance of the termination of membership in a federation, as an exit from a union or as the reduction of the spatial and personal sphere of the host state's jurisdiction.

Which brings us back to the initial question: why use 'consensual secession' as a term for the instances of state formation and not one of the already existing, juridically sanctioned, alternative descriptions? Why insist on consensual secession as a distinct form of secession, in light of the absence of this term in the vocabulary of secessionists and anti-secessionist alike? This question presents itself not just in the case of Serbia and Montenegro – represented in Table 19.1 – whose Constitutional Charter granted both members not an entitlement to 'secede' but, rather, a right to initiate the process of 'stepping out' of the state union, including a right to make a final decision on the issue, depending on the outcome of a mandatory, unit-wide referendum. It also appears in the cases of Singapore (where the rest of the host state survived, in a pretty much unaltered form), as well as Québec (whose potential secession from the rest of Canada would not, not initially at least, lead to the further territorial 'fraying' of the Canadian federation).

In the case of Singapore, the Agreement that preceded its secession from Malaysia explicitly referred to its '*separation*', but the future Asian tiger became independent not by means of secession but in virtue of the Malaysian Prime Minister's announcement – '*declar*[ing] and *proclaim*[ing] . . . that . . . Singapore *shall cease to be* a State of Malaysia and *shall forever be* . . . sovereign . . . and independent of Malaysia'. In the case of Québec, a clear majority in favour of its independence from Canada will (according to the framework established by the Supreme Court) entitle its representatives to '*propose* secession' to federal government and other participants in the confederation, thus putting them under obligation to 'contemplate [its] possibility' as part of good faith constitutional negotiations (Secession Reference 1998: para. 97). From the perspective of the Canadian constitutional order, the emergence of Québec as a fully sovereign and independent state would not count as an instance of 'secession', but rather of a *constitutional revision*, which 'the people of Canada – 'acting through their various governments', 'has within its power to effect . . . within Canadian territory' (ibid: para 85).

## Conclusion

Contingent on the content of individual scholars' private definitions, consensual secession is always more than simply the least-worst mode of state formation. Its intelligibility cannot be divorced from the background understandings of how idealized manifestations of collective self-determination relate to the allegedly brute (f)act of secession, nor from the categorical distinctions that separate secession from the dissolution of a sovereign state, its partition or devolution – nor, ultimately, from the preconceptions about the character of *territorial separation*: a broader category to which each of these modes of state formation belong.

From the perspective of secession which coincides with an entitlement to the so-called external self-determination, the question of whether those vested with it managed to achieve its substance (i.e. an internationally recognized, fully independent and sovereign state) unilaterally or consensually is theoretically uninteresting as well as ethically irrelevant. From the perspective of situations in which no such right exists, references to secession as either consensual or uni-lateral encourage us to consider the former as legitimate and the latter as illegitimate, without taking into account important ethical considerations, which have to do not with the consent of the host state (or of 'international community'), but with the consent of the governed.

With this in mind, 'consensual secession' might best be understood not simply as a 'much contested concept' (cf. Pavković 2015) but also as a scholarly *gesture*: as a move which allows the students of secession (irrespective of the disciplinary vantage point from which they approach this phenomenon) to direct the attention of their audiences away from the questions about domestic constitutionality of secession, away from the questions about the character, intensity and effects of external involvement in the process of state formation and away from the consider-ation of the degree of support which an act of secession ought to enjoy in order to be considered legitimate – both within the seceding region, as well as within the non-seceding part of the host state itself. However understood theoretically, consensual secession cannot but function as a rhetorical weapon.

# References

Anderson, G. 2013, 'Secession in International Law: What Are We Talking About?', *Loyola of Los Angeles International and Comparative Law Journal* 35(3): 343–388.

Coggins, B. 2013, 'The History of Secession: An Overview', in A. Pavković and P. Radan (eds), *The Ash-gate Research Companion to Secession*, Farnham: Ashgate.

Commission of Rapporteurs. 1921, 'Report Presented to the Council of the League by the Commission of Rapporteurs', League of Nations Council Document B7.

Congress, U. S. 1776, 'Declaration of independence' Available in: http://memory. loc. gov/cgi-bin/ampage.

Crawford, J. 2006, *Creation of States in International Law*, Oxford: Oxford University Press.

Cushman, B. 2018, 'Federalism', in K Oren and J. Compton (eds), *The Cambridge Companion to the United States Constitution*, Cambridge: Cambridge University Press.

Declaration of Independence 1776. In Armitage, D. 2007, *The Declaration of Independence*, Cambridge, MA, Harvard University Press, pp. 165–71.

Easton, D. 1975, 'A Re-Assessment of the Concept of Political Support', *British Journal of Political Science* 5(4): 435–457.

Griffiths, R. 2019, 'Dynamics of secession and state birth', in G. Visoka, J. Doyle and E. Newman (eds), *Routledge Handbook of State Recognition,* London: Routledge.

Harrison, R. 2003, *Hobbes, Locke, and Confusion's Masterpiece: An Examination of Seventeenth-Century Political Philosophy*, Cambridge: Cambridge University Press.

Jameson, F. 2005, *Archaeologies of the Future: The Desire Called Utopia and Other Science Fictions*, London: Verso.

Kattan, V. 2018, 'Partition', in A. Peters (ed), *Max Planck Encyclopaedia of Public International Law*, Oxford: Oxford University Press.

Locke, J. 1980 (first published 1690), *Second Treatise on Government*, C. B. Macpherson (ed), Indianapolis: Hackett Publishing.

Manela, E. 2007, *Wilsonian Moment: Self-Determination and the International Origins of Anticolonial National-ism*, Oxford: Oxford University Press.

Michaels, R. 2021, 'Notes on Territory', in J. D'Aspremont & J. Haskell (eds), *Tipping Points in International Law*, Cambridge: Cambridge University Press.

Mill, J. S. 2015 [1859], *On Liberty, Utilitarianism, and Other Essays*, Oxford: Oxford University Press.

Mukerji, C. 2010, 'The Territorial State as a Figured World of Power: Strategies, Logistics, and Impersonal Rule', *Sociological Theory* 28(4): 402–424.

Neep, D. 2017, 'State-Space beyond Territory: Wormholes, Gravitational Fields, and Entanglement', *Journal of Historical Sociology* 30(3): 466.

O'Leary, B. 2007, 'Analysing partition: Definition, classification and explanation', *Political Geography,* 26(8): 886–908.

Oxford English Dictionary. 2020, 'Secession, n.', Oxford: Oxford University Press. www.oed.com/view/Entry/174475. Accessed 23 January 2020.

Pavković, A. 2015, 'Secession as a Much-Contested Concept', in D. Kingsbury & C. Laoutides (eds), *Territorial Separatism in Global Politics: Causes, Outcomes and Resolution*, London: Routledge.

Pavković, A. & Radan, P. 2007, *Creating New States: Theory and Practice of Secession*, Farnham: Ashgate Publishing

Pavković A. & Radan, P. (eds.) 2011, *The Ashgate Research Companion to Secession*, Farnham: Ashgate Publishing

Peters, A. 2017, Populist International Law? The Suspended Independence and the Normative Value of the Referendum on Catalonia' in EJILTalk!: Blog of the European Journal of International Law https://www.ejiltalk.org/populist-international-law-the-suspended-independence-and-the-normative-value-of-the-referendum-on-catalonia/

Scottish Government. 2019, 'Scotland's right to choose: putting Scotland's future in Scotland's hands'. Available at https://www.gov.scot/publications/scotlands-right-choose-putting-scotlands-future-scotlands-hands/pages/3/#:~:text=This%20is%20because%20the%20United,different%20constitutional%20settlements%20and%20rights.

Siroky, D. 2013, 'Explaining secession', in A. Pavković & P. Radan (eds), *The Ashgate Research Companion to Secession*, Farnham: Ashgate.

Skinner, Q. 1989, 'The State', in D. Ross, Q. Skinner & J. Tully (eds), *Political Innovation and Conceptual Change*, Cambridge: Cambridge University Press.

Sloterdijk, P. 2016. Foams: Spheres Volume III: Plural Spherology, Cambridge, Ma: MIT Press.

The Supreme Court of Canada. 1998, Reference re Secession of Quebec.

The Supreme Court of the United States. 1868, Texas v. White. 74 US 700.

Walker, N. 2018. 'Teleological and reflexive nationalism in the new Europe', in J. Jordana et al. (eds), *Changing Borders in Europe,* London: Routledge.

Webster's International Dictionary. 1913. https://www.webster-dictionary.org/definition/consent (accessed on December 2 2022).

Westen, P. 2003, *The Logic of Consent: The Diversity and Deceptiveness of Consent as a Defense to Criminal Conduct*, Aldershot: Ashgate.

Williams, R. 2015, 'Consensus', in *Keywords: A Vocabulary of Culture and Society: New Edition*, Oxford: Oxford University Press.

Wolf, E. 2010, *Europe and the People without History*, Berkeley: University of California Press.

# 20

# DECLARATIONS OF INDEPENDENCE

## A classification

*Argyro Kartsonaki and Aleksandar Pavković*

In his seminal work *The Declaration of Independence*, David Armitage (2007) notes that the 1776 US Declaration of Independence (officially entitled "A Declaration by the Representatives of the United States of America, in General Congress Assembled") brought about a new genre of political writing, marked by "generic promiscuity" (Armitage 2007, 15). It combined the elements of:

a    a declaration of independence ("We, therefore, the representatives of the United States of America . . . solemnly Publish and Declare . . . that these United Colonies are . . . Free and Independent States") (Armitage 2007, 179);

b    a declaration of rights ("We hold these Truths to be self-evident, that all Men are created equal, that they are endowed by their Creator with certain unalienable Rights") (Armitage 2007, 165);

c    a political manifesto made up by "a list of grievances . . . that publicly explained to the world the grounds for a revolutionary action" (Armitage 2007, 15).

The first element of the Declaration announces that now the United States of America are an independent state. The second element, the declaration of rights, stipulates the principles which justify – i.e., legitimize – the creation of the new state. The third section lists grievances – harms and injustices committed by the host state and its agents – that explain why the host state (Great Britain) had lost the authority to govern over the people of the colonies, whom it had (allegedly) systematically harmed. By incorporating these elements in order to justify independence, the 1776 US Declaration created a blueprint for DoIs that secessionists would replicate for centuries.

Dols of unilaterally seceding states, since their "birth" in 1776 with the US DoI, have had at least two interrelated objectives: the delegitimization of the existing host state's rule over the seceding territory (Nardin 2015, 100), and the legitimization of the new, emergent state that is seceding from the existing one. Listing grievances – injustices and harms suffered by the population of the emergent states – has been the standard way of delegitimizing the existing state and of legitimizing the new state: as in the 1776 US Declaration, the new state is presented as the only remedy to the listed grievances.

DOI: 10.4324/9781003036593-24

In the process of the dissolution of the USSR and SFR Yugoslavia from 1990 onwards, a number of federal and sub-federal units abandoned the objective of delegitimizing the old (host) state in their declarations or acts of independence. In some cases, DoIs focused exclusively on the legitimization of the new states, rather than the delegitimization of the old one (Kartsonaki and Pavković 2021). This was achieved by announcing or establishing state institutions which were taking over the state functions of the old state, and/or by announcing the new state's commitments to several internationally sanctioned principles and reaffirming their willingness to join international organizations. This kind of legitimization of the new state in a DoI often culminated in a request or appeal to other states and international organizations to recognize the independence of the new state.

In this chapter we propose a categorization of DoIs based on the strategies of delegitimization and legitimization. We distinguish the following four sub-genres of declarations of independence: grievance declarations, institutionalizing declarations, commitment declarations and restoration declarations. *Grievance declarations* are those in which the list of grievances dominates the DoI, suggesting or stating that the declaration is issued as a (or the) remedy to the grievances listed. These declarations name violations the host state committed against the seceding unit – including human rights abuses, acts of genocide, discrimination and breach of agreements – justifying their call for international recognition on remedial grounds. *Institutionalizing declarations* are those whose primary function is to establish, or announce the establishment of, state institutions and their powers, and/or appoint office holders. This type of DoI emphasizes the institutional capacity of the emergent state without mentioning any grievances against the former host state. It seeks recognition of its independent statehood solely on the basis of its institutional capabilities to create a functional state. These capabilities are assumed to be equal to other recognized independent states. *Commitment declarations* declare the commitments of the new state without necessarily naming or establishing state institutions; for example, commitments to create an appropriate political system (commonly a variant of liberal democracy), to seek membership to international organizations and to pursue cooperation and extensive relations with other states. Commitment declarations call for international recognition of newly seceded states based on their commitment to socialization within the international community, which is constituted by states committed to a liberal democratic (multiparty) system. *Restoration declarations* are not declarations of independence per se, but declarations that independent statehood is being or has been restored. With restoration proclamations, the independent state, which lost its independence involuntarily, is now independent again, regaining its legal or constitutional framework which had been previously removed or extinguished. A few DoIs are mere announcements of independence, with no further content which would allow the classification into one of the sub-genres; those DoIs, which lack a manifesto or a program, cannot be classified into any one of these sub-genres. Table 20.1 provides a list with the DoI we analysed.

With our categorization, we hope to shed light on how secessionists promote a self-constructed image of themselves and their actions in order to gain international support for their secession, and how the rhetoric they use has changed over time with the dominance of liberal democratic discourse in international affairs. Given the rise of secessionist groups around the world, it is imperative to understand the utility and purpose of DoIs, even if they appear to be just one of the tools secessionists use to reach uncontested statehood. In fact, DoIs are necessary instruments for those secessionists who attempt to secede unilaterally, without the consent of their host state: there is no other way of publicly announcing their act of secession or their intention to gain independence for the new state but through a declaration of independence. In a case of non-negotiated, unilateral secession, only the secessionists can (and do) publicly announce their secession – no one else is in position to do so; and any such declaration or public announcement is in fact their DoI. It was perhaps this necessary link between the act of secession and its announcement in the form of a DoI that led Jacques Derrida (1986, 9) to say that "[o] ne cannot decide . . . whether independence is stated or produced by this utterance [i.e. the declaration]" (Derrida 1986, 9).

This chapter is structured as follows. In the next section, we explain why it is important to look more closely at the texts of DoIs and what we can learn from them. We then proceed to the analysis of examples of declarations to illustrate the declarations' categories. The chapter ends with conclusions on the interrelation of DoIs and international recognition.

## Why are DoIs important?

After a lull of more than a decade, there has been a renewed interest in the field of secession. Scholars have resumed studying it from different angles, seeking both to theorize secession and to explain its motives, strategies and tactics (Griffiths and Muro 2020). In the field of theory advancement, Sanjaume-Calvet (2020) and Bauböck (2019) presented a realist and a multi-levelled theory of secession, respectively. In explaining the motives for secession, Rodon and Guinjoan (2018) and Hierro and Queralt (2020) introduced an individual-level approach. Rodon and Guinjoan (2018) explained how an individual's national and regional identity, as well as the stance of their close social circle towards secession, affects whether they would support or oppose secession, focusing on the case of Catalonia. Studying the same case, Hierro and Queralt (2020) sought to explain someone's stance towards secession based on the nature of their profession.

From the international-level point of view, and specifically on how secessionists seek international recognition, Griffiths (2021) examined the tactics that seceding units adopt in order to compel the host state and the international community to recognize them and hence obtain sovereign statehood. Coggins (2014) showed how important the support of great powers has been for the attainment of international recognition and also explained why some great powers support some secessionist movements but oppose others (see also Chapters 13 and 23, this book). Also, Roeder (2007), Florea (2014, 2017) and Griffiths (2015, 2017) investigated the importance of administrative units for the emergence and survival of secessionist movements and the acquisition of international recognition. There is also some emerging literature on the tactics of counter-secession (Ker-Lindsay 2012), and on "engagement without recognition" examining how contested states navigate the lack of recognition in their foreign policy (Bouris and Fernández-Molina 2018; Ker-Lindsay 2018; Ker-Lindsay and Armakolas 2020; see also Chapters 25 and 27, this volume).

Overall studies on secession cover the areas of at least four related research fields, including political science, political theory, international relations and international law. Amidst this plethora of secession-related studies, scholarly work on how secessionists promote their claims in their DoIs remains limited. Pavković (2020) discusses the secessionist appeal to the will of the people and the right to self-determination in several post-1945 DoIs. From an international law point of view, Vidmar (2012) discusses the question of the legality of some recent DoIs and their impact on international recognition of new states, without, however, analysing their content. In addition, the Kosovo DoI in 2008 had sparked some attention again from an international law perspective, mainly due to the unparalleled acceptance it received when compared to other unilateral declarations of independence (among others, Muharremi 2008; Sevastik 2008). Nevertheless, a systematic analysis of DoIs as statements of intent that investigates the rhetoric employed for legitimizing secession is missing.

Secession and international recognition of seceded states are multifaceted processes; the abundance of secession-related literature, briefly outlined earlier in this chapter, is indicative of the complexity of these issues. As part of those multifaceted processes, DoIs, and especially Unilateral Declarations of Independence (UDIs), present and forge an image of the aspiring state that speaks both to the population of the emerging state and to other established states from which international recognition is sought. As Knotter (2020) explains, the act of declaring independence is a part of a ritual with communicative, transcendental and communitarian purposes. We further Knotter's argument by offering a content analysis of the texts of DoIs in the context of their communicative strategies aiming at international recognition. Through DoIs, secessionists escalate their demands to statehood level, and DoIs are the tools with which they legitimize their claims and may attribute a certain type of identity to their aspiring state.

In creating a dataset of UDIs issued after 1945, we used the following selection criteria selection. First, the issuing body of a UDI should be the "legitimate authority" of the seceding entity. That would mean either an elected body of representatives drawn from the seceding entity, or a regional government or a movement that manifestly enjoyed the support of the population as demonstrated either through official or unofficial elections or referendum. By choosing our sample in this way, we sought to avoid the "internet-only DoIs", i.e., DoIs issued online by individuals, proclaiming independence of certain regions without enjoying popular support or having no role in the institutional and political structures of the seceding region.

Second, we refer to UDIs taking place without the consent of the host state. Therefore, negotiated secessions and declarations issued after state dissolutions are not included. In consequence, we included the UDIs of Yugoslav and Soviet federal and sub-federal units which declared independence before the dissolution of Yugoslavia and the Soviet Union respectively.

Third, we do not include cases of decolonization. Contrary to unilateral secession, decolonization is an established right in international law regulated according to the *uti possidetis* principle (UN Charter 1945, Ch. XI–XIII; UNGA 1960; UNSC 1975). It specifically refers to the obligation of the old, mainly European, empires to relinquish their overseas protectorates and mandates after the end of the Second World War, and it was reserved for territories emerging from what has been called as salt-water decolonization, i.e., for colonized territories usually separated by the host state by sea (Hilpold 2009; Cassese 1995). It envisaged a specific course of action, based on the consent of the parent state, which bequeathed independence to these territories after negotiations, or voluntarily placed them under the International Trusteeship System (UN Charter 1945: Ch. XII, Art. 77). Decolonization therefore is regulated by international law, whereas secession and specifically unilateral secession is not. Admittedly, in some cases the secessionists in their UDIs and elsewhere attempt to connect their demands for independence to decolonization, referring to the host state as a colonizer state. This is a secessionist tactic seeking to give legitimacy to secessionist demands seeking to maximize their chances for recognition. Table 20.1 in the annex presents our dataset of post-1945 UDIs.

## Statement of rights

Irrespective of their sub-genre, DoIs tend to put forward general statements of rights in order to legitimize their claims to independence by reference to allegedly universal and established rights. For example, the 1776 US Declaration refers to the rights of individuals to life, liberty and pursuit of happiness, claiming that only by dissolving all bonds with Great Britain, the "good people" of the 13 colonies will be able to pursue them. In the post-1945 period, these rights are explicitly stated for the same purpose in the Proclamation of Independence of Biafra in 1967 and the 2017 Proclamation of the Restoration of Independence of Ambazonia. Apart from those, other DoIs in the post-1945 period do not attempt to legitimize the declarations by reference to these or other rights of individuals.

In the post-1945 period, the reference to individual rights is replaced by a new collective right – that of self-determination – which is allegedly held by groups of individuals called "peoples" or "nations". In addition to the right held by peoples, the post-1945 declarations also refer to the "will of the people", that is, the will of that group of individuals on behalf of whom the declaration is made. The two – a collective right and a collective will – have become the principal legitimizing devices used in the post-1945 declarations of independence. Thus, the will of the people to be independent legitimizes declaring independence and establishing an independent state: this is what the people in question will, and their will overrides any other principle or consideration.

The concept of the will of the people originates in the idea of the "general will" found in the works of Jean-Jacques Rousseau, in particular in his *Social Contract* of 1762. One of its first legislative expressions is found in article 6 of the *Declaration of the Rights of Man and the Citizen* passed by the National Assembly in Paris in August 1789 (Declaration of the Rights of Man and the Citizen 1789). The concept is closely linked with the concept of popular sovereignty – the rule of the people – and thus with democracy either in its direct, plebiscitary form or its indirect, representative forms (assemblies, parliaments): plebiscites or representative assemblies are believed to express the will of the people who are voting in the plebiscite or represented in an assembly. This suggests that the concept of the will of the people does not require or presuppose any specific overt action on behalf of the people whose will is expressed. By proclaiming that "the general will is decided in favor of the Independence of Peru from Spanish domination" (Anna 1975, 221), the Peruvian declaration of 15 July 1821 was probably the first to legitimize state independence by a direct appeal to the will of the people (here "the general will"). In Europe, Prince Ferdinand of the German/Hungarian House of Saxe-Coburg and Gotha-Koháry declared in 1908 the independence of the Kingdom of Bulgaria "in order to respond to the will of the people" (Manifesto, 1908 cited in Strupp 1911, 12).

The phrases "self-determination" and "the right of self-determination" are first found in the writings of German historians in the 1860s (Fisch 2015, 118). These terms gained widespread use in the debates within social democratic and Marxist parties, in particular in the multinational empires of the Habsburgs and the Romanovs. Already in 1916 Lenin linked the right of self-determination to the creation of an independent state and claimed that all peoples, including colonial ones, have that same right. On 15 November 1917, the Soviet government, under his chairmanship, proclaimed "the right of the peoples of Russia to free self-determination, even to the point of separation and the formation of an independent state" (Declaration of the Rights of the Peoples of Russia 1917). On 4 December, the Senate of Finland declared the independence of Finland from Russia, referring to the Finnish people's "right to determine its fate" (Finland Declaration 1917); and on 18 December, Lenin, on behalf of the Soviet Russian government, recognized the Finnish independence "in accordance with the principle of national self-determination" (Lenin 1917). Soon after, on 16 February 1918, the Council of Lithuania proclaimed Lithuanian independence from Russia "on the ground of the recognized right of self-determination" (Lithuania Resolution 1918). Also on 29 October 1918, the Croatian Sabor (parliament) dissolved all state and legal ties between the Kingdom of Croatia, Slavonia and Dalmatia and the Kingdom of Hungary and the Empire of Austria on "the basis of the complete right of national self-determination" (Dokumenti 1920, 195).

Nonetheless, the *right* to self-determination found its first codification in international law only in 1960, in the UN General Assembly *Declaration on Granting Independence to Colonial Countries and Peoples*. The declaration assigns this right in its second article, referring to "all peoples," but provides no clue as to who these peoples are (UNGA 1960). Its article 5 in effect restricts the use of this right to the legitimization of the independence of the European overseas colonies (past and present), and its article 6 rules out its use to legitimize secession from UN member states since "any attempt at the partial or total disruption of the national unity and the territorial integrity of a country is incompatible with the purposes and principles of the Charter of the United Nations" (UNGA 1960, #6). In spite of these limitations found in the *Declaration*, the right of self-determination, attributed to "all peoples" in post-1960 UDIs, is conceived so as to legitimize the creation of independent states out of the territories which were not independent before, regardless of whether these were European colonies or not. As a universal human right, possessed of all peoples, this instrument of legitimization of independence itself appears to be independent of the contingencies of history, ethnicity or geography – and, in a sense, from the will of any one "people" alleged to possess the right. Even those "peoples" (if any) who do not will their independence still possess the right to self-determination.

Nevertheless, unlike the 1776 US Declaration, most post-1945 DoIs do not feature a separate statement of the rights or of the will of the people. Instead, either the preamble or the last clauses of these DoIs simply state that the declaration is made on the basis of the right of self-determination and/or the will of the people. In contrast to the 1776 US Declaration, in these DoIs it is not deemed necessary to explain the source or the nature of the right or of the will. These legitimizing devices appear to have become the standard or conventional discourse of post-1945 DoIs which require no explanation or elaboration.

By referring to the will of the people to declare independence, the DoIs appear to suggest that this is the choice that the people have made; it appears that this normative choice has been elaborated and justified in the post-1980 choice or democratic normative theories of secession. As elaborated in detail in Chapter 14 on normative theories in this volume, the right to self-determination is a subject of theoretical discussion of another type of normative theories – the national theories which argue that nations or "encompassing groups" exclusively possess this right. Another type of normative theory – remedial rights theory – provides a theoretical discussion of some (but not all) of the grievances which are listed in the DoIs and are analysed in the following section.

## Grievance declarations

Grievance declarations are the dominant type of unilateral declarations of independence, as references to grievances against the host state are to be found in the majority of them (Kartsonaki 2020). By stating grievances against the host state, a DoI is offering a reason for rejecting its rule as unjust, harmful and constraining. The need for this group to create its own state thus arises as the only possible remedy for these grievance(s). The general scheme of argumentation can be represented as follows:

> X is a harm or injustice committed by the host state against the population of this territory; this is a harm or injustice that no legitimate state should be (or is) allowed to commit; hence, the host state is not the legitimate state of the population/territory in question.
>
> *(Kartsonaki and Pavković 2021)*

The first post-1945 grievance declaration is probably that of Austria issued in April 1945 by the Communist Party, Christian Socialist Party (Austrian People's Party) and the Social Democratic Party, all of which had consistently opposed the Nazi rule (Blaustein et al. 1977, 34–35). The Austrian Declaration of Independence is preceded by a proclamation of independence which lists grievances, primarily the misdeeds of Nazi Germany. First, its incorporation into the

German Reich (Anschluss) in 1938 was being carried out by "highly treasonable terrorism of Nazi-Fascist minority" and imposed "military and warlike occupation" (Blaustein et al. 1977, 34). Further, the removal of institutions of the state aiming "to dissolve of the unified historical existence of Austria and to destroy it completely"; the degradation of the capital, Vienna, to a provincial town and the federal provinces into "impotent administrative districts"; the "economic and cultural robbery of Vienna and Austrian federal states, robbing the Austrian people of "all independent disposal of the natural resources of its prosperity" and causing "the spiritual and cultural resources of Austria to be atrophied" (Blaustein et al. 1977, 35). The final list of grievances relates to the war: the National Socialist government of Germany had driven the people of Austria "into a senseless and hopeless war of conquest which had sacrificed "nearly the whole of the youth and manhood of our people mercilessly" (Blaustain et al. 1977, 35).

Another declaration that stands out among other grievance declarations is the third declaration of independence of Bangladesh in April 1971, as it introduces the grievance of genocide. The declaration states that "in the conduct of a ruthless and savage war the Pakistani authorities committed and are still continuously committing numerous acts of genocide and unprecedented tortures, amongst others on the civilian and unarmed people of Bangladesh" (Bangladesh Declaration 1971, 1). This is the first declaration of independence in which the phrases "genocide" and "acts of genocide" are used in the list of grievances which lead to the declaration. In this case, genocide and acts of genocide were not cited as stand-alone reasons or grounds for the declaration. Rather, they were part of the measures that "the Pakistan Government" enacted which denied the elected representatives the opportunity (and the right) to meet, establish a constitution and constitute a government: "the Pakistan government by levying an unjust war and committing genocide and by other repressive measures made it impossible for the elected representatives of the people of Bangladesh to meet and frame a Constitution, and give to themselves a Government" (Bangladesh Declaration 1971, 1).

Other grievances that are listed in the Bangladesh Declaration of 1971 are the "illegal and arbitrary" postponement for "an indefinite period" of the Assembly elected for the purposes of framing the Constitution (Bangladesh Declaration 1971, 1). Declaring and waging an unjust and treacherous war is another grievance. Finally, the declaration also accused the host state of preventing the representatives of the Bengali people from performing their political and legal obligations. This can be interpreted as a denial of the right to establish state institutions and government. If so, the declaration is intended to remedy this wrong by being presented as an interim or provisional constitution which sets up the offices of the government of the new state and appoints its office holders.

Apart from the Bangladesh proclamation, declarations of independence of Biafra (1967), Aceh (1976), Western Sahara (1976), Turkish Republic of Northern Cyprus (1983) and South Ossetia (1991), as well as that of Ambazonia (2017), Catalunya (2017) and many others, also list a variety of grievances, in some cases referring to the intentional homicide of civilians by the host state agents. Grievance declarations thus seek to delegitimize the host state, listing the injustices committed against the seceding group by the host state. A (new) state, independent of the state-perpetrator of human rights abuses, is presented as the only possible remedy or prevention of these abuses.

## Commitment declarations

The commitment DoIs shift the attention from the host state to the new one. They do not highlight the violations the host state carried out against the seceding population, but they bring forward pledges the new aspiring state will fulfil when it becomes independent. By committing to a specific political system, a set of citizens' rights and a wide spectrum of cooperation with other states and membership to international organizations, they represent manifestos of liberal democracy and international cooperation.

Characteristic examples of commitment declarations are those of Slovenia and Croatia in 1991 and Kosovo in 2008. All three declarations commit to adhering to internationally recognized norms, including democracy, rule of law and respect of human rights of all their citizens. The Slovenian Declaration, for instance, proclaims that Slovenia is "a rule-of-law and social state with a market economy which is adapted to [the demands of] the environment" and commits to respect "the rights of men and civil liberties ... the European achievements of industrial democracy, above all, social-economic rights, the rights of the employed to participate in decision-making, trade union rights, the inviolability of property" (Slovenia Declaration 1991, #5). They also guarantee a variety of rights – including civil and political rights – to minorities. The Croatian Declaration specifically commits to respect "all human and civil rights" of the Serbs and other national minorities (Croatia Declaration 1991, #3), although soon after the Declaration, the Yugoslav wars broke out. The Croatian and Slovenian declarations also define their political systems as "multiparty", while the Kosovo declaration defines the new state as democratic, multi-ethnic and secular; the latter, unlike the former, also commits to implementing the international plan of state-building in Kosovo proposed by the UN special envoy Martti Ahtisaari.

These three declarations also advance a discourse of "belonging", referring to their entitlement and willingness to join regional and international organizations as well as the commitment to establish good relations with all their neighbours, including the former host state or its successors. Slovenia, for instance, expressed its aspiration "to become a member of the United Nations Organization, to join the process of OSCE, the Council of Europe, the European Community and other associations of states" and to respect the foundation documents of these and other organizations. Second, being a stand-alone (*samosvojna*) and independent state "should be understood as a condition for entering new integrations within former Yugoslav and within the European frameworks". Third, Slovenia would seek to realize these associations with other sovereign states "through agreements, in a peaceful way, through negotiations and dialogue" (Slovenia Declaration, #2). Fourth, the Republic of Slovenia wanted "to strengthen economic, cultural, political, financial and all other relations [with the international community]" and also expected other "states [to] actually recognize it in accordance with international law" (Slovenia Declaration, #2).

This discourse of belonging is accompanied by an assertion of belonging to a certain geographical sphere, i.e., all three declarations make clear that they deem to belong to the European family of states. The Croatian Declaration referred to the historical continuity of their state and pronounced that the Croat nation has been "one of the oldest state-making historical nations of Europe" (Croatia Declaration 1991, #1), firmly anchoring Croatia into the European family. In addition, Kosovo announced that it would seek membership in the EU and will implement the reforms necessary for the "Euro-Atlantic integration" (Kosovo Declaration 2008, #6). The Kosovo declaration commits to good relations with all its neighbours, including Serbia, and also commits to working towards reconciliation with the peoples of its former state. The Kosovo Declaration also invites missions ("presence") of international organizations (including NATO) in Kosovo – the missions which had been in place in Kosovo since the end of NATO intervention in Kosovo in 1999. This commitment is not to be found in any other DoI prior to the Kosovo one.

This type of DoIs resembles manifestos of liberal democracy and international cooperation. They pledge to adhere to the internationally recognized norms of democracy, rule of law and human rights, and they put forward a discourse of "belonging" to a family of states defined by these norms as well as by region, history and language. They call for international recognition of the seceded state based on their commitment to its socialization, avoiding any mention of its rupture with the host state and the controversial issue of breach of the host state's territorial integrity (Kartsonaki and Pavković 2021).

## Institutionalizing declarations

Institutionalizing declarations create a set of state institutions and symbols for the seceding state. What distinguishes them from the commitment declarations is the emphasis they put on the capacities of the secessionists to create a functional state. Contrary to the commitment type, institutionalizing declarations do not necessarily promote a discourse of belonging to an international society or adherence to international norms.

An example of a "pure" institutionalizing declaration is the Armenian one, issued by the Supreme Soviet of the Armenian Soviet Socialist Republic on 23 August 1990. It contains no grievance and no explicit commitment to specific policies; it only specifies the institutions and powers of the new state. The declaration states that this is "the beginning of the process of establishing independence" (Armenia Declaration 1990, 1).

The Armenian declaration creates state institutions in several steps. The first step relates to the symbols of the state: the name of the state is now changed into the Republic of Armenia (or, in short, Armenia), and the state is to have a flag, an anthem and a coat of arms. The second step is to determine the scope, the nature and the bearer of state power: state power has the supremacy over any other, and it wields sovereignty, independence and plenipotentiary authority. The bearer of that power is the people of Armenia, who exercise it directly and through its representative organs. Third, everyone living in Armenia is given the citizenship of the state, and Armenians not living in it have right to citizenship. The fourth step consists of the creation of the armed and security forces which are to provide for the security of the Republic and protect its borders. Fifth, the Republic is proclaimed a subject of international law, which conducts its own foreign policy establishing direct relations with other states and national-state units of the USSR as well as international organizations. Sixth, the people of Armenia take possession of all its natural wealth, "the land, the earth's crust, airspace, water, and other natural resources, as well as economic and intellectual, cultural capabilities are the property of its people" (Armenia Declaration 2). Seventh, the Declaration creates anew the entire economic and financial system of the Republic, "its own money, national bank, finance-loan system, tax and custom service" (Armenia Declaration 2). The Declaration also creates a new political system, including "the separation of legislative, executive, and judicial powers; a multi-party system; equality of political parties under the law; depolitization of law enforcement bodies and armed forces". This system guarantees "freedom of speech, press, and conscience". Finally, the Declaration creates the Republic's "own system of education and of cultural and scientific development"; and it guarantees the use of Armenian as "the state language in all spheres of [its] life" (Armenia Declaration 2). In summary, the Declaration creates the institutions and state symbols, proclaims the state's supreme power and its bearer, the people of Armenia, and then creates the institutions for coercion and state protection, of foreign policy and foreign relations, of economic and financial system, of the political system and of educational and scientific/cultural institutions.

This declaration is not the first which creates or establishes institutions of the seceding state. The Proclamation of Independence of Bangladesh of April 1971, discussed in the "Grievance declarations" section, also announced the establishment of new institutions, outlined their powers and announced the appointment of office holders. The Armenian Declaration of Independence, however, follows the template of sovereign institution-building found in a series of preceding declarations about sovereignty by union republics of the USSR, including Russia, Moldova, Ukraine, Belarus and Turkmenistan. These declarations also establish the name of the state, proclaim the possession of the three central state symbols (flag, anthem and coat of arms), proclaim the "narod" or people of the state as the bearer of sovereignty, establish citizenship, claim possession of the natural resources and protection of the borders, establish representational, coercive, armed, financial/economic and educational institutions and proclaim the majority language the official language of the state. They differ from the 1990 Armenian Declaration in one key feature: these are declarations of (or about) sovereignty and not of independence. One could perhaps argue that all of those sovereignty declarations, at least of the union republics, are in effect, but not in name, declarations of independence which studiously avoid the word "independence"; a number of them (for example, that of Belarus) also assert the right of the sovereign state to enter into associations of states and propose to engage in negotiations for a new association of states.

This suggests that, contrary to the commitment DoIs, which were addressed to the established liberal democratic states of Europe and North America, the target audience of the Armenian Declaration and the preceding declarations of sovereignty was the other federal units and the central authorities of the USSR. Through these declarations, the other federal units and the central administration were informed of the new – sovereign and supreme – powers of the federal units making these declarations and were requested to adjust their actions and policies accordingly. Overall, the institutionalizing declarations emphasize the capacity of the secessionist unit to create a functional state in sole control of its territory and population; it is on this basis that they request international recognition of independence.

## Restoring independence

Restorations of independence technically are not declarations of independence, but declarations that independent statehood is being reinstated: the state, which lost its freedom involuntarily, is now independent again, regaining its legal status or constitutional framework. The aim, however, remains the same as in the DoIs: a unit that belonged to a certain state seeks independence from it. In post-1945 world, restoring the sovereign powers of states that had only a few decades earlier lost these powers through incorporation into larger states was quite rare. One of the early restoration of independence declarations was the 1945 Declaration of Independence of Austria mentioned earlier in this chapter. However, the Baltic republics' declarations appear to be the first declarations of independence issued by an existing legislative body of a federal unit, elected through regular elections. The absence of elaborate justifications in the document of the restoration acts suggests that they were treated as regular and not extraordinary procedures of these legislative bodies, on par with a series of other preceding and subsequent legislative acts. In this sense, these declarations were normalizing secession in the form of restoration of previous sovereign powers.

The 11 March 1990 proclamation of the Supreme Council of the Lithuanian republic on the restoration of its sovereign power can be regarded as a representative case of this sub-genre: its exclusive focus is on the restoration of statehood. The Proclamation starts as follows:

> Expressing the will of the People, the Supreme Council of the Republic of Lithuania decides and solemnly proclaims that the realization of the sovereign rights of the State of Lithuania, violated by alien power in 1940, is being restored, and from now on Lithuania will again become an independent state.
>
> *(Lithuania Act 1990, 1)*

It also affirmed that

> The Act of the Lithuanian Council on Independence of February 16, 1918 and the
> Resolution of the Constituent Seimas of May 15, 1920 on the restoration of a dem-
> ocratic State of Lithuania have never lost their legal force and are the constitutional
> basis of the State of Lithuania. The territory of the State of Lithuania is integral and
> indivisible; the Constitution of any other state does not apply to it.
>
> *(Lithuania Act 1990, 1)*

The Lithuanian state also proclaims its "adherence to universally recognized principles of international laws . . . and guarantees the rights of individuals, citizens, and ethnic communities."
By this act of restoration, the Supreme Council "begins to achieve its full sovereignty" (Furtado
and Chandler 1992, 182). The restoration, thus, consists primarily in the denial of the loss of
the legal force of the previous legal acts.

This proclamation is followed by the resolution of the Supreme Soviet of the Estonian Socialist Soviet Republic on the State Status of Estonia of 30 March 1991. The resolution states that
the occupation of Estonia by the Soviet Union on 17 June 1940 has not terminated the existence
of the Republic of Estonia. In view of the "manifestly expressed will of the Estonian people to
restore the independence and the legitimate state power," the Supreme Soviet of Estonia proclaims the occupation by the Soviet Union illegal and "proclaims the restoration of the Republic
of Estonia" (Estonia Declaration 1991, 1). The third declaration of Latvia is much longer and
detailed than the first two and lists several grievances, primarily illegal acts and acts of armed
aggression committed against the Republic of Latvia. Then it restores articles 1, 2, 3 and 6 of
the 1922 constitution of that state (Latvia Restoration of Independence 1990).

Furthermore, the Supreme Council of Georgia, based on the will of the people expressed
in the referendum of 31 March 1991, "resolve[d] and publicly declare[d]" the restoration of the
state independence based on the Declaration of Independence of 26 May 1918 (Georgia Restoration 1991). The Act of Restoration of State Independence of Georgia provides a detailed
narrative of historical grievance first against Tsarist Russia and then against the Soviet Union
("Soviet Russia" in the text) which in 1921 occupied Georgia by armed aggression. Since Georgia did not capitulate and did not voluntarily join the Soviet Union, the Act claims that its original Declaration of Independence and constitution are "in legal force" today (at the time when
the declaration was issued). Following this, the Act proceeds to establishing the competence and
scope of the state of Georgia; it proclaims the supremacy of the Constitution of Georgia over its
territory as well as the inviolability and indivisibility of the territory of Georgia. The restoration
act thus contains an institutionalizing or state-building aspect as well as a list of grievances.

The Azerbaijan declaration on the restoration of independence was passed on 30 August
1991 (following the failed coup of 20 August in Moscow against USSR President Gorbachev)
by the Supreme Soviet of the Soviet Socialist Republic of Azerbaijan. Similar to the other restoration declarations, this declaration in its first sentence proclaims that it is expressing the will of
the people of Azerbaijan, and in its last sentence it declares the restoration of state independence
of their state. In one sentence only it notes the existence of the independent Republic of Azerbaijan which was recognized "by the international community" from 1918 to 1920 (Azerbaijan
Declaration 1991). There is, however, no further mention of this state or its legal framework
in the declaration. In contrast to the Baltic states and the Georgian Act of Restoration, the
Azerbaijan Declaration does not specify which legal acts of the previous state are restored or are
proclaimed to be in force. In addition, the declaration's commitment to friendly relations with
all republics of the USSR is unprecedented at least among the restoration declarations and so

is the declaration's purported role in bringing together "all patriotic forces" (Azerbaijan Declaration 1991). The principal focus of the declaration appears to be the defence or protection of the restored state: it proclaims the inviolability and indivisibility of its borders and is committed to removing any threat to the security of the state. Like Georgia, Azerbaijan at the time of the declaration faced a secessionist challenge, in this case from the Armenian enclave of Nagorno Karabakh, and a consequent secessionist war.

Restoration declarations announce a change in the state of affairs re-establishing the statehood of a unit that was independent but had involuntarily lost its freedom. With the declaration, this unit regains its legal or constitutional framework. In that sense, these are normalizing declarations, not focusing on any rupture with the host state but proclaiming the return to normality and the restoration of an already existing state.

## Conclusion

DoIs have various purposes: the most obvious one is the declaration that a unit is now a free and independent state, and as such it seeks recognition from the international society of other sovereign states. DoIs may also have other equally important purposes: to make the secessionist cause known as widely as possible both within the region and outside and to attract international attention and support even if the official recognition is not immediately forthcoming. Overall, DoIs seek to legitimize secession both internally and internationally. This chapter has argued that there are different sub-genres of DoIs that pursue the same goal of international recognition or attention through different pathways.

We identified four sub-genres of DoIs. First, grievance declarations focus on the abuses the seceding population (has) suffered and condemn the host state as the perpetrator of these abuses. Second, commitment declarations put forward the common principles the seceding unit shares with existing states and explain why they belong to the group of independent states. Third, institutionalizing declarations demonstrate the capacity of the secessionists to create a functional state in control of its territory and population. Fourth, restoration declarations re-establish lost statehood.

These types of declarations are not mutually exclusive. Elements of grievance, for example, are to be found in other types of declarations as well. In fact, all four sub-genres are found in the 2017 Ambazonian Declaration, entitled "Proclamation Restoring the Independence of the Former British Trust Territory of the Southern Cameroon and Asserting its Sovereign Statehood". One of the lengthiest existent DoIs, the Declaration: copies the 1776 US Declaration statement of rights; lists, at great length, grievances against the former colonizers and the host state, the Republic of Cameron (including its alleged "genocidal project"); proclaims the restoration of independence (under the new name of Ambazonia); creates a series of institutional offices and names their office holders; sets down at length the borders of the state; commits to a parliamentary system, protection of human rights and to joining a variety of international and regional organizations; and, imitating the 2008 Kosovo Declaration, invites "the presence" of international organizations, including international military forces.

Nonetheless, we hope that our classification of DoIs offers a more nuanced understanding of how secessionists forge the image of their new state and how they project it to both internal and international audiences. Most importantly, the exclusive reliance on the grievance model, set by the 1776 US Declaration, appears to be abandoned in the post–Cold War era. The secessionists lost interest in denouncing the host state for its abuses and started to present their state as a functional, co-operative and socialized state committed to international principles of co-operation and friendly relations among states. Restoration declarations follow this pattern too, by reinstating an existing state rather than denouncing the host state. We observe therefore a shift in the focus of the declarations, from the host state to the seceding unit. DoIs are now championing independence not (only) because the seceding group was wronged, but also because it deserves its new state.

# References

Anna, T. E. 1975, 'The Peruvian Declaration of Independence: Freedom by Coercion', *Journal of Latin American Studies*, 7: 221–248.

Armenia, Declaration. 1990, *Declaration of the Independence of Armenia*, Supreme Council of the Armenian Soviet Socialist Republic: Yerevan.

Armitage, D. 2007, *The Declaration of Independence*, Harvard University Press: Cambridge, MA.

Azerbaijan, Declaration. 1991, *Declaration of the Supreme Soviet of the Republic of Azerbaijan about a Restoration of Independence of the Republic of Azerbaijan*, Supreme Council of Azerbaijan: Baku.

Bangladesh, Declaration. 1971, *The Proclamation of Independence of Bangladesh*, Constituent Assembly of Bangladesh: Mujibnagar.

Bauböck, R. 2019, 'A Multilevel Theory of Democratic Secession', *Ethnopolitics*, 18: 227–246.

Biafra, Declaration. 1967, 'Declaration of Independence of Biafra', C. O Ojukwu (ed.) 1969, *Biafra Selected Speeches and Random Thoughts of Chukwuemeka Odumegwu Ojukwu*, Harper & Row: New York: 191–196.

Blaustein, A. P., Sigler, J., Beede, B. R. 1977, *Independence Documents of the World*, Ocean Publications: New York.

Bouris, D. & Fernández-Molina, I. 2018, 'Contested States, Hybrid Diplomatic Practices, and the Everyday Quest for Recognition', *International Political Sociology*, 12: 306–324.

Cassese, A. 1995, *Self-Determination of Peoples, a Legal Reappraisal*, Cambridge University Press: Cambridge.

Catalunya, Declaració. 2017, *Declaració dels Representants de Catalunya* (The Declaration of the Representatives of Catalunya), Catalan Parliament: Barcelona.

Coggins, B. 2014, *Power Politics and State Formation in the Twentieth Century: The Dynamics of Recognition*, Cambridge University Press: New York.

Croatia, Declaration. 1991, *Declaration on the Proclamation of the Sovereign and Stand-Alone Republic of Croatia* (Deklaracija O Proglašenju Suverene I Samostalne Republike Hrvatske), Sabor Republike Hrvatske & Narodne Novine: Zagreb: 31.

Declaration of the Rights of Man and the Citizen. 1789, 'Déclaration des Droits de l'Homme et du Citoyen', 30 September AE/II/1129, Paris: National Assembly.

Declaration Rights of the People of Russia. 1917, 'Declaration of the Rights of the People of Russia', www.marxists.org/history/ussr/government/1917/11/02.htm, accessed 20 November 2021.

Derrida, J. 1986, 'Declarations of Independence', *New Political Science*, 7: 7–15.

Dokumenti. 1920, *Dokumenti o postanku Kraljevine Srba Hrvata i Slovenaca 1914–1919*, (Documents concerning the origin of the Kingdom of Serbs, Croats and Slovenes 1914–1919) compiled by F. Šišić, Matica Hrvatska: Zagreb.

Estonia, Declaration. 1991, *Estonian Supreme Council Decision on the Estonian National Independence*, Supreme Council of the Republic of Estonia: Tallinn.

Finland, Declaration. 1917, *To the People of Finland*, The Senate of Finland: Helsinki.

Fisch, Jörg, 2015. *The Right of Self-Determination of Peoples: The Domestication of an Illusion*, Cambridge University Press: Cambridge.

Florea, A. 2014, 'De Facto States in International Politics (1945–2011): A New Data Set', *International Interactions*, 40: 788–811.

Florea, A. 2017, 'De Facto States: Survival and Disappearance (1945–2011)', *International Studies Quarterly*, 61: 337–351.

Furtado Ch., F. & Chandler, A. 1992, *Perestroika in the Soviet Republics: Documents on the National Question*, Westview Press: Boulder.

Georgia Restoration. 1991, *Act of Restoration of the State Independence of Georgia*, The Supreme Soviet of the Republic of Georgia: Tbilisi.

Griffiths, R. D. 2015, 'Between Dissolution and Blood: How Administrative Lines and Categories Shape Secessionist Outcomes', *International Organization*, 69: 731–751.

Griffiths, R. D. 2017, 'Admission to the Sovereignty Club: The Past, Present, and Future of the International Recognition Regime', *Territory, Politics, Governance*, 5: 177–189.

Griffiths, R. D. 2021, *Secession and the Sovereignty Game*, Cornell University Press: Ithaca.

Griffiths, R. D. & Muro, D. (eds.) 2020, *Strategies of Secession and Counter-Secession*, Rowman and Littlefield International: London.

Hierro, M. J. & Queralt, D. 2020, 'The Divide over Independence: Explaining Preferences for Secession in an Advanced Open Economy', *American Journal of Political Science*, Online first, https://doi.org/10.1111/ajps.12549.

Hilpold, P. 2009, 'The Kosovo Case and International Law: Looking for Applicable Theories', *Chinese Journal of International Law*, 8: 47–61.

Kartsonaki, A. 2020, 'Remedial Secession: Theory, Law and Reality', in R. Griffiths & D. Muro (eds.), *Strategies of Secession and Counter-Secession*, Rowman and Littlefield International: London.

Kartsonaki, A. & Pavković, A. 2021, 'Declarations of Independence after the Cold War: Abandoning Grievance and Avoiding Rupture', *Nations and Nationalism*, 27: 1268–1285.

Ker-Lindsay, J. 2012, *The Foreign Policy of Counter Secession: Preventing the Recognition of Contested States*, Oxford University Press: Oxford.

Ker-Lindsay, J. 2018, 'The Stigmatisation of De Facto States: Disapproval and "Engagement without Recognition"', *Ethnopolitics*, 17: 362–372.

Ker-Lindsay, J. & Armakolas, I. 2020, 'Kosovo, EU Member States and the Recognition-Engagement Nexus', in I. Armakolas & J. Ker-Lindsay (eds.), *The Politics of Recognition and Engagement: New Perspectives on South-East Europ*, Palgrave Macmillan: Cham.

Knotter, L. 2020, 'Why Declare Independence? Observing, Believing, and Performing the Ritual', *Review of International Studies*, 47(2): 252–271.

Kosovo Declaration. 2008, *The Declaration of Independence of Kosovo/Deklarata E Pavarësisë Së Kosovës*, Assembly of Kosovo: Prishtina.

Latvia, Restoration of Independence. 1990, *Declaration of the Supreme Council of the Latvian SSR of the Restoration of Independence of the Republic of Latvia*, Supreme Council of the Latvian SSR: Riga.

Lenin, U. V. 1917, *The Soviet of People's Commissars. No. 101*, Chairman of the Soviet of People's Commissars: Petrograd.

Lithuania, Act. 1990, *Act on the Re-Establishment of the State of Lithuania/Aktas dėl Lietuvos nepriklausomos valstybės atstatymo*, The Supreme Council of the Republic of Lithuania: Vilnius.

Lithuania, Resolution. 1918, *Resolution*, The Council of Lithuania: Vilnius.

Muharremi, R. 2008, 'Kosovo's Declaration of Independence: Self-Determination and Sovereignty Revisited', *Review of Central and East European Law*, 33: 401–435.

Nardin, T. 2015, 'The Diffusion of Sovereignty', *Journal of European Thought*, 41: 89–102.

Pavković, A. 2020, 'Self-Determination or the Will of the People: Declaration of Independence and the Paradox of "Alien-Determined Self-Determination"', in M. Qvortrup (ed.), *Nationalism, Referendums and Democracy: Voting on Ethnic Issues and Independence*, 2nd edition, Routledge: Abingdon, Oxon; New York: 120–140.

Rodon, T. & Guinjoan, M. 2018, 'When the Context Matters: Identity, Secession and the Spatial Dimension in Catalonia', *Political Geography*, 63: 75–87.

Roeder, P. G. 2007, *Where Nation-States Come From*, Princeton University Press: Princeton.

Sanjaume-Calvet, M. 2020, 'Moralism in Theories of Secession: A Realist Perspective', *Nations and Nationalism*, 26: 323–343.

Sevastik, P. 2008, 'Secession, Self-Determination of "Peoples" and Recognition – the Case of Kosovo's Declaration of Independence and International Law', in O. Engdahl & P. Wrange (eds), *Law at War: The Law as It Was and the Law as It Should Be*, Martinus Nijhoff: The Netherlands.

Slovenia, Declaration. 1991, 'Declaration on Independence/Deklaracija ob neodvisnosti, Ljubljana: Government of the Republic of Slovenia/', Ljubljana: Uradni List Republike Slovenije, 25 June 1991: 1.

Strupp, K. 1911, 'Unabhängigkeitserklärung Bulgariens: Proklamation des Fürsten Ferdinand vom 22 September/5 Oktober 1908', Urkunden zur Geschichte des Völkerrechts II, Gotha: Friedrich Andreas Perthes.

UN Charter. 1945, 'Charter of the United Nations [Online]', www.un.org/en/documents/charter/index.shtml

UNGA. 1960, 'General Assembly Resolution 1514 (XV)'. Declaration on the Granting of Independence to Colonial Countries and Peoples. United Nations General Assembly [Online], www.sfu.ca/~palys/UN-Resolution%201514.pdf

UNSC. 1975, 'Resolution 384', United Nations Security Council [Online], www.un.org/en/ga/search/view_doc.asp?symbol=S/RES/384(1975)

Vidmar, J. 2012, 'Conceptualizing Declarations of Independence in International Law', *Oxford Journal of Legal Studies*, 32: 153–177.

Western Sahara, Proclamation. 1976, *Letter of Proclamation of the Independence of the Sahrawi Democratic Arab Republic* (Western Sahara Declaration of Independence), The Provisional National Saharawi Council: Bir Lehlu.

# ANNEX

Table 20.1 Dataset's declarations of independence (post 1945)

| Secessionist Unit | Host State | Year of DoI | Issuing Body | Place of DoI |
|---|---|---|---|---|
| Austria | Germany | 1945 | Socialist Democratic, Christian Socialist Party and Communist Party of Austria | Vienna |
| Katanga | Congo | 1960 | College of Ministers of Katanga | Elisabethville |
| Biafra | Nigeria | 1967 | The governor of East Region (Biafra) Lt.Col. Ojukwu | Enugu |
| Bangladesh | Pakistan | 1971 | Constituent Assembly of Bangladesh | Mujibnagar |
| West Papua (Irian Jaya) | Indonesia | 1971 | Seth Jafet Rumkorem (Brigadier-General) | Victoria |
| Aceh | Indonesia | 1976 | Tengku Hasan M. di Tiro Chairman, National Liberation Front of Acheh | Sumatra |
| Western Sahara | Morocco | 1976 | The Provisional National Saharawi Council representing the will of the people of the Sahrawi Democratic Arab Republic | Bir Lehlu |
| Turkish Republic of North Cyprus | Republic of Cyprus | 1983 | Turkish Cypriot Parliament | Nicosia |
| Armenia | USSR | 1990 | The Supreme Council | Yerevan |
| Bougainville | Papua New Guinea | 1990 | Francis Ona, Interim President of the Republic of Bougainville | Arawa |
| Latvia | USSR | 1990 | Supreme Council of the Latvian SSR | Riga |
| Lithuania | USSR | 1990 | The Supreme Council of the Republic of Lithuania | Vilnius |

| Secessionist Unit | Host State | Year of DoI | Issuing Body | Place of DoI |
|---|---|---|---|---|
| Rehoboth Basters | Namibia | 1990 | Kaptein's Council and the Assembly | Rehoboth |
| Croatia | SFR Yugoslavia | 1991 | Sabor Republike Hrvatske | Zagreb |
| Slovenia | SFR Yugoslavia | 1991 | Government of the Republic of Slovenia | Ljubljana |
| SR Macedonia | SFR Yugoslavia | 1991 | President of the Republic of Macedonia | Skopje |
| Kosovo | SFR Yugoslavia | 1991 | Central Board of the Parliament of the Republic of Kosovo | Kacanik |
| Serbian Krajina | Croatia | 1991 | Great National Assembly of the Serbian District of Slavonia, Eastern Slavonia, Baranja and Western Srem | Knin |
| Nagorno Karabakh | Azerbaijan | 1991 | Joint session of the Nagorno Karabakh Oblast and Shahoumian regional councils | Stepanakert |
| South Ossetia | Georgia | 1991 | Supreme Council of the Republic of South Ossetia | Tskhinvali |
| Transnistria | Moldova | 1991 | Supreme Council of the Pridnestrovskaia Moldavskaia Respublika | Tiraspol |
| Azerbaijan | USSR | 1991 | The Supreme Council | Baku |
| Chechnya | USSR (Russia) | 1991 | The President and the Parliament of Chechnya | Gorki |
| Georgia | USSR | 1991 | The Supreme Council | Tbilisi |
| Kazakhstan | USSR | 1991 | The Supreme Council | Almaty |
| Uzbekistan | USSR | 1991 | President of the Republic | Tashkent |
| Moldova | USSR | 1991 | Parliament of Moldova | Kishinev |
| Estonia | USSR | 1991 | Supreme Council of the Republic of Estonia | Tallinn |
| Belarus | USSR | 1991 | Supreme Council of Belarus | Minsk |
| Kyrgyzstan (Kyrgyz Republic) | USSR | 1991 | The Supreme Council | Bishkek |
| Tajikistan | USSR | 1991 | The Supreme Council | Dushanbe |
| Turkmenistan | USSR | 1991 | The Supreme Council | Ashgabat |
| Ukraine | USSR | 1991 | The Supreme Rada | Kiev |
| Bosnia and Herzegovina | SFR Yugoslavia | 1992 | Alija Izetbegović, Chairman of the Presidency of Bosnia and Herzegovina | Sarajevo |
| Republika Srpska | Bosnia and Herzegovina | 1992 | Assembly of the Serbian people in Bosnia and Herzegovina | Banja Luka |
| Caprivi Strip | Namibia | 1997 | Third National Convention of the United Democratic Party of the Caprivi Strip Held at Katima Mulilo | Katima Mulilo |

*(Continued)*

*Table 20.1* (Continued)

| Secessionist Unit | Host State | Year of DoI | Issuing Body | Place of DoI |
|---|---|---|---|---|
| Abkhazia | Georgia | 1999 | President of the Republic of Abkhazia; Speaker of the People's Assembly of the Republic of Abkhazia; Deputies of the People's Assembly of the Republic of Abkhazia | Sukhumi |
| Kosovo | Serbia | 2008 | Assembly of Kosovo (or elected representatives of Kosovo) | Prishtina |
| Azawad | Mali | 2012 | National Movement for the Liberation of Azawad | Gao |
| Donetsk | Ukraine | 2014 | People's Council of Donetsk Region | Donetsk |
| Lugansk | Ukraine | 2014 | Chairman of the People's Council of the Lugansk People's Republic | Lugansk |
| Ambazonia (British Southern Cameroons) | Cameroun | 2017 | The Governing Council of the Southern Cameroons/ Ambazonia Consortium United Front | Buea |
| Catalonia | Spain | 2017 | Catalan Parliament | Barcelona |

# 21

# VIOLENT AND NONVIOLENT TACTICS OF SECESSION

*Kathleen Gallagher Cunningham and Caitlin McCulloch*

Struggles over the issue of national self-determination are the lead causes of civil war in the international system. Major conflicts such as the secession wars of South Sudan and Eritrea captured global interest. However, the majority of struggles for greater local power do not develop into civil wars. This chapter explores tactical variation in self-determination movements, examining changes in tactical choice over time, as well as delineating incentives that drive self-determination movements to use different tactics. We advance three major sources of input for tactical decision-making – dynamics factors within movements, factors related to the host or parent state that the movement is challenging, and factors related to the international community.

We illustrate these dynamics in the case of the Irish self-determination movement in Northern Ireland, highlighting change over time in tactic use, and the catalysts for driving these tactic changes. We finish with an exploration of currently open questions in the field, again using the Irish self-determination movement to highlight the importance of these possible future avenues of research.

## What are movements for self-determination?

Movements for self-determination are ethnonational groups that make claims for greater autonomy based on this identity. More than 150 such movements exist today.[1] Self-determination movements make a wide range of claims. At the extreme, such groups are "secessionist", i.e., they are seeking an internationally recognized independent state. There is an ongoing secessionist movement in Scotland that seeks independence from the United Kingdom. Some of these groups make limited claims, like the Berber in Algeria who seek autonomy, while others, like the Catalan movement in Spain, have increased their demands over time to full secession.

Many such movements make a diversity of demands, with diverse organizations representing different ideas about the ideal type and scope of self-government. Our focus in this chapter is on movements that share a basis for their claims in ethnic or nationalist distinctiveness. This means that secession or autonomy movements that do not have this basis are not included.

These movements are present around the globe, with the highest concentration in Asia (which has the largest population), and fewer movements in Africa and Latin America. These movements exist in both economically developed and underdeveloped states, and in both

DOI: 10.4324/9781003036593-25

democratic and non-democratic states. Over time, we have observed more movements for self-determination, with a sharp spike in the 1990s when several large polities disintegrated, resulting in new states with ethnonationalist minority groups.

## What tactics are available?

This chapter considers a wide range of tactics that self-determination movements use. Broadly speaking, these can be divided into three categories: conventional politics, nonviolent action, and violent action.

## *Conventional politics*

Many self-determination movements engage in what we consider *conventional politics*. That is, these movements form political parties, contest elections, and hold offices of power. Many federal systems have purposively integrated self-determination movements in this way. For example, India's federal system includes a variety of types of sub-national units (states, territories) that devolve some power and facilitate local mobilization around group identity. Even in non-federal states, such as the United Kingdom, we see regional parliaments (for Northern Ireland, Scotland, and Wales) that facilitate regional parties.

Participation through electoral politics is a clear example of conventional politics being employed by self-determination movements. Yet not all countries have meaningful elections or stable political party systems. Self-determination movements can also represent their interests using alternative conventional means such as participating in governance through appointment at the local or national level. For examples, the Berbers in Algeria were integrated in the government in the mid-to-late 1990s, including being given a governmental body to promote the Berber language and having their culture enshrined in the Algerian constitution (Benrabah 2007).

Additionally, self-determination movements may use legal means to press their governments for increasing autonomy. For instance, indigenous groups in Canada have successfully pushed for increased indigenous sovereignty in British Columbia after a decades-long legal battle, including increased sovereign land rights (Fisher 2021).

## *Tactics of violence*

Violent tactics also take a number of forms. First, we see a great deal of variation in the targets of violence. Historically, organizations in self-determination movements have engaged in *violent attacks* against security forces, property, civilians, or other organizations in the same movement. For example, organizations in the Corsican movements in France frequently attacked property in resort areas on the island, only occasionally targeting people. In contrast, organizations in the Naga movement in India frequently target competing Naga organizations with violent attacks.

When violence is directed at security forces or civilians, these attacks can be fatal or non-fatal. Examples of non-fatal attacks on security forces can look like the clash of the Movement for the Actualization of the Sovereign State of Biafra (MASSOB) with the Nigerian police in 2011 when protests turned violent (Nkwopara 2011). Non-fatal attacks on civilians cover instances like the MASSOB's acid attacks on civilians in 2006 (Enugu 2006), where MASSOB attacked census staff with acid and machetes. Additionally, MASSOB has perpetrated fatal attacks on the security forces both in direct clashes with the police (Reuters 2006) and when protests have grown more violent. This serves as an example of mixed tactic use over time, with MASSOB using violence against multiple different actors but also engaging in nonviolent protest.

Movements for greater self-determination have also engaged in *terrorism*. We define *terrorist* as "those who employ a systematic campaign of indiscriminate violence against public civilian targets to influence a wider audience" (Fortna 2015: 522). The Revolutionary Armed Forces of Colombia (FARC) used gas and incendiary bombings in the early 2000s, including their launching of mortars at the presidential inauguration ceremony of 2002 and their bombing of the Club El Nogal in 2003, which killed a combined 46 and injured more than 200 (Fox 2012).

Finally, another common violent tactic is participation in *civil war*, where the movement organizes an armed opposition to the state. Unlike low-level violence or terrorism, civil war also requires that the state respond with force. Scholars agree that a civil war must be between a recognized state (such as Angola) and an organized opposition (such as UNITA in Angola) that leads to a certain number of battle-related deaths.[2] Often these conflicts can be complex, with more than one organized opposition actor.[3]

## Tactics of nonviolence

This chapter examines three types of tactics that are all considered nonviolent or "not-violent": nonviolent direct action (including but not limited to mass nonviolent mobilization), international diplomacy, and local governance behavior by self-determination movements.

*Nonviolent direct action* includes a number of tactics employed at the individual and group levels. Each of these tactics is designed to undermine the authority of the state, cause disruption, and call attention to movement goals. Gene Sharp, in his 1973 study of nonviolence, identified nearly 200 discrete tactics. These can be meaningfully grouped into a few categories of tactics such as economic noncooperation, political noncooperation, protests, nonviolent intervention, and social noncooperation.

Mass use of these tactics is not common among self-determination movements. More commonly, such movements use a variety of these tactics over time and often use multiple types of nonviolent action. There are several illustrations of nonviolence in self-determination movements. For instance, the movement for secession in East Timor regularly used mass nonviolence, including nonviolent protest. Other groups, such as the Nagas in India, rely on the use of bandhs, or general strikes, to support their movement.

Self-determination movements also engage *in formal and informal diplomacy* with the international community. Huang (2016: 90) defines this as "a rebel group's conduct of foreign affairs during civil war for the purpose of advancing its military and political objectives". For example, the East Timor Action Network engaged in lobbying of the US government in their quest for independence from Indonesia (Weldemichael 2013).

*Local non-state actor governance* (typically used by rebel groups) is also used by self-determination movements to both undermine state authority and to shore up local support. Such "rebel governance" has several forms. Rebels seeking self-determination have used local electoral politics, created political institutions, developed judicial systems, and provided access to healthcare and education. For example, the Tigray People's Liberation Front in Ethiopia ran a system of local courts (called the *firdi baito*) (Loyle 2020). The National Resistance Movement in Uganda created a village committee system that involved both civilian participation and democratic process (Kasfir 2005).

## Trends in tactics

The subsequent set of figures shows trends in the tactics over time. Figure 21.1 shows the number of organizations in self-determination movements actively engaging in conventional politics. This data, from the Strategies of Resistance Data Project (SRDP, Cunningham et al. 2020), includes when an organization registers as a political party, participates in an election, or participates in an electoral campaign. Both national and local elections are included. Organizations in self-determination movements frequently use conventional politics, though we see a peak in the mid-2000s and a decline since then.

Figure 21.2 shows trends in violent activity both against the state (panel 1) and against civilians (panel 2) over time by organizations in self-determination movements (data from SRDP). Organizations such as the Free Aceh Movement (GAM) in Indonesia and the National Democratic Front of Bodoland (NDFB) in India were employing violence against the state in the early 2000s. The Tamil Tigers (LTTE) in Sri Lanka used violence against civilians. Yet, we see a marked decline in the use of violence against states and civilians over time by organizations in self-determination movements. Both conventional and violent political activity appear to drop off to some extent after the mid-2000s. This may be related to the greater use of nonviolent tactics during that time (see Figure 21.5), but could also be the product of declining salience of these identities over time.

Yet, Figure 21.3 paints a different picture. This figure includes only rebel groups in civil wars over secession (Fortna 2015), and only up to 2003. We see a steady increase over time in the number of rebels that use terrorism in pursuit of their political goals. Among the terrorism users in the early 2000s are groups such as the Kurdish Worker Party (PKK) in Turkey and the Abu Sayyaf group in the Philippines.

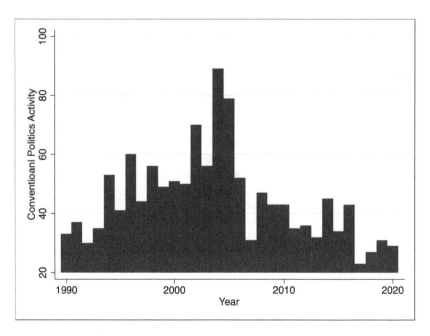

*Figure 21.1*  Conventional political activity at the organization level

*Source*: Cunningham, Dahl, and Frugé (2020).

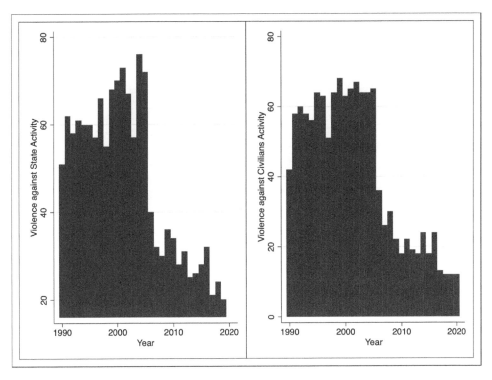

*Figure 21.2*   Violent activity at the organizational level

*Source*: Cunningham, Dahl, and Frugé (2020).

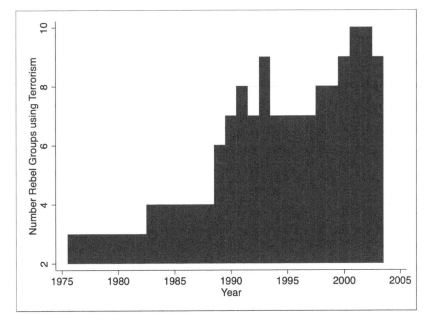

*Figure 21.3*   Terrorist activity in secessionist rebel groups

*Source*: Fortna (2015).

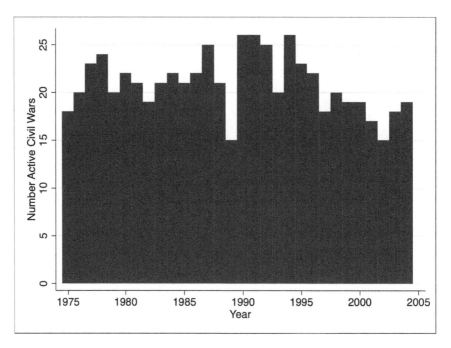

*Figure 21.4*   Civil war activity over self-determination

*Source*: Pettersson et al. (2021).

This increase in the use of terrorism is not a function of more secessionist wars. Figure 21.4 shows the number of ongoing civil wars over self-determination over time (data from Uppsala Conflict Data Program, Pettersson et al. 2021).

The trends in violent activity show a decline in organizational use of violence for all self-determination movements, but a relatively steady number of civil wars over the time period displayed and an increasing use of terrorism in these wars.

Figure 21.5 shows trends in the overall use of nonviolence by self-determination organizations over time (from SRDP). This includes economic noncooperation, political noncooperation, nonviolent intervention, protests, and social noncooperation.[4] We see a similar peak to the conventional political activity, with high levels in the mid-2000s, but a less steep drop over time after that. One comparison to note is that between this figure and Figures 21.1 and 21.2, there is a much higher rate of organizations using nonviolent tactics as opposed to violence or conventional politics.

Figure 21.6 shows trends in the use of both diplomacy (panel 1) and governance, specifically health and education (panel 2), provided by separatist rebel groups. This data is from the Rebel Governance Dataset (Huang 2016) and runs through 2006. The data includes information on which rebels ever use these tactics; thus, the graph represents the number of diplomacy-using or governance-using rebel groups in each year. The number of rebels that engaged in diplomacy and provided governance rose steadily to a peak in the 1990s and has declined since then. These include rebels such as the Bougainville Revolutionary Army (BRA) of Bougainville in Papua New Guinea, using diplomacy, and Polisario of the Western Sahara in Morocco, providing education to civilians.

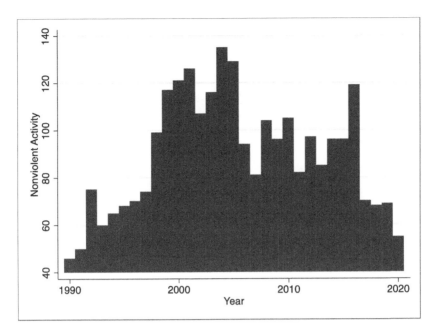

*Figure 21.5* Nonviolent activity at the organizational level

*Source*: Cunningham, Dahl, and Frugé (2020).

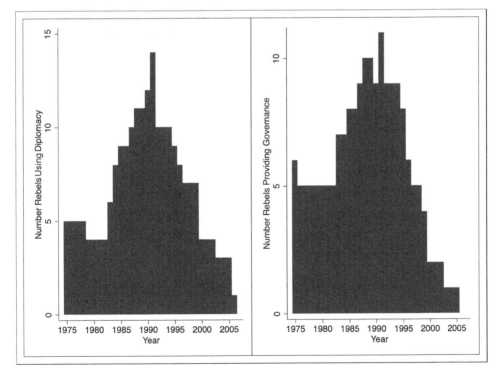

*Figure 21.6* Rebel diplomatic and governance activity

*Source*: Huang (2016).

## Incentives to use different tactics

Decisions about tactical choice are complex, often including internal debate within a movement, and these decisions are sensitive to changing conditions on the ground. Here, we consider three sources of input into these decision-making processes. These are factors that occur within the movement, factors related to the state that the self-determination movement is challenging, and factors related to the international community.

## *Internal (within the movement)*

There are several ways that the inner dynamics of self-determination movements might impact their tactical choices. First, specific organizations may alter their tactics when there are multiple organizations competing for supporters, local or international attention, or preferential treatment from the host state. One permutation of this that we have seen among studies of "terrorist" groups is out-bidding, where organizations use increasingly violent tactics to attract supporters (Crenshaw 1981; Findley and Young 2012). Intense rivalry among armed groups has also been associated with greater targeting of civilians (Metelits 2009; Cunningham et al. 2012). Yet, organizations may also try to differentiate themselves by exercising restraint and working to be seen as a nonviolent alternative within a self-determination movement that has multiple violent organizations.

Direct competition is not the only way that internal dynamics can affect tactical choices. As organizations evaluate which tactics are mostly likely to be effective (and which ones they can reasonably pull off), they will consider the shared pool of possible supporters within the population of the self-determination group. Cunningham et al. (2017) show that some tactics can be viewed as complementary with others. For example, if an organization in a self-determination movement is engaging in frequent protests, other organizations in that same movement are more likely to use tactics such as blockades. We have also seen that terrorist tactics can diffuse from one rebel group to another (Schutte and Weidmann 2011) and among ethnic groups (Polo 2020). The use of nonviolent tactics also spreads spatially (Gallo-Cruz 2012; Gleditsch and Rivera 2017). Thus, we see complex interdependences amongst self-determination movements with multiple organizations.

Change in leadership of a movement using violence has been seen as a critical opportunity for a change in tactics, whether de-escalation (Dudouet 2013) or the outright settlement of a war (Zartman 1989). Leaders who come to power in a rebel group via election are more likely to come to the negotiating table in civil conflict (Cunningham and Sawyer 2019), and this leadership type may impact the menu of tactics available to a rebel group. Additionally, rebel group leaders may have their own personal preferences for tactics their group uses. Historically, we have seen that some social movement leaders are deeply committed ideologically to nonviolent resistance. Even beyond beliefs, the experiences of leaders in self-determination groups may affect their receptivity to different tactics. For example, work on leaders of country states shows that those with military service but no combat experience are more likely to favor going to war (Horowitz et al. 2015).

## *Vis-à-vis the state*

Three factors related to the self-determination movements' host state can affect the movement's preferences over tactics: (1) opportunities to pursue change through state institutions (i.e., institutional access), (2) repressive actions/policies perpetrated by the state, and (3) past accommodations of the movement by the state.

## State institutions

State institutions vary widely, and self-determination movements pursue autonomy in a variety of regime types (democratic, mixed, and autocratic regimes), and in states with varying degrees of political and economic development and stability. A number of movements operate in economically developed democracies, such as the Scottish in the United Kingdom, the Catalan movement in Spain, or the Nagas in India. Yet many other states that face challenges over self-determination are authoritarian or have more closed political systems, such as Myanmar and China.

The structure of state political institutions shapes the means through which self-determination groups are likely to access power. For example, some governments reserve special seats in the legislature for minority populations. Colombia, for instance, reserved seats for indigenous populations. Other states offer paths to greater autonomy through changes to the federal system, as we see in Belgium. Critically, the structure of political competition can create incentives for self-determination groups to use conventional political behavior – such as running candidates or forming political parties. Operating in a democratic state does not preclude the use of violence, as we saw with the Québec movements in Canada in the 1970s.[5] These institutional opportunities are also likely to intersect with the size of the group population (Posner 2004). Many self-determination groups are relatively small, such that a direct proportional representation of their interests would leave them out of power.

## Repression

Repression of self-determination movements also affects their tactical choice. There is a large literature on the effects of repression on political mobilization more broadly (see Chenoweth et al. 2017 for a good summary), and there are a number of ways that repression can incentivize or disincentivize tactics. Moore (1998) advanced a "substitution hypothesis", arguing that repression of one tactic will cause a movement to substitute another. The overall effects of repression appear to be highly conditional. For example, the intensity of repression used is conditioned by the regime type of the state (Davenport and Armstrong 2004), and this in turn can affect responses to repression.

The effects of repression are also contingent upon the nature of the movement the state focuses on. Better-organized nonviolent movements appear more resilient in the face of repression compared to less organized movements, and thus we might expect these more resilient movements to stay the course, while others turn to violence or demobilize (Sutton et al. 2014). Repression of nonviolent resistance can also promote greater resistance when repression "backfires" (Francisco 1995; Martin 2007). Backfire occurs when the repression of protests generates international outcry and leads to greater support of the movement.

## Past accommodation

In addition to repression, states engage in a number of accommodative actions and policies for self-determination movements. For example, Norway created a local parliament for the indigenous Saami focused on cultural preservation. Settlements of civil war often include autonomy for self-determination movements, such as the creation of the Autonomous Region in Muslim Mindanao in the Philippines for the Moro self-determination movement.

Like repression, accommodation can also have a mixed effect on tactical choice depending on the degree to which the accommodation met self-determination movement demands and how much buy-in is achieved among the group. Accommodations achieved through civil war settlement necessarily induce a change in tactics away from violence. If accommodation creates new opportunity structures for groups (such as a local parliament), self-determination movements are likely to shift effort into conventional political behavior. However, limited accommodations may inspire some in a self-determination movement to press harder for change, perhaps escalating their claims or shifting to different tactics (Walter 2009).

## Vis-à-vis the international community

Several aspects of the international community may impact how self-determination movements choose tactics. Here, we consider two key elements: the dynamics of international recognition, and the impact of geopolitics on support for self-determination movements.

### Haphazard politics of recognition

While secession is incredibly uncommon, it does occur. The most recent full secession is the creation of South Sudan. The South Sudanese secession was agreed to in 2005 as part of the civil war settlement, the Comprehensive Peace Agreement/Naivasha Agreement, and the later Eastern Sudan Peace Agreement. The Bougainville region in Papua New Guinea voted in 2019 in a non-binding referendum to secede and has begun negotiations with the state about formally separating. Such events do not follow a predictable pattern with respect to the tactics used. The Bougainville vote and the South Sudan vote both followed bloody civil wars. Montenegro's independence from Serbia in 2006, however, occurred without violent conflict. East Timor's separation from Indonesia is held up as an example of the success of mass nonviolence (Chenoweth et al. 2011), but it was also preceded by a long internal war.

A key factor that has been identified as relevant for successful secession is recognition by a major power state, such as the United States (Coggins 2014). Yet, there appears to be a similarly haphazard response by these states, with little discernable pattern of why or when recognition occurs. Even when a movement is not officially recognized, external states take a number of actions that can support what Huddleston (2021) calls "latent sovereignty", encouraging and enabling self-determination movements. Critically, the varied response of the international community to separatist civil wars, nonviolent campaigns, and even rights campaigns means that there is always a possibility that any specific self-determination movement will gain support, incentivizing the use of unconventional tactics like violence and nonviolent action (Fazal and Griffiths 2014).

### Geopolitics

The broader geopolitical struggles in the international system can also impact tactical choices of self-determination movements. The most recent example of this is in the post-9/11 world. The American "War on Terror" after the attacks on September 11, 2001, lead to a more expansive classification of non-state actors as "combatants" if they engaged in terrorist violence (O'Connell 2004). The intensity of the US response to terrorist threats, and international collaboration around this, disincentives the use of violent tactics for self-determination movements. Historically, we see the impact of the Cold War on tactical choice as well, in terms of the willingness of groups to use violence when supported by external major power states (Kalyvas and Balcells 2010).

Change in norms in the international community can also affect the appeal of different tactics (Griffiths 2021). Increasing attention to human rights, for example, can incentivize movements to avoid violence (Cunningham 2021). International sympathy for self-determination movements is also conditional on what the state is doing. Jo (2015) shows that rebel groups are attuned to these changes in norms and work to comply with international laws.

## The Provisional IRA, Sinn Féin, and tactic shifts over time

The case of the Provisional Irish Republican Army (PIRA) and the Sinn Féin party offers an illustration of the complex and evolving mixture of tactics that separatist groups can pursue over time. First, we discuss a brief chronology of their shifts in and out of violent activity and electoral competition. This highlights the PIRA's declining use of violence (English 2003) – culminating in the official end of its armed struggle (O'Neill 2005). Then, we analyze the pressures which caused this shift, as well as the contexts which allowed it given the literature discussed earlier. We address concerns that the PIRA and Sinn Féin are (or were) separate entities and note the splintered Irish nationalist movement and the role this tactic shift played in some of that splintering. We close with a discussion of how important this case is for exploring emerging new tactics in an overall movement.

### *Timeline of tactic use*

While Sinn Féin began in many ways from an organizing document written by Arthur Griffith in 1904, it did not become a political party until 1907 (Feeney 2003). It was always organized around Irish nationalism, but initially it focused on electoral success, not violence. Over time it fluctuated in both importance and orientation, and when the IRA became an illegal organization, it strategically chose to take Sinn Féin over – "as a political party Sinn Féin was legal, therefore it would be the mouthpiece for the IRA and the IRA's public face" (Feeney 2003: 190).

The IRA shifted heavily towards political training and campaigning in the early 1960s, with Sinn Féin and the IRA continuing to entirely overlap, including their leaders. This shift towards politics was prompted by both recruitment issues (Feeney 2003) as well as leadership pressure (Drake 1991) and came with a focus on helping other groups with nonviolent protest, which proliferated with the increase of media attention (Feeney 2003: 228). This ended in 1970, with the failure of Sinn Féin to make any political headway and a corresponding dive of the IRA deeper into armed conflict (Jackson 2006).

From 1970 onward, Sinn Féin reverted to an extension of the armed wing with the meteoric rise of the more extreme Provisionals within the group. A leading Sinn Féin organizer of the time said that Sinn Féin's role was "agitation and publicity" (Feeney 2003: 260), not political action but rather closer to a propaganda office (Rafter 2005). Sinn Féin picketed police and army barracks and organized protest marches, but it did not politically campaign; so, while it did not pursue conventional political tactics, it did pursue other nonviolent tactics simultaneous to the PIRA's armed struggle.

In 1974, Sinn Féin organized a boycott of the assembly elections and began to present policies, a notable shift towards actual political participation even if it was political participation by abstention. This was also one of the peaks of the PIRA violence and terrorist action, with a barrage of bombing attacks in Britain (Edwards 2014). During this time, the groups remained deeply linked, with the PIRA chief of staff writing a report which stated that Sinn Féin should "come under [PIRA] Army organisers at all levels" (Feeney 2003: 282). This statement reflected reality, with Gerry Adams simultaneously vice-president of Sinn Féin and a leading member of the PIRA Army Council (Feeney 2003).[6]

The hunger strike of the PIRA prisoners, led by Bobby Sands, drew positive attention to the PIRA. When Sands was elected to a parliamentary position, it threw Sinn Féin more deeply into actual electoral politics, not simply policy positions, and legitimized the PIRA (Drake 1991; Feeney 2003). While violence continued (in 1981 the PIRA claimed 70 lives) during the hunger strike, rioting and demonstrations were a major focus of PIRA attention. The leadership of the PIRA was additionally concerned about the rise of Sinn Féin, wondering if the military campaign would need to be tailored to elections (Feeney 2003: 324), and with electoral success, Adams argued that there should be further investment in political campaigning.

Multiple authors argue that Adams was a key figure balancing the military and electoral tactics of the group – pushing for electoral investment but simultaneously recognizing armed struggle as "necessary and morally correct" (Feeney 2003: 327; Whiting 2016), and a broader shift towards a new and younger leadership impacted the PIRA's tactical preferences (Drake 1991; Smith 2002). Adams faced several internal struggles, and after May 1985, the IRA ramped up military action again to satisfy the armed wing that the primacy of Sinn Féin did not mean the armed struggle was lost. This included the PIRA's use of "proxy bombs", bombs where civilians were forced to deliver the device to its detonation area (Drake 1991).

By the late 1980s, the PIRA's war of attrition was wearing on the population, and the PIRA took community feeling towards its violence seriously (Brooks 2021). The existence and prominence of Sinn Féin meant there were public faces on whom to take out that outrage (Feeney 2003: 339). Sinn Féin begin back-channel negotiations with the more moderate Social Democratic and Labour Party (SDLP). Over time, from the mid-1980s to the mid-1990s, Sinn Féin slowly began to reframe armed struggle as an outdated tactic (Alonso 2016, 2001) and to distance itself from it (Whiting 2016). Even while the IRA continued notable attacks on the European mainland (Jackson 2006), the group outlook on conflict was shifting. Back-channel diplomacy with the British saw ups and downs, but external actors such as the United States and President Clinton put pressure on the British (Whiting 2016), and simultaneously popular support shifted against terrorism further, even in the Irish Republican base (Feeney 2003: 419). In 1998, multiparty peace talks led to the Good Friday Agreement, and a lasting ceasefire was declared.

The PIRA pushed forward with decommissioning – with further pressures coming in the form of Adams's leadership of Sinn Féin, the 9/11 attacks, their reframing of terrorist acts (Whiting 2016), as well as the British willingness to tolerate further autonomy and power in the hands of the PIRA to the point of it being called a "pseudo-state" by some scholars (Bean 2008). More violent splinter groups (including, notably, the Real IRA) emerged as the PIRA and Sinn Féin focused on the use of nonviolent and electoral tactics (O'Neill 2005).

This chronology has encapsulated a wide variety of tactics, including armed conflict/terrorism, nonviolent protest, hunger strikes, election boycott, and enthusiastic electoral participation. Here we offer three snapshots to help summarize the major tactics used by the group.

In the early to mid-1970s, the group focused much of its significant organizational energy on terrorist activity, including the previously mentioned Birmingham pub bombings (Edwards 2014), and was an important group for evolution of terrorist tactics (Jackson 2006). While Sinn Féin existed, it served mostly as a mouthpiece for the PIRA and did not seem to have its notable political power.

In the late 1980s and early 1990s, Sinn Féin leaders like Adams were balancing a more extreme portion of the group with a public which was tiring of armed action by simultaneously ramping up both the use of armed conflict and the investment in electoral policy and nonviolent action. This led to mixed terrorist actions and movement on political issues. The transition from terrorism to conventional politics did not occur instantly, and there was an extended period where the group was using both tactics, as well as nonviolent actions (Alonso 2016).

After the Good Friday discussions, and ceasefires, while threats of returning to violence were used, the movement continued to transition to conventional political competition. On July 28, 2005, the PIRA released a statement declaring an official end to their armed campaign (O'Neill 2005).

## Factors influencing the tactic shifts

The tactic shifts of the PIRA/Sinn Féin clearly had multiple important driving factors, and scholars do not agree on which factors were most important for motivating tactic shifts. This case study concentrates on what factors drove the PIRA/Sinn Féin to shift towards nonviolent tactics from 1989 onward to its continued participation in electoral politics.

Internal to the movement, there was change in leadership and shifting civilian support. Organizational elites were key to driving the group towards electoral participation. Gerry Adams, especially, emerges as an important moderate figure who strongly supported a shift towards electoral tactics, and a major figure in the peace talks. Adams rode the delicate balance of recognizing armed struggle as a "necessary" and morally correct option with electoral realities for many years (Morrison and Gill 2018; Whiting 2016; Feeney 2003; Alonso 2001).

Civilian support for violence waned over the late 1980s, with a strong core of Irish Republicans remaining supportive, but civilians more peripheral to the group turning against the violence (Brooks 2021; Guelke 2017: 559; Feeney 2003). The PIRA regularly killed Irish civilians by mistake, and were both aware of community backlash due to that and temporarily ceased violence in direct response to that backlash (Moloney 2002). Community credibility was important to the PIRA, and with much success, they rhetorically framed themselves as morally correct in their fight for self-determination. Sinn Féin were therefore seen as rehabilitated "peacemakers" and received a public opinion boost for turning towards elections rather than violent action (Alonso 2016; Whiting 2016). Additionally, the members of the PIRA grew increasingly older demographically, and younger people are more likely to commit or support violent action (Gill and Horgan 2013).

Internal factors were clearly not the only factors which enabled a shift from violence to electoral politics. The British state was changing its own orientation towards greater autonomy, and there was growing support in London for offering limited autonomy. The British secretary of state for Northern Ireland from 1989 to 1992, Peter Brooke, notoriously compared the PIRA to the independent movement in Cyprus in 1989, offering them both credibility and the possibility of negotiation of autonomy (Ni Aodha 2019), and their power was tolerated within certain limits by the British government (Bean 2008). The British government also willingly engaged in back-channel diplomacy with the movement, leaving open the possibility of the ultimate peace agreement. The peace agreement itself has been seen as giving the group political legitimacy and allowing it to exist as a functional political party (Richards 2001).

External actors were also a factor, especially the United States. President Bill Clinton's "decision to approve a visa to the U.S. in 1994 awarded Adams legitimacy as a credible political actor" (Whiting 2016). Additionally, a visiting ANC (African National Congress) delegation to Belfast in 1998 described Adams as an Irish Mandela (Crawshaw 1998). Several scholars argue that the internationalization of the issue brought by international attention lent the PIRA/Sinn Féin both legitimacy and leverage and kept the peace process moving in their favor (Alonso 2016; Feeney 2003). As previously mentioned, geopolitical issues such as 9/11 were indeed influential in the case of the PIRA for pushing them further towards decommissioning in an effort to differentiate themselves from terrorist actors (Alonso 2016; Feeney 2003).

There are other contexts which scholars suggest may have made these catalyst events more effective, such as internal organizational cohesion. Some scholars suggest that internal governance structures are key to restructuring as a political party (Manning 2007 applied to the PIRA in Whiting 2016), and the PIRA/Sinn Féin were notorious for having a strong internal organization (Jackson 2006). However, the internal structure of the PIRA did not shift with the Good Friday Agreement, so it is hard to understand how that could be the catalyst to prompt tactic change.

In short, many of the variables identified earlier as motivating tactic shifts in these groups are at play in the PIRA/Sinn Féin case, and the pressure of these joined variables pressed the self-determination group to transition to electoral participation.

## IRA group splintering

With the PIRA and Sinn Féin embracing the ceasefire, two smaller, more violent groups split off: the 32 County Sovereignty Movement and the Real IRA (Whiting 2016). These groups joined other violence-using splinter groups such as the Continuity IRA and the Republican Sinn Féin (Tonge 2004). These groups and their splintering from the main force have been confirmed by multiple scholarly works as being due to their unwillingness to give up violent tactics and the "treasonous" dropping of the tactic of abstention (Whiting 2016; Tonge 2004). These groups are smaller, with less sustained public support, and correspondingly are less able to inflict large-scale casualties (Tonge 2004).

## The PIRA–Sinn Féin relationship

The connections between Sinn Féin and the PIRA have fluctuated over time, and many in the Sinn Féin leadership refuse to admit involvement in the PIRA; however, this chapter has treated them as a continuous group. This is for two major reasons: significant overlap in membership and leadership, well supported by many scholarly works despite the denials of Sinn Féin leadership; and the shared strategic thinking between the two groups. Overlapping leadership in the PIRA and Sinn Féin is recorded from the 1960s to the end of the armed conflict in 2005. Gerry Adams and Martin McGuinness are identified as long-term PIRA leaders in multiple sources (Feeney 2003; Alonso 2016). While the two arms of the movement have waxed and waned in power, documents over time have additionally referred to them as joined (Feeney 2003). This has been so despite Adams's protestation that "Sinn Féin is not the PIRA" (Alonso 2016) and of his own lack of involvement in the PIRA (Cowan 2002). Additionally, the groups share strategies – in documents from the 1970s IRA, the council which guides it referred to Sinn Féin as a submissive organization whose tactics were decided by the PIRA (Feeney 2003). This is also a symbiotic organizational relationship – Morrison, the man in charge of publicity in Sinn Féin, admitted that his party used its relationship with the PIRA to manipulate media coverage (Alonso 2016). Simultaneously, Sinn Féin has supported the PIRA, serving as a propaganda device (Feeney 2003) and deflecting accusations of misconduct, such as around the PIRA role in Colombia (Holland 2002). This indicates, for the period of time focused on in our chronology, that the two operated as separate wings of the same organization with a high degree of integration.

## The importance of the PIRA and Sinn Féin

The PIRA and Sinn Féin present a confluence of several factors explored elsewhere in this chapter, leading to definitive tactic shifts for a self-determination group. It provides evidence of a wide range of tactics used, highlights that a period of mixed tactics may occur, and shows that it is possible for violent self-determination groups to shift their tactics to nonviolent action, such as electoral participation, successfully.

## Conclusion

We conclude here by highlighting how this chapter points to two further areas of inquiry. First, the case shows a relatively slow transition from predominantly violent tactics, to mixed (violent, nonviolent, and conventional) tactics, to predominantly conventional tactics. Yet there is little reason to think this pathway represents a common linear progress that movements take. In fact, the roots of the Irish Republican movement were, in part, in the Irish Civil Rights Movement

(Bosi 2006). How does this compare to other self-determination movements that experience shifts among tactics? Do movements hit a tipping point with respect to a certain type of tactic (such as conventional politics)?

A second area for further inquiry related to the relationship between movement leaders and civilian supporters. Gerry Adams is seen as responding to trends in popular support as well as the preferences of PIRA militants. Was the support base for the PIRA/Sinn Féin uniquely powerful in this respect? Would Adams, or another leader in his place, be less responsive to civilian preferences if conventional political competition was not on the horizon? More research on the nature of connections between movement leaders, trends in civilian preferences over tactics, and organizational responsiveness to civilians is needed.

## Glossary

**Nonviolence**  a tactic of disruption employed to achieve a political aim.

**PIRA**  the Provisional Irish Republican Army, which fought for unification of Northern Ireland with the Republic of Ireland.

**Self-determination movement**  ethnonational groups that make claims for greater autonomy based on this identity.

**Sinn Féin**  the political party affiliated with PIRA

**Tactics**  a specific type of behavior used to pressure the state for change related to a political aim.

**Violence**  a tactic of physical harm employed to achieve a political aim.

## Notes

1 A number of projects seek to identify these groups around the world. This chapter uses the Center of International Development and Conflict Management Peace and Conflict Report list. This list has not been updated over time. A more expansive list can be found in the SDM data (Sambanis et al., 2018).
2 Thresholds include 25 a year at the lowest and 1,000 over the war at the highest.
3 For example, the splintered ethnic self-determination groups in Burma have simultaneously fought a civil war against the state and fought amongst themselves.
4 Economic noncooperation includes strikes, tax refusal, or consumer boycotts; protests include rallies, protests, or demonstrations; nonviolent intervention includes sit-ins, occupations, or blockades; social noncooperation includes hunger strike, self-immolation, or other self-harm; political noncooperation includes boycotts of election or withdrawals from political office or coalition in the government.
5 See also Chenoweth (2013) on the use of terrorism in democracies.
6 This is controversial, with Adams claiming he was never a part of the PIRA.

## References

Alonso, R. (2001). 'The modernization in Irish republican thinking toward the utility of violence', *Studies in Conflict & Terrorism* 24(2): pp. 131–144.

Alonso, R. (2016). 'Terrorist skin, peace-party mask: The political communication strategy of Sinn Féin and the PIRA', *Terrorism and Political Violence* 28(3), pp. 520–540.

Bean, S. (2008). *The New Politics of Sinn Féin*. Liverpool: Liverpool University Press.

Benrabah, M. (2007). 'Language-in-education planning in Algeria: Historical development and current issues', *Language policy* 6(2): p. 225.

Bosi, L. (2006). 'The dynamics of social movement development: Northern Ireland's civil rights movement in the 1960s', *Mobilization: An International Quarterly* 11(1): pp. 81–100.

Brooks, R. (2021). 'Tying the hands of militants: Civilian targeting and societal pressures in the provisional IRA and Palestinian Hamas', *Journal of Global Security Studies*: pp. 1–22.

Chenoweth, E. (2013). 'Terrorism and democracy', *Annual Review of Political Science* 16: pp. 355–378.

Chenoweth, E., E. Perkoski, and S. Kang. (2017). 'State repression and nonviolent resistance', *Journal of Conflict Resolution*, 61(9): pp. 1950–1969.

Chenoweth, E., M. J. Stephan, and M. Stephan. (2011). *Why Civil Resistance Works: The Strategic Logic of Nonviolent Conflict*. Columbia (New York City, NY): Columbia University Press.

Coggins, B. (2014). *Power Politics and State Formation in the Twentieth Century: The Dynamics of Recognition*. Cambridge (Cambridge, UK): Cambridge University Press.

Cowan, R. (2002). 'Adams denies IRA links as book calls him a genius', *The Guardian,* 30 September.

Crawshaw, S. (1998). 'The ANC Approves Brothers in Arms In change's embrace', *The Independent,* 2 May.

Crenshaw, M. (1981). 'The causes of terrorism', *Comparative Politics*, 13(4): pp. 379–399.

Cunningham, K. G. (2021). 'Tactical efficacy in self-determination disputes'. Ms.

Cunningham, K. G., K. M. Bakke, and L. J. M. Seymour. (2012). 'Shirts today, skins tomorrow: Dual contests and the effects of fragmentation in self-determination disputes', *Journal of Conflict Resolution* 56(1): pp. 67–93.

Cunningham, K. G., M. Dahl, and A. Frugé. (2017). 'Strategies of resistance: Diversification and diffusion', *American Journal of Political Science* 61(3): pp. 591–605.

Cunningham, K. G., M. Dahl, and A. Frugé. (2020). 'Introducing the strategies of resistance data project', *Journal of Peace Research* 57(3): pp. 482–491.

Cunningham, K. G., and K. Sawyer. (2019). 'Conflict negotiations and rebel leader selection', *Journal of Peace Research* 56(5): pp. 619–634.

Davenport, C., and D. A. Armstrong. (2004). 'Democracy and the violation of human rights: A statistical analysis from 1976 to 1996', *American Journal of Political Science* 48(3): pp. 538–554.

Drake, C. J. (1991) 'The provisional IRA: A case study', *Terrorism and Political Violence*, 3(2), pp. 43–60.

Dudouet, V. (2013). 'Dynamics and factors of transition from armed struggle to nonviolent resistance', *Journal of Peace Research* 50(3): pp. 401–413.

Edwards, R. (2014). 'The Birmingham bombings 40 years on: What can we learn from IRA terror?', *The Telegraph*, 21 November.

English, R. (2003). *Armed Struggle: A History of the IRA*. London: Macmillan.

Enugu, C. (2006). 'Nigerian separatists attack census staff with acid', *Reuters*, 23 March.

Fazal, T. M., and R. D. Griffiths. (2014). 'Membership has its privileges: The changing benefits of state-hood', *International Studies Review* 16(1): pp. 79–106.

Feeney, B. (2003). *Sinn Féin: A Hundred Turbulent Years*. Madison, WI: University of Wisconsin Press.

Findley, M. G., and J. K. Young. (2012). 'More combatant groups, more terror?: Empirical tests of an outbidding logic', *Terrorism and Political Violence* 24(5): pp. 706–721.

Fisher, M. (2021). 'Indigenous people advance a dramatic goal: Reversing colonialism', *The New York Times*, 17 June. Accessed 9/2/21: www.nytimes.com/2021/06/17/world/canada/indigenous-kam-loops-graves.html

Fortna, V. P. (2015). 'Do terrorists win? Rebels' use of terrorism and civil war outcomes', *International Organization* 69(3): pp. 519–556.

Fox, E. (2012). 'Were the FARC behind the Bogota bombing?', *InSight Crime*, 16 May.

Francisco, R. (1995). 'The relationship between coercion and protest: An empirical evaluation in three coercive states', *Journal of Conflict Resolution* 39(2): 263–282.

Gallo-Cruz, S. (2012). 'Organizing global nonviolence: The growth and spread of nonviolent INGOS, 1948–2003', Erickson N. S. and Kurtz, L. R. (Eds.) *Nonviolent Conflict and Civil Resistance (Research in Social Movements, Conflicts and Change, Vol. 34)*. Bingley: Emerald Group Publishing Limited, pp. 213–256.

Gill, P., and Horgan, J. (2013). 'Who were the volunteers? The shifting sociological and operational profile of 1240 provisional Irish Republican Army members', *Terrorism and Political Violence* 25(3): pp. 435–456.

Gleditsch, K. S., and M. Rivera. (2017). 'The diffusion of nonviolent campaigns', *Journal of Conflict Resolution* 61(5): pp. 1120–1145.

Griffiths, R. D. (2021). 'Secessionist strategy and tactical variation in the pursuit of independence', *Journal of Global Security Studies* 6(1).

Guelke, A. (2017). 'Britain after Brexit: The risk to Northern Ireland. *Journal of Democracy* 28(1): pp. 42–52.

Holland, Jack. (2002). 'Gerry and the peacemakers: Protectors of the process', *Irish Echo*, 1–7 May.

Horowitz, M. C., A. C. Stam, and C. M. Ellis. (2015). *Why Leaders Fight*. Cambridge, UK: Cambridge University Press.

Huang, R. (2016). *The Wartime Origins of Democratization: Civil War, Rebel Governance, and Political Gegimes*. Cambridge, UK: Cambridge University Press.

Huddleston, R. J. (2021). 'Foulweather friends: Violence and third party support in self-determination conflicts', *Journal of Conflict Resolution* 65(6): pp. 1187–1214.

Jackson, B. (2006). *Training for Urban Resistance: The Case of the Provisional Irish Republican Army*. Santa Monica, CA: RAND Corporation.

Jo, H. (2015). *Compliant Rebels*. Cambridge, UK: Cambridge University Press.

Kalyvas, S. N., and L. Balcells. (2010). 'International system and technologies of rebellion: How the end of the Cold War shaped internal conflict', *American Political Science Review* 104(3): pp. 415–429.

Kasfir, N. (2005). 'Guerrillas and civilian participation: The national resistance army in Uganda, 1981–86', *Journal of Modern African Studies* 43(2): pp. 271–96.

Loyle, C. E. (2020). 'Laws and order: The impact of rebel governance on post-conflict rule of law' Presented at the Online Peace Science Colloquium. September 25, 2020.

Manning, C. (2007). 'Party-building on the heels of war: El Salvador, Bosnia, Kosovo and Mozambique', *Democratisation* 14(2): pp. 253–272.

Martin, B. (2007). *Justice Ignited: The Dynamics of Backfire*. Lanham, MD: Rowman & Littlefield.

Metelits, C. M. (2009). 'The consequences of rivalry: Explaining insurgent violence using fuzzy sets', *Political Research Quarterly* 62(4): pp. 673–684.

Moloney, E. (2002). *The Secret History of the IRA*. W. W. Norton & Company: New York City, NY.

Moore, W. H. (1998). 'Repression and dissent: Substitution, context, and timing', *American Journal of Political Science*: pp. 851–873.

Morrison, J. and P. Gill (2018). *100 Years of Irish Republican Violence: 1916–2016*. Oxfordshire, UK: Routledge.

Ni Aodha, G. (2019). 'The "unfortunate" 1989 interview with Northern Ireland secretary Peter Brooke', *The Journal.Ie*, 29 December.

Nkwopara, C. (2011). 'Angry reactions trail Police, MASSOB clash', *All Africa*, 31 May.

O'Connell, M. E. (2004). 'Enhancing the status of non-state actors through a global war on terror', *Columbia Journal of Transnational Law* 43: pp. 435–458.

O'Neill, P. (2005). 'I.R.A. statement on end to armed campaign', *The New York Times*, 28 July.

Pettersson, T., S. Davis, A. Deniz, G. Engström, N. Hawach, S. Högbladh, M. Sollenberg, and M. Öberg. (2021). 'Organized violence 1989–2020, with a special emphasis on Syria', *Journal of Peace Research* 58(4): pp. 809–825.

Polo, S. M. (2020). 'How terrorism spreads: Emulation and the diffusion of ethnic and ethnoreligious terrorism', *Journal of Conflict Resolution* 64(10): pp. 1916–1942.

Posner, D. N. (2004). 'The political salience of cultural difference: Why Chewas and Tumbukas are allies in Zambia and adversaries in Malawi', *American Political Science Review* 98(4): pp. 529–545.

Rafter, K. (2005). *Sinn Féin 1905–2005: In the Shadow of Gunmen*. Dublin, Ireland: Gill & MacMillan.

Reuters. (2006). 'Violence mars Nigerian census', *Reuters*, 23 March.

Richards, A. (2001). 'Terrorist groups and political fronts: The IRA, Sinn Féin, the peace process and democracy', *Terrorism and Political Violence* 13(4): pp. 72–89.

Sambanis, N., M. Germann, and A. Schädel. (2018). 'SDM: A new data set on self-determination movements with an application to the reputational theory of conflict', *Journal of Conflict Resolution* 62(3): pp. 656–686.

Schutte, S., and N. B. Weidmann. (2011). 'Diffusion patterns of violence in civil wars', *Political Geography* 30(3): pp. 143–152.

Sharp, G. (1973). *The Politics of Nonviolent Action*. Boston, MA: Porter Sargent.

Smith, M. L. R. (2002). *Fighting for Ireland?: The Military Strategy of the Irish Republican Movement*. Abingdon, UK: Routledge.

Sutton, J., C. R. Butcher, and I. Svensson. (2014). 'Explaining political jiu-jitsu: Institution-building and the outcomes of regime violence against unarmed protests', *Journal of Peace Research* 51(5): pp. 559–573.

Tonge, J. (2004). 'They haven't gone away, you know'. Irish Republican 'dissidents' and 'armed struggle', *Terrorism and Political Violence*, 16(3): pp. 671–693.

Walter, B. F. (2009). *Reputation and Civil War: Why Separatist Conflicts Are So Violent*. Cambridge, UK: Cambridge University Press.

Weldemichael, A. T. (2013). *Third World Colonialism and Strategies of Liberation: Eritrea and East Timor Compared*. Cambridge, UK: Cambridge University Press.

Whiting, S. (2016). 'Mainstream revolutionaries: Sinn Féin as a "normal" political party?', *Terrorism and Political Violence*, 28(3): pp. 541–560.

Zartman, W. (1989). *Ripe for Resolution: Conflict and Intervention in Africa*. Oxford: Oxford University Press.

# 22

# REMOVING THE GOVERNMENT OF THE HOST STATE

## Outside military intervention

*Shpend Kursani*

This chapter aims to spell out a process of how outside military intervention in secessionist conflicts is instigated. It is not a recipe for how to invite outside military intervention to support secessionists. As the chapter attempts to show, inviting outside military intervention in supporting secessionists to remove their host states, while continuing to keep them at bay, involves a process that is not in complete control of either the secessionists or the outside interveners. An oft-ignored party in inviting outside military intervention also involves the host state itself, which is not in complete control of instigating outside military intervention either. Therefore, in attempting to bring to light the process of how the host state government is removed by outside military support, the chapter takes a tripartite focus in analyzing parties in conflict, namely the host state, the secessionist entity, and the outside intervener involved in the conflict.

The chapter first outlines the general patterns of outside support to territorial contenders from the available data. It then moves on to analyze the process of outside military intervention in two cases: Turkey's intervention in Northern Cyprus, and NATO's intervention in Kosovo. In both cases, the chapter examines and attempts to outline the following processes which take place in instigating outside military intervention: (1) the parent state's attempt to unilaterally centralize power; (2) the minority's withdrawal from the host state as a result; (3) the minority's ability to sustain the withdrawal and resistance with outside help prior to outside military intervention; and (4) the final instigation of outside military intervention. It does so by paying attention to primary sources drawn from the letters addressed to the UN by three parties under analysis: the host state, the secessionists, and the outside interveners. Though not a primary objective of the chapter, the evidence points to secessionists' agency in attracting outside support. They do not seem to be simply stand-by observers waiting to be "chosen" as objects by outside military interventionists that come to their aid. Instead, they play an active role in instigating outside military intervention – sustained withdrawal and violence from and against the host state, with prior direct and indirect support playing a considerable role.

## Patterns of violence and outside intervention

Leaving the process of decolonization aside, according to Griffiths and Wasser (2019), between 1946 and 2001 there have been 136 secessionist movements around the world. Moreover, the post–World War II period has witnessed, on average, more than 50 active secessionist movements

DOI: 10.4324/9781003036593-26

every single year (Fazal and Griffiths, 2014; see also Cunningham, 2013). Pointing out the number of secessionist movements outside the colonial context is important because while the decolonization process has run out of steam, demands for self-determination and independent statehood have not. Rarely are such cases that do not fall under the "colonial countries and peoples", in the wording of the 1960 UNGA's declaration on decolonization stipulates (UNGA, 1960), granted independent statehood. If "countries" or "peoples" do not fall under the ambiguous conception of colonization, the gate to become an independent and sovereign member of the international society of states remains rather narrow (Österud, 1997).

Secessionist movements use different strategies to remove their parent state from the territory they claim *ought* to be independent, while ultimately aiming for a universally recognized independence. From a broad perspective of strategies, they can be categorized into peaceful and violent ones. Taking a quick look at Griffiths and Wasser's (2019) 136 secessionist movements, close to one-third have resorted to violence in an attempt at removing their host states (see Figure 22.1). It becomes apparent that while secessionism has been active mainly in the non-Americas, the violent ones have clustered around southeastern Europe (particularly around the process of Yugoslavia's dissolution), the Middle East, and South-East Asia.

Although limited in the period they cover, Bélanger et al. (2005, p. 439) suggest that secessionists hardly receive outside support. They argue that for existing states, the stability of international order is so vital that "states have traditionally maintained an anti-secessionist bias in order to preserve the status quo" (Bélanger et al., 2005, p. 439). However, to test this observation, I use a combination of UCDP/PRIO data, such as their Armed Conflict Dataset, version 21.1 (Pettersson et al., 2021), and their External Support – Disaggregated/Supporter Level Dataset (Högbladh et al., 2011) to investigate some patterns of external support. I also look at whether outside support to territorial contenders has been lethal, i.e., through the provision of troops and weapons, or non-lethal, such as economic and other types of non-lethal support as measured by the aforementioned datasets. The analysis suggests that there have been 72 (internal) territorial conflicts, of which 71% received no outside support while the other 29% did. Moreover, most of those that have received outside support have received lethal types, pointing at the intensity of support for that one-third that receive it (see Table 22.1).

The number of territorial contenders that receive outside support, especially of lethal types, should not be ignored. For as Grant (2014) suggests, the use of armed force in aid of secession,

*Figure 22.1 (Non)violence in secessionist attempts (1946–2011)*

Source: Author's illustration, using the list of secessionist movements from Griffiths and Wasser (2019).

*Table 22.1* Number of territorial contenders receiving outside support

|  | Supported | Unsupported | Total |
|---|---|---|---|
| With lethal and non-lethal | 21 | 51 | 72 |
| Percentage | 29% | 71% | 100% |
| With lethal only | 15 | 57 | 72 |
| Percentage | 21% | 79% | 100% |

*Source*: Author's creation, using the Armed Conflict Dataset version 21.1 from Pettersson et al. (2021) and Högbladh, Pettersson, and Themnér (2011)

*Table 22.2* Number and type of supporters to non-state territorial contenders

|  | State Actors | Non-State Actors | IOs | Total |
|---|---|---|---|---|
| With lethal and non-lethal | 45 | 64 | 4 | 113 |
| Percentage | 40% | 57% | 3% | 100% |
| With lethal only | 27 | 15 | 1 | 43 |
| Percentage | 63% | 35% | 2% | 100% |

*Source*: Author's creation, using the Armed Conflict Dataset version 21.1 from Pettersson, T. et al. (2021) and Högbladh, Pettersson, and Themnér, L. (2011).

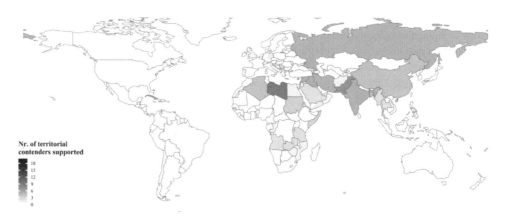

*Figure 22.2*   State supporters of territorial contenders (1975–2009)

*Source*: Author's illustration, using the Armed Conflict Dataset version 21.1 from Pettersson et al. (2021) and Högbladh, Pettersson, and Themnér (2011).

including in aid of colonized people, despite many debates on the issue, has not found general support among the community of states. Therefore, I also investigate actors providing both lethal and non-lethal support. The 21 of the 72 territorial contenders that receive outside support do so from 113 external actors, 57% of which are non-state actors, such as diaspora or other non-governmental organizations; 3% of which are International Organizations (IOs), such as NATO or the African Union; and 40% of which are state actors (see Table 22.2). As this chapter further shows in its analysis, non-state actor support to secessionists can be crucial when the latter attempts to engage in violent attempts at removing the host state. Figure 22.2

further provides an overview of state actors who have supported territorial contenders by lethal or non-lethal means. Figure 22.2 does not depict IO support, such as NATO support to Kosovo. In all, it appears that while the majority of actors providing support to territorial contenders within existing states are non-state actors, state actors remain involved quite considerably in aiding such territorial contenders.

# Northern Cyprus

## *Host state's unilateral attempts to centralize*

The Republic of Cyprus was established as an independent state in 1960 after a series of treaties, most of which were signed between the United Kingdom (as the island's colonizer), the Kingdom of Greece, and the Republic of Turkey on the one hand, and the island's Greek and Turkish communities' representatives, on the other (Camp, 1980). Cyprus's independence, however, did not come on the spur of the moment. Several years before the island's independence, the Greek Cypriots had begun an armed struggle aiming to end British colonial rule and achieve *enosis* – the island's unification with Greece (Castleberry, 1964). In an atmosphere of armed rebellion of the mid- and late 1950s, the Turkish Cypriots, which represented around 20% of the island's population, formed their armed resistance group in opposition to *enosis* but in support of *taksim* – the island's partition (Castleberry, 1964). Several rounds of negotiations took place in the late 1950s between the island's Greek and Turkish communities, as well as the United Kingdom, Greece, and Turkey, in London and Zürich. The negotiations produced a series of treaties and the final constitution of Cyprus based on which it was to become independent.

The treaties leading up to the creation of an independent republic, in effect, were a compromise solution between the five signatories. By accepting the island's independence, the Greek Cypriots compromised on *enosis*, while the Turkish Cypriots compromised on *taksim*. The treaties also came to be the basis of Cyprus's constitution, which, among others, prohibited the island's partition or unification with another state (i.e., Treaty of Guarantee, 1960 see Article 1). The Treaty of Alliance – signed by Greece, Turkey, and Cyprus, also envisaged maintenance of some 950 and 650 Greek and Turkish contingents, respectively, which would participate in the Tripartite Headquarters on the island and secure the latter's independence and constitutional order (Treaty of Alliance, 1960; see Additional Protocol No.1). What appeared to be the main compromise accepted by the Greek side is the power-sharing terms which gave the Turkish Cypriots veto powers over some legislation, and guaranteed their representation in the government, reflecting to some extent the proportion of both communities' population on the island (Bölükbaşi, 1998; Pegg, 1998).

However, soon after the establishment of an independent republic, the President of Cyprus at the time, Makarios (a Greek Cypriot), began to criticize the treaties and the constitution of Cyprus, to which he was one of the signatories. According to the *New York Times* at the time, Makarios claimed that he had been "foiled by the determination of the Turkish minority to use the powers given them in the Constitution" which allegedly were separating the communities (New York Times, 1964, p. 38). He moved to propose a list of 13 amendments to the constitution, which included the abolition of the Turkish Cypriots' veto powers as well as revising the representation of the Turkish Cypriots in government and the armed forces, among others (Ker-Lindsay, 2011). A closer analysis of his 13-point plan suggests that Makarios attempted to unilaterally centralize state power at the hands of the majority Greek Cypriots at the expense of the Turkish Cypriots. Makarios tried to consult and, ideally, receive the consent of both Greece and Turkey for his plan, but both rejected Makarios's plan as dangerous (Ker-Lindsay, 2011). Despite the rejection by the key guarantor powers as well as the representatives of the Turkish Cypriots on the island, in November 1963, Makarios set his plan in motion to unilaterally change the crucial provisions of the constitution touching upon the guaranteed rights of the Turkish Cypriots.

## *Withdrawing from the host state: organized parallelism and violence*

Makarios's unilateral attempt to change the character of the republic triggered a series of events that, most importantly, triggered a wide variety of actions on regional as well as international levels. In protest against Makarios's 13-point plan, Turkish Cypriots decided to withdraw from state institutions, leaving the Greek Cypriots as the sole caretakers of the state administration over the entire island (Bahcheli, 2000). Communal hostilities, for the most part, drew the Turkish Cypriots towards their rural centers where they could better be able to protect themselves (Morag, 2004). During the initial period of hostilities, two organized armed groups (re-)emerged on the island, the EOAK – the Greek Cypriot militia group – and the TMT – the Turkish Cypriot militia group – both of which had been active during the armed struggle of the pre-independence period (Kliot and Mansfield, 1997). By 1967, the enclaves under the TMT's control had largely turned into Turkish Cypriots' *de facto* separate administration (Hadjipavlou-Trigeorgis and Trigeorgis, 1993) while occupying only around 4% of the entire island (Morag, 2004).

In the course of hostilities, killings and atrocities began to mark the intercommunal violence on the entire island – and they were to last for over a decade. This is evidenced, among others, by numerous letters addressed, especially by Turkey, to the UN Security Council (UNSC) (i.e., UNSC S/5731, 1964). The Greek Cypriots and Greece were also vociferous from their perspective. The Greek Cypriot leadership was not denying the gravity of the situation and the harm being inflicted on both Turkish and Greek Cypriots. However, they consistently framed the Turkish rebellion as one being "terrorist" in nature, and that the Greek Cypriots were simply fighting against such acts of terror (i.e., UNSC S/6212, 1965, p. 1).

The government of Turkey also addressed several complaints about the economic blockade and pressure which had been put on the Turkish community in Cyprus since December 1963, pointing at the "refusal of the Greek Cypriot government to permit the importation of the relief materials and food supplies sent by the Turkish Red Crescent" (UNSC S/5958, 1964, p. 1). The division between the two communities only grew, and it not only pitted them against each other per se but also led to the development of parallel existence of each community (see UNSC S/6168, 1965).

The Turkish Cypriot withdrawal was sealed with the establishment of the Provisional Turkish Cypriot Administration (PTCA) on 28 December 1967 (Göktepe, 2005). The government of Greece condemned the measure (UNSC S/8324, 1968), while the government of Turkey suggested that the establishment of the PTCA "is the direct consequence of the actions and policies of the Greek Cypriot Administration" (UNSC S/8327, 1968, p. 1). Fazil Küçük, the Turkish Cypriot leader, also reiterated that the Turkish Cypriots refused to function on an ad hoc basis and that the latter has found "itself forced to provide for its own public services in view of the all-out attacks waged against the Turkish community by the Greek-Cypriot regime" (UNSC S/8327, 1968, p. 2).

## *Sustaining withdrawal and resistance: prior outside aid*

The Turkish Cypriot withdrawal and parallel existence on the island alongside the mounting power of the Greek Cypriots were in many ways facilitated by some sustained outside help from Turkey. In a letter addressed to the UNSC on 26 December 1963, the Greek Cypriot-led government accused the government of Turkey of "the acts of (a) aggression, and (b) intervention in the internal affairs of Cyprus by the threat and use of force against its territorial integrity and political independence" which Turkey had allegedly perpetrated a day preceding the letter (UNSC 8/5488, 1963, p. 113). Similarly, in another letter aired on 4 June 1964, the Greek Cypriot-led government outlined details of Turkey's attempts at training the Turkish Cypriot rebels as well as sending additional force in aid of the latter (see UNSC S/5742, 1964).

In a score of subsequent letters, the Greek Cypriots, as well as Greece, pointed out "incontestable" allegations that arms from Turkey were being "clandestinely" being sent to the Turkish Cypriots (UNSC S/6173, 1965; see also UNSC S/6334, 1965). In effect, the Turkish Cypriots had partially removed the host-state government in small pieces of enclaved territory, which can only be understood considering Turkey's military, economic, and political aid to them. However, while such outside help facilitated the maintenance of Turkish Cypriots' resistance and parallel existence, it appears that they could not govern themselves separately in small, enclaved territories that they occupied.

## Instigation of the outside military intervention: removing the host state

In 1967, at the height of the intercommunal violence in Cyprus, Greece fell under a military regime. As soon as it took power over Greece, the Greek Junta, led by Colonel George Papadopoulos, immediately launched negotiations with Turkey, whereby the Greek Cypriot *enosis* could be achieved in exchange for a Turkish military base to be established on Cyprus (Kıralp, 2017). But the idea suited neither Turkey nor the Turkish Cypriots. A few months after the military junta took over Greece, Fazil Küçük, with the help of Turkey, addressed his concern to the UNSC about the Greeks' explicitly stated aim for "the union of the whole and undivided Cyprus with the motherland, without any intermediary stage" (UNSC, 1967, p. 2). Küçük's letter further went on to state that such a measure was in breach of Cyprus's agreed-upon constitution of 1960.

On 15 July 1974, the Greek Junta organized a coup in Cyprus, whereby Makarios was replaced by an extreme Greek *enoist*, Nikos Sampson (Kliot and Mansfield, 1997). The coup against Makarios had been instigated, exactly because of his reluctance at that point, to accelerate the process of *enosis* (Bölükbaşi, 1998; Bahcheli, 2000). Turkey's intervention on the island became imminent. Two days after the coup in Greek-Cypriot-held Cyprus, Bülent Ecevit, Turkey's Prime Minister at the time, in a letter to the Secretary-General of the UNSC on 17 July 1974, elaborated Turkey's and the Turkish Cypriot community's concerns and dismay about the possibility of *enosis* to occur on the island and stated that these and other aforementioned concerns "made active intervention possible" (UNSC S/11341, 1974, p. 2). On 20 July 1974, Turkey began its military intervention in Cyprus.

Turkey's initial military intervention in Cyprus effectively removed the host-state government from only 2% of the island's territory – namely, the corridor connecting the Kyrenia/Girne mountain range with Nicosia (Kıralp, 2017, p. 601). Several negotiations were held between Greece and Turkey, supported by the United States and the United Kingdom, whereby Turkey demanded a federal solution of two communities in Cyprus. Talks failed on 13 August 1974, whereby Turkey immediately launched the second phase of its intervention and expansion on the island, removing the host state's government control from over 36% of the island's territory (Dodd, 2010). Turkey's second phase of intervention saw a massive amount of population transfers. Some 150,000–200,000, or 30% to 40% of the Greek Cypriots moved from the northern part of the island to its southern part, while around 46,000–65,000, or 38% to 54%, of the

Turkish Cypriots, moved from the southern part of the island to the north (Morag, 2004; Dodd, 2010). What had been previously referred to as the division between the Turkish and Greek communities on the island switched into the division between the northern administered area of the Turkish Cypriots and the southern administrated area of the Greek Cypriots. Turkey's intervention removed the host state's government from now Turkish-Cypriot-governed northern part of the island, which continues to the present day. Northern Cyprus declared its independence in 1983, which to this day remains recognized only by a single UN member – Turkey.

## Kosovo

### *Host state's unilateral attempts to centralize*

Separatist voices and movements in Kosovo have existed at varying points in time during the existence of the Socialist Federal Republic of Yugoslavia (SFRY) under the rule of the Communist Party of Yugoslavia. They became more vociferous, and eventually violent, only after the breakup of the socialist federation in the early 1990s. Six republics constituted the SFRY. Very early on, Serbia, one of SFRY's constituent republics, promulgated laws for its internal administrative organization as early as 1945. According to the 1945 internal administrative reforms, Serbia's territory was decided to be organized such that two provinces were created, Vojvodina and Kosovo (Osmani and Manaj, 2014). However while the former was designated as a single territorial unit with its autonomous administrative structures, Kosovo was not – it had remained without autonomous administration (Vickers, 1998).

The SFRY's constitution was marked with an incredibly high number of changes and amendments (Roberts, 1978). The three most notable constitutional changes and amendments that took place are those of 1963, where Kosovo was upgraded from an autonomous region to an autonomous province within the Republic of Serbia – on par with Serbia's other province, Vojvodina (Judah, 2008). Further changes were those of 1968, which granted Kosovo's majority population some level of language rights, namely the use of the Albanian language, and rights on the use of Albanian symbols. The 1968 amendments also made the Communist Party in Kosovo independent from that of Serbia (Pula, 2004). Most notable were the 1974 constitutional changes in Yugoslavia, which, in effect, strengthened the constituent republics' powers at the expense of the federation. They also increased the powers of Serbia's two provinces, Vojvodina and Kosovo, making them enjoy autonomous governance very close to the other six republics of the SFRY had (Silber and Little, 1997).

Despite the improved political status of Kosovo over the years under the SFRY, and the federal investments in the province's industrial base, education, healthcare, and such, Kosovo did not quite catch up economically with the other parts of the SFRY. Kosovo continued to be the poorest region of the federation. In 1979 the per capita income was only 30% of the federation's average (Arhsien and Howells, 1981). In the environment where Yugoslavia began to face economic crisis as well as Kosovo's continued underdevelopment, coupled with Tito's death in 1980, problems emerged. In March–April 1981, Kosovo Albanians, mainly students, some organized under Marxist-Leninist organizations, gathered in massive numbers to protest the poor conditions at the university and in the province overall. Soon they turned into what Sabrina Ramet calls "anti-Serbian rioting" (Ramet, 2002, p. 6), where nationalist demands for an independent republic and, at times, its unification with Albania were also chanted (Judah, 2008). At the same time, Serbs had been already leaving Kosovo before the spring 1981 demonstrations of Albanians in Kosovo, and the 1981 demonstrations further increased Serb fears over the demands that the Albanians were making (Arhsien and Howells, 1981). The 1981 Kosovo

Albanian disturbances opened the way for Belgrade to return to repressive measures, initially by purging the leadership in Kosovo of its Communist Party ranks (Artisien, 1984).

Belgrade's repressive policies, according to Ramet (2002), only intensified the Albanian–Serb tensions in the province throughout the 1980s. Nationalist voices had been growing throughout Yugoslavia, but notable were those of Albanians and Serbs in Kosovo. Kosovo Serbs were not at ease with the demographic changes that had been taking place in Kosovo, where, by 1981, close to 80% of the province's population were Albanian (Kosovo Agency of Statistics, 2018). By the mid-1980s, Kosovo Serb elites, impatient with loss of power in Kosovo due to Yugoslavia's constitutional changes, were pleading with Serbia's Communist Party in Belgrade to make and enforce constitutional changes and revert the power balance in the province, at the expense of what Albanians had gained in 1974 (Silber and Little, 1997). In April 1987, the Serbian Communist Party leader, Slobodan Milosevic, went to Kosovo where, in front of a large Serbian crowd, wearing the mantle of the Serbs defender, promised those who had gathered the changes they were seeking (Silber and Little, 1997). The road was set for Milosevic to attempt centralization of Serbia's power over its two provinces, and in particular over Kosovo.

In March 1989, Serbia – increasingly under Milosevic's growing power – changed its constitution. The representatives of Kosovo's Assembly ratified Milosevic's demands to change Serbia's constitution, but only under the pressure and intimidation of the Yugoslav National Army "tanks and the Serbian police surrounding the building [which had been also] deployed throughout Kosovo" (Silber and Little, 1997, p. 69). The centralization of Serbia, by way of limiting powers of Kosovo's government and removing the latter's veto powers, had occurred under the environment when Milosevic, with massive Serb popular support, had already toppled regimes in Montenegro and the two autonomous provinces (Hayden, 1992, p. 7).

### Withdrawing from the host state: organized parallelism and violence

Serbia's singlehanded attempt to centralize its rule over its two provinces, and notably over Kosovo, while successful, was met with resistance by Kosovo Albanians. Their resistance manifested in different forms throughout the 1990s, but they could be characterized by two overarching phases. The first was the peaceful phase of withdrawal from the host state. The second was the phase of violent resistance while the withdrawal from the host state continued acutely.

The first step the Kosovo Albanians took at the inception of their peaceful resistance was to massively protest across Kosovo to reject Serbia's centralized rule over Kosovo. The demonstrations were soon brutally crushed by police forces (Judah, 2008). The second step was their attempt to, at least in declaratory fashion, try seceding, initially from Serbia, by declaring Kosovo a republic within the Yugoslav Federation in July 1990, and later from the Yugoslav Federation, by secretly adopting the "Constitution of the Republic of Kosovo" as an independent state in September 1990 (Pula, 2004). Until this point, the question of Kosovo's independence from the SFRY had not been a mainstream one among Kosovo Albanians. However, the massive popular support given to the September 1990 constitution, in a referendum that the Kosovo Albanians had organized independently, made the question of Kosovo's independence something that the overwhelming majority of the Kosovo Albanian population were set to work for.

Coming to grips with the reality that no state, other than Albania, was recognizing their declared "Republika e Kosovës", Kosovo Albanians withdrew from the host state – one which was relatively Serb dominated after the secession of Slovenia, Croatia, Macedonia, and Bosnia and Herzegovina during the early 1990s. Kosovo Albanians resorted to a "parallel system" which was to last for almost a decade. The parallel system meant that Kosovo Albanians' life ran "independently" from their host state's laws and wishes to the extent they could (see Pula, 2004,

p. 797). On several occasions in the UN forums, Yugoslavia[1] recognized that the Kosovo Albanians had withdrawn from their host state. In a letter to the United Nations Office at Geneva of 10 March 1993, Yugoslavia acknowledged that the Kosovo Albanians "refuse to recognize the laws and decisions of state organs of the Republic of Serbia . . . and the Federal Republic of Yugoslavia" (E/CN.4/1993/116, 1993, p. 3). In another letter dated 6 December 1995 to the UN Secretary-General, Yugoslavia noted that the political leadership of Kosovo Albanians is "an ardent advocate of segregation" as it "prohibits the entire Albanian minority population from being associated with" state and other institutions of Yugoslavia (UNGA A/C.3/50/12, 1995, p. 2). Kosovo Albanians' withdrawal from the host state was not simply a voluntary resistance tactic, but non-withdrawal would have meant that the Albanians would have to work for Serbian-ruled educational, media, and cultural institutions, from which the former were laid out from key positions (Kostovicova, 2005).

After the mid-1990s, different small armed groups began to emerge in different parts of Kosovo (see Norris, 2005), opening the door to the phase of violent resistance while maintaining the parallel system. Popular support for armed resistance, which until the mid-1990s had not been prominent, continued to grow after Kosovo had not been included in internationally mediated peace processes between warring parties in other parts of Yugoslavia (Croatia and Bosnia) in the mid-1990s (Perritt, 2008). The largest of armed resistance groups, which later came to dominate the armed resistance in Kosovo, was the Kosovo Liberation Army (KLA). While active before, the KLA made its first public appearance in 1997 (Norris, 2005). Armed resistance became necessary, "according to the KLA, by Serbia's thorough repression of Kosovo's majority Albanian population and its denial of that population's political sovereignty" (Herscher, 2013, p. 83). While the KLA began attacking some Serb positions in 1997, its armed campaigns against Serb police and their stations throughout Kosovo grew massively in 1998 (Herscher, 2013). Serbian police and paramilitary forces took aggressive steps to annihilate the KLA, something which only backfired. For example, according to Perritt (2008), Serbia's attacks against the KLA were so indiscriminate that they led to the deaths of many unarmed civilians, including women and children. Accounts of Serbia's indiscriminate approach to annihilating the KLA in areas where they had been suspected to be operating were given also by many Yugoslav Army volunteers engaged in the late-1990s war in Kosovo (see Herscher, 2013). Such an approach alerted the international community, which began to turn their attention to Kosovo, and while blaming all sides in the conflict, they certainly kept the host state government responsible, as many reactions by states in the UN and other forums attest (see UNSC S/1999/96, 1999; UNSC S/1999/107, 1999)

## Sustaining withdrawal and resistance: prior outside aid

It is difficult to understand the Kosovo Albanian withdrawal and parallel existence alongside repressive measures of Serbia without meaningful help that the Kosovo Albanian resistance had been receiving. Unlike the Turkish Cypriots that had Turkey's direct support since the inception of the conflict on the island, the Kosovo Albanian outside support during peaceful and violent phases of the resistance has been diverse. A sustained and meaningful outside aid came from the growing number of Albanian diaspora in the western countries, especially young men who were leaving Kosovo during the 1990s to, among others, also escape conscription in the Yugoslav Army. According to some accounts, the emerging Kosovo Albanian diaspora during the 1990s account for close to 60% of all waves of Albanian migrants after World War II (King and Vullnetari, 2009). The Kosovo Albanian parallel system, in addition to levying and collecting taxes on and from Albanians in Kosovo, also levied a 3% tax on income specifically for those working abroad (IICK, 2000).

Outside support from the Albanian diaspora seems to have also frustrated Yugoslavia, as noted in many letters of complaints they had been dispatching to the UN. For example, as early as 1995, Yugoslavia dispatched a letter to the UN Secretary-General, complaining that the Kosovo Albanians have been receiving funds from abroad, which they levy as taxes, to run "the self-pro-claimed 'Republic of Kosovo'" (UNGA A/C.3/50/12, 1995, p. 3). The letter also blames "some foreign Governments that are host to a large segment of Albanian immigrants from Kosovo . . . not willing to prevent such activities" (UNGA A/C.3/50/12, 1995, p. 3).

The diaspora support became crucial, especially during the period of violent resistance. Alba-nian diaspora across different western countries had established the "Homeland Calling" fund to aid the armed resistance. The organizations from which the armed resistance in Kosovo came to grow in the 1990s were those who were originally based in West Germany in the 1980s (Pavk-ović, 2000). As one of the fundraising activists in the United States had stressed, "It is each and every patriot's duty to support the KLA" (Koinova, 2013). There is little doubt that the Kosovo Albanian diaspora funds committed to sustaining the armed resistance were crucial. As soon as the KLA began to intensify its activities in 1998, the UNSC adopted Resolution 1160, which condemned the use of excessive force by Serbian police against civilians on the one hand, as well as "acts of terrorism by the Kosovo Liberation Army" on the other, it decided

> that all States shall . . . prevent the sale or supply to the Federal Republic of Yugoslavia, including Kosovo, by their nationals or from their territories . . . of arms and related *matériel of all types*, . . . and shall prevent arming and training for terrorist activities there.
>
> *(UNSC S/RES/1160, 1998, p. 2, emphasis in original)*

Another actor to play a crucial role in aid of Kosovo Albanians throughout the 1990s, and espe-cially during the violent resistance period, was Albania and various actors from within it. Albania was one of the first countries to address the Kosovo Albanian struggle in Kosovo after the rise of Milosevic to power. As early as 2 February 1990, Albania's Foreign Minister at the time, Reis Malile, sent a telegram to the Secretary-General of the UN wanting to draw the international community's attention to the "tragic events in Kosova (Yugoslavia)" (UNSC S/21132, 1990, p. 1). Albania was also one of the first countries to demand deployment of UN forces in Kosovo, as evidenced by the latter's note of 24 April 1993 to the UNSC (UNSC S/25662, 1993, p. 1). Yugoslavia's responses to Albania's letters of support to Kosovo Albanians conveyed Yugoslavia's views of Albania inciting acts of aggression in support of secessionists in another state's territory (i.e., UNSC S/25711, 1993).

Albania's support to Kosovo Albanians became even more crucial when it comes to main-taining the former's phase of violent resistance during the late 1990s. It has been widely sug-gested that when the state collapsed in Albania in the spring of 1997, substantial arms from Albania made their way into Kosovo (see Norris, 2005; Perritt, 2008). In many of its letters to the UNSC, Yugoslavia complained about Albania serving as a safe haven for the KLA. For example, in a letter dated 2 September 1998 to the UNSC, Yugoslavia's representative claimed that Albania had already made facilities available to "terrorists, who call themselves the 'Kosovo Liberation Army'" whereby many of these facilities serve as "boot camps and bases" (A/53/341, 1998, p. 3). In another letter dated 16 December 1998 to the UNSC, Yugoslavia raised the concern that armed groups "numbering hundreds of terrorists attempted on three occasions to cross over from Albania" (UNSC S/1998/1177, 1998, p. 2). The commission established to implement the UNSC Resolution 1160 indicated that Albania was in breach of the said Reso-lution, as it expressed concern over Albania's continuous violations of the Resolution (UNSC

S/RES/1160, 1998, p. 5). Having outside prior outside support to sustain the withdrawal from the host state and resistance was crucial in laying the grounds for the actions of the host state to "invite" outside military intervention.

## Instigation of the outside military intervention: removing the host state

The Kosovo Albanian armed resistance groups, primarily the KLA's tactics, managed to place Kosovo as an intense diplomatic subject not only in the UN but also among the majority of the Great Powers gathered under the "Contact Group", including Russia.[2] Whether it was an intended tactic or not is difficult to judge, but the KLA's "hit-and-run attacks" continuously invited the indiscriminate response on the part of Yugoslav and Serb police and paramilitary forces, who did not spare civilians or entire villages (Naidu, 1999). On 23 September 1998, the UNSC adopted Resolution 1199, calling on parties fighting in Kosovo to a ceasefire (UNSC S/RES/1199, 1998). However, the ceasefire was not being upheld by either of the parties, and the conflict between the Yugoslav forces and the KLA only intensified, leading to an increased number of civilian casualties. Impatience among the international community (mainly of the West) only grew – their inability to stop the conflict with condemnation letters and statements became apparent. Less than a month later, US Ambassador Richard Holbrook went to Belgrade, where he negotiated and agreed with Milosevic to withdraw, or rather decrease, the number of military forces in Kosovo – else, NATO would authorize airstrikes against the Yugoslav forces (Williams and Scharf, 2002).

However, as Norris (2005, p. xxi) suggests, the KLA "quickly exploited the agreement and took control of military positions abandoned by the Serbs". Impatient with KLA's armed resistance, and by way of indiscriminately attempting to fight the KLA, on 15 January 1999, the Yugoslav police and paramilitary forces killed 45 ethnic Albanians in Racak, which became known as the "Racak Massacre". The Racak Massacre invited wide-ranging condemnations against Yugoslavia and its leadership. Two days after the Racak Massacre, on 17 January 1999, Yugoslavia dispatched a letter to the UNSC, which one could say only indicates Yugoslavia's indiscriminate impatience with the KLA tactics. Its letter suggests that the Yugoslav "police had to respond to such terrorist savagery, in line with their powers" (UNSC S/1999/516, 1999, p. 2). The letter also blames William Walker, the head of the OSCE Verification Mission in Kosovo, who visited the crime scene of Racak on the day it had occurred, suggesting that Walker was making threatening suggestions on what needed to be done next (UNSC S/1999/516, 1999).

At the same time, on 30 January 1999, NATO addressed a threatening letter to Slobodan Milosevic, asking him to bring those responsible for the Racak Massacre to justice and that Yugoslavia's authorities must fully cooperate with the International Criminal Tribunal for the former Yugoslavia (UNSC S/1999/107, 1999). NATO's letter to Milosevic also stated that unless Yugoslavia complies with the 25 October 1998 commitments to "ending of excessive and disproportionate use of force in accordance with these commitments", among others, NATO was ready "to take whatever measures are necessary . . . to avert a humanitarian catastrophe, by compelling compliance with the demands of the international community and the achievement of a political settlement" (UNSC S/1999/107, 1999, p. 4). NATO's letter to the UNSC also stated that it "will take all appropriate measures in case of a failure by the Kosovar Albanian side to comply with the demands of the international community" (UNSC S/1999/107, 1999, p. 4).

While talks between the Kosovo Albanian delegation and the Republic of Serbia delegation commenced in Rambouillet, the latter refused to sign a document which they claimed they had not agreed upon. In a letter dated 7 Match 1999 to the UNSC, through the Yugoslav representation in the UN, the President of the Republic of Serbia called the Rambouillet peace process a "great sham stage-managed by the United States" (UNSC S/1999/245, 1999, p. 2). The letter moreover stated that it was cynical that the Kosovo Albanian separatists "are requested to sign the agreement they had made themselves, namely, to agree to the occupation of Kosovo and Metohija by [NATO]" (UNSC S/1999/245, 1999, pp. 2–3). Importantly, given Serbia's refusal to agree with the Rambouillet Accords, Russia, as a member of the Contact Group, also refused to agree on it. However, there was also no consensus among the ranks of the KLA to sign the Rambouillet agreement, for it protected Yugoslavia's and Serbia's sovereignty over the entity. Nevertheless, the Albanian delegation, which included also the KLA, signed the agreement, opening the way for NATO to start its air strikes against Yugoslavia on 24 March 1999.

The NATO airstrikes, which lasted for over 70 days, led to the Kumanovo Agreement signed between the International Security Force (KFOR) under NATO command and Yugoslavia (and Serbia), which sealed the host state's removal from its province's territory. What finally "triggered" NATO's assault over Yugoslavia in supporting the Kosovo Albanian secessionists to remove their host state is not as clear-cut as what triggered Turkey's intervention in Cyprus. Perhaps the European Council's reaction to and support of the NATO airstrikes just two days after they had commenced could bring to light some answers. On 26 March 1999, the European Council deposited a letter to the UNSC (through Germany), in which they stated: "[w]hile the Kosovo Albanians signed the Rambouillet Accords, Belgrade's forces poured into Kosovo to start a new offensive" (UNSC S/1999/342, 1999, p. 2). The Racak Massacre, among others, also featured in the letter, where the European Council's latter claimed that the EU is

> under a moral obligation to ensure that indiscriminate behaviour and violence, which became tangible in the massacre at Racak in January 1999, are not repeated. . . . Aggression must not be rewarded. An aggressor must know that he will have to pay a high price. That is the lesson to be learnt from the twentieth century.
> *(UNSC S/1999/342, 1999, p. 3)*

In line with the Kumanovo Agreement, Yugoslavia withdrew the entire state and security apparatus from Kosovo, paving the way for the UN administration to be established on Kosovo's territory. Within a day after the Kumanovo Agreement was reached, the UNSC passed Resolution 1244, agreeing with Yugoslavia's departure, putting Kosovo under the UN administration with KFOR to secure peace in the territory under NATO's command. Kosovo declared, for the second time, its independence in 2008, which remains recognized by slightly over half of the UN member states.

## Conclusion

The chapter has attempted to shed some light on some aspects of outside military intervention in aid to secession, which has previously been researched at length. Pavković and Radan (2007) have already suggested that violent conflict in secessionist cases increases the risk of outside intervention. However, this chapter undertook a tripartite focus on the secessionists, outside interveners, and an oft-ignored part in the research – the host state itself. In doing so, it suggested that the process of instigating outside military intervention is in control of none of the three parties involved alone and that such a process is a lengthy one, if not also very costly for the sides involved. The argument that the chapter has outlined is that first, the host state unilaterally attempts and does centralize its power over the minority, or the minority's region, by removing some of the latter's powers and rights within the host state. Second, and as a result, the minority withdraws from the host state by establishing a parallel system of existence – defying the host state's unilaterally established, centralized, constitutional regime. Third, and importantly, the withdrawn minority sustains such defiance with, what I have called here, prior outside help, usually from non-state actors, such as diaspora, or neighboring states concerned with the withdrawn minority's struggle.

The host state's stubborn insistence on maintaining its centralized powers over the minority becomes marred with violence. The minority eventually begins to violently resist the host state's repressive attempts to ascertain the centrality and the dominance of the state. The minority's ability to maintain the violent resistance is difficult to understand without the continued prior outside help they receive throughout the process of withdrawal and armed resistance. Finally, what instigated Turkey's fully fledged military intervention in Cyprus or NATO's intervention in Yugoslavia have their differences. Crucial appears to be the combination of the minority's assertive armed resistance, through prior outside help, and the parent state's indiscriminate reaction to the former, leading to increased civilian casualties and increased attention by regional and international actors.

Although not its objective, what becomes apparent from the analysis and discussion, the chapter can indicate that secessionists may have much greater agency in "inviting" outside military intervention than previously assumed. Outside military intervention is not only a calculation of the intervener. The secessionists in the two cases analyzed here use various peaceful and armed resistance tactics to invite attention, and help, from abroad. The host state simply gets "trapped" in the obsession with state centrality and minority's armed resistance. In other words, secessionists are not simply chosen by outsiders; they choose to engage in such tactics that only exploit their host states' stubbornness to suppress them – leading to regional and/or international actors to intervene. Whether it is the outside interveners' self-interest to intervene can surely not be ruled out. In line with the argument developed here, however, given that they have not intervened much earlier, the outside interveners seem to also not be in complete control of the choice of whether and when to intervene.

## Notes

1 Hereinafter, Yugoslavia refers to Serb-dominated Serbia and Montenegro, which is what remained after the dissolution of the Socialist Federal Republic of Yugoslavia.
2 The "Contact Group" included a forum of the following powers: France, Germany, Italy, Russia, the United States, and the United Kingdom.

## References

A/53/341. 1998, 'Letter Dated 2 September 1998 from the Chargé d'affaires a.i. of the Permanent Mission of Yugoslavia to the United Nations Addressed to the Secretary-General', United Nations. Available at: http://daccess-ods.un.org/access.nsf/get?open&DS=A/53/341&Lang=E.
Arhsien, P.F.R. & Howells, R.A. 1981, 'Yugoslavia, Albania and the Kosovo Riots', *The World Today*, 37(11):419–427.
Artisien, P.F.R. 1984, 'A Note on Kosovo and the Future of Yugoslav-Albanian Relations: A Balkan Perspective', *Soviet Studies*, 36(2):267–276.
Bahcheli, T. 2000, 'Searching for a Cyprus Settlement: Considering Options for Creating a Federation, a Confederation, or Two Independent States', *Publius: The Journal of Federalism*, 30(1):203–216.
Bélanger, L., Duchesne, É. & Paquin, J. 2005, 'Foreign Interventions and Secessionist Movements: The Democratic Factor', *Canadian Journal of Political Science / Revue canadienne de science politique*, 38(2):435–462.
Bölükbaşi, S. 1998, 'The Cyprus Dispute and the United Nations: Peaceful Non-Settlement Between 1954 and 1996', *International Journal of Middle East Studies*, 30(3):411–434.
Camp, G.D. 1980, 'Greek-Turkish Conflict over Cyprus', *Political Science Quarterly*, 95(1):43–70.

Castleberry, H.P. 1964, 'Conflict Resolution and the Cyprus Problem', *The Western Political Quarterly*, 17(3):118–130.

Cunningham, K.G. 2013, 'Actor Fragmentation and Civil War Bargaining: How Internal Divisions Generate Civil Conflict', *American Journal of Political Science*, 57(3): 659–672.

Dodd, C.H. 2010, *The history and politics of the Cyprus conflict*. Houndmills, Basingstoke, Hampshire; New York: Palgrave Macmillan.

E/CN.4/1993/116. 1993, 'Letter Dated 10 March 1993 from the Permanent Representative of the Federal Republic of Yugoslavia to the United Nations Office at Geneva Addressed to the Assistant Secretary-General for Human Rights', United Nations. Available at: http://daccess-ods.un.org/access.nsf/get?open&DS=E/CN.4/1990/SR.39&Lang=E.

Fazal, T.M. & Griffiths, R.D. 2014, 'Membership Has Its Privileges: The Changing Benefits of Statehood', *International Studies Review*, 16(1):79–106.

Göktepe, C. 2005, 'The Cyprus Crisis of 1967 and Its Effects on Turkey's Foreign Relations', *Middle Eastern Studies*, 41(3):431–444.

Grant, T.D. 2014, 'Armed Force in Aid of Secession', *Military Law and Law of War Review*, 53(1):69–98.

Griffiths, R.D. & Wasser, L.M. 2019, 'Does Violent Secessionism Work?', *Journal of Conflict Resolution*, 63(5):1310–1336.

Hadjipavlou-Trigeorgis, M. & Trigeorgis, L. 1993, 'Cyprus: An Evolutionary Approach to Conflict Resolution', *The Journal of Conflict Resolution*, 37(2):340–360.

Hayden, R. 1992, 'The Beginning of the End of Federal Yugoslavia: The Slovenian Amendment Crisis of 1989', *The Carl Beck Papers in Russian and East European Studies*, 1001:1–37.

Herscher, A. 2013, *Violence taking place the architecture of the Kosovo conflict*. Stanford: Stanford University Press.

Högbladh, S., Pettersson, T. & Themnér, L. 2011, 'External Support–Disaggregated/Supporter Level Dataset', in *International Studies Association Convention in Montreal*, Montreal: Swedish National Data Service. Available at: https://snd.gu.se/en/catalogue/study/ext0034.

IICK. 2000, *The Kosovo report*. Oxford and New York: The Independent International Commission on Kosovo. Available at: https://reliefweb.int/sites/reliefweb.int/files/resources/6D26FF88119644CFC1256989005CD392-thekosovoreport.pdf.

Judah, T. 2008, *Kosovo: What everyone needs to know*. Oxford: Oxford University Press.

Ker-Lindsay, J. 2011, *The Cyprus problem what everyone needs to know*. Oxford: Oxford University Press. Available at: http://public.eblib.com/choice/publicfullrecord.aspx?p=689300.

King, R. & Vullnetari, J. 2009, 'Remittances, Return, Diaspora: Framing the Debate in the Context of Albania and Kosova', *Southeast European and Black Sea Studies*, 9(4):385–406.

Kıralp, Ş. 2017, 'Cyprus between Enosis, Partition and Independence: Domestic Politics, Diplomacy and External Interventions (1967–74)', *Journal of Balkan and Near Eastern Studies*, 19(6): 591–609.

Kliot, N. & Mansfield, Y. 1997, 'The Political Landscape of Partition', *Political Geography*, 16(6): 495–521.

Koinova, M. 2013, 'Four Types of Diaspora Mobilization: Albanian Diaspora Activism For Kosovo Independence in the US and the UK', *Foreign Policy Analysis*, 9(4):433–453.

Kosovo Agency of Statistics 2018, *Statistical Yearbook of the Republic of Kosovo 2018*. Prishtina.

Kostovicova, D. 2005, *Kosovo: The politics of identity and space*. London; New York: Routledge.

Morag, N. 2004, 'Cyprus and the Clash of Greek and Turkish Nationalisms', *Nationalism and Ethnic Politics*, 10(4):595–624.

Naidu, M.V. 1999, 'NATO'S War on Yugoslavia: Issues, Actors, and Prospects', *Peace Research*, 31(2):1–23.

New York Times 1964, 'Cyprus Problem = Makarios Problem', *The New York Times*, 18 October. Available at: www.nytimes.com/1964/10/18/archives/cyprus-problem-makarios-problem.html.

Norris, J. 2005, *Collision course: NATO, Russia, and Kosovo*. Westport: Praeger.

Osmani, J. & Manaj, R. 2014, *Ndarja Administrativo-Territoriale e Kosovës 1944–2010*, Special Edition. Prishtina: Kosova Academy of Sciences and Arts (42).

Österud, Ö. 1997, 'The narrow gate: Entry to the club of sovereign states', *Review of International Studies*, 23(2):167–184.

Pavković, A. 2000, *The Fragmentation of Yugoslavia: Nationalism and War in the Balkans*. London: Palgrave Macmillan UK.

Pavković, A. & Radan, P. 2007, *Creating new states: Theory and practice of secession*. Hampshire: Ashgate.

Pegg, S. 1998, *International society and the de facto state*. Aldershot: Ashgate.

Perritt, H.H. 2008, *Kosovo liberation army: The inside story of an insurgency*. Urbana; Chicago: University of Illinois Press.

Pettersson, T. et al. 2021, 'Organized Violence 1989–2020, With a Special Emphasis on Syria', *Journal of Peace Research*, 58(4): 809–825.

Pula, B. 2004, 'The Emergence of the Kosovo "Parallel State," 1988–19921', *Nationalities Papers*, 32(4): 797–826.

Ramet, S.P. 2002, *Balkan babel: Disintegration of Yugoslavia from the death of Tito to ethnic war*. Boulder: West-view Press.

Roberts, A. 1978, 'Yugoslavia: The Constitution and the Succession', *The World Today*, 34(4): 136–146.

Silber, L. & Little, A. 1997, *Yugoslavia: death of a nation*. New York: Penguin Books.

Treaty of Alliance. 1960, 'Greece–Turkey–Cyprus: Treaty of Alliance', United Nations Peacemaker. Available at: https://peacemaker.un.org/cyprus-greece-turkey-alliance60.

Treaty of Guarantee. 1960, 'United Kingdom of Great Britain and Northern Ireland, Greece and Turkey and Cyprus: Treaty of Guarantee', United Nations Peacemaker. Available at: https://peacemaker.un.org/cyprus-greece-turkey-guarantee60.

UNGA. 1960, 'Declaration on the Granting of Independence to Colonial Countries and Peoples', United Nations. Available at: https://undocs.org/en/A/RES/1514(XV).

UNGA A/C.3/50/12. 1995, 'Letter Dated 6 December 1995 from the Chargé d'affaires a.i. of the Permanent Mission of Yugoslavia to the United Nations Addressed to the Secretary-General', United Nations. Available at: http://daccess-ods.un.org/access.nsf/get?open&DS=A/C.3/50/12&Lang=E.

UNSC. 1967, 'Letter Dated 30 June 1967 from the Permanent Representative of Turkey Addressed to the Secretary-General', United Nations. Available at: http://daccess-ods.un.org/access.nsf/get?open&DS=S/8028&Lang=E.

UNSC 8/5488. 1963, 'Letter Dated 26 December 1963 from the Permanent Representative of Cyprus addressed to the President of the Security Council', United Nations. Available at: http://daccess-ods.un.org/access.nsf/get?open&DS=S/5488&Lang=E.

UNSC S/1998/1177. 1998, 'Letter Dated 16 December 1998 from the Chargé D'Affaires a.i. of the Permanent Mission of Yugoslavia to the United Nations Addressed to the Secretary-General', United Nations. Available at: http://daccess-ods.un.org/access.nsf/get?open&DS=S/1998/1177&Lang=E.

UNSC S/1999/96. 1999, 'Letter Dated 29 January from the Permanent Representative of the of the United Kingdom of Great Britain and Northern Ireland to the United Nations Addressed to the President of the Security Council', United Nations. Available at: http://daccess-ods.un.org/access.nsf/get?open&DS=S/1999/96&Lang=E.

UNSC S/1999/107. 1999, 'Letter Dated 30 January 1999 from the Secretary-General of the North Atlantic Treaty Organization Addressed to the President of Yugoslavia', United Nations. Available at: http://daccess-ods.un.org/access.nsf/get?open&DS=S/1999/107&Lang=E.

UNSC S/1999/245. 1999, 'Letter Dated 7 March1999 from the Chargé d'affaires a.i. of the Permanent Mission of Yugoslavia to the United Nations Addressed to the President of the Security Council', United Nations. Available at: http://daccess-ods.un.org/access.nsf/get?open&DS=S/1999/245&Lang=E.

UNSC S/1999/342. 1999, 'Letter Dated 26 March 1999 from the Permanent Representative of Germany to the United Nations Addressed to the Secretary-General', United Nations. Available at: http://daccess-ods.un.org/access.nsf/get?open&DS=S/1999/342&Lang=E.

UNSC S/1999/516. 1999, 'Letter Dated 17 January 1999 from the Chargé D'Affaires a.i. of the Permanent Mission of Yugoslavia to the United Nations Addressed to the Secretary-General', United Nations. Available at: http://daccess-ods.un.org/access.nsf/get?open&DS=S/1999/516&Lang=E.

UNSC S/5731. 1964, 'Letter Dated 1 June 1964 from the Permanent Representative of Turkey Addressed to the President of the Security Council', United Nations. Available at: http://daccess-ods.un.org/access.nsf/get?open&DS=S/5731&Lang=E.

UNSC S/5742. 1964, 'Letter Dated 4 June 1964 from the Permanent Representative of Cyprus addressed to the President of the Security Council', United Nations. Available at: http://daccess-ods.un.org/access.nsf/get?open&DS=S/5742&Lang=E.

UNSC S/5958. 1964, 'Letter Dated 10 September 1964 from the Permanent Representative of Turkey addressed to the Secretary-General'. United Nations. Available at: http://daccess-ods.un.org/access.nsf/get?open&DS=S/5958&Lang=E.

UNSC S/6168. 1965, 'Letter Dated 28 January 1965 from the Permanent Representative of Turkey to the Secretary-General', United Nations. Available at: http://daccess-ods.un.org/access.nsf/get?open&DS=S/6168&Lang=E.

UNSC S/6173. 1965, 'Letter Dated 4 February 1965 from the Permanent Representative of Cyprus to the Secretary-General', United Nations. Available at: http://daccess-ods.un.org/access.nsf/get?open&DS=S/6173&Lang=E.

UNSC S/6212. 1965, 'Letter Dated 2 March 1965 from the Permanent Representative of Cyprus addressed to the Secretary-General', United Nations. Available at: http://daccess-ods.un.org/access.nsf/get?open&DS=S/6212&Lang=E.

UNSC S/6334. 1965, 'Letter Dated 6 May 1965 from the Permanent Representative of Cyprus to the Secretary-General', United Nations. Available at: http://daccess-ods.un.org/access.nsf/get?open&DS=S/6334&Lang=E.

UNSC S/8324. 1968, 'Letter Dated 5 January 1968 from the Permanent Representative of Cyprus Addressed to the Secretary-General', United Nations. Available at: http://daccess-ods.un.org/access.nsf/get?open&DS=S/8324&Lang=E.

UNSC S/8327. 1968, 'Letter Dated 8 January 1968 from the Permanent Representative of Turkey Addressed to the Secretary-General', United Nations. Available at: http://daccess-ods.un.org/access.nsf/get?open&DS=S/8327&Lang=E.

UNSC S/11341. 1974, 'Letter Dated 17 July 1974 from the Permanent Representative of Turkey to the United Nations Addressed to the Secretary-General', United Nations. Available at: http://daccess-ods.un.org/access.nsf/get?open&DS=S/11341&Lang=E.

UNSC S/21132. 1990, 'Letter Dated 7 February 1990 from the Permanent Representative of Albania to the United Nations addressed to the Secretary-General'. United Nations. Available at: https://documents-dds-ny.un.org/doc/UNDOC/GEN/N90/030/70/pdf/N9003070.pdf?OpenElement.

UNSC S/25662. 1993, 'Letter Dated 24 April 1993 from the Permanent Representative of Albania to the United Nations Addressed to the President of the Security Council', United Nations. Available at: https://documents-dds-ny.un.org/doc/UNDOC/GEN/N93/238/43/pdf/N9323843.pdf?OpenElement.

UNSC S/25711, 1993. 'Letter Dated 30 April 1993 from the Charge D'Affaires a.i. of the Premanent Mission of Yugoslavia to the United Nations Addressed to the President of the Security Council', United Nations. Available at: http://daccess-ods.un.org/access.nsf/get?open&DS=S/25711&Lang=E.

UNSC S/RES/1160, 1998. 'Resolution 1160 (1998)', United Nations. Available at: http://unscr.com/en/resolutions/doc/1160.

UNSC S/RES/1199, 1998. 'Resolution 1199 (1998)', United Nations. Available at: http://unscr.com/en/resolutions/doc/1199.

Vickers, M. 1998, *Between Serb and Albanian: A history of Kosovo*. New York: Columbia University Press.

Williams, P.R. & Scharf, M.P. 2002, *Peace with justice?: War crimes and accountability in the former Yugoslavia*. Lanham: Rowman & Littlefield.

# 23

# INTERNATIONAL POWER POLITICS AND SECESSION

*Milena Sterio*

## Introduction

The right to self-determination refers to a people's right to choose its political, economic, and social status. This principle is enshrined in various international law documents and also present in state practice – in particular, the principle of self-determination was the theoretical underpinning of decolonization in the 1960s and 1970s. Self-determination is intrinsically linked to the process of secession, whereby the theoretical underpinning of some secessions may be found in the idea of external self-determination. More recently, questions have arisen regarding the scope of the principle of self-determination, and its applicability in the non-decolonization context, to some secessionist struggles. In particular, it remains uncertain that international law itself can provide satisfactory answers to outcomes of different secessionist struggles across the globe, and it may be necessary to analyze the role of power politics in (de)legitimizing secessionist movements. This chapter will first analyze the history of the self-determination principle, before turning to an analysis of its beneficiaries, its contours, and its link to the disputed process of secession. It will then turn to an analysis of the role of power politics in secessions, while concluding that almost all successful secessionist movements have enjoyed the support of at least some great powers.

## History of self-determination

The right to self-determination dates back to the end of the eighteenth century, when it was expressed in the American and French Revolutions as a principle which would guarantee democratic consent of the people within an emerging state entity (Franck 1998). In the nineteenth century, the right to self-determination was used as the driving ideology behind Latin American decolonization (Alvarez 1909). After World War I, President Woodrow Wilson of the United States relied on the principle of self-determination to argue in favor of the creation of nation-states, following the dissolution of the Austro-Hungarian and Ottoman Empires, as corresponding to the will of their respective peoples. During the same time period, Vladimir Lenin, the leader of the Soviet Union, also relied on the principle of self-determination to explain the necessity for peoples to exercise their free will and rid themselves of bourgeois oppression. During World War II, self-determination was relied upon by the Nazi leadership in

DOI: 10.4324/9781003036593-27

order to justify the reunification of the German people (Sterio 2018a). Although leaders relied on self-determination as a political ideology prior to the creation of the United Nations (UN), self-determination did not morph into a legal principle until the promulgation of the United Nations Charter (UN Charter).

Article 1 of the UN Charter provides that one of the main purposes of the UN is to "develop friendly relations among nations based on respect for the principle of equal rights and self-determination of peoples." The UN Charter thus affirmed self-determination as one of the foundational principles binding all UN member states. Post-UN Charter, additional international law documents have reaffirmed the principle of self-determination. Article 1 of the International Covenant on Civil and Political Rights (ICCPR) confirms that all peoples have the right to self-determination, and that "[b]y virtue of that right they freely determine their political status and freely pursue their economic, social and cultural development" (ICCPR 1966: art. 1). The 1960 Declaration on the Granting of Independence to Colonial Countries and Peoples contains identical language in its Article 2 (UNGA 1960). And the 1970 so-called Friendly Relations Declaration further enshrined the legal principle of self-determination within the UN system, by declaring that colonized peoples have the right to self-determination under the UN Charter, and that all states have a duty to refrain from forcible actions which would deprive peoples of their right to self-determination. However, the Friendly Relations Declaration posits the right to self-determination within the decolonization paradigm and bestows it only on peoples whose governments are not representative of their interests:

> Nothing in the foregoing paragraphs shall be construed as authorizing or encouraging any action which would dismember or impair, totally or in part, the territorial integrity or political unity of sovereign and independent States conducting themselves in compliance with the principle of equal rights and self-determination of peoples as described above and thus possessed of a government representing the whole people belonging to the territory without distinction as to race, creed or colour.
>
> *(UNGA 1970)*

In fact, several scholars have interpreted the Friendly Relations Declaration as affirming the right to self-determination in the decolonization context only, arguing that the Declaration does not confer a broader right of self-determination for groups or peoples whose governments act adequately to protect their interest (Sterio 2013; Horowitz 2003).

In the post-decolonization era, other scholars have advanced the argument that international law has evolved to embrace the right to self-determination outside of the decolonization paradigm. First, scholars have argued that the Friendly Relations Declaration provisions, read in context with the ICCPR and the International Covenant on Economic, Social and Cultural Rights, as well as in the context of subsequent UN declarations in the 1990s, which have all affirmed the right to self-determination, demonstrates that the right exists for both colonized and non-colonized peoples (Sterio 2013; Hanna 1999). Scholars have also argued, similarly, that oppressed groups may be treated as if they were pseudo-colonies. "If the government is not representative, the oppressed group may be treated as if they were under colonial domination and will have the right to self-determination. In essence, they will be considered a pseudo-colony" (Hanna 1999). Second, scholars have advanced the idea that all peoples should have the right to self-determination through meaningful choice and democratic processes. According to this argument, international law has evolved to reflect a commitment to democracy, which entails the recognition of full participatory rights for groups within established states (Orentlicher 2003). State practice, beginning in the late twentieth century, also reflects the same idea – the willingness of the international community to examine self-determination claims through the lens of democratic principles. For example, the UN Security Council authorized a military intervention in Haiti in 1994, in order to restore Haiti's legitimately elected president. There has been widespread international support for plebiscites in the context of self-determination claims in order to ascertain the will of the people, in East Timor, South Sudan, Québec, and Scotland. Several separatist groups have relied on the international law right to self-determination in their independence quests, including in Québec, the republics of former Yugoslavia, South Ossetia, and Abkhazia. Finally, some scholars have attempted to separate legitimate self-determination claims from illegitimate ones, by arguing that the right to self-determination only attaches to peoples with territorial claims to well-defined territorial units (Oeter 2014). In sum, support exists among scholars as well as within state practice for the argument that the principle of self-determination applies in both the colonial and non-colonial paradigms.

The International Court of Justice (ICJ) has addressed the principle of self-determination in several cases. In the East Timor case, Portugal, East Timor's last colonizer, sued Australia, arguing that the latter did not have the legal right to enter into a treaty with Indonesia over Timorese natural resources because Portugal was the true sovereign of East Timor, and not Indonesia, which had illegally occupied the island (ICJ 1995). The ICJ refused to solve the dispute, and thus avoided ruling on whether the people of East Timor had the right to self-determination, by invoking the so-called indispensable third-party doctrine. In this case, the ICJ thus set aside the opportunity to develop normative law on self-determination. In the Kosovo advisory opinion, the ICJ similarly avoided making proclamations on the issue of self-determination:

> The Court is not required by the question it has been asked to take a position on whether international law conferred a positive entitlement on Kosovo unilaterally to declare its independence, or, a fortiori, on whether international law generally confers an entitlement on entities situated within a State unilaterally to break away from it.
>
> *(ICJ 2010: para. 56)*

Instead, in this case, the ICJ decided that the Kosovar unilateral declaration of independence was not adopted in violation of international law, without addressing other related issues of self-determination and secession.

In the Western Sahara Advisory Opinion, the ICJ determined that the people of Western Sahara had the right to self-determination, but it refused to rule on the legality of the Moroccan and Mauritanian territorial claims to this region. In this opinion, the ICJ implied that the principle of territorial integrity may prevail over self-determination claims, where there is solid evidence of the existence of a territorial claim over a particular region, despite the fact that such a region does not wish to be governed by the entity asserting the territorial claim (ICJ 1975). The ICJ did not, however, explain how such conflicts between territoriality and self-determination could be resolved, nor did it shed further light on external self-determination or secession.

Finally, in the "Wall" case, the ICJ affirmed the existence of the right to self-determination for the Palestinian people (ICJ 2004). This case is significant because in it the ICJ recognized the right to self-determination for a non-colonized people (although Palestinians represent an occupied people, whose situation can be equated to that of a colonized people).

In light of these decisions, it may be concluded that the ICJ has recognized the right to self-determination for colonized and occupied peoples, but that it has not provided clarification as to how to resolve tensions between territoriality and self-determination, and whether the right to self-determination firmly applies in the non-decolonization and non-occupation paradigms.

In sum, although international law recognizes the right to self-determination for colonized peoples, it is disputed whether international law also recognizes this right outside of the decolonization paradigm, and, if the right exists, who its beneficiaries are and what the contours of the right might be. The next two sections discusses these two complex issues.

## The definition of a "people" for the purposes of self-determination

International law posits that "peoples" have a right to self-determination. However, the term "people" has not been defined in any international treaties or other documents. Most scholars agree that the term connotes a group with a common identity and link to a specific territory, and that "peoplehood" entails the fulfillment of a subjective and an objective element. First, the subjective element consists of a commonly held belief by members of a group that they constitute a unit. Second, the objective element examines whether members of a group share commonalities, such as the same language, culture, ethnicity, political will, and a territorial claim (Scharf 2003).

It is important to distinguish peoples from minority groups. The latter have been defined as a group numerically inferior to the rest of the population of a state, in a non-dominant position, whose members – being nationals of the state – possess ethnic, religious, or linguistic characteristics differing from those of the rest of the population and show, if only implicitly, a sense of solidarity, directed towards preserving their culture, religion, or language (Capotorti 1977).

Several different international law instruments protect minority rights. Article 27 of the ICCPR provides that "persons belonging to such minorities shall not be denied the right . . . to enjoy their own culture, to profess and practice their own religion, or to use their own language" (ICCPR 1966: art. 27). The UN's Human Rights Committee has clarified, in a general comment regarding Article 27, that states have a positive obligation to protect minority rights, and that "[t]he protection of these rights is directed towards ensuring the survival and continued development of the cultural, religious and social identity of the minorities concerned" (HRC 1994: 108). In addition to the ICCPR, the so-called Copenhagen Document protects minority rights by stating that "[p]ersons belonging to national minorities have the right freely to express, preserve and develop their ethnic, cultural, linguistic or religious identity and to maintain and develop their culture in all aspects" (Copenhagen Conference 1990: para. 32). Minority rights are also protected by the Framework Convention for the Protection of National Minorities, which guarantees to ethnic minorities the right to equal treatment before the law, as well as additional rights to use their language and develop their culture, ethnic identity, religion, and traditions (Framework Convention 1995: arts 4, 5, 10, 34).

Several considerations are important to note regarding the distinctions which exist between minority groups and peoples. First, one such main distinction between minority groups and peoples is that the former live within a mother state which is representative of their interests; such minority groups thus do not need to exercise autonomy or self-determination vis-à-vis the larger mother state. Minority rights in general are instead focused on the preservation of the group's identity and culture, and not on its political rights. "Minority rights protect the existence of national, religious, linguistic or ethnic groups, facilitate the development of their identity and ensure that they can fully and effectively participate in all aspects of public life within the state" (Weller 2008). Second, minority groups do not necessarily have territorially linked autonomy claims. Unlike peoples, which are typically viewed as a whole or entire group within a specific territorial unit, minorities may constitute territorially dispersed pockets or smaller subgroups of a whole people. Third, indigenous groups may qualify as peoples or minority groups: some indigenous groups may identify as a single people and lay a particular territorial claim to a region within a larger mother state, while other such groups may be too small or too territorially dispersed to constitute a people (Sterio 2018a). Finally, some groups, although inhabitants of a particular territory, may not identify as a people and may thus be dispossessed of a valid self-determination claim. For example, although the population of Gibraltar inhabits a particular territorial unit, this population has not exercised a particular self-determination claim. In fact, the distinction between minority groups and peoples is crucial in international law, as it limits the applicability of the principle of self-determination; otherwise, if non-people were also entitled to self-determination, "there would be no limit to fragmentation, and peace, security and economic well-being for all would become ever more difficult to achieve" (Weller 2008).

In sum, the principle of self-determination under international law applies to peoples only and does not extend to minorities or other groups. Although "people" is undefined in international treaties or other documents, sufficient consensus exists in the international community to delineate which groups qualify as peoples and to thereby limit the applicability of the principle of self-determination. An additional way in which the application of the principle of self-determination has been curtailed is through the distinction between so-called internal versus external self-determination, which will be discussed directly in the next section.

## Internal v. external self-determination

Self-determination of peoples can be achieved in various ways: through autonomy, self-government, free association, or, in the most extreme cases, through separation from the mother state and the formation of a new state. Self-determination thus exists on two levels: through internal means of expressing autonomy, and through external means of secession. Many peoples have been able, through recent history, to exercise internal self-determination within a larger mother state. Examples include the Québécois in Canada, as well as the Scots in the United Kingdom. In addition, it may be argued that peoples and other groups have been allowed to exercise internal self-determination through autonomy within larger federal states, such as in Brazil, and in the former Soviet Union and Yugoslavia, prior to their dissolutions (Sterio 2013). The most prevalent modes of internal self-determination include autonomy, protectorates, trusteeships, and free association.

Autonomy typically entails the formation and existence of a provincial government, but it is also possible to achieve autonomy through the free exercise of political, social, educational, linguistic, and cultural rights for the relevant people (Hannum 1990). Peoples which enjoy meaningful autonomy within their larger mother states are deemed to have their internal self-determination rights fulfilled. In addition, autonomy can also take the form of a protectorate, trusteeship, or free association. A protectorate is a dependent territory which possesses local autonomy and a degree of independence while remaining a territorial unit of a larger mother state (Crawford 2006). A protectorate is different from a colony, because the former has local rulers who were freely chosen or elected. Examples of protectorates include Guam, Mariana Islands, Puerto Rico, and the Virgin Islands (all protectorates of the United States). A trusteeship is a former colonial unit, administered by another state in the best interest of its people and for the sake of preserving international peace and security. The trusteeship system was created after World War II, within the auspices of the UN, as a management system of colonial units which were working their way toward independence. Palau was the last trust territory to gain independence in 1994, and the trusteeship system has since been dismantled. To the extent that trusteeship encompassed the free will of the governed people, it could have been viewed as a legitimate form of internal self-determination (Sterio 2018a). Finally, free association is a relationship in which a typically smaller state chooses to delegate certain sovereign functions to a larger state. It can also be viewed as a meaningful form of internal self-determination if it is based on the free will of the smaller state's people. Free association is a common form of political self-expression for micro-states, which may not have the territorial or economic capacity to exist completely independently. Examples of free association include the Cook Islands and Niue, which are associated with New Zealand, and Palau, the Marshall Islands, and the Federated States of Micronesia, which are associated with the United States (Dumienski 2014). Additional examples of free association involve five European micro-states: Andorra, which has delegated national defense to Spain and France; San Marino and Monaco, which have delegated defense to Italy and France respectively; Vatican City, whose defense is ensured by Italy and Switzerland; and Lichtenstein, whose diplomatic relations are conducted by Switzerland. Finally, similar examples exist in Oceania: Pacific Island nations of Kiribati and Samoa have delegated their national defenses to Australia and New Zealand respectively, and Nauru, which has delegated its national defense to Australia (Sterio 2018a). It may be noted that free association, unlike autonomy through a provincial government, a protectorate, or a trusteeship, is different as it represents a form of self-determination which blends internal and external self-determination. In fact, the associated state functions as an independent state but voluntarily cedes parts of its sovereignty to another state. Free association is similar to other modes of internal self-determination if one assumes that it is based on the free will of the relevant people, as all modes of internal self-determination described earlier assume that the relevant people has expressed its will as to how it wishes to govern itself. As a general matter, internal self-determination is well accepted in international law and less controversial than external self-determination.

The right to external self-determination entails a separation of the people from the mother state. This version of self-determination is controversial and has not been explicitly recognized as legal outside of the decolonization paradigm. No international treaty or document addresses the distinction between internal and external self-determination directly, but most international law scholars agree that the right to external self-determination accrues only as a last resort, in most extreme situations where a people's right to internal self-determination is not respected by the mother state (Scharf 2003). Precedent for this distinction between internal and external self-determination exists in case law. The Aaland Islands case decided within the auspices of the League of Nations, the Québec secession case decided by the Supreme Court of Canada, the Badinter Commission opinions on the rights of various republics in the wake of the dissolution of the former Yugoslavia, and the ICJ's Kosovo advisory opinion all shed light on this important distinction between internal and external self-determination.

The Aaland Islands are a small island nation geographically situated between Sweden and Finland. When Finland became an independent nation following World War I, the Aaland Islands became a part of Finland. Aalanders claimed that they were ethnically Swedish and expressed a desire to separate from Finland and join Sweden. The case ended up before the League of Nations, which formed a special Commission of Rapporteurs in order to resolve the dispute. The Commission of Rapporteurs held that the Aalanders had various autonomy rights within Finland, and that their right to separate from Finland had thus not been triggered. The Commission suggested that such a separation through secession would be available as "a last resort when the State lacks either the will or the power to enact and apply just and effective guarantees" for minority group rights (ICR 1921). Without adopting the jargon of internal versus external self-determination, the Commission of Rapporteurs, in effect, held that groups have the right to internal self-determination within their existing mother state, and that only in cases where this right is not being respected by the mother state do such group rights to external self-determination accrue.

A similar view was espoused more recently by the Supreme Court of Canada in the Québec case. The francophone Québécois population of Canada had been demanding greater autonomy throughout the second half of the twentieth century. In a 1995 referendum, the Québécois voted by an extremely slim margin to remain a part of Canada. In light of the close referendum result, the Canadian Parliament requested the Supreme Court of Canada to issue an opinion on the legality of a proposed secession of Québec. The Court defined internal self-determination as "a people's pursuit of its political, economic, social and cultural development within the framework of an existing state," and external self-determination as arising "in only the most extreme cases" when a people's right to internal self-determination is being totally frustrated (Secession Reference 1998: paras 126, 135). In addition, the Court was careful to analyze the right to self-determination within the context of the principle of territorial integrity of existing states. The Court thus emphasized that the any right to self-determination "must be sufficiently limited to prevent threats to an existing state's territorial integrity or the stability of relations between sovereign states" (Secession Reference 1998: para. 130). The Court concluded that the right to self-determination must be exercised internally, while protecting the territorial integrity of existing states, and that only in extreme cases may a people accrue the right to external self-determination. Because the Court concluded that the Québécois' rights to internal self-determination were being respected by Canada, the Court declined to elaborate on circumstances where a non-colonized and non-occupied people would have such a right to external self-determination.

The Badinter Commission adopted a similar view in its opinions issued in the context of the dissolution of Yugoslavia. In its *Opinion No. 2*, the Commission held that international law "does not spell out all the implications of the right to self-determination" and that the right "must not involve changes to existing frontiers at the time of independence" (Trifunovska 1994: 474). In the Kosovo Advisory Opinion, the ICJ declined to address the contours of the right to self-determination. Instead, the Court held that the Kosovar Albanians' unilateral declaration of independence in and of itself did not violate any specific international law norms (ICJ 2010). However, the Court did not declare whether Kosovar Albanians had the right to external self-determination through remedial secession.

In light of these cases, it may be argued that international jurisprudence suggests that the right to external self-determination should be viewed as a measure of last resort, and that the right to self-determination ought to be exercised internally, within the confines of the existing mother state, whenever possible. Recent international reactions to the attempted secessions of Catalonia and Kurdistan also confirm this skeptical view of external self-determination. In both cases, the attempted separations were widely condemned and criticized, while the territorial integrity of Spain and Iraq respectively were emphasized and protected (Sterio 2018b). In sum, at best, it may be argued that only some non-colonized peoples whose rights to internal self-determination have been completely frustrated and abused by their mother state may claim the right to external self-determination through remedial secession. The following section will discuss the difference between the principle of self-determination and the process of secession.

## Self-determination and secession: a right and a process?

A traditional view of international law separates the legal principle of self-determination from the state formation process of secession; while self-determination is a legal right which attaches to specific peoples, secession is a factual issue which is not regulated by international law. The following section will discuss the relationship between the right to self-determination and the process of secession.

Secession is a process of state formation which entails the separation of a portion of an existing state in order to form its own state. Successful secessions have been rare in history; some examples include the secessions of Bangladesh (East Pakistan) from Pakistan in 1971, Eritrea from Ethiopia in 1991, and the Baltic States from the former Soviet Union in 1990. Secessions have been traditionally viewed as a question of fact, evidenced by the existence of a new state which has encompassed the seceding entity (Sterio 2018a). The Badinter Commission also confirmed that secessions are questions of fact. According to this factual view of secession, international law has little to do with regulating the process: secessionist struggles are issues of domestic law, and only if a secessionist movement is able to establish control over a specific territorial area and achieve separation from the mother state will international law and relations begin to apply.

Scholars have cited the Bangladesh separation from Pakistan as an example of an effective secession, not because the people of Bangladesh had a legal right to secede, but because they were able to de facto separate from Pakistan and form their own state. "What brought about the recognition of the new entity by the international community was simply the principle of effectiveness. Bangladesh had emerged as an uncontested new State on the international stage" (Tomuschat 2006). In addition, Eritrea's separation from Ethiopia has been viewed as a successful secession, because Eritrea had been entitled to internal autonomy rights within Ethiopia, which the latter reneged upon, and because a subsequent Ethiopian government itself recognized the Eritrean right to independence. "[T]he whole process of secession was oriented towards remedying the wrong suffered by the population as a consequence of the Ethiopian decision to do away with the autonomy they had been promised to enjoy" (Tomuschat 2006). Finally, the case of Kosovo has been analyzed by some as another example of an effective secession (Walter 2014). Yet, in all three cases, internationally recognized states were overwhelmingly reluctant to acknowledge specific claims of external self-determination or to recognize the legal right to secession.

Some scholars have, more recently, discussed secession as a legal right – either from a philosophical standpoint (Brilmayer 1991; Buchanan 1991; Orentlicher 1998), or as a remedial process, justified in instances where the relevant people has been irreparably harmed. The "right" to remedial secession flows from the right to external self-determination, and scholars who advocate in favor of this view argue that both international human rights norms and *jus ad bellum* interventionist rules apply to protect the people whose rights have been abused by its mother state, and which has thereby accrued to right to seek external self-determination through remedial secession.

> It appears that the grounds with the potential to justify the assertion of a right of secession are exactly the same as those which members of the international community may invoke in their quest to assist an oppressed minority against a tyrannical government. . . . On the basis of this deductive reasoning, remedial secession should be acknowledged as part and parcel of positive law.
>
> *(Tomuschat 2006)*

The best illustration of this type of reasoning may be the 1999 NATO-led military campaign against the Federal Republic of Yugoslavia (FRY), to protect Kosovar Albanians from abuses inflicted upon them by the FRY government. This military intervention, justified on the grounds of humanitarian law, ultimately paved the way for the Kosovar Albanians to unilaterally declare Kosovo's independence from the FRY. Some scholars have advanced the argument that states should be able to intervene and use force against another state in order to support a secessionist movement if and when the threshold of humanitarian intervention has been reached. "Essentially, the conditions upon which the permissibility of humanitarian intervention depends, and the conditions under which a group suffering grave discrimination may invoke a right to self-determination and secession, must be the same" (Tomuschat 2006).

Moreover, those who embrace the linkage between self-determination and secession posit that secession cannot be formalistically viewed as a factual process and that, instead, if one accepts that non-colonized oppressed peoples have the right to external self-determination, such peoples also have the right to secession. This argument can be deduced from an analysis of the Friendly Relations Declaration, which provides that states whose governments are representative of all peoples have the right to be free from territorial interference. Conversely, the Declaration can be interpreted to indicate that states which lack such legitimacy are not immune from secessionist claims. "These Declarations [the Friendly Relations Declaration and the Vienna Declaration] indicate that secession may be legitimate in very limited circumstances and that a case by case analysis is necessary to determine whether the right to self-determination includes the right to secede" (Hanna 1999). This type of reasoning is also present in the Canadian Supreme Court's opinion regarding the possible secession of Québec. In its opinion, the Court equated the situation of oppressed peoples, who are blocked from a meaningful exercise of internal self-determination, with that of colonized and subjugated peoples which clearly have the right to external self-determination. The Court thus insinuated that, in some circumstances, an oppressed people would have the right to exercise external self-determination and thus secede from its mother state (Secession Reference 1998). Scholars have posited that states which engage in massive human rights violations, such as abusing peoples and depriving them of meaningful internal self-determination, lose sovereignty over parts of their territory. Secession thus arises as a remedial right, in situations where "a given human community suffers unbearable persecution" (Tomuschat 2006).

Despite all this, it may be concluded that international law embraces the principle of self-determination, but that it remains doubtful whether positive law recognizes a "right" to secession as a component of the right to external self-determination. Thus, while self-determination and secession remain linked, it would be accurate to conclude that present-day international law distinguishes between the legal principle of self-determination and the factual process of state formation through secession.

The following section will address the right to external self-determination, through remedial secession, through the prism of power politics. In fact, it may be argued that international law does not provide satisfactory answers to the question of why some peoples have been able to exercise external self-determination and to secede from their mother states, and that it is power politics which provides better explanations for the different outcomes of various secessionist struggles across the globe.

## External self-determination/secession and power politics

As described earlier, international law is somewhat inconclusive on the contours of the right to external self-determination. Although it is clear in international law that peoples have a right to self-determination, it remains uncertain whether non-colonized peoples have the right to external self-determination outside of the decolonization or occupation contexts. In fact, it may be argued that power politics play a tremendous role in determining the outcomes of such external self-determination quests, and that virtually all peoples which have been successful in achieving external self-determination have enjoyed the support of one or more great powers.

Great powers are the most powerful states in the international arena; these include the veto-holding members of the Security Council (United States, United Kingdom, France,

Russia, and China), as well as additional economic and military powerhouses, such as Germany, Japan, and India, and non-declared nuclear states such as Pakistan and Israel. It may be argued that rogue nations, such as Iran or North Korea, also belong to the great powers "club," due to their unpredictable foreign policy and volatile leadership (Sterio 2013). Great powers have been historically able to exercise tremendous influence on the outcome of various self-determination struggles.

First, a self-determination-seeking people needs to prove that it has been oppressed by its mother state, in a manner which clearly demonstrates that the mother state is unwilling to grant this people internal self-determination. Only peoples which are able to draw international attention to their suffering at the hands of their mother states have traditionally been able to garner support for their independence-seeking cause. For example, the world was appalled at the suffering of the Kosovar Albanians inflicted against them by the Milosevic-led Serbian authorities. Similarly, the East Timorese were able to depict decades of human rights abuses by the Indonesian government, and the South Sudanese were able to highlight abuses committed by the Khartoum government and government-directed militias (Sterio 2013). Yet, great powers play an important role in the media and in the way that conflicts are portrayed. For example, great powers may portray the secessionist group as the culprit in a civil war, or they may label the mother state as a human rights oppressor. For a self-determination-seeking group, it is crucial to garner the support of some of the great powers, which will then shape the appropriate narrative of the group as the victim deserving of external self-determination.

Second, most peoples which have been able to exercise external self-determination have done so when the mother state's central government has been weakened. In fact, none of the peoples who have succeeded in asserting their rights to self-determination has been governed by a strong, powerful government. For example, central governments in Serbia, Indonesia, or Sudan had been plagued by decades of unrest and violence, which contributed to their lack of stability and power. If great powers choose to support the secessionist group logistically, strategically, politically, or militarily, this will contribute further toward weakening the mother state's central government and will facilitate the exercise of external self-determination (Sterio 2013).

Third, most successful self-determination-seeking peoples have been able to attract the support of and involvement of international organizations, such as the UN. Great powers can influence major international organizations into becoming involved in a conflict, in a manner which ultimately contributes to the secessionist group's chances of success. Organizations such as NATO, the UN, and the European Union were present in Kosovo for many years. Similarly, the UN was present in East Timor and South Sudan. The involvement of such international organizations, with the support and encouragement of some of the great powers, can contribute toward the weakening of the mother state's sovereignty and power over the secessionist group and region (Sterio 2013). Finally, almost all successful self-determination-seeking groups have been able to garner the support of some of the great powers. Kosovar Albanians were directly supported by the United States; such American support may have encouraged other nations to also recognize Kosovo as an independent state. Similarly, during the Cold War, most western great powers supported Indonesia, which was perceived as an ally against Vietnam and other pro-Communist countries in Asia. Post–Cold War, western great powers embraced the plight of the East Timorese and became willing to accept their quest for independence from Indonesia. Finally, post–September 11, great powers began to fear the rise of the Islamic state of Sudan; they thus embraced the plight of the South Sudanese and supported this group's quest for independence, in a geopolitical maneuver which would weaken Sudan (Sterio 2013). Even the idea of humanitarian intervention remains embedded in this idea of approval by great powers. Humanitarian intervention is always organized, structured, financed, and led by some of the great powers. Other countries do not have enough power and leverage on the international scene. Often, a humanitarian intervention in support of a secessionist people against its central government contributes to such a people's success in its exercise of external self-determination through the process of secession (Sterio 2013). Thus, almost all successful external self-determination peoples have been supported by at least some great powers. The converse is true as well: most unsuccessful self-determination entities have faced the opposition of some of the great powers. For example, the people of Catalonia have not been successful in achieving external self-determination, as this would entail separation from Spain, a European power supported by virtually all western great powers. The Kurds have similarly failed in their attempts to separate from Iraq, as the latter has enjoyed the support of most great powers (Sterio 2018b). And secessionist conflicts remain "frozen" in former Soviet states and regions, such as Nagorno-Karabakh, South Ossetia, and Abkhazia, where these struggles face the opposition of Russia, one of the most important great powers.

It may be relevant to inquire into the great powers' motivation to support some secessionist movements. One plausible explanation is that great powers tend to support secessionist movements when it is in their geopolitical interest to do so. Examples of this include Kosovo, East Timor, and South Sudan. In the case of Kosovo, western great powers, and mainly the United States, decided to support Kosovar Albanians in order to weaken Serbia and its potential expansion in the Balkans region. In the case of East Timor, western great powers decided to support this people's self-determination cause after the end of the Cold War, when Indonesia, the former Timorese mother state, seemed less crucial as an ally against Russia. And in the case of South Sudan, in the post–September 11 era, western great powers determined to weaken the potentially strong Muslim country of Sudan (Sterio 2018a). In addition, great powers may also derive some of their motivation in choosing to support a self-determination-seeking group from their fear of offending another great power. For example, in the cases of Chechnya, South Ossetia, and Abkhazia, it may be argued that western great powers are unwilling to become involved at the risk of offending Russia (Sterio 2018a). In sum, it seems clear that great powers' support is crucial for any independence-seeking movement, and that great powers act or abstain in the international arena based on their own geopolitical interests. However unsatisfactory this may be, it appears that the outcomes of external self-determination quests through remedial secession are dependent on support by some great powers.

## Conclusion

The right to self-determination remains a fundamental principle of international law and affirms a people's right to auto-govern and freely decide its political fate. Peoples can exercise self-determination internally, through autonomy, or externally, through secession from their mother state. International law is unclear on whether the right to self-determination can be exercised externally, through remedial secession, outside of the decolonization paradigm. Instead, it appears that it is the role of power politics, and in particular the involvement of great powers, which determines the outcome of secessionist struggles. In order for any people to be able to exercise its right to external self-determination through remedial secession, such a people must garner the support of at least some great powers. Conversely, the opposition of great powers may prevent some secessionist movements from successfully achieving independence.

# References

Alvarez, A. 1909, "Latin America and International Law", *American Journal of International Law*, 3: 269.

Brilmayer, L. 1991, "Secession and Self-Determination: A Territorial Interpretation", *Yale Journal of International Law*, 16: 177.

Buchanan, A. 1991, *Secession: The Morality of Political Divorce from Fort Sumter to Lithuania and Quebec*, Boulder: Westview Press.

Capotorti, F. 1977, *Study on the Rights of Persons Belonging to Ethnic, Religious and Linguistic Minorities*, UN Doc. E/CN.4/Sub.2/384/Rev.1.

Copenhagen Conference 1990, "Copenhagen Conference of the Human Dimension of the CSCE", *International Legal Materials*, 29: 1305.

Crawford, J. 2006, *The Creation of States in International Law*, 2nd ed., Oxford: Oxford University Press.

Dumienski, Z. 2014, *Microstates as Modern Protected States: Towards a New Definition of Micro-Statehood*, Occasional paper, Reykjavik: Centre for Small State Studies – Institute of International Affairs – University of Iceland.

Framework Convention 1995, "Framework Convention for the Protection of National Minorities", *International Legal Materials*, 34: 351.

Franck, T. 1998, "The Emerging Right to Democratic Governance", *American Journal of International Law*, 92: 46.

Hanna, R. M. 1999, "Right to Self-Determination in In Re: Secession of Quebec", *Maryland Journal of International Law*, 23: 213.

Hannum, H. 1990, *Autonomy, Sovereignty, and Self-Determination*, Philadelphia: University of Pennsylvania Press.

Horowitz, D. L. 2003, "A Right to Secede?", in S. Macedo & A Buchanan (eds), *Secession and Self-Determination*, New York: New York University Press: 50.

HRC 1994, *Human Rights Committee, General Comment 23*, UN Doc. A/49/50 (Vol. 1).

ICCPR 1966, "International Covenant on Civil and Political Rights, 1966", *United Nations Treaty Series*, 999: 171.

ICJ 1975, "International Court of Justice", *Western Sahara, Advisory Opinion, International Court of Justice Reports*, 12.

ICJ 1995, "International Court of Justice", *East Timor (Portugal v. Australia), International Court of Justice Reports*, 90.

ICJ 2004, "International Court of Justice", *Legal Consequences of the Construction of a Wall in the Occupied Palestinian Territory (Advisory Opinion), International Court of Justice Reports*, 136.

ICJ 2010, "International Court of Justice, 2010", *Accordance with International Law of the Unilateral Declaration of Independence in Respect of Kosovo, Advisory Opinion, International Court of Justice Reports*, 403.

ICR 1921, International Commission of Rapporteurs, 1921, "Report: The Aaland Islands Question", League of Nations Council Document B7: 21/68/106.

Oeter, S. 2014, "The Role of Recognition and Non-Recognition with Regard to Secession", in C. Walter, A. von Ungern-Sternberg & K. Abushov (eds), *Self-Determination and Secession in International Law*, Oxford: Oxford University Press: 45.

Orentlicher, D. 1998, "Separation Anxiety: International Responses to Ethno-Separatist Claims", *Yale Journal of International Law*, 23: 1.

Orentlicher, D. 2003, "International Responses to Separatist Claims: Are Democratic Principles Relevant?", in S. Macedo & A. Buchanan (eds), *Secession and Self-Determination*, New York: New York University Press: 19.

Scharf, M. P. 2003, "Earned Sovereignty: Judicial Underpinnings", *Denver Journal of International Law and Policy*, 31: 373.

Secession Reference 1998, "Supreme Court of Canada", *Reference re Secession of Quebec* [1998] 2 S.C.R. 217.

Sterio, M. 2013, *The Right to Self-Determination under International Law: "Selfistans," Secession and the Rule of the Great Powers*, Abingdon: Routledge.

Sterio, M. 2018a, *Secession in International Law*, Northampton: Edward Elgar.

Sterio, M. 2018b, "Self-Determination and Secession Under International Law: The Cases of Kurdistan and Catalonia", *American Society of International Law Insight*, 22(1), 8 January, <www.asil.org/insights/volume/22/issue/1/self-determination-and-secession-under-international-law-cases-kurdistan>

Tomuschat, C. 2006, "Secession and Self-Determination", in M. G. Kohen (ed), *Secession: International Law Perspectives*, Cambridge: Cambridge University Press: 23.

Trifunovska, S. 1994, *Yugoslavia Through Documents: From its Creation to Its Dissolution*, Dordrecht: Martinus Nijhoff Publishers.

UNGA 1960, United Nations General Assembly, Declaration on the Granting of Independence to Colonial Countries and Peoples, Resolution 1514 (XV), 14 December.

UNGA 1970, United Nations General Assembly, Declaration on Principles of International Law Concerning Friendly Relations and Co-operation Among States in Accordance With the Charter of the United Nations, annex to Resolution 2625 (XXV), 24 October.

Walter, C. 2014, "The Kosovo Advisory Opinion: What It Says and What It Does Not Say", in C. Walter, A. von Ungern-Sternberg & K. Abushov (eds), *Self-Determination and Secession in International Law*, Oxford: Oxford University Press: 13.

Weller, M. 2008, *Escaping the Self-Determination Trap*, Leiden: Martinus Nihjoff Publishers.

# 24

# SURVIVING WITHOUT RECOGNITION

## De facto states

### Helge Blakkisrud

Not all bids for secession result in clear-cut success or failure. Some end up as stalled, incomplete processes where secessionists have secured control over a given territory and population but are denied recognition. Such secessionist entities that exist "in empirical terms but have not been recognized by the international community" (Lynch 2004: 145) are commonly referred to as "de facto states" (Pegg 1998). These are states-in-the-making, stuck in the limbo between reintegration and independence. Unless the parent state – the state formation that the de facto state wants to break away from – consents to secession, the prospects for widespread international recognition are not good at all. With the odds stacked against them, how can de facto states manage to survive?

Realizing that the process of gaining international recognition is unlikely to move forward in the near future, today's de facto states increasingly emphasize *engagement* as a means of boosting their *external* legitimacy (see Eiki Berg's contribution, Chapter 25 in this volume). Even more important, however, is cultivating *internal* legitimacy:

> While internal legitimacy is important for any state, it is particularly important for unrecognized states, whose lack of external legitimacy has made claims to internal legitimacy integral to their quest for recognition.
>
> *(Bakke et al. 2014: 591)*

Such internal legitimacy can be further divided into *output legitimacy*, i.e., the capacity to provide physical and economic security and fulfill core state functions; and *input legitimacy*, based on a sense of identification, identity, and community (Kostovicova 2008; Berg 2013). In the following I explore the challenges involved in developing such internal legitimacy through a review of the literature on state- and nation-building in situations of incomplete, stalled secession.

## Defining unrecognized secessionist statehood

The study of unrecognized statehood still suffers from lack of agreement on *terminology* and *definitions*. Over the years, these entities have been referred to, *inter alia*, as "pseudo-states" (Kolossov and O'Loughlin 1998), "unrecognized states" (Caspersen 2012), "quasi states" (Kolstø 2006), "para-states" (Pełczyńska-Nałęcz et al. 2008), and "contested states" (Geldenhuys 2009) (for an

DOI: 10.4324/9781003036593-28

overview of definitions and attributes, see Kursani 2021: 757). Increasingly, there seems to be convergence around "de facto states," a term introduced by Scott Pegg (1998). Whereas some might argue that all states exist "de facto," and that it is their lack of international recognition that makes these entities stand apart, Pegg's point is that, despite the international community's stubborn insistence that these are not states *de jure*, these entities do physically exist.

Views on statehood were traditionally based on capacity to govern; this led to the concept of empirical statehood. The 1933 Montevideo Convention defined a "state" as a legal entity having (1) a permanent population, (2) a defined territory, (3) a government, and (4) the capacity to enter into relations with other states. Since the establishment of the UN, however, emphasis has shifted from capacity to govern to international recognition (that is, from empirical to juridical statehood). De facto states fail on this last criterion, but insist on their right to exist based on empirical statehood (Pegg 1998; Caspersen 2012).

Various attempts have been made to draw a line distinguishing such de facto states from more short-lived secessionist conflicts and struggles for regional devolution of power. According to Pål Kolstø's influential definition, a "de facto state" must meet the following criteria:

1   Its leadership must be in control of (most of) the territory it lays claim to.
2   It must have sought, but not achieved, international recognition as an independent state.
3   This condition of non-recognition must have persisted for a minimum of two years.

(Kolstø 2006: 725–726)

Kolstø has since modified the second criterion to include de facto states that are recognized by their patron – the external state that acts as protector of the de facto state – and "a handful of other states" (Kolstø 2020: 141). Most observers would nevertheless agree that entities like Kosovo (currently recognized by 97 of the 193 UN member states) or Palestine (recognized by 138) are too widely recognized to be lumped together with the de facto states. Taiwan is closer in terms of international recognition – currently recognized by only 14 UN member states – but this state entity is usually excluded from the de facto state category, being a previously fully recognized state, which lost that status, rather than the other way around (moreover, as reflected in Taiwan's official name, the Republic of China, it does not perceive itself as a secessionist entity).

How many de facto states are there? That depends on the definition applied. Adopting a fairly liberal approach, Adrian Florea argues that, since the end of World War II, there have been 40 cases in all, 24 of which still are in existence (Florea 2020: 1016). Shpend Kursani holds that there have been 30, with 12 still existing (Kursani 2021). With Kolstø's more restrictive definition, however, there are currently just eight (see Table 24.1). Whereas Florea, for example, would argue that Gaza is a de facto state within Palestine, and Palestine is a de facto state within Israel, Kursani would not recognize Gaza – and Kolstø would not recognize either of the two as cases of de facto statehood.

As can be deduced from Table 24.1, most post–Cold War de facto states came into being as a result of the breakup of two European multi-ethnic socialist federations, the Soviet Union and Yugoslavia. In the former Yugoslavia, there are no longer any de facto states that satisfy Kolstø's definition – Republika Srpska Krajina was reincorporated into Croatia by military means, Republika Srpska was, as a result of the Dayton Accords, forced to join the Federation as a constituent member of Bosnia and Herzegovina, and Kosovo is currently recognized by approximately half of the members of the UN. In contrast, in the post-Soviet space there are still six de facto states according to this definition; only one, Chechnya, has ceased to exist, after being reintegrated by force into the Russian Federation. Moreover, Somaliland and the Turkish

*Table 24.1* Former and existing post–Cold War de facto states

| | Proclaimed independence | War of secession | Parent state | Patron state | Dissolved | International recognition as of 2021 |
|---|---|---|---|---|---|---|
| Abkhazia | 1992 | 1992–1993 | Georgia | Russia | | Nauru, Nicaragua, Russia, Syria; Venezuela |
| Chechnya | 1991 | 1994–1996 | Russia | – | 2000 | |
| Donetsk People's Republic (DPR) | 2014 | 2014– | Ukraine | Russia | | Russia |
| Eritrea | 1991 | 1961–1991 | Ethiopia | – | | Full |
| Kosovo | 2008 | 1998–1999 | Serbia | USA | | 97 UN members |
| Luhansk People's Republic (LPR) | 2014 | 2014– | Ukraine | Russia | | Russia |
| Nagorno-Karabakh | 1992 | 1988–1994 | Azerbaijan | Armenia | | None |
| Republika Srpska | 1992 | 1992–1995 | Bosnia | Serbia | 1995 | |
| Republika Srpska Krajina | 1991 | 1991–1992 | Croatia | Serbia | 1995 | |
| Somaliland | 1991 | 1986–1991 | Somalia | – | | None |
| South Ossetia | 1992 | 1992 | Georgia | Russia | | Nauru, Nicaragua, Russia, Syria, Venezuela |
| Tamil Eelam | 1994 | 1983–2009 | Sri Lanka | – | 2009 | |
| Transnistria | 1991 | 1992 | Moldova | Russia | | None |
| Turkish Republic of Northern Cyprus (TRNC) | 1983 | 1967–1974 | Cyprus | Turkey | | Turkey |

*Sources*: Pender (2018); Spanke (2019); Berg and Vits (2020); Turp-Balazs (2020); Kursani (2021).

Republic of Northern Cyprus (TRNC) have successfully maintained their de facto statehood for decades.

In order to consolidate the gains from the war of secession, de facto state authorities must engage in state- and nation-building (Kolstø and Blakkisrud 2008). Scholars disagree on the quality of these processes in the case of de facto statehood. One strand describes the de facto states as "failed states." Kolstø has argued that "the modal tendency . . . is weak state-building" (Kolstø 2006: 727): de facto states generally teeter on the brink of collapse (see also Lynch 2004). However, another strand highlights the remarkable resilience of de facto states (e.g., Pegg 1998; Berg 2012), with some entities having survived for decades. The two strands reflect the paradox of living with non-recognition. On one hand, de facto states strive to project the image of being successful states-in-the-making: they hold elections, collect taxes, provide social infrastructure, and maintain security. On the other hand, the lack of international recognition means that they at any moment risk being reabsorbed into the parent state by force.

Surviving without recognition is hardly feasible without the backing of an external bene-factor, a patron state (Kolstø 2006; Blakkisrud and Kolstø 2012; Caspersen 2012; Dembinska and Campana 2017). Among the existing de facto states, the only exception to this "rule" is Somaliland – but there, the parent state itself is exceptionally weak, which reduces the need for a patron (Johnson and Smaker 2014). De facto states would turn to the patron for security guar-antees: enlisting a powerful ally can shift the military (im)balance and security deficit in relation to the parent state (Blakkisrud and Kolstø 2011: 185). Moreover, patrons can provide financial aid and investments, as well as social infrastructure that the de facto states cannot afford, or are not able to acquire due to the lack of international recognition.

Some observers see such reliance on a patron as testimony to the failure of de facto state projects – proof that they cannot manage to create a self-sufficient state. Others pass an even harsher verdict, arguing that de facto states are mere puppets in the hands of a patron state puppeteer, existing solely because they serve the geopolitical interests of the patron (see, e.g., Cornell and Starr 2009).

With the gradual development of a more nuanced understanding of the dynamics of de facto state conflicts, however, scholarly studies have increasingly emphasized the role of local agency both as regards the origins of secessionist conflicts and their continued existence (see, e.g., O'Loughlin et al. 2014; Markedonov 2015; Dembinska and Campana 2017; Blakkisrud et al. 2021; Hoch and Kopeček 2020). According to Silvia von Steinsdorff (2012: 201), "different from what parent states and some international observers often claim, the [de facto] entities' governments are no mere pawns, instrumentalized arbitrarily by the patron states."

## Output legitimacy: state-building

Output legitimacy is a function of the de facto state authorities' ability to establish territorial control, maintain order and safety, develop state institutions, and provide basic public services to the de facto state population (Dembinska and Campana 2017: 263).

### *Territorial control and borders*

The first step toward establishing de facto statehood consists in securing physical control over territory. According to Kolstø's definition, the de facto state authorities must be in control of (most of) the territory they lay claim to. But where to draw the new borders? History shows that entities that arise from a "segmented state" – entities that already possess some sort of territorial autonomy – have greater chances of establishing viable statehood (Roeder 2007). This is also true for de facto states.

For example, within the Soviet Union, Abkhazia and Chechnya enjoyed status as autonomous republics, and South Ossetia and Nagorno-Karabakh were autonomous oblasts. In the Horn of Africa, Eritrea emerged from what had been a segmented state, 1952–1962, and (the formerly British) Somaliland had enjoyed five days of independent statehood before joining Italian Somaliland to form Somalia in 1960 (Geldenhuys 2009: 129). Both Eritrea and Somaliland had colonial histories distinct from those of their parent state. Although they did not arise straight from a segmented state, they had recent experience of having had separate borders, institutions, and administrations. The chances of surviving the first critical years and consolidating de facto statehood appear much higher for those who can draw on this kind of institutional and infrastructural capacity.

Former administrative status is neither sufficient (as witnessed by the case of Chechnya) nor a precondition for success. TRNC – the oldest de facto state still in existence – has shown that it is possible to carve out functioning de facto statehood across (previous) administrative borders and social infrastructure. However, it makes the initial phase of establishing state structures more complicated – and thus much more difficult to sustain. The fate of Srpska Krajina illustrates this: this entity was an awkward construction consisting of two geographically separated territories with no recent history of autonomy (the fact that they at one stage had been part of the semi-autonomous Austrian Military Frontier was of little help when now trying to define borders or set up institutions). In less than four years, Srpska Krajina collapsed, being reintegrated into Croatia through the military Operation Storm.

Closely related to establishing control over territory is taking charge of the external borders – especially the new de facto border with the parent state. The latter will in practice be identical to the ceasefire line/line of contact. If international actors have been involved in putting an end to the hot phase of the war, this line is often monitored by a peacekeeping mission. In Cyprus, for example, ever since the partition of the island in 1974, the UN has controlled the demilitarized "Green Line" buffer zone that separates TRNC from the Republic of Cyprus. Alternatively, there may be various combinations of international, regional, and local peacekeepers. In the case of Abkhazia, until the 2008 Russo–Georgian War, a contingent of UN observers oversaw a peacekeeping mission under the aegis of the Commonwealth of Independent States (CIS) (in practice staffed by Russian soldiers). Regardless of the composition, such international presence can serve as a tripwire, providing the de facto state with an additional line of defense.

The emergent *civilian* border regime will depend on how post-war dynamics between the secessionists and parent state authorities evolve. The de facto border may be hermetically closed and heavily fortified, as with the "Administrative Borderline" between Nagorno-Karabakh and Azerbaijan proper, from the conclusion of the 1994 ceasefire until the 2020 Second Karabakh War. Here, contact was limited to occasional shelling and snipers shooting across the border, with no possibility for the local population to cross physically from one side to the other. At the other end of the spectrum is the Transnistrian-Moldovan de facto border, where the border regime is so "normalized" that many people commute on a daily basis to work in the opposite entity.

## Military security

At the outset of a war for independence, secessionist leaders are seldom able to enlist regular military units for their cause. Instead, they must rely on various irregular entities, paramilitary units, and guerillas under the command of local warlords. Once the hot phase of the war has ended, a crucial step toward establishing de facto statehood is to take control over these irregular formations (Kolstø 2006; Dembinska and Campana 2017). Otherwise, there is a real danger of local warlords and field commanders undermining the viability of de facto statehood. The case of Chechnya may serve as an example. Here, although civilian government was established in the aftermath of the 1996 Khasavyurt ceasefire agreement, President Aslan Maskhadov failed to disarm the field commanders who had fought alongside him during the First Chechen War (1994–1996). As a result, Maskhadov's government gradually lost control over the territory, with warlords seeking to consolidate their local fiefdoms by engaging in smuggling, kidnapping, and other criminal activities. Soon Maskhadov's government wielded effective control only over the capital region. And when two of the unruly warlords in 1999 launched an attack on neighboring Dagestan, another federal unit of Russia, it served as a pretext for the Russian government to launch the Second Chechen War, a war that spelled the end to the Chechen de facto statehood.

In most cases, de facto state authorities will seek to coopt field commanders and warlords into the new state structures, and to integrate their armed entities into a nascent national army. The case of Nagorno-Karabakh illustrates this process of gradually winding up the power of military leaders. Samvel Babayan, a hero and key commander during the war of secession, was made Minister of Defense after the 1994 ceasefire. For several years, civilian authorities turned a blind eye to Babayan using his position as local strongman to monopolize lucrative parts of the shadow economy. Only in 1999 did President Arkady Ghukasyan feel strong enough to confront Babayan and dismiss him from the government. The following year, Babayan was arrested after a failed assassination attempt on Ghukasyan. The removal of Babayan marked a crucial step toward facilitating civilian control and introducing a more accountable regime in Nagorno-Karabakh (de Waal 2003).

However, even if de facto state authorities succeed in establishing control over the legitimate use of force, that does not resolve the long-term security challenges associated with de facto statehood. A ceasefire is not a peace agreement: without the backing of the international system's "protective norm of nonintervention" (Caspersen 2012: 77), there is a constant threat that the parent state will attempt to reincorporate the secessionist entity by military means. As a result, the de facto state must remain on permanent war footing.

This "security deficit" comes at a cost: de facto state authorities must allocate a disproportionate share of their usually meager fiscal resources to maintain outsized armed forces. With a population of 144,000 (prior the 2020 Second Karabakh War), Nagorno-Karabakh had a standing army of no less than 20,000 men. Or take the Horn of Africa: even though Somalia is a largely failed state and its government is facing more pressing issues than secessionist Somaliland, the Somaliland de facto state authorities still, some 30 years after seceding, devote 35% of the state budget to security, leaving sectors like health, education, and infrastructure with 9.6%, 4.7%, and 4.5%, respectively (Republic of Somaliland 2020: 5).

Moreover, although the status quo often is seen as working in favor of the de facto states (the longer they survive, the more "legitimate" their claim to statehood appears to be), when it comes to defense and military matters, time often works *against* the de facto states. Their paramilitary units may have managed to push back the parent-state forces during the war of secession, but the lack of international recognition often makes it difficult to maintain the local "balance of terror" with the parent state – the de facto states have neither the resources nor access to procure state-of-the-art equipment. Nagorno-Karabakh's disastrous defeat in the 2020 Second Karabakh War demonstrates this. At the time, the local army in Nagorno-Karabakh still relied largely on weapon systems inherited from the Soviet Union, whereas Azerbaijani authorities for years had invested in an ambitious modernization and rearmament program. Close integration with the patron-state army, equipped with more state-of-the-art Russian military hardware, proved insufficient: when the conflict flared up in the fall of 2020, the tactics and weapon systems that had ensured success in the war of secession proved seriously outdated in encounters with Azerbaijani drones. Although the de facto borders were heavily fortified, the Nagorno-Karabakh Defense Army was not prepared for high-tech warfare, and defenses quickly collapsed. In the end, only Russia's intervention saved the de facto state from being fully reabsorbed into Azerbaijan.

Some de facto states seek to outsource security to the patron state. If the patron has extended formal recognition, it may establish military bases in the de facto state – and if not, military assistance may still be provided by deploying peacekeeping forces. Sometimes the patron also assumes responsibility for border protection and control. In the TRNC, the estimated 30,000 soldiers of the Cyprus Turkish Peace Force Command (from Turkey) dwarf the TRNC's own standing forces of 9,000 men. In Abkhazia and South Ossetia, the authorities have agreed to the establishment of Russian military bases and the gradual integration of military structures.

## Institution building and elections

In parallel to introducing effective control over territory and borders, de facto state leaders must establish the institutional fixtures of statehood, that is, develop administrative capacity and governance structures. This is easier for de facto states that originate from a segmented state, as these already have some existing structures on which to build: the regional assembly can be transformed into the national parliament, the regional administration can form the backbone of the new ministerial structure, and so on.

Irrespective of their origins, however, all de facto states will invest heavily in emulating regular, recognized statehood – adopting constitutions, electing presidents and MPs, and setting up an elaborate governmental apparatus (Bakke et al. 2014; Berg and Mölder 2012; Kolstø and Blakkisrud 2012). Not only is such institution-building important as regards establishing effective rule throughout the de facto state, it is also seen as a critical test of statehood (Isachenko 2008; Ó Beacháin et al. 2016). Whereas failed states – states that for various reasons lack the capacity to govern their territory and population – risk little in terms of international sanctions, de facto states bear the burden of proof: they need to demonstrate their capacity to govern in order to have a chance of winning acceptance, and eventually, they hope, recognition.

In some cases, developing institutional capacity has been coupled with the notion of "earned sovereignty." Whereas secessionist demands are normally framed in terms of demands for remedial secession, the process leading up to the (partial) international recognition of Kosovo helped to fuel the idea that sovereignty could be "earned" (Bolton and Visoka 2010). Based on an understanding of "standards" as being a prerequisite for "status" (read: international recognition), many de facto states officially embraced democratization (Caspersen 2011; Kolstø and Blakkisrud 2012; Smolnik 2012).

In fact, a couple of de facto states even outperform their parent states when it comes to democracy development (see Table 24.2). In stark contrast to the image of de facto states as "criminalized badlands," Freedom House in its 2021 annual ranking characterizes TRNC as "free" and Abkhazia, Nagorno-Karabakh, and Somaliland as "partly free" (Freedom House 2021). Such rankings have enabled Nagorno-Karabakh and Somaliland to argue that reunification with their "not free" parent state would mean a setback for the de facto population in terms of political as well as civil rights. This is not to say that *all* de facto states are blossoming democracies: the two latest additions to the family, the Donetsk People's Republic (DPR) and Lugansk People's Republic (LPR), end up outside the Freedom House 1–40 scale, with a negative score (−1) on political rights (see Table 24.2).

While elections and participation may contribute to strengthen internal legitimacy, as for international recognition, "earned sovereignty" proved to be a dead end: no other de facto states

*Table 24.2* Global freedom scores 2020

| De facto state | Political rights (1–40) | Civil liberties (1–60) | Parent state | Political rights (1–40) | Civil liberties (1–60) |
|---|---|---|---|---|---|
| Abkhazia | 17 | 23 | Georgia | 23 | 37 |
| DPR and LPR★ | −1 | 5 | Ukraine | 26 | 34 |
| Nagorno-Karabakh | 16 | 19 | Azerbaijan | 2 | 8 |
| Somaliland | 18 | 24 | Somalia | 1 | 6 |
| South Ossetia | 2 | 8 | Georgia | 23 | 37 |
| Transnistria | 8 | 12 | Moldova | 26 | 35 |
| TRNC | 28 | 50 | Republic of Cyprus | 38 | 56 |

★ Freedom House scores the two de facto states in Donbas together as "Eastern Donbas."

*Source*: Freedom House 2021

were offered the same road map toward internationally recognized statehood as Kosovo was. As a result, the leaders of some de facto states began questioning the wisdom of further democratization. Faced with external existential threats, they argue that de facto states simply cannot afford the luxury of pluralism: de facto states need to present a united front to the outside world (Caspersen 2008, 2011; Kolstø and Blakkisrud 2012). Accordingly, in recent years, several de facto states have witnessed a partial democratic backsliding.

Still, while the quality of democratic procedure may be found wanting by international actors, de facto states, whether "free," "partly free," or "not free," insist on maintaining formal democratic procedures. With the exception of Somaliland, which, after an extended hiatus, finally organized multiparty parliamentary elections in 2021 (the previous elections had taken place in 2005), all regularly organize elections to the executive and legislative branch – the rationale being that the popular vote will strengthen the internal and external legitimacy of the powers-that-be as well as the de facto state project as such.

## *Economic reconstruction*

Once the "rally-round-the-flag" effect and euphoria of having "won" the war of secession begin to wear off, the population will start expecting the de facto authorities to deliver not only physical security, but also a range of public services. However, de facto statehood and lack of international recognition make it very difficult to live up to such expectations.

The local economies are frequently severely disrupted by the war of secession. Beyond wartime destruction and the fact that old economic ties are severed by the new de facto border, the lack of international recognition introduces further constraints. International organizations and states alike will be hesitant to get involved in humanitarian aid and reconstruction without the explicit approval of the parent state. De facto state authorities thus face more challenges in reviving the post-war economy and developing a tax base than most other post-conflict societies. Their emerging economies have been described as "often devastated, informal, or illicit" (Johnson and Smaker 2014: 5; see also Caspersen 2012; Pegg 1998); Kolstø asserts that the "modal tendency" among de facto states is a "weak economy" (Kolstø 2006: 723).

In the immediate post-war phase, when de facto state authorities must tackle empty state coffers, a banking system that at best is cut off from the international market (more often simply non-existent), and with most or all traditional trade links disrupted, the authorities as well as the population must be creative in their coping strategies. In this phase, the economy will almost by default depend on smuggling and shuttle trade to cover some of the most basic needs and, hence, come to include large grey and black sectors. This situation has lent credence to the image of de facto states as "criminalised, war-lord-controlled, ethnic fiefdoms" (Caspersen 2008: 115) and "racketeer states" (Lynch 2004: 59). However, if de facto states survive these first chaotic years, they will necessarily have to develop mechanisms for regulating economic activity in order to fund an army, post-war reconstruction, and, eventually, the revival of the public sector (Blakkisrud and Kolstø 2011). Gradually, with increased centralized regulatory capacity and an evolving legislative base, the domestic market will become more "normalized."

Shopping streets in downtown Sukhumi (Sokhum) or Northern Nicosia (Lefkoşa), cities that by now have served as capital cities for their de facto states for close to 30 and 50 years, respectively, look deceptively normal at first glance. One does not need to stray far or dig deep, however, to discover the harsh realities of living in an unrecognized state cut off from the globalized economy. For example, for years, the hundreds of thousands of tourists visiting Abkhazia annually had to bring cash with them, as the de facto state was cut off from the international banking system and the use of ATMs (this changed only relatively recently, with Russian banks making inroads into the de facto state).

## Providing public services

As to the range of services provided, de facto states can generally ill afford to maintain a social infrastructure that can compete with that of the parent state. This is not only a matter of funding, but also the size of the population and the dearth of qualified personnel. South Ossetia may offer primary healthcare, but there is no way that an entity of this size can manage to provide a full range of specialist medical services. Similarly, while the former pedagogical institute in Tiraspol was turned into a "state university" by the stroke of a pen, the authorities cannot provide all the types of higher education needed to keep their de facto state running. The solution is often to tap into the social and educational institutions of the patron.

De facto states also find themselves cut off from all kinds of international infrastructure. Local telecommunications operators and internet providers must rely on patron or parent-state country codes and licenses (the TRNC country code is +90 – the same as for Turkey, while DPR and LPR for a long time continued to use +380, the country code of Ukraine). Likewise, de facto states are barred from international aviation. Several Turkish companies now fly on TRNC, but, in order not to violate international travel regulations, all flights must touch ground in Turkey before proceeding to a third country. When in 2011 Nagorno-Karabakh announced plans to re-open the airport in Stepanakert, Azerbaijani authorities were not interested in showing the same flexibility, threatening to shoot down any plane approaching the airport, military or civilian.

## Trade and investment

Moreover, all international economic engagement continues to be constrained by the de facto states not being subject to any international regimes and regulations (Blakkisrud et al. 2021). As long as the economy is based on subsistence farming and petty trade, lack of international recognition is less of an immediate problem, but for more developed economies dependent on trade with the outside world, the lack of status creates problems for everything from foreign direct investments and credits to export licenses and market access.

Regarding trade, de facto state authorities must either rely on middlemen or reach some sort of understanding with the parent state (Blakkisrud et al. 2021; Prelz Oltramonti 2015). For example, Transnistria, which inherited an export-oriented economy, has had to agree to the use of Moldovan tariff stamps, and local businesses engaged in exports must register in Moldova proper in return for continued access to international markets. More recently, the Transnistrian authorities agreed to be part to Moldova's Deep and Comprehensive Free Trade Area (DCFTA) agreement with the European Union (in effect since 2016), which allows Transnistrian firms to export to the EU under Moldova's quotas. Other parent states have been less forthcoming than Moldova, however.

With very limited or no access to foreign investments, de facto state authorities are hard pressed to come up with the capital necessary to revive and develop the economy. Often, they face a difficult choice between selling out cheap to patron state-based businesses or having no investments at all. In heavily industrialized Transnistria, the major industrial enterprises that form the backbone of the economy have ended up in Russian hands. In Abkhazia, where the ethnic Abkhazians doggedly defend their independence, the authorities have, to the great frustration of the Russian patron, refused to allow the sale of land to foreigners – thereby forfeiting badly needed investments in the important tourist business. The poor access to aid and credits facilitates a reliance on distorted economic practices (Prelz Oltramonti 2015). This is clearly subversive to the state-building project – but at the same time unavoidable.

Of crucial importance here is the parent state's reintegration strategy. Does it want to lower the threshold for reintegration by engaging in economic interaction (while running the risk of strengthening the economic base of the secessionists)? Or does it prefer to "starve out" the de facto authorities by imposing economic blockades and sanctions? Georgian authorities have tried both strategies in relation to the two secessionist entities on Georgian territory. In the aftermath of Abkhazia's war of secession, Georgia convinced the CIS – including Abkhazia's future patron, Russia – to impose an economic blockade on Abkhazia. And yet, Tbilisi for a long time quietly accepted the development of a flourishing market for contraband at the de facto border with South Ossetia, seeing the Ergneti Market as a conflict-reducing mechanism. Even today the Georgian government follows a two-pronged approach: on one hand, it insists that all economic activity in the "occupied territories" be pre-approved by Georgian authorities, imposing sanctions on international companies that do not abide by this (Ó Beacháin et al. 2016). On the other hand, from 2018 Georgia has pursued a policy of building trust through engagement, focusing on enhanced opportunities for economic interaction and education (Office of the State Minister of Georgia for Reconciliation and Civic Equality 2018).

One way to compensate for the lack of regular international support and investments is to mobilize ethnic kin abroad. Several de facto states can draw on strong, prosperous diaspora communities willing to invest in their cause. The Armenian diaspora has played a crucial role in developing the local infrastructure in Nagorno-Karabakh, but also other entities have benefitted greatly from their diaspora populations. However, such support "comes with a price tag" (Caspersen 2012: 112–113). In the case of Somaliland, it has been argued that the diaspora involvement in domestic politics is so strong that it potentially challenges the state-building project (Bradbury 2008: 175–176).

## Fiscal policy

Lack of recognition also creates hurdles for developing an independent fiscal policy, as no one outside the borders of the de facto state will accept a locally issued currency as legal tender. However, having a "national" currency is often seen as symbolically important in trying to demonstrate statehood, and some de facto states have adopted their own currency for use in domestic transactions. In Transnistria, the de facto state authorities introduced Transnistrian rubles, and Somaliland shillings are used in Somaliland. Others have adopted an intermediary position: Abkhazia has for years had a national bank, but the local currency it issues, the *apsar*, is not used in everyday transactions: it has purely symbolic value. Instead, Abkhazian authorities, like most of their de facto state colleagues, have opted to rely on the currency of the patron.

Economic statistics and performance indicators are likely to be politicized (Broers 2015). Parent states will refer to weak economic indicators as proof of the failure of the de facto state project and often cite too low figures – whereas the de facto authorities will tend to exaggerate grossly. Overall, however, it is exceedingly difficult for de facto state authorities to promote economic development beyond a certain threshold. Some insist on developing an independent tax base; others have made themselves highly dependent on the support of their patron. In the 2021 South Ossetian state budget, for example, more than 80% of the projected income was to be covered by Russian transfers (RES 2020). Some de facto states also try to sell a story of *relative* success. While life in Transnistria may be hard, Transnistrian authorities have insisted that the situation in Moldova proper is worse (see, e.g., Blakkisrud and Kolstø 2011; Berg 2013: 486).

In general, however, it is difficult to reconcile economic development and prosperity with continued unrecognized statehood. As a result, the de facto state authorities may try to offset the negative impact of low living standards, limited range of public services, and lack of material success by compensatory measures in the form of promoting nation-building and patriotism.

## Input legitimacy: nation-building

Most de facto states are fairly small in size and population (see Table 24.3). They have already lost part of their pre-war populations due to warfare and ethnic cleansing, and constantly run the risk of further outmigration and brain drain due to the post-war barriers to human and economic development that de facto statehood entails. The de facto authorities must therefore convince their citizens that secession is the only way forward.

Most de facto states come about as a result of the mobilization of ethnic grievances: already before the onset of the war of secession there was a clearly defined "we" seeking to escape from the alleged discrimination suffered under the rule of the central authorities. Secession is thus carried out in the name of the titular nation of a would-be nation state – such as the Chechens in Chechnya and the Abkhazians in Abkhazia.

*Table 24.3* Size and demographic change

| | Area (km²) | Pre-war population | Current population estimates** | Current ethnic composition, estimates |
|---|---|---|---|---|
| Abkhazia | 8,665 | 525,000 | 245,800 (2019) | 51% Abkhaz, 19% Georgian, 17% Armenian, 9% Russian |
| DPR | 7,853 | 2,666,000 | 2,270,900 (2019) | n.a.*** |
| LPR | 8,337 | 1,781,000 | 1,452,900 (2019) | n.a.*** |
| Nagorno-Karabakh | 3,170* | 189,500* | 120,000 (2021) | 100% Armenian |
| Somaliland | 176,119 | n.a. | 4,171,000 (2020) | 100% Somali |
| South Ossetia | 3,900 | 98,500 | 53,500 (2015) | 90% Ossetian, 7% Georgian |
| Transnistria | 4,163 | 730,000 | 465,200 (2019) | 34% Russian, 33% Moldovan, 27% Ukrainian |
| TRNC | 3,355 | 196,300 | 370,000 (2017) | 95% Turkish |

* Between 1994 and 2020, the Nagorno-Karabakh Republic controlled 11,458 km², but in the 2020 Second Karabakh War, it lost more than two-thirds of this territory. Pre-war population figure is based on the borders of the autonomous oblast.

** Population statistics are at least as politicized as economic statistics. Estimates here are based on data provided by the de facto states.

*** Since DPR and LPR have not published the results of their 2019 censuses, there is no reliable information on current ethnic breakdown.

*Sources:* Demoskop (2013); Artsakh Republic National Statistical Service (2015); Hatay (2017); Berg and Vits (2020); Gosudarstvennyi komitet Respubliki Abkhazia po statistike (2020); Prime Minister of the Republic of Armenia (2021).

Alternatively, mobilization may be ideologically and/or geopolitically inspired. In Transnistria, for example, the secessionist movement was based on ideological bonds to the Soviet project, and resistance to Romanization and the possibility of unification with Romania (Dembinska 2019). With a population consisting of three almost equally sized communities of Russians, Moldovans, and Ukrainians (see Table 24.3), the authorities have emphasized historical-territorial bonds and a supra-ethnic identity (Blakkisrud and Kolstø 2011).

Regardless of ethnic makeup, after the establishment of de facto statehood, the authorities will invariably embark on a process of consolidating the state through reinforcing the national community by means of "symbols, propaganda, history writing, and the cultivation and 'invention' of traditions and national customs" (Kolstø 2006: 730). The war of secession itself functions as a powerful foundational myth, a catharsis transforming the once-oppressed ethnic minority into a state-bearing nation.

Just like secessionist movements that result in international recognition, the de facto state secessionists will promptly introduce the traditional paraphernalia associated with statehood: flag, national anthem, a coat of arms, etc. They institute new holidays, ceremonies, and celebrations, and erect monuments devoted to the struggle for independence and the great sons of the nation – while discarding old ones associated with the parent state and their shared past. They will also start rewriting history to back the new status as an "independent" state, casting the current de facto state as "natural" and legitimate.

While de facto state conflicts are sometimes described as "frozen" (see, e.g., Dembinska and Campana 2017; Kazantsev et al. 2020), the processes of identity formation and self-identification are always dynamic. By cultivating an image of the parent state as "the Other," the shared community that once existed across the de facto border gradually drifts apart, with new, post-secession generations growing up with little or no firsthand knowledge of the people and society on the other side of the new divide. The malleability of such post-secessionist identity projects can be illustrated by how TRNC school history textbooks in the early 2000s, in anticipation of potential EU membership, shifted from an ethnic Turkish/Ottoman narrative to a territorial Cypriot one – and then, once it became clear that the Greek Cypriot "no" in the 2004 referendum on reunification meant that the door to the EU was closed, again reverted to a narrative underlining Turkishness (Dembinska 2017).

Also when it comes to the nation-building project, non-recognition enters the picture, however. The de facto state authorities will seek to strengthen the bonds between the population and the de facto state by instituting citizenship and issuing passports, but the latter have limited practical value – such passports may serve as a domestic ID card, but they will not be valid as travel documents beyond the de facto border. In order to be able to travel, citizens of de facto states will have to acquire dual citizenship. Usually, the patron state will step in. This not only resolves a pressing problem for the de facto state authorities, it may also serve the interests of the patron: If a substantial share of the de facto state population becomes citizens of the patron state, its involvement in the peace processes set up to regulate the secessionist conflict will appear more natural and legitimate. In order to prevent this, parent states will sometimes issue passports to persons residing in the secessionist entity. For example, the Republic of Cyprus offers Cypriot, and, by implication, EU citizenship, to TRNC citizens (Krasniqi 2019: 308; see also Dembinska 2017).

As for representatives of the parent state population living on the territory claimed by the secessionists, these are frequently subject to expulsion or, if they are allowed to stay on after the war of secession, to political marginalization. For example, the pre-war population of the Soviet Nagorno-Karabakh Autonomous Oblast had been 76.9% Armenian and 21.5% Azeri. During the subsequent war, the entire Azeri population – not only in Nagorno-Karabakh proper, but also in the surrounding Azeri-populated regions that ended up on the Armenian-controlled side of the ceasefire line in 1994 – were forced to leave. According to a 2005 census, there were only six ethnic Azeris left in the Nagorno-Karabakh Republic. Similarly, after the 2008 Russo–Georgian War, most of the ethnic Georgians who had remained on lands controlled or claimed by South Ossetia left: the share of ethnic Georgians dropped from 29% before the war of secession in 1991–1992 to 7% today (see Table 24.3).

The second option, marginalization and disenfranchisement, can be illustrated by the Abkhazian approach to the local Georgian population. In the late Soviet period, ethnic Georgians had made up almost half the population (46%, according to the 1989 census). During the war, an estimated 250,000 people, mostly Georgians, fled Abkhazia, but the Gali region in the southeast remained compactly Georgian-populated. Whereas today the two other large ethnic minority groups, Armenians and Russians, are generally accepted and integrated, ethnic Georgians (now comprising 19% of the population) are still viewed as a potential fifth column (Kolstø and Blakkisrud 2013). Almost three decades after the end of the war of secession, the question of whether to issue passports to the Georgian population, thus inviting them into the de facto citizenry, remains highly controversial.

An alternative strategy for dealing with the remnants of parent-state presence is to redefine these groups. In the case of the Georgians in Abkhazia's Gali region, the de facto authorities insist that these are not Georgians but Mingrelians, who in Georgia are defined as a Georgian regional sub-identity. When the Georgian government complains about the de facto state authorities violating the human rights of ethnic Georgians in Abkhazia, Abkhazian authorities counter by arguing that it protects the ethnic identity of the Mingrelians, who in the Georgian-controlled part of Mingrelia are alleged to be threatened by the assimilationist policies of Georgia. Similarly, in Transnistria, the authorities have insisted that local Moldovans continue to use the Cyrillic alphabet, driving a wedge between them and the Moldovans across the Dniester, who switched to the Latin alphabet in 1989.

## Concluding remarks

Despite all the talk about globalization and the erosion of the state, internationally recognized statehood "remains the top prize: it legitimizes the struggle for independence, offers protection for inhabitants, and confers prestige and power on leaders" (Caspersen 2008: 113). Statehood may be taken for granted or seen as increasingly irrelevant for those who enjoy it. For those who do not, it remains a coveted dream. However, living with non-recognition has shown that the old maxim that "possession is nine-tenths of the law" does not extend to de facto statehood.

Based on an examination of Eurasian de facto states, Tomáš Hoch and Vincenc Kopeček (2020) argue that the existence of de facto states is temporary and transitional: sooner or later, they will be reintegrated in the parent state, absorbed by the patron state, or eventually end up gaining international recognition. The 2020 war in Nagorno-Karabakh, which almost wiped out this de facto state, underscores the precariousness of living with non-recognition – even the best-functioning de facto states may be overrun by their parent without much protest from international actors or organizations. Nevertheless, contrary to what might have been expected, the de facto states that came into being at the end of the Cold War and survived the fateful first years have demonstrated remarkable longevity. Two post–Cold War de facto states, Eritrea and Kosovo, have achieved internationally recognized statehood (although in the latter case, without gaining a seat in the UN); others, like Chechnya and Srpska Krajina, were reabsorbed by the parent state – but most continue to hang on to their de facto statehood.

New generations have grown up and come of age without knowing any other reality than de facto statehood. For every decade that passes, reintegration into the parent state becomes more challenging as pre-war ties and memories of a shared community fade. However, given the uncertainty and disadvantages associated with living with non-recognition, the authorities must convince their populations that the sacrifices they have to make will remain meaningful. Ultimately, de facto state legitimacy hinges on the population "believing in the state and its right to exist" (Bakke et al. 2014: 593). Only by successfully consolidating internal legitimacy may de facto states hope to survive in the hostile environment attendant on the continued lack of international recognition.

# References

Artsakh Republic National Statistical Service. 2015, Naselenie (gorodskoe, sel'skoe) po natsional'nosti, polu i vozrastu. http://stat-nkr.am/files/publications/2016/Mardahamar_2015_rus/MAS_2/5_1_187_188.pdf (accessed August 5, 2022).

Bakke, K.M., O'Loughlin, J., Toal, G. & Ward, M.D. 2014, 'Convincing state-builders? Disaggregating internal legitimacy in Abkhazia', *International Studies Quarterly*, 58(3): 591–607.

Berg, E. 2012, 'Parent states versus secessionist entities: Measuring political legitimacy in Cyprus, Moldova and Bosnia & Hercegovina', *Europe–Asia Studies*, 64(7): 1271–1296.

Berg, E. 2013, 'Merging together or drifting apart? Revisiting political legitimacy issues in Cyprus, Moldova, and Bosnia and Herzegovina', *Geopolitics*, 18(2): 467–492.

Berg, E. & Mölder, M. 2012, 'Who is entitled to "earn sovereignty"? Legitimacy and regime support in Abkhazia and Nagorno-Karabakh', *Nations and Nationalism*, 18(3): 527–545.

Berg, E. & Vits, K. 2020, 'Exploring de facto state agency: Negotiation power, international engagement and patronage', in: Baldacchino, G., & Wivel, A. (eds) *Handbook on the Politics of Small States*. Cheltenham: Edward Elgar, 379–394.

Blakkisrud, H., Gelashvili, G., Kemoklidze, N. & Kolstø, P. 2021, 'Navigating de facto statehood: Trade, trust, and agency in Abkhazia's external economic relations', *Eurasian Geography and Economics*, 62(3): 347–371.

Blakkisrud, H. & Kolstø, P. 2011, 'From secessionist conflict toward a functioning state: Processes of state- and nation-building in Transnistria', *Post-Soviet Affairs*, 27(2): 178–210.

Blakkisrud, H. & Kolstø, P. 2012, 'Dynamics of de facto statehood: The South Caucasian de facto states between secession and sovereignty', *Journal of Southeast European and Black Sea Studies*, 12(2): 281–298.

Bolton, G. & Visoka, G. 2010, 'Recognizing Kosovo's independence: Remedial secession or earned sovereignty?', *SEESOX Occasional Paper*, 11.

Bradbury, M. 2008, *Becoming Somaliland*, Bloomington, IN: Indiana University Press.

Broers, L. 2015, 'Resourcing de facto jurisdictions: A theoretical perspective on cases in the South Caucasus', *Caucasus Survey*, 3(3): 269–290.

Caspersen, N. 2008, 'Separatism and democracy in the Caucasus', *Survival*, 50(4): 113–136.

Caspersen, N. 2011, 'Democracy, nationalism and (lack of) sovereignty: The complex dynamics of democratisation in unrecognised states', *Nations and Nationalism*, 17(2): 337–356.

Caspersen, N. 2012, *Unrecognized States: The Struggle for Independence in the Modern International System*, Cambridge: Polity Press.

Cornell, S. & Starr, S.F. (eds) 2009, *The Guns of August 2008: Russia's War in Georgia*, Armonk, NY: M.E. Sharpe.

Dembinska, M. 2017, 'The imagined "other" and its shifts: Politics and identifications in Turkish Cyprus', *National Identities*, 19(4): 395–413.

Dembinska, M. 2019, 'Carving out the nation with the enemy's kin: Double strategy of boundary-making in Transnistria and Abkhazia', *Nations and Nationalism*, 25(1): 298–317.

Dembinska, M. & Campana, A. 2017, 'Frozen conflicts and internal dynamics of de facto states', *International Studies Review* 19(2): 254–278.

Demoskop. 2013, Vsesoyuznaya perepis' naseleniya 1989. www.demoscope.ru/weekly/ssp/resp_nac_89.php?reg=0 (accessed August 5, 2022).

De Waal, T. 2003, *Black Garden: Armenia and Azerbaijan Through Peace and War*, New York: New York University Press.

Florea, A. 2020, 'Rebel governance in de facto states', *European Journal of International Relations*, 26(4): 1004–1031.

Freedom House. 2021, Global freedom scores. https://freedomhouse.org/countries/freedom-world/scores (accessed August 25, 2021).

Geldenhuys, D. 2009, *Contested States in World Politics*, Basingstoke: Palgrave Macmillan.

Gosudarstvennyi komitet Respubliki Abkhazia po statistike. 2020, https://ugsra.org/ofitsialnaya-statistika.php?ELEMENT_ID=415 (accessed August 5, 2022).

Hatay, M. 2017, *Population and politics in North Cyprus*, Oslo/Nicosia: PRIO & Friedrich-Ebert-Stiftung.

Hoch, T. & Kopeček, V. (eds) 2020, *De facto States in Eurasia*, New York: Routledge.

Isachenko, D. 2008, 'The production of recognized space: Statebuilding practices of Northern Cyprus and Transdniestria', *Journal of Intervention and Statebuilding*, 2(3): 353–368.

Johnson, M. C. & Smaker, W. 2014, 'State-building in de facto states: Somaliland and Puntland compared', *Africa Today*, 60(4): 3–23.

Kazantsev, A., Rutland, P., Medvedeva, S. & Safranchuk, I. 2020, 'Russia's policy in the "frozen conflicts" of the post-Soviet space: From ethno-politics to geopolitics', *Caucasus Survey*, 8(2): 142–162.

Kolossov, V. & O'Loughlin, J. 1998, 'Pseudo-states as harbingers of a new geopolitics: The example of the Transdniestr Moldovan Republic (TMR),' *Geopolitics*, 3(1): 151–176.

Kolstø, P. 2006, 'The sustainability and future of unrecognized quasi-states', *Journal of Peace Research*, 43(6): 723–740.

Kolstø, P. 2020, 'Biting the hand that feeds them? Abkhazia–Russia client–patron relations', *Post-Soviet Affairs*, 36(2): 140–158.

Kolstø, P. & Blakkisrud, H. 2008, 'Living with non-recognition: State- and nation-building in South Caucasian quasi-states', *Europe–Asia Studies*, 60(3): 483–509.

Kolstø, P. & Blakkisrud, H. 2012, 'De facto states and democracy: The case of Nagorno-Karabakh', *Communist and Post-Communist Studies*, 45(1–2): 141–151.

Kolstø, P. & Blakkisrud, H. 2013, 'Yielding to the sons of the soil: Abkhazian democracy and the marginalization of the Armenian vote', *Ethnic and Racial Studies*, 36(12): 2075–2095.

Kostovicova, D. 2008, 'Legitimacy and international administration: The Ahtisaari Settlement for Kosovo from a human security perspective', *International Peacekeeping*, 15(5): 631–647.

Krasniqi, G. 2019, 'Contested states as liminal spaces of citizenship: Comparing Kosovo and the Turkish Republic of Northern Cyprus', *Ethnopolitics*, 18(3): 298–314.

Kursani, S. 2021, 'Reconsidering the contested state in post-1945 international relations: An ontological approach', *International Studies Review*, 23(3): 752–77.

Lynch, D. 2004, *Engaging Eurasia's Separatist States: Unresolved Conflicts and de facto States*, Washington, DC: United States Institute of Peace Press.

Markedonov, S. 2015, 'De facto statehood in Eurasia: A political and security phenomenon', *Caucasus Survey*, 3(3): 195–206.

Ó Beacháin, D., Comai, G. & Tsurtsumia-Zurabashvili, A. 2016, 'The secret lives of unrecognised states: Internal dynamics, external relations, and counter-recognition strategies', *Small Wars & Insurgencies*, 27(3): 440–466.

Office of the State Minister of Georgia for Reconciliation and Civic Equality. 2018, *A Step to a Better Future*. https://smr.gov.ge/uploads/prev/Concept_EN_0eaaac2e.pdf (accessed November 23, 2021).

O'Loughlin, J., Kolossov, V. & Toal, G. 2014, 'Inside the post-Soviet de facto states: A comparison of attitudes in Abkhazia, Nagorno-Karabakh, South Ossetia, and Transnistria', *Eurasian Geography and Economics*, 55(5): 423–456.

Pegg, S. 1998, *International Society and the de facto State*, Aldershot: Ashgate.

Pełczyńska-Nałęcz, K., Strachota, K. & Falkowski, M. 2008, 'Para-states in the post-Soviet area from 1991 to 2007', *International Studies Review*, 10(2): 370–387.

Pender, K. 2018, 'Abkhazians appreciate Syrian recognition, no matter the circumstances', *Eurasianet*, July 16. https://eurasianet.org/abkhazians-appreciate-syrian-recognition-no-matter-the-circumstances (accessed August 3, 2022).

Prelz Oltramonti, G. 2015, 'The political economy of a de facto state: The importance of local stakeholders in the case of Abkhazia', *Caucasus Survey*, 3(3): 291–308.

Prime Minister of the Republic of Armenia. 2021, Press releases. www.primeminister.am/en/press-release/item/2021/03/25/Nikol-Pashinyan-meeting/ (accessed August 5, 2022).

Republic of Somaliland Ministry of Development. 2020, Citizen's budget 2020. https://slmof.org/wp-content/uploads/2020/01/Citizines-Budget-2020.pdf (accessed August 25, 2021).

*RES*. 2020, Proekt gosbyudzheta Yuzhnoi Osetii na 2021 god. http://cominf.org/node/1166533566 (accessed September 8, 2021).

Roeder, P. G. 2007, *Where Nation-States Come from: Institutional Change in the Age of Nationalism*, Princeton, NJ: Princeton University Press.

Smolnik, F. 2012, 'Political rule and violent conflict: Elections as institutional mutation in Nagorno-Karabakh', *Communist and Post-Communist Studies*, 45(1–2): 153–163.

Spanke, T. 2019, *Nurturing Dependence: The Role of Patron States in the State and Institution Building Processes of De Facto States*. PhD Dissertation. London: LSE.

Steinsdorff, S. von 2012, 'Incomplete state building – incomplete democracy? How to interpret internal political development in the post-Soviet de facto states', *Communist and Post-Communist Studies*, 45(1–2): 201–206.

Turp-Balazs, C. 2020, 'Serbia's campaign to reduce the number of countries which recognise Kosovo is working', *Emerging Europe*, January 16. https://emerging-europe.com/news/serbias-campaign-to-reduce-the-number-of-countries-which-recognise-kosovo-is-working/ (accessed August 4, 2022).

# 25

# ENGAGEMENT WITHOUT RECOGNITION

*Eiki Berg*

## De facto states positioning within the current international order

Since the end of World War II, the international community has clearly voiced strong support to existing sovereign states and placed emphasis on maintaining respect for their territorial integrity, even in cases where some of them have largely ceased to exist in empirical terms. Indeed, fundamental preoccupations of political order and stability underpin the international community's resistance to secession, thus nurturing failed states whose capacity to act independently from external assistance has become questionable. Yet there are stubborn self-determination claimants that do not fit into the decolonisation normative framework because they do not qualify as "non-self-governing territories" entitled to pursue independent course. As they lay claims on territories legally possessed by their "juridical parents", they give almost no chance to power-sharing schemes or tailor-made self-governance forms, to protect the established international order. Perhaps the most vocal in their demands are *de facto* states (Pegg 1998) – a small subset of the much larger category of secessionist movements, or territorial contenders (Lemke and Crabtree 2020), distinguished mainly by their higher degrees of territorial control, state capacity, and persistence, though unaccepted as such by the wider international society of states. Although some studies have estimated around 30 such entities that have emerged in the post–World War II international order (see Florea 2014; Kursani 2021), it would be fair to keep this figure below ten today. Neither do entities with limited control over their claimed territories such as Western Sahara and Palestine deserve to be called *de facto* states, nor is this term appropriate for entities with little capacity to independently act such as South Ossetia or rebellious regions with unconsolidated statehood such as Donbas self-proclaimed ephemeral states: Donetsk and Lugansk Peoples Republics. Most often *de facto* states are treated as places that, legally speaking, do not exist. Because granting international recognition to a breakaway region (in other words legitimising *de facto* authorities and legalising *de facto* state institutions) can undoubtedly trigger fears of a domino effect in other secessionist conflict areas.

*De facto* states are typically seen as marginal actors in the international system, which are either viewed with hostility or ignored by the vast majority of sovereign states. They are usually labelled as "pariahs, excluded from the mainstream channels of international diplomacy, existing in conditions beyond the pale of normal international intercourse" (Bartmann 2004:12). Given that argumentation of parent states (the recognised sovereign state the *de facto* state is trying to secede

DOI: 10.4324/9781003036593-29

from) has largely been accepted – "the entities are illegal, they represent a *de facto* occupation, they are based on ethnic cleansing and their leaderships lack any popular legitimacy" (Caspersen 2012:41), this predetermines the overall negative attitude towards them. More often than not, this pariah status brings with it political isolation: the absence of official bilateral representation and exclusion from intergovernmental organisations; economic isolation, in the form of sanctions aimed at restricting the flow of goods and services to and from the *de facto* state; and, finally, sociocultural isolation which excludes contestants from sporting events or restricts its nationals' ability to travel abroad (Geldenhuys 2009:47). All this speaks to the generally unfavourable legal conditions and widespread political disengagement that *de facto* states face in the postcolonial international system in particular.

Although, Caspersen may note that any international engagement with *de facto* states has been deemed unlawful (2012:31) and that therefore "the default position has been non-engagement" (2012:40), in reality, "the *de facto* states have not been either consistently ignored or comprehensively embargoed by the international community" (Lynch 2004:112). Even within the context of the generally strong support for the *status quo* in international relations, Pegg (1998:177) argues that *de facto* states have been treated "in three main ways: actively opposing them through the use of embargoes and sanctions; generally ignoring them; and coming to some sort of limited acceptance of their presence". He also notes that the fact that Northern Cyprus can be cited in all three of these "categories shows that they are not necessarily mutually exclusive" (Pegg 1998:181). To this list of three main approaches, Lynch (2004:104) argues that parent states may not only show active opposition but also make attempts to eliminate the *de facto* state by force. While this option being equally possible and rather frequently used – to name here the eradication of the Republika Srpska-Krajina (1995), the Chechen Republic of Ichkeria (2000), Tamil Eelam (2009) and the military advance against the Nagorno-Karabakh Republic (2020) – it is not only most decisive but also most costly, especially in terms of humanitarian consequences, death toll, and destruction. If not trying to uproot *de facto* states from the earth and not recognising them as full-fledged states, then what remains is some sort of engagement which may take different forms.

The idea that *de facto* states can receive varying levels of acceptance from international society is not new. Berg and Toomla (2009), for example, focus on multiple variables derived from political, economic, and public spheres to reveal both the international community's willingness to integrate *de facto* states and, correspondingly, the willingness of *de facto* states to open up to the outside world. They argue that their composite "normalisation" measure can tell us more about the relative differences in treatment than can measures of either internal or external sovereignty. Thus, even though Taiwan is gradually losing international recognition (−6, 2016–2021) while Kosovo is gradually gaining it (+4, 2016–2021),[1] the approach from the rest of the world to both of them is quasi-recognition. A bit surprisingly, Northern Cyprus (recognised only by Turkey) is tolerated by the international community more than partly recognised Abkhazia (recognised by Russia, Venezuela, Nicaragua, Nauru, and Syria). The rest of the *de facto* states such as Abkhazia, Transnistria, and Somaliland remain in the boycott zone, with Nagorno-Karabakh receiving the lowest score. Not a single *de facto* state under scrutiny was found to be completely negated by international society because of its illegality (Berg and Toomla 2009:31–33).

In a similar way, Pegg and Berg's (2016) research indicates that at least some of the traditional narrative on how sovereign states deal with *de facto* states needs to be revised. They were able to trace some evidence of the traditional hostility toward *de facto* states, particularly in the active and global US diplomatic campaign to discourage recognition of Abkhazia after the 2008 Russo–Georgian War. Yet, instead of active opposition through the use of embargoes and sanctions, they repeatedly found the United States offering various forms of diplomatic support to ease the economic isolation of Turkish Cypriots, thus making it hard to sustain the argument that *de facto* states are ignored. Perhaps the closest any *de facto* states came to a hostility view was Nagorno-Karabakh, where its *de facto* leaders were seldom granted contact of any form with US diplomats. Albeit within the general context of non-recognition, US diplomatic cables revealed broad, sustained, and often friendly US interactions with Somaliland and Northern Cyprus. Apparently, *de facto* states were not treated as homogenous entities, and US foreign policy was quite capable of discriminating between them (Pegg and Berg 2016:283).

Other research by Berg and Pegg (2018) demonstrates that the driving force behind US engagement with *de facto* states can be a strategic calculus or dedication to bring about political change by aiding moderates and marginalising hardliners in conflict-prone societies. By engagement, the United States has sought to increase its leverage and footprint in relation to important events that affect its national interests. The three clearest examples of this were the Turkish Cypriots voting to approve the UN-sponsored peace process in Cyprus (2004), the Russo–Georgian War (2008), and Somaliland's presidential election crisis (2008–2010). The fact that Turkish Cypriots, in contrast to Greek Cypriots, said yes to the Annan Peace Plan signified to the United States and other European powers that they deserved to be rewarded with a de-isolation outlook that was expressed most explicitly from 2005 to 2007. In order to counterbalance the increasing Russian influence in the South Caucasus, the US government brought Abkhazia more into focus in 2009. Somaliland saw positive support combined with various forms of threats and pressure in 2007–2009 to its more systematic state-building in the volatile security environment of the Horn of Africa. Interestingly, this research also revealed that parent state sensitivities were not the primary driver of US engagement decisions with *de facto* states (Berg and Pegg 2018:394).

Likewise, Raul Toomla (2016) tests whether there are necessary and sufficient causes that might lead to a *de facto* state having foreign representations on its soil. His approach focuses on bilateral relations that are easier to achieve than multilateral involvements carried out by international organisations – hence, this demonstrates how confirmed states accept *de facto* states and how much they engage with them. In the end, he concludes that having economic ties, a powerful patron state and basic democratic freedoms is a sufficient combination of established conditions to informally engage with a *de facto* state (Toomla 2016:331). However, this informal interaction may entail some sort of formal act that can be interpreted as implied recognition that gives rise to intense speculation. Although "recognition is understood to have occurred only when a state explicitly informs the rest of the world that it has happened" (Ker-Lindsay 2015:276), there are actors that take a careful look at whether the emphasis is set on the words of "non-recognition" or "engagement". Bruno Coppieters (2019:245) for instance, argues that "non-recognition and engagement" prioritises first of all non-recognition of breakaway regions and only then accepts engagement initiatives that foreshadow reunification attempts through creation of common security mechanisms and trade regimes. Only "engagement without recognition", *stricto sensu*, is based on the status-neutral position to seek for pragmatic solutions that do not affect any status claims (Coppieters 2019:252). Previous studies have also shown that even if there are necessary conditions available for establishing different forms of interaction between confirmed states/international organisations and *de facto* states, these engagement records vary across the time and cases, and suffer from recognition implications, perceived or not (see e.g. Axyonova and Gawrich 2018; Kyris 2018).

## De facto state engagement – why so, and so what?

James Ker-Lindsay and Eiki Berg (2018:335) define engagement without recognition "as a mechanism that provides for varying degrees of interaction with *de facto* states while maintaining the position that they are not regarded as independent sovereign actors in the international system". Most often, engagement with *de facto* states includes interactions with the parent state and interactions with the wider international community while leaving out *de facto* states' links with their patrons (Caspersen 2018:375–376). By differentiating various forms of engagement ranging from diplomatic and trade connections to contacts between people and authorities, this opens up new opportunities for conflict management. Caspersen (2018:377) also suggests distinguishing between "engagement with individuals and with institutions, and between what could be termed hard and soft engagement". In her view, hard engagement may result in improvements in state capacity, whereas soft engagement is limited to educational and peo-ple-to-people exchanges. This explains why on certain occasions parent states and *de facto* states either approve or resist engagement activities – on the one hand, parent states dislike everything that bolsters state-building in territories they had laid claim to; on the other hand, *de facto* states resist everything that aims for a return to *status quo ante*.

If *de facto* states and other such entities are not disappearing, then the international com-munity will have to deal with them on different matters. The United States, at least, regularly engages these entities on a wide variety of different subjects. Although it does not recognise them, its interactions with *de facto* states are not uniformly hostile. They are sometimes warm, friendly, and supportive (Berg and Pegg 2018:404). Although US engagement with *de facto* states may be varied and opportunistic, its implementation in practice has demonstrated clear alter-natives to isolationist measures and shown the limited utility of relying exclusively on punitive sanctions in order to cope with the collision of hard facts on the ground, and international norms and principles. It has also illustrated some of the opportunities that may exist to bring adversaries closer to each other's incompatible positions even when dealing with contested or unrecognised sovereignty. Limited and flawed though it may be, third parties including the United States seem not to have any better options than to engage with *de facto* states and promote stability in the short term and hopefully increase the prospects for conflict resolution in the longer term (Berg and Pegg 2018:405), because "isolation does not push you toward reconciliation, but to other forms of survival" (from an interview in de Waal 2018:58).

Engagement with "adversarial governments" has in fact always rested on a strategic mode of US action, in which the building of interactions was instrumental in affecting changes in the target state (Lynch 2002). In this way, engagement was seen as a foreign-policy strategy of establishing contacts and building close ties with the government/civil society of the target state (Smith 2005). It had a great potential as a tool for modifying the behaviour of regimes with which the United States significantly disagreed (Haass and O'Sullivan 2000). Undermining illiberal practices and promoting change became *leitmotif* of engagement, while interactions with despicable regimes or activities under unusual legal and political circumstances remained unhindered (Smith 2005). Rather than the threat of punishment, engagement has relied on the promise of rewards to influence the target's behaviour (Schweller 2005). Its toolbox contains both economic (trade, aid, and credits) and political (implied recognition) incentives; it may open up official channels of communication or remain merely at the people-to-people contact level. Overall, the widespread opinion is that engagement provides alternatives to punitive poli-cies, and that this approach can be also tested in *de facto* states which otherwise try to overcome isolation and siege mentality by establishing even closer relations with their external patrons (Berg and Pegg 2018:389)

Cooley and Mitchell (2010) drew their inspiration for engagement without recognition advocacy from the simple argument that if one is not trying to integrate these breakaway regions with the actors, institutions, and norms of the international community, then one cannot address the problems of clientelism, isolation, and dependency and thus prevent their fall into the patrons' unconditional domain. Thus, engaging *de facto* states should be seen as consistent with support for democratic governance (Broers 2005:68) – engagement enables the development of genuinely participatory and pluralist politics which may favour pro-settlement forces if played out correctly. It should affect the domestic political balance of power by aiding moderates and marginalising hardliners (Lobell 2013:262–263) – doing business with *de facto* state authorities has the potential to bring about regime change through the backdoor. Berg and Pegg (2018:395) found that other factors explaining shifts in attitudes and the prevalence of a positive engagement mood had to do with the fact that parent states either did not exist or actively supported engagement or had devised their own engagement strategy to be deployed alongside US efforts. As long as engagement does not constitute recognition, and that recognition cannot be construed from any particular form of interaction, a wide range of initiatives can be undertaken (Ker-Lindsay 2015:269). In theory, engagement without recognition calls for a number of openings through which *de facto* states' political elites, business leaders, and civil society can build ties to people in the rest of the world. In practice, engagement without recognition as a policy approach has a varied track record from the actions on the ground.

The European Union, for instance, has been equally engaged with some *de facto* states, especially with Kosovo, Taiwan, Northern Cyprus, Transnistria, Abkhazia, and Somaliland. Today, most of the EU member states recognise independent Kosovo; still, five of them do not. In order to satisfy a "Group of Five", Kosovo is not seen as a full-fledged country. While not contradicting its one-China policy and undivided-Cyprus policy, the EU has kept its "diplomatic" presence in the form of European Economic and Trade office in Taipei, and considered Northern Cyprus as part of the EU where the application of the *acquis* has been temporarily suspended due to the ongoing conflict. The EU has also extended its DCFTA with Moldova to Transnistria (Berg and Vits 2022) and assists Somaliland in state-building and counter-terrorist activities (Pegg and Kolstø 2015). As EU access to Nagorno-Karabakh has been largely impossible due to Azerbaijan's tough resistance, then the biggest engagement challenges are posed by Abkhazia. Here, the EU's policy of "non-recognition and engagement" from 2009 onwards has reflected a clear stand on defending Georgia's territorial integrity in its secessionist conflicts, differentiating between Georgia's conflict with Abkhazia and South Ossetia, and at the same time demonstrating a willingness to engage with the populations of *de facto* states through confidence-building measures (Coppieters 2019:241). The European Special Representative for the South Caucasus (EUSR) installed by the European Council, has attempted to deal with *de facto* authorities on an informal level while keeping some ties of information and exchange open, most intensively at the time of Peter Semneby, 2006–2011 (Harzl 2018:45). The need for de-isolation and entering into a "structured dialogue" with *de facto* authorities in the South Caucasus was also suggested by Sabine Fischer (2010), a member of the European Union Institute for Security Studies, an EU think tank. Likewise, the report from the Centre for East European and International Studies (ZOIS) has recently focused on educational issues to enhance the EU profile in Northern Cyprus, Transnistria, and Abkhazia (von Löwis and de Waal 2020). This all suggests mitigating the isolation of *de facto* states while pulling these entities slightly out of their patrons' dominance.

The search for international and regional stability is an important factor explaining the EU's policies on non-recognition, its neutral position regarding the question of status, and also in its recognition policies (Coppieters 2019:251), depending on the specific circumstances for various policy applications. What EU approaches have in common is that they start from the assumption that maintaining isolationist policies vis-à-vis these entities is counterproductive (Harzl 2018). They also repudiate the notion that *de facto* authorities are merely puppets in the hands of their patrons, which are unable or incapable of formulating autonomous political decisions. Although these *de facto* states may be different, they have some capacities to act independently (Berg and Vits 2020). Furthermore, these approaches articulate the need to promote inter-societal dialogue, people-to-people contacts, as well as academic mobility. Thus, the argument follows that "a limited exchange with the *de facto* state is the only way to keep the vision of conflict transformation alive" (Harzl 2018:52), notwithstanding the risk of implied recognition and legit-imising the *de facto* authorities. Benedikt Harzl (2018:67) even suggests the establishment of a status-neutral field presence in the form of the EU information office in Abkhazia, just like the American Institute in Taiwan, which is an example of "privatised" diplomatic and consular ties. A stronger EU presence in the form of liaison offices that can be used "both to deliver more assistance and to demand commitments from the *de facto* authorities" is also supported by Thomas de Waal (2018:4).

## Enabling and constraining factors for engagement

It is not unusual to meet hostility towards acts of unilateral secession and to see a deep reluc-tance by the parent state to interact with *de facto* authorities. International community is mostly on the side of a parent state, as stability and order rule out sovereignty claims voiced by out-laws. It is valid to claim that fear of legitimising the status of *de facto* states holds the rest of the world back from establishing more or less meaningful types of interactions. This is also because engaging with *de facto* states can be viewed as a violation of the principle of safeguarding the territorial integrity of UN member states. There is obviously a tension between territorial integrity and self-determination norms which set obstacles to engagement policies (Caspersen 2018:375). The non-permissive legal and political environment stigmatises breakaway regions as occupied and under the control of illegitimate regimes. Even if, in a manner of speaking, "de facto authorities", applied to the non-recognised entity, may be acceptable as a reference point for interaction between secessionists and international organisations and/or third parties, then the narratives of "illegal occupation" and "illegal annexation" restrict the potential scope for engagement (Coppieters 2018:357). By presenting the question of secession as an act of military foreign occupation, parent states are able to advance an argument against engagement within the confines of international law (Harzl 2018:9). However, talking about engagement of the "Area under the Turkish occupation" is a no-go to Turkish Cypriots, who might consider this as a non-recognition of Northern Cyprus (the northern half of an island controlled by *de facto* authorities).

Ker-Lindsay (2018:366) explores the stigmatisation of *de facto* states and how this affects the interaction with external actors. His systemic factors reveal the existence of a UN Security Council resolution condemning the unilateral declaration of independence (e.g. of Northern Cyprus) and the states following suit; contextual factors test the willingness of parent states to accept interaction between the *de facto* state and third countries; and finally, national factors explain stigmatisation with the fact that the parent state has an ongoing secessionist dispute of its own. This resonates with Harzl's (2018) view that the international community, more than great powers seen individually, cares a lot about the potential reaction of the parent state. There is significant variation across different cases in terms of how willing parent states are to countenance engagement with *de facto* states on their sovereign territory. Parent states are often equipped with UN Security Council resolutions as guiding legal framework that condemns foreign occupations and ethnic cleansings and affirms the territorial integrity principle. If they do accept engagement, then it is mostly within an explicit framework of conflict resolution and territorial integrity, with limits on capacity-building, and always coordinated through the parent state (Caspersen 2018:379–380). This ensures that parent states have full control over coercive measures, sometimes gradually turning the screw, or in other occasions being more permissive to third parties' interactions. Azerbaijan, Cyprus, and Georgia, on the one hand, have earned the reputation of being the most restrictive parent states jealously guarding their privileged position before international law and treating attempts to engage their secessionist entities as implied recognition. Moldova, on the other hand, has demonstrated a more relaxed attitude concerning third party interactions with Transnistria, even to the extent that US diplomats and EU officials are seen frequently meeting *de facto* authorities in Tiraspol (MFA of PMR 2021).

To illustrate this claim, four UN Security Council resolutions (UNSC S/RES/822 1993; UNSC S/RES/853 1993; UNSC S/RES/874 1993; UNSC S/RES/884 1993) have called for the withdrawal of local Armenian forces from the parts of Azerbaijan proper they occupied till the end of 2020. The Azerbaijani side tried to isolate Nagorno-Karabakh in all possible ways: denying entry visas to all third country nationals who had visited Nagorno-Karabakh with some added on the Interpol list for this alleged misconduct; prohibiting economic activities in breakaway region; and discouraging any effort to promote international engagement with Karabakhi Armenians.

The Greek Cypriot government, for their part, has to a large extent succeeded in isolating their northern counterpart internationally: Northern Cyprus exports to the EU are banned by a 1994 European Court of Justice ruling; there are no direct flights (except via Turkey); and regular mail has to be sent to the address "Mersin 10, Turkey". Cyprus has usually relied on UN Security Council Resolutions confirming the territorial integrity of the Republic of Cyprus (UNSC S/RES/353 1974; UNSC S/RES/360 1974), and which view the Turkish Republic of Northern Cyprus as an illegal entity and urge other states not to recognise it (UNSC S/RES/541 1983; UNSC S/RES/550 1984). In the official view, attribution of any kind of validity to any law, court, or other organ of Northern Cyprus must be avoided to safeguard the internationally recognised Republic of Cyprus (see also Ker-Lindsay 2012).

Finally, Georgia's Law on Occupied Territories from 2008 depicts the Russian Federation as a military occupying force and therefore bans economic activities in Abkhazia and South Ossetia by all domestic and foreign companies, and prohibits foreign citizens to travel without authorisation of the Georgian authorities (Parliament of Georgia 2008). The supplementary documents from the government of Georgia – such as the Strategy on Occupied Territories: Engagement through Cooperation (Government of Georgia 2010c), the Action Plan for Engagement on the Implementation of the Strategy (Government of Georgia 2010a), and the Modalities for Conducting Activities in the Occupied Territories (Government of Georgia 2010b) – all acknowledge that engagement is an inevitable component of conflict resolution and the restoration of Georgian territorial integrity. Yet they also reflect concerns that engagement by international state and non-state actors could lead to "creeping recognition" (Fischer 2010).

As demonstrated in this section, parent states see engagement closely linked to the principle of territorial integrity. At the same time, *de facto* states prioritise engagement with the wider international community (Caspersen 2018:377). Thus, it is not only parent states that may constrain engagement activities if not meeting their expectations; *de facto* states are equally important players in this game, since "creeping re-integration" is definitely not something that brings them closer to international recognition. Caspersen (2018:375) argues that the *de facto* state position is affected both by the declared self-determination goal and the degree of support received from a patron state. A self-determination claim that foresees self-proclaimed entities becoming full-fledged states or unification with the patron state has more difficulties to accommodate engagement through the parent state than is the case with (con-)federal arrangements where secessionists may satisfy with an equal standing. As *de facto* states are usually struggling with the parent states' orchestrated isolation regime and hostility exposed by the international community, then this leads to an enduring "do or die" dilemma where *de facto* states either seek protection from external patrons ("do") or face the prospect of forceful reintegration back into their parent states ("die") (Berg and Vits 2018). Although essential for *de facto* states' survival, heavy reliance on the patron state's support comes at a price. This may have also negative policy implication because the engagement strategy may be rejected on the grounds that it usually offers merely a fraction of what *de facto* states get from their patrons in the form of "recognition", financial assistance, and security.

It would be fair to say that *de facto* states are not thrilled about the engagement perspective because this may lead to "creeping re-integration". *De facto* authorities look suspiciously at freedom of travelling, working, or using public services in parent states. Statements reaffirming international support for parent states' territorial integrity in broad policy language are received by *de facto* authorities as objectionable and discouraging their participation. The fact that *de facto* state engagement has been made conditional to the parent state's explicit approval – which stipulates what kind of activities are tolerated and what not, and that interactions are limited to individuals and civil society organisations, and not really engaging *de facto* authorities – all makes engagement without recognition hardly attractive as a policy initiative in the eyes of secessionists. This may actually work in Northern Cyprus, where EU accession in the case of reunification of the island is still regarded as an equally motivating perspective compared to the "splendid isolation" or increased Turkish dominance. Also, Transnistrian authorities have demonstrated their willingness to align with their parent state's conditionality in return for gaining access to foreign markets. However, there are still more *de facto* states which see these moves as downgrading their hard-won independence. Even the most isolated ones may be satisfied with the connections and assistance that patron states provide to them. The heavy cost of breaking free from the parent state is still remembered and never equalled with the potential loss of hard-won sovereignty to the patron state.

However difficult engagement may look in essence, both from the parent state and the *de facto* state perspective, complete ignorance is simply impossible. What several accounts from the past reveal is that the involvement of *de facto* states in direct talks, while contentious, are more often appreciated than not (Berg and Vits 2020:384). At the same time, all the ongoing negotiation formats seem to be stuck on questions related to the status of the participants, and on who and how should be involved in the talks in the first place. When progress is made, it is usually limited to smaller issues, mostly involving social, economic or cultural matters; while the spill-over towards bigger, more fundamental political and diplomatic issues is slow or even non-existent. Negotiations present the parent states with serious dilemmas: in order to have negotiations, one needs to acknowledge the existence of the other side, and the validity of their claims. As the negotiation positions are diametrically opposing, with one side oriented towards reintegration and the other towards secession, the process develops a zero-sum character for both. In this case, keeping the communication channels open becomes even more important than achieving a specific end result, which explains why small agreements on technical issues can be hailed as significant progress and reveals the logic of continuing (international) pressure for talks even when previous rounds have ended in failure. Here, *de facto* states have more to win than to lose: prolonged negotiations give time to adopt constitutions, build state institutions, and consolidate internal legitimacy. Consequently, their agency increases, and their positions in the negotiation process will harden (Mazur 2014).

## Proved track records and conditions for success

Third-party engagement may succeed only if there is sufficient space for innovative manoeuvring among facts and norms, if there is external interest and capacity to pursue conflict management, if the parent state grants approval, if the engagement toolbox and implementation mechanisms look both attractive and credible to *de facto* authorities, and, finally, if all this does not inspire the patron state to introduce countermeasures. In 2009, Abkhazia was given the opportunity to engage with the West on a number of political, economic, social, and cultural issues, while leaving recognition of Abkhazia as an independent state off the table. The overall aim was to maintain trust between the West and the local Abkhaz population, open a new international path that avoided leaving all "Abkhazian eggs in the Russian basket", and support the idea of Georgia as a role model that would become a political-economic magnet for residents of Abkhazia. Contrary to expectations, however, the implementation of the EU's non-recognition and engagement policy alienated many Abkhazians. In other words, the EU's engagement with Abkhazia was doomed to fail (Berg 2015).

The reasons for policy failure were quite indicative. First, the twin pillars of non-recognition and engagement did not support each other as readily as the third parties may have hoped, given their willingness to follow Georgia's lead in setting the parameters of non-recognition. Georgians themselves had gone back and forth between both occupation and engagement rhetoric while leaving an impression of undecidedness: any possible signal of concessions in *de facto* state engagement would have likely caused domestic outcries that ought to be avoided at any cost. While stigmatising contested territories as occupied and under the control of illegitimate regimes, Georgia enacted legislation that criminalised unauthorised visits and contacts with *de facto* state officials and civil society organisations, thereby posing serious obstacles to confidence building. According to the EU perspective, neither Abkhazia nor South Ossetia were "disputed territories" anymore – they had been recognised by their patron state and four other UN members – nor was the EU in a position of convincing Georgians that these were not occupied territories.

Second, EU and US commitment to implementing its engagement strategy remained short of the requisite level. Abkhazia rejected this engagement strategy on the grounds that it offered merely a fraction of what it receives from Russia. The EU and US emphasis has always been more on humanitarian programmes than on structural development. There has been very little that attracts Abkhazians to the EU – the DCFTA is hardly a proper measure to facilitate the export of tangerines and hazelnuts via Tbilisi. At the same time, all contacts and collaborative proposals with the rest of the world had to go through Tbilisi, and de-isolation became exclusively linked with resolution to the conflict. Western diplomats were never able to sort out the details of implementation: how to pay local implementers without making direct bank transfers, or how to decide which documents Abkhazian residents could travel with to participate in confidence-building programs abroad. By contrast, Russian–Abkhazian relations reached a new level in November 2014, when the two parties signed a Treaty of Alliance and Strategic Partnership, and then again in 2020, when the parties agreed upon "The Formation of a Common Socio-Economic Space Between the Russian Federation and the Republic of Abkhazia on the Basis of the Harmonization of Legislations".

Third, the concept of an engagement strategy is a Western intellectual product. Abkhazia's adversary, Georgia, is a pro-Western country with strong ambitions to join transatlantic security structures and the European community. This contradicts the view of Russia, Abkhazia's hegemonic ally that claims prominence in the post-Soviet space. There is no reason to believe that the Western approach, which after all still backs Georgia's territorial integrity claims and makes engagement conditional, can be fruitfully planted in Abkhazian ground. Moreover, Russia is closer to the Abkhazian people in terms of everyday language use and culture than the EU and the United States. When an engagement strategy stipulates the need to diversify Abkhazia's foreign relations, Abkhazians automatically translate this into the language of increasing EU and US leverage, which again equates to meeting Georgia's demands. Of course, none of this means that Abkhazia's "strategic partnership" with Russia better serves its interests as an aspiring sovereign state. Abkhazian leaders do not wish to recognise (or, perhaps, do not care) that whatever sovereignty they possess can easily melt away. At the same time, with the strong polarisation that currently exists in Western–Russian relations, even if the EU and the United States were now to modify its engagement strategy to fully accommodate Abkhazian interests, it would most likely still be unable to serve as a basis for conflict resolution.

Other than Abkhazia, the EU has had difficulties in organising even the smallest of activities with Nagorno-Karabakh and the Donbas Republics. The Azerbaijani and the Ukrainian government have each tried to isolate their breakaway regions at all costs and have lobbied for international support for restoring its own territorial integrity. The Second Karabakh War in September 2020 proved the seriousness of Azerbaijani's stance and left no space for innovative thoughts in presenting the EU or the United States as a third party engaging with *de facto* authorities for the sake of "changing the course" and providing alternatives to isolation. Whereas there is some understanding in EU and US policy circles for Abkhazia's incompatible position with Georgia, all invitations by the EU to explore potential engagement in Donbas thus far have been unsuccessful. Moreover, the *de facto* authorities in DPR and LPR do not think they need the EU to balance the overwhelming Russian dominance, while Kyiv has not accepted territorial losses and expects this problem to be solved sooner rather than later without the EU's help. Transnistria, on the other hand, is economically dependent on EU trade links. Following this logic, trade between the EU and Transnistria has become an important tool of engagement. Due to economic incentives offered by the DCFTA with Moldova, Transnistria has exploited pragmatism (Berg and Vits 2022) and now values its access to European markets in a way that is compatible to its appreciation of military-political or sociocultural connections with Russia. In addition, both the strategic calculus of the EU and the operational constraints set by Moldova coincide with each other – engagement is valued by the EU authorities and agreed upon with the Moldovan government.

At first glance, there is a good reason to believe that EU's "non-recognition and engagement" policy of 2009 remains a modest attempt to make a truly influential shift in conflict dynamics, thus probably not to be revised in future or to be practiced elsewhere. Surprisingly little has been reported about follow-up activities, except some retrospective accounts of informal negotiations and policy initiatives (de Waal 2018) as well as engagements in the field of higher education (von Löwis and de Waal 2020). One may easily get the impression that engagement without recognition has never been a consistent strategy but remains an ad hoc approach, changing as the issues and problems related to *de facto* states are step-by-step uncovered. The most recent EU initiative, called *EU4Dialogue in DG NEAR*, seems to support the aforementioned claim. It is a regional programme for the period 2021–2024, with a budget of 15 million EUR, that aims "to support the overall diplomatic efforts towards peace and stability through enhanced dialogue and people-to-people contacts across the divides" (Annex 3). The programme will engage the CSOs and individuals in conflict regions to help facilitate exchanges and improve overall social conditions. It is designed to be flexible to seize opportunities and adjust to changing environments. The three components – "Supporting Understanding between Conflict Parties", "Support to Conflict Transformation in the South Caucasus and the Republic of Moldova", and "Improving Exchanges across the Divide through Education and Culture" – reveal that *de facto* state engagement can appear in various forms and related to different circumstances also in the future, but one should not expect to see it evolving as a result of coordinated actions with strong institutional backing and financial support. Most importantly, there are not and will not be official policy guidelines prescribing meaningful actions to be taken in order to engage *de facto* states with the rest of the world.

Although often welcomed when real and persistent conditions are met, *de facto* state engagement *per se* may still have some unintended consequences. If not implicit recognition of secessionist entities, then creeping legitimation of *de facto* authorities is what makes third-party policymakers concerned before designing formulas for engagement. Indeed, any type of engagement potentially advances the *de facto* state's institutional capacity, which then might be exploited to further back its claim for self-determination. Previous experiences with *de facto* states show that whatever approach the third party chooses, they risk strengthening and entrenching these entities rather than bringing them closer to the reintegration agenda of the parent states. Unintended consequences have diminished the effect of engagement without recognition in terms of conflict management. These aspects considered, policymakers in this area are faced with apparently unsurmountable obstacles.

Micro-level research has revealed several conditions for success in the engagement practice of third parties. Sebastian Relitz (2021:227) shows in his work on Abkhazia that engagement based on needs-driven approach and implemented indirectly and informally may offer some insights worth considering. Indirectly, it means that third-party engagement practices are carried out through other institutions or international NGOs. The EUSR, for instance, is involved in high-level political dialogue taking place both in Abkhazia and during Geneva International Discussions, thus disconnecting the headquarters in Brussels from direct policymaking. Informality goes hand-in-hand with the facilitation of dialogue and confidence-building measures. This depends on a small number of professionals and their intrinsic motivations to promote capacity-building initiatives for the local population in the non-political sphere, such as small-scale business, rural development, and the field of education. This is where the EU has more to gain in terms of increased leverage and reputation. Instead of keeping emphasis on the humanitarian assistance or conflict management, a third party such as the EU has more to gain if proposed engagement benefits the local population, is positively viewed by *de facto* authorities, and is tolerated both by parent and patron states. Let us not overlook the facts that *de facto* authorities are in a position to approve any engagement of third parties; that without local CSOs and expert communities, it is not possible to implement any engagement project on the ground; and that the parent state has to be informed about concerted actions and ensured that *de facto* state engagement does not bring these breakaway regions closer to international recognition. Furthermore, third parties are advised not to act explicitly against the patron state's interests, as the latter is a potential veto player and may block international engagement in embryo.

In Relitz's (2021:228) view, engagement may easily fail to develop more in the direction of needs-driven interventions, and if so, the objectives of engagement without recognition policy approach would remain unattained. To be correct, non-recognition still prevails and meets its objectives, but engagement fails to take off and bring along a positive change in conflict dynamics. In this case one should not expect to see alternatives to patron dominance evolving; instead, one should be satisfied with the status quo. In a short- or even long-term perspective, this may be in the interest of all possible stakeholders. Parent states maintain their monopoly of claiming sovereignty over a breakaway region and do not need to worry about "creeping recognition". *De facto* states continue their reliance on patron states' support and forget about "creeping reunification". Patron states enjoy the leverage they have on the parties to the conflict and their external supporters and prefer things staying as they currently are. Even third parties, whose operational code is "engagement without recognition", may at times consider *de facto* state engagement (without strategic prerequisites) more challenging to the international order than keeping the secessionist threat localised and in isolation from major trends.

# Note

1 Kosovo's number of recognitions is contested matter as according to Serbian claims, many countries have withdrawn their recognition.

# References

Annex 3 to the Commission Implementing Decision on the ENI East Regional Action Programme for 2019. http://c_2019_5639_f1_annex_en_v2_p1_1041967.pdf (europa.eu).

Axyonova, V. & Gawrich, A. 2018, 'Regional Organizations and Secessionist Entities: Analysing Practices of the EU and the OSCE in Post-Soviet Protracted Conflict Areas', *Ethnopolitics*, 17(4): 408–425.

Bartmann, B. 2004, 'Political Realities and Legal Anomalies: Revisiting the Politics of International Recognition', in T. Bahchelli, B. Bartmann & H. Srebrnik (eds.), *De Facto States: The Quest for Sovereignty*, Oxon: Routledge, 12–31.

Berg, E. 2015. 'Was the West's Engagement with Abkhazia Doomed to Fail?'. *PONARS Eurasia Policy Memo* No. 375. http://www.ponarseurasia.org/memo/was-west-engagement-abkhazia-doomed-fail.

Berg, E. & Pegg, S. 2018, 'Scrutinizing a Policy of "Engagement without Recognition": US Requests for Diplomatic Actions with *De Facto* States', *Foreign Policy Analysis*, 14(3): 388–407.

Berg, E. & Toomla, R. 2009, 'Forms of Normalization in the Quest for De Facto Statehood', *The International Spectator*, 44: 27–45.

Berg, E. & Vits, K. 2018, 'The Do-or-Die Dilemma Facing Post-Soviet De Facto States', *PONARS Eurasia Policy Memo* No. 527

Berg, E. & Vits, K. 2020, 'Exploring *De Facto* State Agency: Negotiation Power, International Engagement and Patronage', in G. Baldachhino & A. Wivel (eds.), *Research Handbook on the Politics of Small States*, Cheltenham: Edward Elgar Publishers, 379–394.

Berg, E. & Vits, K. 2022, 'Transnistria's European Drive: A Means to What End?', *Geopolitics*, 27(3): 852–874.

Broers, L. 2005, 'The Politics of Non-Recognition and Democratization', *Accord*, 17: 68–71.

Caspersen, N. 2012, *Unrecognized States: The Struggle for Sovereignty in the Modern International System*, Cambridge: Polity Press.

Caspersen, N. 2018, 'Recognition, Status Quo or Reintegration: Engagement with De Facto States', *Ethnopolitics*, 17(4): 373–389.

Cooley, A. & Mitchell, L. A. 2010, 'Engagement without Recognition: A New Strategy toward Abkhazia and Eurasia's Unrecognized States', *The Washington Quarterly* 33: 59–73.

Coppieters, B. 2018, '"Statehood", "De Facto Authorities" and "Occupation": Contested Concepts and the EU's Engagement in its European Neighbourhood', *Ethnopolitics*, 17(4): 343–361.

Coppieters, B. 2019, 'Engagement without Recognition', in G. Visoka, J. Doyle & E. Newman (eds.), *Routledge Handbook of State Recognition*, London and New York: Routledge, 241–255.

De Waal, T. 2018, *Uncertain Ground: Engaging with Europe's De Facto States and Breakaway Territories*, Washington, DC: Carnegie Europe.

Fischer, S. 2010, *The EU's Non-Recognition and Engagement Policy towards Abkhazia and South Ossetia*, Brussels: European Union Institute for Security Studies.

Florea, A. 2014, 'De Facto States in International Politics (1945–2011): A New Data Set', *International Interactions*, 40(5): 788–811.

Geldenhuys, D. 2009, *Contested States in World Politics*, Basingstoke: Palgrave.

Government of Georgia 2010a, *Action Plan for Engagement: Office of the State Minister for Reintegration 6 July*. www.iccn.ge/files/action_plan_for_engagement_gog.pdf.

Government of Georgia 2010b, *On Approval of Modalities for Conducting Activities in the Occupied Territories of Georgia*, Tbilisi, No. 320. www.europarl.europa.eu/meetdocs/2009_2014/documents/dsca/dv/dsca_20110315_13/dsca_20110315_13en.pdf.

Government of Georgia 2010c, *State Strategy on Occupied Territories: Engagement through Cooperation*. http://gov.ge/files/225_31228_851158_15.07.20-StateStrategyonOccupiedTerritories-EngagementThrough Cooperation(Final).pdf.

Haass, R. N. & O'Sullivan M. L. (eds.) 2000, *Honey and Vinegar: Incentives, Sanctions and Foreign Policy*. Washington, DC: Brookings Institution Press.

Harzl, B. 2018, *The Law and Politics of Engaging De Facto States: Injecting New Ideas for an Enhanced EU Role*, Washington, DC: Centre for Transatlantic Relations.

Ker-Lindsay, J. 2012, *The Foreign Policy of Counter Secession: Preventing the Recognition of Contested States*, Oxford: Oxford University Press.

Ker-Lindsay, J. 2015, 'Engagement without Recognition: The Limits of Diplomatic Interaction with Contested States', *International Affairs*, 91: 267–285.

Ker-Lindsay, J. 2018, 'The Stigmatisation of De Facto States: Disapproval and "Engagement without Recognition"', *Ethnopolitics*, 17(4): 362–372.

Ker-Lindsay, J. & Berg E. 2018, 'Introduction: A Conceptual Framework for Engagement with De Facto States', *Ethnopolitics*, 17(4): 335–342.

Kursani, S. 2021, 'Reconsidering the Contested State in Post-1945 International Relations: An Ontological Approach', *International Studies Review*, 23(3): 752–778.

Kyris, G. 2018, 'Sovereignty and Engagement without Recognition: Explaining the Failure of Conflict Resolution in Cyprus', *Ethnopolitics*, 17(4): 426–442.

Lemke, D. & Crabtree C. 2020, 'Territorial Contenders in World Politics', *Journal of Conflict Resolution*, 64(2–3): 518–544.

Lobell, S. E. 2013, 'Engaging the Enemy and the Lessons for the Obama Administration', *Political Science Quarterly*, 128: 261–287.

Lynch, D. 2004, *Engaging Eurasia's Separatist States: Unresolved Conflicts and De Facto States*. Washington, DC: United States Institute of Peace Press.

Lynch, M. 2002, 'Why Engage? China and the Logic of Communicative Engagement', *European Journal of International Relations* 8:187–230.

Mazur, N. 2014, 'The Visible Effects of an Invisible Constitution: The Contested State of Transdniestra's Search for Recognition through International Negotiations', Indiana University, Maurer School of Law. Available at: www.repository.law.indiana.edu/etd/6/

MFA of PMR 2021, 'The President of the PMR Held a Meeting with the Head of the EU Delegation to the Republic of Moldova', 22 April. https://mfa-pmr.org/en/node/8480.

Parliament of Georgia 2008, *Law of Georgia on Occupied Territories* No 431, 23 October. https://matsne.gov.ge/en/document/view/19132?publication=6.

Pegg, S. 1998, *International Society and the de Facto State*. Aldershot: Ashgate.

Pegg, S. & Berg E. 2016, 'Lost and Found: The WikiLeaks of *De Facto* State-Great Power Relations', *International Studies Perspectives*, 17(3): 267–286.

Pegg, S. & Kolstø P. 2015, 'Somaliland: Dynamics of Internal Legitimacy and (Lack of) External Sovereignty', *Geoforum*, 66: 193–202.

Relitz, S. 2021, *The Practice of Engagement without Recognition: A Promising Approach to Conflict Resolution in De Facto States?: The Case of the European Union in Abkhazia*. Doctoral thesis, University of Jena, Jena.

Schweller, R. L. 2005, 'Managing the Rise of Great Powers: History and Theory', in A. I. Johnston & R. S. Ross (eds.), *Engaging China: The Management of an Emerging Power*, New York: Routledge, 1–31.

Smith, K. E. 2005, 'Engagement and Conditionality: Incompatible or Mutually Reinforcing', in R. Youngs (ed.), *Global Europe: New Terms of Engagement*, London: The Foreign Policy Centre, 23–29.

Toomla, R. 2016, 'Charting Informal Engagement between De Facto States: A Quantitative Analysis', *Space and Polity*, 20(3): 330–345.

UNSC S/RES/353 1974, 'Cyprus', *United Nations*. http://unscr.com/en/resolutions/353.

UNSC S/RES/360 1974, 'Cyprus' *United Nations*. http://unscr.com/en/resolutions/360.

UNSC S/RES/541 1983, 'Cyprus', *United Nations*. http://unscr.com/en/resolutions/541.

UNSC S/RES/550 1984, 'Cyprus' *United Nations*. http://unscr.com/en/resolutions/550.

UNSC S/RES/822 1993, 'Armenia-Azerbaijan (30 Apr)', *United Nations*. http://unscr.com/en/resolutions/822.

UNSC S/RES/853 1993, 'Armenia-Azerbaijan (29 July)', *United Nations*. http://unscr.com/en/resolutions/853.

UNSC S/RES/874 1993, 'Armenia-Azerbaijan (14 Oct)', *United Nations*. http://unscr.com/en/resolutions/874.

UNSC S/RES/884 1993, "Armenia-Azerbaijan (12 Nov)', *United Nations*. http://unscr.com/en/resolutions/884.

Von Löwis, S. and de Waal, T. 2020, 'Higher Education in Europe's Unrecognised Territories: Challenges and Opportunities', *ZOiS Report* 2.

# 26

# SECESSION AND DIPLOMACY

## Playing the state, proving the nation

*R. Joseph Huddleston and Caroline Hall*

### Why study secessionist diplomacy?

The list of manifold challenges facing a secessionist movement is daunting. In some cases, it faces war with the incumbent state, in which case the aspiring state must recruit, train, and supply a military to fight the state, as well as convince its population to take the risk. In most cases, it must also build and maintain essential state institutions like courts, elections, education, and healthcare. Secessionist movements range in form from nascent nationalist movements with little form or structure to full-fledged regional governments vying for independence. Neither war nor comprehensive governance is common to all secessionist groups, but each faces the eventual requirement of convincing the international community of nation-states to embrace it as a new member. This acceptance is the only item that necessarily requires third-party action – it is, in fact, defined by it – but secessionist groups and other aspiring states still reach out for external assistance at every stage of conflict, from early protests against an incumbent state to staffing whole ministries that lobby for recognition of their successful territorial consolidation.

While there is still much to explore about how secessionist movements conduct diplomacy, no one questions the importance of a well-planned diplomatic strategy as part of a larger pathway towards statehood. We know that self-determination groups prioritize diplomacy at every stage of conflict (Coggins 2015), and that successful rebel groups often pour resources into building and maintaining a diplomatic presence abroad (Huang 2016). We know that secessionists believe international legitimacy is crucial to their eventual success (Coggins 2014; Stewart 2018) and that their leaders think carefully and strategically about managing their international image (Bob 2005), through both traditional channels (Huang 2016; Malejacq 2017) and more modern forms like social media (Jones and Mattiacci 2017; Loyle and Bestvater 2019; Mattiacci and Jones 2020). Moreover, short of recognition, there is an enormous range of positions third parties will take towards secessionist polities. Even if third parties do not recognize them – the most likely outcome for any secessionist group – they still may maintain deep ties with them in what has come to be known as "engagement without recognition" (Cooley and Mitchell 2010; Ker-Lindsay and Berg 2018).[1] Moreover, they change their levels and types of this engagement as a result of what happens in the conflict (Huddleston 2021).

Engaging the world they wish to join is a matter of paramount concern for any successful secessionist government. Yet it is still a relatively understudied aspect of secession. Scholars of secession and recognition tend to train their lenses on how third parties make decisions vis-à-vis

DOI: 10.4324/9781003036593-30

secessionists, not on how secessionists themselves craft their diplomatic strategies. The language used in scholarship on state-secessionist interactions naturally tends to foreground the third-party perspective – including "engagement without recognition", for example. Secessionists aim to join this club of "engagers", and the literature on recognition of secessionists has made sense of it by filling out our understanding of the interests, constraints, and diplomatic methods of external actors.

However, through careful study of diplomacy by secessionists themselves, we can develop new theory about both secession and diplomacy. By most accounts, it resembles the picture that diplomacy scholars of the last century have painted of state-to-state diplomacy. However, for the secessionist, diplomacy also plays additional functions. This chapter will explain how, placing secessionist diplomacy within the context of diplomatic studies writ large as well as exploring why diplomacy is and must be different for groups seeking statehood. Finally, it concludes with a discussion of several open questions about aspiring state diplomacy.

## Diplomacy for the state and diplomacy for the secessionist

Early writings on diplomacy were practical, defining it primarily as a sort of negotiation. Writing in 1917, Satow briefly said it is "the conduct of business between states by peaceful means" (1979, 3), and in 1939, Nicolson called it the "management of international relations by negotiation . . . the method by which these relations are adjusted and managed by ambassadors and envoys" (1950, 15). Theorists have since expanded beyond the practice of state "diplomatists". Hedley Bull's definition includes a wider variety of actors and more dimensions: diplomacy can take place between any "independent political community and another"; it includes formulation and execution of policy, bilateral and multilateral relations, intelligence gathering, and both ad hoc and institutionalized relations (Bull 1977, 160). He points out an inborn normative assumption: diplomacy "presupposes that there exists not only an international system but also an international society" (161). Jönsson and Hall (2005) further break down diplomacy both as an institutional type connecting nodes in the international system and as a symbolic, repetitive ritual, the atomic interactions of international society. Or, as Pouliot and Cornut say, "Diplomacy is both a category of practice and a category of analysis . . . a conceptual building block of a theoretical system" (2015, 299). In the same way that the basic unit of society is the direct person-to-person interaction, the basic unit of international relations is this polity-to-polity interaction. Diplomacy, the real exchange of words and understandings between polities – and by extension, all the preparation behind that act – is the unspoken interactive foundation underlying the "international system".

The international order is maintained by the bilateral and collective interactions between the representatives of the nations of the world, in a system that has evolved to preserve the status quo and, in theory, minimize the use of violence as a means of resolving conflict between polities. Referring to Numelin's 1950 study of intertribal diplomacy (Numelin 1950, cited in Bull 1977), Bull argues that diplomacy studies in IR should cease assuming the state as the central actor (1977, 158). While the diplomacy scholars publishing since then have not insisted that the practice of diplomacy is reserved for states – for example, Pouliot and Cornut (2015), Gilboa (2008), and Jönsson and Hall (2005) all take both state and non-state actors as key theoretical subjects – most empirical work exploring diplomacy still looks to the state as the central case. Still, modern frameworks are well suited for incorporating the outreach of secessionists, as the traditional emphasis on state government agents emphasized by Coggins (2015, 100) is no longer the norm in diplomacy studies. For example, Pouliot and Cornut (2015) note the "polylateral" diplomatic practices of states, which interact with many kinds of non-state actors.

To consider secessionist diplomacy is to consider a strategic, political, and practical framework of a polity attempting a transition in type, a change in membership status that necessarily entails a change in diplomatic form. So, what is that form before and during such a transition? To answer the question, it worth delving into the component parts of diplomacy. Bull's exhaustive chapter on state diplomacy is still an appropriate starting point (Bull 1977, 156–177). Bull specifies that diplomacy includes: (1) formulation and execution of a state's external policy; (2) gathering and assessing information about the international milieu; (3) "communication to other governments and peoples" to explain and justify policy and secure cooperation or neutralize opposition through reason, persuasion, threat of force, and coercion; and (4) both "diplomatic" functions between states and consular functions between state and citizen. Diplomacy takes place bilaterally and multilaterally, in both ad hoc and institutionalized manners, and with both state actors and "peoples" – the "active elements of the country's political life" (159). Diplomacy functions to facilitate communication, negotiate agreements, gather intelligence, minimize friction, and "symbolize the existence of the society of states" (166).

As a cursory demonstration of how secessionist diplomacy fulfills Bull's principles, consider the early South Ossetian fight for autonomy. The Ossetian National Council was the main body through which South Ossetians made known their political demands on greater autonomy in 1918 (Saparov 2014, 68). The South Ossetians saw Georgians as "others", and they did not believe the Georgian government had rightful claim to Ossetian territory. The council engaged in diplomatic efforts early on, communicating its desires to the Georgian government in several Council congresses, asking for the "question of South Ossetia" to be left open in the Georgian constitution formation process, and acknowledging the lack of decisive action regarding South Ossetian autonomy during these congresses (Saparov 2014, 68). The Council asked for Russian to be made an official language and for a special court to be created, composed of Ossetians that would try cases committed in ethnic Ossetian-inhabited territory (Saparov 2014, 68). The Council also sent representatives to meet with Russian Bolsheviks at the 1919 Paris Peace Conference, and there they declared their preference to "join the newly created Russian state as an independent member of the federation" (Tskhovrebov 1981, 93, quoted in Saparov 2014, 69). This early example of the use of third-parties as interlocutors of secessionist demands would become common, a response to the difficulty secessionists face in finding official platforms to explain their political perspective, goals, and grievances.

Following Bull, practice theorists such as Pouliot and Cornut (2015) or Sending, Pouliot, and Neumann (2015, 6) boil down diplomacy to three components: the process of claiming authority and jurisdiction; the relational interface between polities; and the politics of both representation and governing. Or, as Cornut (2015) writes, diplomats manage three roles simultaneously: "knowledge producer, representative of their country, and bureaucrat in a hierarchical institution" (386). Secessionist diplomats – and diplomats for other self-determination groups, governments in exile, and decolonization movements – take on these roles and others. They are knowledge creators, representatives, and bureaucrats, but they also play the roles of activist, fundraiser, media spokesperson, lobbyist, and liaison of all manner of parties they deem helpful to their goals. In addition to all the functions of diplomacy in a recognized state, the secessionist state's diplomatic arm is oriented for ensuring survival, if only in the form of the de facto state,[2] and for international legitimization of their claim. Moreover, secessionist governments recognize that diplomatic interactions are the ligaments of international society, as well as a standard institution of governance, and many secessionist groups invest in diplomatic outreach right away.

These additional goals and roles distinguish the secessionist diplomatic framework from that of established states. Diplomacy serves to both preserve earned domestic sovereignty and justify international sovereignty, both to enable the state to exist and to argue that it exists. That is, secessionist foreign ministries do indeed serve the conventional diplomatic roles of knowledge creation, representation, and bureaucratic function, but at a more basic level, they exist to enable the survival of the state and legitimize themselves before would-be peer audiences.

## Diplomacy for legitimization and diplomacy for survival

Diplomacy for the secessionist group serves many purposes, some that resemble those of states' diplomatic operations, and others that do not. The most obvious distinction is that secessionist groups have a lower baseline goal for diplomacy. Aspiring and recognized states both orient diplomacy towards demonstrating sovereignty and control, representing their positions in relevant venues, gathering intelligence, and managing their images, but the stakes, constraints, and available tools and venues differ entirely.

Coggins's foundational chapter on "rebel diplomacy" gives the broad definition of diplomacy as "strategic use of talk" (Coggins 2015, 100). Secessionist diplomacy is often done on an ad hoc basis early on, with minimal strategy, and diplomats recruited based on their wealth, fame, connections, or international standing, as in the Somaliland case (Pegg 2020). This can be seen in the early diplomatic efforts in Artsakh in 1987, in which a petition to unite the region with Armenia was sent to and ignored by Mikhail Gorbachev, spurring escalation in political and diplomatic actions by Armenian supporters (Özkan 2008).

The line between "harder" conventional diplomatic operations and a "softer" improvisational approach can be blurry. Still, the types of diplomacy "rebel" groups, including secessionists, use can be subdivided into essentially three categories. First is conventional diplomacy, consisting of permanent offices, career representatives who work in one capital or region, and a sustained objective of getting meetings with government officials to advocate their case. Second is public diplomacy, "using the media and other channels of communication to influence public opinion in foreign societies" (Gilboa 2008, 58). Secessionist governments hire public relations firms and lobbyists to influence the state in an official capacity, as well as encourage private actors to influence the narrative of the conflict.[3] The third type of diplomacy is advocacy building, and it is more specific to secessionists (and rebel groups in conflict). This includes fostering activist networks in influential third-party countries, private fundraising for both state-building and military objectives, and relations with diaspora communities around the world, whose support is often crucial in early stages of conflict.

State diplomats are the "eyes, ears, and mouthpieces" of their governments, with either permanent offices or regular circuits established to maintain the information exchange with important third-party governments. They provide the secessionist groups' perspective whenever possible, as "intuitive semioticians" speaking the common language of diplomacy to signal their membership in the international society (Jönsson and Hall 2005, 75), even if they go unrecognized. They fill the same intelligence-gathering role as other diplomats, keeping tabs on factors important to their diplomatic strategies – military capability, domestic politics, public sentiment, economic constraints, and leadership changes – and using this information to draw inferences about intention and craft an overall strategy (Trager 2017, 21). Secessionist diplomats who work in conventional channels play these same roles.

What can differ is what form that channel takes. Secessionist governments face the difficult logistical question of how to get face-to-face time with key decision makers. They set up permanent offices in foreign capitals, but those offices may lack official status, and those diplomats may lack the legal protection that recognized state diplomats are afforded. Or they may have an office with an official invitation from a host government, even while official recognition is lacking. They may be hosted in the offices of sponsoring state governments, as Sahrawi diplomats are hosted by the Algerian embassy in Washington, D.C.[45] Likewise, patron states may employ their diplomatic missions to provide a reliable platform for secessionist representatives, as the Turkish government does for the Turkish Republic of Northern Cyprus (TRNC) (Moss 2020). They also recruit diaspora members near important government centers to be on "standby" as spokespersons for their governments, which may be done on a shoestring budget or entirely voluntarily.[6]

Similarly, secessionist movements emerging out of preestablished, functional regional governments will often institutionalize diplomacy as part of a broader effort to internationalize their presence. The Public Diplomacy Council of Catalonia (DIPLOCAT), for example, was specifically founded to serve this purpose, "addressing international audiences with the aim of establishing a dialogue and positively influencing the image they have of Catalonia" (DIPLOCAT 2019). DIPLOCAT actively reaches out to public and private sector organizations to advance its mission, and it publicizes its diplomatic strategy, including digital communication and formalizing the official use of social media tools. The Catalonian sits on the advisory board of the organization, alongside other high-ranking foreign affairs officials within the Catalonian government. It thus uses its legitimate standing as a recognized autonomous government to bolster its standing in laying the groundwork for independence claims.

Looking to Krasner's (1999) properties associated with sovereignty – "territory, recognition, autonomy, and control" (220) – recognition is predicated on third-party actions, and while territory, autonomy, and control can be consolidated with no outside support, most successful secessionists heavily utilize material and strategic assistance. Secessionists in the Turkish Republic of Northern Cyprus (TRNC), South Ossetia, Abkhazia, Artsakh, Transnistria, and other de facto states have all relied heavily on support from neighboring patron states (Otarashvili 2017), as have other self-determination groups like the Polisario Front (Reuters 2020). For example, Şan Akca's taxonomy of external support of rebel groups (including secessionists) names 11 different types of direct and indirect support (2016, 8), each addressing different strategic considerations.

Calling back to one of the three components of diplomacy outlined by Pouliot and Cornut (2015) or Sending, Pouliot, and Neumann (2015, 6), claiming jurisdiction can be just as challenging as claiming legitimacy and also requires an aspect of the latter in order for it to succeed. External support may actually be detrimental in these cases. In South Ossetia in 2018, there were reports that Russian and de facto authorities in occupied South Ossetian territory were moving the fences that demarcate the border between Georgia and South Ossetia further into Georgian territory, as well as human rights abuses by Russian authorities near these borders (Khatchvani 2019). In cases like these, external support is to the detriment of the legitimacy of secessionist claims, if it shows they are incapable of policing their borders (or their allies).

Still, outside support at every stage of secessionist conflict is crucial for establishing both domestic sovereignty and international sovereignty. In the rare cases that secessionists manage to secure international recognition from other countries, they have usually already gained control and autonomy in the territory in question (Coggins 2011). In this way, external support is crucial to both the building of the de facto state and the entry of the state into the system. Despite this, some secessionists receive generous external support from ethnically tied neighbors – for example, in Artsakh – but have failed to achieve international recognition despite establishing governmental institutions and informal foreign relations with several states.[7]

As both an institution and a practice, secessionist diplomacy serves these two overarching goals of legitimization and survival at the same time as it serves the general purpose of representation. Secessionist governments build their diplomatic operations to both demonstrate sovereignty and argue for their own existence. They "play the state" in the hopes that if they do so long enough, some third parties will eventually switch to a stance of official recognition.

Mampilly (2015) calls this showcasing of government functions that mimic other sovereign states "performative sovereignty". These actions are publicized to project legitimacy, build the case for recognition by showing to the world that they can democratically govern their territory and population and adhere to international law, and therefore earn statehood.[8]

While domestic sovereignty can be achieved by the secessionist state largely on its own, full sovereignty requires external support, both material and political. Stated simply, sovereignty is something achieved (by the secessionist) and something given (by states). A common belief in the Somaliland MFA is that as long as it continues to remain a stable, functioning democracy in a region surrounded by weak states and conflict, and as long as third-party governments know this is the case, at some point neighboring countries will decide that recognition of their independence is advantageous.[9] In this way the internal and external elements of sovereignty and legitimacy interact – governments recognized as legitimate by international actors are likely to have strong claims to legitimacy at home. However, these two dimensions also operate independently. As a de facto state, Somaliland is characterized by internal legitimacy but not external – strong support from its populace, but refusal of recognition from international actors. On the other hand, states mired by protracted conflict often retain recognition by the international community, even as domestic legitimacy evaporates. Somalia remains internationally recognized as a single state, despite three decades of conflict, competing authorities across the country, and a comparatively peaceful political order in secessionist Somaliland.

Secessionists send representatives and set up offices to keep up the image of the sovereign state and take part in the international society described by Bull (1977). Their goal is to continually make the case that they are modern states and would be valuable members of the international community, because they follow international law (Fazal 2018; Jo and Thomson 2014) and can run effective institutions, such as public service provision (Stewart 2018), courts (Loyle 2021), and elections (Casey and Minder 2021). The Republic of Artsakh, for example, boasts that it has an elected President and a National Assembly and touts the fact that Freedom House rates it as "more free" than both Armenia and Azerbaijan in the past (Freedom House 2021). Its long-standing official newspaper *Azat Artsakh* broadcasts this information (in Armenian, Russian, and English), and it is distributed through diplomatic channels whenever possible.

However, a crucial barrier to the success of secessionist diplomacy is access to key diplomatic forums, namely bilateral meetings and IGOs. One way to secure access is the through the patron state – Russia for South Ossetia, or Turkey for the TRNC. These states may provide a diplomatic outlet for unrecognized governments to fill all the conventional roles of diplomacy – knowledge producer, representative, and bureaucrat – as well as that of advocacy. Turkish diplomatic missions often include a TRNC diplomat, compelling interaction with the TRNC by many third parties. Secessionists emerging from regional governments – e.g. Catalonia or the Kurdish Regional Government – may have long-standing relations with other states and IGOs that preceded efforts towards independent statehood. IGOs themselves are key forums for contesting statehood, as they can either coordinate positions among member states or take their own positions. For example, Kyris and Luciano (2021) explain how regional parliaments have played a key role in shaping state positions on unrecognized governments. Member states use parliamentary instruments to compel discussion of unrecognized state issues during sessions, and even pass resolutions, as well as to distinguish parliamentary positions from that of the executive branch. For example, the European Parliament (EP) adopted positions encouraging all EU members to officially recognize Kosovo and Palestine, even while the European Council opposed outright recognition (Kyris and Luciano 2021, 5). Within these interstate bodies, secessionist foreign ministries invest in maintaining influence with state representatives. KRG representatives regularly meet with UN delegations in Baghdad (Kurdistan24 2019), and many in Somaliland's foreign ministry consider the African Union and Pan-African Parliament the most likely venue for discussions or resolutions leading to bilateral recognition.[10]

On the other hand, an important factor distinguishing secessionist foreign ministries from those of recognized states is that, in the quest to justify their independent existence, there are no "small audiences". While they certainly prioritize facetime with official national government officials, secessionist and self-determination diplomats take meetings with small-town mayors (SPS 2013), provincial legislators (SPS 2018), think tanks and activists (Abellán and de Miguel 2017), and practically any other person or entity that is conceivably influential.[11] Secessionist diplomats may assist in drafting resolutions of support to be introduced in national and regional legislatures,[12] as well as encourage and support the development of advocacy organizations in influential countries.[13]

It is part of a strategy to influence foreign countries' domestic politics through as many avenues as possible. Towards this end, they may spend significant time addressing audiences through other media outlets. Although the Polisario Front is a decolonization movement, not a secessionist movement, the range of roles their diplomats take abroad provides an illustrative case. Huddleston (2019) discusses one Polisario diplomat making an appearance on *France24* to counter the Moroccan foreign minister's accusation that the Polisario had been receiving equipment and training from Iran and Hezbollah (Al-Jazeera 2018). The Polisario representative in Australia regularly pens op-eds in Australian and New Zealand news outlets, and has a regular circuit of meetings with university student groups, non-profits, and activist groups (Fadel 2021). In the goal of fostering international legitimacy of their claims, they spend significant time on providing their perspective in hopes that it will appear alongside that of the incumbent state. Mattiacci and Jones (2020, 871) describe the public diplomacy campaigns states employ to manage their image during active repression and conflict, including avoiding accountability for militia violence against civilians and otherwise striving to "achieve plausible deniability". Much of their theory could just as easily be ascribed to secessionist governments and their public diplomacy efforts. Media exposure is seen to have an important effect on policy choices in third-party governments, so they spend time fostering a favorable narrative.

Although Bob (2005) developed his theoretical framework of "marketing rebellion" before the advent of social media, communication strategies developed for traditional press, radio, and TV news outlets have been propelled significantly by the global reach of social media. For example, secessionist groups have made extensive use of Twitter since its founding. In fact, Loyle and Bestvater's study on rebel use of social media finds that, of all "rebel" groups, secessionists are the most likely to use Twitter, and they primarily use it to broadcast to international audiences "to self-promote and report on their operations" (2019, 572). For secessionist groups or governments with strong domestic sovereignty – such as Abkhazia, Somaliland, and Catalonia – this often takes the form of announcements of official meetings with diplomats and dignitaries of recognized states, as well as regular articulation of their right to independence. Secessionists with lower domestic sovereignty, such as West Papua or Tibet, use social media to generate international awareness of claims to independence and the wrongdoing of the incumbent state.[14]

In the same way evolving communications technology has catalyzed changes in diplomatic outreach of secessionists, so too have shifts in the global order. New states have come in waves. Between 1945 and 1960, 36 former colonies emerged as new states. The 1990s witnessed the USSR dissolve into 15 independent countries, Yugoslavia into another 5, the breakup of Czechoslovakia, and the union of East and West Germany. Namibia broke away from South Africa, Eritrea from Ethiopia, and Micronesia, Palau, and the Marshall Islands from the United States. Other campaigns of independence faltered, by contrast. The Sahrawi Republic saw its bids for recognition rapidly decline, losing 38 recognizers following the end of the Cold War and the

Polisario ceasefire agreement with Morocco (Huddleston 2021, 792). The same seismic shift in the world order finally opened the doors for some independence movements while closing the door for others, but it nevertheless demonstrated the importance of system-wide shifts in power relations in determining the success or failure of individual movements.

The long-term aim of every secessionist diplomatic operation is international sovereignty in its maximal form – international recognition and membership in the system. However, survival of the movement, support of the government, and entrenchment of the secessionist state in the system, even unrecognized, are all important goals that play prominent roles in diplomacy. Given the seeming permanence or "stickiness" of some de facto states, one might conceive of international sovereignty as more than just whether external actors are willing to officially recognize secessionists who manage to achieve domestic sovereignty. Huddleston (2020) argues for a continuous conceptualization of international sovereignty more rooted in the extent to which third-parties support secessionist and self-determination groups' domestic control. If external actors actively buy into the existence and performed authority of unrecognized states, it creates a stable new status quo (Buzard, Graham, and Horne 2017; Huddleston 2021). Therefore, although recognition is *the* key to attaining that valuable legal membership in the international system, there is good reason for secessionist diplomacy to concentrate not only on recognition, but on entrenchment of a status quo of partial statehood. A threat to such a status quo may be interpreted as a real security threat, as demonstrated by the Japanese government's 2021 annual defense report, which wrote that the security of Taiwan was "directly connected" to Japanese security (Reynolds 2021).

Depending on their advantages in conflict, self-determination and secessionist entities may also expend significant efforts providing normative or legal arguments *against* the status quo, trying to move influence against the incumbent government. Turning back to Western Sahara, a major component of Polisario diplomacy that has developed in the last decade has been repeatedly taking resource exploitation cases to the European Union, which does not officially recognize Moroccan sovereignty over Western Sahara but still allows European companies to exploit the resources or strategic positioning of the territory, through fishing, coastal access, and use of airspace (Dudley 2018). They were inspired by a Palestinian international strategy supporting lawsuits in intergovernmental and domestic courts,[15] as well as earlier East Timorese claims on resource exploitation rights (Simpson 1994, 337).

Secessionist governments may also successfully make the case that they are better security partners than their incumbent states.[16] The domestic sovereignty of the Kurdish Regional Government (KRG) – its successful democratic institutions, domestic legitimacy, and high degree of security – allows its diplomats to make a strong case around the world that it offers a strategic post in the region unmatched by any recognized state. The United States has invested heavily in the region, bolstering domestic sovereignty and setting the region up for long-term survival, at least as an autonomous region (Faidhi Dri 2021). It is an open question as to whether this kind of investment in a status quo of engagement and support without recognition is better or worse for secessionists' long-term goal of membership in the international system. As Caspersen argues, "International recognition, in a legal sense, does not creep" (2018, 4), and long-term engagement may be an equilibrium stable enough that no third party is willing to upset it without a strong catalyzing event. In the KRG's case, a strong showing in an independence referendum was clearly not that event (Kaplan 2019). Likewise, in its relations with Ethiopia and Kenya and with key regional institutions, namely the African Union (AU) and Intergovernmental Authority for Development (IGAD), the government of Somaliland continually pressures its neighbors to recognize its relatively high security level in a volatile region. It maintains that Somaliland has been a "responsible actor" for "maintenance of the regional and global security", and Somaliland diplomats regularly draw the explicit contrast with Somalia's unrelenting and unsuccessful fight against terrorist organizations (Aden 2021).

When secessionist governments are able to make these credible claims as protectors and providers of regional security, they also build out their diplomatic arms to encourage economic integration, even incorporating ministries of finance and development into their foreign policy outreach. Taiwan is perhaps the best known and most successful case of a de facto state (although not secessionist), heavily incorporating economic integration into both its foreign policy and diplomatic approach, particularly in manufacturing (Yip 2020). For its part, Somaliland's government has cultivated close ties to the Taiwanese government, inviting investment in infrastructure from there, as well as from the United Arab Emirates, which has poured money into much of the recent construction of the port at Berbera (Garowe 2021). Somaliland's diplomats have repeatedly made the case to Addis Ababa that Ethiopia will benefit from having access to another major port in addition to its agreement in Djibouti, and offer access, as well as other trade agreements, without requiring recognition.[17] For its part, the TRNC faces a more hostile set of circumstances for fostering economic ties, given that it has been under EU sanctions since 1984 (Talmon 2001). This has encouraged the government to tie its economic policy – as well as its security policy – into those of Turkey, arguably to the detriment of Greece, recognized Cyprus, and the EU. It has also taken advantage of the combination of proximity to the EU and freedom from EU regulations to establish itself as a popular tourist destination in the Mediterranean for gambling, beaches, and other ocean activities, taking advantage of exchange rates favorable to tourists carrying Euros.

Every secessionist and self-determination government wants full recognition and membership in the international system. However, their diplomatic ministries know – from international law, from other secessionist outcomes, from scholarship, and from their own experience – that recognition is a far-appearing goal on the horizon with an uncertain path between this point and that. As such, as much as they pursue long-term goals of recognition, their short-term diplomatic strategies encourage investment in the situations they have already built. The Polisario Front and Sahrawi Republic do not even explicitly pursue recognition anymore, focusing instead on the implementation of the 1991 referendum agreement that created the UN Mission for the Referendum in Western Sahara (MINURSO). Somaliland's government has the explicit goal of recognition, but according to interviews with Somaliland diplomats, much of its MFA's attention now goes to encouraging a deepening and hardening of de facto interdependence globally and regionally.

## Discussion

As a topic of study, secessionist diplomacy still poses many unanswered questions to the fields of IR and conflict studies. Scholars have generally analyzed third-party support of secessionists from the perspective of the would-be supporters and recognizers, their interests, strategies, and relationships with other powers. This chapter, and volume, presses researchers to train their focus on the secessionists themselves – how they persuade, compel, and compete in the club of states to advance their sovereignty. But many questions remain. What outcomes does secessionist diplomacy yield? Where and when does it tend to succeed and fail? Do secessionists invest more into bilateral relations, or do regional organizations offer a better platform? Many of the "broad strokes" questions about the diplomacy of self-determination remain open.

These aspiring states deploy representatives and set up permanent diplomatic offices in capital cities around the world, often before they even set up schools or clinics for their own civilians, seeing that the capacity to interact with world governments is an early investment into state capacity. Moreover, secessionists perceive of diplomatic outreach both as a means to an end – procuring international support and promoting awareness of their success – and as an end in itself – diplomacy is "what states do" (Huang 2016). From the policy perspective, successful diplomacy provides alternatives to violent confrontation, serving as the catalyst of peace and ceasefire agreements that have historically drawn ends to horrific bloodshed and then sustained the new peace. Yet it can also drastically worsen conflict, inviting arms and actors to flow and weakening chances for peaceful resolution, or else freezing conflict in states of irresolution.

As Rosenau stated, "What makes actors effective in world politics derives not from the sovereignty they possess or the legal privileges thereby accorded them, but rather lies in relational phenomena, in the authority they can commend and the compliance they can thereby elicit" (Rosenau 1990, 40). Secessionist MFAs have absorbed this lesson more than most recognized state entities. The international system is a status quo–preserving system. In more than one sense, all states are "stability-seeking" powers,[18] seeking reliable, predictable regional politics. They are concerned that to recognize a secessionist group that successfully seizes territory is to set a harmful precedent (Coggins 2011). However, that concern is less shared for many forms of engagement short of recognition and support for domestic sovereignty of secessionist governments (Huddleston 2020). This leaves a wide opening for secessionist governments to appeal to third parties to influence their fates in other ways – investment in infrastructure, security and economic partnerships, IGO policy – that still serve to secure their fate in some sense.

Although secessionists all share an aspiration for international sovereignty through recognition, the very act of employing state-like diplomatic machines demonstrates their sovereignty without it, and establishes relations that knit them into the fabric of the international society. Diplomacy is as much a "ritual" as it is an institution (Jönsson and Hall 2005), and diplomats are the sinews of this society, the conduits of communication through which information is exchanged, offers and arguments are made, and signals are broadcast. The international order is maintained by diplomacy, and insofar as the international status quo shifts via consensus, that consensus is articulated by diplomats. Secessionist governments hoping to steadily shift the status quo towards their position, step by reluctant step, know that their presence is required in front of decision makers in influential major and regional powers and international organizations. Moreover, they are aware of the importance of the narratives surrounding their disputes, so they invest resources in cultivating a favorable narrative in official channels and encourage nationals and diaspora members to bring such messaging to lower-level channels. In this way, they press the international consensus towards one that accepts, even strengthens, their hold of their territory. Although diplomatic recognition may be the stated goal of international outreach (Caspersen 2018), "engagement without recognition" often supplants it as an intermediary status quo goal for self-determination groups (Ker-Lindsay and Berg 2018). Diplomatic efforts also focus on conveying the group's availability as valuable military and economic partners to international actors or as providers of regional stability (Buzard, Graham, and Horne 2017; Huddleston 2021), securing their survival as de facto authorities.

In this way, international legitimacy of self-determination groups is quite nuanced, comprising both the *de jure* legitimacy of the recognition of key actors and the *de facto* legitimacy revealed in cooperation between those same governments and international bodies and the non-state actors in question. Diplomatic efforts of secessionist actively seek both forms. In so doing, these actors encounter a basic tension between diplomatic strategies that build international legitimacy and those that secure their survival by making themselves invaluable partners to important powers. Understanding this tension – and understanding the short- and long-term goals they develop in response – remains a crucial task at hand for the field of IR and conflict studies, and a critical open question as to how international actors, such as the United States or the EU, can better influence the outcomes of these intractable conflicts.

# Glossary

**Advocacy-building diplomacy**   diplomatic activities intended to build awareness and advocacy movements in the civil societies of other countries.

**Aspiring state**   a separatist, secessionist, or self-determination movement with the goal of creating a new state recognized by the other nation-states of the world and/or by the United Nations.

**Conventional diplomacy**   diplomatic activities carried out in an official capacity, on behalf of the secessionist state, before the receiving state's government, including officials from legislative and executive branches, especially foreign ministry officials.

**De facto state**   a state with domestic sovereignty but without universal international recognition, so that the government has an effective monopoly on violence within the territory it claims and/or holds, even while third-party countries do not officially recognize its status.

**Domestic sovereignty**   sovereignty over the intrastate functions of governance, potentially including security, policing, judicial functions, elections, and public services.

**Engagement without recognition**   when a state maintains relations with a secessionist government or de facto state, even while it maintains a foreign policy of non-recognition.

**IGO**   intergovernmental organization. An organization composed of sovereign states, established by treaty or charter, intended to serve common interests and tend to international legal disputes.

**International sovereignty**   sovereignty over international functions of governance, including international security and diplomacy, usually established by the official recognition of other states.

**MFA**   Ministry of Foreign Affairs. The branch of government, usually under the executive branch, that handles matters of foreign policy towards other states.

**Polity**   any group of people who have a collective political identity, are organized in some form of institutional social relations, and are able to mobilize resources towards political goals.

**Public diplomacy**   diplomatic activities that are intended to speak directly to foreign publics and that usually influence government policy.

**Recognition**   When a state's government establishes the policy that it considers another state's government sovereign over its claimed territory, and considers it to be an equal, sovereign member of the international system.

**Secessionist movement**   a political movement vying for the establishment of a new sovereign state on a territory currently under another state's sovereign domain.

**Self-determination**   the principle that all peoples have a right to freely choose their sovereign and international political status with no interference from other states, as well as to choose the form and function of the government.

# Notes

1 See Eiki Berg, Chapter 25 in this volume, for an exhaustive treatment of this topic.
2 See Helge Blakkisrud, Chapter 24 in this volume, on surviving without recognition.
3 See Part V of this volume, especially James Ker-Lindsay's Chapter 27.
4 Personal interview, Sahrawi Diplomat, 14 January 2019.

5 The Polisario Front is technically not a secessionist entity, but an anti-colonial movement. However, we refer to it repeatedly because its diplomatic operations serve all the same purposes as other cases discussed here.

6 Personal interview, Somaliland Diplomat, 29 February 2020.

7 At one point, Artsakh has had permanent representatives stationed in Armenia, Russia, the United States, France, Australia, Germany, and Lebanon (NKR 2008).

8 This theme arose repeatedly in interviews with Somaliland, Turkish Cypriot, and Sahrawi diplomats.

9 Personal interview, Somaliland Diplomat, 3 May 2021.

10 Personal interview, Somaliland Diplomat, 3 May 2021.

11 As one recent example, the town of Martakert in Artsakh signed a memorandum of cooperation with the Lebanese town of Bourj Hammoud to officially establish relations between the two towns. See News.am (2018).

12 Personal interview, Sahrawi Diplomat, 14 January 2019.

13 For example, the Sahrawi Association in the USA and Cantabria por el Sáhara in Spain, or the Somaliland advocacy organization Not4Gotten in the UK.

14 Respectively: @Abkhaziagovge, @somalilandmfa, @catalgov, @FreeWestPapua, @freetibetorg.

15 Personal interview, Sahrawi Diplomat, 2 January 2019.

16 See Milena Sterio, Chapter 23 in this volume, on international power politics and secession.

17 Personal interview, Somaliland Diplomat, 3 May 2021.

18 Paquin's term (Paquin 2010).

# References

Abellán L. and de Miguel R. (2017). Key Catalan Ideologue Met with Julian Assange in London. *El Pais*, 13 November. Available at: https://english.elpais.com/elpais/2017/11/13/inenglish/1510565565_636373.html (accessed 8 January 2022).

Aden N. (2021). Somaliland's Foreign Policy Strategy: Exploring Plausible Options to Statehood Status. *Intergovernmental Research and Policy Journal*. Available at: https://irpj.euclid.int/articles/somalilands-foreign-policy-strategy-exploring-plausible-options-to-statehood-status/ (accessed 24 July 2021).

Al-Jazeera. (2018). Morocco Cuts Diplomatic Ties with Iran over Western Sahara Feud. Available at: www.aljazeera.com/news/2018/5/1/morocco-cuts-diplomatic-ties-with-iran-over-western-sahara-feud (accessed 21 July 2021).

Bob C. (2005). *The Marketing of Rebellion: Insurgents, Media, and International Activism.* New York, NY: Cambridge University Press.

Bull H. (1977). *The Anarchical Society: A Study of Order in World Politics.* New York: Columbia University Press.

Buzard K., Graham BAT., and Horne B. (2017). Unrecognized States: A Theory of Self-Determination and Foreign Influence. *The Journal of Law, Economics, and Organization* 33(3), pp. 578–611. DOI: 10.1093/jleo/eww017.

Casey N. and Minder R. (2021). Spain Hoped Catalonia's Separatists Would Fade: They're Gaining Ground. *The New York Times*, 19 February. Available at: www.nytimes.com/2021/02/19/world/europe/spain-catalonia-independence.html (accessed 8 January 2022).

Caspersen N. (2018). Recognition, Status Quo or Reintegration: Engagement with De Facto States. *Ethnopolitics* 17(4), pp. 373–389. DOI: 10.1080/17449057.2018.1495360.

Coggins B. (2011). Friends in High Places: International Politics and the Emergence of States from Secessionism. *International Organization* 65(3), pp. 433–467.

Coggins B. (2014). *Power Politics and State Formation in the Twentieth Century: The Dynamics of Recognition.* New York: Cambridge University Press.

Coggins B. (2015). Rebel Diplomacy: Theorizing Violent Non-State Actors' Strategic Use of Talk. In: Arjona A., Kasfir N., and Mampilly Z. (eds.) *Rebel Governance in Civil War.* Cambridge: Cambridge University Press, pp. 98–118. DOI: 10.1017/CBO9781316182468.005.

Cooley A. and Mitchell LA. (2010). Engagement without Recognition: A New Strategy toward Abkhazia and Eurasia's Unrecognized States. *Washington Quarterly* 33(4), pp. 59–73. DOI: 10.1080/0163660X.2010.516183.

Cornut J. (2015). To Be a Diplomat Abroad: Diplomatic Practice at Embassies. *Cooperation and Conflict* 50(3), pp. 385–401. DOI: 10.1177/0010836715574912.

DIPLOCAT. (2019). *Strategic Plan of the Public Diplomacy Council of Catalonia 2019–2022*. Barcelona: Public Diplomacy Council of Catalonia. Available at: https://diplocat.cat/media/upload/arxius/publicacions/pla-estrategic-Diplocat_2019-2022-en.pdf (accessed 30 December 2021).

Dudley D. (2018). EU Fisheries Deal with Morocco Sparks Criticism over Inclusion of Western Sahara Waters. *Forbes*, 24 July. Available at: www.forbes.com/sites/dominicdudley/2018/07/24/eu-fisheries-morocco-western-sahara/ (accessed 8 January 2022).

Fadel K. (2021). Time to Undo Trump's Legacy in Western Sahara. *On Line Opinion*. Available at: www.onlineopinion.com.au/view.asp?article=21697 (accessed 8 January 2022).

Faidhi Dri K. (2021). Washington to Encourage US Investment in Kurdistan Region: Top Official. *rudaw. net*, 9 March. Available at: www.rudaw.net/english/kurdistan/300920213 (accessed 8 January 2022).

Fazal T. (2018). *Wars of Law: Unintended Consequences in the Regulation of Armed Conflict*. Ithaca, NY: Cornell University Press.

Freedom House. (2021). *Nagorno-Karabakh: Freedom in the World 2021 Country Report*. Freedom House. Available at: https://freedomhouse.org/country/nagorno-karabakh/freedom-world/2021 (accessed 8 January 2022).

Garowe. (2021). UAE and Ethiopia Sign $1bn Deal on Construction of Road to Somaliland's Berbera Port. *Garowe Online*, 5 August. Available at: www.garoweonline.com/index.php/en/world/africa/uae-and-ethiopia-sign-1bn-deal-on-construction-of-road-to-somaliland-s-berbera-port (accessed 8 January 2022).

Gilboa E. (2008). Searching for a Theory of Public Diplomacy. *The Annals of the American Academy of Political and Social Science* 616(1), pp. 55–77. DOI: 10.1177/0002716207312142.

Huang R. (2016). Rebel Diplomacy in Civil War. *International Security* 40(4), pp. 89–126. DOI: 10.1162/ISEC_a_00237.

Huddleston RJ. (2019). Can John Bolton Thaw Western Sahara's Long-Frozen Conflict? *Foreign Policy*. Available at: https://foreignpolicy.com/2019/05/09/can-john-bolton-thaw-western-saharas-long-frozen-conflict-morocco-western-sahara-polisario-minurso-sahrawi-republic/.

Huddleston RJ. (2020). Continuous Recognition: A Latent Variable Approach to Measuring International Sovereignty of Self-Determination Movements. *Journal of Peace Research* 57(6). Available at: https://papers.ssrn.com/abstract=3331944 (accessed 10 February 2019).

Huddleston RJ. (2021). Foulweather Friends: Violence and Third Party Support in Self-Determination Conflicts. *Journal of Conflict Resolution* 65(6). DOI: 10.1177/0022002721993226.

Jo H. and Thomson CP. (2014). Legitimacy and Compliance with International Law: Access to Detainees in Civil Conflicts, 1991–2006. *British Journal of Political Science; Cambridge* 44(2), pp. 323–355. DOI: https://doi.org.ezproxy.shu.edu/10.1017/S0007123412000749.

Jones BT. and Mattiacci E. (2017). A Manifesto, in 140 Characters or Fewer: Social Media as a Tool of Rebel Diplomacy. *British Journal of Political Science*, pp. 1–23. DOI: 10.1017/S0007123416000612.

Jönsson C. and Hall M. (2005). *Essence of Diplomacy*. London: Palgrave Macmillan UK. DOI: 10.1057/9780230511040.

Kaplan ML. (2019). Foreign Support, Miscalculation, and Conflict Escalation: Iraqi Kurdish Self-Determination in Perspective. *Ethnopolitics* 18(1), pp. 29–45. DOI: 10.1080/17449057.2018.1525164.

Ker-Lindsay J. and Berg E. (2018). Introduction: A Conceptual Framework for Engagement with De Facto States. *Ethnopolitics* 17(4), pp. 335–342. DOI: 10.1080/17449057.2018.1495362.

Khatchvani, T. (2019). Russia's new strategy in Georgia: Creeping Occupation. *LSE Human Rights Blog*, London School of Economics. Available at: https://blogs.lse.ac.uk/humanrights/2019/02/05/russias-new-strategy-in-georgia-creeping-occupation/ (accessed 5 May 2022)

Krasner S. (1999). *Sovereignty: Organized Hypocrisy*. Princeton, NJ: Princeton University Press.

Kurdistan24. (2019). KRG President Meets UN Security Council, Vows to Mend Ties with Baghdad, Protect Kurdish Rights. *Kurdistan 24*. Available at: www.kurdistan24.net/en/story/20021-KRG-President-meets-UN-Security-Council,-vows-to-mend-ties-with-Baghdad,-protect-Kurdish-rights (accessed 5 January 2022).

Kyris G. and Luciano B. (2021). Collective Recognition and Regional Parliaments: Navigating Statehood Conflict. *Global Studies Quarterly* 1(3), p. ksab011. DOI: 10.1093/isagsq/ksab011.

Loyle C. (2021). Rebel Justice during Armed Conflict. *Journal of Conflict Resolution* 65(1), pp. 108–134.

Loyle C. and Bestvater S. (2019). #rebel: Rebel Communication Strategies in the Age of Social Media. *Conflict Management and Peace Science* 36(6).

Malejacq R. (2017). From Rebel to Quasi-State: Governance, Diplomacy and Legitimacy in the Midst of Afghanistan's Wars (1979–2001). *Small Wars & Insurgencies* 28(4–5), pp. 867–886. DOI: 10.1080/09592318.2017.1322332.

Mampilly Z. (2015). Performing the Nation-State: Rebel Governance and Symbolic Processes. In: Arjona A., Kasfir N., and Mampilly Z. (eds.) *Rebel Governance in Civil War*. Cambridge: Cambridge University Press, pp. 74–97. DOI: 10.1017/CBO9781316182468.004.

Mattiacci E. and Jones BT. (2020). Restoring Legitimacy: Public Diplomacy Campaigns during Civil Wars. *International Studies Quarterly* 64(4), pp. 867–878. DOI: 10.1093/isq/sqaa065.

Moss S. (2020). Turkey to Fund Data Center in Internationally Unrecognized Northern Cyprus. *Data Center Dynamics*, 24 December. Available at: www.datacenterdynamics.com/en/news/turkey-fund-da-ta-center-internationally-unrecognized-northern-cyprus/ (accessed 8 January 2022).

News.am. (2018). Karabakh's Martakert, Lebanon's Bourj Hammoud Sign Memorandum of Cooperation. *Armenia News*, 18 May. Available at: https://news.am/eng/news/451940.html (accessed 8 January 2022).

Nicolson H. (1950). *Diplomacy*. Institute for the Study of Diplomacy (ed.). Washington, DC: Institute for the Study of Diplomacy, School of Foreign Service, Georgetown University.

NKR. (2008). Permanent Representations. Available at: https://web.archive.org/web/20110526135731/http:/www.nkr.am/en/permanent-representations/104/ (accessed 8 January 2022).

Numelin R. (1950). *The Beginnings of Diplomacy: A Sociological Study of Inter-Tribal and International Relations*. Oxford: Oxford University Press.

Otarashvili M. (2017). *Russia's Quiet Annexation of South Ossetia Continues*. 11 April. Foreign Policy Research Institute. Available at: www.fpri.org/article/2017/04/russias-quiet-annexation-south-osse-tia-continues/ (accessed 8 January 2022).

Özkan B. (2008). Who Gains from the "No War No Peace" Situation? A Critical Analysis of the Nagorno-Karabakh Conflict. *Geopolitics* 13(3), pp. 572–599. DOI: 10.1080/14650040802203919.

Paquin J. (2010). *A Stability-Seeking Power: U.S. Foreign Policy and Secessionist Conflicts*. Montréal: McGill Queens University Press.

Pegg S. (2020). Somaliland. In: Visoka G., Doyle J., and Newman E. (eds.) *Routledge Handbook of State Recognition*. London; New York: Routledge, Taylor & Francis Group.

Pouliot V. and Cornut J. (2015). Practice Theory and the Study of Diplomacy: A Research Agenda. *Cooperation and Conflict* 50(3), pp. 297–315. DOI: 10.1177/0010836715574913.

Reuters. (2020). Algeria Rejects Trump's Stance on Western Sahara. *Reuters*, 12 December. Available at: www.reuters.com/article/algeria-westernsahara-usa-idUSKBN28M0MZ (accessed 8 January 2022).

Reynolds I. (2021). Japan Mentions Taiwan Stability in Defense Paper for First Time. Available at: www.japantimes.co.jp/news/2021/07/13/national/japan-taiwan-defense-paper/ (accessed 23 July 2021).

Rosenau J. (1990). *Turbulence in World Politics: A Theory of Change and Continuity*. Princeton, NJ: Princeton University Press.

San-Akca B. (2016). *States in Disguise: Causes of State Support for Rebel Groups*. Oxford: Oxford University Press. Available at: www.oxfordscholarship.com/view/10.1093/acprof:oso/9780190250881.001.0001/acprof-9780190250881 (accessed 16 December 2018).

Saparov A. (2014). *From Conflict to Autonomy in the Caucasus: The Soviet Union and the Making of Abkhazia, South Ossetia and Nagorno Karabakh*. 0 ed. Abingdon, UK: Routledge. DOI: 10.4324/9781315758992.

Satow EM. (1979). *Satow's Guide to Diplomatic Practice*. 5th ed. London; New York: Longman.

Sending OJ., Pouliot V., and Neumann IB. (eds.). (2015). *Diplomacy and the Making of World Politics*. Cambridge, UK: Cambridge University Press.

Simpson G. (1994). Judging the East Timor Dispute: Self-Determination at the International Court of Justice. *Hastings International and Comparative Law Review* 17(2), p. 27.

SPS. (2013). Western Sahara: Saharawi Delegation Received by Mayor of Sesto Fiorentino. *Sahara Press Service*, 20 November. Available at: https://allafrica.com/stories/201311201467.html (accessed 8 January 2022).

SPS. (2018). Saharawi National Council Speaker in a Working Visit to Spanish Cantabria Province. *Sahara Press Service*, 21 November. Available at: www.spsrasd.info/news/en/articles/2018/11/21/18457.html (accessed 8 January 2022).

Stewart M. (2018). Civil War as State-Making: Strategic Governance in Civil War. *International Organization* 72(1), pp. 205–226. DOI: https://doi.org/10.1017/S0020818317000418.

Talmon S. (2001). The Cyprus Question before the European Court of Justice. *European Journal of International Law* 12(4), pp. 727–750. DOI: 10.1093/ejil/12.4.727.

Trager R. (2017). *Diplomacy: Communication and the Origins of International Order*. Cambridge: Cambridge University Press. DOI: 10.1017/9781107278776.

Tskhovrebov VD. (1981). *Iz Istorii Iugo-Osetinskoi Organizatsii KP Gruzii (1917–1925)*. Tskhinvali: Iryston.

Yip H. (2020). Taiwan Shows How to Carefully Snip Chinese Economic Ties. *Foreign Policy*, 24 July. Available at: http://foreignpolicy.com/2020/07/24/taiwan-china-economic-ties-decoupling/ (accessed 8 January 2022).

# PART V

# Counter-secession strategies

# 27

# COUNTERING SECESSION

*James Ker-Lindsay*

The way in which states respond to acts of secession and then try to prevent secessionist territories from being accepted on the international stage has traditionally been subject to relatively little academic attention (Ker-Lindsay, 2012). In part, this was because there were relatively few such entities on the world stage. However, there has been a growth in the number of secessionist territories seeking recognition (Griffiths, 2016, 2021). This means that there is a growing interest in both academic and policy circles in the ways that states respond to acts of separatism, both in terms of being a domestic challenge and, more importantly, as a matter of foreign policy. Specifically, how do they signal to the wider international community that the act of secession is opposed? And how do they formulate their diplomatic strategies to counter efforts by the seceding territory to gain recognition or even legitimisation?

In broad terms, a counter-secession strategy needs to be built on four elements. First, the state must make it clear to the international community that it rejects the act of secession and that it continues to claim sovereignty over the seceding territory. This can be done in several ways. For instance, the declaration of independence can be annulled. The parent state – as the country that the seceding territory is breaking away from is often known – can continue to maintain institutions, even nominal ones, with responsibility for the area that has seceded. This ensures that there is no question about the ongoing claim to sovereignty. Secondly, steps must be taken to ensure that the territory is not recognised by other countries and that it is not permitted to join international organisations and bodies. The third element is to prevent legitimisation. Even if a territory does not gain formal recognition, it can achieve a high level of international acceptance. Preventing this can often be just as important as stopping formal recognition. Fourthly, an ongoing effort must be made to shore up the legitimacy of the claim to the secessionist territory. This can be done through legal routes, such as international court cases undermining the breakaway territory's claim to effective independence. Taken together, these measures can create a broad and inclusive counter-secession strategy.

## Formulating a counter-recognition strategy

Before examining how states implement counter-recognition strategies, it is important to consider how such strategies are formulated. First, in many cases, such strategies will be a significant part of a country's foreign policy. An act of secession is almost always viewed as a fundamental

DOI: 10.4324/9781003036593-32

threat to the state. It will therefore often have a central part in its external relations. Indeed, it may become the overarching national issue.

This strong reaction may be driven by a wide variety of factors (Ker-Lindsay, 2013). For instance, the territory in question may have important economic value to the state. It may be a centre of industrial activity or rich in natural resources. Alternatively, it may have cultural of historical significance to the nation. Sometimes a policy of counter-secession will be driven by a fear of contagion. While the territory in question may not have intrinsic worth, there is a fear that if it is allowed to secede, then other regions will follow. Alternatively, a country may be unable to accept the loss of a part of its territory and will want to hold on to a region, even if it is causing considerable problems, for no other reason than it sees itself as a part of the geographical whole. States have a certain image of themselves, and their citizens often understand the country in a particular geographic way.

In many, if not most, cases of unilateral secession, the campaign to prevent the recognition of the breakaway territory will become the single most important foreign policy objective of the state. It will therefore often involve much of the state's domestic and foreign administrative apparatus. In some cases, a formal body will coordinate the state's responses. At other times, it may be a looser arrangement. While various parts of the government may have a role to play in the process, the most significant actor is most usually the foreign ministry (Ker-Lindsay, 2012). As expected, this will involve officials at all levels, from the foreign minister downwards. It will also involve the country's embassies abroad. The problem is that operating an extensive diplomatic operation and associated public diplomacy campaign is very expensive. Indeed, it is beyond the means of many states. A more focused effort is therefore used in many cases. In particular, the permanent mission to the United Nations in New York may become the hub for diplomatic activity, as it provides a way to engage with the senior representatives of almost every other state relatively easily and effectively (Grant, 2009). In this context, the annual General Assembly is an especially important focus of activity, as it provides a chance for direct bilateral meetings with other heads of governments. As well as the traditional methods of diplomatic activity, states may also employ other partners to help them make their case. For instance, many countries engaged in counter-recognition efforts employ the services of major lobbying firms to act on their behalf. Well-organised and highly motivated diaspora communities in the right countries, armed with the right information and messages, can also play an important part in counter-recognition activities (Ker-Lindsay, 2012).

As for developing the strategy itself, there is considerable variation across states. Some countries have an extremely well-designed strategy in place and take an uncompromising approach. Cyprus is a very good case in point. It resists any and every attempt to recognise or even tacitly accept the existence of the 'Turkish Republic of Northern Cyprus'. By way of contrast, Serbia has tended to take a more uneven approach towards Kosovo. In the aftermath of Kosovo's declaration of independence, in February 2008, the Serbian government developed a very strong strategy to prevent recognition. However, five years later, it appeared as if it had all but given up on trying to stop states from recognising Kosovo. That in turn changed back to a stronger counter-recognition strategy following a successful initiative to prevent Kosovo from joining the UN Educational, Scientific and Cultural Organisation (UNESCO), in 2015. Since then, Serbia has again been trying to prevent Kosovo from being recognised and from joining international organisations. Indeed, it has gone even further than this and started persuading countries to rescind their recognition. This has seemingly produced some significant results. As of early 2022, the Serbian Foreign Ministry has seemingly persuaded well over a dozen countries to reverse the decision on recognition and declare that they still recognise Kosovo to be a part of Serbia; at least pending a final agreement between Belgrade and Pristina. Having reached a high of around 113 UN members, Kosovo is now recognised by around 98 UN member states.

## Maintaining a claim to the territory

The first step in any serious counter-recognition strategy is to maintain a claim to the territory in question. This element of the counter-recognition strategy is in fact absolutely vital to any wider strategy of counter-recognition. While it may seem a rather futile gesture in the face of an act of unilateral secession, especially when there is no realistic prospect of reasserting sovereignty in the short or medium term, it sends a crucial signal to the wider international community that the act of secession has not been accepted, even tacitly, by the parent state. This is important, as it has long been accepted that a state facing an act of secession will often take many years, if not decades, before it formally recognises that a part of its territory is irretrievably lost. However, long before it openly and formally accepts that the territory is lost, the parent state will start to signal that it has effectively accepted the secession of the territory. In the intervening period between secession and formal acceptance, many third parties will closely watch the behaviour of the parent state before deciding how to respond to a secessionist entity (Lauterpacht, 1947). If it looks as if the loss of the territory has been accepted in all but name, then it is likely that external parties will start to interact with the territory. This in turn will thereby erode the parent state's claim to the territory. For this reason, any state that wishes to fight an act of secession must ensure that outside actors are left with absolutely no doubt about its ongoing claim to sovereignty over the territory in question.

The assertion of sovereignty can be done in a variety of different ways. One of the first steps, and perhaps the most important, is to challenge the purported secession. Any unilateral declaration of independence (UDI), and any acts deriving from it, must be rejected. Sometimes, this can be done through a simple statement issued by the parent state. At other times, it may be a more formal procedure, such as a resolution by the national parliament. At the same time, and to reinforce the point, states will sometimes bring criminal charges against key officials considered to be responsible for the act of secession. For example, three officials held responsible for Kosovo's declaration of independence – the President, the Prime Minister and Speaker of the Assembly – were all charged with treason by the Serbian government (Reuters, 2008). More recently, following Catalonia's declaration of independence, in October 2017, the Spanish government charged Carlos Puigdemont, the President of Catalonia, as well as other members of the regional government with rebellion. This eventually resulted in jail terms for the accused (New York Times, 2019). As well as these direct efforts to challenge an act of secession, steps may also be taken to undermine the legitimacy of such officials in other ways; such as by issuing warrants for their arrests on other charges, including allegations of having committed war crimes. Such actions can be useful in terms of the wider counter-recognition strategy, as they can then be used as further evidence by the parent state that the secessionist territory is either morally illegitimate or built on illegal foundations. Again, Serbia has been very active in this regard. A number of senior Kosovo officials have been detained by other countries on warrants issued by Serbia through Interpol (Balkan Insight, 2017).

As well as the immediate response to a declaration of independence, states will often maintain an ongoing claim to the territory in a variety of other ways. In some instances, the state will maintain the formal representation of the territory in state institutions and retain nominal structures of governance over the breakaway area. For example, it may continue to recognise the existence of municipal and regional councils, even though these have no direct authority over the territory in question. Likewise, they may continue to recognise the existence of elected officials for the region in question. This could include continuing to hold elections for mayors, councillors and even members of the national parliament. This approach is very prevalent in Cyprus, where exiled voters from towns and districts not under the effective control of the state continue to elect officials and send representatives to the national parliament to represent those areas. Tied to this, the government may also try to maintain a sense of community amongst the erstwhile inhabitants of the territories. For instance, as internally displaced persons, they may be given special privileges and tax breaks. In some cases, this status is even hereditary. This can mean that after a generation or two, there are more people who hail from the region than were originally displaced. Allied to this, the ongoing claim to ownership of property in the breakaway territory will be recognised and may even be accepted as collateral for bank loans, albeit under-written by the government (Gurel et al., 2012). On top of this, there are a multitude of other ways that states can reinforce the claim to territory, both domestically and internationally. Even ensuring that the territory is included on television weather broadcasts sends the message that the territory is still regarded as an integral part of the state. All this in turn reinforces the message that the territory is still claimed and that the act of secession is still opposed.

## Preventing bilateral recognition and membership of international organisations

The second element of any counter-recognition strategy is preventing the breakaway territory from gaining formal international acceptance, either by preventing bilateral recognition or by stopping the territory in question from joining international organisations. While maintaining a claim to the territory represents the foundation of any counter-recognition strategy, this ele-ment is the cornerstone of actual counter-recognition practice. Needless to say, states facing acts of secession will usually channel considerable resources into fighting their cause on the interna-tional stage. Indeed, as already noted, preventing the recognition of the breakaway territory will often be the single overriding objective of the state's entire foreign policy. For example, when Cyprus joined the European Union, it was regarded as the single-issue member state because of its focus on the 'national issue' (Ioannides, 2017).

In terms of the actual objectives of a counter-recognition strategy, as one would expect the prevention of bilateral recognition by other states is usually seen as the single most important activity for a state engaged in a counter-recognition effort. In this regard, it is widely understood that parent states start with an overwhelming advantage in the modern international system. Whereas in the nineteenth century, territories that had broken away and had managed to assert effective independence were usually recognised as states, since the end of the Second World War this mode of thinking has changed dramatically (Fabry, 2010). The emphasis on the territorial integrity of states has taken on a greater emphasis in international affairs. And while many will also point to the emergence of self-determination as a norm of international politics, in reality the application of this concept in a manner that leads to the creation of new sovereign states has been applied in a very narrow set of circumstances, most usually relating to the independence of overseas colonial territories. This gives the parent state a powerful platform on which to begin their efforts.

While the parent state has a strong advantage in secessionist disputes, in many cases it will in fact try to downplay the act of secession. Rather than present the situation as a domestic act of rebellion by the inhabitants of the secessionist territory, a parent state will instead emphasise that the breakaway entity is the product of an illegal act of aggression by an external state. This is very prevalent in the cases of Cyprus and Georgia. Both usually seek to present the situation as one of invasion and occupation of the seceded territories, rather than secession. This approach offers two important benefits. In the first instance, it is used to emphasise that there is no intrinsic reason why the internal parties of the conflict cannot resolve their differences and live together. It is the outside actor that is ultimately responsible for the situation. Secondly, as it is generally recognised that statehood requires that the state be truly independent of outside control (Craw-ford, 2006) rather than a puppet entity, this approach is explicitly designed to fundamentally undermine the claim to statehood by the breakaway territory.

Given these factors, in most cases of secession, the chances of widespread bilateral recognition are relatively low. Nevertheless, states cannot afford to neglect a counter-recognition campaign. As noted, to do so may suggest that they had relinquished their claim to the territory. However, given the expense of doing so, it becomes readily apparent that any such efforts need to be focused. It is simply not possible to lobby every country on a permanent, or even on a regular, basis. To this end, there is a clear hierarchy of states that need to be engaged. As one may expect, the prime targets in any strategy are the five permanent members of the UN Security Council – China, France, Russia, the United Kingdom, and the United States. By virtue of their position to shape the Security Council, discussed later in this chapter, as well as their wider standing in international affairs, these great powers invariably play an overarching role in preventing the wider acceptance of an act of secession (Sterio, 2013; Coggins, 2014). Beyond these five states, counter-recognition efforts will then be focused on other key actors, such as regional powers or states that have a degree of influence over other countries. For example, in the EU context, Germany is an important actor. In the Islamic world, Saudi Arabia is often seen as a vital player. Britain still has a network of contacts with the countries that are members of the Commonwealth, just as Spain and France are seen to have a degree of influence over Latin America and the Francophone countries, respectively. Beyond that, states will also try to solicit support from other countries that are also facing a separatist threat. Of course, in such circumstances, it is not just about lobbying these states not to recognise the territory in question. A major part of any counter-recognition strategy will also focus on co-opting them as active campaigners to persuade others not to recognise the breakaway state. For example, Serbia sees Spain as an important partner in its counter-recognition efforts, and Madrid has taken a very hardline position on Kosovo in EU settings (Ferrero-Turrión, 2020).

The second strand of the formal counter-recognition strategy involves preventing the secession territory from joining international and regional organisations, or from becoming increasingly engaged with such bodies. Obviously, the most significant of these bodies is the United Nations. Indeed, the UN has now become crucial to any recognition battle. For the seceding territory, membership offers a way to full international acceptance. Although it must be underlined that the United Nations cannot recognise states, membership of the UN is often understood to amount to 'universal recognition' – even though not all members if the UN are recognised by every other member. In the case of the UN, membership is extremely hard to secure if the circumstances of membership are in any way contentious (see Grant, 2009). The requirement that any application for membership must be endorsed by the Security Council means that the five permanent members hold a veto over the process. Thereafter, admittance is contingent on a majority vote from the General Assembly. Here, it is a numbers game. A territory needs 97 votes of the current 193 members of the UN. This is where bilateral recognitions really matter. All this effectively means that the chances of a territory joining the UN prior to the express recognition by the parent state are negligible. Indeed, the only country in the modern era to have unilaterally seceded and gone on to join the UN, the People's Republic of Bangladesh, only did so once Pakistan, its former parent state, agreed to recognise it; this despite the fact that it had already been recognised by the four of the five permanent members of the Security Council, the United States, Russia, Britain and France (Musson, 2008).

In reality, in cases of contested secession, preventing UN membership is fairly easy to achieve. To this extent, a far more important goal is to secure a UN security Council resolution calling on states not to recognise the territory as an independent state. Perhaps more than any other step that can be taken, a resolution endorsing collective non-recognition can shape the overall international response to a secessionist territory. However, due to the major veto-wielding powers, this is not always possible. For example, in the case of South Ossetia and Abkhazia, which had seceded from Georgia, and were recognised by Russia in 2008, Moscow was in a position to block any resolutions condemning either the purported act of secession by the territories or its own decision to recognise their independence. But even if a formal act of condemnation is blocked in the Security Council, the UN can still play an important role in counter-recognition efforts through the General Assembly. For example, while Moscow was able to block a draft Security Council resolution condemning a referendum on the status of Crimea, which was designed to pave the way for the territory's secession and subsequent annexation by the Russian Federation in March 2014, just weeks later the General Assembly was able to pass Resolution 68/262 on the 'Territorial Integrity of Ukraine' by 100 votes in favour versus 11 against, with 58 abstentions and 24 absentees.

While formal membership of the United Nations may not be possible, there are in fact various other ways in which de facto states can engage with the UN. One possibility is to apply to become a non-member observer state. Unlike full membership, this does not require support from the Security Council. Instead, it can be granted by the General Assembly. Such a status can be incredibly powerful in terms of reinforcing the perception that the territory in question is a state. Moreover, history has shown that almost every state that has achieved this status has eventually gone on to achieve full membership. Once again, given that this requires a simple majority of UN members, bilateral recognitions are vital. In addition, the UN also consists of a multitude of other bodies. Here the potential opportunities for membership are much greater. For example, the voting method used for membership of the World Bank and the International Monetary Fund is weighted towards the world's wealthiest countries. This meant that Kosovo – which was supported by many of the world's leading economies, such as the United States, Germany, France, Britain and Japan, amongst others – was able to join both bodies a year after declaring independence. In other cases, there is no right of veto. In these cases, the sheer weight of numbers is sufficient. As membership of these other bodies can be important in terms of adding legitimacy to a territory, the campaign for membership can become very hard fought. This was seen in Kosovo's unsuccessful bid to join the UN Educational, Scientific and Cultural Organisation (UNESCO), in 2015. Serbia engaged in a sustained diplomatic effort to prevent its membership. As a result, several countries that had already recognised Kosovo – such as Egypt, Japan and South Korea – abstained in the vote, therefore ensuring the bid failed (B92, 2015). More recently, in 2018, Kosovo's bid to join Interpol, the international police body, was also thwarted following a concerted Serbian campaign to prevent membership (Balkan Insight, 2019).

As well as the UN bodies and organisations, there are a whole host of other international and regional organisations that states can potentially join. These too become key battlegrounds. Senior officials from parent states will therefore often try to attend major meetings on international bodies, precisely to engage in lobbying activities. However, there is a vast disparity in terms of the formal requirements for membership. In some cases, international organisations deliberately try to avoid becoming entangled in recognition disputes and therefore insist that UN membership be a formal requirement for accession. For instance, this is the case with the Organisation of Islamic Cooperation (OIC). In other cases, there appears to be a presumption that a new member will also be a member of the United Nations, but this is not formally set out. This appears to be the case with the European Union, where there has been a debate as to whether Kosovo can join even if it is still not a member of the UN (EU Official, comment to the author). In other organisations, the terms of membership are less clear. For example, the EU is a member of some international bodies, even though it is not a state. This precedent can in turn provide enough ambiguity to allow states that do not enjoy full recognition to be accepted by non-recognising members. For example, the fact that the EU is a member of the European Bank for Reconstruction and Development (EBRD) appears to have been enough to persuade several members that did not recognise Kosovo to vote in favour of its member-ship, and for some others to abstain, when the issue came before the organisation in 2012. Of course, where there is sufficient political will, steps can be taken to include territories that have not been recognised as members in the proceedings of some international organisations. For example, despite its prohibition on allowing membership for non-UN members, the OIC has admitted Northern Cyprus and Kosovo as observers. For these reasons, parent states may often try to engage with international and regional organisations, which can become important bat-tlegrounds for recognition struggles.

## Preventing legitimisation

Although preventing the formal recognition of a secessionist territory by other states and stop-ping it from securing membership of key international organisations are crucial elements of any counter-recognition strategy, there is more to it than this. As emphasised, it is extremely difficult for a breakaway territory to gain widespread recognition. In this regard, a far greater challenge is to prevent the gradual acceptance of a secessionist entity by other states. While recognition is rare, such territories slowly come to be accepted by the international community (Berg and Toomla, 2009). This can happen in a variety of ways. While it will usually be mini-mal, sometimes such legitimisation can be extensive and amount to recognition in all but name (Ker-Lindsay, 2015). For example, Greece maintains extremely close economic and political relations with Kosovo, even though it formally maintains its policy of non-recognition (Arma-kolas, 2020). There may be good reasons for this. For instance, there may be matters that require a degree of formal engagement, such as the protection of citizens living in the territory or the prevention of organised crime and terrorism.

In broad terms, legitimisation comes in many shapes and forms. One important area is eco-nomic interaction between the breakaway territory and the wider world. This is seen by parent states as particularly problematic, as this can provide financial stability for the secessionist entity, thus providing the foundations for long-term sustainability. Eventually, this can even make the breakaway territory viable as an entity. For this reason, efforts are often made to ensure that the territory in question remains economically isolated. This may mean trying to prevent direct trade between the territory and the outside world, even though these restrictions can often be easily circumvented with the support of a patron state. It can also mean trying to prevent the development of transportation links, such as direct flights into the territory. Again, while these can often be worked around, such as by flying from within a patron state, as happens between Turkey and Northern Cyprus, it provides an added layer of complication for the breakaway territory that hinders its links with the outside world. The parent state will also try to ensure that the territory remains isolated in many other ways. For example, steps will often be taken to ensure that the breakaway territory cannot participate in various educational and cultural activities. In this context, one of the most heavily contested areas of activity is participation in sporting activities. While there are many who argue that sports should be above politics, in reality the presence of teams from a secessionist territory in international sporting events can be an immensely powerful symbol of their acceptance on the world stage. For this reason, Serbia fought extremely hard to prevent Kosovo from participating in international football competi-tions and taking part in the Olympic Games. Despite a sustained effort, Belgrade eventually lost both efforts. Kosovo participated at the 2016 Olympic Games in Rio de Janeiro and took part in the qualifications for the 2018 football World Cup.

As can be seen, parent states will regard this 'creeping legitimisation' as a major concern. Indeed, given the relatively unlikely prospect that the territory will gain formal recognition, it may even come to be seen as a far more central worry than the possibility of formal recognition. Therefore, at the same time as operating formal diplomatic efforts to prevent recognition, parent states will also often engage in efforts to prevent any gradual acceptance.

Given the range of activities that can be viewed as conferring a degree of acceptance on the secessionist territory, preventing legitimisation usually requires a far greater range of interventions than preventing recognition. Of course, formal diplomacy will play a part. However, parent states will also engage in wider public diplomacy. In some instances, efforts will be made to launch campaigns to inform public opinion about the issue. Again, this may also be done through formal foreign ministry channels. For example, embassies will often keep a close watch on the domestic situation in the country where they are based and may make representations to national governments when they see something that they believe challenges their sovereignty. They may also take steps to enforce their sovereignty in other ways. This may include efforts to try to prevent figures from the breakaway territory from speaking at universities and other public settings. For example, the Abkhaz State University has found it difficult to build wider European ties because of objections from Georgia (Coppieters, 2021). But such efforts may also involve a greater variety of actors than the foreign ministry. Again, professional lobbyists and diaspora groups may play their part. So too can other parts of the government, such as information and communications agencies, which can organise efforts to 'enlighten' wider international opinion. For instance, in Cyprus, the government's Press and Information Office has been active in producing literature to 'enlighten' international audiences about the 'invasion and occupation' of Cyprus.

While it is understood that preventing a secessionist territory from gaining wider legitimisation is an important element of any counter-recognition strategy, this can bring other, potentially greater, problems. While parent states will want to make sure that secessionist entities do not gain gradual acceptance on the world stage, they must be equally careful not to isolate the territories too much. Keeping secessionist territories wholly apart from the international community will often force them to deepen their relationship with a patron state (Berg and Vits, 2020). This in turn makes a settlement all the more difficult, as it not only erodes any trust between the secessionist entity and the parent state, but it can also increase the levels of influence of the patron, which often has little to gain from a settlement that would inevitably erode its influence over the situation. For this reason, it is increasingly recognised by external observers that the notion of 'engagement without recognition', as the method of allowing limited external interaction with unrecognised states is now generally known, can be an important tool of conflict management (Berg and Ker-Lindsay, 2019). Nevertheless, most parent states remain inherently cautious about external engagement with a breakaway territory in any form, viewing this as a slippery slope towards general acceptance.

## The role of international legal and judicial bodies

The fourth and final pillar of an effective counter-recognition strategy is the use of legal and judicial routes to prevent recognition and legitimisation. These can have very significant effects. A review of such activities show that this route can focus on either challenging the right of independence or cementing the view that the case in question is really about invasion and occupation by an external actor. In the case of the former – challenging the right of independence – the most important case to date was the International Court of Justice (ICJ) advisory opinion on Kosovo. Initiated by Serbia, the UN General Assembly voted to refer the legality of Kosovo's unilateral declaration of independence to the International Court of Justice. The case attracted significant international attention and was the first and only time that all five permanent members of the Security Council had participated in a case before the Court (for an analysis of this case, see Milanovic and Wood, 2015). In the end, the Court opted for a very narrow reading of the question put before it. It decided that the formal declaration of independence did not contravene general international law. However, and importantly, the court deliberately avoided taking a position on whether Kosovo was in fact a state. Likewise, it did not take a position on whether the states that had recognised Kosovo had, in doing so, breached their obligation to respect the territorial integrity of Serbia (International Court of Justice, 2010). In this regard, the opinion effectively amounted to a stalemate. Third countries could read it as they wanted.

Another option is to argue that the territory is under occupation, rather than secessionist in nature. One of the most important cases in this context was the Loizidou at the European Court of Human Rights. The proceedings were initiated by Titina Loizidou, a Greek Cypriot who had been displaced during the Turkish invasion of the island in 1974. She argued that she had been illegally deprived of the use of her property. The Court agreed and awarded compensation, Importantly, the judges ruled that Turkey was liable, as Northern Cyprus was not a sovereign state. Instead, the Turkish Cypriot administration amounted to a subordinate administration of Turkey (ECHR, 1995). This was a crucial case, as it cemented the position of the Cypriot government that the Cyprus Problem was not in essence a secessionist dispute. It was a case of invasion and occupation by an external party. A second useful example was the case before the European Court of Justice (ECJ) regarding direct trade with Northern Cyprus. This centred on proceedings brought by a Cypriot company in the British courts and led to the end of direct commercial contacts between the European Union and the TRNC (Talmon, 2001).

Notably, the Government of the Republic of Cyprus has never initiated a case directly. As officials point out, it is unnecessary. The illegality of the Turkish Cypriot declaration of independence and the TRNC has been recognised by the Security Council. Indeed, officials note that it would in fact be highly counterproductive to pursue a case elsewhere, such as before the ICJ. Even with seemingly clear-cut cases, there is a significant risk. There is always the potential for a legal surprise. For this reason, legal avenues, while potentially beneficial, have to be handled carefully. They are often riskier than they might seem – although the pay-offs if they are successful can be significant.

## Conclusion

How states counter secession is a growing area of interest for academics and policymakers. As noted, there are four key strands of any policy. First, the claim to the territory must be maintained. This includes making it clear that the act of secession is opposed and laying claim, even if nominally, to the territory. Secondly, steps must be taken to prevent recognition or the admission of the breakaway territory into regional and international organisations. A third element is to prevent the wider acceptance or legitimisation of the territory, not just in terms of political acceptance, but also in terms of preventing it from being integrated into cultural and sporting organisations and events and into the international economy. Finally, the legality of the decision to secede needs to be challenged, ideally with a view to ensuring that the breakaway state comes to be seen as the mere occupied proxy for another state.

These strategies naturally change and evolve with time. Immediately following a declaration of independence, the focus will be on asserting a claim and ensuring that the territory is not recognised. Once the immediate prospect of recognition has declined, the effort is then likely to shift towards preventing legitimation and trying to undermine the claim to statehood. Rather than spending time, effort and, often, large sums of money on a major diplomatic campaign to prevent recognition in the immediate phase, a more sustainable long-term strategy can be developed. However, the campaign can never be entirely ignored. If the parent state becomes too lax, then this may be read as a sign that it has effectively given up and may open the way for third countries, if not to recognise the secessionist territory, then at least to increase the extent and scope of their engagement with it.

Steps to prevent the recognition or wider acceptance of breakaway territories need to be formulated according to a wider strategy for managing the conflict in its broader dimensions. Isolating such territories not only makes a settlement less likely, as the seceding territory will have an increasingly negative view of the parent state, but it also forces it to have to build even closer relations with a patron state that may have little if any interest in seeing the conflict resolved. On top of this, we also must accept that sometimes such counter-secession strategies are not in fact aimed at reunification – although this will obviously be the stated aim. Instead, the strategy is aimed at showing a domestic audience that the government is continuing its efforts to bring about a settlement of the conflict. In this sense, not all counter-secession strategies are quite as firmly aimed at counter-secession as they may seem.

# References

Armakolas, I. 2020, 'Greece: Kosovo's Most Engaged Non-Recogniser', in A. Ioannis & J. Ker-Lindsay (eds.), *The Politics of Recognition and Engagement: EU Member State Relations with Kosovo*, Basingstoke: Palgrave Macmillan.

B92. 2015, 'Kosovo's Bid to Join UNESCO Fails; Details of Voting Emerge', November 9.

Balkan Insight. 2017, 'Kosovo Asks Interpol to Cancel Serbian Warrants', February 20.

Balkan Insight. 2019, 'Kosovo Withdraws Application to Join Interpol', October 15.

Berg, E. & Ker-Lindsay, J. (eds.). 2019, *The Politics of International Interaction with De Facto States*, Abingdon: Routledge.

Berg, E. & Toomla, R. 2009, 'Forms of Normalisation in the Quest for De Facto Statehood', *The International Spectator*, 44 (4).

Berg, E. & Vits, K. 2020, 'Exploring De Facto State Agency: Negotiation Power, International Engagement and Patronage', in G. Baldacchino & A. Wivel (eds.), *Handbook on the Politics of Small States*, Cheltenham: Edward Elgar.

Coggins, B. 2014, *Power Politics and State Formation in the Twentieth Century: The Dynamics of Recognition*, Cambridge: Cambridge University Press.

Coppieters, B. 2021, 'A Struggle over Recognition and Nonrecognition: The Internationalization of the Abkhaz State University', *Nationalities Papers*, 1–22.

Crawford, J. 2006, *The Creation of States in International Law*, 2nd Edition, Oxford: Oxford University Press.

European Court of Human Rights. 1995, *Loizidou v. Turkey* Judgment (no. 15318/89, Preliminary Objections), March 23.

Fabry, M. 2010, *Recognizing States: International Society and the Establishment of New States since 1776*, Oxford: Oxford University Press.

Ferrero-Turrión, R. 2020, 'Spain: Kosovo's Strongest Opponent in Europe', in I. Armakolas and J. Ker-Lindsay (eds.), *The Politics of Recognition and Engagement: EU Member State Relations with Kosovo*, Basingstoke: Palgrave Macmillan.

Grant, T. D. 2009, *Admission to the United Nations: Charter 4 and the Rise of Universal Organization*, Leiden: Martinus Nijhoff.

Griffiths, R. D. 2016, *Age of Secession: The International and Domestic Determinants of State Birth*, Cambridge: Cambridge University Press.

Griffiths, R. D. 2021, *Secession and the Sovereignty Game*, Ithaca: Cornell University Press.

Gurel, A., Hatay, M., & Yakinthou, C. 2012, *Displacement in Cyprus: Consequences of Civil and Military Strife*, Nicosia: PRIO, Peace Research Institute, Oslo.

International Court of Justice. 2010, 'Accordance with International Law of the Unilateral Declaration of Independence in Respect of Kosovo', *Advisory Opinion*, July 22.

Ioannides, I. 2017, 'Cyprus and EU Enlargement to the Western Balkans: A Balancing Act', *Southeast European and Black Sea Studies Journal*, 17 (4): 631–647.

Ker-Lindsay, J. 2012, *The Foreign Policy of Counter Secession: Preventing the Recognition of Contested States*, Oxford: Oxford University Press.

Ker-Lindsay, J. 2013, 'Understanding State Responses to Secession', *Peacebuilding*, 2 (1).

Ker-Lindsay, J. 2015, 'Engagement without Recognition: The Limits of Diplomatic Interaction with Contested States', *International Affairs*, 92 (2).

Lauterpacht, H. 1947, *Recognition in International Law*, Cambridge: Cambridge University Press.

Milanovic, M. & Wood, M. (eds.). 2015, *The Law and Politics of the Kosovo Advisory Opinion*, Oxford: Oxford University Press.

Musson, J. 2008, 'Britain and the Recognition of Bangladesh in 1972', *Diplomacy and Statecraft*, 19 (1).

*New York Times*. 2019, 'Catalan Separatist Leaders Get Lengthy Prison Terms for Sedition', October 14.

Reuters. 2008, 'Serbia Charges Kosovo Leaders with Treason', February 18.

Sterio, M. 2013, *The Right to Self-determination under International Law: "Selfistans", Secession and the Rule of the Great Powers*, Abingdon: Routledge.

Talmon, S. 2001, 'The Cyprus Question before the European Court of Justice', *European Journal of International Law*, 12 (4).

# 28

# SECESSIONIST DE-MOBILIZATION

## From 'exit' back to 'voice'

*Karlo Basta*

Scholars know a great deal about secessionist escalation.[1] This focus on mobilization for independence is understandable: the territorial status quo bias of the international system puts a premium on 'diagnosing' challenges to the territorial integrity of states. Understanding what causes the escalation of secessionist activity is thus important for both policymakers and scholars. On a more banal note, dramatic showdowns between independence movements and the state may fascinate scholars more than the less exciting task of cooling a febrile political atmosphere. Yet, this analytic focus on secessionist build-up means that we know almost nothing about how or why secessionist movements scale back their activity.[2]

Secessionist *demobilization* emerges as a concern only where a serious challenge to the territorial status quo – either by *peaceful* means (e.g. referenda or civil disobedience campaigns) or violent ones (a full-scale civil war or a low-level campaign of violence) – fails in attaining its goal.[3] If a movement succeeds in obtaining independence, the issue of de-escalation is moot.[4] But if a referendum fails to secure a majority for independence, or a secessionist army loses a war of independence, secessionist elites must decide whether or not to suspend or abandon their pursuit of independent statehood.

This chapter develops a conceptual map meant to facilitate research into secessionist demobilization. I begin with two key features that characterize any secessionist situation. The first has to do with the divisions within any potentially secessionist community. Support for independence is variable – it must be fostered and sustained in order for independence to have a chance of success.[5] Yet, constituencies for independent statehood are ideologically heterogeneous. Their members disagree about the legitimacy of the common state and the desirability or feasibility of independence. A significant proportion of the population will either oppose independence or be indifferent to it. The key task of secessionist activists is to win over a sufficiently large proportion of that population (Roeder 2018).[6] The process of mobilization is simultaneously one of (public *and* private) persuasion, ideological homogenization, and escalation of collective emotions.

Those elements of the process of mobilization relate to the second feature of any secessionist situation. Once an organization or a societal segment abandons the territorial status quo in favour of independence, they cross *a dual – cognitive and social – threshold*. The cognitive threshold relates to the discursive logic of endorsing secession: it only makes sense to pursue independence if one believes that the status quo is not only intolerable, but *unfixable in the foreseeable future*.

DOI: 10.4324/9781003036593-33

The shift represents a material, cognitive, and emotional investment that is difficult to reverse.[7] Abandoning independence once one has endorsed it is thus psychologically costly. Embracing secession also entails crossing a *social* threshold. Mobilizing for independence is a collective and public performative act. Public commitments are difficult to reverse. Once support for secession crosses the hegemonic threshold (Lustick 2001), any organization or individual contemplating public reversal will face serious countervailing pressure. For individuals, that might entail potentially costly reputational damage and social ostracism. Organizations are likely to experience loss of support and membership, or, in the case of violent struggles, direct violent attacks. De-escalation is thus socially costly as well.

Secessionist reversals are not impossible, of course, but this starting point suggests why they may be politically demanding. To what extent this is the case depends on a set of additional factors. The first is the *purpose* of secession. If the goal of independence is to address a set of instrumental issues such as the security or safety of a population, credibly removing the threat might neutralize the secessionist claim. If, on the other hand, the goal is to achieve recognition, particularly after an impression has been created that such recognition is impossible within the confines of the existing state, de-escalation becomes more difficult.

The second variable is the character of the secessionist movement. A unified movement with a strong organizational backbone is more capable of stepping back from the brink than an internally fragmented one. At the same time, however, an excessively fragmented movement may be so internally destructive as to completely dissolve popular support for secession, making de-escalation easier. The third factor of importance is the behaviour of anti-secessionist actors, most notably the central government. The centre's response to the failure of the secessionist movement will provide differentiated incentives to de-escalation, depending on the combination of sticks and carrots offered. Inflexibility toward the weakened secessionist movement may make stepping back from the brink more difficult. Concessions may make it easier for the pragmatic secessionists to deescalate.

## Secessionist turn as a cognitive and social threshold

Successful secessionist movements normally gather support over long time periods.[8] The main reason is the difficulty of lining up an otherwise heterogeneous population behind a common project. Most *potentially* secessionist communities are differentiated along multiple lines, including class, ideology, and party affiliation, among others. People who see themselves as belonging to the same national community will thus often disagree on the best institutional expression of that community.[9] Members of the same sub-state nation will hold divergent attitudes toward the state and the necessity and possibility of independence.

A useful way of categorizing these differences is by differentiating among three discrete segments of any sub-state nation according to Albert Hirschman's exit/voice/loyalty schema (Hirschman 1970). The first segment consists of people who consider the state to be fully and unconditionally legitimate, and are likely to oppose secession on principle. In Hirschman's terms, they exhibit *loyalty* toward the state. The second segment includes those attentive to how the state acknowledges their identity and facilitates the protection of their interests as members of a discrete nation. Their support for the common state is contingent. Their political modus operandi is *voice* – they seek to align the existing system with their preferences. They do not support independence, but are not opposed to it in principle. The final segment encompasses those members of sub-state nations who consider the common state to be illegitimate and unreformable. They reject voice in favour of exit – the pursuit of independent statehood.

Membership in these three 'camps' is not fixed. For secessionists, the key goal is to shift those who believe that their interests and identities can be accommodated within the common state from the 'voice' to the 'exit' camp (Basta 2021; Roeder 2018). The target of this agitation are organizations, individuals, and – at the intermediate level – networks in which those individuals are embedded.[10] Proponents of independence may seek to shift the goals of regional parties from institutional reform to secession, and they may look to convince, cajole, or pressure individuals into supporting the secessionist cause.

If secessionists harness sufficient organizational resources and win the backing of a substantial segment of the regional population, they may mount a major challenge to the institutional status quo – for example, through a referendum or a violent uprising – in order to achieve independence. If they fail in their bid, they face the prospect of having to suspend or abandon the goal of independent statehood. To return to Hirschman's metaphor, at the point of failure, secessionist leadership may need to revert from exit to voice. Yet here, Hirschman's framework starts to lose analytical traction. For Hirschman, shifts between exit and voice, in either the market or political setting, are relatively frictionless.[11] If one abandons a product in favour of a superior one, nothing stops that person from returning to the original product once its supplier has addressed the flaws that prompted the shift. Likewise, if a person defects from their preferred political party in one election, there are few costs associated with voting for the same party by the next vote. Yet, this journey from voice to exit and back to voice is not as smooth when it comes to the dynamics of secession.

Successful mobilization for independence constitutes the crossing of a qualitative threshold that makes reversals costly. The threshold in question has two related, if distinctive, components. The first is a cognitive-discursive one. In order to endorse secession, people must first find it *necessary*. Secession is a radical political option, akin to revolutions and civil wars. It is certain to produce economic costs (Reynaerts and Vanschoonbeek 2016) and may result in physical harm for those who pursue it (Cunningham, Dahl, and Frugé 2019). Secessionist movements are unlikely to obtain international recognition due to the territorial status quo bias of the international system (Coggins 2011). Moreover, the pursuit of independence may be socially unacceptable since it implies a set of psychological dispositions – intemperance and *unreasonableness* – that are normally disparaged both by mainstream ideologies such as liberalism, and many religious traditions, all of which advocate patience and moderation (Feit 2018).

In order to neutralize these concerns, secessionist narratives must portray the institutional status quo not only as insupportable from the perspective of the potentially seceding community, but *irreparable at any future point*. To return to Hirschman, a persuasive secessionist narrative must demonstrate why voice is no longer feasible, and – more to the point – why it will not *become* feasible, at least not within a reasonable amount of time (Basta 2020). This temporal aspect of the narrative is crucial. It makes no sense to adopt secession as a political goal if one believes that there is potential to reform the system in favour of the claimant community within an acceptable period of time.[12] Only if the door to institutional reform to remedy the situation is *permanently* closed – if voice cannot improve the system's 'performance' – does it make sense to resort to secession.

Put differently, once a community has transitioned from voice to exit – from federalism, say, to secession – its members signal a decisive break with status quo politics. They will have created a threshold that is not easy to reverse in discursive terms. If the stated reason for embracing secession is that the common state is *permanently closed* to any advancement of the claimant community's interests, then reversing course (transitioning from exit to voice) implies that the community was mistaken in its original evaluation or that its claim was not genuine. This is difficult to acknowledge, particularly in light of the public and performative character of secessionist mobilization, the subject of the rest of this section.

The second component of the threshold constituted by successful secessionist mobilization is social. Mobilization for independent statehood is an inherently *public* act. The most effective way of convincing large numbers of people to support independence is not through one-on-one persuasion, though that approach has its use in the early stages of mobilization. Claim-making through public spectacle and performance is a far more effective and efficient method of mobilizing people behind a common goal (García 2016). In peaceful secessionist bids, this means turning out large masses of people in demonstrations and claiming the public space (Hau 2016; Parravano et al. 2015). In violent secessions, the purpose of the violence is less to achieve independence by seizing power than to attain what Roeder calls 'programmatic coordination'. Its goal is propagandistic, which is to say, performative (Roeder 2018: 152).

Equally important is the role played by social pressure. Some individuals will make up their minds to support secession not because they have weighed the arguments in favour of or against it as isolated individuals, but as a consequence of what others around them say and do. Especially relevant are actions of individuals in one's workplace, family, and friendship networks. This claim finds support in the literature on social influence (Cialdini and Goldstein 2004; Crano and Seyranian 2007; Moscovici 1980; Noelle-Neumann 1974).[13] While some members of the relevant community may embrace secession because they were persuaded by the case advanced by the partisans of independence, others will do so because they do not wish to be ostracized or isolated, especially once secession becomes the dominant political option in their networks. According to Moscovici's theory of minority influence, persuasion should be more important in the early stages of mobilization (when secession is not yet a dominant position) and social pressure in the later ones (when a tipping point is reached whereby public expression of support for independence becomes the norm) (Moscovici 1980).

Once this dual threshold has been crossed, it becomes difficult to backtrack, even if the secessionist bid has been defeated. A secessionist leader seeking to revert to the politics of voice will find themselves in the minority amid a society mobilized for independence. They will face multiple points of resistance to course reversal – from members of their own organization (who might oppose de-escalation out of genuine commitment or because they wish to improve their organizational position); other secessionist organizations or factions; the independence-minded public; and their personal networks. Their attempt to return to the politics of voice may be characterized as a betrayal of the movement's principles and may incur a range of penalties. The social threshold thus constitutes a lock-in mechanism that makes it difficult to de-escalate. The social threshold is reinforced by the cognitive-discursive one – the turning-point narrative that can be plausibly used to delegitimize attempts to stand down from the brink. This dual threshold renders de-escalation difficult, but not impossible. The next section foregrounds three issues that have a bearing on just how difficult the path from exit back to voice may be.

## The political playing field and secessionist de-escalation

### *The purpose of secession*

A frequently overlooked facet of secession is the variety of purposes that it serves in different contexts. While some secessions are primarily expressive, others are instrumental.[14] The goal of expressive secession is to ensure that state institutions appropriately signal the identity of the claimant group – something that presumably cannot happen satisfactorily within the framework of the state from which secession is sought. By contrast, the aim of instrumental secession is to protect the interests – such as the material well-being, physical security, or the culture – of the population in question.[15] Clearly, secessionist movements may combine both sets of arguments, but there is an analytical difference between a movement whose aim is primarily to protect a population from an immediate and rescindable threat, and one whose target population is not under any meaningful physical or existential threat, but where the aim of secession is totemic.

For example, the Biafran secession was a response to the combined effects of the political marginalization of Igbo officers and politicians in the context of early-post-independence struggles, and of anti-Igbo pogroms in areas where the Igbo were in the minority. Biafran secession was thus largely a defensive reaction to an immediate physical threat to the seceding entity's population. By contrast, Slovenia's secession was in no meaningful sense equivalent. We can project onto the 1990 independence referendum the outcomes that followed over the coming years in Croatia, Slovenia, and Bosnia. Nevertheless, no national community in the former Yugoslavia, with the exception of Kosovo Albanians and Kosovo Serbs, was prior to the war either systematically persecuted and repressed, or had its immediate material well-being meaningfully compromised. The conflict played out largely in the domain of expressive values.

Instrumental secessions are arguably more reversible than ones where the totemic importance of independent statehood outweighs the instrumental benefits (or costs) thereof. The discursive reason is that a secession aiming to redress a sudden (rather than cumulative) but radical threat to the physical well-being of a population may be plausibly reversed if and when the threat is credibly removed, either by the offending party or via international intervention. In the case of Biafra, the end of anti-Igbo pogroms would have been something of the kind. Indeed, Igbo secessionism lay dormant until decades later, and even then was far from dominant in the Igbo community and is apparently still subject to an instrumental calculus. Where independent statehood, however, has been endorsed by a significant proportion of the population not on instrumental but on symbolic/expressive grounds, reversals become more difficult. Where expressive goals of secession are combined with heightened and enduring concern for the physical safety of a community, we should expect reversals to be particularly difficult.

## The character of the secessionist movement

One of the key elements that might influence the likelihood of de-escalation relates to the organizational features of the secessionist movement. The major issue here is the degree of fragmentation and internal competition among the secessionist organizations, be they political parties, armed groups, or cultural or religious organizations. Scholars of ethnic conflict have argued persuasively that much of what passes for inter-group conflict is the consequence of competition for power among various factions *within* a community (Brubaker and Laitin 1998; Chandra 2005; Horowitz 1985; Moore et al. 2014; Rabushka and Shepsle 1972). The same goes for the resolution of ethnic and nationalist conflagrations. In her account of peace settlements, Kathleen Gallagher Cunningham finds that internally fragmented movements are more prone to mutual conflict. Where this is the case, peace is more difficult to achieve: even though the state is more likely to accommodate fragmented communities, the high likelihood of internal conflict makes the situation difficult to manage in the aggregate (Gallagher Cunningham 2014: 171).

While Gallagher Cunningham's work does not explain secessionist de-escalation, her argument has important implications for outcomes of secessionist struggles. Intense political competition within a community is likely to exacerbate the social threshold problems associated with secessionist de-escalation. An organizationally cohesive movement, one that possesses the organizational means to stave off intra-group challenges and does not have to contend with competing entities, should be able to either suspend or reverse the secessionist drive. Post–Civil War Nigeria offers an indicative example. The Ohanaeze Ndi Igbo, the sole organization claiming to represent the Igbo people – the backbone of the Biafran project – monopolized the articulation of the community's grievances after the 1967–1970 war. The organization insisted on voice – the participation in the post-war Nigerian federal and power-sharing institutional framework – rather than rupture (Onuoha 2014: 11–12). This outcome was facilitated by the decisive military defeat of the Biafran secessionist project in 1970, and by the readiness of the Nigerian government to forgo open retribution against the Igbo and institutionalize ethnic accommodation (Simpson 2014: 348).[16] The key element, however, was the organizational cohesion of the movement.

By contrast, the more fragmented framework of Catalan politics in the aftermath of the unsuccessful bid for unilateral independence in October 2017 did not facilitate a similar abandonment of secessionist goals. Here, the fragmentation of the political space into two large independentist camps, one around the Republican Left of Catalonia (ERC) and the other around the former Catalan president Carles Puigdemont and his Together for Catalonia (JxCat) party, made it difficult to de-escalate. No party could step back from the independentist project without being charged by the other with betraying national interests, especially given the two parties' electorates overlap to a significant degree.

At the other extreme, the secessionist organizational space can become so fragmented as to facilitate de-escalation. In the 1980s and early 1990s Punjab, the movement for an independent Khalistan splintered into a multitude of armed groups, none of which was capable of effectively controlling its purported constituents – the Sikhs of Punjab and beyond. Various armed groups fought each other and brutalized the local population until whatever legitimacy the secessionist cause enjoyed evaporated (Jetly 2008: 68, 72; Van Dyke 2009: 987, 990–991). This made it easier for moderate Sikh politicians to de-escalate and return to the politics of voice.

Thus, de-escalation may be facilitated either by an organizationally integrated or highly fragmented secessionist movement. Where the movement is fragmented into only a few entities of similar strength, the balance of power may make it more difficult to ramp down secessionist rhetoric and action. None of the major organizations can safely return to the politics of voice without the risk of being outflanked by their competitors. If multiple secessionist organizations are competing in the electoral arena, de-escalation might cost them votes. If they are waging armed struggle for independence, they might lose support among their fighters who might defect to the more militant organization.[17] The specific pathway will depend on other factors, including the scale and scope of the defeat, the potential threat to members of the organization and their followers, and the perceived likelihood of achievement of the stated goal in the near future.

## Actions of the status quo actors

Central governments and other players favouring the territorial status quo play a pivotal role in shaping the possibility of secessionist demobilization.[18] Central governments are particularly important since they can either facilitate or block the international recognition of a seceding territory (Griffiths and Muro 2020) and can withhold or extend institutional concessions short of independence. Once a secessionist bid has failed, the central government's strategy of managing the aftermath will shape the relative attractiveness of exit and voice. There are at least three feasible strategies central authorities may pursue to facilitate secessionist de-escalation. They can *facilitate voice and foreclose exit*; they can *foster voice and allow for exit*, or they can *foreclose both voice and exit*. Each strategy should have different implications for the likelihood of secessionist de-escalation.

The first option entails the continuation, expansion, or implementation of institutional mechanisms that protect a particular community's interests and/or express its identity. These mechanisms may include territorial or non-territorial autonomy, consociational arrangements, and electoral rules that permit political organization along identity lines. In situations where kin states are involved, the centre might facilitate the institutionalization of relations between the community and the kin state.[19] Demonstrating the efficacy of voice by accommodating some of the claimant community's demands should make it easier for moderates among secessionists to argue in favour of de-escalating political efforts after a failed attempt to achieve independence. Yet, as the previous section notes, competition within the secessionist camp may reduce their incentives to do so, as can expressive motives for secession.

Secessionist moderates will be further helped if the central government – or its external allies – increase the future costs of secession by demonstrating a credible commitment to preventing exit in the future. This can be done in a variety of ways, ranging from the prospect of deploying overwhelming force to prevent secession; through constitutional or statutory measures (Canada's Clarity Act is a prime example, though constitutional clauses prohibiting secession may have a similar function); and through policy measures (Spain facilitated the outflow of enterprise headquarters as the Catalan government prepared for the 2017 referendum). The central government can also seek to suppress secessionist activity by effective use of force and surveillance in anticipation of a renewed secession bid (Williams 2021).

An additional element that raises the costs of continued pursuit of independence is the commitment of the relevant external actors to the preservation of the existing borders of a given country. In 2017 Iraq's allies and neighbours, including notably the United States, Turkey, and Iran, opposed the Kurdish initiative for independent statehood (Kaplan 2019). In Bosnia and Herzegovina, the 1995 NATO deployment that ended the war and the clear commitment by key external players likewise suggested prohibitively high costs of further pursuit of secession by the Bosnian Serbs. This combination may enhance the political attractiveness of abandoning or suspending the pursuit of independence.

The second strategy central governments may opt for combines voice and exit. In the aftermath of secession bids, central governments will be tempted to erect barriers to any future secession attempt. Nevertheless, in democratic multinational states, the central government may choose not to close off institutionalized paths to independence.[20] In response to the 2014 Scottish referendum, the UK government and main opposition parties committed to enhancing Scotland's autonomy while opting not to establish statutory barriers to any future exercise of Scotland's right to decide.

These kinds of scenarios are rare, but there is some merit in considering their implications for the possibility of de-escalation, especially in light of arguments in favour of constitutionalizing the right to secession (Sorens 2012: 121). On the one hand, expanding the opportunities for voice ought to facilitate de-escalation by reducing grievances. Indeed, retaining the possibility of exit – though it is a different matter altogether whether such a possibility remains as default (because the government chooses not to implement policies to prevent it) or by design (because the centre formalizes it as a constitutional option) – may contribute to the political acceptability of the territorial status quo. If a more radical wing of the secessionist movement argues that the window of opportunity may close for good if it is not exploited, more moderate secessionists might point to the continued feasibility of pursuing independence via institutionalized means at some future point.

Yet, leaving the path to secession open may remove an important incentive to de-escalate in those instances where the political dynamic inside the secessionist camp fosters continued activity. Here, however, we have little empirical precedent, so a counterfactual exercise must take the place of examples. If a fully mobilized movement fails in obtaining independence in a referendum, but the outbidding process among well-entrenched political parties prevents de-escalation, the absence of major political costs may result in renewed attempts to hold a referendum. In fact there were demands for a new referendum soon after the 1980 Québec vote.[21] Only the force of personality of the Parti Québécois' leader, René Lévesque, convinced the party membership to stand down and deradicalize (Fraser 2001: ch. 18).

Finally, the central government may attempt to limit possibilities of both voice and exit in an effort to stamp out the secessionist threat altogether.[22] The centre might, for example, refuse to extend any institutional or policy concessions to the restive community, thus reducing the efficacy of the voice option. This could happen in both authoritarian and democratic settings. In the latter, a majoritarian political system might marginalize a minority community by default. The same result could obtain from integrative political institutions that undercut the claimant community's ability to organize along identity lines – including electoral laws that either prohibit or disincentivize 'ethnic' parties, and territorial reforms that subdivide relevant communities into multiple geographic units. This deliberate foreclosing of voice may then be combined by policies that increase the cost of exit along the lines previously outlined.

This *suppressive* strategy may succeed in deescalating the secessionist struggle in the short term by denying secessionist elites the institutional tools through which they might continue pursuing independence, and by demoralizing the movement by increasing the costs of that pursuit. Sri Lanka's approach to Tamil demands for self-determination in the wake of the civil war exemplifies this approach. While Tamils in Sri Lanka's North do have political parties representing them, these parties' demands for greater autonomy have been largely ignored. Moreover, the decisive defeat of the Tamil secessionist army leaves no doubt about the costs of renewed attempts to establish an independent state.

Indeed, for the time being, the strategy has resulted in secessionist de-escalation, with the Tamil National Alliance (TNA) advocating self-rule for the Tamil community and abandoning independence (Rasaratnam 2016: 226). The central government's lack of responsiveness to demands for national autonomy, however, may over the long term foster a renewed commitment to secession (Lecours 2021). TNA's constituents have viewed the coalition's abandonment of exit in favour of voice with suspicion (Rasaratnam 2016: 227). If the aim of the suppressive strategy is to keep the dissatisfaction of a particular community from boiling over into secessionist action, it may be effective for a time. However, this strategy may not permanently extinguish the claim for independent statehood.

## Secessionist demobilization as an opportunity

The paucity of explanatory work on secessionist demobilization presents a major opportunity for new research. This chapter points to several paths down which scholars interested in the politics of secession might venture. Most importantly, it foregrounds the emergent properties of secessionist mobilization and the implications these properties have for the likelihood of demobilization, or, to return to Hirschman's metaphor, the likelihood of transitioning from the politics of exit back to the politics of voice. Successful secessionist mobilization entails the crossing of a cognitive and social threshold. This process is difficult to reverse – it is subject to a ratchet effect similar to one that Ian Lustick identifies in his work on state contraction (Lustick 2001). When a secessionist bid fails, organizations that spearheaded it must decide whether to abandon their goal or whether to continue pursuing it. Secessionist threshold as conceptualized in this chapter is a social and political fact with significant implications for the probability of secessionist reversals. Future research ought to conceptualize it with greater precision, and operationalize and test its impact.

The chapter foregrounds the importance of three additional characteristics of any secessionist situation in understanding the dynamics of secessionist demobilization. The first is the purpose of secession. There is no *a priori* reason to assume that the political purpose of independence is constant across cases. In some instances, the goal might be primarily instrumental, whereas elsewhere it might be more expressive.[23] This purpose may influence the 'porousness' of the secessionist threshold, and the relative difficulty or ease of course reversal for secessionist organizations. The second characteristic has to do with the organizational structure of the independence movement. A unified and organizationally disciplined movement might find it less politically costly to transition from exit to voice than one where multiple factions compete for the support of the same constituency. Here, there is room for exploring an additional dimension – the type of citizen–party linkages characterizing the movement (Kitschelt 2000). Clientelist secessionist parties may be in a better position to control the process of de-escalation than programmatic ones where the linkages between parties and citizens are more fluid and less predictable (Siroky et al. 2021).

Finally, policies deployed by opponents of secession may also shape the possibility of de-escalation. The chapter foregrounds ways in which central governments may shape the efficacy of voice and cost of exit in order to incentivize secessionist demobilization. In addition to central authorities, future research ought to consider a range of other players, both international (including foreign governments and corporations, bond-rating agencies, intergovernmental bodies, diasporas, and illicit networks), and domestic (parties and movements operating in the restive region but opposing independence, labour unions, businesses, media organizations, and the religious establishment, among others). The web of international connections for a given multinational state is particularly important in understanding the structural advantages of some central governments vis-à-vis secessionist movements. The government of a country that is tightly embedded within the political and economic networks of key global or regional players will find it easier to increase the costs of exit – via lower likelihood of international recognition – than governments of countries that lack 'friends in high places' (Coggins 2011).

The dearth of research into secessionist demobilization should suffice to attract greater scholarly attention to it. There is, however, another reason to turn the analytical lens toward secessionist reversals: understanding *de*-escalation can shed light on the process of escalation. Indeed, real-world political reversals often provide scholars with opportunities to re-evaluate their knowledge of a particular phenomenon (the fall of communism and the Arab Spring, for instance, helped regenerate authoritarian regime theories). In the case of secessionist dynamics, mobilization thresholds come into full relief only when one considers attempts to reverse across them. Broadening our knowledge of secessionist de-escalation has the potential to improve our understanding of mobilization for independence.

## Notes

1 See work on the political strategies of secessionist mobilization (Roeder 2018); the role of framing in secessionist escalation (Elias 2018; Giuliano 2011; Huszka 2014); the possible role of 'foreclosed paths' to greater autonomy (Della Porta, O'Connor, and Portos 2019; Lecours 2021); how loss of autonomy influences the likelihood of mobilization (Germann and Sambanis 2020; Siroky and Cuffe 2015; Sorens 2012: 62); the emergent properties of secessionist mobilization (Basta 2020; Beissinger 2002); how kin states and diasporas facilitate independence bids (Jenne 2007; Koinova 2011; Saideman and Ayres 2000); and how patterns of inequality shape secessionist escalation (Deiwiks, Cederman, and Gleditsch 2012; Rode et al. 2018). This is in addition to the large scholarship on institutional accommodation and integration and their role in secessionist struggles.
2 This situation reflects the state of affairs in the much more developed social movement literature. There, too, we know far more about what makes people take up a particular cause than what makes them abandon it (Fillieule 2015; Kamenitsa 1998).
3 For an important conceptualization of different paths to independence, see Griffiths and Wasser (2019).
4 Except in those instances, such as Cyprus, where the process leads to reunification of de facto separate entities, but in those instances, the pattern of political and social activism is substantively and qualitatively different.

5 Of course, there is such a thing as secession-by-default. This is the situation where a multinational state breaks up, perhaps despite the wishes of most of its population. In those circumstances, some communities may find themselves with a new state without having wished for it or mobilized for it.

6 What constitutes a sufficient proportion of the population is both contested and contextual.

7 In part this reflects the entrapping logic of 'sunk costs' – the investment of money, time, and effort that might make it difficult for an individual to reverse a course of action even when that course has been shown to be irrational or wasteful (Arkes and Blumer 1985; Staw 1976). For the application of this idea to secessionist movements, though again with reference to escalation rather than de-escalation, see Ferreira (2021). The cognitive effort required in order to make a particular decision might have a similar effect – predisposing individuals to continue pursuing a 'failing' course of action (Cunha and Caldieraro 2009). Finally, while most of this work assumes an individualized process, we should not discount, in the context of collective action, the way in which members of a community might consider the sunk costs undertaken by their co-nationals (Olivola 2018).

8 Consider the following communities whose secessionist bids attracted significant following at least a generation after the establishment of the state from which independence was sought: the Tamils of Sri Lanka, the Acehnese of Indonesia, the various movements in India's Assam, the Croats in Yugoslavia, the Irish within the United Kingdom, the Confederate States of America, the Catalans in Spain, and the Kurds in Turkey. Of course, this does not mean that secessionist movements never arise soon after the establishment of statehood (as they did in Biafra and Katanga, for example), but the balance of historical evidence points to the slow-burn tendency.

9 Jaime Lluch demonstrates the degree and the kind of internal differentiation in the case of the political parties in Quebec and Catalonia (Lluch 2014). The by-now-standard Moreno-Linz question implies it among the general population of minority territorial units (Moreno 2006). The same observation about intra-group differentiation is implicit in the work on ethnic outbidding (Chandra 2005; Horowitz 1985; Rabushka and Shepsle 1972).

10 On the role played by network nodes in the process of persuasion, see Druckman, Levendusky, and McLain (2018) and Schaffer and Baker (2015).

11 Hirschman does not explicitly discuss the switch from exit to voice as much as one from boycott to voice (Hirschman 1970: 86). He does discuss asymmetries of re-entry that are in some sense the functional equivalent to secessionist demobilization discussed here (Hirschman 1970: 89). Ultimately, though, the dynamic between voice and exit in his work suggests a relatively flexible boundary between the two in both directions: 'exit has an essential role to play in restoring quality of performance of government, just as in any organization' (Hirschman 1970: 117). The implication is clear – by improving its performance, an organization can restore its legitimacy and effect 're-entry'.

12 What constitutes an 'acceptable' period, and whether the system is reformable is, of course, a matter of political contestation rather than an obvious feature of the political landscape.

13 For similar claims in sociology and political science, see Granovetter (1978), Kuran (1991), and Lustick and Miodownik (2020).

14 For an elaboration of the instrumental/symbolic dichotomy, see work on electoral politics (Hamlin and Jennings 2011), and the territorial dimension of nationalist claims (Basta 2021; Kelle 2017).

15 Secessionist claims can, of course, serve as a bargaining chip in achieving concessions short of independence.

16 Conciliatory institutional measures were combined with punitive policies against the Igbo, including the way in which the currency issue (Owen 2009: 577) and the property 'abandoned' by Igbo (Nwangwu et al. 2020: 538) were settled.

17 An interesting example is the divide that caused the Irish Civil War (Kissane 2005). The Irish uprising did result in the creation of the Irish Free State, but the logic of intra-Irish conflict is similar to one under discussion.

18 The central government is far from the only player favouring the continuation of the common state. Others include 'unionist' political parties, organizations, and individuals in the seceding territory; social actors that might oppose independence, including a variety of local and international business interests; or foreign allies of the state in question, including, in the aftermath of civil wars, external powers that stopped the conflict and implemented the peace.

19 As in Northern Ireland and South Tyrol.

20 A violent secession bid would be unlikely to result in the central government being sanguine about a similar attempt in the future, given the costs and the political implications of not attempting to put in place barriers to renewed push.

21 The reason for the radicalization was the politically combustible patriation of the Canadian constitution without the approval by Quebec. Lévesque believed that a renewed secession bid was going to marginalize the PQ politically and thus believed that the pursuit of another referendum so soon after the 1980s one would in effect destroy the movement.

22 Due to space constraints, this chapter does not discuss other forms of 'managing' secessionist movements, including through either negative (repression) or positive (cooptation/subsidization) incentives. They clearly have a role to play in the outcomes.

23 The distinction is primarily analytical – most situations will feature both angles. However, it should be possible to establish empirically whether a given movement prioritizes expressive or instrumental dimension.

# References

Arkes, H. R. and Blumer, C. (1985). "The Psychology of Sunk Cost." *Organizational Behavior and Human Decision Processes*, 35(1), pp. 124–140.

Basta, K. (2020). "'Time's Up!': Framing Collective Impatience for Radical Political Change." *Political Psychology*, 41(4), pp. 755–770.

———. (2021). *The Symbolic State: Minority Recognition, Majority Backlash, and Secession in Multinational Countries*. Kingston: McGill-Queen's University Press.

Beissinger, M. R. (2002). *Nationalist Mobilization and the Collapse of the Soviet State*. Cambridge: Cambridge University Press.

Brubaker, R. and Laitin, D. (1998). "Ethnic and Nationalist Violence." *Annual Review of Sociology*, 24, pp. 423–452.

Chandra, K. (2005). "Ethnic Parties and Democratic Stability." *Perspectives on Politics*, 3(2), pp. 235–252.

Cialdini, R. B. and Goldstein, N. J. (2004). "Social Influence: Compliance and Conformity." *Annual Review of Psychology*, 55(1), pp. 591–621.

Coggins, B. (2011). "Friends in High Places: International Politics and the Emergence of States from Secessionism." *International Organization*, 65(3), pp. 433–467.

Crano, W. D. and Seyranian, V. (2007). "Majority and Minority Influence." *Social and Personality Psychology Compass*, 1(1), pp. 572–589.

Cunha, M., Jr. and Caldieraro, F. (2009). "Sunk-Cost Effects on Purely Behavioral Investments." *Cognitive Science*, 33(1), pp. 105–113.

Cunningham, K. G., Dahl, M., and Frugé, A. (2019). "Introducing the Strategies of Resistance Data Project." *Journal of Peace Research*, 57(3), pp. 482–491.

Deiwiks, C., Cederman, L., and Skrede Gleditsch, K. (2012). "Inequality and Conflict in Federations." *Journal of Peace Research*, 49(2), pp. 289–304.

Della Porta, D., O'Connor, F., and Portos, M. (2019). "Protest Cycles and Referendums for Independence: Closed Opportunities and the Path of Radicalization in Catalonia." *Revista Internacional de Sociología*, 77(4), pp. 1–14.

Druckman, J. N., Levendusky, M. S., and McLain, A. (2018). "No Need to Watch: How the Effects of Partisan Media Can Spread via Interpersonal Discussions." *American Journal of Political Science*, 62(1), pp. 99–112.

Elias, A. (2018). "Making the Economic Case for Independence: The Scottish National Party's Electoral Strategy in Post-Devolution Scotland." *Regional & Federal* Studies, 29(1), pp. 1–23.

Feit, M. (2018). "Intimations of Democratic Impatience: The Book of Job." *Political Theology*, 19(5), pp. 421–438.

Ferreira, C. (2021). "Entrapped in a Failing Course of Action: Explaining the Territorial Crisis in 2017 Catalonia." *Regional & Federal Studies*, online first, pp. 1–20.

Fillieule, O. (2015). "Demobilization and Disengagement in a Life Course Perspective." In: D. Della Porta and M. Diani, eds., *The Oxford Handbook of Social Movements*. Oxford Handbooks in Politics & International Relations. Oxford: Oxford University Press.

Fraser, G. (2001). *René Lévesque & the Parti Québécois in Power*. Montreal: McGill-Queen's University Press.

Gallagher Cunningham, K. (2014). *Inside the Politics of Self-Determination*. New York: Oxford University Press.

García, C. (2016). "Using Street Protests and National Commemorations for Nation-Building Purposes: The Campaign for the Independence of Catalonia (2012–2014)." *The Journal of International Communication*, 22(2), pp. 229–252.

Germann, M. and Sambanis, N. (2020). "Political Exclusion, Lost Autonomy, and Escalating Conflict over Self-Determination." *International Organization*, 75(7), pp. 178–203.

Giuliano, E. (2011). *Constructing Grievance: Ethnic Nationalism in Russia's Republics*. Ithaca: Cornell University Press.

Granovetter, M. (1978). "Threshold Models of Collective Behavior." *American Journal of Sociology*, 83(6), pp. 1420–1443.

Griffiths, R. D. and Muro, D. (2020). "Introduction." In: R. D. Griffiths and D. Muro, eds., *Strategies of Secession and Counter-Secession*. London: Rowman & Littlefield International; ECPR Press.

Griffiths, R. D. and Wasser, L. M. (2019). "Does Violent Secessionism Work?" *Journal of Conflict Resolution*, 63(5), pp. 1310–1336.

Hamlin, A. and Jennings, C. (2011). "Expressive Political Behaviour: Foundations, Scope and Implications." *British Journal of Political Science*, 41(3), pp. 645–670.

Hau, M. F. (2016). "Nation Space, and Identity in the City: Marking Space and Making Place in Barcelona." *Etnofoor*, 28(2), pp. 77–98.

Hirschman, A. O. (1970). *Exit, Voice, and Loyalty: Responses to Decline in Firms, Organizations, and States*. Cambridge, MA: Harvard University Press.

Horowitz, D. L. (1985). *Ethnic Groups in Conflict*. Berkeley: University of California Press.

Huszka, B. (2014). *Secessionist Movements and Ethnic Conflict: Debate-Framing and Rhetoric in Independence Campaigns*. New York: Routledge.

Jenne, E. K. (2007). *Ethnic Bargaining : The Paradox of Minority Empowerment*. Ithaca: Cornell University Press.

Jetly, R. (2008). "The Khalistan Movement in India: The Interplay of Politics and State Power." *International Review of Modern Sociology*, 34(1), pp. 61–75.

Kamenitsa, L. (1998). "The Complexity of Decline: Explaining the Marginalization of the East German Women's Movement." *Mobilization: An International Quarterly*, 3(2), pp. 245–263.

Kaplan, M. L. (2019). "Foreign Support, Miscalculation, and Conflict Escalation: Iraqi Kurdish Self-Determination in Perspective." *Ethnopolitics*, 18(1), pp. 29–45.

Kelle, F. L. (2017). "To Claim or Not to Claim? How Territorial Value Shapes Demands for Self-Determination." *Comparative Political Studies*, 50(7), pp. 992–1020.

Kissane, B. (2005). *The Politics of the Irish Civil War*. Oxford: Oxford University Press.

Kitschelt, H. (2000). "Linkages between Citizens and Politicians in Democratic Polities." *Comparative Political Studies*, 33(6–7), pp. 845–879.

Koinova, M. (2011). "Diasporas and Secessionist Conflicts: The Mobilization of the Armenian, Albanian and Chechen Diasporas." *Ethnic and Racial Studies*, 34(2), pp. 333–356.

Kuran, T. (1991). "Now Out of Never: The Element of Surprise in the East European Revolution of 1989." *World Politics*, 44(1), pp. 7–48.

Lecours, A. (2021). *Nationalism, Secession, and Autonomy*. Oxford: Oxford University Press.

Lluch, J. (2014). *Visions of Sovereignty: Nationalism and Accommodation in Multinational Democracies*. Philadelphia: University of Pennsylvania Press.

Lustick, I. S. (2001). "Thresholds of Opportunity and Barriers to Change in the Right-Sizing of States." In: B. O'Leary, I. Lustick, and T. M. Callaghy, eds., *Rightsizing the State: The Politics of Moving Borders*. Oxford: Oxford University Press.

Lustick, I. S. and Miodownik, D. (2020). "When Do Institutions Suddenly Collapse? Zones of Knowledge and the Likelihood of Political Cascades." *Quality & Quantity*, 54(2), pp. 413–437.

Moore, G., Loizides, N., Sandal, N. A., and Lordos, A. (2014). "Winning Peace Frames: Intra-Ethnic Outbidding in Northern Ireland and Cyprus." *West European Politics*, 37(1), pp. 159–181.

Moreno, L. (2006). "Scotland, Catalonia, Europeanization and the 'Moreno Question.'" *Scottish Affairs*, 54(1), pp. 1–21.

Moscovici, S. (1980). "Toward a Theory of Conversion Behavior." In: L. Berkowitz, ed., *Advances in Experimental Social Psychology* 13:209–239. New York; London: Academic Press.

Noelle-Neumann, E. (1974). "The Spiral of Silence a Theory of Public Opinion." *Journal of Communication*, 24(2), pp. 43–51.

Nwangwu, C., Onuoha, F. C., Nwosu, B. U., and Ezeibe, C. (2020). "The Political Economy of Biafra Separatism and Post-War Igbo Nationalism in Nigeria." *African Affairs*, 119(477), pp. 526–551.

Olivola, C. Y. (2018). "The Interpersonal Sunk-Cost Effect." *Psychological Science*, 29(7), pp. 1072–1083.

Onuoha, G. (2014). "The Politics of 'Hope' and 'Despair': Generational Dimensions to Igbo Nationalism in Post-Civil War Nigeria." *African Sociological Review/Revue Africaine de Sociologie*, 18(1), pp. 2–26.

Owen, O. (2009). "Biafran Pound Notes." *Africa: Journal of the International African Institute*, 79(4), pp. 570–594.

Parravano, A, Noguera, J. A., Hermida, P., and Tena-Sánchez, J. (2015). "Field Evidence of Social In-fluence in the Expression of Political Preferences: The Case of Secessionists Flags in Barcelona." *PLoS One*, 10(5), pp. 1–26.

Rabushka, A. and Shepsle, K. A. (1972). *Politics in Plural Societies: A Theory of Democratic Instability*. Columbus, OH: Merrill.

Rasaratnam, M. (2016). *Tamils and the Nation: India and Sri Lanka Compared*. London: Oxford University Press.

Reynaerts, J. and Vanschoonbeek, J. (2016). "The Economics of State Fragmentation: Assessing the Economic Impact of Secession: Addendum." SSRN Scholarly Paper ID 2804901. Rochester, NY: Social Science Research Network.

Rode, M., Pitlik, H., Mas, B., and Ángel, M. (2018). "Does Fiscal Federalism Deter or Spur Secessionist Movements? Empirical Evidence from Europe." *Publius: The Journal of Federalism*, 48(2), pp. 161–190.

Roeder, P. G. (2018). *National Secession: Persuasion and Violence in Independence Campaigns*. Ithaca: Cornell University Press.

Saideman, S. M. and Ayres, R. W. (2000). "Determining the Causes of Irredentism: Logit Analyses of Minorities at Risk Data from the 1980s and 1990s." *Journal of Politics*, 62(4), pp. 1126–1144.

Schaffer, J. and Baker, A. (2015). "Clientelism as Persuasion-Buying: Evidence from Latin America." *Comparative Political Studies*, 48(9), pp. 1093–1126.

Simpson, B. (2014). "The Biafran Secession and the Limits of Self-Determination." *Journal of Genocide Research*, 16(2–3), pp. 337–354.

Siroky, D. S. and Cuffe, J. (2015). "Lost Autonomy, Nationalism and Separatism." *Comparative Political Studies*, 48(1), pp. 3–34.

Siroky, D. S., Mueller, S., Fazi, A., and Hechter, M. (2021). "Containing Nationalism: Culture, Economics and Indirect Rule in Corsica." *Comparative Political Studies*, 54(6), pp. 1023–1057.

Sorens, J. (2012). *Secessionism: Identity, Interest, and Strategy*. Montreal: McGill-Queen's University Press.

Staw, B. M. (1976). "Knee-Deep in the Big Muddy: A Study of Escalating Commitment to a Chosen Course of Action." *Organizational Behaviour and Human Performance*, 16(1), pp. 27–44.

Van Dyke, V. (2009). "The Khalistan Movement in Punjab, India, and the Post-Militancy Era: Structural Change and New Political Compulsions." *Asian Survey*, 49(6), pp. 975–997.

Williams, R. (2021). "Turning the Lights on to Keep Them in the Fold: How Governments Preempt Secession Attempts." *Conflict Management and Peace Science*, online first, pp. 1–25.

# 29

# THE STRATEGIES OF COUNTER-SECESSION

## How states prevent independence

*Peter Krause*

The majority of states in the world today were created via secession, including 106 out of 156 new states formed since 1931 (Coggins, 2011). Although the birth of these new nation-states is cause for celebration by those who struggled for autonomy, most states in the international system eye secession as a source of instability. Since World War II, a majority of civil wars have been secessionist (Fearon and Laitin, 2003). Many of the world's most economically and militarily powerful states currently face one of the over 60 ongoing secessionist movements (Griffiths and Martinez, 2021) – China with Xinjiang, France with Corsica, Spain with Catalonia and the Basque region, Russia with Chechnya, and the United Kingdom with Scotland, among others. Whether they are currently confronting an active struggle or not, states may reject secession abroad lest it establish precedent for groups with potentially separatist identities at home (Walter, 2009).

Although the majority of states in the world today were created via secession, the majority of secessionist movements (63%) have failed to gain independence (Coggins, 2014). This is no accident. Most movements fail because the states who host them successfully prevent their independence via numerous counter-secession strategies. In fact, the 63% figure *significantly* underestimates the success rate of counter-secession. There are over 300 nations today that lack sovereign states, and untold thousands more groups whose identities never became nationalist and/or separatist. State attempts to alter identities and demographics have played a key role in snuffing out potential secessionists before they materialize (Minahan, 2002). Of the minority of nations that have mobilized for autonomy, most have lost violent and/or nonviolent struggles with the state and have ultimately not been formally recognized by the international community. Independence is not won cheaply, and existing states will fight to maintain their borders throughout the four phases of secession: identity formation, group mobilization, (un)armed struggle, and international recognition.

Counter-secession is far more common than secession, yet studies of the latter are far more common than those of the former. "Secession" yields 259,000 results in Google Scholar, whereas "countersecession" and "counter-secession" combined yield only 800 results. By comparison, "terrorism" yields 1,830,000 results while "counterterrorism" and "counter terrorism" yield 370,000 results. The "counter-" concepts, perhaps understandably, receive less scholarly attention, but secession's ratio to its "counter"-part is more than 65 times larger than that of terrorism. Despite the fact that some studies of counterinsurgency and colonialism focused on

DOI: 10.4324/9781003036593-34

secessionist movements may not show up in a basic search, it is clear that counter-secession remains an undertheorized and understudied phenomenon.

Thankfully, there are a small but growing number of quality studies focused on counter-secession (Ker-Lindsay, 2012; Griffiths and Muro, 2020; Muro and Woertz, 2018). Nonetheless, we lack a comprehensive presentation of states' full repertoire of counter-secession strategies, including their causal logic and illustrative examples across time and space. This chapter aims to provide such an overview of counter-secession strategies, connecting them to the key phases of secessionist struggles while detailing when and how states employ them.

First, this chapter will explain how and why secession occurs, identifying the four key phases of the process. Next, it presents a typology and description of the eight most common and significant counter-secession strategies. The chapter concludes by suggesting directions for future research based on this typology of counter-secession strategies.

## How secession occurs: four phases from identity formation to international recognition

To understand how states attempt to prevent secession – the formal withdrawal of a territory and its people from their sovereign authority – we must first understand how the phenomenon occurs. There is no single blueprint, but secession attempts usually progress through four phases: identity formation, group mobilization, (un)armed struggle, and international recognition (see Figure 29.1). As I discuss in more detail later, these phases overlap and do not always occur in this exact order, but most secessionist movements follow this path in some form.

### *Identity formation*

Groups rarely attempt (let alone achieve) secession without first developing a common ethnic, religious, and/or national identity tied to a piece of territory over which they do not – but yearn to – exercise sovereignty. Nationalism often has roots in pre-existing ethnicities and languages (Smith, 1995), although as Gellner (1983: 48–49) explains,

> Nations as a natural, God-given way of classifying men, as an inherent though long-delayed political destiny, are a myth; nationalism, which sometimes takes pre-existing cultures and turns them into nations, sometimes invents them, and often obliterates pre-existing cultures: that is a reality.

| Phase 1 | Phase 2 | Phase 3 | Phase 4 |
| Identity Formation | Group Mobilization | (Un)armed Struggle | International Recognition |

*Figure 29.1*   The four phases of secession
*Source:* Conceptualized by the author and created by Caroline Denning (used with permission).[1]

Individuals have multiple ethnic, religious, ideological, and civic identities, but individual and state actions – through education, cultural programs, and state laws – have a significant influence on which become national identities and which do not. For example, individuals living in the Levant at the beginning of the twentieth century were politically part of the Ottoman Empire, spoke languages including (Ottoman) Turkish, Arabic, Armenian, and Hebrew, and worshipped as Muslims, Christians, and Jews. Some of those identities subsequently became the basis for nation-states (e.g. Turkish, Jewish, Armenian), others became the basis for nationalisms that failed (e.g. pan-Arab nationalism), and others became supporting parts of the national identities of successful states in the region (e.g. Islam), including new national identities that were created by colonial powers and local elites (e.g. Jordanian, Iraqi, Lebanese).

There was no guarantee that these were the national identities that would emerge from the remains of the Ottoman Empire in the twentieth century. The actions of powerful states and motivated community leaders transformed the Bedouin on the east bank of the Jordan River into Jordanians, individuals from Baghdad, Basra, and Mosul into Iraqis, and Jews around the world into Zionists emigrating to the Palestine Mandate (Alon, 2009; Avineri, 2017; Tripp, 2002). Without those identities, these states would not have emerged and/or endured, and these individuals and their territory would have been absorbed by other established nation-states.

## Group mobilization

Second, the national group must mobilize by forming political parties, armed groups, and/or other organizations to actively advocate for self-determination. Secession involves an existing state losing control over part of its territory and the citizens who live there, along with the associated tax revenue, strategic location, and political influence. State governments come in many shapes, sizes, and ideologies, but one thing they can all agree on is that they will not willingly give up territory and the power that comes with it. National groups must therefore organize themselves into a cohesive secessionist movement to effectively contest state authority. This is a challenge on multiple levels. It represents a collective action problem for the group, as all would benefit from an autonomous nation state, but those who organize to fight for it will pay a disproportionate share of the costs, especially because such advocacy can lead to jail time and death at the hands of a resistant host state. Sometimes the challenge is not that groups cannot find leaders, but rather that they have too many. Fragmented national movements with multiple significant organizations face internal competition, infighting, and the lack of a cohesive message and strategy, as have the Palestinians and the Kurds (Krause, 2017). Mobilizing the nation into a cohesive movement with a strong organization to lead it is therefore a crucial phase for secessionists.

## (Un)armed struggle

Third, because the host state rarely simply grants the wishes of newly mobilized secessionist organizations, they often undertake a nonviolent and/or violent struggle with the host state, sometimes for generations. Some scholars suggest that nonviolent campaigns are more effective (Chenoweth and Stephan, 2011), although this is not necessarily the case for nationalist struggles, which represent the highest stakes for state governments. The secessionists' resources, the host state's regime type, and the presence of foreign support all help dictate the (non)violent nature of the struggle and its ultimate outcome. Victories on the battlefield (e.g. Saratoga for the Americans, Dien Bien Phu for the Vietnamese, Afabet for the Eritreans) or in the city square (e.g. anti-USSR protests in the Baltics in 1991, recent protests in Hong Kong) can help generate momentum and international support for independence even if the secessionists fail to overpower the state and establish autonomy on their own.

## *International recognition*

Finally, usually after a period of struggle with the host state, some secessionist movements gain enough international support to be recognized by the United Nations and formally secede to become a new state.[2] Support for recognition is built not only through successful (un)armed struggle with the host state, but also through connections with foreign states on the grounds of ethnic or ideological solidarity, a shared host state enemy, appeals to norms of self-determination, and direct diplomacy. A number of national movements, from the Algerians to Vietnamese, have had foreign delegations in multiple states. These delegations engage with local politicians and their constituents to convince them of the worthiness of the secessionists' cause and the benefits of an alliance with their new state-to-be. Should they convince the five permanent members of the Security Council not to veto their application, then receive supporting votes from 9 of the 15 UN Security Council members, then receive support from two-thirds of the UN General Assembly, they finally become a new state.

## How counter-secession turns the phases of secession into chokepoints

The four phases illustrated in Figure 29.1 also represent four major chokepoints for states to prevent secession from within their borders. If a group does not develop a nationalist and/or separatist identity, then they will not want to secede in the first place. If a national group is unable to mobilize to create a cohesive movement with strong political organizations to lead it, then it will be unable to effectively advocate and struggle for independence. If a mobilized movement cannot effectively contend with its host state in armed or unarmed struggle, then it will likely remain a repressed people without independence. And even if a group succeeds in the first three phases, it cannot achieve de jure secession and sovereignty without formal recognition from the United Nations. So although most states in the world today are the result of secessionist movements, the majority of would-be secessionists are selected out at each phase of this process, leaving us today with thousands of potential separatist groups, hundreds of nations, 60 active secessionist movements, 14 ongoing secessionist civil wars, and four newly independent secessionist states since 2000 (East Timor, Montenegro, Kosovo, and South Sudan).

This winnowing of secessionists as they run the gauntlet to freedom is no coincidence, but rather largely the result of host states actively working to prevent their departure. As illustrated in Figure 29.2, states employ a variety of counter-secession strategies at each phase of the struggle. These strategies can occur simultaneously, but they are usually aimed at thwarting one of the four phase objectives: preventing the formation of a separatist identity, demobilizing the secessionist group, defeating the group in (un)armed struggle, and blocking international recognition.

The state usually has to succeed at only one of these chokepoints to prevent secession and win, whereas the secessionists ultimately have to be successful at all four. The main exception is that states sometimes "win" the direct struggle with a secessionist movement in the third phase and nonetheless see the movement recognized by the international community, as with Indonesia and East Timor.[4] But the international community generally will not recognize a new state for a group that lacks a separatist identity or is not mobilized, and many who are (e.g. the Kurdish, Catalan, and Sahrawi movements) have failed to clear this last hurdle. The next section details the precise counter-secession strategies that states use to both preempt and prevent independence.

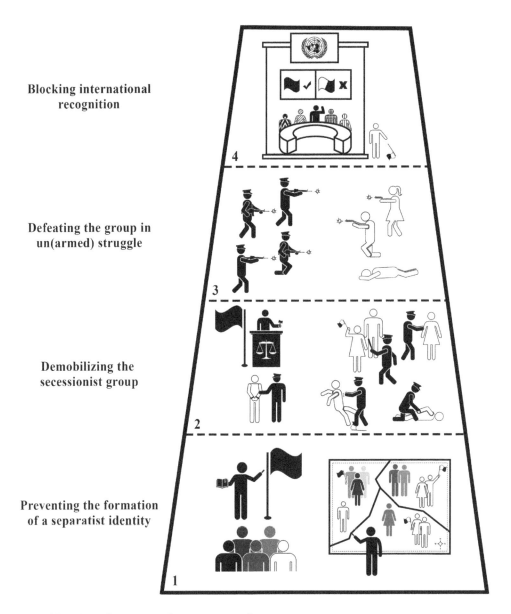

*Figure 29.2* How the state gauntlet prevents secession

*Source:* Conceptualized by the author and created by Caroline Denning (used with permission).[3]

## The strategies of counter-secession

The ever-shrinking cone of secessionist movements in Figure 29.2 is testament to the ability of states to thwart secession in a variety of ways at each phase of the process. States have political, legal, economic, and military tools to prevent secession, and a number of counter-secession strategies make use of more than one of them. These tools include administrative organization of the state and its territories to forestall secession (political), making it illegal to protest or operate a secessionist political party (legal), cutting or increasing government funding to a restive region (economic), and employing various forms of violent repression (military). The key actors that can be targeted are the population that supports secession and would become the citizens of the new state, the secessionist movement organizations and those who lead them, and the foreign states who make legal and political decisions to support and/or recognize the new state. As detailed in Figure 29.2, counter-secession strategies often shift their focus in this fashion as the struggle progresses – from population, to movement, to foreign states.

Counter-secession strategies can begin before there is even an organized struggle in order to prevent a cohesive secessionist movement from crystallizing. As described in Table 29.1, this can take the form of shifting the demographic geography of a region to prevent the existence of a contiguous, cohesive population that seeks autonomy, or drawing administrative boundaries so as to head off future political challenges. Once a population begins to mobilize, the state can attempt to ban its political parties or repress it through increased policing. If a robust secessionist movement emerges, states may attempt to separate civilian supporters from the secessionist groups physically and/or economically, employ large-scale violent repression with the military, or engage in (coercive) diplomacy with foreign states to prevent recognition of the movement's legitimacy.

Many of these strategies have both an accommodationist and a coercive variant, in that states can employ them to offer benefits and/or impose costs, all in pursuit of maintaining their territorial integrity. Concessions in the form of favorable policies to the would-be secessionists – recognition of their language, land redistribution, repatriation, legalization of their parties, funding their schools, permitting their protests, and granting regional autonomy – can happen as part of any strategy and at any phase to prevent secession. Strategies need not happen during these exact phases or in this exact order, but many strategies do become more or less viable depending on the timing and context.

Table 29.1 previews the eight main strategies of counter-secession, including their causal logic, historical examples, and relevant scholarship. Below, each strategy is presented in greater depth alongside a discussion of its successful and unsuccessful use across time and space.

## Cultural assimilation: building a common national identity, weakening secessionist identities

Whether a state's identity is based on a single ethnicity (e.g. Albania and Japan) or is multinational (e.g. Brazil and Canada), all states educate their populations about their country's history, instill common values, and promote literacy in one or more languages. As Brown explains, "Public education in Malaysia . . . is promoted as a nation-building tool, seeking to inculcate a sense of Malaysian-ness and patriotism" (Brown, 2007). These actions help create a cohesive society of connected citizens, but they also implicitly or explicitly represent a counter-secession strategy. By fostering a shared civic – if not also ethnic and national – identity, the state creates social bonds that make individuals less likely to want to leave, while simultaneously weakening alternative national identities that could become the basis for secession.

Cultural assimilation is the earliest and most preventative counter-secession strategy, as it helps ensure that most of the religious, ethnic, ideological, and regional identities that exist are not mobilized on separatist lines. As Gellner argues, nationalism is the belief that the political and national unit should be congruent; cultural assimilation is often about convincing one's people that they already are (Gellner, 1983). In theory, every US state – not to mention every religious and ethnic group – could attempt to secede. In practice, however, there has been only one robust attempt a century and a half ago, with insignificant secessionist organizations in just a few states today (e.g. Alaska and Texas). For all of its current internal discord, the United States

*Table 29.1* States' repertoire of counter-secession strategies

| Strategy | Tactics and causal logic | Historical examples | Relevant scholarship |
|---|---|---|---|
| Cultural assimilation | Strengthen the common aspects of the dominant state identity and weak separatist identities through education, promotion, or restriction of language, religion, culture | "Russification" in Russia/USSR, American assimilation of immigrants and Native Americans in the nineteenth and twentieth centuries | Brown (2007); Darden and Mylonas (2016) |
| Administrative organization | Change internal administrative lines to divide the population and prevent the rise of a proto-state; alternatively, concede some regional autonomy in exchange for loyalty to the state government | United Kingdom and Uganda/Buganda (1958–62); Post-Soviet Secessionism (1990s); Nigeria and Republic of Biafra (1967–70); Gran Colombia (1828–30) | Ratner (1996); Forsberg (2013); Griffiths (2015) |
| Civilian displacement | Physically disperse or detain civilians from the national group to separate them from each other and/or their movement; move non-separatist civilians in to change regional demographics | Morocco and Western Sahara (1975); China and Xinjiang (1940s–present); USSR and Chechnya (1944) | Toft (2002); Burds (2007) |
| Banning secessionist political activity | Make secession illegal and ban its organizations from the political process, making it more challenging to build a robust secessionist movement by raising the costs of advocacy and decreasing support for secessionism among the population | Batasuna Party in Spain (2003); Bulgaria and United Macedonian Organization (2001); Cameroon and Southern Cameroons National Council (2001); China and Taiwan (2005) | Ginsburg and Versteeg (2018); Bourne (2020) |
| Fragmenting the secessionist movement | Divide the secessionist movement by fostering personal and organizational splits, discriminately cracking down on strongest group to allow the emergence of internal rivals | Israel and the PLO/ Hamas (1980s); France and the FLN (1954–1962) | Lawrence (2010); Cunningham (2011); Pearlman (2011); Krause (2017) |
| Economic coercion | Restricting flow of wealth and resources to the secessionist territory and/or population to weaken it via blockades, boycotts, and sanctions; offering enhanced access to food, jobs, and education in exchange for loyalty to the state | British and Malaya (1948–1960); France and Algeria (1959–1962); Nigeria and Republic of Biafra (1967–70); Bangladesh and Shanti Bahini (1972) | Muro and Woertz (2018); Huysmans and Crombez (2020); Thomas and Falola (2020) |
| Violent repression | Weaken and coerce the secessionist movement by increasing policing of secessionist populations, violent repression of protests, arresting movement leaders, and military assaults on secessionist areas and organizations | Ethiopia and Eritrea (1961–1991); India and Kashmir (1989–1994); Sri Lanka and the Tamils (2008–2009); British in Northern Ireland (1969–2007) | Spruyt (2005); Butt (2017) |
| Blocking international recognition | Forcing unilateral attempts at secession, pressuring states, regional bodies, and international organizations to not recognize the secessionists as a legitimate movement or as a new state | Pakistan and Bangladesh (1971–1979); UK and Northern Cyprus (1983); Serbia and Kosovo (2008–present) | Ker-Lindsay (2012); Coggins (2014); Siroky et al. (2020) |

faces little risk of regional secession, in no small part because of its triumph in the struggle to instill a single national identity ("*the* United States") that trumped multiple regional ones ("*these* United States").

This general pattern applies to identities across the globe. Griffiths identified 403 secessionist movements between 1816 and 2011, a number of which were the same group pushing for secession at different times (Griffiths, 2016). Compare that to the tens of thousands of sub-state administrative districts in the world today, 6,800 languages spoken, 12,583 ethnic groups, and 10,000 religions, and it becomes clear that the number of possible secessionist identities is exponentially higher than the number of those that have materialized (Loh and Harmon, 2005).

States are more likely to culturally assimilate their populations when they face "an external threat of territorial conquest or externally supported secession" (Darden and Mylonas, 2016). These concerns drove "Russification" across the Russian and Soviet Empires from the late nineteenth century onwards. Nonetheless, states don't always effectively pursue cultural assimilation for all of their citizens, as demonstrated by the splintering of Yugoslavia in the 1990s into multiple states whose separate national identities were never extinguished, despite attempts to create a new supra-ethnic Yugoslav national identity (Banac, 1988).

## Administrative organization: redrawing lines, devolving authority

Secession is about changing international boundaries. One of the most effective ways to prevent a change in international boundaries *among* states is to manipulate internal boundaries *within* a state. States constantly redraw administrative boundaries – and the authority that goes with them – regardless of the presence of secessionist movements. The never-ending debate in the United States over gerrymandering and redistricting at the state and local level reveals how contentious these fights are, as the placement of lines significantly shapes political power and opportunity.

The same is true for secession. As Griffiths argues, "Secessionist movements that do not cohere with any administrative region are the least likely to be granted independence" (Griffiths, 2015: 732). Under the international legal principle of *uti possidetis*, new states must have – and maintain – their borders at the time of independence to avoid instability and irredentism (Ratner, 1996). States therefore can (re)draw their internal boundaries to divide and disempower would-be secessionist groups, ensuring that they lack a contiguous, homogenous territory where they can gain political control and develop a proto-state. The Nigerian government redrew its internal boundaries in 1967 to dilute the concentration of pro-secessionist Igbos and separate them from the main oil reserves in the region, which helped the government prevent the development of a Biafran proto-state and its ultimate secession. The development of a proto-state increases the probability that secessionist movements will achieve independence by 37%, and there have only been *three* cases of successful secession since 1816 without a proto-state (Griffiths, 2015). Administrative organization and authority is therefore a true chokepoint for counter-secession.

Administrative organization can also be utilized as a strategic concession. In this scenario, the state grants a certain region greater autonomy in the hope that its associated population and movement will be satiated short of secession, as with the British and Buganda in 1961. Some studies suggest that these concessions make conflict less likely without necessarily creating a domino effect for other would-be secessionists (Forsberg, 2013; Madiès et al., 2018), although regions that have had autonomy in the past are more likely to seek secession in the future (Siroky and Cuffe, 2015). Should a state be faced with a robust secessionist movement in a contiguous region that it cannot otherwise thwart, the state may also utilize its variation in administrative status to allow one region to secede, while holding onto other regions that lack its same level of administrative autonomy – thus avoiding an unlimited precedent.

This was Moscow's strategy at the end of the Cold War, as it ultimately allowed union republics like Ukraine and the Baltics to secede, while it held the line and denied non-union republics like Chechnya. Moscow did not face a robust secessionist challenge from a number of other ethnic minorities, like the Tatars, who lacked a cohesive identity and movement because of the Soviet strategies of administrative organization that prevented a contiguous, homogenous Tatarstan. The Soviet Union's breakup thus revealed how administrative organization can prevent secessionist identities and movements from emerging (Tatars), thwart others that do (Chechnya), while limiting the concession of independence to those whose identity and geographical concentration become too strong to stop (Ukraine).

## Civilian displacement: dispersing and diluting populations

Redrawing internal borders is one way to prevent the concentration of a secessionist population in a recognized region; another is to change the demographics within the region itself. States can do this by dispersing the (would-be) secessionist population into other areas, or diluting their dominance over a given area by settling individuals from other populations.[5] Dispersed populations are the least likely to make secessionist claims and the least likely to succeed, whereas geographically concentrated groups are the most likely to make and achieve secessionist claims due to their higher legitimacy and capacity (Toft, 2002).

Civilian displacement via dispersion can and has been used at any phase of secessionism, from preventing the coalescing of a nationalist identity and movement, as with the Tatars, to weakening the support of insurgent groups amidst an ongoing war, as with the Chechens. In terms of preventing identity formation and a robust movement,

> The borders of contemporary Tatarstan are the product of Soviet social engineering, designed to divide the Muslim peoples by linguistic and cultural criteria into separate territorial administrative units that could be controlled from Moscow. These borders were explicitly intended to prevent the formation a large Turkic-Muslim nation in the Volga region. As of 1989, this engineering had succeeded in keeping Tatars a minority in Tatarstan: they constituted 48.5 percent, while ethnic Russians constituted 43.2 percent of the region's 3.6 million population. The Tatars were a dispersed ethnic group whose members were scattered across the Russian Federation: 68 percent lived outside their titular republic.
>
> *(Toft, 2002: 105)*

In terms of countering uprisings and conflict, in 1944 the Soviet Union initiated the forced population transfer of almost 500,000 Chechens from the Checheno-Ingush Autonomous Soviet Socialist Republic to the Kazakh SSR and Kyrgyz SSR after four years of sporadic resistance by the Chechens. The Soviets justified the population transfer on the basis that it was necessary to defuse ethnic tensions, stabilize the political situation in the region, and prevent the Chechens from rallying for autonomy and sovereignty (Burds, 2007).

Dilution can happen via state-directed settlement into the disputed area of a population that does not share the secessionist group's identity or support its objectives. The Green March of hundreds of thousands of Moroccan civilians (with military support) in 1975 was such an attempt to control the "Spanish Sahara" by diluting the dominance of the native Sahrawi in the territory and keep it – or add it, depending on one's perspective – as part of Morocco (Weiner, 1979). Since the 1940s, China has encouraged Han Chinese mass migration into Xinjiang, purposely changing the regional demographics to prevent the growth of a strong Uyghur identity and a robust movement for independence. These tactics of civilian displacement have regularly been labeled "ethnic cleansing" by the international community, but many states continue to employ them in the belief that demography is destiny when it comes to (preventing) secession.

## Banning secession: making secessionist parties and secession itself illegal

If states cannot prevent the emergence of a nationalist, separatist identity, then they may make secession illegal and ban its advocates from the political process. The act of banning secessionist organizations makes it more challenging to build a robust secessionist movement, as the basic actions of assembly, monetary donation, and participating in elections become crimes. When states criminalize secession, they raise the costs of advocacy and hope to decrease support for secession among the population. However, states also make extralegal (i.e. violent) confrontation more likely, because the secessionists who remain believe they have no choice but to work against the system, rather than through it.

Democracies are less likely to ban organizations simply for being secessionist, as that potentially violates norms of free speech and assembly codified in both national laws and the UN Declaration of Human Rights (Bourne, 2020). For this reason, the European Council on Human Rights struck down a 2001 Bulgarian ban on the United Macedonian Organization/Ilinden-Pirin, ruling that a secessionist agenda *in the absence of association with violence or other undemocratic objectives* is not illegitimate. Therefore, most bans by democracies are not of secession *per se*, but rather of organizations who are "anti-system," "anti-democratic," or have links to violence as a result of their pro-secessionist stance. States found it easier to make the secessionist connection to violence after 9/11: For the first time since the fall of its dictator in 1975, Spain banned a party in 2003 for its connections to the terrorist group Basque Homeland and Liberty (ETA), after Batasuna had participated in elections for the previous 20 years.

Nondemocracies also criminalize links to violence, but have less of a problem banning secession itself. In 2001, the Cameroon government declared the Southern Cameroons National Council (SCNC) illegal for its nonviolent advocacy for secession of Anglophile Cameroons (Konings and Nyamnjoh, 1997). Turkey has banned ten parties for "threatening national unity" and promoting Kurdish nationalism, and is in the process of seeking to ban yet another – the People's Democratic Party (HDP) (BBC, 2021). In 2005, China passed an explicit anti-secession law aimed at Taiwan, which threatened war should Taiwan move for de jure independence (Cody, 2005).

Only 30% of states today ban secession, whereas 67% are silent on the issue, though many of the latter implicitly reject secession by supporting the integrity of the state in their constitutions (Ginsburg and Versteeg, 2018). What about the final 3%? A very small number of states have explicitly legalized secession under certain conditions – usually involving clear referenda – including Ethiopia, France (before 1995), St. Kitts and Nevis, and Uzbekistan (Ginsburg and Versteeg, 2018). Nonetheless, the letter and spirit of the law often differ. Although Ethiopia has some of the clearest legal language allowing its many constituent nations to secede, in reality the central government has violently worked to prevent any attempts at secession (Habtu, 2005). States may also make specific concessions to secessionist movements – like Canada with Québec and the United Kingdom with Scotland – hoping to ultimately retain them with a renewed commitment to the state. However, making secession explicitly legal unsurprisingly makes it more likely, and so is often a last ditch attempt at counter-secession (Ginsburg and Versteeg, 2018).

### *Fragmenting the secessionist movement: divide and conquer*

When states cannot or will not effectively ban nationalist organizations from existing, they often seek to encourage division among them to prevent a cohesive secessionist movement. Divide and conquer was perhaps the most common colonial strategy, and it endures to this day as a key counter-secession strategy. National movements that lack unity (Pearlman, 2011) or a single dominant organization to lead them (Krause, 2017) are far less likely to be successful. They spend their time and resources competing with (and even killing) each other for movement leadership, because the movement leader at the moment of secession is most likely to become the head of the new state, with all of the accompanying political and economic spoils (Krause, 2017). This endemic infighting wastes scarce resources and ensures that the movement lacks a cohesive strategy and clear message for engaging with the host state and the international community.

States know this, and they employ a variety of tactics to foment rifts in the secessionist movements they face. States may play on personal rivalries or pit groups against each other in elections to create division. States may also selectively repress the strongest secessionist group – which pose the greatest current threat – to allow weaker rivals to rise and challenge the hegemon. In the 1980s, Israel harshly cracked down on PLO-affiliated groups while allowing the growth of Islamists in Gaza. Although Islamic Jihad and Hamas ultimately became the two largest security threats to Israel, their emergence in the 1990s split the Palestinian national movement, leading to infighting that significantly blunted the Palestinian national movement's international support and political effectiveness.

In some cases, states offer carrots rather than sticks to divide the opposition. As Cunningham suggests, states may "divide and concede" rather than divide and conquer, offering concessions to individual leaders or organizations to help cement existing splits, encourage an end to their resistance, and even bring certain factions over to the side of the state (Cunningham, 2011). Secession cannot happen without organizations emerging to advocate for it, but the only thing as problematic as no organizations may be too many. When they are unable to prevent the emergence of secessionist groups, states will work hard to divide and defeat them.

### *Economic coercion: squeezing a movement and its people*

States have significant economic leverage over secessionist movements within their borders. State governments control the collection and distribution of tax revenue, as well as the legal and physical access for trade across both international and internal state borders. When facing a secessionist challenge, states can thus turn these spigots on or off to economically coerce secessionist movements and their local population. Sanctions in the form of regional boycotts, blockades, and general isolation from government funding and international trade and investment can weaken a secessionist movement and its popular support (Woertz, 2017). Although not utilized as often as it was by colonial powers in the nineteenth and twentieth centuries, economic coercion remains a common strategy of counter-secession today.

Economic coercion varies in a deterrent or compellent nature depending on the phase of the secession process, but it is always about manipulating costs and benefits to incentivize a region to remain. Before a struggle even begins, states can build in expensive exit clauses to deter secession by making it too economically costly (Huysmans and Crombez, 2020). More directly, China has imposed sanctions on Taiwan (both import and export), harassed and intimidated Taiwanese business people, and pursued economic disruption, damage, and sabotage (Tanner, 2007). Once conflict begins, states may switch to compellence and increase the economic pressure accordingly. Amidst the Nigerian-Biafran Civil War, Nigeria enacted a military blockade of all food and military supplies to the eastern state, resulting in mass starvation and death amongst Biafran soldiers and civilians. Throughout much of the conflict, the Biafran Organization of Freedom Fighters (BOFF) faced a shortage of armaments and foreign aid, and thus was at a significant disadvantage militarily compared to the federal army, which ultimately triumphed (Thomas and Falola, 2020).

Economic coercion involves carrots as often as or more often than it does sticks, either as an implied benefit of remaining in the state or as additional economic concessions granted to preempt the emergence of a secessionist movement or weaken its support. To counter the insurgency in Malaya, the British-backed government initiated a variety of development and assistance programs, including the Rural Industrial Development Authority, the rejuvenation of the Malayan Labor Movement, and the "new villages" project. These had the primary objective of bringing stability to Malaya, but also the added benefit of taking popular support away from the insurgents (Komer, 1972). In 1997, Bangladesh was able to quell Shanti Bahini's demands for independence with an autonomy deal that included significant economic incentives channeled through a new regional council. This council was provided with multiple sources of income to fund the decisions of the tribal leadership, including the right to oversee the provision of business transactions (Rashiduzzaman, 1998).

Although economic incentives worked in the cases of Malaya and Bangladesh, they failed in Algeria. Under President Charles De Gaulle's leadership in 1959, France offered humanitarian aid and assistance to local communities as part of the Plan de Constantine, a five-year economic and infrastructure program aimed at rebuilding popular support for the colonial government from the native Muslim population. The plan promised to increase Algeria's national revenue, expand educational opportunities for children, and create new residential areas, but also resulted in the uprooting of villages and housing of civilians in abject conditions. These policies somewhat improved relations with the native population, but ultimately failed to counter the political strength of the National Liberation Front (FLN), which won the population's support and Algeria's independence in 1962.

## Violent repression: deploying the police and military

Violent repression is typically not the first tool used by the host state, although its more public and destructive nature means that it is often the first evidence outsiders see of "counter-secession." If the state fails to prevent the emergence of a separate national identity or secessionist movement, however, it will often employ force via the police and/or the military to physically repress and eliminate the secessionist population and its organizations. Secession rarely destroys a state, given that it entails removing some but not all of its territory. Nonetheless, it can seriously threaten a state's security by altering its borders, removing its resources, and creating a new, autonomous rival – often close to its capital. When the threat is significant and/or the state has a fragmented governing coalition, the state is likely not only to employ counter-secession, but to do so violently (Butt, 2017; Spruyt, 2005).

States have a number of choices concerning the targets and severity of their repression. Do they discriminately target secessionist organizations only, or do they indiscriminately attack their supporting civilian populations as well? Do they focus on arrests or military offensives? If the latter, is it limited operations or all-out war? The strategy of violent repression is, first and foremost, to protect the state and prevent its defeat by the secessionists. Second, the state aims to weaken the capabilities of and support for the secessionist movement, both by eliminating its current members and deterring future ones from joining. Third, the state aims to send the message of its strong opposition to the international community, who might otherwise believe they could support the secessionists at low cost.

Violent repression, while almost always brutal, has been effective on a number of occasions. After Kashmiri nationalists backed by Pakistan launched a secessionist rebellion in 1987, India responded with heavy-handed repression. By 1993, there were 175,000 soldiers and 30,000 paramilitary personnel in the province who were emboldened to "shoot and kill, and search and arrest without a warrant, all under immunity from prosecution" (Butt, 2017: 113). The conflict further soured parts of the Kashmiri population and Pakistan against India, but India's violent repression helped avoid secession. Sri Lanka's violent crackdown against the Tamils in 2008–2009 and the British in Northern Ireland from 1969 to 2007 were similarly successful in utilizing arrests and military offensives to prevent secession.

Military force is often the last resort for a reason – it is frequently used once the secessionists are strong, and it therefore does not always work. In response to the 1970 Pakistani election of the Awami League, who supported East Pakistan/Bengali autonomy, President Yahya Khan declared martial law. West Pakistani soldiers implemented Operation Searchlight, which targeted and massacred hundreds of thousands of Bengali civilians, but West Pakistan lost the conflict and Bangladesh seceded. In a more protracted struggle, Ethiopia violently repressed the Eritrean national movement for 30 years before the secessionists defeated them on the battlefield in 1991 and gained their independence two years later (Iyob, 1995). In some cases, a state's violent repression can backfire, as heavy-handed actions can hurt the state's credibility or spark intervention on behalf of the national movement, as happened in Kosovo in 1998–1999 (Kuperman, 2008).

## Blocking international recognition: you're not a state unless (most) other states say so

Existing states get to decide which prospects get to join their club. Secessionist movements can establish various types of de facto autonomy, but if they want de jure secession and statehood, then they need international recognition. Host states who want to prevent secession from their territory can therefore pressure other states against formally recognizing the secessionist movement, whether unilaterally or via international organizations like the United Nations. A lack of recognition deprives the secessionists not only of status, but also of standing to formally conduct arms deals, trade, taxation, and other aspects of sovereign rule.

The most important state for enabling or blocking recognition is the host state itself. If the host state is not engaging in significant and egregious human rights abuses, it is fairly likely that the international community will side with them in refusing international recognition of the secessionists – as occurred with Catalonia and Crimea in recent years. The only state to have unilaterally seceded (i.e. without acquiescence from the host state) and subsequently joined the United Nations was Bangladesh in 1979 (Siroky et al., 2020). Regions that attempt unilateral secession most commonly go unrecognized, even if they have established a proto-state, like Somaliland. The most successful recent unilateral secessionist territory, Kosovo, still is not a UN member due to blocking by Russia, China, and their allies. Although Kosovo has been recognized by a slight majority of states in the world, it will likely take improved recognition and an agreement with its former host state, Serbia, before it becomes a UN member.

As demonstrated in the Kosovo example, after the host state it is the great powers who play the central role in preventing or enabling international recognition, both due to their significant influence over allies and their powerful positions at the UN. Indeed, Bangladesh received recognition despite Pakistan's objections because the permanent members of the UN Security

Council unanimously agreed to recognize it. Most of the time, the opposition of a single great power is enough to block recognition, as the British demonstrated with their efforts to block international recognition of Northern Cyprus (Ker-Lindsay, 2017). In general, states are more likely to recognize if it helps their security situation by not threatening them domestically or internationally and/or threatening their rivals (Coggins, 2011).

## Conclusion

Most states in the world today were formed via secession, including 31 of 34 new states added since 1990. What is most surprising is not how many successful secessionist movements there are, but rather how few. The vast majority of secessionist efforts fail – and even more never get off the ground – due in large part to the concerted efforts of host states to maintain their territorial integrity. Counter-secession is more common than secession, given the aforementioned successes in preventing separatist identities and movements from emerging in the first place. Yet we have a growing but scattered understanding of the many strategies of counter-secession employed by states.

Understanding the four main phases of secession – identity formation, group mobilization, (un)armed struggle, and international recognition – and when states employ various strategies within and between them is an important first step to a comprehensive analysis of counter-secession. Meta-analyses of state strategies not only can provide a more complete picture of secessionist struggles from start to finish, but they can also help address the selection effects inherent to the fact that most secessionist movements do not progress from one phase to the next.

The four phases and eight strategies detailed here represent a first cut. Although they capture a common trajectory that resonates with secessionist challenges and counter-secession efforts across time and space, there is much to be gained from challenging, rearranging, and building on the typology. Do states have comprehensive counter-secession grand strategies that utilize each of these approaches at different phases of the struggle? How do certain strategies complement or contradict each other, and under what conditions? Under what conditions do states attempt to counter secession by tolerating or even cooperating with insurgents, rather than directly combatting them? (Staniland, 2021). These are some of the many important questions that remain largely unanswered. I hope that this chapter's collective presentation of counter-secession strategies can help provide a foundation for their analysis.

## Notes

1 Previously printed in Krause, P. (2022). The strategies of counter-secession: How states prevent independence. *Nations and Nationalism*, 28(3), 788–805. https://doi.org/10.1111/nana.12822, John Wiley and Sons, reused with permission. United Nations logo from https://pngimg.com/images/logos/un.
2 Before 1945, recognition came via the League of Nations or dyadic recognition by a critical mass of neighboring and/or powerful states.
3 Previously printed in Krause, P. (2022). The strategies of counter-secession: How states prevent independence. *Nations and Nationalism*, 28(3), 788–805. https://doi.org/10.1111/nana.12822, John Wiley and Sons, reused with permission. United Nations logo from https://pngimg.com/images/logos/un, machine gun from www.clipartmax.com/middle/m2i8H7K9A0G6H7b1_machine-gun-war-deadly-weapon-military-army-sig-sauer-m400-price/, gavel from www.clipartmax.com/middle/m2i8K9i8N4K9K9b1_legal-hammer-black-shape-gavel-silhouette/, scales from www.clipartmax.com/max/m2K9A0m2b1d3N4H7/, book from www.clipartmax.com/middle/m2i8K9H7G6d3A0N4_book-black-and-white-transparent/.
4 This is nonetheless rare. From 1931 to 2002, 13 out of 15 secessionist movements that won wars gained independence, whereas only 4 out of 22 who lost wars did (Coggins, 2011: 445).

5  Having co-ethnic settlers in a disputed area also makes it more likely that the state will claim the territory and have its claim respected by others (Krause and Eiran, 2018).

# References

Alon Y. (2009). *The Making of Jordan: Tribes, Colonialism and the Modern State.* New York: Palgrave Macmillan.

Avineri S. (2017). *The Making of Modern Zionism: The Intellectual Origins of the Jewish State.* New York: Basic Books.

Banac I. (1988). *The National Question in Yugoslavia: Origins, History, Politics.* Ithaca: Cornell University Press.

BBC. (2021). Turkey Moves to Ban Pro-Kurdish HDP Opposition Party. *BBC News,* 17 March.

Bourne A. (2020). *Democratic Dilemmas: Why Democracies Ban Political Parties.* New York: Routledge.

Brown G.K. (2007). Making Ethnic Citizens: The Politics and Practice of Education in Malaysia. *International Journal of Educational Development* 27(3), pp. 318–330.

Burds J. (2007). The Soviet War against "Fifth Columnists": The Case of Chechnya, 1942–4. *Journal of Contemporary History* 42(2), pp. 267–314.

Butt A.I. (2017). *Secession and Security: Explaining State Strategy against Separatists.* Ithaca: Cornell University Press.

Chenoweth E., and Stephan M.J. (2011). *Why Civil Resistance Works: The Strategic Logic of Nonviolent Conflict.* New York: Columbia University Press.

Cody, E. (2005). China Sends Warning to Taiwan With Anti-Secession Law. *The Washington Post,* 8 March.

Coggins B. (2011). Friends in High Places: International Politics and the Emergence of States from Secessionism. *International Organization* 65(3), pp. 433–467.

Coggins B. (2014). *Power Politics and State Formation in the Twentieth Century: The Dynamics of Recognition.* Cambridge: Cambridge University Press.

Cunningham K.G. (2011). Divide and Conquer or Divide and Concede: How Do States Respond to Internally Divided Separatists? *The American Political Science Review* 105(2), pp. 275–297.

Darden K., and Mylonas H. (2016). Threats to Territorial Integrity, National Mass Schooling, and Linguistic Commonality. *Comparative Political Studies* 49(11), pp. 1446–1479.

Fearon J., and Laitin D. (2003). Ethnicity, Insurgency, and Civil War. *The American Political Science Review* 97(1), pp. 75–90.

Forsberg E. (2013). Do Ethnic Dominoes Fall? Evaluating Domino Effects of Granting Territorial Concessions to Separatist Groups. *International Studies Quarterly* 57(2), pp. 329–340.

Gellner E. (1983). *Nations and Nationalism.* Ithaca: Cornell University Press.

Ginsburg T., and Versteeg M. (2018). From Catalonia to California: Secession in Constitutional Law. *Alabama Law Review* 70(4), pp. 923–986.

Griffiths R. (2015). Between Dissolution and Blood: How Administrative Lines and Categories Shape Secessionist Outcomes. *International Organization* 69(3), pp. 731–751.

Griffiths R. (2016). *Age of Secession: The International and Domestic Determinants of State Birth.* Cambridge: Cambridge University Press.

Griffiths R., and Martinez A. (2021). Local Conditions and the Demand for Independence: A Dataset of Secessionist Grievances. *Nations and Nationalism* 27(2), pp. 580–590.

Griffiths R., and Muro D. (eds.). (2020). *Strategies of Secession and Counter-Secession.* London: Rowman & Littlefield International Ltd.

Habtu A. (2005). Multiethnic Federalism in Ethiopia: A Study of the Secession Clause in the Constitution. *Publius: The Journal of Federalism* 35(2), pp. 313–335.

Huysmans M., and Crombez C. (2020). Making Exit Costly But Efficient: The Political Economy of Exit Clauses and Secession. *Constitutional Political Economy* 31(1), pp. 89–110.

Iyob R. (1995). *The Eritrean Struggle for Independence: Domination, Resistance, Nationalism, 1941–1993.* Cambridge: Cambridge University Press.

Ker-Lindsay J. (2012). *The Foreign Policy of Counter Secession: Preventing the Recognition of Contested States.* Oxford: Oxford University Press.

Ker-Lindsay J. (2017). Great Powers, Counter Secession, and Non-Recognition: Britain and the 1983 Unilateral Declaration of Independence of the "Turkish Republic of Northern Cyprus". *Diplomacy & Statecraft* 28(3), pp. 431–453.

Komer R.W. (1972). *The Malayan Emergency in Retrospect: Organization of a Successful Counterinsurgency Effort.* 1 January. Santa Monica, CA: RAND Corporation.

Konings P., and Nyamnjoh F.B. (1997). The Anglophone Problem in Cameroon. *The Journal of Modern African Studies* 35(2), pp. 207–229.

Krause P. (2017). *Rebel Power: Why National Movements Compete, Fight, and Win*. Ithaca, NY: Cornell University Press.

Krause P., and Eiran E. (2018). How Human Boundaries Become State Borders: Radical Flanks and Territorial Control in the Modern Era. *Comparative Politics* 50(4), pp. 479–499.

Kuperman A. (2008). The Moral Hazard of Humanitarian Intervention: Lessons from the Balkans. *International Studies Quarterly* 52(1), pp. 49–80.

Lawrence A.S. (2010). Triggering Nationalist Violence: Competition and Conflict in Uprisings against Colonial Rule. *International Security* 35(2), pp. 88–122.

Loh J., and Harmon D. (2005). A Global Index of Biocultural Diversity. *Ecological Indicators* 5(3), pp. 231–241.

Madiès T., Rota-Grasiozi G., Tranchant J.-P., et al. (2018). The Economics of Secession: A Review of Legal, Theoretical, and Empirical Aspects. *Swiss Journal of Economics and Statistics* 154(1), p. 19.

Minahan J. (ed.). (2002). *Encyclopedia of the Stateless Nations: Ethnic and National Groups around the World*. Westport, CT: Greenwood Press.

Muro D., and Woertz E. (eds.). (2018). *Secession and Counter-Secession: An International Relations Perspective*. Barcelona: CIDOB.

Pearlman W. (2011). *Violence, Nonviolence, and the Palestinian National Movement*. New York: Cambridge University Press.

Rashiduzzaman M. (1998). Bangladesh's Chittagong Hill Tracts Peace Accord: Institutional Features and Strategic Concerns. *Asian Survey* 38(7).

Ratner S. (1996). Drawing a Better Line: UTI Possidetis and the Borders of New States. *The American Journal of International Law* 90(4), pp. 590–624. American Society of International Law.

Siroky D., and Cuffe J. (2015). Lost Autonomy, Nationalism and Separatism. *Comparative Political Studies* 48(1), pp. 3–34.

Siroky D., Popovic M., and Mirilovic N. (2020). Unilateral Secession, International Recognition, and Great Power Contestation. *Journal of Peace Research* 58(5), pp. 1049–1067.

Smith A. (1995). *Nations and Nationalism in a Global Era*. Cambridge: Polity.

Spruyt H. (2005). *Ending Empire: Contested Sovereignty and Territorial Partition*. Ithaca, NY: Cornell University Press.

Staniland P. (2021). *Ordering Violence: Explaining Armed Group-State Relations from Conflict to Cooperation*. Ithaca: Cornell University Press.

Tanner M. (2007). Economic Coercion: Factors Affecting Success and Failure. In: *Chinese Economic Coercion Against Taiwan*. 1st ed. A Tricky Weapon to Use. Santa Monica, CA: RAND Corporation, pp. 11–32.

Thomas C.G., and Falola T. (2020). The Secession of Biafra, 1967–1970. In: *Secession and Separatist Conflicts in Postcolonial Africa*. Calgary: University of Calgary Press.

Toft M. (2002). Indivisible Territory, Geographic Concentration, and Ethnic War. *Security Studies* 12(2), pp. 82–119.

Tripp C. (2002). *A History of Iraq*. Cambridge: Cambridge University Press.

Walter B. (2009). *Reputation and Civil War: Why Separatist Conflicts Are So Violent*. Cambridge: Cambridge University Press.

Weiner J. (1979). The Green March in Historical Perspective. *Middle East Journal* 33(1), pp. 20–33.

Woertz E. (2017). Economic Aspects of Counter Secession Strategies. In: *Secession and Counter-Secession: An International Relations Perspective*. Barcelona: Barcelona Centre for International Affairs, pp. 99–106.

# 30

# HOW PARENT STATES PREVENT RECOGNITION

*Scott Pegg*

## Introduction

Secession remains a pervasive feature of the contemporary states system. On one commonly used benchmark, the number of UN member states increased from 159 in 1990 to 193 in 2023. While not all this increase was due to secession or dissolution, much of it was, including the dissolutions of the former Soviet Union and the former Yugoslavia as well as the secessions of Eritrea from Ethiopia and, most recently, South Sudan from Sudan. Griffiths (2021: 14) estimates that there has been an average of 52 secessionist movements per year in the post-1945 period. Just looking at the much smaller subset of referendums on secession, in recent decades we can see the legally accepted but ultimately unsuccessful independence referendums in Québec (1995) and Scotland (2014), the legally accepted and successful independence referendum in South Sudan (2011), the largely ignored but overwhelmingly popular independence referendum in Somaliland (2001) and a similar one that might actually lead to independence for Bougainville (2019) as well as the hotly contested and sharply disputed referendums in Catalonia (2017) and Iraqi Kurdistan (2017).

While there are several examples where parent states have given their blessing or consent to state dissolution (e.g., former Czechoslovakia, Egypt and Syria, Senegal and Gambia) or allowing secessionists to be recognized and form new states (e.g., Eritrea, Montenegro, South Sudan), this consent is typically not forthcoming because "any new state constitutes a subtraction in territory from at least one existing state" (Griffiths 2021: 18). This chapter explores the various strategies and tactics available to sovereign states in seeking to prevent recognition of their secessionist challengers.

The chapter proceeds as follows. The next section sets out several caveats or qualifications to the analysis pursued here. We then turn to the international normative environment which is generally quite favorable for existing sovereign states. The following section highlights parent state options for counter-recognition strategies to pursue. We then highlight some of the limits to parent states' ability to defeat secessionist movements decisively. A conclusion summarizes the main findings.

## Caveats/limitations/qualifications

The view presented here is a broad one from the proverbial 35,000 feet up in the air. Given the pervasiveness of secession in the modern era, there are a wide variety of parent states facing

DOI: 10.4324/9781003036593-35

secessionist challenges. The Republic of Cyprus and Somalia might have similar inclinations toward their respective secessionist challenges (the Turkish Republic of Northern Cyprus and the Republic of Somaliland) but Nicosia is far richer, better qualified, and dramatically more capable to act against its secessionist challenger than Mogadishu is. A military dictatorship like Burma will have a different set of options in responding to its secessionist challengers from what a stable democratic state like Canada or the United Kingdom will have. European Union member states facing secessionist bids will probably have more options available to them than small Pacific Island states.

Correspondingly, there are a wide variety of secessionist movements, some of which pursue their aims via civil wars and others of which pursue their aims via the ballot box. Griffiths (2021: 31–37), for example, identifies six distinct types of secessionist movements, which he terms democratized, indigenous legal, weak combative, strong combative, decolonial and de facto, and acknowledges that there is hybridity within and between these categories and movement between them as local conditions change.

Parent state-secessionist dynamics also change over time. China and Taiwan were more evenly balanced economic, military and political competitors in the 1980s than they are today. Somalia and Somaliland were in broadly similar places for most of the 1990s. Since then, however, Somaliland has largely consolidated peace and made significant progress in democratization, while Somalia has not. State strategies also change. Georgia, for example, has alternated between more and less accommodative strategies vis-à-vis Abkhazia (Berg and Pegg 2020). This chapter offers a broad-based view of how parent states in general try to prevent secessionist challengers from being recognized. Some of the dynamics it highlights will not be relevant for specific cases.

Another caveat to acknowledge here concerns the international recognition regime. How existing states decide based upon what criteria (or no criteria) whether to recognize aspiring states has changed and evolved throughout the history of the modern states system (Fabry 2010; Griffiths 2021; Pegg 1998/2019). The international recognition regime has evolved over time, and there is no reason to expect that it cannot evolve again in new or different directions. Indeed, several creative and innovative suggestions have been put forward in this regard (Englebert 2009; Fabry 2010; Griffiths 2021; Herbst 2000). This chapter focuses on the post-1945 international recognition regime currently in existence and does not examine past or future alternatives to it.

Finally, as Ker-Lindsay (2012) notes in his seminal work on this topic, there is an analytical distinction that can be made between parent states contesting secession and parent states seeking to prevent recognition. As he explains, "The opposition to an act of secession is rooted to the real or perceived intrinsic importance that a specific territory has for the state. It is about substance" (Ker-Lindsay 2012: 70). In contrast, preventing recognition

> is about process. It is about maintaining a claim to the territory to construct a bargaining position that will determine the eventual settlement of the dispute . . . the prevention of recognition is about maintaining the diplomatic upper hand. Ultimately, it is all about leverage.
>
> *(Ker-Lindsay 2012: 70)*

This chapter focuses on parent states trying to prevent recognition.

## A favorable international normative environment

At first glance, the international normative environment might appear quite favorable to secessionist aspirations. After all, the principle of self-determination was incorporated into Articles 1(2) and 55 of the UN Charter. More famously, UN General Assembly Resolution 1514 of

1960 ("A Declaration on the Granting of Independence to Colonial Countries and Peoples") decisively proclaimed that "All peoples have the right to self-determination; by virtue of that right they freely determine their political status and freely pursue their economic, social and cultural development." It went on to emphasize that "inadequacy of political, economic, social or educational preparedness should never serve as a pretext for delaying independence."

Yet, that same resolution subsequently qualifies the right to self-determination by mandating that "Any attempt aimed at the partial or total disruption of the national unity and the territorial integrity of a country is incompatible with the purposes and principles of the Charter of the United Nations." As Emerson (1971: 459) wryly observed, "what is stated in big print – as in the reiterated United Nations injunction: All peoples have the right to self-determination – is drastically modified by what follows in small print." The subsequent history of self-determination since 1945 can be succinctly summarized in two main parts. First, an attempt to extend the principle quickly to all "salt-water" or "blue-water" colonies under European colonial rule. Second, an attempt to sharply delimit the number of eligible "selves" to just former European colonies and a few small exceptions such as territories under military occupation or *apartheid* rule to minimize the potential for disruption that a more generalized right to self-determination could bring (Pegg 1998/2019: 138–139).

Parallel developments occurred in terms of territorial integrity. From the Treaty of Westphalia (1648) through to at least the turn of the twentieth century, "territorial change was seen as a normal, indeed inevitable, part of international relations" (Pegg 1998/2019: 120). After 1945, the international community attempted to freeze the political map of the world and sanctify the existing distribution of territorial borders as inviolable and permanent. There are several explanations for this. First, territorial disputes were previously a major source of inter-state war. Removing territorial change from the international agenda is certainly one major explanation for the sharp decline in inter-state war since 1945 (Mueller 2004). Second, the number of nations (4,000–8,000 on some estimates) vastly exceeds the number of sovereign states in the world today (less than 200). Almost all states contain multiple ethnicities or nationalities within their borders and are thus potentially vulnerable to secessionist challenges. Third, the fixed territorial borders regime has a wonderful simplicity about it. One would struggle mightily to define where Yorubaland begins and ends, but the border between Benin and Nigeria can be delimited precisely. Finally, secession is arguably a poor solution to many state problems that could potentially be solved by measures far less disruptive to domestic and international peace.

The result is a post-1945 international normative environment that is highly conservative and status quo biased in favor of existing sovereign states and against their secessionist challengers. The rights of self-determination and territorial integrity ostensibly compete with one another, but the post-1945 international system and, particularly, the post-1960/postcolonial system has come down overwhelmingly in favor of the right to territorial integrity. As Österud (1997: 168) observes,

> There is still some proliferation of new political entities recognized as states, but this is mainly limited to the successors of Communist multinational states and to a few leftovers from European overseas empires. Otherwise, club membership is closed in favor of the territorial integrity of established states.

Importantly, the role that parent states play in keeping club membership closed is crucial. With a few historical exceptions like Manchukuo and the South African Bantustans (Griffiths 2021: 25), international practice has been quite clear and consistent. When parent states consent to secessionists breaking away, the rest of the international community supports that decision.

Thus, shortly after Sudan recognized South Sudan, it received widespread international recognition from other states and was rapidly admitted as a full member state of the African Union and the UN. Conversely, parent state objections typically result in a powerful veto denying recognition to the secessionist entity. In Griffiths's (2021: 44) phrasing, "In the normative collision between self-determination and territorial integrity . . . secessionists have numerous cards to play (decolonization, human rights, etc.), but states have the ace: the principle that sovereign territory is inviolate." Perhaps the most extreme example of this is Somalia, which has not had a viable central government since 1991 and yet is still able to use its juridical sovereignty to deny recognition to the much more empirically effective Somaliland. As Geldenhuys (2009: 146) explains,

> Although devoid of empirical statehood, Somalia has retained its juridical statehood – a feature that has allowed it to effectively veto Somaliland's progress to confirmed statehood. African countries have allowed this absurdity by their dogmatic commitment to the phantom state of Somalia over the factual state of Somaliland.

Some might argue that this portrayal of the international normative environment might be accurate for the Cold War era, but surely things have changed with the rapid increase in the number of sovereign states since the end of the Cold War. Intuitively, this seems to make sense. UN membership increased from 159 member states in 1990 to 184 member states in 1993. Such a fundamental spike of 25 new UN member states in three years must surely indicate changed international practice. For better or worse, this does not appear to be the case. Fabry (2012: 664) maintains that "Rather than making any notable dents in the previously established recognition practice, the end of the Cold War in fact extended it beyond the ex-colonial world." In his view,

> The break-ups of the Soviet Union in 1991 and Czechoslovakia in 1992 might have commenced as separatist bids by some of their constituent units, but foreign recognition of the successor states came only once the respective central governments had agreed to the dissolution of the unions.
>
> *(Fabry 2012: 664)*

The former Yugoslav republics were not recognized until outside powers came to regard Yugoslavia "as a case of dissolution legally equivalent to the consensual dissolution of the USSR or Czechoslovakia" (Fabry 2012: 665).

Even regarding the still contested recognitions of Abkhazia, Kosovo and South Ossetia,

> the leading recognizing powers took great care in all three cases to reject the applicability of their decision to other situations of unilateral secession, and they have since approached those other situations as if no acknowledgment of the three territories had taken place.
>
> *(Fabry 2012: 661)*

Looking specifically at Kosovo, Klich (2021) similarly maintains that "Although there was disagreement by the major powers about Kosovo's right to self-determination, the one component of this question upon which a consensus was clear was that Kosovo did not set a precedent." Fabry's (2012: 665) concise conclusion is that:

> in the post-Cold War period territorial integrity continued (1) to be protected normatively against non-consensual changes from inside as well as outside; and (2) to prevail

over the self-determination of peoples in the sense in which this idea had been understood in nineteenth and earlier twentieth-century recognition practices.

Crawford (2007: 415) similarly concludes that

> State practice since 1945 shows the extreme reluctance of States to recognize or accept unilateral secession outside the colonial context. That practice has not changed since 1989, despite the emergence during that period of twenty-three new States. On the contrary, the practice has been powerfully reinforced.

Ker-Lindsay (2012: 173) also maintains that the dissolutions of the Soviet Union, Yugoslavia and Czechoslovakia and the emergence of Eritrea and East Timor

> served to reinforce the idea that there was no general right of self-determination leading to statehood unless it was done with the permission of the parent state, or in cases where there was a defined constitutional or legal right to independence for the seceding entity.

Thus, the continued persistence of an international normative environment which prioritizes territorial integrity over self-determination, and which grants parent states effective veto power over the emergence of new states within their territory constitutes the most powerful advantage parent states have at their disposal when trying to deny recognition to secessionist challengers. Within this broadly supportive international context, though, parent states also regularly must make choices about which strategies they want to pursue when dealing with secessionist challengers. We turn to those options now.

## Counter-recognition strategies: choices and options

Potentially, parent states have two options available to them that can decisively end secessionist conflicts (Berg and Pegg 2020: 53). First, they can crush the secessionist movement. Relatively recent examples of parent states pursuing this strategy include Croatia forcibly eradicating the Serbian Republic of Krajina (1995), Russia forcibly eradicating Chechnya (1999), Sri Lanka forcibly eradicating Tamil Eelam (2009) and Azerbaijan substantively eradicating much of Nagorno-Karabakh (2020) before agreeing to a ceasefire that preserved the existence of a much smaller Nagorno-Karabakh. Although the humanitarian costs of such a strategy can be devastatingly high, the international community is generally quite permissive about allowing parent states to attempt forcible eradication. As Ker-Lindsay (2012: 57) puts it, "successful efforts to retake secessionist territory have produced relatively little by way of criticism."

Barbara Walter's (2006) empirical work suggests that the number of potential secessionist challengers that governments face determines how willing they will be to fight or to accommodate any individual secessionist challenge. In her explanation, "governments are significantly more likely to fight against a particular separatist group if the *number of future challengers* and the potential *long-term losses* from future challenges are high" (Walter 2006: 314, emphasis in original). Walter is correct, but there are two huge limits to forcible eradication that deter most parent states from pursuing it. First, for democratic states facing secessionist challengers like Canada, Spain or the United Kingdom, forcible eradication is politically unacceptable to their populations and off the table as an option. The cure is seen as far worse than the disease. Second, many other parent states simply do not have the ability to pursue such a strategy. Georgia might want to forcibly eradicate Abkhazia, but it does not possess the requisite military strength needed to do this. Burma has tried repeatedly to eradicate its Chin, Karen and Shan secessionist challengers but has not yet been able to do so. Most parent states are either unable or unwilling to pursue forcible eradication.

Second, parent states can decisively end secessionist movements by recognizing the secessionists and allowing them to leave. Ethiopia recognizing Eritrea (1993), Serbia recognizing Montenegro (2006) and Sudan recognizing South Sudan (2011) are all relatively recent cases where parent states have chosen to grant their consent to secessionist movements on their territory leaving. As noted earlier, with rare exceptions, such consensual secessions are almost always followed by widespread sovereign recognition from the rest of the international community and ultimately punctuated by the new state's formal admission as a full member of the UN, as happened most recently with South Sudan in 2011. Yet, most parent states remain unwilling to pursue this option.

If granting recognition to secessionists and forcibly eradicating them are not viable options for most parent states, then those states typically try to prevent recognition of the secessionist entities operating on their territories. Ker-Lindsay (2012: 70–76) identifies five not mutually exclusive reasons why parent states seek to prevent recognition. First, parent states might want to preserve the option for a future negotiated settlement or peaceful reintegration of the secessionist territory. Second, they might want to keep their military options open. Azerbaijan is a paradigmatic example here. It was unable to pursue a military solution against Nagorno-Karabakh for the first two decades of its existence. Gradually, over time, Azerbaijan successfully converted its oil revenues into military capabilities, which it then employed against Nagorno-Karabakh in 2020. Third, parent states might want to prevent recognition to try to achieve a more orderly secession on terms more favorable to them. Ker-Lindsay (2012: 73) suggests Serbia exemplifies this strategy vis-à-vis Kosovo. Most Serbs acknowledge Kosovo's independence is irreversible but believe that its desire for Serbian consent and the various material, economic and diplomatic benefits that would flow from full UN membership (Fazal and Griffiths 2014) provide leverage to them in determining the specific terms of Kosovo's secession. Fourth, parent states might not have a specific end goal in mind but seek to prevent recognition to maintain the status quo and buy themselves time to pursue whatever option they choose later. Finally, some parent states may seek to prevent recognition as a form of punishment against a secessionist entity that has embarrassed them through its desire to leave. Ker-Lindsay suggests the Republic of Cyprus may exemplify this motivation. In his view, their campaign to isolate and sanction the Turkish Republic of Northern Cyprus (TRNC) can be seen as "an act of empowerment in the face of defeat" and a means to restore a sense of honor and self-esteem (Ker-Lindsay 2014: 43).

Before getting into various options that states can choose from when pursuing non-recognition, it is first worth highlighting just how wide the range of choices available to parent states is. Looking just at de facto states, only one of the six types of secessionist movements in Griffiths's (2021) classificatory scheme, Berg and Pegg (2020) find significant variation between what they term Moldova's strategy of "open engagement" with Transnistria, Georgia's strategy of "tentative engagement" with Abkhazia and the Republic of Cyprus' strategy of isolation and sanctions against the TRNC. To illustrate the wide variety of choices parent states can make, it is worth examining the highly divergent and contrasting strategies pursued by Chisinau and Nicosia.

Among other things, Moldova has placed no restrictions on the movement of people between Moldova and Transnistria. Regular bus services running every 30 minutes connect Chisinau with Tiraspol. Moldova's national football team plays some of its home matches in Transnistria's Sheriff stadium. Moldova has recognized Transnistrian university diplomas and its car license plates. It has also recognized Transnistria's right to establish and maintain international contacts in economic, scientific-technical and cultural areas. Moldova has encouraged US diplomats to meet with Transnistrian leaders, and it has allowed Transnistrian companies to export goods with customs stamps bearing the inscription "Republic of Moldova, Tiraspol Customs" (Berg and Pegg 2020: 54–56).

In stark contrast, the Republic of Cyprus has repeatedly sought to isolate, sanction and embargo Northern Cyprus. Among others, the Republic of Cyprus has secured a series of UN Security Council Resolutions, including UNSC Resolutions 186 (1964), 353 (1974), 360 (1974), 541 (1983) and 550 (1984) which have variously recognized the now exclusively Greek Cypriot administration as the government of Cyprus, confirmed the territorial integrity of the Republic of Cyprus, declared the attempt to create a Turkish Cypriot state invalid and called upon other states not to recognize "any Cypriot state other than the Republic of Cyprus." Nicosia has also succeeded in getting the Universal Postal Union to declare TRNC postage stamps as illegal and invalid, which means that all mail to and from Northern Cyprus must be routed through Turkey; and in getting the International Civil Aviation Organization (ICAO) to not recognize Ercan Airport which means that all tourist flights to and from Northern Cyprus must also originate from or stop in Turkey. Passengers arriving via Ercan Airport or any Turkish Cypriot maritime port are deemed to have "illegally entered" the Republic of Cyprus. Nicosia has also pursued cases in the European Court of Justice that have significantly strengthened the economic embargo against the TRNC and used its European Union membership to veto EU proposals that it sees as favorable to Northern Cyprus. Nicosia regularly objects to any Turkish Cypriot participation in international sporting or cultural events, and it has succeeded in getting countries like the United States to always use quote marks when referring to any TRNC officials or institutions as in "central bank" or "prime minister." It also deems the "universities" in Northern Cyprus illegal and campaigns internationally against their degrees being recognized or accorded any form of legitimacy (Berg and Pegg 2020: 61–63, 65).

The discussion of the divergent approaches taken to secessionist challengers by Chisinau and Nicosia illustrates the wide variety of options that parent states can choose from when pursuing strategies of non-recognition vis-à-vis their secessionist challengers. Many parent states probably find themselves somewhere between these two extremes of open engagement and severe isolation. Parent states also find themselves shifting strategies over time, becoming more accommodative or punitive in response to domestic or international developments. Georgia's relations with Abkhazia illustrate both more of a middle-ground approach than that pursued by either Chisinau or Nicosia and one that has also shifted and changed over time (Berg and Pegg 2020: 56–58). Some parent states might wish to pursue certain options but lack the capabilities needed to do so effectively. We turn now to a series of classic or typical strategies parent states pursue to prevent recognition of secessionist challengers, before examining alternative forms of "engagement without recognition" that parent states can also choose to pursue if they want.

As Ker-Lindsay (2012: 77–78) emphasizes,

> The first step in any counter-recognition strategy is to stake an ongoing claim to sovereignty over the territory in question . . . any silence about an act of secession may possibly be read as de facto acceptance of the loss. . . . Thereafter, the claim to sovereignty must be continually reinforced.

Parent states will frequently use language like "the occupied territories" or "so called" or "self-proclaimed" to signify their continued claim over territories that violent secessionists or de facto states control, and they will emphasize their democratic credentials to counter the claims of peaceful or indigenous secessionist movements.

After continuously asserting and reasserting the parent state's ongoing claim to sovereignty, the next step is to prevent other states from recognizing the secessionists. Parent states draw heavily here on the favorable international environment described earlier. As Ker-Lindsay (2012: 79) observes, "As one might expect, respect for the principle of the territorial integrity of states, and the illegality and unacceptability of unilateral secession under international law, is often a central argument in these efforts."

Preventing other states from recognizing secessionist claims takes place at multiple different levels. At the global level, given its paramount importance in ratifying confirmed and widely accepted statehood, many parent states seek UN resolutions supporting them and/or weakening secessionist claims like those described earlier in the Cyprus case. While securing such resolutions is difficult because they require the affirmative vote or at least abstention of all five permanent Security Council members, once such a resolution is in place, "any attempt to reverse it can be blocked by just one permanent member" (Ker-Lindsay 2012: 133).

Even more important than such resolutions, though, is getting the support of one or more permanent Security Council members to block any secessionist's acceptance as a full UN member. As Griffiths (2021: 19) points out, "the defining feature of joining the sovereignty club is obtaining a full seat" in the UN General Assembly. That is why Klich (2021) defines de facto states in terms of not having recognition "which is sufficient to gain entry into the United Nations." Such a definition removes what Caspersen (2012: 10) terms the "borderline cases" of Kosovo and Taiwan from debate. Although Kosovo is now recognized by around 100 countries and Taiwan is now recognized by only 14 countries, neither entity is a sovereign state under Klich's definition because neither of them have recognition "sufficient to gain entry into the United Nations." What does this require? Article 4(2) of the UN Charter mandates that the General Assembly votes on applicants following a recommendation from the Security Council. Thus, any permanent member of the Security Council can veto the necessary recommendation to the General Assembly, as Russia currently would with Kosovo and China would with Taiwan. As Riegl and Doboš (2018: 463) observe, "any entity's bid for sovereign statehood and full international recognition can be blocked by any UNSC permanent member."

Below the level of the UN, parent states also use their membership in regional international organizations to thwart secessionist ambitions. Somalia, for example, has repeatedly blocked attempts to have discussions about Somaliland at the African Union. Since 2004, the Republic of Cyprus has used its EU membership to veto several proposed initiatives pertaining to Northern Cyprus. As Berg (2013: 480) emphasizes, "lifting the EU trade embargo on the north or opening Ercan International Airport are matters requiring the sovereign consent of the Greek-Cypriot member state, consent that is regularly denied by Cyprus." Parent states also try to block secessionist challenges from participating in regional international organizations. Somalia, for example, has blocked Somaliland from participating as an observer in both the African Union and the Intergovernmental Authority on Development (IGAD), an important regional grouping in the Horn of Africa. China has allowed Taiwan to participate as a full member of the World Trade Organization (WTO) under the name "Chinese Taipei" since 2002, but it has fiercely resisted Taiwan's renewed campaign for observer status at the World Health Organization in the wake of its generally successful response to the COVID-19 pandemic.

Bilaterally, parent states also try to prevent recognition of their secessionist challenger by any other state. China, for example, has been using its increasingly powerful diplomatic, military and economic leverage to get countries to switch recognition from Taipei to Beijing. Looking just at sub-Saharan Africa as an example, over the past 15 years, Burkina Faso, Chad, Gambia, Malawi, São Tomé and Principe, and Senegal have all switched diplomatic recognition from Taipei to Beijing. Taiwan is now left with just one diplomatic ally in sub-Saharan Africa,

Eswatini (formerly Swaziland). Even better than getting states to un-recognize your secessionist challenger is getting them to not recognize it in the first place. Somalia has been entirely successful in this regard, as no state has recognized Somaliland. After Georgia saw Abkhazia pick up a few recognitions from Latin American states like Nicaragua and Venezuela and from Pacific Island states like Nauru and Vanuatu, it "intensified its counter-recognition policies and . . . opened an unprecedented number of new embassies and established diplomatic ties, especially in Latin America, the Pacific region, and Africa" to try to prevent any future such recognitions (Ó Beacháin, Comai and Tsurtsumia-Zurabashvili 2016: 454).

Beyond merely seeking to prevent recognition of their secessionist challengers, parent states also often seek to deny them various other opportunities for international interactions. In addition to the various forms of economic isolation that the Republic of Cyprus maintains, Somalia has formally objected to DP World's foreign direct investment to expand Berbera's port in Somaliland. Somalia's Ministry of Ports and Marine Development declared the deal facilitating DP World's investment in Berbera as "non-existent, null and void" in 2018 (Berg and Pegg 2020: 60), but construction on the port and its associated infrastructure proceeds today. Georgia complained severely about the opening of a Benetton shop in Sukhumi, Abkhazia, in 2009, and its complaints forced McDonald's to abandon plans to open a restaurant in the same city in 2013 (Ó Beacháin, Comai and Tsurtsumia-Zurabashvili, 2016: 454). Parent states also often try to deny their secessionist challengers the opportunity to participate in international cultural or sporting events, fearing that such participation amounts to legitimizing these entities. As Ker-Lindsay (2012: 181) explains,

> The degree of 'name recognition' that emerges from participating in major sporting and cultural events is so great – perhaps even greater, in public opinion terms, than membership of many political bodies – that these events have become key battlegrounds in the recognition contest.

Beijing allows Taiwan to participate in the International Olympics as "Chinese Taipei," but most secessionist movements are relegated to events such as the Confederation of Independent Football Associations (CONIFA) World Football Cup, an international football tournament for stateless peoples and regions which is unaffiliated with the Federation of Independent Football Associations (FIFA), which organizes the much-better-known World Cup. where soccer powers like Argentina, Brazil, Cameroon, France, Germany, Mexico and Nigeria compete. In contrast, CONIFA features teams like Abkhazia, Darfur, Kurdistan Region, Matabeleland, Northern Cyprus, Somaliland and Tibet.

Griffiths (2021: 33) points out that "individual states have substantial latitude in their response to secessionist demands." As the previous discussion of Moldova illustrates, not all parent states wish to pursue isolationist or exclusionary strategies against their secessionist challengers. Instead, parent states might wish to continue engaging their secessionist challengers without recognizing the legitimacy of their secessionist claim. Democratic states facing secessionist bids regularly do not seek to isolate or punish secessionists to demonstrate that everything is fine in Québec or Scotland and hence there is no reason for them to want to secede in the first place. Parent states like Moldova can also come to see isolation as a self-defeating strategy. It is hard to entice the population in secessionist areas to want to reintegrate with your state if you are constantly vilifying them and denigrating their legitimacy. The trust required for peaceful compromise solutions is probably not being built by pursuing such strategies. Beyond this, isolation can also force secessionist groups into a much deeper embrace of the external friends or patrons they do have. Georgia regularly criticizes Abkhazia for its excessive dependence on

Russia, and Cyprus similarly critiques the TRNC's excessive dependence on Turkey, but the isolationist policies they have pursued have contributed to that dependency. If, for example, Ercan Airport was recognized by the ICAO as a safe and functional airport (which it is), then Northern Cyprus would certainly have direct flights from Germany, the United Kingdom and other European countries and not depend entirely on flights to and from Turkey. Allowing civil society in Abkhazia (Hoch, Kopeček and Baar 2017) to interact regularly with EU counterparts might open some space for cooperation or compromise that is not created by isolating Abkhaz civil society. For parent states that seek to encourage peaceful reunification and find isolation a counterproductive strategy, the good news is that the possibilities for "engagement without recognition" are almost endless. As Ker-Lindsay (2015: 285) explains, "as long as it keeps insisting that it has not in fact recognized it, a state can even go so far as to interact with a contested state as though it were recognized in all but name."

## Limits to states' ability to defeat secessionist movements

The international normative environment described earlier in this chapter and the substantial, material benefits that come with recognized statehood (Fazal and Griffiths 2014) tilt the playing field heavily in favor of parent states when it comes to denying recognition to secessionist challengers. Yet, denying recognition to secessionists and successfully resolving secessionist conflicts are two quite different things (Berg and Pegg 2020). Post-1945 parent states almost always succeed at the first task but have a much more checkered or problematic track record when it comes to the second task. Specifically, parent states encounter four major problems that limit their ability to defeat secessionist movements decisively.

First, however favorable the international normative environment remains, parent states still operate in an anarchical international system where they often have limited abilities to transform regional or global balances of power. Parent states may be militarily weaker than their secessionist challengers. They might also be hindered in their ability to change dynamics on the ground by a powerful external patron state that supports the secessionists. As Berg and Pegg (2020: 64) put it, "However unjust their creation was in the eyes of the parent state, Northern Cyprus and Abkhazia now feature defined frontiers which are easy for organized military forces to defend at relatively low cost." Turkey has supported Northern Cyprus for decades now, and there is no reason to believe it cannot continue supporting the TRNC for decades to come. Although its support is far more ambiguous and open to interpretation, the United States has similarly provided enough support to Taiwan to preserve its existence since 1979. Theoretically, Riegl and Doboš (2018: 462) demonstrate that the success or failure of secessionist bids are determined by "the strongest, highly committed, external actor." In their view, "even a vastly superior external actor in terms of power, with low- or medium-level involvement, can be in an inferior position in influencing an outcome of the conflict in the event that the comparatively weaker actor is highly committed" (Riegl and Doboš 2018: 447). Thus, the United States is a stronger power than Russia, but Russia's much greater degree of commitment to securing outcomes favorable to it in Crimea and eastern Ukraine has determined the course of events there. For Riegl and Doboš (2018: 463), "Normative and effectiveness criteria thus play only secondary roles that become important once the external actors are uninterested in the case or as foreign policy tools." The international normative environment generally enables parent states to prevent secessionist bids from being recognized, but the anarchical nature of the international system often denies them the ability to defeat secessionist movements decisively.

Second, secessionist disputes are never "frozen conflicts" (Broers 2013: 70; Lynch 2002: 835). They are constantly evolving and changing. In some cases, entire generations of people have now grown into adulthood in secessionist-controlled territories and have no memory whatsoever of life under the parent state. Burmese secessionists who might have been more willing to negotiate with the previous democratic regime have now hardened their attitudes against the brutal repression of the current military dictatorship. Secessionists in places like Abkhazia, Northern Cyprus and Somaliland have now grown accustomed to changing their leaders via the ballot box. It is hard to imagine them ever agreeing to reunification with the parent state outside of a similarly democratic process. Many secessionist groups have developed internal legitimacy with the populations they claim to represent, and they have, in some cases, delivered reasonably good governance to those populations. As Klich (2021) puts it, "Those excluded entities outside the gates have proven to be much more resilient and persistent than initially predicted, and some have become key players in regional power balances, a fact acknowledged by major international club members." The internal growth, development and legitimacy of some secessionist movements and the governance they provide is a second reason parent states have trouble decisively defeating them.

Third, for parent states, preventing legitimization, or what Berg and Toomla (2009) term normalization, "is often a far greater challenge than preventing formal recognition" (Ker-Lindsay 2012: 175). Many third parties do not view secessionists with the same degree of animosity that their parent states view them, and they do not believe, sincerely or cynically, that isolating and sanctioning them is the most productive way forward. As Ker-Lindsay (2012: 175) explains, "Many countries, while opposing unilateral acts of secession and insisting that they will not recognize the territory in question, are willing to engage with the territory in a variety of ways that fall short of actual recognition." Greece, for example, has not recognized Kosovo because it has concerns about the precedent this could set for Northern Cyprus, but it generally maintains friendly relations with Kosovo and has extensive economic interactions with it. Ethiopia, similarly, has not recognized Somaliland but has partnered with it on the DP World deal expanding Berbera's port and developing the "Berbera corridor" to serve Ethiopia's import and export needs (Stepputat and Hagmann 2019). Ethiopian Airlines currently operates two roundtrip flights a day between Addis Ababa and Hargeisa. Taiwan's uncertain legal status did not prevent it from becoming the world's 17th-leading exporter and importer of world merchandise trade in 2019 (WTO 2020: 82) or the world's 12th-leading exporter and importer of world merchandise trade in 2019 if intra-EU trade is excluded (WTO 2020: 83). Taiwan was the world's ninth-largest exporter and importer of manufactured goods in 2019 (WTO 2020: 95). International oil companies have signed contracts with the Kurdistan Regional Government (KRG) in Iraq despite serious constitutional questions over whether the KRG can legally sign such contracts (Voller 2013). Just as parent states can extensively engage secessionists without recognizing them, so too can third parties. Many external actors including sovereign states, transnational corporations and non-governmental organizations are quite willing to engage secessionist regions without recognizing them, and this degree of acceptance makes it more difficult than it otherwise would be for parent states to defeat secessionists.

Finally, secession remains an attractive and inspiring goal that continues to motivate large numbers of people in all regions of the world. Sovereign states have been largely successful in denying secessionists recognition, but they have struggled in vain to extinguish their hopes and dreams. Secession must seem to parent states like a horror movie where no matter what you do to try to kill the monster, the monster keeps coming back to life. The United Kingdom (UK), for example, probably thought it had decisively defeated Scottish secessionism after Scots voted 55% to 45% to remain in the UK in September 2014. At a minimum, they thought the question of Scottish independence had been shelved for at least a generation. Yet, the UK's own decision in the "Brexit" referendum to leave the European Union in June 2016 against the wishes of its Scottish voters has now brought the question of Scotland's independence from the UK squarely back onto the agenda. Similarly, although the Iraqi Kurds badly miscalculated the vehement hostility of the international reaction to their independence referendum in September 2017, the desire for an independent Kurdish state remains keenly felt throughout the region (Palani et al. 2019). Secessionist sentiment waned to some extent with Burma's transition to democracy, but it has now reemerged strongly after the country's return to military dictatorship. The desire for independence and a state to call one's own remains a powerful motivating force, even if it has lain dormant for years or decades. Parent states have been much more successful at preventing recognition than they have been at preventing the desire to be recognized.

## Conclusion

Despite the widespread variation in secessionist movements, Griffiths (2021: 4) argues that

> at the strategic level, all contemporary secessionist movements are alike. Their settings may look different, but the strategic playing field is the same. All of them need to compel and persuade their home state and/or the international community to recognize them.

As this chapter has demonstrated, most parent states are able to resist the temptation to recognize their secessionist movements and allow them to leave consensually. Griffiths's first option is thus largely closed to most secessionists. That typically leaves them pursuing the second option of trying to appeal directly to the international community. Despite the significant increase in the number of UN member states since the end of the Cold War, the international normative environment remains strongly skewed against secession. When self-determination and territorial integrity come into conflict, territorial integrity almost always wins. This is the principal reason why parent states are usually successful in preventing recognition of their secessionist challengers.

Beyond the generally favorable normative environment, parent states typically choose to pursue various strategies of non-recognition at the global, regional and bilateral levels to further protect themselves against any possible loss of sovereign territory. Although all parent states and all secessionist movements maneuver on the same strategic playing field, "their tactics vary according to local conditions" (Griffiths 2021: 31). Parent state capabilities vary dramatically, and options available to powerful parent states might not even be contemplated by weaker ones. Parent states also have considerable flexibility in deciding how accommodative or engaging they want to be with their secessionist challengers or how confrontational and isolationist they wish to be with them. They often change their strategies over time in response to domestic, regional or international developments.

Whatever mix of strategies parent states choose to pursue, they are almost always successful at preventing recognition of secessionist movements without their prior consent or blessing. They are much less successful, though, at decisively defeating secessionist movements (Berg and Pegg 2020). This duality looks set to persist. The anarchic international system, secessionists' ability to deliver reasonably tolerable levels of governance and economic development to their populations, the willingness of external actors to engage secessionist movements without recognizing them and the continuing normative appeal of secession to marginalized peoples around the world make secession an extremely difficult enemy to defeat once and for all. Parent states can largely run the table on preventing recognition, but they struggle with limited success to deny secessionists some degree of normalization, legitimization or what Ker-Lindsay (2012: 16) terms "Taiwanization."

The analysis put forward in this chapter supports Fazal and Griffiths's (2014: 98) prediction that the combination of the increased tangible and material benefits of sovereign statehood, the continued normative consensus against unilateral secession and the international community's somewhat patchy or not entirely consistent emphasis on democratization means that "[s]ecessionism might become more peaceful, but also more persistent, populating an area of not-quite-international relations with a growing number of would-be states eager to work with and through international institutions." That might not be the best possible future one could imagine, but it is also far from the worst. It may also be the best we can hope for in this age of secession.

## Glossary

**De facto state**   a secessionist entity that controls territory, provides governance, secures popular legitimacy and persists over time, but whose desire for widespread recognition of its proclaimed sovereignty is entirely or significantly rejected by the international community. Examples include Abkhazia, Somaliland and Transnistria.

**Parent state**   the widely recognized sovereign state that a secessionist entity is trying to secede from. Examples include Spain (Catalonia) and the United Kingdom (Scotland).

**Patron state**   a widely recognized sovereign state that provides critical support to a secessionist movement. Examples include Armenia (Nagorno-Karabakh) and Turkey (Northern Cyprus).

## References

Berg, E. (2013). Merging together or drifting apart? Revisiting political legitimacy issues in Cyprus, Moldova, and Bosnia and Herzegovina. *Geopolitics*, 18(2), pp. 467–492.

Berg, E. and Pegg, S. (2020). Do parent state strategies matter in resolving secessionist conflicts with de facto states? In R. D. Griffiths and D. Muro, eds., *Strategies of Secession and Counter-Secession*. London: Rowman and Littlefield/ECPR Press, pp. 52–68.

Berg, E. and Toomla, R. (2009). Forms of normalization in the quest for de facto statehood. *The International Spectator*, 44(4), pp. 27–45.

Broers, L. (2013). Recognizing politics in unrecognized states: 20 years of enquiry into the *de facto* states of the South Caucasus. *Caucasus Survey*, 1(1), pp. 59–74.

Caspersen, N. (2012). *Unrecognized States: The Struggle for Sovereignty in the Modern International System*. Cambridge: Polity Press.

Crawford, J. (2007). *The Creation of States in International Law*. 2nd ed. Oxford: Oxford University Press.

Emerson, R. (1971). Self-determination. *American Journal of International Law*, 65(3), pp. 459–475.

Englebert, P. (2009). *Africa: Unity, Sovereignty, and Sorrow*. Boulder: Lynne Rienner Publishers.

Fabry, M. (2010). *Recognizing States: International Society and the Establishment of New States since 1776*. Oxford: Oxford University Press.

Fabry, M. (2012). The contemporary practice of state recognition: Kosovo, South Ossetia, Abkhazia, and their aftermath. *Nationalities Papers*, 40(5), pp. 661–676.

Fazal, T. M. and Griffiths, R. D. (2014). Membership has its privileges: The changing benefits of statehood. *International Studies Review*, 16(1), pp. 79–106.

Geldenhuys, D. (2009). *Contested States in World Politics*. New York: Palgrave Macmillan.

Griffiths, R. D. (2021). *Secession and the Sovereignty Game: Strategy and Tactics for Aspiring Nations*. Ithaca: Cornell University Press.

Herbst, J. (2000). *States and Power in Africa: Comparative Lessons in Authority and Control*. Princeton: Princeton University Press.

Hoch, T., Kopeček, V. and Baar, V. (2017). Civil society and conflict transformation in de facto states: The case of Abkhazia. *Problems of Post-Communism*, 64(6), pp. 329–341.

Ker-Lindsay, J. (2012). *The Foreign Policy of Counter-Secession: Preventing the Recognition of Contested States*. Oxford: Oxford University Press.

Ker-Lindsay, J. (2014). Understanding state responses to secession. *Peacebuilding*, 2(1), pp. 28–44.

Ker-Lindsay, J. (2015). Engagement without recognition: The limits of diplomatic interaction with contested states. *International Affairs*, 91(2), pp. 267–285.

Klich, S. (2021 forthcoming). *De Facto State Identity and International Legitimation*. London: Routledge.

Lynch, D. (2002). Separatist states and post-Soviet conflicts. *International Affairs*, 78(4), pp. 831–848.

Mueller, J. (2004). *The Remnants of War*. Ithaca: Cornell University Press.

Ó Beacháin, D., Comai, G. and Tsurtsumia-Zurabashvili, A. (2016). The secret lives of unrecognized states: Internal dynamics, external relations, and counter-recognition strategies. *Small Wars and Insurgencies*, 27(3), pp. 440–466.

Österud, Ö. (1997). The narrow gate: Entry to the club of sovereign states. *Review of International Studies*, 23(2), pp. 167–184.

Palani, K., Khidir, J., Dechesne, M. and Bakker, E. (2019). The development of Kurdistan's de facto statehood: Kurdistan's September 2017 referendum for independence. *Third World Quarterly*, 40(12), pp. 2270–2288.

Pegg, S. (1998/2019). *International Society and the De Facto State*. London: Routledge.

Riegl, M. and Doboš, B. (2018). Power and recognition: How (super)powers decide the international recognition process. *Politics & Policy*, 46(3), pp. 442–471.

Stepputat, F. and Hagmann, T. (2019). Politics of circulation: The makings of the Berbera corridor in Somali East Africa. *Environment and Planning D: Society and Space*, 37(5), pp. 794–813.

Voller, Y. (2013). Kurdish oil politics in Iraq: Contested sovereignty and unilateralism. *Middle East Policy*, 20(1), pp. 66–82.

Walter, B. F. (2006). Building reputation: Why governments fight some separatists but not others. *American Journal of Political Science*, 50(2), pp. 313–330.

World Trade Organization (WTO). (2020). *World Trade Statistical Review 2020*. Geneva: World Trade Organization.

31

# MANAGING SELF-DETERMINATION STRUGGLES THROUGH DECENTRALIZATION

*Andreas Juon and Kristin M. Bakke*

## Introduction

Among policymakers, decentralization has long been considered a measure for managing struggles over self-determination. An increasing number of states rely on decentralization – including federalism and regional autonomy arrangements – in attempts to reconcile minority demands for self-determination with concerns over territorial integrity (Brancati 2008; Cederman et al. 2015; Germann & Sambanis 2021; Keil & Anderson 2018; Wolff 2009). By dividing power between tiers of government, decentralization bears the promise of a compromise solution. Such intentions are apparent where decentralization is adopted in the aftermath of violent conflict. Iraq, for example, accepted far-ranging autonomy for Kurdistan to address Kurdish calls for self-determination. Similarly, Bosnia and Herzegovina has recognized Serb autonomy in the formerly separatist Republika Srpska. Far from isolated, these cases represent a widening pattern of decentralization as a means to meet self-determination demands – and prevent violent conflict.

A similar rationale has spurred moves towards decentralization in attempts to prevent violent conflict in the first place. Post-Franco Spain adopted a highly decentralized system to counter Basque and Catalan secessionism. In the 1990s, the United Kingdom erected devolved government structures to address calls for self-determination in Scotland. Meanwhile, Canada has used decentralization to defuse demands for Québec independence.

Yet, these cases illustrate not only that decentralization is frequently used to manage self-determination struggles, but also why its merits remain contested. In spite of their decentralized status, both Kurdistan and Catalonia held contested independence referenda in 2017 (Griffiths 2017). Having already organized one failed independence referendum in 2014, the Scottish Nationalist Party is now demanding another attempt. Bosnia has avoided civil war recurrence. Yet, Serb nationalist parties continue to agitate for secession. In sum, decentralization appears to be a double-edged sword: It may defuse tensions by awarding self-rule to minorities. Yet, there is no guarantee that empowered regional elites will not ask for more.

This chapter discusses the continuing debate on how decentralization affects secessionism. Its assessment builds on previous comprehensive reviews (e.g., Ghai 2000; Keil & Anderson 2018; McGarry & O'Leary 2005, 2011; Watts 1998). It complements these by providing updated evidence from the newest studies. In so doing, it highlights three of the most significant recent theoretical and methodological developments: (1) the endeavor to account for the difficult

DOI: 10.4324/9781003036593-36

circumstances in which decentralization is often adopted, and the increased attention given to (2) its societal context and (3) its specific institutional design. Together, it is argued, these developments hold the promise of transcending the still indeterminate 'pro and con' debate on how decentralization affects secessionism.

This chapter proceeds as follows. In the next section, the concept of decentralization is discussed, after which the contrary arguments on how it affects secessionism are considered. The aforementioned new theoretical developments are then discussed, followed by the chapter's conclusion.

## Concepts of decentralization

This chapter proceeds from a broad concept of decentralization. It is concerned with institutional arrangements that transfer at least minimal powers of self-rule to lower-tier territorial units (such as cantons, provinces, regions, and states) (Keil & Anderson 2018; McGarry & O'Leary 2005; Rodden 2004; Treisman 2007). Some scholars rely on a more restricted concept, sometimes used interchangeably with 'federalism' and focus on a smaller list of federal states that has remained largely unchanged since the Second World War (Elazar 1987; McGarry & O'Leary 2011) – though inclusion on this list varies based on definitional criteria. In contrast to federalism, which entails a formal division of power enshrined in a state's constitution and is often conceived as a binary concept (Rodden 2004), decentralization implies a spectrum, encompassing territorial autonomy arrangements of various scope and depth (Treisman 2007). A broader concept enables this chapter to consider the accelerating spread of decentralization to non-Western regions and many post-conflict cases (Hartzell & Hoddie 2008). Both usually stop short of formal federalism.

As defined at the beginning of the chapter, decentralization encompasses a wide spectrum of arrangements. Federations divide sovereign powers between tiers of government. In Riker's (1964: 11) classic definition:

> A constitution is federal if (1) two levels of government rule the same land and people, (2) each level has at least one area of action in which it is autonomous, and (3) there is some guarantee . . . of the autonomy of each government in its own sphere.

That is, the division of powers within federations is based on constitutional guarantees that cannot be unilaterally revoked by either side (Hechter 2000: 139; McGarry & O'Leary 2011; Rodden 2004; Watts 1998). Federations often combine self-rule with extensive shared rule, whereby the various levels pursue common ends while retaining their 'respective integrities' (Elazar 1987; cf. Watts 1998). While the precise list of federations varies between different scholars (Elazar 1987; McGarry & O'Leary 2011; Watts 1998), it is often seen as including the United States, Switzerland, Mexico, India, and Russia (Elazar 1987; McGarry & O'Leary 2011). A comparably shallower arrangement is devolution, whereby the central government awards limited decision-making autonomy to subnational governments, yet explicitly retains the right to unilaterally rescind autonomy, alter and override policies, or even to change internal boundaries (McGarry & O'Leary 2011). A prominent example of such arrangements are the devolved administrations in Scotland and Wales in the UK.

Decentralized arrangements can be symmetrical or asymmetrical. Asymmetrical arrangements mean that only some of the state's territorial units – states, regions, provinces – attain guarantees for autonomy. Examples include autonomous regions such as Karakalpakstan in Uzbekistan, Gorno-Badakhshan in Tajikistan, and the Caribbean Coast Autonomous Regions in Nicaragua (McGarry & O'Leary 2011). Asymmetric autonomy is often conceded in peace treaties, for example Kosovo's decentralized districts, the region of Bougainville in Papua New Guinea, and Aceh in Indonesia (Hartzell & Hoddie 2008; Wolff 2009). Finally, asymmetry may be the result of intergovernmental bargaining, even where all territorial units formally enjoy uniform rights. This is the situation in Canada, where Québec has taken advantage of more opportunities for self-governance than the other provinces (Basta 2018).

Decentralization can involve the transfer of different types of competencies (Bakke 2015; Falleti 2005; Hooghe et al. 2016; Keil & Anderson 2018; Rodden 2004; Treisman 2007).[1] First, *policy* autonomy refers to the authority of decentralized government tiers to independently formulate their own policies. This is maximized where their exclusive ability to craft policy is expansive (including, for example, cultural, welfare, and economic matters) and free from central government vetoes. Second, *fiscal* autonomy refers to devolved competencies or fiscal guarantees that enable decentralized government to finance its operations. This includes powers to set major taxes, keep income arising on its territory, and borrow on financial markets (Hooghe et al. 2016; Treisman 2007). Alternately, fiscal autonomy also refers to de-facto financial resources that become available to decentralized government as a result of these institutional arrangements (Rodden 2004; Treisman 2007). Third, *political* autonomy refers to whether decentralized executives and legislatures are independently chosen by the population within their territory (Hooghe et al. 2016; Wibbels 2005). These different competencies can coincide, but they do not have to.

Similar to previous reviews (Ghai 2000; McGarry & O'Leary 2005, 2011), this conceptualization excludes three related but distinct concepts. First, it excludes *personal autonomy*, where diversity is accommodated on an individual basis. Second, it excludes *corporate autonomy*, whereby competencies are devolved to specific ethnic groups. As secessionism often revolves around territorial homelands, both omissions make substantial sense. Third, arrangements of deconcentration and delegation are also excluded.[2] These territorially devolve competencies, but do not create separate subnational governments. Hence, they are less relevant to addressing self-determination struggles.

In sum, the concept of decentralization refers to diverse institutional arrangements with varied competencies. It is not a binary concept. As discussed in the section on recent research approaches, these differences are important for how decentralization affects secessionism. Not only may its different forms exert diverging effects, but these may also vary between different underpinning social and economic contexts. As such, increased attention to specific institutional arrangements helps reframe the overarching, but still indeterminate, debate on the pros and cons of decentralization, to which the next section turns.

## How decentralization affects secessionism

This section elaborates on the 'pro and con' debate. One sub-section each is dedicated to theoretical arguments and evidence in favor of *and* against the merits of decentralization as a tool for managing self-determination struggles.

### *Arguments in favor of decentralization*

There are three broad types of arguments in favor of decentralization as a tool of managing self-determination struggles. First and foremost, it alleviates minority groups' grievances. These arise when minorities perceive their political rights as unjustly violated by the central government (Cederman et al. 2015; Gurr 2000; Østby 2008; Petersen 2002). Decentralization addresses such concerns by giving minority groups 'the means – legal, political, and material – to protect and promote their cultural practices' (Gurr 2000: 165) – assuming that the minority groups are concentrated within subnational territorial units. Thereby, it helps minorities satisfy their culturally heterogeneous preferences, which often play a central role in motivating secessionism (Hechter 2000). Additionally, by decentralizing power to regional governments, it also provides minorities with a greater stake in government, encourages higher participation, and makes policy more congruent with their preferences (Brancati 2008; Cederman et al. 2015).[3] In this way, decentralization might avert calls for outright secession in the first place (Bächtiger & Steiner 2004; Brass 1974; Kohli 2004) and, in Bermeo's (2002) words, be 'peace preserving'.

A second argument in favor of decentralization centers on its potential to reassure minorities. This is especially relevant in (post-)conflict contexts. Such situations are often characterized by security dilemmas, whereby mobilized minorities fear future repression if they lay down arms (Fearon 1998; Lake & Rothchild 2005; Posen 1993; Weingast 1998). Decentralization points to a way out of this dilemma. It mitigates commitment problems by raising the costs for central government to renege on its promises (Hartzell & Hoddie 2008; Mattes & Savun 2009; Saideman et al. 2002; Walter 2009). Additionally, decentralization can make minority groups more confident that they will remain politically represented and that their vital concerns are protected (Cederman et al. 2015). For instance, a minority group could use 'its' region's decentralized institutions to 'check any efforts by their competitors to win full control of the apparatus of the state' (Hartzell & Hoddie 2008: 66). In this way, decentralization might help de-escalate ongoing and potentially violent secessionist conflicts.

A third argument in favor of decentralization highlights how it affects elite incentives for secessionist mobilization. Where decentralization is based on homogeneous units, it may accentuate intra-group differences, split self-determination movements, and create incentives for mobilization on intra-ethnic issues (Filippov et al. 2004; Ghai 2000; Horowitz 1985). Where decentralization splits a minority into multiple subunits, it may create incentives for between-subunit competition, while reducing between-group competition (Horowitz 1985). Additionally, decentralization may 'dilute' conflict by directing it at multiple subnational centers (ibid.; Cohen 1997; Saideman et al. 2002) – although possibly this means merely that conflict takes a different form (cf. Cunningham & Weidmann 2010). In the long term, by creating opportunities for local-level interactions, decentralization may also habituate political elites into dealing with each other at the subnational level (Hartzell & Hoddie 2008; Horowitz 1985). Especially where regional leaders are included in national-level institutions, this may encourage institutionalized bargaining and encourage compromise, rather than escalation (Filippov et al. 2004). In this way, decentralization might reduce elite incentives to mount bids for self-determination, direct them to politicize other issues, or at least discourage destabilizing forms of bargaining.

## *Evidence in favor of decentralization*

There is considerable evidence that decentralization may reduce minority groups' willingness to secede. In several prominent cases, including Canada, Switzerland (Bächtiger & Steiner 2004), and India (Brass 1974; Kohli 2004), decentralization has defused cultural issues and addressed grievances. Bermeo (2002) finds that federalism is consistently associated with less discrimination, grievances, and armed rebellion. Decentralization may also have defused secessionism in diverse and difficult contexts such as post-Franco Spain, Bosnia, and Nigeria (Ghai 2000; Hechter 2000; Horowitz 1985). Cross-national evidence indicates that it can, indeed, prevent both violent (Cederman et al. 2015) and nonviolent (Germann & Sambanis 2021) self-determination conflicts. For post-conflict environments in particular, Hartzell and Hoddie (2008) find that it is part of a package of mutually reinforcing security guarantees (cf. Mattes and Savun 2009; Walter 2002). Other studies offer cause for more limited optimism. In separate investigations, Cohen (1997), Hechter (2000), and Saideman and colleagues (2002) show that decentralization in the form of federalism is associated with fewer armed rebellions. However, they also find that it increases the frequency of low-level conflict. Using agent-based modeling, the results by Lustick and colleagues (2004) also indicate that decentralization decreases violent conflict but increases overall mobilization. Given evidence that violent secessionist movements may be less success-ful in attaining independence (Griffiths & Wasser 2019), these findings are less determinate as regards the overall effects of decentralization. However, they further underline arguments that decentralization may at least render self-determination struggles less violent.

## Arguments against decentralization

In spite of its demonstrated advantages, there are also counter arguments against the merits of decentralization for managing secessionism. First, decentralization can provide territorially con-centrated minority groups with increased capabilities, which they could exploit in secessionist bids. By awarding them autonomous institutions within 'their' regions, it increases the ability of minority elites to overcome coordination problems (Bunce 1999; Kymlicka 1998; Riker 1964; Roeder 1991; Snyder 2000). Where it awards them local media platforms and subnational security forces, it increases their relative capabilities vis-à-vis the central government (Brancati 2008; Cornell 2002). By demarcating specific territories, decentralization provides secessionists with ready-made 'proto-states' (Cornell 2002). By allowing minority elites to build experience in governing, decentralization may make independence more feasible (Brancati 2006; Roeder 1991). Finally, decentralization provides transnational kin states with a local collaborator on the ground (Bunce 2007; Cornell 2002). In sum, according to this first argument, decentraliza-tion makes secession easier should minorities desire it (Chapman & Roeder 2007; McGarry & O'Leary 2005, 2009; Rothchild & Roeder 2005; Snyder 2000). Hence, it may be a slippery slope and represent only an intermediate step on the way to secession (Bunce 2007; Bunce & Watts 2005; Cornell 2002; Kymlicka 1998; Lake & Rothchild 2005). Accommodated groups may settle for decentralization in the short term but renege in the long term. Once the insti-tutional resources provided by decentralization are consolidated, they might exploit these to mount a renewed secessionist challenge in the future.

A second, and more contested, point made by the critics of decentralization is that it may also increase the *willingness* of minorities to secede. In one variant of this argument, when minorities realize they are able to successfully manage their own affairs, demands for independence may grow (Kymlicka 1998). In another variant, decentralization is argued to reinforce inter-ethnic differences (Bunce 1999; Christin & Hug 2012; Roeder 1991; Snyder 2000), prevent the for-mation of a 'unity feeling' (Elkins & Sides 2007), and encourage ethnocentric behavior. This effect may be compounded where decentralization allows minorities to pass legislation that actively promotes their customs – the very steps that may alleviate minority grievances with respect to protecting their culture – and thereby further reinforce subnational identities (Bunce 1999; Roeder 1991).

Third, decentralization may privilege access to political power for radical political elites. These may demand ever deeper decentralization or outright secession (Brancati 2006). Decen-tralization may also focus the policy agenda on segmental issues and encourage the perception of politics as a zero-sum game between different ethnic groups (Roeder 2007). Thereby, it may create incentives for governing minority elites to mobilize on an ethnic basis. For minority elites outside of government control, it may encourage participation in destabilizing outbidding processes (Roeder 2007), which may lead even moderate leaders to make extreme demands and pull extremists into politics.

## Evidence against decentralization

The critics of decentralization point to a number of cases where it failed to inhibit secessionism. A frequently discussed set of cases are the former socialist federations. Numerous studies argue that the USSR's decision in the 1920s to opt for a decentralized state structure entailed grave, unintended consequences decades later. Whereas nationalist movements were initially subdued by Communist party hegemony, they emerged as powerful actors during the 1980s, as central state strength waned, and successfully exploited existing decentralized structures for their self-determination struggles (Beissinger 2002; Bunce 1999; Cornell 2002; Roeder 1991).

Some scholars allege that regional autonomy in the USSR not only provided minority groups with increased capabilities, but also increased their willingness to secede. Roeder (1991: 204) argues that Soviet ethnofederalism 'perpetuated or strengthened ethnic differences' and thereby laid the foundation for subsequent self-determination movements. Similarly, Suny (1993: 126) argues that the USSR's system 'fostered the development of conscious, secular, politically mobilizable nationalities'. A key piece of evidence that is in line with such a mechanism is that the earliest secessionist mobilization occurred among the USSR's most affluent groups whose cohesion was increased by decentralized institutions (Beissinger 2002; Roeder 1991, 2007).

While the relationship between decentralization and secessionism in the former socialist federations, such as the USSR, is strong at the surface, several points of contention remain. A first is the issue of reverse causality. Rather than causing secessionism, decentralization might have been adopted *in response* to pre-existing secessionist threats. Indeed, as prominently argued, had the Soviet leadership around Lenin opted for a unitary system instead, the USSR might have collapsed earlier (McGarry & O'Leary 2005, 2009). In response, however, some critics of decentralization argue that the USSR's decentralization was mostly unrelated to actual minority demands and frequently happened top-down at 'Stalin's whim' (Cornell 2002).

A second concern is whether the former socialist federations hold external validity for other decentralization efforts. Many scholars argue that they were 'sham' federations that did not entail real autonomy for minorities amid Communist Party hegemony (McGarry & O'Leary 2005). They further hold that the most violent secessionism in the region originated from the *absence* of real autonomy, compounded by the lack of ethnic homogeneity in many autonomous regions (Ghai 2000; McGarry & O'Leary 2005, 2009). Additionally, the USSR's homeland ethnofederalism is very rarely used (Anderson 2016), and evidence from these cases may hence not be applicable to other contexts.

Critiques of decentralization also point to the frequent breakdown of other decentralized states as evidence against its merits. These include Ethiopia (where Eritrea broke away in 1991), Pakistan (Bangladesh broke away in 1971), Malaysia (Singapore broke away in 1965), and Serbia and Montenegro (Montenegro broke away in 2006) (Lake & Rothchild 2005). A cross-regional comparative analysis of 13 post-socialist states by Bunce and Watts (2005) indicates that majority–minority conflict was more likely in states that inherited extensive federal or autonomy arrangements, such as Azerbaijan, Georgia, Russia, and Yugoslavia. In a within-case analysis, Cornell (2002) concludes that separatism in the South Caucasus emerged only in autonomous areas. Studying ethnic mobilization in Russia since the 1990s, Treisman (1997) finds that the most autonomous ethno-regions were emboldened by their powers to engage in secessionism and seek further concessions.

These case-based observations are complemented by some cross-regional studies that reach less optimistic results than those cited in the previous sub-section. Several studies find no coherent effects of decentralization, at least in the form of federalism, on ethnic conflict, including secessionism (Pospieszna & Schneider 2013; Selway & Templeman 2012). Others find that decentralization may fuel secessionist conflict, especially if coupled with inter-regional inequalities (Deiwiks et al. 2012) or if a large number of units is controlled by minorities (Christin & Hug 2012). Finally, there is some evidence that federalism may have negative effects on state cohesion, as given by minority attachment to the state (Elkins & Sides 2007).

As this section shows, there are strong arguments and evidence on either side in this 'pro and con' debate. The next section turns to approaches that bear the promise of overcoming this indeterminacy.

## Recent research approaches

In this section, three recent research approaches are reviewed that promise to overcome the indeterminacy of the 'pro and con' debate. These highlight (1) the difficult circumstances in which decentralization is often adopted, and its variable effects, depending on (2) the societal context in which it is embedded and (3) on its specific institutional design.

### *Accounting for the origins of decentralization*

A first set of studies advances the debate on how decentralization affects self-determination struggles by explicitly addressing the conditions under which it is adopted in the first place. Considering this first step is important, as it may critically affect subsequent self-determination struggles. The starting point for such arguments is that decentralization is the outcome of a bargaining process between subnational minority groups and the central government of their resident state (Cetinyan 2002; Jenne 2007). A key assumption is that the preferences of these actors diverge: minority groups prefer greater autonomy, whereas central governments prefer less. This means that, at the equilibrium, a minority group's attained decentralization is influenced by its relative capabilities, which shape the pressure it can exert on the central government.

This bargaining logic helps clarify the risks of ignoring the origins of decentralization, even when researchers focus on its subsequent effects (Sambanis & Milanovic 2014; but see Brancati 2006; Bunce & Watts 2005). First, weak and ethnically heterogeneous states disproportionately often concede decentralization in the first place. Yet, the same characteristics – state weakness and heterogeneity – make these states especially prone to secessionism. Second, decentralization may also work less well in such difficult contexts (McGarry & O'Leary 2005, 2011). Third, within these states, large, culturally dissimilar, and mobilized minorities are most likely to attain decentralized status (McGarry & O'Leary 2005, 2011). Yet precisely the same types of groups are the ones most likely to give rise to secessionist movements as well (Bunce 2007; Deiwiks et al. 2012; Dikshit 1975; Watts 1998). Hence, any correlation between decentralization and secessionism might arise from ignoring such state- and group-level selection effects.

Recent research has explored several options to address this endogeneity problem. A first is to try to control for the severity of 'baseline' secessionist risks. The increasing availability of fine-grained measures of decentralization makes such approaches more feasible (cf. Hooghe et al. 2016). However, accounting for all factors that might influence a minority's bargaining power is difficult, and existing approaches yield highly diverging findings (Anderson 2016). A second option are comparisons within a world region that hold constant a range of such confounding factors. This is the approach that many aforementioned studies of the former socialist states have taken (cf. Bunce & Watts 2005). Yet, while these findings may offer greater internal validity, they suffer in terms of external validity.

A third option are instrumental variable approaches. Intuitively, these attempt to ignore variation in decentralization that is caused by factors that also affect secessionism. In one pioneering study, Brancati (2006) relies on UK colonial legacies, a country's physical size, and the presence of non-contiguous territories to instrument for decentralization in a given country. These characteristics influence a country's decentralization levels but might not directly affect whether it sees future secessionism. More recently, Cederman and colleagues (2015) instrument for decentralization at the group level. Focusing on sub-Saharan Africa and Southeast Asia, they find that large groups in former British colonies are more likely to 'inherit' autonomy, whereas no similar pattern exists for former French colonies. Exploiting this variation, they find a pacifying effect of decentralization. In spite of these advances, and as pointed out by Sambanis and Milanovic (2014), coming up with an instrument that convincingly meets the exclusion restriction is extremely difficult.

In sum, much progress has been made to address the origins of decentralization in cross-national studies. In spite of the remaining challenges, it is already a contribution 'simply' to draw attention to this endogenous relationship. Future research in this vein promises to yield more robust findings on how decentralization affects secessionism in 'the average case' and, thereby, weigh in on the 'pro and con' debate.

## Societal context

Rather than focusing on its 'average' effects, a second option is to change the question from *whether* decentralization works to manage self-determination struggles to the *conditions under which* it does (Bakke 2015; Bakke & Wibbels 2006; Brancati 2006; Cederman et al. 2015; Christin & Hug 2012; Hale 2004; Sambanis & Milanovic 2014; Siroky & Cuffe 2015). The key intuition in these approaches is that the same decentralized arrangements may produce different results in different contexts. Three types of factors have received particular attention: first, societal structure; second, the form of intergovernmental bargaining; and third, the temporal context under which decentralization is adopted.

A key societal factor that moderates the effect of decentralization is a country's degree of ethnic heterogeneity. There are different arguments here. On the one hand, decentralization is often adopted to address the challenges posed by diversity. Yet, it may work less well in the most diverse contexts. This might apply to states that lack a clearly dominant 'Staatsvolk' (McGarry & O'Leary 2005, 2011), where minorities lack nested identities (Dikshit 1975; Ghai 2000; McGarry & O'Leary 2011; Lake & Rothchild 2005), or where there is no antecedent sense of nationhood (Ahuja & Varshney 2005). In such cases, majority groups may be less willing and able to peacefully deal with challenges from below (Bunce 2007; Lake & Rothchild 2005). Where this situation is not mitigated by integrative civic networks (Varshney 2002), the resulting distrust may complicate compromises and encourage destabilizing bargaining. At the local level, ethnic heterogeneity might further be associated with low support for decentralization by internal minorities and discrimination against them, and thereby similarly be prone to renewed tensions (Cunningham & Weidmann 2010). On the other hand, in the absence of ethnic diversity, the redistributive debate that is bound to emerge from any decentralized arrangement may be a cause of intergovernmental conflict in its own right and not be a price worth paying (cf. Rodden 2002; Wibbels 2005). In ethnically heterogeneous countries, the benefit of decentralization may outweigh such distributional concerns, but in ethnically homogenous countries, it may not (Bakke 2015). Though there is no consensus yet on how ethnicity mitigates the effects that decentralized institutions' effect on the likelihood of secessionist conflict, there is a growing consensus that it does.

Another prominently discussed structural factor is the spatial distribution of economic inequalities. A long literature has stressed that the combination of decentralization with inter-regional inequalities may stoke secessionist sentiment. Several studies show that regional inequalities may contribute to the emergence of nationalism (Gourevitch 1979), as citizens in both rich and poor regions develop grievances over the distribution of resources (Horowitz 1985). One cross-national study finds that decentralization coupled with regional inequalities indeed fuels secessionism (Deiwiks et al. 2012). Important here is that different societal contexts will condition specific institutional effects. As Bakke (2015) shows, fiscal autonomy specifically may foster grievances among comparably poor groups, who then lack the financial resources to handle their increased competencies (cf. Bakke & Wibbels 2006). In contrast, the very same institutional arrangement may help stem grievances among wealthier groups, who have the fiscal means to exercise self-rule.

A second set of studies focus on how the incentives of national and regional leaders shape intergovernmental bargaining. A key factor is the presence of regionalist parties before decentralization is instituted. In such cases, regionalist parties may capture decentralized government tiers (Brancati 2006, 2008). In turn, they may also use access to regional government to deepen cleavages and advocate policies that harm other regions. Such processes may be particularly pronounced amid democratic transitions where regional elections precede national ones (Bunce 2007; Linz & Stepan 1992). Recognized by Riker already in 1964, a number of studies in the federalism literature see political parties as central to integrating tiers of government (e.g. Rodden & Wibbels 2002; Filippov et al. 2004; Bednar 2009). Drawing on this literature, Bakke (2015) shows that co-partisanship between regional and central governments may critically moderate how decentralization affects secessionism in a given region. In particular, ties between regional and central party leaders may prevent at least the violent escalation of self-determination conflicts.

A third moderating aspect that has received increasing attention is the embeddedness of decentralization in specific temporal sequences. One factor is whether secessionist conflict has already escalated into violence when decentralization is adopted. In such cases, minorities may hold lower trust and render decentralization less stable (McGarry & O'Leary 2011). Prior violence may also contribute to polarization and leave behind an infrastructural legacy conducive to conflict recurrence – it may be too little, too late (Cederman et al. 2015). In these difficult circumstances, combining decentralization with power-sharing at the center may help alleviate minority concerns (ibid.; McGarry & O'Leary 2005, 2011; Wolff 2009). A related factor is changes in decentralization levels over time (Germann & Sambanis 2021; Siroky & Cuffe 2015). Where minorities have become used to significant autonomy, its withdrawal may spark or escalate self-determination struggles. Finally, the sequencing whereby specific competencies are decentralized may also shape relations between the subnational and central government in a path-dependent way (Falleti 2005). This might similarly moderate the trajectory of self-determination movements as well.

In sum, while there is no broad consensus on any particular factor, these studies advance the understanding of how the effects of decentralization might be moderated by its societal context, thereby moving away from the either/or nature of the long-dominant 'pro and con' debate. Perhaps most importantly, they outline the specific structural, actor-related, and temporal conditions under which decentralization might be more, or less, fruitfully used to manage secessionism.

## *The institutional design of decentralization*

A third approach is concerned with underlying institutional design – and refrains from conceptualizing (and operationalizing) decentralization as a binary. Existing research has focused on three aspects of institutional design: the number and size of decentralized units, their boundaries, and their competencies.

First, a long-standing literature has highlighted that decentralized arrangements with a low number of units, for instance bi-regional federations, are more likely to break down (Watts 1998). Such a bifurcated state structure might entail political polarization (Dikshit 1975). For example, this may have encouraged secessionist sentiment in the Nigerian first Republic, that was composed of three ethnonational regions (Ghai 2000). Other scholars highlight the destabilizing potential if there is one oversized decentralized entity. For example, this applied to several cases affected by secessionism, including Pakistan, Nigeria in the 1960s, Yugoslavia, the USSR, and Czechoslovakia (Dikshit 1975; Hale 2004). In such constellations, the large unit is powerful enough to 'vie in strength with many or all of the others combined'. For example, it is capable to blackmail the central government and possibly restore domination over minority-dominated areas (cf. Filippov et al. 2004). In turn, this might reduce minorities' trust in the stability of the decentralized system and enhance their motivation to secede (Dikshit 1975: 239). Consistent with such arguments, Hale (2004) finds that ethnofederations with one core region were far more likely to break down than those arrangements without such a core. However, proposals to abolish dominant core regions, such as Pakistan's large Punjab province, are often controversial, and their implementation might entail new inter-ethnic tensions (Adeney 2012).

A second design factor are decentralized units' territorial boundaries and their relation to ethnic settlement patterns. One aspect is whether decentralized entities are ethnically homogeneous. On the one hand, the grievance-alleviating effect of decentralization whereby decentralization dissuades secessionist sentiment, for example by addressing minorities' cultural preferences, depends on at least moderate homogeneity of units (Bakke 2015; Elkins & Sides 2007). On the other hand, homogeneous units are also associated with the alleged identity-hardening effect of decentralization (Christin & Hug 2012; Horowitz 1985; Roeder 2009) – although studies have also suggested that homogeneous units may accentuate subethnic divisions where groups possess multiple intra-ethnic cleavages (Horowitz 1985; cf. Ahuja & Varshney 2005; Chandra 2005). A related aspect is a minority group's degree of fragmentation across decentralized units. Subdividing groups across multiple units may decrease secessionist mobilization, especially where a group has little or no internal divisions, as was the case with the Hausa settling in Nigeria's northern region (Horowitz 1985; cf. Filippov et al. 2004). Yet a problem with such proposals is the feasibility of establishing them. Only few decentralized states exist where the boundaries of the subnational units were consciously redrawn to split up groups internally, often due to fierce resistance (Anderson 2016) and fears of ensuing communal tensions (Adeney 2012). In spite of these concerns, more systematic attention to the territorial boundaries underlying decentralization attempts seems desirable, starting with detailed data on the composition of federal units (Christin & Hug 2012; Cunningham & Weidmann 2010).

A third design factor refers to the specific competencies of decentralized units. Most fundamentally, the effects of various competencies may differ in how they affect conflict. For instance, many ethnically based secessionist movements are culturally defined, and in such cases, cultural autonomy may be more important than other aspects, although it might not be equally important in all self-determination struggles (Bakke 2015). Even variation within a specific type of competencies may have far-reaching consequences. For example, as the political economy literature highlights for intergovernmental cooperation on economic reforms, fiscal decentralization based on transfers may create incentives for distributional struggles between regions. Conversely, it may enable reform and yield better relations between government tiers where it awards taxing autonomy instead (Rodden 2002; Wibbels 2005). Finally, awarding asymmetric competencies to a single unit may affect overall stability, as it might entail backlashes – both from the state's dominant group, such as the English speakers in Canada (Basta 2018; Ghai 2000; Kymlicka 1998) and from minority groups in other units that desire similar powers (Cunningham &

Weidmann 2010). For instance, the formally privileged status of Kashmir in India has led to widespread resentment among other states (Ghai 2000). There are numerous other competency aspects to consider, but the key point here is that the debate about decentralization's effect on secessionism is meaningful only if it is about the specifics of the institutional design.

In sum, while there is no consensus around a particular institutional design of decentralization, there is growing agreement that this matters greatly for how it affects secessionism. By highlighting these crucial differences, and spawning comparative work along these lines, future research in this approach has the potential of further advancing the debate on how decentralization affects secessionism.

## Conclusion

This chapter has provided an updated discussion of recent research on decentralization and secessionism. It has revisited the still indeterminate debate on the merits of managing secessionism through decentralization. Based on this, it has highlighted three recent research approaches that offer the potential of transcending this debate. First, there is increasing attention to the origins of decentralization. This enables conceiving of decentralization as a bargaining outcome and directs attention to the difficult context under which it is often adopted in the first place. Thereby, such approaches entail the opportunity of attaining more robust relationships between decentralization and secessionism for the 'average case'. Second, recent work highlights the critical role of societal context – such as ethnic heterogeneity, economic inequality, the form of intergovernmental bargaining, and preceding conflict – which moderates how decentralization affects secessionism. Third, scholars increasingly theorize and investigate the institutional design of decentralization – including the number of territorial units, their boundaries, and their concrete competencies. These approaches hold the potential of going beyond the 'pro and con' debate altogether. Instead, they direct attention to how decentralization interacts with the societies it governs and the differences between its various institutional subtypes.

## Notes

1  A fourth type, given by Treisman (2007), is constitutional decentralization, which refers to the degree to which subnational governments can veto the decision by the superordinate government. Often, this is seen as part of the shared-rule dimension of decentralization, which is discussed later in this chapter regarding the institutional specifics of decentralization.
2  See www1.worldbank.org/publicsector/decentralization/admin.htm (accessed: 19.4.2021).
3  Both arguments draw on the classic fiscal federalism literature (Tiebout, 1956; Oates, 1972).

## References

Adeney K. (2012). A Step Towards Inclusive Federalism in Pakistan? The Politics of the 18th Amendment. *Publius: The Journal of Federalism* 42(4), pp. 539–565.

Ahuja A and Varshney A. (2005). Antecedent Nationhood, Subsequent Statehood: Explaining the Relative Success of Indian Federalism. In: Roeder PG and Rothchild (eds) *Sustainable Peace: Power and Democracy after Civil Wars*. Ithaca, London: Cornell University Press, pp. 241–264.

Anderson L. (2016). Ethnofederalism and the Management of Ethnic Conflict: Assessing the Alternatives. *Publius: The Journal of Federalism* 46(1), pp. 1–24.

Bächtiger A and Steiner J. (2004). Switzerland: Territorial Cleavage Management as Paragon and Paradox. In: Amoretti UM and Bermeo NG (eds) *Federalism and Territorial Cleavages*. Baltimore, MD: Johns Hopkins University Press, pp. 27–54.

Bakke KM. (2015). *Decentralization and Intrastate Struggles: Chechnya, Punjab, and Québec*. Cambridge: Cambridge University Press.

Bakke KM and Wibbels E. (2006). Diversity, Disparity, and Civil Conflict in Federal States. *World Politics* 59(1), pp. 1–50.

Basta K. (2018). The State between Minority and Majority Nationalism: Decentralization, Symbolic Recognition, and Secessionist Crises in Spain and Canada. *Publius: The Journal of Federalism* 48(1), pp. 51–75.

Bednar J. (2009). *The Robust Federation.* Cambridge: Cambridge University Press.

Beissinger MR. (2002). *Nationalist Mobilization and the Collapse of the Soviet State.* Cambridge; New York: Cambridge University Press.

Bermeo NG. (2002). The Import of Institutions. *Journal of Democracy* 13(2), pp. 96–110.

Brancati D. (2006). Decentralization: Fueling the Fire or Dampening the Flames of Ethnic Conflict and Secessionism? *International Organization* 60(3), pp. 651–685.

Brancati D. (2008). *Peace by Design.* Oxford: Oxford University Press.

Brass P. (1974). *Language, Religion and Politics in North India.* New York, London: Cambridge University Press.

Bunce V. (1999). *Subversive Institutions: The Design and the Destruction of Socialism and the State.* Cambridge studies in comparative politics. Cambridge, UK ; New York: Cambridge University Press.

Bunce V. (2007). *Minority Politics in Ethnofederal States: Cooperation, Autonomy or Secession?* Einaudi Center for International Studies Working Paper Series 08–07. Cornell University.

Bunce V and Watts S. (2005). Managing diversity and sustaining democracy in the postcommunist world. In: Roeder PG and Rothchild (eds) *Sustainable Peace: Power and Democracy after Civil Wars.* Ithaca, London: Cornell University Press, pp. 133–158.

Cederman L-E, Hug S, Schädel A, et al. (2015). Territorial Autonomy in the Shadow of Conflict: Too Little, Too Late? *American Political Science Review* 109(2), pp. 354–370.

Cetinyan R. (2002). Ethnic Bargaining in the Shadow of Third-Party Intervention. *International Organization* 56(3), pp. 645–677.

Chandra K. (2005). Ethnic parties and democratic stability. *Perspectives on Politics* 3(2), pp. 235–252.

Chapman T and Roeder PG. (2007). Partition as a Solution to Wars of Nationalism: The Importance of Institutions. *American Political Science Review* 101(4), pp. 677–691.

Christin T and Hug S. (2012). Federalism, the Geographic Location of Groups, and Conflict. *Conflict Management and Peace Science* 29(1), pp. 93–122.

Cohen FS. (1997). Proportional versus majoritarian ethnic conflict management in democracies. *Comparative Political Studies* 30(5), pp. 607–630.

Cornell SE. (2002). Autonomy as a Source of Conflict: Caucasian Conflicts in Theoretical Perspective. *World Politics* 54(2), pp. 245–276.

Cunningham KG and Weidmann NB. (2010). Shared Space: Ethnic Groups, State Accommodation, and Localized Conflict1: Ethnic Groups, State Accommodation, and Localized Conflict. *International Studies Quarterly* 54(4), pp. 1035–1054.

Deiwiks C, Cederman L-E and Gleditsch KS. (2012). Inequality and conflict in federations. *Journal of Peace Research* 49(2), pp. 289–304.

Dikshit RD. (1975). *The Political Geography of Federalism: An Inquiry into Origins and Stability.* Delhi, Bombay, Calcutta, Madras: The Macmillan Company of India Limited.

Elazar DJ. (1987). *Exploring Federalism.* Alabama: University of Alabama Press.

Elkins Z and Sides J. (2007). Can institutions build unity in multiethnic states? *American Political Science Review* 101(4), pp. 693–708.

Falleti TG. (2005). A Sequential Theory of Decentralization: Latin American Cases in Comparative Perspective. *American Political Science Review* 99(3), pp. 327–346.

Fearon JD. (1998). Commitment Problems and the Spread of Ethnic Conflict. In: Lake DA and Rothchild D (eds) *The International Spread of Ethnic Conflict: Fear, Diffusion, and Escalation.* Princeton, NJ: Princeton University Press, pp. 107–126.

Filippov M, Ordeshook PC and Shvetsova O. (2004). *Designing Federalism: A Theory of Self-Sustainable Federal Institutions.* New York: Cambridge University Press.

Germann M and Sambanis N. (2021). Political Exclusion, Lost Autonomy, and Escalating Conflict over Self-Determination. *International Organization* 75(1), pp. 178–203.

Ghai Y. (2000). Autonomy as a Strategy for Diffusing Conflict. In: Stern PC and Druckman D (eds) *International Conflict Resolution After the Cold War.* Washington, DC: National Academies Press, pp. 483–530.

Gourevitch PA. (1979). The Reemergence of "Peripheral Nationalisms": Some Comparative Speculations on the Spatial Distribution of Political Leadership and Economic Growth. *Comparative Studies in Society and History* 21(3), pp. 303–322.

Griffiths RD. (2017). Kurdistan and Catalonia Are Voting on Independence. Welcome to the Age of Secession. *Washington Post*, 23 September.

Griffiths RD and Wasser LM. (2019). Does Violent Secessionism Work? *Journal of Conflict Resolution* 63(5), pp. 1310–1336.

Gurr TR. (2000). *Peoples Versus States: Minorities at Risk in the New Century*. Washington, DC: US Institute of Peace Press.

Hale HE. (2004) Divided We Stand: Institutional Sources of Ethnofederal State Survival and Collapse. *World Politics* 56(2), pp. 165–193.

Hartzell C and Hoddie M. (2008). *Crafting Peace: Power-Sharing Institutions and the Negotiated Settlement of Civil Wars*. University Park: Penn State University Press.

Hechter M. (2000). *Containing Nationalism*. Oxford, England; New York: Oxford University Press.

Hooghe L, Marks G, Schakel AH, et al. (2016). *Measuring Regional Authority: A Postfunctionalist Theory of Governance, Volume I*. Oxford: Oxford University Press.

Horowitz DL. (1985). *Ethnic Groups in Conflict*. Berkeley, Los Angeles, London: University of California Press.

Jenne EK. (2007). *Ethnic Bargaining: The Paradox of Minority Empowerment*. Ithaca: Cornell University Press.

Keil S and Anderson P. (2018). Decentralization as a tool for conflict resolution. In: Detterbeck K and Hepburn E (eds) *Handbook of Territorial Politics*. Cheltenham: Edward Elgar Publishing, pp. 89–104.

Kohli A. (2004). India: Federalism and the Accommodation of Ethnic Nationalism. In: Amoretti UM and Bermeo NG (eds) *Federalism and Territorial Cleavages*. Baltimore, MD: Johns Hopkins University Press, pp. 281–300.

Kymlicka W. (1998). Is Federalism a Viable Alternative to Secession? In: Lehning PB (ed) *Theories of Secession*. European Political Science Series. London; New York: Routledge, pp. 109–148.

Lake DA and Rothchild D. (2005). Territorial Decentralization and Civil War Settlements. In: Roeder PG and Rothchild D (eds) *Sustainable Peace: Power and Democracy after Civil Wars*. Ithaca, London: Cornell University Press, pp. 109–132.

Linz JJ and Stepan A. (1992). Political Identities and Electoral Sequences: Spain, the Soviet Union, and Yugoslavia. *Daedalus* 121(2), pp. 123–139.

Lustick IS, Miodownik D and Eidelson RJ. (2004). Secessionism in Multicultural States: Does Sharing Power Prevent or Encourage It? *American Political Science Review* 98(2), pp. 209–229.

Mattes M and Savun B. (2009). Fostering Peace after Civil War: Commitment Problems and Agreement Design. *International Studies Quarterly* 53(3), pp. 737–759.

McGarry J and O'Leary B. (2005). Federation as a Method of Ethnic Conflict Regulation. In: Noel S (ed) *From Power Sharing to Democracy. Post-Conflict Institutions in Ethnically Divided Societies*. Montreal & Kingston, London, Ithaca: McGill-Queen's University Press, pp. 263–296.

McGarry J and O'Leary B. (2009). Must Pluri-national Federations Fail? *Ethnopolitics* 8(1), pp. 5–25.

McGarry J and O'Leary B. (2011). Territorial Approaches to Ethnic Conflict Settlement. In: Cordell K and Wolff S (eds) *Routledge Handbook of Ethnic Conflict*. Routledge handbooks. London: Routledge, pp. 249–265.

Oates WE. (1972). *Fiscal Federalism*. New York: Harcourt Brace Jovanovich.

Østby G. (2008). Polarization, Horizontal Inequalities and Violent Civil Conflict. *Journal of Peace Research* 45(2), pp. 143–162.

Petersen RD. (2002). *Understanding Ethnic Violence: Fear, Hatred, and Resentment in Twentieth-Century Eastern Europe*. Cambridge: Cambridge University Press.

Posen BR. (1993). The Security Dilemma and Ethnic Conflict. *Survival* 35(1), pp. 27–47.

Pospieszna P and Schneider G. (2013). The Illusion of "Peace Through Power-Sharing": Constitutional Choice in the Shadow of Civil War. *Civil Wars* 15(sup1), pp. 44–70.

Riker WH. (1964). *Federalism: Origin, Operation, Significance*. Boston: Little, Brown and Company.

Rodden J. (2002). The Dilemma of Fiscal Federalism: Grants and Fiscal Performance around the World. *American Journal of Political Science* 46(3), p. 670.

Rodden J. (2004.) Comparative Federalism and Decentralization: On Meaning and Measurement. *Comparative Politics* 36(4), p. 481.

Rodden J and Wibbels W. (2002). Beyond the Fiction of Federalism: Macroeconomic Management in Multitiered Systems. *World Politics* 54(4), pp. 494–531.

Roeder PG. (1991). Soviet Federalism and Ethnic Mobilization. *World Politics* 43(2), pp. 196–232.

Roeder PG. (2007). *Where Nation-States Come from: Institutional Change in the Age of Nationalism*. Princeton, NJ: Princeton University Press.

Roeder PG. (2009). Ethnofederalism and the Mismanagement of Conflicting Nationalisms. *Regional & Federal Studies* 19(2), pp. 203–219.

Rothchild D and Roeder PG. (2005). Dilemmas of State-Building in Divided Societies. In: Roeder PG and Rothchild (eds) *Sustainable Peace: Power and Democracy after Civil Wars*. Ithaca, London: Cornell University Press, pp. 1–26.

Saideman SM, Lanoue DJ, Campenni M, et al. (2002). Democratization, Political Institutions, and Ethnic Conflict: A Pooled Time-Series Analysis, 1985–1998. *Comparative Political Studies* 35(1), pp. 103–129.

Sambanis N and Milanovic B. (2014). Explaining Regional Autonomy Differences in Decentralized Countries. *Comparative Political Studies* 47(13), pp. 1830–1855.

Selway J and Templeman K. (2012). The Myth of Consociationalism? Conflict Reduction in Divided Societies. *Comparative Political Studies* 45(12), pp. 1542–1571.

Siroky DS and Cuffe J. (2015). Lost autonomy, nationalism and separatism. *Comparative Political Studies* 48(1), pp. 3–34.

Snyder J. (2000). *From Voting to Violence: Democratization and Nationalist Conflict*. New York, London: W.W. Norton & Company.

Suny RG. (1993). *The Revenge of the Past*. Stanford: Stanford University Press.

Tiebout CM. (1956). A Pure Theory of Local Expenditures. *Journal of Political Economy* 64(5), pp. 416–424.

Treisman D. (2007). *The Architecture of Government. Rethinking Political Decentralization*. New York: Cambridge University Press.

Treisman DS. (1997). Russia's "Ethnic Revival": The Separatist Activism of Regional Leaders in a Post-communist Order. *World Politics* 49(2), 212–249.

Varshney A. (2002). *Ethnic Conflict and Civic Life: Hindus and Muslims in India*. New Haven, CT: Yale University Press.

Walter BF. (2002). *Committing to Peace: The Successful Settlement of Civil Wars*. Princeton, NJ: Princeton University Press.

Walter BF. (2009). *Reputation and Civil War: Why Separatist Conflicts Are So Violent*. Cambridge, UK; New York: Cambridge University Press.

Watts RL. (1998). Federalism, Federal Political Systems, and Federations. *Annual Review of Political Science* 1(1), pp. 117–137.

Weingast BR. (1998). Political Institutions: Rational Choice Perspectives. In: Goodin RE and Klingemann H-D (eds) *A New Handbook of Political Science*. Oxford: Oxford University Press, pp. 167–190.

Wibbels E. (2005). *Federalism and the Market: Intergovernmental Conflict and Economic Reform in the Developing World*. Cambridge: Cambridge University Press.

Wolff S. (2009). Complex Power-sharing and the Centrality of Territorial Self-Governance in Contemporary Conflict Settlements. *Ethnopolitics* 8(1), pp. 27–45.

# PART VI

# International law and secession

# 32

# SELF-DETERMINATION AS THE BASIS FOR A RIGHT TO SECESSION

*Brad R. Roth*

## Introduction

The international system unequivocally embraces the maxim: "All peoples have the right to self-determination; by virtue of that right they freely determine their political status and freely pursue their economic, social and cultural development" (ICCPR 1966: art. 1; ICESCR 1966: art. 1). Although dispositive in cases of "salt water colonialism," this maxim has far less definitive application to other contexts. Geographically concentrated ethnic minorities within the integral territories of existing states have frequently invoked this seemingly straightforward statement, essentially to no avail. Even on the rare occasions when these communities have achieved their goal of sovereign independence, the international system has gone to great lengths to avoid attributing that success to the self-determination right.

Nonetheless, one cannot gainsay the relevance to secession questions of the international legal doctrine of self-determination of peoples. The self-determination principle is deeply embedded in the fabric of the present international peace and security order. "Remedial secession," even though it has never been overtly accepted as an international right, abstractly follows as a corollary, and therefore cannot be excluded as a legal consequence. A latent doctrinal entitlement of geographically discrete and manifestly subjugated political communities makes itself felt, however indirectly, in disputes about the territorial integrity of existing states.

This chapter will begin by exploring the conceptual relationship between "the principle of equal rights and self-determination of peoples" (UNC 1945: art. 1(2)) and the sovereign equality of states (UNC 1945: art. 2(1)) within the post–World War II global legal framework, tracing its development, within a generation, into the basis for a definitive repudiation of colonial subjugation. It will then discuss the challenges that the presence within existing states of geographically concentrated and manifestly subjugated minority groups poses to the prevailing framework. The chapter will go on to examine how the breakup of the Socialist Federal Republic of Yugoslavia (Yugoslavia) prompted the international system to accommodate non-consensual territorial fragmentation in an ad hoc manner – first in response to the initial outbreak of hostilities in the early 1990s, and then in the further case of Kosovo – rendering the territorial integrity norm partially unsettled (or, if one prefers, open-textured).

DOI: 10.4324/9781003036593-38

Brad R. Roth

# Peoples, states, and non-self-governing territories in the UN Charter scheme

The United Nations (UN) Charter purports to have been authored not by governmental officials or administrative apparatuses, or even by "states," but by "peoples" (UN 1945: preamble). To be sure, one can reasonably take a cynical view of such rhetoric: those who participated in the treaty's drafting and entry into force were not only at great remove from ordinary folk, but they in many cases were not even indirectly accountable to popular will. Yet this styling of the document is not trivial: it speaks to the conceptual framework that underlies the normative system.

Although states are routinely described as entities possessed of "(a) a permanent population; (b) a defined territory; (c) government; and (d) capacity to enter into relations with other states" (Montevideo Convention 1933, art. 1), they are more usefully understood as abstractions – units of a conceptual order, to which are ascribed characteristic legal properties. States do not "exist" in the way that physical objects exist; their existence, in legal terms, is an artifact of other international actors' explicit or implicit acknowledgment (express "recognition" typically being a sufficient, but not necessary, condition). The rights, obligations, powers, and immunities of statehood do not automatically attach to any territory and population under the effective control of an independent government, nor are they automatically vitiated where the territory and population cease to be subject to a unified system of effective authority (Roth 2010). Thus, a state is best thought of as a territorially based political community on which the international system has conferred the status of sovereign equality.

In this scheme, governments (i.e., ruling apparatuses) are agents rather than principals; not only specific administrations, but whole constitutional orders can come and go without affecting the state's international legal personality, and without affecting the legal status of obligations that previous governments incurred in the state's name. Those who assert rights, incur obligations, and confer immunities on behalf of the territorial units purport to do so on behalf of the permanent populations that those units encompass.

From the international system's perspective, the legal validity of a purported exercise of state power is predicated, at any given moment, on external acknowledgment of the putative officials' standing to speak for the political communities to which international legal personality is ascribed. Historically, the presumptive criterion for acknowledging that standing has been effective control through internal processes – the will of the political community being associated with widespread popular acquiescence rather than with the workings of institutions and processes designed to ensure accountability (Roth 1999). Ideological pluralism in the international order, especially during the UN system's first four and a half decades, ensured that a one-party regime that tolerated no organized opposition could speak as authoritatively for the underlying political community as could a liberal-democratic order, and that the outcome of a coup, insurrection, or civil war could confer standing on a governmental apparatus as validly as the outcome of a "free and fair" election.

It is in this jurisprudential light that the expression, "We, the Peoples of the United Nations," needs to be interpreted. That the expression cannot be taken at face value does not imply that it should not be taken seriously. Putting aside its ethereal preamble, the Charter's core normative provisions disclose the centrality of this theme. "The Organization is based on the principle of the sovereign equality of all its Members" (UNC 1945: art. 2(1)), in service of the purpose, *inter alia*, "[t]o develop friendly relations among nations based on respect for the principle of equal rights and self-determination of peoples" (UNC 1945: art. 1(2)). The equal status of member states thus implements the equal rights and self-determination of the political communities, the self-determination of which the states are presumed to manifest.

From the outset, however, the problem of colonialism confounded this elegant scheme. (It is perhaps telltale that the term is avoided throughout the document.) In particular, the colonial possessions of the Second World War's winners (as distinct from those of the losers, addressed in the Charter's detailed Trusteeship provisions) required elaborate rationalization. The Charter identified "territories whose peoples have not yet attained a full measure of self-government," with the colonial powers accepting "as a sacred trust" the promotion "to the utmost" of "the well-being of the inhabitants," and pledging "to develop self-government" among the ruled in accordance with "their varying stages of advancement" (UNC 1945: art. 73).

Mass resistance in the global South resolved this anomaly within a mere 15 years. The UN General Assembly's 1960 decolonization resolutions constitute a *de facto* Charter amendment. Resolution 1514 (XV), passed by a vote of 89–0–9, ascribed to "dependent peoples," in the name of self-determination, a "right to complete independence," and called for immediate steps to this end "in Trust and Non-Self-Governing Territories or all other territories which have not yet attained independence." It expressly rejected as a rationale for delay any supposed "[i]nadequacy of political, economic, social or educational preparedness" of the subjected populations, and demanded immediate cessation of all "repressive measures" against independence efforts (UNGA 1960a). The UN's repudiation of colonialism was from that moment definitive.

Two new issues, however, arose on the heels of this development. First, the definition of "Trust and Non-Self-Governing Territories or all other territories which have not yet attained independence" is by no means self-evident. Portugal, in particular, had refused this characterization of its overseas colonies, insisting that they be regarded as integral sovereign territories. In addition to specifically repudiating Portugal's claim in Resolution 1542 (XV), the General Assembly, by a vote of 69–2–21 (with Portugal and South Africa opposed), passed Resolution 1541 (XV) for the purpose of establishing criteria for the application of its decolonization demands.

Although adverting expressly to territories "known to be of the colonial type," the General Assembly spoke expansively of any "territory which is geographically separate and is distinct ethnically and/or culturally from the country administering it" and which is subject to "administrative, political, juridical, economic, or historical" factors that "arbitrarily place it in a position or status of subordination" (UNGA 1960b). These territories' inhabitants would have an option on sovereign independence, and their expression of a preference for a status short of sovereignty was to be subjected to special scrutiny.

The second issue concerned the application of the independence criteria to the inhabitants of "geographically separate" and "ethnically and/or culturally distinct" territories within the ex-colonies' externally imposed and arbitrarily drawn boundaries. The archetypical case was that of Katanga province within the emergent Democratic Republic of the Congo. If Congo-Leopoldville was entitled to independence from Belgium, might not Katanga have a right to independence from Congo-Leopoldville? Postcolonial governments regarded this prospect as a major threat, both to their nation-building projects and to their efforts to resist what they perceived to be "divide-and-conquer" strategies of the withdrawing colonial powers.

The position of Resolution 1514 (XV) was unequivocal: "Any attempt aimed at the partial or total disruption of the national unity and the territorial integrity of a country is incompatible with the purposes and principles of the Charter of the United Nations." Whatever might be said abstractly about territories "arbitrarily place[d] it in a position or status of subordination," the UN intended to draw the line at the transformation of overseas colonies into independent states, while reaffirming the inviolability of the boundaries of existing and emergent states alike.

The International Court of Justice in 1986 affirmed the principle of *uti possidetis*, "which upgraded former administrative delimitations, established during the colonial period, to international frontiers," even though "[a]t first sight this principle conflicts outright with another one, the right of peoples to self-determination." As the Court pointed out,

> The essential requirement of stability in order to survive, to develop and gradually to consolidate their independence in all fields, has induced African States judiciously to consent to the respecting of colonial frontiers, and to take account of it in the interpretation of the principle of self-determination of peoples.
>
> *(ICJ 1986: paras 23–25)*

The reconciliation of the self-determination and non-fragmentation norms has been most prominently articulated in the UN General Assembly's 1970 Declaration explicating and extending the "friendly relations" language of Charter Article 1(2). The Friendly Relations Declaration (UNGA 1970), upon reiterating the absolute-sounding self-determination language of the 1960 decolonization resolutions, inserted the famous "safeguard clause":

> Nothing in the foregoing paragraphs shall be construed as authorizing or encouraging any action which would dismember or impair, totally or in part, the territorial integrity or political unity of sovereign and independent States conducting themselves in compliance with the principle of equal rights and self-determination of peoples as described above *and thus possessed of a government representing the whole people belonging to the territory without distinction as to race, creed or colour.*
>
> *(UNGA 1970, emphasis added)*

This verbiage allowed the self-determination doctrine to be invoked not only in respect of territories that were literally non-self-governing, but also against vestiges of colonialism as manifested in Rhodesia (where colonial settlers had unilaterally declared independence in 1965 to thwart decolonization) and South Africa (a long-independent state that had imposed *apartheid* to perpetuate colonial subjugation by internal means). The safeguard clause's language has since been routinely reiterated (typically stripping from "without distinction" the specifications of "race, creed, or colour"; see Vienna Declaration 1993; UNGA 1995).

Insofar as the elaborations contained in Resolution 1541 (XV) and the Friendly Relations Declaration lend moral persuasiveness to the independence entitlement derived from the principle of self-determination, they do so at the expense of undermining the simplicity and certainty that was widely desired. Why, after all, should salt water be the exclusive indicator of geographical separateness? What are the implications for "ethnically and/or culturally distinct" territories, integral to existing states, that are nonetheless "arbitrarily place[d] in a position or status of subordination"? What about existing states that can be said, even from ideologically and culturally diverse perspectives, to lack "a government representing the whole people belonging to the territory without distinction"?

These questions inevitably linger. They become all the more salient after the end of the Cold War era, as the international system's studied agnosticism about the legitimacy of governing arrangements – save for the definitive exclusion of Axis-era fascism, colonialism, and *apartheid* – gives way to a more exacting conceptualization of a state as manifesting the self-governance of "the whole people belonging to the territory without distinction."

## Peoples, ethnic and cultural minorities, and human rights

The story of self-determination's application to decolonization is remarkably free of any engagement with ethnonationalism, notwithstanding the concept's origins in the project of liberating "nations" – understood in ethnic terms – from their subjection to multinational empires such as Austria-Hungary. In the famous words of Woodrow Wilson's Point X (of the Fourteen Points) of January 8, 1918: "The peoples of Austria-Hungary, whose place among the nations we wish to see safeguarded and assured, should be accorded the freest opportunity of autonomous development" (Wilson 1918: 691).

Wilson's articulation of the self-determination imperative contained within it the same tensions and dilemmas that to this day plague any effort to apply it outside of the colonial context. Wilson averred that

> all well-defined national aspirations shall be accorded the utmost satisfaction that can be accorded them without introducing new or perpetuating old elements of discord and antagonism that would be likely in time to break the peace of Europe and consequently of the world.
>
> *(Brown 1920: 235)*

Yet, as was pointed out contemporaneously, all of the key terms amount to question-begging. As one commentator put it:

> [I]f a plebiscite is to be had, it is not at all easy to find a proper territorial basis without danger of a political gerrymander that may work grave injustice. If a race is in a minority, how shall it be permitted to vote? As a separate unit? Or in districts where it begins to assert a bare majority? Or in districts where it enjoys a marked predominance?
>
> *(Brown 1920: 237)*

Worse still:

> [I]n any attempt to satisfy "the well-defined national aspirations" of a given people . . . it is obvious that a considerable racial minority must always be left united with another race. The question then becomes . . . whether it is more just to leave Hungarians and Saxons under Roumanian rule, or Roumanians under the domination of Magyars and Saxons.
>
> *(Brown 1920: 237)*

The post–World War I settlement addressed the limits of ethnonational self-determination by establishing ad hoc treaty rights for the minority collectivities left subject to the sovereignty of emergent states that were designed to fulfill the aspirations of their ethnic majorities. As has been noted, "the Great Powers were happy to interfere in the internal affairs of 'new' states but allowed no meddling in their own affairs" (Mazower 1997: 53). Even so, this "interference" was largely ineffective, except in the dark sense that irredentist neighboring states – especially Germany – exploited supposed violations of the treaty rights of their cross-border co-ethnics to rationalize aggressive postures. As one observer summarized the lesson in the Second World War's aftermath, in reference to Hitler's ally in Czechoslovakia's Sudetenland, "Every protected minority will ultimately find its Henlein" (Mazower 1997: 58).

The UN Charter-based order adopted neither the identification of "peoplehood" with ethnicity nor the attribution of any element of international legal personality to minority communities as such. The international human rights system developed within the UN system set about to confer rights on individuals in consideration of their minority status, rather than on minority collectivities. In addition to protecting individuals against discrimination on the basis of "race, colour, . . . language, religion, [or] national . . . origin" (ICCPR 1966: art. 26), the

International Covenant on Civil and Political Rights (ICCPR) guarantees to "persons belonging to . . . ethnic, religious or linguistic minorities" the right "to enjoy their own culture, to profess and practise their own religion, or to use their own language" (ICCPR 1966: art. 27). Apart from the special case of indigenous peoples (UNGA 2007), the international system makes no effort to accord rights to sub-state collectivities *per se*, such as a designated share of authority over decisions distinctively affecting their collective interests.

This individualistic approach avoids various pitfalls, including an onus to establish invidious distinctions between "national" minorities entitled to collective rights and "non-autochthonous" minorities entitled only to individual rights (Ramet 2006: 560). On the other hand, conferral of individual rights arguably fails to bring about genuine equality for minorities within a state that privileges, whether concretely or merely symbolically, the ethnic majority's language, culture, religion, or history.

The end of the Cold War era occasioned some revisiting of this orthodoxy, introducing the prospect that international organizations will place their weight behind autonomy arrangements for minorities that are geographically concentrated within states' integral territories. As Malcolm Shaw has noted, European documents, such as the Council of Europe's 1995 Framework Convention for Protection of National Minorities, "while extremely cautiously formulated and accompanied by significant provisos," introduce "a territorial dimension into minority rights within the territorial framework of independent states" (Shaw 1997: 486). But while many states have established consociational arrangements of various sorts, including territorial autonomy, to assure that minorities are more palpably "at home" in the national territory, international law does not thus far mandate any such arrangements.

Still less has international legal right of "peoples" to "freely determine their political status" been applied in favor of secessionist claims of a geographically concentrated ethnic minority. Even in the case of indigenous peoples, where the international community belatedly (and over substantial resistance from states that had previously emerged from colonialism) came to ascribe collective rights on the rhetorical basis of the right of peoples to self-determination,[1] the announced right to determine "political status" pointedly (and, at best, paradoxically) excludes any impairment of existing states' "territorial integrity or political unity" (UNGA 2007: art. 46).

Except in the context of indigenous peoples, where the group's incorporation into the state is too patently tainted by historical impositions to be treated as unproblematic, the fundamental difficulty of the self-determination right lies in identifying the right-bearer. This problem is reflected in the domestic court decision dealing most elaborately with the international law of self-determination: the Canadian Supreme Court's advisory opinion on the prospect of Québec secession.

Although insistent that the self-determination right remains applicable outside the colonial context, entailing even recourse to secession "as a last resort" (SCC 1998: para. 134), the Canadian high court held that the right could not be invoked to justify the unilateral secession of Québec. In arriving at this judgment, the court managed to sidestep the elemental question of whether the "people" entitled to self-determination was comprised of (a) the entire Québec population, (b) the entire Québec population minus the indigenous communities; (c) Francophone Québécois, or (d) all Francophone Canadians, irrespective of provincial residence – or, indeed, (e) the Canadian population as a whole:

> Although much of the Quebec population certainly shares many of the characteristics of a people, it is not necessary to decide the "people" issue because, whatever may be the correct determination of this issue in the context of Quebec, a right to secession only arises under the principle of self-determination of peoples at international law where "a people" is governed as part of a colonial empire; where "a people" is subject

to alien subjugation, domination or exploitation; and possibly where "a people" is denied any meaningful exercise of its right to self-determination within the state of which it forms a part. In other circumstances, peoples are expected to achieve self-determination within the framework of their existing state. A state whose government represents the whole of the people or peoples resident within its territory, on a basis of equality and without discrimination, and respects the principles of self-determination in its internal arrangements, is entitled to maintain its territorial integrity under international law and to have that territorial integrity recognized by other states.

(SCC 1998: para. 154)

Thus, the court predicated Canada's international legal right to maintain its territorial integrity on its manifest satisfaction of the conditions of the Friendly Relations Declaration's safeguard clause. Governance in the interests of and with the participation of all parts of the population "without distinction" – which must be construed to mean "without invidious distinction," rather than without inclusionary quotas or other special rights and statuses (which exist in Canada) – obviates the question of any discrete group's peoplehood. (It also helpfully obviates the need to ascertain the rights of minority communities within Québec itself in the event of a secession, including the status of challenges to Québec's own territorial integrity.) As long as there is no manifest subordination of any discrete collectivity, there is no need of further designations.

This disposition raises the intriguing question of whether "peoplehood" itself is a category constituted, not by a group's intrinsic characteristics, but by the contingencies of power relations. The political salience of characteristics such as ethnicity varies widely with historical circumstance. Arguably, a geographically concentrated minority population becomes a distinct "people" when, and only when, it finds itself, on a long-term and intractable basis, subject to "administrative, political, juridical, economic, or historical" factors that "arbitrarily place it in a position or status of subordination" (Roth 2018).

Be this as it may, the full implications of the right of peoples to self-determination remain unresolved. As reflected in the Supreme Court of Canada's opinion in *Reference re Secession of Quebec*, the doctrine's animating logic does not exclude the prospect of it being authoritatively applied to call for remedial secession of an integral territory, given some set of facts in which all indicators are favorably aligned.

## The Yugoslav dissolution of 1991–1992 and the Badinter Commission opinions

The international system is remarkably slow to acknowledge secession. This can partly be attributed to the traditional rule against "premature recognition," which regards external recognition of a breakaway territory as a presumptive violation of the non-intervention norm. Even though this rule is said to give way once the central government's armed efforts to re-establish control have ceased or become manifestly hopeless (Lauterpacht 1947: 12), external recognition of the seceding entity tends to occur only after the central government has formally relinquished the rebellious territory (Crawford 1997: para. 26). An example is the international recognition of Eritrea, which occurred only after Ethiopia's formal relinquishment in 1993, despite far earlier establishment of the "facts on the ground"; Somaliland remains generally unrecognized, notwithstanding three decades of effective self-government.

This is not to say that internal movements' secession efforts constitute a violation of international law. In the traditional understanding, the international legal order regulates external involvement in secession disputes, but presumptively neither forbids nor validates internal efforts at secession (ICJ 2010: para. 80). Historically, secessionists have assumed the risk of forcible suppression (subject to the constraints of human rights and humanitarian law) and, where successful by their own efforts (without inadmissible foreign assistance), have reaped the reward of international acceptance.

This traditional approach, however, represents what many observers condemn as an outdated conception of international law's relationship to internal conflict. In this conception, the international order was principally concerned with peace among rather than within states, and regarded external involvement in internal conflict as the problem rather than the solution. Internal conflict over the terms of public order within an existing state took on the imagined character of a trial by ordeal – the principal international concerns being that the winner be determined by authentically internal means and that rival foreign powers be prevented from exacerbating the conflict in pursuit of their own advantage.

The end of the Cold War occasioned greater optimism about the role of international law in resolving internal conflict. Among officials, jurists, scholars, and practitioners who emphasized human rights over non-intervention, the imperative of respect for the outcomes of trials by ordeal seemed discordant with the rule-of-law project. The same aspiration that undergirded advocacy for an international "democratic entitlement" to resolve governmental legitimacy contests (Fox 1992; Franck 1992) led to a disposition to establish a legal pathway by which secession could be peacefully achieved and internationally secured without the consent of the pre-existing state. Yet this disposition encountered the confounding elements that are, as discussed previously, endemic to such controversies.

The crisis in Yugoslavia unfolded in this context. On June 25, 1991, Slovenia and Croatia – component republics of the Yugoslav federation – declared independence. Slovenia's ensuing seizure of border posts in its territory from the Yugoslav People's Army (JNA) prompted a brief armed conflict, but a cease-fire shortly followed, and Slovenia's path to independence – though formally delayed by the terms of the July 7, 1991, Brioni Accords – was from then on essentially unimpeded.

Croatia's independence effort, however, prompted much more serious difficulties. Forces representing Croatia's Serb minority (somewhat over 12% of the population), geographically concentrated in the central region of Krajina and the northeastern regions of Western and Eastern Slavonia, were in armed rebellion against the elected nationalist Croatian government – rebellion facilitated by units of the Serb-dominated JNA stationed in Croatian territory. Pro-independence governments in Macedonia and in Bosnia and Herzegovina were also laying the groundwork for secession, meaning that four of the six Yugoslav republics, comprising a majority (over 56%) of the federation's population, were seeking to withdraw from Yugoslavia. With the federal government's constitutional processes deadlocked, Serbia's partisans within federal institutions resorted to unconstitutional measures to seek to maintain the federation on Serbia's terms or, failing that, to annex to Serbia substantial Croatian and Bosnian territories bearing concentrated Serb populations.

As the war in Croatia intensified, with the preponderance of atrocities being committed by Serb irregulars, the European Community determined to adopt legal positions toward these developments by establishing on August 27, 1991, a panel of five constitutional-court judges: the Conference on Yugoslavia Arbitration Commission, known by the name of its chair, French Constitutional Council President Robert Badinter. Beginning in late 1991, this panel issued a series of judgments that came to be treated as authoritative not only by the EC and its member states, but ultimately by the international community as a whole.

A traditional reading of international legal norms in force in 1991–1992, as described earlier, would have counseled withholding judgment on the fate of Yugoslavia, letting the violence run its course without interference and accepting whatever configuration might ultimately emerge. Yet the Badinter Commission understandably saw its mission as precisely the opposite: to use law to preempt a violent solution. To do so, it concocted a blend of constitutional-law and international-law principles in order to draw a line against the ethnonational project that the judges evidently deemed, on moral and political grounds (and not without justification in those terms), to be most at fault for the descent into violence: the Serb nationalist movement.

A peculiarity of this situation was that EC diplomacy had already staked out a position that the Commission could scarcely have been expected to undercut. The very EC ministerial meeting that formed the Commission simultaneously announced the EC's "determination never to recognise changes of frontiers which have not been brought about by peaceful means and by agreement," seemingly unconscious of the irony that in so stating, it was itself recognizing a non-consensual change of frontiers: the transfer of sovereignty over (in substantial part, predominantly Serb-inhabited) territory from Belgrade to Zagreb. The EC ministers condemned as "deeply misguided" the effort of Serb insurgents to address anticipated problems of "the new constitutional order through military means," while not condemning Croatian forces' use of military means to re-establish control over rebel-held territory. They further characterized the JNA's "active support to the Serbian side" as an "illegal use" of Yugoslav forces (Hill & Smith 2000: 363). These statements, which prejudged all of the major legal questions, were consistent with earlier pronouncements of the Conference on Security and Cooperation in Europe (Weller 1992: 574).

Accordingly, the central theme of the Commission's approach was to characterize Yugoslavia not as a state in civil war, beset by multiple contested efforts at secession, but as a federation undergoing a non-consensual "dissolution." The critical move came in the Commission's *Opinion No. 1*, dated November 29, 1991. There, the Commission asserted:

> [I]n the case of a federal-type State, which embraces communities that possess a degree of autonomy and, moreover, participate in the exercise of political power within the framework of institutions common to the Federation, the existence of the State implies that the federal organs represent the components of the Federation and wield effective power.
>
> *(Trifunovska 1994: 416)*

In assessing the facts on the ground at that time, the Commission found that:

> The composition and workings of the essential organs of the Federation . . . no longer meet the criteria of participation and representativeness inherent in a federal State;

> The recourse to force has led to armed conflict from the different elements of the Federation which has caused the death of thousands of people and wrought considerable destruction within a few months. The authorities of the Federation and the Republics have shown themselves to be powerless to enforce respect for . . . ceasefire agreements.
>
> *(Trifunovska 1994: 417)*

Since the very existence of the Yugoslav state presupposed functioning federal institutions, the Commission reasoned, the collapse of these institutions and the recourse to force entailed nothing less than "a process of dissolution" of the Yugoslav state into its component republics. The Yugoslav state was thereby said to be losing its international legal personality, with the six republics collectively succeeding to that personality.

In its *Opinion No. 2* and *Opinion No. 3*, issued on January 11, 1992, the Commission made further determinations that flowed directly from the first judgment. According to the Commission, with the disappearance of central authority, the republics' territorial relations *inter se* were to be governed (even before the territories' objective emergence as states, let alone any formal external recognition) by the venerable principle of *uti possidetis*, which in the decolonization context had ascribed to the newly independent states their previous colonial boundaries (Trifunovska 1994: 480).

These judgments deviated from the traditional approach of international law to internal conflict in the following respects:

First, the judgments treat federal states as though their international legal personality differs from that of unitary states. But federal or unitary institutional configuration is an artifact of the state's constitutional order, which that state may alter or overthrow in the exercise of its "inalienable" sovereign prerogative. A federal state is traditionally considered to "constitute a sole person in the eyes of international law" (Montevideo Convention 1933: art. 2).

Second, the Commission departs from a consistent pattern of state practice and *opinio juris* in identifying a loss of governmental coherence with a loss of state coherence. Quintessentially, Somalia and Lebanon have experienced long periods during which they have lacked an effective central government while rival authorities have maintained zones of control, but it has never been suggested that these states had "dissolved."

Third, whereas the Commission deems an inability to maintain effective control and to quell violence in the national territory as indicative of dissolution of Yugoslavia. This turns on its head the traditional rule against "premature recognition" that resists acknowledging new sovereignty arrangements until they have been irreversibly established on the ground. Moreover, the Commission tellingly applies no such standard of effectivity to the governments of the emergent successor states – in particular, Croatia and, subsequently, Bosnia and Herzegovina, both of which would manifestly have failed such a test.

Fourth, the Commission imported the principle of *uti possidetis* from the decolonization process, in which the newly decolonized entities were liberated from the colonial powers rather than de-linked from one another. In the colonial context, *uti possidetis* preserved the status quo *inter se*, whereas here it produced a drastic shift in power relations among the emergent states' constituent groups. And whereas the application of *uti possidetis* discourages violence across boundary lines, it may actually encourage violence within them, by validating forcible efforts to re-establish a territorial integrity that has been effectively lost (Roth 2015: 394–403).

The Commission showed little appreciation of the controversy that represented the very core of the conflict. From one perspective – that of the republics' ethnic majorities – the Yugoslav Federation was a voluntary and contingent union of six established territorial entities, each of which would naturally succeed to statehood within their inviolable boundaries should the Federation fail. From another perspective – that of the Serb minorities in Croatia and Bosnia – Yugoslavia was a single, multinational state whose internal boundaries had been indispensably predicated on the unity of – and balance of federal rights among – the encompassed ethnic communities (Radan 1999). As one commentator has noted, "While all Yugoslav constitutions affirmed the various nations' right to self-determination, including the right of secession, a fundamental ambiguity remained as to whom exactly this right belonged – to South-Slavic Yugoslav *ethnoi*, or the *demoi* of Yugoslavia's component republics" (Oklopčić 2013: 520).

The Commission undoubtedly saw itself as favoring what appeared as a territorial or "civic" brand of nationalism over a straightforwardly ethnic brand. But in this particular context, such a disposition merely guaranteed that upon dissolution, the ethnonational aspirations of the dominant groups within these intra-state boundaries would be the ones satisfied, to the exclusion of those of the territorial minorities.

Thus, the Commission adopted a framework that led it inexorably to condemn both for-cible efforts of the JNA to maintain Yugoslavia's territorial integrity and forcible efforts of JNA-backed Serb irregulars to breach Croatia's (and, subsequently, Bosnia's) territorial integrity, while affirming the legal validity of forcible efforts to maintain the territorial integrity of the republics, even prior to any official categorization of the republics as sovereign states. The con-ferral or withholding of "recognition" was treated as an ancillary question, subject to further considerations; the lawfulness *vel non* of the use of force turned exclusively on what was taken to be the objective dissolution and emergence of sovereign entities.

The Commission managed to accomplish all of this without relying on the doctrine of self-determination of peoples. The independence of the republics within their pre-established borders was said to follow, not from a right of self-determination, but merely from principles associated uniquely with a federal state's dissolution.[2] Meanwhile, whatever might be said for the right to self-determination on the part of Serbs within Croatia and Bosnia and Herzegovina (to which the Commission spoke in the vaguest possible terms), this right could not be imple-mented through forcible changes in the republic boundaries. Croatia's Serbs might well have wondered why, if Croatia could be supported in its secession from Yugoslavia, a Croatian Serb republic (Republika Srpska Krajina) could not equally be supported in its effort to secede from Croatia; the answer given was that Croatia was not seceding, but rather *succeeding* to a share, demarcated by the republic borders, of the legal personality of the dissolved Yugoslav federation.

The Commission's determinations resonated sufficiently with the international community that the practice of states and intergovernmental organizations quickly came to conform to them. The conduct of the Serb nationalist movement during the conflict up to that point – and even far more in the period immediately to follow – conjured up memories of the long-repu-diated Axis-era fascism. Although the international community notoriously underperformed in defending the proclaimed territorial inviolability of the republics, it never ceased to affirm that inviolability as a matter of *opinio juris*.

As ad hoc responses to pressing concerns of situational political morality, the Commission's determinations may have much to recommend them. Complicated though the Yugoslav situa-tion was, a strong argument can be made against attributing moral equivalence to the claims of the conflicting parties. But as statements of *lex lata*, the Commission's conclusions are difficult to defend. And as statements of *lex ferenda*, they tend to substitute one form of arbitrariness for another.

Perhaps the best that can be said for the Commission's stance is that it assumed the circum-stances to be so thoroughly *sui generis* that the determinations could be expected to have no substantial effect on future cases. Although this assumption has thus far proved correct as a tech-nical matter, the willingness of the international community to break with the past practice of withholding recognition from breakaway entities cannot help but unsettle the previously fixed expectations about the international system's approach to secession questions.

## The great equivocation: the ICJ's Kosovo advisory opinion

The quintessential test case of self-determination as the basis for a right to secession is that of Kosovo. Here lay a culturally, linguistically, and historically distinct minority, geographically concentrated within a discrete fragment of integral sovereign territory (Albanians constituting over 85% of the provincial population), having suffered manifest predation at the hands of an ethnonationally oriented state. And indeed, Kosovo represents an example of an effective seces-sion, against the will of the pre-existing state, that has achieved widespread (though by no means universal) international recognition.

The Badinter Commission's theory of Yugoslav dissolution characterized Yugoslavia as having been constituted by its six republics, not its eight administrative entities (notwithstanding the allocation to Kosovo of a seat on the eight-member Yugoslav State Council). Thus, Kosovo, a province endowed with autonomous status under the 1974 Yugoslav Constitution, was understood to be an integral part of the Republic of Serbia, and thus of a new state emerging from Yugoslavia's dissolution, the (Serbia-dominated) Federal Republic of Yugoslavia – Serbia and Montenegro (FRY).

The Serbian government of Slobodan Milosevic, posturing in support of a supposedly beleaguered Serb provincial minority as well as in vindication of Kosovo's historic status (dating to an epic 1389 battle) as "the cradle of Serb civilization" (Singh 2000: 2), withdrew the province's autonomy in 1989. The ensuing pattern of harsh discrimination against the province's large majority of ethnic Albanians precipitated a crisis by the late 1990s, as an ethnic-Albanian insurgency was met by ever more ruthless counterinsurgent efforts (Independent International Commission on Kosovo, 2000). In the face of Security Council deadlock after the FRY had failed to heed Security Council resolutions calling for an end to the violence and had refused to accede to terms posed by Western powers at the Rambouillet peace conference, North American Treaty Organization forces commenced a 79-day bombing campaign that, while initially triggering exacerbation of counterinsurgent atrocities (including forcible displacement, or "ethnic cleansing"), ultimately resulted in the withdrawal of FRY forces.

Although the Security Council never affirmed the lawfulness of the NATO intervention, it effectively placed Kosovo under an international trusteeship, precluding all FRY exercise of territorial control. Security Council Resolution 1244 nonetheless pointedly "reaffirm[ed] the commitment of all Member States to the sovereignty and territorial integrity of the Federal Republic of Yugoslavia." The resolution incorporated by reference terms of the Rambouillet "accords" that established provisional self-government while leaving the territory's final status to future negotiations. The result was an interminable impasse between a new, more rule-of-law-oriented Serbian government (which in 2006 consented to Montenegrin independence) that was willing to accept almost any outcome short of secession and a Kosovar leadership that would accept nothing less.

In 2008, the Kosovars' elected leadership, acting expressly outside (because *ultra vires* of) its role within the UN-sponsored Provisional Institutions of Self-Government, unilaterally declared independence. Serbia responded with a request to the UN General Assembly – approved by a vote of 77–6, with 74 abstentions – for an International Court of Justice (ICJ) Advisory Opinion on whether the declaration was "in accordance with international law" (UNGA 2008).

The phrasing of the question, evidently designed to avoid confrontation with the states that had immediately recognized Kosovo, allowed the Court conveniently to skirt the issues of the territory's international legal status and the unilateral declaration's international legal consequences. The question, as posed, has an all-too-simple answer: Apart from cases in which the declarations are intertwined with extrinsic violations of international legal norms (such as resistance to decolonization or a foreign state's inadmissible use of force), a unilateral declaration of independence per se is not subject to international legal regulation. The non-regulation of such efforts has not been a mere omission or gap in the law, but rather an affirmative consignment of such matters to the domestic jurisdiction – which has meant, historically, that they were permitted to be worked out internally by force.

Under ordinary circumstances, a secessionist local regime runs the risk that the central government will have recourse to forcible suppression in furtherance of the state's sovereign prerogative to maintain its territorial integrity. In this case, the Security Council had disabled Serbia's forcible response, thereby shielding the local authorities from that risk, even while having purported to reaffirm Serbia's territorial integrity. The *ultra vires* nature of the Kosovo leadership's act under UN protection might have been thought to call into question whether the declaration was "in accordance with international law," were the Court disposed to address the merits.

The unsettled state of the legal doctrine dictated otherwise. The Court limited itself to noting that states have expressed "radically different views" on: (1) "[w]hether, outside the context of non-self-governing territories and peoples subject to alien subjugation, domination, and exploitation, the international law of self-determination of peoples confers upon part of the population of an existing State a right to separate from that state"; (2) "whether international law provides for a right of 'remedial secession' and, if so, in what circumstances"; and (3) "whether the circumstances which some participants maintained would give rise to a right of 'remedial secession' were actually present in Kosovo" (ICJ 2010: para. 82). These "radically different views" were evidenced by the abundant contrasting submissions of interested states (Milanović 2015).

## Conclusion: the unsettled question of remedial secession

The doctrinal relationship of self-determination to secession is a conundrum. All peoples have the right to determine their political status, and yet, in the famous formulation of Ivor Jennings, "the people cannot decide until somebody decides who are the people" (Vidmar 2013: 243). Outside the decolonization context, the distinctness of a "people" (*qua* political community) is a fraught question. Affinities associated with ethnicity, culture, history, language, and religion have variable political relevance, and can exclusively ground territorial units only when grotesque measures are taken to impose a demographic coherence on the geography. Absent such coherence, each new reconstitution of national territory reproduces the problem of majorities and minorities, often in an intensified form.

The international system thus maintains its strong presumption in favor of maintaining states' territorial integrity. Still, contemporary statehood finds its justification in its purporting to manifest the self-determination of the territorial population as a whole. Where a particular existing delimitation dooms a territorially concentrated ethnic minority to subordination and predation within an inalterably adverse national political community, adjustments need to be made. Where such issues defy internal resolution, the international system cannot be spared the task of arbitrating the question. That it does so ad hoc, rather than on the basis of consistent and coherent norms, reflects multifarious harsh realities rather than any failure of ingenuity at the international level.

## Notes

1 The 2007 UN Declaration on the Rights of Indigenous Peoples distinctively specifies the following collective rights: "the right to participate in decision-making in matters which would affect their rights, through representatives chosen by themselves in accordance with their own procedures, as well as to maintain and develop their own indigenous decisionmaking institutions" (UNGA 2007: art. 18); the right to be consulted "in good faith" prior to the implementation of legislative or administrative measures affecting them (UNGA 2007: art. 19); "the right to the lands, territories and resources which they have traditionally owned, occupied or otherwise used or acquired" (UNGA 2007: art. 26); the right to restitution of confiscated land, territory, and resources "or, when this is not possible, just, fair and equitable compensation" (UNGA 2007: art. 28).

2 The Commission's *Opinion No. 4*, issued on January 11, 1992, taking note of the Bosnian Serb community's express rejection of Bosnian independence and desire in that event to establish a separate republic within Serb-dominated territory, concluded that "the will of the peoples of Bosnia-Hercegovina to

constitute the [Republic] as a sovereign and independent State cannot be held to have been fully established." But curiously, its proposed solution was "a referendum of all the citizens of the [Republic] without distinction." (Trifunovska 1994: 488) The non sequitur was entirely overlooked: the first sentence invoked "the will of the peoples" severally, whereas the second evidently eschewed (ethnic) peoplehood as a relevant category, indicating that the will of a simple majority of individual citizens can override a dissenting "people," however cohesive.

# References

Brown, P. 1920, "Self-Determination in Central Europe", *American Journal of International Law*, 14: 235.

Crawford, J. 1997, *State Practice and International Law in Relation to Unilateral Secession*, Report for the Department of Justice of Canada, <https://is.muni.cz/el/1422/jaro2006/MP803Z/um/1393966/INTERNATIONAL_LAW_AND_UNILATERAL_SECESSION.pdf>

Fox, G. 1992, "The Right to Political Participation in International Law", *Yale Journal of International Law*, 17: 539

Franck, T. 1992, "The Emerging Right to Democratic Governance", *American Journal of International Law*, 86: 46

Hill, C. & Smith, K. (eds), 2000, *European Foreign Policy: Key Documents*, London: Routledge.

ICCPR 1966, International Covenant on Civil and Political Rights, 1966, *United Nations Treaty Series*, 999: 171

ICESCR 1966, International Covenant on Economic, Social, and Cultural Rights, 1966, *United Nations Treaty Series*, 993: 3

ICJ 1986, International Court of Justice, *Case Concerning the Frontier Dispute (Burkina Faso/Republic of Mali)*, *International Court of Justice Reports* 554

ICJ 2010, International Court of Justice, 2010, *Accordance with International Law of the Unilateral Declaration of Independence in Respect of Kosovo*, Advisory Opinion, *International Court of Justice Reports* 403

Independent International Commission on Kosovo 2000, *The Kosovo Report: Conflict, International Response, Lessons Learned*, Oxford: Oxford University Press.

Lauterpacht, H. 1947, *Recognition in International Law*, Cambridge: Cambridge University Press.

Mazower, M. 1997, "Minorities and the League of Nations in Interwar Europe", *Daedalus*, 126(2): 47

Milanović, M. 2015, "Arguing the Kosovo Case", in M. Milanović & M. Wood (eds), *The Law and Politics of the Kosovo Advisory Opinion*, Oxford: Oxford University Press: 21–59.

Montevideo Convention 1933, Montevideo Convention on the Rights and Duties of States, 1933, *League of Nations Treaty Series*, 165: 19

Oklopčić, Z. 2013, "Beyond Empty, Conservative, and Ethereal: Pluralist Self-Determination and a Peripheral Political Imaginary", *Leiden Journal of International Law*, 26: 509.

Radan, P. 1999, "Yugoslavia's Internal Borders as International Borders: A Question of Appropriateness", *Eastern European Quarterly*, 33: 137

Ramet, S. 2006, *The Three Yugoslavias: State-Building and Legitimation, 1918–2005*. Bloomington: Indiana University Press.

Roth, B. 1999, *Governmental Illegitimacy in International Law*, Oxford: Oxford University Press.

Roth, B. 2010, "Secessions, Coups, and the International Rule of Law: Assessing the Decline of the Effective Control Doctrine", *Melbourne Journal of International Law*, 11: 393

Roth, B. 2015, "The Virtues of Bright Lines: Self-Determination, Secession, and External Intervention", *German Law Journal*, 16: 384

Roth, B. 2018, "The Relevance of Democratic Principles to the Self-Determination Norm", in P. Hilpold (ed.), *Autonomy and Self-Determination in Europe and in Global Perspective*, Cheltenham: Edward Elgar Publishing: 56–76

SCC 1998, Supreme Court of Canada, *Reference re Secession of Quebec*, *Supreme Court Reports*, 2: 217–297

Shaw, M. 1997, "Peoples, Territorialism, and Boundaries", *European Journal of International Law*, 8: 478

Singh, S. R. 2000, "The Kosovo Crisis and the Quest for Diplomatic Solution', *India Quarterly*, 56: 1

Trifunovska, S. 1994, *Yugoslavia Through Documents: From Its Creation to Its Dissolution*, Dordrecht: Martinus Nijhoff Publishers.

UNC 1945, United Nations Charter, 1945, www.un.org/en/about-us/un-charter/full-text

UNGA 1960a, United Nations General Assembly, Declaration on the Granting of Independence to Colonial Countries and Peoples, G.A. Res. 1514 (XV), 15 December 1960.

UNGA 1960b, United Nations General Assembly, Principles Which Should Guide Members in Determining Whether or Not an Obligation Exists to Transmit Information under Article 73(e) of the Charter, G.A. Res. 1541 (XV), 15 December.

UNGA 1970, United Nations General Assembly, Declaration on Principles of International Law Concerning Friendly Relations and Co-Operation Among States in Accordance With the Charter of the United Nations, annex to Resolution 2625 (XXV), 24 October.

UNGA 1995, United Nations General Assembly, Declaration on the Occasion of the Fiftieth Anniversary of the United Nations, G.A. Res 50/6, 24 October.

UNGA 2007, United Nations General Assembly, Declaration on the Rights of Indigenous Peoples, GA Res. 61/295, 13 September.

UNGA 2008, United Nations General Assembly, Request for an Advisory Opinion of the International Court of Justice on Whether the Unilateral Declaration of Independence of Kosovo Is in Accordance with International Law, G.A. Res. 63/3, 8 October.

Vidmar, J. 2013, *Democratic Statehood in International Law: The Emergence of New States in Post-Cold War Practice*, Oxford: Hart Publishing Co.

Weller, M. (1992). "The International Response to the Dissolution of the Socialist Federal Republic of Yugoslavia", *American Journal of International Law*, 86: 569.

Wilson, W. 1918, "Address of the President", *Congressional Record*, 8 January, 690–693.

Vienna Declaration 1993, World Conference on Human Rights, Vienna Declaration and Programme of Action, UN Doc A/CONF.157/23, 12 July.

# 33

# THE ACQUISITION OF INDEPENDENCE AND INTERNATIONAL BOUNDARIES

*Suzanne Lalonde*

The very first line of the Preamble to the Charter of the United Nations (UN Charter) proclaims the determination of the "peoples of the United Nations" to prevent the "scourge of war". This foundational commitment is given form in Article 1, which sets out the purposes of the Organization and identifies as its first priority the maintenance of international peace and security (Article 1(1)). In pursuit of this central purpose, Article 2 sets out seven guiding "Principles" and at the top of the list, affirms "the principle of the sovereign equality of all its Members" (Article 2(1)). As a necessary corollary, paragraph 4 of Article 2 imposes on all Members the obligation "to refrain in their international relations from the threat or use of force against the territorial integrity or political independence of any state" (Article 2(4)).

These fundamental Charter provisions reflect the deep-rooted conviction that the best guarantee of peace lies in protecting the independence of existing States. Since boundaries evidence the extent of State sovereignty and authority, the protection of international boundaries has assumed a crucial role in the international system (Shaw 1996: 77). Zacher underlines this vital nexus between territorial stability and international peace. "The development of a norm concerning respect for states' territoriality is particularly important because scholars have established that territorial disputes have been the major cause of enduring interstate rivalries, the frequency of war, and the intensity of war" (Zacher 2001: 215–216). It is this reality that led Lord Curzon to famously declare in 1907, that "[f]rontiers are indeed the razor's edge on which hang suspended the modern issues of war and peace" (Curzon 1908: 7).

Thus, for Jennings, territorial stability and territorial change lie at the heart of the whole problem of the legal ordering of international society (Jennings 1963: 87). Shaw also affirms that notwithstanding the development of international standards in, for example, human rights, minority rights, and environmental law, and despite the evolution of international organizations, "the fundamental orientation of international law still focuses upon territorial sovereignty. Accordingly, the principle of the stability of boundaries constitutes an overarching postulate of the international legal system" (Shaw 1996: 81). While some other kinds of legal ordering need to be capable of constant change to meet new needs, Jennings emphasizes that "in a properly ordered society, territorial boundaries will be among the most stable of all institutions" (Jennings 1963: 70).

Shaw acknowledges, however, that the push for change is constant, but insists that territorial change should only occur in a clear, secure, and regulated manner and cautions that such change should not be too easily accomplished even within established guidelines, "for territorial change

DOI: 10.4324/9781003036593-39

tends to bring with it political disruption which one would be loath to accept too glibly or in too facile a manner" (Shaw 1996: 81–83). The Court of Arbitration echoed this warning in the *Dubai/Sharjah* case, pointing out that "the re-opening of the legal status of the boundaries of a State may give rise to very grave consequences, which may endanger the life of the State itself" (Court of Arbitration 1981: 578).

It is against this entrenched commitment to safeguard territorial stability that claims to self-determination and secession will be considered and more specifically, how territorial limits are determined in such contexts. For the way in which international law reacts is intrinsically connected to the circumstances surrounding the accession to independence (Corten 1999: 408). Where there exists a positive right to independence, international rules and principles will dictate a specific territorial outcome. In the absence of a clearly established right to independence, the question of the determination of the new international boundaries is fraught with uncertainty.

In an attempt to provide a comprehensive overview, three different "contexts" in which independence can be attained will be examined: claims to external self-determination, unilateral secession, and the dissolution of existing States. In each case, the source of the right will be identified and/or a summary explanation of the concept will be provided. On the basis of these understandings, the principal international boundary rules and principles relevant in each case will be identified and analyzed to show how international law regulates the determination of boundaries in each of these scenarios so as to ensure that any change to the territorial framework does not threaten the stability of the international order.

# Self-determination

## *The right to external self-determination of the people of a sovereign independent State*

### *Source and content of the right*

Nicholson broadly defines self-determination, in a political sense, as a "people's capacity to make choices about external status or internal development" (Nicholson: Chapter 1, this volume). Referring to its overt nature as a political principle and its obvious antecedents in the principle of nationality, Crawford stresses that in the years after 1945, which he refers to as the dawn of modern international law, "the question whether self-determination was a legal right or principle was a divisive issue" (Crawford 2006: 108):

> Self-determination as a legal right or principle threatened to bring about significant changes in the political geography of the world . . . As an overtly political principle, it raised concerns about the character of international law and the justiciability of political disputes.
>
> *(Crawford 2006: 108)*

These concerns no doubt account for the rather prudent references to self-determination in the UN Charter. The term appears only twice: in Article 1(2), where one of the purposes of the United Nations is stated to be the development of "friendly relations among nations based on respect for the principle of equal rights and self-determination of peoples", and in Article 55, where the same formula is used to express the general views of the United Nations in the fields of social and economic development and respect for human rights.

These Charter articles are understood to affirm the sovereign equality of existing States, and in particular, the right of the people of a State (understood as its entire population), to choose its own form of government without external intervention. Crawford confirms this interpretation: "In this case, the principle of self-determination normally takes the well-known form of the rule preventing intervention in the internal affairs of a State, a central element of which is the right of the people of the State to choose for themselves their own form of government" (Crawford 2006: 126).

## The territorial implications of the right to external self-determination of the people of a sovereign independent State

A number of international legal rules and principles guarantee the territorial extent of a sovereign independent State, chief among them the principle of territorial integrity. For Blay, territorial integrity refers to the territorial "oneness" or "wholeness" of the State (Blay 2010: online), while for Lauterpacht, it is "synonymous with territorial inviolability" and thus protects the territorial framework of an independent State (Lauterpacht 1952: 154). Under Article 2(7) of the UN Charter, States are guaranteed exclusive jurisdiction within national borders and under Article 2(4), as we have seen, the use of force against the territorial integrity or political independence of any State is prohibited. The territorial integrity principle is thus the foundation stone upon which rests the entire international legal order (Simpson 1994: 340).

Other rules specifically protect the sanctity of established boundaries. Lachaume argues, for instance, that the inviolability of frontiers is a recognized and uncontested principle of international law even though international texts and documents have rarely made express reference to it (Lachaume 1980: 79). The inviolability principle safeguards the territorial extent of independent States by prohibiting incursions by the sovereignty of other States through sporadic and temporary violations of boundaries.

The principle of the intangibility of frontiers, for its part, implies that existing boundaries, whether established by international agreement or through effective occupation, cannot be called into question through the use of force. The two concepts of inviolability and intangibility are undoubtedly closely linked insofar as they both prohibit unilateral violations of the boundaries of another State. Yet they are not interchangeable:

> [T]he only specific meaning of the intangibility principle seems to me to be . . . that States must not dispute the validity of the title on the basis of which the boundary is established, even if this title appears somewhat questionable . . . In other words, while the inviolability principle protects territorial integrity, the intangibility principle protects the territorial unit.
>
> *(Charpentier 1980: 163, author's translation)*

Other manifestations of the principle of the finality and stability of established boundaries include the boundary exception to the fundamental change of circumstances rule (Vienna Convention 1969: Article 62) and the rule that a succession of State does not affect a boundary or the regime of a boundary established by treaty (Vienna Succession Convention 1978: Article 11). International tribunals have also established, notably in the *Temple of Preah Vihear* case (ICJ 1962: 34), that the interpretation of boundary treaties is influenced and guided by the principle of stability (Lalonde 2002: 143–150).

## The right of external self-determination of colonial/non-self-governing peoples

### Source and content of the right

In the decades following the adoption of the UN Charter, the General Assembly endeavored to flesh out the rather terse references to self-determination in Articles 1(2) and 55 and to broaden the scope of the principle. On 14 December 1960, the General Assembly adopted Resolution 1514(XV), the Declaration on the Granting of Independence to Colonial Countries and Peoples (Colonial Declaration), which states as its political objective the speedy and unconditional end of colonialism. The preamble to the Colonial Declaration emphasizes "the need for the creation of conditions of stability and well-being and peaceful and friendly relations based on respect for the principles of equal rights and self-determination of peoples" and refers to the "yearning for freedom in all dependent peoples" and the movement to independence overseen by the UN for Trust and Non-Self Governing Territories. To this end, Article 2 unequivocally declares that "[a]ll peoples have the right of self-determination" (UNGA 1960).

However, the concern for stability evidenced in the Preamble is operationalized in three of the seven articles of the Colonial Declaration. Article 4 commands that armed action and repressive measures directed against dependent peoples cease "in order to enable them to exercise peacefully and freely their right to complete independence and *the integrity of their national territory shall be respected*" (emphasis added). Article 6 addresses potential threats from within and declares that "[a]ny attempts aimed at the partial or total disruption of the national unity and *the territorial integrity of a country* is incompatible with the purposes and principles of the Charter of the United Nations" (emphasis added). Article 7 further enjoins all States to strictly observe the provisions of the UN Charter and the Colonial Declaration "on the basis of equality, non-interference in the internal affairs of all States, and respect for the sovereign rights of all peoples and their territorial integrity" (UNGA 1960).

### The territorial implications of the right to external self-determination of colonial/non-self-governing peoples

While the application of the self-determination principle to non-self-governing territories, understood as a right to independence, is indisputable, Shaw argues that the basis of the principle in the colonial context has been transformed "from the personal concept implicit in the political definition of self-determination to the strict territorial concept of international practice" (Shaw 1986: 102). The "self" of self-determination is to be understood in spatial terms as a right accruing to a colonial people within the framework of an existing colonial territorial unit, and "not on the basis of ethnic, cultural, historical or other factors" (Corten 1999: 104, author's translation).

This territorial definition of the right to self-determination is grounded in Article 6 of the Colonial Declaration, which, together with Chapters 11 (Non-Self-Governing Territories) and 12 (International Trusteeship System) of the UN Charter, has been interpreted as condemning the dismemberment of colonial units prior to independence. Administering powers are thus under an obligation to maintain the unity of a non-self-governing entity to ensure that the inhabitants exercise their right to self-determination as a single indivisible unit and to guarantee that the wishes of the whole of the population are implemented. It was on this basis that actions by the United Kingdom concerning islands belonging to the colonies of Mauritius and the Seychelles and France's policy on Mayotte, were condemned by the Security Council and General Assembly (Lalonde 2002: 155–158 for further examples).

For most non-self-governing territories in the twentieth century, certainly in Africa, independence was achieved not through revolution (as was the case in nineteenth-century Latin America) but by virtue of grants of independence by the former metropolitan powers. Independence was devolved to a territorially defined colony, irrespective of whether its territorial limits were the product of international or internal administrative acts. Not only did the "non-dismemberment" obligation contribute to the preservation of the territorial status quo, but the *nemo dat quod non habet* principle would also have guaranteed the continuity of existing boundaries. This principle, invoked by the arbitrator in the *Island of Palmas* case (PCA 1928: 11), provides that a "predecessor State may transfer to the successor State only the territorial extent of its own competence" (Shaw 1986: 234). In the context of the decolonization of Africa, therefore, the newly independent States acquired from the metropolitan powers only so much territory as they had themselves possessed. To that extent, the *nemo dat* principle contributed very substantially to the preservation of existing boundaries in Africa.

Thus, within the colonial context, the territorial framework of the non-self-governing entity was, with only a few exceptions, "substantially accepted as the identification pattern for the exercise of the right to self-determination" (Shaw 1982: 71). Once independence was achieved, international law, including the UN Charter and Article 6 of the Colonial Declaration, protected the territorial expression of the new State from internal and external forces (Crawford 1979: 101–102). This territorial interpretation of the right of self-determination in the colonial period ensured that it coexisted, without contradiction, with the principle of territorial integrity.

### The right of external self-determination of peoples subject to foreign domination and of peoples subject to systemic discrimination by their own government

#### Source and content of the right

A decade after the Colonial Declaration was adopted, the General Assembly not only reaffirmed its commitment to the UN Charter's principles, but expanded their application beyond the colonial context. The preamble and the operative paragraphs of the Declaration on Friendly Relations reiterate the UN's commitment to the principle of equal rights and self-determination of peoples: "[A]ll peoples have the right freely to determine, without external interference, their political status and to pursue their economic, social and cultural development" (UNGA 1970). However, while the Declaration on Friendly Relations proclaims that the right of self-determination inures to all peoples and not merely to non-self-governing peoples, it also attests to the priority afforded the territorial integrity principle and the international community's constant preoccupation with ensuring territorial stability:

> Nothing in the foregoing paragraphs shall be construed as authorizing or encouraging any action which would dismember or impair, totally or in part, the territorial integrity or political unity of sovereign independent States conducting themselves in compliance with the principle of equal rights and self-determination of peoples as described above and thus possessed of a government representing the whole people belonging to the territory without distinction as to race, creed or colour.
> *(UNGA 1970)*

This "safeguard clause" testifies to the continued relevance of the Committee of Jurists' conclusion in their 1920 report on the Aaland Islands dispute:

> Positive international law does not recognize the right of national groups to separate themselves from the State of which they are a part by the simple expression of a wish, any more than it recognizes the right of other States to claim such a separation.
> *(ICJ 1920: 2)*

The justification for this rule was subsequently provided by the Commission of Rapporteurs in their own report on the Aaland Islands dispute:

> To concede to minorities, either of language or religion, or to any fractions of a population the right of withdrawing from the community to which they belong, because it is their wish or their good pleasure, would be to destroy order and stability within States and to inaugurate anarchy in international life; it would be to uphold a theory incompatible with the very idea of the State as a territorial and political unity.
> *(ICR 1921: 4)*

However, the "safeguard clause", along with other important provisions in the Declaration, have been interpreted as legitimizing independence for minority groups within sovereign independent States in certain situations akin to colonialism. The precise scope of this postcolonial right of external self-determination was extensively analyzed by the Supreme Court of Canada in 1998 in *Reference re Secession of Quebec*, which Crawford describes as "[t]he most significant modern discussion" of the issue (Crawford 2006: 119).

The Supreme Court begins its discussion of the "Scope of the Right to Self-determination" by asserting that the principle has evolved within a framework of respect for the territorial integrity of existing States (Secession Reference 1998: para. 127). The Court then states:

> The recognized sources of international law establish that the right to self-determination of a people is normally fulfilled through *internal* self-determination – a people's pursuit of its political, economic, social and cultural development within the framework of an existing state. A right to *external* self-determination (which in this case potentially takes the form of the assertion of a right to unilateral secession) arises in only the most extreme of cases and, even then, under carefully defined circumstances.
> *(Secession Reference 1998: para. 126, emphasis in the original)*

The right of colonial peoples to exercise their right to self-determination by "breaking away from the 'imperial' power", according to the Court, is now "undisputed" (Secession Reference 1998: para. 132). In its opinion, the other "clear case" where a right to external self-determination accrues is where a people is "subject to alien subjugation, domination or exploitation outside a colonial context". This recognition, according to the Court, finds its roots in the Declaration on Friendly Relations, including in paragraph (b) under the heading "The principle of equal rights and self-determination of peoples":

> (b) To bring a speedy end to colonialism, having due regard to the freely expressed will of the peoples concerned; and bearing in mind that subjection of peoples to alien subjugation, domination and exploitation constitutes a violation of the principle, as well as a denial of fundamental human rights, and is contrary to the Charter.

The Supreme Court refers to a third circumstance where the right of self-determination may ground a right to independence. The Court explains that the underlying rationale for this third category is that, "when a people is blocked from the meaningful exercise of its right to self-determination internally, it is entitled, as a last resort, to exercise it by secession" (Secession Reference 1998: para. 134). "Clearly, such a circumstance parallels the other two recognized situations in that the ability of a people to exercise its right to self-determination internally is somehow being totally frustrated" (Secession Reference 1998: para. 135).

Crawford describes this third category as "remedial secession" and asserts that it springs from the "safeguard clause" in the Declaration on Friendly Relations and its broader formulation in Article I(2) of the 1993 Vienna Declaration, which requires that governments represent the whole people belonging to their territory "without distinction of any kind" (Vienna Declaration 1993).

> The question is whether these paragraphs envisage what may be termed "remedial secession" in the case of a State that does not conduct itself in compliance with the principle of equal rights and self-determination of peoples; e.g., in the case of total denial to a particular group or people within the State any role in their own government, either through their own institutions or the general institutions of the state. At least it is arguable that, in extreme cases of oppression, international law allows remedial secession to discrete peoples within a State.
>
> *(Crawford 2006: 119)*

However, as Higgins notes, there can be no *legal entitlement* to independence when there is representative government (Higgins 1994: 117). This was ultimately the conclusion of the Canadian Supreme Court with respect to Québec (Secession Reference 1998: para. 136). Crawford emphasizes that according to "the formula" in both instruments,

> a State whose government represents the whole people of its territory without distinction of any kind, that is to say, on a basis of equality, and in particular without discrimination on grounds of race, creed or colour, complies with the principle of self-determination in respect of all of its people *and is entitled to the protection of its territorial integrity*.
>
> *(Crawford 2006: 118–119, emphasis added)*

Thus, international law does not at present recognize a right to independence – understood as a *legal entitlement* – for national groups within sovereign States possessed of a government representing the whole people without discrimination.

## The territorial implications of the right to external self-determination of peoples subject to foreign domination and of peoples subject to systemic discrimination by their own government

What are the territorial consequences of the right to external self-determination recognized in the two specific contexts described earlier? The rules dictating the territorial outcome where a non-self-governing territory accedes to independence have already been canvassed in the preceding section. The same rules and considerations apply where a people subjected to foreign subjugation, domination or exploitation exercises its right to external self-determination. As in the colonial context, the subjugated entity is the self-determination unit and exercises its legal entitlement to independence within the political and geographical boundaries that define it. This outcome is also guaranteed under the humanitarian law of occupation, which provides that an occupying power does not acquire sovereignty over the territory it controls. Military or hostile occupation is deemed to be temporary and consequently, the occupying power is obligated to preserve the *status quo ante* (ICRC 2012). Once it has exercised its right to external self-determination and regained its statehood, the unit then benefits from the right to territorial integrity and other international guarantees.

In the case of oppressed peoples, Crawford insists that the issue is the same: "At the root, the question of defining 'peoples' concerns identifying the *categories of territory* to which the principle of self-determination applies *as a matter of right*" (Crawford 2006: 126, emphasis added). International practice, he asserts, identifies such categories "plainly enough"; in general, they are "those territories established and recognized as separate political units" (Crawford 2006: 127). Among them, he lists

> *other territories forming distinct political-geographical areas*, whose inhabitants are arbitrarily excluded from any share in the government either of the region or of the State to which they belong, with the result that the *territory* becomes in effect, with respect to the remainder of the State, non-self-governing.
>
> *(Crawford 2006: 127, emphasis added)*

Higgins justifies this territorial approach to identifying the self-determination unit as necessary to prevent "fragmented chaos" (Higgins 1963: 104).

The fact that an oppressed people inhabiting a distinct political-geographical unit has a *legal entitlement* to independence, recognized in law and by the international community, will have significant territorial consequences, for its right to self-determination preempts claims by the parent State to its integrity. As with colonial or subjugated peoples with whom they are equated (Secession Reference 1998: para. 135), the inhabitants of these distinct territorial units are entitled to attain statehood within their bounded space.

The *uti possidetis juris* principle, for instance, may afford it some measure of territorial protection. The modern formulation of the principle is traditionally associated with the decolonization of Central and South America in the nineteenth century. In the decades following independence, the young Republics agreed in some cases to adopt as their new international boundaries former Spanish administrative lines. This practice was referred to as the implementation of the *uti possidetis juris, ita possideatis* principle ("as you possess, so may you continue to possess"). When in the twentieth century the member States of the Organization of African Unity (OAU) pledged themselves to respect the colonial boundaries existing at the time of independence (OAU 1963; Cairo Resolution 1964), the International Court of Justice (ICJ) and many commentators viewed their commitment as further evidence of the role of *uti possidetis* in the process of decolonization.

It has been argued that, despite the weight of significant learned commentary, the principle of *uti possidetis juris* had much less influence on the independence process and the determination of boundaries in the colonial context than has been attributed to it (Lalonde 2002: 24–60 and 103–137). While pronouncements by the ICJ have undoubtedly endowed the *uti possidetis* principle with some normative status in the law of decolonization, we have argued that cases and State practice reveal that at its strongest, *uti possideti juris* constitutes a presumption in favor of the continuity of the pre-independence borders of non-self-governing units that have successfully attained independence. We have deplored the tendency to treat *uti possidetis* as an all-embracing expression of the various legal rules and principles that contribute to the resolution of boundary issues in the colonial context.

The critical point, however, is that the principle has been deemed to provide a stabilizing solution for the determination of the boundaries of a self-determination unit, possessed of a *legal entitlement* to independence, upon its accession to statehood. In the case of systemic discrimination by a parent State, the "unit" entitled to exercise its right to self-determination externally will be geographically defined and will constitute a political entity in its own right. Shaw's analysis of the evolution of the right of self-determination in the colonial context from a political to a territorial concept therefore holds true in this modern context as well: the "self" of self-determination must also in these circumstances be understood in spatial terms (Shaw 1986: 102). Thus, in the absence of a negotiated settlement, the *uti possidetis juris* principle can ensure that the "territorial unit" entitled to independence accedes to statehood with its former internal boundaries intact. The territorial extent of the newly independent State will then be guaranteed by the rules we have discussed, including territorial integrity and the intangibility of frontiers.

## Unilateral secession

### *Scope of the concept*

The right of a people to self-determination is so widely recognized in international conventions that the principle has now acquired the status of a general principle of international law (Cassesse 1995: 171–172). However, the principle of self-determination has evolved within a framework of respect for the territorial integrity of existing States. As the Supreme Court of Canada emphasizes,

> [t]he various international documents that support the existence of a people's right to self-determination also contain parallel statements supportive of the conclusion that the exercise of such a right must be sufficiently limited to prevent threats to an existing state's territorial integrity or the stability of relations between sovereign states.
>
> *(Secession Reference 1998: para. 127)*

It is indeed clear from the formulations of the principle in international instruments such as the Declaration on Friendly Relations and the Vienna Declaration that the international community expects that in most cases, the right will be exercised "internally", within the framework of existing sovereign States and consistently with the maintenance of the territorial integrity of those States.

Only in "extreme cases" and in "carefully defined circumstances" does international law allow that the right of self-determination may be exercised "externally" and lead to independence: in situations where a people is subjected to colonial rule or foreign military occupation, or where a territorially identifiable "unit" within a sovereign State is oppressed. However, while international law may not grant linguistic, ethnic, or other entities a positive right to independence in the absence of systemic discrimination, nor does it expressly prohibit secession by such peoples, groups, or minorities. International law is neutral with respect to secession, and in certain circumstances, it may well adapt to recognize effective political realities. This legal vacuum has led Franck to conclude that while international law may not confer a positive entitlement to secede unilaterally, peoples have a right, understood as a privilege, to *attempt* secession (Franck 1998: para. 2.11).

Christakis forcefully argues however, that international law not only does not permit unilateral secession, but is in fact hostile to all secessionist endeavors:

> [I]t is wrong to regard international law as affording such an "indirect right", such a "privilege" to secessionist groups. International law neither "permits" nor "authorizes"

secession. Rather what it does . . . is to erect against it important obstacles, by *protecting* the State against secessionist movements. Law is hostile to secession and scarcely "permits" it. It does no more than *take into account reality* when secession succeeds against all odds.

*(Christakis 1999: 82–83, emphasis in original, author's translation)*

The Canadian Supreme Court echoes Christakis' warning, declaring that while international law contains neither a right to unilateral secession nor the explicit denial of such a right,

> such a denial is, to some extent, implicit in the exceptional circumstances required for secession to be permitted under the right of a people to self-determination . . . [I]nternational law places great importance on the territorial integrity of nation states and, by and large, leaves the creation of a new state to be determined by the domestic law of the existing state of which the seceding entity presently forms a part.
>
> *(Secession Reference 1998: para. 112)*

Crawford also contends that a definite pattern emerges from the international responses to unilateral secession and threats of secession in the non-colonial context: "even in cases where there is a strong and continued call for independence, it is a matter for the government of the State concerned to consider how to respond" (Crawford 2006: 417).

Though Cassesse agrees that State practice and the overwhelming view of States remain opposed to secession, and that this is one of the few areas on which full agreement exists among all States, he does emphasize that secession "is a fact of life, outside the realm of law" (Cassesse 1995: 123). As Quaye comments: "The legitimacy of any secessionist movement depends on whether or not that movement succeeds, and, to a certain extent, without any regard to how that success is brought about" (Quaye 1991: 240). Radan also emphasizes that "secession cannot be said to have occurred until the process has been completed by the creation of a new state (Radan 2008: 21). While acknowledging that legal consequences can indeed flow from political facts, the Canadian Supreme Court nevertheless stressed that the principle of effectivity operates very differently from a legal entitlement.

> It may be that a unilateral secession by Quebec would eventually be accorded legal status by Canada and other states . . . but this does not support the more radical contention that subsequent recognition . . . could be taken to mean that secession was achieved under colour of a legal right.
>
> *(Secession Reference 1998: para. 144)*

This analysis is also reflected in the conclusions of the five international experts retained by the Québec government in 1992 to prepare an opinion on various legal questions relating to the territorial limits of an independent Québec (Five Experts Opinion). "[I]n a non-colonial context, the attainment of sovereignty by a territory is merely a question of fact in the eyes of international law: the new State is considered as such if its existence is effective" (Franck et al. 1992: 49). This reality – that the principle of effectiveness governs the success or failure of a unilateral secession – has profound implications for the determination of the eventual boundaries of the seceding entity.

## The territorial implications of unilateral secession

Crawford defines the criteria for statehood in the event of a unilateral secession as "the maintenance of a stable and effective government over a reasonably well-defined territory, to the exclusion of the metropolitan/predecessor State in such circumstances that independence is in fact undisputed or manifestly undisputable" (Crawford 1979: 266). Thus, if a seceding entity succeeds in asserting effective control over the territory it claims, and if the effectiveness of its statehood is recognized by the international community, the newly independent State will benefit from the protection afforded by the principles of territorial integrity, stability, and the inviolability of frontiers. The problem is that such a conclusion does not shed any light on the most critical issue: what happens if the unilateral secession is contested by the parent State and the seceding entity is unable to wrest control from it over the entire territory it claims?

Craven highlights the uncertainty that surrounds a bid for independence in the absence of a recognized legal entitlement. "Generally speaking, unless an explicit process of devolution is at work, the process by which an entity acquires or loses Statehood is shrouded by doubt, both as regards the relevant factual circumstances and as to their legal significance" (Craven 1995: 375–376). Much of this uncertainty stems from the fact that the principle of effectiveness offers no guarantees. While the seceding entity would be seeking to assert effective control, the parent State would, for its part, be entitled to resist such an attempt by all lawful means. International law, as already noted, sides with the territorial integrity of the parent State in such circumstances (in the absence of systemic discrimination) and consequently authorizes it to oppose claims to secession. Furthermore, third-party States are expected to remain neutral, as any assistance proffered to the seceding entity would be deemed an intervention in the internal affairs of the State in question.

While international law may acknowledge political realities once the independence of a seceding entity is firmly established, it will do so only in relation to the territory that the entity effectively controls. Indeed, international law responds in a radically different manner depending on the circumstances surrounding the accession to independence. Either it is a case involving a *right* to external self-determination, wherein accession is based on legitimacy, or it is a case of secession wherein independence is based on *effectiveness*. Corten emphasizes how this critical distinction inevitably affects the consequences of independence, chief among which is the delimitation of new boundaries: "This split, valid for the modes of accession to independence, must also be valid for its consequences, among which must undeniably be included the delimitation of frontiers" (Corten 1999: 407, author's translation). When independence is founded on a legal entitlement, the sequence is a right to external self-determination, therefore a right to the creation of a State, therefore a right to a territory, and therefore a right to definite boundaries (Corten 1999: 408). Independence established on the basis of effectiveness triggers an entirely different sequence: no right to external self-determination, therefore no right to the creation of a State, therefore no right to territory, and therefore no right to definite boundaries, whatever they may be.

While acknowledging that effectiveness governs the outcome of an attempted unilateral secession, some commentators argue that seceding entities benefit from predetermined boundaries. For example, in their 1992 report for the Québec government, the five experts state that when unilateral secession occurs within the framework of a well-defined territorial district, by virtue of the *uti possidetis juris* principle, the former borders of this district automatically become the boundaries of the new State (Franck et al. 1992: 28). Corten persuasively counters, however, that to detach one element in the sequence, namely the determination of boundaries, from the particular mode of accession to independence is illogical and untenable (Corten 1999: 408). The *uti possidetis juris* principle cannot impose such a territorial outcome on a parent State "possessed of a government representing the whole people without discrimination" and thus entitled, under international law, to the integrity of its national territory.

A detailed analysis of the *uti possidetis juris* principle is beyond the scope of this chapter and can be sought elsewhere (Lalonde 2002). However, a critical contention will be briefly considered: that the *uti possidetis juris* mandates respect for a seceding entity's existing boundaries because of its status as a "general principle of international law applicable to situations outside the colonial context". This characterization was espoused by the Badinter Arbitration Commission (Badinter Commission) created to advise the International Conference for Peace in Yugoslavia (1991) and subsequently endorsed by the five international law experts in their 1992 legal opinion for the Québec government.

According to the Badinter Commission, this characterization of the *uti possidetis juris* principle is supported by the 1986 decision of the ICJ in the *Frontier Dispute* case between Burkina Faso and Mali (Trifunovska 1994: 480). In its *Opinion No. 3*, the Commission reproduced the following passage from the ICJ's decision:

> Nevertheless the principle is not a special rule with pertains solely to one specific system of international law. It is a general principle which is logically connected with the phenomenon of the obtaining of independence, wherever it occurs. Its obvious purpose is to prevent the independence and stability of new States being endangered by fratricidal struggles.
>
> *(ICJ 1986: 565)*

It is interesting to note that the Badinter Commission omitted the last few words of the final sentence. The entire sentence reads: "Its obvious purpose is to prevent the independence and stability of new States being endangered by fratricidal struggles *once the administering power has withdrawn*" (emphasis added). Considered in its proper context, it is clear that the ICJ was merely affirming that the *uti possidetis juris* principle was not a special rule that pertained solely to one specific system of international law and therefore could apply to cases of *decolonization* elsewhere than in Latin America. At least four other instances confirm that the ICJ's discussion of the *uti possidetis juris* principle was firmly grounded in the colonial context (Lalonde 2002: 191). It is therefore difficult to draw from the *Frontier Dispute* case any support for the Commission's conclusion that the *uti possidetis juris* principle should govern in situations of unilateral secession.

The five international law experts refer to the same amputated passage in the *Frontier Dispute* case and endorse the Badinter Commission's conclusion that the *uti possidetis juris* is a general principle of international law. They also affirm that its status is no longer simply a matter of judicial interpretation but that, as a result of "recent" events, a general practice accepted as law has crystallized (Franck et al. 1992: 29). However, the State practice identified by the experts – the Soviet, Czechoslovakian, and Yugoslav precedents – does not support the contention that *uti possidetis juris* has become a customary rule of international law in the postcolonial context.

The essence of custom is that it should constitute "evidence of a general practice accepted as law" (ICJ Statute 1945: Article 38(1)(b). While it cannot be denied that with respect to the Soviet Union, the international boundaries of the successor States ultimately largely followed the former internal Soviet limits, this outcome is not, in of itself, sufficient to make of the dissolution of the Soviet Union a clear and incontestable precedent. Not only do the three key instruments in the period of independence (Minsk Agreement 1991; Alma Ata Protocol 1991; CIS Charter 1993) fail to mention the *uti possidetis juris* principle, but more importantly, it is impossible to establish that the former Soviet republics felt compelled to adopt a particular solution in resolving the issue of their mutual boundaries. Rather, the debate surrounding this vital question (Lalonde 2002: 219–220) reveals that for the great majority of the parties involved, only an *agreement* between the republics could guarantee the maintenance of the borders existing within the former Soviet Union (see, for example, the bilateral boundary agreement between Russia and Kazakhstan; Weerts 1999: 119).

As for the Czechoslovakian precedent, Crawford has described the separation of the Czech Republic and Slovakia as "a straightforwardly consensual process at the level of the governments and parliaments concerned" (Crawford 1997: 29). The two constituent republics became separate States after an agreement between them dissolved the Czechoslovakian Federation. Dissolution was achieved by parliamentary action under the Constitution Act of 1992, and by the date agreed upon for independence (1 January 1993), most of the arrangements for the dissolution had been worked out by agreement between the two governments. Certain other changes, including minor exchanges of territory, were subsequently agreed to. As all the issues arising out of the separation were resolved on the basis of the consent of the two parties, little support for a binding rule of *uti possidetis juris* can be garnered from this particular precedent.

Finally, in the case of Yugoslavia, a territorial settlement based on respect for federal administrative borders was imposed upon the constituent republics by the European Community (now European Union) and some major States. However, in Yugoslavia, extraordinary circumstances, rather than any established practice, seem to account for the solution ultimately adopted. Crawford identifies three critical factors that strongly affected the international response to the crisis:

> (1) four of the six republics, containing a substantial majority of the population, were attempting to break away; (2) the constitutional order, under which the constituent republics themselves "participated in the exercise of political power within the framework of institutions common to the Federation" had completely broken down; and (3) Yugoslavia was undergoing large-scale and unrelenting ethnic conflict which threatened to lead and did in fact lead to war crimes and crimes against humanity.
>
> *(Crawford 1997: 28)*

In light of these facts, the five experts' conclusion on the legal status of the *uti possidetis juris* principle in the postcolonial context is overstated. The international practice they rely upon does not appear to fulfill the twin requirements of custom – namely a constant, extensive, and uniform usage coupled with an *opinio juris sive necessitatis* (the conviction that such usage is legally mandatory). Consequently, the *uti possidetis juris* principle cannot be imposed upon a parent State under the mantle of custom. Furthermore, any claim that the Soviet, Czechoslovakian, and Yugoslav precedents are material to the determination of the boundaries of an entity attempting to secede from a sovereign independent State glosses over a critical distinction: all three cases involved the *dissolution* of the predecessor State, a critical factor that will be discussed in the next section. Thus, in the absence of a legal entitlement to external self-determination, an entity's claim to statehood, as well as to its boundaries, will be determined according to the principle of effectiveness, which offers no guarantees.

## Dissolution

### *Scope of the concept*

The principal distinction between dissolution and secession lies in the fact that in a case of dissolution, there is no "parent" State entitled to insist on respect for its territorial integrity. As Crawford explains: "The main difference is that in cases of dissolution, no one party is allowed to veto the process. By contrast, where the government of the predecessor state maintains its status as such, its assent to secession is necessary, at least unless and until the seceding entity has firmly established control beyond hope of recall (Crawford 1997: 17). As discussed, the presumption in favor of the continuity of States and the stability of boundaries means that the outcome of an attempted unilateral secession is weighed in favor of the parent State and against the secessionist endeavor. However, when an entity asserts its independence against a State that is itself in the process of dismemberment (through the effective and simultaneous disassociation of the majority of its constituent territorial units), no such presumption will operate in favor of the sovereignty of the parent State, and the nascent entity will be able to achieve statehood with much greater ease (Craven 1995: 380).

The fundamental difference in how the international community reacts to unilateral secession versus the dissolution of the parent State is clearly evidenced in the Yugoslav context. In its early stages, the Yugoslav crisis was characterized as an attempt on the part of two of Yugoslavia's constituent republics to secede (Slovenia and Croatia). At that juncture, States in the region and beyond categorically refused to recognize the declarations of independence and insisted upon respect for the territorial integrity of the Yugoslav State. This approach was grounded in fears of widening political instability and was also entirely consistent with the restrictive formulations of the right of self-determination discussed earlier. The subsequent shift in favor of recognition occurred only after the Badinter Commission's critical determination in its *Opinion No. 1* that the process unfolding in Yugoslavia was one of dissolution (Trifunovska 1994: 417). This crucial finding informed the entire subsequent handling of the crisis by the international community.

## The territorial implications of the dissolution of the parent state

In advising the International Conference for Peace in Yugoslavia, the Badinter Commission opined in its *Opinion No. 3* that the *uti possidetis juris* principle would act in the context of Yugoslavia to guarantee the internal administrative boundaries of the former republics in advance of formal independence:

> *Third* – Except where otherwise agreed, the former boundaries become frontiers protected by international law. This conclusion follows from the principle of respect for the territorial status quo and, in particular, from the principle of *uti possidetis. Uti possidetis*, though initially applied in settling decolonization issues in America and Africa, is today recognized as a general principle, as stated by the International Court of Justice . . . in the case between *Burkina Faso and Mali*.
>
> *(Trifunovska 1994: 480)*

Reference should be made to our previous explanation that in the *Frontier Dispute* case, the ICJ declared that the *uti possidetis juris* principle was a principle of general application in *decolonization* situations. Arguments were also marshalled to repudiate the characterization of the *uti possidetis juris* as a binding norm of customary international law, imposing a particular territorial outcome on all parties.

Even if one accepts that *uti possidetis* should perhaps be considered in situations of unilateral secession or dissolution, as defined and applied by the Badinter Commission it has been transformed almost beyond recognition. If, as the Commission concluded in its *Opinion No. 1*, the entire constitutional framework was collapsing, by virtue of what principle were the Yugoslav republican borders and only the republican borders entitled to protection? No convincing argument was put forward to justify the conclusion that the right of self-determination of the Serbian minorities, for example, had to be restricted in order to preserve the territorial integrity of Croatia and Bosnia when by their own declarations of independence, the two republics had themselves violated the territorial integrity of the Yugoslav Federation.

The Commission attributed this pre-selection to the operation of the *uti possidetis juris* principle. Yet, as Ratner has pointed out, *"uti possidetis* is agnostic on whether or not secessions or break-ups should occur"* (Ratner 1996: 601). In both Latin America and Africa, two separate and distinct processes were at work: first, the identification of the presumptive units of statehood, whether by virtue of revolution and the principle of effectiveness or by the right of external self-determination of colonial peoples; and second, the determination of the boundaries of those entities through the application of various principles, including *uti possidetis*. In the absence of any legitimizing principle, *uti possidetis* does not itself provide any criteria for deciding which entity should benefit from international legal protection. As a distinct and territorially defined administrative unit, the 91% Albanian majority in the former Autonomous Province of Kosovo could also have benefited from the presumption. This difficulty is highlighted by Angelet:

> The principle of *uti possidetis* can only fulfil its stabilizing role on condition that the beneficiary of the principle is designated beforehand: in the absence of this designation, the *uti possidetis* principle could generate a multitude of solutions depending on whether independence is proclaimed at one or the other level of organization of the predecessor State. Yet, outside the decolonization context, international law does not designate such beneficiaries.
>
> *(Angelet 1999: 219, author's translation)*

When the entire fabric of a State unravels, existing boundaries necessarily deserve consideration and some deference, but decision-makers should have the opportunity to consider whether significantly better lines can be drawn to promote long-term peace and stability. Existing boundaries and administrative limits at all levels should be evaluated as to their suitability as international frontiers in terms of the age of the line, the process by which the line has been drawn, and the viability of the entities on either side of the line. Alternatives should be considered to take into account minorities trapped within the emerging States and the respect of human rights. If international entities decide to intervene and to guarantee the boundaries of specific internal units in the context of the dissolution of a State, then that decision – if agreed to or enforced – may have operative effect. The crux of the matter is not to confuse this political process with a pre-existing requirement under international law to protect a select category of internal boundaries.

## Conclusion

A central value and fundamental organizing principle of the international legal order is the need to guarantee territorial stability for the sake of peace. This fundamental priority was perhaps first recognized in 1909 by the Permanent Court of Arbitration in the *Grisbådarna* case, when it stated that "it is a well established principle of the law of nations that a state of things that actually exists and has existed for a long time should be changed as little as possible" (PCA 1909: 6). Kaikobad has qualified this strong adherence to the territorial *status quo* as a fundamental precept of international law (Kaikobad 1983: 120).

To manage territorial change in a "clear, secure and regulated manner", international law and State practice have strictly defined the circumstances in which a territorially defined unit's right to self-determination can fracture the territorial integrity of a sovereign State. Self-determination, in its external version, has been deemed to confer a *legal entitlement* to independence only in the case of non-self-governing peoples, or peoples subjected to foreign subjugation or systemic discrimination by their own government.

Outside these three strictly defined situations, international law protects and defends the territorial integrity of existing States. Thus, in cases of attempted unilateral secession, no legal entitlement to independence and statehood is recognized. In such situations, the primacy afforded the continuity and integrity of the parent State's territory creates a formidable obstacle to the success of the secessionist endeavor. In situations where the very fabric of a State is disintegrating, the territorial outcome of such a dramatic change in the geopolitical map is not predetermined. Various political solutions and territorial principles will inevitably be considered and the ultimate resolution of the crisis will be driven by the need to re-establish stability and guarantee long-term peace.

# References

Alma Ata Protocol 1991, "Protocol to the agreement establishing the commonwealth of independent states (Alma Ata Protocol)", *International Legal Materials*, 31: 148–154.

Angelet, N. 1999, "Quelques observations sur le principe de l'*uti possidetis* à l'aune du cas hypothétique de la Belgique", in O. Corten et al. (eds.), *Démembrements d'États et délimitations territoriales: l'uti possidetis en question(s)*, Brussels: Bruylant.

Blay, S. K. N. 2010, "Territorial Integrity and Political Independence", *Max Planck Encyclopedia of Public International Law*, available at <https://opil.ouplaw.com/view/10.1093/law:epil/9780199231690/law-9780199231690-e1116>

Cairo Resolution 1964, "Organization of African Unity, *Cairo Resolution*, 1964", reproduced in I. Brownlie (ed) 1971, *Basic Documents on African Affairs*, Oxford: Clarendon Press: 360.

Cassesse, A. 1995, *Self-Determination of Peoples: A Legal Reappraisal*, Cambridge: Cambridge University Press.

Charpentier, J. 1980, "Le problème des enclaves", in *Société française pour le droit international – Colloque de Poitiers*, *La frontière*, Paris: Éditions A. Pedone: 41–56.

Christakis, T. 1999, *Le droit à l'autodétermination en dehors des situations de décolonization*, Paris: La documentation française.

CIS Charter 1993, "Charter of the Commonwealth of Independent States", *International Legal Materials*, 34: 1293.

Corten, O. 1999, "Droit des peuples à disposer d'eux-mêmes et *uti possidetis*: deux faces d'une même médaille?", in O. Corten et al. (eds), *Démembrements d'États et délimitations territoriales: l'uti possidetis en question(s)*, Bruxelles: Bruylant: 403–435.

Court of Arbitration 1981, "The Dubai/Sharjah Boundary Arbitration", *International Law Reports*, 91: 543–701.

Craven, M. 1995, "The European Community Arbitration Commission on Yugoslavia", *British Yearbook of International Law*, 66: 333–413.

Crawford, J. 1979, *The Creation of States*, Oxford: Clarendon Press.

Crawford, J. 1997, "State Practice and International Law in Relation to Unilateral Secession: Report", submitted to the Canadian Federal Government, 19 February 1997, <https://is.muni.cz/el/1422/jaro2006/MP803Z/um/1393966/INTERNATIONAL_LAW_AND_UNILATERAL_SECESSION.pdf>

Crawford, J. 2006, *The Creation of States*, 2nd ed., Oxford: Oxford University Press.

Curzon, G. N. 1908, *Frontiers* (Romanes lecture delivered at Oxford University, 2 November 1907), 2nd ed., Oxford: Clarendon Press.

Franck, T. M. 1998, "Supplément au dossier: Rapports d'experts de l'*amicus curiae*", Tab 3, para. 2.11, in The matter of the *Reference re Secession of Quebec*.

Franck, T. M. et al. 1992, "L'intégrité territoriale du Québec dans l'hypothèse de l'accession à la souveraineté", in *Commission parlementaire d'étude des questions afférentes à l'accession du Québec à la souveraineté*, volume 1, Québec: Secrétariat du Québec aux affaires canadiennes.

Higgins, R. 1963, *The Development of International Law Through the Political Organs of the UN*, London: Oxford University Press.

Higgins, R. 1994, *Problems and Process: International Law and How We Use It*, Oxford: Clarendon Press.

ICJ 1920, International Committee of Jurists, 1920, "Advisory Opinion Upon the Legal Aspects of the Aaland Islands Question", *League of Nations Official Journal*, Special Supplement No. 3: 2.

ICJ 1962, International Court of Justice, 1962, *Case Concerning the Temple of Preah Vihear (Cambodia* v. *Thailand)*, *International Court of Justice Reports* 4.

ICJ 1986, International Court of Justice, *Case Concerning the Frontier Dispute (Burkina Faso/Republic of Mali)*, *International Court of Justice Reports* 554.

ICJ Statute 1945, *United Nations Charter and Statute of the International Court of Justice*, 1945, *United Nations Treaty Series* 1: XVI.

ICR 1921, International Commission of Rapporteurs, 1921, "Report: The Aaland Islands Question", League of Nations Council Document B7: 21/68/106.

ICRC 2012, International Committee of the Red Cross, 2012, "Contemporary Challenges to IHL–Occupation: Overview", available at <www.icrc.org/en/doc/war-and-law/contemporary-challeng-es-for-ihl/occupation/overview-occupation.htm>

Jennings, R. Y. 1963, *The Acquisition of Territory in International Law*, Manchester: Manchester University Press.

Kaikobad, K. H. 1983, "Some Observations on the Doctrine of Continuity and Finality of Boundaries", *British Yearbook of International Law*, 54: 119–141.

Lachaume, J.-F. 1980, "La Frontière: Séparation", in *Société française pour le droit international – Colloque de Poitiers, La frontière*, Paris: Éditions A. Pedone: 77–94.

Lalonde, S. 2002, *Determining Boundaries in a Conflicted World: The Role of Uti Possidetis*, Montreal: McGill-Queen's University Press.

Lauterpacht, H. 1952, *Disputes, War and Neutrality*, 7th ed., London: Longmans, Green & Co.

Minsk Agreement 1991, "Agreement Establishing the Commonwealth of Independent States", *International Legal Materials*, 31: 138–141.

OAU 1963, "Organization of African Unity, *Charter*, 1963", *United Nations Treaty Series*, 479: 39.

PCA 1909, Permanent Court of Arbitration, *The Grisbådarna Case (Norway v. Sweden)*, available at <https://sites.dundee.ac.uk/dolfin/wp-content/uploads/sites/95/2018/05/1-Permanent-Court-Of-Arbitra-tion-Maritime-Boundary-Ruling.pdf>

PCA 1928, Permanent Court of Arbitration (Max Huber Arbitrator), *Island of Palmas (or Miangas) (The Netherlands/The United States of America*, *Reports of International Arbitral Awards* XI: 1.

Quaye, C. O. 1991, *Liberation Struggles in International Law*, Philadelphia: Temple University Press.

Radan, P. 2008, "Secession: A Word in Search of a Meaning", in A. Pavković & P. Radan (eds), *On the Way to Statehood: Secession and Globalisation*, Aldershot: Ashgate Publishing Limited: 17–32.

Ratner, S. 1996, "Drawing a Better Line: *Uti Possidetis* and the Borders of New States", *American Journal of International Law*, 90: 590–624.

Secession Reference 1998, Supreme Court of Canada, *Reference re Secession of Quebec* [1998] 2 S.C.R. 217.

Shaw, M. N. 1982, "Territory in International Law", *Netherlands Yearbook of International Law*, 13: 61–91.

Shaw, M. N. 1986, *Title to Territory in Africa: International Legal Issues*, Oxford: Clarendon Press.

Shaw, M. N. 1996, "The Heritage of States: The Principle of *Uti Possidetis Juris* Today", *British Yearbook of International Law*, 67: 75–154.

Simpson, G. J. 1994, "Judging the East Timor Dispute: Self-Determination at the International Court of Justice", *Hastings International and Comparative Law Review*, 17: 323–348.

Trifunovska, S. 1994, *Yugoslavia Through Documents: From Its Creation to Its Dissolution*, Dordrecht: Martinus Nijhoff Publishers.

UNGA 1960, United Nations General Assembly, Declaration on the Granting of Independence to Colonial Countries and Peoples, Resolution 1514 (XV), 14 December.

UNGA 1970, United Nations General Assembly, Declaration on Principles of International Law Concerning Friendly Relations and Co-Operation Among States in Accordance With the Charter of the United Nations, Annex to Resolution 2625 (XXV), 24 October.

Vienna Convention 1969, "*Vienna Convention on the Law of Treaties, 1969*", *United Nations Treaty Series*, 1155: 331.

Vienna Declaration 1993, World Conference on Human Rights, 1993, *Vienna Declaration and Programme of Action*, 12 July, A/CONF.157/23.

Vienna Succession Convention 1978, *Vienna Convention on succession of States in respect of treaties*, 1978, *United Nations Treaty Series* 1946: 3.

Weerts, L. 1999, "Heurs et malheurs du principe de l'*uti possidetis*: le cas du démembrement de l'U.R.S.S.", in O. Corten et al., *Démembrements d'États et délimitations territoriales: l'uti possidetis en question(s)*, Bruxelles: Bruylant: 79–142.

Zacher, M. W. 2001, "The Territorial Integrity Norm: International Boundaries and the Use of Force", *International Organization*, 55: 215–250.

# 34

# INTERNATIONAL LAW AND THE BREAK-UP OF YUGOSLAVIA

## *Thomas D. Grant*

Seldom has secession or the break-up of States, or for that matter the creation of a new State, occasioned formal legal proceedings that address international law aspects of those events in more than incidental ways. Laden as it is with politics, self-determination, too, is oftener addressed as a political principle than as a subject amenable to regulation under law. The break-up of Yugoslavia, however, occasioned the use of formal procedures of law at the international level in a number of attempts to place that prolonged, multi-stage, and deplorably violent process under legal rules. The break-up of Yugoslavia affords, to an unusual extent, an opportunity to consider self-determination and secession as matters of law and not of politics alone.

A large jurisprudence, an extensive state practice, and volumes of scholarly writing have addressed the many dimensions of international law relevant to the break-up of Yugoslavia (Radan 2002). The present chapter, which supplies an overview only, proceeds under five topical heads: the independence and recognition of States; federalism and international law; succession; international dispute settlement; and criminal law.

## Independence and recognition

A striking result of the break-up of Yugoslavia was the emergence in the territory of that State of a series of new States. Yugoslavia – or the Socialist Federal Republic of Yugoslavia (SFRY), to give the full title of that State before it broke up – was a federation consisting of six constituent units, called "republics" under the SFRY's Constitution of 1974. After two of the republics, Croatia and Slovenia, declared that they no longer formed part of Yugoslavia, a cascade of crises began, eventually leading to the worst violence that Europe had witnessed since the Second World War.

International law, like any legal system, needs to say who or what entities are legal persons, legal personality being the capacity of an entity to hold legal rights and be subject to legal obligations in a given legal system. States, notwithstanding the importance of other actors, especially individual human beings, remain the principal legal persons in the international legal system. International law therefore needs to say what entities are States. Having no central organ entrusted to answer that question comprehensively, international law has approached the matter in a largely decentralized way. It has determined what entities are States through the individual decisions that existing States reach as to whether or not to recognize an entity as a State

DOI: 10.4324/9781003036593-40

(Oppenheim 1992: § 39). Through the aggregate practice of States recognizing, or withholding recognition, a collective position is discerned and the claim to statehood – that is to say, the claim to constitute an international legal person – is either accepted or not.

Following the declarations of independence of Croatia and Slovenia and of two further SFRY republics – Macedonia, and Bosnia and Herzegovina – the question arose as to whether to recognize these entities, or to withhold recognition, and if the former, *when* to recognize them.

## The initial independence declarations

Slovenia's parliament voted on September 27, 1990, to disapply federal legislation in Slovenia. On December 23, 1990, Slovenia held a referendum in which the voters chose independence. The day before, Croatia had subordinated SFRY law to Croatian law (Weller 1992: 569). Croatia and Slovenia declared themselves independent in June 1991. Macedonia declared itself independent in September 1991, Bosnia and Herzegovina in March 1992. Bosnia's declaration followed a referendum that expressed support for independence but that Serbs in the republic boycotted.

The United States, the European Communities (EC), the Commission on Security and Cooperation in Europe (CSCE), and others outside Yugoslavia did not encourage the republics to pursue independence. To the contrary, the international position in 1990 and through much of 1991 was to favor the integrity of Yugoslavia in its existing borders. The European Communities (EC), alarmed by events in Yugoslavia, in August 1991 convened a conference. At the United Nations (UN), the Soviet Union said that Yugoslavia demonstrated "how dangerous is the growth of separatism and national extremism, not only for each individual country, but for entire regions" (Weller 1992: 579).

The preference for preserving the integrity of Yugoslavia notwithstanding, the break-up of the country continued apace.

## Recognition and collective response

By a Declaration dated December 16, 1991, the EC Conference on Yugoslavia invited "all Yugoslav Republics" to state by December 23 whether they wished to be recognized as independent States. According to the Declaration, "The Community and its Member States confirm their attachment to the principles of the Helsinki Final Act and the Charter of Paris, in particular the principle of self-determination" (Trifunovska 1994: 431). The Declaration further set out Guidelines for the recognition of new States. The Guidelines stated that the EC member States were willing to recognize new States "subject to the normal standards of international practice and the political realities in each case". The Guidelines required, as a prerequisite to recognition, that each republic accept "the appropriate international obligations and have committed [itself] in good faith to a peaceful process and to negotiations" (Trifunovska 1994: 431). The Guidelines further required that a republic, in order to be considered for recognition, respect human and minority rights, as well as accept the principle that existing boundaries are inviolable. The Guidelines did not invite consideration of requests by groups or territories other than the constituent republics.

To render advice in the application of the Guidelines, the EC Council of Ministers established an Arbitration Commission. Known as the "Badinter Commission" after the head of the French constitutional court, Robert Badinter, who chaired it, this body functioned through the summer of 1993 – that is, through the initial period of the break-up of Yugoslavia – and served as a sort of juristic adjunct to the Conference on Yugoslavia. More an advisory body than a classic arbitral mechanism, the Commission produced a series of opinions addressing the ongoing break-up (Pellet 1992). Among other matters, the Badinter Commission considered whether republics that had declared independence satisfied the Guidelines for recognition.

In *Opinion No. 1*, adopted on January 11, 1992, the Badinter Commission said that "the existence or disappearance of the State is a question of fact . . . the effects of recognition by other States are purely declaratory" (Trifunovska 1994: 416). The Commission here articulated a distinct view, which has been the prevalent one in modern international law, that, by recognizing an entity as a State, other States express a judgment about the facts of the situation; they do not through the act of recognition constitute a State where none had existed before (Grant 1999: 1–12). In *Opinion No. 5*, adopted the same day, the Commission concluded that Croatia had satisfied the EC Guidelines, subject to the republic amending its constitutional law in order to implement protections for the Serb ethnic population (Trifunovska 1994: 490). *Opinion No. 7* concluded that Slovenia, too, met the Guidelines; the Commission drew attention in this regard to Slovenian laws protecting Italian and Hungarian minorities in that country (Trifunovska 1994: 500).

More fraught was the situation in Bosnia and Herzegovina. The Badinter Commission, in *Opinion No. 4*, also dated January 11, concluded that the rejection of independence by the Serb ethnic population of that republic cast significant doubt on whether "a sovereign and independent State" had been "fully established" (Trifunovska 1994: 488). The Commission returned to the question of Bosnia in the summer and, in *Opinion No. 8*, which it adopted on July 4, 1992, noted that a referendum had resulted in an overwhelming majority for independence and that all of the Member States of the EC already had recognized Bosnia (Trifunovska 1994: 636).

As the practice in regard to Bosnia showed, by no means did the Commission's findings bind the States concerned. The EC States recognized Bosnia *after* the Commission had concluded in *Opinion No. 4* that Bosnia was not yet an appropriate object of recognition and *before* the Commission had returned to the matter in *Opinion No. 8*. Inversely, the Commission had determined that the former Yugoslav republic of Macedonia had given satisfactory undertakings in regard to its territorial limits and hostile propaganda against a neighbor, Greece (Trifunovska 1994: 495); but even so, States delayed recognizing that country, and the UN placed a special qualification on its eventual membership, a matter to which this chapter turns later.

With regard to Croatia and Slovenia, too, the Badinter Commission's advice had not been followed by every EC Member State. Germany announced that it was recognizing the two republics before the Commission delivered its first opinions (Crawford 1996: 482). States in the EC and others voiced criticism at the time toward Germany and other States that had recognized Croatia and Slovenia ahead of the group as a whole (Grant 1999: 145–208). The criticism suggests, perhaps, that an expectation had taken hold, in Europe at least with regard to the events at hand, that the recognition of new States should no longer be unilateral or entirely discretionary. To the extent that States did adhere to a collective approach, this appears to have been chiefly on prudential grounds, not considerations of legal duty. Nevertheless, the attempt among EC States to impart some regularity to their response, in particular their use of a legal advisory commission, contrasts with other modern episodes of the emergence of new States.

## Kosovo independence and the ICJ advisory opinion

Kosovo, under the Yugoslav constitution of 1974, had not been a republic. It had been an autonomous province of a republic, Serbia. In 1989, Serbia declared a state of emergency, effectively terminated Kosovo's autonomy and began a crackdown against individuals and institutions in the province (ICTY 2009: paras 217–221). The violent early stages of the break-up of Yugoslavia in 1991–1992 overshadowed events in Kosovo, but the situation there did not resolve itself.

In 1998, the situation in Kosovo worsened considerably. Security forces and the army of the Federal Republic of Yugoslavia (FRY) escalated their actions against Kosovar separatists. Civilian casualties increased. The Security Council and the Organization for Security and Co-operation in Europe (OSCE), together with a Contact Group consisting of the United Kingdom, the United States, France, Germany, Italy, Russia, and the EU, sought to induce Serbia to curtail its operations in the province. Serbia refused. The Security Council, by turns, condemned Serbia and called for a ceasefire (Krieger 2001: 128). The Security Council in October 1998 endorsed an OSCE verification mission for Kosovo (Weller 1999: 191). Serbia stymied the deployment of the mission.

A massacre of civilians at the town of Račak on January 15, 1999, in retrospect, appears to have been a turning point (Krieger 2001: 195). The Contact Group convened talks at Rambouillet and Paris in February 1999, and these led to a draft interim arrangement, under which Kosovo would exercise substantial self-government in Serbia. The Kosovars, though opposed to the continued sovereignty of Serbia over Kosovo, accepted the interim arrangement. Serbia rejected it, and Serbia's operations in Kosovo escalated further still. A quarter of the population of the province by then had been displaced by the violence. NATO commenced an air campaign against Serbia on March 24, 1999, Operation Allied Force. One NATO country reckoned that Kosovo had faced an "impending humanitarian catastrophe" (ICJ 2000: para. 2.12).

The NATO campaign concluded on June 10, 1999. By Resolution 1244 (1999) of June 10, 1999, the Security Council demanded the "verifiable phased withdrawal from Kosovo of all [Yugoslav] military, police and paramilitary forces" and authorized the deployment to Kosovo of an international military and international civil apparatus. In effect, the province from that point onward was under international control.

Under SCR 1244 (1999), Serbia no longer had an administrative or security presence in the province but remained notionally the sovereign. The international civil apparatus shared Kosovo's administration with local authorities who were organized as "provisional democratic self-governing institutions" (Krieger 2001: 365). The international apparatus carried out practically all functions at first, with a transition taking place over time toward the local authorities. NATO and the EU furnished security and police (ICJ 2010: paras 95–100). On February 17, 2008, after prolonged efforts to reach a final settlement of affairs between Kosovo and Serbia failed, Kosovo declared independence.

A newcomer to the legal issues surrounding the break-up of Yugoslavia is likely to be surprised when reading the Advisory Opinion of the International Court of Justice (ICJ) of July 22, 2010 in regard to Kosovo, for, though this is a legal instrument with a seemingly natural connection to those matters, it says little about Kosovo's separation from Serbia or third States' recognition of the new state of affairs that emerged after the declaration of independence. Instead, in keeping with its judicial function, the Court focused on the specific question that the General Assembly had put to it, the legality of the *declaration* by which the creation of a new State had been announced (ICJ 2010: 51). Further specifying the terms, the Court clarified that the declaration emanated, in fact, not from the provisional institutions of self-government of Kosovo that the UN Security Council had established but, instead, from a popular conclave outside the structure of those institutions (ICJ 2010: para. 54, paras 102–109).

The Court was clear that general international law contains no prohibition against making a declaration of independence. Territorial integrity, an important principle of international law, entails that a State is not to be divided by force from *outside* the State: it is a principle addressing *international* relations (ICJ 2010: paras 80–81). Accordingly, an attempt within a State to separate from it, while no doubt of concern to the public law of the State, is not as such regulated by international law. It is when an independence movement attains sufficient indicia of statehood that other States may begin to consider recognizing it as a State. The participation of the aspiring new State in processes of international law thus begins. This is the purport of the ICJ's observation that Kosovo's declaration of independence was "not intended . . . to take effect within the legal order created for the interim phase [under SCR 1244 (1999)]"; the declaration was intended, instead, to invite other States to consider Kosovo as an actor in the international legal order (ICJ 2010: paras 105, 121).

Though the ICJ identified these as issues that the General Assembly had not called on to address (ICJ 2010: para. 83), a number of States used the proceedings to ventilate their legal positions in regard to secession and recognition. Some of the States supporting Kosovo suggested that a right of "remedial secession" applies in situations in which gross human rights violations practically rule out the continued participation of a territory in the State to which it belongs (ICJ 2009b: 33–34; ICJ 2009c: para. 3.17). Cyprus, which opposed Kosovo's separation, advanced that there is no such right, even in extreme cases (ICJ 2009a: para. 144). Other States that opposed Kosovo's separation, however, seemed to remain open to the possibility that, *in extremis*, self-determination might entail a right to secede (ICJ 2009d: paras 86–88). Serbia advanced its view as to the legal effects (or non-effects) of recognition and as to the criteria of statehood in international law (ICJ 2009e: paras 501–523). The United Kingdom drew attention to the large number of States already having recognized Kosovo at the time of the proceedings and to their diversity (ICJ 2009f: para. 6).

Some academic writers have suggested that NATO's intervention in Kosovo should be understood as an armed support for the secession of that territory from the State to which it belonged (Falk 1999: 850; Ruys 2018: 904). Serbia, for its part, brought claims against NATO member States at the ICJ, including claims alleging unlawful intervention in the domestic affairs of a State (Serbia, Application). None of Serbia's claims prevailed (ICJ 2004: 328). NATO and its Member States were clear that humanitarian considerations, as well as the need to stop conflict and instability from spreading to neighboring countries, motivated their action (Kritsiotis 2000: 339–345).

At any rate, the interim character of the arrangements under SCR 1244 (1999) left the door open to the FRY to achieve the long-term continuation of its sovereignty in Kosovo, an opening absent in forcible separations of territory. Russia, for example, in seizing Crimea, gave that territory's sovereign, Ukraine, no interim (ICJ 2019: 588–589, 603).

Serbia and Russia, as of 2021, continued to oppose Kosovo's admission to the UN. They expressed dismay that the break-up of Yugoslavia had not stopped at the independence of the six republics that were formerly constituents of the SFRY. Academic Steven Ratner, writing in the 1990s, had referred to "the temptation of ethnic separatists to divide the world further along administrative lines" (Ratner 1996: 591). Across a range of international institutions and processes, however, Kosovo has gained acceptance as an independent State. There has been so far, no *reductio absurdum* of independence claims. Arguably the first chapter in the long crisis of Yugoslavia's break-up, Kosovo seems also to have been the last.

## Separation by consent

Not all steps in the break-up of Yugoslavia involved armed conflict and contested legal claims. The FRY, under a new Constitutional Charter, had renamed itself in February 2003 the Union of Serbia and Montenegro. In a referendum on May 21, 2006, the citizens of Montenegro indicated support for independence. Montenegro declared itself independent on June 3, 2006. Serbia without incident continued as a UN Member. The UN on June 28, 2006 admitted Montenegro as a new Member.

Thus, each of the republics that formerly had comprised the SFRY, and Kosovo, a formerly autonomous province of one of those republics, came to be independent States.

A significant number of new States emerged in the world after 1945 through essentially consensual acts. In the break-up of Yugoslavia, the emergence of Montenegro resembled that wider practice, to an extent. However, it was the exception to what otherwise to date has been among the most violent episodes of State creation in the UN Charter era.

★ ★ ★

As the preceding summary suggests, it was through more than one process that new States came to independence in the former SFRY. There was the consent-based separation of Montenegro from the federal union that it had formed with Serbia. There was the unilateral act of independence leading to the emergence of Kosovo. As for the other new States, which had emerged in the first years of Yugoslavia's break-up, these had resulted from the dissolution of the federal institutions of the SFRY, a distinct process to which this chapter now turns.

## Federalism and international law

The break-up of Yugoslavia called on those States and international organizations that attempted to ameliorate its effects to consider the relation between federalism and international law. As noted earlier, the SFRY was a federal State. International law says nothing to define with precision how powers are allocated between the central (or "federal" government) of a federal State and its constituent units, but international practice, at least incidentally, acknowledges the existence of federal States. Some treaties mention them. The autonomy of the units that comprise a federation may have consequences in regard to the fulfillment by the federation of obligations under international law. The break-up of Yugoslavia illustrates that the federal form also may have consequences for the legal relations of States that emerge when a federation disappears.

### *The fate of the SFRY*

A lawyer's definition of secession covers the non-consensual, unilateral separation of a territory to form a State. Doubt arises as to whether the independent States that emerged in 1991–1992 in the territory of the SFRY did so from a separation of that kind. The doubt arises from the manner in which the federal institutions of the SFRY came to an end.

The Badinter Commission observed that "the form of internal political organization and the constitutional provisions [of a State] are mere facts" – i.e., international *legal* rules exist and operate on their own plane, and so domestic arrangements, such as national constitutions, do not change the international ones. The Commission's observations here accorded with practice: in other settings, such as Somalia, even a prolonged governmental vacuum has not resulted in the disappearance of the State as an international legal person as far as courts and international organizations are concerned. However, after a point, domestic arrangements do have salience for claims regarding the existence of a State. Because, for purposes of international legal relations, one expects a government to exist in a State and for that government to hold "sway over the population and the territory," the absence of a government may affect whether a State still exists (Trifunovska 1994: 416).

The Commission elaborated on the relation between the governing arrangements in a federation and the existence of a State:

> [the federal-type State] embraces *communities* that possess a degree of autonomy and, moreover, *participate in the exercise of political power* within the framework of institutions

common to the Federation . . . [T]he existence of the State implies that *the federal organs represent the components* of the Federation and wield effective power.

*(Trifunovska 1994: 416, emphasis added)*

As of the end of 1991 and early 1992, the Badinter Commission observed that the federal organs of the SFRY "no longer [met] the criteria for participation and representativeness inherent in the Federal State"; "[t]he authorities of the Federation and the Republics ha[d] shown themselves to be powerless to enforce respect for the . . . ceasefire agreements concluded under the auspices of the European Communities or the United Nations Organization". From those observations, the Commission concluded that, as of January 11, 1992, the SFRY was "in the process of dissolution" (Trifunovska 1994: 417).

The Commission returned to the matter six months later. According to the Commission, in its *Opinion No. 8*:

> [T]he existence of a federal state, which is made up of a number of separate entities, is seriously compromised when a majority of those entities, embracing the greater part of the territory and population, constitute themselves as sovereign states with the result that federal authority may no longer be effectively exercised.

*(Trifunovska 1994: 635)*

The Commission observed that the federal organs of the SFRY were, by that date, defunct. All national territory and population were "now entirely under the sovereign authority of . . . new States". No "common federal bodies" existed. The Commission concluded that "the process of dissolution of the SFRY . . . is now complete and . . . the SFRY no longer exists" (Trifunovska 1994: 636).

An important element in the Commission's reasoning was that even the core of the former SFRY – the territory of Serbia and its close ally Montenegro – no longer participated in that State: the two republics had "constituted a new state, the 'Federal Republic of Yugoslavia'" (Trifunovska 1994: 636). The dissolution of the SFRY, with that development in view, was indeed "complete."

The legal characterization of these events as of 1992, however, remained unsettled. The new State to which the Commission referred – the FRY – did not accept that the SFRY had disappeared. It was the FRY's view that a series of secessions had diminished the SFRY's territory but that the FRY was the same entity, for international law purposes, as the SFRY. The Badinter Commission rejected this position, as had the UN Security Council, to which the Commission referred in its reasoning (Trifunovska 1994: 636). The Commission's understanding was eventually affirmed, but, through the 1990s, the FRY's insistence that the SFRY still existed gave rise to practical problems of State succession, including in regard to the application of treaties, representation at the UN, and the disposition of international boundaries, matters on which the remainder of this chapter will address.

Before turning to State succession, some further words are in order about federalism – in particular about the use of federal and kindred arrangements to address the aftermath of Yugoslavia's break-up.

## The federal settlement in Bosnia and Herzegovina

The break-up of Yugoslavia took place through the disappearance of a federation, but, among the new States that resulted, two new federal States came into being. The new State consisting of Serbia and Montenegro – the FRY – has already been mentioned, from which the smaller

497

part later peacefully separated. Of greater interest for its relative novelty is the federal settlement adopted under international auspices in Bosnia and Herzegovina.

A General Framework Agreement adopted in December 1995 at Dayton set out the legal framework for peace. Central to the framework was a new constitution. Incorporated into the Agreement as Annex 4, the Constitution of the Republic of Bosnia and Herzegovina is a federal constitution. Under the Constitution, the State is comprised of two main territorial "Entities": the Republika Srpska and the Federation of Bosnia and Herzegovina. The Constitution allocates minimal powers to the federal (i.e., central) government of the State and includes safeguards to prevent either of the constituent Entities from impinging too much on any "vital interest" of the other. The nomenclature is somewhat infelicitous, one of the constituents of a federal republic being a "Republika" and the other a "Federation," but it reflects underlying realities: the Republika is a pragmatic acknowledgement of the interests of ethnic Serbs who had opposed the creation of a Bosnian State from the outset; the Federation is an expedient to preserve an alliance between Bosnian Muslims and Croats who comprise the main groups in that Entity.

The Brčko District, a municipal area between the two Entities, is under a distinct legal regime created, in part, through an arbitral process, which this chapter will touch on next.

The implementation of the federal constitution in Bosnia has presented considerable difficulty. The integrity of the constitutional order there has relied for over a quarter century on a robust international presence. Nevertheless, the federal settlement seems to have supplied the flexibility its authors intended and thus continues to serve as the legal basis for public order in the State. Parties since then have entertained federal constitutions in other places that have experienced secessionist conflict, such as Cyprus and the Solomon Islands, which suggests, perhaps, that ready alternatives are not at hand.

## Further fault lines and new solutions

When it appeared some years after its independence that ethnic divisions might destabilize Macedonia, new governmental arrangements were negotiated. These did not call for federal institutions as such. However, the Ohrid settlement of August 2001, which stipulated the new arrangements, called for a "revised Law on Self-Government . . . that reinforces the powers of elected local officials and enlarges substantially their competencies" (Ohrid Framework Agreement 2001).

A hallmark of federalism, locating government closer to the people governed, was a solution to which parties in the former Yugoslavia turned in several forms. Thus, as States emerged from the break-up of the SFRY, which had been one of Europe's main examples of a federal State, new federations and other autonomy regimes came on the scene. The resilience of these approaches to government continues to be tested in the former Yugoslavia and in other parts of the world where parties have decentralized their constitutions in response to internal crisis.

## Succession

As mentioned earlier, the dissolution of the SFRY gave rise to questions of State succession. Succession of States means the replacement of one State by another in the responsibility for the international relations of territory, a definition expressed in the 1978 Vienna Convention on Succession of States in Respect of Treaties, Article 2(1)(*b*) (Vienna Succession Convention 1978). That instrument has not achieved wide subscription. Even among the States that have adopted it, the convention emphasizes the role of agreed solutions: the convention sets out general rules binding on its adherents, but it provides for those States, within the bounds of other international legal obligations, to agree otherwise. Two elements are visible here, both qualifying the Convention's general rules: the element of agreement, and that of prior obligation. The Badinter Commission, when it addressed succession, acknowledged both.

## Agreed solutions and accordance with international law

"[I]t is incumbent upon the Republics," the Badinter Commission said in January 1992, "to settle such problems of state succession as may arise from this process [of dissolution] in keeping with the principles and rules of international law, with particular regard for human rights and the rights of peoples and minorities" (Trifunovska 1994: 417). The Commission reiterated the point in July 1992, adding that the successor States in the former SFRY were to reach a settlement in equitable fashion and under agreed procedures – "subject only to compliance with the imperatives of general international law" (Trifunovska 1994: 640).

So, too, did the Commission, in its *Opinion No. 15*, call on the successor States to observe their conventional (i.e., treaty) obligations. The apportionment of assets and liabilities of the National Bank of Yugoslavia (NBY) and of the successor States' banks was subject to the international agreements of the NBY and of an agreement that the NBY and other Yugoslav banking institutions had entered in 1988 with foreign commercial banks (Trifunovska 1999: 1250–1253). Thus, the expectation was that the successor States to the SFRY would settle issues of succession amongst themselves fairly, and, also, that whatever settlement they agreed, it would accord with international legal obligations of the States involved.

The Badinter Commission, in its *Opinion No. 11*, adopted on July 16, 1993, set out specific dates for the succession of States following the break-up. The Commission reasoned that the date of succession corresponds to that of independence. According to the Commission, for Croatia and Slovenia the date of succession was October 8, 1991; for Macedonia, November 17, 1991; and for Bosnia and Herzegovina, March 6, 1992 (Trifunovska 1994: 1019). The FRY raised "particular problems" because it claimed to continue the SFRY but all international bodies "which [had] had to state their views on this issue" said that "this [was] not a position that [could] be upheld" (Trifunovska 1994: 1019). After further consideration, the Commission concluded that the date of succession of the FRY was April 27, 1992 – the date on which Serbia and Montenegro adopted a new constitution and after which international bodies referred to the "*former* SFRY" (Trifunovska 1994: 1019, emphasis added). The Commission added, consistent with its approach to succession overall, that all its findings as to dates of succession were subject to the successor States agreeing otherwise (Trifunovska 1994: 1020).

Settlement of issues of State succession arising out of the break-up of Yugoslavia has involved tremendous complexity and special arrangements, as well as attempts to apply general approaches. Some issues have stubbornly resisted settlement, even as the independent successor States enter their fourth decade (Tams 2016). Two high-profile issues that *were* resolved, or largely so, may be addressed here briefly – the relation of the FRY to the UN; and the borders of the new States.

## The UN membership question

Some of the States that emerged from the break-up of Yugoslavia were admitted as Members of the UN without serious incident. Croatia, Bosnia and Herzegovina, and Slovenia were admitted on May 22, 1992. Macedonia, with complications that this chapter addresses in the section on international dispute settlement, was admitted on April 7, 1993. Montenegro, as noted earlier, was admitted in 2006 following its peaceful separation that year from the State Union of Serbia and Montenegro. All were admitted as new States, no general rights of membership having survived their emergence from the SFRY upon that State's dissolution.

The FRY, by contrast, though having emerged as a new State in 1992, disputed its status. It maintained through the 1990s that it was *not* a new State, but, instead, the continuation of the SFRY – and, thus, entitled to the SFRY's seat at the UN. As the ICJ later noted, "the legal situation that obtained within the United Nations [with respect to the FRY] . . . remained ambiguous and open to different assessments" (ICJ 2004: ¶ 64). The situation at last was settled when the Organization admitted the FRY as a new Member on November 1, 2000. This is the UN membership that the Union of Serbia and Montenegro continued after 2003 and Serbia, after 2006.

## Succession, State borders, and other territorial regimes

Newly independent States in several parts of the world have disputed the precise disposition of their external boundaries. In most cases, however, boundary disputes have not concerned very substantial territories. The avoidance of wide-ranging boundary disputes owes in large part to the acceptance in international practice that pre-existing administrative boundaries supply the basis for new international boundaries. Described under the rubric *uti possidetis juris*, which international courts and tribunals accept as a principle of customary international law (ICJ 1986b: ¶ 20), this practice is particularly salient when a federal State disaggregates into its former constituent units. Such units already had boundaries for purposes of the law of the federation and, typically, each exercised wide-ranging powers within its territory.

Not all parties to the break-up of Yugoslavia, however, observed the principle that new States presumptively succeed to the existing boundary settlements. The Serb minorities in Croatia and Bosnia, backed by the FRY government, endeavored in fact to enforce a new settlement. No significant change to a boundary was achieved in this way.

The stability of pre-independence territorial boundaries in Yugoslavia also extended to other boundaries and jurisdictional regimes. The (peaceful) settlement of the Croatia–Slovenia maritime dispute supplies a notable illustration. The two States consented under a 2009 Agreement to submit to arbitration certain issues concerning their maritime boundary. The arbitral tribunal in the case, in its Final Award, dated June 29, 2017, among other holdings, determined that boundaries established under treaties that the SFRY had entered into before its dissolution are not affected by State succession (PCA 2017: para. 9). The tribunal also noted the Badinter Commission's holding in regard to *uti possidetis* and the inter-republican boundaries within the SFRY: those boundaries, too, remain unchanged, despite the political upheavals taking place around them. There was also a dispute in regard to the Bay of Savudrija/Piran, which Croatia said is a juridic "historic bay" with limits that had been defined under the SFRY. The tribunal determined that the status of the bay indeed survived the succession of States and it remained internal waters "within the pre-existing limits" (PCA 2017: paras 883, 885; Vidas 2018).

★ ★ ★

The federal structure of Yugoslavia perhaps deepened the fault lines along which that State's break-up took place, but federalism also supplied a set of boundaries that, if they had been given proper respect, might have stabilized the state of affairs without the prolonged violence and disputation that in fact ensued. As the Badinter Commission observed in its *Opinion No. 3*, *uti possidetis* "applies all the more readily" in view of Article 5 of the former SFRY constitution, which stipulated that no republic boundary was to be changed without consent (Trifunovska 1994: 480). The Commission's observation about the constitutional law of the SFRY was consistent with earlier jurisprudence, the ICJ having said that pre-independence internal law is the relevant source when defining a boundary under the *uti possidetis* principle (ICJ 2005:110; ICJ 1992: 559).

## International dispute settlement

In addressing the complex disputes that attended the break-up of Yugoslavia, an extraordinary array of dispute settlement mechanisms were employed, not only by the States themselves but also by other States and by international organizations that took an interest in the future of the region. This chapter already has mentioned the Security Council's attempts to avert a break-up of Yugoslavia and the efforts of the EC's Badinter Commission to regulate the break-up with fact-finding and legal analysis.

Distinct from efforts to address the situation globally, parties in the former Yugoslavia turned to adjudication and arbitration in order to settle particular disputes. Parties brought cases under several of the main international dispute settlement procedures, including at the ICJ and the Permanent Court of Arbitration; the *Genocide* cases at the ICJ are among the highest profile in the history of that court. Other mechanisms were called into being to address specific problems arising in the break-up. For example, a special arbitration, stipulated under the peace settlement for Bosnia, addressed the troubled city of Brčko.

Negotiation, itself potentially a mechanism of dispute settlement, also came into play, though negotiated settlements in some instances took decades to reach.

Perhaps most strikingly, in two parts of the former Yugoslavia – in Bosnia and Herzegovina and in Kosovo – territorial administration was placed under international control as part of a comprehensive effort at stabilization. Though not always described as an example of dispute settlement, the placing of these parts of the former Yugoslavia under internationalized regimes may be addressed as part of the multifaceted effort to resolve the difficulties that the break-up of Yugoslavia entailed.

## Genocide cases

Bosnia and Herzegovina, on March 20, 1993, instituted proceedings at the ICJ against the FRY, as that State was called at the time. Bosnia and Herzegovina opened by likening the FRY's alleged conduct to the genocide perpetrated by the Nazis during World War II. However, jurisdiction of a court such as the ICJ at the inter-State level depends upon the consent of States to submit to its jurisdiction. The gravity of a claim does not in itself create jurisdiction where none otherwise exists (ICJ 2012: 139). Bosnia's claims against the FRY were followed by some of the most extended and complex skirmishes over jurisdiction in the history of the ICJ. The FRY argued, *inter alia*, that Bosnia lacked standing to bring claims, due to alleged infirmities surrounding its emergence as an independent State; that the conflict in Bosnia was internal only and, lacking an international dimension, was not a proper subject for an inter-State claim; and that the Genocide Convention – which contained the sole jurisdictional basis for Bosnia's claims – did not apply to the FRY, on grounds that Bosnia's succession to the Convention, if effective at all, was effective only after the events that Bosnia's claims addressed. The ICJ, with minor exceptions, rejected the FRY's jurisdictional arguments (ICJ 1996: 623) and proceeded to adjudicate the merits.

In its merits judgment, which it delivered in February 2007, the Court found that Serbia, which since the start of proceedings had re-constituted itself as "Serbia and Montenegro", and then as "Serbia", had breached its obligation to Bosnia under the Genocide Convention to prevent the crime of genocide (ICJ 1996: para. 471 (5)). The Court further held that Serbia was obliged to transfer to the ICTY for trial individuals accused of genocide (ICJ 1996: para. 471 (6), (8)). Serbia was not, in the Court's judgment, legally responsible for committing genocide, for conspiring to commit or inciting genocide, or for being complicit in that crime (ICJ 1996: para. 471 (2), (3), (4)).

A central issue in the *Bosnian Genocide case* was the attribution (or "imputation") to Serbia of conduct of Bosnian Serb forces. The ICTY Appeals Chamber in the *Tadić case* in 1999 had suggested that "overall control" by a State over the conduct of another actor – such as the Appeals Chamber held the FRY to have exercised over the Bosnian Serb forces – may suffice to impute that actor's conduct to the State (ICTY 1999: paras 99–145). The ICJ, however, when addressing imputation years before in *Nicaragua v. United States*, had indicated a more specific and exacting test, one of "effective control" (ICJ 1986a: 64–65). In the *Bosnian Genocide case*, the ICJ adhered to the *Nicaragua* test. The ICJ reasoned that the ICTY Appeals Tribunal had been dealing with a different legal question, not sufficiently analogous to give an answer to that which Bosnia's claims had raised. The Appeals Tribunal had had to determine whether the armed conflict in Bosnia was international for purposes of the ICTY's jurisdiction over allegations against individuals for criminal offenses; the tribunal concluded that Serbia's involvement was enough to have made the conflict international. The ICJ, by contrast, had to determine whether the conduct of a combatant force is to be imputed to a foreign State for purposes of determining the international legal responsibility of the State for breaches against another State (ICJ 2007: 208–211). The ICJ concluded that Serbia's influence over the Bosnian Serbs did not suffice to attach responsibility to Serbia.

Some years after Bosnia instituted proceedings at the ICJ, Croatia did so as well. Like Bosnia, Croatia invoked the Genocide Convention against Serbia (ICJ 1999). As with the *Bosnia and Herzegovina v. Serbia* case, Croatia's case gave rise to extended and complex exchanges over jurisdiction and admissibility, with Serbia arguing – ultimately without success – to avoid the application of the Genocide Convention. In proceeding to exercise jurisdiction over Croatia's claims, the ICJ cautioned, however, that the existence of substantive obligations – such as those contained in customary international law – does not in itself constitute a mechanism by which to adjudicate claims of breach. Croatia's claims against Serbia could proceed before the Court only to the extent that they fell within the compromissory clause (jurisdictional clause) of the Genocide Convention (ICJ 2015: 47–48, 2008: 464). The *Genocide* cases serve as a reminder that there is no general international jurisdiction to deliver binding judgments over claims concerning secession or self-determination.

In the merits phase of Croatia's case, the Court found that the conduct of the SFRY army and of Serb forces in Eastern Slavonia, Western Slavonia, Banovina/Banija, Kordun, Lika, and Dalmatia satisfied the *actus reus* element of genocide (ICJ 2015: 117–118). In this part of its judgment, the ICJ thus carried out fact-finding and took judicial notice of events that had taken place in Croatia. However, the Court concluded that the evidence failed to establish that Serbia had had the intention to commit genocide (ICJ 2015: 128). To constitute a breach of the Genocide Convention, both conduct and intent must be present, and, so, the Court rejected Croatia's claim. Serbia counterclaimed that Croatia had violated the Genocide Convention in its conduct toward the Serb ethnic minority in Croatia. The ICJ judged that Croatia committed no internationally wrongful act in relation to the Convention and so rejected Serbia's counterclaim (ICJ 2015: 152–153).

The Court took as settled that "Serbs living in Croatia . . . constitute a 'national [or] ethnical' 'group' within the meaning of Article II of the Genocide Convention" (ICJ 2015: 130) a holding consonant with the Badinter Commission's conclusions in regard to that minority population over twenty years before.

## Supervised independence as dispute settlement mechanism

The parties to the conflict in Bosnia and Herzegovina engaged in nearly four years of negotiations before concluding the General Framework Agreement, which this chapter touched on earlier. The challenge had been to arrive at a settlement that satisfied the demands and concerns of the three principal ethnic groups of the country (Szasz 1996). The further challenge was to prevent a later breakdown of the settlement embodied in the Agreement. Thus, the United States, the EU, and other third parties took an extraordinary step: they constituted a series of mechanisms for ongoing oversight and management of the peace settlement. A military force, police forces, and administrative elements were installed. A High Representative, in practice an EU national, was given extensive powers. Academic writers have compared these arrangements to protectorates in the age of imperialism (Fox 2008; Stahn 2008; Wilde 2008).

There was also an EU Administrator for Mostar, under an interim Statute for the City (Trifunovska 1999: 438–439); and, in Croatia, a managed process to reintegrate Eastern Slavonia, Baranja, and Western Sirmium into the country following the attempted secession there by Serb ethnic forces (Trifunovska 1999: 657–659). As addressed in the next sub-section, Brčko, which was subject to an arbitral proceeding to decide its final disposition, was placed under an International Supervisor.

Kosovo, too, as this chapter noted previously, was placed under international administration, but this was under a regime distinct from that in Bosnia. The UN Security Council, by Resolution 1244 (1999) of June 10, 1999, authorized the creation of an international military presence – the NATO Kosovo Force or "KFOR" – and an international civil presence – the United Nations Interim Administration Mission in Kosovo or "UNMIK". The Security Council adopted SCR 1244 under Charter Chapter VII and, in so doing, expressed its determination "to resolve the grave humanitarian situation" to which the armed conflict in Kosovo had given rise. The Security Council described the arrangement that it created as a "*transitional* administration" (emphasis added) with the purpose of "establishing and overseeing the development of provisional democratic self-governing institutions". In this way, in addition to supplying stability and administering the territory for the time being, the Security Council assigned the interim administration a development function with a view to the completion of its mission at some future date. The date remained indeterminate. As the ICJ observed in its 2010 advisory opinion, the eventual outcome in Kosovo remained to be decided through negotiation (ICJ 2010: 444).

The uncertainties surrounding SCR 1244 notwithstanding, the resolution was clear as to the central problem: it required the FRY to get out. A formal FRY sovereignty remained, but the effective machinery of administration, and in particular the tools of coercion, would now change hands. The Security Council was also clear that, whatever the exact contours of a final settlement, Kosovo would have "substantial autonomy and self-government."

In November 2005, the UN Secretary-General appointed Martti Ahtisaari, former President of Finland, as Special Envoy for the negotiations as to the final status of Kosovo. The Special Envoy indicated, in February 2007, that despite intensive negotiations, the parties were unable to reach an agreement. The Special Envoy concluded that negotiations had been exhausted and that "the only viable option for Kosovo is independence, to be supervised for an initial period by the international community" (Ahtisaari, M. 2007: paras 3, 5). A further attempt was made to bring the parties to agreement on Kosovo's future status, this time under a Troika comprising the European Union, the Russian Federation, and the United States. Despite the Troika's efforts, which ran from August 9 to December 3, 2007, no agreement was reached (Troika 2007). This chapter already has addressed the independence of Kosovo which followed, a unilateral act outside the international framework that the Security Council had fashioned in the hope that the parties would have reached a settlement on agreed terms.

## Brčko

Brčko, a city and administrative district in the northeast part of Bosnia and Herzegovina, under the terms of the Dayton settlement was provisionally associated with the Serb Entity, the Republika Srpska, but the settlement stipulated that an arbitration tribunal would determine Brčko's final disposition. Ethnic cleansing had shifted the composition of Brčko from predominantly Bosnian Muslim and Croat to Serb. The settlement obliged the authorities of the Republika Srpska to allow displaced inhabitants to return. The tribunal found that as of 1998 those authorities by and large had not done so (ATD 1999: 540–541). The tribunal found that this and other failures to accord with the peace settlement were attributable to Slobodan Milosevic, the FRY leader (ATD 1999: 540).

The arbitral tribunal's Final Award, adopted March 5, 1999, created "a new multi-ethnic democratic government to be known as 'The Brčko District of Bosnia and Herzegovina'". The Final Award indicated that "sovereignty" over the District would be in the hands of the central government of the Republic of Bosnia and Herzegovina, but that its territory would be treated simultaneously as belonging to the Republika Srpska and to the Bosnian-Croat federal Entity, the Federation (ATD 1999: 539). An idiosyncrasy arising from this arrangement is that, if one were to have added together the surface areas of the Serb Entity, the Bosnian-Croat Entity, and the District *before* the award, and then added their areas *after* the award, as the award defines them, then the latter sum would be larger than the former.

Neither of the Entities comprising the Republic exercises effective authority over the District. The authority of the Republic there is heavily restricted too. An international supervisory regime applies to the District. The International Supervisor, who also serves as the Principal Deputy High Representative for Bosnia and Herzegovina, exercises substantial powers, including the power to issue "remedial orders" in the event of noncompliance in Brčko with the terms of the Final Award (ATD 1999: 539). Unlike most arbitral tribunals, which are *functus officio* after delivery of a final award, the Brčko Tribunal continued in existence, in readiness to address contingencies that might arise in the District (ATD 1999: 539).

Though unusual in the time since 1945, the approach taken to Bosnia's Brčko District finds analogy in earlier practice. For example, the Principal Allied and Associated Powers after World War I vested in a Conference of Ambassadors the authority to carry out a procedure, similar to arbitration, to determine the final disposition of the Jaworzina district (PCIJ 1923: 29) To address Brčko, the arbitral tribunal itself employed yet another modality that evokes an earlier period of international relations, international administration, albeit on a more modest scale than elsewhere in the former Yugoslavia, including in Bosnia as a whole. The remedial powers of the International Supervisor further suggest that dispute settlement is an underlying purpose of international administration in this form.

## *Macedonia*

Macedonia, an SFRY republic home to multiple ethnic groups and among the least-developed parts of the former federation, might have seemed at risk of violence, but, in fact, Macedonia remained peaceful in the first years of independence. The difficulty for Macedonia from the start was its name. The republic's neighbor to the south, Greece, objected that, by using the name, which is the same as that of Greece's northern region, the new State implied a territorial claim against Greece. Countries delayed recognizing Macedonia, and the UN admitted it as a Member under a conditional formula unprecedented in UN practice. Under SCR 817 (1993), Macedonia was to be "provisionally referred to for all purposes within the United Nations as 'the former Yugoslav Republic of Macedonia' pending settlement of the difference that has arisen over the name of the State" (Trifunovska 1994: 883–884). Emphasizing strict adherence to this formula, the UN treated "the" as the first part of the new Member's name, and following English alphabetization, Macedonia was seated next to Thailand (Wood 1997: 240).

The Badinter Commission in January 1992, when considering Macedonia's independence, however, concluded that that State had "renounced all territorial claims of any kind in unambiguous statements binding in international law" and that "the use of the name 'Macedonia' cannot therefore imply any territorial claim against another State" (Trifunovska 1994: 495). The Commission had taken note of Macedonia's "formal undertaking . . . to refrain . . . from any hostile propaganda against any other State" (Trifunovska 1994: 495). That EC Member States delayed recognizing Macedonia reflects that the decision whether to recognize a new State remains a matter of discretion – and that observance of the Badinter Commission's findings went only so far (Ioannides 2010). States outside the EC, too, delayed recognition, evidently on similar grounds. The United States when indicating its intention to delay recognition noted the name dispute (*Digest of U.S. Practice in International Law*, 1991–1999: 1147) as did Australia (Hewitson 1992: 417). Within the EC, France recognized Macedonia in 1992 but did not open diplomatic relations until the end of 1993, the latter delay entailing no particular legal position but communicating a degree of reserve (Annuaire français 1992: 1146, 1994: 1070).

Notwithstanding widespread recognition of Macedonia and normalization of diplomatic ties, the difficulty over the name escalated in 2008. The occasion was Macedonia's failure to gain admission to NATO. Greece, a NATO member, apparently had objected to Macedonia's admission. By an Interim Accord of September 13, 1995, Greece had legally committed itself not to object "to the application by or the membership of" Macedonia in international organizations of which Greece is a member, subject to a reserved right to object "if and to the extent [Macedonia] is to be referred to in such organization or institution differently than in" SCR 817. Macedonia brought a claim against Greece at the ICJ for Greece's alleged failure to respect the Interim Accord. Greece argued that Macedonia, through various means, was seeking to establish in international usage a name other than the one that the Security Council had designated; and, therefore, that Greece was at liberty to exercise its reserved right to object to Macedonia's accession to NATO. Greece's argument also relied on procedural rules of NATO, by which the Alliance reaches decisions on accession by consensus and without provision for a formal veto. The ICJ accepted neither argument. Greece, the Court held, had breached its obligation under the Interim Accord. Macedonia had requested, as further relief, that the Court direct Greece to "cease and desist" from any steps that might frustrate Macedonia's NATO aspirations, relief that the Court declined to grant.

Academic writers have given considerable attention to the FRY's relationship with the UN. The case of Macedonia and Greece at NATO has remained comparatively obscure. That case illustrates, however, that the break-up of Yugoslavia affected more than one of the organized structures of international relations. The stress of the break-up had wide-ranging effects.

By a Final Agreement of June 17, 2018, Macedonia and Greece settled the name difference. The former Yugoslav republic since then, in accordance with Article 1(3)(a) of the Final Agreement, has been called *erga omnes* (i.e., for all purposes, and not just in the UN), "Republic of North Macedonia," short form "North Macedonia" (Final Agreement 2019: 1089). North Macedonia acceded to NATO on March 27, 2020 (NATO 2022).

## *Other bilateral issues*

This chapter already has mentioned the Croatia-Slovenia maritime boundary arbitration. Outstanding bilateral issues between Kosovo and Serbia also have occasioned resort to international dispute settlement mechanisms. Serbia's claim of sovereignty over its former province remains an irritant, but, in 2020, under the Washington Agreement, which US Special Envoy Richard Grenell mediated, the parties agreed to implement earlier agreements re-opening highway and rail links between the countries' respective capitals. They also agreed to enhanced regional economic cooperation and the mutual recognition of diplomas and professional certificates. Kosovo affirmed its obligation to implement a judgment of its Constitutional Court in favor of the Serbian Orthodox Church (Muharremi 2021).

## Criminal law

Armed conflict in parts of Croatia and throughout Bosnia and Kosovo at different times resulted in human suffering on a massive scale. The proceedings that Bosnia and Croatia instituted against Serbia for genocide have been noted in this chapter already. Those were inter-State claims. Distinctly, international criminal law concerns the responsibility of *individuals* for criminal acts. In *Prosecutor v. Milutinović and others*, the Trial Chamber of the ICTY upheld allegations of atrocities in Kosovo (ICTY 2009). Serbia's President, Slobodan Milosevic, was the original first-named defendant. Other notable rulings were the conviction in 1998 of Bosnian Serb commander Radislav Krstić for the genocide perpetrated in July 1995 at Srebrenica; convictions in 2001 of three Bosnian Serbs for ethnic cleansing in Bosnia, in the course of which they used rape as "an instrument of terror"; and the convictions of two Croatian generals in 2011 in connection with ethnic cleansing operations against ethnic Serbs in Croatia's Krajina region in the early 1990s (see generally Adams 2018). The ICTY determined that there had been no unlawful targeting in the NATO air campaign in 1999 in Kosovo and Serbia and, so, no charges were brought in that connection.

The last prosecution to commence before the tribunal was of a former interior minister of Macedonia, against whom crimes were alleged in connection with the fighting in 2001 between Macedonia's security services and Albanian guerrillas. The tribunal acquitted him.

Violence against individuals is not a necessary concomitant to secession, or, for that matter, to the seizure of territory in acts of international aggression. However, mass atrocities took place in Bangladesh and Biafra in the course of secessionist conflicts, and serious human rights abuses have attended the forcible separation of Crimea. In the modern experience, such episodes of territorial mutation have been sanguinary. A salient feature of the break-up of Yugoslavia and its aftermath has been the development of a criminal jurisprudence addressed to individual perpetrators in that setting.

## References

Adams, A. 2018, "The Legacy of the International Criminal Tribunals for the Former Yugoslavia and Rwanda and Their Contribution to the Crime of Rape", *European Journal of International Law*, 29: 749–769.

Ahtisaari, M. 2007, Report of the Special Envoy of the Secretary-General on Kosovo's Future Status, S/2007/168, Mar. 26.

Annuaire français 1992, *Annuaire français de droit international public* 1992, vol. 38.

Annuaire français 1994, *Annuaire français de droit international public* 1994, vol. 40.

ATD 1999, "Arbitral Tribunal for Dispute Over Inter-Entity Boundary in Brčko Area, Final Award", *International Legal Materials*, 38: 536.

Crawford, B. 1996, "Explaining Defection from International Cooperation: Germany's Unilateral Recognition of Croatia", *World Politics*, 48: 482–521.

*Digest of U.S. Practice in International Law*, 1991–1999, Washington: Office of the Legal Adviser, U.S. Department of State.

Falk, R. A. 1999, "Kosovo, World Order, and the Future of International Law", *American Journal of International Law*, 93: 847–857.

Final Agreement 2019, "Final Agreement for the Settlement of the Differences as Described in the United Nations Security Council Resolutions 817 (1993) and 845 (1993), Termination of the Interim Accord of 1995, and the Establishment of a Strategic Partnership Between the Parties," Annex I to A/73/745 – S/2019/139, 2019, *International Legal Materials*, 58: 1084–1100.

Fox, G. H. 2008, *Humanitarian Occupation*, Cambridge: Cambridge University Press.

Grant, T. D. 1999, *The Recognition of States*, Westport: Greenwood Publishing Group.

Hewitson, P. (ed.) 1992, "Australian Practice in International Law 1992", *Australian Yearbook of International Law*, 14: 375–691.

ICJ 1986a, International Court of Justice, *Military and Paramilitary Activities in and against Nicaragua (Nicaragua v. United States of America)*, International Court of Justice Reports 14.

ICJ 1986b, International Court of Justice, *Case Concerning the Frontier Dispute (Burkina Faso/Republic of Mali)*, International Court of Justice Reports 554.

ICJ 1992, International Court of Justice, *Land, Island and Maritime Frontier Dispute (El Salvador/Honduras: Nicaragua intervening)*, International Court of Justice Reports 559.

ICJ 1996, International Court of Justice, *Application of the Convention on the Prevention and Punishment of the Crime of Genocide (Bosnia and Herzegovina v. Yugoslavia), Preliminary Objections*, International Court of Justice Reports 623.

ICJ 1999, International Court of Justice, Croatia, Application Instituting Proceedings, https://icj-cij.org/public/files/case-related/118/7125.pdf

ICJ 2000, Netherlands Prelim. Objections, *Legality of Use of Force (Serbia and Montenegro v. Netherlands)*.

ICJ 2004, International Court of Justice, *Legality of Use of Force (Serbia and Montenegro v. Belgium)*, International Court of Justice Reports 328.

ICJ 2005, International Court of Justice, *Case Concerning the Frontier Dispute (Benin/Niger)*, International Court of Justice Reports 110.

ICJ 2007, International Court of Justice, *Application of the Convention on the Prevention and Punishment of the Crime of Genocide (Bosnia and Herzegovina v. Serbia and Montenegro)*, International Court of Justice Reports 43.

ICJ 2008, International Court of Justice, *Application of the Convention on the Prevention and Punishment of the Crime of Genocide (Croatia v. Serbia), Preliminary Objections*, International Court of Justice Reports 464.

ICJ 2009a, Cyprus Written Statement (*Kosovo* advisory proceedings), April 17, 2009.

ICJ 2009b, Germany Written Statement (*Kosovo* advisory proceedings), April 17, 2009.

ICJ 2009c, Netherlands Written Statement (*Kosovo* advisory proceedings), April 17, 2009.

ICJ 2009d, Russian Federation Written Statement (*Kosovo* advisory proceedings), April 17, 2009.

ICJ 2009e, Serbia Written Statement (*Kosovo* advisory proceedings), April 17, 2009.

ICJ 2009f, United Kingdom Written Comments (*Kosovo* advisory proceedings), July 17, 2009.

ICJ 2010, International Court of Justice, *Accordance with International Law of the Unilateral Declaration of Independence in Respect of Kosovo, Advisory Opinion* International Court of Justice Reports 403.

ICJ 2012, International Court of Justice, *Jurisdictional Immunities of the State (Germany v. Italy: Greece Intervening)*, International Court of Justice Reports 136.

ICJ 2015, International Court of Justice, *Application of the Convention on the Prevention and Punishment of the Crime of Genocide (Croatia v. Serbia)*, International Court of Justice Reports 47.

ICJ 2019, International Court of Justice, *Application of the International Convention for the Suppression of the Financing of Terrorism and of the International Convention on the Elimination of All Forms of Racial Discrimination (Ukraine v. Russian Federation)*, International Court of Justice Reports 558.

ICTY 1999, International Criminal Tribunal for the Former Yugoslavia, *Prosecutor v. Tadić, IT-94-1-A*, <www.icty.org/x/cases/tadic/acjug/en/tad-aj990715e.pdf>

ICTY 2009, International Criminal Tribunal for the Former Yugoslavia, 2009, *Prosecutor v. Milan Milutinović, et al, IT-05-87-T0*, <www.refworld.org/cases,ICTY,49a7bf602.html>

Ioannides, M. 2010, "Naming a State", *Max Planck Year Book of United Nations Law*, 14: 521–522.

Krieger, H. (ed.) 2001, *The Kosovo Conflict and International Law: An Analytical Documentation 1974–1999*, Cambridge: Cambridge University Press.

Kritsiotis, D. 2000, "The Kosovo Crisis and NATO's Application of Armed Force against the Federal Republic of Yugoslavia", *International & Comparative Law Quarterly*, 49: 330–359.

Muharremi, R. 2021, "The 'Washington Agreement' between Kosovo and Serbia", *American Society of International Law Insight*, 25(4): Mar. 12, <www.asil.org/sites/default/files/ASIL_Insights_2021_V25_I4.pdf>

NATO 2022, North Atlantic Treaty Organization, Relations with the Republic of North Macedonia, <www.nato.int/cps/en/natohq/topics_48830.htm>

Ohrid Framework Agreement 2001, <https://peacemaker.un.org/fyrom-ohridagreement2001>

Oppenheim, L. 1992, *International Law*, 9th ed., London: Longman.

PCA 2017, Permanent Court of Arbitration, *Republic of Slovenia/Republic of Croatia*, PCA Case No. 2021–04, Final Award, June 29, 2017.

PCIJ 1923, Permanent Court of International Justice, *Question of Jaworzina (Polish-Czechoslovakian Frontier), Advisory Opinion*, 1923 P.C.I.J. (ser. B) No. 8 (Dec. 6).

Pellet, A. 1992, "The Opinions of the Badinter Arbitration Committee. A Second Breath for the Self-Determination of Peoples", *European Journal of International Law*, 3: 178–185.

Radan, P. 2002, *The Break-up of Yugoslavia and International Law*, London: Routledge.

Ratner, S. R, 1996, "Drawing a Better Line: *Uti Possidetis* and the Borders of New States", *American Journal of International Law*, 90: 590–624.

Ruys, T. 2018, "Criminalizing Aggression: How the Future of the Law on the Use of Force Rests in the Hands of the ICC", *European Journal of International Law*, 29: 887–917.

Stahn, C. 2008, *The Law and Practice of International Territorial Administration: Versailles to Iraq and Beyond*, Cambridge: Cambridge University Press.

Szasz, P. 1996, "Introductory Note," *International Legal Materials*, 35: 75.

Tams, C. J. 2016, "State Succession to Investment Treaties: Mapping the Issues", *ICSID Review: Foreign Investment Law Journal*, 31: 314–343.

Trifunovska, S. 1994, *Yugoslavia Through Documents: From Its Creation to Its Dissolution*, Dordrecht: Martinus Nijhoff Publishers.

Trifunovska, S. 1999, *Yugoslavia Through Documents: From Its Dissolution to the Peace Settlement*, The Hague: Martinus Nijhoff Publishers.

Troika 2007, Troika on Kosovo 2007, Report of the Troika on Kosovo, Dec. 4, S/2007/723, annex.

Vidas, D. 2018, "The Delimitation of the Territorial Sea, The Continental Shelf, and the EEZ," in A. G. Oude Elferink, T. Henriksen and S. V. Busch (eds.), *Maritime Boundary Delimitation: The Case Law. Is it Consistent and Predictable?*, Cambridge: Cambridge University Press: 33–61.

Vienna Succession Convention 1978, *Vienna Convention on succession of States in respect of treaties*, United Nations Treaty Series 1946: 3.

Weller, M. 1992, "The International Response to the Dissolution of the Socialist Federal Republic of Yugoslavia", *American Journal of International Law*, 86: 569–607.

Weller, M. 1999, *The Crisis in Kosovo 1989–1999*, Cambridge: Documents & Analysis Publishing Ltd.

Wilde, R. 2008, *International Territorial Administration: How Trusteeship and the Civilizing Mission Never Went Away*, Oxford: Oxford University Press.

Wood, M. C. 1997, "Participation of Former Yugoslav States in the United Nations and in Multilateral Treaties", *Max Planck Year Book of United Nations Law*, 1: 231–257.

# 35

# ARTICLE 50 OF THE TREATY ON EUROPEAN UNION

## "Seceding" from the European Union

*Nikos Skoutaris*

### Introduction

Unlike breach, withdrawal from an international treaty is in principle a lawful act and not too uncommon an act (Helfer 2005). Article 54 of the Vienna Convention on the Law of the Treaties (Vienna Convention) allows a State to withdraw from a treaty either in conformity with the relevant provisions or by consent of all parties. Article 4 of the Vienna Convention, however, clarifies that the Convention "applies only to Treaties which are concluded by States after the entry into force of the present Convention" (Vienna Convention 1969). This means that the European Union (EU) Member States that had ratified the Convention have had an undeniable right to withdraw from the EU since at least "the first 'new' treaty amending the original ones (i.e. the Single European Act) entered into force in 1987 (the Convention entered into force on 27 January 1980)" (Closa 2017: 188).

Notwithstanding, the implicit existence of such right of withdrawal from the voluntary union of States predated the ratification of the Vienna Convention. This is evident from the fact that nobody contested the right of the United Kingdom (UK) to withdraw from the Common Market if the British electorate had decided so in the first "Brexit" referendum in 1975 (Tatham 2012: 144). Moreover, Greenland managed to withdraw from the EU following its 1982 referendum and three years of subsequent negotiations that led to a very different relationship with the EU. Although Greenland was not a (Member) State itself, its withdrawal – following a democratic vote of its inhabitants – underlined the fact that the EU was a voluntary union of States and peoples from where participating entities could leave. This was also the view of several national constitutional actors. For instance, the German Constitutional Court in its famous ruling on the Maastricht Treaty proclaimed that EU "membership may . . . be terminated by means of an appropriate act being passed" (Re Maastricht Treaty 1993). A similar view was adopted by the Czech Constitutional Court in its ruling on the Treaty of Lisbon (Re Treaty of Lisbon 2008).

In any case, the Treaty of Lisbon, which entered into force in 2009, clarified beyond any doubt that such right of withdrawal exists. Article 50 of the Treaty on European Union (TEU) explicitly allows a Member State "to withdraw from the Union in accordance with its own constitutional requirements". This provision could be seen as a *lex specialis* to the aforementioned general international law rule provided in the Vienna Convention. From an EU law point of

DOI: 10.4324/9781003036593-41

view, however, the EU is also a "community of unlimited duration, having its own institutions, its own personality, its own legal capacity [and] real powers stemming from a limitation of sovereignty or transfer of powers from the [Member] States" (Costa v. ENEL 1964). To the extent that Article 50 of the TEU allows the withdrawal of a Member State from the EU and the abrupt end to the symbiotic relationship of its legal order with that of the EU, it is also a process that bears significant resemblance with secession. In fact, Garben has suggested that the right to secede under Article 50 is "[the only undeniable legal limit that Member States have at their disposal against competence creep under the current Treaty framework" (Garben 2020). It serves as an important reminder that Member States have the power to put an end to the federalist "Sonderweg" of "an ever closer union" (Weiler 2009).

This chapter offers a concise analysis of Article 50 as a constitutional clause that allows the secession of a constituent part of a voluntary union of States. It does so by explaining its unilateral and unconditional character; reviewing the procedural stages it foresees and the legal arrangements it triggers; and, in the context of the UK, referring to the possibility of re-accession to the EU either by the UK itself or one of its constituent nations.

## Article 50(1) of the Treaty on European Union: unilateralism and national constitutional requirements

Friel distinguishes three categories of withdrawal models in federal or quasi-federal systems (Friel 2004). The state primacy or sovereignty model provides every constituent unit with an unqualified right to secede. The federal primacy model prohibits secession, while the federal control model provides a right to withdrawal subject to certain conditions. The first paragraph of Article 50 provides that "any Member State may decide to withdraw from the Union in accordance with its own constitutional requirements." The second one allows the relevant Member State to notify the EU Council of its decision, while the third makes clear that the withdrawal may take place even if there is no agreement between the withdrawing Member State and the remaining ones. Therefore, the Article 50 right clearly belongs to the state primacy model since it is characterised by unilateralism.

As the Court of Justice of the European Union (CJEU) has confirmed in *Wightman v. Secretary of State for Exiting the European Union*, "the decision to withdraw is for [a] Member State alone to take, in accordance with its constitutional requirements, and therefore depends solely on its sovereign choice" (Wightman v. Secretary of State 2018: para. 50). It "is totally independent of the will of the EU [and] the remaining Member States" (Closa 2017: 193–194). Such unilateralism is very different from what, the Canadian Supreme Court, in *Reference re Secession of Quebec*, has held. There, the Court made clear that "the unambiguous expression of a clear majority of Quebecers that they no longer wish to remain in Canada" would give rise to "the constitutional duty to negotiate" secession (Secession Reference 1998: para. 104).

Having said that, the unilateral nature of the right to secede from the EU seems to face at least one limitation at the national constitutional level. As already mentioned, pursuant to Article 50(1), the withdrawal of a Member State should take place in accordance with its own constitutional requirements. This idea that such a fundamental political choice about the constitutional future of a Member State and the Union should be respecting the national constitutional rules is in conformity with the composite, intertwined and multi-level character of the European constitution (Besselink 2007; Claes 2006; Pernice 1999; Ziller 2005). Pernice has explained that the constitution of Europe is "made up of the constitutions of the Member States bound together by a complementary constitutional body consisting of the European Treaties" (Pernice 1999: 707). However, "the relation between the EU and national constitutions should not be viewed as a conglomerate of autonomous, more or less, detached systems which relate to each other at different 'levels'" (Besselink 2007: 6). Instead, it should be viewed as a "mutually assumed relationship" "where one part cannot function without the other" (Besselink 2007: 6). At the very core of this composite constitution lies the idea of constitutional tolerance (Weiler 2009: 7). This is *par excellence* depicted in Article 4(2) of the TEU, which provides that the "Union shall respect . . . Member States' national identities, inherent in their fundamental structures, political and constitutional, inclusive of regional and local self-government". This means that the starting point of how the EU accommodates major constitutional events such as the decision to withdraw from the Union is and should be with respect to the relevant Member States' position, the processes that take place within it, and their outcomes (Peers 2012: 59). Having said that, there is a limit to such relative heteronomy and deference. This can be found in the foundational values enshrined in Article 2 of the TEU. Those are common values to the Member States, but more importantly, they are set as the requirements for accession and EU membership pursuant to Article 49 of the TEU, and the breach of which could lead to the triggering of the Article 7 sanction procedure.

More importantly, for the purposes of this chapter, within the context of the Brexit negotiations, the EU-derived obligation for respect of the national constitutional requirements gave rise to a significant legal question in the UK. According to the uncodified and idiosyncratic British constitution, it was not entirely clear which constitutional actor possessed the right to trigger Article 50. Was it the Government using its undeniable prerogative/executive power to represent the UK in the international plane? Or was it the sovereign UK Parliament – the main locus of the British constitutional and political order.

This genuine question of separation of powers was adjudicated in *R (Miller) v. State for Exiting the European Union* (R (Miller) v. Secretary of State 2018). There, the UK Supreme Court decided that the UK Government could not rely on executive powers in the area of international relations to trigger Article 50. Instead, in accordance with the principle of parliamentary sovereignty, which lies at the heart of the uncodified British constitution, the UK Parliament had to enact relevant legislation authorising the Government to trigger the withdrawal process, which they subsequently did (European Union (Notification of Withdrawal) Act 2017). With their decision, the majority of the Supreme Court judges highlighted the prominent constitutional role of the British legislature where sovereignty lies. At the same time, they made clear that such a role is not shared with the regional parliaments. The 11 judges of the Supreme Court unanimously rejected the argument put forward by the devolved governments that Westminster had become constitutionally bound to ask for the consent of the Scottish Parliament in order to start the withdrawal process.

Eeckhout and Frantziou convincingly argue, however, that it is not sufficient to follow the constitutionally prescribed procedure only at the start of the withdrawal process (Eeckhout & Frantziou 2017: 710). A "constitutionalist interpretation [of Article 50] requires deep and genuine respect for the withdrawing Member State's constitutional requirements" (ibid) throughout the process of withdrawal. In the UK context, such respect led the Supreme Court in *R (Miller) v. The Prime Minister (Lord Advocate Intervening)* to find that the UK Government had illegally prorogued Parliament in autumn 2019 when they used the standard and ancient legislative procedure of prorogation as a tool to prevent Members of Parliament from intervening prior to the UK's departure from the EU on 31 October 2019. According to the unanimous decision of the Court, respect to parliamentary sovereignty and democratic accountability meant that a prorogation is unlawful when it has "the effect of frustrating or preventing, without reasonable justification, the ability of Parliament to carry out its constitutional functions as a legislature and as the body responsible for the supervision of the executive." (R (Miller) v. The Prime Minister 2020: para. 50).

Finally, the requirements of the British constitutional order that is founded on the principle of parliamentary sovereignty included the need for Parliament to approve the Withdrawal Agreement.

> Under the UK constitution, [the decision to withdraw] is conditional on ultimate parliamentary approval, and it is only at the end of the Article 50 negotiations, when the terms of withdrawal are clear, that there can be a final decision on such withdrawal. Even if there is no withdrawal agreement, it is but Parliament which can decide, at the end of the two-year process, that the UK leaves the EU. That means that, under UK constitutional law, withdrawal is a process requiring a series of steps.
>
> *(Eeckhout & Frantziou 2017: 710)*

Indeed, after one of the most tumultuous periods in modern British politics, Parliament managed to approve the revised Withdrawal Agreement by passing the necessary implementation legislation – the EU (Withdrawal Agreement) Act 2020.

At the other end of the spectrum, the composite nature of the EU constitution is also evident by the fact that the fulfilment of the condition to respect the "national constitutional requirements" may also be judicially reviewed by the CJEU (Tridimas 2016: 303). Having said that, one has to accept that the ability of the CJEU to judicially review "national constitutional requirements" would be extremely modest. In essence, its role would be limited to ensuring that the relevant withdrawal would not be grossly violating the common constitutional traditions of the Member States per Article 6(3) of the TEU and the foundational values of the European constitutional order as provided by Article 2 of the TEU. If that was to be proved, the EU would be faced with the following paradoxical scenario: its judicial branch would be blocking the withdrawal of a Member State due to breaches of constitutional principles that could have anyway led to a suspension of its membership rights according to Article 7.

## Article 50(3) of the Treaty on European Union: the (un)conditional nature of Article 50

Apart from unilateral withdrawal, the exercise of the right to withdraw pursuant to Article 50 is also unconditional in that it "is not subjected to any preliminary verification of conditions nor is it even conditional on the conclusion of the agreement foreseen in the provision" (Closa 2017: 195). Article 50(1) allows a Member State "to withdraw from the Union in accordance with its own constitutional requirements". Article 50(3) foresees that the withdrawal can take place two years after the Member State has notified the EU of its intention to leave even if no withdrawal agreement has been achieved by then. Once the notification of Article 50 has been submitted, the withdrawal of a Member State is certain – even in a disorderly fashion that could harm the political and economic interests of both the EU and the withdrawing State – unless revoked by the State itself.

This is in marked contrast with the majority of constitutional provisions that regulate secessions. Most of them provide for conditions with regard to the organisation of a referendum that could potentially lead to secession and/or foresee an *inter partes* agreement as an important step to finalise the process. For instance, a referendum for the reunification of Ireland can only be organised if "it appears likely to [the UK Secretary of State] that a majority of those voting would express a wish that Northern Ireland should cease to be part of the United Kingdom and form part of a united Ireland" (Northern Ireland Act 1998: Schedule 1). Article 113 of the Constitution of Saint Kitts and Nevis allows for the secession of Nevis Island following a process that is prescribed in a very detailed manner by that provision. In Liechtenstein, pursuant to Article 4(2) of its Constitution, secession can only be regulated by law or by treaty, while Article 39(4)(e) of the Ethiopian constitution allows for it "when the division of assets is effected in a manner prescribed by law".

The CJEU went a step further in underlining the unconditional and Member State–driven nature of the Article 50 process.

> A Member State that has reversed its decision to withdraw from the European Union is entitled to revoke that notification for as long as a withdrawal agreement concluded between that Member State and the European Union has not entered into force or, if no such agreement has been concluded, for as long as the two-year period laid down in Article 50(3), possibly extended in accordance with that provision, has not expired.
>
> *(Wightman v. Secretary of State 2018: para. 69)*

To the extent that such decision is unequivocal and unconditional, "the sovereign nature of the right of withdrawal enshrined in Article 50(1) supports the conclusion that the Member State concerned has a right to revoke the notification of its intention to withdraw from the European Union" (Wightman v. Secretary of State 2018: para. 57).

The fact that the right to withdraw from the EU is unconditional, however, does not mean that the political will and aims of the withdrawing Member State are the sole defining factors in how this process is shaped. For instance, pursuant to Article 50(3), the consent of the remaining Member States is necessary if the period of negotiations is to be extended. Indeed, the UK managed to successfully extend this period three times after the remaining 27 Member States unanimously agreed to it. More importantly, the agreement of the qualified majority of the Council members after obtaining the consent of the European Parliament is also needed for reaching an agreement on the terms of the orderly withdrawal, as we shall see in the next section.

## Articles 50(2) and (4) of the Treaty on European Union: negotiating a withdrawal agreement

### *The negotiations*

Paragraphs 2 and 4 of Article 50 set some brief procedural requirements concerning the negotiations for the orderly withdrawal of a Member State. According to them, after a Member State notifies the European Council of its intention to withdraw, the latter sets its negotiating guidelines. The guidelines frame the aims of the EU in those negotiations and provide for clear instructions to the negotiator, which is the EU Commission under Article 218(3) of the Treaty on the Functioning of the European Union (TFEU). Article 50(2) of the TEU states that the overall aim of the negotiations is to reach a settlement with the withdrawing Member State on "the arrangements for its withdrawal, taking account of the framework for its future relationship with the Union". Such agreement is to be concluded by the Council (of Ministers) of the EU using qualified majority voting after obtaining the consent of the European Parliament. Article 50 "thereby makes clear that, on the Union side, the process is driven by its institutions, and not by the Member States themselves" (Hillion 2018: 32).

Although the wording of Article 50(2) is rather opaque (Hillion 2015), the EU's official position has always been that negotiations with a withdrawing Member State should follow a certain sequence:

first, the terms of its withdrawal have to be agreed; and after its official withdrawal, the future relationship between the withdrawn Member State and the rest of the EU can be settled (European Council 2017). Until the official withdrawal of a Member State, EU law continues to apply to and within it, both when it comes to rights and obligations as if it has not triggered Article 50. The only exception to this rule is provided in Article 50(4). According to it, the withdrawing Member State cannot participate in the discussions and decisions of the Council (of Ministers) and the European Council that affect the position of the EU in the negotiations concerning its withdrawal.

The fact that the withdrawing Member State does not take part in the formulation of the EU position with regard to the withdrawal negotiations has an important constitutional consequence. EU law principles that bind the institutions and the Member States when conducting their actions in the EU plane are not applicable to the withdrawing State during the negotiations for its orderly withdrawal. In particular, Herbst and Hofmeister have convincingly explained that the principle of loyal cooperation binds only the EU and not the withdrawing State during those negotiations (Herbst 2005: 1758; Hofmeister 2010: 598).

The aforementioned procedural rules, stages, and milestones were followed during the Brexit negotiations. On 29 March 2017, in accordance with Article 50(2), the then Prime Minister, Theresa May, notified the President of the European Council of the UK's intention to leave the EU (May 2017). In response, the European Council published its negotiating guidelines a month later (European Council 2017). There, the EU made clear that although the future relationship with the UK would be taken into account, the negotiations under Article 50 would aim at the terms of the UK's orderly withdrawal. According to the EU, the main issues that had to be sorted out related to the rights of British citizens residing in the EU, EU citizens residing in the UK and their families; the financial settlement; and the status of three territorial borders: the one on the island of Ireland; the one between the UK Sovereign Base Areas in Cyprus and the Republic of Cyprus; and the one between Gibraltar and Spain.

At the end of 2017, the UK and the EU, in their Joint Report, managed to reach a political agreement on the terms of the UK's withdrawal (Joint Report 2017). The EU published a draft of the Withdrawal Treaty on 28 February 2018 (Draft Withdrawal Agreement 2018a). But it was only in November 2018 that the UK Government managed to reach an agreement with the EU (Draft Withdrawal Agreement 2018b). Given that Prime Minister May had failed to secure the British legislature's consent in three consecutive attempts, it was obvious that her position had become untenable. The following summer she resigned and was succeeded by Boris Johnson. "With a further change in Prime Minister and the EU willing to reopen negotiations on the text of the Irish Protocol, a revised Withdrawal Agreement [was] endorsed by EU leaders on 17 October 2019" (Armstrong 2021: 412).

## *The withdrawal agreement*

"Article 50 confers an 'exceptional horizontal competence', enabling the Union to negotiate and conclude the withdrawal agreement deemed to encompass 'all matters necessary to arrange the withdrawal'" (Hillion 2018: 40). Despite the wide scope of this exceptional competence, Tridimas notes that "in concluding the withdrawal agreement the EU . . . is bound to respect the EU Treaties and higher ranking constitutional norms of EU law" (Tridimas 2016: 311). In fact, the CJEU has held that the obligations imposed on the EU by an international agreement cannot have the effect of prejudicing the constitutional principles of EU law, which include the principle that all EU acts must respect fundamental rights (Kadi v. Council and Commission 2008: para. 285). This means that the terms of the orderly withdrawal of a Member State should not be violating the Article 2 values.

Indeed, the Withdrawal Agreement that the EU and the UK endorsed in 2019 is a wide-ranging international treaty that settles a number of issues arising from Brexit (UK's Withdrawal Agreement 2019). Part One provides for legal definitions and the territorial scope. Part Two addresses the rights of EU citizens living in the UK, UK citizens living in the EU and their families. Part Three sets out how the application of EU law in the UK will be phased out after the end of the transition period. Part Four provides for the rules applying to the transition period that ended on 31 December 2020. Part Five sets out the financial settlement; while Part Six includes, *inter alia*, rules on the main decision-making body (the Joint Commission) and dispute settlement. In order to appreciate the width of this horizontal competence, three areas regulated by the Withdrawal Agreement need to be noted: (1) the transition, (2) the rights of Brexit Citizens and (3) the Protocol on Ireland/Northern Ireland. What is evident from this examination is that the end result of the Article 50 procedure is an arrangement that aims at effectively absorbing the tensions created by the secession of a constituent part from the Union.

## Transition

The transition period lasted from 31 January 2020 when the UK officially withdrew from the EU until 31 December 2020. Pursuant to Article 127 of the UK's Withdrawal Agreement, EU law was applicable to and in the UK during the transition period. The reason why the EU and the UK agreed that EU law would enjoy extra-territorial application in Britain for a period of 11 months was to ensure that the UK and EU negotiators would have some breathing space to find a mutually acceptable arrangement for the future UK–EU relationship. This was particularly important given that the official negotiations for the future relationship could start only after the UK had left the EU. Moreover, during the transition period, the UK had the time to negotiate trade agreements with third countries that would enter into force after the transition period ended per Article 129 of the Withdrawal Agreement, thus creating some form of continuity in the trade relations of the UK with the rest of the world. Although Article 132 of the UK's Withdrawal Agreement provided the UK with the right to extend this period for up to two years, they refrained from doing so.

Interestingly, it had been suggested that a transition period is outside the Article 50 competence "because this aspect of the Withdrawal Agreement governs the relationship between the two sides after Brexit day" (Peers 2020: 126). However, the view that prevailed was that "a transitional arrangement [is] legitimately conceived as one of the (indeterminate) 'arrangements for withdrawal' envisaged" by the said Article (Hillion 2018: 43). Given that the official negotiations for a future relationship could start only after the UK had withdrawn from the EU, a reading of Article 50 that excluded the possibility of a transitional arrangement would have led to a period where there would have been no legal relationship between the UK and the EU (Peers 2020: 126). Such an outcome would increase the fissures created by the secession and sits very uncomfortably with the obligation of the EU to develop "a special relationship with neighbouring countries" pursuant to Article 8 of the TEU. Conversely, a withdrawal agreement that provides for such a "bridging" arrangement is one that takes into account the future relationship between the withdrawing State and the Rest of the EU, as Article 50 requests and allows the EU and the withdrawing State to transition smoothly to a new stage in their peaceful neighbourly relations.

## Brexit citizens

Despite the polarised rhetoric concerning free movement of persons during the Brexit referendum, the UK and the EU managed to agree fairly quickly on the issue of post-Brexit citizens' rights. Accordingly, EU citizens lawfully residing in the UK and UK citizens lawfully residing in the EU (and their family members) at the end of the transition period (31 December 2020) retained their rights of residence and work, and most notably the right to equal treatment as currently derived from EU law.

In the December 2017 Joint Report, the UK and the EU pointed out that the Withdrawal Agreement should "enable the effective exercise of rights derived from Union law and based on past life choices" (Joint Report 2017: para. 6). Articles 9 to 39 of the Withdrawal Agreement enshrine those rights through direct references to the relevant primary and secondary EU legislation. In particular, Article 13 provides that Brexit Citizens retain their residence rights, while Article 15 clarifies that those who have resided legally for a continuous period of five years are deemed permanent residents. More importantly, Article 12 prohibits any discrimination based on the nationality of those Brexit Citizens.

Such an arrangement, that preserves the EU-derived rights to a population that would have otherwise lost them due to the consequences of a political decision, underlines the wide nature of Article 50 of the TEU as a clause that can be used to absorb the tensions created by secession. In fact, by providing that the CJEU will continue to adjudicate on the rights of Brexit Citizens even after the end of the transition period, the Withdrawal Agreement goes a step further in ensuring legal certainty. According to Article 158 of the Withdrawal Agreement, the UK courts will be able to send preliminary references related to Brexit citizens' rights. This avenue of judicial assistance will be available for any litigation that has started up to eight years after the end of the transition period. The only difference between this voluntary procedure and the one described in Article 267 of the TFEU is that the UK courts of last instance will not be obliged to refer. In that way, the Court of Justice will be able to influence British legal life for a number of years after Brexit, at least with regard to the very sensitive issue of citizens' rights, and ensure that Brexit citizens do not suffer from a political decision they could not influence.

## Protocol on Ireland/Northern Ireland

The withdrawal of the UK from the EU raised unique and complex legal and practical issues with regard to the Irish border, many of which are linked to the Belfast/Good Friday Agreement of 1998. These issues include the question of the territorial border; the threat to the island of Ireland as a single economic area; the rights of Irish passport holders in the North; practical questions that are directly related to the thousands of people who cross the border every day to work and have access to childcare and healthcare, among other activities.

Knowing the devastating impact that the hardening of the border might have had on the fragile politics of the post-conflict society, the UK and the EU committed themselves to keep the territorial border between an EU Member State – the Republic of Ireland – and a future third country frictionless. Such commitment, however, did not stop the UK Government from deciding that the UK should withdraw from the single market and the EU customs union after the end of the transition period. Those two somehow contradictory political goals led the Brexit negotiations to be haunted by an almost unsolvable riddle. How could the UK leave the single market and the EU customs union but keep the Irish territorial border free of any physical infrastructure without jeopardising the integrity of the EU project?

That riddle had two possible solutions. The UK as a whole could opt for a relationship with the EU that would be much closer than the one described in its red lines. Alternatively, the UK could accept that Northern Ireland would have a much closer relationship with the EU than the rest of the territory comprising the UK. The former approach was largely the one adopted in the draft Withdrawal Agreement negotiated by Theresa May and endorsed by the European Council on 25 November 2018 (Draft Withdrawal Agreement 2018b). However, her inability to convince the majority of MPs to support it led to her demise. The latter was initially suggested by the Commission in February 2018 and ultimately accepted – albeit in a revised form – by Boris Johnson's administration in October 2019 (UK's Withdrawal Agreement 2019).

The final Brexit deal is almost identical to Theresa May's except for one significant change: the fabled backstop (and the changes in the non-legally binding political declaration). The arrangement for Northern Ireland is a differentiated arrangement for the region that could only collapse should the regional parliament decide so, or if a future arrangement supersedes it. The major difference with the February 2018 EU proposal for a Northern Ireland-specific arrangement is that the current deal recognises that, *de jure*, Northern Ireland remains within the UK customs union (Irish Protocol 2019: art. 4). Notwithstanding, EU customs legislation continues to apply to the region even after the end of the transition period (Irish Protocol 2019: art. 5(3)). Similarly, Articles 30 and 110 of the TFEU (Irish Protocol 2019: art. 5(5)) that prohibit customs duties and discriminatory internal taxation on imported goods from EU Member States and a significant part of the EU *acquis* on the free movement of goods remain applicable with regard to Northern Ireland (Irish Protocol 2019: art. 5(4)), as is the case for EU law provisions concerning VAT and excise (Irish Protocol 2019: art. 8). This makes the region *de facto* part of the EU customs territory in the sense that this crucial part of the law of the EU internal market enjoys extra-territorial application over this area.

In practice, this hybrid regime means that after the end of the transition period, trade between the two shores of the Irish Sea is not frictionless any more. According to Article 263 of the Union Customs Code, goods that are taken out of Northern Ireland and sent to Great Britain have to be covered by a pre-departure declaration. The situation is significantly more complicated for trade flows in the opposite direction: from Great Britain to Northern Ireland. Apart from complying with EU import formalities including entry summary declarations and customs declarations, traders may also face tariffs if the relevant goods are not wholly obtained in the UK. Concerning checks and controls of product safety, these are based primarily on risk analysis. Having said that, when it comes to live animals, animal products, and plants, systematic sanitary and phytosanitary checks take place at entry points to secure the integrity of the Union's single market (Irish Protocol 2019: art. 5(4)).

As of mid-2022, those unavoidable frictions were largely addressed by allowing for grace periods. With regard to food, for instance, major retailers do not need to comply with all the EU's usual certification requirements when importing goods from the rest of the UK. However, once those grace periods expire, there is the fear that the systems of those supermarkets and other retailers would be overwhelmed by the existence of complex bureaucratic requirements. But, if one puts aside the bureaucratic and administrative costs that companies in Northern Ireland face, the arrangement may allow the province to have the best of both worlds, as it remains *de jure* part of the UK customs territory but applies *de facto* EU customs and free movement of goods legislation. This hybrid model that the UK and the EU opted for allowed the UK political elites to accept what was in essence an arrangement that was very similar to what the Commission initially proposed in February 2018 (Draft Withdrawal Agreement 2018a). More importantly, it allowed the UK and the EU to provide for an imaginative solution to a problem created by this *sui generis* secession.

## Article 50(5) of the Treaty on European Union: re-joining the EU

On 31 January 2021 at 23:00 UK time, the United Kingdom officially withdrew from the European Union after 47 years of membership in this supranational organisation. According to the Court of Justice in *Wightman v. Secretary of State for Exiting the European Union*, up until that moment, the UK could have revoked its Article 50 notification and remained part of the Union "under terms that [were] unchanged as regards its status as a Member State" (Wightman v. Secretary of State 2018: para. 74). From an EU membership point of view, the importance of this moment could not go unnoticed. The moment the UK was no longer bound by the EU Treaties, it became a third State. According to Article 50(5), this means that if its political elites and the UK electorate experience a damascene conversion and decide to re-accede to the EU, they would have to follow the procedure prescribed in Article 49.

Article 49 provides that "[a]ny European State which respects the values referred to in Article 2 and is committed to promoting them may apply to become a member of the Union". After receiving such an application, the Council has to unanimously decide on opening the Accession negotiations after consulting with the Commission and receiving the consent of the majority of the component members of the European Parliament. The negotiations are compartmentalised in chapters and are driven by soft law instruments in the form of bilateral accession partnerships and progress reports (Hillion 2011: 187; 2015: 126). Once there is an agreement that the candidate State has complied with all the relevant conditions contained in all the negotiating chapters, an Accession Treaty is drafted. Article 49(2) TEU provides for all "[t]he conditions of admission and the adjustments to the Treaties on which the Union is founded, which such admission entails". The signatories are the Union Member States and the candidate State. The Member States have to ratify the Accession Treaty in accordance with their respective constitutional requirements. Innocuous as it may sound, this might prove a cumbersome process given some recent constitutional developments. For instance, the amended Article 88–5 of the French Constitution provides that the ratification of an Accession Treaty could be submitted to referendum unless the Parliament decides differently with an enhanced majority of three fifths.

The same process would apply to Scotland as well if in the future, it becomes an independent State that wishes to join the EU. That marks a significant shift in the debate on Scottish independence. Back in 2014, when the independence referendum took place, a significant number of academics and politicians, including the Scottish Government (Scottish Government 2013: 216–224), argued that the continuous EU membership of Scotland could be secured by using Article 48 which governs the Treaty amendment procedure, and not Article 49 that allows European States to accede to the Union. They based their argument on the fact that unlike normal acceding independent States, Scotland was already part of the EU legal order. Notwithstanding the legal value of this argument (Skoutaris 2017), following the withdrawal of the United Kingdom including Scotland from the EU, this question has become a moot point.

The situation is different in the case of Northern Ireland, however. The secession of Northern Ireland would not lead to the creation of a new (Member) State. Instead, it would trigger the territorial expansion of an EU Member State – the Republic of Ireland – to which EU law already applies in accordance with Article 52.

"Westminster has formally conceded that Northern Ireland can secede from the United Kingdom to join a united Ireland, if its people, and the people of the Irish Republic, voting separately, agree to this" (McGarry 2010: 148). Article 1 of the legally binding British-Irish Agreement, which is part of the Belfast/Good Friday Agreement and registered with the Secretariat of the United Nations, recognises such right in no uncertain terms. In particular, the UK and the Republic of Ireland:

(i) recognise the legitimacy of whatever choice is freely exercised by a majority of the people of Northern Ireland with regard to its status, whether they prefer to continue to support the Union with Great Britain or a sovereign united Ireland;

(ii) recognise that it is for the people of the island of Ireland alone, . . . to exercise their right of self-determination on the basis of consent, freely and concurrently given, North and South, to bring about a united Ireland, if that is their wish, accepting that this right must be achieved and exercised with and subject to the agreement and consent of a majority of the people of Northern Ireland; . . .

(iii) affirm that if, in the future, the people of the island of Ireland exercise their right of self-determination on the basis set out in sections (i) and (ii) above to bring about a united Ireland, it will be a binding obligation on both Governments to introduce and support in their respective Parliaments legislation to give effect to that wish (Belfast/Good Friday Agreement 1998).

Those international legal obligations concerning the status of Northern Ireland have also been enshrined in UK legislation. Section 1 of the Northern Ireland Act 1998 is a rare example of a provision of a constitutional statute explicitly recognising the right of secession of a region. Schedule 1 of the Northern Ireland Act describes under which circumstances a referendum for the reunification of Ireland can and should be called by the UK Secretary of State. Recently, in *Re McCord*, the High Court of Justice in Northern Ireland discussed and clarified the aforementioned Northern Ireland Act provisions (Re McCord 2018). It held that the Secretary of State has

> a discretionary power to order a border poll under Schedule 1 paragraph 1 even where she is not of the view that it is likely that the majority of voters would vote for Northern Ireland to cease to be part of the United Kingdom and to become part of a united Ireland.
>
> *(Re McCord 2018: para. 18)*

However, if it appears to her that a majority would be likely to vote for a united Ireland, then, she is under a duty to call a poll (Re McCord 2018: para. 20).

A similar statutory duty for calling a referendum on Irish unification does not exist on the other side of the Irish border. If one looks at the Irish Constitution, and especially at the text of the revised Articles 2 and 3, they would realise that there is nothing that explicitly states that the Taoiseach or any other institution and/or office holder is obliged by the Constitution, and the duties of their office, to pursue a United Ireland. The procedure for holding a referendum in the Republic of Ireland can be found in Article 46 of its constitution, and the Referendum Acts. In sum, the proposal must be supported by both houses of the *Oireachtas*, submitted to and approved by the electorate and signed into law by the President. So, in purely legal terms, the decision to propose a referendum on unity lies with the parliament, while the approval or rejection of the Irish unification proposal rests with the electorate. Overall, there is a clear and well-founded constitutional pathway for the secession of Northern Ireland from the United Kingdom and the unification of the island of Ireland, and as such the return of Northern Ireland as part of the EU.

From an EU law point of view, the reunification of Ireland could follow the precedent of the German reunification, where the application of the *acquis* was extended to East Germany without an amendment of the primary legislation, as agreed in a special meeting of the European Council in Dublin on 28 April 1990. The necessary acts of secondary law were adopted on the basis of delegation of powers to the Commission, in order to ensure that the EU legislative process would be able to effectively respond to the speed of historical events. The difference is that, in the case of Germany, the *acquis* did not apply at all in the East before the reunification. In Northern Ireland, even after the expiry of the Brexit transition, a substantial part of EU law will continue to enjoy extraterritorial application due to the Protocol on Ireland/Northern

Ireland attached to UK's Withdrawal Agreement. To this effect, the European Council agreed the following statement in the minutes to the agreement on the Brexit negotiating guidelines on 29 April 2017:

> The European Council acknowledges that the Good Friday Agreement expressly provides for an agreed mechanism whereby a united Ireland may be brought about through peaceful and democratic means; and, in this regard, the European Council acknowledges that, in accordance with international law, the entire territory of such a united Ireland would thus be part of the European Union.
>
> *(European Council 2017)*

## In lieu of a conclusion

Schütze has convincingly argued that the EU is an "(inter)national phenomenon [standing] on – federal– middle ground" between national and international law (Schütze 2009: 73). One of the consequences of this is that the application of every constitutional principle and phenomenon that we are used to experiencing at the national level is conditioned upon the insistent realities of a project whose constitutive fundament lies in public international law. Democracy offers a good example of this point. Although it is undoubted that liberal democracy is a common principle of all 27 Member States and that, pursuant to Article 10 of the TEU, the "functioning of the Union sh[ould] be founded on representative democracy" the application of the democratic principle at the EU level takes place in a rather uncommon fashion. If one extends this argument to the right to secede (from the EU), one sees that its application has been adapted to reflect the voluntary character of this union of States. In sum, Article 50 of the TEU undoubtedly provides for a right to secede from the EU. Its actual application, however, is rather different from what we are used to at the national level. The right is unconditional and unilateral; its application follows the logic of the European intertwined and composite constitution by requesting respect to the national constitutional requirements; while the main aim of its several procedural stages is to lead to an arrangement that would absorb the tensions created by the exercise of such right. This is to be expected from a constitutional order that has a municipal character but remains a voluntary union of sovereign States.

## References

Armstrong, K.A. 2021, "(Br)Exit from the European Union–Control, Autonomy and the Evolution of EU Law", in P. Craig & G. de Búrca (eds.), *The Evolution of EU Law*, 3rd ed., Oxford: Oxford University Press: 399–430.

Belfast/Good Friday Agreement 1998, "The Belfast Agreement, Ref: Cm. 3883", <www.gov.uk/government/publications/the-belfast-agreement>

Besselink, L.F.M. 2007, *A Composite European Constitution/Een Samengestelde Europese Constitutie*, Groningen: Europa Law Publishing.

Claes, M. 2006, *The National Courts' Mandate in the European Constitution*, Oxford: Hart Publishing.

Closa, C. 2017, "Interpreting Article 50: Exit, Voice and . . . What About Loyalty?", in C. Closa (ed.), *Secession from a Member State and Withdrawal from the European Union*, Cambridge: Cambridge University Press: 187–214.

Costa v. ENEL 1964, Court of Justice of the European Union, *Costa v. ENEL*, Case no. 6/64, EU:C:1964:66.

Draft Withdrawal Agreement 2018a, "Draft Agreement on the Withdrawal of the United Kingdom of Great Britain and Northern Ireland from the European Union and the European Atomic Energy Community", 19 March 2018, <www.gov.uk/government/publications/draft-withdrawal-agreement-19-march-2018>

Draft Withdrawal Agreement 2018b, "Draft Agreement on the Withdrawal of the United Kingdom of Great Britain and Northern Ireland from the European Union and the European Atomic Energy Community, as Agreed at Negotiators' Level", 14 November, https://ec.europa.eu/info/publications/

draft-agreement-withdrawal-united-kingdom-great-britain-and-northern-ireland-european-un-
ion-and-european-atomic-energy-community-agreed-negotiators-level-14-november-2018_en

Eeckhout, P. & Frantziou, E. 2017, "Brexit and Article 50 TEU: A Constitutionalist Reading", *Common Market Law Review*, 54: 695–734.

European Council 2017, "European Council (Art. 50) Guidelines for Brexit Negotiations, <www.consil-ium.europa.eu/en/press/press-releases/2017/04/29/euco-brexit-guidelines/>

European Union (Notification of Withdrawal) Act 2017, *European Union (Notification of Withdrawal) Act 2017*, c.9, <www.legislation.gov.uk/ukpga/2017/9/contents/enacted>

Friel, R. J. 2004, "Providing a Constitutional Framework for Withdrawal from the EU: Article 59 of the Draft European Constitution", *International & Comparative Law Quarterly*, 53: 407–428.

Garben, S. 2020, "Collective Identity as a Legal Limit to European Integration in Areas of Core State Powers", *Journal of Common Market Studies*, 58: 41–55.

Helfer, L.R. 2005, "Exiting Treaties", *Virginia Law Review*, 91(7): 1579–1648.

Herbst, J. 2005, "Observations on the Right to Withdraw from the European Union: Who are the 'Masters of the Treaties?", *German Law Journal*, 6: 1755–1760.

Hillion, C. 2011, "EU Enlargement", in P. Craig & G. de Búrca (eds.), *The Evolution of EU Law*, 2nd ed., Oxford: Oxford University Press: 187–216.

Hillion, C. 2015, "Accession and Withdrawal in the Law of the European Union", in A. Arnull & D. Chalmers (eds.), *The Oxford Handbook of European Union Law*, Oxford: Oxford University Press: 126–151.

Hillion, C. 2018, "Withdrawal under Article 50 TEU: An Integration-Friendly Process", *Common Market Law Review*, 55: 29–56.

Hofmeister, H. 2010, "Should I Stay or Should I Go?–A Critical Analysis of the Right to Withdraw from the EU", *European Law Journal*, 16: 589–603.

Irish Protocol 2019, "Protocol on Ireland/Northern Ireland, Agreement on the withdrawal of the United Kingdom of Great Britain and Northern Ireland from the European Union and the European Atomic Energy Community", 12 November, *Official Journal*: 2019/C 384I/1.

Joint Report 2017, Joint Report from the Negotiators of the European Union and the United Kingdom Government on Progress during Phase 1 of Negotiations under Article 50 TEU on the United Kingdom's Orderly Withdrawal from the European Union, 8 December, <https://ec.europa.eu/info/publications/joint-report-negotiators-european-union-and-united-kingdom-government-progress-during-phase-1-negotiations-under-article-50-teu-united-kingdoms-orderly-withdrawal-european-union_en>

Kadi v. Council and Commission 2008, Court of Justice of the European Union, *Kadi v. Council and Commission*, Joined Cases no. C – 402/05 P and C – 415/05 P, ECLI:EU:C:2008:461.

May, T. 2017, Prime Minister's Letter to Donald Tusk Triggering Article 50, 29 March 2017, <www.gov.uk/government/publications/prime-ministers-letter-to-donald-tusk-triggering-article-50>

McGarry, J. 2010, "Asymmetrical Autonomy in the United Kingdom", in M. Weller & K. Nobbs (eds.), *Asymmetric Autonomy and the Settlement of Ethnic Conflicts*, Philadelphia: University of Pennsylvania Press: 148–181.

Northern Ireland Act 1998, Northern Ireland Act 1998, c.47, <www.legislation.gov.uk/ukpga/1998/47/contents>

Peers, S. 2012, "The future of EU Treaty Amendments", *Yearbook of European Law*, 31: 17–111.

Peers, S. 2020, "The End–or a New Beginning? The EU/UK Withdrawal Agreement", *Yearbook of European Law*, 39: 122–198.

Pernice, I. 1999, "Multi-Level Constitutionalism and the Treaty of Amsterdam: European Constitution Making Revisited", *Common Market Law Review*, 36: 703–750.

R (Miller) v. Secretary of State 2018, United Kingdom Supreme Court, *R (Miller) v Secretary of State for Exiting the European Union* [2018] A.C. 61.

R (Miller) v. The Prime Minister 2020, United Kingdom Supreme Court, *R (Miller) v. The Prime Minister (Lord Advocate intervening)* [2020] A.C. 373.

Re Maastricht Treaty 1993, German Federal Constitutional Court, *Re Maastricht Treaty*, Cases 2 BvR 2134/92, 2 BvR 2159/92, part II.

Re McCord 2018, High Court of Justice in Northern Ireland, *Re McCord* [2018] NIQB 106.

Re Treaty of Lisbon 2008 Czech Constitutional Court, *Re Treaty of Lisbon*, Judgment Pl. ÚS 19/08: 1 2008/11/26.

Schütze, R. 2009, *From Dual to Cooperative Federalism: The Changing Structure of European Law*, Oxford: Oxford University Press.

Scottish Government 2013, Scotland's Future: Your Guide to an Independent Scotland, <www.gov.scot/resource/0043/00439021.pdf>

Secession Reference 1998, Supreme Court of Canada, *Reference re Secession of Quebec* [1998] 2 S.C.R. 217.

Skoutaris, N. 2017, "Territorial Differentiation in EU Law: Can Scotland and Northern Ireland Remain in the EU and/or the Single Market?", *Cambridge Yearbook of European Legal Studies*, 19: 287–310.

Tatham, A.F. 2012, "Don't Mention Divorce at the Wedding, Darling!: EU Accession and Withdrawal After Lisbon", A. Biondi, P. Eeckhout & S. Ripley (eds.), *EU Law After Lisbon*, Oxford: Oxford University Press: 128–154.

Tridimas, T. 2016, "Article 50: An Endgame without an End?", *King's Law Journal*, 27(3): 297–313.

UK's Withdrawal Agreement 2019, "Agreement on the Withdrawal of the United Kingdom of Great Britain and Northern Ireland from the European Union and the European Atomic Energy Community", 12 November, *Official Journal*: 2019/C 384I/1.

Vienna Convention 1969, Vienna Convention on the Law of the Treaties, 23 May, 1155 U.N.T.S. 331.

Weiler, J.H.H. 2009, "In Defence of the Status Quo: Europe's Sonderweg", in M. Wind & J. H. H. Weiler (eds.), *European Constitutionalism Beyond the State*, Cambridge: Cambridge University Press: 7–26.

Wightman v. Secretary of State 2018, Court of Justice of the European Union, *Wightman v. Secretary of State for Exiting the European Union*, Case no. C-621/18, ECLI:EU:C:2018:999.

Ziller, J. 2005, "National Constitutional Concepts in the New Constitution for Europe", *European Constitutional Law Review*, 1: 247–271 and 452–480.

# PART VII

# Constitutional law and secession

# 36

# ANTI-SECESSION CONSTITUTIONALISM

*Rivka Weill**

## Introduction

For a state to exist, it must assert effective control over people, territory, and a legal system. Declarations of independence are typically an *assertion* of such control, even when it is not yet backed by facts on the ground. Only after acquiring such control – often by winning a war of independence against internal and/or external forces – the state may find the resources and time to engage in constitution making. This may explain why constitutions are often adopted later than declarations of independence (Weill 2021).

Scholars have long asserted that the resulting constitutional documents typically don't expressly include a right of state members to secede, nor do they forbid it (Monahan et al. 1996; Coggins 2011). Some suggested that this silence is coincidental; had the framers of constitutions entertained the matter, they would have explicitly included a constitutional right permitting state members to secede (Norman 1998). Reality supposedly reinforces this notion. After all, secessionist parties operate in democratic countries. Some scholars interpret this as proof that states tolerate and even allow secessionist tendencies (Norman 2003; Jovanović 2011). This interpretation is also backed by a rationale that, if democratic legitimacy is based on popular consent and majority rule, state members should not be forced to remain under state authority if they desire to form their own state. Thus, many argue that this constitutional silence on secession should be interpreted as implicit permission to secede. In the landmark decision of the Canadian Supreme Court, which deals with the question of whether Québec may constitutionally secede from Canada, scholars find support for a variant of this approach (Secession Reference 1998). They read it as judicial endorsement of the position that secession aligns with constitutionalism but may be brought about via a constitutional amendment (Barber 2018).

While scholars perceive states as open to the possibility of secession, they accept that democratic states are often militant about their democratic regimes. Many states do not tolerate political parties that endorse terrorism or racism or seek to replace democracy with totalitarian rule. This militant stance is justified by democratic theory (Loewenstein 1937a, 1937b). Democracy should not commit suicide by enabling its internal enemies to take over, exploiting its tolerance and openness to diverse and even competing views on what constitutes the common good.

Yet, this prevailing scholarly treatment of secession did not align with the facts on the ground (Weill 2018). Rather, the overwhelming majority of states' constitutions ban secession.

DOI: 10.4324/9781003036593-43

Surprisingly, this is the prevalent approach of democratic and semi-democratic countries, not just totalitarian regimes.[1] States use the most unconventional methods at their disposal to not just prevent but prohibit secession: (1) they ban secessionist political parties from participating in elections; and (2) they adopt constitutional eternity clauses, which declare the unity of the nation and/or its territorial integrity unamenable. Furthermore, militant democracy that is typically associated only with bans on political parties is also about treating certain constitutional values as eternal, and unamenable. In fact, bans on political parties and eternity clauses should be treated as mirror images of one another (Weill 2017). Militant democracy is thus not just about protection of democratic values as we customarily justify it. It is used primarily to protect territorial integrity and prevent secession.

In response, secessionists must resort to extra-constitutional means to achieve their goals. States, thus, challenge secessionists to prove the intensity of their preferences and test their willingness to pay the prices of breaching the law. States try to dissuade secessionists from embarking on the secessionist process to begin with.

This chapter discusses the following questions: (1) What is secession for constitutional law purposes? (2) How is the secessionist struggle affected by and framed within a global discourse of rights? (3) How do constitutions treat secession? (4) Why did the literature miss the prevalence of anti-secession constitutionalism? (5) Why do constitutions include a total ban on secession? (6) What processes may legitimize secession? (7) How does international law cooperate with constitutional law to discourage secession? And, finally, (8) what are the lessons for comparative constitutional law? Secession is an especially worthy subject for rigorous constitutional study. It requires us to rethink our most basic understanding of constitutionalism.

## What is secession from a constitutional law perspective?

As is discussed elsewhere in this book, there is no uniform definition of secession (Radan, Chapter 3, this volume). International law scholars may define secession differently from constitutional law scholars. This chapter defines secession as a *combined* challenge to the state's control over both its citizenry and territory. Loss of only one of these components does not qualify (Brilmayer 1991; Weill 2018). As states must assert effective control over citizens and territory to exist, the combined challenge requires the rump state to redefine its constitutional governing arrangements. Arrangements that promote internal autonomy and enhance or protect minorities' unique identities fall short of secession, so long as states retain the internal control necessary to undo them.

This definition leads to three primary types of secessions:

1   *Classic secession* – This occurs when part of the citizenry wishes to depart with part of the state's territory and *establish its own independent state.* Had the Scots in the United Kingdom (UK) in 2014, or the Catalans in Spain in 2017, achieved independence, their case would have amounted to a classic form of secession.
2   *Irredentist secession* – This occurs when part of the citizenry wishes to depart with part of the territory to *join another existing, typically neighboring, state.* Often, the citizens want to restore a previous status quo or become part of the majority in the other state, while in their mother state they belong to a minority along ethnic, religious, or cultural lines. Russia attempted to portray the Crimea crisis of 2014 as a case of irredentist secession, in which ethnic Russians – the majority of Crimea's population – wished to secede from Ukraine in order to restore the previous status quo. However, most Western states believe that Russia forcefully annexed Crimea. Russia's all-out war against Ukraine in 2022 only reinforces this

Western conviction (Weill 2022). It should further be noted that often it is difficult to distinguish classic secessionist attempts from irredentist ones in the early stages of the conflict, since different factions within the secessionists may desire different ends.

3   *Partition of states* – When states completely dissolve and new states form instead, it poses an *ex-ante* challenge to a state's control over its citizenry and territory and amounts to secession. This was true of Yugoslavia's breakup and the Soviet Union's dissolution in the 1990s.

When the people departing the state are not its citizens or when the state has never annexed the territory involved, then the state has practically acknowledged that such departure does not challenge its core identity and constitutional governing arrangements. It may subsequently lose control over an occupied territory or people it never treated as its citizens. Yet, this loss will not amount to secession; this territory or people never belonged to the state to begin with. Thus, states' constitutional arrangements do not typically rigorously defend against such loss (Weill 2018).

Those who inquire about how the international community through international law should respond to secession may decouple these cases. They may define secession differently. They may differentiate between the first two scenarios, because only in the classic form of secession does the new emerging entity desperately need the international community's recognition to succeed. In the case of irredentist secession, the departing entity already enjoys the backing of an existing state with which it merges, even if the international community objects to the new territorial arrangement. International law scholars may further distinguish the third case from the first two cases because, in cases of partition, no rump state is left. This gives rise to a host of new questions about international recognition of new states and (dis)continuity of the former rump state's international rights and obligations. However, this chapter discusses constitutional treatment of secession. Thus, it treats all three forms of loss of citizens plus territory as secession.

## How is the secessionist struggle affected by the global discourse of rights?

Secession is a seismic force that has been shaping world history since antiquity. Those seeking to secede are primarily driven by identity politics. They may be a minority in their mother state based on ethnic, religious, or even political views but believe that they can become part of the majority through secession. They may seek to better control the public sphere than is achievable in their mother state in matters such as national holidays, dominant language, and culture. In essence, they aim to redefine minority–majority relationships through secession.

The quest to secede may have been present at the state's establishment, because the state formed without accounting for the population's ethnic or religious characteristics. This is typical in cases of decolonization. When forming the colonies, the colonial powers divided land between themselves, focusing on their own interests rather than those of the native populations. Later, decolonization followed this pre-existing colonial oft-arbitrary land division (Ratner 1996). Alternatively, internal and external migration may provoke secessionist impulses by concentrating minorities in certain state territories, thereby either changing or threatening to change the population's identity.

Secessionists act on their ambition when they feel that secession is both attainable and sustainable. It may be attainable if secessionists judge that the international community is more open to such challenges to state sovereignty. The secessionists may interpret the international community's advocacy of minorities' rights as an invitation to push this agenda further in the direction of self-rule. They may believe that independence is more sustainable, because globalization has opened international trade and allows even small entities to survive with their considerably smaller economies. Democracy's global spread has supposedly made the world a safer place. Democratic states' reluctance to go to war between themselves contributes to secessionists' belief that independence is a less risky endeavor worth pursuing.

While secessionists seek to redraw state boundaries, the mother state may oppose secession for a variety of legitimate interests. At times, secession may threaten the state's very existence because the new boundaries are more difficult to protect or involve loss of access to natural resources, including water or gas. States may also feel obligated to protect the citizens who reject secession from becoming unwillingly trapped in a new state arrangement. Since secession may involve a power struggle between different populations within the state, members of the mother state's majority may fear becoming a minority under a new state arrangement. They may dread facing subsequent persecution, infringement of rights, and even loss of life.

## How do constitutions treat secession?

The constitutions of the overwhelming majority of states ban secession *explicitly*. This constitutional ban is typical of both democratic and non-democratic states alike. Only a small percentage of states do not address the secessionist challenge in their constitutions. Extremely few states allow for secession in their constitutions.

The constitutional approach to secession of the 192 states which were members in 2018 of the United Nations (UN) may be summarized as follows:

1  *Ban* – A total of 152 countries, representing 79% of UN members, explicitly ban secession in their constitutions. This ban is commonplace in all types of political regimes. In fact, among democratic and semi-democratic countries, 74% explicitly ban secession (Weill 2018: 913). The constitutional ban on secession is even more prevalent, if we were also to include judicial inferences of the implicit existence of such prohibition from the constitutional text.
2  *Silence* – Only 28 countries, representing 14.6% of UN members, do not explicitly protect territorial integrity or national unity in their constitutions and are in that sense silent on the topic (Weill 2018: 912).
3  *Permission* – Only 7 countries, representing 3.6% of UN members, supposedly allow secession by including an explicit secession clause setting the prerequisites to achieve secession.
4  *Unclear* – A total of 5 states, representing 2.6% of UN members, are difficult to classify. Bosnia and Herzegovina explicitly left the question of the constitutionality of secession to the discretion of its Constitutional Court. The UK also seems exceptional. It enabled a referendum on Scottish independence in 2014 and legislated a secession process for Northern Ireland (Weill 2018: 912–913). Yet, it has prevented Scotland from holding an additional referendum on secession since Brexit. Denmark, Iceland, and Vanuatu provide constitutional procedures for territorial change without embodying a conflicting constitutional language that protects territorial integrity. However, it is not clear whether their constitutional provisions apply to secession that involves the withdrawal of *both* territory and citizens.

How do states ban secession in their constitutions? States not only predominantly ban secession, but in fact exploit their most unconventional constitutional tools to prevent it. A total of 103 states, constituting 54% of UN member states, include an explicit constitutional ban on secessionist political parties from participating in elections. Of democratic and semi-democratic states, 47% explicitly ban secessionist political parties (Weill 2018: 935). This, in turn, prevents secessionists from reaching the levers of power and initiating legislation or constitutional amendments to achieve secession.

In the 103 states, the ban may come in the following three forms:

1   An explicit constitutional ban of political parties that threaten territorial integrity or national unity and sovereignty exists in 56 countries (54.4%). For example, Article 68 of the Turkish Constitution states: "The statutes and programs, as well as the activities of political parties shall not be contrary to the independence of the State, its indivisible integrity with its territory and nation."

2   An explicit requirement that political parties must be nationally based and rejection of any form of regional or sectorial political party, exists in 34 countries (33%). For example, Article 55(4) of the Ghana Constitution states: "Every political party shall have a national character, and membership shall not be based on ethnic, religious, regional or other sectional divisions." It further states in Article 55(7):

> For purposes of registration, a prospective political party shall furnish the Electoral Commission with a copy of its Constitution and the names and addresses of its national officers; and shall satisfy the Commission that – **a.** there is ordinarily resident, or registered as a voter, in each district of Ghana, at least one founding member of the party; **b.** the party has branches in all the regions of Ghana and is, in addition, organised in not less than two-thirds of the districts in each region; and **c.** the party's name, emblem, colour, motto or any other symbol has no ethnic, regional, religious or other sectional connotation or gives the appearance that its activities are confined only to a part of Ghana.

3   An explicit requirement that political parties respect the constitution or must not pursue aims forbidden under criminal law. In other constitutional provisions and/or the criminal code, territorial integrity is protected. This is an indirect ban on secessionist political parties. This type of political ban exists in 13 countries (12.6%) (Weill 2018: 935–937).

In their struggle to maintain territorial integrity and prevent secession, states employ another unconventional constitutional tool. A total of 108 states – 56% of the UN's members – treat territorial unity and/or national unity as unamendable and eternal constitutional values. This is true also of 48% of the democratic or semi-democratic countries. Such eternity clauses are intended to trigger the "unconstitutional constitutional amendment" doctrine, under which courts declare any contrary constitutional amendment invalid. These constitutional provisions, in turn, may enable the courts to prevent secessionist regions from even holding referenda on independence to begin with. The Italian and German Constitutional Courts have done so regarding Veneto, in 2015, and Bavaria, in 2016, respectively (Corte Const. 2015; BVerfG 2016).

These constitutional eternity clauses come in the following two forms (Weill 2018: 951–952):

1   An explicit eternity clause protecting territorial integrity from amendment exists in 43 states (40%). For example, Article 89 of the French Constitution states: "No amendment procedure shall be commenced or continued where the integrity of national territory is placed in jeopardy."

2   A declaration that territorial and national integrity are eternal, permanent, and unchangeable constitutional values stated in constitutional preambles, state duties, and/or fundamental principles exists in 65 states (60%) (Weill 2018: 951–952). For example, Article 2 of the Spanish Constitution states: "The Constitution is based on the indissoluble unity of the Spanish Nation, the common and indivisible homeland of all Spaniards."

These two constitutional tools are unconventional, because they instigate a democratic paradox. States prevent peaceful legislative and/or constitutional change from occurring, in contradistinction to the nature of democracy as a free marketplace where competition over ideas takes place and governance is based on the consent of the governed. Supposedly, democratic processes should enable even secession, if agreed upon between the two opposing sides on the secession question. Yet, the aforementioned constitutional provisions try to prevent secession from ever obtaining such agreement. Too frequent or wide employment of these unconventional tools threatens the very democratic nature of the state. Thus, these tools should be treated as last-resort nuclear weapons, intended to deter secessionist forces rather than be used.

Despite their unconventional character, about 70% of the UN members have at least one of these two constitutional weapons: a ban on secessionist political parties and/or a shield of eternity status granted to protect territorial integrity (Weill 2018: 962). About 40% of the countries employ both mechanisms. Of democratic and semi-democratic countries, 62% have at least one of these mechanisms, and 32% have both (Weill 2018: 962).

## Why did the literature miss the prevalence of anti-secession constitutionalism?

There are various factors that mislead and hide the prevalence of anti-secession constitutionalism:

1   *Indirect Text* – Constitutional provisions do not typically discuss secession per se. They prefer to express their desire to protect territorial integrity and/or national unity. Thus, people who search for the word "secession" in constitutions will emerge empty-handed. Furthermore, constitutions often express their disavowal of secession indirectly by banning regional or sectorial political parties. They do not add that these provisions are aimed at preventing secession. Rather, it is inferred. At times, the eternal protection of territorial integrity appears in preambles and general principles that scholarship has traditionally dismissed as merely aspirational and non-binding. To expose the true extent of states' defense mechanisms, one needs to approach the text with a theory in mind of the tools that states are likely to employ to prevent secession.

2   *A Common False Narrative of Democracy's Defense Mechanisms* – The story that democratic states tell themselves and the world at large is that they act militantly and exploit tools that are borderline non-democratic only to protect their democratic nature. They are democratic, but not suicidal. This narrative distinguishes modern democracies from totalitarian regimes' forceful reign, while establishing their superiority compared to the naïve democratic regimes that fell prey to totalitarian impulses during World War II (Fox & Nolte 1995). Thus, scholars typically associate the ban on political parties with protection of democracy, not prevention of secession. This narrative becomes even more pressing when international courts, such as the European Court of Human Rights, forbid states from banning *peaceful* secessionist political parties (Ilinden v. Bulgaria 2005; Case of the Socialist Party of Turk 2013). This "militant democracy" narrative, which singles out only the protection of democracy as justifying bans on political parties, leads scholars to assume that, even when textual constitutional provisions ban secession, they are dead letters, not enforced.

3   *Missed Nexus between Democracy's Defense Mechanisms* – Scholars not only misunderstand militant democracy, but also associate it only with a ban on political parties, thus missing the importance of eternity clauses. Indeed, Karl Loewenstein's plea to democracies to be militant on the eve of World War II focused primarily on promoting such bans against the imminent threat of fascism and Nazism. As a Jew, he fled from Germany to the United States and

developed his militant democracy theory in two watershed articles in 1937 (Loewenstein 1937a, 1937b).However, bans on political parties and eternity clauses are mirror images (Weill 2017). They are both constitutional tools aimed to protect society's core values from change. They simply kick in at different times to protect the constitutional status quo. The ban serves as the front guard of democracy, preventing those who do not accept the system's basic values from reaching representative bodies and initiating constitutional change from within. An eternity clause is the rear guard, intended to invalidate amendments that have already been ratified yet challenge the system's core values. Supposedly, the ban on political parties is a constitutional provision that may be amended and, as such, fundamentally differs from an eternity clause. In essence, however, the ban is more about eternity and absolute entrenchment than any eternity clause because those who challenge the core values identified in the ban would never obtain the power to initiate a constitutional amendment. In fact, Loewenstein intended to protect access to the different levers of political power, supporting a broader array of tools than just a ban on political parties (Weill 2020). In passing, he even mentioned the need to make the processes of amending the constitution more stringent. Only when understanding the theoretical connection between the ban on political parties and eternity clauses and examining constitutional texts with the two mechanisms in mind, does the extent of democracies' fight against secession reveal itself.

4   *The Impact of Canada's Landmark Secession Decision* – In the Canadian Supreme Court's constitutional decision dealing with a possible secession of Québec, the Court held that Canada's Constitution did not allow for a unilateral secession of Québec. Yet, it did rule that secession is possible through constitutional amendment (Secession Reference 1998). This decision created the false impression among leading comparative constitutional scholars that constitutions are typically silent on secession, as is true regarding Canada. It further convinced scholars that secession does not necessitate a revolutionary new beginning but may be achieved via a constitutional amendment. However, the Canadian constitutional silence on the topic is not the typical constitutional approach to secession at the global level. Furthermore, the Supreme Court's decision, which allows for secession via a constitutional amendment, is exceptional in comparative constitutional law (Weill 2018: 979–984). As this chapter has elaborated, most states forbid constitutional amendments that may legitimize secession.

5   *Confusing Practice* – When examining states' constitutional behavior, their actual practice makes it difficult to construct a unifying theory. There are many secessionist political parties operating in various states despite the ban on secessionist political parties. States do not target every secessionist political party, because they want to enable people to steam out their frustration and soften their agendas through the operation of regular politics (Bligh 2013). In other words, they rely on the fact that political actors who enjoy the benefits of being part of the system, such as representatives' special status, are often less inclined to destroy the system, according to the epithet that the most dangerous people are those with the least to lose. Thus, states are strategic about the use of the ban. They try to tailor its use to combat parties that are neither too small to be threatening nor too big to be squashed by the ban, as is evident in recent years in Ukraine, Belgium, Bulgaria, Spain, and Turkey (Weill 2018).

6   *Doublespeak* – Many states engage in various forms of doublespeak. They ban political parties on grounds of racism or terrorism when, in fact, they target these parties for their secessionism. States "say" in their constitutional texts that they protect territorial integrity, yet set constitutional procedures for pursuing territorial change in the same breath. They do not explicate whether these procedures apply to secession, which involves the withdrawal of both citizens and territory. For example, Article 2 of the Burundi Constitution states: "The national territory of Burundi is inalienable and indivisible." Yet, Article 295

provides a procedure for territorial change: "Any cession, exchange, or adjunction of territory is only valid with the consent of the Burundian People called to pronounce itself by referendum." At the same time, Article 299 also forbids constitutional amendments geared towards secession: "No procedure of revision may be retained if it infringes the national unity, the cohesion of the Burundian People, the secularity of the State, the reconciliation, the democracy or the integrity of the territory of the Republic."

A minority of states "say" that they allow secession, yet set such procedural hurdles that secession becomes all but impossible to achieve. Such procedural hurdles primarily include the need to attain the endorsement of supermajorities and/or national referenda. This is not merely a theory. The Constitution of St. Kitts and Nevis, for instance, enables secession of Nevis. In 1998, 61.7% of the Nevis electorate voted to secede but did not attain the threshold requirement of a two-thirds majority.

Only when all these intermediate mechanisms fail to suppress secession does the extent of democracies' fight against secession become apparent. Spain's overtaking of the Catalans brutally showcased this. After the Catalan Parliament unilaterally declared independence in 2017, the Spanish central government dismantled Catalonia's legislative and executive branches. It called for renewed elections after jailing central figures of the Catalan independence movement on charges of sedition, rebellion, and misuse of public funds. However, Spain is no outlier. Its struggle only exposed what democracies desperately try to hide; they do not tolerate secession any more than do totalitarian regimes (Weill 2018: 940).

## Why do constitutions include a total ban on secession?

States are not overly concerned by loss of population, even through *en masse* emigration. Nor do they dismiss a possible redrawing of their boundaries, though they may not be thrilled about it. However, they do treat the combined threat of losing citizens plus territory – that is, secession – quite differently. Supposedly, states could have been satisfied with a ban against unilateral secession but allow for secession if the mother state and the departing one agree upon it. Yet, they ban even consensual secession between the two parties by forbidding amendment of their constitutions to reflect such consent. Two rationales can be offered for the existing prevalence of *total* bans on secession:

1   *Strategic* – States try to maximize the chances that secession will not occur while minimizing the unavoidable costs incurred in preventing secession. They do not want their own public and the international community to perceive their actions as totalitarian by squashing peaceful attempts to secede. At the same time, they carefully lay out the tools to prevent secession from ever gaining momentum. Democracies have successfully created an "acoustic separation" where secessionists understand that they are being targeted because they are secessionists, while the world at large believes that the democracies' fight against them is driven by the will to prevent racism, terrorism, and the like.[2] If democracies fail in their utilization of tools to prevent secession from gaining momentum, then democracies want to approach the negotiation table with the upper hand. The total ban on secession enables them to extract the best deal vis-à-vis the secessionists, because nothing is conceded ahead of the negotiation (Sunstein 1991; Weill 2018).

2   *Basic Norm* – Constitutions may have no choice but to totally ban secession. Many scholars distinguish between the original constituent power that adopted the initial constitutional document and the derivative constituent power in charge of amending the constitution

(Weill 2014). The latter power of amendment is considered inferior to the superior power of initial constitutional adoption. The amendment power is provided for in the constitution. As such, it is subject to the limitations imposed by the text. This, in turn, enables the justification of eternity clauses and the derivative judicial doctrine, which empowers courts to declare a constitutional amendment unconstitutional, even though it passed in accordance with the constitutional amendment process. The courts may find the amendment unconstitutional, because it negates the content of an eternity clause, which identified constitutional rights and values that may not be amended (Weill 2014). Yet, this explanation leaves constitutional framers with the choice of whether to set (explicitly or implicitly) eternity clauses and which values to protect as untouchable.

How is secession different? Arguably, the constitutional amendment power is on par with the original constitution making power with the former not inferior to the latter. An inferior power may not establish norms that can become part of a higher normative document – a constitution. Constitution-making power may not be delegated to inferior bodies.[3] Yet, constitutions assume the identity of the people who author the text. Moreover, since the constitution is typically the supreme legal document prevailing over regular enactments, the constitution-making body is the ultimate sovereign body in the legal system (Weill 2006, 2021).

While every amendment seeks to change a constitution's content, secession is a challenge of a different sort. It seeks to redefine the identity of the constitution-making body in the state. Secessionists seek to break out of the state's hold, arguing that they are entitled to create a new independent state or join another existing state. Since they do not accept the constitution-making body's authority to rule them, the constitution cannot establish a secession process for them. Furthermore, by definition, a negotiation process over secession highlights the state's potential to dissolve by defining two parties – secessionists, on the one hand, and the *rest* of the state – rather than the *whole* state – on the other. It cannot be constitutionally enshrined *ex ante*, because it undermines any state's effort to engage in nation-building. Simply put, it would mean that no unified nation is ever truly formed.

Secession's legitimacy cannot be derived from a document authored by "We the People," when secessionists do not consider themselves members. A constitution's total ban on secession reflects this, in turn. It reveals that popular sovereignty is a territorial concept. It is not composed of people alone, as customarily thought. Rather, popular sovereignty is composed of a combination of people plus territory. The loss of only one component does not redefine popular sovereignty. Losing both requires the rump state to embark on a new constitutional beginning. It is undisputed that secession entails a new constitutional beginning for the departing state. However, this chapter argues that secession requires the *rump state* to embark on a new constitutional beginning, as well (Weill 2018: 978–985). Thus, secession is typically, by nature, an exercise in revolutionary constitutionalism in the Kelsenian sense (Kelsen 1945).

## What processes may legitimize secession?

### Constitutional processes for territorial change

Very few states provide an explicit secession process in their constitutions. Table 36.1 summarizes the data. Of the seven states, three engage in explicit constitutional doublespeak, allowing for secession yet vowing to protect territorial integrity. It is, thus, difficult to predict how the legislative, executive, and judicial bodies will treat attempts to secede in these states. Ethiopia cannot be counted on to tolerate secession in light of its totalitarian regime.

Table 36.1 Procedure in constitutional secession clauses

| State | Doublespeak | Process |
|---|---|---|
| Ethiopia | Authoritarian regime | Approval by a two-thirds majority of the members of the Legislative Council of the People "concerned" + majority vote in referendum (Ethiopia Constitution, art. 39). |
| Liechtenstein | | "A majority of the citizens residing there who are entitled to vote." Secession shall be regulated by law or treaty. "A second ballot shall be held in the commune after the negotiations have been completed" (Liechtenstein Constitution, art. 8). |
| St. Kitts and Nevis | | Two-thirds of all the elected Assembly members + the bill has been approved in a referendum held in Nevis by not less than two-thirds of all the votes validly cast on that referendum (St. Kitts and Nevis Constitution, art. 113). |
| Slovakia | Declare territorial integrity indivisible + Ban secessionist political parties | National Referenda |
| South Africa | Declare territorial integrity indivisible | National legislation |
| Sudan | | The process provided: "**1.** Six months before the end of the six-year interim period, **2.** The people of Southern Sudan shall either: **a.** confirm unity of the Sudan . . . or **b.** vote for secession" (Sudan Constitution, art. 222). |
| Republic of Uzbekistan | Declare territorial integrity indivisible + Ban secessionist political parties | "The Republic of Karakalpakstan shall have the right to secede from the Republic of Uzbekistan on the basis of a nation-wide referendum held by the people of Karakalpakstan" (Republic of Uzbekistan Constitution, art. 74). |

There is no uniform process provided for secession. Few states are satisfied with endorsement of the people in the seceding area. Most maintain control over the process through demands for national legislation. Most also require either the endorsement of all the people through national referenda or some form of supermajority consent. These requirements make it extremely difficult for secessionists to achieve secession since secession is more likely to be opposed at the national level. South Sudan is exceptional. It utilized the constitutional secession clause to achieve secession, because the process reflected a compromise mechanism adopted after a bloody civil war. Sudan accepted, from the very start, that it could not engage in nation-building in the interim six-year era, between the constitution's adoption and the vote on secession.

Forty-eight states provide processes for territorial change in their constitutions. However, it is not clear whether these processes are applicable to a secession that involves withdrawal of people in addition to territory. Moreover, 45 of these states also protect territorial integrity in their constitutions, so that any territorial change also requires a constitutional amendment. Constitutional amendment, in turn, usually involves meeting supermajority requirements. Furthermore, 42 of

*Table 36.2* Constitutional procedure for territorial change

| No. of States | % of UN States | Legislative Approval Required | Referenda Approval Required | Supermajorities Requirements | Constitutional Amendment Requirement |
|---|---|---|---|---|---|
| 15 | 7.8% | Yes | No | No | Yes |
| 6 | 3.1% | Yes | No | Supermajority of entire legislature | Yes |
| 13 | 6.8% | Yes | National referendum | No | Yes |
| 7 | 3.7% | Requires enactment of law | National referendum | Supermajority in national referendum | Yes |
| 7 | 3.7% | Requires enactment of law | Approval of concerned or interested population in referendum | No | Yes |

*Source*: Data from Weill (2018).

these states protect territorial integrity and/or national unity through bans on political parties and/or eternity clauses, so that it is not at all clear whether any constitutional amendment, if ratified, would pass judicial scrutiny.

Putting all these reservations aside, Table 36.2 summarizes the data on the types of processes needed to achieve territorial change in these states. All of these states retain control over the process through a demand for approval of the legislative body, not leaving this crucial decision to the discretion of the executive branch within its treaty power prerogatives. Some even demand not mere legislative approval, but the actual passage of legislation. Most demand the people's endorsement in referenda, in addition to legislative consent. Most also mandate either some form of supermajority requirements and/or the holding of national referenda, thereby making territorial change more difficult.

Of the 48 countries analyzed in Table 36.2, only Denmark, Iceland, and Vanuatu do not require constitutional amendment to affect territorial change.

## Consent of two new peoples

When constitutions do provide a process for territorial change, they often seek the consultation of national referenda, or of the people in the area that want to secede. However, except for non-revolutionary secession (discussed in the next sub-section), secession should involve the consent of potentially *two new peoples*: the people in the area seeking to secede, and the population residing in the rest of the state. Each must separately engage in constitution-making, and their bilateral consent is needed to avoid conflicting claims to sovereignty over people and territory in the seceding area.

Beyond the theoretical exploration described earlier, which reconceptualizes popular sovereignty as a territorial concept, support for this position may be found in the American *Texas v. White* decision, given in the aftermath of the Civil War. Texas seceded from the United States in early 1861 and fought the Civil War as a member of the Confederate States of America (CSA). Following the CSA's defeat in the Civil War, the Reconstruction administration in Texas initiated proceedings for the recovery of bonds, which were issued by the federal government to Texas. These bonds were transferred during the Civil War to private citizens. The

Reconstruction administration, and later the elected administration, argued that the transfer of bonds was invalid. While the transfer required the governor's signature before the Civil War, the secessionist Texan legislature annulled this requirement, knowing that the US Treasury would not pay for bonds that would fund the rebellion. Thus, the private citizens acted in bad faith when purchasing the bonds without the governor's signature and/or did not pay full consideration for them.

For Texas to succeed in its lawsuit, it had to establish that the Supreme Court had jurisdiction to hear the dispute. This then raised the question of whether Texas was a state of the Union at the time the case was initiated and heard. If it was not, the Court was bound to dismiss the case for lack of jurisdiction. The majority of the Supreme Court ruled that Texas had never seceded from the Union and that therefore the Court had jurisdiction to hear the case. In delivering the opinion of the majority, Chief Justice Chase said:

> [T]he Union was solemnly declared to "be perpetual." . . . the Constitution was ordained "to form a more perfect Union." It is difficult to convey the idea of indissoluble unity more clearly than by these words. What can be indissoluble if a perpetual Union, made more perfect, is not? . . . The Constitution, in all its provisions, looks to an indestructible Union, composed of indestructible States. When, therefore, Texas became one of the United States, she entered into an indissoluble relation. All the obligations of perpetual union, and all the guaranties of republican government in the Union, attached at once to the State. The act which consummated her admission into the Union was something more than a compact; it was the incorporation of a new member into the political body. And it was final. The union between Texas and the other States was as complete, as perpetual, and as indissoluble as the union between the original States. There was no place for reconsideration, or revocation, except through revolution, or through consent of the States.
>
> *(Texas v. White 1869: 725–726)*

The Court read the American Constitution's preamble, which provides for a "more perfect Union," as an implicit eternity clause that forbade secession, despite the Constitution's silence on secession. It even used language that suggests that Chase was relying on the notion that a constitution may have an unamendable, fundamental core set of values/rights that the judiciary may identify by inference from reading all its provisions. Chase identified the prohibition on secession as forming such a core value. This is why Chase spoke of "the Constitution, in all its provisions." This decision transpired a century before the Indian Supreme Court articulated a similar doctrine, stating that the Indian Constitution has a "basic structure" that may not be altered (Kesavananda Bharati v. Kerala 1973), though the dominant academic approach believes that the Indian Court, rather than the American one, invented this doctrine.

Moreover, the Court explained that secession requires a constitutional revolution, because it challenges and redefines the political body. Chase further conceded that achieving consensual secession required "the consent of the states." He thus acknowledged that the secession process posits the secessionists (as one people) on the one hand and the rest of the country (as the other people) on the other hand.

The Court ruled out the possibility that secession may be achieved through a constitutional amendment. It spoke of finality, perpetuity, perfection, and indissolubility – the linguistic characteristic of constitutional eternity clauses. Chase further stated that the Constitution intended to form a more perfect Union than the original Articles of Confederation. The original pact required unanimous consent of the States for change.

## *Non-revolutionary secession*

Can secession be achieved via a constitutional amendment? The decision of the Canadian Supreme Court in *Reference re Secession of Quebec* declared that unlateral secession is constitutionally forbidden. However, the Court recognized that secession may be achieved through a constitutional amendment. Though referenda have no binding status, the Supreme Court recommended the use of a consultative referendum and demanded a "clear question" and a "clear majority vote" in the secessionist province as preconditions for negotiations to facilitate secession through a constitutional amendment. However, the Court cautioned that negotiations may fail to achieve secession, even if secession had the requisite popular support.

Following the Court's decision, Canada's federal government passed the Clarity Act, in which it committed not to negotiate on terms of secession with any province unless the House of Commons determined that, as set out in section 2(4), "there has been a clear expression of a will by a clear majority of the population of that province that the province cease to be part of Canada." Section 2(2) stated that this demanded considering among others: (1) "the size of the majority," (2) "the percentage of eligible voters voting in the referendum," and (3) the opinions of all relevant political actors. This Act thus left ample room for broad exercise of discretion on whether the Canadian government will agree to negotiate at all.

Québec countered with its own Clarity Act (Bill 99), which asserted its sovereignty and control over the referendum process. By the terms of the Preamble to Bill 99, Québec interpreted the federal Clarity Act as an affront to its right to control its destiny. Section 4 of Bill 99 declared that a simple majority of the votes cast would be sufficient to trigger the secession process.

Canada's constitutional development is unique, and its decision should not serve as a precedent for comparative purposes (Weill 2018). Canada's constitution is utterly silent on secession and territorial unity. This is an approach not shared by most other countries. Throughout its history, Canada also sought to disguise radical constitutional changes as mere evolutionary developments, with its latest revolutionary development culminating in acquisition of full independence by the severance of the remaining constitutional ties with the UK, as recently as 1982. Other states prefer to make secessionists pay by outlawing secession, thus revealing the true revolutionary nature of the secessionists' action. Canada's Constitution also grants each province unique rights to initiate constitutional change. The Supreme Court's decision to recognize Québec's right to initiate a secession process aligns with this initiation right, as the Court explicitly highlighted (Secession Reference 1998: 257). Not least, Québec has never consented to the Canadian Charter of Rights and Freedoms, which was imposed on it. In fact, Québec's assertion that it has sovereign power to control secession in Bill 99 explicitly relied on the Charter's compulsory nature. Furthermore, Canada has provided its provinces a form of a nullification right that enables them to overcome the Charter of Rights through the override power. This override power authorizes the provincial legislatures to legislate in derogation of fundamental freedoms and rights provided in the Charter, including freedom of religion, freedom of expression, life, liberty, and equality. This, too, attests to the unique identity of Canada's constitution-making body.

The Canadian Supreme Court states that the negotiations over secession are to take place "by the representatives of two legitimate majorities, namely, the clear majority of the population of Quebec, and the clear majority of Canada as a whole, whatever that may be" (Secession Reference 1998: para. 93). The Court uses a vague language of "whatever that may be" and does not clarify what constitutes "Canada as a whole." However, it seems unlikely that Québec's population will be represented twice – both as the secessionist party and as a component of "Canada as a whole." Rather, "Canada as a whole" would probably stand only for the population that would remain within Canada after Québec would secede, if allowed. However, the Canadian constitution does not provide such a track for constitutional amendments. Thus, though the Court's decision posits that secession may be achieved through constitutional amendment, this disguises the true revolutionary nature of secession in the Canadian context.

Secession can be non-revolutionary from a constitutional perspective only when it does not challenge popular sovereignty and the identity of the constitution-making body. When the original, pre-secession sovereign body in a given territory has not engaged in a nation-building enterprise to begin with, secession does not require a new constitutional beginning and break with the past for either party involved. Thus, it may be accomplished simply through a constitutional amendment. The governing model in these cases is loose and treaty-like and functions like a confederation. To protect the sovereignty of the member sub-units, this governing model allows them two powers: (1) veto right over constitutional amendments; and (2) nullification power over the application of the common/federal law in their territory. Such a treaty-like governing model is more common as a transition period, during the early stages of forming a federal state or during the early phases of acquiring a new territory. For example, the American Articles of Confederation fulfilled this model, until the US adopted its constitution and transitioned to a federal system. Sudan after its civil war has not engaged in nation-building, after adopting its new constitution in 2005, because it allowed an interim period within which South Sudan may decide to secede (which it did). Though the European Union is an international framework, it is unique in its resemblance to a quasi-state and seems to fit this model (Weill 2018: 982). This explains why Brexit could have been achieved unilaterally, under Article 50 of the Treaty of the European Union.

## How do constitutional law and international law cooperate to combat secession?

Interestingly, international law and constitutional law seem to complement and reinforce each other in combating secession. Just like the constitutional law of member states, international law seeks to prevent secession in order to promote peace and protect the territorial integrity of member states. It, too, prompts secessionists to act outside the law, if they dare embark on secession. This strategy seems to work. When international law allows secession, as is true in cases of decolonization or foreign rule (UNGA 1960), the secession's success rate is 77%. In contrast, when international law requires potential secessionists to promote internal rights of self-determination within an existing state but does not recognize their external right to express self-determination by establishing an independent state, their success rate is only 16% (Weill 2018: 978; Fazal & Griffiths 2008).

Kosovo is a prime example of international law's efforts to keep secession outside international law. Many scholars expected the International Court of Justice to recognize a remedial right to secede in cases of great infringement of human rights in the Kosovo case, given Serbia's infringement of human rights. Instead, the Court merely declared that Kosovo's unilateral declaration of independence *did not violate* international law (ICJ 2010). Initially, international law sought to prevent Serbia and Kosovo from undertaking unilateral acts under a UN interim administration, which did suspend Serbia's sovereignty over Kosovo but also denied Kosovo the right to secede unilaterally. In its declaration of independence, however, Kosovo explicitly stated that because the interim administration failed, it declared independence (Weill 2018: 981). It did not assert that it has the right to secede under international law. This would have forced the Court's hand to determine whether Kosovo had the right to secede. Thus, Kosovo did not risk an outright rejection of its right to secede, but also paid the price for acting outside international law. In fact, it is not yet a recognized member in the UN.

## What are the lessons for comparative constitutional law?

The story told in this chapter should warn against utopian stories of constitutionalism, which do not align with reality. Democracies, no less than authoritarian regimes, combat secession using their most potent unconventional constitutional tools. Although we customarily associate militant democracy with bans on political parties, militant democracy also utilizes constitutional eternity clauses. Both mechanisms serve not only to protect democratic values but to guarantee the territorial integrity of the state and the unity of its nation. In fact, the overwhelming majority of states worldwide utilize militant democracy tools to prevent secession. To understand states' motivation for this all-out war against secession, we must reconceptualize popular sovereignty as a territorial concept – composed of citizens plus territory. This, in turn, explains why secession typically requires a revolutionary constitutional beginning, and may not be achieved via a constitutional amendment. Since secession redefines the identity of the constitution-making body – "We the Territorial People" – it cannot be legitimized from within the constitutional system. This chapter thus argues that the American post–Civil War *Texas v. White* decision is more representative of comparative constitutional law on the subject, than Canada's *Reference re Secession of Quebec* decision.

## Notes

* I thank Peter Radan and my daughter, Elisheva Feintuch, for very helpful comments. This research is supported by the Israel Science Foundation (grant no. 3080/21). For elaboration on the different themes presented in this chapter, see Weill (2018).
1 I relied on the Economist Intelligence Unit's Democracy Index and Freedom House's Country Scores. If one or both indexes found a country to be authoritarian or not free, I treated it as non-democratic.
2 The term acoustic separation is taken from Dan-Cohen (1984).
3 There is a vast literature that argues that constitutional amendment power is inferior to constitution-making power. See Weill (2014).

## References

Barber, N. W. 2018, *The Principles of Constitutionalism*, Oxford: Oxford University Press.
Bligh, G. 2013, "Defending Democracy: A New Understanding of the Party-Banning Phenomenon", *Vanderbilt Journal of Transnational Law*, 46: 1321.
Brilmayer, L. 1991, "Secession and Self-Determination: A Territorial Interpretation", *Yale Journal of International Law*, 16: 177.
BVerfG 2016, BVerfG 2 BvR 349/16, Dec. 16, 2016.
Case of the Socialist Party of Turk. 2013, Case of the Socialist Party of Turk. (STP) v. Turk., App. No. 26482/95, Eur. Ct. H.R. Rep. (2013).
Coggins, B. L. 2011, "The History of Secession: An Overview," in A. Pavković & P. Radan (eds), *The Ashgate Research Companion to Secession*, Great Britain: Ashgate: 23–43.
Corte Const. 2015, Corte Const., 23–37, 2015.
Dan-Cohen, M. 1984, "Decision Rules and Conduct Rules: On Acoustic Separation in Criminal Law", *Harvard Law Review*, 97(3): 625.
Fazal, T. & Griffiths, R. 2008, "A State of One's Own: The Rise of Secession Since World War II", *The Brown Journal of World Affairs*, 15(1): 199.
Fox, G. H. & Nolte, G. 1995, "Intolerant Democracies", *Harvard International Law Journal*, 36(1): 1.
ICJ 2010, International Court of Justice, *Accordance with International Law of the Unilateral Declaration of Independence in Respect of Kosovo*, Advisory Opinion International Court of Justice Reports 403.
Ilinden v. Bulgaria 2005, *Case of the United Macedonian Organisation Ilinden–Pirin and Others v. Bulgaria*, App. No. 59489/00, Eur. Ct. H.R. Rep. (2005).
Jovanović, M. A. 2011, "To Constitutionalize or Not? Secession as Materiae Constitutionis", in A. Pavković & P. Radan (eds), *The Ashgate Research Companion to Secession*, Farnham: Ashgate: 345–363.

Kelsen, H. 1945, *General Theory of Law and State*, trans. by A. Wedberg, Cambridge: Harvard University Press.

Kesavananda Bharati v. Kerala 1973, Supreme Court of India, *Kesavananda Bharati v. Kerala*, (1973) 4 SCC 225; AIR 1973; SC 1461.

Loewenstein, K. 1937a, "Militant Democracy and Fundamental Rights, I", *American Political Science Review*, 31(3): 417–432.

Loewenstein, K. 1937b, "Militant Democracy and Fundamental Rights, II", *American Political Science Review*, 31(4): 638–658.

Monahan, P. J., Bryant, M. J. & Coté, N. C. 1996. "Coming to Terms with Plan B: Ten Principles Governing Secession," *C. D. Howe Institute, Comment*, 83: 1.

Norman, W. 1998, "The Ethics of Secession as the Regulation of Secessionist Politics", in M. Moore (ed), *National Self-Determination and Secession*, Oxford: Oxford University Press: 34–62.

Norman, W. 2003, "Domesticating Secession", in S. Macedo & A. Buchanan (eds), *Secession and Self-Determination*, New York: New York University Press: 193–237.

Ratner, S. R. 1996, "*Drawing a Better Line: Uti Possidetis and the Borders of New States*", *American Journal of International Law* 90: 590.

Secession Reference 1998, Supreme Court of Canada, *Reference re Secession of Quebec*, [1998] 2 S.C.R. 217.

Sunstein, C. R. 1991, "Constitutionalism and Secession", *University of Chicago Law Review*, 58: 633.

Texas v. White 1869, *Texas v. White*, 74 U.S. 700 (1868).

UNGA 1960, United Nations General Assembly, Declaration on the Granting of Independence to Colonial Countries and Peoples, Resolution 1514 (XV), 14 December.

Weill, R. 2006, "Shouldn't We Seek the People's Consent? On the Nexus between the Procedures of Adoption and Amendment of Israel's Constitution", MISHPAT U'MEMSHAL 10: 449 (2007) [Hebrew].

Weill, R. 2014, "The New Commonwealth Model of Constitutionalism Notwithstanding: On Judicial Review and Constitution-Making", *American Journal of Comparative Law*, 62: 127.

Weill, R. 2017, "On the Nexus of Eternity Clauses, Proportional Representation, and Banned Political Parties", *Election Law Journal*, 16(2): 237.

Weill, R. 2018, "Secession and the Prevalence of Both Militant Democracy and Eternity Clauses Worldwide", *Cardozo Law Review*, 40(2): 905.

Weill, R. 2020, "Global Constitutional Strategies to Counter-Secession", in R. D. Griffiths & D. Muro (eds), *Strategies of Secession and Counter-Secession*, London: Rowman & Littlefield: 84–99.

Weill, R. 2021, "Acontextual Constitutionalism and the Relationship between the People, Constituent Power and the State: On Nicholas Barber's 'The Principles of Constitutionalism'", *Jerusalem Review of Legal Studies*, 24(1): 94.

Weill, R. 2022, "'We the Territorial People' and the Russia-Ukraine War", *VerfBlog*, 2022/5/07, <https://verfassungsblog.de/we-the-territorial-people-and-the-russia-ukraine-war/>

# 37

# CONSTITUTIONAL LAW AND SECESSION IN THE UNITED STATES

*Roman J. Hoyos*

In 2006, the Alaska Supreme Court considered whether the state's lieutenant governor was justified in refusing to certify a proposed secession initiative for circulation. The question the initiative posed was:

> Shall the State of Alaska obtain independence from the United States of America, and become an independent nation, if such independence is legally possible, and if such independence is not legally possible under present law, shall the State of Alaska seek changes in existing law and Constitutional provisions to authorize such independence, and then obtain independence?
>
> *(Kohlhaas v. State 2006: 716)*

The Court affirmed the lieutenant governor's decision, holding that secession was unconstitutional. Four years later, the Court again affirmed the lieutenant governor's decision to keep a revised secession initiative from circulating. Reviewing the jurisprudence of secession, the Court wrote:

> The constitutionality of secession was "intensely debated and . . . unresolved" until the end of the Civil War. As President Abraham Lincoln stated in his first inaugural address, "A disruption of the Federal Union heretofore only menaced, is now formidably attempted." President Lincoln tried to persuade the country to reject threats of secession from southern states, arguing that "no State, upon its own mere motion, can lawfully get out of the Union, – that *resolves* and *ordinances* to that effect are legally void," and that "the Union of these States is perpetual." While a state's ability to secede was an unsettled question before the end of the Civil War, subsequent United States Supreme Court opinions have concluded that secession is clearly unconstitutional, and Lincoln's belief in a perpetual Union is reflected in what we have described as "a plenitude of Supreme Court cases holding as completely null" the acts of secession by Confederate states.
>
> *(Kohlhaas v. State 2010: 109–110, emphasis in original)*

DOI: 10.4324/9781003036593-44

The Alaska Court neatly and succinctly captured the history of jurisprudence of secession. But while it accurately described its origins as "unresolved," it erred in holding that secession is now "completely null." While it is now clear that no state has a constitutional right to unilateral, or at-will, secession, bilateral secession – a negotiated agreement between a state and the United States – remains a constitutional possibility. This is apparent in the Alaska Court's quotation of Lincoln's First Inaugural Address, that "no State, *upon its own mere motion*" can secede. Thus, to the extent that the secession initiative advocated bilateral secession, its constitutional status should have posed no bar to being placed on the ballot.

The *Kohlhaas* cases highlight the central constitutional question of secession. Nevertheless, the constitutional law of secession in the United States is more than simply a question of whether a state has a constitutional right to secede. That law, which grew out of the secession of southern slaveholding states, deals with the nature of executive power and how presidents can respond to a live secessionist movement, congressional power to restore loyal, or republican, government, and the jurisdictional scope of the governments of states that attempt, but ultimately fail, to secede. These questions (and others) were worked out in hundreds of cases in state and federal courts over several decades. In fact, the last US Supreme Court opinion on the issue was handed down in 1895. This chapter will focus on three key components that laid the basic foundation for the US constitutional law on secession – Lincoln's deft approach to exercising his executive authority, the Supreme Court's response to and elaboration of executive power with respect to secession, and *Texas v. White*, the Supreme Court's most notable statement on secession as a constitutional right.

## Presidential (in)action

The typical starting point for understanding the constitutional law of secession is Abraham Lincoln's First Inaugural Address, which placed great emphasis on the perpetuity of the union. But as Kenneth Stampp has pointed out, for the most part, Lincoln's Inaugural Address did not break new ground (Stampp 1978: 5). In many ways, it was firmly grounded in President Andrew Jackson's Proclamation on Nullification. There was one crucial difference, however, and that was how each interpreted the "more perfect Union" clause of the US Constitution's Preamble. For Jackson, the clause identified the principles of unity and prosperity as linked aims of the new Constitution. By contrast, Lincoln argued that the clause identified perpetuity as the guiding principle.

Jackson's Proclamation emphasized the idea of unity as central to the creation and prosperity of the Union. It was unity that had succeeded in gaining independence from Great Britain, and it was unity that led to recognizing the ineffectiveness of the Articles of Confederation. The new nation created by the Constitution of the United States created, first, a government, as opposed to a mere league as suggested by compact theorists, and, second, a prosperous nation. It was only after the creation of a new national government in 1789 that the United States found "prosperity at home and high consideration abroad" (Jackson 1832: 1204).

The success of the new constitution was achieved by resting the authority of the federal government and its several branches upon the people themselves, rather than upon the states. One of the central problems of the government created by the Articles of Confederation was that its policies could be implemented only with the aid of the states themselves. It was "the wisdom of our country as to substitute for that confederation a form of government, dependent for its existence on the local interest, the party spirit of a State, or of a prevailing faction in a State". The unity created by the new constitution was best exemplified in the elections of the president and vice president. "We are ONE PEOPLE in the choice of the President and Vice President," said Jackson. Secession could not be a constitutional right, then, because it would undermine the very purpose for which the new Constitution was created – prosperity through unity, or "a more perfect Union" (Jackson 1832: 1211).

While Lincoln's First Inaugural echoed much of Jackson's Proclamation, he nonetheless replaced Jackson's emphasis on unity with perpetuity. Lincoln linked the perpetual union clause in the Articles of Confederation to the "more perfect Union" clause of the Preamble. However, as Stampp pointed out, the perpetual union clause in the Articles of Confederation was not included in the Constitution, despite being included in an early draft by the Philadelphia Convention's Committee of Detail. He suggests that the delegates may have felt sheepish about including it considering that they were endeavoring to destroy and replace the perpetual union created by the Articles of Confederation. More generally, however, Stampp has questioned whether the relationship between union and perpetuity is a necessary one. "It is more than a metaphysical quibble to question whether, in a political system, perpetuity is a necessary attribute of perfection," he wrote (Stampp 1978: 10). Consent, unity, prosperity, and the power to execute the law directly upon individuals, rather than having to go through the states – all part of Jackson's Proclamation – were preconditions for a more perfect Union, and perhaps for perpetuity, as well.

However, Lincoln may have been uncomfortable with Jackson's emphasis on unity and prosperity as the primary justifications for the Union. Resting the case for union on prosperity may have implicitly recognized slavery as a source of national prosperity. That would not have been problematic for Jackson, but it would have certainly been a problem for Lincoln. While Lincoln disclaimed an intent to interfere with slavery as it existed in the states, he was certainly opposed to its expansion. Perpetuity, then, perhaps offered a more slavery-neutral constitutional principle that could justify the Union and recognize slavery where it existed, while keeping its expansion negotiable, as Lincoln explained elsewhere in the Address.

Understood this way, perpetuity was a meta-constitutional principle that prefigured prosperity. Perpetuity could foster continual engagement and negotiation of even the most divisive issues. Secession would not end the division; it would simply transform it into an international problem. It wasn't secession *ad infinitum* that was necessarily the problem, but new international competition for continental resources between a slaveholding republic and a non-slaveholding republic, which could in turn re-introduce European competitors for continental expansion. A perpetual union was thus a prerequisite for prosperity, while "Plainly, the central idea of secession is the essence of anarchy" (Lincoln 1861: 268).

But Lincoln's First Inaugural Address was not only concerned with identifying a background constitutional principle for rejecting the right of secession. He was also working within a particular legal context with respect to executive authority. Although believing secession to be unconstitutional, President Buchanan had taken the approach that he had no power to interfere with secession one way or another. He refused to receive the commissioners that the seceding states had sent to discuss their terms of secession. But he also took no action to prevent secession, even declining to resupply a US fort.

Buchanan was supported in this effort by an opinion written by his Attorney General Jeremiah Black. For Black, the question of secession was one for Congress to consider, not the President. As Black explained to Buchanan:

> If one of the States should declare her independence, your action cannot depend upon the rightfulness of the cause upon which such declaration is based. Whether the retirement of a State from the Union be the exercise of a right reserved in the Constitution, or a revolutionary movement, it is certain that you have not in either

case the authority to recognize the independence or to absolve her from her federal obligations. Congress, or the other States in convention assembled, must take such measures as may be necessary and proper. In such an event, I see no course for you but to go straight onward in the path you have hitherto trodden – that is, execute the laws to the extent of the defensive means placed in your hands, and act generally upon the assumption that the present constitutional relations between the States and the Federal Government continue to exist, until a new order of things shall be established either by law or force.

*("Power of the President in Executing the Laws" Black 1860: 523–524)*

While Black's opinion has generally been construed as a justification for executive non-interference with secession, read carefully, it also provided a guide to executive action. Reading it from the perspective of the firing on Fort Sumter, in fact, it appears that President Lincoln could well have used it as a guide to manipulate South Carolina into the firing, and into justification for executive action in response to secession.

Black's opinion had determined that the President's action could only be limited to defensive actions, particularly with respect to the protection of federal property, such as "forts, arsenals, magazines, dock yards, navy yards, customs houses, public ships, and other property which the United States has bought, built, and paid for" ("Power of the President in Executing the Laws" Black 1860: 520–521). In his First Inaugural, Lincoln explained that

In doing this there needs to be no bloodshed or violence, and there shall be none unless it be forced upon the national authority. The power confided to me will be used to hold, occupy, and possess the property and places belonging to the Government and to collect the duties and imposts; but beyond what may be necessary for these objects, there will be no invasion, no using of force against or among the people anywhere (Lincoln 1861: 266).

Moreover, he continued,

Where hostility to the United States in any interior locality shall be so great and universal as to prevent competent resident citizens from holding the Federal offices, there will be no attempt to force obnoxious strangers among the people for that object. While the strict legal right may exist in the Government to enforce the exercise of these offices, the attempt to do so would be so irritating and so nearly impracticable withal that I deem it better to forego for the time the uses of such offices (Lincoln 1861: 266).

These statements are consistent with Black's opinion.

Lincoln's attempt to resupply Fort Sumter could be read as simply an attempt to "execute the laws to the extent of the defensive means placed in your hands," as Black suggested. Nevertheless, it led to the firing on a fort, "bought, built, and paid for" by the United States, and its subsequent capture by the State of South Carolina. This gave Lincoln the defensive justification he needed to respond lawfully and militarily to secession, allowing him to invoke the 1795 and 1808 militia and insurrection acts. Secession had ceased to be a mere debate between "the exercise of a constitutional right reserved in the Constitution, or a revolutionary movement"; it was now an armed conflict. Once South Carolina fired on the attempted resupply of Fort Sumter, the entire justification for executive action was made. An armed insurrection now existed, and Lincoln set about creating a military response.

## The *Prize Cases* and executive power

Congress remained out of session after the firing on Fort Sumter. That left only the executive branch to take action, which Lincoln did by invoking the militia and insurrection acts to call out the militia, declare martial law, and blockade southern ports. Most of his early actions, at least on suspending the writ of habeas corpus and imposing a blockade upon southern ports, were subsequently ratified by Congress. And the Supreme Court appeared to have had little interest in standing in the way. But the fact that Lincoln walked a fairly tight legal line effectively made congressional and judicial support all the easier. Nevertheless, as J. G. Randall once explained, "Being a domestic conflict, yet with all the proportions of a foreign war, the struggle naturally engendered legal complications which would be confusing to an outside observer" (Randall 1926: 48).

This is not to say that there was no resistance to Lincoln's early actions. In 1861, Supreme Court Chief Justice Roger B. Taney pushed back against Lincoln's declaration of martial law and suspension of the writ of habeas corpus in Maryland (not one of the seceding states) in his *Ex parte Merryman* opinion, now celebrated by civil libertarians (Ex parte Merryman 1861). However, in 1864, in another habeas case during the war, *Ex parte Vallandigham*, the Supreme Court rejected an appeal from a conviction by a military commission (Ex parte Vallandigham 1864). While the Supreme Court came to its decision on legalistic grounds, the district court identified the pragmatic reasons for the Supreme Court's avoidance of the issue.

> I have referred thus briefly to the present crisis of the country as having a bearing on the question before the court. It is clearly not a time when any one connected with the judicial department of the government should allow himself, except from the most stringent obligations of duty, to embarrass or thwart the executive in his efforts to deliver the country from the dangers which press so heavily upon it.
>
> *(Ex parte Vallandigham 1863: 922)*

In 1866, the Supreme Court effectively confirmed this wartime consideration in *Ex parte Milligan*, after the war:

> During the late wicked Rebellion, the temper of the times did not allow that calmness in deliberation and discussion so necessary to a correct conclusion of a purely judicial question. *Then*, considerations of safety were mingled with the exercise of power; and feelings and interests prevailed which are happily terminated. *Now* that the public safety is assured, this question, as well as all others, can be discussed and decided without passion or the admixture of any element not required to form a legal judgment. We approach the investigation of this case, fully sensible of the magnitude of the inquiry and the necessity of full and cautious deliberation.
>
> *(Ex parte Milligan 1866: 109, emphasis added)*

While the majority ultimately rebuked Lincoln's suspension of the writ of habeas corpus and use of military commissions to try civilians, *Ex parte Milligan* has had a complicated history. One scholar has argued that Lincoln actually understood the law at the time better than did Justice Davis, author of the majority opinion (Winger 2020; Mackey 2020). Historian Michael Les Benedict has suggested that Chief Justice Salmon Chase's concurring opinion has in some ways been more influential (Benedict 2020). While Davis's majority opinion has been revered for its broad statements regarding civil liberty, Chase's opinion was more sensitive to the realities of civil liberty in 1866. While southern courts were open and functioning, for instance, they were largely controlled by ex-Confederates, and were being used to harass and imprison freed people, Union soldiers, and southern loyalists. Chase's opinion held out the possibilities of military commissions and suspensions of the writ of habeas corpus in such situations (Haggerty 2020). Moreover, the more existential the crisis for the nation, the more the Court has preferred to defer the decisions made by the other branches (Benedict). As secession is the most existential crisis, it is not clear how much of a role *Ex parte Milligan* would play in the throes of a second secessionist movement. It is entirely possible that Lincoln's (or Chase's) approach would ultimately prevail, and a president given a broader scope of action than the *Ex parte Milligan* opinion might otherwise suggest.

While Lincoln's suspension of the writ of habeas corpus was perhaps his most controversial act, his blockade of southern ports was the trickier question, as it implicated not only constitutional law, but international law and politics as well. Lincoln faced twin problems with the blockade. First, he had to avoid stepping on Congress's power to declare war. Second, he had to avoid entering into a public war that might invite European nations to support the Confederacy. His blockade of southern ports seemed to be a *de facto* declaration of war, by treating secessionists as belligerents. And capturing neutral vessels of foreign nations could invite those nations to take sides with the Confederacy. Lincoln's blockade was considered by the Supreme Court in the *Prize Cases*, where the Court offered its first major statement on the nature of the attempted secession, and the president's power to respond to it, in a seemingly "obscure and narrow judicial decision about naval operations" (Lee 2008).

The *Prize Cases* has produced confusion ever since the opinion was handed down. Many contemporaries, for instance, believed that the opinion recognized secession (Nicoletti 2017). Modern scholars, by contrast, have been perplexed by the legal basis of the Court's opinion. According to Stephen Vladek, for instance, "Grier's majority opinion dances around whether it's the Constitution that's doing the work, whether it's the statutes that are doing the work, or whether it's international law that's doing the work" (Vladek 2008: 87). This confusion is due to the complexity of the issues the Court was dealing with, and its attempt to weave these bodies of law together.

"The right of prize and capture," or the capture of a neutral vessel on the high seas, the Supreme Court explained, "has its origin in the '*jus belli*' [i.e. laws of war], and is governed and adjudged under the law of nations." In other words, prize is a matter of international law. As a legal matter, there are two elements to claim prize, "a war must exist *de facto*, and the neutral must have knowledge or notice of the intention of one of the parties belligerent to use this mode of coercion against a port, city, or territory, in possession of the other" (The Prize Cases 1862: 666). The key question in the *Prize Cases* concerned the first element – whether a war existed. The claim to a prize, then, seemed to be an implied recognition of the legitimacy of secession, as only sovereigns could be subject to the law of nations.

The first step for the Court in trying to avoid the law of nations problem was to distinguish between public wars between two sovereigns, and civil wars. The *Prize Cases* was one of the first opinions to attempt to flesh out this distinction. As the concept of civil war took shape in the age of revolution, it was coming to mean a war within a state between parties competing for control of a state. Secession challenged this conception, as it was an attempt to sever a state, not gain control over it (Armitage 2017). However, the Court, like Lincoln, decided that secession was an internal, or civil, war, a war within a state, not between states. But a war nonetheless, for purposes of international law.

But was it a war according to the Constitution? Only Congress has the power to declare war. If it does not, or if a president takes war-like measures before Congress declares war, can a war exist as a legal or constitutional matter? The Court had already answered that question in its phrasing of the elements of prize: the question was whether a war existed *de facto*, not *de jure*. The Court defined "war" broadly, as "That state in which a nation prosecutes its right by force," not simply whether Congress had issued a formal declaration. The Court then determined that it was "bound" to take judicial notice of "its actual existence [a]s a fact in our domestic history." Ultimately, the question of whether a war exists "is a question to be decided *by him* [i.e. the President], and this Court must be governed by the decisions and acts of the political department of the Government to which this power was entrusted." The blockade proclamation thus constituted "conclusive evidence to the Court that a state of war existed" (The Prize Cases 1862: 666, 671). This was not a case where the Court was simply taking the president's word for it. The proclamation of blockade was conclusive only in combination with the judicial notice of the "actual existence" of war following the firing on Fort Sumter.

But there was yet another problem: Lincoln rested his blockade authority on his duty as president to execute the laws of the United States. How could waging a war against states of the Union be considered executing the laws?

J. G. Randall once explained that "There are varying degrees of disturbances with which a government may be confronted: riot, insurrection, rebellion, civil war" (Randall 1926: 60). There can be subtle shading between these types of disturbances. But, it is possible for a riot or an insurrection to grow into a civil war. As the Supreme Court explained, "Insurrection against a government may or may not culminate in an organized rebellion, *but a civil war always begins by insurrection* against the lawful authority of the Government" (The Prize Cases 1862: 666, emphasis added). What distinguishes a civil war from other types of "disturbances" is scale and organization. Once it reaches the level of war, then the tools of war, including the law of war, apply. But using such tools does not change the character of the disturbance, which remains a domestic war.

The origination of secession in insurrection had important legal consequences. It enabled the president to invoke the militia and insurrection acts to call out the militia and deploy military and naval forces "to suppress insurrection against the government of a State or of the United States." As the armed conflict moved from insurrection to rebellion and finally to civil war, as "the number, power, and organization" of the insurrectionists intensified, the president's power to take military action to suppress the initial insurrection without a formal declaration of war remained intact. Once the insurrection reaches the point of civil war, the president, as part of his or her power to suppress an insurrection, also realizes the power to invoke the *jus belli*, and to treat the insurrectionists as belligerents, which includes the right to capture and prize. This was what Randall referred to as the "insurrection theory" of the war (Randall 1926: 63). So, the question is not whether it is international, constitutional, or positive law that is doing the work, but how they work together to explain the president's duty to respond to an existential crisis created by attempted unilateral secession.

In short, then, the president has no power to recognize the unilateral secession of a state or group of states. More than that, the president has an affirmative duty to continue to execute the laws in those states claiming to have seceded. In that sense, the *Prize Cases* rejected the approach that President Buchanan and Attorney General Black adopted. Because a civil war is a domestic disturbance, originating in insurrection, the president can use the tools and laws of war to perform their duty to put down the insurrection/secession/civil war. However, the president cannot initiate an offensive military action against a state attempting unilateral secession. The military actions may only be defensive, only a response to the president's attempt to perform his or her duty to execute the laws. Black, Lincoln, and the Court in the *Prize Cases* all took that position, as did Congress in ratifying Lincoln's actions once it was able to convene.

## *Texas v. White* and the right of secession

While the *Prize Cases* held that the president could not decide the question of secession, it implied that unilateral secession was not a constitutional right by recognizing the president's duty to execute the laws in the states purporting to secede. However, the Court did not reach directly the question of secession's constitutionality. *Texas v. White* is the Supreme Court's major statement on the right of secession. Scholars are split on the Court's opinion. While Herman Belz has described Chief Justice Salmon "Chase's analysis of the constitutional meaning of statehood [as] the most searching and comprehensive examination of the subject in constitutional law to that time" (Belz 1993: 129–130), Peter Radan sees it as rightly relegated to a mere footnote (Radan 2006: 205). It would be fair to say that Radan captures the prevailing view among modern scholars.

*Texas v. White* was not the first case to raise the secession question. In *Georgia v. Stanton*, decided the year before *Texas v. White*, the Court determined that that the status of the seceded states was a political question, and thus that the Court had no jurisdiction to determine the constitutionality of the Reconstruction Acts of 1867, which had imposed military rule upon the southern states. In some respects, *Georgia v. Stanton* was the better case to decide the secession question. But it was also the more politically charged, as it dealt with one of the most controversial congressional Reconstruction policies. It also raised a separation of powers issue that was absent in *Texas v. White*. So, there were serious practical political problems in offering an opinion on secession in *Georgia v. Stanton*. Interestingly, Chase concurred in *Stanton*'s result but did not elaborate his disagreement with the reasoning behind the *Stanton* opinion (Georgia v. Stanton 1867: 70). It is possible to think of his *Texas v. White* opinion as an elaboration of his concurring opinion in *Georgia v. Stanton*.

The specific legal question in *Texas v. White* was whether Texas was a *state* for purposes of the Supreme Court's original jurisdiction. But there was an array of ancillary questions. If Texas was a state, had it remained a state despite its secession ordinance? If not, was its status restored *a fortiori* by military defeat, the end of the war, or at some other point? If it was not a state, when did it lose its status as a state, and who could restore it, and how? For Justice Grier in his dissent, the question was easily resolved. As a textual matter, a *state* is defined in the Constitution as having representation in Congress. As Texas had no representatives in either house, Texas was not a state. This was the easiest, more straightforward path to the question presented. It was agnostic on the secession question, and required no great inquiry into constitutional theory. In contrast to Grier, Chase took a winding tour through political and constitutional theory. He began by distinguishing a state from its government, which he used in combination with perpetuity to develop an *imperio in imperium* conception of the federal union, or the idea that "The Constitution, in all its provisions, looks to an indestructible Union, composed of indestructible States" (Texas v. White 1869: 725).

The bulk of the scholarly focus on Chase's opinion deals with his idea of perpetuity. On this point, Chase mostly restates Lincoln's arguments from his First Inaugural Address. Like Lincoln, Chase connects the perpetuity clause in the Articles of Confederation to the "more perfect Union" clause in the Preamble to the Constitution of the United States. Stampp's critique of Lincoln's First Inaugural also applies to *Texas v. White*. Another problem with Chase's perpetuity claim is that even Chase himself, like Lincoln, does not hold that the Union is totally indestructible. States may leave the Union, but only with permission of the states that remain (Texas v. White 1869: 726). If consensual secession is a legitimate constitutional possibility, then destruction of the Union is possible.

Chase would have been on firmer ground had he relied upon the Constitution's "more perfect Union" clause and contrasted it with the Articles of Confederation. The West Virginia

Supreme Court identified such a path to perpetuity. In the first post-war case to consider the right to secession, the West Virginia Supreme Court argued that "Government is a necessity of man's nature, and not a mere caprice, however wisdom and experience may mould its structure or vary its application. Its perpetuity springs from its continued necessity, and is therefore an essential element of its nature" (Hood v. Maxwell 1866: 242). The West Virginia Supreme Court's connection between necessity and perpetuity was closer to Jackson's connection of prosperity to union than to Lincoln's tenuous textual conception of perpetuity. It also more accurately captured the reason for replacing the union created by the Articles of Confederation with the union created by the Constitution of the United States. The Articles were abandoned when the government it created could no longer meet the needs for which it was created. The war had clearly demonstrated the continuing vitality of the union created by the Constitution (Hyman 1975).

But while the perpetuity argument answered the question of whether a state could leave the Union, it did not quite answer the question of whether a state could lose its status as a state as a result of its attempt to secede.

Rather than starting with the Constitution and its conceptualization of a state, as Grier did, Chase started with a more philosophical inquiry into the idea of a state. His key point was that there is a distinction between a state and its government. A state consists "of people, territory, and government" (Texas v. White 1869: 720). For Chase, the philosophical and the constitutional conception of the state shared these same basic characteristics. "This is undoubtedly the fundamental idea upon which the republican institutions of our own country are established" (Texas v. White 1869: 721). Chase then described the process by which Texas seceded from the Union to demonstrate that it was a governmental decision, and that the state itself, the sovereign, the people, remained.

Justice Grier was critical of Chase's conception of the secession process. For Grier, it was significant that the states used the constitutional convention as the means of secession. The convention had been understood as the institutional embodiment of the people's sovereignty since the American Revolution. Thus, Grier concluded, it was the people, in the exercise of their sovereignty, who had decided to secede (Texas v. White 1869: 740). So, Chase's distinction between state and government did not quite do the work that Chase seemed to hope for.

However, the convention's place in the American constitutional order was in the midst of change. John Alexander Jameson had just published the first legal treatise on constitutional conventions the year before *Texas v. White*. Jameson argued that the convention was not the embodiment of the people's sovereignty, but merely another branch of government (Jameson 1867). Chase did not cite Jameson's treatise, but he may well have been influenced by it. The treatise was well noted, and well received by the legal press and major legal commentators, including Thomas Cooley, whose own treatise on state constitutional law was published the same year as *Texas v. White* (Cooley 1868).

The debate between Grier and Chase thus exposed a conceptual shift in thinking about political ideas. Shortly before the war, Francis Lieber had pointed out that the term *sovereignty* was underdeveloped, a result of being both new and vague. For Lieber, the more appropriate concept was *nation*, which he viewed as a moral good, responsible, in his view, for the progress of civilization (Lieber 1861). Lieber was also skeptical of the idea of *popular sovereignty*, which had grown in prominence in the first half of the nineteenth century, largely in conversation with the widespread use of constitutional conventions for constitutional reform. While Lieber appreciated the political value of conventions, he rejected the idea that they represented some vague and undefined popular sovereign. The ideas of *sovereignty* and *popular sovereignty* were thus in flux in 1868, moving from the conception reflected in Grier's dissent to that reflected in Chase's opinion. Grier was using the term *sovereignty* in the sense of popular sovereignty, and its particular pre-secession meaning, as the people's power to make their own constitutions. By contrast, Chase was using it in a more modern, abstract sense to describe the foundation of state authority.

For Chase, the people, the territory, and the need to govern remained, despite the attempted secession. In other words, the state's civil jurisdiction remained as the war determined the secession question. By separating out a state's civil jurisdiction from its acts in support of secession, Chase created space to recognize the continuing "separate and independent existence" of the states (Texas v. White 1869: 725). As he explained later in his opinion,

> acts necessary to peace and good order among citizens, such for example, as acts sanctioning and protecting marriage and the domestic relations, governing the course of descents, regulating the conveyance and transfer of property, real and personal, and providing remedies for injuries to person and estate, and other similar acts, which would be valid is emanating from a lawful government, must be regarded in general as valid when proceeding from an actual, though unlawful, government; and that acts in furtherance or support of rebellion against the United States, or intended to defeat the just rights of citizens, and other acts of like nature, must, in general, be regarded as invalid in void.
>
> *(Texas v. White 1869: 733)*

Here, he seemed to be building upon his earlier circuit opinion in *Shortridge v. Macon*, in which he held that the interest on debt incurred before secession in a state attempting secession during war could be recovered after the war. "Legal rights," he wrote, "could neither be originated nor defeated by the action of the central authorities of the late rebellion" (Shortridge v. Macon 1867: 23). And in a circuit opinion after *Texas v. White*, Chase reiterated the point that if courts failed to recognize the civil jurisdiction of states during secession, "the effect must be to annul all official acts performed by these officers." He continued that, "It is impossible to measure the evils which such a construction would add to the calamities which have already fallen upon the people of these states" (In re Griffin 1869: 25). The states, then, remained sovereign in their ability to govern for purposes unrelated to secession and war. But no portion of its sovereignty could decide a state's relationship to the Union. To the extent that popular sovereignty existed, it was the people of the nation, not the state or a convention.

Because there was no bilateral agreement between the states desiring to secede and those remaining in the Union, the states were at no time out of the Union. The attempted secession had simply left "a State deprived of all rightful government, by revolutionary violence." In such a condition, "[i]t was necessary that the old constitution should receive such amendments as would conform its provisions to the new conditions created by emancipation, and afford adequate security to the people of the State," Chase wrote (Texas v. White 1869: 730). The states themselves, as states, as political communities, remained intact, as indestructible states within an indestructible Union. Their failed attempt to secede left the state, and its civil jurisdiction, intact, but the government in need of reform, which was the responsibility of Congress and its duty to ensure republican *government* in the states. Congress exercised its responsibility in the Reconstruction Acts, which sought only the reorganization and restoration of the state *governments*, not the states themselves.

## Consolidating *Texas v. White*

*Texas v. White* was not the last secession case the Court heard. One of the major questions following *Texas v. White* was whether the states' police power remained intact during the war. At least one state court after *Texas v. White* refused to recognize the continuation of its state's civil jurisdiction until it regained its legal status (Ex parte Bibb 1870). The Supreme Court, however, built upon a distinction that Chase identified in *Texas v. White* between *de facto* and *de jure* governments. Although, the state governments ceased being *de jure* governments, they remained *de facto* governments for purposes of civil government. Only those acts carried out in support of secession or war were nullified; the states' general non-war-related police powers remained intact. As Justice Field explained in *Horn v. Lockhard*, abandoning the tentative tone in *Texas v. White*,

> The existence of a state of insurrection and war did not loosen the bonds of society, or do away with civil government, or the regular administration of the laws. Order was to be preserved, police regulations maintained, crime prosecuted, property protected, contracts enforced, marriages celebrated, estates settled, and the transfer and descent of property regulated precisely as in time of peace.
>
> *(Horn v. Lockhard 1873: 580)*

Law and governance goes on even in the midst of an attempt secession. Litigation over secession and its effects continued in the Supreme Court until the 1890s, when the Court, seemingly exhausted from the cases, simply quoted Field's opinion in *Horn v. Lockhard* as "the well-settled doctrine" concerning secession (Johnson v. Atlantic 1895: 645). It was by that point that the question concerning the constitutionality of unilateral secession and the effects of a failed such secession could be said to be resolved.

# References

Armitage, D. 2017, *Civil Wars: A History in Ideas*, New York: Alfred A. Knopf.

Belz, H. 1993, "Deep-Conviction Jurisprudence and *Texas v. White*: A Comment on G. Edward White's Historicist Interpretation of Chief Justice Samuel Chase", *Northern Kentucky Law Review* 21: 117–131.

Benedict, M. 2020, "*Ex Parte Milligan* in Context and History: From Reconstruction to the War on Terror", in S. Winger & J. White (eds), Ex Parte Milligan *Reconsidered: Race and Civil Liberties from the Lincoln Administration to the War on Terror*, Lawrence: University Press of Kansas: 305–326.

Cooley, T. 1868, *A Treatise on the Constitutional Limitations Which Rest upon the Legislative Power of the States of the American Union*, Boston: Little, Brown.

Ex parte Bibb 1870, *Ex parte Bibb*, 44 Ala. 140 (1870).

Ex parte Merryman 1861, *Ex parte Merryman*, 17 F. Cas. 144 (1861).

Ex parte Milligan 1866, *Ex parte Milligan*, 71 U.S. 2 (1866).

Ex parte Vallandigham 1863, *Ex parte Vallandigham*, 28 F. Cas. 874 (1863).

Ex parte Vallandigham 1864, *Ex parte Vallandigham*, 68 U.S. 243 (1864).

Georgia v. Stanton 1867, *Georgia v. Stanton*, 73 U.S. 50 (1867).

Haggerty, M. 2020, "To Leave Behind the law of Force: Salmon Chase and the Civil War Era", in S. Winger & J. White (eds), Ex Parte Milligan *Reconsidered: Race and Civil Liberties from the Lincoln Administration to the War on Terror*, Lawrence: University Press of Kansas: 222–242.

Hood v. Maxwell 1866, *Hood v. Maxwell*, 1 W.Va. 219 (1866).

Horn v. Lockhard 1873, *Horn v. Lockhard*, 84 U.S. 570 (1873).

Hyman, H. 1975, *A More Perfect Union: The Impact of the Civil War and Reconstruction on the Constitution*, Boston: Houghton Mifflin Company.

In re Griffin 1869, *In re Griffin*, 11 F. Cas. 7 (1869).

Jackson, A. 1832, "Proclamation", in J. D. Richardson (ed), *A Compilation of the Messages and Papers of the Presidents, Volume III*, New York: Bureau of National Literature, Inc, 1897: 1203–1219.

Jameson, J. 1867, *The Constitutional Convention: Its History, Powers, and Modes of Proceeding*. New York: C. Scribner and Company.

Johnson v. Atlantic 1895, *Johnson v. Atlantic, G & W.I. Transit Co*, 156 U.S. 618 (1895).

Kohlhaas v. State 2006, *Kohlhaas v. State*, 147 P. 3d 714 (2006).

Kohlhaas v. State 2010, *Kohlhaas v. State*, 233 P. 3d 105 (2010).

Lee, T. 2008, "The Civil War in U.S. Foreign Relations Law: A Dress Rehearsal for Modern Transformations", *St. Louis University Law Review*, 53: 53–71.

Lieber, F. (1861). *What Is Our Constitution, League, Pact, or Government?: Two Lectures on the Constitution of the United States, Concluding a Course on the Modern State*, New York: Board of Trustees.

Lincoln, A. 1861, "First Inaugural Address", in R. P. Basler (ed.), *The Collected Works of Abraham Lincoln, Vol IV*, New Brunswick: Rutgers University Press, 1953: 262–271.

Mackey, T. 2020, *Opposing Lincoln: Clement L. Vallandigham, and the Legal Battle over Dissent in Wartime*, Lawrence: University Press of Kansas.

Nicoletti, C. 2017, *Secession on Trial: The Treason Prosecution of Jefferson Davis*, New York: Cambridge University Press.

Black, J. 1860, "Power of the President in Executing the Laws", Opinion of the U. S. Attorney General, 9, p. 516.

The Prize Cases 1862, *The Prize Cases*, 67 U.S. 635 (1862).

Radan, P. 2006, "'An Indestructible Union . . . of Indestructible States': The Supreme Court of the United States and Secession", *Legal History*, 10: 187–205.

Randall, J. 1926, *Constitutional Problems Under Lincoln*, New York: D. Appleton and Company.

Shortridge v. Macon 1867, *Shortridge v. Macon*, 22 F. Cas. 20 (1867).

Stampp, K. 1978, "The Concept of Perpetual Union", *The Journal of American History*, 65: 5–33.

Texas v. White 1869, *Texas v. White*, 74 U.S. 700 (1869).

Vladek, S. 2008, "Re-Thinking the Prize Cases: Some Remarks in Response to Professor Lee", *St. Louis University Law Review*, 53: 85–91.

Winger, S. 2020, "The Least Naive Position: The Lincoln Administration and International Law in American Wars on Terror", in S. Winger & J. White (eds), Ex Parte Milligan *Reconsidered: Race and Civil Liberties from the Lincoln Administration to the War on Terror*, Lawrence: University Press of Kansas: 243–276.

# 38

# CONSTITUTIONAL LAW AND SECESSION IN AUSTRALIA

*Thomas D. Musgrave*

## Introduction

Federalism, as Dicey has noted, "is the natural condition of states which desire union and do not desire unity" (Dicey 1927: lxxv). When regional attachments clash with national attachment, this inherent aspect of federations can lead to centrifugal pressures, with the possibility of disintegration should one of the component parts of the federation decide to secede (Craven 1986: 4, 7). A decision to secede, when it has been endorsed in a referendum by a majority of voters, evokes a fundamental issue for liberal democratic federations. Should the expressed will of the electorate of a component part of a federation be given effect, on the basis of the legitimising force of the democratic process? Or should the expressed will of that electorate not be given effect, in that it represents only the position of a minority of the total population of the federation, and secession necessarily affects the federation as a whole? (Musgrave 2003: 95). This issue was at the heart of the attempted secession of Western Australia. A referendum had been held in Western Australia which clearly and unequivocally endorsed the secession of the state from the Australian federation, prompting the government of Western Australia to submit a petition to secede to the British Parliament. The petition was opposed by the Australian government. This chapter will examine how the attempted secession of Western Australia was dealt with, in the context of the Australian Constitution.

## The formation of the Australian federation

The British first arrived in Australia in 1788 and established the colony of New South Wales. By the mid-nineteenth century, there were six separate British colonies in Australia, viz. New South Wales, Victoria, Queensland, South Australia, Tasmania and Western Australia. The six colonies each had their own separate government and laws. The five eastern colonies had become self-governing entities in the 1850s. Western Australia, on the other hand, did not become a self-governing entity until 1890. New South Wales and Victoria were the two largest colonies in terms of population and economic development. The colonies adopted policies which protected and fostered their individual commercial and economic interests. The imposition of tariffs on goods which crossed inter-colonial borders was the principal means of doing this. Tariffs provided the colonial governments with the bulk of their revenue, but they had the negative effect of restricting inter-colonial trade and commerce.

DOI: 10.4324/9781003036593-45

Although the colonies were self-governing, they were nevertheless subject, by virtue of the doctrine of parliamentary sovereignty, to the overriding control of the British Parliament, otherwise known as the Imperial Parliament. The relationship of the Imperial Parliament to the colonial parliaments was explicitly set out in the *Colonial Laws Validity Act* 1865 (Imp) (28 & 29 Vict. c 63). Section 2 of the Act declared that when a colonial law was "repugnant" to an Act of the Imperial Parliament which extended to that colony, the colonial law was "absolutely void and inoperative" to the extent of the repugnancy.

The idea of uniting the colonies into a single entity developed slowly in the mid-nineteenth century. Initially, there was considerable opposition, particularly amongst the smaller states, who feared that they would be dominated by the two largest colonies of New South Wales and Victoria, and further that they would be deprived of their considerable revenue in the form of inter-colonial tariffs. Given that the colonies were each possessed of a separate parliament, laws, and regional identity, those advocating the union of the colonies recognised that only a federal arrangement would be possible (Craven 1986: 14).

By the 1880s the attitude of the smaller colonies began to change and the idea of federation became increasingly popular. In 1889, the Premier of New South Wales, Sir Henry Parkes, called for the convening of a national convention of colonial parliamentary representatives, in order to draft a constitution providing for a federal structure. This convention took place in 1891. A draft constitution was drawn up, setting out a federal structure, based on a combination of British and American constitutional principles. This draft constitution was further refined at the conference of 1897–1898.

The colonies of New South Wales, Victoria, South Australia, and Tasmania then held referendums in 1898, in order to obtain popular support for the proposed federation. Queensland and Western Australia did not participate in this referendum process. Pursuant to the referendum results, some modifications to the draft constitution were made. Once this had been done, referendums were again held in 1899, with Queensland participating this time. In each instance, the referendum result was in favour of federation.

The colonies themselves did not have the constitutional power to unite in a federation. Their constitutions only empowered them to govern within the existing context of their own territory. In order to alter their constitutional status and unite in a federation, it was necessary for the colonies to request legal intervention from the Imperial Parliament, which, as noted earlier, exercised ultimate control over its colonial possessions by virtue of the doctrine of parliamentary sovereignty. A petition was drafted by each of the five eastern colonies and presented to the Imperial Parliament, requesting that the Parliament enact legislation adopting the draft constitution and thereby create the Australian federation (La Nauze 1972: 248). After making a number of amendments, the Imperial Parliament duly enacted the draft constitution, thereby creating the Australian federation and transforming the colonies into states within the federation. The federation was to be known as the Commonwealth of Australia. The *Commonwealth of Australia Constitution Act 1900* (Imp) (63 & 64 Vict. c 12) was adopted on 5 July 1900. It received royal assent on 9 July 1900. Section 3 of the Act stated that the Commonwealth would come into being on a day proclaimed by the Queen. This was subsequently declared to be 1 January 1901.

## The Australian Constitution

The *Commonwealth of Australia Constitution Act 1900* contains a preamble and nine sections. The preamble and the first eight sections are referred to as the "covering clauses". They do not form part of the Australian Constitution. The ninth section is entitled "The Constitution". It is only this part of the British statute which comprises the Australian Constitution. The Constitution is comprised of 128 sections, divided into eight chapters. The eight chapters deal, respectively, with the federal parliament, the federal executive, the federal judiciary, finance and trade, states, new states, miscellaneous, and alterations to the Constitution.

Chapter 1 of the Constitution created a bicameral parliament, comprised of an Upper House, known as the Senate, and a Lower House, known as the House of Representatives. Laws may be formulated in both Houses, although a money bill cannot originate in the Senate. The allocation of legislative powers between the federal parliament and the states is addressed in Chapter 1. The federal parliament was granted a limited number of specific heads of power, in sections 51 and 52, and the residuum was granted to the states. Most of the powers granted to the federal parliament are concurrent, so that both the federal parliament and the state parliaments can enact laws on these subject matters. In the event of a conflict between a federal law and a state law on the same subject matter, section 109 provides that the federal law will prevail to the extent of the inconsistency.

The very important issue of trade and commerce was dealt with in Chapter 4. The thrust of the Chapter was to create a single and unified economic unit comprising the entire country. Section 92 provided that trade between the states is to be "absolutely free". This means that there can be no tariffs between the states. Section 90 granted the federal parliament exclusive jurisdiction to determine whether tariffs are to be imposed on goods imported from overseas. As a result, it has been the federal parliament which decides whether the federation will adopt a policy of free trade or protectionism with regard to such goods.

Section 128 addresses the issue of amendments to the Constitution. Given that the *Commonwealth of Australia Constitution Act 1900* which created the Australian Constitution was a British statute, amendments to that statute would need to be effected by the Imperial Parliament. However, an amending formula was built into the statute, whereby it could be amended solely within the Australian context, without the necessity of resorting to the Imperial Parliament. Section 128 requires that any proposed amendment to the Constitution first obtain an absolute majority of votes in both houses of parliament. The proposed amendment must then be presented by way of referendum to the electors of the states. A majority of electors in a majority of the states, as well as a majority of electors throughout the country, must approve the proposed amendment in order to effect a change to the Constitution.

## Western Australia joins the federation, reluctantly

Unlike the five eastern colonies, Western Australia was reluctant to join the new federation. It had expressed doubts about doing so both at the constitutional conference of 1891 and at that of 1897–1898. Western Australia did not take part in the referendums of 1898 and 1899, and was not a party to the petition requesting the Imperial Parliament to enact the draft constitution into law (Musgrave 2003: 96). When the Imperial Parliament adopted the *Commonwealth of Australia Constitution Act 1900* on 5 July 1900, Western Australia had still not held a referendum on whether to join the federation.

There were a number of reasons for Western Australia's misgivings. Whereas the five eastern colonies had become self-governing entities in the 1850s, Western Australia did not become self-governing until 1890. Western Australia was consequently reluctant to relinquish to a central government any of the political power which it had only so recently acquired (Besant 1990: 226–227). There was also the issue of the "tyranny of distance". Western Australia was isolated from the eastern colonies by an enormous "sea of sand", which resulted in there being very little affinity between the traditional Western Australian "sandgropers" and their eastern counterparts. But the most important reason for Western Australia's reluctance to join the federation involved economic considerations. Approximately half of Western Australia's revenues came from inter-colonial tariffs from mining and agriculture, which formed the basis of Western Australia's economy (Shaw 1961: 195). Were those tariffs to be removed, the economy of Western Australia would be seriously crippled. Yet this was precisely what section 92 of the Australian Constitution proposed to do, declaring that inter-state trade and commerce must be "absolutely free".

In spite of these reservations, Western Australia did join the federation, albeit at the last moment. Considerable pressure had been brought to bear to ensure that it did so. This pressure came primarily from two sources, viz. the Eastern Goldfields Reform Association and the British Colonial Secretary, Joseph Chamberlain.

Gold had been discovered in and around Kalgoorlie in 1893, and this had resulted in an influx of fortune-seekers throughout the 1890s. Between 1890 and 1900 Western Australia's population increased from 47,000 to 179,000 (Besant 1990: 228, fn. 42). Whereas the long-time residents of Western Australia were essentially isolationist in character, this was not true of the newcomers, most of whom had come from the eastern colonies and who retained strong affinities with those colonies (Musgrave 2003: 97). The reluctance of the long-time residents of Western Australia to be a part of the federation was thus counterbalanced by the newcomers, who did very much want to become a part of the proposed new federation. The newly arrived goldminers formed the Eastern Goldfields Reform League, with the aim of seceding from Western Australia and joining the Australian federation. As Western Australia's prosperity depended to a considerable degree on the income derived from the Goldfields, its secession from Western Australia would have been disastrous to the colony.

It was at this point that the British Colonial Secretary, Joseph Chamberlain, brought his own pressure to bear on the government of Western Australia. On 27 April 1900, he sent a telegram to the acting Governor of Western Australia, darkly alluding to the secessionist movement and counselling the government that in these circumstances it would be advisable for the colony to join the federation (Besant 1990: 228; La Nauze 1972: 260). Under these pressures, the government of Western Australia did reluctantly agree to federate, and a referendum was hastily organised for 31 July 1900 (*Australasian Federation Enabling Act* 1900, 63 Vict. No. 55, Statutes of Western Australia).

The issue then arose as to who should be permitted to vote in the referendum. It was argued that the Goldfields newcomers were not "true" Western Australians, and therefore should not be allowed to determine the political future of Western Australia (Watt 1958: 64; Besant 1990: 228). But, eventually it was decided that any person who had been resident in Western Australia for the previous 12 months should be permitted to vote (Musgrave 2003: 98). As a result, many persons in the region of the Goldfields were enfranchised, and their vote swung the result in favour of joining the federation. "Had the electoral roll not been changed, it is questionable whether an affirmative vote would have been obtained at all or whether that vote would have been sufficient to legitimate the entry of Western Australia into the federation" (Musgrave 2003: 98). The *Commonwealth of Australia Constitution Act* had already been enacted by the Imperial Parliament when the referendum was held in Western Australia, which explains the unusual wording of the preamble and covering clause 3 with regard to Western Australia.

## Western Australia's unhappiness with the federation

As noted previously, Western Australia's reluctance to join the federation was to a large degree economic in nature. Western Australia did not want to give up the income it derived from inter-colonial tariffs, as these tariffs comprised approximately one half of the colony's revenue.

But the tariffs would be abolished under the proposed Constitution, by virtue of section 92. In order to induce Western Australia to join the federation, a special provision was added which mitigated the impact of section 92 on Western Australia. Section 95 provided for a partial five-year exemption to Western Australia from the effects of section 92. By virtue of section 95 Western Australia could be entitled to impose interstate tariffs for a period of five years, with the tariffs imposed being reduced by 20% each successive year. The exemption from the effects of section 92 would therefore terminate after five years (Watt 1958: 64).

The exemption provided by section 95 came to an end in 1906. From this point onward Western Australia experienced the full impact of section 92. It could no longer impose tariffs on its agricultural produce which, together with mining, was the primary mainstay of the Western Australian economy. Consequently, the government of Western Australia was deprived of a great part of its habitual revenue. Moreover, the federal government, which had exclusive control of international tariffs by virtue of section 90, had become increasingly committed to a policy of protectionism, imposing federal tariffs on imported manufactured goods. This meant that Western Australian farmers could no longer purchase manufactured goods, such as farming machinery, from abroad, since the federal tariffs now made the purchase of those goods prohib-itive. Section 92 compounded this situation, because any developing industries in Western Aus-tralia were simply not able to survive in the open Australian market against the more established industries of the eastern states (Musgrave 2003: 99). The response of the Western Australian Legislature was to adopt a resolution in 1906, declaring that federation had "proved detrimental to the best interest" of the state, and calling for a referendum to canvass public support for "the possibility of a withdrawal from such a union" (Western Australia, Legislative Assembly 1906 Debates Volume 29, page 1871). However, nothing came of this resolution.

Many Western Australians were convinced that the economic problems experienced by Western Australia were endemic, because they were entrenched in the provisions of the Con-stitution. Those problems could not actually be resolved unless and until the Constitution itself was amended. In 1924 the federal government appointed a Royal Commission to investigate, *inter alia*, the economic difficulties of Western Australia.

This Commission recommended that changes be made to the Constitution. But a second Royal Commission, appointed in 1927, recommended in 1929 that no alterations be made to the Constitution. Many Western Australians concluded that not only was the Constitution structured in a way which seriously disadvantaged the economic interests of Western Australia, but that this economic harm would continue indefinitely unless that structure was fundamentally changed.

Matters came to a head with the onset of the Great Depression in 1929. The Depression had a devastating impact on Western Australian farmers, who watched as the price of primary products, and in particular wheat, fell precipitously on the world market (Robertson 1974: 416). The Western Australian electorate grew increasingly angry at both the Commonwealth and the state governments, neither of which seemed able to do anything to alleviate their plight.

The unhappy voters dealt first with the state Labor government. In the election of April 1930 the state government was defeated in favour of a coalition of the Country and National parties. Dissatisfaction with the Commonwealth government led to the formation, in May 1930, of the Dominion League of Western Australia. The Dominion League was politically non-aligned, and was therefore able to appeal to voters across the entire political spectrum. It had one purpose only, viz. to effect the secession of Western Australia from the federation. The Dominion League argued that only by so doing could the problems of Western Australia be effectively resolved. The League grew rapidly in popularity amongst a large part of the Western Australian electorate (Besant 1990: 236). At the same time the new Premier, Sir James Mitchell, declared that he was personally in favour of secession. By December 1932, the Western Australian government had enacted the *Secession Referendum Act* 1932, which specified in section 2 that a referendum on secession would be held on the same day as the next general election (23 Geo. 5, Statutes of Western Australia, no 47, 201). Section 6 of the Act set out the question on secession:

> Are you in favour of the State of Western Australia withdrawing from the federal Commonwealth established under the Commonwealth of Australia Constitution Act (Imperial)?

The election and the referendum took place on 8 April 1933. The referendum result was overwhelmingly in favour of secession. Almost two-thirds of the electorate voted for secession: the vote was 138,653 in favour and 70,706 against (*Secession Act* 1934, 25 Geo. 5, Statutes of Western Australia No. 2, The Second Schedule, s 7). Although the Coalition government was defeated in the election, the incoming Labor government declared that it would take "all necessary steps to give effect to the majority decision of the people" (Watt 1958: 55, quoting the *Sunday Times*, 9 April 1933).

## The petition to secede

The new government then proceeded to canvass the alternatives for secession. There were three possible courses of action: a unilateral declaration of independence, recourse to the amending formula of section 128, and a petition to the Imperial Parliament to amend the *Commonwealth of Australia Constitution Act* 1900.

The first two options were quickly ruled out. Western Australia certainly did not want to sever its connection with the United Kingdom, with whom it conducted the bulk of its trade. The goal of the Dominion League, whose very name bespoke loyalty to the Crown, was rather to achieve the status of a separate dominion for Western Australia within the British Empire.

Resort to section 128 was also a non-starter. Although a majority of Western Australians had voted in favour of secession, the formula set out in section 128 required that there be a majority of voters throughout Australia, in a majority of states. This clearly would never be achieved. It was simply unthinkable that a majority of voters throughout Australia, in a majority of states, would vote in favour of the dismemberment of the federation.

The government of Western Australia therefore chose the third option, which was to petition the Imperial Parliament to amend the *Commonwealth of Australia Constitution Act* 1900. As this Act was a British statute, the Imperial Parliament had full power, by virtue of the doctrine of parliamentary sovereignty, to amend the statute as it saw fit. This meant that it could alter the Act to remove Western Australia from the Australian federation and then enact legislation which would recreate Western Australia as a separate, self-governing dominion within the British Empire (Musgrave 2003: 108). Accordingly, the parliament of Western Australia adopted the *Secession Act* 1934 (25 Geo 5, Statutes of Western Australia). This Act authorised the presentation to the Imperial Parliament of a petition to secede. Given that two-thirds of the Western Australian electorate had voted in favour of secession, the government of Western Australia was confident that the Imperial Parliament would grant the petition.

The petition was presented to the Imperial Parliament in November 1934. But to the surprise of the Western Australian delegation, the Imperial Parliament responded by advising the delegation that the petition would not be considered until it first determined whether the petition was properly receivable. To this end, the Imperial Parliament convened a Joint Select Committee of six members, three of whom were drawn from the House of Lords and three from the House of Commons. The most prominent member of the Committee was the Law Lord, Lord Wright (Musgrave 2003: 109).

## The legal issues

In 1901, the Premier of Western Australia, Sir John Forrest, declared that "an Act of the Imperial Parliament could sever Western Australia from the federation in the same way that an Act of the Imperial Parliament had joined it to the federation" (Musgrave 2003: 110). But in 1935, when Western Australia presented its petition to the Imperial Parliament, this statement was no longer accurate. The constitutional relationship between the United Kingdom and the dominions had been continuously evolving since 1901, and by 1926 a constitutional convention had crystallized which now governed the relationship. This convention constrained the Imperial Parliament from enacting legislation relating to the affairs of a dominion only when that dominion had specifically requested the Imperial Parliament to do so. Although an obligatory rule, a constitutional convention was non-legal in nature, and therefore not enforceable by legal action. The obligatory force of a convention depended upon political considerations, rather than legal ones (Wheare 1953: 10, 19; Keith 1933: 99).

The *Balfour Declaration* of 1926 formally recognised that the relationship between the United Kingdom and the dominions was now governed by this convention:

> Their position and mutual relation may be readily defined. They are autonomous communities within the British Empire, equal in status, in no way subordinate one to another in any aspect of their domestic or external affairs, united by a common allegiance to the Crown, and freely associated as members of the British Commonwealth of Nations . . . . Every self-governing member of the Empire is now the master of its destiny. In fact, if not always in form, it is subject to no compulsion whatever.
>
> *(Report of the Imperial Conference 1926, Summary of Proceedings (1926) Cmd. 2768, 12–36, c. VI, I.)*

The provisions of the *Balfour Declaration* were subsequently embodied as law in the 1931 *Statute of Westminster* (22 Geo V, c 4). The primary thrust of the *Statute* was set out in section 4:

> No Act of Parliament of the United Kingdom passed after the commencement of this Act shall extend to a Dominion as part of the law of the Dominion unless it has expressly declared in that Act that that Dominion has requested, and consented to the enactment thereof.

The necessary corollary to this provision was that a dominion parliament could now enact valid legislation which was contrary to legislation enacted by the Imperial Parliament. This was explicitly so stated in section 2 of the *Statute of Westminster*. As a result, the provisions of the *Colonial Laws Validity Act* 1865 (Imp) (28 & 29 Vict. c 63) would no longer apply to any legislation enacted by a dominion after the *Statute* came into force.

The *Statute of Westminster* also addressed issues raised by the division of legislative power in federal dominions. Section 9 was of particular importance to Australia. Section 9(1) declared that the Commonwealth Parliament was prohibited from legislating on any matter which fell solely within the constitutional authority of the states:

> Nothing in this Act shall be deemed to authorise the Parliament of the Commonwealth of Australia to make laws on any matter within the authority of the States of Australia, not being a matter within the authority of the Parliament or Government of the Commonwealth of Australia.

Section 9(2) further elaborated on the content of section 9(1):

> Nothing in this Act shall be deemed to require the concurrence of the Parliament or Government of the Commonwealth of Australia in any law made by the Parliament of the United Kingdom with respect to any matter within the authority of the States of Australia, not being a matter within the authority of the Parliament or Government of the Commonwealth of Australia, in any case where it would have been in accordance with the constitutional practice existing before the commencement of this Act that the Parliament of the United Kingdom should make that law without that concurrence.

In other words, the receivability of the petition was contingent on whether the issue of secession was one which came within the sole authority of the states, or whether it was a matter which fell within the constitutional authority of the Commonwealth.

But even if the petition was receivable under section 9, there was a further problem, which arose by virtue of section 10. Sections 2 and 4 of the *Statute*, as noted earlier, specified that a dominion parliament could enact valid legislation which was contrary to legislation enacted by the Imperial Parliament, and that no legislation enacted by the Imperial Parliament would apply to a dominion unless that dominion had expressly so consented. However, section 10(1) declared that these two provisions would apply only to those dominions which had adopted the *Statute of Westminster* as a part of their own law. When Western Australia presented its petition to the Imperial Parliament in 1934, the *Statute* had not yet been adopted in Australia. It was therefore doubtful that the *Statute* could be utilised in determining the receivability of the petition.

If the *Statute* was not applicable, it would then be necessary to go behind the *Statute*, to the constitutional convention upon which the *Statute* had been based. But the Joint Select Committee would still be faced with the same fundamental question, viz. whether the petition was receivable "in the context of the Australian Federation, where jurisdiction was divided between two levels of government" (Musgrave 2003: 114). But unlike the *Statute of Westminster*, the *Balfour Declaration* had not explained how the constitutional convention it embodied was to apply to federal dominions.

Moreover, although the *Statute of Westminster*, or at the very least the constitutional convention upon which it was based, would provide the constitutional basis for determining whether the petition of Western Australia was receivable, the Imperial Parliament could always choose to act outside that framework, by virtue of the doctrine of parliamentary sovereignty. It was axiomatic that neither the *Statute* nor the constitutional convention could fetter the doctrine of parliamentary sovereignty, but rather were subject to it. Consequently, the *Statute* and the convention could always be undone by the Imperial Parliament, should it decide to do so.

## The decision of the joint select committee

The Joint Select Committee heard submissions from Western Australia and the Commonwealth over a period of four weeks, from 27 March to 17 April 1935. It handed down its decision on 22 May 1935, in a report of 13 paragraphs. The decision of the Committee was entitled the *Report by the Joint Committee of the House of Lords and the House of Commons Appointed to Consider the Petition of the State of Western Australia* (The Report 1934–1935).

The Committee set out its role in paragraph 1. This was simply to determine whether the petition of Western Australia was "proper to be received". The Committee noted in paragraph 6 that only the Imperial Parliament could amend the *Commonwealth of Australia Constitution Act*, as requested by the petition. This was because the *Constitution Act* itself did not provide for any mechanism for secession, and the amendment procedure of section 128 did not extend to the preamble and covering clauses of the Act, which referred, *inter alia*, to Western Australia.

In paragraph 2 of the Report, the Committee affirmed the doctrine of parliamentary sovereignty, declaring that the Imperial Parliament was empowered "to legislate for the whole Empire". However, it then declared that it would make its decision "in accordance with long-established and clearly understood constitutional principles". The Committee thereby signalled that it would adhere to the constitutional principles which had developed between the United Kingdom and the self-governing dominions. Its rationale for doing so was set out explicitly in paragraph 12. Only by adhering to the constitutional principles, the Committee declared, could "the legal competence" of the Imperial Parliament "be reconciled with the fundamental conception" of the dominions "as autonomous communities".

In determining whether the petition was receivable, the Committee had to establish the basis upon which it would do so. As noted previously, section 10 of the *Statute of Westminster* declared that the *Statute* would be applicable only with respect to those dominions whose parliaments had adopted it. As this had not yet occurred in Australia, it was questionable whether the Committee could refer to the *Statute* in resolving the matter. The Committee did not explicitly answer this question. However, the wording of the Report seems to indicate that the Committee did not formally base its decision on the *Statute*, but rather simply on the constitutional convention. In paragraph 7, for example, the Committee declared that the Imperial Parliament would act in accordance with "a well established convention of the constitutional practice governing the relations between the parliament of the United Kingdom and the other parliaments of the Empire". Likewise, in paragraph 12, the Committee referred to the "established constitutional conventions". But although the Committee did not explicitly base its decision on the *Statute*, it did refer to the *Statute*, in paragraph 10, for confirmation of its decision, based on its interpretation of the convention. It also pointed out, in paragraph 2, that the constitutional principles governing the relationship of the Imperial Parliament to the self-governing dominions had been given "formal and statutory approval in the *Statute of Westminster*".

The fundamental question before the Committee was to determine how these constitutional principles applied to the receivability of the petition, given the federal nature of the Australian Commonwealth. On the one hand, the petition of Western Australia had received the support of a very large majority of the Western Australian electorate, but, on the other hand, it was opposed by the Commonwealth government. The receivability of the petition in these circumstances could be resolved only by determining whether secession was a matter which came within state jurisdiction, or whether it was a matter which came within federal jurisdiction.

The Committee began by pointing out, in paragraph 7 of the Report, that the constitutional convention governing the relationship between the Imperial Parliament and the dominion parliaments applied to a request from a dominion "speaking with the voice which represents it as a whole and not merely at the request of a minority. Consequently, it would ordinarily be the federal government of a dominion, speaking for the country as a whole, which would be the appropriate level of government to make a petition to the Imperial Parliament. This did not mean, however, that there could not also be petitions from a state government to the Imperial Parliament, as the Committee pointed out in paragraph 9:

> This division (of powers) is one which, in the opinion of the Committee, cannot be ignored in considering the application of the general constitutional principles governing the intervention in the affairs of any self-governing member of the British Empire.

But a petition from a state government could be properly receivable, according to the Committee, only when the subject matter of the petition fell within state powers. The subject matter in this case, however, did not fall within state powers, as the Committee pointed out in paragraph 11. When the British Parliament enacted the *Commonwealth of Australia Constitution Act* which brought the Australian federation into being, the Imperial Parliament thereby gave "effect to the voice of the people of the continent of Australia, and not to the voice of any State or States" (The Report 1934–1935: para. 11, x). It was only "when invoked by the voice of the people of Australia" that the Imperial Parliament could "properly vary or dissolve that Federal Union" (The Report 1934–1935: para. 11, x). The secession of one state from the federation was therefore necessarily a matter which concerned the people of the entire federation. Consequently, a referendum in one state, no matter how large the vote of that state's electorate, could not be determinative of the matter. Only if the people of the entire federation had expressed a willingness to vary or dissolve the federation could this occur. Any request to do so, as the Committee pointed out in paragraph 7, had to emanate from a dominion "speaking with the voice which represents it as a whole and not merely at the request of a minority".

The Committee concluded in paragraph 13 that secession was not a matter which fell within the state's jurisdiction, and therefore that the petition of Western Australia to the Imperial Parliament was not receivable. In the words of the Committee, Western Australia, as a state, was "not concerned with the subject-matter of the proposed legislation" and therefore the Imperial Parliament did not have jurisdiction to enact the request "except upon the definite request of the Commonwealth of Australia, conveying the clearly expressed wishes of the Australian people as a whole".

## Conclusion

The attempted secession of Western Australia from the Australian federation well exemplifies the problem which invariably arises in a liberal democratic federation when faced with the threat of secession. Should effect be given to the expressed will of a majority of the electorate within the component part, given a clear and unequivocal referendum result in favour of secession, or should effect be given to the will of the electorate of the entire federation, given that secession will necessarily affect the entire federation?

In the case of the petition of Western Australia, the Joint Select Committee did recognise that the petition of the government of Western Australia conveyed "the wishes of the people of Western Australia, as ascertained in a referendum organised by the State authorities" (The Report 1934–1935: para. 3, vii). But although the Committee acknowledged this expression of the democratic will of the electorate of Western Australia, it decided that the will of one component part of the federation could not in itself be decisive of the outcome. The electorate of one state was not entitled to decide whether their state would or would not remain in the federation (Musgrave 2003: 125). Secession, the Committee concluded, was a matter which necessarily affected the entire federation. Therefore, any change to the composition of the federation could only be effected by "the definite request of the Commonwealth of Australia conveying the clearly expressed wish of the Australian people as a whole" (The Report 1934–1935: para. 13, x).

## References

*Australasian Federation Enabling Act* 1900, (63 Vict. No. 55, Statutes of Western Australia).
Balfour Declaration 1926, *Balfour Declaration* (*Report of the Imperial Conference* 1926, *Summary of Proceedings* (1926) Cmd. 2768, 12–36, c. VI, I.).

Besant, C. 1990, "Two Nations, Two Destinies: A Reflection on the Significance of the Western Australian Secessionist Movement to Australia, Canada and the British Empire", *University of Western Australia Law Review*, 20: 209.

*Colonial Laws Validity Act* 1865 (Imp), (28 & 29 Vict. c 63).

*Commonwealth of Australia Constitution Act* 1900 (Imp), (63 & 64 Vict. c 12).

Craven, G. 1986, *Secession: The Ultimate States Right*, Melbourne: Melbourne University Press.

Dicey, A. V. 1927, *The Law of the Constitution*, 8th ed., London: MacMillan.

Keith, A. 1933, *The Constitutional Law of the British Dominions*, London: MacMillan.

La Nauze, J. A. 1972, *The Making of the Australian Constitution*, Melbourne: Melbourne University Press.

Musgrave, T. 2003, "The Western Australian Secessionist Movement", *Macquarie Law Journal*, 3: 95.

Robertson, J. 1974, "1930–1939", in F. Crowley (ed.), *A New History of Australia*, Melbourne: Heinemann: 416.

*Secession Act* 1934, (25 Geo. 5, No. 2, Statutes of Western Australia).

*Secession Referendum Act* 1932, (23 Geo. 5, No. 47, Statutes of Western Australia).

Shaw, A. 1961, *The Story of Australia*, London: Faber.

*Statute of Westminster* 1931 (22 Geo V, c 4).

The Report 1934–1935, *Report by the Joint Committee of the House of Lords and the House of Commons Appointed to Consider the Petition of the State of Western Australia* (United Kingdom Parliamentary Papers of the House of Commons (1934–1935) Volume VI, No. 88).

Watt, E. 1958, "Secession in Western Australia", *University Studies in Western Australian History*, 3: 43.

Western Australia, Legislative Assembly 1906 Debates, Volume 29, 1871.

Wheare, K. 1953, *The Statute of Westminster and Dominion Status*, 5th ed., London: Oxford University Press.

# 39

# THE LAW OF SECESSION IN CANADA

*Alyn James Johnson*

## Introduction

In 1996, the Canadian government sought an advisory opinion from the Supreme Court of Canada on the question of whether the province of Québec could unilaterally secede from the country under either domestic or international law. The unanimous Supreme Court responded two years later with the remarkable *Reference re Secession of Quebec* (*Secession Reference*). On the international law front, the Court affirmed well-established principles: self-determination is an internal matter for sovereign states to manage on their own except in a narrow range of circumstances where a group of people are subject to colonial rule or are subject to ongoing oppression or a systematic frustration of their aspirations (Secession Reference 1998: paras 126–138). These narrow circumstances were inapplicable to the situation of Québec, leading to the conclusion that unilateral secession could not proceed legally under the auspices of international law. On the domestic law front, on the other hand, the Court broke new ground by recognizing an orderly procedural framework, grounded within the unwritten "internal architecture" of the Canadian Constitution, allowing for secession. This framework could be activated by a formal, democratically sourced request to secede by one province, and would impose a legal duty on all provinces and the national government to negotiate in good faith to resolve the situation.

The following discussion of this landmark decision focuses only on the domestic law analysis and is prefaced by a brief consideration of the relevant historical context of the secession movement in Québec. It should be noted at the outset that the *Secession Reference* deals with the legality of a recognized political unit (i.e. a province) separating from the rest of Canada, and does not explore the question of secession involving a sub-regional territory.

## Historical context: the constitutional alienation of Québec

The "Dominion" of Canada was created by the British Parliament through the *British North America Act, 1867* (later renamed the Constitution *Act, 1867*). The new country consisted of a central government and four provinces (that number has since grown to ten), with legislative power carefully divided between a national Parliament and provincial legislatures. While it is possible to discern a centralist slant in the founding document, a strong provincial rights movement developed shortly thereafter, and the Judicial Committee of the Privy Council

DOI: 10.4324/9781003036593-46

ultimately interpreted the *Constitution Act, 1867* as creating two "supreme" and "autonomous" levels of government (Hodge v. The Queen 1883: 132; Liquidators of the Maritime Bank v. Receiver-General 1892: 442; Russell 2004: 34–52).

While struggles between the national and provincial levels of government have remained a constant and divisive feature of the Canadian political landscape to the present day, this federal dynamic became considerably more complex beginning in the 1960s, in a period known as the "Quiet Revolution," when a very strong nationalist movement grew in Québec. Québec is one of the original founding provinces, and is the historical home of the French Canadians, or "Québécois," who have always made up the majority of the province and are Canada's largest ethnic minority. Québec itself is one of Canada's largest provinces, containing approximately one quarter of the total population of the country in the latter part of the twentieth century.

In political terms, Québec nationalism expressed itself in two main ways – a more moderate emphasis on changes to the division of legislative powers between the central government and the provinces under the Constitution to accommodate Québec's distinct society, and a more radical drive for independence. In 1976, a Parti Québécois (PQ) government committed to sovereignty was elected in the province, and PQ governments proceeded to hold popular referendums on the separation of Québec from Canada in 1980 and 1995. While both referendum results were against sovereignty, the margin dramatically decreased in the later referendum. The results were 60% to 40% against in 1980 and 50.6% to 49.4% against in 1995.

The substantial increase in support for Québec nationalism between the two referendums can be sourced in the *Constitution Act, 1982* – a set of major amendments enacted by the British Parliament in 1982 that were the product of several decades of intermittent and at times acrimonious attempts to patriate the Canadian Constitution from Great Britain, institute an amending formula acceptable to all provinces and the central government, and make alterations to the division of legislative powers. By 1982, an entrenched bill of rights – the *Canadian Charter of Rights and Freedoms* (Charter 1982) – was added to the package of constitutional reforms, as well as a recognition and affirmation of certain Indigenous rights.

Glaringly absent from the 1982 constitutional amendments, however, was unanimity. The final package was accepted by only nine out of the ten Canadian provinces, plus the national government. Given the scope of the amendments (the *Charter* (1982) fundamentally altered the relationship between courts and legislatures; the amending formula locked in a broad range of structures for the foreseeable future) anything less than unanimity was arguably illegitimate. The Québec government refused to accept the constitutional settlement due in large part to unsatisfied demands for greater legislative control over certain areas of culture and the economy and an express veto over future amendments affecting the province. An additional very important factor accounting for Québec's refusal to sign on to the constitutional reform package was the very aggressive negotiation tactics of the central government of Prime Minister Pierre Elliott Trudeau, who, while Québécois, vehemently rejected the vision of Québec nationalism stemming from the "Quiet Revolution." Trudeau favoured a vision of a "pan-Canadian nationalism" foregrounding a country of citizens with strong ties not to provincial governments but to a powerful central government (Russell 2004: 79–81, 107–126; Johnson 2004: 249–251).

The effect of the 1982 amendments on Canadian national unity cannot be overstated. Québec, one of Canada's largest provinces, containing Canada's largest ethnic minority, was outside of the constitutional settlement. The province's ethnic distinctiveness was thus inscribed into the very fabric of the Constitution in the most divisive way imaginable. Peter Hogg observes that "the outcome of the constitutional changes of 1982 was a diminution of Québec's powers and a profound sense of grievance in the province" (Hogg 2007: 4.1(c)), and Sujit Choudhry and Jean-François Gaudreault-DesBiens's comment that "there is a hole in the pan-Canadian constitutional patriotism that the *Charter* inspires, and that hole is Québec" (Choudhry & Gaudreault-DesBiens 2007: 169). The lasting influence of Québec's constitutional alienation continues to the present day (Ballingall 2019; England 2021).

Between 1985 and 1992, significant attempts were made by Trudeau's successor, Prime Minister Brian Mulroney, to accommodate Québec and thereby repair the damage to the Constitution. Very protracted, very divisive, and very public constitutional negotiations enveloped the country for many years, leading first to the spectacular last-minute failure of the Meech Lake Accord (1987–1990), a failure that was perceived as a "humiliation" by segments of the Québec population (MacLauchlan 1997: 164), and then to the miserable and largely inevitable defeat of the subsequent Charlottetown Accord (1991–1992). The country emerged from this experience bruised and divided, and nationalist and separatist sentiment in Québec increased dramatically, culminating in the razor-thin margin of just over 1% in the 1995 referendum on secession. The 1995 vote was immediately preceded by draft Québec legislation providing that a successful referendum would lead to a unilateral declaration of independence, and immediately followed by clear indications from the PQ government that another referendum would be likely when conditions were propitious (MacLauchlan 1997: 160).

## The unwritten constitution and the procedural framework for secession

Given the turbulent context outlined in the previous section, there is little doubt that the Supreme Court of Canada was faced with a political and constitutional crisis when it turned to answer the Canadian government's 1996 request for an advisory opinion on the legality of secession. The resulting *Secession Reference* proved to be a remarkable exercise in judicial statecraft. This statecraft can be assessed based on the extent to which the Court remained firmly within its institutional role – that of interpreting the law and the Constitution – yet nevertheless was able to offer a divided nation a constructive way forward that soothed rather than inflamed national tensions. Three areas of judicial statecraft are particularly noteworthy: first, the appointment of an *amicus curiae* to represent Québec; second, the refusal to be limited by the narrow scope of the questions posed by the Canadian government; and third, the use of unwritten constitutional principles to enunciate a procedural framework governing secession. Each of these three areas will be discussed in this chapter under separate headings, followed by a brief consideration of the political aftermath of the decision which revealed an important shortcoming in the Court's analysis.

## *The* amicus curiae

An initial and very significant problem faced by the Court was the Québec government's refusal to participate in the proceedings. Québec took the very public position that the courts had no jurisdiction in determining the future of the province, which could be decided only by an expression of the will of the people through a referendum (MacLauchlan 1997: 159–160, 163–164; Radmilovic 2010: 852–853). This position appeared to have some resonance, with opinion polls suggesting that a significant proportion of the Québec population disapproved of the national government's decision to seek a judicial opinion on the question of secession (MacLauchlan 1997: 163; Radmilovic 2010: 852–853). Furthermore, in the earlier decision of *Re: Objection by Québec to a Resolution to Amend the Constitution*, condemned by many observers as being unsound in law and governed by a nationalist political bias, the Supreme Court notoriously denied Québec a declaration that the 1982 amendments, being made without the province's consent, were unconstitutional (Des Rosiers 2000: 178–180; Russell 2004: 128–129; Choudhry & Gaudreault-DesBiens 2007: 176–178). The refusal of Québec to participate in the secession proceedings thus threatened their entire legitimacy. The Court responded to this situation by appointing a prominent Québec lawyer and supporter of the sovereignty movement as *amicus curiae* to argue the case for secession (Radmilovic 2010: 852–853). This move shrewdly avoided a situation where Québec's alienation would be inscribed in the very raw materials giving rise to the advisory opinion. The anti-secession cause was very fully represented before the Court by the national government and by numerous intervenors including four provinces and territories, four Indigenous groups, a minority rights group, and a group representing women's interests (MacLauchlan 1997: 170–173; Dawson 1999–2000: 14–26). Québec representation was essential, and the *amicus curiae* solved the problem.

## The reference questions

The reference questions posed by the Canadian government were all directed to the legality of unilateral secession, and in oral argument, the Attorney General of Canada strongly urged the Court to confine its opinion to the unilateralism question (Factum 1996: 38–39). This focus on unilateral secession arose because, as noted previously, the Québec government proceeded on the basis that a referendum in favour of secession would lead to a declaration of independence regardless of any subsequent interactions with the rest of Canada. Nevertheless, the Court astutely recognized the political danger of being forced to operate in such a narrow space that the result would seem pre-determined. A negative answer on unilateralism seemed likely, and without more, such an answer would further accentuate Québec's already severe sense of alienation. Indeed, a national institution, with judges appointed by the national government, and with a decision on record widely criticized as being biased in favour of the national government, would have found as a matter of law that the province was imprisoned within the very 1982 framework to which it did not consent. The Court controlled this situation by going beyond the posed question on unilateralism and addressing instead the larger possibility of secession under the Constitution. This larger focus enabled an opinion that offered something to both secessionist and anti-secessionist forces. While one could argue that a court should not expand the scope of an advisory opinion beyond stated questions, such a conservative approach seems inappropriate in the context of a political and constitutional crisis where a full and well-reasoned analysis is essential.

## The foundational unwritten principles of the constitution

The broader question of the legality of secession led the Court to the emphatic conclusion that the "Constitution is not a straitjacket," and that fundamental changes, including secession, are indeed possible:

> The Constitution is the expression of the sovereignty of the people of Canada. It lies within the power of the people of Canada, acting through their various governments duly elected and recognized under the Constitution, to effect whatever constitutional arrangements are desired within Canadian territory, including, should it be so desired, the secession of Quebec from Canada.
>
> *(Secession Reference 1998: paras 85, 150)*

The legal path to secession, however, had to go through rather than around the Constitution – a legal secession would have to proceed pursuant to a formal constitutional amendment (Secession Reference 1998: para. 84).

The critical issue for the Court was determining the appropriate amending formula to handle a change of such magnitude. The *Constitution Act, 1982* specifies that "Amendments to the Constitution of Canada shall be made only in accordance with the authority contained in the Constitution of Canada" (s. 52(3)). Most of the parties arguing anti-secessionist positions, and a majority of legal commentators writing at the time, placed great emphasis on the specific amending formulas set out in Part V of the *Constitution Act, 1982*, with many viewing Part V as a "comprehensive code" governing fundamental changes (MacLauchlan 1997: 173–174; Webber 1997: 288–291, 317; Dawson 1999–2000: 20, 37; Leclair 2002: 398). Yet this "comprehensive code" approach had very significant weaknesses. Most obviously, as the Court itself observed, Part V "is silent as to the ability of a province to secede from Confederation" (Secession Reference 1998: para. 84). Additionally, a close analysis of the various amending formulas in Part V reveals that entirely predictable subjects are covered, for example, changes to the Supreme Court of Canada and the Senate (which had been discussed in the past) and alteration to provincial boundaries and the addition of new provinces (which had actually occurred in the past). These are subjects that Robert Howse and Alissa Malkin convincingly characterize as part of the natural process of "nation-building" and not "nation-breaking" (Howse & Malkin 1997: 192–193). Part V, in other words, can reasonably be read as applying to amendments that occur within the existing federal structure of Canada, but less convincingly read as applying to amendments that involve a fundamental alteration of that structure.

The Court's solution to the problem of determining the appropriate amending formula governing secession was to look deep into the foundations of the Canadian political system. The logic here appears impeccable: the constitutional structure holding the country together would provide the appropriate basis on which to take the country apart. In particular, the Court focused on the dynamic interrelationship of four essential unwritten constitutional principles: democracy, federalism, the rule of law, and the protection of minorities (Secession Reference 1998: para. 49). The *Secession Reference* situates these principles within a cogent theory of unwritten constitutionalism, and arguably provides the most remarkable and extensive expression of such a theory ever enunciated by a common law court:

> Our Constitution has an internal architecture, or what the majority of this court in *OPSEU v. Ontario (Attorney General)* called a "basic constitutional structure" (OPSEU v. Ontario 1987: 57). The individual elements of the Constitution are linked to the others, and must be interpreted by reference to the structure of the Constitution as a whole. As we recently emphasized in the *Provincial Judges Reference*, certain underlying principles infuse our Constitution and breathe life into it. Speaking of the rule of law principle in the *Manitoba Language Rights Reference*, (Manitoba Reference 1985: 750), we held that "the principle is clearly implicit in the very nature of a Constitution." The same may be said of the other three constitutional principles we underscore today.
>
> Although these underlying principles are not explicitly made part of the Constitution by any written provision, other than in some respects by the oblique reference in the preamble to the *Constitution Act, 1867*, it would be impossible to conceive of our constitutional structure without them. The principles dictate major elements of the architecture of the Constitution itself and are as such its lifeblood.
>
> *(Secession Reference 1998: paras 50–51)*

On a practical level, unwritten principles can "assist in the interpretation of the text and the delineation of spheres of jurisdiction, the scope of rights and obligations, and the role of our political institutions," and critically, "may in certain circumstances give rise to substantive legal obligations . . . which constitute substantive limitations upon government action" (Secession Reference 1998: paras 52, 54).

The *Secession Reference* provides a detailed discussion of each of the four relevant unwritten principles (Secession Reference 1998: paras 55–82), and then applies them to determine the appropriate amending formula to govern the issue of secession. The analysis logically begins with the democratic principle. As noted earlier, the Québec government took the public position that secession was a matter for the people of the province to decide, with a referendum providing the appropriate mechanism. The principle of democratic self-determination also figured prominently in the arguments of the *amicus curiae*, and while democracy was conspicuously absent in the arguments advanced by the national government and the various intervenor provinces, the Court itself proved to be very sympathetic to the normative force of a popular referendum, observing that:

> Our political institutions are premised on the democratic principle, and so an expression of the democratic will of the people of a province carries weight, in that it would confer legitimacy on the efforts of the government of Quebec to initiate the Constitution's amendment process in order to secede by constitutional means.
>
> *(Secession Reference 1998: para. 87)*

This passage is critical in recognizing the force of the democratic principle, but also in locating it within a larger legal context. Secession, while clearly possible if grounded in the legitimacy stemming from an expression of democratic will, must proceed through "constitutional means."

Under the Court's interpretation of the "architecture" of the Constitution, the operation of the democratic principle, while providing succour to the secessionist cause, is channelled and contained by the principles of federalism and the rule of law, both emphasized in argument by the Attorney General of Canada and the Attorneys General of the provinces of Saskatchewan and Manitoba. Federalism leads to the existence of "different and equally legitimate majorities in different provinces and territories and at the federal level," enabling "citizens to participate concurrently in different collectivities" (Secession Reference 1998: para. 66). The democratic principle thus does not begin and end in a single referendum. Other expressions of the democratic principle within the context of Canadian federalism over the years have woven a complex tapestry of pre-existing legal obligations that must be held to constrain the will of each participant:

> Constitutional government is necessarily predicated on the idea that the political representatives of the people of a province have the capacity and the power to commit the province to be bound into the future by the constitutional rules being adopted. These rules are "binding" not in the sense of frustrating the will of a majority of a province, but as defining the majority which must be consulted in order to alter the fundamental balances of political power (including the spheres of autonomy guaranteed by the principle of federalism), individual rights, and minority rights in our society.
>
> *(Secession Reference 1998: para. 76)*

The Court's methodology in the *Secession Reference* is consistently to stress that the relevant unwritten principles "function in symbiosis" such that "[n]o single principle can be defined in isolation from the others, nor does any one principle trump or exclude the operation of any other" (Secession Reference 1998: para. 49). This "symbiosis" provides the legal basis for the Court's pre-eminent exercise in statecraft, for the result favoured neither secessionist nor anti-secessionist forces, and instead aligned the parties in a dialogic process. The embeddedness of the democratic principle within the legal context of a federal state provides a clear negative answer to the question of the legality of unilateral secession (Secession Reference 1998: para. 104). But while Québec's sovereignty, including the potency of any expression of democratic sovereign will, is constrained, the Court is equally clear that the other members of the Canadian federation (the provinces and the national government) cannot simply ignore a democratically sourced desire to secede and do not have a simple veto or block on the legitimate aspirations of a province. Instead, a dialogue must ensue:

> The federalism principle, in conjunction with the democratic principle, dictates that the clear repudiation of the existing constitutional order and the clear expression of the desire to pursue secession by the population of a province would give rise to a reciprocal obligation on all parties to Confederation to negotiate constitutional changes to respond to that desire. . . . The corollary of a legitimate attempt by one participant in Confederation to seek an amendment to the Constitution is an obligation on all parties to come to the negotiating table.
>
> *(Secession Reference 1998: para. 88)*

Clearly, the unwritten constitutional obligations arising from the "symbiosis" of the foundational principles flow in more than one direction. Unilateral secession is not legal, but secession itself is a legal possibility that must be respected and acknowledged by all members of the federation where the appropriate democratic credentials are in place.

The constitutional duty to negotiate recognized by the Court, which constrains all of the parties, is informed by the fourth unwritten principle relevant to the issue of secession – that of the protection of minorities. Negotiations would have to "address the interests" of "other participants, as well as the rights of all Canadians both within and outside Quebec" (Secession Reference 1998: para. 92). The reference here to "other participants" must be taken to include the Indigenous groups and the women's and minority advocacy groups that appeared as intervenors in *Secession Reference*. Significant portions of the landmass of Québec would likely be subject to complex territorial and treaty-related claims on the part of Indigenous peoples in the event of any attempt at secession, and those interests would have to be taken into account (Secession Reference 1998: para. 139; Howse 1997: 210; Morse 1999–2000: 116–124). At the time of the 1995 referendum, several Indigenous groups in Québec held their own referendums with results firmly (in the area of 90%) rejecting any kind of separation of the province from the rest of Canada (Morse 1999–2000: 124).

The preceding analysis suggests that the law governing secession in Canada is overwhelmingly procedural in nature. A referendum in favour of secession, followed by a formal request to amend the Constitution, will trigger a duty to negotiate on the part of all of the parties to the federation. This is ultimately a political process and is not susceptible to judicially imposed, substantive limitations other than the governing proposition that the necessary negotiations "must be conducted with an eye to the constitutional principles we have outlined, which must inform the actions of *all* the participants in the negotiation process" (Secession Reference 1998: para. 94, emphasis in original). The referendum itself must be "free of ambiguity," based on a "clear" question, and backed by a "clear" majority (Secession Reference 1998: paras 87, 93), but the Court does not quantify the requisite clarity further, suggesting that these too are matters to be determined politically. The one other requirement that is placed on the duty to negotiate is that it must be conducted in good faith:

> Refusal of a party to conduct negotiations in a manner consistent with constitutional principles and values would seriously put at risk the legitimacy of that party's assertion of its rights, and perhaps the negotiation process as a whole. Those who quite legitimately insist upon the importance of upholding the rule of law cannot at the same time be oblivious to the need to act in conformity with constitutional principles and values, and so do their part to contribute to the maintenance and promotion of an environment in which the rule of law may flourish.
>
> *(Secession Reference 1998: para. 95)*

The Court specifies that the ultimate arbiter of the conduct of the negotiations will be the domestic and international political community, not the courts (Secession Reference 1998: paras 102–103). Somewhat paradoxically then, Canada's highest court establishes a law of secession that appears to be unenforceable in a court of law. The Court provides the legal framework within which the political players are to operate.

It is appropriate to pause at this point and note that some legal scholars have strongly criticized the Court for straying from its appropriate institutional role and making illegitimate use of unwritten principles, constitutional architecture, and a fabricated duty to negotiate rather than relying on the authoritative written amending formulas set out in Part V (Hurlburt 1998–1999: 184–188; Monahan 1999–2000: 75–79; Cameron 2002: 104–113). Three responses to these critiques should be made. First, as previously noted, Part V does not offer any clear path forward – there is neither an express reference to secession nor a serviceable analogue in the textual amending formulas. Second, the Court did not manufacture its account of the "internal architecture" of the Constitution for the purposes of managing the secession crisis. Quite the contrary, numerous high-profile decisions (many cited in the *Secession Reference* itself) over the previous decade had begun the process of mapping out the structure of the Constitution and the "imperatives" that could be drawn from unwritten principles (Johnson 2019; Walters 2008). This body of case law provides a firm jurisprudential basis for the discussion of constitutional structure and the deployment of unwritten principles that leads to the recognition of a duty to negotiate.

The third argument against those commentators arguing that the Court strained its proper role under the Constitution is precisely the proceduralism of the solution to the secession issue. Such proceduralism is a testament to a restrained rather than an illegitimate exercise of judicial power. The Court did not favour either the secessionist or the anti-secessionist position, or unduly interfere with the operation of political players, and rather recognized a dialogic framework that enabled political players to address their differences. This appears to be the very epitome of a respectful exercise of judicial statecraft. Indeed, Nathalie Des Rosiers hails the *Secession Reference* as offering a "brilliant process-oriented response":

> The decision of the Court seeks to foster a public debate on the issue of the treatment of minorities and on the duty of participants in a democracy to acknowledge the desire for change of the other partner. I view this not as giving the solution but at helping the participants to come to grips with the frailties of their positions. It educates the public on the issues of principle involved and it educates the parties of the weaknesses of their positions, but it gives them a chance to move beyond such difficulties. In fact, it enhances the discussion process among the players.
>
> *(Des Rosiers 2000: 182)*

The Court arguably provided a very potent, well-considered, and timely reminder to a country in danger of coming apart that dialogue and negotiation are the very essence of a federal democratic state. In this sense, the duty to negotiate, far from being an illegitimate judicial fabrication "in which the law played little or no part" (Cameron 2002: 104), appears to be exactly what the *Secession Reference* claims it is: a "substantive legal obligation" drawn directly from the "internal architecture" of the Constitution.

## Political aftermath and the problem of quantifying a "clear" referendum

With the exception of an important skirmish between the national government and the Québec government in 2000, the intensity of the secessionist threat appeared to decline after the Supreme Court delivered its opinion. Québec nationalism remains a very potent political force in the country and has a very powerful influence on national and provincial politics, but the movement to actually break up the country has never regained the momentum it had on the eve of the *Secession Reference*. There are doubtless many factors involved in this decline of secessionist sentiment, including a pressing national preoccupation with economic stability and the retirement of the influential and charismatic Québec leader, Lucien Bouchard. Nevertheless, the Court's opinion almost certainly played some role in lowering the temperature from its height in 1995–1996. Both the Canadian government and the Québec government in fact appeared to be relatively satisfied with the opinion (Russell 2004: 245). Each side, in other words, could find a degree of victory and public vindication in a ruling that rejected unilateral secession but offered an ordered process for achieving a legal secession. Peter Hogg, a leading constitutional scholar, observes that "Without this ruling, it is by no means obvious that the federal government and the other provinces would be prepared to negotiate the break-up of their country" (Hogg 2007: 5.7(a)). With the ruling, and with a complex round of negotiations set as a mandatory part of any future secession process, both sides perhaps inevitably took a step back from the precipice.

The single skirmish noted at the beginning of this section involved two pieces of legislation, the first passed by the national Parliament, and the second by the Québec legislature. The *Clarity Act*, enacted by Parliament in 2000, provides that the Canadian government cannot enter into negotiations on a formal request by a province to secede unless the House of Commons first determines that both the content of the underlying referendum question and the margin of victory are sufficiently "clear." On the first point, the legislation specifies that a "clear" question must contain a "direct expression" of a will to secede and not just a mandate to negotiate, and additionally, the question cannot obscure or confuse a "direct expression" of a will to secede through reference to other possible economic or political arrangements with Canada (Clarity Act 2000: s. 1(4)). On the issue of the margin of victory necessary for a "clear" result, the legislation specifies that the size of the majority and the percentage of eligible voters participating "shall" be taken into account (Clarity Act 2000: s. 2(2)).

While the *Clarity Act* can be said to provide a political mechanism to address substantive issues that the Supreme Court did not resolve (beyond stating that the referendum question and the margin of victory must be "clear" and "free of ambiguity"), the legislation appears to inject a significant degree of unilateralism into the secession process that arguably frustrates the dialogic thrust of the *Secession Reference*. Unilateralism is contrary to the Court's understanding of the obligations that flow from the structure of the Constitution, pursuant to which no party can simply secede, and no party has a veto over the ability of a province to secede. By giving the House of Commons the power to make a political call on whether a referendum is legitimate, the *Clarity Act* indirectly provides one party with a veto. One could counter that the House of Commons is a national political institution and thus the perfect forum to debate the legitimacy of a referendum question and a referendum result. However, most of the members of the House of Commons representing Québec voted against the legislation, meaning that the procedure put in place by the *Clarity Act* may simply reproduce regional alienation and potentially short-circuit the entire process set out in the *Secession Reference*.

Because the Supreme Court found that the Constitution requires that a dialogic process must precede secession, and also found that a formal request for an amendment grounded in an expression of democratic will (i.e. a referendum) must precede the dialogic process, it follows that the terms governing the adequacy of the referendum should be specified by law – by the courts in their role as neutral arbiters of the Constitution – rather than by political players. Thus, the *Secession Reference* arguably needed to go beyond the imprecise language of "clear" and "free of ambiguity" and provide substantive guidance sufficient to enable a referendum to unfold without becoming mired in disagreement. It is worth noting that neither of the 1980 and 1995 Québec referendum questions would meet the definitions set out in the *Clarity Act* (Hogg 2007: 5.7(a)). If these questions were deficient, the Court should have said so. The Court was also aware of the close result of the 1995 referendum and again should have provided at least some guidance in qualifying an adequate majority.

The Québec government, for its part, read the *Clarity Act* as an aggressive statement, and immediately responded with the even more aggressive *Act respecting the exercise of the fundamental rights and prerogatives of the Québec people and the Québec State* (Bill 99 2000) This legislation baldly states that a referendum would be valid under Québec law with a vote of 51% (Bill 99 2000: s. 4), thereby directly challenging the national government. The Québec legislation went even further and appeared to directly challenge the *Secession Reference* on the issue of unilateral secession by stating that "The right of the Québec people to self-determination is founded in fact and in law," and that "The Québec people has the inalienable right to freely decide the political regime and legal status of Québec" (Bill 99 2000: ss. 1–2). When the *Clarity Act* is read in the context of the responding Québec legislation, with the latter upping the ante considerably and threatening a new round of rising tensions, serious doubts about the practical wisdom of the former enactment arise. The *Secession Reference* cooled the political climate somewhat, and the *Clarity Act* unnecessarily raised temperatures again. Both statutes remain in force to the present day, but the brief skirmish of 2000 did not gain further momentum.

While the *Secession Reference* was occasioned by the threat of Québec separatism, there is nothing in the decision itself to limit its application to that province only. Should other provinces in Canada seek to separate, the appropriate constitutional processes would be those set out by the Supreme Court, and the response of the national government to an attempt to secede would also likely be informed by the *Clarity Act* (unless that enactment is repealed). This observation regarding the broader application of the *Secession Reference* is not entirely of abstract or theoretical interest, for in recent years separatist movements have gained support in the western Canadian province of Alberta, and also to a lesser extent in the neighbouring western province of Saskatchewan (Flanagan, Mintz & Morton 2020; Wagner 2021). These movements, which have waxed and waned several times over the last two decades, have been fuelled by a combination of rich reserves of natural resources, a sense of a lack of political power over these resources, and a general sense of alienation due to a perceived centralist bias in the national government. The existence of a detailed precedent on secession from the country's highest Court will likely serve as a check on these movements by providing some certainty about the difficult constitutional processes ahead.

# Conclusion

Canadian law recognizes a procedure governing secession grounded in the "internal architecture" of the Constitution. The Supreme Court of Canada maps out this procedure in the *Secession Reference*, stressing the dynamic interaction of four foundational unwritten principles: democracy, federalism, the rule of law, and the protection of minorities. A legitimate secession is initiated through an exercise of the democratic principle within a given province but must be perfected through a process that respects the operation of the other principles. The province seeking to secede must make a formal request for an amendment to the Constitution, and then must engage in negotiations with the other parties to the federation. The duty to negotiate is ultimately binding on these other parties as well and must be pursued in good faith by each participant. An important shortcoming of the opinion, which has come to light due to the subsequent *Clarity Act*, is the failure of the Court to adequately quantify the components of a legitimate referendum (question and necessary majority) that could support a request for secession. While the Court's overall approach is procedural, it would appear that in this particular area substantive guidance is needed in order to avoid having individual parties short-circuit the process before it can even begin.

A final observation that should be made is that although the focus of the present chapter is on the law of secession in Canada, the *Secession Reference* could well have application to other democratic jurisdictions structured by a federal constitution. Importing Canadian law to another country would likely depend on two important considerations: first, whether the receiving legal system has a written Constitution addressing secession; and second, whether the receiving legal system is open to unwritten as well as written constitutional norms. The Supreme Court of Canada's opinion flows from a Constitution that does not expressly address secession, and from a Constitution that has an enforceable unwritten "internal architecture."

# References

Ballingall, A. 2019, "How Secularism Became Quebec's Religion: The Distinct Path to Bill 21", *Toronto Star*, 5 April 2019.

Bill 99 2000, *Act Respecting the Exercise of the Fundamental Rights and Prerogatives of the Québec People and the Québec State*, R.S.Q. c E-20.2.

Cameron, J. 2002, "The Written Word and the Constitution's 'Vital Unstated Assumptions'", in P. Thibault, B. Pelletier & L. Perret (eds.), *Essays in Honour of Gérald-A Beaudoin*, Cowansville: Éditions Yvon Blais, 91

Charter 1982, *Canadian Charter of Rights and Freedoms, Constitution Act, 1982*, being Schedule B to the *Canada Act 1982* (U.K.), 1982, c 11, Part I.

Choudhry, S. & Gaudreault-DesBiens, J.-F. 2007, "Frank Iacobucci as Constitution Maker: From the Québec Veto Reference to the Meech Lake Accord and the Québec Secession Reference", *University of Toronto Law Journal*, 57: 165.

Clarity Act 2000, *An Act to Give Effect to the Requirement for Clarity as Set Out in the Opinion of the Supreme Court of Canada in the Quebec Secession Reference*, S.C. 2000, c. 26.

Constitution Act 1867, *Constitution Act, 1867*, 30–31 Vict, c 3 (U.K.).

Constitution Act 1982, *Constitution Act, 1982*, Being Schedule B to the *Canada Act 1982* (U.K.), 1982, c 11.

Dawson, M. 1999–2000, "Reflections on the Opinion of the Supreme Court of Canada in the Québec Secession Reference", *National Journal of Constitutional Law*, 11: 5.

Des Rosiers, N. 2000, "From Québec Veto to Québec Secession: The Evolution of the Supreme Court of Canada on Québec-Canada Disputes", *Canadian Journal of Law and Jurisprudence*, 13: 171.

England, E. 2021, "The Constitutional Amendments in Quebec's Bill 96: Whose Consent is Needed?", 3 August 2021, <https://constitutionalstudies.ca/2021/08/11094/#:~:text=On%20May%2013th%2C%202021%2C%20the%20Quebec%20government%20introduced,language%20of%20Qu%C3%A9bec%E2%80%9D%20in%20the%20Quebec%20National%20Assembly>

Factum 1996, "Factum of the Attorney General of Canada," (1997) IN THE MATTER OF Section 53 of the Supreme Court Act, R.S.C. 1985, Chap. S-26; AND IN THE MATTER OF a Reference by the Governor in Council concerning certain questions relating to the secession of Québec from Canada, as set out in Order in Council P.C. 1996–1947, dated the 30th day of September.

Flanagan, T., Mintz, J. M. & FL Morton (eds) 2020, *Moment of Truth: How to Think about Alberta's Future*, Toronto: Sutherland House.

Hodge v. The Queen 1883, Judicial Committee of the Privy Council, *Hodge v. The Queen* (1883) 9 A. C. 117.

Hogg, P. 2007, *Constitutional Law of Canada*, 5th ed., Scarborough: Carswell.

Howse, R. & Malkin, A. 1997, "Canadians Are a Sovereign People: How the Supreme Court Should Approach the Reference on Québec Secession", *Canadian Bar Review*, 76: 186.

Hurlburt, W. H. 1998–1999, "Fairy Tales and Living Trees: Observations on Some Recent Constitutional Decisions of the Supreme Court of Canada", *Manitoba Law Journal*, 26: 181.

Johnson, A. J. 2019, "The Judges Reference and the Secession Reference at 20: Reassessing the Supreme Court of Canada's Unfinished Unwritten Constitutional Principles Project", *Alberta Law Review*, 56: 1077.

Johnson, P.-M. 2004, "The Place of Québec in North America", *Canada-United States Law Journal*, 30: 245.

Leclair, J. 2002, "Canada's Unfathomable Unwritten Constitutional Principles", *Queen's Law Journal*, 27: 389.

Liquidators of the Maritime Bank v. Receiver-General 1892, Judicial Committee of the Privy Council, *Liquidators of the Maritime Bank of Canada v. Receiver-General of New Brunswick* [1892] A.C. 437.

MacLauchlan, H. W. 1997, "Accounting for Democracy and the Rule of Law in the Québec Secession Reference", *Canadian Bar Review*, 76: 155.

Manitoba Reference 1985, Supreme Court of Canada, *Reference re Manitoba Language Rights* [1985] 1 S.C.R. 721.

Monahan, P. 1999–2000, "The Public Policy Role of the Supreme Court of Canada in the Secession Reference", *National Journal of Constitutional Law*, 11: 65.

Morse, B. 1999–2000, "How Would Quebec's Secession Affect Aboriginal Peoples and Aboriginal Rights?", *National Journal of Constitutional Law*, 11: 107.

OPSEU v. Ontario 1987, Supreme Court of Canada, *OPSEU v. Ontario (Attorney General)* [1987] 2 S.C.R. 2.

Radmilovic, V. 2010, "Strategic Legitimacy Cultivation at the Supreme Court of Canada: Quebec Secession Reference and Beyond", *Canadian Journal of Political Science*, 43: 843.

Russell, P. H. 2004, *Constitutional Odyssey: Can Canadians Become a Sovereign People?*, 3rd ed., Toronto: University of Toronto Press.

Secession Reference 1998, Supreme Court of Canada, *Reference re Secession of Quebec* [1998] 2 S.C.R. 217.

Wagner, M. 2021, *No Other Option: Self-Determination for Alberta*, London: Domino Effect Publishing.

Walters, M. D. 2008, "Written Constitutions and Unwritten Constitutionalism", in G. Huscroft (ed.), *Expounding the Constitution: Essays in Constitutional Theory*, New York: Cambridge University Press: 245.

Webber, J. 1997, "The Legality of a Unilateral Declaration of Independence under Canadian Law", *McGill Law Journal*, 42: 281.

# 40

# CONSTITUTIONAL LAW AND SECESSION IN CHINA

## A historical outline

*Yan Xiang and Yawen Zhang*

### Introduction

It is clear from the texts of the current Constitution of the People's Republic of China (1982), the Anti-Secession Law of the People's Republic of China (2005), and the Law of the People's Republic of China on Safeguarding National Security Law in the Hong Kong Special Administrative Region (2020), that current constitutional arrangements in China demonstrably oppose secession. However, these arrangements have deeply historical origins. This chapter traces the historical origins of the antagonism towards secession in China's long philosophical and legislative tradition. Analysis of the historical practices and perspectives from which the Chinese anti-secession position has been derived and established reveals that the dominant historical elements found to be underlying this position are the ideology of Great Unity (*dà yī tǒng*), and a millennia-long commitment to a unitary system of authority and power in the interests of peace and stability. The chapter reviews the constitutional thought and practice relating to anti-secessionism in modern China in light of these elements so as to provide a greater understanding of the more recent historical development of the anti-secession position in modern Chinese constitutional law, including the current constitutional system of the People's Republic of China. Far from anti-secessionism being a recent addition to the modern Chinese constitutional system, the current system simply exemplifies China's deeply historical antipathy to any territorial division or secession.

### The historical origins of anti-secession thought

Where does the Chinese anti-secession position come from, and why is contemporary China so adamantly opposed to secession in its constitutional arrangements? This chapter attempts to answer these questions.

Prior to the attempt to imitate Western constitutionalism in the late Qing dynasty (1840s–1920s), no constitution, such as the term means now, had ever been promulgated in the historical evolution of China (Chen 2018). There is no instance of constitutionalism in ancient China, as is found in Europe and North America. However, if a constitution can be defined as a statement of the basic organizational forms of the state or other important social and political systems, rather than as a legal instrument for safeguarding fundamental individual rights, then

DOI: 10.4324/9781003036593-47

China can be seen as having a deeply rooted constitutional tradition. Furthermore, this tradition is the driving force behind the development and implementation of modern China's various anti-secession constitutions because of two key aspects of this tradition, both dating back to ancient China: the ideology of Great Unity, and the commitment to a unitary governing system.

## The ideology of Great Unity

Most scholars in China and abroad recognize the importance of the Great Unity paradigm in Chinese political culture (Pines 2000). The influence of this idea is extremely far-reaching: it has permeated the basic conceptions of the Chinese state throughout its history (He 2011). The idea was mainly formed during the Spring and Autumn Period and the Warring States Period of the Dong Zhou dynasty (770–221 BC), two of the most chaotic periods in Chinese history. At the same time, these periods were also eras in which many schools of thought developed and competed. There were fierce conflicts over many issues between these different schools, but all agreed on the need to safeguard China's unity (Chen 2012). Thinkers of distinctly different ideological inclinations unanimously accepted political unification under a single monarch of the entire known civilized world – "All-under-Heaven" (*tianxia*) – as the only feasible means to put an end to perennial war (Pines 2012).

Confucius (551–479 BC) was probably the first to outline the advantages of ruling according to the idea of Great Unity (Pines 2000). He was emphatic that state order needed to come from a core of unitary power, believing that:

> When the Way prevails in the world, rites, music, and punitive expeditions proceed
> from the Son of Heaven. When the Way no longer prevails in the world, rites, music,
> and punitive expeditions proceed from the feudal lords.
>
> *(Confucius 2007: 115)*

Confucius was not the only thinker who sought a remedy for the political and social disintegration of perennial wars. Mozi (476–390 BC), a proponent of the ideal of "universal love" (*jiān'ài*), also held that there was only one remedy for universal disorder: the establishment of a universal ruler. In "Elevating Uniformity" he stated that, without this, the "[g]ood ways were concealed and nobody taught them to others. The disorder in All under Heaven reached the level of birds and beasts" (Mozi 2007: 56).

After Confucius and Mozi, new generations of thinkers further developed the idea of Great Unity. Mencius (Mengzi) (385–303 BC), the most prominent of Confucius's disciples, used the expression "united under one's way" for Great Unity (Mengzi 2016). This referred specifically to state unification. Laozi (c. 600s–400s BC), the founder of Daoism, also referred to a sense of oneness, saying:

> There is a thing formed in chaos existing before Heaven and Earth. Silent and solitary,
> it stands alone, unchanging. It goes around with peril. It may be the Mother of the
> world. Not knowing its name, I can only style it the "Dao".
>
> *(Laozi 2012: 108)*

This oneness referred to the epistemological unity of the universe, to the single progenitor of "myriad things", and, more importantly, to the principle of the construction of the single unitary state.

The *Lüshi Chunqiu*, a classic encyclopedia of state governance compiled in the mid-third century BC and known in English as *Master Lü's Spring and Autumn Annals*, echoed Laozi's oneness thinking, explaining the need for unity of rule as follows: "The state needs the ruler, thereby it is unified. All under Heaven upholds oneness, thereby unifying the realm. Oneness means proper government; doubleness means chaos" (Lü 2016: 173). State unification and ensuring ruling order all under heaven was, therefore, the ultimate goal of the "Son of Heaven". When this title was taken up by the Chinese emperors (Pines 2000), it became their goal as well.

These ideas about Great Unity from Legalism, Taoism, Confucianism and Mohism, provided abundant resources for the formation of the Chinese empire's political understanding of Great Unity (Jiang 2016), and the great unified empire established by the Qin (221–207 BC) and Han dynasties (202 BC–220 AD) made the idea of Great Unity from the pre-Qin period a reality (Pines 2012). From the Qin and Han dynasties on, the concept of a united China became the fundamental ideological path for Chinese rule for successive dynasties (Wang 2019). Even though there were periods of division in China during the Wei, Jin, Southern, and Northern dynasties between 220 AD and 589 AD, and the Five Dynasties and ten states between 907 AD and 979 AD, all the contending regime leaders took the reunification of China as their overarching ambition (Pan, Yang & Wu 2014).

The recurring cycle from disintegration to reunification in Chinese history has thus derived its driving force from a unitary ideology (Xu 2015). Because of the influence of this ideology, secessionist and separatist attempts have faced systematic resistance throughout the centuries. The unitary ideology delegitimized any separatist tendency or theory, and provided a ready source for political mobilization against separatism and secession. Since only he who could unify the realm could become a "True Monarch" or "True Son of Heaven", submission of the people to a ruling dynasty depended on whether it could achieve territorial unification. The inability to complete an effective unification of China was considered an unforgivable failure of those in power, making them unable to command the general obedience of the people (Pines 2012). Unification thus was not only an ideological concept; it also constituted the most important content of ancient Chinese constitutional arrangements because unification was the major sign of the legitimacy of a political regime. Within this unitary worldview, only a unified state and a unified authority could provide legitimacy to a regime.

Unification, however, did not mean mono-ethnicity. Both Chinese and "barbarians" (non-Chinese) are discussed in Great Unity thought. In the process of pursuing China's Great Unity, interaction and exchanges among all ethnic groups were considered inevitable and likely to become more frequent. The idea of Great Unity provided a conceptual canopy under which many different peoples could be brought together in an integrated way (Kim 2018). As Emperor Taizong of the Tang dynasty (c. 600–700 AD) declared: "Since antiquity has honored the Chinese and looked down on barbarians; I alone love them as one. Therefore, their tribes follow me like father or mother" (Lewis 1990: 150). Ethnic minorities formed the elites who were in charge of government power during the dynasties of the Wei-Jin period (386–534 AD), the Yuan dynasty (1271–1368), and the Qing dynasty (1636–1921), further supporting this idea of national unity as integration or incorporation. The Mongolian Kublai Khan (1216–1294), the founding emperor of the Yuan dynasty, even put forward the idea of One Family in the *tianxia* system to support his claim to the throne (Yan 2018) and did not seek to erase the ethnic distinctions under Mongol rule (Kim 2018).

## The desire for a unitary system

After Emperor Qin Shi Huang (259–210 BC) reunified China and established an unprecedented empire in 221 BC, the unitary state system became the overwhelming norm for subsequent dynasties (Gu 1985). According to Fei's statistics, in the 4,000 years from the Xia dynasty (2070–1600 BC) to the revolution of 1911, China's periods of division added up to around 650 years, accounting for only about 15% of the 4,000 years. If the calculations are taken from the unification under Qin Shi Huang in 221 BC to 1911 instead, the periods of division amount to only around 100 years, accounting for less than 5% of that entire period (Fei 2003). Unification has been a persistent aim and characteristic throughout China's history.

## The impact of the environment on the formation of the unitary system

China's desire for and development of a unitary system was not only deeply influenced by the idea of Great Unity. It was also closely related to the special ecological environment and geographical location of that part of east Asia in which the Chinese people lived (Xu 2015). As an old saying goes in China, a state must rely on its mountains and rivers. In ancient China, thanks to the flat terrain and fertile soil of China's central plains, the traditional rural economy of small self-sufficient villages, or a "smallholder economy", arose (Ni 2003). However, this most typical ancient Chinese mode of agricultural living was highly susceptible to natural disasters. This meant that people needed to learn to "tame" the Yellow River and other rivers that irrigated the land and fed the population as well as bringing natural disasters and destroying their homes and villages (Su 2018). In addition to dealing with floods and other disasters, farmers living in the central plains also needed to deal with the invasion of northern nomads. Since the Shang and Zhou dynasties (1600–256 BC), the Huaxia people of the central plains had experienced military conflict with these northern nomads (Zhao 2002). To manage both the flooding issue of the plains' rivers and navigate the clashes between the central plains' civilization and the northern pastoral civilization, the unified deployment capabilities of a central government were needed. In other words, if the dynasties of the central plains wanted to resist nomad invasion, they required a unitary political and social core as the driving power of society. A cohesive unitary state system therefore became the optimal solution for solving both natural disasters and the invasion problem (Su 2018). However, diverging from the strategy of the Qin dynasty, which built the Great Wall to keep out the Huns, the Han dynasty sought peace with the Huns by marriage and integration. China's unitary state system can therefore also be seen as based on the physical nature and strategic needs of China's traditional agricultural economic structure (He 2018).

## The anti-secession approach in the unitary system

Within the Chinese unitary system, control over all social communities had to be realized within the unitary power structure (Chen 2018). In such a structure, secession could not be tolerated, since it was generally believed that if secession was allowed, the ruler who had failed to attain or maintain unity would not have been a "true Son of Heaven" and therefore not a legitimate ruler, and the unitary state order would crumble (Pines 2012). However, while the unitary state system necessarily opposed secession, it didn't require all the regions of the state to have a uniform government structure. Multi-level differences were allowed within the system.

The commandery system that had been implemented in the central plains region during the Qin dynasty played the crucial function of integrating the different localities of the country into an overarching entity (Su 2018). Under the commandery system, local officials were directly appointed and removed by the emperor, thus establishing a highly centralized power base. However, the *Jimi* system, the ruling policy for border minority regions implemented from the Qin and Han dynasties, meant that the central plains rulers effectively appointed the leaders of ethnic minorities as the important local officials, allowing them to rule their areas according to their traditional customs. Compared with the commandery system, the *Jimi* system meant only formal submission of the border ethnic minorities: as outer areas, they therefore had only a loose connection with the central government (Zhao 2018). Since such vassal territories were generally geographically far from the central authority, they were not ruled directly and required only the vassal territory's formal recognition of unification (Kim 2018).

The coexistence of regions with different levels of governance that was allowed in this model of the unitary state fashioned a unified political order based on difference (Tanigawa 1971). The foundation of China's constitutional tradition has thus been a form of unification in which regional differences were accepted as part of integration, but could never be used as a justification for secession (Pines 2012).

## Anti-secession constitutional thought and practice in modern China

Although there was a word for "constitution" in ancient China – *xiàn fǎ* – its conception was essentially different from the conception of modern constitutions as the products of Western revolutions. The term "constitution" in ancient China was mainly applicable to three broad situations: first, general laws or decrees; second, the laws made by the monarch; third, the implementation and promulgation of the law (Chen 2018). The modern understanding of a constitution as the foundational law of a state was only introduced into China during the late Qing dynasty (1840–1912) in an attempt to imitate constitutionalism in Europe. In attempting to match European constitutional culture with China's semi-colonial and semi-feudal society, Chinese intellectuals created a unique body of modern constitutional thought and practice for China (Zhang 2004). Notably, since China's modern constitution was born in the context of invasion by foreign powers, frequent wars, and compensation for territorial cession, China's constitution(s) were committed to the pursuit of safeguarding national sovereignty, limiting territorial cession, and saving the country from foreign subjugation. Because of the occasional confrontation with Western powers and their attempts to take over Chinese territory, the need to defend national sovereignty and territorial integrity runs through the whole course of the development of modern Chinese constitutional law. As a result, almost all modern Chinese constitutional thought and practice rejects any form of secession.

Anti-secession constitutional thought first explicitly emerged in modern China in the nineteenth century. In 1840, China lost the first Opium War to Great Britain, to whom China then ceded Hong Kong. Afterwards, China was defeated in a series of battles with Western powers, with whom they were forced to sign multiple unequal treaties. This series of defeats and treaties seriously violated China's commitment to national sovereignty and territorial integrity, and hurt Chinese intellectuals' sense of national self-respect (Zhang 2012). In fact, both the constitutional reformers who supported China's imperial system and the revolutionaries who advocated the establishment of a democratic republic aimed to safeguard state unification, and opposed secession.

Among the constitutional reformers, Emperor Guangxu, political thinker and reformer Kang Youwei, and Kang's prominent disciple Liang Qichao endeavored to maintain state unity and territorial integrity through the establishment of a reformed constitutional system. Similarly, Sun Yat-Sen, founder of the Kuomintang (KMT), and leader of the 1911 revolution that ended China's last imperial dynasty, also maintained the firm stance of state unity and territory integrity.

Sun advanced a systematic, comprehensive political doctrine that included the following three anti-secession aspects. First, unification was to be recognized as the dominant direction of China's historical development, and the common consciousness of the Chinese people. As Sun wrote:

> China's territory has been unified for thousands of years. Although they had separated, it would not be long before they recombine into a unified state. In the recent five hundred years, the land of the eighteen provinces is almost as solid as the Chalice of Eternal Stability, and there is no danger of division.
>
> *(Sun 1981: 223)*

In 1922, in the *Sun-Joffe Manifesto*, Sun stated that "China is a unified state, the idea has been firmly imprinted in our historical consciousness, which enables us to be preserved as a unified state, despite many destructive forces" (Sun 1985: 528).

Second, the constitutional state of China must be a unified one; if it was not unified, the state would be in chaos. Sun believed that unification (or reunification) was the foundation of a state's prosperity:

> All provinces in China have always been unified in history. They are not separated or cannot be unified. Moreover, when they were unified, they were governed, while whenever they were divided, they were chaotic. The reason why the United States is prosperous and strong is the reunification, not the division of the states. For an originally unified state, the provinces as its component should not be separated. China's current temporary inability to reunify is caused by the secessionist regime of the military.
>
> *(Sun 1986: 304)*

In his 1923 Declaration of Peaceful Reunification, Sun said:

> After the reunification is achieved, all subsequent developments and revolutions are possible. Finance, industry, and education could all flourish. The national will would be free, and not be distorted by force.
>
> *(Sun 1985: 51)*

Third, unification would be conducive not only to the happiness and tranquility of the Chinese people, but also to peace and development in Asia. Arguing from a historical perspective, Sun claimed secession brought great suffering to the people:

> There have been more than dozens of dynasties in the history of China. Whenever the dynasty changed, there were temporary secessions, when the people were destitute living on the edge of starvation.
>
> *(Sun 1986: 373)*

Sun summed up the Chinese people's hopes for reunification in remarkably simple language: "Unification is the hope of all Chinese people. If China is unified, the people of the whole state will enjoy the blessings; if not, the people will suffer" (Sun 1986: 373). At the same time, while Sun recognized that a reunified China would be a vast state, he believed that a unified and stable China would have a positive impact on the peace and development of the world, especially in and around Asia: "If the Chinese people do not have the ability to reunify, East Asia will be in turmoil, and the world cannot be peaceful" (Sun 1986: 364).

Chen Duxiu, a founder of the Communist Party of China (CPC) and a contemporary of Sun, also advocated state unification against secession. Chen believed that state unification and opposition to secession were fundamental to the survival of China as a state and as a nation. In the publication *Guide Weekly*, he wrote that most Chinese people wanted reunification because it brought peace:

> Only when the military power and political power are unified, a central government that can unify the state could be formed, and then domestic peace can be achieved, so everyone must be unified.
>
> *(Chen 1922)*

According to Chen, the mass of the Chinese people urgently wanted the secessions caused by warlords to stop. Reunification was seen as the path to peace in their war-torn country.

## Anti-secession in early modern Chinese constitutional practice (1911–1949)

The importance of safeguarding the unity of the Chinese state and maintaining its territorial integrity continued to be emphasized in the constitution-making of the post-imperial, republican period, echoing this historical theme of anti-secessionism. This can be seen in the steps taken towards developing a modern Chinese constitutional law and practice during the republican period.

### *The first constitutional acts: the period of the provisional government of the Republic of China (1911–1912)*

The 1911 revolution launched by Sun Yat-Sen and the KMT successfully ended the imperial regime of more than two millennia, opening a completely new republican epoch in China. In the aftermath of the revolution, the Provisional Constitution of the Republic of China was promulgated by the Republic's Provisional Senate. To ensure the fruits of the revolutionary reunification of China, Article III of Chapter I of the provisional constitution stipulated that the territory of the Republic of China included 22 provinces, inner and outer Mongolia, Tibet, and Qinghai (Chinghai) (Provisional Senate of the ROC 1912).

This was the first time in Chinese history that China's territorial boundaries had been set down in the form of a modern foundational constitution. The purpose was not just to formally found the modern Chinese unitary state and promote the Chinese people's sense of belonging to that state, but to publicize China's territorial scope to the world, and its intention to maintain and defend its national sovereignty and territorial integrity, and oppose secession.

### *The Beiyang government (1912–1928)*

On 13 February 1912, Sun Yat-Sen stepped down as the provisional president to be replaced by former imperial military officer Yuan Shikai, who established the Beiyang (Beijing) government. On 31 October 1913, the Constitution Drafting Committee of the National Assembly passed the Draft Constitution of the Republic of China. The first article of the draft stipulated that "the Republic of China will always be a unified democratic country" (Constitutional Drafting Committee 1913: 2). Article II also specified that "the territory of the Republic of China, based on its inherent territory . . . cannot be changed without a law" (Constitutional Drafting Committee 1913: 2). Unlike the Provisional Constitution, the Draft Constitution also emphasized that the Republic of China's territory was based on its "inherent" territory. The purpose of this was to declare national sovereignty, independence, and territorial integrity through the highest form of political contract, effectively denying any legal standing to domestic secessionist forces. However, Yuan intervened in the constitution-making process by promulgating the Provisional Constitution of the Republic of China (1914), replacing the above Draft. Article I of the Provisional Constitution provided that the Republic of China was to be organized by "the Chinese people". The Chinese people here included not only those of the Han majority, but also ethnic minorities such as Tibetans, the Hui, the Manchus, and Mongolians. Article III also affirmed that the territory of the Republic of China was the territory of the Qing dynasty, thus confirming the succession of the Republic to the territory covered by the Qing empire (Provisional Constitution Conference of the ROC 1914).

After Yuan's death in 1916 and a period of political disintegration, in 1923, warlords led by Cao Kun, a military leader who once served in the Beiyang Army, took control of Beijing and instituted the Constitution of the Republic of China (1923) (Constitutional Conference of the ROC 1923). Article I of this constitution proclaimed China as a unitary state and declared that the Republic of China would always be a unified democratic state. Article III, furthermore, repeated the provisions of the 1912 Provisional Constitution that the territory of the Republic of China should be according to its inherent territory, and its division could not be changed outside of the law (Constitutional Conference of the ROC 1923).

During the period of the Beiyang government, various warlords fought for power. After each successively gained power, they promulgated various constitutions to clarify the state's territorial scope and sovereignty. Although the instrumental nature of their constitutions was obvious at the time, the constitutional stipulation of maintaining state unification and defending territorial sovereignty remained the same.

## The Nanjing National Government (1928–1949)

For nearly his entire life, Sun Yat-Sen fought for the establishment of a unified and independent China. However, in the face of the failure of the second revolution in 1913 and his Constitutional Protection Movement, Sun realized that it was not feasible to unify the state by opposing one warlord or supporting another. Nevertheless, in a manifesto jointly issued in 1923 by Sun and the Soviet special envoy Adolf Joffe, state unification was singled out as one of the principal goals of the Chinese revolution. Sun died in 1925 without realizing this goal. He was succeeded by General Chiang Kai-shek, who shared Sun's ideal of Chinese unification. Chiang's Northern Expedition, launched in 1926, successfully reunited a large part of China (Zhang 2012), and in 1928 Chiang established the seat of Chinese government in Nanjing, creating the Nanjing National Government, which claimed sovereignty over the same territory as the Qing empire.

In 1931, the KMT government under Chiang promulgated the Provisional Constitution of the Republic of China's Tutelage Period. Article I emphasized that the territory of the Republic of China included the provinces and Tibet, with an added declaration that Mongolia and Tibet were inseparable sacred territories of China. Article LXXX further explained the regional governing system in the border areas of Mongolia and Tibet that allowed them to be separately prescribed by law according to their local situations (National Assembly of the ROC 1931).

These provisions indicate that the state system built during the Nanjing National Government was intended as a model of multi-ethnic governance under a unified system of one-party order.

In the same year, the Communist Party of China (CPC), under Mao Zedong and Zhu De, established the Jiangxi Soviet in Ruijin as the Chinese Soviet Republic (CSR), providing it with its own constitutional document, the Constitutional Outline of the Chinese Soviet Republic of 1931. Taking the USSR as a model, this document granted full autonomy to all ethnic minorities living in China, including all Mongolians, Muslims, Tibetans, Miao, Yao, Koreans, and other minorities, and recognized their right of complete separation from China. Article XIV of the Constitutional Outline stated that ethnic minorities were to enjoy the full right to self-determination, i.e., they could join the Union of Chinese Soviets, or secede from it and form their own state (First National Congress of the Chinese Soviet 1931).

In the historical context of the 1930s, the CPC was regarded as a branch of the Communist International (Comintern), which promoted Leninist views on national issues and advocated national self-determination for the people in Mongolia, Tibet, and Xinjiang (Liu, 2011). Regardless of the overall conditions in China, the Constitutional Outline copied the USSR federal constitution, which (in theory) allowed for the secession of major federal units. In reality, to have implemented the Soviet federal model in a situation in which ten (or more) warlords controlled various regions and provinces would have led to the violent disintegration of the Chinese state, leaving the Chinese people in turmoil. By the time the Second Sino–Japanese War broke out, the CPC had in effect abandoned the Soviet federal model as a blueprint for the organization of the Chinese state. Permission to secede from a Soviet China proved short-lived.

In the summer of 1937, the Imperial Japanese Army surrounded the Beijing area and crossed the famed Lugou Bridge into southwestern Beijing, signaling Japan's full-scale aggression against China (Zhang 2012). In response, the KMT and CPC ended their civil war and created an anti-Japanese united front, calling for close cooperation with all elements, classes, and nations in the fight against fascism. At the same time, the two parties came to view state unification as the primary premise for national self-determination. In the 1938 Declaration of KMT Provisional National Congress, the KMT specifically emphasized that:

> [A]ll ethnic groups in China were oppressed by Japan. The national self-determination promoted by the Japanese is nothing more than temptation and incitement, and the result can only bring secession of China's territory. Therefore, our compatriots must be deeply aware that only the fight against the invading Japanese army can relieve oppression, and to form a free and unified Republic of China in which all ethnic groups can freely unite.
>
> *(Rong & Sun 1985: 466–468)*

In October 1938, at the Sixth Plenary Session of the Central Committee of the CPC, Mao declared that under the principle of united resistance against the Japanese, ethnic minorities such as Mongolians, Tibetans, Miao, Yao, and other minorities would be allowed to manage their own affairs, but all ethnic groups would be included within the unitary state. This could be considered as the turning point of the CPC's policy on the national issue (Xu & Luo 2011). At this point, the CPC replaced the Leninist principles of national self-determination, right to secession, and federalism, as emphasized in the past under the Soviet federal model, with the principle of regional national autonomy in ethnic minority areas (Xiao 1999), within a unified China.

Similarly, Article IV of the Draft Constitution of the Republic of China (1936) promulgated by the KMT, defined the territory of the Republic of China by listing the following as belonging to China: provinces Jiangsu, Zhejiang, Anhui, Jiangxi, Hubei, Hunan, Xichuan, Xikang,

Hebei, Shandong, Shanxi, Henan, Shaanxi, Gansu, Qinghai, Fujian, Guangdong, Guangxi, Yunnan, Guizhou, Liaoning, Jilin, Heilongjiang, Rehe, Chahaer, Suiyuan, Ningxia, Xinjiang, Mongolia, Tibet, and other territories originally belonging to China (National Assembly of the ROC 1936). Although clumsy, this was a constitutional response to, and political declaration against, the Japanese invasion and subsequent loss of territory. The CPC, then cooperating with the KMT in the fight against Japan, was given control over the area at the borders of the Japanese-occupied territories. The CPC's 1941 Administrative Program of Shaan-Gan-Ning Border Region further affirmed the fundamental constitutional provision that China's territories could not be divided. Article II of the Program stated: "We adhere to unity with friendly parties, friendly armies, and all the people in the border region, and oppose capitulation, secession, and retrogression" (Central Bureau of Shaan-Gan-Ning Border Region 1941: 1).

Although the KMT government lost the War of Liberation (1945–1949) to the CPC and had retreated to Taiwan, its leader Chiang Kai-Shek continued to uphold the principle of absolute unification. Because of this adherence, many scholars consider the cross-strait disputes between the PRC and Taiwan as being over the distribution of political power, not China's territorial sovereignty and integrity (Dang 2014).

## Anti-secession constitutional system in the PRC (1949–present)

The successful unification of China was one of the CPC's greatest achievements, and an important source of legitimacy. After founding the People's Republic of China (PRC) in 1949, the CPC proceeded to address the secession problems of Taiwan, Hong Kong, and Macau left over by history and wars, forging an anti-secession constitutional legal system. This anti-secession legal system is a complex body of law incorporating the constitution and its code, constitutional law, criminal law, and other administrative laws. The following analyzes the constitutional code and constitutional laws that form part of this complex system.

### *Anti-secession in the constitutional code of the PRC*

Since 1949, the Common Program of the Chinese People's Political Consultative Conference (CPPCC 1949) has promulgated one constitutional document and the National People's Congress (NPC) has formulated four. At the constitutional code level, safeguarding state unity, sovereignty, and territorial integrity forms the basic spirit of all five documents (Xu 2005).

The first constitutional document, the Common Program of the CPPCC in 1949, specifically stipulated the implementation of state unification, opposition to ethnic secession, and adherence to national sovereignty and territorial integrity (CPPCC 1949: art. LIV). In the first constitution of the PRC, ratified in 1954, there were no specific provisions regarding secession, but the basic principle of protecting sovereign integrity had obvious anti-secession implications (NPC 1954: art. XX). The constitutions enacted in 1975 and 1978 retained this basic principle.

The preamble of the PRC's constitution of 1982, currently in effect, states that it is the lofty duty of the entire Chinese people – including their compatriots in Taiwan – to accomplish the great task of reunifying the motherland. Article XXVIII upholds the maintenance of public order and the suppression of criminal activities that endanger state security; Article XXIX stipulates the tasks of the armed forces regarding resistance to foreign aggression, participation in national reconstruction, and defense of the motherland. Article LII states that Chinese citizens have an obligation to maintain national unification and defend the motherland (NPC 1982). Although none of these constitutional provisions directly use the term "anti-secession", they uniformly reflect the legislative intent to safeguard state unification and thereby oppose secession.

## Anti-secession in the constitutional laws of the PRC

The PRC is a multi-ethnic unitary state composed of 56 ethnic groups, with Han nationality as the main ethnic group (Chen 2020). Provincial administrative divisions include 23 provinces, five ethnic minority autonomous regions, four municipalities, and two special administrative regions (SARs) directly under the administration of the Chinese central government. The Law of Regional National Autonomy of the PRC (LRNA) aims at addressing the balance between ethnic diversity and central unification while upholding territory integrity. The preamble of the LRNA mandates the safeguarding of national autonomous areas under the leadership of the central power, while Article II states that all national autonomous areas are inalienable parts of the PRC (NPC 1984).

The LRNA also provides a legal framework to facilitate ethnic minority autonomy. This specifies the right of ethnic minorities to administer their internal affairs, and their adherence to the principles of equality, unity, and common prosperity, for all nations within China and bestows considerable political, economic, and cultural rights on ethnic minorities (Xia 2009). Nevertheless, according to the LRNA, the organs of self-government of the national autonomous areas, as local organs of state power, must place the interests of state power above anything else, and prohibit any acts that may undermine the unity of the nationalities or instigate national division (NPC 1984: art. V).

The PRC's constitution of 1982 also specifically provides for a "One Country, Two Systems" principle. Article XXXI states that:

> The state may establish administrative regions when necessary. The system to be instituted in special administrative regions shall be prescribed by law enacted by the National People's Congress in the light of specific conditions.
>
> *(NPC 1982)*

However, this single law is not sufficient to meet the PRC's current goals of strengthening national unification and maintaining territorial security. Therefore, based on China's unitary system, specific laws for the SARs have been introduced, including the Basic Law of the Hong Kong Special Administrative Region (NPC 1997), and the Basic Law of the Macau Special Administrative Region (NPC 1999). With the implementation of the "One Country, Two Systems" approach and the smooth return of Hong Kong and Macau and their establishment as special administrative regions, a new legal relationship between the central government and SARs as special entities within the state has been established. This allows the two SARs to maintain their existing capitalist system for 50 years, while upholding the state sovereignty, unity, and territorial integrity of China.

In order to strictly abide by the "One Country, Two Systems" policy, the Hong Kong Basic Law and Macau Basic Law provide the two special entities with a high degree of specific autonomous scope under the constitutional framework (Leng 2011). As prescribed in these laws, the two SARs are responsible for their own internal affairs, including the judiciary and courts of final appeal, immigration and customs, public finance, currencies, and extradition. However, diplomacy and military defense are the reserved power of the central government in Beijing (NPC 1997). The Basic Laws of both SARs state in their preambles that upholding national unification and territorial integrity is essential for maintaining their prosperity and stability as inalienable parts of China. Thus, the specific provisions of the Basic Laws reflect the principle of safeguarding Chinese national sovereignty and unity.

These provisions were strengthened in 2020 when the 20th meeting of the Standing Committee of the 13th National People's Congress of the PRC passed the Safeguarding National

Security Law for the Hong Kong SAR to prevent and punish crimes that attempted to undermine national unity, subvert state power, organize territorial activities, or collude with foreign forces to jeopardize national security in the Hong Kong SAR. Chapter III of this law provides detailed provisions against crimes relating to secession: anyone organizing, planning, committing, or participating in an act of secession in Hong Kong or any other part of the PRC commits a criminal offense (NPC Standing Committee 2020: art. XX). In addition to compulsory punishment measures, the law defines the obligations of the citizens of Hong Kong, based on the combined principles of "One Country, Two Systems" and "Hong Kong people ruling Hong Kong." Article VI reiterates the constitutional obligation of all Chinese citizens to abide by this law to safeguard national sovereignty, unity, and territorial integrity and not engage in any activity that endangers national security (NPC Standing Committee 2020).

The policy attitude of the PRC towards Taiwan also reflects China's primary objective of maintaining national unity and resisting secession. The Anti-Secession Law of the People's Republic of China (ASL), adopted on 14 March 2005, provides the legal framework for the policy. The promulgation of ASL was China's response to rising pressure for Taiwan's independence, considered a long-term threat to Chinese reunification. It is also a legal response to proposals by Taiwan separatists to amend the Constitution of the Republic of China to achieve their goal of independence. In setting a legal framework to prevent Taiwan from seceding from China, the ASL strictly abides by the NPC's 1982 constitution, which declares Taiwan to be an inalienable part of Chinese territory, and reiterates the legislative will to preserve the sovereignty and territorial integrity of China as expressed in the 1982 Constitution (NPC 2005: art. II).

The ASL consists of ten articles that stipulate not only social, economic, and cultural measures to be taken to maintain peace and prosperity between the two sides of the Taiwan Strait, but also non-peaceful and the other measures to protect China's sovereignty and territorial integrity. In this way, the ASL adopts a "carrot" and "stick" approach (Zou 2005). The "carrot" is to achieve reunification with Taiwan and the end of political conflicts through consultations and negotiations on an equal footing, and the "stick" is found in the military option to protect China's sovereignty and territorial integrity if Taiwan declares independence from China, or engages in any major incident entailing secession from China. The key function of the ASL is to provide a mechanism to channel the soft/hard approaches into one legal framework representing the PRC's Taiwan policy and to reinforce the PRC's legitimacy in its approach to the Taiwan secession issue (You 2006).

Since the founding of the PRC in 1949, China has thus gradually established a specific and relatively comprehensive anti-secession constitutional system whose primary goal is safeguarding national unity and territorial sovereignty. From the basic provisions of the 1982 constitution that firmly safeguard state sovereignty and territorial integrity, to the implementation of the Law of Regional National Autonomy of the PRC, the Basic Law of Hong Kong SAR, the Basic Law of Macau SAR, and the Anti-Secession Law of the PRC, the current constitutional framework supports the unitary system of ancient China. Maintaining state unity remains the primary principle, while allowing for various degrees of autonomy according to local special circumstances.

## Conclusion

From the first provisional constitution in 1912 to the last constitution of the Republic of China in 1946, all of China's early modern constitutional documents have emphasized maintaining the territorial integrity of China, thereby rejecting secession. Anti-secession has also been a theme of the PRC's constitutional system since its establishment in 1949. All constitutional documents promulgated by the PRC have emphasized the protection of China's state sovereignty and territorial integrity, embodying an anti-secession constitutional standpoint. In addition, constitutional laws covering regional autonomy and SARs have also stipulated the indivisibility of China's state territory. The constitutional thought and practice of modern China has thus always reflected an anti-secession position. Furthermore, this anti-secession position can be found throughout the thought and practice of pre-modern, imperial China in the persistent idea of Great Unity, which has provided the philosophical and ideological foundation for China's unitary state system to this day. The current anti-secession constitutional position of China thus has deep roots in Chinese philosophical and legal traditions and state practices.

# References

Central Bureau of Shaan-Gan-Ning Border Region 1941, "Administrative Program of Shaan-Gan-Ning Border Region", (*Shaan-Gan-Ning Bianqu Shizheng Gangling*), *Jiefang*, 128: 0–2.

Chen, D. 1922, "Ben Bao Xuanyan" (Publishing Words), *Xiangdao* (*The Guide Weekly*). <www.cnbksy.com/literature/browsePiece?eid=null&bcId=null&pieceId=1f18eb4b4288f2b20a60177be3317a06&ltid=7&activeId=61b99476f74f7f4c5346b32c&downloadSource=GENERALSEARCH>

Chen, J. 2020, "Regional Ethnic Autonomy: Thinking and Actions on the Reconstruction of a Unified Multi-Ethnic Country By the CPC", *International Journal of Anthropology and Ethnology*, 4(8): 1–16.

Chen, X. 2012, *Zhongguo Fazhi Shi* (*Chinese Legal History*), Wuhan: Wuhan University Press.

Chen, X. 2018, *The Study of Chinese Constitutional Culture*, New York: William S. Hein & Co., Inc. & Wells Information Service Inc.

Confucius 2007, *The Analects of Confucius*, New York: Columbia University Press.

Constitutional Conference of the ROC 1923, *Constitution of the Republic of China (1923)* (*Caokun Xianfa*), <https://en.wikisource.org/wiki/Constitution_of_the_Republic_of_China_(1923)>

Constitutional Drafting Committee 1913, *Draft of the Constitution of the Republic of China (1913)* (*Tiantan Draft Constitution*) (*Tiantan Xiancao*), <www.cnbksy.com/search/detail/7eddfd4cffb9495f8b2d596b313d9808963314a6c631ea8b277b87a05d014d0b/12/6122619223b09976743ae0f8>

CPPCC 1949, *Common Program of the Chinese People's Political Consultative Conference* (*Zhongguo Renmin Zhengzhi Xieshang Huiyi Gongtong Gangling*), <www.lscps.gov.cn/html/20990>

Dang, X. 2014, *Fan Fenlie Guojia Fa Yunxing Jizhi Yanjiu* (*Research on the Operation Mechanism of Anti-Secession Law*), Lanzhou: Lanzhou University Press.

Fei, X. 2003, *Zhonghua Minzu De Duoyuan Yiti Geju* (*The Pattern of Pluralism and Integration of the Chinese Nation*), Beijing: Central University for Nationalities Press.

First National Congress of the Chinese Soviet 1931, "Constitutional Outline of the Chinese Soviet Republic (1931)", (*Zhonghua Suweiai Gongheguo Xianfa Dagang*), *Zhongguo Chulu Yanjiu*, 1(1): 131–136.

Gu, B. 1985, "Zailun Zhonghua Minzu De Gongtongxing", (On the Commonality of the Chinese Nation), *Xinjiang Shehui Kexue* (*Xinjiang Social Science*), 3: 1–9.

He, X. 2011, "Dayitong Linian Yu Zhongguo Shaoshu Minzu", (The Idea of Great Unity and Chinese Ethnic Minorities), *Yunnan Shehui Kexue* (*Yunnan Social Science*), 5: 91–96.

He, Y. 2018, *Zhongguo Gudai Nongye Wenming* (*Ancient Chinese Agricultural Civilization*), Nanjing: Jiangsu Renmin Chubanshe (Jiangsu People's Publishing House).

Jiang, Y. 2016, *Shijie Wenming Shiyu Xia De Zhonghua Wenming* (*Chinese Civilization from the Perspective of World Civilization*), Shanghai: Fudan University Press.

Kim, Y. 2018, *A History of Chinese Political Thought*, Cambridge: Polity Press.

Laozi 2012, *Tao Te Ching*, Changchun: Jilin University Press.

Leng, T. 2011, "On the Fundamental Characteristics of the 'One Country, Two Systems' Policy", *Academic Journal of "One Country, Two Systems"*, 1: 49–54.

Lewis, M. 1990, *Sanctioned Violence in Early China*, Albany: State University of New York Press.

Liu, X. 2011, "Zhongguo Guojia Xingtai Zhuanxing De Bianjiang Zhi Wei" (The Frontier Dimension of China's National Form Transformation), *Wenhua Zongheng*, 6: 10–13.

Lü, B. 2016, *Lü Shi Chun Qiu*, Beijing: Zhong Hua Shuju.

Mengzi 2016, *Mengzi*, Beijing: Shidai Huawen Shuju.

Mozi 2007, *Mozi*, Beijing: Zhong Hua Shuju.

National Assembly of the ROC 1931, The Provisional Constitution of Republic of China's Tutelage Period (*Zhonghua Minguo Xunzheng Shiqi Yuefa*), <https://china-journal.org/2016/05/31/provisional-constitution-of-the-republic-of-china-1931/>

National Assembly of the ROC 1936, The Draft Constitution of the Republic of China (1936) (*Zhon-ghua Minguo Xianfa Caoan*, also known as *Wu Wu Xian Cao*), <http://orcp.hustoj.com/wp-content/uploads/2016/01/1935-Draft-of-the-Constitution-of-the-Republic-of-China.pdf>

Ni, X. 2003, 'Nonggeng Jingji Dui Zhongguo Chuantong Wenhua Tezheng Xingcheng De Yingxiang' (The Influence of Agricultural Economy on the Formation of Chinese Traditional Cultural Charac-teristics), *Jiangsu Guangbo Dianshi Daxue Xuebao* (*Journal of Jiangsu Radio & Television University*), 14(5): 53–55.

NPC 1954, The Constitution of the PRC (1954), <www.lawinfochina.com/display.aspx?id=14754&lib=law>

NPC 1982, The Constitution of the PRC (1982) (*Zhonghua Renmin Gongheguo Xian Fa*), <www.lawinfochina.com/display.aspx?id=1&lib=law&SearchKeyword=constitution&SearchCKeyword=>

NPC 1984, Law of Regional National Autonomy of the PRC (*Zhonghua Renmin Gongheguo Minzu Quyu Zizhi Fa*), <www.lawinfochina.com/display.aspx?id=43&lib=law&SearchKeyword=&SearchCKeywor d=%c3%f1%d7%e5%c7%f8%d3%f2%d7%d4%d6%ce>

NPC 1997, The Basic Law of Hong Kong SAR of the PRC (*Zhonghua Renmin Gongheguo Xianggang Tebie Xingzheng Qu Jiben Fa*), <www.lawinfochina.com/display.aspx?id=1210&lib=law&Search Keyword=&SearchCKeyword=%cc%d8%b1%f0%d0%d0%d5%fe%c7%f8%bb%f9%b1%be%b7%a8>

NPC 1999, The Basic Law of Macau SAR of the PRC (*Zhonghua Renmin Gongheguo Aomen Tebie Xing-zheng Qu Jiben Fa*), <www.lawinfochina.com/display.aspx?id=531&lib=law&SearchKeyword=&-SearchCKeyword=%cc%d8%b1%f0%d0%d0%d5%fe%c7%f8%bb%f9%b1%be%b7%a8>

NPC 2005, National People's Congress of the People's Republic of China, Anti-Secession Law of the People's Republic of China (*Fan Fenlie Guojia Fa*), <www.lawinfochina.com/display.aspx?id=3970&lib=law&SearchKeyword=&SearchCKeyword=%b7%b4%b7%d6%c1%d1%b9%fa%bc%d2%b7%a8>

NPC Standing Committee 2020, Safeguarding National Security law in Hong Kong SAR (2021), (*Zhon-ghua Renmin Gongheguo Xianggang Tebie Xingzhengqu Weihu Guojia Anquan Fa*), <www.lawinfochina.com/display.aspx?id=33019&lib=law&SearchKeyword=&SearchCKeyword=%ce%ac%bb%a4%b9%fa%bc%d2%b0%b2%c8%ab%b7%a8>

Pan, W., Yang, W. & Wu, L. 2014, *Jianming Zhongguo Chuantong Wenhua* (*Concise Chinese Traditional Cul-ture*), Wuhan: Huazhong University of Science and Technology Press.

Pines, Y. 2000, "'The One That Pervades the All' in Ancient Chinese Political Thought: The Origins of 'The Great Unity' Paradigm'", *Toung Pao*, 86(2): 280–291.

Pines, Y. 2012, *The Everlasting Empire: The Political Culture of Ancient China and Its Imperial Legacy*, New Jersey: Princeton University Press.

Provisional Constitution Conference of the ROC 1914, *The Provisional Constitution of the Republic of China (1914)* (*Zhonghua Minguo Yuefa*), <https://archive.org/details/cu31924023469822/page/n5/mode/2up>

Rong, M. & Sun, C. 1985, *All Previous Congress Information of Chinese KMT*, Beijing: Guangming Daily Press.

Su, L. (2018). *The Constitution of Ancient China*. New Jersey: Princeton University Press.

Sun, Y.-S. 1981, *Sun Yat-Sen Complete Works*, Volume I, Beijing: Zhonghua Book Company.

Sun, Y.-S. 1985. *Sun Yat-Sen Complete Works*, Volumes VI–VII, Beijing: Zhonghua Book Company.

Sun, Y.-S. 1986, *Sun Yat-Sen Complete Works*, Volumes IX–XI, Beijing: Zhonghua Book Company.

Tanigawa, M. 1971, *Sun Yat-Sen and Three Notable Chinese Characteristics within the Chinese Constitutions*, Kuramae Tokyo: Chikuma Shobō.

Wang, R. 2019, "Reconstruction of the 'Unified' Narrative of Chinese History", *Dongfang Xuekan*, 4: 13–20.

Xia, C. 2009, "Autonomous Legislative Power in Regional Ethnic Autonomy of the People's Republic of China: The Law and Reality", in J. C. Oliveira & P. Cardinal (eds), *One Country, Two Systems, Three Legal Orders – Perspectives of Evolution*, Berlin: Springer: 541–563.

Xiao, J. 1999, *The National Style of Chinese Nation*, Beijing: Minzu Press.

Xu, C. 2005, "On the Legislative Basis and Nature of the Anti-Secession Law", *Academic Journal of Zhong-zhou*, 3: 94–96.

Xu, J. & Luo, S. 2011, *A Brief History of China's Ethnic Policy*, Yinchuan: Ningxia People's Publishing House.

Xu, L. 2015, "The Influence of the 'World View of Great Unity' on China's Border Governance", *Journal of National Institute of Administration*, 6: 29–32.

Yan, Q. 2018, "The Great Unity and the Formulation of the Chinese National Community Conscious-ness", *Journal of Southwest University for Nationalities*, 5: 16.

You, J. 2006, "China's Anti-secession Law and the Risk of War in the Taiwan Strait, *Contemporary Security Policy*, 27(2): 237–257.

Zhang, J. 2004, *Chinese Constitutional History*, Changchun: Jilin People's Press.

Zhang, Q. 2012, *The Constitution of China: A Contextual Analysis*, Oxford: Hart Publishing.

Zhao, L. 2002, "Agricultural and Nomadic Nations: Conflict, Conflation & Their Historical Effect", *Wuhan University Journal (Humanity Science)*, 55(6): 700–706.

Zhao, X. 2018, "'The 'Limited Expansionism' in Ancient China and the 'Order of China in Asia'", *Jinan Journal*, 234(7): 106–118.

Zou, K. 2005, "Governing the Taiwan Issue in Accordance with Law: An Essay on China's Anti-Secession Law", *Chinese Journal of International Law*, 4(2): 455–463.

# 41

# CONSTITUTIONAL LAW AND SECESSION IN THE UNITED KINGDOM

*Aileen McHarg\**

## Introduction

The United Kingdom (UK) is a multinational – or, more accurately, plurinational (Keating 2001; Tierney 2005) – State with four distinct territorial units. Although formally understood as a unitary State (i.e., it has a single source of sovereign authority, located in the UK, or Westminster, Parliament), it was formed through a series of unions between England and its smaller neighbours – consensual, if unequal, in the case of Scotland; forced in the case of Wales and Ireland (now Northern Ireland), albeit with the formal consent of the Irish Parliament. This historical development has left a legacy of distinct sub-state national identities, and asymmetric governance, most recently in the establishment of devolved legislatures and governments for Scotland, Wales, and Northern Ireland from 1999, giving the UK characteristics of a union State – or a State of unions – rather than a purely unitary State (Rokkan & Urwin 1982; Mitchell 2009).

In each case, formal enlargement of the State was marked by the enactment of so-called "Acts of Union" by the Westminster Parliament (and for Scotland and Ireland, parallel legislation by their own Parliaments, which then ceased to exist): the Laws in Wales Acts 1535/42; the Union with Scotland Acts 1706/7; and the Union with Ireland Acts 1800/1. The constitutional status of the union legislation is disputed. There is some support for the proposition that the 1707 Union was constitutive of a new State, and hence that its terms are binding on the UK Parliament (see, e.g., MacCormick v. Lord Advocate 1953). But the dominant view – recently confirmed by the Northern Ireland Court of Appeal in *Re Allister* (NICA 2022) in relation to the Irish Acts of Union – is that their terms are freely amendable, certainly expressly, and potentially also by implication.

Thus, while the Union is declared in all three sets of legislation to be indissoluble, these Acts have in practice proved to be no barrier to secession. In 1922, the Irish Free State was established, consisting of 26 counties of Ireland. In addition, the Northern Ireland Act 1998 explicitly contemplates the possibility of the remaining six counties of Northern Ireland leaving the UK to become part of a united Ireland, while in September 2014 an independence referendum was held in Scotland.

In that referendum, a majority of voters opted to remain in the UK, as did a majority of Northern Ireland's voters in a so-called "border poll" held in 1973.[1] However, the UK's withdrawal from the European Union (Brexit) has led to active contemplation of Irish unification, and active discussion of the process by which that might be secured (see, e.g., Murray & O'Donoghue 2019; Constitution Unit 2021), albeit there is not yet majority support for it. Similarly, in Scotland, where opinion polls indicate that support for leaving or remaining in the UK is now finely balanced, Brexit has fuelled the case for a second independence referendum, which has been actively sought by the Scottish National Party (SNP)–led Scottish Government since 2017.

In this chapter, I will discuss each of these secession or putative secession processes in turn. As will be seen, each is very different. In the case of Ireland, secession began in a revolutionary act, which provoked a violent reaction, and eventually led to a negotiated settlement. In Northern Ireland, a (limited) right to secede is legally recognised and (partially) legally regulated in domestic constitutional law, and underpinned by an international agreement. In Scotland, the 2014 independence referendum was consensual and legally sanctioned, but essentially ad hoc.

Nevertheless, the differences between them are – in strictly constitutional terms – less significant than they might appear. On the one hand, all three are, or are capable of being, constitutionally valid secession processes because, in the UK's uncodified and famously flexible constitutional order, the only absolute constitutional requirement is the agreement of the Westminster Parliament. Thanks to the doctrine of parliamentary sovereignty, it is free to make or unmake the borders of the State as it sees fit.[2] On the other hand, prior legal recognition of secession claims is also less important than it might appear, as Parliament cannot (as a matter of domestic law) be bound to uphold them. The sovereignty of Parliament thus constitutes both an opportunity for, and an obstacle to, secessionist movements. It also means that there is no single legal pathway to secession, nor any particular set of terms on which it must take place; what matters ultimately is the political pressure that can brought to bear on the UK Parliament in order to secure its consent. Even so, there may be a case for more consistent legal recognition and regulation of secession rights, which I will briefly consider in the concluding section.

For reasons of space, I will not discuss secession by either Wales[3] or England.[4] Notwithstanding their different constitutional histories, Welsh claims for independence are likely to be handled in much the same way as for Scotland (Evans 2020). As for England, in the unlikely event that a sufficient majority of voters ever wishes to leave the Union, such is English dominance of representation in the UK Parliament (533/650 seats in the House of Commons) that the necessary constitutional consent is likely to be relatively easily secured.

## The secession of Ireland

The roots of the Irish secession can be traced to the Union of 1800/1 itself (McLean & McMillan 2010: 75–85). Although the Irish Parliament had voted for the Union, its membership was limited to Anglicans; hence, the vast majority of Irish people – both Catholics and non-conforming Protestants – were not represented in the decision.[5] McLean and McMillan describe Catholic emancipation as an unspoken term of the Union (McLean & McMillan 2010: 75), but this was immediately breached by the refusal of the King, George III, to agree to it. Catholic emancipation was eventually achieved in 1829, but by then the Union was seen as illegitimate by the majority in Ireland (Mansergh 1940: 298; McLean & McMillan 2010: 85), and by the 1840s campaigns were underway to repeal it.

Nationalism in Ireland initially took a constitutional form, aimed at establishing "Home Rule" (devolution) within the UK. Bills were introduced to establish a devolved Parliament for Ireland in 1886 and 1893, but both were defeated. In stark contrast to attitudes in Ireland, majority public opinion in Great Britain considered the maintenance of the Union as essential to the authority of the State and the integrity of the British Empire, even if this conflicted with the will of the majority in Ireland (Dicey 1886: ch. VIII; Mansergh 1940: 296). A third Home

Rule Bill was introduced in 1912, and enacted in 1914, thanks to the fact that the Irish Parliamentary Party held the balance of power in the House of Commons, and that the House of Lords' veto had been removed by the Parliament Act 1911. However, the Act was immediately suspended upon enactment due to opposition by Protestant Unionists, who formed a majority in the North East of Ireland, and the outbreak of the First World War. Ulster Unionists – with the support of the Conservative Opposition, the Army, and even the King – regarded the 1914 Act as illegitimate, because it proposed a fundamental constitutional change which had not been subject to specific popular approval either via a general election or a referendum,[6] and they were prepared to threaten armed insurrection to oppose it (McLean & Lubbock 2010; Saunders 2013; Reid 2017).

The 1916 Easter Rising marked the turn from constitutional to revolutionary nationalism. The brutal suppression of the Rising by the British Government, combined with growing international support for self-determination of nations, promoted by US President Woodrow Wilson, persuaded the majority of Irish people that something stronger than Home Rule was required (Reid 2017; O'Donoghue 2019). In the December 1918 UK General Election, the republican party, Sinn Féin, swept aside the pro-Home Rule Irish Parliamentary Party, winning 73 out of 101 seats in Ireland. Instead of taking their seats at Westminster, Sinn Féin MPs constituted themselves as the first Dáil Éireann on 21 January 1919, and issued a declaration of independence, ratifying the Easter 1916 Proclamation of an Irish Republic.

The revolutionaries expected to receive a sympathetic hearing for their case for self-determination at the Versailles Peace Conference, but were in fact unsuccessful. The British Government also refused to recognise the Dáil and its accompanying institutions (including a provisional government, court system, and police force – Mitchell 2002: 73–75), and declared it illegal in September 1919. The British response thereafter was twofold. On the one hand, an attempt to suppress the revolution through force, met by the countervailing force of the Irish Republican Army (IRA). On the other hand, the enactment of further Home Rule legislation – the Government of Ireland Act 1920 – this time establishing separate parliaments for northern and southern Ireland.

Neither strategy was successful. Although the Dáil and provisional government were forced underground, they did not cease to operate (Mitchell 2002: 75–80), and while the use of force failed to destroy the IRA, it did destroy the remaining legitimacy of the British State in Ireland (Townsend 2002: 11–12). Sinn Féin candidates swept the board (outside Ulster) at elections to the Parliament of Southern Ireland held under the 1920 Act in May 1921, promptly constituting themselves as the second Dáil. However, the British Government's actions were sufficient to stop the revolutionary institutions operating effectively, nor could the IRA defeat the British forces (Mitchell 2002: 82–83).

By June 1921, stalemate had been reached. The British Government entered into talks with the provisional government, leading to a truce in July, and the agreement of an Anglo-Irish Treaty in December 1921, providing for the creation of an Irish Free State with Dominion status (see Torrance 2021b). The Irish Free State (Agreement) Act 1922 provided for the establishment of a provisional parliament and government, which drafted, in negotiation with the British authorities, a constitution for the Irish Free State. The constitution was approved by an Act of the provisional parliament, the Constitution of the Irish Free State (Saorstát Éireann) Act 1922, and subsequently by the UK Parliament in the Irish Free State (Constitution) Act 1922, and the Irish Free State came formally into being by Royal Proclamation on 6 December 1922.

While constitutional legitimacy was secured, from the British point of view, through the enactment of the Agreement and Constitution Acts, the reality of the situation might be thought to be rather different: that the British had been forced to accept the *de facto* legitimacy of the revolutionary institutions and to come to terms with them (the language of a "treaty" suggesting an agreement between separate States). Indeed, the Irish Supreme Court held, in *Byrne v. Ireland*, that the constitution of the Irish Free State was enacted by the provisional parliament, not by Westminster (Byrne v. Ireland 1972).

But the provisional government did not secure all that it wanted. For one thing, it was forced to accept the partition of Ireland. The Anglo-Irish Treaty maintained what Torrance calls the "polite fiction" (Torrance 2020: 29) of Irish unity by providing that the whole of Ireland would secede from the UK, but gave the Parliament of Northern Ireland one month to decide whether it wished to withdraw from the Irish Free State and remain part of the UK, which it duly did on 7 December 1922. For another, Dominion status did not mean complete independence. Although no longer part of the UK,[7] the Irish Free State remained part of the British Empire, and the drafters of the constitution were forced to accept the authority of the Crown and the Judicial Committee of the Privy Council, as well as the overriding legislative authority of the Imperial Parliament. In fact, the concessions exacted – in particular, the oath of loyalty to the Crown required of members of the Free State Parliament – led to a civil war (from June 1922 to May 1923) between pro- and anti-Treaty factions.

Nevertheless, Dominion status did give a substantially greater measure of autonomy than Home Rule would have done, and provided a pathway towards full independence (see Coffey 2016; Mohn 2016). The Statute of Westminster 1931 ended the right of the UK Parliament to legislate for the Dominions without their consent, and removed the supremacy of Imperial law, thus enabling the Free State Parliament to amend the Free State constitution and facilitating the dismantling of the Treaty settlement. A new constitution was adopted in 1937, which declared Ireland an independent sovereign State, and it finally adopted the description of a republic, thereby withdrawing from the Commonwealth, in 1949 – given recognition by the UK Parliament in the Ireland Act 1949.

## Northern Ireland and Irish unification

The other concession made by the republican negotiators – the partition of Ireland – has, however, proved to be more enduring, with Northern Ireland reaching its centenary as a distinct territorial and political unit in 2020. Section 1(1) of the Northern Ireland Act 1998 declares that

> Northern Ireland in its entirety remains part of the United Kingdom and shall not cease to be so without the consent of a majority of the people of Northern Ireland voting in a poll held for the purposes of this section.

However, section 1(2) goes on to state that

> if the wish expressed by a majority in such a poll is that Northern Ireland should cease to be part of the United Kingdom and form part of a united Ireland, the Secretary of State shall lay before Parliament such proposals to give effect to that wish as may be agreed between Her Majesty's Government in the United Kingdom and the Government of Ireland.

These statutory provisions reflect the "principle of consent" contained in the 1998 Belfast/Good Friday Agreement, signed by the Governments of the UK and Ireland, plus the political parties in Northern Ireland. This ended three decades of euphemistically-named "Troubles"; i.e., violent conflict between Irish republican paramilitaries seeking to establish a united Ireland, loyalist paramilitaries seeking to preserve the Union, and British security forces. The principle of consent means that

> it is for the people of the island of Ireland alone, by agreement between the two parts respectively and without external impediment, to exercise their right of self-deter- mination on the basis of consent, freely and concurrently given, North and South, to bring about a united Ireland if that is their wish, accepting that this right must be achieved and exercised with and subject to the agreement and consent of a majority of the people of Northern Ireland.
>
> *(Secretary of State for Northern Ireland 1998: Article 1(ii))*

The origins of the principle of consent are, though, much older. As indicated in the previous section, during the revolutionary period, Protestant Unionists in Ulster claimed their own right of self-determination, backed up by the threat of force, to resist subjection to an all-Ire- land Parliament (see McLean & Lubbock 2010; Reid 2017), and exercised their right, via the Parliament of Northern Ireland, under the Anglo-Irish Treaty, to refuse to consent to join the Irish Free State.

The status of Northern Ireland as part of the UK, and a guarantee that its status would not change without the consent of the Parliament of Northern Ireland, was affirmed in section 1(2) of the Ireland Act 1949. This was enacted to give reassurance to Unionists in the wake of the Republic of Ireland's final rupture from the UK and its territorial claim to the whole of the island of Ireland contained in Articles 2 and 3 of the 1937 Constitution (Mansergh 1991: 339–341). That this was about bolstering Northern Ireland's place in the Union, rather than paving the way for secession, is underlined by the fact that republican (i.e. pro-unification) political organisations (even non-violent ones) were banned under successive Special Powers Acts enacted by the Parliament of Northern Ireland (Murray 2021: 110). The location of the principle of consent in the Parliament, rather than directly with the people, of Northern Ireland further cemented the Union, given that its electoral arrangements artificially reduced Nationalist representation (Murray 2021: 110).

In section 1 of the Northern Ireland Constitution Act 1973, the right to consent was trans- ferred from the (by now abolished) Parliament of Northern Ireland to the people of Northern Ireland voting in a referendum. There was, though, no *right* to a referendum; the decision to hold a poll was left entirely to the discretion of the UK Government, subject only to the stip- ulation that there had to be at least ten years between votes. Again, therefore, the aim of the border poll held in March 1973 was to reassure Unionists, and take the issue of the border out of political contention, ahead of efforts to establish new devolved institutions on a power-shar- ing basis. But while it manifestly failed to do so, given the almost complete boycott of the poll by Northern Ireland's Catholic population, it did confirm the idea that sovereignty, at least in a political if not strictly legal sense, lay with the people of Northern Ireland, rather than the Westminster Parliament (Mitchell 2009: 181).

Given their political motivation, unsurprisingly, neither the 1949 Act nor the 1973 Act specified what would happen in the event that there was majority support for changing North- ern Ireland's constitutional status. However, in December 1973, the Sunningdale Agreement, between the British and Irish Governments and political parties in Northern Ireland, stated for the first time that, if there were a majority vote for a united Ireland, the British Government would support that wish. This position was reiterated in the 1985 Anglo-Irish Agreement, and again in the 1993 Downing Street Declaration, in which the UK Government also reaffirmed that it had "no selfish strategic or economic interest in Northern Ireland".

By the time of the 1998 Belfast/Good Friday Agreement, then, it was clearly accepted that Northern Ireland could leave the UK, but what the Agreement made explicit was acceptance of a principle of *parallel* consent to Irish unification north and south of the border, thus accommodating both Unionist and Nationalist views as to the location of constitution power on the island of Ireland (Murray 2021: 109–115). A key breakthrough was the Irish Government's commitment to amend the Irish Constitution to remove its territorial claim to Northern Ireland, which had hitherto impeded Irish acceptance of a Northern veto (see Boland v. An Taoiseach 1974; McGimpsey v. Ireland 1990). The 1998 Agreement was itself confirmed through referendums in both Ireland and Northern Ireland, again reinforcing the principle of consent.

It is, however, important not to overstate the significance of the principle of consent. For one thing, it does not connote a *general* right to self-determination. The UK Supreme Court in *R (Miller) v. Secretary of State for Exiting the European Union* held that it does not extend to a right of consent to constitutional change in general, nor does it encompass any alternative constitutional futures outside the UK (R (Miller) v. Secretary of State 2018: para. 135). The choice is to remain part of the UK, or to join a united Ireland.[8]

In addition, the principle of consent is unlikely to be legally enforceable. The referendum commitment in section 1 of the Northern Ireland Act 1998 can be understood as a manner and form constraint on the sovereignty of the Westminster Parliament, which *may* be enforceable so long as it remains on the statute book. However, this is an unorthodox view of the doctrine of parliamentary sovereignty for which there is little authority, and in any case, there is nothing to stop the provision itself from being repealed or replaced – as of course happened to the earlier constitutional guarantees in the 1949 and 1973 Acts. The underpinning commitments in the Belfast/Good Friday Agreement are also unlikely to be directly enforceable, either in international or domestic courts (Constitution Unit 2021: para. 4.10), though there is likely to be substantial international pressure to comply with them, not only from Ireland but also, in particular, from the United States.

Further, there is substantial uncertainty surrounding the operation of the principle of consent. Schedule 1 to the 1998 Act provides that a unification referendum may be held in two sets of circumstances. First, the Secretary of State for Northern Ireland (i.e., a UK Government Minister)[9] has discretion to hold a poll at any time. Second, (unlike under the 1973 Act) a poll *must* be held[10] "if at any time it appears likely to [the Secretary of State] that a majority of those voting would express a wish that Northern Ireland should cease to be part of the United Kingdom and form part of a united Ireland". In either case, polls may be held no more frequently than every seven years. However, it is not clear on what basis the Secretary of State is to form a judgment as to whether a referendum is either mandatory or desirable. And the statute is silent on a range of other key issues, including the franchise, the question to be asked, the voting threshold, and the conduct of the referendum (see Murray and O'Donoghue 2019; Constitution Unit 2021). It has, though, been persuasively argued that only a simple majority requirement would be compatible with the Belfast/Good Friday Agreement's commitment that either a united Ireland or the status quo must be treated as equally valid outcomes (Murray & O'Donoghue 2019: 181–182; Constitution Unit 2021: para. 4.33).

Successive Secretaries of State have refused to be drawn on their approach to these matters, and the Northern Ireland Court of Appeal, in *Re McCord* (NICA 2020), recently rejected a challenge seeking to force the UK Government to draw up and publish its referendum policy. The court emphasised the value of political flexibility in judging when and on what terms a referendum should be held. However, it also repeatedly emphasised that the Secretary of State's powers "must be exercised honestly in the public interest with rigorous impartiality in the context that it is for the people of Ireland alone to exercise their right of self-determination" (NICA

2020: paras 67, 82). This means, for example, that the Secretary of State could not, in the face of rising support for unification, decide to hold a discretionary poll with the sole purpose of delaying a mandatory poll for a further seven years (NICA 2020: para. 66).

The requirement for concurrent (though not necessarily simultaneous) consent north and south of the border creates additional uncertainties and challenges, as does the appropriate sequencing of referendums and negotiations over the terms of unification (including any necessary changes to the Irish Constitution) (Constitution Unit 2021: Part II).

In the event of a vote in favour of unification, legislation would be required in both the UK and Ireland to give effect to it. The 1998 Agreement requires the UK Government both to introduce *and support* legislation in the UK Parliament, but only the former obligation appears in the Northern Ireland Act, given the constitutional sensitivities around interference with proceedings in Parliament pursuant to Article 9 of the Bill of Rights of 1689, which precludes any proceedings in Parliament being impeached or questioned in any court. Should either the UK or Irish legislature fail to enact the necessary legislation, they would be in breach of the 1998 Agreement; if only one were to do so, Northern Ireland would once again become a disputed territory (Constitution Unit 2021: paras 4.56–4.52).

Whatever the outcome of a unification referendum, the 1998 Agreement creates two continuing obligations. First, whichever government has sovereignty in Northern Ireland must act with rigorous impartiality between, and secure parity of esteem for, both Unionist and Nationalist communities. Second, the right of the people of Northern Ireland to hold either British or Irish identities and citizenship, or both, must be respected (Secretary of State for Northern Ireland 1998: Articles 1(v) and 1(vi)). Thus, in the event of unification, these provisions would give the UK Government a continuing role in upholding the rights of British citizens in Ireland (Murray & O'Donoghue 2019: 188).

## Scottish independence

There is no equivalent for Scotland of section 1 of the Northern Ireland Act 1998. Yet it is central to contemporary Scottish nationalist thinking that Scots have a right to self-determination, deriving from a distinctive Scottish constitutional tradition based on popular rather than parliamentary sovereignty (see, e.g., Scottish Government 2019: 5). There is scant *legal* authority for this proposition (McHarg 2020: 433–437), nor is it likely that the right of self-determination in international law would encompass a right for Scotland to become independent. As the Canadian Supreme Court held in *Reference re Secession of Quebec* (Secession Reference 1998), where national minorities already enjoy a high degree of *internal* self-determination, such as is manifestly the case in relation both to Québec and to Scotland (albeit Scottish autonomy within the UK is not constitutionally guaranteed),[11] they do not also have a right to *external* self-determination. Nevertheless, there is plenty of *political* recognition of Scotland's right to self-determination.

Martin argues that

> since the resolution of the Irish question in 1921, . . . the British Union has been based on an assumption of the separate and collective consent of four constituent parts, each of which is free to withdraw its consent if it wants to.
>
> *(Martin 2021: 7)*[12]

In 1989, the cross-party Scottish Constitutional Convention proclaimed "the sovereign right of the Scottish people to determine the form of government best suited to their needs" (Campaign for a Scottish Assembly 1989), a claim which has been repeatedly endorsed since. The right of the people of Scotland to become independent has also been explicitly endorsed across the political spectrum, both within Scotland (e.g., Smith Commission 2014: para. 18) and by successive UK Prime Ministers over the past 30 years. As in Northern Ireland, devolution referendums held in Scotland in 1979 and 1997, and above all the 2014 independence referendum itself, provide powerful evidence of the existence of a *de facto* constitutional right to self-determination, exercisable by the people of Scotland alone.

The 2014 referendum came about essentially by chance, when the pro-independence SNP won an overall majority at the 2011 (devolved) Scottish Parliament elections. This was unexpected both because the proportional electoral system used for Scottish elections makes it difficult for a single party to gain a majority, and because public support for independence at the time was relatively low (between 24% and 35% – Keating & McEwen 2017: 8). Nevertheless, the UK Government accepted that its election victory gave the SNP a mandate to hold an independence referendum, as promised in its manifesto. No doubt an element of political calculation was involved: unionists expected an easy victory, and hence to take the idea of independence off the political agenda (Keating & McEwen 2017: 2). However, Ciaran Martin, the civil servant in charge of the UK Government's referendum negotiations, argues that it was inconceivable to UK Government ministers that the mandate could be ignored (Martin 2021: 12).

The UK Government did, though, dispute the Scottish Government's claim that it had the competence, within the terms of the devolution legislation set out in the Scotland Act of 1998, to organise a lawful referendum, arguing that only the UK Parliament had the authority to do so (UK Government 2012). This claim in turn was legally controversial (Torrance 2021a: chs 3 and 5), though it was generally agreed that it would be preferable to avoid the issue being settled in court. After months of negotiation, the UK and Scottish Governments signed the Edinburgh Agreement in October 2012 (UK Government/Scottish Government 2012). The UK Government agreed to amend the Scotland Act temporarily (by Order in Council under section 30 of the Act) to make it clear that the Scottish Parliament had power to legislate for a referendum, but subject to the oversight of the UK Electoral Commission, and conformity with UK electoral law. This enabled the Scottish Parliament to determine the date of the referendum, the question to be asked, the franchise, and the detailed campaign rules via the Scottish Independence Referendum (Franchise) Act 2013 and the Scottish Independence Referendum Act 2013.

After a long referendum campaign, 55% of the electorate voted No to independence. Although the process was essentially improvised, informed opinion concluded that it had worked well, with a very high level of civic engagement and no serious violence (Tierney 2015). While independence supporters may have lost the vote, they won the campaign (Mitchell 2016), cementing the independence question at the heart of Scottish political debate, as well as the SNP's dominance of Scottish electoral politics.

Had a majority voted for independence, the effect of the referendum would have been advisory only: further UK legislation would clearly have been required in order for Scotland to become independent. The Edinburgh Agreement committed both sides to respect the result, but this was not legally binding, and no pathway to independence was set out. The Scottish Government's position was that Westminster should pass enabling legislation, allowing the Scottish Parliament to make the necessary preparations for independence, including adopting an interim constitution, and to make the formal declaration of independence (Scottish Government 2014), but it is unclear whether the UK Government would have agreed. Some argued that there ought to be a second referendum on the terms of independence agreed between the two governments (see, e.g. Murkens et al. 2002: 31–35), but this did not find general favour, given the distorting effect that it might have on the initial vote and subsequent negotiations (Martin 2021: 34). Had

Scotland become independent, it is likely that the rest of the UK would have been treated as the continuing State, but an alternative analysis suggested that Scottish independence should be treated as a dissolution of, rather than secession from, the UK, thus creating two continuing States (Bell 2016). However, this, like other terms of independence, would have essentially been a matter for negotiation.

The opportunity was not taken after the 2014 vote to clarify either the circumstances in which a future Scottish independence referendum would be held, or the process to be followed. The circumstances leading to, and the conduct of, the 2014 referendum thus stand as powerful political precedents for what should happen in future, but they are not legally binding.

In fact, as already noted, Brexit ignited the case for a second referendum much sooner than expected. Given the centrality of the issue of maintaining an independent Scotland's membership of the European Union during the 2014 campaign (Douglas-Scott 2016), and the UK Government's refusal to make any concessions to the fact that a majority of Scottish voters opted to remain in the EU,[13] the Scottish Government regarded Brexit as a "material change in circumstances" justifying a second independence referendum. An initial request was made in March 2017 for another section 30 Order to allow the Scottish Parliament to enact the necessary legislation, and in December 2019, a request was made for a permanent transfer of competence to hold an independence referendum and powers to prepare for independence, along with statutory recognition of Scotland's right to self-determination, and a statutory duty on both the UK and Scottish Governments to co-operate in the implementation of a vote for independence (Scottish Government 2019). In anticipation of a second referendum, the Scottish Parliament enacted general framework legislation for regulating referendums in the Referendums (Scotland) Act of 2020, and in March 2021 a draft Bill was published to apply that framework to an independence referendum (Scottish Government 2021).

In its 2019 paper, the Scottish Government insisted both that the Scottish people had a right to self-determination, and that it had a mandate – given a majority of pro-independence parties in the Scottish Parliament (the SNP and Scottish Green Party) – to hold a referendum. That mandate was reinforced at the May 2021 Scottish Parliament elections. This time, though, the mandate has not been treated as decisive. UK Government ministers have given various reasons for rejecting the request for another referendum. Then Prime Minister Theresa May, in 2017, simply said "now is not the time", given the need to complete the Brexit process (others have cited the need to tackle the Covid-19 pandemic or the climate emergency). Her successor, Boris Johnson, claimed that the 2014 referendum was a "once in a generation event" (a period apparently varying anywhere between 25 and 50 years). Other ministers have stipulated the need for clear and consistent majority support for independence in opinion polls (see generally Torrance 2021a: ch. 6).

These responses are inconsistent, lacking any foundation in principle, and indeterminate in content, but what they have in common is the implicit insistence that it is for the UK Government, not the Scottish Government, to determine when – and whether – a second referendum should take place. A similar lack of principle and consistency can be seen in proposals by unionists to change the rules for a second referendum – whether to insist on a special majority, to change the question, or to alter the franchise – all of which smack of attempted gerrymandering.

In the face of UK Government intransigence, the Scottish Government has few options. It could attempt to legislate unilaterally for a referendum, but at the risk of legal challenge to the *vires* of such legislation, legislative override by the UK Parliament, a boycott by unionists, and/ or refusal by the UK Government to co-operate in the event of a vote for independence. Other non-referendum pathways to independence all suffer from similar problems (McCorkindale & McHarg 2021).

The independence process in Scotland is thus at a stalemate; likely to be broken only by a decisive change in public opinion for or against independence, or a change in political fortunes, either at the UK level – giving the SNP leverage to negotiate a second referendum – or in Scotland – taking demand for a second referendum off the agenda.

## Conclusion: regulating secession in the United Kingdom's constitution

The independence debate in Scotland is caught between rival claims to constitutional legitimacy and constitutional legality of a kind that proved disastrous in Ireland a century ago, and which the Belfast/Good Friday Agreement and Northern Ireland Act 1998 sought to resolve for Northern Ireland with – so far – a considerable degree of success. It is, however, striking how little read-across there is from the Northern Ireland settlement in debates about independence for Scotland. This raises the question whether there should be more systematic and consistent legal recognition and regulation of secession rights across the UK, and in fact several proposals have been made to that effect.

As Barber argues (Barber 2015: 5), most of the standard arguments against constitutionalising secession rights are inapplicable in the UK, given that the principle, and many of the contentious issues, about by whom and where the right to self-determination should be exercised have already been settled in practice. Nor can it reasonably be argued that constitutional regulation of secession has, in and of itself, been a destabilising force in Northern Ireland. By contrast, the absence of a clear constitutional path to independence in Scotland *is* destabilising. It enables the Scottish Government to maintain the threat of independence while avoiding a vote which it is not guaranteed to win. Meanwhile the perception that Scots' democratic rights are being denied may itself fuel support for independence.

There are, however, two major problems with proposals for a UK "Clarity Act"[14] (setting out, for example, when and by whom a referendum may be triggered, and the conditions for a successful secession vote). First, in the middle of a dispute about whether there should be a second Scottish independence referendum, it is likely to be difficult, if not impossible, to secure agreement on a set of secession rules. If permissive, they would hand a victory to the Scottish Government; if restrictive, they might be perceived as being intended simply to frustrate aspirations for independence. Secondly, a uniform solution would have to be consistent with the terms of the Belfast/Good Friday Agreement, yet a seven-year period between votes, and a duty to trigger a referendum based on bare-majority support for secession, are unlikely to commend themselves to unionists elsewhere in the UK.

Should the UK survive its current secessionist pressures, it may be that agreement can be reached at some point in the future on a set of rules which combine a reasonable degree of certainty and stability in the exercise of secession rights. But consistent regulation across all parts of the State seems unrealistic in light of the deep-seated asymmetry of the UK's territorial constitution.

In June 2022, after this chapter had been submitted, Scotland's Lord Advocate, at the request of the Scottish Government, and in an attempt to break the political stalemate, made a reference to the UK Supreme Court, asking whether the Scottish Parliament had the competence to legislate unilaterally for a second independence referendum. In November 2022, the Supreme Court ruled that such legislation would be ultra vires, and that the people of Scotland do not enjoy a right to external self-determination under international law (*Reference by the Lord Advocate of Devolution Issues Under Paragraph 34 of Schedule 6 to the Scotland Act 1998* [2022] UKSC 31). Scotland's constitutional pathway towards independence therefore remains uncertain.

# Notes

* I am grateful to Oran Doyle for his comments on an earlier draft of this chapter, and for sharing with me, in draft, a paper that addresses similar issues (see Doyle 2022).
1 In the poll, 99% voted to remain in the UK, but the poll was boycotted by the (minority) Nationalist community.
2 In *Madzimbamuto v. Lardner Burke*, concerning the legality of the unilateral declaration of independence by the government of Southern Rhodesia in 1965, the Judicial Committee of the Privy Council made clear that the UK Parliament was not obliged to accept it (Madzimbamuto v. Lardner-Burke 1969).
3 Support for secession in Wales is much lower than in Scotland or Northern Ireland, albeit also increased since Brexit, and independence is being considered as a possible constitutional future for Wales by the Independent Commission on the Constitutional Future of Wales established by the (unionist) Welsh Government in November 2021.
4 English independence is currently very much a fringe movement. However, there has in recent years been a growth in English national consciousness, one manifestation of which is greater relaxation about the break-up of the UK through independence for the minority nations. See Henderson & Wyn Jones (2021).
5 The franchise had been extended in 1793, but property qualifications still privileged Anglicans over Catholics and other Protestant denominations.
6 Such was his opposition to Home Rule that the eminent Victorian jurist, A.V. Dicey – hitherto the arch-defender of the unlimited sovereignty of Parliament – was converted to the case for a (UK-wide) referendum before a Home Rule Bill could be regarded as constitutionally acceptable (see McLean 2010).
7 The name of the state was formally changed to the United Kingdom of Great Britain and Northern Ireland by the Parliamentary and Royal Titles Act 1927.
8 Support for an independent Northern Ireland, as an alternative to Dublin rule, has been a minor strand within Unionist constitutional thinking (see Mitchell 2009: 68–69, 177).
9 Notably, the devolved Northern Ireland Assembly has no formal role to play in authorising a referendum, though a vote in the Assembly is likely to carry considerable political weight – Constitution Unit 2021: paras 8.26–8.31).
10 More accurately, the Secretary of State must lay a draft Order in Council before Parliament providing for a poll to be held, but technically this could be vetoed by either House of Parliament (Northern Ireland Act 1998, s.96(2)), albeit this is highly unlikely in practice. I am grateful to Oran Doyle for drawing this to my attention.
11 The Scotland Act 2016, s. 1, states that the devolved institutions in Scotland are "a permanent part of the United Kingdom's constitutional arrangements" which "are not to be abolished except on the basis of a decision of the people of Scotland voting in a referendum." However, these provisions are almost certainly not legally enforceable.
12 For Scotland, as for Ireland, this was not always the case: the 1715 and 1745 Jacobite Rebellions were brutally suppressed by the British authorities.
13 In stark contrast to Northern Ireland, where the Northern Ireland Protocol to the EU Withdrawal Agreement makes special arrangements to keep the province inside the EU single market and customs union.
14 The terminology, but not necessarily the content, is borrowed from Canada (see Johnson, Chapter 39, this volume).

# References

Barber, N. W. 2015, "The Constitutional Regulation of Scottish Secession", Oxford Legal Studies Research Paper No 38/2015.
Bell, C. 2016, "International Law, the Independence Debate, and Political Settlement in the UK", in A. McHarg et al. (eds), *The Scottish Independence Referendum: Constitutional and Political Implications*, Oxford: Oxford University Press: 197.
Boland v. An Taoiseach 1974, Supreme Court of Ireland, *Boland v. An Taoiseach* [1974] I.R. 338.
Byrne v. Ireland 1972, Supreme Court of Ireland, *Byrne v. Ireland* [1972] I.R. 241.
Campaign for a Scottish Assembly 1989, *A Claim of Right for Scotland.*

Coffey, D. 2016, "1916, 1921 and the 'Destruction of the Legal Unity of the British Empire'", *Dublin University Law Journal*, 39: 333.

Constitution Unit 2021, *Working Group on Unification Referendums on the Island of Ireland: Final Report*, London.

Dicey, A. V. 1886, *England's Case Against Home Rule*, Richmond: The Richmond Publishing Co. Limited (reprinted from the 1886 edition in 1973).

Douglas-Scott, S. 2016, "Scotland, Secession and the European Union", in A. McHarg et al. (eds), *The Scottish Independence Referendum: Constitutional and Political Implications*, Oxford: Oxford University Press: 175.

Doyle, O. 2022, "Leaving the Union: Constitutionalising Secession Rights in the United Kingdom", *Federalismi.it* (Special Issue: The Constitutional Implications of Brexit), 10: 222.

Evans, G. 2020, "Debating Welsh Independence: The Political and Constitutional Pathways to a Referendum", *United Kingdom Constitutional Law Blog*, 29 July 2020.

Henderson, A. & Wyn Jones, R. 2021, *Englishness: The Political Force Transforming Britain*, Oxford: Oxford University Press.

Keating, M. 2001, *Plurinational Democracy: Stateless Nations in a Post-Sovereignty Era*, Oxford: Oxford University Press.

Keating, M. & McEwen, N. 2017, "The Scottish Independence Debate", in M. Keating (ed), *Debating Scotland: Issues of Independence and Union in the 2014 Referendum*, Oxford: Oxford University Press: 1.

MacCormick v. Lord Advocate 1953, Inner House of the Court of Session, *MacCormick v. Lord Advocate* [1953] S.L.T. 396.

Madzimbamuto v. Lardner-Burke 1969, Judicial Committee of the Privy Council, *Madzimbamuto v. Lardner-Burke*, [1969] A.C. 645.

Mansergh, N. 1940, *The Irish Question 1840–1921*, London: George Allen & Unwin Ltd.

Mansergh, N. 1991, *The Unresolved Question: The Anglo-Irish Settlement and Its Undoing 1912–72*, New Haven: Yale University Press.

Martin, C. 2021, *Resist, Reform or Re-Run? Short- and Long-Term Reflections on Scotland and Independence Referendums*, Oxford: Blavatnik School of Government, University of Oxford.

McCorkindale, C. & McHarg, A. 2021, "Constitutional Pathways to a Second Independence Referendum", in E. Hepburn et al. (eds), *Scotland's New Choice: Independence after Brexit*, Edinburgh: Centre on Constitutional Change: 34.

McGimpsey v. Ireland 1990, Supreme Court of Ireland, *McGimpsey v. Ireland* [1990] I.R.L.M. 440.

McHarg, A. 2020, "The Declaration of Arbroath and Scots Law", in K. P. Müller (ed.), *Scotland and Arbroath 1320–2020*, Berlin: Peter Lang GmbH: 423.

McLean, I. 2010, "The Contradictions of Professor Dicey", in I. McLean (ed.), *What's Wrong with the British Constitution?*, Oxford: Oxford University Press: 128.

McLean, I. & Lubbock, T. 2010, "The Curious Incident of the Guns in the Night Time", in I. McLean (ed.), *What's Wrong with the British Constitution?*, Oxford: Oxford University Press: 100.

McLean, I. & McMillan, A. 2010, "1707 and 1800: A Treaty (Mostly) Honoured and a Treaty Broken", in I. McLean (ed.), *What's Wrong with the British Constitution?*, Oxford: Oxford University Press: 47.

Mitchell, A. 2002, "Alternative Government: 'Exit Britannia' – the Formation of the Irish National State, 1918–21", in J. Augusteijn (ed), *The Irish Revolution 1913–1923*, Basingstoke: Palgrave: 70.

Mitchell, J. 2009, *Devolution in the UK*, Manchester: Manchester University Press.

Mitchell, J. 2016, "The Referendum Campaign", in A. McHarg et al. (eds), *The Scottish Independence Referendum: Constitutional and Political Implications*, Oxford: Oxford University Press: 75.

Mohn, T. 2016, "The Irish Question and the Evolution of British Imperial Law 1916–22", *Dublin University Law Journal*, 39: 405.

Murkens, J. E. K. et al., 2002, *Scottish Independence: A Practical Guide*, Edinburgh: Edinburgh University Press.

Murray, C. R. G. 2021, "The Constitutional Significance of the People of Northern Ireland", in O. Doyle, A. McHarg & J. E. K. Murkens (eds), *The Brexit Challenge for Ireland and the United Kingdom: Constitutions Under Pressure*, Cambridge: Cambridge University Press: 108.

Murray, C. R. G. & O'Donoghue, A. 2019, "Life after Brexit: Operationalising the Belfast/Good Friday Agreement's Principle of Consent", *Dublin University Law Journal*, 42: 147–190.

NICA 2020, Northern Island Court of Appeal, *Re McCord (Border Poll)* [2020] NICA 23.

NICA 2022, Northern Island Court of Appeal, *Re Allister and Others for Judicial Review* [2022] NICA 15.

O'Donoghue, M. 2019, "'Ireland's Independence Day': The 1918 Election Campaign in Ireland and the Wilsonian Moment", *European Review of History*, 26: 834.

R (Miller) v. Secretary of State 2018, United Kingdom Supreme Court, *R (Miller) v. Secretary of State for Exiting the European Union* [2018] A.C. 61.

Reid, W. 2017, "Democracy, Sovereignty and Unionist Political Thought during the Revolutionary Period in Ireland c.1912–1922", *Transactions of the Royal Historical Society*, 27: 211.

Rokkan, S. & Urwin, D. W. 1982, "Introduction: Centres and Peripheries in Western Europe", in S. Rokkan & D. Urwin (eds), *The Politics of Territorial Identity: Studies in European Regionalism*, London: Sage Publications Ltd: 1.

Saunders, R. 2013, "Tory Rebels and Tory Democracy: The Ulster Crisis, 1900–14", in R. Carr & B. W. Hart (eds), *The Foundations of the British Conservative Party: Essays on Conservatism from Lord Salisbury to David Cameron*, London: Bloomsbury Academic: 65.

Scottish Government 2014, *The Scottish Independence Bill: A Consultation on an Interim Constitution for Scotland*.

Scottish Government 2019, *Scotland's Right to Choose: Putting Scotland's Future in Scotland's Hands*.

Scottish Government 2021, *Draft Independence Referendum Bill*.

Secession Reference 1998, Supreme Court of Canada, *Reference Re Secession of Quebec*, [1998] 2 S.C.R. 217.

Secretary of State for Northern Ireland 1998, *The Belfast Agreement: An Agreement Reached at the Multi-Party Talks on Northern Ireland*, Cmnd 3883.

Smith Commission 2014, *Report of the Smith Commission for Further Devolution of Powers to the Scottish Parliament*.

Tierney, S. 2005, *Constitutional Law and National Pluralism*, Oxford: University Press.

Tierney, S. 2015, "Direct Democracy in the United Kingdom: Reflections from the Scottish Independence Referendum", *Public Law*: 663.

Torrance, D. 2020, *Parliament and Northern Ireland, 1921–2021*, House of Commons Library, CBP 8884.

Torrance, D. 2021a, *Scottish Independence Referendum: Legal Issues*, House of Commons Library, CBP 9104.

Torrance, D. 2021b, *The Anglo-Irish Treaty, 1921*, House of Commons Library, CBP 9260.

Townsend, C. 2002, "Historiography: Telling the Irish Revolution", in J. Augusteijn (ed), *The Irish Revolution 1913–1923*, Basingstoke: Palgrave: 1.

UK Government 2012, *Scotland's Constitutional Future: A Consultation on Facilitating a Legal, Fair and Decisive Referendum on Whether Scotland Should Leave the United Kingdom*, CM 8203.

UK Government/Scottish Government 2012, *Agreement between the United Kingdom Government and the Scottish Government on a Referendum on Independence for Scotland*.

# 42

# CONSTITUTIONAL LAW AND SECESSION IN SPAIN

*Elisenda Casañas-Adam*

## Introduction

This chapter will discuss the Spanish constitutional framework and the debates surrounding its application to attempts to secede from the Spanish state. For this, it will begin with a brief discussion of origins of the Spanish Constitution of 1978, with a focus on the territorial question and the establishment of the State of the Autonomies. Next, it will discuss the attempts to begin a secession process by the Basque Country, and the ongoing Catalan secession process. It will then move on to consider the concept of the 'Right to Decide' as an alternative to the right to self-determination in this context, and the different legal avenues used by these movements to try to secure a referendum on independence. The final section will discuss the response of the central authorities and the case law of the Constitutional Court in this context, with some considerations looking to the future. Overall, it will argue that the questions of whether, and if so, how, secession is possible under the Spanish Constitution in response to sustained and democratically expressed support for such an option in a sub-state nation or unit has not yet been successfully resolved.

## The Spanish Constitution of 1978: context and relevant provisions for the secession debate

The Spanish state was constructed through the union of independent crowns going back to the fifteenth century, and the territorial organisation of the state has been a source of ongoing conflict throughout Spanish constitutional history. The current 1978 Constitution was the result of the consensus between different political forces in a peaceful transition to democracy after 40 years of dictatorship, including representatives of Spain's three historical nations, Catalonia, the Basque Country and Galicia (Ferreres Comella 2013). The Constitution provided for a new territorial model, known as the 'State of the Autonomies', which is also a reflection of this compromise, enabling the establishment a quasi-federal system with some elements of recognition of the plurinational nature of the state (Aja Fernandez 2014). This model has developed into a fully decentralised state composed of 17 Autonomous Communities (ACs), each with their corresponding parliament and government, regulated in their Statute of Autonomy. The resolution of conflicts between the AC's and the central authorities over the interpretation of the

DOI: 10.4324/9781003036593-49

Constitution is conferred on the Constitutional Court, which has played a fundamental role in the establishment of the system (Casañas-Adam 2017). As part of this framework, however, there is no specific reference to secession or to the self-determination of Spain's sub-state nations or territories. In this sense, there is neither a secession clause nor a procedure enabling a sub-state unit to secede from the rest of Spain, but this is also not explicitly prohibited in the constitutional text. A suggestion that a secession clause be included during the constituent debates of 1978 was rejected by a majority of MPs participating in the drafting process.[1] As a result, the question of whether secession of a sub-state nation or unit is possible under the Spanish Constitution, and if so, what are the legal avenues thought which it can be attained, is the object of ongoing political and academic debate.

More specifically, debates about secession, self-determination and the Spanish Constitution revolve around three different sets of constitutional provisions. The first of these sets of constitutional provisions are those set out in the Constitution's Preliminary Title, which establish the foundations of the constitutional system (Ferreres Comella 2013). Three of its sections are central to this debate: Art. 1.1, establishes Spain as a *social and democratic State*, subject to the rule of law' (. . .); Art. 1.2 states that 'National *sovereignty is vested in the Spanish people*'; and Art. 2 of the Constitution states that it is based on 'the indissoluble *unity of the Spanish Nation*, the common and indivisible homeland of all Spaniards' but at the same time 'recognizes and guarantees the right to *self-government of the nationalities* and regions of which it is composed and the solidarity among them all'. The term 'nationality' was included as a compromise term to give some recognition to the minority nations in the Constitution, in acknowledgement of the plurinational nature of the State. However, various scholars have highlighted that the final version of this provision, and in particular the reference to the 'indissoluble unity of the Spanish nation', was imposed on the drafters through the central government in response to initial proposals that simply referred to the self-government of nationalities and regions (López Bofill 2019). This a clear reflection of the influence of the previous regime on the constituent process, and of the strongly contrasting views on the territorial model at that time. The inclusion of the emphasis on political unity was therefore aimed at avoiding any future interpretations that might bestow sovereignty on any other nation than the Spanish nation, thus opening the door to legitimising secession.

To date, there is also no constitutional or legal definition of the term 'nationality' as included in Art. 2 of the Constitution. The opportunity for the Constitutional Court to provide an interpretation this section in accordance with Spain's plurinational reality arose in the context of a challenge to a reform of Catalonia's Statute of Autonomy in 2010, which included the statement in its Preamble that 'the Catalan Parliament had defined Catalonia as a nation'. However, although the court acknowledged that Catalonia could be considered a nation in the wider sociological or political sense, it distinguished this from the strict legal-constitutional sense.[2] It then went on to state that in this (legal-constitutional) sense, 'the Constitution does not recognize any other than the Spanish nation' (FJ 12). This interpretation, and the court's unfortunate statement, denied any legal relevance to the status of Spain's historical nations under the Constitution, and therefore provided the basis for arguments that there are no distinct sub-state peoples or nations in Spain who could be entitled to secede. This interpretation, however, stands in stark contrast with comparative scholarship on western plurinational states which commonly focuses on Spain as one of its main examples (Keating 2001, Tierney 2004).

As the two most significant secessionist attempts in Spain since 1978 have involved proposals for a sub-state referendum on the constitutional future on an AC, the second set of constitutional provisions that are of relevance for debates on secession are those that provide the constitutional regulation of referendums. Here two sections are of particular significance. The first of these sections confers *exclusive competence* on the State over the '*Authorization* of popular consultations through the holding of *referendums*' (Art. 149.1.32). In addition, there is a general provision enabling the central government to submit political decisions of special importance to *all citizens* in a consultative referendum (Art. 92.1). However, the Constitution also provides for the celebration of referendums at the AC level, for the enactment or amendment of a Statute of Autonomy (Arts. 151.2.iii, 152.2). In this context, the debates revolve around the potential for ACs to be recognised or conferred competences to hold a referendum or another form or citizen consultation that could enable the corresponding AC citizens to express their views, or make a decision, on the AC's secession.

The third set of provisions that are of relevance for the question of secession in the aforementioned context are the procedures for reform of the Constitution itself. The Constitution provides two different procedures for its amendment, which depend on the object and scope of the proposed reform (Ferreres Comella 2013). The more rigid procedure, which applies to a total reform (the drafting of a new Constitution) or to the reform of certain core elements, requires the approval by two-thirds of both chambers of the central parliament (Congress and Senate) in two successive parliaments (the first must be dissolved after the vote and new elections held) and ratification by referendum by all Spanish citizens (Art. 168). This procedure would apply to any attempts to reform Arts. 1 and 2, and therefore to any attempt to amend the conferral of sovereignty on the Spanish people or the reference to the 'indissoluble unity of the Spanish Nation'. The insurmountable barriers involved in this process are also highlighted as another example of the pressures and concerns for safeguarding unity in the constitutional drafting process (López Bofill 2019). The amendment of the rest of the Constitution's provisions, including those relating to the State of the Autonomies, requires a majority of three-fifths of each chamber and, if one-tenth of the members of one chamber requests it, ratification by referendum (Art. 167). The ACs' participation in the constitutional reform process is limited to being able to propose a reform of the Constitution, either by filing a Bill directly to the central parliament or by requesting the central government to do so (Arts. 167 and 87). Indeed, despite the involvement of the Senate in both processes, it is generally accepted that, as currently organised, this is not a chamber of territorial representation. For those who argue that secession is not possible under the Constitution in its current form, the amendment process is the only option available for any sub-state referendums and/or secession processes, but there are also significant debates about at what stage, or in what order, these should be carried out.

## Secessionist challenges: from the Basque Country to Catalonia

Since the drafting of the 1978 Constitution, Spain has faced two significant challenges of the 'sovereigntist' nature, directed at securing a degree of rupture or 'secession' of one part of the Spanish territory from the rest of the state. In both cases, the challenge was led by the democratically elected AC institutions, therefore reflecting strong citizen support in the corresponding AC, and resulting in a conflict between the AC and central authorities. The first of these arose in the Basque Country, when the Basque Government put forward what became known as the *Ibarretxe Plan* (named after the then President of the Basque Government, who was behind it). The initial aim of the plan was to draft a new 'political statute' for the Basque Country, which would give it a 'confederal' legal-political status within Spain, to be negotiated and agreed with the Spanish authorities (Keating and Bray 2006, López Basaguren 2009). However, while the draft was approved by the Basque Parliament, it was defeated by a substantial majority in the Spanish Congress. The Basque Government then moved to promote the holding of a referendum on the political status of the Basque Country, and the Basque Parliament enacted a 'Statute of Consultations' to that end, which was struck down by the Constitutional Court.[3] Ibarretxe then called for early elections to reinforce his position but did not obtain a majority to form government again, and the process came to an end.

The second and more long-standing 'sovereigntist' challenge arose in Catalonia and is still ongoing at the time of this writing (Bossacoma Busquets and López Bofill 2016, Alberti Rovira 2019). Support for independence in Catalonia started increasing significantly after the Constitutional Court invalidated part of its reformed Statute of Autonomy and became the objective of its governing institutions after the Catalan elections of 2012. In 2013, the Catalan Parliament adopted the 'Declaration of Sovereignty and the Right to Decide of the Catalan People', initiating a process to try to reach an agreement with the central authorities to hold an independence referendum.[4] An initial attempt to hold the referendum in 2014 was deemed unconstitutional and therefore became a 'citizen's participation process', resulting in a low turnout. In response, the Catalan Government announced that the 2015 elections would be treated as a referendum and when the pro-independence parties won the majority of seats (but not of votes), the Catalan Parliament passed a resolution declaring the start of the independence process.[5] The President of the Catalan Government then announced that a binding referendum on independence would be held on 1 October 2017. In preparation for an eventual vote in favour of independence, the Catalan Parliament passed two laws, the 'Law creating an independent republic' and the 'transition law', to provide for the period of transition to an independent state.[6] The referendum of 1 October went ahead, despite being suspended by the Constitutional Court and the Spanish Government sending riot police to intervene and remove ballot boxes from polling stations. On 10 October, the President of Catalonia declared the independence of Catalonia but suspended its effects, and just over two weeks later, the Catalan Parliament – without the representatives from most of the unionist parties, who left in protest – voted to approve a resolution declaring independence from Spain.

The response of the Spanish authorities to the Catalan process and referendum is well known (Bossacoma Busquets 2021). On the day of voting on the independence resolution in the Catalan Parliament, the Spanish Government declared the suspension of Catalan self-government, in application of Art. 155 of the Spanish Constitution, dissolved the Parliament, and called new elections for the end of the year. The leaders of the Catalan independence process, including those from its institutions of self-government and civil society organisations, either left Spain for self-exile or were tried for rebellion, sedition and misuse of public funds, resulting in prison terms ranging from 9 to 13 years. However, the two successive elections to the Catalan Parliament held after the referendum (2017 and 2021) have again returned a pro-independence majority committed to the holding of another referendum and securing independence. On the other hand, a change in the governing party in the central institutions in 2017 led to a more conciliatory approach, followed by the restarting of negotiations and the pardon of those convicted for their role in the referendum. But the strong disagreement between the central and Catalan authorities on the compatibility of holding an independence referendum with the constitutional framework remains, highlighting that the crisis is not yet resolved.

## Potential basis for, and avenues to, secession under the Spanish Constitution

In response to the central authorities' refusal to engage with their requests, a distinctive feature of sovereignist or secessionist processes in the Spanish context is that they have been based on the construction of a new democracy-based 'right to decide' of the citizens on sub-state units in democratic systems (López 2011, Ridao Martin 2014, Barceló Serramaleda 2015, Barceló Serramaleda et al. 2015). This new right was initially referred to in the Basque process and was then further developed and became central to Catalonia's requests for a referendum, with a strong presence in social mobilisations, institutional action and scholarly work alike. In this context, the 'right to decide' is defined as the right of the citizens of Catalonia to express themselves collectively on the possible secession of the Catalan territory from Spain, and to have their view taken into consideration in the determination of Catalonia's constitutional future. While it is defined as a 'right', it is at the same time framed as nothing more than the formulation of pre-existing constitutional rights in a democratic state, and finds its basis in different provisions of the Constitution, such as the regulation of freedom of expression (Art. 20), the right of citizens to participate directly in public affairs (Art. 23) and fundamentally in the democratic principle (Art. 1). The right to decide is therefore understood as distinct from the right to self-determination, which scholars highlight has evolved, in particular in international law, to be understood as applying generally to postcolonial settings. Defined in this way, it builds on the principles and processes that governed the Québec referendums of 1980 and 1995 in Canada, the Canadian Supreme Court's secession reference of 1998, and the Scottish in independence referendum process in 2014 in the United Kingdom.

The 'right to decide' was central to the Basque Parliament's proposed referendum, where one of the questions to be posed to citizens requested their views on reaching an agreement on the exercise of the 'right to decide of the Basque people' (Keating and Bray 2006, López Basaguren 2016). It then featured prominently in the Resolutions of the Catalan Parliament that have paved the way for the secessionist process. In 2012, its Resolution on the General Political Orientation of Catalonia declared that 'Catalonia must commence a new era based on the right to decide' (par. 2).[7] Following this, in its high-profile 'Declaration of Sovereignty and the Right to Decide' in 2013, it declared that, in accordance with the will of the democratically expressed majority of the people in Catalonia, the Parliament of Catalonia agreed to initiate the process to exercise the right to decide, so that the people of Catalonia may decide their collective political future.[8] It was also clearly present in civil society and citizen mobilisations in Catalonia. For example, the first pro-independence march after the Constitutional Court's Statute of Autonomy decision was headed by a banner that read 'We are a nation, we decide' (Guibernau 2012).

However, the right to decide has been criticised by different scholars, including some that are generally supportive of the pro-referendum movement, on various grounds. The main criticisms focus on the indeterminacy or ductility of this right, which sometimes is limited to the right to express an opinion on secession, while in others it appears to extend to the right to break away from the host state, and on its excessive reliance on the principle of democracy above all other constitutional rights and principles (Tornos Mas 2015, Ferreres Comella 2016, Torbisco Casals 2017, Bossacoma Busquets 2020). It has also been argued that it is misleading in the Catalan context, as the claims being put forward are in reality claims for self-determination (Bossacoma Busquets 2020). As the Catalan process developed, and in the light of the refusal of the Spanish authorities to engage with the process, the 'right to decide' also became the basis for the articulation of more radical understandings of its content and role, and of the move to a unilateral pathway to independence.[9] Furthermore, in the final stages of the referendum process, the focus of the Catalan institutions moved from the right to decide to the right to self-determination, while still maintaining the strong democratic basis for their claims.[10] This, therefore, appears to blur the initial distinction between both rights.

It is on the basis of the right to decide that a number of constitutionally compatible mechanisms to allow a Catalan independence referendum to take place were developed. In 2013, the Institute of Autonomic Studies of Barcelona, a prestigious research institute linked to the Catalan Government, highlighted five different procedures through which Catalonia could hold a referendum on its constitutional future, in the exercise of its 'right to decide'.[11] The various options involved varied degrees of legal complexity, and also of intervention of the central authorities in the process, and were drawn from proposals of, and supported by, reputed constitutional law scholars from within and outside Catalonia (Bossacoma Busquets and López Bofill 2016, Ridao Martin 2014, Vintró 2013). Overall, they highlighted that there existed plausible alternative interpretations of the Constitution to the one put forward by the central authorities which would enable, at least, the holding of an independence referendum. In brief, the first mechanism proposed was to base the referendum on the previously enacted Catalan statute on referendums, drafted by the Catalan Parliament to enable it to intervene in this area, and which had been challenged by the central authorities before the Constitutional Court.[12] The second mechanism was to use the procedure for consultative referendums provided for in Art. 92 of the Constitution. The third proposal was to use the constitutional mechanism for the transfer of competences to the Catalan institutions of self-government under Art. 150 of the Constitution. The fourth would be to hold a non-referendary consultation of citizens, therefore avoiding the strict legal requirements for referendums. The fifth and final mechanism proposed was to reform the Constitution to include the provision for consultative referendums for Autonomous Communities. The report then recommended that the Catalan authorities negotiate with the central ones to decide on the most appropriate option.

Taking into consideration the aforementioned proposals, the Catalan Government tried to find a consensual, negotiated and constitutionally compatible avenue to hold its referendum. On 16 January 2014, the Catalan Parliament passed a proposal to request the Spanish Parliament for the transfer of the competence to 'authorise, hold and call consultative referendum so that the Catalans may express themselves on the collective political future of Catalonia'.[13] This was rejected by a majority in the Spanish Parliament, with the Spanish Prime Minister arguing that neither the delegation of competence requested nor the object of the proposed referendum was compatible with the constitutional framework.[14] Due to the central authorities' refusal to enter into a dialogue on the referendum, the Catalan Government decided to hold a non-referendary consultation, which would avoid any requirement for authorisation or intervention by the central authorities. To that end, the Catalan Parliament enacted the Catalan Statute 10/2014 on Non-referendary consultations, which was passed on 19 September 2014. This was followed by the Catalan Decree 129/2014, which called for a non-referendary consultation on the political future of Catalonia. Both the Statute and the Decree were challenged before the Constitutional Court by the Spanish Government, who initially suspended their validity and then struck down most of their provisions. The invalidation of the legal basis for the consultation led to its being converted into a 'citizens participation process', and then to the 'plebiscitary elections' and subsequent adoption of the more radical unilateral referendum route.

In this context, another notable feature of the Catalan process and its articulation of the 'right to decide' was that it was framed by reference to the European Union's broader constitutional framework, seeking to make use of relevant aspects of EU principles and to bring in the EU institutions as intermediaries between Catalonia and the central state (Casañas-Adam et al. 2018). The European focus of the referendum process can be seen in the Catalan Parliament's initial Resolutions, firstly urging the Catalan Government, political forces and social and economic agents to build the maximum consensus 'in dialogue with the international community, the European Union and the Spanish government'; and secondly, in the adoption of the 'Declaration of Sovereignty and the Right to Decide of the people of Catalonia', where 'Europeanism' was included as one of the main principles for the process, stating that 'The founding principles of the European Union will be defended and promoted, particularly the fundamental rights of citizens, democracy, the commitment to the welfare state and solidarity among the various peoples of Europe'.[15] The Catalan Parliament therefore not only framed the referendum as a

European-wide issue but made explicit reference to EU principles as facilitating the process and providing a more flexible and accommodating legal framework, which would be more responsive to Catalan demands. The Catalan Government also appealed directly to the EU Member States and institutions for assistance, and for them to act as mediators between themselves and the Spanish authorities in order to enable the referendum to go ahead. However, as is well known, the EU institutions and representatives took the position that this was an 'internal constitutional issue' for Spain to resolve, and they largely sided with the position of the Spanish authorities (Casañas-Adam et al. 2018).

## The state's response to 'secessionist challenges': the Constitutional Court's case law on secession and the constitution

As seen earlier, the central authorities' main strategy in responding to requests, proposals and initiatives from the ACs in this context was to refuse to engage with them and to challenge any unilateral AC initiative before the Constitutional Court. This placed the resolution of the conflicts arising from the secession attempts in the hands of the Constitutional Court, and it is the court's decisions arising from these processes that set out the current legal position on secession and constitutional law in Spain. Its initial case law on secession arose in the context of the Basque Country, and of the statute legislating for a popular consultation on the future status of the Basque Country enacted by the Basque Parliament in 2008. In response to the challenge by the Spanish Government, the court declared the statute unconstitutional and set out its initial doctrine on the validity of referendums in this context.[16] First, the court declared that only the Spanish Government could authorise a referendum, and in accordance with art. 149.1.32 of the Constitution, there were no implicit AC competences in this area. Furthermore, it declared that a non-binding instrument for popular consultation where the electorate is called on to give its opinion on a matter of political importance will still be a referendum, even if called something different, and the aforementioned requirements will apply. Second, and in response to the reference to the 'right to decide of the Basque people', the court argued that certain matters that affect the foundations of the constitutional order, such as the unity of the Spanish nation (Art. 2) or the conferral of sovereignty on the Spanish people (Art. 1), could not be submitted to referendum, even with the authorisation of the Spanish Government. The reasoning behind this point was that the referendum could not be used to consider issues that would require constitutional reform, as this would alter the corresponding procedure of constitutional reform itself by introducing a referendum at an early stage, which is not provided for in the Constitution (Ferreres Comella 2016). Third, the court noted that there are no material limits to the reform of the Constitution; therefore, the Basque proposal could be accommodated by the constitutional framework, as long as the appropriate procedures for constitutional reform were followed. In this case, the appropriate procedure would be the more rigid procedure in Art. 168 CE.

This was the court's established position on these issues until the 'Catalan Process' generated a series of more recent and extensive case law. The first decision of particular relevance is the initial challenge to the Catalan Parliament's 'Declaration of Sovereignty and the Right to Decide of the People of Catalonia' in 2014 (Fossas Espadaler 2014, Ferreres Comella 2014).[17] In this decision, the court distinguished between two separate parts of the declaration. On the one hand, it invalidated the part that referred to the principle of sovereignty, on the basis that the conferral of sovereignty on the Catalan people contradicted Art. 1 of the Constitution, which establishes that national sovereignty is ascribed to the Spanish people, and Art. 2, which states that the Constitution rests on the indissoluble unity of the Spanish nation. As a consequence, the court declared that a region in Spain cannot unilaterally call a referendum on self-determination to decide on its integration in Spain. Interestingly, the court referred to the Canadian Supreme Court's 1998 secession reference opinion to support its own decision, but as various scholars have highlighted, it did so with some confusion (Ferreres Comella 2014). Indeed, the Spanish Constitutional Court failed to distinguish clearly between the question of whether a region can secede unilaterally, and that of whether it can hold an independence referendum. While the Canadian Supreme court stated that Québec could not secede unilaterally, it did not question the legality of the referendums held unilaterally in the region in 1980 and 1995.

On the other hand, however, the court upheld the part of the declaration on the 'right to decide', with a series of considerations that seemed to point to a change in its approach to these conflicts. For this, the court considered that the reference to this right has to be considered in the light of the general legal context of the declaration, which included a commitment to a number of principles, among them, the principles of legality and dialogue. The court then declared that if the right to decide was a political aspiration to be exercised within the existing legal framework, it was not in violation of the Constitution. The court referred here again to its existing case law, stating that Spain was not a militant democracy, and that all political programmes and aspirations could be defended in the public sphere as long as they were pursued through legal and constitutional procedures. But the court went further, declaring that the problems that arise when a particular territory wants to change its legal status cannot be resolved by the Constitutional Court, and that they must be resolved by the different territorial powers that make up the State of the Autonomies, through dialogue and cooperation. It also noted that a broad understanding of dialogue did not exclude any legitimate institutions or any procedure that respected the constitutional framework. Invoking the constitutional principles of institutional cooperation and loyalty, it stated that if region submitted a proposal for constitutional reform, the Spanish Parliament should 'take it into account' (FJ 4). However, it did not specify what procedures could lead to such a proposal, or the conditions or consequences of this duty of taking such a proposal into consideration.

This decision was well received by both the Spanish and Catalan Governments. The Spanish Government saw it as confirming the court's earlier case law on the need for the Constitution to be reformed for the Spanish authorities to be able to authorise a Catalan independence referendum. The Catalan Government, in contrast, saw this decision as qualifying the court's previous case law on this issue and suggesting that a Catalan independence referendum could be authorised by the Spanish authorities as a first step in the exercise of the 'right to decide'. If a majority of Catalan citizens then expressed a preference for independence, this would then trigger the necessary process of reform of the Constitution that would enable secession to take place. As Ferreres Comella notes, the court did not explicitly address this issue in its decision, therefore leaving room for disagreement on its interpretation (Ferreres Comella 2014).

However, this was only the first in a long line of Constitutional Court decisions on the Catalan process. De Miguel Bárcena documents up 32 different court decisions resulting from the confrontation between the Catalan authorities and the Spanish Government in this context (Miguel Bárcena 2018). These included challenges to the enactment of a Catalan Statute on Non-referendary Consultations, the Decree regulating the holding of a consultation on Catalonia's constitutional future, and the Catalan Government's actions with reference to what became a citizen's participation event. Following these decisions, the court's decision on the challenge to the resolution adopted by the new Catalan Parliament elected via 'plebiscitary elections' is also of notable significance, and its tone and approach to the Catalan process is very different to the one adopted in its other prominent decision just under two years earlier.[18] The court, again, declared the unconstitutionality of the self-recognition of sovereignty by an AC, noting that in the

Constitution, sovereignty is conferred exclusively on the Spanish people, who is indivisible. In response to the democratic arguments in the declaration, it stressed that 'the unconditional primacy of the Constitution also protects the democratic principle, as the safeguard of the integrity of the Constitution must be seen, at the same time, as the preservation of due respect to popular will'(FJ 5). This decision, from the court's perspective at least, put an end to the doubts regarding what were the 'preparatory acts' that could lead to a reform of the Constitution to include the recognition of the right to secession or secession itself. There was no further mention of the need for dialogue and cooperation, or of the constitution requiring the central authorities to take into account the ACs' claims. The court simply stated that the legislative assemblies of the ACs could exercise their right to initiate a constitutional reform process, which would lead to a debate inside and out of the institutions on any political project, including secession. Nonetheless, the realisation of that project would need to follow the established rigid procedure for constitutional reform under Art. 168. In other words, the court went back on its more flexible and conciliatory approach and endorsed the position of the central authorities.

## Academic debates and proposals

The need for constitutional reform using the rigid Art. 168 procedure signifies an unsurmountable barrier not only to secession, but also to hold a referendum consulting citizens of a sub-state unit on their constitutional future (Bossacoma Busquets and López Bofill 2016, Barceló Serramaleda 2020, Payero López 2020). This process would require two double qualified majorities at the central level, plus the members of central parliament and government being prepared to lose their seat in the process. Secondly, it would also require the consultation of all Spanish citizens via a referendum. Therefore, while the Constitutional Court stresses that the pursuit of secession or of other constitutionally transformative projects is not incompatible with the Constitution, and that ACs that want to hold a referendum on secession simply have to follow the constitutional procedures to do so, the near impossibility of pursuing this path for constitutional reform means there are no available avenues for an AC to pursue secession in practice. This is the case even in the context of a clear and sustained, democratically expressed desire to hold an independence referendum by the citizens on a specific AC, articulated through their constitutionally established institutions of self-government. This is particularly problematic in a plurinational quasi-federal system. The court itself appeared to acknowledge this in its 2014 decision, where it called on the political actors to enter into a dialogue to find a solution to the constitutional crisis and stated that if a region submits a proposal for constitutional reform, the Spanish Parliament should 'take it into account'.[19] However, when no cooperation or dialogue followed this decision, and in particular when the central authorities continued to refuse to recognise or engage with the demands for a referendum coming from Catalonia, the court then returned to its more legalistic and restrictive approach.

The Spanish Constitutional Court's position also stands in stark contrast with constitutional a position on secession in other plurinational liberal democracies such as Canada or the United Kingdom, where constitutional avenues have been found to enable sub-state independence referendums to go ahead with the agreement or acquiescence of the central authorities (Oklopcic 2017). It is true, of course, that other constitutional democracies such as Germany or Italy do not allow independence referendums, and that their respective constitutional courts have adopted a case law that is similar to that of the Spanish Constitutional Court (Castellà Andreu 2019b). However, there is a significant difference between these cases and those of the Basque Country and, in particular, Catalonia in Spain, which would appear to make Canada and the UK the most relevant comparators: the strong and sustained support for an independence referendum expressed through the election of pro-independence majorities to their institutions of self-government (López Bofill 2019). This would therefore make Spain the exception in this context, in the sense that Catalan secessionist formations have obtained a substantial majority in five successive elections to the Catalan Parliament (2012, 2016, 2017 and 2021). Again, the Spanish Constitutional Court referred specifically to the Québec secession reference in its 2014 decision, acknowledging therefore its significance in this context, but ultimately leading to a notably different outcome.[20]

As a result of these factors, the question of whether – and if so, how – secession of a sub-state nation or unit is possible under the Constitution is still a matter of political and scholarly debate. There is some academic support for the Constitutional Court's decision, and some positions that go further and argue that it is not possible to include a secession clause in the Spanish Constitution, even if using the appropriate procedure for constitutional reform (Muñoz Machado 2017, Aragón Reyes 2002). Nonetheless, many scholars consider the current constitutional position on secession in Spain unsatisfactory and unsustainable, particularly in the light of the clear and continuous citizen support for an independence referendum in Catalonia. Various scholars have stressed that the Constitutional Court's position that a consultation on the secession of a part of the Spanish territory would require the reform of the Constitution could be further qualified. For example, Tornos argues that a referendum that asks citizens in one part of the state on their desire to secede from the host state does not, as such, imply an amendment of the Constitution, even if it is agreed that a favourable vote will lead to a reform of the constitutional text (Tornos Mas 2015). Bossacoma, on the other hand, highlights that with a more holistic interpretation, focusing also on the principles of democracy, liberty and equality, complemented by other constitutional provisions such as the right to autonomy of nationalities and regions, the constitutional framework could be understood as only prohibiting secessions which are not democratic, liberal and peaceful (Bossacoma Busquets 2020).

Furthermore, for many scholars, what originated as a political crisis in Catalonia has now developed into a constitutional crisis, where the 1978 consensus on the territorial model in the constitution has been lost (Alberti Rovira 2019, Muñoz Machado et al. 2017). The current situation of deadlock seems to begin to point to the very exceptional circumstances where even some of those who were critical of the formulation of the 'right to decide', and of the Basque and Catalan sovereignist processes, have argued for a referendum on Catalan independence to be allowed to take place. For example, Castellà Andreu has stressed that in a situation of grave political and constitutional crisis, where for a long period there is a demand for secession coming from a majority of Catalan society and any attempts to resolve the issue or reform the system fail, the law should not ignore the situation (Castellà Andreu 2019a). In these circumstances, he continues, a political negotiation would be inevitable, and a referendum would be an adequate means to ratify a decision adopted previously by political representatives. Similarly, Ferreres Comella considers that in certain circumstances, an independence referendum could be justified as a practical solution to a serious political problem, and therefore for reasons of political opportunity (Ferreres Comella 2016). Highlighting the divisive effects of such a referendum, he argues that for it to be considered it would require the independence forces to have obtained solid and stable support in ordinary elections in Catalonia.

Some scholars go further and have argued for the 'constitutionalisation' of the right to secede in the Spanish Constitution. Aláez Corral and Bastida Freijedo, for example, have proposed the constitutionalisation of a secession procedure as a means to harmonise the roles of constitutional legality and democracy and therefore as a tool to strengthen the binding force of the Spanish Constitution in the current context (Aláez Corral and Bastida Freijedo 2019). They propose that this be included as a new special amendment procedure or the Constitution, enabling the peaceful and legal external self-determination of existing ACs. There are also broader proposals for the solution of the current deadlock through constitutional reform which would enable a wider range of options to be included in the debate and in a potential referendum (Muñoz Machado et al. 2017). Many scholars argue for a federal reform of the State of the Autonomies, including the recognition of Spain as a plurinational State integrating the national realities of Catalonia and the Basque Country, which could then be subject to a referendum of all the Spanish citizens (Aja Fernandez 2014 and 2020, Tornos Mas 2015 and 2019, López Basaguren 2019; Máiz 2020). Overall, the consensus seems to be that negotiation is the only way out of the crisis, oriented to the construction of a new consensus and an agreement that is satisfactory for all parties involved (see the extensive contributions in Almeda 2021). However, if reaching this agreement is not possible, and support for secession in Catalonia remains high, an independence referendum as an avenue for opening a potential constitutional secession process may be the only democratic outcome.

## Conclusion

The Spanish 1978 Constitution set out the basis for a plurinational devolved state, in response to the desire for autonomy of Catalonia, the Basque Country and Galicia. The lack of explicit regulation of secession, either enabling or prohibiting an AC from breaking away from the Spanish state, has led to an extensive debate over whether, and if so how, this could take place under the constitutional framework. The sovereignist movements led by the institutions of self-government of the Basque Country and, more recently, of Catalonia have focused their demands on the holding of an independence referendum, following the examples of Scotland and Québec. The central authorities' refusal to acknowledge and engage with these requests, based on a restrictive understanding of the constitutional provisions on sovereignty and the unity of the Spanish nation, has resulted in a constitutional crisis where the consensus on the territorial model has been broken. Many scholars have highlighted the current legal position on secession in the Spanish Constitution is unsatisfactory and unsustainable and have put forward various proposals to overcome the current deadlock. At the time of completion of this chapter, the Spanish and Catalan authorities had begun a process of political negotiation to resolve the crisis. What the final outcome will be remains to be seen.

## Notes

1 Diario de Sesiones de la Cortes Generales. Congreso de los Diputados, 91, 16 June 1978, 3427–3435.
2 Constitutional Court Decision 31/2010.
3 Constitutional Court Decision 103/2008.
4 Resolution 5/X of the Parliament of Catalonia, adopting the Declaration of sovereignty and right to decide of the people of Catalonia. Available at www.parlament.cat/document/intrade/7176 (accessed 10 December 2021).
5 Resolution 1/XI of the Parliament of Catalonia, on the Start of the Political Process in Catalonia as a consequence of the electoral results of 27 September. Available at: www.parlament.cat/document/intrade/153127 (accessed 10 December 2021).
6 Law 19/2017, of 6 September, on the Referendum on Self-determination, available at https://exteriors.gencat.cat/web/.content/00_ACTUALITAT/notes_context/Law-19_2017-on-the-Referendum-on-Self-determination.pdf; and Law 20/2017, of 7 September, on juridical transition and the foundation of the republic, available at https://exteriors.gencat.cat/web/.content/00_ACTUALITAT/notes_context/Law-on-Juridical-Transition.pdf (accessed 10 December 2021).
7 Resolution 742/IX of the Parliament of Catalonia, on the general political orientation of the Government of Catalonia. Available at www.parlament.cat/document/intrade/6026 (accessed 10 December 2021).

8  See note 4.
9  See note 5.
10  See note 6.
11  Institut d'Estudis Autonomics, 'Informe sobre els procediments legals a traves dels quals els ciutadans i les ciutadanes de Catalunya poden ser consultats sobre llur futur politic col.lectiu', 2013. Available at http://collectiupraga.cat/wp-content/uploads/2013/09/Informe-consultes-IEA-11.03.2013.pdf (accessed 10 December 2021).
12  The Catalan Parliament enacted a Catalan statute on referendums in 2010 (Catalan Law 4/2010), which included the requirement for any referendum to be held in Catalonia to be authorised by the central Government. This was challenged before the Constitutional Court by the central Government at that time for violation of the constitional provisions on referendums, leading to its initial suspension.
13  Resolution 479/X of the Catalan Parliament, Butlleti Official del Parlament de Catalunya, 239, 17 January 2014.
14  Diario de Sesiones del Congreso de los Diputados, 8 April 2014, 192.
15  See notes 4 and 7.
16  Constitutional Court Decision 103/2008.
17  Constitutional Court Decision 42/2014.
18  Constitutional Court Decision 259/2015.
19  See note 16.
20  See note 16.

# References

Aja Fernandez, E. 2014, *Estado Autonómico y Reforma Federal*, Madrid: Alianz.

Aja Fernandez, E. 2020, "Enfoques sobre el conflicto Catalunya-España", *Revista IDEES*, 45 Special Issue: 1–11.

Aláez Corral, B. & Bastida Freijedo, F. 2019, "Constitutionalizing Secession in Order to Harmonize Constitutionality and Democracy in Territorial Decentralized States Like Spain", in A. Lopez-Basaguren & L. Escajedo San-Epifaneo (eds), *Claims for Secession and Federalism: A Comparative Study with a Special Focus on Spain*, Cham: Springer: 265–285.

Alberti Rovira, E. 2019, "El Conflicto de Cataluña como Crisis Constitucional", *Fundamentos: Cuadernos monograficos de teoría del Estado, derecho público, e historia constitucional*, Num. 10.

Almeda, P. (ed) 2021, *Catalunya-Espanya. Del conflicte politic al diàleg?* Generalitat de Catalunya/IDEES, Barcelona: Catarata.

Aragón Reyes, M. 2002, *Constitución, Democracia y Control*, Mexico: Universidad Nacional Autónoma de México.

Barceló Serramaleda, M. 2015, "The Right to Decide: A Proposal for Its Legal Construction", in J. Gonzàlez-Agàpito (ed), *Perspectives d'Estat. Una Visió Crítica*, <https://perspectives-estat.espais.iec.cat/2015/07/20/dretadecidir/>

Barceló Serramaleda, M. 2020, "El ejercicio del derecho a decidir como solución del conflicto territorial entre Catalunya y España", *Revista IDEES*, 45 Special Issue: 1–9.

Barceló Serramaleda, M., Corretja, M., González Bondia, A., López, J., & Vilajosana, J. M. 2015, *El derecho a decidir. Teoría y práctica de un nuevo derecho*, Barcelona: Atelier.

Bossacoma Busquets, P. 2020, *Morality and Legality of Secession: A Theory of National Self-Determination*, Cham: Palgrave Macmillan.

Bossacoma Busquets, P. 2021, "Self-Determination and Coercion in Spain: The Case of Catalonia", *Revista d'Estudis Autonòmics i Federals*, 34: 291–327.

Bossacoma Busquets, P. & López Bofill, H. 2016, "The Secession of Catalonia: Legal Strategies and Barriers", in X. Cuadras-Morató (ed), *Catalonia: A New State in Europe?*, London: Routledge: 107–148.

Casañas-Adam, E. 2017, "The Constitutional Court of Spain: From System Balancer to Polarizing Centralist", in N. T. Aroney & J. Kinkaid (eds), *Courts in Federal Countries: Federalists or Unitarists?*, Toronto: University of Toronto Press: 367–403.

Casañas-Adam, E., Kagiaros, D. & Tierney, S. 2018, "Democracy in Question? Direct Democracy in the European Union", *European Constitutional Law Review*, 14 (2): 261–282.

Castellà Andreu, J. M. 2019a, "Constitution and Referendum on Secession in Catalonia", in A. Lopez-Basaguren & J. Escajedo San-Epifaneo (eds), *Claims for Secession and Federalism: A Comparative Study with a Special Focus on Spain*, Cham: Springer: 405–422.

Castellà Andreu, J. M. 2019b, "The Reception in Spain of the Reference of the Supreme Court in Canada on the Secession of Quebec", in G. Delledonne & G. Martinico (eds), *The Canadian Contribution to the Comparative Law of Secession*, London: Palgrave Macmillan: 69–86.

Ferreres Comella, V. 2013, *The Constitution of Spain: A Contextual Analysis*, Oxford: Hart.

Ferreres Comella, V. 2014, "The Spanish Constitutional Court Confronts Catalonia's 'Right to Decide' (Comment on the Judgement 42/2014)", *European Constitutional Law Review*, 10: 571–590.

Ferreres Comella, V. 2016, "Cataluña y el Derecho a Decidir", *Teoría y Realidad Constitucional*, 37: 461–475.

Fossas Espadaler, E. 2014, "Interpretar la politica. Comentatio a la STC 422014, de 25 de marzo, sobre la Declaracion de soberania y el derecho a decider del pueblo de Cataluña", *Revista Espanola de Derecho Constitucional*, 34: 273–300.

Guibernau, M. 2012, "The Rise of Secessionism in Catalonia Has Emerged Out of the Will to Decide the Region's Political Destiny as a Nation", *LSE Blog*, 29 May 2012, <https://blogs.lse.ac.uk/europpblog/2012/05/29/catalonia-secession/>

Keating, M. 2001, *Plurinational Democracy: Stateless Nations in a Post-Sovereign Era*, Oxford: Oxford University Press.

Keating, M. & Bray, Z. 2006, "Renegotiating Sovereignty: Basque Nationalism and the Rise and Fall of the Ibarretxe Plan", *Ehtnopolitics*, 4: 347–364.

López, J. 2011, "Del dret a l'autodeterminació al dret a decidir: Un possible canvi de paradigma en la reivindicació dels drets de les nacions sense estat", *Quaderns de Recerca*, 4 (November), Centre Unesco de Catalunya (Unescocat).

López Basaguren, A. 2009, "Sobre referendum y comunidades autonomas: La ley vasca de la 'consulta' ante el Tribunal Constitucional", *Revista d'Estudis Autonòmics i Federals*, 202–240.

López Basaguren, A. 2016, "Demanda de secession en Cataluña y sistema democrático: El *procés* a la luz de la experiencia comparada", *Teoría y Realidad Constitucional*, 37: 163–185.

López Basaguren, A. 2019, "Claims for Secession un Catalonia: Rule of law, Democratic Principle and Federal Alternative", in A. Lopez-Basaguren & L. Escajedo San-Epifaneo (eds), *Claims for Secession and Federalism: A Comparative Study with a Special Focus on Spain*, Cham: Springer: 365–388.

López Bofill, H. 2019, "Hubris, Constitutionalism, and the 'Indissoluble Unity of the Spanish Nation': The Repression of Catalan Secessionist Referenda in Spanish Constitutional Law", *International Journal of Constitutional Law*, 17 (3): 943–969.

Máiz, R. 2020, "Una propuesta desde el federalismo plurinacional", *Revista IDEES*, 45 Special Issue: 1–19.

Miguel Bárcena, J. 2018, "El proceso soberanista ante el Tribunal Constitucional", *Revista Española de Derecho Constitucional*, 113: 133–166.

Muñoz Machado, S. 2017, "Más allá de la intentona independentista", *El Cronista*, 71(2): 6–9.

Muñoz Machado, S., et al. 2017, *Ideas para una reforma de la Constitución* (Report), Madrid: UCM, <https://www.ucm.es/data/cont/media/www/pag-31775//Ideas%20para%20una%20reforma%20constitucional.pdf>

Oklopcic, Z. 2017, "Constitutionalize This: Catalan Referendum as Political Surprise and Theoretical Disruption", *International Journal of Constitutional Law Blog*, 6 October 2017, www.iconnectblog.com/2017/10/constitutionalize-this-the-catalan-referendum-as-political-surprise-and-theoretical-disruption

Payero López, L. 2020, "El diálogo y la negociación: ¿síntomas de debilidad o de salud democrática?", *Revista IDEES*, 45 Special Issue: 1–9.

Ridao Martin, J. 2014, *El dret a decidir. La consulta sobre el futur politic de Catalunya*. Barcelona: Institut d'Estudis Autonòmics.

Tierney, S. 2004, *Constitutional Law and National Pluralism*, Oxford: Oxford University Press.

Torbisco Casals, N. 2017, "National Minorities, Self-Determination and Human Rights: A Critique of the Dominant Paradigms in the Catalan Case", in P. A. Kraus & J. Vergès Gifra (eds), *The Catalan Process: Sovereignty, Self-Determination and Democracy in the 21st Century*, Barcelona: Institut d'Estudis de l'Autogovern: 195–226.

Tornos Mas, J. 2015, *De Escocia a Cataluña. Referendum y Reforma Constitucional*, Madrid: Iustel.

Tornos Mas, J. 2019, "Secession and Federalism: The Spanish Case", in A. Lopez-Basaguren & L. Escajedo San-Epifaneo (eds), *Claims for Secession and Federalism: A Comparative Study with a Special Focus on Spain*, Cham: Springer: 389–404.

Vintró, J. 2013, "La Declaració de sobirania i del dret a decidir del poble de catalunya: un apunt jurídic", *Revista Catalana de Dret Public Blog*, <https://eapc-rcdp.blog.gencat.cat/2013/02/07/la-declaracio-de-sobirania-i-del-dret-a-decidir-del-poble-de-catalunya-un-apunt-juridic-joan-vintro/>

# INDEX

Note: numbers in **bold** indicate a table. Numbers in *italics* indicate a figure.

ANC *see* African National Congress
Anderson, Glen 30, 32–35, 88–89
Andorra 335
Anishnaabe 102, 106; *aki* (the Earth) 105
Anglophile Cameroons 422
Anglo-Irish Treaty 1921 593–595
*annus mirabilis* of 1666 20
Anti-Fascist People's Freedom League, Burma 65
anti-secession 179; China 576–588
anti-secession constitutionalism 525–539;
   comparative constitutional law and 539;
   constitutional bans on 532–533; constitutional
   law and international law combining to combat
   538; constitutional law perspective on 526–527;
   constitutional procedure for territorial change
   **535**, 535; constitutional secession clauses **534**;
   factors that hide prevalence of 530–532; global
   discourse on rights and 527–528; modern
   China 580–585; non-revolutionary 537–538;
   PRC 585–587; processes to legitimize 533–535
Anti-Secession Law (PRC) 576, 587
anti-secessionist: actors 401; bias 315
apartheid 8, 47, 431, 462
Arendt, Hannah 127
Armenia: Artsakh as "more free" than 377;
   Artsakh petition 375; Azeri in 354–355;
   diaspora 352; Karabakhi Armenians 352, **353**,
   365; Nagorno Karabakh 290, **345**, **353**, 354,
   441; as patron state 441; secession referendum
   **235**; Supreme Soviet of the Armenian Soviet
   Socialist Republic 287; USSR and **235**, **294**
Armenian Declaration 1990 287, 288
Armenian language 377, 415
Armitage, David 35, 279
Aronovitch, H. 201
Artsakh: as "more free" than Armenia and
   Azerbaijan 377; petition 375; secessionists in 376
Assam 409n8
aspiring nation: joining the UN 208
aspiring state 157–158, 213; Abkhazia 368;
   declarations of definition of 382; independence
   by 282, 285; secessionist diplomacy and 372,
   373. 375, 380
Atlantic Charter 64–65
Austin, J. L. 19
Autonomous Bougainville Government 238
Autonomous Communities (ACs) Spain 251,
   604, 609
autonomous oblasts 346, 354
autonomy: Aaland Islands 9, 335; achieving
   334; Article 4 and 108; Article 27 and 46;
   asymmetric 445, 452; Berber in Algeria 297;
   birth of nation-states and struggle for 413;
   Catalan Autonomy Statute 253; Catalonia 242,
   243, 244; Checheno-Ingush Autonomous Soviet
   Socialist Republic 421; civil war settlements and
   305; claims for 149; control contrasted against

165; corporate 445; cultural 23, 201, 452;
demands for 152, 153, 154, 216, 420; Dominion
status and 594; East Pakistan/Bengal 425; Eritrea
337; fiscal 445, 451; informal 214; 'inheriting'
450; Irish 308, 309; Law of Regional National
Autonomy of PRC (LRNA) 586, 587; Kosovo
320, 470, 488, 493, 496; Kurdistan 443; Lecours'
work on 156; Luxemburg on 22; paths to 305;
personal 445; policy 445; political 445; regional
23, 229, 418, 419, 443, 448, 588; retracted
or lost 155; right of 10, 92, 102; Scotland
406, 597; self-determination and 21, 61, 333,
340; self-rule and 251; social or political 63;
South Ossetia 374; sovereignty and 376; 'State
of Autonomies' (Spain) 604, 611, 614; static
and dynamic 156; Statute of Autonomy 2010
(Catalonia) 605, 606, 607, 608; territorial and
non-territorial 405; Ukraine's proclamation of
24; use of violence in pursuit of 156; *see also*
indigenous autonomy
autonomy rights 221
Austria: Anschluss **234**; declaration of
   independence from Germany **294**; dissolution
   of ties with Kingdom of Croatia 283; grievance
   declaration of 1945 284; Nazi rule in 284–285
Austria-Hungary 463
Australia 84; Aboriginal community healthcare
   providers 113; colonization of 105;
   *Commonwealth of Australia Constitution Act
   1900* 554–556, 558, 562; Constitution 555;
   constitutional law and secession in 553–562;
   democratized movements among indigenous
   and aboriginal communities in 212; irredentist
   referendums **234**; Kiribati and 335; Macedonia
   and 505; National Congress of Australia's First
   Peoples 111; New South Wales **234**, 553, 554;
   Portugal's lawsuit against 332; Queensland **234**,
   553, 554; *Secession Referendum Act 1932* 558;
   South Australia 553, 554; Tasmania **234**, 553,
   554; *see also* Western Australia
Austrian Declaration of Independence 1945 284, 288
Austrian Military Frontier 346
Austrian People's Party 284
Awami League 98
Azerbaijan: "administrative borderline" between
   Nagorno-Karabakh and 347; Artsakh and 212;
   Artsakh as "more free" than 377; Bunce and
   Watts on 448; declaration on the restoration
   of independence 289–290; failed coup 289;
   modernization and re-armament program of
   348; Nagorno Karabakh and **295**, **345**, 349, **349**,
   351, 363, 365, 433, 434; oil revenues of 434; as
   restrictive parent state 364–365; Second Karabakh
   War and 368; USSR, secession from **295**
Azerbaijan declaration on the restoration of
   independence 1991 289–290
Azeri 354–355

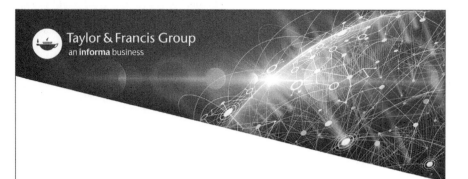